CHURCHILL

ALSO BY ROY JENKINS

Mr Attlee: An Interim Biography

Pursuit of Progress

Mr Balfour's Poodle

Sir Charles Dilke: A Victorian Tragedy

The Labour Case

Asquith

Essays and Speeches

Afternoon on the Potomac?

What Matters Now

Nine Men of Power

Partnership of Principle

Truman

Baldwin

Twentieth-century Portraits

European Diary

A Life at the Centre

Portraits and Miniatures

Gladstone

The Chancellors

Roy Jenkins

CHURCHILL

MACMILLAN

First published 2001 by Macmillan
an imprint of Pan Macmillan Ltd
Pan Macmillan, 20 New Wharf Road, London N1 9RR
Basingstoke and Oxford
Associated companies throughout the world
www.panmacmillan.com

ISBN 0 333 78290 9

A CIP catalogue record for this book is available from
the British Library.

Typeset by SetSystems Ltd, Saffron Walden, Essex
Printed and bound in Great Britain by
Mackays of Chatham plc, Chatham, Kent

Contents

———————

List of Illustrations

Section One

Section Three

Preface

WHEN I COMPLETED the final chapter of this book, at the end of February 2001, I was only a few days younger than was Churchill at the end of his second premiership, forty-six years earlier. Amid all the many who have written on or around Churchill – somewhere between fifty and a hundred – I can at least claim to be the only octogenarian who has ventured into the list. I suppose I can also claim to have had the widest parliamentary and ministerial experience of his biographers.

On the other hand I cannot claim really to have known Churchill. I was introduced to him by my father on a (to me) memorable occasion in 1941 when, the old chamber having been destroyed by bombs, the House of Commons was meeting in its temporary home of Church House in Dean's Yard, Westminster. At around that time I listened to several of his most notable orations, some in Parliament, some broadcast, and throughout the war and its aftermath he was an immanent presence in my life, and in that of my contemporaries.

Seven years after that brief encounter of 1941 I became a young MP and sat in the House of Commons with him for the next sixteen years. With varying degrees of appreciation – I was of course in the opposite party – I observed his performance, first in opposition, then as head of his second government, and finally during the nine years of his parliamentary somnolence. I was aware of witnessing something unique, but also remote and unpredictable. It was like looking at a great mountain landscape, which could occasionally be illuminated by an unforgettable light but could also descend into lowering cloud, from the terrace of a modest hotel a safe distance away. I had no significant conversation with him during those sixteen years. I doubt if he knew who I was, although I became a member of the Other Club (over which he had kept a very tight control) at the end of his life, but only arrived in time to atte? his obituary dinner.

However, although I had many inhibitions about venturing a Churchill biography, the slightness of the acquaintances? not among them. I do not believe that biography demands?

necessarily profits from personal knowledge. It can distort as much as it illuminates. I never saw Charles Dilke or Asquith, but I do not feel that my lives of them suffered from this particular deficiency, any more than I thought that my now fifty-three-year-old piece of juvenilia about Attlee, whom I did know well, was made of higher quality as a result.

Even more obviously than with Dilke and Asquith, I never knew or saw Gladstone. I was at the start very hesitant about engaging with the Grand Old Man of Victorian politics, but that was for the quite different reason that I feared his larger-than-life quality made him too big a subject for me, and in particular that I would be defeated by his absorption in theological and liturgical disputes. Once launched on the project, however, I never regretted having undertaken Gladstone.

Similar inhibitions initially applied even more strongly to Churchill. And the scale of the existing literature about him was several times more formidable than that about Gladstone. Progress from Asquith to Glad-stone to Churchill is exponential. If there is five times as much about Gladstone as about Asquith, there is at least ten times as much about Churchill as about Gladstone. On the other hand, after Gladstone, I had come to be attracted rather than inhibited by big subjects. To have tried to write a full-length book about a medium-grade even if inher-ently interesting subject, say William Harcourt or John Morley, both of whom could do with reappraisals, would be the equivalent of trying to get excited, after a Himalayan expedition, by an amble up Snowdon.

There were two decisive figures who persuaded me to undertake Churchill. The first was Andrew Adonis. He put the issue with almost exactly the same sentiment as that of the preceding sentence. 'After Gladstone,' he said, 'there is one direction, and only one direction to go which will not be an anti-climax, and that is Churchill.' The other influence, even more conclusive if not equally formative, was that of Lady Soames (Mary Churchill). When I was still hesitating she was as generous in encouragement as she has since been in help, although never wanting to see anything that I had written until it was past the point of no recall. 'I would much like another Liberal study of my father,' she enthusiastically said, referring back to Lady Violet Bonham Carter's 1965 *Winston Churchill as I Knew Him*. I only hope that she will ~~n~~ot be as disapproving of some aspects of this book as, despite that ~~bei~~ng essentially favourable (as is this), was Lady Violet (née Asquith) of ~~1~~964 biography of her father.

~~As w~~ith Gladstone, so with Churchill I never had subsequent regrets. ~~I found~~ him even more rewarding as a focus of interest and effort than

I had found Gladstone. Indeed, as will be seen in the last paragraph of the text, in the course of the process I changed my mind about their relative qualities as wholly exceptional specimens of humanity, and would now put Churchill marginally ahead of Gladstone. A sceptic might say this proves nothing more than that I have the self-centredness to regard whatever book I am currently engaged on as being more important than any others. It does not however make me regard the subjects of my absorption with excessive reverence. I have become increasingly convinced that great men have strong elements of comicality in them. This was certainly true of Gladstone and Churchill, and, as an offstage example, it was also true of General de Gaulle, who was two-thirds a political giant and one-third a figure of fun.

I do not claim to have unearthed many new facts about Churchill. With published sources about him on their existing scale this would be almost impossible. Nor am I a great partisan of the 'revelatory' biography. Churchill in life was singularly lacking in inhibition or concealment. There are consequently no great hidden reservoirs of behaviour to be tapped. Nearly all the facts have been provided in the massive eight-volume official biography started by Randolph Churchill but essentially done by Sir Martin Gilbert, with the dates of publication extending from 1966 to 1988. Every student of Churchill's life is necessarily dependent upon these, and perhaps even more upon the *Companion Volumes* of supporting documents, thirteen of them up to 1939, with a further three, re-entitled *War Papers*, taking the documentation to the end of 1941. When this rich seam (for the moment) runs out, the deprivation is quickly felt. Any subsequent writer is deeply in Martin Gilbert's debt.

I also have heavy debts to Andrew Adonis, the source of the already quoted piece of decisive advice. He in addition cast his encyclopaedic and critical eye over every page of the typescript. At one stage last autumn, when I thought that illness might prevent my writing the last eight chapters of the book, I decided that he was the only person who could possibly do it for me. Fortunately that did not prove necessary, but my debt to him nonetheless remains pre-eminent. He alone has impaired my rule that every sentence comes out in my own laborious and almost illegible long-hand. Three or four necessary linking passages of a few hundred words, only lightly amended by me, have come from his pen.

Next my debt is to my secretary, Gimma Macpherson, who a little intermediate help from me transformed the nearly manuscript into typescript, while also exhibiting a lively and encouraging interest in the narrative. Then there are those who, purely voluntarily, read every word of the resultant typescript and made many helpful criticisms and suggestions: Max Hastings; Arthur Schlesinger; the late Lord Harris of Greenwich; and, of course, my wife. Others read individual chapters or groups of chapters.

In addition there are those who might be described as the professional midwives of the book: Michael Sissons, my literary agent who was a part initiator of the idea and an unfailing source of encouragement; Ian Chapman (Junior) and then Jeremy Trevathan at Macmillan who were responsible for seeing it turn into a handsome volume; Peter James who is the prince of detailed editors; Robbie Low who did meticulous work on the reference footnotes; and Elisabeth Sifton of Farrar, Straus and Giroux, New York, who in the course of demanding many clarifications for the American edition also did much to make the text more comprehensible to some British readers.

Roy Jenkins
East Hendred
April 2001

Glossary of Parliamentary Terms

CHURCHILL WAS A great parliamentarian and a member of the House of Commons (with two short intervals) for nearly sixty-four years. As such he naturally used a lot of parliamentary terms which may appear as incomprehensible jargon to non-British readers, and perhaps indeed to many British ones as well. But it would be depressingly denuding to strip his own language or mine in writing about him of such terms. I have therefore decided to attempt a glossary, primarily but not exclusively for American readers, in the hope that this will shed some light on to arcane mysteries.

Constituencies: Relatively small geographical areas from which MPs are elected by a simple plurality. The total number has varied but there have broadly been about 650 for a population which in 1900 was little more than thirty million and in 2000 barely sixty million. Until the Third Reform Act of 1885 nearly all constituencies were two-member, both in the boroughs (towns and cities) and in the (broadly) rural counties. After that most constituencies became single-member, but some two-member exceptions remained and included two of Churchill's constituencies: Oldham in Lancashire from 1900 to 1906 and Dundee in Scotland from 1908 to 1922. In these exceptions candidates habitually had a 'running mate', nearly always of the same party. There has never been a 'locality rule' in British politics. No residential qualification is required and many of the most famous figures have been elected in the course of their careers from a bewildering geographical spread. Latterly this has become more difficult, although not impossible. Neither Margaret Thatcher nor Tony Blair had any connection with their constituencies until they came to represent them in Parliament. Churchill's electoral contests embraced not only Lancashire and Scotland, but also London suburbia, as well as the East Midlands city Leicester and the Abbey division of Westminster, the home ground Parliament itself.

In these circumstances constituency chairmen, voluntar

although often rewarded with knighthoods, were important in keeping non-locally bred MPs in touch with local opinion. There were also, until 1950 when they were abolished, twelve university seats as a little berry on the tree of geographical representation. The electorates here were the graduates of the respective universities.

Constituencies are regularly reviewed by boundary commissions to ensure an approximate equality of electorates in the face of demographic fluctuations. Their boundaries may be redrawn, or the constituencies themselves may be merged or divided, and their names are often therefore changed.

Division: A term used in two senses, although the former appears much more in this book:

(i) a vote in the House of Commons (or occasionally the House of Lords) when members file through either the 'aye' or the 'no' division lobby and have their names recorded by parliamentary clerks. But although the name-checking is done by clerks the actual counting of the votes is done by MPs, two from each side, who stand at the exit doors to each lobby. Anyone calling a division thus has to put in two 'tellers', who do not nominally vote. Confusingly, therefore, the numbers voting on either side should always be augmented by two to give the accurate picture of how the House divided. As divisions are mostly conducted on party lines it is usual to refer to 'the Tory lobby' or 'the Labour lobby' or 'the Liberal lobby'.

(ii) Division is also an alternative name for a constituency, in American terms the equivalent of a Congressional district. In this sense it is natural to talk about the Central Division or the North or West or East or South divisions of a big provincial city.

Parliaments: The House of Commons is elected at a general election for a parliamentary term of five years, and the party leader who is able to command a majority in the Commons is invited by the Sovereign to form a government: this is when a Prime Minister is said to 'kiss hands'. The parliamentary term is divided into annual sessions, each session ending when Parliament is prorogued; at any time within the term, ‑‑rliament may be dissolved and a new general election held. (Both ‑‑ogation and dissolution are in the prerogative of the crown, ‑‑gh in practice the decision is the Prime Minister's.) The period ‑‑ sessions is known as a recess, though the word can also be ‑‑ other periods when the House does not sit. A constituency which loses its MP through death or retirement during the life of a parliament must elect another at a bye-election.

The Address: Each year's session of Parliament begins with a Queen's (or King's) speech, delivered by the Sovereign from the Throne in the House of Lords, but written for her (or him) by the government and is a statement of government legislative and other intentions for the year. The Prime Minister then moves a 'loyal address' thanking the Sovereign for 'the Gracious Speech from the Throne'. The Opposition or an individual member can then put down amendments in the form of 'while thanking Her (His) Majesty for the Gracious Speech regrets' that X or Y is or is not included. If the government is defeated on an amendment to the Address it would be regarded as a central challenge to its authority, calling for either its resignation or a general election.

The Chamber: MPs debate in the Commons chamber, the government side sitting on benches to the right of the Speaker's Chair, the opposition parties to the left. A member who changes his party is thus said to have crossed the floor. Front-benchers (members of the government and their Opposition equivalents) speak from one or other of two despatch boxes; all others speak from the back benches. The government front bench is also known as the Treasury bench. A gangway cuts through the middle of the benches on both sides. Close to the Speaker's chair is the official box, where civil servants may be consulted by government ministers. The division lobbies – two long, narrow corridors – are parallel to but outside the chamber on either side. Arrangements in the House of Lords are similar, except that it has no Speaker and no Speaker's Chair; instead debates are inactively presided over by the Lord Chancellor – or his deputy – seated on the Woolsack.

Procedure: Every bill presented to Parliament goes through several stages. The first reading in the House of Commons is a formal notification of the bill, an announcement of its long title (the bill itself may not yet have been drafted, but it cannot range further than the long title). The second reading is a general debate on the merits of the bill; if defeated on the vote at this stage, the bill cannot be reintroduced in the same session. The bill then goes to the committee stage, when it receives detailed examination clause by clause from a committee of the whole House or (an innovation of the Attlee government) from standing committee consisting of up to fifty members appointe proportion to the party strength in the House. There follows the report stage on the floor of the House, when the bill and any amendments agreed in committee are subjected to further detailed examination. Last there is a third reading, and if the bill is passed it then goes to the House of Lords for similar treatment. A bill passed by both Houses is enacted only when it receives the royal assent.

Prime Minister's questions, recently unhelpfully gladiatorial, are short, regular sessions during which MPs may put questions to the PM.

Proceedings in both Houses are reported verbatim (though often tidied up to produce a greater elegance than the MP actually achieved) in the daily Official Report known as Hansard, after the name of the original printers.

Whips: The Leader of the House, who is a member of the Cabinet, is in charge of the business of the House, but the day-to-day organization of Commons business is in the hands of the party 'whips', one Chief Whip and perhaps eight or ten assistants on each side. On the government side their principal business is to expedite the passing of legislation. They issue a weekly instruction to their supporters about when important votes are likely and into which lobby they should go. These instructions can be defied, although it requires unusual boldness to do so at all frequently.

There are also occasional 'free' (or unwhipped) votes, particularly on private member's bills, which are proposed by backbenchers not ministers and for which limited time is available.

During most of Churchill's career the Whips' Office also had certain extra-parliamentary functions in relation to the proposing of candidates for constituencies and the raising of party funds. These functions have recently fallen into desuetude.

It was also traditionally the case that whips' tasks were workaday, not attracting those who rose high in politics. Latterly, however, both Sir Edward Heath and John Major have come to the premiership through the Whips' Office.

The Franchise: Until the 'Great' Reform Act of 1832 Britain had a pattern of those entitled to vote which was both haphazard and highly restrictive. Even after that it remained restrictive, with only 650,000 ble to vote. In 1867 the Second Reform Act, mainly by giving the vote heads of working-class families in the boroughs, put the number up early 2,000,000. In 1885 it went to about 5,000,000 and remained there until female suffrage began in 1918. Universal votes for all over eighteen (except for peers and lunatics) did not however arrive until 1970.

A further restriction on simple democracy was that the 'business vote' persisted until 1950. This gave a second or even a third or fourth vote to those who occupied business premises away from their homes. Such votes were significant in city centres such as Churchill's 1906–8 Manchester constituency.

The Privy Council is a somewhat archaic survival from the Councils of medieval and early-modern monarchs, which figure much in Shakespeare's historical plays. The Privy Council today has over 600 members and is summoned as a whole only on the accession of a new sovereign. Very small groups of Privy Councillors (the quorum is as low as four) meet with the Queen quite frequently formally to approve orders in council (executive acts) which are decided upon by the government. Of the 600 members of the Privy Council 150 or so are members of the House of Commons. All full ministers automatically become so on appointment and retain the rank for life. Thus Churchill was a Privy Councillor for the last fifty-seven years of his life and I have been one for thirty-seven years. They are addressed as 'Right Honourable' on envelopes and as 'the right honourable gentleman' or 'the right honourable lady' in parliamentary debates. They have traditionally enjoyed some priority in being called to speak in the House of Commons, but that has recently been eroded. As well as ministers and ex-ministers some senior backbenchers have the rank bestowed upon them.

The Lord President of the Council is one of the so-called sinecure offices, allowing membership of Cabinet without fixed duties. The others are the Lord Privy Seal and the Chancellor of the Duchy of Lancaster.

PART ONE

A BRASH YOUNG MAN

1874–1908

A DOUBTFUL PROVENANCE

CHURCHILL'S PROVENANCE WAS aristocratic, indeed ducal, and some have seen this as the most important key to his whole career. That is unconvincing. Churchill was far too many faceted, idiosyncratic and unpredictable a character to allow himself to be imprisoned by the circumstances of his birth. His devotion to his career and his conviction that he was a man of destiny were far stronger than any class or tribal loyalty. There have been politicians of high duty and honour – Edward Halifax and Alec Douglas-Home immediately spring to mind – who did see life through spectacles much bounded by their landed background. But Churchill was emphatically not among them. Apart from anything else, he never had any land beyond his shaky ownership (and later only occupation) of the 300 acres surrounding Chartwell, the West Kent house only twenty-four miles from London which he bought in 1922 and just managed, with financial subventions from friends, to cling on to for the remaining four decades of his life.

The second reason was that the Marlborough heritage was not one which stood very high in esteem, record of public service or secure affluence. The family had a memorable swashbuckling founder in John Churchill, the victor in the first decade of the eighteenth century of the battles of Blenheim, Ramillies, Oudenaarde and Malplaquet, who acquired a fine mansion among other rewards. But even this first Duke, although he inspired Winston Churchill to write four resonant volumes of praise (and of refutation of the historian Thomas Babington Macaulay's criticism) just over 200 years after his death, was as famous for ruthless self-advancement as he was for martial prowess; and the house, as its name of Blenheim *Palace* implies and as its size-enhancing Vanburgh architecture was dedicated to achieving, was showy even by the standards of the time.

Subsequent holders of the dukedom contributed little distinction and much profligacy. In 1882, when the seventh in the line had been reached, Gladstone, who in general had an excessive respect for dukes, claimed that none of the Marlboroughs had shown either morals or principles. Certainly no lustre to the family name was added by the second, third or fourth Dukes. The fifth was a talented gardener, but he seriously dissipated the Marlborough fortune and had to abandon the fine subsidiary estate (now the site of Reading University) where he had exercised his botanical skills. The sixth was almost equally extravagant. The seventh, who was the father of Lord Randolph and hence the grandfather of Winston Churchill, made the nearest approach to respectability and a record of public service. He was an MP for ten years, Lord President of the Council under both Derby and Disraeli in 1867–8, and Lord Lieutenant of Ireland for the last four years of Disraeli's second government.*

As a father this seventh Duke's record was at once more dramatic and more mixed. On the one hand he produced a two-generation dynasty which made the name of Churchill resound throughout Britain's national life in a way that it had not done since the death of the first Duke in 1722. On the other, the resonance, in the case of Lord Randolph, had a distinctly meretricious note to it. And Lord Randolph's elder brother was, in the words of an eminent modern historian, 'one of the most disreputable men ever to have debased the highest rank in the British peerage'.[1] He appropriately bore the name of Blandford, the title of the Marlborough heir, for most of his relatively short life, during which he was expelled from Eton, got caught up in two sexual scandals, one of which involved him in a violent quarrel with the Prince of Wales (in which quarrel the fault may not have been unilateral), and sold off, as a short-term staunching operation, the formidable Marlborough picture collection. About his only constructive act was to install electric light and a rudimentary form of central heating at Blenheim. That was paid for by his second wife, who as a rich American provided sustaining dollars and began a strong Churchill family tradition of looking matrimonially westward. This example was followed by both his son, the ninth Duke, Winston Churchill's cousin and near contemporary, who married two transatlantic heiresses, and by his younger brother (Lord Randolph Churchill), who married one (Winston Churchill's mother). The fortune of the father of Lady Randolph was however a little precarious. Furthermore he was unwilling to contribute much of it to the sustenance of the Churchill family.

* But perhaps his most unusual feat was to cause the 'nodding of Homer' in the shape of the *Dictionary of National Biography*, which falsely listed him in both the full and the concise versions as the *sixth* Duke rather than the seventh.

Since the eighth Duke there have been another three Marlboroughs. Of these subsequent three, while they rose somewhat above the level of the eighth Duke, it is difficult to find much that is positive to say. Winston Churchill's family background, while nominally of the highest aristocracy, was subtly inferior to that of a Cavendish, a Russell, a Cecil or a Stanley.

He was born on 30 November 1874 and, mainly by accident, at the very core of this slightly doubtful purple – in Blenheim Palace, although in a singularly bleak-looking bedroom. The accident arose out of his being two months premature. He should have been born in January in the small but fashionable house in Charles Street, Mayfair which his father had rented to receive him, or more purposefully perhaps to use as a base for the somewhat rackety metropolitan life of which Lord Randolph and his bride of only seven and a half months' standing were equally fond. This house not being ready, they had taken autumn refuge in Blenheim, and, as Lord Randolph put it in a letter to his mother-in-law in Paris, 'She [Lady Randolph] had a fall on Tuesday walking with the shooters, and a rather imprudent and rough drive in a pony carriage brought on the pains on Saturday night. We tried to stop them, but it was no use.'[2] Neither the London obstetrician nor his Oxford auxiliary could arrive in time, although it was over twenty-four hours to the birth from the onset of the labour pains, and the baby was born very early on the Monday morning with the assistance only of the Woodstock country doctor. Both mother and baby survived this paucity of attention perfectly healthily – as did the local doctor, who whether as a result or not was able himself to migrate to a London practice a decade or so later.

Everything to do with Winston Churchill's arrival in the world was done in a hurry. Perhaps Lord Randolph's most remembered phrase (and phrases were his strongest suit) was his description of Gladstone as 'an old man in a hurry'. His own style was at least equally that of a young man in a hurry, almost in a constant frenzy of impatience, and perhaps rationally so, for, although thirty-nine years his junior, he predeceased Gladstone by three years. The hurry was pre-eminently true of his courtship of Miss Jennie Jerome. They first met at a Cowes regatta shipboard party on 12 August 1873 and became engaged to be married three days later.

There then intervened the only period of semi-stasis in the saga. The Jerome family were in fact a very suitable American family for a Marlborough alliance. Leonard Jerome was a New York financial buccaneer. Winston Churchill, in his still highly readable although hagiographic 1905 biography of his father, was to describe Jerome as having 'founded and edited the *New York Times*'.[3] This owed more to family piety than to truth. Jerome had briefly in the course of some financial deals been a part proprietor of the *Times*. But what he was strong in was not newspaper publishing but horse racing, having founded both the Jerome Park track and the Coney Island Jockey Club. There was a touch of Joseph P. Kennedy about him. There was even a suggestion that he named his second daughter after Jenny Lind, the 'Swedish nightingale' (although the spelling was different), who was his current principal *inamorata*. He was pleased at the idea of this second daughter marrying an English duke's son (even if he was not the heir), but not to the extent of being willing, in the joke which John F. Kennedy was to make about his father's financing of the 1960 Presidential campaign, 'to pay for a landslide'. The seventh Duke was at first opposed to the whole idea of the union, being unimpressed by the uncontrolled precipitateness of his son's passion, and believing moreover that 'this Mr J. seems to be a sporting, and I should think vulgar kind of man', who was evidently 'of the class of speculators; he has been bankrupt twice; and may be so again'.[4] Over the autumn the Duke was brought reluctantly to overcome these objections of principle by his son's determination. He was the first but by no means the last of the Marlboroughs to have to deal with the fathers of American heiresses and he set a pattern of believing that the least *consuegros* could do for the honour of such a noble alliance was generously to finance it.

There were however two difficulties. First, Leonard Jerome, true to the Duke's descriptions of the hazards of his occupation, was in a speculative downturn. He had been badly mauled by the plunge of the New York stock exchange of that year (1873). Second, he claimed to hold advanced New World ideas about the financial rights of married women. (This was before the British Married Women's Property Act of 1882 gave women any property rights against their husbands.) The Duke assumed that whatever settlement could be obtained would be under the exclusive control of his son. Jerome thought it should be settled on his daughter. This led to a good deal of haggling which went on into the spring of 1874. Eventually a compromise was reached, by which Jerome settled a sum of £50,000 (approximately £2.5 million at present values), producing an income of £2,000 a year, with a half of both capital and income belonging to the husband and a half to the wife. The Duke settled another £1,100 a year for life on Randolph which gave the couple the equivalent of a present-day income of a little more than £150,000 a year, a sum which guaranteed that they would live constantly above their income and be always in debt.

As soon as this settlement was reached they were married, on 15 April 1874. It cannot be said that the wedding took place *en beauté*. It was not at Woodstock, or in a suitable London church, or a Fifth Avenue equivalent. It was in the British Embassy in Paris. The Jeromes attended and were among the very few witnesses, but neither Marlborough parent did; Blandford represented the family. However there was no ostracism at home. The couple were welcomed at Blenheim and in May were given a public reception in Woodstock, for which small family borough Lord Randolph had been first and fairly narrowly elected a member of Parliament at the general election of February 1874. He was twenty-five years of age at the time both of his election and of the birth of Winston Churchill. Jennie Churchill was twenty.

She had passed most of her adolescence in Paris, which Mrs Jerome appeared to prefer to New York, was considered a beauty and had already attracted much admiration before she met Lord Randolph. Her looks were undoubtedly striking, but what emerges most clearly from many photographs is that she quickly assumed an appearance which was hard, imperious and increasingly self-indulgent. Her performance as a wife, and indeed as a mother, was at least as mixed as that of the seventh Duke of Marlborough as a father. She and Randolph undoubtedly began upon a basis of mutual passion. Although they both liked a fashionable London life she accepted with calmness and even contentment the three years of virtual exile to Dublin which followed from her husband's 1876 quarrel (over a lady, but on his brother's, not his own, part) with the Prince of Wales. Her second son, Jack, was born in the Irish capital at the beginning of 1880. There has long been a strong suggestion that this boy had a different father from Winston Churchill, although this did not prevent the two brothers being close at various periods of their lives, notably in South Africa at the turn of the century and at the peak of Winston Churchill's career in the Second World War, when he accommodated the widowed Jack in 10 Downing Street. The most romantic candidate for alternative parenthood was Count Charles Kinsky, an Austrian diplomat of high aristocratic connection and of a proud elegance reminiscent of Sargent's portrait of Lord Ribblesdale. Lady Randolph was much taken up with him in the early and mid-1880s but the dates are wrong for giving him a procreative role; he did not arrive in London until 1881. If the legitimacy of Jack Churchill is challenged, a more likely candidate seems to be the Dublin-based Colonel John

Strange Jocelyn, who succeeded his nephew as the fifth Earl of Roden later in the year 1880. He was thirty years older than Lady Randolph, but that was no necessary bar.

She looked after her husband rather well during a protracted illness which effectively took him out of politics from the spring to the autumn of 1882, and very well during the last tragic three years or so of disintegration before his death at the beginning of 1895. But the couple were effectively estranged over much of the 1880s, including the years of his short political apogee. She, like Queen Victoria, did not know of his disastrous 1886 resignation from the Chancellorship of the Exchequer until she read it in *The Times*. During these years she had many suitors, more than a few of them probably lovers. They included apart from those mentioned, the Marquis de Breteuil, Lord Dunraven, the French novelist Paul Bourget and King Milan of Serbia. George Moore, the Anglo-Irish novelist, said she had 200 lovers, but apart from anything else the number is suspiciously round. She claimed to have firmly rejected the overtures of Sir Charles Dilke, which however did not prevent Lord Randolph, who appeared mostly to be more tolerant, from attempting to assault him.

After Lord Randolph's death her choice of partners became more bizarre as well as more public. In 1900, at the age of forty-six, she insisted on marrying George Cornwallis-West, a Scots Guards subaltern who was twenty years her junior. The marriage lasted fourteen years before ending in divorce. Cornwallis-West clearly had considerable drawing power, for he then married Mrs Patrick Campbell. Three years later Lady Randolph made a third marriage to Montague Porch, an hitherto quiet Somerset country gentleman who had been a Colonial Service officer in Nigeria and who was even younger than Cornwallis-West. She died in 1921, aged sixty-seven. Porch survived until 1964.

Was Jennie Churchill a better mother than a wife? Her elder son's most famous comment on their early relationship sounds a note at once admiring and wistful. After citing an adulatory passage (in which the most striking phrase was nonetheless 'more of the panther than of the woman in her look') written by the future Lord D'Abernon after first seeing her during the Irish period, Winston Churchill commented: 'My mother made the same brilliant impression upon my childhood's eye. She shone for me like the Evening Star. I loved her dearly – but at a distance.'[5] This was in *My Early Life* (that is up to 1906) which he published in 1930, and is probably the most engaging of all his books, using a light and sparkling note of detached irony. The fact that these sentences were written and published nearly fifty years after the period to which they refer gives them a greater not a lesser validity.

They are moreover borne out by the correspondence of the period. Throughout his two years at his first preparatory school (St George's, Ascot, which appears from the disparately independent testimonies of Churchill himself and of the art critic Roger Fry to have been a place of appalling brutality even by the flogging standards of the age), his subsequent three and a half years at a much gentler Brighton establishment, and then his nearly five years at Harrow, there is a constant hoping for visits which did not take place, of wishing for more attention in the future, and of being shunted around rather than of being automatically welcomed at home for short or long holidays.

The forms of letter address are also interesting. Churchill most frequently began his 'My darling Mummy' and ended more variously. A fairly typical second-year Harrow example was 'Good Bye, my own, with love I remain, Your son Winston S Churchill'. She habitually wrote to him, not too infrequently but mostly shortly, 'Dearest Winston' and ended 'Yr loving Mother JSC'.[6]

There were two competitors for writing to him at least equally or more affectionate letters. The first was the Countess of Wilton, in the relevant years a lady in her mid- to late forties, who wrote often, mostly starting 'Dearest Winston' and ending, more significantly 'With best love, Yr ever affecte. deputy mother, Laura Wilton'.[7] The other was Churchill's nurse, Mrs Everest, who was engaged to look after him (and later his brother Jack) within a month or so of his birth. Elizabeth Everest was from the Medway Towns, and one of her lasting influences was to make Churchill feel that Kent was the best county in England. She would have approved (more than Clementine Churchill did) of his acquiring Chartwell twenty-seven years after her death. Before coming to the Churchills she had looked after the small daughter of a Cumberland clergyman, whom Winston retrieved after twenty years to join him at her graveside.

Mrs Everest obviously possessed among other attributes great descriptive power, for she made life in that northern parsonage so vivid to Churchill that, although vicarious, it was one of his most permanent early memories. There is no evidence that a spousely Mr Everest had ever existed, so that her 'Mrs' was purely honorary, like that of many a housekeeper of the period. Although she had a sister (who was married to a prison warder in the Isle of Wight), to whose house she once took Winston to stay, thus giving him, it has been suggested, his only experience of humble life, she was able to concentrate almost all her affection upon the two Churchill boys. She was the central emotional prop of Winston's childhood, and mutual dependence continued throughout his adolescence. The Randolph Churchills had not kept her on after the end of Jack's childhood, but Winston at least maintained strong contact and visited her several times in her final illness.

Mrs Everest's letters to Churchill typically began (21 January 1891, when he was sixteen) 'My darling Winny' and ended 'Lots of love and kisses Fm your loving old woom'.[8] A typical topping and tailing from him to her (from Harrow, July 1890) was 'My darling Old Woom' and 'Good Bye darling, I hope you will enjoy yourself, with love from Winny'.[9] One other person who used 'Winny' (or 'Winnie') was Count Kinsky. On 5 February 1891 he wrote a letter from the Austro-Hungarian Embassy in Belgrave Square of which the content, as well as the salutations, was not without interest: 'I am sending you all the stamps I could scrape together for the moment. Do you want some more later on? If so say so. How is your old head? I hope all right again. I am off to Sandringham tomorrow until Monday. If I have a good thing racing you shall be on. I am going to lunch with Mama now so must be off. Be a good boy and write if you have nothing better to do ... Yours ever, CK'.[10]

Winston Churchill's non-relationship with his father was even more wistful than was his semi-relationship with his mother. Lord Randolph was too exhilarated by politics during his period of success and too depressed by them (and by his health) during his decline to have much time for parenthood. It is one of the supreme ironies that now, more than a century after his death, he should be best known as a father. In life it was always an intensely personal fame, sought and achieved, which was his forte, just as parenthood or any other form of domestic activity certainly was not. The most poignant comment on Winston Churchill's relations with his father is that which he is reported to have made to his own son, another and by no means wholly satisfactory Randolph, in the late 1930s, when that Randolph was twenty-six or twenty-seven. They had a long and maybe fairly alcoholic dinner together, alone at Chartwell. Towards the end Churchill said: 'We have this evening had a longer period of continuous conversation together than the total which I ever had with my father in the whole course of his life.'[11]

If Lord Randolph does not stand very high as a parent, how does he stand, in the perspective of more than a hundred years, as a politician?

Not much better, in my view. He had the gift of insolence, which can be defined as the ability to think up memorably amusing phrases and the nerve to deliver them without fear. It is by no means a negligible gift, but nor is it of the highest order. It is one which he has shared most notably with Disraeli, Joseph Chamberlain and F. E. Smith (Lord Birkenhead). But all of these were in a different category from him for constructive purpose and consistency of belief. Randolph Churchill had some qualities beyond his insolence to make his words resound and his fame increase. He had a memorable name, an idiosyncratic appearance and a good speaking delivery, whether on a provincial platform or in the House of Commons. He also had strong if sporadic private charm, although intermingled with offensive and often pointless rudeness. But did he have underlying qualities beneath his brash and slightly vulgar charisma which raised his performance above political 'pranks', the designation memorably bestowed upon them by Salisbury, the Conservative leader of the last two decades of the nineteenth century? Or was his record just that of an essentially immature young man without much warmth of heart or depth of brain?

The opinions of his major semi-contemporaries inclined much more in the unfavourable direction. Gladstone, the still more commanding Liberal leader, although he paid a surprising tribute to his 'courtliness', thought that he had not 'a single grain of conviction in him except in the abstract' (whatever the last phrase meant). Arthur Balfour, who had been one of the four members of Lord Randolph's Fourth party,* although always a semi-detached one, said that he had 'the manners of a pirate and the courage of a governess'.[12] Salisbury in 1884 (although subsequently giving him major appointments in his first two governments) thought that Randolph was the antithesis of the Sudanese Mahdi who 'pretends to be half mad and is very sane in reality'.[13] The Mahdi was just about to murder General Gordon, to whom the same remark, either way round for that matter, might have been applied.

The real trouble with Randolph Churchill was that nearly all his political attitudes were dictated by opportunism and not by any coherent corpus of belief. Tory Democracy was his central theme. But he had very little idea of what he meant by it, except that he saw it as a good slogan for self-promotion and for the tormenting of the old guard of

---

* A semi-satirical name for the small Tory ginger group which Lord Randolph Churchill set up in the parliament of 1880. It had only four members and was directed about as much against the Conservative leadership as against the Gladstone government.

his party, first Sir Stafford Northcote and then Salisbury himself. He was a powerful demotic orator but it was never very clear to what end he wished to mobilize his working-class audiences. There was a certain 'instinctive rowdyism', as a *Spectator* obituary put it, about his politics. He liked an occasional provincial riot and a disorderly House of Commons. But his attempts to raise the mob for Toryism were essentially sterile. Salisbury's promotion of 'villa Conservatism' was a great deal more rational as well as more successful because it was based on a real confluence of interest. Combined with the creation of the one-member suburban constituencies, a feature of the 1885 electoral settlement which Salisbury had percipiently negotiated with Gladstone, this made a far greater contribution to the solidity of Conservative representation in England, except for the very bad years of 1906, 1945 and 1997, than any forays which Randolph Churchill was attempting.

Lord Randolph's opportunism produced several bewildering shifts of position. In the autumn of 1883 he delivered a speech in Edinburgh which was so hostile to any extension of the franchise that Arthur Balfour, who was sharing the platform with him, felt it necessary gently to repudiate him before the meeting was over. But within a few months he was denouncing the 'mediocrity of an unchanging mind' and advocating the full assimilation of the county to the borough franchise. They may have had something to do with his seeking a seat in radical Birmingham (Woodstock was due to disappear under redistribution), but it probably owed even more to his most natural recipe for political action which can be summarized as 'if at first you don't succeed, shuffle up the cards and try again'. The Edinburgh speech had generally gone down badly.

Still less consistent was Randolph Churchill's attitude to the dominating Irish question. Ireland became increasingly difficult to govern as part of Britain during the early years of the second Gladstone government. Charles Stewart Parnell, a Protestant landlord paradoxically (for much of the agitation was about religion and land tenure), was proving a powerful new leader of the Irish Nationalist party, adept both at rallying crowds in Ireland and at disrupting the proceedings of the House of Commons in London. The Liberal government tried a mixture of mild land reform and Coercion (that is, giving special police and court powers by legislation). Neither was effective, and these failures began to prepare Gladstone's mind for his dramatic 1885 conversion to Irish Home Rule. The issue was complicated by the fact that, whereas in the other three provinces the mass of the population was Celtic and

Catholic, much of Ulster (then the most prosperous part of the country) was inhabited by Presbyterians of Scottish origin who preferred to be governed from London rather than from Dublin. The Scots Presbyterians were sometimes known as Orangemen after King William of Orange, who had facilitated their settlement following the Battle of the Boyne in 1690.

Lord Randolph became a principal agent of the Conservative alliance with Parnell over the summer and autumn of 1885. This alliance brought down the second Gladstone government and then garnered the Irish vote in England for the Conservatives, particularly in Lancashire. In pursuit of this objective Lord Randolph sought to undermine the 'law and order' decisions of the fifth Earl Spencer, Gladstone's immediately preceding Viceroy in Dublin, and by so doing did much to swing both Spencer and Sir William Harcourt (former Home Secretary and soon to be Chancellor of the Exchequer) to Home Rule. In and out of government Randolph Churchill had opposed Coercion Acts, despite the fact that by 1885 at latest the only realistic alternatives for British policy on Ireland were either Home Rule or a prolonged period of 'resolute government'. Balfour, despite his early sobriquet of 'pretty Fanny', and although he was semi-despised as an uncertain ally by Lord Randolph, had the firmness of mind to see this and the ruthlessness to provide the harsh resolution as Chief Secretary for Ireland from 1887 to 1892. Churchill havered between the two. He had been tolerant of Irish obstruction in the House of Commons, for he liked parliamentary mischief. He had been party to several murky negotiations with Parnell. And he was privately contemptuous of obscurantist Ulster politicians.

When therefore he went to Belfast in February 1886, whipped up religious as well as political intolerance and in a subsequent public letter coined his brilliant but wholly irresponsible slogan 'Ulster will fight; Ulster will be right', there was a widespread suspicion that he was motivated more by opportunism than by principle. And such suspicion would not have been lessened had the terms of a letter which he wrote at the time to his Dublin friend Lord Justice Fitzgibbon been known: 'I decided some time ago that, if the G.O.M. [Gladstone's sobriquet, short for Grand Old Man] went for Home Rule, the Orange card would be the one to play. Please God it may turn out to be the ace of trumps and not the two. . . .'

An even more extreme example of Randolph Churchill's unprincipled audacity had been provided a few years earlier by his exploitation of the Bradlaugh issue at the beginning of the 1880 parliament. The performance on this issue of the majority of the House of Commons was a supreme example of Victorian hypocrisy. The atheist and somewhat self-righteous (but otherwise admirable) Charles Bradlaugh had been elected member for Northampton. A cross-party majority of the House of Commons made asses of themselves by refusing to allow him either to affirm or to take the oath (he was ecumenically willing to do either), despite the fact that he was twice subsequently returned at Northampton bye-elections precipitated by this intolerance, and then compounded rather than mitigated this foolishness by passing a resolution of sympathy and an expunging of these decisions eleven years later when Bradlaugh lay dying.

The greatest responsibility for these parliamentary antics rested upon Lord Randolph Churchill. Caring little for religion himself he saw the issue as an opportunity to run rings around Gladstone, who combined deep Anglican conviction with a growing tolerance. Given the total cynicism of his whole enterprise, Lord Randolph conducted it brilliantly – and, which was the redeeming feature, very funnily. He managed to portray the Grand Old Anglican as having (by supporting Bradlaugh's rights) become converted to atheism, republicanism and contraception, and he did so with such wit and impudence that most of the House laughed with him, and against the Prime Minister, at this preposterous claim. More seriously he took a great deal of the edge of authority off the first couple of years of a government which had just been returned with a majority of over a hundred.

There were some counterbalancing virtues to Lord Randolph. He was by no means such a bad minister as might have been expected. As Secretary of State for India for seven months in the second half of 1885 he was on the whole liked by his officials. They were impressed by his capacity for hard work, his speed of comprehension and his surprising courtesy in dealing with them. He also resisted the will of the Queen to appoint her second son, the Duke of Connaught, most inappropriately as army commander in the Bombay Presidency, and secured, again contrary to the royal wish, the appointment of General Roberts, an altogether more serious soldier, although one always temperamentally committed to a 'forward' policy, to the higher post of Commander-in-Chief in India as a whole. Roberts and the Viceroy, Lord Dufferin, pushed Lord Randolph to the key event of his brief Secretaryship of State, which was the annexation of Upper Burma. This enabled Dufferin to add Ava (the ancient kingdom of which was the core of the added territory) to his title, but to Churchill's record it merely added another contradiction. He had previously been strongly in favour of imperial restraint and economy: he was the only prominent Conservative to oppose Gladstone's bombardment of Alexandria in 1882.

Lord Randolph's India Office term was also marked by his inability to separate imperial administration from the polemics of internal politics. His presentation of the Indian budget to the House of Commons for instance, which was otherwise more lucid and informative than was usual, contained an ill-fitting and violent attack upon Lord Ripon, Dufferin's predecessor, whom Churchill had a few months previously praised in extravagant terms. This caused a mixture of uneasiness and resentment. The nadir was however reached during a speech in Birmingham (where he was unsuccessfully contending the Central division against John Bright) when he denounced the offensive spectacle of 'three Bengali baboos' sitting on Bright's platform in the august surroundings of the neo-Grecian town hall of that city. For the sake of a cheap phrase he exploded his reputation as a friend of educated Indians.

Both these events nevertheless contributed to the satisfaction of his most constant and dominating desire, which was to attract attention. Towards this goal he was greatly aided by the newspapers, who fully recognized his star capacity, even if it was that of a short-term and shooting one. In that November (of 1885) he was graded as 'Class One' by the Central News Agency, a category which he shared only with Gladstone, Salisbury and Joseph Chamberlain. It meant that his platform speeches got almost verbatim reporting, as opposed to the one column which was the ration of Hartington, Dilke, Granville and Spencer, or the half-column which was the standard allocation of Harcourt, Hicks Beach and several other leading politicians.

This *réclame* led to Salisbury somewhat reluctantly giving him the second position in his second government, which was formed in July 1886. 'He feared Lord Randolph Churchill must be Chancellor of the Exchequer and Leader [of the House of Commons], which I did not like,' was Queen Victoria's succinct summary of the position in her journal entry for the 25th of that month.*[14] He was thirty-seven, and was the youngest Chancellor since Pitt in 1782. Gladstone had been almost forty-three when he first occupied the office, although Palmerston had refused it at the age of twenty-five in 1809. Salisbury however regarded Churchill's mental age as well below the evidence of his birth certificate. 'His character', he wrote, admittedly just after Churchill's

* She added: 'He is so mad and odd and has also bad health.'

resignation at the end of the year, 'is quite untamed. Both in impulsiveness and variability and in a tendency which can be described by the scholastic word *vulgaris*, he presents the characteristics of extreme youth.'

Nevertheless Churchill's diligence and even adroitness in leading the House of Commons earned some plaudits. He got the necessary business through and Parliament into a six-month recess by early August. He then occupied the non-parliamentary months in four principal ways. First he went on an 'incognito' tour of Berlin, Vienna and Paris. The alleged incognito of 'Mr Spencer', far from preserving anonymity, greatly increased press interest in his peregrinations, of which the main object appeared to be the stirring up of trouble for his old butt, Stafford Northcote, reincarnated as the Earl of Iddesleigh and installed as Foreign Secretary. Lord Randolph's second activity was the making of three vastly publicized October speeches, one at Dartford in suburban Kent and two at Bradford, where the National Union of Conservative Associations, which he liked to regard as a private army useful for reminding Salisbury of the independent power of his nominal lieutenant, was then meeting. On these various occasions it was the tone rather than the content (which was vague) of his speeches which made him seem as though he was not long destined for office. He spoke as an independent commander who might easily give his troops orders to be off in an opposite direction as soon as he had precisely determined what direction that should be.

His third occupation of the autumn, and one to which he took with ease and relish, was quarrelling with his colleagues. With Lord George Hamilton at the Admiralty and with the great newsagent W. H. Smith at the War Office, there was a certain rational basis for the quarrels. He was determined to slash their expenditure estimates. But he also picked gratuitous quarrels with at least another seven ministers, including Hicks Beach, his immediate predecessor as Tory Chancellor, who had graciously made way for him, and was his most friendlily disposed colleague. And, as though to make sure that he was leaving no one out, he wrote a November letter to the Prime Minister expressing general disillusionment with him, his government and the low intellectual level and class prejudices of the whole Conservative party in the House of Commons.

His fourth activity sounds more constructive but, in view of the logical consequences of the other three, proved equally sterile. He put together by early December a complete budget for presentation in

April. It was a restless budget in the sense that it pulled up almost every plant in the garden, looked at its roots and replanted it in a somewhat different place. But it did not seek to alter the shape of the garden. It contained several attractive measures, including income tax down from eight to fivepence in the pound and the abolition of the tea duty. This was balanced by a mild degree of improvidence (a reduction in the sinking fund for redeeming government debt), some upward tinkering with non-regressive indirect taxes (wine, horses and cartridges), and a readjustment (mainly in favour of younger sons!) of death duties.

It was an extraordinary feat of mechanical self-discipline to have done it all at that stage, and it duly impressed most of his Treasury officials, who (like the India Office ones) found him courteous, comprehending and quick. But it was not a tribute to his political antennae. The idea that a budget could be sealed up nearly half a year in advance, put on ice and taken out in perfect condition and ready for delivery at the last moment was unrealistic even in the days when Chancellors did not deal with macro-economics and when Britain's currency was splendidly isolated. Churchill even made the mistake of taking it to the Cabinet four months in advance, thus sacrificing the Chancellor's normal pre-rogative of presenting his colleagues with a stark and urgent choice of his budget or no budget at all. It was coolly received. The coolness further alienated him from his colleagues. Within a few days he plunged into his 22 December letter of resignation. Almost certainly he intended it as a ploy and not a final act. But Salisbury had already had more than enough. He was a better if quieter tactician than Churchill. And he was not a man to resist the suicide of a nuisance. Lord Randolph was out, and out for good.

There were a few flickerings but not more from the dying volcano during the remaining eight years of his life. 'He was the chief mourner at his own protracted funeral,' was the terrible phrase of Rosebery, always better at phrases than at being Prime Minister (1894–5), about this closing period of Lord Randolph's life. When Lord Randolph died in January 1895, Winston Churchill was just over twenty years of age. He was old enough to have known his father well. But he had not done so. He compensated by enveloping in a roseate glow his almost unknown and, when he did know him, preoccupied, ill-tempered and discouraging parent. His filial biography, mostly written nine or ten years after his father's death, achieved the remarkable feat of being partisan, often unconvincing, yet still fresh and wholly enjoyable to read nearly a hundred years after it was begun. It did a great deal for Lord

Randolph's posthumous reputation, although that already had a curious survival capacity. His reputation, or at least his fame, went on beyond its deserts. A more realistic appraisal is that Lord Randolph had been unique since Pitt in attracting so much political attention while dying so young. But Pitt was Prime Minister for nineteen of his forty-six years. Churchill's proportion of the same lifespan in even subordinate office was confined to eleven months. It could justifiably be said that his career was without rival in making so much noise and achieving so little. The main legacy that he left to his elder son (there was very little money) was a desire to cut a figure, accompanied by a conviction that he too was likely to die young, and that he had therefore better be quick about it.

This was Winston Churchill's somewhat doubtful provenance. Some of the emotional pulls and disappointments of his childhood have already been discussed. It was clearly not a notably cosseted one, and justified John Grigg's claim that Lloyd George's rural Welsh background, even though notably non-affluent, with the early death of his schoolteacher father leaving him dependent upon his village-cobbler maternal uncle, was nonetheless more privileged in matters which count to a child than was the ducal ambience of Winston Churchill.[15] He was lucky in Mrs Everest, perhaps less so in his schools. The brutality of the first one has been described. The second balanced its softness by a lack of intellectual rigour. The third was Harrow. Throughout there is the strong impression that his lack of academic quality was not nearly as great as has generally been presented. He was certainly not a natural classicist. Nor did he balance this deficiency with being a natural mathematician. But he loved narrative history and he had exceptional interest in and aptitude for the use of the English language. This was perceived and appreciated by the more intelligent of his teachers. They may not have recognized his potential ability to compose some of the most resonant speeches in the history of the language. But they did recognize that there was something unusual in him, which was well worth trying to bring out. The most successful of these 'mind-openers' was Robert Somervell, the lower-school English master. As Churchill put it in *My Early Life*, written, to use the phrase of the Harrow school song, forty years on:

> Mr. Somervell – a most delightful man, to whom my debt is great – was
> charged with the duty of teaching the stupidest boys the most disregarded
> thing – namely, to write mere English. He knew how to do it. He taught

it as no one else has ever taught it. . . . As I remained in the Third Fourth [a very disregarded form] three times as long as anyone else, I had three times as much of it. I learned it thoroughly. Thus I got into my bones the essential structure of the ordinary British sentence – which is a noble thing.*[16]

Somervell was not the only master who took a special interest in Churchill. J. E. C. Welldon followed Montagu Butler (the great-uncle of R. A. Butler, who was translated to the Mastership of Trinity College, Cambridge) as headmaster of Harrow in 1886. Churchill apparently first attracted Welldon's attention by faultlessly reciting 1,200 lines of Macaulay's *Lays of Ancient Rome*. For this he gained a prize open to the whole school, although still languishing in the lowest form. The trouble was the classical dominance of the period and Churchill's combination of unwillingness and inability to wrap his mind around Greek and Latin grammar and texts. A little later Welldon attempted to repair this deficiency by giving him special classical tuition for three brief quarter-hours a week. It did not work. Churchill remained impervious to the subtleties of Latin construction. 'Mr Welldon seemed to be physically pained by a mistake being made . . .' the pupil wrote many years later. 'I remember that later on Mr Asquith used to have just the same sort of look on his face when I sometimes adorned a Cabinet discussion by bringing out one of my few but faithful Latin quotations.'[17]

By the time of his special Welldon lessons Churchill had been placed in the army form, in which he spent his last three years at Harrow. This was a segregated mixed-age group, which he says resulted in his being 'withdrawn from the ordinary movement of the school from form to form'. This sudden lurch of a decision appears to have resulted from his lack of obvious scholastic prowess and his growing interest in all things military. This impressed itself on his father, who in a rare visit to his playroom witnessed his collection and deployment of 1,500 lead soldiers. The playroom visit coincided with Lord Randolph's growing conviction that Winston was not clever enough for the Bar. The idea that he was an uninterested and uninteresting dullard was however almost entirely

* Somervell had two sons. One, David Somervell, an Oxford history don, published an exculpatory study of Baldwin in 1953. The other, Sir Donald (later Lord) Somervell, was Solicitor-General under Baldwin before becoming first Neville Chamberlain's and then Winston Churchill's Attorney-General from 1936 to 1945, momentarily Home Secretary in Churchill's 'Caretaker' Tory government of that summer, and finally a Lord of Appeal in Ordinary.

misplaced. He could write very good general essays. His memory was phenomenal, as was shown by his Macaulay feat. And, whenever his enthusiasm was engaged, as it mostly was by history (perhaps particularly military history) and English literature, and was not inhibited by the baleful barriers of classics and mathematics, he performed well. These qualities were perceptively recognized by Welldon, who not only gave him the unsuccessful special lessons but also corresponded with him at length during his subaltern years in India.

Harrow was then a more famous school than it is today. It was much nearer to being on a level with Eton as a ruling-class school. It had not grown out of a religious collegiate foundation as was the case with Eton and Winchester, and was always a 'school' and not a 'college'. This perhaps made it (at least overtly) more Mammon-orientated. But, as it had already produced five Prime Ministers, including the two nineteenth-century stars of Peel and Palmerston, and had in the pipeline another two in the shape of Baldwin and Churchill himself, it had a considerable political record. It did not provide Churchill with many of his close future collaborators: Leo Amery, with whom his relations were always prickly, and David Margesson, the dreaded Chief Whip, were about the nearest (and not very near) to this category. But it did give him both his favourite general of the Second World War (Field Marshal the Earl Alexander of Tunis, as he became) and his favourite private secretary (J. R. Colville). Churchill was not paternally loyal to Harrow: he sent his own son to Eton, without notably fortunate results. But he became sentimentally attached to his old school. After his visit to School Songs there in December 1940, when he was ecstatically received at an emotionally impressionable period of his life, he developed the habit of attending this nostalgic and for him satisfactorily tear-making occasion for most of the remaining twenty-four years of his life.

Harrow was not particularly good at preparing Churchill for the Royal Military Academy at Sandhurst. He had to make three attempts, and was removed after the second failure to a well-known crammer called Captain James, in the Earl's Court Road in London. Although his cramming was delayed for several months by a severe kidney-rupturing accident resulting from jumping (to avoid capture in a game) thirty feet from a bridge in Dorset, the Captain's 'renowned system of intensive poultry farming' eventually worked and Churchill succeeded in being accepted for a cavalry cadetship. This had the advantage of demanding fewer marks than an infantry one, and the disadvantage that life in a cavalry mess was considerably more expensive. Churchill had done well in his history and (more surprisingly) his chemistry papers. In others he had done badly: 'I had to find another useful card.' He chose mathematics over Latin and French, the other possible choices, and by a great act of will he quickly learned enough to qualify. Then this alien knowledge 'passed away like the phantasmagoria of a fevered dream'.[18] But he was in, and he went to the Royal Military Academy in September 1893, remaining there for fifteen months.

Churchill did well at Sandhurst. Although he had just scraped in he passed out eighth in his batch of 150. He also proved himself good on and with horses. He left in December 1894, nine months after the end of Gladstone's last premiership. Lord Randolph, having returned from an unsuccessful health-restoring world trip on Christmas Eve, died on 24 January 1895. Winston Churchill was commissioned as a second lieutenant in the 4th Hussars in February. His pay was little more than £150 a year (although nearly £300 in India, where his regiment was about to go), but he needed at least another £500 (approximately £25,000 at today's values) to live up to the style of the regiment. There was not much money available from his father's estate. He still had his mother, 'forty, young, beautiful and fascinating'[19] as he later described her at that time, but financially another drain, although strong on 'networking' influence. Otherwise he was on his own.

2

SUBALTERN OF EMPIRE AND
JOURNALIST OF OPPORTUNITY

THE 4TH HUSSARS disembarked at Bombay in early October 1896. Churchill thus arrived in India at the high point of empire, eight months before Queen Victoria's Diamond Jubilee. But he was never, either in the way he passed his time or in the assumptions of his thought, a remotely typical junior cavalry officer. He had a high romantic view of the monarchy and the Empire, but for the rest he was almost the antithesis of his kind. He did not welcome an ordered and leisurely life. He was conscious of the inadequacies of his education and intellectual knowledge, and eager to repair them. He was instinctively challenging of the conventional wisdom of the army, and often of the repute and military skills of famous generals. So far from wishing to be accepted as a typical and well-fitting member of the mess, earning plaudits for his good-mannered conformity, his dominating desire was to attract the greatest possible attention to himself, both on the local and on the world scene.

His flamboyant impatience was at least accompanied by enough good sense to see that his future did not lie in diligently awaiting promotion to captain, to major, to colonel, and then maybe to general officer rank. The military virtue which he abundantly possessed was personal bravery. His love of danger gave him a recklessness which was personally admirable but would not, at this stage of his life, have made him a confidence-giving commander of more than a handful of men. His addiction to polo (the only ball game which throughout his life stirred his interest) was almost the only other link with his confrères. But it was an intense effort of competitive willpower rather than a desire for recreational pleasure which drew him to play an obsessively large number of chukkas.

Given this last proclivity India was a happy overseas posting for Churchill. From the moment of his regiment's arrival at Bombay he approached everything with a mixture of zest and bombast. His eagerness to get ashore after a voyage of twenty-three days resulted in the dislocation of his right shoulder in a too impatient effort to lever himself from a plunging launch on to some slippery harbour steps. It could easily be reset, but remained for the rest of his life likely to come out again at unexpected and inconvenient moments. He maintained that it once nearly did so when he made a too expansive gesture in the House of Commons.

On his third night in the sub-continent he, one other subaltern and three more senior officers of the newly arrived regiment were summoned to dine with the Governor of the Bombay Presidency, the appropriately titled Lord Sandhurst. As Churchill wrote over thirty years later, no doubt with a deliberate degree of self-mocking exaggeration:

> His Excellency, after the health of the Queen Empress had been drunk and dinner was over, was good enough to ask my opinion upon several matters, and considering the magnificent character of his hospitality, I thought it would be unbecoming in me not to reply fully. I have forgotten the particular points of British and Indian affairs upon which he sought my counsel; all I can remember is that I responded generously. There were indeed moments when he seemed willing to impart his own views; but I thought it would be ungracious to put him to so much trouble; and he very readily subsided. He kindly sent his aide-de-camp with us to make sure we found our way back to camp all right.[1]

Churchill and the 4th Hussars then entrained for Bangalore, the Aldershot or main military depot of South India, which at a height of 3,000 feet was thought to provide very favourable climatic and other circumstances for regimental life. He settled into a large bungalow with two other subalterns, with all their needs looked after by a fleet of Indian servants. He also settled into a routine of duties which amounted to no more than three hours a day and were all completed by 10.30 a.m. Apart from those early-morning hours and recreational polo in the late afternoon, the rest of the day was free.

The 4th Hussars stayed in India for eight and a half years of this regime, but Winston Churchill effectively stayed for only nineteen months, and into this period he fitted two London leaves of a few months each, three winter visits to Calcutta which involved four days of travel each way, an expedition to Hyderabad as part of a triumphant team in a polo tournament, and participation, away from his regiment, in a hazardous but journalistically productive North-West Frontier expedition.

Even more remarkable than this impressively restless record, however, was how he spent his time during the months of tranquillity at Bangalore. At the same time that he was behaving with the utmost self-confidence to the Viceroy, to the Governor of Bombay and no doubt to his commanding officer, assuming an almost divine right to be present at every scene of military action in the world and pulling both his own and his mother's strings to get to them, he also decided that he was seriously under-educated and ought to do something about it. This was perhaps the moment when Winston Churchill's unique and paradoxical qualities, which were in sum sufficient to make him a very great man, first clearly exhibited themselves. These were his self-confidence and his self-centredness. Convinced that he was (or at least ought to be) a man of destiny, he had no desire to pass his days sharing the intellectual indolence of his fellow subalterns. There was also the insight to realize what he did not know. And there was the willpower, in unfavourable circumstances and by naive methods, to try to correct his deficiencies.

He was fleetingly attracted by the idea of resigning his commission and going to Oxford, where he would by this time have been about five years late. At least it would have been rather less of a drain on the family finances than life in the 4th Hussars. As he put it in a January 1897 letter to his mother (the fully preserved correspondence with whom was at this stage more substantial than during his schooldays): 'I envy Jack the liberal education of an University.* I find my literary tastes growing day by day – and if only I knew Latin and Greek – I think I would leave the army and try and take my degree in History, Philosophy and Economics. But I cannot face parsing and Latin prose again. What a strange inversion of fortune – that I should be a soldier and Jack at college.'[2]

However he received no maternal encouragement to overcome the classical lions standing in his path, and instead set about a determined home university course. Here Lady Randolph did help, not as a postal tutor but as an efficient despatcher of requested books. At first his diet, and therefore his requests, were confined almost exclusively to Gibbon and Macaulay. She sent him the eight volumes of *The Decline and Fall of the Roman Empire*, followed by twelve of Macaulay – eight of history and five of essays. He got through them all, at a steady rather than a galloping rate: 'Fifty pages of Macaulay and 25 of Gibbon every day',

---

* There was a current proposition, which however came to nothing, that Churchill's younger brother, then in his last year at Harrow, should go to Oxford.

he wrote in February. On the whole he was more impressed by Gibbon – Macaulay 'is not half so solid'.[3] But he found virtues in each of them: 'Macaulay crisp and forcible – Gibbon stately and impressive. Both are fascinating and show what a fine language English is – since it can be pleasing in styles so different.'[4] While 'pleasing' may be thought a surprisingly weak word for Churchill to have used in this context, there can be little doubt of the combined and permanent impact of both of them, different although he may have found their styles, upon his writing and his oratory.

When he moved outside this declamatory duo his quest for knowledge continued to be voracious but less discriminatory. He got heavily diverted into and substantially excited by Winwood Reade's *The Martyrdom of Man*, a quasi-philosophical (and anti-religious) work of very doubtful permanent interest or value. Churchill's self-education programme is curiously reminiscent of that of a very different specimen of humanity who nonetheless reached equally high political office, and for whom, nearly fifty years later, Churchill came to have considerable respect, namely Harry S. Truman. Truman as a young man made himself biographically very well read. He was particularly good not only on the history of the American presidency but also on the Roman emperors and on great military commanders of every epoch. But he had gained it all by solitary and untutored reading. As a result he was familiar with the spelling but not the pronunciation of many proper names and could come out with the most surprising versions. That was not exactly Churchill's problem. The officers of the 4th Hussars may not have had much depth of historical or classical knowledge, but they knew what were the accepted pronunciation of the names of those of whom they had heard. However, the analogy did hold in another respect: neither Churchill nor Truman had in their early life anyone to knock the corners off the knowledge they were solitarily and a little laboriously accumulating. Churchill's equivalent of Truman mispronunciations was regarding *The Martyrdom of Man* (which was a great favourite of his colonel) as a major even if misguided book.

For the most part his excursions outside the solid base of Gibbon and Macaulay were better judged and comprised such classics as Adam Smith's *Wealth of Nations*, Charles Darwin's *Origin of Species*, Jowett's translation of Plato's *Republic*, and *The Constitutional History of England* by Henry Hallam (the father of the *jeune homme fatal* who so excited the mutual jealousy of Gladstone and Tennyson). In addition to this formidable course in background knowledge Churchill also set about the pumping into his veins of undiluted (and undigested) political facts. He got his mother to send him twenty-seven volumes of the *Annual Register*, in which, beginning with Disraeli's second government of 1874–80, he studied the bare details of every major parliamentary debate and legislative development of these years of his very early childhood. He then summarized the accounts and gave his own moderately progressive judgements on how he would have spoken and voted on each issue. It was an impressive work of political exegesis, pointing to powerful application, an assurance that he should prepare himself for a great role, and a somewhat unsophisticated view of how best to do so.

This Indian correspondence with his mother was also notable in three other ways. First, his position as an intellectual tyro did not in the least inhibit him from the most sweeping comments on people and issues. Thus on 1 January 1897, during his long train journey back from his Calcutta Christmas, he dismissed the Liberal-appointed Viceroy: 'The Elgins are very unpopular out here and make a very poor show after the Lansdownes. The evil that a Radical Government does lives after it. All the great offices of state have to be filled out of the scrappy remnant of the Liberal Peers. And so you get Elgin Viceroy. They tell me that they are too stiff and pompous for words – and "Calcutta Society" cannot find an epithet to describe them by.'[5]

An irony was that only eight years later, when Churchill became a junior minister in the Campbell-Bannerman government, Lord Elgin was to be his Secretary of State at the Colonial Office. Perhaps Elgin had not taken enough notice of him in Calcutta. But Churchill's Tory partisanship of 1897 led to no admiration for the rising stars of that party. Eight weeks later he wrote:

> Among the leaders of the Tory party are two whom I despise and detest as politicians above all others – Mr Balfour and George Curzon. The one – a languid, lazy, lack-a-daisical cynic – the unmonumental figurehead of the Conservative party; the other the spoiled darling of politics – blown with conceit – insolent from undeserved success – the typification of the superior Oxford prig. It is to that pair all the criminal muddles of the last 15 months should be ascribed.

Their chief he treated somewhat but not much better. 'Lord Salisbury, an able and obstinate man, who joins the brain of a statesman to the delicate susceptibilities of a mule, has been encouraged to blunder tactlessly along until nearly every section of the Union party and nearly every cabinet in Europe has been irritated or offended.'[6]

Following these views it is not perhaps surprising that he wrote on 6 April: 'There are no lengths to which I would not go in opposing [our Machiavellian Government] were I in the House of Commons. I am a Liberal in all but name. My views excite the pious horror of the Mess. Were it not for Home Rule – to which I will never consent – I would enter Parliament as a Liberal. As it is – Tory Democracy will have to be the standard under which I shall range myself.'[7] Three months later, when he was home on a leave obtained remarkably quickly after arriving in India, it was under this standard that he got himself invited to deliver the first platform speech of his life, at a fête of the Primrose League, a Conservative fringe organization, on the edge of Bath. It was a good political speech, well phrased, quite amusing and with plenty of cues for applause. It was substantially reported in the *Bath Daily Chronicle* and nearly as well in the London *Morning Post*. But it did not give much indication that he was 'a Liberal in all but name'. 'The British workman has more to hope for from the rising tide of Tory democracy than from the dried-up drain-pipe of Radicalism'[8] was perhaps the quintessential phrase.

The second topic which dominated his maternal correspondence was money. Here, in contrast with political judgements, it was Lady Randolph who took the lead. Her most reproving letter was dated 26 February (1897), a day after Churchill had blandly denounced Balfour and Curzon. 'It is with very unusual feelings that I sit down to write to you my weekly letter,' it ominously began.

> Generally it is a pleasure – but this time it is quite the reverse. . . . I went to Cox's this morning & find out that not only you have anticipated the whole of your quarter's allowance due this month but £45 besides – & now this cheque for £50 – & that *you knew* you had nothing at the bank. The manager told me they had warned you that they would not let you overdraw & the next mail brought this cheque. I *must* say I think it is *too* bad of you – indeed it is hardly honourable knowing as you do that you are dependent on me & that I give you the biggest allowance I *possibly can*, more than I can afford. . . . If you cannot live on yr allowance from me & yr pay you will have to leave the 4th Hussars. *I cannot* increase yr allowance.[9]

Again on 5 March she reverted to the subject with frank precision: 'Out of £2,700 a year [approximately £135,000 at present-day values] £800 of it goes to you 2 boys, £410 for house rent & stables, which leaves me £1,500 for everything – taxes, servants, stables, food, dress, travelling – & now I have to pay the interest on money borrowed. I *really* fear for the future.'[10] And then she wrote once more on 25 March, no doubt only coincidentally from the Hôtel Metropole, Monte Carlo, saying that his last letter had arrived at 'a bad moment & found me more than usually hard up'.[11] Churchill, probably wisely, allowed these various complaints to flow off his back. The fact that Anglo-Indian mails were delivered only three weeks after despatch took something of the edge off them. By the time they arrived the mood may have changed. Out of these pressures Churchill evolved two firm rules which he followed faithfully for the rest of his life. The first was that expenditure should be determined by needs (generously interpreted) rather than by resources. He stood the famous maxim of Dickens's Mr Micawber on its head. Second, he decided that when the gap between income and expenditure became uncomfortably wide the spirited solution must always be to increase income rather than to reduce expenditure.

Such a buoyant view of financial problems made an important contribution to the third topic in his correspondence with his mother. This was his desire that she should use all possible influence to get him to every scene of military action in the world. This was partly because of a reckless adventurism and partly because of a shrewd appraisal that he could earn £15 or £20 a 'letter' (as articles from a front were then mostly described) for front-line despatches to the *Morning Post* or the *Daily Telegraph*. There is not the slightest evidence that Lady Randolph ever offered her charms to Sir Bindon Blood or Sir Herbert Kitchener (as he then was) or Lord Roberts, which might have been unwelcome to at least two of them, or of her own willingness to accommodate them within George Moore's exaggerated 'two hundred', but there is the strong impression that Winston Churchill wanted her to use every guile to get him to the most exposed positions on the frontiers of empire.

His first experience, however, had been on the shrinking frontiers of the Spanish Empire rather than of the still expanding British ones. In the autumn of 1895, very soon after his Hussars commissioning, he set out for Cuba and the guerrilla war against the local 'rebels' which the Spanish were desultorily waging. His father's old Fourth party colleague Sir Henry Drummond Wolf, who had become ambassador to Madrid, was mobilized to procure access to the battlefields for Churchill and his subaltern colleague Reggie Barnes (later a major-general) to observe the activities of the Spanish forces. Winston Churchill celebrated his twenty-first birthday under mild fire. This he regarded as a very satisfactory concatenation. And his mother had a role on his way there,

for he and Barnes had been met on the quayside in New York by
Bourke Cockran, who had undoubtedly been one of her successful
admirers, and was equally undoubtedly an American turn-of-the-century
politician of interest. He had been elected to the House of Representatives in 1890 and he had made a run to secure the Democratic
Presidential nomination for himself rather than Grover Cleveland in
1892. In 1895 he was in the course of changing sides, and in 1896
supported McKinley, the Republican nominee. He was (needless to say)
rich. He was half an East Coast gentleman and half a Tammany Hall
politico. He was a powerful orator and consummate politician from
whom Churchill learned much, and with whom he continued to corre-
spond long after their quayside encounter.

Cockran made a profound impact upon Churchill. As late as 1932,
when he put together a collection of essays entitled *Thoughts and
Adventures*, Churchill wrote:

> I must record the strong impression which this remarkable man made
> upon my untutored mind. I have never seen his like, or in some respects
> his equal. With his enormous head, gleaming eyes and flexible counten-
> ance, he looked uncommonly like the portraits of Charles James Fox. It
> was not my fortune to hear any of his orations, but his conversation, in
> point, in pith, in rotundity, in antithesis, and in comprehension, exceeded
> anything I have ever heard.[12]

He took Churchill to stay at his Fifth Avenue residence just off the
south-east corner of Central Park, a surprisingly up-town location for
the 1890s on a site from which sprang first the old Savoy Plaza Hotel
around 1900 and then the General Motors complex in 1968. Cockran
gave a stimulating dinner party for Churchill on his first evening ashore,
and generally entertained him so interestingly and generously as to
imbue him with a lasting sense of the excitement of New York. 'This is
a very great country my dear Jack,' he wrote to his brother.[13] And to his
mother: 'They really make rather a fuss of us here and extend the most
lavish hospitality. We are members of all the Clubs and one person
seems to vie with another in trying to make our time pleasant. . . .'[14]
The electricity of New York in that mid-autumn week just before his
twenty-first birthday was probably of even greater significance for his
future life than his baptism of fire in Cuba. The credit for making this
impact so strong upon this future honorary citizen of the United States
must rest largely with Bourke Cockran.

Churchill's second martial venture was with the Malakand Field

Force against rebellious Pathan tribesmen in the Swat Valley close up against the Afghanistan frontier of India. He heard the news of the outbreak of the uprising and of the consequent despatch of a punitive British expedition of three brigades 'on the lawns of Goodwood in lovely weather'* at the end of July 1897. The expedition was to be commanded by the splendidly named Sir Bindon Blood, then a major-general, who, in spite of participating in every campaign from the Zulu War of 1879 to his retirement in 1907, managed to live until the age of ninety-seven, dying five days after Churchill became Prime Minister in 1940. He matched Churchill himself in his ability to combine reckless exposure with extreme longevity. Of more immediate relevance however was the fact that a year or so before Churchill had extracted from Blood at a country-house party a loose promise that if ever he commanded another expedition he would allow the young cornet of Hussars to come with him.

The looseness of the promise did not deter Churchill. Within forty-eight hours of his Goodwood news, having telegraphed Sir Bindon but without a reply, he cut off two weeks of his leave and left Charing Cross Station on the Indian Mail train to Brindisi. 'I only just caught the train; but I caught it in the best of spirits.'[15] He then spent rather over a month in the most hectic travelling. His spirits slightly sagged when he got no telegraphic reply from Blood at either Brindisi or Aden, when the Red Sea was 'stifling', and when the ship provided neither tolerable food nor adequate ventilation. But they rose again when, at Bombay, he received an ambiguously encouraging telegram from Blood: 'Very difficult; no vacancies; come up as a correspondent; will try to fit you in. B.B.'[16] This was enough, supplemented only by a subsequent letter in the same vein, to sustain him for the thirty-six-hour journey to Banga-lore, to persuade his indulgent colonel to let him go (presumably martial spirit and experience in young officers was welcomed), and to send him

---

* It is surprising that, during this English leave, Churchill paid so much attention to race meetings. Apart from this Goodwood excursion he twice wrote in the early spring saying how much he hoped to be back for the Epsom Derby meeting. No doubt it was partly due to his general equine enthusiasm of the period, although subsequently, while he continued for another quarter-century to play polo, he never showed much enthusiasm for racing until his son-in-law Christopher Soames led him back to the sport as a minor owner in the late 1940s. Partly also, no doubt, it was that the cool enclosures at Epsom, Ascot or Goodwood came to epitomize for him the contrast with the hot and dusty Deccan, and that they also provided very good opportunities for 'networking'.

off on a still more formidable journey to the north, accompanied only by what he described as 'my dressing boy and campaigning kit'.

He went to the Bangalore railway station and asked for a ticket to Nowshera, which was the railhead for the Malakand expedition, but which sounded like a more than passable imitation of 'nowhere'. Then, in his own words:

> I had the curiosity to ask how far it was. The polite Indian [booking clerk] consulted a railway time table and impassively answered, 2,028 miles. . . . This meant a five days' journey in the worst of the heat. I was alone; but with plenty of books, the time passed not unpleasantly. Those large leather-lined Indian railway carriages, deeply shuttered and blinded from the blistering sun and kept fairly cool by a circular wheel of wet straw which turned from time to time, were well adapted to the local conditions. I spent five days in a dark padded moving cell, reading mostly by lamplight or by some jealously admitted ray of glare.[17]

His determined desire to see action was incontestable.

What were the motives? Some he shared with most of his (nominal) kind. Cavalry subalterns in the year of the Queen–Empress's Diamond Jubilee and at the peak of empire, were mostly brave, anxious to gain battle experience and to win medals and 'clasps'. But few of them would have exerted themselves, as Churchill did, and travelled almost continuously, as he also did, for nearly five weeks and at their own expense to get to a fighting front. They would have lacked both the energy and the effrontery. Fame was his constant spur, and the best route to this that he saw at the time was through his writing. He was happy, even exhilarated, to run considerable risks to provide himself with good copy. The campaign in which he participated was at once a hazardous and a brutal one. From the point of view of his journalism it was a moderate success. He was accredited both by the (Indian) *Pioneer* and by the *Daily Telegraph*. But the latter paid him only £5 (£250 today) a column as against the £15 or £20 which he had been confidently expecting a few months before.

Much more important than these despatches, however, was the fact that his experiences in and around the Swat Valley led to his first book, accurately rather than imaginatively entitled *The Story of the Malakand Field Force*. He was with Blood and his troops for about six weeks. He got back to Bangalore just after the middle of October (1897). Nearly everybody except Winston Churchill would in these circumstances have been content to relax for a few months, to bore their fellow officers

with their adventures, and to settle back into regimental routine. He, by
contrast, had by the end of the year completed and posted off to his
mother an 85,000-word book (the length of a short novel) on the
campaign. The feat was the more remarkable because he was also
working intermittently during that autumn at his one and only work of
fiction, *Savrola*, which was of about equal length.

Lady Randolph got the book published (very quickly) by Longman
and proof-read (wildly inaccurately) by Moreton Frewen, an Anglo-Irish
gentleman who was married to her sister Clara and was very briefly and
much later MP for County Cork. The book attracted a great deal of
notice, almost all of it favourable, except for complaints about the
misprints and about some very eccentric punctuation, which was also
the responsibility of Frewen. A review in the *Athenaeum* said that 'it
suggests in style pages by Napier punctuated by a mad printer's reader'.
The work of the 'mad printer's reader' at first almost obliterated for
Churchill his pleasure at the general success. 'I scream with disappointment and shame when I contemplate the hideous blunders that deface
it,' he wrote to his mother in May 1898.[18] However the approximately
£600 (£30,000) which it earned constituted a balming poultice. The slim
volume (in contrast with the considerable if eloquent prolixity of nearly
all of Churchill's later works) was an engaging and vividly written piece
of rapportage, showing a strong narrative sense; there was also a by no
means immature reflective chapter at the end. The whole was dedicated
to Sir Bindon Blood. Of course the notice which it attracted, and part
of the praise, stemmed from the resonance of the name Churchill bore.
He even got an admiring letter from the Prince of Wales, not normally
the most dedicated of bibliophiles: 'I have read it with the greatest
possible interest and I think the descriptions and the language generally
excellent. Everybody is reading it, and I only hear it spoken of with
praise.'[19] However, the letter concluded by advising him to 'stick to the
Army' and not rush to add MP to his name.

The writing of his novel straddled that of *Malakand*. He began it on
the stifling voyage back to India for his North-West Frontier excursion.
This was another example of his restless energy even under the most
unfavourable circumstances. He told his mother that he had completed
five chapters before leaving Bangalore for Nowshera. Then it was set
aside. But he returned to it as soon as *Malakand* was out of the way, and
he informed his brother in a letter of 26 May (1898) that he had finished
it. Again it was short, even more so than was *Malakand*. It was originally
to be called *Affairs of State*, a title about as different from *Savrola* as it is

possible to imagine, and it retained this name in his references to it for
at least the first eighteen months from conception. *Savrola* was essentially a British *roman-à-clef* (although it did not require much intelligence to break the key) implausibly set in a Balkan Ruritania. The
heroine Lucile, married to the by no means entirely vicious but out-of-
touch ruler–dictator Morala, is widely thought to have been modelled
on Lady Randolph. His description of her radiance was reminiscent, a
little *mutatis mutandis*, of John Henry Newman's unforgettable description of the position, at once modest and dominating, of St Philip Neri
in sixteenth-century Rome.[20] 'Foreign princes had paid her homage,'
Churchill wrote in *Savrola*, 'not only as the loveliest woman in Europe
but also as a great political figure. Her salon was crowded with the most
famous men of every country. Statesmen, soldiers, poets and men of
letters had worshipped at her shrine.'[21]

Yet the match is not perfect. Lucile is portrayed as more ethereal,
and certainly more chaste, than Lady Randolph. Furthermore, as the
love interest of the novel, at once forced and cardboard-like, involved
her forsaking Morala for the rasher appeal of Savrola, who was undoubtedly Winston himself, the scenario, if authentic, would have been a little
incestuous. This feeling is increased, and becomes practically Hamlet-
like, if Morala, as many sought to do, is identified as Lord Randolph.
One description of him is thought to support this view: 'Her husband
was affectionate and at such time as he could spare from public matters
was at her service. Of late things had been less bright. . . . Hard lines
had come into his face, lines of work and anxiety, and sometimes she
caught a look of awful weariness, as of one who toils and yet foresees
that his labour will be in vain.'[22]

There is a 'nurse', a crucial and continuing presence and influence in
Savrola's life, who is Mrs Everest reincarnated. Savrola himself is an
immensely revealing portrait. He is a patrician on the side of the people.
'Vehement, high, and daring' was his cast of mind. 'The life he lived
was the only one he could ever live; he must go on to the end. The end
comes often early to such men, whose spirits are so wrought that they
know rest only in action, contentment only in danger, and in confusion
find their only peace.'[23]

There was also a streak of cosmic pessimism present in the book,
recalling both Gladstone's essentially fearful religion, inspired by his
apprehension of the awful prospects of mankind, and Balfour's famously
depressive passage when he wrote that 'The energies of our system will
decay, the glory of the sun will be dimmed, and the earth, tideless and

inert, will no longer tolerate the race which has for a moment disturbed its solitude. Man will go down into the pit, and all his thoughts will perish.'[24] Churchill wrote (at the age of twenty-three): 'The cooling process would continue: the perfect development of life would end in death: the whole solar system, the whole universe itself, would one day be cold and lifeless as a burnt-out firework.'[25] Yet, while he might echo the eschatological gloom of two of his illustrious Prime Ministerial predecessors, he (and to some considerable extent they too) had no intention of being inert in advance of the planet becoming so. 'Ambition was the motive force,' Churchill wrote of Savrola, 'and he was powerless to resist it.'[26]

He did not write *Savrola* at all secretly, as many first novelists have done. But he was not a typical first novelist. His letters home were full of the news of its progress. And his fellow officers were kept abreast of his activities. Indeed, according to *My Early Life*, they made several suggestions 'for stimulating the love interest'. Perhaps wisely he did not accept most of the suggestions for increasing the sexual titillation, but nor did he resent them, and the book is dedicated to 'The Officers Of The IVth (Queen's Own) Hussars In Whose Company The Author Lived For Four Happy Years'. The four years had many intervals, but there is nonetheless no reason to doubt the genuineness of the warmth.

Savrola, although almost equally quickly written, was published more slowly (and with fewer misprints) than *Malakand*. It first came out, rather like a Dickens or a Trollope novel (no bad precedents), in serial parts between May and December 1899 in *Macmillan's Magazine*. In book form it first appeared in America in November of that year, and then in England in the February of 1900. It was a good pattern for a semi-established author, which he had certainly become by then, for an intermediate book *The River War*, eschewing the economy of *Malakand* and *Savrola* and running to a full 250,000 words and two volumes, had been published in November 1899. *Savrola* continues to be occasionally read; a new edition came out in 1990. But its continuing mild fame plainly stems from that of Winston Churchill rather than vice versa. It is a respectable, readable and fascinating (because of what later became of its author) piece of juvenilia.

The River War takes us into the next and middle phase of Churchill's career as a soldier and publicist on the frontiers of empire. It was subtitled 'An Historical Account of the Reconquest of the Soudan', and was on an altogether different scale from the other two books. It also made some attempt at objective history as opposed to the simple relating of exploits in which the author had participated. Churchill himself did not appear on the scene until the second volume. The level of dedication was also raised. It was to 'The Marquess Of Salisbury, K.G., Under Whose Wise Direction The Conservative Party Have Long Enjoyed Power And The Nation Prosperity, During Whose Administrations The Reorganization of Egypt Has Been Mainly Accomplished, And Upon Whose Advice Her Majesty Determined To Order The Reconquest Of The Soudan'. There was not much evidence of Churchill's incipient Liberalism in these measured if unusually sycophantic words. They appear, however, to have been occasioned more by direct gratitude than by toadyism. Without Salisbury Churchill would probably not have participated in the campaign at all. The Sirdar (commander) of the Egyptian Army, then Sir Herbert Kitchener, leading the expedition of reconquest against the heir of the Mahdi, whose forces had murdered General Gordon at Khartoum thirteen years earlier, was strongly resistant to having Churchill on his strength. He clearly regarded him as a young whippersnapper who was 'publicity seeking' and 'medal hunting' – two descriptions which Churchill recorded as being unfriendlily applied to him at the time. Churchill in return wrote of the future 'great poster': 'He may be a general – but never a gentleman.'*[27]

During the first half of 1898 Churchill pursued his desire to be part of the Sudan campaign with relentless determination. He was mostly at Bangalore, although in early January he again made the long expedition to Calcutta and was much better received than the year before. Even the previously reviled Elgins (with whom on this occasion he stayed, which may have been the main reason for his change of view) moved up in his estimation. Then, in late February, he travelled to Meerut near Delhi for another polo tournament, and went on from there for the 400 or so miles to Peshawar in the hope of being taken on by General Sir William Lockhart, who was about to conduct the Tirah campaign against another set of rebellious tribesmen on and around the North-West Frontier. This was a disciplinary as well as a physical risk, for it involved the certainty, if General Lockhart was uncooperative, of being late returning to Bangalore from his north Indian polo leave. Lockhart

* This was a judgement which many would have endorsed throughout Kitchener's career, but it was notably contradicted by his behaviour seventeen years later toward Churchill himself. When, at the nadir of his fortunes, the latter was forced out of the Admiralty by the veto of the Tories coming into the Asquith coalition in May 1915, Kitchener, then Secretary of State for War, was the one minister who paid him a visit of condolence.

however was helpful and took Churchill on his own staff as an orderly officer and even allowed him to sprout the red tabs of a staff officer. But the General was less bellicose and therefore less forthcoming in providing Churchill with the action and danger than Blood had been. He even secured a lasting negotiated peace with the tribesmen, and Churchill was back in Bangalore by mid-April, where he remained for two months, getting on with *Savrola* and continuing to send frantic messages to everyone he thought might be of help about his desire to participate in the Sudan campaign. The battle at Atbara had already been won by Kitchener, but Churchill, quite rightly as things turned out, regarded this as only a useful prelude to the engagement with the weight of the Dervish force at Omdurman.

For this he hoped he might still be in time. One advantage of the bloodless Tirah expedition was that it entitled him to another long period of home leave, and he sailed from Bombay on 18 June. Churchill was extraordinarily fortunate in his home leave. Even viceroys normally had to wait two and a half to three years. This was his second return after only twenty months in India. At first he thought he could drop off in Egypt and go straight up the Nile. But by early June he came to accept that this was not possible. He had extracted some sort of promise from Sir Evelyn Wood, the Adjutant-General in London, but he was still well short of acceptance by Kitchener, the commander on the spot.

He was also seized by English nostalgia. 'I cannot give up my fortnight in London,' he wrote to his mother from Bangalore. 'It is worth its minutes in sovereigns.' And then, with an engaging ability to prick the balloon of his own enthusiasm: 'You will probably find that I shall not enjoy it actually vy much. Schopenhauer [perhaps the disadvantage of too much undigested reading] says that if you anticipate you only use up some of the pleasure of the moment in advance. And that therefore things that are greatly looked forward to usually disappoint. . . . Still I shall come and shall hope you will meet me at [Victoria] station.'[28] He was therefore set on a visit to England, and indeed asked whether a political meeting in Bradford (one of his father's favourite stamping grounds) might be organized. But he also kept one foot firmly on his other objective and said that he was 'leaving [my] native servant and campaigning kit in Egypt – tent, saddles, etc'. (Where did they go? Even if the left-luggage office at Port Said accommodated the equipment, what happened to the poor Indian servant, left alone nearly 3,000 miles from home in a country he had never seen before?)

The Tory meeting at Bradford was arranged and took place with some considerable success on 14 July; once again it was very well reported in the *Morning Post*. There is no evidence, however, and some considerable supposition to the contrary, that Lady Randolph had met him at Victoria. Although generally a good correspondent, she was only hesitantly welcoming of his visits to England, partly on the grounds of expense (the return passage cost about £80, the rough equivalent of £4,000 today), and partly because of her fear that he would be too much of a butterfly, alighting briefly on too many different attractive plants rather than sticking to anything long enough for solid achievement.

Furthermore, they had had a very rough epistolary time (about money, needless to say) earlier that year. She wanted to borrow £14,000, no doubt to pay urgent debts. This she could only do with Winston signing certain documents which he judged likely to mean that his ultimate trust-fund income, that is after her death, would be reduced from £2,500 to £1,800. 'I sign these papers', he wrote on 30 January 1898,

> purely and solely out of affection for you. I write plainly that no other consideration would have induced me to sign them. As it is I sign them upon two conditions – which justice and prudence alike demand. *First.* That you settle definitely upon me during your life the allowance of £500 per annum I now enjoy at your pleasure. *Second.* That you obtain a written promise from Jack that on coming of age he will at once identify himself with the transaction, insure his life and divide with me the burden.[29]

The first condition at least was not implemented. It was not so much this as the inherent squalor of financial disputes within families which left the damage. Two days before the letter just quoted he had written semi-tolerantly:

> Speaking quite frankly on the subject – there is no doubt that we are both you and I equally thoughtless – spendthrift and extravagant. We both know what is good and we both like to have it. Arrangements for paying are left to the future. . . . I sympathise with all your extravagances – even more than you do with mine – it seems just as suicidal to me when you spend £200 on a ball dress as it does to you when I purchase a new polo pony for £100. And yet I feel that you ought to have the dress and I the polo pony. The pinch of the whole matter is that we are damned poor.[30]

What he wrote just two months later was much worse: 'You ask me not to allude to the subject of money arrangements – and I agree with you that it is better not to prolong the affair. It has left a dirty taste in my mouth – and yet I would not be other than what I am or do other than I have done. The pain I feel in the matter is that it has brought a disagreeable element into our lives. I fear the effects may be permanent.'[31] No doubt the dispute left a nasty taste in the mouth of Jennie Churchill also, and in that spring she hardly wrote to her elder son. In mid-April he was complaining, but more plaintively than bitterly, about her five-week silence and begging to be restored to her correspondence.

When he got back to England on 2 July she was at great pains, whether or not she met him at the station, to advance both his political and his military desires. As Churchill later put it: 'Many were the pleasant luncheons and dinners attended by the powers of those days which occupied the two months of these frenzied negotiations. But all without avail.' A powerful array of allies was mobilized. It ranged from the Prime Minister, through Lord Cromer, the long-standing and powerful British Agent in Egypt, and Sir Evelyn Wood the Adjutant-General to the less obviously relevant figure of Lady Jeune, the wife of the President of the Probate, Divorce and Admiralty Division of the High Court, who nonetheless seemed to be a key go-between. But the formidable and familiar figure of Kitchener remained for a time determinedly blocking. This atmosphere was succinctly captured in a letter with several surprising features which Wood (whose sister was Parnell's Mrs O'Shea) wrote to Lady Randolph on 10 July:

Dear Jennie [a very familiar form of address for the period]
    The Sirdar declines to take Mr Churchill [a very formal way of referring to a twenty-three-year-old son], and I write to show you the correspondence in order we may concert as to future measures – I will call tomorrow either at 9 on my way home cycling [very good for a senior general in 1898] – or about 10 on my way to office.
    Yrs affect.
    Evelyn Wood.[32]

The 'future measures' would no doubt have been formidable, although they might have been a case of an irresistible force meeting an immovable object, the latter in the shape of Sir H. Kitchener. The stubbornness of his resistance to Churchill was quite remarkable. Not only did he resist his Prime Minister and his local Cairo political superior on the matter, but he also seemed prepared to face a turf war with the army command in London. As Sirdar, his control over appointments in the formations of the Egyptian army was not in dispute. But that army needed to be reinforced for the Sudan campaign with British units, administratively if not operationally responsible not to him but to the Adjutant-General in the Horse Guards in London. He made matters worse by wanting to take Lord Fincastle, the son of an obscure Scottish earl, who had written a rival Malakand book to Churchill's. Wood was coruscating about not accepting this nomination: 'Fincastle had been reported three times "as below average of rank." '* Churchill was of course being very pushy and getting others to push even harder on his behalf, but the whole contretemps is a good example of the animosity which, for at least the first half of his life, his combination of brash bravery and determined publicity-seeking was capable of arousing.

Eventually it was sorted out by the otherwise unfortunate death of a young 21st Lancers subaltern. Maybe even Kitchener had begun to feel that he was over-engaged and was looking for a way out. At any rate it was all settled by 24 July, and a few days later Churchill bounded off on another of his rail and boat trips to the East. This time it was via Marseille, but the boat ('A filthy tramp – manned by those detestable French sailors') lived down to the reputation of that which had taken him to Bombay a year before. However he was always (at that stage in life) willing to put up with discomfort, 'only five nights and four days',[33] in order to get to a scene of action.

He was also good at arranging his outlets. Before leaving London he got the *Morning Post* to agree to pay him £15 a column. This was not wholly compatible with the undertaking given by Lady Jeune in her last ineffective telegraphic appeal to Kitchener: 'Hope you will take Churchill. Guarantee he won't write.'[34] Nevertheless it was fully comprehensible in view of the fairly chilling terms which the War Office laid down for his journey to Cairo and attachment to the 21st Lancers: 'It is understood that you will proceed at your own expense and that in the event of your being killed or wounded in the impending operations, or for any other reason, no charge of any kind will fall on British Army funds.'[35]

Almost as soon as Churchill reported to the colonel of the 21st Lancers at Abbasiya Barracks in Cairo the regiment was off on the long 1,400-mile expedition to the south. He was in Luxor by 5 August, only eight days after leaving London, and at Atbara, the scene of the April battle which had aroused his desire to travel at least 8,000 miles in order to be present at the next engagements against the heir of the Mahdi, by 15 August. From there Kitchener began on the 24th the final advance

* He was nonetheless a holder of the Victoria Cross.

which resulted in the (semi-)victorious Battle of Omdurman of 2
September. At first Churchill was not impressed by his regiment of
attachment. 'The 21st Lancers', he wrote to his mother in late August,
'are not on the whole a good business and I would much rather have
been attached to the Egyptian cavalry staff.'[36]

The officer who was 'attached to the Egyptian cavalry staff' in this
campaign was Captain Douglas Haig. Indeed it is remarkable how many
of the great figures of the First World War were involved in what was
after all a relatively small punitory and pacifying expedition sixteen years
before its outbreak. Captain Rawlinson (later General Lord Rawlinson
and in command of the British Fourth Army in France, which took
much of the brunt of Ludendorff's final and nearly successful offensive
in the spring of 1918) was also on Kitchener's staff. And when on the
eve of the Battle of Omdurman Churchill went for a Nile-side walk he
was hailed from a gunboat 'by a junior naval Lieutenant named Beatty'
(later, with Jellicoe, one of the two most famous British admirals of the
1914–18 war), who tossed a magnum of champagne halfway towards
the shore; Churchill gladly waded up to his knees in order to retrieve it.
Churchill's position after 1914, as a still very young (forty) senior
minister, turned on his vastly greater knowledge of naval and military
commanders than that possessed by any of his ministerial colleagues –
except for Kitchener. But this was by no means a clear advantage. It
bred jealousy at least as much as friendship.

Later Churchill revised substantially upwards his opinion of his
regiment of attachment. 'I never saw better men than the 21st Lancers,'
he wrote on 16 September to his shipboard 'passage from India' friend,
the then Colonel Ian Hamilton, who by his inability to win (maybe
against the odds) in Gallipoli in 1915 was to contribute to one of the
worst downswings in Churchill's mercurial career. 'I don't mean to say
I admired their discipline or their general training – both I thought
inferior. But they were the 6 year British soldier type – and every man
was an intelligent human being that knew his own mind. My faith in
our race and blood was much strengthened.'[37]

This was after their fairly famous if also fairly useless cavalry charge
of 2 September. Great bravery was exhibited. Three Victoria Crosses
were awarded within the regiment. But, as the seventh Marquess of
Anglesey wrote in the fifth and 1982 volume of his definitive *History of
the British Cavalry*: 'As with the charge of the light brigade at Balaclava
forty-four years before the most futile and inefficient part of the battle
was the most extravagantly praised.'[38] It was inefficient because it

resulted in equally heavy casualties on the British as on the Dervish side, and, in circumstances in which they had immensely more troops on the spot but we had 'the maxim gun', this could hardly be accounted a triumph. The 21st Lancers lost one officer and twenty men killed, four officers and forty-six men wounded, all out of a total strength of just over three hundred. In addition, a severe loss for a cavalry regiment, 119 horses were destroyed. Only twenty-three of the opposing forces were killed, which makes somewhat improbable Churchill's claim that, with the pistol which he was using in place of a sword because of his dislocated shoulder, he killed 'several – 3 for certain – 2 doubtful'. However there is no doubt that he acquitted himself with honour and even distinction. As usual he led a charmed life, 'without a hair of my horse or a stitch of my clothing being touched. Very few can say the same.'[39] And a victory was secured, if not by the gallantry of the 21st Lancers, at least by the less reckless deployment of more stolid troops. Omdurman, the capital of the Khalifa Abdullahi, the heir of the twelve-year-dead Mahdi, was occupied within a day or so, and this phase of the campaign was over. The 21st Lancers, and Churchill with them, were stood down and began their journey of return. But, again to quote Lord Anglesey, 'A more ineffective pursuit it is difficult to imagine.'[40] The Khalifa was not captured until over a year later. Churchill made the same criticism at the time, but even more did he criticize Kitchener for his callousness towards the Dervish wounded on the field and for his desecration of the Mahdi's tomb in Omdurman itself (Kitchener made his skull into an inkwell). No doubt at this stage Churchill was, with some reason, hostile to Kitchener. However, in *The River War*, which because of it size and scope was an even more impressive feat of concentrated composition than were his earlier books, he damagingly maintained these criticisms, although softening them with some tribute to Kitchener's general strategic direction.

'The defeat and destruction of the Dervish army was so complete', Churchill wrote semi-ironically in *My Early Life*, 'that the frugal Kitchener was able to dispense immediately with the costly services of a British cavalry regiment. Three days after the battle the 21st Lancers started northwards on their march home.'[41] Churchill made faster progress than most. He had after all only been 'attached' not anchored to the 21st Lancers and the excitement was over. He was back in England by early October and stayed there for two months. He was working hard on *The River War* and also on his own future. He decided to leave the army, which might be an economizing move insofar as it would save the £500 a year of lavish Hussars living. But it was hazardous in that it meant giving up his only regular income and depending entirely upon his growing but still uncertain literary earnings. Its central motivation was to seek a seat in Parliament, which also in the short run involved expense and not income, although in the longer run might be expected to buttress his fame and thus increase both his lecturing and writing value. This it spectacularly did, with the longer run beginning as early as the end of 1901 and continuing for nearly sixty years. But this was far from guaranteed at the time, and the decision to 'send in his papers' must therefore be accounted high- rather than low-stake play. Furthermore he decided to go back for a final three months in India, mainly for polo playing, which was a final bit of Hussar extravagance.

In England that autumn he pursued his political contacts and addressed three Conservative meetings – at Rotherhithe, Dover and Southsea. He wisely cultivated party agents, most notably Captain Middleton (the 'Skipper') at Conservative Central Office, and newspaper proprietors and their editors, being surprisingly impressed by the civility and manners of Alfred Harmsworth, not then Lord Northcliffe. And he a little desultorily courted Miss Pamela Plowden, whom he had met a couple of years before in India. He flickered, much attracted but slightly teasing in his letters, around her flame, but was obviously in no financial position to offer marriage. In 1902 she married the second Earl of Lytton, and survived Churchill by six years. They remained firm friends to the end of his life.

On 2 December Churchill set out on his third (and final; he never went back after his cavalry days) passage to India. By the familiar Brindisi–Bombay route he was in Bangalore a week before Christmas, and stayed there, his last period of regular regimental life, until mid-January 1899, when he set off first to Madras and then to Jodhpur and Meerut for six weeks of polo playing. This culminated, very satisfactor-ily, in the 4th Hussars defeating the 2nd Dragoons in the final and winning the championship. As with the number of Dervishes he had personally shot before Omdurman there is some confusion about how many of the winning Hussar quartet of goals were his. What is certain, however, is that he was a very good member of the team of four. Photographed with the other players, he stands out as looking much the youngest and also the least like a moustachioed stage version of a late-Victorian cavalry officer.

He always had to play with his left arm strapped to his side because of the old shoulder problem. But at Meerut he had complicated the issue by falling downstairs in Sir Bindon Blood's governor's residence. No doubt they had been intensively reminiscing about Malakand days. He sprained both his ankles, was considerably bruised elsewhere and was generally in a state of 'walking wounded'. However his team-mates insisted that he should play. His quality must have been such that it is easy to understand why a man who only liked doing things that he did well and was in general uninterested by balls, moving or still, and never seduced by golf, went on playing polo until the age of fifty, just about when he became Chancellor of the Exchequer.

After Meerut he went for his third winter visit to Calcutta, and this time stayed a week with the newly installed Viceroy, George Nathaniel Curzon, the man he had called 'the spoiled darling of politics . . . the typification of the . . . Oxford prig' two years earlier. Under the influence of the Viceroy's hospitality (or perhaps even more of the notice which it implied), he completely changed his view of the 'very superior person'. '[I] had several long and delightful talks with Lord Curzon,' he wrote on 26 March 1899 in the last letter that he ever sent to his Marlborough grandmother.* 'I understand the success he has obtained. He is a remarkable man – and to my surprise I found he had a great charm of manner. I had not expected this from reading his speeches. I think his Viceroyalty will be a signal success. They are both already vy. popular.'[42] This Calcutta visit was enhanced by the presence of his old headmaster Dr Welldon, who had become bishop there.

He reported on the Curzons in very similar terms to his mother, who at this stage had been seized with the idea of founding a literary magazine. For the general idea he was as enthusiastic as she was, but wanted it to be 'of a certain *dilettante* excellence' which would qualify it to be read 'equally by the educated people of Paris, of Petersburg, of London or New York',[43] and might moreover make the family a much needed £1,000 a year. Almost needless to say it did not. Inappropriately entitled (in Churchill's view) the *Anglo-Saxon Review*, it ceased publication after ten quarterly issues.

So there was no contribution from it to the war chest for a political foray which he had become almost obsessively keen on creating. His urge for politics and his sense of his political vocation were welling up with increasing force. After some pro-Salisbury ('He is a wonderful

---

* She died on 16 April. All his other three grandparents had gone well before. There was nothing in Churchill's heredity to presage his own long life, which in these early years he thought improbable.

man') and anti-Joseph Chamberlain (who was 'losing ground a good deal') remarks, he had justified his judgements by adding in an 11 January letter: 'I feel it instinctively. I know I am right. I have got instinct in these things. Inherited probably. This life is vy pleasant and I pass the time quickly and worthily – but I have no right to dally in the pleasant valleys of amusement. What an awful thing it will be if I don't come off. It will break my heart for I have nothing else but ambition to cling to.'[44]

After Calcutta he returned to Bangalore and his regiment for only four days of settling up, which he was fortunately able to do at a slight profit. He sailed from Bombay on 20 March, just under thirty months since he had first arrived there. Although India was for several years in the early 1930s to dominate his political activity, and considerably to damage his political prospects, he never felt it necessary to refresh his direct knowledge of the sub-continent, which he regarded as a geographical expression and 'no more a country than is the equator'.

He broke his journey home in Egypt and went for nearly two weeks to Cairo, where he installed himself in the Savoy Hotel ('very comfortable though I fear rather expensive'),[45] and endeavoured to do as much checking and further accumulation of knowledge as possible for *The River War*, which was then close to completion. His most valued source was Lord Cromer, the effective head of the government of the country, with whom his relations became at least as good as those with Kitchener were bad; the two may not have been unconnected. Cromer expressed general admiration for the text he had been asked to read, although not without thinking it necessary to put Churchill right on a number of matters. 'My remarks were, I know, severe, and it is very sensible of you to take them in the spirit in which they were intended,'[46] he wrote on 2 April. One of the things about which he put him right was General Charles Gordon, the victim of the Mahdi's revolt of 1884–5, who to most of the British public was the prototype of a *Boys' Own Paper* hero, although to Gladstone little more than an unbalanced and insubordinate junior general. Cromer, fourteen years later, and with Gladstone as well as Gordon dead, inclined very much to the Gladstone view, and semi-converted Churchill to it. After the young author had been given by Cromer first luncheon and then a two-and-a-half-hour critique of his book, he, a little crestfallen, wrote:

What I then learned makes it necessary to considerably modify [one of Churchill's very rare split infinitives] the earlier chapter dealing with the

Gordon episode. I feel that it will be impossible for me to sacrifice all the fine phrases and pleasing paragraphs I have written about Gordon, but Cromer was very bitter about him and begged me not to pander to the popular belief on the subject. Of course there is no doubt that Gordon as a political figure was absolutely hopeless. He was so erratic, capricious, utterly unreliable, his mood changed so often, his temper was abominable, he was frequently drunk, and yet with all he had a tremendous sense of honour and great abilities, and a still greater obstinacy.[47]

There is little room for doubt that Cromer was one of the few people who succeeded in establishing a mixture of moral and intellectual ascendancy over the almost irrepressible Churchill of this period. This comes out well but almost unconsciously from his account of Cromer taking him to see the Khedive. 'I was much amused by observing the relations between the British Agent and the *de jure* Ruler of Egypt. The Khedive's attitude reminded me of a school-boy who is brought to see another school-boy in the presence of the head-master.'[48]

Churchill got back to England via Marseille in mid-April, and almost immediately plunged into politics. First he made full use of his silver spoon to sup with the great and famous. On 2 May he sat down at a Rothschild dinner party with both Balfour and Asquith – and seems to have been less intimidated by these two Prime Ministers-in-waiting than by Cromer: 'A.J.B. was markedly civil to me – I thought – agreed with and paid great attention to everything I said. I talked well and not too much – in my opinion.'[49]

He addressed Conservative meetings in Paddington (his father's old seat) and Cardiff in mid-May. His political attention, however, was becoming concentrated upon Oldham, the strongly cotton-dominated borough in Lancashire just to the north of Manchester. It was a two-member parliamentary seat, one of the thirty or so in this category left over in the broadly single-member seat redistribution of 1885 from what had previously been the old borough pattern. In 1895, it had returned two not very distinguished Conservatives. By 1899 one of them was unwell and wanted to resign. The other (Robert Ascroft) thought Churchill would be a suitable bye-election candidate and junior running mate in a future general election. He summoned Churchill to see him in the House of Commons, and arranged that, as a suitable testing of the waters, Churchill would come to Oldham in June and address a meeting. Churchill agreed with alacrity, as any eager prospective candidate would have done, but proposed that his cousin, the almost equally young Duke of Marlborough, should share the platform with him.

Then Ascroft confused the situation by suddenly dying before the meeting, while his ailing colleague remained alive, although anxious to go. The government party machine thought they might easily lose both seats, and decided they would prefer to concentrate the misery. The unusual event of a double bye-election in a single constituency was therefore decided upon, polling day was fixed for 6 July and Churchill was proclaimed, almost without discussion, as one of the Conservative candidates. He was twenty-four and a half, and his sixty-five-year political career was launched.

3

OLDHAM AND SOUTH AFRICA

AT OLDHAM IN July 1899 Churchill neither distinguished nor disgraced himself. Together with his running mate (than whom he did marginally better) he participated in the loss of two previously Conservative-held seats. But the election came when the government was on an ebb-tide; the result did not greatly surprise the party leaders and managers; and the adverse swing of around 2 per cent was modest for a mid-term bye-election.

Was Churchill an effective candidate? He himself certainly thought so during the campaign. 'My speech last night at the club produced great enthusiasm,' he wrote to his mother on 25 June, 'and there is no doubt that if anyone can win this seat I can.'[1] To Pamela Plowden, who had proved resistant to his efforts to entice her to Lancashire, he wrote on the Sunday before the poll that, while the result was doubtful, 'I personally have made a vy good impression.'[2]

The line-up of candidates was curious. At the 1895 general election both the two elected Tories and the two defeated Liberals had been relatively obscure. This was subject only to the qualification that the subsequently deceased Ascroft, who had headed the poll, running a good 600 votes ahead of his fellow Conservative (Oswald QC), had the working-class pull (and Oldham was very much a working-class borough) of being the highly respected solicitor of the Amalgamated Society of Cotton Spinners, the main local trade union. This connection was probably largely responsible for Churchill's junior partner becoming James Mawdsley, the general secretary of that union in Lancashire. This was at first thought to be a brilliant ploy. The *Manchester Evening News* on 26 June opined that Mr Mawdsley 'may be able to carry [Mr Churchill] into Parliament as the late Mr Ascroft carried Mr Oswald'.[3] (He certainly had the weight to do so. He was an immensely heavy man who succumbed in the course of a year from injuries sustained by sitting in and sundering a china bath.)

The new Conservative pair were given the sobriquet of 'the scion [of the aristocracy] and the socialist', which was thought to be helpful,

although Churchill was a scion with hardly any inheritance, and Mawdsley was a very doubtful socialist. Mawdsley's main contribution to the
platform case seemed to be a reiteration of the somewhat downbeat
mantra that both parties were hypocritical, but that the Liberals were
the worse. Moreover, instead of being perceived as a splendid upholder
of one end of the flag of Tory Democracy, he was more widely thought
of as a class traitor. 'In the end, however,' as Churchill sadly reflected
long subsequently, 'all the Liberal and Radical Trade Unionists went
off and voted for their party, and we were left with our own strong
supporters rather upset by the appearance of a wicked Socialist on their
platforms.'[4]

The Liberal team was more formidable. The senior of the two was
Alfred Emmott, whose family was very much part of the warp and woof
of Oldham, being one of the leading cotton spinners of the town, and
who at the age of forty had already himself served on the town council
for eighteen years and been mayor. He continued as member for
Oldham for twelve years, serving for the last five of these as Chairman
of Committees in the House of Commons, and then becoming a peer,
most unusually combining this with entering the government for the
first time and occupying two successive parliamentary secretaryships
before being promoted to a brief spell of Cabinet membership in
1914–15. Asquith, in a frivolous 'marking as in a [Cambridge] Tripos'
letter at the end of February of the latter year, put him equal bottom
(with four others) in his list of Cabinet effectiveness.

The second and still brighter candidate star (although even he was
to get only equal ninth in the Asquith 'marking') was the then twenty-
nine-year-old Walter Runciman. His family were shipowners and even
wealthier than the Emmotts, but from Tyneside, and no doubt partly
for this reason ran 200 votes behind Emmott. Unlike Emmott he did
not hold Oldham at the 1900 general election, but, subsequently sustained by a bewildering number and spread of other constituencies,
entered the Cabinet on the same day as Churchill in 1908, was President of the Board of Trade both for the first two years of the First
World War and for six years of the National government in the 1930s.
He then crowned his career by producing a plan for the dismemberment of Czechoslovakia which greatly aided the Munich surrender of
1938.

Hovering like a constant cloud over the two Tories throughout the
double bye-election was a Clerical Tithes Bill, which the Salisbury
government had recently introduced. This was a piece of fairly gross

financial favouritism for the Church of England, directly benefiting both the income of the clergy and the revenues of the Church schools. It aroused vehement Nonconformist opposition. Rather as the community charge ninety years later became almost universally known as the poll tax, so its proper name got submerged in the unfriendly catchphrase of the Clerical Doles Bill. Indeed Churchill in his retrospective account appears to have convinced himself that this was its true title, and so referred to it without inverted commas or explanation.

Emmott and Runciman were both Nonconformists. There is no certainty about Mawdsley's religious affiliation, but it is unlikely that he would have been an Anglican. So the only even nominal member of the Church of England involved in the contest was Churchill, and the weight of the controversy therefore fell upon him.* Exceptionally he decided to take cover, and repudiated the bill. This may or may not have won a handful of votes, but it certainly provoked criticism, from Arthur Balfour, the soon-to-inherit crown prince of the Conservative party, and, later, from Churchill himself. Balfour was reported to have said: 'I thought he was a young man of promise, but it appears he is a young man of promises.' And Churchill's own subsequent verdict was: 'Amid the enthusiastic cheers of my supporters I announced that, if returned, I would not vote for the measure. This was a frightful mistake. It is not the slightest use defending Governments or parties unless you defend the worst thing about which they are attacked.'[5]

The last point may have been an exaggerated statement of position, but it was the case that when the votes had been counted, and had revealed a gap of about 7 per cent of the poll between Churchill and the second and defeated Liberal, he left the borough, having made some good local friends but trailing no clouds of national glory: 'I returned to London with those feelings of deflation which a bottle of champagne, or even soda-water, represents when it has been half emptied and left uncorked for a night. No one came to see me on my return to my mother's house.'[6] However there was at least a letter, from the ever urbane (and occasionally kind) if also coolly critical Balfour: 'I hope you will not be discouraged by what has taken place. For many reasons this is a very unpropitious time to fight bye-elections. . . . Never mind, it

---

* This was a little unfair, for he was a very detached member, both in practice and in belief. His most famous aphorism on the subject, pronounced much later was 'I could hardly be called a pillar of the Church, I am more in the nature of a buttress, for I support it from the outside.'

will come right; and this small reverse will have no permanent ill effect upon your political fortunes.'[7]

In spite of this placebo, and a number of other friendly letters from high sources (Salisbury, Joseph Chamberlain, Cromer, General Evelyn Wood) occasioned however less by the loss of the bye-election and more by *The River War*, which he completed in late July, had published in early November and distributed liberally, he did not feel that he had earned any Oldham laurels on which to rest. They were not nearly solid enough, and in any event he was not a rester. He needed yet another theatre of action. During September war in South Africa became imminent. Until 1886, when gold was discovered in the Witwatersrand and Johannesburg moved to becoming the richest mining city in the world, an uneasy balance existed between the Boers and the British in South Africa. The British were mostly in Cape Province and Natal. The Boers dominated the Transvaal and the Orange River Colony, where they carried on a rugged agriculture and lived in close-knit and isolated communities. The majority native tribes were little regarded on either side of the divide. The opening up of the 'Rand' upset the balance. The lure of gold brought an influx of British and other nationalities into the Transvaal. The Boers, who controlled the political process of the province and of the Orange River Colony, treated them as 'Uitlanders' and refused them voting and other rights. Gradually the tension built up. It was exemplified by the reckless adventure of the Jameson Raid in 1895 and by Cecil Rhodes's desire to develop a British imperialism up the whole length of Africa, linked by a Cape-to-Cairo railway, and on 12 October (1899) it led to the outbreak of war between the British and the two Boer republics, a war which proved much more difficult and protracted than the British had expected.

By 14 October* Churchill was embarked on a Castle Line ship and on his way to Cape Town and the front. It was not entirely a question of quick and sudden reaction. Churchill had done a good deal of anticipation and advance planning. In mid-September, fortified by a competing offer from the *Daily Mail*, he had made a remarkably favourable journalistic arrangement with the *Morning Post*. He was to be paid £250 a month for a four-month assignment (the equivalent of a modern salary of £160,000) plus all expenses. And in early October he

---

* Churchill himself (*My Early Life*, p. 244) gives the date of embarkation as 11 October, but it is clear from letters which he wrote, including one 'in the train' (to Southampton) on 14 October, that his memory played him false.

had got Chamberlain, the most dominant of Colonial Secretaries, to commend to Alfred Milner, the most powerful of High Commissioners, 'the son of my old friend'.

When Churchill sailed on the *Dunottar Castle* he was in the company of Sir Redvers Buller, the just-appointed Commander-in-Chief for the war, plus staff, and – personal for Churchill – by a fine consignment of sixty bottles of alcohol together with a dozen of Rose's Lime Juice. This fortfying baggage was interesting not so much for its size, which was quite modest and fitted in with the fact that Churchill never drank quite as much as, not entirely to his displeasure, he was reputed to do, as for the prices which the bill revealed. The claret cost two shillings a bottle, the port three shillings and sixpence, the vermouth three shillings and the Scotch whisky four. The only mildly extravagant items were vintage champagne at nine shillings a bottle and Very Old Eau de Vie at twelve and sixpence.[8]

The voyage was not pleasant. Churchill's constant search for long-distance adventure was made the more impressive by his thoroughly disliking turn-of-the-century liner life, which through a film of nostalgia sounds so attractive. Frequently he was sick. He also hated the constrictions of a ship. 'What an odious affair is a modern sea journey,' he wrote in his first despatch for the *Morning Post*. However the *Dunottar Castle* got him to Cape Town by the end of the month in which the war had started. The war was still nearly 1,500 miles away. He proceeded by train to East London and then by another boat (seasick again) to Durban, to where his ingenuity (shared with two correspondents) got him half a week ahead of the more leisurely progress of Buller and staff.

In the course of the voyage out he had secured from Lord Gerard, a rich, middle-aged but adventurous *bon vivant* who had found his way on to General Buller's staff as an aide-de-camp but was also, a little confusingly, Colonel of the Lancashire Hussars, the promise of a commission in and attachment to that yeomanry regiment.* The

---

* As Churchill accumulated a rich experience of different regiments of the British Army, it is tempting to consider what he did about uniforms. Obviously the 4th Hussars was his anchor. On the North-West Frontier, however, he was attached to the 31st Punjab Infantry and in the Sudan to the 21st Lancers. In South Africa there were the Lancashire Hussars, and, after his escape from captivity, the South African Light Horse. In pre-1914 years he was in the Queen's Own Oxfordshire Hussars (a yeomanry regiment), rising to the rank of major and regularly attending, even when a senior minister, their summer camp, which was conveniently mostly at Blenheim. It was

ambiguity of Churchill's position as half a newspaper correspondent and half a serving officer had been a recurring feature of his previous martial adventures. Nor was it unique to him. It had been equally true of Lord Fincastle VC on the North-West Frontier, and the status of Colonel Rhodes, the correspondent of *The Times* in the Sudan, was not completely clear. As on these previous occasions it certainly did not make Churchill a non-combatant. Had he been so he could hardly have claimed to have killed five and maybe seven Dervishes. But in South Africa the issue quickly assumed a considerable importance.

From Durban Churchill immediately proceeded fifty miles north to Pietermaritzburg. By then the British position in Natal, let alone the prospect for a successful conquest of the Boer republics of the Orange River Colony and the Transvaal, was becoming precarious. Nearly all the Natal British forces were already shut up in Ladysmith (another hundred miles to the north), with the railway line cut at Colenso on the Tugela river. At Estcourt, which was as far north as the British could get unimpeded, Churchill ran into a North-West Frontier acquaintance, Captain (later General) Aylmer Haldane (a cousin of the future Lord Chancellor R. B. Haldane), who was about to be sent with an armoured train, a naval gun and a few scratch companies to probe for a further advance. Churchill readily accepted the opportunity to accompany him. As he was to write in *My Early Life*: 'Nothing looks more formidable and impressive than an armoured train; but nothing is in fact more vulnerable and helpless. It was only necessary to blow up a bridge or culvert to leave the monster stranded, far from home and help, at the mercy of the enemy. This situation did not seem to have occurred to our commander.'[9] Churchill's criticisms of this 'monster' were no doubt justified, although it could be commented that the only rival for vulnerability were great battleships, with the expensive ordering of which, within little more than a decade, he was to have a great deal to do.

---

bearing their insignia that he went to France after his resignation from the government in November 1915. He was then attached to the 2nd Grenadier Guards before commanding a battalion of the Royal Scots Fusiliers. In the Second World War he widened his choice of uniforms even beyond this range, frequently choosing to be an RAF air commodore (a uniform which did not suit him) and appearing at Yalta as a colonel of Hussars. For naval occasions he seemed content with the old sea-dog outfit of an Elder Brother of Trinity House; he never appeared as an admiral. It may be that the early stage of this variety of choice helped to account for the weight of his tailors' bills. In the five years between 1895 and 1900 they amounted to the rough equivalent of a modern £30,000, and were settled very slowly.

The vulnerability of the train proved itself more quickly and decisively than that of the dreadnoughts. After a penetration of about fourteen miles Boer horsemen were sighted on the surrounding hills, and it was decided to withdraw to base at Estcourt. Under sporadic fire the 'monster', with a civilian engine-driver who was anxious to get out of the combat zone, was making a good forty miles an hour when it was suddenly derailed. The engine, which was in the middle of the train, remained on the tracks, but three of the armoured trucks were off and blocking the path home.

Haldane organized return fire against the encircling and heavily bombarding Boers, while Churchill endeavoured to get the wrecked trucks off the track. He established a fine morale-boosting ascendancy over the lightly wounded and anxious-to-flee engine-driver, persuaded him to resume the controls and to move the engine up and down trying with some success to butt the trucks to one side. This enabled the engine and half the train, taking the wounded, to get away and return to Estcourt. Churchill remained at the core of the little battle. Suddenly he found himself confronted at forty yards by the rifle of a Boer horseman:

> That morning [it was 15 November 1899] I had taken with me, Correspondent-status notwithstanding, my Mauser pistol. I thought I could kill this man, and after the treatment I had received I earnestly desired to do so. I put my hand to my belt, the pistol was not there. When engaged in clearing the line, getting in and out of the engine, etc., I had taken it off. . . . The Boer continued to look along his sights, I thought there was absolutely no chance of escape, if he fired he would surely hit me, so I held up my hands and surrendered myself a prisoner of war.[10]

So eventually did half the contingent. They were taken to Pretoria, where Churchill together with other officers was incarcerated in the State Model School, converted into a prison camp.

There was no question but that Churchill had behaved with his usual reckless bravery during the two-hour or so attempt to get the train going again. The only person who queried this was Churchill himself. He defensively quoted 'the great Napoleon' as having said that 'When one is alone and unarmed a surrender may be pardoned.' There were however two ambiguities relating to his capture. The first related to the identity of the Boer sharpshooter who had him so firmly in his sights and whom he might have killed had he not mislaid his pistol. As a result of a chance encounter in London three years later Churchill came firmly to believe that it was General Louis Botha himself. Botha succeeded from the premiership of the Transvaal to that of the new Union of South Africa in 1910 and became the key figure in holding that country staunchly to the British cause in 1914 and in defeating the German forces in South-West Africa in the following year. The idea that they might have met in single combat and that either might have killed the other therefore assumed a strong place in Churchill's dramatic and romantic mind. Alas, it seems to be an unfounded figment. Even Randolph Churchill in the first volume of the mammoth official biography could not sustain it. He thought the most likely explanation was that Botha, who at that stage could not speak English at all fluently, had been misunderstood by Churchill. He had meant to say that he was in general command of the area in which the incident of the armoured train had taken place and not that he was the lone horseman.

The second ambiguity was on what possible ground Churchill could claim to be a non-combatant, immune from capture, or at any rate entitled to immediate release if, by ill-chance, this fate befell him. Yet this case he pursued with considerable implausibility and great persistence. He submitted requests for his release *as a non-combatant* on 18 November, 26 November ('I have consistently adhered to my character as a press representative, taking no part in the defence of the armoured train and being quite unarmed') and 8 December.[11] However he was willing to play both sides of the street, and on 30 November he wrote to the Assistant Adjutant-General at the War Office asking to be classified as a 'military officer', because there had been rumours of an exchange of combatant prisoners and he thought that otherwise he might 'fall between two stools'. His appeal to the Boers of 8 December contained a significant new point: 'If I am released I will give any *parole* that may be required not to serve against the Republican forces or to give any information affecting the military situation.'[12]

At first the Boer Commander-in-Chief appeared absolutely adamant against his release. On 19 November General Joubert telegraphed from Ladysmith to Pretoria: 'I urge you that he must be guarded and watched as dangerous for our war; otherwise he can still do us a lot of harm. In a word, he must not be released during the war. It is through his active part that *one section* of the armoured train got away.'[13] Within a couple of weeks however Joubert changed his mind, and on 12 December, no doubt influenced by Churchill's parole pledge, he wrote: 'If I accept his word, then my objections to his release cease. Seeing that a parole was promised him and that he suggested leaving Africa to return to Europe where he would report and speak only the truth of his experiences – and if the Government accepts this and he does so – then I have no further objections to his being set free, without our accepting somebody else in exchange. . . . PS Will he tell the truth? He will also be a chip off the old block.'*14

Before Joubert's change of mind had begun to be put into effect, Churchill had gone over the fence of the State Model School with the intention of making the 280-mile journey to Portuguese territory at Lourenço Marques. On his own and unable to speak either Afrikaans or Kaffir, although fortified by the surprisingly large sum of £75 in cash (the equivalent of £3,750 today), this was a most hazardous undertaking. It might not however have been any less so with two companions, Captain Haldane and a third man, sometimes referred to as Lieutenant and sometimes as Sergeant Brockie in contemporary accounts. This was the plan up to the moment of escape. Brockie was in fact a regimental sergeant major of the Imperial Light Horse who succeeded in passing himself off to the Boers as an officer and thus was in the State Model School rather than with the other ranks behind barbed wire on Pretoria race-course a mile and a half away. The two companions would probably have provided more of a protection against loneliness than safety against capture, although Brockie's ability to speak both Dutch and Kaffir might have been a help.

The essence of the danger however lay in the presence of Winston Churchill, whether alone or accompanied. His publicity-attracting quality guaranteed that the escape would be immediately reported to the top of the Boer government, and that the most strenuous efforts would be made to ensure recapture. For this reason Haldane and Brockie at first resisted his inclusion in the group. They may also have been influenced by a wonderfully rash and grandiose plan which he and a few other junior officers had been planning and to which he devoted five full pages of *My Early Life*. They would not just get over the fence and slip away. They would overpower the thirty rather dozy police guards, seize their arms, hurry to the race-course, do the same thing there, release the 2,000 other-rank British prisoners and with this sizeable force take over the whole capital city, incarcerate the Kruger government, and hold out for weeks or months, maybe long enough to bring

---

* Both the infelicities in style and any obscurities in substance in this letter can be attributed to it being a translation from the Afrikaans in which it was written.

the war to an end. This wildly optimistic plan was firmly sat upon by the more senior British officers in the State Model School.

Churchill's solitary escape aroused continuing and tangled but largely subterranean controversy. To dispose of the breaking of parole point first: Churchill undoubtedly volunteered undertakings (most notably in his letter of 8 December to the Boer government) which he did not subsequently fulfil. He served against the Republican forces for another seven months until he finally left South Africa on 7 July 1900, and he gave all the information, military and other, to Sir Redvers Buller about the situation in the Transvaal which he possessed.[15] However his offer of parole had not been accepted. He had not been released, even though he might have been. He had escaped. Furthermore, insofar as he was a military officer, he would have been breaking rules if he had given such a parole. It was his duty to try to escape and, if he succeeded, to be available for further service. This led back to the persistent ambiguity about his status, which he was only too keen himself to foster, playing one card or the other according to which best suited his short-term advantage. He hated being a prisoner, even though it was only for twenty-four days. 'In Durance Vile' he headed the relevant autobiographical chapter. He was determined to get out at the earliest possible moment. His impatience, his self-centredness and his conviction that he had to pursue his search for fame on every day of what he believed would be his short life all combined to give him a feeling of almost divine right to immediate freedom.

Nor can it be argued that this ambiguity about parole did much harm to his future relations with the Boer leaders of what became the Union of South Africa. Botha, who had probably at least been loosely in charge of his capture, became a firm friend. And Smuts, then a young Boer general, who later became his favourite Dominion Prime Minister, and almost his favourite adviser of any sort, confined himself to telegraphing laconically on 16 December (1899): 'What truth is there in the rumour that Churchill has escaped but has been caught again?'[16] Joubert, the Commandant of the Boer forces, took at least temporarily a more resentful line: '. . . I wonder whether it would not be a good thing to make public the correspondence about the release of Churchill to show the world what a scoundrel he is'.[17]

The second, more delicate and quietly long-lasting issue was whether Churchill had behaved badly by going off on his own. This was a view taken fluctuatingly if not obsessively by Haldane, by Brockie (killed in a

Rand mine accident within a few years), by Lieutenant Frederick le
Mesurier of the Dublin Fusiliers, who successfully escaped with Haldane
and Brockie three months later (he was killed in the Ypres Salient in
1915), and by Lieutenant Thomas Frankland of the same regiment, who
was also killed in the same year in Gallipoli, and who was closely
associated with both the December and the March escapes.

Haldane's view was much the most tenacious, partly because he lived
much the longest – until 1950, and to illustrate the down as well as the
up fluctuations of the grievance sent Churchill a copy of his 1948
memoirs with a warm inscription. (Frankland had done the same,
although with a less solipsistic book, as long before as Churchill's
marriage in 1908.) The essence of the complaint of General Haldane
(as he had become) was that Churchill when he made his unilateral
break-out had let down the other two by rendering their escape
impossible without a substantial delay, and that he had done so without
consultation. He scouted Churchill's claim that he had got Brockie's
approval for his move, and carried Brockie with him in this. What does
not seem to be in dispute is that the break had been planned for the
previous night, but had been postponed, apparently with tripartite
agreement, until the following evening (12 December) because the
disposition of the guards was unpropitious. Once again the circumstances did not look right, so Haldane and Brockie went to a hurried
dinner, intending to try again later that night. At this stage Churchill
lost patience and went over the fence on his own. There is some
obscurity as to whether he was aware that the second postponement was
intended to be only until later that night; probably so, for he claimed to
have waited for the others, in considerable danger of being apprehended,
for one and a half to two hours on the far side of the fence. This wait
(whatever was its exact length) is borne out by the fact that Haldane
recorded a Pyramus and Thisbe-like conversation with him through the
fence, during which he offered Churchill his compass and some chocolate. What is also obscure is why Haldane and Brockie assumed that
Churchill's having gone over precluded their following; the alarm had
not been raised.

So far there does not seem to be any more conflict of evidence than
that which would be natural between two honest witnesses, of different
temperament, describing a motor accident which they had observed
from opposite sides of the street, particularly if they were recalling it
after a long interval. Haldane's complaint was most clearly set out in a

long (6,000-word) memorandum which he drafted in 1924 and then amplified in 1935.* This reversion to the issue, once after twenty-five years and again after thirty-six, may be held to point to an obsession and to contradict his own statement (in the memorandum) that 'I decided that the less was said the better, which is the policy I have consistently followed in the matter.' On the other hand Haldane never sought to publish the memorandum, not even in his own memoirs. When he died he deposited it, and the rest of his diaries, in the National Library of Scotland, where it can be consulted, although there has never been any attempt to bring it to public notice. The essence of his criticisms were as follows:

[1] I must admit that I was surprised and disgusted to find myself left in the lurch, for Churchill had walked off with my carefully thought-out plan or what he knew of it, and had simply taken the bread out of my mouth.

[2] ... the truth was that at Pretoria I was thinking of *three* individuals and he of *one* man only, himself. ...

[3] Had Churchill only possessed the moral courage to admit that, in the excitement of the moment, he saw a chance of escape and could not resist the temptation to take advantage of it, not realizing that it would compromise the escape of his companions, all would have been well. ... But it was not to be, and the false step, once taken, made the difficulty of retraction, if ever contemplated, a thousand times more difficult, until, as time went on, it became impossible; for what would have been overlooked in the spontaneous admission of an impetuous youth of twenty-five, would have been condemned in the maturer man.[18]

In further mitigation of Haldane's nearly half-century-long keeping of the issue alive, at any rate in his own mind, it can be said that he was subject to successive provocative waves as Churchill continued to publish accounts of these distant events with which Haldane did not agree. Almost immediately after the events described Churchill got his two South African chronicles into the bookshops. *London to Ladysmith via Pretoria* came out in May and sold 14,000 copies. It was followed in October by *Ian Hamilton's March*, which sold 8,000. Then, almost a generation later, he produced at the turn of the years 1923–4 two

---

* This, at least on the face of it, damaging document is published in full in the second part of the *Companion Volume* to the first volume of the official biography (pp. 1099–115). As Randolph Churchill was still in full charge at that stage, it being a year or so before his death, and only approximately the same time after that of Winston Churchill, this was an example of fairness beyond the call of duty.

Strand Magazine articles recounting his escape. These articles undoubtedly provoked Haldane to his 1924 setting out (privately) of the record as he saw it. And in 1930 Churchill produced his much praised and very successful *My Early Life*, in which no fewer than ten (out of twenty-nine) chapters were devoted to South Africa, with four of them specifically on his own capture and escape. While it took Haldane five years to react to this, his 1935 expansion of his 1924 screed may be seen as a disagreeable raking over old ashes, but it must be said in Haldane's defence that these ashes had been far from allowed to lie smouldering by the other principal party.

There was another, earlier incident in Churchill–Haldane relations which may well have left a considerable deposit in Haldane's mind. In 1912 Churchill believed that he had been libelled in *Blackwood's Magazine* on the question of whether he had broken his parole. He swung into heavy action with his close friend F. E. Smith, later Lord Birkenhead, and not the most gentle of KCs, acting for him. They wanted Haldane, then a brigadier-general with a command in Kent, to give evidence for Churchill. Haldane did not want to do so, although he was equally adamant that he would not go into the box against him. A great barrage of persuasion was unleashed against him: a summons from the Admiralty to call there upon the First Lord, as Churchill had become, and pressure to meet Smith to help prepare the statement of case. Haldane took effective evasive action, but found the rumbustious circus approach distasteful. It reminded him of an occasion when Churchill, trying to get himself accepted as part of the Haldane–Brockie break-out party, had mistakenly tried to attract Haldane with the promise of glorious publicity: '[He] held out as a bait that he would take care that, if successful, my name was not hid under a bushel. In other words I should share "in a blaze of triumph" such as, according to the account of his escape in the *Strand Magazine*, he enjoyed on reaching Durban. But advertisement has never appealed to me.'[19]

The last sentence was no doubt honestly modest, but it also revealed a plain soldier's distaste for the publicity rodomontade which always attended Churchill, and maybe a touch of perverse jealousy too. Common involvement in an escape enterprise, even if the parties remain successfully together instead of being separated, is by no means always a recipe for continuing friendship. The Haldane issue cast a nasty private shadow over the otherwise gratifying glamour of Churchill's escape. But there is no clear evidence that Churchill was guilty of anything more than impetuous self-centredness, accompanied by rash courage. And all these three attributes were always very much part of his make-up as a young man. So was luck, and he enjoyed a great deal of this in his solitary journey from the prison camp to Lourenço Marques.

First he walked through the town for half a mile until he struck a railway line, which he hoped was the one east to Delagoa Bay. He wore a brown suit and a slouch hat, and hoped that if he walked with confidence he would be unchallenged. His audacity paid. Then he walked for two hours along the line until he came to a train station, which might have been Eerste Fabriekan, the first of thirteen which, at widely varying intervals, were scattered along the route to the Indian Ocean. His tactic was to jump on a train a short way out of the station just before it had gathered speed. This he accomplished with difficulty, for, partly because of his dislocated shoulder, he was not particularly agile. It was a goods train, mainly carrying empty coal bags back to a colliery area. Among them he enjoyed a comfortable if sooty sleep for a few hours. He was however awake to leave the train well before dawn. This again presented some difficulty. He bounced into a ditch and was lucky to suffer no laming injury. He was then near Witbank, the third of the stations and the centre of a mining district. He had accomplished about 80 miles and had another 200 to go.

Throughout the next long day of South African summer he wandered about, nervous of being seen, without much sustenance or plan. Then at 1.30 a.m. on the second night he came to a colliery with substantial outbuildings. He decided, mainly because he had no alternative, to risk an appeal for help. Perhaps he would find someone who, maybe out of sympathy or avarice (he was more than willing to spend his £75), would not turn him in to the Boer authorities but assist him on his journey. He knocked at a door. This was his outstanding, almost miraculous piece of luck. The man who sleepily answered was an English mine manager named John Howard. Once Howard had busted Churchill's original and wholly unconvincing explanation of his presence and established his true identity and purpose, he took him in and fed him, even supplying him with whisky and cigars, then got a colleague, Dan Dewsnap,* to lower him down the mine shaft, where he remained,

* This was the icing on Churchill's cake of luck. Dewsnap came from Oldham, where his wife still was. When Churchill returned to the town at the beginning of the 1900 general election campaign, he told a great meeting in the Theatre Royal the story of his escape and referred to Dewsnap, and an excited cry of 'His wife's in the gallery,' rang

accompanied by a troop of rats but well provendered, for several days until the excitement and intensive searches occasioned by the discovery of his escape appeared to be abating. Eventually, a full week after his break-out he was with the help of Howard and his friends put in a truck of wool bales which was to be shunted on to a freight train bound for Delagoa Bay. The journey was estimated to take sixteen hours, but in fact it lasted almost four times as long, with many hours of waiting culminating in a final agonizing night (although he managed to sleep through most of it) at the border station of Komati Poort, but on the wrong side of the frontier. Eventually the train chugged on across the border and at Ressana Garcia he saw through a chink, almost as though they were a company of welcoming angels, the elaborate uniforms of Portuguese officials on the platform.

This was how Churchill told the story in *My Early Life*, published thirty years later, although it appears from the 1990s investigations of his granddaughter, Celia Sandys, and published in her *Churchill: Wanted Dead or Alive*, that he was dependent not only upon luck and his own nerve but also upon the attendant activities of Charles Burnham, a local storekeeper and merchant, whose goods provided Churchill's protection and bower. Burnham decided that he ought to come with him on the train, and at various points of hold-up, when Churchill thought he was entirely dependent upon chance, he was in fact dependent upon small bribes judiciously dispensed by Burnham to untie dangerous knots.[20] What however is neither new nor disputed is that, once safely in Lourenço Marques, Churchill with some difficulty roused the British consul and having established his identity was once again well received. Late that same evening he was on a boat to Durban, where he arrived on 23 December.

He was given a resounding welcome and immediately found himself a figure of world fame. 'The blaze of triumph', in which, if accurately reported by Haldane, he had offered the latter a share, was no exaggeration. He made a speech to a large crowd in front of the town hall and he received 'sheaves of telegrams' from many parts of the world before he departed that evening to dine and sleep with the Governor of Natal at Pietermaritzburg. The next day he rejoined General Buller's army. Buller was an admirer, although the feeling was by no means fully reciprocated, in spite of the General's Victoria Cross, which had

---

out. This redoubled the warmth of the welcome for the returning hero. (*My Early Life*, pp. 369–70.)

however been earned many years earlier. Buller was reported (by Churchill) as saying: 'You have done very well. Is there anything we can do for you?'[21] What he did was to give Churchill a lieutenant's commission in the South African Light Horse, without requiring him to give up his *Morning Post* reporting, despite the fact that such duality of function had been forbidden by the War Office. Roberts and Kitchener, who arrived in South Africa in March, the former as Commander-in-Chief and the latter as his Chief of Staff, did not take nearly such an enthusiastic view of Churchill. 'Bobs', the great Field Marshal, was very cool. Their job was to repair the damage of the three British defeats of the December (1899) 'black week' (of General Gatacre at Stormberg, of General Lord Methuen at Magersfontein, and of General Buller at Colenso).

Churchill stayed in South Africa for another six months until Pretoria had been occupied and the war, in his view, had been won. He engaged, and always with gallantry, in a number of serious actions, at Spion Kop, at Hussar Hill, at Potgieter's Ferry and at Diamond Hill. He was among the first into both Ladysmith and Pretoria. Nonetheless it is difficult not to see much of this post-escape period as resembling the transformation scene of a spectacular musical comedy, with a full stage and the characters arriving from all sides, but with Churchill always at the centre. In late January (1900) Lady Randolph turned up, accompanied from Cape Town to Durban by her younger son Jack, and more or less in command of a hospital ship called the *Maine*, for which £40,000 of Anglo-American money had been raised. Unfortunately one of her first patients was Jack, who was lightly wounded on 12 February and needed a month's care. Winston Churchill was disappointed that Pamela Plowden was not of the party. 'Oh why did you not come out as secretary?' he wrote to her on 28 January.[22] On 6 January he had written to his mother about her (Lady Randolph and Miss Plowden were quite close and perhaps both treated Churchill's exuberance with something of the same mixture of admiration and detachment), 'I think a great deal of Pamela; she loves me vy dearly,'[23] which perhaps betrays a certain complacency about his relations with Miss Plowden. She married Lord Lytton within two years.

Lady Randolph was at this time a good deal more urgently intent on matrimony than was Miss Plowden. In mid-March she and her ship sailed off the scene and back to England with a load of wounded. Very soon after her return she married George Cornwallis-West, who was only two weeks older than Winston Churchill. The union, which lasted in a rickety way for thirteen years, did not enhance her general standing.

Meanwhile the musical extravaganza rolled on in South Africa. Among Churchill's performances was a bicycle ride through the centre of Johannesburg in civilian clothes while it was still under somewhat feeble Boer occupation. By this cool expedition he got an important message through to Roberts, who softened towards him as a result. He also helped Roberts by reducing the ludicrous clutter of dukes on his headquarters staff. It put flesh on W. S. Gilbert's *Gondoliers* line of eleven years earlier: 'Dukes were three a penny.' There were indeed three of them there, Norfolk, Marlborough and Westminster. Churchill managed to relieve him of the latter two for most of the time. They accompanied him on an alternating basis on his various expeditions, rather as the Downing Street private secretaries were to do forty years later. 'Enter Churchill, accompanied by two dukes' might have been an appropriate stage direction. When he cantered into Pretoria and visited his old place of incarceration he was accompanied by Marlborough. When travelling down to Cape Town for his voyage home he was breakfasting on the train with Westminster (such were apparently still the amenities of wartime travel) when there was a minor ambush. Churchill, true as ever to his non-combatant status, fired his last anti-Boer shots. It is unlikely they hit anyone.

In these latter months he had however been almost as combative with words as with bullets, but in what was interpreted by many to be a pro-rather than an anti-Boer direction. From Durban he had telegraphed a despatch to the *Morning Post* in January: 'Reviewing the whole situation, it is foolish not to recognize that we are fighting a formidable and terrible adversary. The high qualities of the burghers increases their efficiency. . . . We must face the facts. The individual Boer, mounted in suitable country, is worth from three to five regular soldiers.' And he compounded the sin in some eyes by urging in March that 'A generous forgiving policy must be followed,' even to the Boers in Natal, who had revolted rather than declaring war. 'Peace and happiness can only come to South Africa through the fusion and concord of the Dutch and British races, who must forever live side by side under the supremacy of Britain. . . .'[24] Even with the last phrase this early example of his 'magnanimity in victory' approach produced a storm of criticism.

When he got to Cape Town after the interrupted train journey he paused only to give Sir Alfred Milner, the experienced and normally

self-assured High Commissioner, the benefit of his views, as well as to
have a day's jackal-hunting with him and the attendant Duke of
Westminster, before sailing for home in the *Dunottar Castle*, by chance
the same ship which had brought him out, just over seven months
before. As a young man in a hurry he had certainly not been slothful
during these months. His bravery, his effrontery, his impact had all
been remarkable. At the age of twenty-five he had acquired something
approaching a world reputation. In future whatever he did or said was
sure to attract attention, even if not agreement or admiration.

——— 4 ———
TORY INTO LIBERAL

CHURCHILL LANDED AT Southampton on 20 July 1900. Ten weeks and two days later he was elected member of Parliament for Oldham, still within his twenty-sixth year. He had been unattracted by the offer of an alternative candidature at Southport, on the coast of Lancashire, which had been dangled before him while he was still in South Africa. Southport, with its combination of seaside landladies and early commuting members of the Liverpool commercial classes seeking ozone breezes, sounds a better Conservative proposition than the largely proletarian cotton-spinning town of Oldham. But this was not in fact so. Curzon had been comfortably elected at Southport in 1895, but, when he left to become Viceroy of India in 1898, the bye-election was lost by the Conservatives. The winning Liberal died in the following year and the second bye-election produced a similar result.

Churchill would therefore have gained nothing by being tempted to Southport. But he was not so disposed. He believed in his 'star'. And his star hovered over Oldham. The words of Dan Dewsnap at the Transvaal colliery continued to ring round in his head. 'They'd all vote for you next time,' Dewsnap had said. (In fact they were far from doing so. The swing to Churchill between the 1899 bye-election and the 1900 general election fourteen months later was only about 6 per cent, which was just enough.) But it was his belief more than the facts which counted. He believed that he would always get through, even if by narrow margins. The bullet that cut through the feather of his South African Light Horse hat at Spion Kop would do no more than sartorial harm. The man who opened the door to him at the colliery near Witbank would take him in and not turn him in. The burghers in the streets of Johannesburg would be too preoccupied to notice the passage of a stray cyclist. And so, thus far, it always worked out, including at Oldham. He beat Walter Runciman by 222 votes and squeezed into second place, only sixteen votes behind Emmott, the better-dug-in Liberal, and a crucial 409 votes ahead of his own Tory running mate.

Overall this 'khaki election' allowed the Conservatives to capitalize on the apparent British victory in South Africa (although it was to be another eighteen months before the Peace of Vereeniging with the Boers was signed) and restore their majority to its solid 130-plus level before the erosion of bye-election defeats like those at Oldham in the previous year. Despite the narrowness of the contest there, however, the local campaign was not a particularly rough one. Both Emmott and Runciman were Liberal Imperialists, more inclined to the views of Rosebery and Asquith than to those of Lloyd George or even Campbell-Bannerman. They could not therefore easily be denounced as disloyal pro-Boers, and indeed Churchill himself, while eager to exploit his own adventures, was not disposed to lash himself into a passion of anti-Boer hysteria.

Joseph Chamberlain, the lion of the moment, came to Oldham to deliver over an hour's oration on his behalf. This led to his inviting Churchill for two days to his house in Birmingham, where polling was still continuing, and sending him round to three West Midlands meetings in a special train. The great man put on for him a programme worthy of Lord Beaconsfield's theatrical reception of the young Duke of Portland at Hughenden in 1880. Chamberlain rested in bed all of one day, but got up for dinner to receive the returning political warrior and to regale him with a bottle of 1834 port. With Balfour, Salisbury's nephew and soon-to-succeed crown prince, Churchill's dealings were more mixed, but in outcome at least equally head-turning. He failed to get Balfour to travel the eight miles from his own constituency in Manchester to Oldham, but then responded to a summons from 'King Arthur' to abort a journey to London and immediately return north to Manchester:

> Mr Balfour was addressing a considerable gathering when I arrived. The whole meeting rose and shouted at my entry. With his great air the Leader of the House of Commons presented me to the audience. After this I never addressed any but the greatest meetings. Five or six thousand electors – all men – brimming with interest, thoroughly acquainted with the main objects, crowded into the finest halls, with venerated pillars of the party and many-a-year members of Parliament sitting as supporters on the platform! Such henceforward in that election and indeed for nearly a generation were my experiences.[1]

The new Parliament met for a couple of weeks on 3 December, not only for swearing-in and the election of a Speaker, but for a Queen's speech (not delivered by the declining Sovereign in person) and for eight parliamentary days of substantive debate. They were all devoted in one form or another to matters arising out of the South Africa War, and indeed on the second night of the debate on the address an amendment relating to the terms on which a settlement should be made was moved by Emmott, the senior member for Oldham. It was amazing that Churchill, with the eagerness of the new junior member, let all this pass over his head without attending. He had sailed for New York on 1 December.

This indicated a calm nerve and a determination to stick to his plans, but did not mean that he undervalued his new position. Objectively the standing of an MP was far higher in 1900 than it is today. Britain, although a little shaken by the early defeats of the South African War, was a great and self-confident empire, and one of its proudest possessions was its parliamentary system. Although it had a more restricted franchise than most developed countries, the prestige of its legislature was much higher. It would have been difficult to find any member or aspiring member, not merely Tory or Liberal, but in the nascent Labour party too, and even, paradoxically, quite a few of the Irish Home Rulers as well, who did not instinctively regard the House of Commons as the greatest legislative assembly in the world.

Churchill certainly did. He also regarded membership of it as a natural although highly desirable part of his destiny. Having got there he remained a member with one very brief interval, and a second more worrying one of two years, for sixty-four years, a span which exceeded even Gladstone's sixty-two and a half years. It was therefore doubly odd, that, being delighted in the autumn to add the suffix of 'MP' to his name, he was not also eager to avail himself of the earliest opportunity of sitting on the green benches, from which, apart from Gladstone – the greatest thunderer of the lot – Disraeli, Russell, Palmerston, his father and Joseph Chamberlain had performed.

He was not blasé. But throughout his life he was very realistic about money. He was not exactly grasping, and he had no dominating desire to accumulate for its own sake 'a great stock of scrip or securities' (in the famous phrase he was to use about his friend Birkenhead),* but he was determinedly extravagant without any bedrock of financial support. Most MPs in those days were rich, and the minority who were not were

---

* In his 1933 Foreword to *F.E.*, the first version of the second Earl of Birkenhead's life of his father.

in general naturally austere. Churchill was neither. And MPs were not
then paid.

Churchill, who had already had a good previous financial period, with
the success of several books accompanied by a high *Morning Post* salary
and a low-spending seven months in South Africa, shrewdly decided
that his earning capacity as a celebrity lecturer was at a temporary peak
and that he had better cash in on it. He therefore devoted the last days
of October and the whole of November to an intensive and profitable
British lecture tour. It was arranged through an agent, Gerald Christie,
whom he continued to use for many decades. Churchill managed to
keep a full grip on the equity, which meant the number and cost of the
tickets which could be sold for a particular evening in a particular hall.
As a result, in the meticulous accounts which he kept, his net profits,
which were high, given the money values of the period, both varied
substantially and produced very precise sums, calculated down to shillings and pence.

He limbered up with a visit as a returning alumnus to Harrow on 25
October, but even there he did not allow his nostalgia to prevent his
going away the richer by £27, the equivalent today of £1,350. He also
there learned that his material was out of control – he was of course
talking about his South African adventures – and that he only got
through a quarter of his notes in one and a half hours. He had this
better organized for his real launch, which was at the St James's Hall in
London on 30 October. There he had persuaded Field Marshal Lord
Wolseley, the Commander-in-Chief of the army, to take the chair and
introduce him, and he made the impressive sum of £265 6s 2d (the
rough equivalent of £13,000). He devoted himself throughout to getting
the most eminent of chairmen: Rosebery in Edinburgh, Derby in
Liverpool, Dufferin and Ava in Belfast, Ashbourne, the Irish Lord
Chancellor, in Dublin, and he would have got Joseph Chamberlain in
Birmingham had that weary titan not thought it necessary to take a
post-election Mediterranean holiday; Churchill had there to make do
with Lord Dudley. After the St James's Hall launch he did another
twenty-seven widely scattered engagements in the next thirty-one days.
In effect he had only Sundays off. The star occasions were Liverpool,
which exceeded even the St James's Hall takings, and Cheltenham,
which was not far behind. Glasgow, Birmingham, Brighton, Bristol,
Manchester and Dublin also produced very solid takings. Only the semi-
suburban occasions of Westbourne Park (London) and Windsor failed
(narrowly) to net the equivalent of a modern £3,000. The month

produced an aggregate of £3,782 15s 5d (£190,000). It was a spectacular effort.

Britain having been conquered, America beckoned. The December parliamentary session was sacrificed to Mammon, but Mammon, as can be his way, disappointed, though maybe only by the standards of the Churchill family's maritally based expectations that America would always be more generous than Britain. He did not allow for a difference of emotional reaction to the Boer War. While England was mostly bathed in a lather of jingoism, the United States was at best more detached and at worst saw the British war against the Boer republics as a delayed repeat of its own War of Independence. Also in New York, where he started, there was a residual Dutch feeling among some of the oldest-established families who might otherwise have been expected to be the best upholders of an Anglo-Saxon partnership. This did not however prevent Governor Theodore Roosevelt – just elected Vice-President and only nine months short of succeeding the assassinated McKinley as President – from inviting him to dinner in the Mansion at Albany, the New York State capital, within a few days of his arrival.

There is no record of whether this Albany dinner went badly, but it certainly did nothing to prevent the development of a deep and surprising Theodore Roosevelt animus against Churchill. Scattered over the years his judgements (in correspondence) were always unfavourable. On 23 May 1908, he wrote to his son: 'Yes that is an interesting book of Winston Churchill about his father, but I can't help feeling that about both of them that the older one *was* a rather cheap character.' A few months later Roosevelt wrote to Whitelaw Reid, the proprietor and editor of the *New York Herald Tribune*: 'I do not like Winston Churchill but I suppose I ought to write to him.' (Churchill had just sent Roosevelt a copy of one of his books.) Then in June 1910, when Roosevelt had represented the US government at the funeral of King Edward VII, he wrote to Senator Henry Cabot Lodge: 'I have refused to meet Winston Churchill. . . . All the other public men, on both sides, I was glad to meet.' His sole approach to a counterbalancing remark was on 22 August 1914 when he wrote to Arthur Lee MP (the donor of Chequers): 'I have never liked Winston Churchill, but in view of what you tell me as to his admirable conduct and nerve in mobilizing the fleet, I do wish that if it comes your way you would extend to him my congratulations.'[2]

This chronicle of prejudice was perhaps put into perspective by Mrs Alice Longworth, Roosevelt's daughter, who lived on in Washington well into her nineties and the 1980s, always retaining her edge of sharp comment. Arthur Schlesinger once said to her: 'Why did your father dislike Winston Churchill so much?' 'Because they were so alike,' Mrs Longworth conclusively replied.[3]

Churchill's American lecture agent was not nearly as satisfactory as Christie in London. Major Pond, as he styled himself, although it was not obvious in which campaign he had served, was both tiresomely obtrusive and made bad bargains. By 1 January 1901 Churchill was writing of him (to his mother), 'He is a vulgar Yankee impresario and poured a lot of very mendacious statements into the ears of the reporters. . . .'[4] Pond may have been a scapegoat for Churchill's general dissatisfaction with the tour, but his pejorative use of the word 'Yankee' to his mother was odd. Through a combination of Pond, somewhat disappointing financial returns and audiences more cool about the British cause than he had expected, Churchill's enthusiasm for the United States was less on this trip than it had been five years before. This time he much preferred Canada, where he had better audiences, made more money and spent an enjoyable Christmas with the Governing-General Mintos in Ottawa.* Altogether he felt, paraphrasing Laurence Sterne, that 'they order these things better in Canada'.

Yet the failure of the tour was very relative. He cleared just over £1,600 (£80,000) for two months' effort, about 40 per cent of what he had made in half the time at home. Winnipeg (a clear winner), New York,[†] Philadelphia and Toronto did him the best. He found the grind of one-night performances often more exhausting than rewarding (on one occasion there was no public lecture but he 'was hired out for £40 to perform at an evening party in a private house – like a conjurer'),[5] and he may even have been a little homesick, if not exactly for his 'home', which was never a very strong feature in his life as a young man, at least for the political arena in which he had earned a place and which he had treated so cavalierly in December. 'I shall be home by the 10th of February and am looking forward very much to the beginning of Parliament . . .' he wrote to his mother on 9 January. 'I have got to hate the tour very much indeed, and if it were much longer I do not think I

* Miss Plowden was also a Christmas house guest, but there was a sense of mutual, amicable disengagement.
† Where Mark Twain, then at the height of his fame, presided and introduced the lecturer with the gracious phrase: 'Mr Churchill by his father is an Englishman, by his mother he is an American, no doubt a blend that makes the perfect man.'

would be able to go through with it.'[6] He had counterbalancing achievements, however. He also wrote at about this time: 'I am vy proud of the fact that there is not one person in a million who at my age could have earned £10,000 without any capital in less than two years.'[7] Nor did he, except at the margin, spend this equivalent of a modern half-million pounds on riotous living. He handed it over for investment to Sir Ernest Cassel, the epitome of a successful Edwardian plutocrat and a close friend of King Edward himself. There was always the sense with Churchill, at this stage largely because of the multifarious high-life contacts of his mother, that if he had wanted a music lesson it would have been Sir Edward Elgar who would have been sent for, or, if a little nursing attention had been required Florence Nightingale would have come out of retirement.

The Britain which Churchill re-entered at Liverpool on 10 February was different in one important symbolic respect from the one he had left. Not only had the new century begun (by strict if not popular reckoning) but the Victorian age was over. Queen Victoria had died on 22 January while Churchill was in Winnipeg. He was not shattered by the news. It did nothing to take the edge off his pleasure at $1,150 having been collected at the doors of his lecture that evening, and his first comments (again to his mother) were some friendlily mocking remarks about the self-indulgent lifestyle of the new King. But it did have the quirkily odd result that he, who was for much of his later career to be regarded as the last Victorian left in British politics, had by his eagerness for lecture fees forgone the opportunity to take the parliamentary oath of allegiance to the Queen. When he was first admitted, on 14 February, it was to King Edward VII that he swore his fealty; this was probably appropriate, for in fact he was, and remained, essentially an Edwardian rather than a Victorian.

Four days later he made his maiden speech. This was neither a disaster like Disraeli's notorious 1837 performance, nor a spectacular success like the 1906 polemic of his future friend F. E. Smith. He spoke for half an hour at about 10.30 on a Monday night immediately following David Lloyd George, who was then a thirty-eight-year-old North Wales solicitor and MP of eleven years' standing and some fame and/or notoriety, who had just made a somewhat intemperate pro-Boer speech. This juxtaposition (together with his own *réclame*) ensured Churchill a very full house. At least two newspapers however (the *Standard* and the *Morning Post*) were even more impressed by the attendance in the Ladies' Gallery than on the floor: there was a great turn-up of Conservative *grandes dames*, but they were more matriarchal and auntly than romantically maidenly.

It was a good speech, and it reads well today. Churchill had of course prepared it most carefully and more or less learned it by heart. This was not unusual in a maiden speaker of energy and ambition. What was unusual in Churchill however was that it was a practice that he continued for years to come; indeed the meticulous preparation although not the learning by heart persisted throughout the whole of his career.

What he could not prepare was an appropriate opening comment on Lloyd George's speech. With the thought for this he was most fortuitously provided by his neighbour (Thomas Gibson Bowles, MP for King's Lynn, who also subsequently transferred to the Liberal party) a few minutes before he had to take the plunge. Bowles told him to say that Lloyd George, who had made a violent speech while withdrawing a moderate amendment, would have done better to have moved his moderate amendment without making his violent speech. It was a neat beginning.

Churchill spoke from the corner seat in the bench immediately behind the ministers, which was the place from where his father had latterly but not most successfully performed, and he did so in a full frock coat. The subject was the general conduct of the war in South Africa, and he had four striking passages. Early on he said: 'If I were a Boer fighting in the field – and if I were a Boer I hope I should be fighting in the field . . .'. Then, arguing against a proposition that in a post-war transition to democracy there should be interim military rather than civilian government, he said: 'I have often myself been very much ashamed to see respectable old Boer farmers – the Boer is a curious combination of the squire and the peasant, and under the rough coat of the farmer there are very often to be found the instincts of the squire – I have been ashamed to see such men ordered about peremptorily by young subaltern officers, as if they were private soldiers.' His third point was that it ought to be made 'easy and honourable for the Boers to surrender, and painful and perilous for them to continue in the field'. And the fourth, on which he sat down and therefore, wisely or otherwise, made the final memory of the speech, was to raise the spirit of Lord Randolph Churchill by saying that he was sure that his kindly reception was 'because of a certain splendid memory which many honourable members still preserve'.[8]

Edwardian newspapers, popular and patrician alike, reported Parliament with a detailed interest unimaginable today. Nevertheless, while not making headline news in the way that F. E. Smith's first speech was to do six years later, the welter of comment, largely favourable, aroused by Churchill was exceptional. Many of the cuttings from nineteen different newspapers which he kept among his records were adulatory without qualification. The more interesting were the less typical ones. H. W. Massingham in the Liberal *Daily News* wrote:

> Mr Winston Churchill's reply was in very striking contrast to the speech [Lloyd George's] to which it was indeed only nominally an answer. The personal contrast was as striking as that of treatment and method. Mr George has many natural advantages; Mr Churchill has many disadvantages. In his closing sentences he spoke gracefully of the splendid memory of his father. Mr Churchill does not inherit his father's voice – save for the slight lisp – or his father's manner. Address, accent, appearance do not help him.
>   But he has one quality – intellect. He has an eye – and he can judge and think for himself. Parts of the speech were faulty enough – there was claptrap with the wisdom and insight. But such remarks ['more squires than peasants', 'an honourable peace', etc.] showed that this young man has kept his critical faculty through the glamour of association with our arms.
>   . . . then Mr [Joseph] Chamberlain rose. His speech was an able piece of debating – clear, rasping, coarse in tone, full of points aimed – and successfully aimed – at the average party spirit of his following. . . . But the speech was utterly without elevation – and in insight and breadth of treatment it was far inferior to Mr Churchill's.

The *Manchester Guardian* sketch, written by J. B. Atkins, who had travelled out to South Africa with Churchill, had something of the balanced appraisal of a friendly acquaintance. 'His [Churchill's] was a carefully turned speech, filled with antitheses of a literary flavour. His father, with all his power, had little literary sense, and this possession is all in favour of the young member who started out tonight.' Perhaps the most critical note came from the *Glasgow Herald*:

> Occasionally there were tones and inflections of voice which forcibly recalled his father, Lord Randolph Churchill, but the hon. Gentleman did not show much trace of his parent's brilliancy in debate. . . . Readiness he had in abundance and he may develop well, but to those who remember the electrical effect of the father's maiden speech, the son's first plunge into debate was nowhere near so high a flight.

Immediately after this maiden effort Churchill showed slight signs of parliamentary incontinence and intervened twice in the following week. One of them was a supplementary question which Speaker Gully ruled out of order. This incontinent tendency did not gain momentum. He made two quite notable speeches that spring, one in March and one in May, and was then kept fairly quiet during the remaining three years for which he sat as a Conservative.

In 1901 he made a total of nine Commons interventions, but these were supplemented by about thirty political speeches in the country and a fresh burst of lecturing in the spring – somewhat less profitable than in 1900. The March speech was a debating effort (although nonetheless carefully prepared) on the side of the government. Major-General Colvile had held a fairly disastrous command in South Africa and had first been 'Stellenbosched', in the vivid current word for being sent back to base (the equivalent of *limogé* in French) and then returned to England, from where, in a generous 'old boys' gesture, he had been appointed Commander-in-Chief of the garrison at Gibraltar. Later, however, when more damaging facts about Colvile's inadequacies had come to light, this appointment was rescinded by the War Office. A storm of parliamentary criticism ensued, and it looked as though the government might be defeated by a motion demanding a committee of enquiry. Churchill weighed in with force, arguing that 'the right to select, to promote and dismiss' must be left to the military authorities. Selection was a necessary human process, particularly in the armed forces, and if it were hobbled the army would become a flaccid affair. The speech was the success of the occasion, and Churchill himself believed that he had turned votes and helped to give the government a comfortable majority. He had certainly pleased St John Brodrick, the Secretary of State for War, whose note to him (admittedly sent during the excitement of the debate) contained a fine example of false prophecy: 'May I say you will never make a better speech than you made tonight.'[9]

He did not long retain the War Secretary's favour, for his May speech was an all-out attack on a scheme of army reorganization which was intended to be the *chef d'oeuvre* of Brodrick's Secretaryship of State. It involved an increase in the army estimates by £5 million over the previous year, exclusive of special expenditure in South Africa and China (the Boxer Rebellion). This 'extravagance' set Churchill pietistically off. It was fifteen years since Lord Randolph had made for the cause of military economy 'the greatest sacrifice of any minister of modern times'. 'I am very glad the House has allowed me . . . to lift again the tattered flag that I found lying on a stricken field.'

Fortunately, however, Winston Churchill engaged with issues more serious than this waving of the filial bloody shirt. Brodrick proposed the creation of three army corps of regulars and another three of militia and volunteers in reserve. Churchill was scathing about the three regular corps: 'one is quite enough to fight savages and three are not enough even to begin to fight Europeans'. 'A European War cannot be anything but a cruel heart-rending struggle, which, if we are ever to enjoy the bitter fruits of victory, must demand, perhaps for several years, the whole manhood of the nation, the entire suspension of peaceful industries, and the concentration to one end of every vital energy of the community.' This was a better prophecy than that of Brodrick, about his future speechmaking, and Churchill's aphorism that 'the wars of peoples will be more terrible than the wars of kings' was also very much on the mark.

His other major point – an unorthodox one for a cavalry subaltern – was to proclaim the supremacy in terms of British national interest of the navy over the army:

> The only weapon with which we can expect to cope with great nations is the Navy. . . . And surely to adopt the double policy of equal effort both on Army and Navy, spending thirty millions on each, is to combine the disadvantages and dangers of all courses without the advantages or security of any, and to run the risk of crashing to the ground between two stools, with a Navy uselessly weak and an Army uselessly strong.[10]

This speech, which lasted nearly an hour, was a setpiece oration. He recorded that he had spent six weeks preparing it, much of which must have gone on learning it by heart, for he sent off the text to his friend Oliver Borthwick at the *Morning Post*, requesting a good report, nearly three weeks before the debut. He delivered the speech faultlessly, betraying however to a sharp observer that he was reading from an internal teleprompter by at one stage picking up a book in order to read a long quotation from his father, and then putting the book down again well before the end of the passage. The time of preparation was well spent. The speech not only made a splash at the time, but had several important consequences for Churchill. It gave him a theme which he developed on several speaking and writing occasions in the remainder of the year. It made him an interesting figure to the Liberal party; warm letters were written by such disparate figures on that side of politics as

Sir William Harcourt, W. T. Stead and John Burns.[11] And, most important of all, as he wrote of it, admittedly nearly thirty years later, in *My Early Life*: 'it marked a definite divergence of thought and sympathy from nearly all those who thronged the benches around me'.[12]

As the central interest of the first phase of Churchill's parliamentary career is the build-up to his change of party of May 1904, this speech must be seen as one important early stage of the journey. In some way the process in retrospect seems ineluctable. In another it is subject to a rather awkward question: What would Churchill have done had he been offered a post in the Conservative government? On 11 July 1902, Salisbury resigned and his nephew, Arthur Balfour, moved as effortlessly into the premiership as Asquith was to do in 1908 and Neville Chamberlain in 1937. Perhaps because he had for so long been almost co-head of the government, Balfour made very few changes to its shape. Almost the only one of any importance was his appointment of C. T. Ritchie as Chancellor of the Exchequer in the place of Hicks-Beach, who had insisted on retiring with Salisbury. It was a strange appointment, for neither socially nor intellectually did the worlds of Balfour and Ritchie touch. Balfour thought of him as an effective if unprepossessing man of business who must therefore understand the dark mysteries of finance and economics, about which his own ignorance was profound. But Ritchie was as stubborn as he was unversed in the ways of Balfourian courtesies and ambiguities, and he had become a dogmatic Free Trader. His first and only budget proved a perfect trip-wire for setting off the great Protectionist–Free Trade dispute which was to bedevil the Balfour government and reduce the Conservative position in the next parliament to a rump, just as the great European dispute was to do to the Major government and its aftermath ninety years later.

The Protectionist issue was also to have a profound effect on the career of Winston Churchill. In the summer of 1902, however, that young and thrusting politician was more concerned with the minor changes in the government, or rather with their absence on any scale, than with the possible 'political consequences of Mr Ritchie'.* He had been closely associated over his year and a half in the House of Commons with a group of four other highly privileged young Conservatives. They were all between three and five years older than he was, but none in 1902 was more than thirty-four. They were happy to be

* To anticipate the title of J. M. Keynes's 1926 pamphlet *The Economic Consequences of Mr Churchill*.

known, at once self-mockingly and self-consciously, as the 'Hughligans', after their most intellectually certain and, on the majority of issues, most right-wing member, Lord Hugh Cecil, the fifth son of the old Marquess of Salisbury. Cecil, like Gladstone, sat seriatim for Greenwich and for Oxford University, although in a reverse order from the GOM, and was almost as highly educated, although of a much more sterile and less constructive cast of mind. Of the other members of the coterie there was Earl Percy, the eldest son of the seventh Duke of Northumberland and as a Christ Church 'first' another of those who half made Churchill feel the lack of a university education, although this was already a declining neurosis. Next came Arthur Stanley, a younger son of the sixteenth Earl of Derby who, like Churchill, had gone straight from school into the 'world', although that of diplomacy rather than of the army. He faded politically, and his main middle-life distinction was to be chairman of the Royal Automobile Club for nearly thirty years; he looked rather like an inter-war advertisement for 'Shell Goes Faster'. The remaining member was Ian Malcolm, the very model of a matinée idol, who matched his own looks by marrying Lillie Langtry's daughter. Malcolm and Cecil lost their seats in the 1906 slaughter, as Churchill would have done had he stuck to the Conservative party.

Most of the Hughligans had some fairly intimate association with Balfour, being either his relations or his former private secretaries, which perhaps inhibited them from repeating the wrecking role which their loose inspiration, Lord Randolph Churchill's Fourth party, had performed a generation earlier against both Gladstone and Stafford Northcote (the 1876–85 Tory leader in the Commons). Hugh Cecil, for example, was not able to achieve his full fastidious 'hooligan' potential until nearly ten years later when he played such a leading part in the 'squalid, frigid'* shouting down for a full half-hour of Asquith, as to provoke Will Crooks, a solid Labour trades unionist MP, to exclaim that 'many a man has been certified insane for less than the noble lord has done this afternoon'.[13]

What the Hughligans were really good at was the organization of intimate political dinner parties in the subterranean private dining rooms of the House of Commons. Their aim was to deepen their acquaintanceship with the famous, and perhaps even more to make sure that the famous knew who they were. They cast an eclectic net. They

* The phrase used in Churchill's daily parliamentary letter (as Home Secretary) to the King (*Companion Volume*, II, pt 2, p. 1103).

had Balfour and Campbell-Bannerman, Morley and Hicks Beach, and on one occasion in July 1901, as over-enthusiastic hosts or hostesses are liable to do, they overdid it by inviting both Rosebery and Harcourt, who had not been on speaking terms for seven years, to dine on the same night. It served them right that, Rosebery having been put off (though he had them all for a Sunday at Mentmore a couple of weeks later), Harcourt forgot to turn up.

Nine months later they had a notable dinner with Joseph Chamberlain. With his taste for dramatic entries and exits, he paused at the door as he left them and (at least in the pointed-up memory of Churchill) said, 'You young gentlemen have entertained me royally, and in return I will give you a priceless secret. Tariffs! There are the politics of the future, and of the near future. Study them closely and make yourselves masters of them, and you will not regret your hospitality to me.'[14] As that was thirteen months before Chamberlain's political pattern-shattering speech at Birmingham town hall in favour of Protection and his supremely but justifiably arrogant remark to the Liberal Chief Whip ('You may burn your leaflets; we are going to talk about something else'), the advice was not as trite as it sounds in retrospect. One of those who benefited from it (Cecil was also a Free Trader) was Churchill. He did indeed study tariffs, and made himself a master of the polemics of the subject, but not in a way that Chamberlain would have wished.

The Hughligans were closely linked in the sense that they were much at ease in each other's company, and that friendly relations persisted long after they had lost any political cohesion. Hugh Cecil was a High Tory best man at Churchill's wedding four years after the latter had joined the Liberal party. But such association did not proscribe those who were ambitious (which Churchill most assuredly was) from keeping a watchful and not entirely benevolent eye on the progress of the others. In Balfour's minor reconstruction of the government only Percy got preferment. He became under-secretary at the India Office, and a year later was transferred to the Foreign Office. There can be little doubt that Churchill would at that stage have liked junior office, and probably thought that he deserved it. There is no extant letter of the time, not even to his mother, which discloses his thoughts, but the matter is at once delicately and not too euphemistically dealt with by his son Randolph Churchill in the second volume (and the last which he wrote) of the official biography: 'Balfour did not avail himself of this opportunity to offer Churchill any Ministerial office. So high was Churchill's opinion of his own merits and so considerable had been his early parliamentary success that whatever others may have thought, we may be sure he would have been in no way surprised by inclusion in the ministry.'[15]

So the awkward question is whether a parliamentary under-secretaryship would have kept him within the Conservative party. It would undoubtedly have made him better disposed towards Balfour, and have made it more difficult for him easily to slip his Tory moorings. But there is little enough to suggest that, although like nearly every ambitious politician his lips sometimes slavered and his eye gleamed at the prospects of office, he could be easily bought off. It is unlikely that, in or out of office, he would have been seduced by Chamberlain's Protectionist doctrine. The arguments which Churchill deployed against it, and which he had been developing in correspondence and in speech hints a year or so before its full-scale Birmingham launch in May 1903, point to a profound conviction rather than to any mood of personal pique. He would have been deeply unhappy when in the autumn of 1903 Balfour encouraged the resignation of the three Free Trade ministers – Ritchie, Balfour of Burleigh and Lord George Hamilton – and then found that the Duke of Devonshire too, whom the Prime Minister did not want to lose, insisted on going with them. It is unlikely that, after that, any junior post and probably not even a senior one, would have kept Churchill in a government which was listing heavily towards Protection, and shipping a good deal of electoral water in the process.

Churchill's Conservative infidelity had begun before Balfour became Prime Minister with a typically unrewarding flirtation with that incorrigible political *allumeur* Lord Rosebery. Rosebery announced long in advance that he was going to make a great speech at Chesterfield in mid-December 1901. Its greatness was symbolized by the fact that Asquith and Edward Grey, his two Vice-Presidents of the Liberal Imperialist Council, travelled that far north just to sit upon his platform. And Churchill got into a quiver of excitement about the prospect of its leading to the formation of a middle party. Rosebery was strong on phrases which were memorable rather than meaningful. The Liberal party must pursue a policy of the 'clean slate' and put away 'flyblown phylacteries'. In the meantime 'I must plough my lonely furrow ... but before I get to the end of that furrow it is possible that I may find myself not alone.'[16] But whether this meant that he was going to unfurl a standard to which middle opinion could rally was left totally obscure.

Churchill however continued to hope that the chubby earl would prove decisively responsive. Three weeks later, at the beginning of 1902, Churchill went to speak at Blackpool, against which background (although the tower and the piers had been added in the meantime) his father, eighteen years earlier, had made one of the best of his insolently mocking satires of Gladstone. Lord Randolph's 'chips with everything' speech had described how delegations of working men who came to witness Mr Gladstone at his tree-felling recreation were 'permitted to gaze and worship and adore . . . and each of them presented with a few chips as a memorial of that memorable scene'. And so it was with all those who from different directions had looked to the GOM's 1880 victory and his second premiership for succour. 'To all who leaned upon Mr Gladstone, who trusted in him, and hoped for something from him – chips, nothing but chips – hard, dry, unnourishing, indigestible chips . . .'.[17]

Winston Churchill did not quite emulate such satire, but there were two interesting aspects to *his* Blackpool speech. First, he dropped his handkerchief for Rosebery to pick up, and in the course of so doing provided an insight into his own somewhat romantic criteria for leadership: 'I welcome Lord Rosebery's speech because he is the only man amongst the opposition who has a patriotic mind, and who is in a position to offer responsible criticism. Lord Rosebery possesses the three requirements an English Prime Minister should have. He must have a great position in Parliament, popularity in the country, he must have rank and prestige.'[18]

Second, he made an early (for him) and very tentative foray into social policy. The other (and very different from Rosebery) Liberal who greatly impressed him at this time was John Morley. Churchill was already going through a phase when other pastures were green and where the tea next door was better than in one's own parents' house. When Churchill dined with Morley in that same December of 1901 in a small male party which included Buckle, the editor of *The Times*, J. A. Spender of the *Westminster Gazette* and Lord Goschen (whose availability as a replacement his father had memorably forgotten when he resigned in 1886 and who had still become a somewhat sententious ex-Chancellor of the Exchequer of Free Trade views), his host had greatly commended to him Seebohm Rowntree's study of poverty in York. Churchill quickly bought and read it, and it figured prominently in his thoughts and correspondence over that Christmas and New Year. At Blackpool he said:

I have been reading a book which has fairly made my hair stand on end, written by a Mr Rowntree who deals with poverty in the town of York. It is found that the poverty of the people of that city extends to nearly one-fifth of the population; nearly one-fifth had something between one and a half and three-fourths as much food to eat as the paupers in the York Union. That I call a terrible and shocking thing, people who have only the workhouse or prison as the only avenues to change from their present situation.[19]

Rosebery proved a false siren, as Hugh Cecil, not often wise but so on this occasion, warned Churchill at the turn of the year: '[do not] respond to the Imperialist's invitation until he has built himself a house to entertain you in. Now he has only a share in a dilapidated umbrella.'[20] It was a shrewd piece of metaphorical advice, in spite of houses (as well as money) being attributes of which Rosebery – the lord of Dalmeny, Mentmore, the Durdans, 40 Berkeley Square and a Naples villa – was never short.

Perhaps as a result of Rosebery's perennial inability to provide more than a flickering light but more probably because nearly all political movement tends to be a ratcheting process, with fluctuations of mood and two steps forward being balanced by at least one step back, early 1902 was for Churchill a period of pause in his general pro-Liberal direction. He supported the Tory government's Education Bill of that session, which was a sensible thing to do, for it marked a decisive advance for state secondary education, and offended the Liberals only because the bill also extended state aid to Anglican and Roman Catholic primary schools, and the prejudices of Liberal Noncomformist supporters made the party prefer them to be inefficient rather than subsidized.

His other 1902 piece of anti-Liberalism was less admirable. Almost the only collective achievement of the Hughligans was the blocking of the Deceased Wife's Sister Bill. The question of whether a widowed husband should be legally allowed to marry his sister-in-law was at the time an issue of dispute at least comparable with the age of homosexual consent or the banning of foxhunting a hundred years later. There was a clear Commons (although not Lords) majority in favour of liberalization. But there was a virulent minority, of which Lord Hugh Cecil, on high sacerdotal grounds, was a leading member, who were determined to oppose. He got his little band of five, including Churchill, to exploit a most blatant procedural device. Being at that time all bachelors (Malcolm's Langtry marriage was later in the year) they might not in

any event have been considered best qualified to pronounce on the issue
which, at a time when frequent deaths in childbirth left many modest
families dependent upon an aunt moving in, was of considerable practical concern. Still less did they cover themselves with glory by lingering
so long in the division lobby after a previous vote that, it being a private
member's and not a government bill, time ran out and the majority was
frustrated. It could be argued that these wrecking tactics were suitably
in the tradition of Lord Randolph Churchill's manoeuvring of the
Fourth party to exploit the Bradlaugh issue in the early 1880s. Cecil and
co. earned a rebuke from the Speaker and a good deal of public obloquy.
Lord Randolph's grandson, Randolph Churchill, argued in the second
volume of the official biography, with his tongue presumably firmly in
his cheek, that Winston Churchill was doing no more than following a
family tradition. Three successive Dukes of Marlborough, he pointed
out, had voted against the measure in the Lords. It is tempting to
remark that the family tradition would have suggested there was no
point in marrying a second sister. Whatever fortune the father-in-law
was willing to make available would have been sucked dry in the first
go.

These were Winston Churchill's last throwbacks. Even before Chamberlain flung the Protectionist issue into the centre of British politics,
Churchill was committing himself to a quasi-philosophical position,
profound or naive according to taste, from which he had no intention
of resiling. 'Our planet is not a very big one compared with other
celestial bodies,' he wrote to a constituent in 1902, 'and I see no
particular reason why we should endeavour to make inside our planet a
smaller planet called the British Empire, cut off by impassable space
from everything else.'[21]

Then, ten days after Chamberlain's Birmingham speech in May 1903,
Churchill wrote a letter of intransigent protest and warning to Balfour:

> I am utterly opposed to anything which will alter the Free Trade character
> of this country; & I consider such an issue superior in importance to any
> other now before us. Preferential Tariffs, even in respect of articles which
> we are bound to tax for revenue purpose, are dangerous and objectionable.
> But of course it is quite impossible to stop there and I am persuaded that
> once the policy is begun it must lead to the establishment of a complete
> Protective system, involving commercial disaster, & the Americanization
> of English politics. . . . I should like to tell you that an attempt on your
> part to preserve the Free Trade policy & character of the Tory party
> would command my absolute loyalty. I would even swallow six army

corps – if it would make any difference & sink all minor differences. But if on the other hand you have made up your mind & there is no going back, I must reconsider my position in politics.[22]

This long handwritten letter from a twenty-eight-year-old back-bencher of only two and a half years' standing to a Prime Minister could be admired for boldness or damned for brashness, but it was certainly an example of Churchill's self-confidence and determination always to go straight to the top. In the same week he gilded the lily by writing in similar form to Campbell-Bannerman, the leader of the opposition, urging him to consider in his parliamentary tactics the interests of the Conservative Free Traders, as prospective allies in the fiscal battle. Churchill received courteous but bland replies from both leaders.

Further stages in the evolution of Churchill's political position were marked by two even longer letters which he wrote in the last part of 1903. The first was dated 24 October and was addressed to Hugh Cecil. But it is also marked 'Not Sent'. Whether this reduces its validity is a moot point. It could be argued that it makes it more an unprejudiced mind-steering exercise on Churchill's part. On the other hand when drafted it was presumably intended to be sent, and the fact that Cecil was himself an hysteric, although someone of a very different temperament from Churchill, may account for the occasional hysteria of the tone.

I want to impress upon you that I am absolutely in earnest in what I said to you yesterday & I do not think that anything is likely to happen to turn me.

I understand your plan vy clearly; and it is not mine. I do not want to be enrolled in a narrow sect of latter day Peelites austerely unbending in economics, more Tory than the Tories in other things. I do not intend to be a 'loyal supporter' of the Unionist party [alternative name of the time for the Conservative party] or of this present administration, & I object to be so labelled. . . . to proceed making perfervid protestations of loyalty to the 'party' & yet to trample on the dearest aspirations of the party & thwart its most popular champions is to court utter ruin.

You like this sort of thing. You derive a melancholy satisfaction from the idea of being driven out of politics nursing your wrongs. . . . I think you will have your martyrdom as you wish.

But I do not share this view. I am an English Liberal. I hate the Tory party, their men, their words and their methods. I feel no sort of sympathy with them – except for my own people at Oldham. . . . It is therefore my intention that before Parliament meets [that is in late January or

February] my separation from the Tory party and the Government shall be complete & irrevocable; & during the next session I propose to act consistently with the Liberal party.[23]

His second letter was to his American friend Bourke Cockran, dated 12th December, and contained interesting indications of his confidence that people in his position could secure new constituencies almost as easily as he could command a new horse in the hunting field:

> ... I believe that Chamberlain will be defeated at the General Election by an overwhelming majority. What will happen to the Free Trade Unionists by whose exertions this result will have been largely attained is another matter. . . .
>
> I do not think people like Lord Hugh Cecil and myself will be shut out of Parliament. The freedom which we possess here of standing in any constituency enables those who are well known and looked upon as prominent politicians to find another road back [to] the House of Commons when one particular constituency rejects them. But I fear the rank and file of our small party will suffer terribly – many of them being altogether extinguished and ending their public life once and for all. . . . I have had all sorts of rows and troubles in my own constituency and I am thinking of trying my luck in pastures new. . . .
>
> I wish you would send me some good Free Trade speeches that have been made in America, and some facts about corruption, lobbying, and so forth.[24]

The reference to constituency trouble in this letter was fully justified, for on 23 December his General Purposes Committee in Oldham sent him as a sour Christmas present the news that it had passed the following resolution for submission to a full meeting of the Association on 8 January 1904: 'That this meeting intimates to Mr Winston S. Churchill, MP that he has forfeited their confidence in him as Unionist member for Oldham, and in the event of an election taking place he must no longer rely on the Conservative Organization being used on his behalf'. At the wider January meeting the resolution was endorsed with only one vote to the contrary and a few abstentions. It was however a stand-off rather than a critical situation, for the last thing that Churchill's local Conservative militants wanted was a bye-election, which they were fairly sure they would lose. He was therefore able to offer to resign, but to do so with impunity and to continue to sit in Parliament until the general election.

His reference to 'trying his luck in pastures new' was equally quickly followed up. On 13 January he wrote: 'I lunched with Herbert Gladstone [youngest and most political son of the GOM, who was then Liberal Chief Whip] yesterday and talked to him a great deal about seats.'[25] In some ways, however, the most pregnant sentence in Churchill's letter to Cockran was that demanding 'some facts about corruption, lobbying, and so forth'. It should be seen as an echo of a phrase in his Balfour letter when he wrote of his fear that Protection, besides its economic unwisdom, would lead to 'the Americanization of English politics'. Apart from his belief that Protection would impoverish Britain (and Lancashire in particular) Churchill had a profound conviction that tariffs meant the handing over of fiscal politics to the competing pulls of different industrial interests, and that those with the longest purses and least scruples would get the highest duties. This view intertwined with two other strands – his sense of shock at the poverty (as exposed by Rowntree and others) in which many people in the richest country in the world were condemned to live, and a certain, maybe partly snobbish, repugnance at the plutocratic opulence of many of the 'new men' of Edwardian life – to produce a general radicalization of his politics. This latter feeling was not very different from that which Gladstone, vastly different a character although he was, felt at the ostentation of the 1870s, another decade full of new affluence, as was vividly portrayed in Trollope's least benevolently tolerant novel, *The Way We Live Now*.

Churchill was vulnerable to the charge that it was other people's sumptuousness and material values rather than his own which shocked him. It was for instance within the slipstream of the refreshment of two weeks at Sir Ernest Cassel's villa in the Swiss canton of the Valais ('A large comfortable 4 storied house – complete with baths, a French cook & private land & every luxury that would be expected in England … on a gigantic mountain spur 7,000 feet high and [in] the centre of a circle of the most glorious snow mountains in Switzerland')[26] that he went to Glasgow in November 1904 and delivered one of his strongest speeches in this genre. But he was not alone in practising this dichotomy.* Many of Gladstone's most moralist orations were delivered on forays from the most luxurious of country houses. And if personal

---

* Nevertheless members of the Churchill family did have a certain penchant for riding insouciantly on horses of apparent contradiction. Probably only Lady Randolph (in December 1907, by which time Churchill was subsidizing her rather than vice versa) could have calmly stated that she was proposing to move into the Ritz Hotel in order to save money.

austerity is to be regarded as a necessary foundation for radical impulse some of the most famous battle cries for reform must be invalidated.

On the Glasgow occasion, at a large meeting in the St Andrew's Hall, Churchill attacked the government for becoming increasingly subservient to the capitalist interests in the country. In one of those contrapuntal phrases of which he was so fond, and in the use of which (although with more rotundity) he anticipated the speeches which Theodore Sorensen was fifty years later to write for John F. Kennedy, he said that he was more afraid of the Independent Capitalist Party than of the Independent Labour Party:

> No one seems to care anything but about money today. Nothing is held of account except the bank accounts. Quality, education, civic distinction, public virtue seem each year to be valued less and less. Riches unadorned seem each year to be valued more and more. We have in London an important section of people who go about preaching the gospel of Mammon, advocating the 10% commandments, who raise each day the inspiring prayer 'Give cash in our time, O Lord'.[27]

By this time Churchill had crossed his Rubicon. He did not actually fulfil his promise (or threat) to Cecil that by the beginning of the 1904 session he would be on the opposition benches. But on the Tory benches he became an increasingly isolated figure. On 29 March a parliamentary scene of almost symbolic rejection of Churchill by his old party took place. On the motion for the Easter adjournment (and therefore an occasion for a general review of the political situation), which had been moved by the Prime Minister, Churchill rose to speak (still from the government side of the chamber) immediately following Lloyd George. Balfour rose simultaneously, but to leave the chamber. Churchill was affronted by what he regarded as the Prime Minister's 'lack of deference and respect' to the House. This was being over-sensitive. No doubt some aspects of parliamentary manners were better in those days, but ex-senior ministers, let alone rebellious backbenchers of twenty-nine, have often in recent decades had the experience of a Treasury bench less populated and attentive than they thought was their due. At any rate Churchill's self-importance, no doubt playing on an existing feeling that he was a presumptuous and disloyal young cub, provoked a major Conservative demonstration. The front bench all shuffled quietly out. The backbenchers left with less dignity but almost equal unanimity. Some of them stood noisily at the side of the Speaker's chair and up the steps beside the official box, mockingly barracking their erstwhile colleague.

This Holy Week demonstration of Christian charity had a profound impression on Churchill. It made clear to him how strongly reciprocated was his doubly private (because not sent) expression of hatred of the Tory party to Hugh Cecil of the previous autumn. His angry dismay was little assuaged by his father's old Fourth party colleague, Sir John Gorst, then the nearly seventy-year-old Tory member for Cambridge University, staying behind and rising to protest on possibly excessively nostalgic grounds against Churchill's ostracism ('the hereditary right of the honourable member for Oldham to the respect and consideration of the House ought to have preserved him from such treatment as he received at the hands of his party this afternoon').[28] Gorst's support was not based only on manners and memories of the early 1880s. He followed Churchill across the floor of the House and unsuccessfully contested his home town of Preston as a Liberal in 1910.

Churchill's House of Commons experiences in that spring were traumatic. Three weeks later, on 22 April, he was making one of his most radical early speeches in favour of a private member's bill to improve trades union rights and reverse the immensely harmful (to the unions) decision in the Taff Vale case of 1901; this judgement reversed the presumption which had prevailed since the 1870s, and allowed unions to be sued for damages as a result of strikes. Here he was not as isolated on his own benches as on the previous occasion, for seventeen Conservatives supported the motion put forward by David Shackleton, MP for Clitheroe. But this experience was still more devastating to Churchill. When he had been speaking for forty-five minutes (too long, one is tempted to say) without notes, but with as usual a text completely committed to memory, his internal teleprompter suddenly collapsed. He was on a sentence which began: 'It lies with the government to satisfy the working classes but there is no justification . . .'.[29] That was when amnesia struck. After a brief agony of vainly searching for words, both in his mind and in his pockets, which nonetheless must have seemed like an eternity, he sat down and covered his face with his hands.

This would have been an appalling confidence-shattering experience for anyone. It was especially so for Churchill. The first escalation came from the fact that he was not a nervous young member endeavouring, rather beyond his capacity, to do his duty by his constituents. He was, by his own choice, a high-wire trapeze artist, and the sight of his falling off without a safety net must have been for many an almost irresistible pleasure. Nonetheless the much vaunted collective good feeling of the House of Commons seems for once to have asserted itself, and the

murmurs of supporting sympathy were much stronger than the Tory
jeers. The second escalation was that it was little more than ten years
since many members had observed the appalling mental decline, from
physical causes, of Lord Randolph Churchill, much of the degeneration
exhibiting itself through inability to make coherent speeches. Winston
Churchill had made much of proclaiming that his was a short-lived
family, and that he must get on quickly with the achievement of fame.
But such faintly rhetorical predictions of his own doom were different
from actually exhibiting in public what could easily be an early symptom
of an hereditary decline.

This crisis came when Churchill was negotiating an exceptionally
exposed and dangerous political defile and made his recovery from it
the more remarkable. He had a short period of abject dismay, but then
rallied by attempting to improve his memory by the new system of
Pelmanism (of which nothing ever came) and more practically by
ensuring that in future he always had with him the fullest and most
clearly set-out speech notes.

His next significant action in the House of Commons was silent but
nonetheless eloquent. He decided that it was time to change parties,
and made one of the more dramatic floor-crossings in parliamentary
history. When Parliament resumed after the Whitsun recess he rejected
the unfriendly government benches and took his seat below the gangway
on the Liberal side. This has sometimes been presented as though it
were a gesture based upon an impulse of the moment. But as the seat
upon which he landed, as well as being next to Lloyd George, who had
already become a friendly acquaintance, was the one from which he
thought his father performed in his days of Fourth party mischief,* it is
difficult not to believe that it was more than fortuitously empty, and
that there must have been an element of prearrangement. While there
is room for argument about whether he was ever an engrained philo-
sophical Liberal (but who of the leaders were: was Gladstone, was
Joseph Chamberlain in his radical days, was Lloyd George himself?),
there was no doubt that his new party offered him at the time a more
comfortable beach than the one that he had left.

---

* In fact, this was not so. Lord Randolph had sat in the corner seat of the front bench
below the gangway, which was occupied in the Parliament of 1900 by Henry Labouchère. Lloyd George sat in the corner seat of the second bench below the gangway,
which was where Winston Churchill joined him.

CHURCHILL'S LANDING ON the Liberal shore is reminiscent, mainly because of Gladstone's 1866 use of it in not wholly dissimilar circumstances, of the Virgil passage on Dido receiving the shipwrecked Aeneas at Carthage. Gladstone of course deployed the original Latin before the House of Commons: 'Ejectum littore egentum excepi' (an exile on my shore I sheltered), and added that he hoped the Liberal party would not at any time say of him, 'Et regni demens in parte locavi' (and fool that I was I shared with you my realm). While the Liberal party, unlike Dido, neither exactly fell in love with Churchill (except, maybe, for Violet Asquith) nor gave him half their patrimony, they did treat with remarkable enthusiasm and generosity a latter-day recruit who joined them only at a time when their prospects were already riding high. A constituency (Manchester North-West) which, while far from superficially gilt-edged, was in fact almost perfectly tailored for his short-term enhancement was quickly made available. He went to Manchester and received the endorsement of the Liberal Association there at the end of the same week at which his parliamentary débâcle of 22 April 1904 had occurred. It was a very welcome gleam of light in that mood of temporary darkness. Parties nationally mostly welcome converts, although the local enthusiasm for making room for their candidature can often be markedly low. But there was no problem about making room in Manchester North-West. The seat had a popular local Conservative member in Sir William Houldsworth and the Liberals had allowed him an unopposed return in 1900. Then, with one of Churchill's pieces of luck, Houldsworth announced, three months *after* the new candidate's acceptance of the nomination, that he was retiring.

Nationally the Liberal party in 1904–5 were in a position not very different from that of Tony Blair's Labour party in 1995–6. The government were doing very badly and they were doing well. The byeelections were highly satisfactory. Yet the record of successive defeats was such that the Liberals could not quite believe the favourable

evidence. They had won only a single general election since 1886, and
that the narrow and barren victory of 1892. They had also been through
some very bitter intra-party disputes, and, while they had more experienced ex-ministers than were available to Labour in 1997, there was a
gap of doubt to be bridged as to whether they could form a coherent
and competent administration.

Churchill brought no experience of government, but he brought a
famous name, an ebullient personality and a sense, not entirely complimentary, that he was unlikely to join a losing side. Partly for that last
reason, Churchill's popularity at this stage in his career was by no means
the equivalent of his fame. Although he was often far from easy social
currency, he was invited almost everywhere that he chose to go.
Hospitality to young lions was not the same as voicing consistent
approval of their behaviour. King Edward VII, perhaps the last British
monarch to be an arbiter of fashion, sometime enemy of Lord Randolph
but long-term friend, although probably not more, of Lady Randolph,
provided an elevated one-man map of conflicting attitudes towards their
son. As Prince of Wales he always took an interest in him, frequently
corresponding about his books and his various imperial adventures at
the end of Queen Victoria's reign. Then, as King, he had him to stay at
Balmoral for an autumn week in 1902, which was hardly the royal habit
with young backbenchers of twenty-seven. 'I have been vy kindly treated
here by the King, who has gone out of his way to be nice to me,' he
wrote to his mother. 'It has been most pleasant & easy going & today
the stalking was excellent, tho I missed my stags. You will see the King
on Weds when he comes to Invercauld;* mind you gush to him about
my having written to you saying how much etc etc I had enjoyed myself
here.'[1]

By the next year however he appeared to be relatively out of favour.
'I go to Dalmeny [Rosebery's Firth of Forth house] tomorrow,' he
wrote this time from Invercauld. 'I have put my name down at Balmoral
– but I fear I am still in disgrace.'[2] This by no means amounted to a
severance of relations. The links were too manifold for that. In Novem-

---

* Invercauld Castle, a mere five miles from Balmoral, was rented for several seasons by
Sigmund Neumann (later a baronet), an Anglo-Bavarian banker who did well in South
African diamonds and who most successfully worked his way into the set of King
Edward VII. So determined was he always to be on hand that he also rented Raynham
Hall, the Norfolk mansion of the descendants of 'Turnip' Townshend, which was ten
miles from Sandringham, and in addition took Cecil Lodge on Newmarket Heath.

ber 1904, when Churchill made his anti-plutocracy speech in Glasgow, Lady Randolph was staying at Sandringham in a select and fashionable party organized for the King's sixty-third birthday. 'I read your speech at Glasgow with such interest,' she wrote to him from there with maternal ambiguity. 'I did not discuss it with the King, you will be surprised to hear. I think it was rather a pity your Chairman attacked A[rthur] B[alfour] the way he did.* I see the audience resented it – at least so the papers make out.... Here I am in a hotbed of protectionists.'³

After the change of government in December 1905, Churchill's relations with the King inevitably went on to a slightly different basis, although his status as a junior minister did not make them officially close, and there was still a substantial element, good and bad, of the personal in them. In August 1906, in reply to a somewhat boastful letter from Churchill about the weight of business he had transacted during the session, the private secretary's reply contained an addition in the royal handwriting stating: 'His Majesty is glad to see that you are becoming a *reliable* Minister and above all a serious politician, *which can only be obtained by putting country before Party*.'⁴ His admonitory benignity must be seen against the comprehensive disapproval of the new under-secretary about which the King had written to the Prince of Wales (later King George V) as recently as 19 March that year: 'As for Mr Churchill he is *almost more* of [a] cad in office than he was in opposition.'⁵

Politicians at this period set great store by protestations (at any rate within a charmed circle) that political differences, and even strong public attacks, should make no difference to personal friendship. There was always an element of fiction about this, particularly insofar as it related to the best-established figures, who nominally set most store by it. Churchill had two sets of correspondence during the years of his transition with marquisal grandees both of whom protested the supremacy of friendship over politics. The first was with Salisbury (the lesser fourth, not the Prime Ministerial third marquess) in 1904. However there is not much evidence of subsequent intimacy; Churchill never stayed again at Hatfield during that marquess's lifetime. The second was with Londonderry, who was the nephew of his Marlborough grandmother, to whom Churchill had been close up to her death in

---

* The chairman did nothing which Churchill did not do – and Churchill did it with much more resonance.

1899. This concerned membership of the Carlton Club,* that ever prickly subject for those leaving or joining the Conservative party. Londonderry, who was Lord President of the Council as well as chairman of the Club, wrote that 'whatever course you take politically will I hope never make any difference to our relations',[6] but again there was not much evidence of subsequent closeness.

Paradoxically it was in fact among the 'new men', whose manners were supposed to be less good, that Churchill made and preserved some of the best cross-party relationships. With Lloyd George he enjoyed a deepening friendly acquaintanceship well before he symbolically sat himself down beside him in the House of Commons. Joseph Chamberlain was surprisingly benign towards Churchill's implacable opposition to the cause which was dearest to his heart. When he became aware that Churchill thought he had 'cut' him in the lobby of the House of Commons, he wrote (15 August 1903) quite a long letter of denial; it was his 'short-sightedness' and not any personal hostility: 'you may be certain . . . that I bear no malice for political opposition. I have felt for a long time – in fact from your first confidences to me – that you would never settle down in the position of what is called "a loyal supporter". I do not think there is much room in politics for a dissentient Tory, but Heaven knows that the other side stands much in need of new talent, and I expect you will drift there before very long.'[7] And, a year or so later, when Churchill had completed that drift, Chamberlain had him for a night at Highbury, his Birmingham house, and was most helpful about the biography of Lord Randolph Churchill with which he was currently much occupied.

The third example was the strongest of the lot. Almost as soon as Churchill had settled into the bosom of the Liberal party, F. E. Smith erupted on to the political scene as a swashbuckling Tory barrister–MP from Liverpool. He made his reputation with a coruscating but not maidenly first speech in March 1906, and then proceeded, in spite of a certain underlying (but at the time well-concealed) moderation, to espouse the more extreme course in nearly all the Conservative controversies of the Liberal years. He was for dying in the last ditch and not compromising on resistance to the Parliament Bill which curbed the powers of the House of Lords, and he was depicted as Edward Carson's

* Churchill did not in fact resign from the Club until a year after his crossing of the floor and his adoption as a Liberal candidate. He rejoined after an interval of twenty years.

'galloper' in the virulence of his resistance to Irish Home Rule. In spite of this he became and remained Churchill's closest friend, so much so that, after Smith's premature death in 1930, he was never fully replaced in the sense that Churchill never again had a friend who was an equal as well as a wholly congenial intimate.*

The exception to the 'new man' rule was the ninth Duke of Marlborough. Sunny, as he was known – not particularly matching his temperament but stemming from his early designation of Earl of Sunderland, before he became either Marquess of Blandford or Duke – was a solid Tory on the issues and a junior minister (indeed in the post in which Churchill succeeded him) in the declining years of the Balfour government. But, much to his credit, he never faltered during those years in his family loyalty or genuine friendship towards Churchill, for whom Blenheim remained a safe and welcoming haven. In July 1908 Churchill was even allowed to take Lloyd George to stay there.

However, almost all Conservative government supporters who did not know Churchill, and some of those who did, were much less friendly to him. A good example was provided by J. L. Wanklyn, the Liberal Unionist MP for Central Bradford and a man of such obscurity that he escapes the great catch-all of *Who Was Who*. On 5 February 1904 he wrote:

> 75 Chester Square
> Sir,
>   One of your friends opposite rudely interrupted Mr Wyndham in his speech yesterday afternoon and was told by the Speaker to resume his seat. When I called 'order, order', you had the impertinence to turn round and rebuked me for 'shouting people down'. Permit me to warn you that if I have any more impertinence from a young man like yourself, I shall know how to deal with it. Your conduct in using words like 'lie', 'quack', 'charlatan', 'weak', 'dangerous' of Mr Balfour and of Mr Chamberlain has disgusted most people, as well as
>   Yours truly
>   James Leslie Wanklyn[8]

The same feeling expressed itself in Churchill's being blackballed for the Hurlingham Club, which, as he noted with offence, was almost without precedent as polo players there were both rare and in consequence normally greatly welcomed. This put him into a defensive mood

---

* The nearest approach to an exception was General (Field Marshal from 1941) Jan Smuts (1870–1950), Prime Minister of South Africa 1919–24 and 1939–48.

– about clubs at least – which he expressed by declining an offer to put him up for Brooks's, a good and more traditional alternative to the Carlton, but already at least as Liberal Unionist as Asquithian. 'I do not think while political animosities are so keen that I should care to expose myself to the petty malevolence of the ballot. I was fortunate to be elected to a good many clubs while I was yet unknown. I am disinclined at present to put myself forward for others, though I should greatly like to be a member of Brooks's. . . . I do not think you & your Liberal friends realise the intense political bitterness which is felt against me on the other side.'[9]

His politely rejected proposer was the Master of Elibank, later Liberal Chief Whip, who had been a Churchill fan for some time. He had written to him after the Tory walk-out during his speech of 29 March 1904 to express his resentment 'in common with that of many others' at 'the abominable rudeness with which you were treated in the House yesterday', and had added, striking a more upbeat and probably therefore even more welcome note, 'Your speech was splendid & unanswerable.'[10] However there was in general no lack of Liberal welcome. Although Churchill's natural affiliations might have been expected to be more with the Liberal Imperialists, Asquith, Grey and Haldane, his personal relations at the time of his transition were rather closer with the 'little Englanders'. For John Morley's often quirky personality he had conceived a regard, partly but not wholly literary, second only to his admiration for Rosebery's sterile glamour, and Morley was a benignly unobtrusive godfather to the launching of his Liberal life. Lloyd George, hardly perhaps a little *Englander*, has in this context already been mentioned. But it was Campbell-Bannerman who, even if not the most dominant figure, was the leader of the party and the future Prime Minister who was to give Churchill his first office.

With him Churchill's relations were smooth if not intimate. C.B. had greatly (and publicly) admired an early March (1904) speech of Churchill's attacking a Protectionist Sugar Convention to which the British government had subscribed. He described the speech as 'brilliant' and 'containing the most sustained piece of irony I have ever heard in the House of Commons'.[11] Churchill purred, and replied appreciatively. A month later the leader invited Churchill to a quiet little dinner, which was as good a welcome as could be received by a new recruit to a party, particularly one who at that stage had not actually arrived.

Churchill threw himself into the causes of his new party with all the vehemence of a convert and all the impetuosity of his nature. His speeches indeed were inclined to go over several tops. In May 1905 he delivered in Manchester his classic but hardly moderate denunciation of the party he had only recently left, and of its leader with whom he had enthusiastically stood on a platform in that same city at the beginning of the same parliament:

> The great leader of the Protectionist party, whatever else you may or may not think about him, has at any rate left me in no doubt as to what use he will make of his victory if he should win it. We know perfectly well what to expect – a party of great vested interests, banded together in a formidable confederation, corruption at home, aggression to cover it up abroad, the trickery of tariff juggles, the tyranny of a party machine, sentiment by the bucketful, patriotism by the imperial pint, the open hand at the public exchequer, the open door at the public house, dear food for the million, cheap labour for the millionaire.[12]

Then in late July of the same year, when Balfour was beaten on a snap vote in the House of Commons but declined to resign, Churchill delivered an unrestrained House of Commons denunciation. The Prime Minister had 'flouted the traditions of Parliament and dishonoured the service of the Crown'. Balfour's reply was thought to have inflicted more damage on Churchill than he had himself received from the attack. 'It is not on the whole desirable', the Prime Minister said, 'to come down to this House with invective which is both prepared and violent. . . . If there is preparation there should be more finish, and if there is so much violence there should certainly be more obvious veracity of feeling.'[13] It was the victory of the rapier over the bludgeon.

Moreover it provoked some friendly worry that Churchill was damaging himself by pressing too hard. Even his fan the Master of Elibank was disturbed. He wrote to Churchill with circumlocutory gentleness but with unmistakable intent:

> I cannot but feel that perhaps it is not wise entirely to lose sight of the more tender susceptibilities of that strong and silent element which inevitably must rank amongst your backers in order ultimately to carry you and your policy to success in the Country. The feeling, then, amongst these men, is, I think, not so much that your reference to AJB is overdone as that its continuance may detract, in the public estimation, from the weight and general effect produced by the high level of your speeches on current problems. Honestly, I am inclined to share that view.[14]

The same speech also produced letters of varying remonstrance from Lord Hugh Cecil, his old Free Trade ally and future best man, and Sir Ian Hamilton, an intellectual general who had been his friend from Malakand to Pretoria. Hamilton twisted the knife by telling Churchill how 'exceedingly nice' Balfour had been about him at a recent small party where everybody else (except for Hamilton himself) had been eager to rend him apart. And, at about the same time, but written before the speech, a letter had arrived from Bourke Cockran, who had been in England and always wrote with considerable political sophistication, urging Churchill to silence criticism of his vaunting ambition by announcing that for the next parliament, but not beyond, he would accept no office in a Liberal government. He would fight for their cause, but not expect immediate reward.

Nevertheless, in spite of such over-exuberances, the general standard of Churchill's Free Trade speaking was high. Randolph Churchill in volume two of the official biography somewhat over-eggs the custard by stating baldly that 'By the time of the Election, it is no exaggeration to say that he had become the Opposition's most popular and effective exponent of the Free Trade case.'[15] That accolade must belong to Asquith, who followed Chamberlain round the country answering his detailed points with a relentless combination of statistical memory and command over the rules of logic. Asquith rehabilitated himself with the centre and left of the Liberal party (after his 'heresies' of support for the Boer War), and secured his unchallenged succession to the premiership when Campbell-Bannerman's short reign came to an end. Churchill could not begin to rival Asquith's natural authority in this campaign. Nor was he Asquith's equal in either of the attributes mentioned. But he was a very useful and dashing provider of light cavalry support, and his command over memorable imagery was such as to make his speeches in this campaign retain, if the oxymoron is permissible, a dated freshness. Thus, in the House of Commons on 5 March 1905:

> The main argument against these taxes is based on a great principle, which is that this country should be free to purchase its supplies of food wherever it chooses and whenever it chooses in the open markets of the world. . . . It is a principle of special importance to Lancashire members, who, travelling from one great city to another, see in every valley of that undulating region towns and townships which are the homes of a vast thriving population living on a soil which could not support in decent comfort a twentieth of their number. I have been told that within thirty miles of the Manchester Exchange – I might say of the Free Trade Hall

– there is gathered together the greatest concentration of human beings on the surface of the globe. This mass of people are absolutely dependent for the food they eat and the material they employ upon supplies which reach them mainly from foreign lands. They are dependent on the conditions of a crop at one end of the world, and the state of a market at the other; and yet, upon this artificial foundation, through the inestimable advantages of unfettered enterprise, and of unrestricted sea communication, they have been able to build up a vast industrial fabric, which, it is no exaggeration to say, is the economic marvel of the world.

Then, again, in the same speech, but on a different note:

The dangers which threaten the tranquillity of the modern world come not from those powers that have become interdependent upon others, interwoven by commerce with other States; they come from those powers which are more or less detached, which stand more or less aloof from the general intercourse of mankind, and are comparatively independent and self-supporting. Quite apart from the economic argument, which on this side we regard as sanctioned, we do not want to see the British Empire degenerate into a sullen confederacy, walled off, like a mediaeval town, from the surrounding country, victualled for a siege, and containing within the circle of its battlements all that is necessary for war. We want this country and the States associated with it to take their parts freely and fairly in the general intercourse of commercial nations.[16]

On an earlier occasion, just before crossing the floor and addressing the inaugural meeting of the Free Trade League, he had deployed a similar general argument, but as on the subsequent occasion illustrated by graphic (but different) detail:

why should so many ships come to British ports? Why should we carry on an extensive entrepôt trade? Why should sixty millions' worth of manufactured goods be sent into the United Kingdom, unloaded there, warehoused there, made up into fresh cargoes, loaded into ships again, and distributed at a profit all over the world? Other harbours are as wide and deep as ours; other climates are quite as genial – other skies are just as blue. Why should the world's shipping labour in the chops of the Bristol Channel, or crowd up the dreary reaches of the Mersey? It is because our harbours are more nearly as nature made them; because the perverted ingenuity of man has not been occupied in obstructing them with fiscal stake nets and tariff mud bars. This is why they come.[17]

There is a certain plangent melancholy in recalling the deployment of these simple and classical arguments, of which the essential basis was the confident assurance that the civilized world was a secure place and that Britain had the foremost niche within it. The Edwardian years were the last decade in which they could have been so deployed. Churchill did it with great spirit and conviction, helping to ensure that there was a full-scale national (and up to a point rational) debate on the broad issue; and, although he committed some excesses and made some enemies, he enhanced his value to the Liberal party and, ignoring Bourke Cockran's advice, his claim to significant office in a Liberal government.

These accomplishments were the more remarkable because, during these years of 1903, 1904, and 1905, broadly the twenty-ninth, thirtieth and thirty-first of his life, Churchill had been engaged on a major literary enterprise, both in size and in quality. In the three years of 1898 and 1899 and 1900 Churchill had published no fewer than five books, beginning with the The Malakand Field Force, going on to his very substantial River War, the delayed issuing of his novel Savrola and his two medium pieces of South African War rapportage, London to Ladysmith and Ian Hamilton's March. After this spate there was then a gap of five and a quarter years before the appearance, on 1 January 1906, of the most important, substantial and reputation-enhancing of all his young man's writings. This was his two-volume life of his father. Subsequently he wrote nothing of remotely comparable scope until, in 1923 and on the approach to his fiftieth birthday, The World Crisis, his five-volume history of the First World War, began to appear.

Lord Randolph Churchill had appointed two literary executors, neither of whom would today be easily guessed. The first was the husband of one of his sisters who had sat as Conservative member for High Wycombe before succeeding as the fourth Earl Howe in 1900. The second was another fairly obscure Tory MP, Ernest Beckett, a member of the Yorkshire Post-owning Leeds banking family, who had moved out to the broad acres of the East and North Ridings. Beckett, an uncle of the first Mrs Anthony Eden, sat for Whitby for twenty years before becoming Lord Grimthorpe. Neither of these was particularly keen on entrusting Winston Churchill with the biographical task. They probably thought that any resurrection of Lord Randolph's story was likely to do as much harm as good, and the name and publicity-seeking reputation of Winston Churchill by no means stilled those doubts. However they were persuaded, partly by Lord Rosebery, that a filial attempt at the biographical task should be allowed. The large collection of Lord Randolph's papers (although nothing like the quantity subsequently accumulated by his son), which had spent the seven and a half years since his death in the vaults of the Grosvenor Square branch of the London and Westminster Bank, was made available to Winston Churchill in July 1902.

The terms of Lord Randolph's trust deed were potentially restrictive. Howe and Beckett were to have 'absolute discretion' over what use should be made of the papers. It was however silent on the crucial point of whether, if they appointed a biographer, their 'discretion' should extend to control over what he wrote. There was less ambiguity in the stipulation that no document or letter relating to the India Office (where Lord Randolph had served for seven months) or to the Foreign Office (where he had never served) was to be used in any way without the written consent of 'Her Majesty's Secretary of State for either of the said Departments for the time being'. It was obscure what was to happen if the two Secretaries of State disagreed, or indeed whether 'the time being' meant 1893, when the deed was drawn up, or whatever date at which the question of publication might arise. This point seemed to be half disposed of by Rosebery, who had been Foreign Secretary in 1893, and with whom a copy of the deed had been deposited, assuming a pivotal role, although the two Secretaries of State of 1905, Lansdowne and St John Brodrick, were both consulted before the book was published.

The point about executors' rights over a biographer's content gave rise to more difficulty. In the September, two months after the decision had been made, Winston Churchill found it necessary to write to Beckett:

> I incline strongly to the belief that the duty of the literary executors is discharged 'when to the best of their judgement they have selected a suitable biographer'.* Questions of style, or literary taste, of the scope of work, of the proportion of various incidents in the work, are all matters of opinion, and matters upon which opinion will very often be divided. A syndicate may comprise an encyclopaedia, only a man can write a book.[18]

In spite of this spirited statement of authors' rights, Churchill had to accept a number of powers reserved to the executors, although with the proviso that any unresolved dispute should go either to Rosebery or to the former Chancellor of the Exchequer, Sir Michael Hicks Beach, for

---

* His use of inverted commas implied that he thought he was quoting from his father's trust deed, but this was not so.

arbitration. It never came to that, which was as well, for Rosebery, as usual, proved himself tiresome. He tried to get Churchill (but fortunately not in an arbitral and therefore authoritative capacity) to take out the admirable if slightly high-flown passage on Blenheim with which the book begins.

Still more aggravating was Rosebery's behaviour over the elegant essay on his recollections of Lord Randolph which he wrote for Churchill following a conversation with him, and then refused with a good deal of tergiversation to let him have. Eventually he published it as a monograph nine months after the appearance of Churchill's book, and sent it to him with the typically condescending comment: 'I am sending you an advertisement of your book.'[19] The remark of Randolph Churchill (of the third generation) in the official biography seems to be wholly justified: 'This episode reveals the extraordinarily ambivalent [a generous word] character of Rosebery. He first volunteers information; says he made a note and will send it to Churchill; later says he has burnt it; when Churchill puts down his own recollections of the conversation, Rosebery asks Churchill not to print it; admits he has not burnt his notes, declining to send them to Churchill, but says that if further badgered in the matter he will burn them.'[20] Balfour was also a source of some difficulty, as opposed to the much more co-operative Joseph Chamberlain.

Where Churchill kept his full freedom (appropriately but not necessarily inevitably) was on money. He was to take 'all financial liability and all profits' from the book. The latter proved considerable. He employed as his agent Frank Harris, who had not then achieved the notoriety which the (Paris) publication of his four volumes of *My Life and Loves* was later to bring him, and did very well out of him. Harris negotiated an £8,000 advance (between £400,000 and £500,000 at today's prices) from Macmillans, with whom Churchill had not hitherto published. Furthermore, after Macmillans had earned £4,000 of profit, all further profits were to be split equally between publisher and author. And for that he paid Harris not a full 10 per cent commission, but only 10 per cent on the amount by which Harris had got Macmillans to exceed the £4,000 which had been the offer from Longmans, the publishers of his previous five books. The resultant £400 which Harris received was moreover a once-and-for-all payment; he had no lien on Churchill's subsequent receipts from the book.

Perhaps this handsome deal was a reward for Churchill's good nerve in waiting until he had something substantial to sell. Harris operated only in October 1905, hardly three months before publication and more than three years after Churchill had started work. Overall the pace of that work was impressive. Three years was hardly excessive for a two-volume, 250,000-word book based upon careful research. He had not then taken to his later habits of dictation and employing research assistants. The manuscript of *Lord Randolph Churchill* is all in his own hand, and the work on the documents was also done by himself. Already however he was developing a 'cottage industry' approach to the writing of books. Fully equipped workshops had to be set up. There was one at Blenheim, an ample 'cottage', where Sunny Marlborough placed several rooms and also, in the winter months, good hunters at his disposal. This was appropriate, for most of the papers were in the family palace. The other, less obviously necessary, was at Wimborne House, off Piccadilly, where his Aunt Cornelia, Lord Randolph's sister, a keen Liberal who greatly encouraged Churchill's change of party, was still chatelaine. It was something of a paving pattern for the way in which, nearly fifty years later, he would move his headquarters as leader of the opposition from Hyde Park Gate to the Savoy Hotel when the parliamentary battle became tense.

There is some suggestion however that the actual writing of the book was slow to get going. As late as 25 August 1904, he wrote to his mother from Sir Ernest Cassel's Swiss villa (another 'cottage' workshop, it appears): 'I have been working away at my book and am slowly getting into the stride. But the difficulty of the task impresses me as I proceed.'[21] As the rapid production of his previous books had shown, he was capable of great fluency. But *Lord Randolph Churchill* was better written than any of these. He had shown, in the last lap and with many political distractions, that he could combine speed with quality. And the writing in this book was of very high quality. This is the main reason why, nearly a hundred years after publication and in spite of its two-volume tombstone shape, it retains a high readability.

It had a lot of faults. He treated Lord Randolph more as an icon than as a human being. The book was weak on his private personality, on the reasons for his persistent ill-health and (very understandably) on his relationship with his wife. But its major fault was a perverse desire to prove that the one thing on which Lord Randolph was absolutely consistent was his opposition to Home Rule for Ireland. Such a defence is the more striking because Winston Churchill, in spite of his romantic pietism, was in general willing to evacuate, although often under a smokescreen of selective (and sometimes inaccurate) quotation, untenable pieces of ground. But on Lord Randolph's opposition to Home Rule he wrote: 'to the repeal of the Parliamentary Union he was always unalterably opposed'.* 'No Unionist politician has a clearer record,' he added.[22] It is strange that Winston Churchill, already by the time of publication a committed Liberal and soon to be both a leading member of a Home Rule Cabinet and a truculent opponent of Ulster at the time of the Curragh 'mutiny' of 1914, should have chosen such unpromising terrain on which to dig his father in.

Nevertheless the book ranks as perhaps the best of the consanguineous biographies. Lockhart on Sir Walter Scott and G. O. Trevelyan on Macaulay come to mind as possible rivals, but in both cases the relationship is less close. Cyril Asquith's contribution to the standard life of his father is heavily diluted in the biographical professionalism of his senior collaborator, J. A. Spender. Lady Gwendoline Cecil on Salisbury, Lady Victoria Hicks Beach on St Aldwyn (as her father became) are careful and honest narratives such as any man should be pleased to have a daughter write about him, as, substituting niece for daughter, is Mrs Blanche Dugdale on Balfour. The second Lord Birkenhead's two goes at his father (already cited because Churchill wrote the foreword to the first) were both lively and respectable. But none of them, except Lockhart's and Trevelyan's, was in the same class as Winston Churchill's book. And none of them, when they wrote, was as young, or as much involved in other activities, or dealing with a figure of such little solid achievement as Lord Randolph. It was a major accomplishment, which even had he written nothing further, would have entitled Winston Churchill to a place among the best political writers. Even with his vast subsequent output *Lord Randolph Churchill* is his third-best book, surpassed only by those two brief volumes, *My Early Life* and *Great Contemporaries*.

It was on the whole as well received as it deserved to be. Unfortunately nearly all reviews at the time were anonymous, thereby considerably reducing their interest. The *Times Literary Supplement*, the *Sunday Times* and the *Spectator*, a good spread, were particularly favourable. The *TLS* struck a high note by describing it as 'among the two or three most exciting political biographies in the language', and an interesting one by saying that, while Winston Churchill (like his subject) had hardly

---

* Wilfred Scawen Blunt, who had known Lord Randolph well in the relevant years, wrote a convincing rebuttal of this in a letter to Winston Churchill on 21 January 1906 (*Companion Volume*, II, pt 1, pp. 491–2).

been conspicuous for self-restraint, he nonetheless wrote 'like an historian, and not at all like a man on a party platform'.

The two markedly unfavourable notices were in the *Daily Telegraph* and the *Sun*, the latter title covering a journal with more literary pretension than has its successor today. The *Daily Telegraph* thought the author seemed 'to have been trained in the worst school of American journalism'. The review provoked a letter of protest from the Duke of Marlborough, but more in defence of his uncle Randolph than of his cousin Winston. Marlborough thought he had delivered a knock-out blow by describing the review as 'essentially un-English', but somewhat marred the apparent tolerant effect by explaining to Winston Churchill that he intended this to be a devastating reference to the Jewish ownership of the paper by Levy Lawson, recently created (by Balfour) the first Lord Burnham.

These two onslaughts were balanced by letters of strong appreciation from the disparate band of Rosebery (whose prickles were temporarily in abeyance), Joseph Chamberlain, J. A. Spender (then editor of the *Westminster Gazette)* and W. F. Monypenny, with Buckle the multi-volume biographer of Disraeli. The sales were good but not spectacular – 5,827 in the first four months. Harris had made a better deal for Churchill than for Macmillans.

The timing of the publication of *Lord Randolph Churchill* was in one sense brilliantly done to make the maximum impact, yet it also came in a period too overcharged for Winston Churchill fully to take in its critical acclaim. The Balfour government was the only one of the twentieth century to subside to its end without defeat in a general election or an immediate crisis. Balfour resigned on 4 December 1905. Many thought it was a move of surpassing subtlety, designed to show how the Liberals, rent by dispute and low on ministerial experience, would be unable to form a convincing government. If this was Balfour's calculation it was one of the most disastrous in recent British political history. The electorate, so far from finding the Liberal government unconvincing, were delighted to have a change from the long, tired and latterly bickering years of Conservative rule. And while there were difficulties about Cabinet-making, Edward Grey in particular holding out for some time against serving under Campbell-Bannerman as leader in the Commons as well as Prime Minister, the prospect of refreshing draughts of power after a decade of thirst proved a powerful incitement to unity. The Cabinet list was complete and senior ministers received their seals of office on 11 December, a week after Balfour's resignation.

Churchill was not among them. Bourke Cockran's fear that he would be damaged by premature and excessive reward proved unfounded. Nor was this in any way surprising. Churchill was barely thirty-one years old, wholly without administrative experience, and had only been in his new party for a year and a half. He was however quickly assured of good junior office, and had no anxious period of waiting on tenterhooks. He was indeed offered a nominally higher post than that which, by his choice, he ultimately accepted. On Saturday, 9 December Campbell-Bannerman summoned Churchill to his house in Belgrave Square and offered him the Financial Secretaryship to the Treasury. This was normally regarded as the senior of all the junior minister posts, and the one which led most assuredly to the Cabinet.* It would also have given him the opportunity of working closely under Asquith, already clearly the coming leader, who became Chancellor of the Exchequer. But Churchill's tastes did not lie in the direction of being closely *under* any master, and with a bold stroke he asked if he could instead be under-secretary for the Colonies. Campbell-Bannerman confirmed in a handwritten note later that evening that he could have this nominally lower post.

Strong though his family feeling often was, Churchill was not at all influenced by the fact that he would be succeeding his Marlborough cousin in this job. What he did was to see a fine opening and to go for it with a determined nerve. His Secretary of State was to be the ninth Earl of Elgin, already encountered as Viceroy when Churchill was posted to Bangalore in the late 1890s.

Elgin brought great hereditary distinction to his office. His paternal grandfather, when ambassador to Constantinople, garnered the Elgin marbles and spent too much of the family fortunes on restoring them. His maternal grandfather was the Earl of Durham, the 'Radical Jack' of the Reform Bill and of the Report which paved the way to self-government for Canada. His father had been a notable governor-general in Ottawa before becoming Viceroy of India in 1862 and dying there the following year. He himself was one of the few Whigs to remain with Gladstone after the Home Rule split of 1886, and had followed his father as Viceroy in 1893. Yet, despite this pedigree, Elgin was a man of little drive, utterly lacking in the charismatic arts. He was not in fact elderly, being between fifty-five and fifty-eight during his two and a quarter years as Colonial Secretary, but a combination of his white and fuzzy beard, his

---

* And indeed Reginald McKenna, who got the job *vice* Churchill, was in the Cabinet (as President of the Board of Education) fifteen months ahead of him.

liking for a quiet life, much of it in Scotland, and his inability to keep pace with the restless vigour of his under-secretary gave the impression that he was much older than his years. And he was indisputably a peer, and therefore of course precluded from the proceedings of the House of Commons, where Churchill would be the sole voice of the department. Furthermore, South African business, firmly under the Colonial Office, showed every sign of being a dominating issue in the new parliament. Not only had constitutions to be provided for the defeated Boer republics of the Transvaal and the Orange River Colony (as it was then called), but the question of indentured Chinese labour in the mines of the Witwatersrand, or 'Chinese Slavery' as it soon became in popular parlance, was to be a highly charged election issue. Churchill was opting for prominence and parliamentary opportunity rather than rank, a high-risk strategy, but such was his normal choice at this stage in his life.

Before these possibilities could be exploited the election had to be won, both nationally if the Liberal government was to be more than a small island in a surrounding Tory sea, and locally in North-West Manchester if Churchill's plan for House of Commons prominence was to be fulfilled. The latter in particular looked far from certain. Churchill spent Christmas at Blenheim, having not previously done much at the Colonial Office, except to establish wary relations with Elgin, and to appoint a young civil servant, Edward Marsh (who was in fact a couple of years older than himself), as his private secretary. The relationship with Marsh proved more fructuous than that with Elgin. Marsh, who was a considerable *littérateur* as well as an efficient but unthrusting official, followed Churchill to no fewer than eight departments and remained a great friend and occasional literary adviser until his death in 1953. On the afternoon of 15 December, the day on which he was offered the appointment, he went to see Lady Lytton (Miss Pamela Plowden) in order to get a 'fix' from her on his new master, and was rewarded for his trouble with one of the more perceptive remarks ever made about Churchill. 'The first time you meet Winston', she said, 'you see all his faults, and the rest of your life you spend in discovering his virtues.'[23]

Churchill wrote to Elgin on the day of his appointment, beginning his letter with the respectful archaism of 'My dear Lord', and received a reply (beginning 'Dear Mr Churchill') from the intriguing address of 28 Hyde Park Gate.* Elgin treated Churchill with remarkable tolerance

---

* After the devastating defeat of 1945 Churchill was to live in 28 Hyde Park Gate for the remaining twenty years of his life.

throughout their ill-matched partnership, and responded courteously to repeated attempts by Sir Francis Hopwood, the permanent under-secretary of the department, to get him to discipline his exuberant subordinate. Hopwood's lack of appreciation of Churchill can be gauged from a letter which he wrote to Elgin two years into the life of the government: 'He is most tiresome to deal with and will I fear give trouble – as his father did – in any position to which he may be called. The restless energy, uncontrollable desire for notoriety and the lack of moral perception make him an anxiety indeed!'[24] Elgin's most spirited riposte to Churchill was famous for its laconicism. When, in 1907, the under-secretary wrote a long minute, pontificating on almost all aspects of colonial policy and ending, at once grandiloquently and redundantly, 'These are my views. W.S.C.', the only response from his Secretary of State was a side note: 'But not mine, E.'[25]

Churchill needed the Christmas rest at Blenheim. He had been seriously ill for a couple of weeks immediately preceding the formation of the new government. It was a mysterious illness affecting his tongue, his throat and his heart, and the cure involved 'an American rubber [that is masseuse], a venerable God-fearing old lady – of sovereign virtue' and a period of retirement at Canford Manor (now a school), a country house of the Wimbornes. A public announcement of the illness, without details, prompted several letters of sympathy, including one (slightly cool) on behalf of the King. However by the New Year (aided by the importation of the 'rubber' to Blenheim) he appeared to be quite fit and ready for the Manchester fray.

He issued his election address on 1 January 1906 and proceeded to Manchester a day or two later, ten days before the polling date for the city, one of the earliest in the country. He and Edward Marsh installed themselves in the splendours of the then only seven-years-old redbrick and brown terracotta Midland Hotel. Balfour, the more established star of the Manchester political firmament, who had been member for the East division for twenty-one years, was in the sixty-year-old Italianate and stuccoed Queen's Hotel, where Churchill had recommended his mother, the Midland not having then passed its teething troubles, to stay for the 1900 election. The descent upon the city's hotels of these two very non-Mancunian figures, like world-class opera singers arriving for a gala performance, was almost a caricature of the patrician and non-locally indigenous nature of much of British electioneering in those days, and indeed for another sixty or seventy years subsequently.

Churchill, according to Marsh, further epitomized this sense of separateness, although accompanied by a certain patrician sympathy. He immediately suggested they should go for a walk, and, when they quickly got into mean streets, 'Winston looked about him, and his sympathetic imagination was stirred. "Fancy", he said, "living in one of these streets – never seeing anything beautiful – never eating anything savoury – *never saying anything clever!*"'[26]

Churchill did not allow his new official status to moderate the sharpness of his election address. After dealing reasonably cautiously with a number of points in the Liberal programme, he went off into a denunciation of the previous parliament:

> Jealous of nothing, save the leisure of its members, it has bartered Parliamentary rights for longer holidays and easier hours of session, and shirked urgent public business at the promptings of personal indolence. Viewy, intolerant, dilettante, lax, the tool of Whips and wire-pullers, the lackey of private interests, the Parliament of 1900 has grudged the freedom of speech, conspired against the freedom of trade, parodied the freedom and the dignity of labour.

His caution however showed itself both on Ireland ('I shall support no Irish legislation which I regard as likely to injure the effective integrity of the United Kingdom, or to lead, however indirectly, to Separation') and on Chinese labour in South Africa ('A Liberal Government, while it is forced to bear any part of the responsibility, is bound to do its utmost to restrict such a system, and to put down its abuses').

At the redistribution of 1885 Manchester had been divided into six single-member constituencies, which together with those in the adjacent borough of Salford, separated from the city by historical accident and not by geography or disparateness, constituted a conurban unit of nine seats. Only one of them had elected a Liberal in 1900, and that by the narrowest of margins. In the North division Charles Schwann (soon to become a baronet and to modify his name to the more literarily distinguished form of Charles Swann) had sat fairly quietly since 1886. This was not the most obvious area for the one Liberal redoubt. Much of it later became the marginal (between Labour and Tory) seat of Blackley. But Manchester pre-1914 politics did not follow a classic left–right pattern. Balfour's seat of East Manchester, safe for twenty years, was much more working class than the North-West division which Churchill was successfully hoping to capture. The North-West seat comprised the greater part of the city centre (where there was in those days a substantial business vote) together with the prosperous residential district of Cheetham Hill. It was in this area that the leaders of Manchester's Jewish community were congregated. Its numbers were not vast – of a total electoral role of 11,411 in the constituency it was estimated that 740 were Jewish, of whom 470 lived on Cheetham Hill – but they were an influential group, and it could be cynically alleged that the vigour with which Churchill opposed (and helped to kill) a restrictive Aliens Bill in the session of 1904 was not unconnected with the fact that this was exactly when he alighted on Manchester North-West. Certainly it helped to put him into friendly relations with Nathan Laski, the father of Professor Harold Laski and then probably the most locally influential Jew in Manchester.*

Churchill kept Free Trade in the centre of his campaign and as a result secured the support of most of the textile trade including the former prominent Tory and splendidly named Mr Tootal Broadhurst. The Conservative candidate was a forty-year-old and puritanically evangelical London solicitor named Joynson-Hicks. Churchill was later to sit in Cabinet with 'Jix' (as he was commonly though not often affectionately known), but their occupancy for nearly five years of two of the most senior positions (Chancellor and Home Secretary) in Baldwin's second government did not produce much mutual warmth. Churchill wrote of him in 1932 that 'he runs the risk of being most humorous when he wishes to be most serious'. The main thrust of Hicks's attack was to collect and publish as a leaflet the most disagreeable things which Churchill had in the past said about the Liberal party. Churchill dealt with this robustly, and in a manner reminiscent, although at the same time illustrating their difference of styles, of Gladstone's riposte in 1866 to a similar attack by Disraeli mocking an 1831 high Tory Oxford Union speech by the Liberal leader. Gladstone responded: 'My youthful mind and imagination were impressed with some idle and futile fears which still bewilder and distract the mature

---

* There was however another Jew in Manchester at the time who was to be internationally even more influential. That was Dr Chaim Weizmann, then a lecturer in organic chemistry at the University there and the future first President of Israel. During that election campaign (on 9 January) Weizmann had a seventy-five-minute interview in the Queen's Hotel with the losing Balfour which in the long run was more important for world Jewry than anything which passed between Nathan Laski and the winning Churchill. This interview laid the foundation for what, after a delay of eleven years, became the Balfour Declaration in favour of a Jewish national home in Palestine; it should however be added that Churchill also was mostly very well disposed towards Zionism.

mind of the right honourable gentleman.' Churchill, in 1906, said, 'I said a lot of stupid things when I was in the Conservative party, and I left it because I did not want to go on saying stupid things.'[27]

Churchill had packed meetings throughout the short campaign, and was on powerful swashbuckling form. He was troubled by early suffragette manifestations (Manchester was the home city of the Pankhursts) and was perhaps provoked by them into one or two unwise statements. When asked a direct question about his future voting intentions if elected, he replied: 'The only time I have voted in the House of Commons on this question I have voted in favour of women's suffrage, but, having regard to the perpetual disturbance at public meetings at this election, I utterly decline to pledge myself. . . .' 'I am not going to be henpecked on a question of such grave importance,' was another of his perhaps too vivid ripostes. However the campaign had a fine momentum about it, and by ten o'clock on the evening of Saturday, 13 January he had been declared elected by 5,659 votes to 4,398, a majority of 1,241 (the equivalent of about 6,000 with a modern-sized electorate) on an 89 per cent poll. The results throughout Manchester and Salford were sensational. In place of the eight Tories and one Liberal at the dissolution, there were now seven Liberals, two Labour members and no Tories. It was not possible to measure Churchill's own swing (because of the unopposed return of 1900) but the average for the conurbation was 17.9 per cent as against 10.3 per cent for the country as a whole.

Balfour, despite his official biographer's sober view that he was on sparkling oratorical form during his campaign, was out by the devastatingly large margin of 6,403 to 4,423. Under the much more flexible 'parachutage' constituency conventions of the period, this defeat did not long exclude him from the House of Commons. He was back within six weeks as member for the City of London. But it was a major setback, made the worse by the fact that, as a resigned Prime Minister and a defeated parliamentary candidate, he had to spend the next two weeks during which polling continued in other constituencies travelling the country, from Nottingham to Glasgow, and to several lesser towns as well, and trying to salvage what he could from the Tory wreckage.

Churchill himself spoke at a few more scattered meetings, although going briefly to London on 19 January in order to have his first encounter with General J. C. Smuts. Smuts had written, 'I have come from the Transvaal in the hope that I may have an opportunity to discuss with you the situation in the Transvaal and in South Africa generally.'[28] Churchill then settled back in the capital by the end of the month, ready for the new parliament (which met on 13 February) with its vast Liberal majority, and for energetic (but not exclusive) concentration on the work of his department.

He was still living in bachelor chambers in the 1880s mansion flats of 105 Mount Street, Mayfair, the lease of which he had taken over from his cousin Marlborough nearly six years before, although about to move in the course of the year a half-mile or so to 12 Bolton Street, off Piccadilly, where he stayed until 1909. Politicians in those days lived at once spaciously and close to each other. No. 105 Mount Street was only twelve doors from 127 Mount Street, to which Asquith had retreated, farming out his five young children to a house in Surrey, after the death of his first wife in 1891.

At the end of January 1906 all seemed set fair for Churchill. He had received many letters of congratulation, both on his accession to office and on his Manchester triumph. Yet he might have been wise to pay particular attention to a pre-Christmas epistle from his old collaborator and continuing friend Lord Hugh Cecil, which showed insight unusual from that source:

18 December 1905   Junior Carlton Club
My Dear Winston,
    By 'gaseous' I mean that you have a reputation for shining on a platform & in the House – but as a firework. This has carried you well so far but the further steps require a reputation as a good administrator, a skilled & industrious official – the sort of reputation Edward Grey eminently has – you will remember your father greatly improved his position by his work at the India Office.
    But still more important it is that you should stand well with & be liked by your colleagues. If a man's colleagues are all on his side he runs forward as easily as a bicyclist before the wind. Harcourt cd not be PM because he swore at his colleagues. AJB holds his position as leader almost entirely by the effect of his charm on his front bench & in spite of enormous blunders & no popularity in the country. Hear the words of the sage!
    Yrs.
        Hugh Cecil[29]

6

AN UPWARDLY MOBILE
UNDER-SECRETARY

SOUTH AFRICA DOMINATED Churchill's early ministerial months. This was for two reasons. The one of more long-term significance was the pressing need for a constitutional settlement with the Transvaal, and then, in its train, with the Orange River Colony, the lesser of the two defeated Boer republics. In the three and a half years since the end of the war they had been administered as Crown Colonies under the direct and authoritarian rule of Alfred Milner, who, first appointed in 1897, remained as High Commissioner until June 1905. There was no dispute that the time had come for a new constitutional arrangement. Alfred Lyttelton, Elgin's Conservative predecessor as Colonial Secretary, had prepared a scheme for 'representative' (as opposed to 'responsible') government. The issue was the extent to which the new Liberal government would modify the scheme.

The second issue, that of the employment of indentured Chinese labour in the Rand mines, authorized by the Conservative government in early 1904, became politically even more dominant because of its exploitation by most Liberal candidates (although not by Churchill) as a general election issue second only to Free Trade. This was compounded by battered Conservative counter-exploitation of the difficulties of the Liberal government in bringing to a quick end the system against which Liberal candidates had so loudly fulminated.*

The Chinese labourers were not formally in a condition of slavery, in spite of a free Liberal electioneering use of the word. Indeed Churchill, in response to a Conservative amendment to the Address on

---

* A good example of the political-football nature of the issue was provided by Lloyd George saying during the campaign (10 January 1906): 'What would they say to introducing Chinamen at a shilling a day in the Welsh quarries? Slavery on the hills of Wales! Heaven forgive me for the suggestion'; and by F. E. Smith making devastating use of the remark, and of Lloyd George's attempted denial of it, in his celebrated maiden speech of 13 March.

22 February, invented one of his most famous early phrases by saying
that, while there were many objections to the conditions under which
the Chinese worked in South Africa, 'it cannot in the opinion of His
Majesty's government be classified as slavery in the extreme acceptance
of the word without some risk of terminological inexactitude'.*[1] Nonetheless the conditions under which, by the time of the change of
government, 47,619 Chinese (nearly a third of the total mining work-
force) had been brought to the Transvaal were, even bearing in mind
the contemporary conditions in British coal mines or Lancashire cotton
mills, distinctly shocking. They were required to work ten hours a day
for six days a week. There was at first no minimum wage, then one of
two shillings a day (not, *pace* Lloyd George, one shilling). They lived in
compounds around the mines which they were forbidden to leave
without rarely given forty-eight-hour passes. They were not allowed to
engage in any business, own any property or seek access to any court of
law. They were liable to special punishment for fourteen specified
offences. And in practice although not in strict theory it was made
impossible for them to be accompanied by their families. What differentiated the system from slavery was that they were not bought or sold,
and that they could return to China provided they could raise £17 (the
equivalent of thirty weeks' wages) for the return passage.

The phasing out of the system was to present the Liberal government,
and the Colonial Office in particular, with one of the most intractable
problems of its first year. Even Balfour and Lyttelton had become
uneasy about it during 1905. Many Liberal candidates, who now flooded
the government benches, had made an emotional meal of the issue
during the general election. On the other hand the British population
in the Transvaal, largely identified with the mining interest, for whose
rights the long and expensive war had at least nominally been fought,
and whose views were powerfully represented to London by the new
High Commissioner, Lord Selborne, had persuaded themselves that the
removal of the Chinese would mean the collapse of gold mining and
hence of much of the strength of the South African economy.

The new government at home, while containing some members
who felt strongly on the issue, also contained others who were even
more concerned that it should look responsible, maintain a fair degree
of continuity in external policy, and above all accept the sanctity of

---

* It is commonly but inaccurately thought that he rotundly substituted this phrase when
challenged on his use of the parliamentarily unacceptable world 'lie'.

contracts (including licences already issued for the importation of further consignments of Chinese) and not upset them by retrospective legislation. The 'lawyer ministers', headed by Asquith, were a powerful force on this latter side. The position which Churchill had to defend in the House of Commons was therefore a delicate one, and delicacy was not always his strongest suit.

Constitution-making for the Transvaal proved a more rewarding pursuit. Here there were a couple of main issues lurking under the camouflage of words or phrases which, while they became familiar at the time, do not today automatically illuminate the field of contention. The first was 'responsible' as opposed to merely 'representative' government. The Lyttelton Constitution, as it became known, conceded 'representative' government, meaning that there should be an elected assembly which could give its views, but to which the executive council, continuing to be at least partly nominated by the governor, would not be responsible. 'Responsible' government meant that the composition of the assembly controlled the composition and actions of the executive, in other words roughly the position which prevailed in Britain or perhaps more precisely in Canada, then regarded as the model for self-government under the British Crown, even though a few imperial vetoes persisted there.

The Liberal government, from an early stage and partly under the vigilant pressure of Churchill, was in favour of taking an important step away from Lyttelton and conceding responsible government. But it wanted the palm without the dust, in other words to try to secure a majority for the 'British' (or at any rate the non-Boer) party within the Transvaal. In the Orange River Colony, with an almost unleavened population of rural Boers, this was a hopeless aim, but it was the Transvaal which counted, as Churchill pointed out with his own typical trenchancy of style (no anonymous and anodyne drafting here) in a memorandum dated 30 January (1906):

> It must never be forgotten that the politics of the Transvaal are the politics of South Africa. Johannesburg is the railway, commercial, financial and political nerve-centre of the whole. It is the arena in which all that is most militant in Boer and Briton meet and carry on their perennial duel. The British population of Johannesburg are the representatives and champions of British authority in South Africa. The Transvaal Boers are the representatives and champions of the Dutch. Whatever is done for or against the one or the other is done for or against the whole race in the sub-continent. Cape Colony, Natal, Rhodesia and the Orange River Colony form an audience of vehement and anxious partisans.[2]

The desirability of a 'British' majority was however confused by the wretched Chinese labour problem. What the London government wanted was a Transvaal government which would take the problem off their hands, ideally by being in favour of fairly rapid repatriation, or at least against any further recruitment, but in any event by accepting the responsibility. It was by no means clear that a 'British' majority would conduce to this end. The mainly rural Boer population was neutral in the Chinese argument. The 'British' mining interest, backed by Selborne, was almost obsessive the other way. Churchill, in the same memorandum, rather splendidly transcended this short-term problem, even though it was about to cause him a great deal of trouble in the House of Commons. The new government, he said, came to the issue:

> independent, uncompromised, free to hold the scales even, cut off from neither race, able to work on terms of impartial justice with both. Let not that supreme advantage be thrown away. We cannot take either the one side or the other. We are free from the trammels of the mining interest. Do not let us throw ourselves into the arms of the Boers. Do not let us do anything which makes us the champion of one race, and consequently deprives us *for ever* of the confidence of the other. The question of the constitution ought not to be prejudiced by the desirability of terminating Chinese labour. It should be settled with reference to the general future of South Africa, and not with reference to any particular question of South African politics.[3]

Nevertheless the issues of the electoral roll and of the number and distribution of constituencies assumed great importance in the striking of the appropriate balance between the two communities. 'One vote, one value' became, as Churchill put it, 'the fighting position of the British party'. This motto sounds like a truism, but this was not so in circumstances where the scattered Boers had very large families and the more concentrated and urban British were quite often bachelors seeking a fortune before marriage and, even if accompanied, were mostly content with many fewer children. In most democracies constituency boundaries were determined on a population rather than a voting-roll basis, with in general a bias towards rural areas. The demand for 'one vote, one value', so far from being a truism, therefore challenged this normal pattern in two respects. Nevertheless, it was what, with Churchill's support, was implemented. The Boers, however, got considerable countervailing concessions. The 'military vote' for the members of the remaining British garrison was abolished. There were to be sixty (rather than the Lyttelton-proposed thirty) constituencies. There was to be absolute equality in official transactions between the English and Dutch languages. And there was to be manhood suffrage, without any property qualification.

Churchill was forthrightly on the side of advancing well beyond Lyttelton on all these points, which were being strenuously discussed within the government over and immediately after the general election. He was particularly good at the fluent commitment of his views to paper, although he did not always do so in the most tactful terms, as in an earlier memorandum (of 3 January) on the language issue:

> In Canada as in South Africa, the duality of language is inconvenient; but the difficulty is much more likely to persist in Canada than in South Africa, for in Canada the two races dwell separately in well-marked geographical areas, and local peculiarities are preserved; but in South Africa the two races are intermingled in every town, in every village, almost in every farm. The English language, with its literature and its flexibility, and, above all, its business convenience, must prevail in so universal a competition against a vulgar dialect. The only way in which the *taal* [Afrikaans] can be kept active is by making it a proscribed language, which the Boers could cultivate as an easy method of defying their conquerors. Whatever may happen to South Africa in the future, it will certainly speak English. I am therefore of opinion that absolute duality of language in government and education may, so far as Imperial interests are concerned, be conceded in principle, as it has already been conceded in fact.[4]

The recommendation was clear, sensible and liberal, even if the prophecy was wrong in several respects, and the contempt for the 'vulgar dialect' was brutal. But Churchill was writing an internal government minute in days when Whitehall did not leak.

Churchill's status in policy making was ambiguous. At the end of December (1905) a Cabinet committee of five members had been set up to recommend on these issues of how far there should be an advance from Lyttelton. Churchill was not among the five, who were Loreburn (Lord Chancellor and chairman), Ripon (Lord Privy Seal), Asquith (Chancellor of the Exchequer), Elgin and James Bryce (Chief Secretary for Ireland, and constitutional expert in his own right). It was no doubt considered inappropriate for an under-secretary to be named as a member of a *Cabinet* committee among such luminaries. But Churchill's papers provided much of the agenda and driving force for the committee, and that he almost certainly attended. Such at any rate seem

to be the import of a pregnant letter which Asquith wrote to him on
1 February (1906):

Treasury Chambers

My dear Winston,
    Would it not be a good thing if you could prepare a short reasoned
statement, showing in each case the grounds on which the Committee
arrived at the four conclusions in our report of today?
    It might be an effective aid to the discussion of the matter by the
Cabinet.
    You might perhaps ask Ld Elgin whether he concurs in the suggestion.
    Yrs always,
      H. H. Asquith[5]

This letter from a man who, at that stage and in spite of the 'My dear
Winston', did not know Churchill at all well, but who was widely
regarded as the organizing chief of staff of the benign but easy-going
Campbell-Bannerman premiership, hints at a great deal. Churchill, in
Asquith's cool view, was the best hope for a sinewy and persuasive
paper. He was a much better prospect, in terms of both energy and skill,
than Lord Elgin, or an official. But there was a delicate corner to be
turned in relation to Elgin's susceptibilities, and this Asquith, more
wisely than courageously, hoped would be sorted out by Churchill
himself.

Elgin and Churchill were about as unlike each other as it is possible
to imagine. Churchill lived by phrase-making. He thought rhetorically,
and was constantly in danger of his policy being made by his phrases
rather than vice versa. Elgin eschewed any epigram or rhetorical flourish
and abhorred the fluent flippancy of some of Churchill's minutes.
Indeed fluency of any kind was foreign to Elgin, who practically never
spoke in Cabinet and was inarticulate in the House of Lords. Given
their completely contrasting personae, the two men got on tolerably
well during their tasking twenty-eight months together. This was partly
because they were psychologically non-competitive. However, Elgin was
not a negligible Colonial Secretary. He was liberal in his approach to
Transvaal issues, and therefore more or less at one with Churchill on
that first major test. Elsewhere he was decently conservative, and
therefore popular with the department and with the colonial governors.
He was much more inclined to support the 'man on the spot' than was
Churchill, perhaps because he had five years' experience of being the
(grandest) 'man on the spot' in Calcutta, and by no means always

supported by London. He also handled Churchill with forbearance and some wisdom. He mostly turned him down on 'human rights' issues, when from Kenya to Natal to Ceylon the under-secretary was constantly querying decisions and punishments given locally against individuals. Elgin was much more tolerant of Churchill's presumption than Hopwood, the permanent under-secretary, who, in spite of being a civil servant of exceptional previous and subsequent breadth of experience (he 'pursued' Churchill to the Admiralty and ended as Lord Southborough), did not have the breadth of mind to appreciate the quality beneath Churchill's brashness.

Elgin was, however, determined to be in charge of his department and not to allow himself to be bullied or unduly dazzled by Churchill. While they often disagreed they never quarrelled. But nor did they develop any real affinity. When Churchill went on an extended semi-public, semi-private tour of East Africa for more than four months in the long recess of 1907–8 his absence was more of a relief than a deprivation for Elgin, and would have been even more of a relief had Churchill not kept up a constant bombardment of comment and recommendation sent back to the Colonial Office.* Elgin's written comments on his relationship with Churchill were odd. After they had been together a year he wrote to express his selfish but flattering relief that Churchill had not been promoted and concluded: 'I shall always look back on our co-operation during this year of toil and strife with real gratitude to you, not only for the courage and ability with which you have fought our case – *but for the invariable consideration you have shown for me and my opinions*' (my italics).[6] The last half-sentence, clearly not in the context ironical, would of course have been much more appropriately written from an under-secretary to his Secretary of State than the other way round. And then, just after the end, Elgin wrote to his successor, Lord Crewe, about 'pleasant personal relations' with Churchill and his 'in many ways attractive personality', but concluded, as though caught in a suffocating bear-hug, 'All the same I know quite well that it has affected my position *outside the Office*, and the strain has often been severe.'[7] And when they were officially separated on Asquith's accession to the premiership in April 1908, Churchill on promotion,

---

* One of Hopwood's complaints about him to Elgin was that he kept the accompanying Edward Marsh at work for '14 hours in one day upon these memoranda in the heat and discomfort of the Red Sea' (*Companion Volume*, II, pt 2, p. 730).

Elgin on unwilling retirement, there is no indication that they ever again saw each other during the remaining nine years of Elgin's life.

Churchill's parliamentary performance during this Colonial Office period was mixed, although always attention-attracting. He got through his first debate, that in which he used the unforgettable 'terminological inexactitude' phrase, quite well. Then, a month later on 21 March (1906) he had a near disaster. Alfred Milner, who amalgamated the intellectual certainties and austere self-righteousness of an Enoch Powell with the assured and complacent administrative capacity of a John Anderson (Lord Waverley), had become a viscount in 1902, but made his maiden speech in the House of Lords only at the end of February 1906, eight months after his return from South Africa. Although responsible for more highly controversial decisions than almost any other man in British politics of the time, he carefully cultivated an aura of non-partisanship.

However, Lord Portsmouth, a junior War Office minister, succeeded in extracting from Milner the admission that in South Africa he had agreed to the flogging, unauthorized by any judicial process, of Chinese coolies. This led an elderly radical MP, William Byles, member for Salford North and therefore a close constituency neighbour of Churchill's, to put down a motion of harsh censure upon Milner. The government did not want this carried, but were by no means certain that they could restrain their overflowing and mostly inexperienced backbenches from doing so.

Such a result would have been extremely unwelcome to Asquith and Grey, who held the two premier offices under Campbell-Bannerman and who retained for Milner a Balliol and imperialist respect combined with an element of affection. This makes it remarkable that they (and particularly Asquith, who was rapidly becoming the government's all-purpose 'sledgehammer' in the House of Commons) left it entirely to Churchill to deal with this delicate issue. And it was the more remarkable because Churchill had had to spend the first part of that parliamentary day controverting a mischief-making attempt by no less a figure than Joseph Chamberlain to mock the government on the issue of Chinese labour, and had attacked Chamberlain in typically provocative terms. Two speeches in a single day, one against Chamberlain, the most dominating figure of Edwardian politics (until his stroke four months later), and the other demanding a delicate massaging of rampant radicals, was a strong ration for a junior minister and a clear indication of the high-risk prominence which he had secured by opting to be the sole Commons spokesman of the most exposed department.

For once Churchill's risk-taking did not succeed. He diverted the Byles motion with an innocuous amendment, against the flogging of Chinese but declining 'in the interests of peace and reconciliation in South Africa . . . from passing censure of individuals'. It was his speech and not the tactic which was the trouble. He endeavoured to persuade his militant backbenchers that Milner was not worth censuring, not because of his virtue, but because he was such a burned-out figure of the past. This was offensive and also proved untrue. Nearly ten years later, when Churchill was at one of the nadirs of his fortunes, Milner became a member of Lloyd George's War Cabinet of five, in which government Churchill, despite his great run of success from 1908 to 1914, would have been delighted to accept a subordinate position, as he did when he became Minister of Munitions in June 1917. And nearly twenty years later, when Curzon died, Milner was chosen as Chancellor of Oxford University by acclaim, although dying before he could be inaugurated (and leaving the field open for the election of Lord Cave and the consequent humiliating defeat of Asquith).

Even the faithful Edward Marsh (although then only in the fourth month of his twenty-four years of private-secretarial association with Churchill) described the speech as 'one of WSC's failures': 'it was generally felt to be unbecoming in its tone and was long remembered against him . . . the fault was one of manner . . . of harshness of utterance . . . he appeared to be taunting a discredited statesman with the evil days on which he had fallen'.[8] The passage which caused particular offence was:

> Lord Milner has gone from South Africa, probably for ever. The public service knows him no more. Having exercised great authority he now exerts none. Having held high employment he now has no employment. Having disposed of events which have shaped the course of history, he is now unable to deflect to the smallest degree the policy of the day. Having been for many years . . . the arbiter of the fortune of men who are 'rich beyond the dreams of avarice' he is today poor, and I will add honourably poor. After twenty years of exhausting service under the Crown he is today a retired Civil Servant, without pension or gratuity of any kind whatever . . . Lord Milner has ceased to be a factor in public events.[9]

He then compounded the offence by comparing the position of Milner with that of the atheist Bradlaugh in 1880 and Parnell in 1887 when the Pigott forgeries, which implicated the Irish leader in agrarian crime, were believed by the majority of the House of Commons. It was the patronizing nature of his defence of a man who, at the time, was widely regarded as much greater than himself which rankled, and which stirred up authorities from the Warden of All Souls (Sir William Anson) to the King. The Warden wrote of the speech as a 'pompous and impertinent' effusion from a 'young jackanapes'.[10] Edward VII wrote to Lady Londonderry that 'the conduct of a certain relation of yours is simply scandalous'.[11]

A more serious although much more politely phrased appraisal and rebuke came from Lord Selborne, former Unionist First Lord of the Admiralty, who had been despatched to South Africa to replace Milner in 1905. He endeavoured to work with the new Liberal government, although his main contribution was to send them some fairly sententious pieces of advice, to which he no doubt thought he was entitled by his seniority (Edward Grey had been his fag at Winchester). To Churchill he wrote on 15 April:

> As regards the Milner debate, I fully realize that your intention was to parry the blow aimed at him by his enemies; but if you put yourself in the place of South African Britishers, as in your dispassionate critical nature you can, you will not be surprised at their attitude towards HMG [His Majesty's Government]. It is true to say that the South African British as a whole idolize Milner, and to them it is absolutely impossible to conceive how any man can propose anything in the nature of a vote of censure on him unless he is a traitor. . . . I think the danger of a really serious breach of sentiment between the Liberal Party and the South Africa British is a very real one, and one which exercises me deeply.[12]

While there can be no doubt that the March speech did Churchill's standing widespread and substantial harm, it was counterbalanced by another South African parliamentary occasion, when at the end of July he persuaded the House of Commons to pass the new Transvaal constitution by a vote of 316 to 83. That counts as one of the most resonant and successful of his early speeches, rightly earning a place in anthologies of his life's orations. The most famous passage of this speech was the one in which he directly addressed the leading members of the opposition:

> They are the accepted guides of a party which, though in a minority in the House, nevertheless embodies nearly half the nation. I will ask them seriously whether they will not pause before they commit themselves to

violent or rash denunciations of this great arrangement. I will ask them, further, whether they will not consider if they cannot join with us to invest the grant of a free constitution to the Transvaal with something of a national sanction. With all our majority we can only make it the gift of a party; they can make it the gift of England. And if that were so, I am quite sure that all those inestimable blessings which we confidently hope will flow from this decision will be gained more surely and much more speedily: and the first real step will be taken to withdraw South African affairs from the arena of British party politics, in which they have inflicted injury on both political parties and in which they have suffered grievous injury themselves.[13]

This sounds on the borders of pretentiousness for such a young and often deliberately provocative minister. But the speech was apparently not ill received on this occasion, although it is noticeable that the only two letters of warm congratulation which find their way into the Churchill archive both come from men who had not actually heard the debate. They were however from welcome sources – General Sir Ian Hamilton and the old (ex-Viceroy) Marquess of Ripon.

This success allowed Churchill to begin with good morale his first long recess as a minister. There was no question of such a state of achievement justifying an idle holiday. He departed from London on 12 August, although not until he had procured an invitation from Kaiser Wilhelm II to attend German army manoeuvres near Breslau in early September, which involved the most complicated arrangements about suitable uniforms, on which he consulted that great expert King Edward VII. He went first to Deauville and then to his familiar haunt of Sir Ernest Cassel's Swiss villa. From Deauville he reported to his private secretary: 'I have been vy idle here & vy dissipated – gambling every night till 5 in the morning. I have made a little money – had made a lot.'[14] (He told his brother that he had come away with a net £260, the equivalent of more than £12,000 today.) Dissipated he may have been, but not idle. On 15 August he sent to the King a *pièce justificative* of nearly 4,000 words of the policy towards the Transvaal, handwritten on thirty-five sheets of octavo paper. And when the royal private secretary wrote back from Marienbad with the assurance that the King had read it with interest but also with some polite scepticism, a further instalment of nearly the same length was sent from Switzerland. The reply to that was shorter, even curt, but the royal scepticism persisted: 'The King still fears however that you are somewhat sanguine in your prognostications.'[15]

Churchill also found holiday time for a substantial letter to the Prime Minister, in reply to which Campbell-Bannerman (also in Marienbad) noted, 'You are with your usual energy making good use of the holidays.'[16] This however was not an ironic put-down, for the content of the Prime Minister's letter was substantial and its tone friendly, although he also passed on from the King a warning that Churchill should not be too 'communicative and frank' with the Kaiser when he encountered him at the manoeuvres. The giving of this royal warning was clearly the first that Campbell-Bannerman had heard of the martial expedition of his junior subordinate. It may be thought that so unusual and delicate a holiday recreation would have required prior Prime Ministerial sanction, and the fact that it was not sought yet another indication of Churchill's bumptious self-confidence, as well as of the relaxed regime which prevailed under Campbell-Bannerman.

The friendliness of the Prime Minister's letter did not however presage an early promotion for Churchill. This was what he inevitably most wanted. He was like a bird which was bound to beat its wings against whatever ceiling was placed above it. The Cabinet, so that he could express his views in the flesh and on all subjects of policy, and not merely on colonial policy on paper, was the goal. It was not that he was unhappy in his present job. Indeed at one stage he canvassed (to his mother at least) the prospect that he might be asked to join the Cabinet while remaining number two at the Colonial Office. (Poor Elgin, is one's natural reaction. Churchill made his life difficult enough as it was. To have had his 'subordinate' sitting with him in Cabinet, and no doubt sounding off far more frequently than he himself did, would surely have made it impossible.) However this did not happen, although Asquith, a month or so before he became Prime Minister on 8 April 1908, seriously discussed it with the King, who was against the proposal, arguing that Queen Victoria had vetoed a similar proposition (for the Foreign Office) made by Rosebery in favour of Edward Grey.

The King, according to Asquith's subsequent account to his wife, made no attempt to contest the claim to promotion of Churchill, about whom he was 'quite warm in his praise', provided it was in 'some real Cabinet office'. Asquith himself said that Churchill had 'every claim to Cabinet rank', citing in his favour the curious argument that 'he had behaved very well when twice passed over for ... [men] of "inferior claims"'.[17] The argument was curious because it is difficult to see why Churchill, still only thirty-three years old and a Liberal recruit of only three years' standing, should have been expected to behave badly, or how exactly he would have done so, except in the privacy of his own tantrum, had he been so disposed. The conversation is nonetheless an interesting indication of how quickly Churchill had persuaded even such a coolly phlegmatic figure as Asquith, who subsequently became fond of Churchill's company although always inclined affectionately to mock his extravagances, to agree with his own valuation of his talents.

The two promotions over Churchill's head of men of 'inferior claims' were first McKenna, in January 1907, who, as a result of Bryce becoming ambassador in Washington and Birrell succeeding him as Chief Secretary for Ireland, succeeded Birrell as President of the Board of Education; and second Lewis (widely known as 'Lulu') Harcourt, the dedicated former private secretary over many years to his 'great gladiator' father Sir William, who was for no very obvious reason transformed in March 1907 from being a First Commissioner of Works outside the Cabinet to bearing the same title within the Cabinet.

McKenna, as long as the Asquith premiership lasted, ran a fluctuating two-horse race with Churchill. McKenna was not at all like Churchill. He was prim, even prissy, efficient but with almost nil charisma, yet always getting jobs above his obvious deserts, and even when he ceased to get (or at least to accept) them, being considered for a possible return to the Exchequer by Prime Ministers as late as Baldwin and Neville Chamberlain. He was to be First Lord of the Admiralty when Churchill, in alliance with Lloyd George, was an 'economist' on naval expenditure. And he was to be Home Secretary when Churchill, becoming First Lord in his place in 1911, suddenly discovered the merits of battleships. McKenna was also Chancellor, and not a bad one, for the seventeen months of the 1915–16 Asquith coalition, an office which it took Churchill nearly another decade to attain. Moreover, his young wife, formerly Pamela Jekyll, whom McKenna married in April 1908, quickly became a bridge-playing favourite of Asquith's, whereas Clementine Hozier, who became Mrs Winston Churchill five months later, with all her many virtues, never had any special appeal for the Prime Minister in the spacious days of that brilliant government when social proximity to 10 Downing Street counted for a good deal. McKenna was long a formidable if unexciting rival to Churchill. 'Lulu' Harcourt was not in that category. A rich, aesthetic radical who always tended to the leftward side in Cabinet disputes, he was a successful Colonial Secretary in 1910–15 before going back to the Office of Works to make way for Bonar Law in the Asquith coalition. He died young and suspiciously after a homosexual scandal in 1922.

During the latter months of 1907, Churchill was very much a man who had achieved the potentialities of his present office and was awaiting a wider opportunity. This no doubt accounted for the relative calmness of mind with which he approached his four-month Mediterranean islands and East African tour. The calmness did not preclude the outpouring of the memoranda which provoked Sir Francis Hopwood, but it did mean that, having first balanced his Silesian experiences of the previous year by attending French army manoeuvres in Champagne, this time accompanied by his new friend F. E. Smith, he was able to enjoy the last but one autumn in British parliamentary history without a meeting of the House of Commons (the final one – so far, at least – was in 1913) with no fear of being dangerously away from the field of action. There is a sense, although without any documentary evidence, that he already had a firm understanding with Asquith about his future prospects.

This did not extend to knowing exactly what office was to bring him into the Cabinet. There were at least four at issue, apart from entering the Cabinet without a change of job: the first was replacing Elgin as Colonial Secretary; the second was the Admiralty, where the First Lord was Churchill's uncle, Lord Tweedmouth, who was in the course of going mildly off his head; the third was the Local Government Board, with presumably another equivalent post for the current occupant, the by then highly conservative John Burns, who nonetheless trailed clouds of proletarian glory; and the fourth was the Board of Trade, which was about to be vacated by Lloyd George on his promotion to the Exchequer.

Churchill expressed to Asquith a firm preference for continuing at the Colonial Office. The surprises were that he did not clutch at the Admiralty, the hope of which three and a half years later was to bring him importunately to pursue Asquith to a holiday house in Scotland, and the vehemence of his dislike for the Local Government Board. 'I refuse to be shut up in a soup kitchen with Mrs Sidney Webb'[18] (of whom more later) was the aphorism with which Edward Marsh credited his opposition to this post. More significant, for an aphorism has the limitations of an aphorism and few were more addicted to them than was Churchill, were the rash and intractable terms in which he wrote about this considerable office to Asquith: 'There is no place in the Government more laborious, more anxious, more thankless, more cloaked with petty and even squalid detail, more full of hopeless and insoluble difficulties. . . .'[19] He also professed himself untrained for and, by implication, incompetent at conducting a detailed domestic policy bill through Parliament.

This was the more surprising because of the enthusiasm with which he accepted Asquith's finally firm offer of the Board of Trade, and even more of the early-welfare-state manner in which he there discharged his duties during the next twenty-one months. During this period Churchill became not only Lloyd George's successor in the department but also his enthusiastic adjutant in formulating the social policy which was a central part of the New Liberalism as opposed to the old Gladstonian tradition of non-interference in 'condition of the people' matters. For Churchill there was only one disadvantage to the Board of Trade at this stage in his career. Under the old anomalies in the official salary structure (Baldwin, ex-Prime Minister, was an even worse victim when he became Lord President in 1931), it carried a salary of £2,500 as against the £5,000 of Secretaries of State and other more traditional offices. And money was nearly always a problem for Churchill. Otherwise the horizon was set fair for him in April 1908.

PART TWO

THE GLOW-WORM GLOWS:
THE MORNING WAS GOLDEN

1908–1914

7

Two Hustings and an Altar

CHURCHILL'S LIFE WAS rarely without drama, but the spring of 1908 provided it on an unusually generous scale. In mid-March he sat next to and was engrossed by Clementine Hozier at a London dinner party.* On 8 April he was formally offered the Presidency of the Board of Trade, making him, at thirty-three, the youngest member of a Cabinet since Hartington in 1866, and one of a select few who throughout the whole history of British Cabinet government have secured such preferment in their early thirties: Pitt, Palmerston, Peel, Gladstone, Harold Wilson – and William Hague. For the weekend of 11–12 April he persuaded his mother to invite Clementine Hozier and her mother (like Lady Randolph an experienced runner in the adultery stakes) to Salisbury Hall, her rented Hertfordshire house. These two days turned his dinner-party infatuation with Miss Hozier into a serious and, as it turned out, immensely durable interest.

---

* He had encountered her once previously, four years earlier at a ball. According to Miss Hozier's account, given well after she had become Mrs Churchill, 'he never [then] uttered a word and was very gauche . . . he never asked me for a dance, he never asked me to have supper with him – he just stood and stared'. The 1908 dinner party was given by Lady St Helier, formerly Lady Jeune, who ten years before had been so helpful in getting Churchill to the Sudanese campaign and the Battle of Omdurman. Among the guests were his great new friend F. E. Smith plus wife; Churchill's uncle Lord Tweedmouth, First Lord of the Admiralty and former Chief Whip, who had eased his passage to the Liberal party; Sir Henry Lucy, foremost of parliamentary sketchwriters, whose appraisals did much to make or break House of Commons reputations; Ruth Moore, an American lady who was soon to marry the future Lord Lee of Fareham and to provide much of the money which was to enable her husband to restore Chequers and give it to the nation as a country house for Prime Ministers; and Sir Frederick Lugard, the great West African colonial administrator, and his wife, who was an independent colonial expert under the name of Flora Shaw. Miss Shaw was the least pro-Churchill of this company, and the evening did nothing to improve her opinion of him. She was his other table neighbour; he arrived late, in the middle of the main course, and never turned from Miss Hozier and in her direction. The whole occasion was as though, with perfect foresight, nearly every participant had been chosen to contribute a tableau in a pageant of Churchill's life.

Immediately after this he had to leave for Manchester. In accordance with an archaic rule which had begun in 1705 and continued until 1919, and then in a modified form until 1926, a newly appointed Cabinet minister had to seek re-election by his constituency. Often this was allowed to happen unopposed by the opposition party, but not so in Churchill's case. There, on 23 April, against the confident expectations which he had expressed a week before in a letter to Miss Hozier, he was defeated by 429 votes and the opposition of the fox-terrier-like Joynson-Hicks. This was a setback, but fortunately far from a fatal one. Churchill was a famous figure whose rumbustious politics appealed to Liberal activists in the constituencies. Four days after the defeat he claimed that he had received approaches from eight or nine safe seats where bye-elections were impending or could be procured. Dundee, the Tayside city of jute, linen, shipbuilding, jam and cakes, was certainly available, and the local Liberals welcoming. It was to that haven that Churchill, with a fine sense of the political unity of the United Kingdom, quickly bounded across the Scottish border. He was returned with a satisfactory plurality (but well short of an absolute majority of the votes) on 9 May. Only then, after his 'big dipper' of a spring, was he able to concentrate on his new department – although without losing touch with or interest in Miss Hozier.

What had gone wrong in Manchester to undermine his confidence of 16 April that the 'Jews, Irish, Unionist Free Traders – the three doubtful elements – wh were all alleged to be estranged, have come or are coming back into line, & I have little fear of their not voting solidly for me on Friday'?[1] Maybe the Jews and the Unionist Free Traders did, although the latter were not so estranged from their normal party as they had been when Joseph Chamberlain was at the height of his rampant campaigning. The Irish apparently did not, even though Churchill attempted to encourage them by securing Asquith's permission to say that Home Rule would be an issue to be dealt with in the second term of the Liberal government. Against this had to be set the unpopularity of the government's Nonconformist-inspired Education Bill of the 1907 session with Roman Catholics (as with Anglicans), and the position was certainly not redeemed by the even more unpopular Licensing Bill. The Catholic diocesan for Manchester was the Bishop of Salford, and he pronounced adversely to Churchill on the Sunday before the poll.

The degree of obedience to such pulpit fatwas was however doubtful, even when religion played a much greater part in politics than it does today, just as views on how any particular group vote tends to be based more on gossip than on statistics. At least equally weighty factors were the intervention of an independent socialist candidate, who took 276 votes, and a general ebbing of radical enthusiasm two and a quarter years after the 'new dawn' of 1906. Joynson-Hicks, who had a flatly partisan political style, denounced the government in phrases which, *mutatis mutandis*, are always wearily familiar. They had 'in the space of two short years . . . alienated our colonies, thrown away the fruits of the Transvaal war, attempted to gerrymander our Constitution, increased our taxation, flouted our religious convictions, let loose chaos and bloodshed in Ireland and are now setting out to attack every trade and institution not prepared to obey the rattle of the Radical drum'.[2] There is nothing to suggest that Churchill was either a bad or, on this ebb-tide, a particularly skilful candidate. He had a swing against him of 6.6 per cent, somewhat but not much above the going rate for bye-elections that winter and spring. He took his defeat very well. In a letter thirteen days later, and with only a side-swipe at 'those sulky Irish Catholics' who he claimed had changed sides at the last moment, he wrote: 'The Liberal party is I must say a good party to fight with. Such loyalty and kindness in misfortune I never saw. I might have won them a great victory from the way they treat me.'[3]

In Dundee, where his percentage of votes cast was in fact nearly three points lower than in Manchester, the seat was regarded as 'safe for life' and the contest was considered to have proceeded satisfactorily. (The British electoral system is not without its vagaries.) The 56 per cent who voted against Churchill were happily (for him) and almost evenly split between Conservative and Labour candidates, with a maverick fourth candidate, in the shape of one Edwin Scrymgeour, running as a 'prohibitionist' (of alcohol) and taking 2.5 per cent of the vote. It was this 'cloud no bigger than a man's hand' which most needed watching, for it was Scrymgeour, with his views unchanged, and anathema to Churchill, the latter having in the meantime become a still better target for prohibitionists, who after fourteen and a half years and another four elections showed that 'safe for life' was a relative rather than an absolute term, and defeated Churchill in 1922.

Dundee in 1908 provided big audiences and Churchill provided resonant orations, the most notable of them cast in an anti-socialist direction, which was a shift of emphasis for him. In the Caird Hall in the core of the city he began with a passage of raillery which partly foreshadowed some of his 1945–50 extravagances, although without the reference to the Gestapo, of which neither he nor anyone else had heard: 'Translated into concrete terms, Socialist society is a set of disagreeable individuals who obtained a majority for their caucus at some recent elections, and whose officials now look upon humanity through innumerable grilles and pigeon holes and over innumerable counters, and say to them "tickets please".'[4] Then, in a more famous passage, he attempted his own definition of what separated progressive Liberalism from socialism, and did so with impressive contrapuntal oratory, which however owed more to careful preparation than to spontaneous inspiration:

> Socialism seeks to pull down wealth; Liberalism seeks to raise up poverty. Socialism would destroy private interests; Liberalism would preserve private interests in the only way in which they can be safely and justly preserved, namely by reconciling them with public right. Socialism would kill enterprise; Liberalism would rescue enterprise from the trammels of privilege and preference.[5]

On 10 May Churchill's train south rounded the curve out of Dundee station into the long but slow straight of the Tay bridge before gathering speed across the Kingdom of Fife and crossing the other Firth before Edinburgh and on to London. It was then a ten-and-a-half-hour journey, but it is doubtful if even Churchill's impatience grudged the time. He had put constituency problems behind him for a few years, and did not much return except for a few days each autumn, in the interval between then and the first 1910 general election. Dundee, in spite of its fine site, was not a heartstrings-clutching place for Sassenachs. I remember one of his successors as member for that city (John Strachey) telling me that some of the most pleasurable moments of his life were those when he settled into his seat over the Tay estuary – going south. Churchill on that May morning had every reason to regard his achievement with satisfaction and his prospects with exhilaration. But, although it was never his habit to set any limit to the ceiling of his ambition, it cannot have occurred to him that it would be exactly thirty-two years to the day that he would become Prime Minister, or in what desperate circumstances he would achieve that goal.

Meanwhile Miss Hozier had been spending a spring month with her mother partly in the Black Forest to collect her sister Nellie (later Romilly) from a tuberculosis clinic and partly in Milan – to buy clothes. Worldly old Lady St Helier, her great-aunt and Churchill's enthusiastic patron, thought her mother must have been mad to take her abroad at such a promising time. From both destinations Clementine wrote to Churchill letters of regret at being away and of fascinated interest in the Manchester and Dundee contests. Maybe her mother had a better nerve and a surer matrimonial judgement than did her great-aunt.

The mother, Lady Blanche Hozier (née Ogilvy) was the eldest child of the tenth Earl of Airlie. She had made a late and by no means satisfactory marriage to Henry Hozier in 1878. It was not obviously satisfactory because he was over forty, just divorced and of neither equivalent birth nor secure wealth. He had, however, been a successful Brigade of Guards officer, had considerable entrepreneurial talent, and was generally a man of interest and charm. Clementine, although somewhat frightened of Hozier also became extremely interested in him before his death in 1907. The trouble was not his birth or his personality, but that he was fundamentally non-uxorious, although little less so than was his wife. The marriage broke up in 1891, and Lady Blanche subsequently lived in straitened circumstances, sometimes in Seaford in Sussex, sometimes across the Channel in Dieppe, sometimes at Abingdon Villas in far Kensington, which was not then a fashionable address. Any impression of high affluence given by the clothes-buying descent upon Milan was false: it was probably because that city was then cheap.

While there is no doubt that Lady Blanche was Clementine's mother, it is unlikely that Henry Hozier was her father. It requires no prurient searching out of old scandals to take this view. Mary Soames, Clementine Churchill's surviving daughter, put it bluntly in her (1998) introduction to her finely edited volume of the letters which her parents exchanged with each other over fifty-six years: 'In her later life Clementine became convinced that she was not the child of Henry Hozier. . . .'[6] Who then was her father? Certainty is elusive, for here again Lady Soames is blunt: 'There is no doubt that Blanche Hozier was promiscuous; and at the time when her husband was threatening to divorce her, gossip had it that she had at least nine lovers.'[7] The most likely candidates for the paternal role seem to have been Bertram Mitford (1837–1916), who became the first Lord Redesdale in 1902, and Captain William Middleton (1846–92). Mitford was a member of the diplomatic service as a young man and served in Russia, China and Japan. He was offered the ambassadorship at St Petersburg in 1871, but preferred a spell of London life and was appointed secretary to the Office of Works by Disraeli in 1874, in which year he was married to Blanche's younger sister, an earlier Clementine, and retained that post until 1886, the year of his possible daughter's birth. In the 1890s he was briefly Conservative member of Parliament for Stratford-upon-Avon, but his interests were becoming increasingly literary. He had written several good travel books out of his experiences as an attaché, and devoted many years to an autobiography, which Edmund Gosse said, with an element of hyperbole, 'will long be read and always be referred to'.

In his later guise as Redesdale he also translated important foreign texts and makes a surprise appearance in this capacity in Asquith's letters to Venetia Stanley.* He was very deaf in the last decade of his life, but he retained something of a boulevardier's zest. Gosse's essay on him in the *Dictionary of National Biography* concludes with the following vignette:

> As a human being, Lord Redesdale was a sort of Prince Charming; with his fine features, sparkling eyes, erect and elastic figure, and in the last years, his burnished silver curls, he was a universal favourite, a gallant figure of a gentleman, solidly English in reality, but polished and sharpened by foreign society. To see him stroll down Pall Mall, exquisitely dressed, his hat a little on one side, with a smile and a nod for everyone was to watch the survival of a type never frequent and now extinct.[8]

His second son, who succeeded him in the title, was caricatured as Uncle Matthew or 'Farve' in the novels of his granddaughter, Nancy Mitford.

Middleton, known as 'Bay' because his colouring was reminiscent of such horses, had a much shorter life and provides less interesting detail. He was an officer in the 12th Lancers who was killed steeplechasing at the age of forty-six. He had been a close friend of Lady Randolph's in Ireland in the early days of her marriage, as indeed had been Lady Blanche, but the two women had drifted apart until their children's romance brought them together again. It is remarkable that the offspring of two such old libertines should have made one of the most famously long-lasting and faithful marriages in history.

Clementine Hozier in 1908 and at the age of twenty-two was not at all as this somewhat rackety background may make her sound. There were many contemporary references to her great beauty, which does not however entirely come through in photographs. But there is no reason to doubt that she had a firm, sensitive, rather nervous, almost

---

* On 10 July 1914, already three weeks after the Sarejevo assassination and with the Irish crisis boiling up to its height, Asquith wrote: 'Before going to bed I started on the first volume of Chamberlain's (the German) Kant, translated by old Redesdale, who gave it to me the other day.'

fawn-like appearance (but certainly not elfin-like, for she was tall), totally unlike the self-indulgent lusciousness of her mother-in-law to be. In contrast with Lady Randolph at any stage in her life, she conveyed a virginal impression. But while this was probably technically accurate she was not exactly an ingénue straight from the schoolroom. She had made three engagements (to be married), two of them to the same man and semi-secret. He was Sidney Peel, a grandson of the formidable Sir Robert and a devoted swain of hers. He was nearly fifteen years her senior and was a friendly comfort rather than an electric spark to her. The other was Lionel Earle, a civil servant of good provenance and considerable wealth, who, although older than Peel, probably did excite her. This engagement was made public, and indeed wedding presents had begun to arrive before her doubts set in. A kind friend made the mistake of inviting them both, accompanied by Lady Blanche, to spend a fortnight at his property in Holland. This proved too much and Clementine, with strong will, went back to her somewhat humdrum life in Dieppe or London and (in the latter) to giving French lessons at half a crown an hour.

By the rules of the Edwardian matrimonial market it was therefore more than time that she settled down. But so it also was for Winston Churchill who, although not taller than her, was eleven and a half years older. Unlike 'Miss Beale and Miss Buss' he had not been entirely immune to Cupid's darts. But nor had these darts played any very dominating part in his life. He was emphatically not a ladies' man. He did not dance, and he was bad at routine dinner-party conversation. Unless his female neighbours could inspire him to talk, preferably about himself, although with the future of the world as the next best thing, he mostly ignored them. The course of his warm but hardly obsessive relationship with Pamela Lytton has already been charted. Then there was a lady called Muriel Wilson, a daughter of the rich Hull shipowning family at whose Tranby Croft house in the East Riding the great 'baccarat scandal' involving King Edward VII and Colonel Gordon-Cumming had taken place in 1891. She and Churchill had a relationship of half-mocking, half-sexual friendship. In the early autumn of 1906 they had gone (chaperoned of course) on a comprehensive motor tour of central Italy – Bologna, Ravenna, Rimini, Urbino, Perugia, Siena – during which he had written to his mother of 'the tranquil *banalité*' of his relations with her. She was good at keeping her end up at flirtatious teasing, and when, in the spring of 1907, there were rumours that he was about to marry Miss Botha, the well-favoured daughter of

Churchill's captor in Natal, who had accompanied her father to London for an Imperial Conference, Muriel Wilson wrote from the South of France, where in preference to the Yorkshire Wolds she seemed to spend most of her time, with a good balance between mild jealousy and mockery: 'I hear you are engaged to Miss Botha – is this true? . . . I look forward to a peaceful old age here in the sun & surrounded by the blue sea, & *you* I hope – & Miss Botha, and all the little Bothas will come & see me & my garden (I shall be like Alice Rothschild) & I will have a luncheon party to meet you – other old crocks like ourselves – & the Prime Minister will write his name in our Visitors' Book. . . .'9

Miss Botha was gossip columnists' fantasy – they already existed in the 1900s, if not quite so intrusively as today. There was one other and much more mysterious amorous sortie. Ethel Barrymore was a distinguished American-born actress of the period, five years younger than Churchill, who was in London in 1896–8, although subsequently only occasionally for 'star' appearances. Nearly all biographies of Churchill state firmly that he proposed marriage to Miss Barrymore, but none of them say when or provide any other supporting detail. In the official biography Randolph Churchill, who is normally rich in supporting sources, here provides none. He confines himself to saying that Miss Barrymore long afterwards confirmed orally to him that 'she had been much attracted to Churchill', and that he had sent her a telegram for her eightieth birthday. That anniversary was of course many decades later, and one is left wondering whether, without doubting the formal truth of the reiterated statement, this was just a 'stage-door johnnie' infatuation of the late 1890s, when Churchill was certainly in no position seriously to envisage marriage, or whether it was just a late-night single extravagant declaration on his part, without expectation, or perhaps even desire, of acceptance.

The other name which needs to be inserted into this framework is that of Violet Asquith, the Prime Minister's daughter. She was at least near to being in love with Churchill, although not he with her. This did not prevent a considerable friendship, in spite of Churchill's deep post-1915 disenchantment with her father, from persisting far into their old ages. Once again, however, as with Ethel Barrymore, there are mysterious elements, not here arising from any lack of documentation. It is copious, particularly on Miss Asquith's side, but contradictory.

Lady Violet Bonham Carter, as she had by then become, by virtue of a combination of her 1916 marriage to Maurice Bonham Carter and her father's 1925 earldom, published in 1965, six months or so after

Churchill's death, and under the title of *Winston Churchill as I Knew Him*, one of the best and most perceptive of the many Churchill books. It was highly personal and dramatic. It begins with a memorable description of her first meeting with him, in the summer of 1906, when he was thirty-one and she nineteen. She is precise about who gave the dinner, where it took place, and who were the other guests:

> I found myself sitting next to this young man who seemed to me quite different from any young man I had ever met. For a long time he remained sunk in abstraction. Then he appeared to become suddenly aware of my existence. . . . he burst forth into an eloquent diatribe on the shortness of human life, the immensity of possible human accomplishment – a theme so well exploited by the poets, prophets and philosophers of all ages that it might seem difficult to invest it with a new and startling significance. Yet for me he did so, in a torrent of magnificent language which appeared to be both effortless and inexhaustible and ended with the words I shall always remember: 'We are all worms. But I do believe that I am a glow-worm.' By this time I was convinced of it – and my conviction remained unshaken throughout the years that followed.[10]

When she got home she told her father that 'for the first time in my life I had seen genius'. Asquith looked tolerantly amused and said (at least in her memory of nearly sixty years later): 'Well, Winston would certainly agree with you there – but I am not sure whether you will find many others of the same mind. Still, I know exactly what you mean. He is not only remarkable but unique.'[11]

The first contradiction is that in a most meticulously edited collection of her diaries and letters which came out in 1996 there is no reference of any sort to the occasion. It is impossible to believe that it did not take place. The detail and general plausibility are far too great for that. But it is nonetheless odd that such a dramatic event in her life should not have found a place in her voluminous contemporary writing, and possible therefore to think that there was an element of retrospective romanticism about her later account.

This is of relevance in comparing her 1965 reaction to the appearance of Clementine Hozier upon the scene with what she wrote at the time. In *Winston Churchill as I Knew Him* Violet Bonham Carter wrote of the Churchill marriage: 'His wife was already my friend. . . . She had come out a few years before me, and as I gazed upon her finished, flawless beauty and reflected on her wide experience of the world I was just stumbling into, I felt an awestruck admiration. Awe vanished, admiration stayed, and with it began a friendship which no vicissitude has ever shaken.... I soon discovered that she was in fact a better natural Liberal than Winston, and this discovery brought me much relief on her behalf.'[12]

What Violet Asquith wrote at the time was however a good deal less blandly enthusiastic. On hearing of the engagement she had an exchange of letters with her friend Venetia Stanley, who was Clementine's first cousin, although it was with Venetia's sister, Sylvia Henley, that Clementine had the stronger and longer-lasting friendship. Violet Asquith wrote:

> The news of the clinching of Winston's engagement to the Hozier has just reached me from him. I must say I am much gladder for her sake than I am sorry for his. His wife could never be more to him than an ornamental sideboard as I have often said & she is unexacting enough not to mind not being more. Whether he will ultimately mind her being as stupid as an *owl* I don't know – it is a danger no doubt – but for the moment she will have a rest at least from making her own clothes & I think he must be a *little* in love. Father thinks that it spells disaster for them both.... I don't know that it does that. He did not *wish* for – though he needs it badly – a critical reformatory wife who would stop up the lacunas in his taste etc. & hold him back from blunders.... I have wired begging them *both* to come here [Slains Castle, Aberdeenshire] on the 17th – won't it be amusing if they do? Father is a little chilly about it – & W. generally, & Margot [the second Mrs Asquith] has an odd theory that Clementine is *mad*! which she clings to with tenacity in spite of my assurance that she is sane to the point of dreariness.[13]

Venetia Stanley wrote two days later, probably (it being a Sunday) without having got Violet's letter: 'Aren't you thrilled about Winston. How I wonder whether Clementine will become as much of a Cabinet bore as Pamela [McKenna], I don't expect she will as she is too humble. Poor Pamela I'm afraid will be awfully bored at no longer being the only young Liberal matron. I had a very ecstatic letter from Clemmie saying all the suitable things. I wonder how stupid Winston thinks her.'[14]

This was not the most generous or charitable exchange, but nor should it be seen as deeply shocking or proof of the hypocrisy of future friendship. If private comment about third parties were always to be revealed, especially when made under the stress of a particular mood or a sudden piece of news, there are many of us who would fall by the wayside. It is tempting to see them as two ugly sisters who had been upset by the success of Cinderella. And no doubt Violet was moved by elements of jealousy. But she was far from ugly, had a lot of *amitiés amoureuses*, and was at the time greatly enjoying the first burst of the Prime Minister's daughter. And Venetia, while far from conventionally beautiful, had a magnetic ability to enliven a conversation or an occasion, and had plenty of admirers, including within a few years the Prime Minister himself. Furthermore she had no particular affiliation with Churchill, except as an exhilarating half-member of their 'set'.

His pursuit of Clementine, although probably firmly decided upon in the spring, and in no way strongly resisted, was not brought to a conclusion until just after the end of the parliamentary session. This was symbolic. Throughout her long marriage she was to experience no more than the most mild and infrequent gusts of feminine rivalry. But she was nonetheless up against a most formidable competitor for his attention, and that was his attachment to what was always to him the great game of politics. Even when his mind was set upon what turned out to be a most felicitous marriage, his equivalent of Francis Drake's bowls on Plymouth Hoe, in the shape of his first session as a Cabinet minister, had first to be completed.

Parliament adjourned that year rather early – on 1 August – and, with Miss Hozier on the Isle of Wight at the Cowes regatta for the first week of the month, Churchill went to stay at a house in Rutland which his cousin Freddie Guest had rented, and which was burned down while he was there. He retreated to Nuneham Park near Oxford in some disarray. Eddie Marsh, who had been with him in Rutland, had lost all his own clothes as well as Churchill's working papers. Nuneham was then the house of a Cabinet colleague, 'Lulu' Harcourt, and was a convenient staging post both for the Oxford wedding of Churchill's younger brother Jack to Lady Gwendeline Bertie, daughter of the Earl of Abingdon (which example may have been a subsidiary factor urging him towards matrimony), and for Blenheim, to where he proposed to move and to have a rendezvous with Clementine on Monday, 10 August. This was a change from the original plan, which had been to spend a few days at Salisbury Hall with Lady Randolph, as in April. Churchill however became very keen to get Clementine to Blenheim, and indeed to use the grand background for his proposal of marriage, which was made and accepted on Tuesday the 11th.

She was at first resistant to the Blenheim plan, thinking that it would involve a large and smart house party, but was somewhat reassured when told that it would merely be the Duke, who had recently been left by his Vanderbilt wife and whom Clementine never came to like, the increasingly inevitable F. E. Smith (she never much liked him either, although she did like his wife, formerly Margaret Furneaux) and one of Churchill's Board of Trade private secretaries (not Marsh, whom she did come much to like but who was presumably exhausted by his experiences in the fire). Her attitude to this more departmental secretary, who subsequently became Sir William Clark and British High Commissioner in Ottawa and then Pretoria, is not recorded, and she was in any event presumably too taken up with Churchill (as he was with her) and with the charting of her future life to be greatly concerned with the fellow guests. There was again a certain symbolism for the future about her being surrounded for these two crucial days by two of her husband-to-be's closest friends, neither of whom she ever came remotely to cherish. It was also interesting that Churchill, who had too high an opinion of his own quality to be unduly impressed by wealth or grandeur (as opposed to liking being made comfortable by them), should have been so eager for the Blenheim backcloth, particularly as he must by then have been aware that she was one of the last people to be swept away by it. It was probably more for his own sense of appropriateness that he wished it to be there. He had been born in Blenheim, he had written much of his then most successful book there and he was to write another (of four volumes) about the founder of the great house, and he was to be buried in a churchyard on the edge of the park. To become engaged to be married there fitted in with his sense of pattern and continuity.

The betrothal achieved, they went first to call on Lady Blanche in the modest Abingdon Villas house and then for a postponed few days to Lady Randolph at Salisbury Hall. From there the engagement was announced on 15 August, and the wedding was set for 12 September, at St Margaret's Westminster. It was very much an 'out-of-season' date, but they nonetheless managed to assemble 1,300 guests. Except for Lloyd George, who was the only one outside the family to sign the register, most major politicians were away, so that it could not in this respect rival Asquith's wedding to Margot Tennant, fourteen years before, when Gladstone, Rosebery and Balfour had all signed. There was however something appropriate about Lloyd George, with whom Churchill's alliance was then very close, being in solitary splendour. It was also not untypical that Churchill was reported as being in animated political conversation with him in the vestry. The formidable Bishop Edwards of St Asaph officiated and Dean Welldon of Manchester (formerly Churchill's headmaster at Harrow and then Bishop in Calcutta) gave the address. Venetia Stanley was among the bridesmaids.

The *Tailor and Cutter* added to the gaiety of the occasion by describing Churchill's clothes as 'one of the greatest failures as a wedding garment we have ever seen, giving the wearer a sort of glorified coachman appearance'. On the contrary, Churchill looked untypically glossy for the event, and his best man, Lord Hugh Cecil, much closer to an attendant coachman.

8

THE SORCERER'S APPRENTICE
AT THE BOARD OF TRADE

────────────

BY THE TIME THAT Churchill got back from his honeymoon – a few pietistic days at Blenheim, followed by further fairly short visits to Lake Maggiore and Venice – he was near to completing six of the twenty-two months that he was to spend at the Board of Trade. It was an ambivalent department, half rooted in history and half concerned with workaday matters which made it not very different from the Local Government Board, against which he had pronounced himself so intransigently.

He had an illustrious list of predecessors in the office – Huskisson, Gladstone, Cardwell, John Bright, Joseph Chamberlain and, immediately, Lloyd George. They had not all taken to their appointment with enthusiasm. Gladstone, admittedly when he was made Vice-President in 1841 rather than President in 1843, had complained that, while he had hoped to be concerned with the affairs of men, he found himself set 'to governing packages'. And in those days the Board of Trade was at least as concerned as was the Treasury with raising the national revenue, three-quarters of which came from import and excise duties. After Gladstone himself, pulling exceptionally in double harness with Disraeli, had in the 1850s made the Treasury pre-eminent and the budget into a great national event, this was no longer so, and most subsequent Presidents occupied the office with at least the hope and often the reality that it was a staging post to something else, preferably the Chancellorship of the Exchequer.

This was certainly the case with Lloyd George, whose departure towards that (often mistaken) politicians' heaven of the Treasury had made the vacancy for Churchill. Nonetheless the responsibilities and powers of the Board of Trade were considerable, even if something of a ragbag. They included company registration and regulation, patents and designs, merchant shipping, railways, trade and labour statistics, conciliation in industrial disputes, and advice to the Foreign Office in commercial negotiations. As John Grigg put it in the second volume of his life of Lloyd George, 'state intervention and control had been reduced to a minimum, but such powers as were retained to ensure the smooth, orderly working of capitalism were largely exercised by the Board of Trade'.[1]

Lloyd George in exercising these multifarious powers had pursued a very cool strategy, which balanced two different sides of his kaleidoscopic nature. First he took an almost naive pleasure in being a minister of the crown. He did not quite emulate John Burns, who, on being appointed the first 'working man' Cabinet member in 1905, is reputed to have said to Campbell-Bannerman: 'Sir 'Enry, you never did a more popular thing in your life.'[2] But Lloyd George's first speech as a minister, in the Caernarvon Guildhall, had more than a touch of 'local boy makes good' pride about it. This gave him a great desire to make a conventional success of being a minister, and led him to set about his departmental duties in a quietly conciliatory way. On the other hand he knew that he could never satisfy his consuming appetite for power by success with company law or marine regulations, and therefore balanced his capacity as a neat administrator, delegating a lot of detailed work, with a determined programme of barnstorming general speeches.

This was somewhat different from Churchill's approach, eagerly though at that stage he sought Lloyd George as an ally, and equal though was his appetite for power. Churchill was pleased but not dazzled by becoming a senior minister at the age of thirty-three. He thought it, if not exactly his birthright, at least a proper reward for his individual talents building upon an hereditary propensity to rule. Also he was a more energetic intervener in questions of detail. His natural instinct was to shake any apple tree within reach and to get as much fruit off it as he possibly could. At first, to vary the fructiferous metaphor, he feared that Lloyd George had taken 'all the plums' out of the Board of Trade pudding. In fact, however, he probably got more out of it in his twenty-two months there than his predecessor had done in his twenty-eight. But he did it, paradoxically, by freely accepting a role as Lloyd George's number two in a partnership of constructive radicalism, two social reforming New Liberals who had turned their backs on the old Gladstonian tradition of concentrating on libertarian political issues and leaving social conditions to look after themselves.

It was not difficult for Churchill, even with his vaulting ambition, to accept a junior partnership with a man who was eleven and a half years his senior and who had been a Liberal MP for thirteen years before him. There is much fascination in the Lloyd George–Churchill relationship, which, through a series of very differing phases, was to last another thirty-five years after the one stepped into the other's shoes at the Board of Trade.* They were the two British politicians of genius, using the word in the sense of exceptional and original powers transcending purely rational measurement, in the first half of the twentieth century. As a result they were the two outstanding Prime Ministers, although in terms of solid (peacetime) achievement Asquith runs at least equal, rather as Peel did with Gladstone and Disraeli in the Victorian age. Churchill was substantially the greater man both because of the wider range outside politics of his interests and accomplishments and because his central achievement in 1940 and 1941 was of a higher order than Lloyd George's in 1917 and 1918, brought off against heavier odds, and still more vital to the future of the world. Furthermore, although Churchill could indulge in some violent lurches of view, both on issues and on people, he had more fixity of purpose and coherence of belief than did Lloyd George: more principle and less opportunism would be another way of putting it.

Yet Lloyd George was undoubtedly stronger in a number of significant qualities than was Churchill, and one, and perhaps the most remarkable, of his strengths was that he could long exercise an almost effortless authority over Churchill. Churchill himself, never one to write himself down, bore most eloquent witness of this after a meeting with Lloyd George, the first for some time, during Churchill's Chancellor-

---

* An interesting aspect of the relationship was their terms of epistolary address, one to the other. Churchill, largely because of the vividness of his father's memory, was more frequently addressed by his christian name than was any other leading politician except for Austen Chamberlain, where the same consideration applied with even greater force. But Lloyd George, who was not in any event a great letter writer, did not begin to address him as 'My dear Winston' (as opposed to 'My dear Churchill') until the end of 1908, which was well after Asquith, for example, had started doing so. Lloyd George, by contrast, was very rarely referred to by his christian name – Tories preferred to deprive him of one-half of his surname and to refer to him patronizingly as 'George'. Churchill claimed to be one of the few people who called him 'David'. But such a form of address did not appear in a letter until the autumn of 1910, after Churchill had been to stay with him at Criccieth house. Letters may not tell the whole story, for in early 1914 Churchill claimed they were so close that for ten years hardly a day had gone by without their having half an hour's talk together. 'How bored you must both be,' was Augustus Birrell's splendidly balloon-pricking response to this information. Asquith was literally never, outside his antecedent family, addressed as 'Herbert', his intended christian name. All his colleagues called him 'Asquith' or 'Prime Minister' or 'HHA' or latterly 'the Chief'. His second wife called him by his second given name of 'Henry', which she thought was more chic.

ship in the late 1920s. Churchill had sought the meeting because he wanted to check with Lloyd George some points for his last volume of *The World Crisis*. This part of the meeting, Robert Boothby, then Churchill's parliamentary private secretary, recorded as having gone well. Lloyd George answered all his questions. Then Churchill added: 'Within five minutes the old relationship between us was completely re-established. The relationship between Master and Servant. And I was the Servant.'[3] No doubt Churchill said it with his tongue at least half in his cheek. But it must have had an element of truth, and anyone who could make Churchill even pretend to a relationship of servitude was clearly a most formidable figure.

By that time Lloyd George had been out of office for six years, and had another seventeen years of political sterility before him. During the 1930s both his powers and his judgement waned, although at least as late as the 1940 Norway debate he could make an occasional devastating speech. His reputation had been considerably tarnished by a semi-adulatory visit which he had paid to Hitler in the summer of 1936. Some saw him in 1940 as a possible British Pétain. However, Churchill, partly no doubt out of nostalgic sentiment but partly also for reasons of safeguarding his flanks, was playing with the idea of making him either ambassador in Washington (following the death of Lord Lothian) or Minister of Agriculture, in which area Lloyd George was thought to have become an expert as a result of growing apples on the semi-suburban hills of Surrey. Perhaps fortunately by that stage, neither job came off.

Lloyd George's superiorities were not just those of personality. He was in most circumstances a more persuasive – and certainly a more spontaneous – speaker than Churchill. He could get himself more into the working of the minds of his audiences. Churchill spoke at his listeners. Lloyd George wrapped himself around them. He was also, and by much the same token, a far better listener, and partly as a result of his Celtic intuition had more understanding of what was going on in the minds of his interlocutors. This last point was of considerable practical significance in the context of the Board of Trade in 1908. Lloyd George was a brilliant industrial conciliator, and continued to exercise his art in this field up to and beyond his accession to the premiership, rather like an instrumentalist who had become a major conductor but liked occasionally reverting to giving a virtuoso perform-ance on his old fiddle or other musical tool. Churchill's limitation as a conciliator in the judgement of a not ill-disposed Board of Trade official was simply that 'he talked too much'. He did not give the parties an opportunity to get alongside each other. Nevertheless he saw the resolution of industrial disputes as an important part of his Board of Trade function, and did manage to achieve several important settlements.

What however seized his imagination about the Board of Trade was the opportunity offered to make his mark as a social reformer. In a ranging letter to Asquith on 14 March 1908 (that is before he had either been offered or accepted the Board of Trade), he had written: 'Dimly across gulfs of ignorance I see the outline of a policy which I call the Minimum Standard. It is national rather than departmental. I am doubtful of my power to give it concrete expression. If I did, I expect before long I should find myself in collision with some of my best friends – like for instance John Morley, who at the end of a lifetime of study & thought has come to the conclusion that nothing can be done.'[4] Nine months later however he had come to see his way much more clearly and was less worried about offending Gladstone's vicar in the Cabinet. In another important letter to Asquith, this one brimming with self-confidence and setting out (on 29 December 1908) the results of his Christmas holiday thoughts, he wrote:

I have been revolving many things during these few days of tranquillity & I feel impelled to state to you the conviction that for a long time past has been forming in my mind. There is a tremendous policy of Social Organization. The need is urgent and the moment ripe. Germany with a harder climate and far less accumulated wealth has managed to establish tolerable basic conditions for her people. She is organized not only for war, but for peace. We are organized for nothing except party politics. The Minister who will apply to this country the successful experiences of Germany in social organization may or may not be supported at the polls, but he will at least have left a memorial which time will not deface of his administration. . . . We have at least two years. We have the miseries which this winter is inflicting upon the poorer classes [who] back us. And oddly enough the very class of legislation which is required is just the kind the House of Lords will not dare to oppose.* The expenditure of

* The relevance of the first consideration is that 1908–9 was a period of what was then called 'bad trade' but would now be designated 'economic recession'. Unemployment nearly doubled to 7.2 per cent and industrial bargaining was almost all about how much wage reduction was acceptable and not about wage increases. The government (except perhaps for Churchill) noted these adverse developments with regret but without accepting responsibility for them. Even Lloyd George in his ground-breaking 1909

less than ten millions a year, not upon relief, but upon machinery & thrift-stimuli would make England a different country for the poor. And I believe that once the nation begins to feel the momentum of these large designs, it will range itself at first with breathless interest & afterwards in solid support behind the shoulder of the Government. Here are the steps as I see them.

1. Labour Exchanges and Unemployment Insurance:
2. National Infirmity Insurance etc:
3. Special Expansive State Industries – Afforestation – Roads:
4. Modernized Poor Law ie classification:
5. Railway Amalgamation with State Control and guarantee:
6. Education compulsory till 17.

I believe there is not one of those things that cannot be carried & carried triumphantly & that they would not only benefit the state but fortify the party. But how much better to fail in such noble efforts, than to perish by slow paralysis or windy agitation.

I say – thrust a big slice of Bismarckism over the whole underside of our industrial system, & await the consequences whatever they may be with a good conscience.[5]

This letter was boundingly uninhibited for a minister in the lower half of the Cabinet to send to a Prime Minister who was more famous for his critical appraisals than for his naive enthusiasms. It set out, even if without great precision, an itemized programme of 'New Liberalism'. Even more did it proclaim the doctrine that it was the duty of a government, particularly one with a big majority, to use the golden hour for decisive legislation rather than to believe that the main use of electoral victory should be to do nothing to impair the prospect of another victory at the next election.

Churchill's first legislative task at the Board of Trade was to get through Lloyd George's Port of London Bill, which set up a unified

---

budget spoke of 'bad trade' as though it were much more an act of God than something with which the government could or should deal. Churchill's point about the House of Lords was based on the second chamber having destroyed the principal 'political' bills of the first two sessions of the new parliament, the Education and the Licensing Bills. Neither was particularly popular except with Nonconformist Liberal activists. On the other hand the Lords had not interfered with the Trades Disputes Bill, which gave to the trades unions an immunity from the law which would have horrified Mrs Thatcher (and did at the time half horrify Asquith and Haldane). Until the rejection of the budget of 1909 the peers chose their targets carefully and even a little cynically, with more regard for populism than for blind independence.

authority for the whole tidal stretch of the Thames, and was 'absolutely non party'. So at least Churchill assured Lord Salisbury in a December 1908 letter, successfully urging him to ease its passage through the Lords. This enabled Churchill to begin the new year of 1909 by appointing his junior minister, Hudson Kearley, soon to be Lord Devonport, as the first chairman of the new Authority. Kearley had been one of the earliest of the chain grocers, but there is a feeling that, although he had suited Lloyd George well,* Churchill was glad to be rid of him and to have Jack Tennant, the Prime Minister's brother-in-law, in his place. Churchill also had the good luck to have as his permanent secretary at the Board Sir Hubert Llewellyn Smith, one of the greatest constructive civil servants of his day. Lloyd George for part of his period there had Sir Francis Hopwood, who would not have been a helpful partner for Churchill. Churchill also recruited a young William Beveridge to the staff of the department. And on some of the schemes he maintained close and friendly touch with Sidney Webb, who acted as a conduit of communication with his wife, currently on the point of completing the famous Minority Report of the Royal Commission on the Poor Law (February 1909). Beatrice Webb, famous also for the asperity of her diary comments on individuals, was in the course of revising substantially upwards her opinion of Churchill. When she had first met him, as long ago as 8 July 1903, she had written damningly:

> Went in to dinner with Winston Churchill. First impression: restless, almost intolerably so, without capacity for sustained and unexcited labour, egotistical, bumptious, shallow-minded and reactionary, but with a certain personal magnetism, great pluck and some originality, not of intellect but of character. More of the American speculator than the English aristocrat. Talks exclusively about himself and his electioneering plans, wanted me to tell him of someone who would get statistics for him. 'I never do any brainwork that anyone else can do for me' – an axiom that shows organizing but not thinking capacity. Replete with dodges for winning Oldham against the Labour & Liberal candidates. But I dare say he has a

* Lloyd George was always partial to shopkeepers (and their wives), although with in general a preference for drapers rather than grocers. But he was close enough to Kearley to go on a long Christmas motor tour with him to Nice and back in 1907. Kearley, as Devonport, achieved an approach to a place in history when Ben Tillett, during the great dock strike of 1911, used an oration on Tower Hill to call upon 'God almighty to strike Lord Devonport dead'. He survived until 1934.

better side, which the ordinary cheap cynicism of his position and career covers to a casual dinner acquaintance.

Bound to be unpopular, too unpleasant a flavour with his restless self-regarding personality and lack of moral or intellectual refinement. . . . No notion of scientific research, philosophy, literature or art, still less of religion. But his pluck, courage, resourcefulness and great tradition may carry him far, unless he knocks himself to pieces like his father.[6]

Nearly a year later, when the Webbs swallowed their prejudices (Sidney in general agreed with Beatrice on persons, she following him more on facts and policies) to the extent of inviting him to one of their relatively austere but lion-cultivating political dinners, she was if anything more critical. That evening they had the new Liberal recruit with Lloyd George, the Herbert Gladstones, the G. M. Trevelyans and the Charles Mastermans, to their Embankment house near the Tate Gallery.

> On my other side sat Winston Churchill. The impression he makes is an unpleasant one: he drinks too much, talks too much and does no thinking worthy of the name. Such ideas as he has are a good jumble of old-fashioned Radicalism and mere Toryism; at present, wishing to be advanced, old-fashioned Radicalism is in the ascendant. He is completely ignorant of all social questions and does not know it. He is chock full of prejudices and catchwords, and constantly strives for new and effective ways of stating these. He has no sympathy with suffering, no intellectual curiosity, he is neither scientific nor benevolent. I tried the 'national minimum' on him, but he was evidently unaware of the most elementary objections to unrestricted competition and was still in the stage of 'infant-school economics'. . . .*
>
> Lloyd George is altogether superior both in character and in intellect to Winston Churchill or Herbert Gladstone.[7]

Four and a half years later, however, there was a very different note. For 16 October 1908 she wrote:

> On Sunday we lunched with Winston Churchill and his bride – a charming lady, well-bred and pretty, and earnest with it, but not rich, by no means a 'good match', which is to Winston's credit. Winston had made a really eloquent speech on the unemployed the night before and he has mastered the Webb scheme, though not going the whole length of compulsory labour exchanges. He is brilliantly able – more than a phrase-monger, I think – and definitely casting in his lot with constructive state action. No doubt he puts that side forward to me, but still he could

---

* Compare Churchill's letter to Asquith of twenty-one months later.

not do it so well if he did not agree somewhat with it. After lunch Lloyd
George came in and asked us to breakfast to discuss the insurance
scheme. . . . He [Lloyd George] is a clever fellow, but has less intellect
than Winston, and not such an attractive personality – more of the
preacher, less of the statesman.[8]

The contrasting appraisals, particularly on the relative merits of
Churchill and Lloyd George, may be thought just as indicative of the
unsteadiness of Mrs Webb's personal judgement as of the statesmanlike
evolution of Churchill. But he had certainly improved his social-reform
credentials, which was not surprising in view of the three schemes to
which he devoted his central departmental attention. The first was the
Trades Board Bill, designed to deal with the problem of 'sweated
labour', mainly in the small garment-making workshops of the East End
of London and of Leeds and Manchester. The problem was exacerbated
by the heavy immigration from eastern Europe into these areas which
was a feature of the period. The Home Office, which controlled the
factory inspectorate, had a tradition of cautious conservatism upon the
issue, which Herbert Gladstone as Home Secretary had no will to
contradict. Although he was on many issues friendly to the Labour
party, on this he remained true to his father's distrust of 'constructive
radicalism'.

When Churchill made the running, however, those manning the
walls of Jericho on both government and opposition benches proved
disposed to crumble. 'The Trades Board Bill has been beautifully
received and will be passed without a division,' he wrote to his wife on
28 April 1909. 'A. Balfour and Alfred Lyttelton were most friendly to
it. . . .'[9] It was a modest bill covering only 200,000 workers, of whom
nearly three-quarters were female, and applied only to a few specified
trades, for which tripartite boards (employers, workers' representatives
and a few independents) with the power to fix minimum rates for both
timework and piecework were set up. Four years later, a good example
of effective gradualism, the scope of the legislation was extended to
cover five more trades and an additional 170,000 employees.

The second of these measures, and the one which brought him
closest to the Webbs, although they and the whole social-reform thrust
were also much in favour of Trade Boards, was that of setting up a
network of labour exchanges. These, it was strongly believed at the
time, could by increasing the fluidity of the labour market make a
significant impact on unemployment – the main preoccupation of 1908
and of 1909, until trade began to revive towards the end of the latter

year and performed very strongly in the remaining five and a half years of Liberal government. It was an early instance of using supply-side rather than macro-economic measures to deal with the problem, although Churchill, who was at this stage something of a Keynesian before Keynes, would have been willing to embrace more general counter-recession measures. He did achieve one minor success in this direction when, in September 1908, he persuaded McKenna as First Lord of the Admiralty to take account of unemployment levels in shipbuilding when timing the placing of his naval orders.

Churchill saw his policy on labour exchanges as being almost umbilically linked with the introduction of a scheme of unemployment insurance. By the end of 1908 he was able to present the Cabinet with well-worked-out and fairly detailed proposals on these two issues. No doubt the coherence of the proposals owed a good deal to the tidy but innovating skills of Llewellyn Smith and Beveridge. There is nonetheless a strong impression that Churchill was effectively in charge of his department and using his officials with just the right mixture of driving force and respect for practical problems. The labour-exchanges proposal proceeded smoothly. A bill was introduced in May 1909 and successfully carried through during that session. The first exchanges opened on 1 February 1910, at the beginning, as it happened, of Churchill's last month at the Board of Trade. Apart from conducting the legislation through Parliament he took a close personal interest in the results on the ground. In the autumn of 1909 he somewhat incongruously combined another visit to German army manoeuvres with the inspection of their 'labour bureaux' at Frankfurt and Strasbourg (Alsace being then in its period of Wilhelmine annexation to Germany). And on 1 February, accompanied by Clementine, he made a tour of the first seventeen exchanges which came into operation in London.

Unemployment insurance presented greater problems and advanced at a much slower pace. There was some Cabinet opposition, and he wrote in exasperation to his wife on 27 April (1909) of 'that old ruffian Burns and that little goose Runciman' as being knots of resistance, 'and I could not get any decision yesterday from the Cabinet'.[10] Asquith, however, he thought was firm on his side. This was only two days before Lloyd George's budget, most famous of the century, and it was therefore understandable both that the Cabinet had its mind upon other things and that Lloyd George was not ready with the details of his parallel health insurance scheme. Churchill himself indeed had the sense to see that the government could not have two charge-imposing bites at

the insurance cherry, and that he must therefore wait until Lloyd
George was ready. Unemployment insurance did not become law until
December 1911, by which time he had not merely left the Board of
Trade, but had passed through the Home Office and was two months
into his time as First Lord of the Admiralty. Nonetheless it was very
much Churchill's scheme, with the details fully worked out under his
Presidency. It was to cover a substantial but limited group of workers
numbering about three million in the industries then most liable to
cyclical fluctuation: building and construction, engineering, and shipbuilding, although with provision for possible future extension. The
benefits were seven shillings and sixpence (37.5 pence, about the equivalent of a modern £18.50) a week for the first five weeks without work,
tapering down to six shillings a week for the next five weeks, and five
shillings a week for a final five weeks. The costs were to be met by a
compulsory deduction of twopence a week from wages, a penny a week
from the employer and a subvention of another penny a week from the
Treasury.

Together these three measures gave Churchill a substantial record as
a social reformer. Insurance temporarily became for him an almost
sacred principle and led him, with his relentless urge to phrase-making,
to coin a slogan which offers serious rivalry in the higher meaningless-
ness to a famous mantra enunciated by his 'squalid nuisance' of the
Second World War, Aneurin Bevan. 'The language of priorities is the
religion of socialism,' Bevan was to proclaim in 1949. Churchill, forty
years before, had announced with equal resonance that 'Insurance
brought the miracle of averages to the rescue of the masses.'[11] It was
also true that he always spoke of the deprivation which he was eager to
relieve in a peculiarly *de haut en bas* way, in this respect striking a very
different note from Lloyd George. With Churchill there was often a
great deal about humble families and cottage homes. On the other hand
he firmly dismissed a Llewellyn Smith recommendation that entitlement
to benefits should depend upon diligent sobriety. 'I do not like mixing
moralities and mathematics,' he robustly said.[12] But his approach,
although liberal, was highly patrician. There was never any attempt to
pretend that his own often urgent need for large sums of money in
order to sustain his extravagances bore any relation to the problems of
the deserving poor. He did not pretend to understand these from the
inside, merely to sympathize with them from on high. He was of a
different order, almost of a different race.

In this respect he was in reality little separate from most antecedent and subsequent social reformers, from Joseph Chamberlain (in his radical days) to Bevan himself, with his National Health Service achievement. They were both almost as naturally patrician, and separated in their lifestyle, from those whom they were endeavouring to help as was Churchill. But Churchill was more instinctively frank about his degree of separation. And it could be further argued that several of those who had more direct experience of deprivation, John Burns at the time under discussion or Philip Snowden in the 1920s, when they had the power to do anything about it were far more stony-hearted towards the relief of suffering. It was also the case that Churchill soon forgot about social reform when he left first the Board of Trade and then the Home Office and became engaged with the problems of the Admiralty, the romance of the Fleet and, as he increasingly saw it, the German naval challenge. 'Departmentalitis' is however a disorder from which many others have suffered, and to which someone of Churchill's enthusiastic, egocentric and almost obsessive temperament was obviously likely to be prone. Churchill was not unique in finding the detailed problems of one department quickly becoming remote when those of another are pressing.

General political issues, however, rarely failed to engage Churchill and during his Board of Trade years he managed to ruffle the feathers of a number of his colleagues and of the King. His dismissive comment on Burns and Runciman has already been cited. He also had acrimonious exchanges of letters in May 1908 with Crewe (who had succeeded Elgin at the Colonial Office) about his (Churchill's) intervention in a Commons colonial debate – which he claimed he had done only at the request of the Prime Minister;* and in December of the same year with Edward Grey over his attempt to use the Paris Embassy to organize a whole series of political conversations with French politicians far beyond Board of Trade responsibilities during a visit he planned for the following month. King Edward became sufficiently upset by speeches which Churchill made at Leicester in September 1909 and at Manchester in March 1910, to cause his private secretary to write letters of remonstrance. And after the first general election of 1910 Margot Asquith (although very doubtfully speaking on behalf of her husband,

---

* It was a good example of Churchill's indestructible bounce that less than three weeks after this sharp exchange of letters he was writing to Crewe (presumably in the latter's capacity as the Secretary of State of his private secretary's 'home' department) more or less demanding that Eddie Marsh be given the upper-middle grade honour of CMG.

who had however himself written a letter of rebuke to Churchill after an Edinburgh speech in July 1909 – his indiscretions were geographically well spread) contributed a letter at once hysterical, contradictory and purporting to convey royal views. If only Churchill would 'thrive on being liked instead of loving abusive notice and rotten notoriety' he would vastly improve his position in the eyes of 'the best elements both in politics & society'.[13]

Churchill's main extra-departmental foray in the first years of his Cabinet career was one which, quite soon afterwards, came to seem dripping with paradox. In firm alliance with Lloyd George, and with practically no one else, he mounted a bitter battle against what the two of them denounced as the extravagant warship-building programme of the First Lord of the Admiralty, the prim and stubborn Reginald McKenna. In early December 1908, McKenna, who in spite of his previous if brief Treasury experience had become very much an admirals' First Lord, brought forward his naval estimates for the year 1909–10. These provided for a total expenditure of £36 million,* an increase of 180 per cent on Lord George Hamilton's £13.25 million, which had been a factor in provoking Lord Randolph's 1886 resignation. Perhaps of more impact was the fact that the estimates provided for the laying down of six dreadnoughts, the new type of battleship which had been the gift to mankind of Admiral Lord Fisher, First Sea Lord (the professional head of the navy) from 1904 to 1910. Unfortunately he gave it not merely to the British branch of that species but to the German and, a little later, to the Austrian and Italian branches as well, and thereby gave a great boost to competitive construction. Security could not just be allowed to rest upon a major stock of previous types of capital ship, in which the British were strong, but also involved keeping up with the Hohenzollerns, from a new start-line of *circa* 1906.

Churchill, although he was within a few years to be responsible for (and passionately committed to) taking the peacetime naval estimates up to £53.5 million, was at this stage unconvinced not merely by McKenna's detailed proposals, but also of the basic concept of a German

---

* These and other figures relating to the pre-1914 period of 'great armaments', with Churchill first on one side and then on the other, should be seen against the present cost of approximately £600 million for one US Stealth bomber. Adjusted by the usual rough but useful factor of fifty for the change in the value of money, this means that one such bomber at the start of the twenty-first century costs a third as much as, at the end of the first decade of the century, McKenna contemplated spending upon the entire British fleet.

threat. In August 1908 he interrupted his engagement festivities to go to Swansea on Saturday the 15th and there proclaimed a doctrine which was as welcome to the anti-armaments wing of the Liberal party as it was sceptical about a German menace. 'I think it is greatly to be deprecated that persons should try to spread the belief in this country that war between Great Britain and Germany is inevitable,' he said. 'It is all nonsense. There is no collision of primary interests – big, important interests – between Great Britain and Germany in any quarter of the globe.' 'There is no feeling of ill-will towards Germany,' he continued. 'I say we honour the strong, patient, industrious German people.'[14]

This inspired the old radical iconoclast Henry Labouchère to send him congratulations, a wedding present and the specific statement that 'you and Lloyd George seem to me the only members of the Cabinet that are not afflicted by the armament craze'.[15] And Lloyd George himself, who was fortuitously in Hamburg, wrote to say, 'Your Swansea speech was tiptop and pleased the Germans immensely.'[16] This praise also pleased Churchill immensely. He was going through a pro-German phase, stemming to some extent from the notice which the Kaiser took of him, but more because of his admiration for their social security schemes. And more important still was his desire to cement a radical partnership with the Chancellor of the Exchequer. Lloyd George of course had almost an obligatory departmental duty to criticize McKenna's estimates. Churchill, without such a duty, was happy to join him as an enthusiastic freebooter. Within the Cabinet they were supported on the merits by Morley, Burns and Harcourt, although these three, as Asquith noted, were not anxious to be too much identified with the two flashing (and some thought flashy) radical stars. However the two were delighted to be associated with each other, and Lloyd George wrote Churchill a significant letter before setting off for a Christmas holiday at the appropriately chosen Prince de Galles Hotel at Cannes:

> I cannot go away without expressing to you my deep obligation for the assistance you rendered me in smashing McKenna's fatuous estimates & my warm admiration for the splendid way in which you tore them up.
>
> I am a Celt & you will forgive me for telling you that the whole time you were raking McK's squadron I had a vivid idea in my mind that your father looked on with pride at the skilful & plucky way in which his brilliant son was achieving victory in a cause for which he had sacrificed his career & his life.[17]

Victory, however, was an optimistic description of what had been or was to be achieved. The battle was not fully joined until February 1909. In the early part of the month a long-range paper bombardment took place. As so often both Churchill's energy and his effrontery were amazing. At the beginning of the month he circulated an argumentative and detailed Cabinet paper of approximately 2,000 words, replete with tables of analysis of German naval expenditure and comparisons with exact relative strengths. In my Cabinet experience I never saw a paper of such detailed yet centrally challenging argument produced by one minister against the recommendations of another whose responsibilities were not even contiguous to his own. McKenna, not unnaturally, responded with an equally detailed if somewhat less spirited refutation. Churchill got a new Cabinet paper produced in which McKenna's arguments were down one side of a two-column format, with his own counter-arguments down the other side. 'I venture to submit to the Cabinet these notes upon the First Lord's Memorandum in a form which renders reference easy,' he calmly and almost condescendingly began.[18]

Churchill, however, was more provocative than persuasive. The three wobbly supporters became still more wobbly, Asquith became impatient and even Lloyd George began to seek a middle way. On 20 February Asquith, writing to his wife, said: 'The economists are in a state of wild alarm, and Winston and Ll.G. by their combined machinations have got the bulk of the Liberal press into the same camp. . . . They (the two) go about darkly hinting at resignation (which is bluff) and there will in any case be a lot of steam let off, and at any rate a temporary revival of the old pro-Boer animus. I am able to keep a fairly cool head amidst it all, but there are moments when I am disposed summarily to cashier them both.'[19] This last thought was not to be taken seriously, for there were many more moments when Asquith saw the disadvantages of such drastic action. It was as much bluff as were their resignation hints.

The crux came at a Cabinet on 24 February. Asquith described it in terms which were as illuminating about his methods of Cabinet management as they were of the over-exposed segment in which Churchill and, to a lesser extent, Lloyd George had allowed themselves to be isolated. 'A sudden curve developed of which I took immediate advantage, with the result that strangely enough we came to a conclusion which satisfied McKenna and Grey and also Ll.G. and Winston.'[20] Four dreadnoughts were to be laid down immediately and another four if and when the need was proved. As could easily have been foretold this was held to have become the case by late July. The two 'economists', as they were known in those days, not because of their expertise in the 'dismal science' but because they were against naval (or military) extravagance, had fought a remarkably ineffective battle. Their opponents had asked for six ships. The 'economists' tried to hold out for four. And the result of the 'compromise' was eight.

This defeat of the economists in February made it the more necessary that the budget of 1909 – due on 29 April and to be Lloyd George's first – for reasons both of practical finance and of the Chancellor's prestige should be a major event, and that it most certainly was. Quite apart from Lloyd George's personal position, it was also essential that the Cabinet as a whole should regain the initiative. At the end of its third year a government with a huge majority was becoming both becalmed and unpopular. The bye-election record during 1908 was disastrous. It was not just North-West Manchester. There were also Conservative gains in Ashburton, Ross-on-Wye, both Peckham and Shoreditch in London, Newcastle-on-Tyne, and Pudsey in Yorkshire. They were as widespread as they were numerous. Most legislation was sterile. Major bills passed overwhelmingly in the Commons were thrown out or emasculated in the Lords, and the government appeared to have little idea what to do about it, other than for the House of Commons futilely to pass the Campbell-Bannerman resolutions of protest against the Lords in June 1907.

The budget, apart from the practical need to increase the revenue by what sounds the puny sum of £16 million, but which amounted to an increase of 11 per cent, seemed to offer the best way out of this impasse. This could be on either of two plausible assumptions. The first was that the House of Lords, intimidated by a constitutional convention already more than 250 years old, would not dare to veto a Finance Bill. The best way therefore to get through any controversial social or political advance was to use the budget so that it achieved more than the raising of a given amount of revenue. The second and alternative tactic was to make the budget so provocative that it would be a bait luring the peers to their destruction. The government would then have a much more popular rallying cry on which to fight an election than the wrongs of Nonconformist schoolteachers or the evils of too many pubs.

Some have unconvincingly argued that such a subtle plot was always in the mind of the Chancellor, and maybe of the Prime Minister too. A peers' rejection of a Finance Bill was thought too unlikely – they would never dare. Asquith in particular persisted during the summer and early autumn, when the Finance Bill was slowly grinding its way through the Commons, in treating a Lords' rejection as unthinkable. 'That way revolution lies,' he said in Birmingham on 17 September. And in at least the early stages of the budget battle the indications are that the Chancellor also regarded his proposals as a way of circumventing the veto rather than as a preliminary to destroying it. He may at most have thought of the options as in the nature of a two-way bet, but with a peers' rejection very much in the nature of a place rather than a win.

Perhaps a bare outline of the taxation proposals which caused such reaction, small though they are by today's standards, should first be recalled. The Chancellor set himself to raise an additional £16 million mainly to pay for battleships and for social benefits. And as the cost of both was likely to be on a mounting curve it was important to use measures from which the yield was likely to increase in the future. The first was the only one which contradicted this rule. It was the familiar Chancellor's comfort of reducing the sinking fund, which however did stand unusually high, by £3 million. The second was to raise death and associated duties so as to bring in another £4 million in the current year and £6.5 million in the future. The third was the adjustment of income tax (mainly upwards) so as to bring in another £3 million. For the first time a differential between earned and unearned income was introduced. The rate of tax on earned income remained at one shilling (ninepence up to £2,000); on unearned it was increased to one shilling and twopence (the equivalent of 6p in the pound today). Fourth was the introduction of a super-tax (or surtax as it came subsequently to be known). This was to be charged at the rate of sixpence in the pound on the amount by which all incomes of £5,000 or more exceeded £3,000. It was to bring in £500,000 in the current year and £2.3 million in the following years. Of all the Chancellor's proposals this was the most pregnant with social change, although this was not appreciated at the time, and it was not the proposal which aroused the most controversy.

This distinction was reserved for the land taxes, the fifth major item in the budget. Under this heading came a tax of 20 per cent on the unearned increment in land values (to be paid either when the land was sold or when it passed at death); a capital tax of a halfpenny in the pound (approximately 0.2 per cent) on the value of undeveloped land and minerals; and a 10 per cent reversion duty on any benefit which came to a lessor at the end of a lease. All told, the land taxes were estimated to bring in only £500,000 in the current year, but with a substantial but vague increase in subsequent years. In fact the most that they yielded was a vast wave of apprehension and hostility among the landowning classes. They never produced more than £1.5 million a year, and by a final irony were quietly repealed in the 1920 budget in the Chancellorship of Austen Chamberlain (who had been the leading parliamentary opponent of the budget of 1909) and under the premiership of Lloyd George himself.

The sixth group of higher 1909 taxes related to alcohol and tobacco. The cost of licences for the sale of liquor was increased so as to bring in an extra £2.6 million. The excise duty on spirits was up by enough to increase the revenue by £1.6 million and the price of a measure of whisky by a halfpenny. Tobacco was to contribute another £1.8 million. The seventh major item was directed towards motorists and other petrol-driven road users, who were for the first time becoming of taxable importance. There was to be a graduated scale for motor-car licences, rising according to horsepower from two to forty guineas (the latter a very large sum at present values) and a tax of threepence a gallon on petrol. These yields (estimated at £750,000) were to be put into a special Road Fund for highway construction and could not be counted as a contribution to closing the budgetary gap. The same consideration applied to a new mineral-rights duty of a shilling in the pound with the proceeds going to the creation of a Miners' Welfare Fund. Such were the main provisions of the 'People's Budget' which produced the bitterest political warfare and the most prolonged constitutional crisis since the Great Reform Act of 1832.

Churchill felt some ambiguity about this budget. Unusually it was subjected to detailed prior examination and argument in the Cabinet. In the six weeks leading up to its introduction no fewer than fourteen Cabinets were largely devoted to its discussion. Lloyd George had to do without a Chancellor's normal and valuable weapons of surprise and urgency, with the disclosure of his hand to his colleagues taking place so late that there is hardly time for them to do anything about it. Throughout this Cabinet marathon the impression is that Churchill was uncharacteristically quiet.* He was not a carping critic of the Chancellor like Haldane, McKenna, Runciman and Harcourt. Nor was he haughtily but more silently disapproving like Grey and Crewe. But how much positive support did he give? Certainly not as much as Asquith, who (much more characteristically) was almost as silent, but used his

---

* A main reason why it is an impression rather than a recorded fact is that there were no Cabinet minutes in those days.

position and authority to do occasional summings up in the Chancellor's favour which were based more on resolve than on a counting of heads.

Long afterwards Lloyd George indicated that he had thought Churchill somewhat 'Blenheim-minded' at the time, although much closer to the event (May 1909) he led his intimate friend D. R. Daniel to record him as saying, 'I should say that I have Winston Churchill with me in the Cabinet, and above all the Prime Minister has backed me up through thick and thin with splendid loyalty.'* The likely truth is that Churchill was subject to conflicting pulls. He valued his alliance with Lloyd George, he was still anxious to reinforce his radical credentials, and once a battle had been joined he was a natural partisan, although also with a certain capacity to see beyond the confines of the battlefield. On the other hand he had a lot of rich friends and relations. In the latter category it was his Wimborne cousin, Ivor Guest, currently Liberal MP for Cardiff District (that is suburbs) and later Lord Lieutenant of Ireland, who caused more trouble than his other cousin the overtly Conservative Sunny Marlborough. As dukes went, Marlborough remained relatively restrained. He was of course against the budget, but he did not rival his confrère the Duke of Beaufort, who said he would 'like to see Winston Churchill and Lloyd George in the midst of twenty couples of dog hounds', or even the Duke of Buccleuch, who gave the budget as his reason for cancelling his habitual guinea subscription to a Dumfriesshire football club. Guest, in spite of being a son of Churchill's radical Aunt Cornelia, was a core member of a group of about thirty rich Liberal MPs who expressed reservation about the land taxes in a deputation to the Prime Minister. He went further and privately threatened to resign his seat. This dismayed Churchill, who wrote (to his wife): 'This is a great worry to me. It would ruin his career – and cost me a friend and ally.'[21]

Guest's particular trouble was that his father had made over his property to him two years before, when a survival of only one year after transfer was required. The budget extended that to five years, and Guest greatly doubted whether the first Lord Wimborne had the extra years in him. In fact he did (he lived until 1914), Guest stayed as a Liberal

---

* Daniel's memoir is doubly protected by being both unpublished (although in the National Library of Wales) and written in Welsh. For the unlocking of this semi-secret source, however, I am indebted not to my own Welshness – I unfortunately belong to the non-Welsh-speaking majority in Wales – but to John Grigg, who employed an expert translator. (See Notes on Sources in his second volume: *Lloyd George: The People's Champion*.)

MP, was appointed (with a peerage of his own, Ashby St Ledgers, under which title he sat until his father's death) to the not inappropriate office of Paymaster-General in 1912 and went on to preside at Viceregal Lodge, Dublin over the disastrous Anglo-Irish year of 1916. In a further irony one of his younger brothers, Freddie Guest, became Lloyd George's Chief Whip for most of both his wartime and peacetime Coalition government.

Churchill did not enjoy such conflicting pulls, but he was not a man to let them deflect him from a central political purpose. He swallowed his doubts and, whether or not he had been much help during the Cabinet arguments, he threw himself whole-heartedly into the propaganda battle for the budget. On 22 June he accepted the presidency of the Budget League, an organization set up as a riposte to the newly formed Budget Protest League under Walter Long, and thereafter took a vigorous and mostly helpful part in public advocacy of Lloyd George's proposals in the country. Once he had committed himself to the task his oratory was unrestrained. It was, for instance, at one of the meetings set up by the Budget League – in Edinburgh on 17 July – that he incurred the unusual penalty of a direct letter of rebuke from the generally easy-going Prime Minister himself. Furthermore this was followed up by the Cabinet, four days after the speech, taking the even more unusual step of formally rebuking him for 'purporting to speak on behalf of the Government' in a way that was 'quite indefensible and altogether inconsistent with Cabinet responsibility and Ministerial cohesion'.[22]

What had provoked Asquith and his colleagues to this portentous reaction was Churchill's statement that a peers' rejection would be followed by a dissolution of Parliament. Like many complained-of statements, it was true, and exactly foreshadowed what happened. But it appeared objectionable, first because it ran counter to Asquith's tactic of treating a throwing out of a Finance Bill by the Lords as so constitutionally monstrous as to be unimaginable; and second because it presupposed the automatic consent of the Sovereign to a dissolution. As one had not in fact been denied to a Prime Minister since 1834, and then with unfortunate consequences for the Crown, the point was fairly academic. But it had nonetheless provoked a letter of protest to Asquith from Lord Knollys, the Liberal (with both a large and a small l) royal private secretary, which rather wearily began: 'The King desires me to say it is painful to him to be continually obliged to complain of *certain* [my italics] of your colleagues.'[23]

This got Asquith on a sensitive spot, because he for once agreed with the complaint and Churchill became the unfortunate victim of uttering premature truth which provoked a royal letter that the Prime Minister was not disposed to refute. Churchill at this stage did have a remarkable capacity for upsetting Buckingham Palace. His next major speech in the country, at Leicester on 4 September, resulted in Knollys (on instructions) writing a letter to *The Times* dissociating the King from the constitutional doctrine there expressed. Asquith on this occasion was not agitated, and Churchill himself, in Strasbourg for the German army manoeuvres, while agitated was unrepentant. 'He [Knollys] and the King must really have gone mad,' he wrote to his wife.*24 Churchill was always a firm monarchist, but when, in his years of glorious sunset, bland remarks were made about his having 'devotedly served' six Sovereigns, 'provoked and disputed with' might in the case of at least two of the six, have been a more accurate if less roseate phrase.

Between those two Churchill speeches, there was the still more memorable and, from a royal point of view at least, more objectionable Limehouse oration of Lloyd George. Greatly occupied with the long struggle to get the Finance Bill through the House of Commons, the Chancellor had been very abstemious throughout the summer months about indulgence in one of his favourite pastimes, that of popular oratory. But on 30 July he made up for this austerity. He went to the East End of London and addressed 4,000 people in a large meeting-hall cum entertainment centre called the Edinburgh Castle. Churchill accompanied him and sat upon the platform. The tone of Lloyd George's remarks and of his seduction of the audience are well illustrated by the following passage dealing with the new mineral-rights duty directed to the setting up of a Miners' Welfare Fund.

> Have you been down a coal mine? I went down one the other day. We sank down into a pit half a mile deep. We then walked underneath the mountain, and we had about three-quarters of a mile of rock and shale above us. The earth seemed to be striving – around us and above us – to crush us in. You could see the pit props bent and twisted and sundered, their fibres split in resisting the pressure. Sometimes they give way, and then there is mutilation and death. Often a spark ignites, the whole pit is

* Churchill had talked about press proprietors repaying Balfour for peerages he had bestowed upon them by printing his vapid orations at length. Knollys was instructed publicly to protest on the highly formal point that peerages emanated from the sovereign and not from the Prime Minister of the day.

deluged in fire, and the breath of life is scorched out of hundreds of breasts by the consuming flame. . . . Yet when the Prime Minister and I knock at the doors of these great landlords, and say to them: 'Here, you know these poor fellows who have been digging up royalties at the risk of their lives, some of them are old, they have survived the perils of their trade, they are broken, they can earn no more. Won't you give them something towards keeping them out of the workhouse?' They scowl at us. We say 'Only a halfpenny, just a copper.' They retort 'You thieves!' . . . If this is an indication of the view taken by these great landlords of their responsibility to the people who, at the risk of life, create their warmth, then I say their day of reckoning is at hand.[25]

In this and other passages of the famous oration points were given particular pungency by equating the mean and selfish plutocrats with ducal grandeur. 'A fully fledged duke costs as much to keep up as two dreadnoughts, and dukes are just as great a terror and last longer' was one of his happiest taunts. Churchill, in spite of his Marlborough cousin and his Westminster friend, did not detach himself from ducal teasing. Yet it would have been impossible to imagine him deploying an argument in the way that Lloyd George did. This was not because he wished to pull his punches – even against dukes. His language was sometimes more violent, for there was always a sybilline seductiveness about Lloyd George's attacks. And Churchill could sometimes be just as mocking, as when he replied at Burnley in December 1909 to a speech that Curzon had delivered on Churchill's old stamping ground of Oldham the night before. Curzon had said, quoting Ernest Renan he claimed, that 'all civilization had been the work of aristocracies'. 'They liked that in Oldham,' Churchill replied. 'There was not a duke, not an earl, not a marquis, not a viscount in Oldham who did not feel that a compliment had been paid to him.'[26] Yet the passage in which Lloyd George made his East End audience, the great majority of whom (for cockneys were mostly non-travellers in those days) had never been nearer to a coalfield than Paddington Station or a West Kent hop-field, feel the tensions and terrors of life underground could never have been done by Churchill. He might have extolled the place of coal and consequently of miners in Britain's island story of rise to national wealth and greatness. He would have done it with phrases more elevated than Lloyd George's, but in the abstract. He would never have made his audience feel the menace of the great weight of earth above and the testing almost to destruction of the pit props.

King Edward, despite his general benignity, was less moved by the pressure on the pit props than was the Limehouse audience, and Asquith found him (at Cowes) unusually displeased and growling. In a sense this took the pressure off Churchill, who was, in royal eyes, only the junior partner in such stirring up of class feeling. What effect this oratory had upon the Conservative peers is uncertain. They were moving almost ineluctably towards rejection of the Finance Bill by the end of the summer. Lansdowne, their leader, had said a little ambiguously on 16 July that they could not swallow it whole 'without wincing'. Churchill at Edinburgh the next day had with juvenile boisterousness (maybe encouraged by the birth of his first child six days before) misinterpreted 'wincing' as 'mincing' and had told Lord Lansdowne that he would have 'to eat his mince'.

Before the time for the test of the peers' nerve arrived, the Finance Bill had to complete its almost incredibly laborious progress through the Commons. This was accomplished only on 20 November, after seventy parliamentary days devoted to the bill, 554 divisions upon it, and almost no summer recess. On the following evening, when the Chancellor gave a celebratory dinner to those ministers who had assisted in the passage, Churchill was included although his division record (198, below even the Prime Minister's 202) was the worst of all those present.* This was despite a curious Tory complaint raised on the floor of the House, that during the all-night sitting of 17–18 August Churchill had been present 'in his pyjamas'. The presumption must be that he was wearing them under his outer garments to enable him to sleep more comfortably between divisions. But, as his son Randolph reasonably pointed out, Churchill never wore or possessed pyjamas in his life. Perhaps it was some early version of his Second World War siren suits that he was trying out.

The Lords were not dilatory in organizing a 'first-class funeral' for the bill. They devoted five parliamentary days to a second-reading debate and then threw it out by a majority of 350 to 75 on 1 December. This could be seen as a slight improvement on the 1893 rejection of the second Home Rule Bill, when a vote of 419 to 41 killed the last hope of Anglo-Irish reconciliation within a common polity. No prominent Conservative except for Balfour of Burleigh cast a vote in favour of the budget, although many of the wisest warned against the folly of what was being done and abstained. Perhaps the most sombre and percipient of the

* J. A. Pease, the Chief Whip, was appropriately top with a score of 518, Lloyd George achieved a very respectable 462.

warnings came from the normally obscure Lord Reay. 'Oligarchies', he said, 'were seldom destroyed and more frequently committed suicide.'[27]

It was immediately clear, as Churchill had been rash enough to predict at Edinburgh, that there was no alternative to an early dissolution of Parliament. Asquith announced this on the day following the Lords vote, and prorogation took place on the day after that. Polling was spread over the fortnight beginning 15 January 1910, but the campaign had begun before Christmas. It began heavily for Asquith because on 15 December his private secretary had been sent for by Lord Knollys,* his royal vis-à-vis, and solemnly informed that the King would not agree to the coercion of the Lords by a mass creation of Liberal peers until after a *second* general election. This sat ill with the Prime Minister's own declaration, only five days before, that 'we shall not hold office unless we can secure the safeguards which experience shows us to be necessary for the legislative utility and honour of the party of progress'.[28] The position was not made easier by his being either constrained or deciding on his own volition to keep this bad news secret throughout the campaign.

Churchill was certainly not told. Apart from anything else, he did not at that stage carry a reputation as a good repository of secrets. Equally certainly, however, he was one of the minority of ministers who had rejoiced at the rashness of the Lords. Lord Crewe, generally considered the epitome of solid if unexciting probity, had made a very interestingly precise statement in winding up for the government the rejection debate. 'The great *majority* [my italics] of the ministers, including the Chancellor of the Exchequer, had hoped to the last that the bill would pass.'[29] He would hardly have used the carefully qualified statement had there not been a minority holding the opposite view, and Churchill has the first claim to have been part of it. Wilfred Scawen Blunt, rich Sussex squire, Arabist, honorary Irish Nationalist and well-known *coureur*, who in spite of his extravagance of behaviour and of opinion often provides a good window on to Churchill, shines a confirming shaft of light. In his diary for 2 October 1909, he records him as saying that 'his hope

---

* Knollys himself almost certainly regretted having to convey this decision, and would not have hardened it. He is recorded as having told the Clerk to the Privy Council 'very gravely and emphatically that he thought the Lords mad'. (There were a lot of charges of madness associated with the urbane and liberal Knollys that autumn. Three months before Churchill had thought him and the King mad. Perhaps these judgements were more an indication of the febrility of the time than of individual sanity.)

and prayer was that they [the peers] would throw out the Bill, as it would save the Government from certain defeat if the elections were put off'.[30] His hope and prayer having been granted, Churchill took to the hustings not only with gusto, a quality in which he was rarely lacking, but also with a somewhat misplaced optimism, both for the result and for an early resolution of the constitutional issue.

9

A YOUNG HOME SECRETARY

CHURCHILL DID VERY well in the first 1910 election. He rightly assumed victory in Dundee, and handsomely secured it. He led his Labour running mate by a short head of 382, which was just enough for his prestige, while between them they crushed the Unionists by more than two to one. Scrymgeour, the cloud 'no bigger than a man's hand' which was eventually to produce a deluge, doubled his vote, but still had only 15 per cent of Churchill's.

This electoral security allowed Churchill to range around both Scotland and England as a political star. He was glad to be away from Dundee. As he had written to his wife from the Queen's Hotel (now happily no more), during a three-month-earlier constituency visit: 'This hotel is a great trial to me. Yesterday morning I had half-eaten a kipper when a huge maggot crept out & flashed his teeth at me! Today I could find nothing nourishing for lunch but pancakes. Such are the trials which great & good men endure in the service of their country!'[1] The experience was by no means unfamiliar to other peripatetic politicians in the first two-thirds or even three-quarters of the twentieth century, although Churchill's reaction to it was typically more extravagant than most.

He spoke much in Lancashire where, in spite of his 1908 defeat he was thought to have a special pull, and covered Scotland from Inverness to the central belt. He encouraged the Liberal activists by publishing a 150-page booklet entitled *The People's Rights*, which mainly comprised previously delivered speeches. His oratory was fairly unrestrained but he nonetheless received the accolade of a New Year's day request from the Prime Minister that he should cross the Firth of Tay and deliver a speech in his East Fife constituency. However, it was only when the election was over that Churchill delivered his most extreme anti-hereditary-peerage pronouncements in the form of a Cabinet paper calling for the complete abolition of the House of Lords. The Liberal party had lost its great 1906 majority and had to settle down to an equality of seats with the Conservatives, but nonetheless to a position in

which, because of the balancing force of the Irish Nationalists and the
Labour party, it was only they who could govern. Asquith, a bit *piano*
throughout the campaign, was in the aftermath at the worst phase of his
peacetime premiership. These were the circumstances in which, on 14
February (1910), still (just) at the Board of Trade, Churchill circulated
a Cabinet memorandum stating:

> The time has come for the total abolition of the House of Lords.
> Powerful sections of the Conservative party are now engaged in cutting
> that assembly to ribbons. Many Conservatives have frankly abandoned
> the hereditary principle. Scarcely a voice in any party is raised on behalf
> of the existing institution. We cannot as a Liberal party stand outside this
> spontaneous repudiation of hereditary and aristocratic privilege. Still less
> can we stand by and watch inertly the attempt to replace hereditary
> privilege by other and more objectionable forms of securing Conservative
> predominance.

He announced that there was much to be said for unicameralism. 'I
would not myself be frightened by having only one [chamber].' However
he recognized 'the soothing effect [of a second chamber] upon large
classes, who fear that their special interests may be ill-treated by the
modern House of Commons'. Moreover the Cabinet would never agree
on total abolition, 'and at this juncture unity is vital'. Therefore, 'both
on merits and tactics', he was prepared to support an entirely reconstituted second chamber, a detailed plan for which he proceeded to set out
with all the crisp certainty of an efficient housekeeper compiling a
grocery list. It should have only 150 members. A hundred of them
should be elected by 'fifty great two-member constituencies'. Only those
who had a record of service such as ten years in one or other House or
long municipal experience or the occupancy of 'certain great offices'
should be eligible to stand. They would be elected for eight years,
'retiring by halves'. These hundred should then proceed to co-opt
another fifty, but doing so by a method which reflected 'the strict party
proportion' of the elected hundred. The new chamber would have no
power over money bills but could delay other legislation for two years,
after which, if disagreement persisted, there should be a joint session of
both Houses, and the issue resolved by a simple majority vote in the
combined sitting.[2]
 Churchill's proposals for House of Lords reform made no progress.
They were too drastic for the Cabinet's moderates, notably Grey and
Crewe. And they were also unwelcome to most radicals, both in the

Cabinet and on the back benches, who wanted no diversion from the battle of the veto. They wanted to keep the House of Lords as indefensible as possible so as to strengthen the case for giving it minimum power. Several of Churchill's proposals on powers, which were less original, did however find their way into the Parliament Act.

His crisp, even crude certainty, as illustrated both by this memorandum and by an equally incisive letter (about the order in which the vital government business of budget and 'veto' should be taken) which he wrote to the temporarily dithering Prime Minister four days later, did not prevent his transfer to a position much closer to the scene of constitutional action. Some reconstruction of the government was naturally due after the general election. Asquith thought Churchill deserved promotion. On 1 February he wrote to him from the South of France, where he had retired for post-election restoration, and offered him, in flattering terms, the Irish Office. He began by praising Churchill's work during the election: 'Your speeches from first to last have reached high-water mark, and will live in history.' Then he stressed the importance of the job. 'Twice in my experience, it has been held, under not more arduous conditions, by men (on each side) of the weightiest calibre – Balfour and Morley.' Then he added, 'I don't press it on you,' but strongly implied that the alternative was to stay at the Board of Trade and carry on 'your great projects' there.[3] Churchill was not at all put off by this. He wrote back politely declining the Irish Office, but straightforwardly asking for either the Admiralty or the Home Office (in that order). He sustained his claim to one of these offices in a very bold and not over-modest manner for a young man of thirty-five:

> It is fitting, if you will allow me to say so – that Ministers should occupy positions in the Government which correspond to some extent with their influence in the country. No Minister holding an office of the second class can play a large part without producing awkward and doubtful relations with some of his colleagues in more important positions. . . . At a time so critical & with struggles so grave impending, there should be a generous appreciation of the real forces which contribute to the strength of the party & of your government.[4]

Churchill did not get the Admiralty. Asquith had no wish to replace McKenna at that stage. But he did get the Home Office. Herbert Gladstone bore a great name and had been a good Chief Whip in difficult days of Liberal opposition. He had made the alliance with Labour party which contributed considerably to the vast majo

1906, although later, in the years of Liberal decline, some saw it as a fatal letting of the Trojan horse through the walls. But he had been a patchy Home Secretary, and in particular was thought by both Asquith and the King to have mishandled a typical Home Office storm out of a clear sky which had blown up in the previous September and concerned the delicate question of whether the Roman Catholic bishops should be allowed to carry the Host in public procession through the streets of London. Asquith was more than ready to ship him off to South Africa as the first Governor-General of the newly created Union and to ennoble him as Viscount Gladstone, the first peer in his family, even though his father had bestowed coronets upon more than a hundred others.

Churchill was the youngest occupant of the somewhat portentous post of Secretary of State for the Home Department since Sir Robert Peel in 1822, and has not since been superseded in youthfulness. The Home Secretary is nominally the senior Secretary of State. This is for no more profound reason than that when the unified function of Secretary of State was definitively divided into two in 1782, the Home Secretary being Lord Shelburne and the Foreign Secretary being Charles James Fox, the former took precedence as a peer. This persists in court but not in government list precedence, where both the Foreign Secretary and the Chancellor normally but not invariably come above the Home Secretary. What is however of more potential significance about the Home Secretaryship is that it is like a plank of wood out of which all other domestic departments have been carved. Ministries like Agriculture, Environment and Employment have left big holes in the coverage of the Home Office. Apart from its central responsibility for police, prisons and the state of the criminal law it also retains a pile of semi-archaic responsibilities, often merely for the reason that no one has thought it worth while to put in a bid for yet another item on the Home Office's original list. In this way a Home Secretary finds himself looking after wild birds in Scotland and determining what towns should be allowed to call themselves cities in England and Wales. The more serious matters which greatly occupied Churchill's mind during the brief but tumultuous twenty months which he spent as Home Secretary were a mixture of the permanent preoccupations of the office and of those which have since faded away. In the former category were prison reform, the fire service, immigration and naturalization law, betting and gaming, drugs, the supervision of local authority and voluntary society provision for children in care, election law, and above all the holding of the delicate balance between individual liberty and the proper authority of the state. In the latter and more evanescent category were the final decision in whether or not death sentences should be carried out, women's suffrage, the regulation of hours of work in shops and safety in mines.

There was also, spanning the two categories, a loose Home Secretarial responsibility for the second tier of the government's relations with the Sovereign. The first tier, the serious policy discussions, the weekly audiences and, as we have seen, the royal complaints about the demagogic behaviour of individual ministers, was obviously in the hands of the Prime Minister. But Home Secretaries are a sort of assistant representative of the government to the Palace. Their presence used to be required at royal births. They still read the oath at the swearing in of bishops, with the prelate's hands clasped in those of the Sovereign. They are present at the dubbing of knights. They receive, with the Sovereign, the Prime Minister and the Foreign Secretary, visiting heads of state. In my day, fifty-five years after Churchill, the role was symbolized by the fact that I wore a cutaway morning coat at least every two weeks, whereas when I was subsequently promoted to be Chancellor of the Exchequer I never once put on such a garment in the course of two and a half years. And in Churchill's own case it was fortified by two special factors.

First, although not in order of time, was the prosecution for criminal libel of one Edward Mylius, who had put into written form an improbable rumour which had been circulating for some time that King George V (who succeeded his father in May 1910), while serving as a junior naval officer with the Mediterranean Fleet, had contracted a secret marriage with one of the daughters of the Commander-in-Chief at Malta. This, if true, would of course have made bigamous his marriage with Queen Mary and their offspring, including two subsequent kings, illegitimate. It was therefore a serious matter. The Palace advisers were divided as to whether to sue. The King might have had to go into the witness box to sustain such an action. Churchill took personal charge of the case, and was robustly, even rashly, in favour of facing the risks. As often, his nerve worked. At the trial on 1 February 1911, the King was not subpoenaed. Mylius was imprisoned and the rumour was scotched. This produced a significant store of royal gratitude to set against som distinctly less favourable judgements of Churchill in the mind of th somewhat stolid monarch. But at least some of the Home Secretary's colleagues thought that in this, as on some surrounding issues, he had shown more combative enthusiasm than calm judgement.

The second special link between Churchill as Home Secretary and both King Edward and King George was the traditional daily parliamentary letter from the government front bench to the Sovereign. In Queen Victoria's reign this chore was meticulously discharged by Prime Ministers who were in the House of Commons: Russell, Palmerston, Disraeli and Gladstone all did it. Salisbury, as a peer, could not report on Commons business, no more could Rosebery, but various Commons leaders – Hicks Beach, Randolph Churchill, W. H. Smith, Arthur Balfour – did it in their place, and Balfour continued with the practice when he became the first Commons Prime Minister since Gladstone, but cursorily, for his intellectual processes did not engage with those of King Edward. Campbell-Bannerman attempted the task, but although his habits of mind and behaviour were much closer to those of his Sovereign, both liking French novels and French cuisine, tempered by stately walks along the promenade at Marienbad, his energy was constantly strained by the demands of the premiership. In those pre-secretariat days the Prime Minister had also the responsibility of reporting by hand to the King on Cabinet proceedings, and his efforts here aroused frequent complaints of inadequacy. He therefore delegated the daily parliamentary letter to the Home Secretary, which was a practice continued by Asquith.*

Churchill, it need hardly be said, approached the task with gusto. It was a considerable and mostly pointless burden for a busy Cabinet minister, involving getting off each night a substantial budget on what had happened in the House of Commons during the day. Both Gladstone and Churchill, and maybe others too, habitually wrote it sitting on the front bench. It would have been a nightmare for a non-fluent minister. That was not a problem for Churchill. What he did was to pour out a stream of uninhibited consciousness interspersed with whatever aphorisms came into his mind as he went along. He mentioned speeches, elevating those of his friends, particularly those on the opposition benches such as F. E. Smith and Lord Hugh Cecil, but also freely expressing his own views both on the merits of issues and on the performance of individuals. Letters began and ended appropriately: 'Mr

---

't has long since been further downgraded, with a whip who is also a royal household ...ctionary today performing the duty.

Secretary Churchill with his humble duty . . .' through to, for example, 'All of which is now submitted by Your Majesty's faithful servant and subject,' but in between he wrote almost as he might have done to his brother or another minister. The whole exercise enscapulated his attitude to the monarchy: a great respect for the institution, which was contained in the forms of address, combined with a total confidence and freedom in the expression of his own views on a basis of Whiggish equality.

Between 21 February and his death on 6 May of the same year, King Edward received twenty-seven of these letters. They were mostly of a length of 400–500 words and therefore amounted to a considerable test of energy at the end of full days as well as between them constituting the nucleus of a long pamphlet or even of a short book. King Edward never registered any objection to their buoyantly opinionated tone (how thoroughly did he read them?), although, when controversy later arose at the effect of Churchill's letters on his heir, Knollys, probably knocking off a few corners, indicated that King Edward 'did not always appear pleased with certain occasional passages in them'.[5] Nonetheless they made very good gossipy reading and ought to have amused King Edward more than anything which had come from the staid pen of Herbert Gladstone. Thus on 11 March 1910 Churchill wrote: 'Friday was consumed in a very thin discussion of the remaining Army Estimates required at the present. The House assumed that listless air which indicated that the questions of interest lay outside the debates. Captains and Majors talked mildly to each other and the other Members took refuge in the smoking rooms.'[6] And on 6 April, apropos a speech of Lloyd George's, he suddenly plunged off into a comparison between him and Joseph Chamberlain:

> There are some vy deep strong points of resemblance. . . . Mr Churchill has often been powerfully struck with them. They appear in manner, in view, in mood and in expression. Mr Churchill has seen a photograph of Mr Lloyd George taken about ten years ago without his moustache, which really presented an extraordinary resemblance in type to the Chamberlain of the early eighties. And certain it is that both, though strong radicals by temperament, have possessed in a peculiar degree the power of pressing the springs which activate the ordinary Conservative mind.[7]

After the death of King Edward, Parliament remained adjourned fo[r] nearly a month. When it resumed, on 4 June 1910, Churchill revert[ed]

to his letter-writing habit, but now of course to the new King, George
V. Churchill, who was to compose the formidable total of eighty-four
parliamentary letters (apart from another eighteen to the King on other
subjects) over the next fourteen months, did not noticeably change his
style to meet the less sophisticated character of the new monarch. There
may have been a few less jokes, but there was not much in it. However,
all appeared to run smoothly over the summer and indeed over the
dissolution of Parliament in late November, after the rejection by the
House of Lords of the government's 'veto bill' and the second 1910
general election, with its almost exact confirmation of the result of the
first. Soon after there arose a truly bizarre incident. Churchill wrote
describing a debate on a Labour amendment to the Address covering
what was then loosely called the 'right to work'. He added three slightly
sententious but hardly revolutionary sentences of his own. The whole
produced the most ludicrous overreaction from the tyro King, which
rumbled on for a full week, consuming reams of paper and many hours
of the time of the King, the Prime Minister, the Home Secretary and
their respective private secretaries. Despite its absurdities, however, the
incident shone several shafts of light and is worth attention.

Churchill's complained-of passage ran as follows:

> Mr O'Grady, an advanced Labour politician from Leeds, put his party's
> point of view in a moderate and persuasive speech. . . . He was seconded
> by Mr Clynes, a Manchester Labour man and one of the best of them, a
> quiet intelligent hard-working member. The President of the Local Govt
> Board replied. Mr Burns as usual dealt faithfully with his former col-
> leagues. He opposed the Motion on the grounds that it would discourage
> thrift and prevent employers from keeping on good men in times of
> trouble as they often do now. . . .
>
> The subject is a very great one and cuts down to the foundation of
> things. Mr Churchill has always felt that it ought to be possible with our
> present science and civilization to mitigate the violent fluctuation of trade
> by some resource to public works of a reproductive character which could
> be carried on placidly in good times and actively in bad.
>
> As for tramps and wastrels there ought to be proper Labour Colonies
> where they could be sent for considerable periods and made to realize
> their duty to the State. Such institutions are now being considered at the
> Home Office. It must not however be forgotten that there are idlers and
> wastrels at both ends of the social scale.[8]

The next move was a letter which Lord Knollys was required to send
the Prime Minister's principal private secretary: 'The King thinks

that Mr Churchill's views, as contained in the enclosed, are very socialistic. What he advocates is nothing more than workshops which have been tried in France [by Louis Blanc in 1849] and have turned out a complete failure. . . . HM considers it quite superfluous for Churchill, in a letter of the description he was writing to him, to bring in about "idlers and wastrels at both ends of the social ladder [*sic*]".'[9]

Asquith caused this letter to be sent on to Churchill, who responded, direct to the King, in a manner at once affronted, spirited and strongly argumentative:

Mr Secretary Churchill with his humble duty to YM. He has received with deep regret the expression of YM displeasure wh has reached him through the PM upon a phrase wh occurred in his Parly letter of Friday last. Mr Churchill has never been offered any guidance as to the form wh such letters shd take and he consequently pursued the course he had been accustomed to follow when His late Majesty was on the Throne, namely with deep respect to write freely and frankly upon the events, issues and feelings of the debates in the H. of C. His late M on several occasions conveyed to the Home Secy His approval of the form and style of these letters, wh were frequently of a discursive character and frequently contained expressions of personal opinion upon the subjects under discussion. Mr Ch now gathers that YM desires that he should confine himself to a narrative of the debates. He is of course most anxious to meet YM wishes in every respect: and in this case the result will be a lightening of his labours wh at this season are severe. He ventures however to point out that very excellent summaries of the debates, far better than he could write in the time and space available, appear in all the newspapers, and that the use of the Parly letter has greatly diminished from this modern cause. . . . Mr Ch will also feel a serious difficulty in writing these letters in the future after what has occurred, for fear that in a moment of inadvertence or fatigue some phrase or expression may escape him wh will produce an unfavourable impression on YM. He therefore wd earnestly desire that YM wd give commands that the duty shd be transferred to some other Minister who wd be able to write with the feelings of confidence in YM gracious and indulgent favour wh Mr Ch deeply regrets to have lost.'[10]

Three comments, in ascending order of importance, immediately spring to mind. First, Churchill, always it must be remembered writing these letters by hand, never felt forced by anger, propriety or subservience to eschew his time-saving abbreviations. Second, he might have been better advised to have left out his by implication disparagin comparison between the King and his father, particularly as Knollys did not sustain his roseate recollection of King Edward's favour. Third, he was a master of dumb insolence, of a sort which even the most contemptuous and experienced of sergeant majors, dealing with the most callow of young officers, would have found it difficult to emulate. Moreover King George V, inexperienced a sovereign though he might then have appeared, was nine years older than Churchill.

The outcome of this bombardment, as might have been expected, was a stand-off. Knollys replied to Churchill making one or two argumentative points of his own but essentially saying: 'The King directs me to add that your letters are always instructive and interesting and he would be sorry if he were to receive no further ones from you in the future. At the same time he would not wish you to continue them if you feel disinclined to do so.'[11] Knollys also sent Churchill's letter to Asquith's secretary, saying, 'I don't think the tone of the letter is quite a proper one nor has he taken the matter in the right way.'[12] A day later Churchill had a further go at Knollys (whatever his Home Office or other government press of business he always had indefatigable energy for carrying on a correspondential dispute at length and with urgency), his main complaint being that the King's rebuke was 'utterly undeserved on this occasion, and bore no proportion to any error unconsciously committed'. Furthermore it ought to have been delivered direct and not through the Prime Minister.[13]

Knollys's final shot (to Asquith's principal secretary) was at once niggling towards Churchill and historically defensive about his having 'sneaked' to 10 Downing Street. 'I enclose you Mr Churchill's reply,' he wrote. 'He means it to be conciliatory I imagine, but he is rather like "A Bull in a China Shop".... Queen Victoria always used to send remonstrances to Lord Palmerston through Lord John Russell.'[14]

In general Knollys comes out of this correspondence rather below his reputation for urbane liberalism (although he was of course always an agent rather than a principal), and Churchill emerges well up to his habit of irrepressible combativism. He wrote to King George V another sixty-seven parliamentary letters. At first they were shorter and even a little boring. But he soon regained his exuberance, and his gift for phrase-making could rarely be suppressed into blandness. Soon he was ministerially telling the King of a House that was 'curiously listless and for the most part vy empty' because 'private members, however loudly they assert their rights to speak, cannot command audiences'.[15] And royal relations were restored by King George's gratitude for Churchill's aggressive and successful handling of the Mylius affair over the turn of the year 1910–11.

In a considerable part of his Home Office administration Churchill continued with his Board of Trade reforming zeal. This showed itself in at least four ways. First, he was the driving force behind the Mines Act of 1911. It did not actually get to the statute book until McKenna had become Home Secretary, and even during Churchill's time there the detailed piloting of the bill, as was natural, was in the hands of Charles Masterman, his parliamentary under-secretary.* But it was Churchill who, as was recognized by the Chief Inspector of Mines, provided the essential impetus and the authority to secure time for the bill in a very crowded parliamentary session. The mining industry was then central to the British economy. It employed over a million men, and its large exports were a crucial element in the country's foreign earnings.

It was also a desperately dangerous industry. This was highlighted in 1910 by two major colliery disasters. At one, in Cumberland, there was a death-roll of 132, and at the other, near Bolton in the Lancashire coalfield, no fewer than 320 men were killed. But even in years which were spared these devastating explosions of underground gas, there was a steady casualty rate, the cumulative effect of small collapses of roof or the running out of control of the primitive cages which took men down deep into the earth, of approximately a thousand a year. This was a degree of risk which would be totally unacceptable in any modern industry. It meant that when a man came to the end of a working life of fifty years as a collier he had survived a rather over one-in-twenty chance of being killed, and had almost certainly suffered at least one quite severe injury. It was towards repairing this appalling record that

---

* Masterman was a remarkable junior minister, having some of the characteristics of Edward Boyle (1923–81). They were both chubby-cheeked intellectual ministers, they both wrote and talked well, they were both enthusiastic in their politics, but more devoted to their beliefs than to their careers – the one a Christian socialist in the Liberal party and the other much the same in the Conservative party. And they both died young in their fifties. It was as well that Masterman did not attach too much importance to his career, for he was singularly unlucky in it. He was once unseated on petition, then lost three bye-elections in a row when he was promoted to the Cabinet in 1914, and after nine months of this humiliation eventually had to resign. He won a Manchester seat in 1923, but lost it a year later. He was Churchill's almost exact contemporary in spite of his subordinate role. On the whole they got on well together, although Masterman could be critical of his Secretary of State's attitude and beliefs. Whatever else he was Churchill was not a Christian socialist.

the Mines Bill was largely directed. It lifted the minimum age for
employment in the pits from thirteen to fourteen. It raised the standard
of training and qualification for managers, foremen and inspectors in
the mines. It set up stricter regulation of the system of haulage and
coal-cutting machinery as of the use of electricity underground. To
make a reality of this, the size of the mining inspectorate was substantially increased, and the provision by the companies of ambulance and
rescue services was made obligatory. In other words it was a thoroughly
bureaucratic measure, such as would today be bitterly criticized by free-
marketeers, particularly if it emerged from the European Commission.
It was however very popular with the Labour party of the day, and was
described by Ramsay MacDonald, about to become the party's leader,
as 'a boon to our mining community'.

The second measure was a Shops Bill designed to improve the
conditions of the 1.5 million, even more than in coalmining, employed
in retail outlets. This was not an original inspiration of Churchill's, for
a very similar measure had been introduced by Herbert Gladstone in
1909 but had foundered under the pressures of that Finance Bill-
dominated session. Even in 1911 (it had again been crowded out in the
1910 session) it was badly emasculated in committee. The shopkeepers'
lobby was a powerful one and had a lot of influence in the Liberal party.
Churchill got through one early closing day a week and a statutory
mealtime respite for employees, but lost his provisions for a maximum
of sixty hours of work, for the restriction of overtime and for Sunday
closing. He referred bitterly to it as 'a mere piece of salvage from a
wreck', but he accepted the placebo of the presidency of the Early
Closing Association, and held it, a little incongruously, into the Second
World War.

His third legislative activity as Home Secretary was a carry-over from
his days at the Board of Trade, and had nothing to do with his
departmental responsibilities. The National Insurance Act, which
became law in the summer of 1911, had Lloyd George as the sponsoring
minister. Churchill nonetheless played the major role in steering Part
II, which dealt with unemployment insurance provisions, through the
House of Commons. This was appropriate both because he had prepared nearly all this part of the legislation before leaving the Board of
Trade, and because, as he told the House on 25 May: 'There is no
proposal in the field of politics that I care about more than this great
insurance scheme.'[16] Even so, it was a tribute to his bounding energy
t on top of the responsibilities of a major department and while also

taking a full part in the proceedings on the Parliament Bill, which was that summer's centre of controversy, he should in addition have made time for this legacy of his recent past.

Churchill's main non-legislative Home Office achievement was in the field of prison reform. It was non-legislative because, although he devoted some of his long summer holiday of 1910 to writing for Asquith a memorandum which was in effect an outline of a full-scale Criminal Justice Bill, he failed to get a place for it in the crowded next session, and after that his mind moved from prisons to warships. Fortunately in the circumstances he had decided, as soon as he got to the Home Office, to do all that he could by administrative action to improve prison conditions.

This was not because he correctly foresaw legislative frustration but much more because he feared the early fall of the government and wished to make some quick mark. The result of the first 1910 election had left the Liberals staggering. Asquith's mental balance was normally much steadier than was his after-dinner physical balance. But for a few weeks even he lost his normal calm sagacity. In fact, with their Labour and Irish allies, neither of whom in the circumstances had any alternative to sustaining the government, the Liberals had a secure majority of 124 ('What would Dizzy have said with [such] a majority?'[17] Admiral Fisher wrote in one of his explosive letters to Churchill on 2 March). And even Margot Asquith, with her occasional core of insight surrounded by a penumbra of nonsense, wrote to Churchill of the need 'to keep our tails up . . . because our Prime Minister has made a mistake'[18] – in hesitating over whether he could govern with the new House of Commons. The fact was that the Liberal Cabinet, having been used to their vast independent majority, were unnecessarily thrown off balance by having to accommodate themselves to living in virtual coalition circumstances. Once they had one so, however, they performed more effectively than did the Attlee government after they too lost their equally vast majority in 1950.

This mood of indecisive apprehension at least had the benefit of galvanizing Churchill into a period both of pontificating general advice and of high departmental activity on prisons. He pursued a policy of 'total ignoral' (to use a happy phrase of George Brown, a considerable politician of fifty years later) of the quietist advice given him in an otherwise sensible farewell letter from his predecessor. 'As regards prisons it won't be a bad thing to give a harassed department some rest,' Herbert Gladstone wrote on 19 February.[19] This was a prescription s totally alien to Churchill's temperament that it was a waste of time to write it, even had the recipient been more disposed to take notice of his predecessor. The convert from Toryism ought to have been grateful for Gladstone's helpfulness, as Liberal Chief Whip, in getting him a constituency in 1904–5, but Churchill's attitude to Liberalism never bore much respect for the Gladstonian tradition, and in any event it is perhaps a Home Office habit for reforming Secretaries of State to be impatient of the caution of their predecessor.

The conventional wisdom is that Churchill's twenty-four-day experience in a Boer prisoner-of-war compound gave him a peculiar sympathy and even identification with all prisoners. This is an implausible or at best an inadequate explanation of his reforming zeal on the subject. Twenty-four days, with sights always on the strong possibility of an early escape, is hardly the psychological equivalent of a long period of incarceration; and there is also the consideration that there was no 'dishonour' (a concept to which Churchill was always sensitive) about this imprisonment. It was more that he naturally had a lively sympathy for the underdog, particularly against the middle-dog, provided, and it was quite a big proviso, that his own position as a top-dog was unchallenged. He propounded a doctrine which was to be reinterpreted with approval by his successor but seventeen as Home Secretary (R. A. Butler) in the House of Commons forty-seven years later: 'The mood and temper of the public with regard to the treatment of crime and criminals is one of the unfailing tests of the civilization of a country.'[20]

Churchill began, in typically dramatic form, on his sixth evening as Home Secretary, by attending the opening night of John Galsworthy's proselytizing play *Justice*, and taking with him the impressively named Sir Evelyn Ruggles-Brise, chairman of the Prison Commissioners, who had the seniority of being an Asquith appointment from nearly twenty years earlier. The play, with its indictment of the dead hand of penal policy, and particularly of solitary confinement, made a powerful impact upon Churchill, and maybe upon Ruggles-Brise too, although the latter might have thought that he knew more about prison life than did Galsworthy.

He also asked for (and readily obtained) a memorandum of advice for the ubiquitous and loquacious Wilfred Scawen Blunt, who a couple of decades before had served a two-month sentence in Galway and Kilmainham gaols for Irish political offenders – but who had been subjected, unlike Parnell a few years earlier and although a very distinct member of the upper classes, to both hard labour and solitary confinement. Armed with Galsworthy, Blunt and, most importantly, his own prior beliefs, Churchill proceeded to mount a strong attack on various prison practices. First, in March, he announced that political prisoners were to be treated differently from those imprisoned for 'dishonesty or cruelty or other crimes implying moral turpitude'. On the other hand there were 'those whose general character is good and whose offences, however reprehensible, do not involve personal dishonour'.[21] The respective categories were at once imprecise, involving highly subjective judgements, and very Churchillian. But his objectives were not difficult to recognize, even if more difficult to define, and were of considerable practical importance at a time when many militant suffragettes were inviting and receiving sentences of imprisonment. Henceforward they and other 'political' prisoners were allowed to wear their own clothes and to have supplies of books and food sent in, although the food was not much use if they were on hunger strike. He also endeavoured to make prison more tolerable for the general run of prisoners. Solitary confinement was severely limited, occasional concerts and lectures were provided, and prisoners' aid on discharge was improved.

Fundamentally, however, his policies were based on a deep scepticism about the value of prison either as a deterrent to crime or as a reformative influence on prisoners. The main thrust of his penal policy was therefore directed to keeping people out of gaol. Although the numbers in prison at any one time were then many fewer than today, there was a vast turnover of those – mainly drunks and debtors, including those who could or would not pay fines – who were incarcerated for as few as four or five days. His drive to keep debtors and drunks as well as young persons aged between sixteen and twenty-one out of prison led to dramatic falls in the numbers passing through the system. As a result of measures he initiated the numbers imprisoned for non-payment of fines dropped from nearly 100,000 in 1908–9 to fewer than 2,000 in 1918–19. Over the same period there was also a reduction of over two-thirds in the number of boys in prison. Churchill was sensitive to the malign results of early acclimatization to the indignities of prison, believing that, searing though these were, familiarity bred a certain contempt, and that the deterrent effect diminished. He also found it inappropriate that anyone sent to prison for even the shortest sentence should go through the same humiliating formalities of admission – fingerprinting, photographing for permanent rogues' gallery recording, being driven off in a Black Maria – as was a major criminal sentenced to a long term of penal servitude.

Altogether Churchill's attitude to punishment made him a 'soft' Home Secretary, both in instinct and in policy implementation. As such he was subject to much obloquy from those in press and Parliament who later came to be known as the 'hangers and floggers'. If it was a question of debate in the House of Commons he robustly rebutted his assailants, as when he commuted the sentence on seven young offenders whom he had encountered in Pentonville prison. Earl Winterton, who was then himself not far beyond the age range of a young offender, even though he had been an MP since 1904 (and was to remain one until well into my early House of Commons years), led a fierce Tory attack. 'I was very glad of the opportunity of recommending the use of the prerogative in these cases,' Churchill replied, 'because I wanted to draw the attention of the country . . . to the evil by which 7,000 lads of the poorer classes are sent to gaol every year for offences for which, if the noble lord had committed them at college, he would not have been subjected to the slightest degree of inconvenience.'[22]

Churchill was also open to the hazards of ungrateful prisoners or ex-prisoners not living up to his hopes for them, and to subsequent campaigns of mockery enthusiastically conducted by his opponents in both press and Parliament. It is a scenario familiar to most Home Secretaries. The particular note of 'told you so' hilarity associated with the famous case of the 'Dartmoor Shepherd' was however at least as much the fault of Lloyd George as of Churchill. For some curious reason (perhaps he was trying to get more prison money out of him), the Home Secretary took the Chancellor of the Exchequer on a visit to the famous and already antiquated penal establishment in Devon. The two radical stars there encountered a sixty-eight-year-old prisoner called David Davies whose gentleness of demeanour was epitomized by his having become the shepherd of the prison flock; according to Churchill, he had the unusual gift of calling individual sheep by name. Davies was serving three years' penal servitude for stealing a few shillings from a church poor box and had also been sentenced to ten years of preventive detention.

His case, not unnaturally, at least on the surface, made a shocking impression on both Chancellor and Home Secretary. Churchill had Davies released on probation and placed on a farm in North Wales. Lloyd George, more rashly, made a much publicized speech about him, giving him the mnemonic sobriquet of the 'Dartmoor Shepherd' and contrasting his lot with that of the lordly descendants of the 'plunderers of the poor' on a much larger scale who were currently living off the fat of the land while holding the people's government to ransom. Unfortunately Mr Davies, who had served a total of thirty-eight years since 1870, had got habituated to a prison rather than a more normal agricultural pattern of life. He stayed only one night on the farm near Wrexham, broke into a nearby home and was quickly back in gaol. Churchill was too self-confident to be deflected from his policies by such minor mishaps.

The responsibility of final decision in death-penalty cases caused him unease. Forty-three capital sentences were pronounced during Churchill's twenty months at the Home Office, and they all came up for individual decision by the Secretary of State. Until the abolition of capital punishment in 1965 it was the practice to keep in an alcove to the right of the Home Secretary's desk a chart, somewhat in the form of a billiard marker, on which a disc for each sentenced man (or occasionally woman) was moved from day to day, along a track beginning with the sentence and ending with the date of projected execution. The Home Secretary was thus daily reminded of how long still remained for his decision. The device avoided the danger of a hanging taking place inadvertently through his preoccupation with other matters. It also cast a constant sombre pall over the room – a gloomy enough if impressive chamber in an 1861 building in any event – as well as weighing heavily on the mind of any sensitive holder of the office. Nor was there any respite, for the pattern of an average of one death sentence every two weeks almost guaranteed that, as each case was disposed of, in one way or another, the macabre board was always reinforced.

These cases consumed a disproportionate and oppressive expenditure of Home Secretaries' time. Even the almost brutally rumbustious Harcourt disliked them in the 1880s. Asquith brooded over them with distaste in the 1890s. And so did Churchill at the end of the next decade. The tradition was that within the department only the permanent under-secretary assisted the Home Secretary in his lonely decision from which there was no return, although the trial judge might also be consulted.

Churchill used the prerogative of mercy in twenty-one of the forty-three cases. The other twenty-two he let die. To some of them he devoted immense attention, arguing the case out in lengthy memoranda which, while nominally addressed to the permanent under-secretary, S

Edward Troup,* were in fact mind-clearing exercises for himself. He agonized, but not quite as much as did the Foreign Secretary, to whom he delegated this and a few other parts of his function when he was away on a long holiday over the late summer and early autumn of 1910. (Delegation to a minister of such seniority was made necessary by the fiction that the Secretaryship of State was a single and indivisible entity and that therefore, while one Secretary of State could act for another, a junior minister in his own department could not do so.) Edward Grey wrote to Churchill from Balmoral on 21 August that year, telling him that no new facts had turned up in either of the two cases with which he had been left and that he had therefore followed Churchill's provisional recommendation that 'the law should take its course', but adding: 'I think this part of your job is beastly & on the night before the two men were hung I kept meditating upon the sort of night they were having, till I felt as if I ought not to let them hang unless I went to be hung too.'[23]

Churchill agreed to the extent that he much later recorded (in a 1935 *News of the World* article) that 'of all the offices I have held this was the one that I liked the least,' and he left no doubt that the death-penalty decisions contributed heavily to this adverse judgement. On the other hand his freedom from replicating Grey's night of guilt came partly from his belief that a lifetime of incarceration was worse than forced extinction. He had never shielded himself from sudden death. On one occasion when, against the advice of both the permanent undersecretary and the trial judge, he had hesitatingly decided upon a reprieve (and commutation to a life sentence), he was curiously relieved when the convicted man quickly committed suicide. It was as though he regarded the outcome as the best of both worlds and that the prisoner had proved himself a man.

He was never an abolitionist. When in 1948 the House of Commons first voted against the death penalty, but was frustrated in the implementation of its view for nearly another twenty years by a combination of the opposition of the Lords, the equivocal attitude of the Labour government then in office and the search for compromise by

---

* Troup, who seems in general to have been an admirable permanent secretary (see in particular pp. 196–7 below), was responsible for a very good comment on the interaction of Churchill and the Home Office: 'Once a week or oftener, Mr Churchill came into the Office bringing with him some adventurous or impossible projects; but after half an hour's discussion something was evolved which was still adventurous, but not impossible' (quoted in Martin Gilbert's summary volume, *Churchill: A Life*, p. 225).

Conservative governments in the 1950s, Churchill spoke movingly (and distastefully) of his 1910–11 experiences; but he voted in favour of retention. Less creditable was his address at about the same time (1948) to a Conservative Women's Conference, long an inflammatory audience on matters of penal policy. There, with a touch of hyperbole, he compared the alleged indifference to 'crimes of robbery and violence' of the abolitionist Labour backbenchers (there were quite a few Tories too) with their responsibility for 'at least half a million deaths in the Punjab alone' as a result of the precipitate withdrawal from India. But his main criticism was the weakness of the government in leaving to an unwhipped vote 'this grave decision on capital punishment to the most unrepresentative and irresponsible House of Commons that ever sat at Westminster'.[24] But he was never really at ease in opposition (or with Conservative women – Clementine was even less so), and he could hardly have been expected to be favourable to that swollen 1945 majority which was the symbol of the nation's temporary rejection of his unique services. His late-1940s partisanship bore little relation to the essentially moderate policy which he was to pursue when he returned to office in 1951–5.

Back in 1910, however, capital punishment was an issue of little controversy. Of far greater moment was the campaign for women's suffrage, where Churchill soon found himself in the eye of the storm. For once this was not because of the strength of his opinions. In rare contrast to Asquith (anti) and Grey (pro), Churchill took a middle course: he favoured an early extension of the vote to some women, but only if it could be achieved without undue political disturbance (meaning, as he urged in private, only if it could be done without harming Liberal electoral prospects, such as might be the result of a high property qualification). A reform to meet these objectives was almost impossible to devise; and as the partisan motive was equally impossible to articulate in public, he was reduced to equivocations such as those he was reported as using at Dundee during the December 1910 general election:

> [Mr Churchill] was still of opinion that the sex disqualification [from voting] was not a true or logical disqualification, and he was therefore in favour of the principle of women being enfranchised. But he declined utterly to pledge himself to any particular Bill . . . and it was very desirable that they [the suffragettes] should not build any undue hopes on any words he might say.[25]

This was not a temptation to which Mrs Pankhurst and her suffra-gette followers succumbed. On the contrary, they targeted his meetings and movements for especial disruption in their increasingly violent campaign. During the first 1910 general election he was attacked by a young woman with a dog-whip at Temple Meads Station, Bristol. More challenging for Churchill as Home Secretary was the policing of suffragette demonstrations and the treatment of hunger-striking suffragettes in prison, responsibility for both of which fell to him. In both repects he generally avoided excessive heavy-handedness. But there were difficult moments, particularly after 'Black Friday' (18 November 1910), when inept policing of a demonstration in Parliament Square resulted in six hours of street fighting and 200 arrests. To minimize the repercussions, most of those arrested were released without charge. This only further inflamed the militants, who alleged a cover-up. Four days later a scuffle took place on the steps of 10 Downing Street, ending with Churchill barking instructions to the police ('Take that woman away. She is obviously the ringleader'), which soon added to the folklore of Churchill assuming personal command at the scene of police operations.

The suffragettes dogged Churchill throughout his Home Secretary-ship. Successive attempts at a legislative *via media* foundered, and by the end of 1911 internal Liberal divisions on the issue became so serious that Churchill warned Asquith, with characteristic extravagance of simile, that unless he took a grip soon his government might 'come to grief in [an] ignominious way, and perish like Sisera at a woman's hand'.[26] Churchill's proposed solution was a referendum on the issue, as a device to enable the competing camps to fight it out to a resolution without endangering the government's survival. This found no favour with Asquith, and women's suffrage remained unresolved, amid periodic crises, until the outbreak of war pushed it into temporary limbo (along with Irish Home Rule) in 1914.

His holiday in the first summer of his Home Secretaryship is of considerable 'pattern of life' interest. It was a Mediterranean cruise, taking in Monte Carlo but mainly in Greek and Turkish waters, and was a very typical Churchill enterprise in several ways. First, it was a very long holiday, more than six weeks, taken by one of the least lazy of men in one of the most responsible of offices. This was mostly his habit. He fostered his unflagging energy by changes of scene and of pattern of life. He never did nothing: his relaxations were above all conversation, with a high ratio of talking to listening, over long indulgent meals, painting (after 1915), such idiosyncrasies as bricklaying (from a still later stage) and bezique (from earlier but becoming obsessive in later life). But he always worked ferociously when he was not doing anything else, whether at his ministerial duties or at his books, at least fourteen of which were 'proper' ones (as opposed to collections put together by others), and as several were multi-volumed (some too much so) this amounted to a total output of thirty-one volumes. The constant frenzy of activity which produced these formidable results required the solacing accompaniments of changes of scene and rhythm. It was the same when he was Chancellor of the Exchequer, and also writing two books in the 1920s. His frenetic activity during the parliamentary sessions was matched by equally strenuous but different activities during holidays, mostly at Chartwell, and often even longer than the legendary ones which his head of government, Stanley Baldwin, took at Aix-les-Bains. And still more strikingly was it so even in the desperate days of 1940 and the scarcely less demanding ones of 1941, when, without remission of effort, his whole entourage had to be moved for weekends to Chequers or, when the moon was full, to Ditchley, in north Oxfordshire.

Second, the 1910 holiday was typical because of his means of transport and choice of host. Churchill always liked to travel in comfort and arrive to luxury, and if possible, as with this cruise, to combine both. One of his aphorisms of a decade or so later was that the advantage of knowing Philip Sassoon (minor politician and owner and re-creator of Lympne, the Kent house of dash and style which looked across Romney Marsh to France) was that it was like always going by a train with a pullman car. And he was often not fastidious about who provided the pullman. On this 1910 occasion it was Count Arnold Maurice de Forest, generally and not wholly reassuringly known as 'Tuty'. Forest was the adopted son of the great Austro-French financier Baron Hirsch, and hence very rich. He was nonetheless a keen Liberal, who had unsuccessfully contested Southport at the first 1910 election, and been elected for West Ham North in the summer of 1911 after Masterman was unseated on petition.

Forest had married a daughter of the Lord Gerard who had promised Churchill a commission in the Lancashire Yeomanry on their *Dunottar Castle* voyage to South Africa in 1899. Unfortunately Forest's relations with that family did not go smoothly, and he was one of the few men who have sued their mother-in-law for slander. This was in the year after his provision of the magic carpet for the Churchills to visit the near Orient, and although Forest employed four King's Counsel,

including Sir Edward Clarke and F. E. Smith, his case collapsed before
luncheon on the first day. King George V, whose judgements were
sometimes narrow but who could also have an earthy force, was
recorded by Lord Derby as having commented to him on 20 August
1911 (that is just after he had been relieved of the threat of having to
agree to a mass creation of peers): 'There was only one name I told
[Asquith] whatever happened I should refuse to accept – and that was
de Forest.'[27]

Forest went through further vicissitudes. Churchill put him up for
membership of various clubs but he was always blackballed. Forest then
changed his name to Bendern. He survived until 1968, having for nearly
the last four decades of his life become a citizen of Liechtenstein. He
was one of the several louche (and in this case slightly mysterious)
characters for whom Churchill had a partiality. He liked bounders, and
was content in the summer of 1910 to spend six weeks in the close
company of one and to accumulate a substantial debt of hospitality to
him. Clementine Churchill's acquiescence is more surprising, for she
was in general more fastidious in her judgement of such people than
was her husband. Later in life, if she could not dissuade her husband
from their company, she at least absented herself. But on this eastern
Mediterranean cruise she was present for the whole time. As only two
years before the Churchills had spent most of their honeymoon at
Forest's Moravian castle, she may have felt it ungracious to rebel so
soon against her host's company.

Churchill did not of course devote his long holiday to sightseeing
and sunbathing. His attitude to recreation in such circumstances was
neatly captured by Asquith on another cruise (this time on the Admiralty
yacht) nearly four years later: 'Winston never set foot on shore at
Syracuse, but dictated in his cabin a treatise (which I am about to read)
on the world's supplies of oil.'[28] Nor was Asquith left short of reading
matter on Churchill's departmental interests following the earlier cruise.
Soon after his return Churchill sent the Prime Minister an immense
memorandum setting out his views and projects for every aspect of the
Home Office's penal responsibilities. Asquith wrote to Venetia Stanley
on one occasion that 'Winston thinks with his mouth,' and there was no
doubt that from about this time onwards the Home Secretary began to
occupy a great deal of Cabinet time with his views on almost every
subject under discussion. But Asquith's comment was not entirely fair,
for certainly on departmental matters, and to some considerable extent
on more general ones too, he supported his mouth with his pen.

Even so, Churchill had a somewhat slackwater period in the early autumn of 1910. Then in November there began the series of events which alienated (on a semi-permanent basis) from Churchill the Lib–Lab left which, as exemplified by Beatrice Webb, had been becoming so much more favourable to him during his Board of Trade and early Home Office days. These events also led to Asquith coming gradually, throughout the first eight months of 1911, to feel that the Home Secretaryship was not the right position for Churchill. The slackwater was induced by the course of the constitutional crisis, which from the budget of 1909 to the peers' reluctant acceptance of the Parliament Bill in August 1911 had become an underground stream for nearly half a year following the death of King Edward, and from Churchill having been semi-excluded from the subterranean processes. A cross-party constitutional conference was set up on 16 June (1910) in an attempt to protect King George V from beginning his reign with a major crisis.

Asquith, Lloyd George, Crewe and Birrell were the government members. Balfour, Lansdowne, Austen Chamberlain and the Earl Cawdor – the last now a totally forgotten figure, except through his forebear in *Macbeth* – represented the opposition. Churchill, as Home Secretary and in view of at least his own estimate of his political weight, might have expected to be included, but there is no evidence that he made much fuss about this. The conference in any event got nowhere, although it met intermittently (and fairly friendlily) over that summer and early autumn. The essential blockage was Home Rule. Lansdowne, although he could be moderate as he showed in the final round of the Parliament Bill in August 1911, and even courageously iconoclastic as in his 'peace letter' to the *Daily Telegraph* in 1917, was determinedly against Home Rule, and not only from an Ulster point of view. As a large southern Irish landlord (his inherited titles included the earldom of Kerry), he believed doggedly in upholding the rights of the Protestant Ascendancy in Leinster, Munster and Connaught and not merely, like Bonar Law, in defending the interests of the Scots Presbyterians in Ulster. The conference foundered upon the rock of his quiet intransigence.

Alongside these formal and unsuccessful negotiations, Lloyd George, with one of his Celtic streaks of lightning through the sky, was formulating his idea of a grand coalition, by which both major parties would shed their extremist wings and come together in a government which would, to quote Churchill's phrase of nearly two years before, 'thrust a big slice of Bismarckism over the whole underside of ou industrial system'. Lloyd George's scheme provided in the Conservatives' favour for a stronger navy, compulsory military training and, maybe, Tariff Reform. The Liberals were to get Home Rule, Welsh Church Disestablishment and a curbing of the powers of the House of Lords.

Perhaps more important, as with most political deals, was the allocation of offices. Asquith was to remain Prime Minister but to be sent up to the House of Lords, allowing Balfour to assume the leadership of the House of Commons and the chairmanship of the Committee of Imperial Defence. Lansdowne was to revert to the Foreign Office, which he had occupied between 1900 and 1905. Austen Chamberlain was to be First Lord of the Admiralty. What was there for Churchill, who because of both his cross-party friendships (particularly with F. E. Smith, who was the principal Tory intermediary in this portion of the scheme) and his lack of ideology (although not of polemics) was a natural proponent of coalition? He was also anathema to most Tories. There is some evidence (mainly from the diaries of Lucy (Mrs Charles) Masterman, who could only have been a secondary source) that they would have demanded his exclusion, and that Lloyd George, for the greater glory of his grand scheme, would have acquiesced in such a veto. This view was to be given retrospective plausibility by the extreme Tory hostility even to Churchill's demoted inclusion in the 1915 Coalition. Mrs Masterman further recorded that this hostility put Churchill off the scheme.[29] His general enthusiasm for coalition was not strong enough to survive his own exclusion. There is some contrary evidence, however, that the War Office was marked down for him.

None of this was put to the test. Balfour, great proponent and practitioner of coalition although he was to be in his fifteen years of life after death (as Tory leader) from 1915 to 1930, eventually killed it on the advice of his Chief Whip (Akers-Douglas). The Tory backbenchers, Akers-Douglas said, would not have it, and Balfour was not prepared to be a latter-day Peel and split his party, as had occurred in 1846. So, by the mid-autumn of 1910, both parties reverted to their battle stations, and prepared for the second general election of the year, made inevitable by the insistence of successive monarchs that two spins of the electoral wheel were necessary before they would agree to a coercion of the peers. It was a form of mild torture inflicted upon both politicians and the electorate, never previously known, although 1830 and 1831 were close rivals, as were the three successive autumn elections of 1922, 1923 and 1924, and was subsequently repeated only in 1974.

Asquith, fortified by a secret promise, wrung from a reluctant King, that if this second election confirmed the result of the first one in January there would be royal assent to a mass creation of Liberal peers, announced the dissolution of Parliament on 18 November and the election was over a week before Christmas. Not unnaturally in the circumstances it was an apathetic contest. One in six of those who had voted in January declined to do so again. Fifty-four seats changed hands. The government did badly in Lancashire and the West Country (where they lost five Devon seats) and well in London. But these were cross-currents in a basically static sea. The overall picture was that Liberals lost three seats and the Conservatives one, while both the Labour party and the Irish Nationalists picked up two each. The government were marginally stronger vis-à-vis the opposition and marginally weaker vis-à-vis their allied parties. But these ripples were as nothing compared with the fact that the result of the first 1910 election had been indisputably confirmed. A third election was clearly out of the question. What remained to be settled was whether the government got their Parliament Bill with or without a mass creation of peers, and this took nearly another eight months to resolve.

10

FROM PRISONS TO WARSHIPS

FOR CHURCHILL THE second 1910 election did not go quite so well as the first. Rather uncharacteristically he refused a challenge from Bonar Law to go back to North-West Manchester and there to engage with him in a knightly combat 'to the death', death being interpreted as an understanding that the loser would not seek re-entry to the new parliament. It was an extreme example of politicians treating constituencies as being as transferable as professional footballers. The seat, lost by Churchill in 1908, had been won back for the Liberals in the first 1910 election, but no one seemed to take much notice of the sitting MP. He was not the problem. It was rather that Churchill having got his 'seat for life' in Dundee had no desire to return to the hazards of Cheetham Hill. But Bonar Law was sacrificing at least as much. Dulwich was as safe as Dundee (and a good deal more convenient) but he nonetheless responded to a party call to head the campaign in Lancashire.

Law was beaten and, freed from his offer not to go elsewhere by Churchill's failure to respond, had to seek refuge in Bootle, an unlikely although at that time secure Tory haven. Churchill's refusal of one-to-one combat on an exposed ridge, rather like his maybe imagined direct encounter with Louis Botha in 1899, was in some ways surprising. It might have been expected to appeal to his romanticism. And had he accepted it he would have changed the history of the Conservative party. Law, kept out of the House of Commons, could not have succeeded Balfour as leader in the autumn of 1911. He could not have mounted his campaign of intransigence over Ulster in 1912–14, which brought the threat of civil war in Britain nearer than at any time since the seventeenth century. He could not have vetoed Churchill's continuing at the Admiralty in May 1915, and sullenly but not finally resisted his return to government as Minister of Munitions in 1917. And he would not have been in a position to bring down the Lloyd George coalition in 1922, and to condemn Churchill to two years in the political wilderness.

Churchill won in Dundee (as he would have done in Manchester) but he had 1,500 fewer votes than in the previous January and suffered a swing against him of 7 per cent as compared with a Scottish average of just over 1 per cent. The indefatigable Scrymgeour crept up by another 300 votes to a fifth of Churchill's total. As ten months before, Churchill's campaigning was widespread and his oratory often pungent. But his role was less central because, as he firmly acknowledged in another of his remarkably self-confident, even faintly patronizing, letters to the Prime Minister on 3 January 1911, 'You seemed to be far more effectively master of the situation & in the arguments than at the January Election, & yr speeches stood out in massive pre-eminence whether in relation to colleagues or opponents.'[1]

In this letter Churchill took a very firm position on bringing the peers to justice:

> We ought as early as possible to make it clear that we are not a bit afraid of creating 500 Peers – if necessary: that we believe ourselves beyond doubt possessed of the power, & will not shrink from using it. Such a creation wd be in fact for the interest of the Liberal party & a disaster to the Conservative party. It would be possible to make a list of men whose local and civic reputations stood so high with both parties in cities & counties that all attempts to ridicule their character or to compare them unfavourably with the present nobility wd fall vy flat. We should at a stroke gain a great addition of influence in the country. The wealth & importance of British society cd easily maintain 1000 notables – much more easily than 300 a century ago. . . . One thing we must not put up with is any dilatory vapourings in the Lords about constitutions in general. If the Bill does not make proper progress *we should clink the coronets in their scabbards!* [my italics] . . .

Then he turned from clinking to appeasing:

> After the veto has been restricted I hope we may be able to pursue *une politique d'apaisement*. . . . I trust that some of the disappointment of defeat may be mitigated by a liberal grant of Honours (following the precedent of the last Coronation) to prominent members of the Opposition. Privy Councillorships for Bonar Law and FE: the Order of Merit for Joe [Chamberlain]; a proportion of Tory Peers and Baronets; something for the Tory Press. . . .
>
> Then on policy. We shd offer to confer with the Conservatives not only on the Reform of the Lords but on Ireland. I would like to come to an understanding with Balfour about the Navy. . . . The sharp edge should be taken off the [sale of alcohol] licence duties where they are reall

cutting too deep. Death duties ought not to fall on landed estates more than once in 25 years. We ought to pursue a national and not a sectional policy: & to try to make our prolonged tenure of power as agreeable as possible to the other half of our fellow countrymen. You will have the power to do all this because of the unshakeable confidence which the Liberal masses will give to the leader who restricts the veto of the Lords by strong and fearless action. . . . These are my feelings at the present juncture, wh I put before you in all sincerity and knowing that you will share many of them, & that you will not resent the expression of any.'[2]

At the conclusion of this remarkable missive, Churchill added, 'I was interrupted in copying out this letter* by the Stepney affair from wh I have just returned.' The Stepney affair was the infamous battle of Sidney Street. This was a dramatic but (had the Home Secretary not elevated it) relatively minor clash between police and criminals who might or might not have been dedicated anarchists but who were certainly recent immigrants. The latter consideration introduced a xenophobic element into the argument, which was exacerbated by the fact that Churchill, with an election pending in the most Jewish and therefore immigration-friendly division of Manchester, had taken such a hostile attitude to the restrictive Aliens Bill of 1904. Three and a half weeks before Sidney Street, a gang of Latvians were found by the police trying to tunnel into a jeweller's shop in Houndsditch. They retaliated violently, killed two policemen, wounded another and got away. They found a relatively safe house in Sidney Street, Stepney, and the police did not again make contact with them until the evening of 2 January. Early the next morning the Home Secretary's authority for the rein-forcement of the police with a more powerfully armed platoon of Scots Guards from the Tower of London was sought. In view of previous

* There is a mild mystery about the timing of this letter. It was dated 3 January (a Wednesday) and written, as were several of Churchill's more swashbucklingly radical pronouncements, on Blenheim Palace paper. But on 3 January, which was the date of the Sidney Street escapade, he began the day at his house in London and was given the news of the build-up of the East End confrontation while in his bath, which was as frequent a place for him to receive important news as was Blenheim as a launching pad for his radical thunderbolts. He then went to the Home Office and received more information before deciding to insert himself into the scene of action. There is also the question of what he meant by 'copying out this letter'. No doubt he wished to keep a copy of such an important communication, but it might have been expected that he would have delegated this task to Edward Marsh or some lesser official. And if one of them provided the version which went to Asquith surely Churchill's time-saving abbreviations would have been expanded.

police casualties this was not unreasonable and Churchill immediately gave his consent. The trouble was that he then could not resist going to see the fun himself. He and his less than martial private secretary, Eddie Marsh were driven there from the Home Office in mid-morning. Both of them top-hatted and Churchill made more conspicuous by a fine astrakhan-collared overcoat, they provided a wonderful photographic opportunity, which was duly exploited.

There is some uncertainty as to whether Churchill attempted to give operational commands. To the police he almost certainly did not, although the officer in charge of a fraught operation, in which yet another policeman was killed and two wounded, must have found it more inhibiting than encouraging to have to perform in the presence of such an elevated superior. On the other hand when the house caught fire the officer in charge of the fire brigade detachment which was present did seek Churchill's instructions, and was told to let it burn down. This may well have been sensible in view of the dangerous criminals within. Eventually two charred bodies were found, but this left one or two of the Latvians unaccounted for. Two weeks later Churchill had to give evidence at an inquest, not a natural duty of a Home Secretary, and then when the new House of Commons met was subject to one of Balfour's more successful pieces of cool raillery. 'I understand what the photographer was doing,' he said, 'but what was the right honourable gentleman doing?'[3]

The significance was that the whole vastly publicized affair fortified Churchill's already incipient reputation for being far from a calm and judicious Home Secretary. He was perceived more as a trigger-happy boy scout, or at best a junior officer, who wished to behave in the streets of London as though he was still with the Malakand Field Force or on the armoured train in Natal. And this came at a time when exceptional industrial tensions made a steady hand at the Home Office more than usually necessary. Before the second 1910 election there was the Tony-pandy affair, which became adversely and unfairly remembered against Churchill in Labour and trades union circles. It may indeed have made a considerable contribution to the Labour party's hazardous neutrality between Halifax and Churchill as a successor to Chamberlain in May 1940.

Yet until the end of 1910 Churchill's Home Office administration was not at all trigger-happy in relation to industrial disputes. In May there had been a potentially explosive dock strike at Newport, Monmouthshire. One of the Newport shipowning companies, Houlder

Brothers, took an inflammatory attitude and proposed to import fifty-five 'blackleg' stevedores to load their held-up ship. They were to some extent supported by the secretary of the Shipping Federation but not by the manager of the Newport docks. The arrival of this imported non-union labour seemed certain to provoke a stormy and probably violent reaction from the picketing Newport dockers. This threw into a great state the mayor of the town and his Watch Committee (as police authorities in boroughs were called in those days). They were not particularly sympathetic to Houlders, but they were very conscious of their own responsibilities for preserving public order, and were not merely deeply concerned by the objective prospects of a serious breach but also intimidated by threats of retaliation against the strikers from Houlders. The attitude of F. H. Houlder, the senior partner, was well expressed in his view that 'in the Argentine they managed these things better: they would send artillery and machine guns, and give proper protection to their subjects'.[4] The mayor consequently bombarded the Home Office with urgent requests for 300 Metropolitan policemen and for 300 troops as well.

Both the organization of the police and the legal responsibility for avoiding civic commotion were very locally diffused at the time. Troops could be sent only at the specific request of the civil authority on the ground, which in effect meant the mayor as chief magistrate. The post therefore carried more responsibility than in the almost purely orna-mental municipal role which it subsequently assumed until the London election of 2000. Furthermore, if the mayor was to manage without the military, his local police resources were very limited. Newport would not have had a total borough strength of more than 150 in its indepen-dent police force of the time. The mayor was therefore reduced to scraping around for neighbourly loans. 'All local resources exhausted,' he telegraphed to the Home Office permanent secretary on 21 May, 'and am promised tomorrow sixty men from Bristol and forty from Merthyr, and am hoping to get forty from Glamorgan County and like number from Monmouthshire County: but these latter eighty are doubtful as demonstration is to be made in Cardiff tomorrow and Cardiff City can render no assistance.'[5]

Sir Edward Troup, at the receiving end in London and acting throughout on Churchill's general instructions, behaved with great sense and coolness. Meeting Houlder had a salutary effect on him. 'If [he] bullied his stevedores as he tried to bully me, it is no wonder there was a strike!' he reported to Churchill. This was after Houlder had arrived at Troup's private house at about 10.45 p.m. 'He seemed to have dined and was much excited.'[6] And a day later Troup telegraphed very firmly to the Shipping Federation: 'The Secretary of State can only repeat that if you land men at Newport or bring them into docks in present circumstances you will incur very grave responsibility.' However via the permanent secretary of the War Office, of which organization, after he had failed to rouse them over the weekend, Troup did not have much opinion ('If the "possible invader" lands on Saturday afternoon, the W.O. will read the telegrams announcing his landing on Monday morning'), he arranged for General Officer Commanding (GOC) at the garrison town of Chester to set the requested troops on standby.

Their deployment did not prove necessary. On Churchill's direct initiative, and drawing on his previous departmental experience, a Board of Trade conciliator (Mitchell) was sent to Newport, and at a quadripartite meeting in the town hall (mayor, Mitchell, 'masters' and 'men') secured a settlement within about six hours of his arrival. True to his role as a caricature of a minor capitalist, Houlder repudiated it and was still intent on bringing in his blacklegs. However, he was sufficiently isolated to be brought into line, and the tension subsided on 24 May. Newport had experienced its most exciting time since the Chartist riot there of 1839, and Churchill's Home Office had played a steady, even a distinguished, role. The Home Secretary himself might have played a more 'hands on' and maybe an equally steadying part had he not left England for a Whitsun holiday in Switzerland and Venice on 21 May. His subsequent communications took the form of: 'Telegrams tomorrow will find me at Grand Hotel, Goschenein. . . . We do not reach Venice till Wednesday.'[7] His changes of scene were sacrosanct, but his energies were rarely diverted into sandcastles rather than statecraft, and the policy of his permanent secretary in London, who operated within his general direction, and to some extent under his inspiration, could certainly not have been accused of being over-excited or trigger-happy.

Tonypandy, a Rhondda mining town or village twenty-five miles to the north-west of Newport, became a much more notorious name in industrial history and on the escutcheon of Churchill. Some said that this was partly because it was one of the few Welsh place-names which the English found it easy to pronounce (although Newport cannot have given much difficulty), and in any event they mostly mispronounce Tonypandy, with a long rather than a short 'o'. It was probably more because it was at the epicentre of the raw but renowned industria͏ͭ communities into which from about 1840 onwards the exploitation of the rich coal-seams transformed a forty-five-mile-wide swathe of hitherto sylvan fastnesses running from the east of Carmarthenshire through Glamorgan to the middle of Monmouthshire.

In early November 1910, a convoluted dispute about the relative payment for working difficult and easier coal-seams broke out in the Rhondda and Aberdare valleys, bringing about 25,000 men out on strike (a tenth of the total then employed in the whole South Wales coalfield). This led to a tense situation at several collieries in the locality, and eventually to fairly serious window-breaking and looting of shops in the small centre of Tonypandy. This began on the night of Monday, 7 November, and although the Chief Constable of Glamorgan had, according to a report of Churchill's to the King, no fewer than 1,400 constables at his disposal, a cornucopia compared with that of his poor cousin of Newport, he decided to apply direct to the GOC Southern Command for troop reinforcement. There are several points here. First, just as the miners were gradually (and certainly by 1926) coming to be regarded as the most battle-hardened troops of industrial labour, so by a sort of symbiotic relationship the Glamorgan County Constabulary came to assume some of the characteristics of the crack battalion of the countervailing forces. As I recall from my childhood they had, like members of the Prussian Guard, silver spikes on their helmets, a form of aggressive decoration eschewed by the lesser Monmouthshire force. However, to judge from their Chief Constable's application, the Glamorgan nerve was not quite up to their insignia.

The second point of interest is why the Glamorgan Chief Constable was able to go direct to Southern Command while the Newport one had to go through both his mayor and the Home Office. The answer is partly that there was no mayor and corporation covering the Rhondda, merely a humble urban district council, and partly that the Chief Constables of counties were 'gentlemen' and those of boroughs were 'players' – professional policemen – and in pre-1914, even pre-1939, England gentlemen were accorded much greater authority.

Fortunately the general put in charge of the operation – Nevil Macready – was a very sensible man, who was anxious to co-operate with the more cautious view of the Home Office. The infantry, advancing from Salisbury Plain, were at first halted by Churchill at Swindon, and the cavalry allowed no nearer the scene of potential battle than Cardiff. A little later Churchill agreed to the cavalry advancing to Pontypridd, at the junction of the Aberdare and Rhondda valleys.

However, as the rioting persisted over several days and nights, with damage to sixty-three shops and one man killed, but accidentally in a scuffle rather than by punitive action, Churchill did eventually allow a detachment of the Lancashire Fusiliers into the valley, where indeed they remained for nearly a year. They never engaged with the strikers. The battle, such as it was, was fought by the Glamorgan Constabulary, reinforced by some London policemen (the Metropolitan Police, under Churchill, saw quite a lot of non-metropolitan England and Wales) with rolled-up mackintoshes as their hardly lethal weapons. There were no serious casualties, apart from the one man who died before either the Metropolitan Police or the military reinforcements arrived.

On any objective analysis it is difficult to fault Churchill in the Rhondda for any sin of aggression or vindictiveness towards labour. Indeed at the time he was more criticized from the opposite direction. *The Times* thundered at his weakness. Yet there are lines of attack to which some politicians, whether or not they are 'guilty as charged', are peculiarly vulnerable because they seem to fit in with their general character and behaviour. Thus a charge of trickiness in Lloyd George or indolence in Baldwin or indiscretion in Hugh Dalton clung to them like a spot of grease on a pale suit. And there was always sufficient of the 'galloping major' about Churchill to make it easy to assume that he was acting with over-boisterous irresponsibility, power having gone to his head.

The contrast with Asquith is instructive. In the second year of his Home Secretaryship, seventeen years earlier, Asquith had to deal with a public-order problem very similar to that which arose at Tonypandy. A Yorkshire mining strike led to a riotous situation at some collieries around Wakefield. The local magistrates applied for reinforcements. Asquith sent them 400 Metropolitan policemen. The situation continued to deteriorate and the magistrates with increasing strenuousness asked for these to be strengthened by troops. Asquith reluctantly agreed to the deployment of a platoon of infantry. On about the fourth day, at a colliery called Featherstone and under the pressure of a menacing crowd, they opened fire. Two civilians were killed. For a time thereafter Asquith was subject to sporadic protests at public meetings. 'Why did you murder the miners at Featherstone in '92?' was a typical taunt. 'It was not '92, it was '93' was his coolly weary and over-precise reply.[8] But Featherstone never stuck to him as Tonypandy did to Churchill. On the other hand Asquith's 'wait and see' of March 1910 did stick. He in fact used the phrase, in relation to the government's plans for a 'veto bill' not in a hesitant or apologetic form but growlingly with a hint of menace. Later however it was pressed into frequent service as a phrase encapsulating his inactivity. Churchill was never accused of waiting and seeing but rather of leaping before he looked.

The Sidney Street escapade, coming six weeks or so after Tonypandy, was Churchill's great mistake. It gave a retrospective justification to suspicions of rashness. And this was reinforced by his behaving much less circumspectly than previously in the wave of industrial strife, which together with the crunch of the constitutional crisis and the hottest weather of the century beset the country in the summer of 1911. This began with a seamen's and firemen's strike in mid-June, which itself was fairly quickly settled, and favourably to the strikers. The wave of sympathetic and emulatory disputes, mainly in transport of one sort or another, ran on throughout July and well into August, when it culminated in the big bang of a national railway strike called on 15 August for the following evening. Churchill, who until nearly then and no doubt encouraged by Troup, had behaved with the restrained caution which he had displayed in 1910, at that stage seemed to go into overdrive.

The situation on Merseyside, where a dockers' strike dragged on much longer than in London, became tense. The lord mayor of Liverpool and the mayor of Birkenhead applied not only for troops but for a warship in the Mersey (to do quite what was by no means clear). Churchill arranged for the provision of both. The result was a minor shooting incident on 14 August with no deaths but eight injured. There were pretty bad nerves all round (no doubt it is easier to say this today than on the Liverpool waterfront at the time). Lord Derby as the local magnate wrote to Churchill that 'in forty-eight hours all poor people will be face to face with starvation and God alone knows what happens when the moment arrives'.[9] And on the next day King George V telegraphed to Churchill: 'Accounts from Liverpool show that the situation there more like revolution than a strike.'[10]

When the railway strike became imminent Churchill secured the suspension of the rule that troops could be deployed (for purposes of local and industrial order) only upon a specific requisition from a civic authority. Briefly thereafter the industrial battlefield became an armed camp. There were battalions in Hyde Park, and singularly unfortunately from the point of view of Churchill's reputation with the radical press, they occupied all the railway stations of Manchester without any request from that city's lord mayor. This alienated C. P Scott, the Jehovah-like editor of the *Manchester Guardian*, who had hitherto been one of Churchill's warmest supporters. When the railway strike became actual the two radical stars of the government devoted themselves to different roles, Lloyd George to conciliation, Churchill to intimidation. 'The railway strike will now be fought out,' the latter telegraphed to the King on 18 August.[11]

It might have been held that this was a deliberate and brilliant deployment of their respective talents. Lloyd George had the more constructive role. He settled the strike (mainly by getting the main railway companies – there were then nine – to recognize and deal with the trades unions) by 20 August, while Churchill went on fulminating. In a House of Commons speech defending his actions on the 22nd he spoke in apocalyptic terms of the threat 'in that great quadrilateral of industrialism, from Liverpool and Manchester on the west to Hull and Grimsby on the east, from Newcastle down to Birmingham and Coventry in the south ... of a swift and certain degeneration of all the means, of all the structure, social and economic, on which the life of the people depends'. He compared the threat with the breaching of the great Nimrod dam on the Euphrates when 'the enormous popula-tion who lived by that artificial means ... were absolutely wiped from the book of human life'.[12]

It was flaming hyperbole, which would have merited an earlier version of G. K. Chesterton's brilliant satirical verses entitled 'Chuck it Smith' mocking the claim of Churchill's friend F. E. (later Lord Birkenhead) that the Welsh Church Disestablishment Bill had 'affronted the con-science of every Christian community in Europe'. Asquith did not like hyperbole, and my strong but unsubstantiated guess is that the moment (mid-August 1911) when he heard (or read) this speech was the moment when he decided that Churchill, although his force and talents were such that there was no thought of dropping him from the government, was not best suited to the Home Office at a time when unusual tensions, industrial and political, were beginning to threaten the hitherto rela-tively placid life of liberal England.

Fortunately for Churchill, as at any rate it appeared at the time, his own mind was simultaneously beginning to range beyond the Home Office. On top of the Coronation and the heat, the strikes and the victory over the peers, that summer had also seen a qualitative change in the international climate. On 1 July, a German 'gunboat' arrived off the Moroccan port of Agadir, a location which the French regarded as well within their sphere of interest and within a country over which they were about to proclaim a protectorate. It never fired its guns, and there was little indication of any intention to do so. Its despatch to Agadir was a gesture, but a provocatively flamboyant one, with if anything more of an effect on the British than on the more closely concerned French. They fairly quickly came to an accord with the Germans, who recognized France as the predominant European power in Morocco.

The British were peculiarly sensitive to any naval challenge. Sending gunboats to intimidate had, at least since Palmerston, been a British near monopoly. There were no signs of great popular excitement comparable with the Disraeli-encouraged 'by jingo if we do' mood of 1878, but the effect of the incident on some members of the political class, and above all on Churchill, was dramatic. After the Agadir incident he would no longer have contemplated making his calming Swansea speech of August 1908 or of fighting his battle in alliance with Lloyd George against McKenna's naval estimates of 1909. In *The World Crisis* (the relevant volume was published in 1923) he went out of his way to recant on that issue: 'although the Chancellor of the Exchequer and I were right in the narrow sense [of facts and figures], we were absolutely wrong in relation to the deep tides of destiny'.[13]

This conversion in 1911 however produced no immediate break with Lloyd George. Instead Churchill contributed to getting the Chancellor to insert in his annual Mansion House speech to the financial leaders of the City of London a robust warning to Germany which was as surprising from Lloyd George at the time as it was a remarkable foretaste of his dogged militarism of five years later. 'I would make great sacrifices to preserve peace,' Lloyd George somewhat routinely began.

> But if a situation were to be forced upon us in which peace could only be preserved by the surrender of the great and beneficent position Britain has won by centuries of heroism and achievement, by allowing Britain to be treated where her interests were vitally affected as if she were of no account in the Cabinet of nations, then I say emphatically that peace at that price would be a humiliation intolerable for a great country like ours to endure.[14]

Quite how vitally British interests were affected in Morocco may be open to dispute, but there was no doubt about the significance of this speech, fully appreciated and resented in Berlin, from the man who had previously been thought of as the leading 'pacifist' minister. The effect of Agadir upon Churchill was still more profound than that upon Lloyd

George. From that moment onward Churchill's mind was never long free of military matters (taking the adjective also to embrace naval ones) until well into the 1920s. They dominated his remaining thirteen weeks at the Home Office. At first there was a natural correspondence between his departmental responsibilities and his military excitement. The industrial unrest meant that, perhaps a little over-enthusiastically, he was sending troops around the country. When however the industrial unrest subsided towards the end of August, the weight of his energies did not return to the more civilian side of Home Office business. He had long had a strong if fluctuating military interest. It had shown itself in his childhood passion for the deployment of lead soldiers – although many who have not subsequently shown much martial spirit have shared that enthusiasm – then in his determination to witness (and to write about) every possible imperial campaign, and again in his finding time in his busy early summers as a minister to put in a week's annual service with the Oxfordshire Hussars. These camps mostly took place conveniently in the park at Blenheim, and there was some doubt (in Clementine Churchill's mind at any rate) as to whether the opportunity they provided for hard drinking and high-stake gambling with F. E. Smith and other less famous amateur officers was not as great an incentive as was the military training.

However she should not have been in doubt about how much one part of his mind was stirred by the soldier's art. He had written to her on 31 May 1909 from such a military encampment and after a field day in which the senior commanders had in his view shown much deficiency:

> Do you know I would greatly like to have some practice in the handling of large forces. I have much confidence in my judgment on things, when I see clearly, but on nothing do I seem to *feel* the truth more than in tactical combinations. It is a vain and foolish thing to say – but *you* will not laugh at it. I am sure I have the root of the matter in me – but never I fear in this state of existence will it have a chance of flowering – in bright red blossom.[15]

This undercurrent of Bonapartism he on the whole kept strictly under control during his voyage to radicalism. But it was always latently present, and the Agadir incident and his changed perception of the German threat which it rightly or wrongly provoked acted like a prince's kiss on the sleeping beauty.

In the first volume of *The World Crisis* (perhaps with a little retrospective touching up) Churchill described an excited scene in Edward Grey's

room on 25 July 1911.* He and Lloyd George had been hastily
summoned back from a walk in St James's Park to join the Foreign
Secretary: 'His [Grey's] first words were: "I have just received a communication from the German Ambassador so stiff that the Fleet might
be attacked at any moment. I have sent for McKenna to warn him." '[16]
Thereafter Churchill was a changed man. The security of the nation
became dominant in his mind, almost an obsession. Within a few days
he had organized a special military guard on the stores of naval cordite
in London. Within three weeks – weeks of great industrial and political
tension – he had composed and circulated to the members of the
Committee of Imperial Defence a major memorandum in which he
postulated a full-scale war, and sought with considerable prescience to
chart its early course. The basic assumptions were that Britain would
ally itself with France and that the two western powers would be
supported by Russia in a continent-wide struggle against Germany
supported by Austro-Hungary. Germany, because its army was both
bigger than that of France (2.2 million against 1.7 million) and of 'at
least equal quality', could be expected to seize the initiative and to do so
by advancing through Belgium. By the twentieth day the Germans
would break through the line of the Meuse and the French would be
forced back on Paris and the south. The British would help to redress
the balance by immediately sending a regular force of 107,000 (very
precise) to France and by moving 100,000 troops of the British Army in
India (not the Indian Army), who should reach Marseille on the fortieth
day, which was when the French could first hope to turn the tide.[17]
(The Battle of the Marne, one of the great military recoveries in history,
in fact took place between 6 and 10 September 1914, between the
thirty-seventh and the forty-first days after French mobilization.).

   This remarkable document was obviously all Churchill's own work.
Apart from anything else there was no official in the Home Office who
would have had either the knowledge or the duty to assist him in its
preparation. The immediate effect of Churchill's paper is difficult to
gauge. There were no direct written responses to it. Probably most of
the members of the Committee of Imperial Defence, if they read it
through, dismissed it, although quite tolerantly, as another example of

* It was however in the Foreign Secretary's room in the House of Commons rather than
in the high-ceilinged splendour of the Secretary of State's room in the Foreign Office,
from which Grey, three years later, imagined he could see 'the lights going out all over
Europe'.

'Winston being over-excited'. It was not however just a one-off extravaganza. During the next four weeks he wrote substantial foreign and
military policy letters to Grey (on 30 August), to Lloyd George (on 31
August), to Asquith (on 13 September), to McKenna (on that same day)
and to Lloyd George again (on 14 September).

The shift of his interests therefore preceded his change of posts. The
knowledge that Asquith, after the industrial excitements of August, was
moving towards the need for a calmer man at the Home Office would
not have disturbed him, provided that he could get the alternative job
that he wanted. This was the Admiralty. It was not a presumptuous
desire, for the Admiralty, although it carried substantial special perquisites, was not senior to the Home Office, indeed was a very mild step
downwards, and he had in any event been semi-offered the First
Lordship in 1908 and had asked for it (equally with the Home Office)
in 1910. But in 1911, when Asquith decided that he wanted a shake-up
at the Admiralty just as much as he wanted a calm-down at the Home
Office, there was competition as to who would effect the shake-up.

The main object of the shake-up was to create a War Staff at the
Admiralty, such as had already been imposed on the War Office, and to
make the admirals co-operate more with that other service department
rather than operating in sublime or complacent isolation. One obvious
instrument for this was Haldane, who had done precisely this job at the
War Office. He had the further attribute of being the Prime Minister's
oldest friend in politics, but that, as there are many examples to show,
is not always the strongest qualification for preferment. His disadvantages were that he had become a peer in the previous spring and it was
held, by Churchill at least, that such a crucial post should be in the
Commons; that Haldane's direct transfer from the War Office would
be rubbing the nose of the navy in their need to come up to the army's
standard of organization; and above all that Churchill had expressed an
insistent wish for the job.

Asquith, in that last long recess before he acquired his own Thames-
side establishment at Sutton Courtenay, was at Archerfield near North
Berwick, a house lent by one of his Tennant brothers-in-law. He had
invited the Churchills to stay for a few days in late September. Haldane
had his own house at Cloan in Perthshire and undertook the substantial
journey from there to see the Prime Minister.* His description of events

---

* Presumably in an early motor car. It was nearly fifty miles with a ferry crossing of

imported a sense of almost physical rivalry into the competition. 'As I entered the approach,' Haldane wrote, 'I saw Winston Churchill standing at the door. I divined that he had heard of possible changes and had come down at once to see the Prime Minister. It was as I thought. Churchill was importunate about getting himself to the Admiralty. . . . Obviously Churchill had been pressing hard. I returned to Cloan and came back the next day. Churchill was still there, and the Prime Minister shut me up in a room with him.'[18]

Haldane was right that Churchill greatly wanted the Admiralty, but the impression he conveyed of Churchill's having inserted himself into the house and intimidated the Prime Minister by his importunities is more a reaction to his own disappointment than an accurate picture. Asquith, who was never frightened by Churchill – amusement was his more frequent attitude – would hardly have invited him to stay at that point of decision unless he had effectively made up his mind in advance that he was to have the post. Shutting them up in a room together was a typical Asquith ploy, and not an unsuccessful one. They established a *modus vivendi* (there would not have been much point in a reshuffle to bring about better co-ordination between the services if the First Lord of the Admiralty was to be at daggers drawn with the War Secretary). They worked together well until Haldane became Lord Chancellor in the following year.

Eventually they were to be fellow victims of a Tory exclusion order as a condition for the formation of the first War Coalition in 1915. Haldane was dropped altogether. Churchill was heavily demoted. It is an ironic thought that the heads of the two ministers who had done more than any others to prepare the services for war should have been chopped off by the party which was demanding the war's more vigorous prosecution. A further irony was that Haldane, thought of with his Liberal Imperialist past as one of the more right-wing members of the Asquith government, became *Labour* Lord Chancellor in 1924, at the end of which same year Churchill, Lloyd George's partner in militant radicalism between 1905 and 1911, became *Conservative* Chancellor of the Exchequer.

-th of Forth, and the fact that he did the round trip again on the following day points considerable eagerness on his part.

11

'The Ruler of the King's Navee'

The Admiralty, apart from affording Churchill the excitement of commanding great forces, brought with it two fine perquisites. The first was Admiralty House, at the top of Whitehall, which made the First Lord with only the Prime Minister, the Chancellor of the Exchequer and the Lord Chancellor a ministerial possessor of an official residence, and Admiralty House was in some ways the finest of the four. The second was the Admiralty yacht, a lavishly fitted-up craft of 4,000 tons and with a crew of 196, appropriately (in Churchill's case) named *Enchantress*, for such she was for him. During his nearly three peacetime years as First Lord he spent an aggregate of eight months in her, visiting every ship and naval facility in the Mediterranean as in home waters, and doing much of his paperwork afloat, as well as using the ship for extensive sightseeing holidays, sometimes with the Prime Minister and a suitably chosen Asquithian party on board.

Churchill became so absorbed in his new department and the cocoons that it provided for his life that he had less time to spare for general politics and other ministers' business than when he had been at either the Board of Trade or the Home Office. There was however one exception, and that was the Home Rule controversy and the near rupture of the constitution to which it led. With that for him hereditary subject Churchill was fully engaged, sometimes truculently, sometimes seeking compromise.

Surprisingly the Churchills did not move into Admiralty House until eighteen months after it had been put at their disposal. It was semi-free, which meant that when he occupied it his salary, which at the Home Office and the Admiralty had been elevated from the 'miserable' £2,500 of the Board of Trade to £5,000, was abated by £500 as a token but not negligible rent (£25,000 at present prices). The rub lay in this grand house being thought to require twelve servants, none of which, apart from perhaps a doorman, as is the way in official residences, was provided at public expense. And the Churchills, right through from their marriage three years before, had been mild

financially embarrassed. His large earnings of 1900–1, even in the care
of Sir Ernest Cassel, had been exhausted during his back-bench and
junior-minister years. And although in the 1920s he was vigorously to
exploit his pen whether in or out of office, he did practically no
profitable writing during his years as a Liberal minister. There was a
trickle of royalties from previous books, but apart from them and a few
dividends he had to try to live on his salary, which was never enough
for him. There was no risk of bankruptcy, but he was always up against
the margin, with a lot of unpaid bills lying around. Churchill did not
greatly mind this, but Clementine hated it, and her dislike was redoubled when she thought that the problem was exacerbated by the loss in
gambling sessions of money they could not afford. She was too wise a
wife to do much preaching, but she was always a force on the side of
caution and economy.

When they returned to London after their marriage excursions they
settled temporarily into Churchill's little bachelor house in Bolton
Street off Piccadilly. Then in early 1909 they took a fairly short
(eighteen-year) lease on 33 Eccleston Square and moved in, after a good
deal of refurbishment, some of it economically done, in May of that
year. It was a spacious and conveniently sited house, though neither
elegant nor spirit-lifting, any more than was the locality. Pimlico –
divided from Belgravia by the railway lines running into Victoria Station
and separated from Westminster proper by the greater gap of the one
having a uniform mid-nineteenth-century layout and the other, around
the Abbey, having a much earlier history and architecture – was built on
land most of which was waste until 1835, and looks and feels like it.
The Churchill acquisition, however, with its basement and four storeys
above the ground, was a more than adequate family house, with space
for moderate-scale entertaining, and at least one special amenity, a large
first-floor library (two rooms knocked into one) that Churchill had
made for himself. There was also good nursery space, which was as well
for their first two children were born there, Diana in July 1909 and
Randolph in May 1911.

Diana was launched with a fleet of family godparents, headed by the
Duke of Marlborough. Randolph had fewer, but his two godfathers
were more political. There was the rapidly becoming inevitable F. E.
Smith and there was Edward Grey, with whom Churchill began a new
closeness during that summer of 1911. In most ways Grey was not a
natural Churchill friend, being almost the antithesis of Smith, far from
swashbuckling and verging on the priggish. When the move to Admir-

alty House eventually took place, Grey, a widower from the death of his
first wife in 1906 until his second marriage to Pamela Glenconner in
1922 and without any firm London base, became the Churchills' tenant
at 33 Eccleston Square. Churchill was drawn to him because they
increasingly agreed with each other's 'hard' foreign policy line:
Germany was the growing menace and Britain must if necessary be
prepared to counter this by fighting on the side of France. Churchill
also found it useful to have a ministerial ally of such a different style
from his own flamboyance; and he was grateful to Grey for throwing
the cloak of his high respectability over him in Cabinet. It was well
summed up by a postscript to a letter he wrote to Clementine on 25
June 1911: 'Do ask Grey to be godfather – I am sure it is a vy good
idea, & will give him great pleasure. I am always hearing nice things he
has said about me. He likes and wistfully admires our little circle. What
do you think?'[1]

Churchill was an enthusiastic and loving father, although the pitch of
his expectations, for Randolph in particular, became too high, and his
relations with these two children were less close and satisfactory than
with the subsequent ones, Sarah (born October 1914) and Mary (born
September 1922). Clementine had difficult and exhausting deliveries,
and required several months of convalescence, mostly away from London. The Eccleston Square establishment, nursery apart, was run with a
staff of one manservant, a female cook and two maids, which relative
austerity was a main reason why Admiralty House appeared formidably
expensive. What is less clear is why they changed their minds in the
spring of 1913. There is no particularly revealing piece of correspondence. The likelihood is that Churchill always wanted to make the move
and to enjoy the historic grandeur of Admiralty House, and that
Clementine realistically appreciated that the best she could do was to
mount a delaying action and at the end of the day to hope for a semi-
compromise. This was exactly what happened. It was agreed that they
would take over the official house except for the grandest state rooms
or the principal floor (which might have been thought to destroy part
of the point of the move), the exclusion of which would allow the
servant complement to be reduced from twelve to nine. Wisely she
ensured that, when the move took place, Churchill was safely out of the
way in the Admiralty yacht, and then, rather surprisingly, for she was
never such an Asquith favourite as either her sister-in-law Goonie
Churchill or her sister Nellie Romilly, let alone her cousin Venetia
Stanley, made the actual transition via the Asquith house at Sutton

Courtenay. She left Eccleston Square for the last time on a Saturday morning, spent two days of intensive golf with the Asquiths and returned early on the Monday for her first full immersion in Admiralty House.

The acquisition of a country house was not at this stage within the range even of Churchill's extravagance. And, indeed, he would not have had much time for one, for, as he subsequently recorded in the first volume of *The World Crisis*: 'Saturdays, Sundays and any other spare day I spent always with the Fleets at Portsmouth or at Portland or Devonport, or with the Flotilla at Harwich. Officers of every rank came on board to lunch or dine and discussion proceeded without ceasing, on every aspect of naval war and administration.'[2] From the context it appears that he was probably referring only to the spring of 1912, when there was a great naval assembly along the middle south coast of England. However his total of eight months afloat during these years meant a strong pattern of *Enchantress* expeditions even at less concentrated times. During his years as First Lord, Blenheim did not figure nearly as much as previously, and he very rarely stayed in other people's houses. Almost all of his always prolific correspondence was dated from either the Admiralty or *Enchantress*.

Clementine *per contra* paid a lot of country or seaside visits. The Stanleys' houses at Alderley and Penrhos, a cottage on Wilfred Scawen Blunt's estate behind Brighton and even a hotel at Crowborough were all in this category, and sometimes, a little later, beach holidays for the infant children. These included some throwbacks to her peripatetic and money-saving childhood – Seaford and Dieppe – and some less nostalgic places, the Astor house at Sandwich Bay and a commercially rented one at Overstrand near Cromer. Her sister-in-law and her children were frequent companions. Churchill came for occasional days or short weekends. Even in bad English summer weather he quite liked a short burst of beach life, provided the sand was of a consistency which made possible the construction of elaborate castellated fortifications. Even so, he was quickly back off to London. During these Admiralty years, more perhaps than at any other phase in his career, even including 1940–1, he was a driven man. 'At least fifteen years of consistent policy were required', he wrote in *The World Crisis*, 'to give the Royal Navy the widely extended outlook upon war problems and of war situations without which seamanship, gunnery, instrumentalisms of every kind, devotion of the highest order, could not achieve their due reward. Fifteen years! And we were only to have thirty months!'[3] Driven men are not often the most balanced. But they are generally the most dedicated. As a result holidays of any length which he and his wife spent together during those years on the threshold of Armageddon – though for most people they were far less consciously so than in 1936–9 – took the form of *Enchantress* cruises, twice to the Mediterranean, more often in British home waters.

What were the problems to which Churchill was so desperate to apply himself in the thirty months? They fell into two categories. In the first were the broadest issues of Britain's politico-military orientation, with which Churchill instinctively and inevitably became embroiled. While his perspective was greatly influenced by the different offices for which he was from time to time responsible, he was never one to confine his eyes to the narrow ground beneath his feet. He always looked up to the high trees, although viewing them with considerable difference of angle according to the departmental platform from which he looked. His appraisal of Britain's naval requirements underwent a violent change between 1909 when he opposed McKenna and 1911–14 when (opposed *inter alia* by McKenna) he pushed the estimates up to a level far beyond what McKenna or Goschen or, most of all, Lord Randolph Churchill would have regarded as the boundaries of the tolerable. And then, ten years later, when he assumed his first Conservative office in the surprisingly elevated rank of Chancellor of the Exchequer, he for the third time nearly broke up a government on the issue of naval expenditure. The first time he had been in favour of less, the second time of more, and on this future third occasion of less again. He would of course have claimed that circumstances had changed, significantly between 1909 and 1913–14, and vastly between then and 1925. Nevertheless it was an example of zigzagging on a formidable scale.

Of more direct relevance to his pre-1914 performance was the fact that, after 1911, and unlike most of his colleagues, he had come to regard a major European war as more likely than not, and to believe that, if it came, Britain's interest and honour lay in fighting on the side of France against Germany, and not in seeking a handwashing neutrality. This is subject to two qualifications. The first relates to a very uncharacteristic minute which he addressed to Grey and Asquith on 23 August 1912. It was occasioned by the decision of the French to concentrate their considerable fleet in the Mediterranean and to leave the Channel coast and the Atlantic seaboard to the British navy, which in turn was considerably reducing its Mediterranean presence. It was a

disposition which could not have occurred without the Anglo-French
Entente of 1904 and the subsequent staff talks. But Churchill was at
pains to stress that these fleet deployments were autonomous and could
have been sensibly made by France if Britain did not exist or vice versa.
Therefore, he claimed, but with a peculiar lack of conviction, that
Britain maintained its freedom of choice if it came to war between
France and Germany. It was Churchill writing for the record (although
for what purpose is not clear) and in doing so losing all his habitual
verve and persuasiveness. He doubtfully believed what he was saying,
and being normally the least dissimulating of men it immediately
showed itself in a hobbled and convoluted style.

The second qualification is that his belief in the likelihood of war,
and in a British duty to be involved if it came, should not be equated
with a desire for it. On 15 September 1909 (admittedly nearly two years
before the beginning of his full *Götterdämmerung* period) he had written
to his wife from Würzburg, where he was attending the German army
manoeuvres: 'I think another 50 years will see a wiser & a gentler world.
But we shall not be spectators of it. Only the P.K. [puppy kitten – their
name for Diana] will glitter in a happier scene. How easily men could
make things much better than they are – if they only all tried together!
Much as war attracts me & fascinates my mind with its tremendous
situations – I feel more deeply every year – & can measure the feeling
here in the midst of arms – what vile and wicked folly & barbarism it
all is.'[4] This letter is balanced by a passage from Edward Grey's
memoirs, which is the more interesting because of the generally unreveal-
ealing nature of those two volumes. Referring to the late summer of
1911, when the repercussions of Agadir were rumbling on, Grey wrote:

> One other colleague, not tied to London by official work, kept me
> company for love of the crisis. . . . Let me not be supposed to imply that
> Churchill was working for war, or desired it. . . . It was only that his high-
> mettled spirit was exhilarated by the air of crisis and high events. His
> companionship was a great refreshment, and late in the afternoon he
> would call for me and take me to the Automobile Club, which was but
> thinly populated, like other clubs, at that season. There, after what had
> been to me a weary, perhaps anxious, day he would cool his ardour and I
> revive my spirits in the swimming bath.[5]

This budget of quotations should perhaps be rounded off (although
it involves moving forward a few years and should be taken with the
pinch of salt which this source always requires) from Margot Asquith's

diary for the evening of 4 August, the day of the outbreak of the Great War, as it was known until 1939. 'We were at war. I left [the room] to go to bed, and, as I was passing at the foot of the [10 Downing Street] staircase, I saw Winston Churchill with a happy face striding towards the double doors of the Cabinet room.'[6] The reality no doubt was that Churchill was always on a delicate hinge between excitement at the prospect of great military clashes and apprehension at their consequences. He was never indifferent to human suffering, and was always as a strategist and even as a tactician a 'light casualty' man. He would not have enjoyed being Haig on the Somme or the supreme commander of either the German or the Russian armies in the mass slaughter of which Stalingrad was the epitome. But he was not intimidated by the prospect of war. Rather was he exhilarated by it, and to this extent Mrs Asquith was for once right.

This combination of attitudes, to cast the net of comparison even further forward, made him, by one of the great good chances of history, the perfect man for 1940 and 1941. It required immense courage and great self-confidence to fight on, but it did not require brutal stolidity, for the battles that had to be fought in those years when Britain stood alone were knife-edged ones but were not comparable in slaughter with what had happened in the First World War on the Western Front, let alone the Eastern Front, or what was immediately pending on the Russian Front in the Second World War. One of the factors which may have fostered Churchill's improbable but long-continuing post-war friendship with Montgomery was that the Field Marshal, vainly self-righteous and narrowly puritanical though he was, had been a wonderful instrument of the Prime Minister's desire for victories without heavy slaughter. And then in the last (1950s) phase of Churchill's power, perfectly rationally, horror at the awfulness of the prospect overtook any possible excitement at the clash. It was one thing to launch a dashing cavalry charge at Omdurman in 1898 and another to dice with H-bombs in the Cold War tension of 1953 and 1954. Churchill ended by trying (unsuccessfully in direct terms) to use his great martial prestige to save the world from mutually assured destruction.

None of these projections into the future or conflicting emotional pulls of the time interfered with Churchill's 1911–14 determination to maintain and enhance British naval superiority. He was also resolved to do it in terms not just of gross numbers of ships but also of efficiency of training, equipment and command. He was a bold and controversial First Lord. Yet, in spite of being an object of Tory obloquy, he did not have great trouble across the floor of the House of Commons. This was because he took a firm 'big navy' view, which commanded Conservative support and broadly outweighed (for three and a half years at least) any adverse view which his somewhat abrupt changes of high naval command might otherwise have provoked. His House of Commons speeches up to the outbreak of war, particularly those moving the naval estimates, attracted more Liberal than Conservative discontent. Nevertheless his performance at the Admiralty was always a high-wire act and one without a safety net. If his major decisions on command or equipment had gone seriously and manifestly wrong, his 'heart in the right place' desire for a strong navy would not have saved him from Tory wrath. And if he had lost the support of the Prime Minister, and at least the acquiescence of the solid centre of the Liberal Cabinet, all his fame and brilliance would not have saved him from being left on an isolated ridge without support from either side.

The command changes which he made were at once determined and complicated. He inherited a First Sea Lord in the shape of Admiral Sir Arthur Wilson, who was as dourly monosyllabic as his predecessor until January 1910, Sir Jackie (now Lord) Fisher, had been extravagantly ebullient. Churchill never liked silent men, and the commanders of the Second World War who could not express themselves fluently around the dining table at 10 Downing Street or Chequers were (sometimes unfairly) ill judged by him. They matched his own irrepressible conversational exuberance so badly as to make him feel ill at ease, maybe even a little vulgar, and were therefore valued below their deserts.

Wilson was however a harder nut to crack, on account of their relative prestige, than any general or admiral whom Churchill ran across in 1940–5. He was a VC, notably unselfseeking (he several times refused a peerage) and very popular in a gruff way ('old 'Ard 'Art' was his sobriquet), with all ranks of the Royal Navy. Moreover Wilson was thirty-two and a half years Churchill's senior. He was due to retire in the spring of 1912, but that was not fast enough for the new First Lord. This was because Wilson was totally opposed to the main purpose for which Churchill had been sent to the Admiralty, which was the creation of a Naval War Staff comparable with that which Haldane had instituted for the army. The object was to get away from the position, as Churchill put it, in which 'all plans were locked up in the mind of one taciturn admiral'.[7] Wilson was that admiral. In addition he was against the two main changes of naval strategy which the government thought necessary. The first was to accommodate the army plans for the transhipment of seven divisions to France in the first days of a European war, and the second was to move from a policy in the event of war of 'close blockade' of German ports to one of intercept on the high seas of any ship attempting to supply the enemy (a change generally held to be made necessary by the development of the torpedo, which rendered stationary ships sitting targets). Churchill got Wilson out by mid-November 1911, on, as he put in *The World Crisis*, 'friendly, civil but at the same time cool terms'.[8] The unexpected twist in this saga was that when, in May 1915, Fisher having flounced, Wilson was offered a return to the post of First Sea Lord he wrote to Asquith saying that he would accept it only 'under Mr Churchill'.*[9]

In place of Wilson, Churchill uncharacteristically made a compromise appointment. Sir Francis Bridgeman was promoted (reluctantly on his part) from Commander-in-Chief of the Home Fleet to First Sea Lord, and Prince Louis of Battenberg was moved into position as Second Sea Lord to be Bridgeman's successor. The Third Sea Lord was allowed to continue but the Fourth was also shunted. Sir George Callaghan replaced Bridgeman as Commander of the Home Fleet and Sir John Jellicoe, judged to be too junior for the full role, was made his second-in-command. Rear Admiral David Beatty, the provider of Nile-side champagne in 1898, was brought into Churchill's private office as his Naval Secretary. Thus were Jellicoe and Beatty, the two most famous naval commanders of the 1914 war, moved into positions from which they could further advance. These changes were announced on 26 November, five weeks after Churchill had taken up his new office, and were received with mild and tentative disapproval by the naval lobby, which was strong on the Conservative benches[†] and in parts of the press. The changes were not denounced, but pursed lips expressed the fear, or the hope, that Churchill's rashness would soon get him into trouble.

---

* There must at the time have been a cult of senility or a shortage of middle-aged admirals for the reappointment of a seventy-three-year-old officer to be seen as the best replacement for the unbalanced resignation of a seventy-four-year-old one.
† Here they included the irremediably disputatious Admiral Lord Charles Beresford. Beresford had managed over the previous thirty-seven years to alternate rising naval commands with being in and out of the House of Commons and using it as a platform for explosive speeches on Admiralty policy. He was currently (at the age of sixty-five) MP for Portsmouth but had previously had brief snatches as member for Waterford, St Marylebone, York and Woolwich, as well as advancing up the naval ladder to become Commander-in-Chief of the Channel Fleet.

In fact the appointments erred on the side of caution and respect for seniority. Bridgeman, even had he been in robust health, which he was not, would probably have been too conventional and maybe too old (he was only six years younger than Wilson) to have suited Churchill. Within a year he was eased out (on the nominal ground that his health had permitted him to attend only three out of six meetings of the Committee of Imperial Defence and that on one even of those three occasions he was 'forced to leave from sudden fainting'). Bridgeman did not go quietly and the second change produced the hostile criticism from Bonar Law, Beresford and the rest which the first had just avoided. Churchill might have done better to have gone for Prince Louis of Battenberg, who was then his choice for First Sea Lord, at the first rather than the second bite. Prince Louis, who after a very literal anglicization of name during the 1914 war became the first of the Mountbatten line, being the father of Lord Louis (later Earl) of that clan and the great-uncle of Prince Philip, had been born in Graz in Austria but had assumed British nationality on joining the Royal Navy at the age of fourteen in 1868. He spoke with a heavy Germanic accent (somewhat but presumably not vastly stronger than that of King Edward VII). He was an impressive figure of a man and a competent admiral who had the sophistication to co-operate well with Churchill.*

Nevertheless it did not in the long run work out altogether well, because British xenophobia after the outbreak of war with Germany – even dachshunds were in danger from some 'patriots' – helped to force his resignation at the end of October 1914. It was also the case that Admiral Callaghan was held to be no good as the war commander of the Home Fleet. This was on the grounds of age – he was sixty-two. Churchill was then able to replace him with Jellicoe, well prepared as a result of a year as Callaghan's deputy and two years as Second Sea Lord for the crucial and awesome role in which he was 'the only man who could lose the war in an afternoon'. This ceaseless shuffling of the top naval commanders was hardly designed to inspire confidence either in naval planning or in Churchill's judgement. Behind all these dispositions of personnel there was a lurking presence, half offstage and half onstage. This was Admiral of the Fleet Lord Fisher, who had been First Sea Lord from 1904 to 1910, when at the age of almost seventy he had supposedly retired to Lucerne. Almost everything he did was conducted

* The photograph of them together has a balanced urbanity which contrasts with the potentially explosive tensions shown in that of Churchill with Admiral Lord Fisher.

with a mixture of dudgeon and enthusiasm. He was arguably half mad, but he had a streak of narrow genius in him, and is widely regarded (even in retrospect) as the greatest naval administrator since Nelson. He had been born in Ceylon in 1841 and had a cast of features which suggested a more exotic provenance than the impeccable British background of his captain of infantry father and his mother, who is described in the *The Dictionary of National Biography* as being 'of New Bond Street, London'. Certainly his appearance was sufficiently compelling and idiosyncratic to persuade Jan Morris to write a portrait seventy-five years after his death which was entitled *Fisher's Face* and is in effect an extended love letter.

Fisher had first met Churchill at Biarritz during a spring holiday in 1907 and clearly saw in him a young junior minister of high interest and rising quality. He began to favour him with his brand of eccentric correspondence as early as 27 April of that year. They each, across a gap of thirty-four years' difference in age, recognized an exceptional human being in the other. Their mutual fascination, for it was not exactly friendship, survived a considerable conflict of interest when Churchill opposed McKenna's naval estimates for 1909. Fisher, the king of the dreadnoughts, was determined to get eight of them. But he also wanted to keep as striking a young minister as Churchill within the orbit of his influence. The balance of their early relationship was probably that Churchill was even more flattered by the attentions of the old, gnarled and famous Admiral than vice versa.

Fisher's letters were on the borders of hysteria, although they could also contain nuggets of very good sense. They typically ended with salutations like 'Yours to a cinder', 'Yours till Hell freezes' or 'Yours till charcoal sprouts', which led Churchill to write in the first volume of *The World Crisis*, 'Alas there was a day when Hell froze and charcoal sprouted and friendship was reduced to cinders.'[10]

That day was however more than three years away when Churchill became First Lord. Fisher engineered a successful 'lovers' tiff' in the spring of 1912, when he disapproved of some appointments of Churchill's and wrote woundingly about them. However, as he no doubt intended, this was no more than a ploy which led to his being invited to join a party on the Admiralty yacht at Naples a month later and to propound his views not only to Churchill but to the Prime Minister as well, if he could get either of them to listen. His degree of success is not recorded, but relations with the First Lord were fully restored, and Fisher did a lot of dancing (at which he was very good) in the somewhat unappetizing pre-breakfast hour with the twenty-five-year-old Violet Asquith.

Churchill had three times to recommend the appointment of a new First Sea Lord, but it was only on the third occasion, after Prince Louis had been forced out, that he brought back Fisher, who was by then seventy-three, a decision which was to have the most disastrous consequences for Churchill's own career. However, as we are informed also in *The World Crisis*, Churchill got very close to asking Fisher rather than Bridgeman to replace Wilson in 1911. The new First Lord had summoned Fisher from Lucerne to give him advice, and this led, whether accidentally or not is unclear, to their spending three days together in a Surrey country house. 'I find Fisher a veritable volcano of knowledge and of inspiration,' Churchill later wrote. 'On the way up to London ... I was on the brink of saying "Come and help me", and had he by a word seemed to wish to return, I would surely have spoken. But he maintained a proper dignity, and in an hour we were in London. Other reflections supervened, adverse counsels were not lacking, and in a few days I had definitely made up my mind to look elsewhere for a First Sea Lord.'[11]

The 'adverse counsels' would have related to Fisher's divisiveness. During his previous tenure he had succeeded, ably assisted by Lord Charles Beresford on the other side, in making almost every officer throughout the service into either a dedicated pro-Fisher man or an equally dedicated anti-Fisher one. This had led to his leaving, despite his great achievements, under something of a cloud in 1910. So Churchill reluctantly steered away from a reimportation of the Fisher–Beresford quarrel into the Admiralty. But he remained very much under the old Admiral's spell, got him in 1912–13 to preside over a Royal Commission on Oil Supply, a crucial subject at the time, and in addition accepted a great deal of *sub rosa* advice from him, often preferring Fisher's views on strategy, equipment and personnel to that of his official advisers. This did not conduce to harmonious working of the chain of command, and there is no doubt that in many ways the Sea Lords found Churchill a difficult political chief with whom to work.

There was a further destabilizing factor in the shape of Sir Francis Hopwood, Churchill's old enemy from Colonial Office days. For some extraordinary reason Churchill had allowed Hopwood to follow him to the Admiralty. He was not the permanent secretary – that was and long remained an experienced and widely trusted official bearing the surprising name of Sir Graham Greene – but in 1912 Hopwood became a Civil Lord, mainly concerned with detailed financial control. This made him a member of the Board of Admiralty, and thus privy to most gossip about Churchill's relations with his admirals. This he determinedly passed on, in a snake-in-the-grass way, to Lord Stamfordham, the King's more Tory private secretary. (Lord Knollys, the more Liberal one whom he had inherited from King Edward, and whose style never suited King George, had gone at the end of 1911.) Fortunately the 'Sailor King' never showed much desire to get involved in Admiralty feuds, and in particular turned Bridgeman down fairly flat when he tried to raise royal sympathy for his supersession at the end of 1912.

Churchill's position as First Lord was therefore from the outset replete with hazard, not only because of what he saw as the great challenge of the Kaiser's High Seas Fleet, but also from perils nearer home. It was a tribute to his courage and self-confidence that he achieved so much while exposed to two-way fire, with many pacifist-inclined Liberal MPs (a tendency also well represented in the Cabinet) on one side of him, and on the other his unpopularity with the Tories and the suspicion which this, together with his brashness, aroused among Conservative-inclined senior naval officers.

Part of the suspicion he assuaged by his extraordinary success in pushing the naval estimates from the £39 million which he inherited from McKenna up to and through the £50 million barrier. He also paid more attention to (and secured more improvement in) lower-deck pay and conditions than had any First Lord for a long time. In addition he drove through two major technical changes, which had their own risks. The first was development of the 15-inch battleship gun in place of the 13½ inch, which was a more hazardous and a more qualitative change than it sounds, because it increased the 'punch' power from 1,400 pounds of explosive to one of approximately 2,000 pounds. Had however the new weapon proved ineffective because over-ambitious, this would have left the navy with the worst of both worlds.

The second was setting in train the conversion of the whole fleet from coal to oil, with great potential benefits, but again with the considerable risks of transition. This conversion was essential to increase battleship speed to the 25 knots that was necessary if the Germans were to be outmanoeuvred, although of course they quickly did the same. It had the benefit of leading to an immensely profitable British government-controlling investment in the Anglo-Persian Oil Company, where an initial outlay of £2.2 million, later increased to £5 million, soon became worth £50 million and later much more. It also greatly increased the cleanliness of life afloat and the speed of refuelling.

All this was done within the framework of a naval policy designed to show the Germans that, whatever they built, Britain would build more. The slow progress of a battleship from its start as an item in the following year's naval estimates to becoming a hull on a shipyard slipway to being commissioned and available for fighting service meant that, even with a welter of available information, it is difficult to give an accurate summary of the relative British and German fleet strengths during the Churchill Admiralty years. The figures are shrouded in almost as dense a sea mist as were the ships themselves when they opaquely manoeuvred around each other in grey northern waters. The obscurity worked in favour of higher rather than lower expenditure.

Probably the best snapshot is that when Churchill became First Lord there were twelve British dreadnought battleships in service (including the Lord Nelson class, which were strictly pre-dreadnought, although in some respects even stronger) as against eight German. There were also six hulls already laid down, another two on the point of being so, and another four already provided for in the 1911–12 estimates. For the future, Churchill thought that if the Germans had adhered to their six-year programme of two–two–two–two–two–three, he would have been content to build four–three–four–three–four–three. If however, as they did by virtue of the new Naval Law of April 1912, the Germans went up to three–two–three–two–three–two, he would insist on going up to five–four–five–four–five–four, so as to maintain a 60 per cent superiority. There were a lot of naval vessels afloat other than dreadnought battleships, but as attention was so much concentrated upon the dreadnoughts at the time it is simpler to use them as a crude index of relative strength. Another factor affecting British appraisal of the strength of the German threat was the deepening of the Kiel Canal to accommodate the biggest ships, which was announced in 1909 and completed in June 1914. This gave the Germans much greater flexibility in the deployment of their big ships between the Baltic and the North Seas. These appraisals led Churchill to maintain McKenna's estimates for 1912, which provided for five Queen Elizabeth class battleships (dreadnoughts with 15-inch guns and other improvements) of the hitherto and unprecedented displacement of 27,500 tons plus another one of the same size paid for by Malaya. In 1913 he provided for another five of the same type and in 1914 for the same dose again, plus another one which might or might not be forthcoming from Canada. None of these latter groups came into service until well into the First World War, but they loomed over the last years of the peace, and set the terms of engagement or non-engagement for the wartime stand-off of the grand fleets, broken during 1914–18 only by the inconclusive Battle of Jutland in June 1916. There were two pre-war attempts at a 'naval holiday', to use the jargon of the time. But, when they failed, both sides went on building. It was an extravagant policy, although it kept a lot of shipyards on Clyde and Tyne echoing to the noise of riveting machinery. It did not seem to give Britain any great margin of superiority, and it certainly did not prevent war. But at least it meant that, when war came, Britain did not lose it at sea, although it did not clearly win it there either.

12

CHURCHILL IN ASQUITHLAND

CHURCHILL'S ABILITY TO pursue his big-navy policy, which became central to his whole political identity, depended essentially on his relations with his principal Cabinet colleagues. How did they develop during this period? The two most important ministers after the Prime Minister were Lloyd George and Edward Grey. This was partly because of the strength of their sharply contrasting personalities. They were neither of them commonplace men, and the resignation of either would have seriously destabilized the government. The only subsequent occasions when the two offices have been in equally balanced but contrasting hands have been (a little marginally) in the Baldwin government of 1924–9 with Churchill himself at the Treasury and Austen Chamberlain in the Foreign Office; and (more clearly) in that part of the Attlee government (1947–50) when the two posts were held by Stafford Cripps and Ernest Bevin.

Until the summer of 1911 Churchill had been much closer to Lloyd George than to Grey. They were radical allies and their flamboyant and mercurial temperaments were better matched. From then onwards Churchill's new closeness to Grey tilted the balance away from Lloyd George. Churchill came to regard Grey as a natural senior partner in the Cabinet: he supported Grey's underlying if not explicit commitment to France, and Grey supported Churchill's demands for ever larger naval estimates. And they were both eager, Grey a little warily, Churchill with less inhibition, to cement the confluence of interest with personal warmth. But it was not a deep-seated friendship based on natural affinity. They were colleagues and allies of circumstance. After they left the Asquith governments, Churchill in 1915, Grey in 1916, neither happily, they hardly saw each other during the remaining seventeen years of Grey's life.

With Lloyd George the previous pulls of interest were reversed. A free-spending First Lord of the Admiralty is a natural antagonist for a Chancellor of the Exchequer. Furthermore Lloyd George thought that Churchill had lost interest in the subjects which had brought them together and that he had become obsessed with the navy. He is recorded as having mocked him for becoming a 'water creature'. 'You think we all live in the sea, and all your thoughts are devoted to sea life, fishes and other aquatic creatures. You forget that most of us live on land.'[1] Nevertheless the natural affinity between Lloyd George and Churchill remained a strong countervailing force. And in 1912–13 it was strengthened by a temporarily dominating political contretemps. This was the Marconi scandal, which nearly destroyed Lloyd George's career. It also involved one other minister (Rufus Isaacs) as well as one ex-minister (the Master of Elibank) and drew Churchill, without the remotest justification, into its miasma.

Herbert Samuel as Postmaster-General had in March 1912 concluded with the Marconi Company an agreement for wireless telegraphy stations throughout the Empire. The allegation of impropriety arose because the managing director of the Marconi Company was Geoffrey Isaacs, a brother of Rufus Isaacs, the Attorney-General. This was accompanied by rumours that three ministers had made a great killing out of speculation in Marconi shares. Samuel was totally innocent. He had never touched any such share, and the main reason for trying to implicate him was the anti-Semitic overtones which hung around the issue. To bring together one Samuel and two Isaacses in a skein of transactions bordering on the world of high finance was an irresistible attraction for Hilaire Belloc, G. K. Chesterton and his brother Cecil. They were skirmishers around the case, as well as being, in the first two cases at least, the best rhymsters of the period, and were obsessed with what they saw as the conspiracies of international Jewry.

Rufus Isaacs was the primary purchaser and he passed on significant packets of shares to the Master of Elibank (Liberal Chief Whip at the time of the transaction)* and to Lloyd George. Elibank had speculated partly on his own behalf and partly with Liberal party political funds, which latter fact of course added piquancy to the steaming dish. But much the biggest target was Lloyd George, the Chancellor who was the scourge of the propertied classes and the symbol (up to a point at any rate) of Nonconformist Celtic purity against the self-indulgent greed of

* 'The Master' had resigned from the government in August 1912, when he was created Lord Murray of Elibank. He soon afterwards departed on an extended business visit to the slightly improbable destination of Bogotá (Colombia) and was unavailable to the Select Committee which investigated the affair. This led to 'gone to Bogotá' becoming a derisory anti-Liberal catchphrase.

metropolitan plutocracy. He was a most succulent bird to have caught, comparable with throwing a net around Gladstone or Baldwin or Cripps, and the lips of many Tories slavered at the prospect of the meal ahead. In fact none of the ministers had dealt in the shares of the British Marconi Company, which alone was a beneficiary of the contract. But they had speculated in those of its separate American cousin. Although no profits from the British company came to the shareholders in the American company, its shares nonetheless tended to rise or fall, sympathetically if irrationally, with those of the British company. In the outcome none of the ministers, and not even Liberal party funds, made money out of a series of complicated transactions. But the intention had been to secure speculative gains from volatile, high-profile shares, even if the execution had been incompetent.

The main fault of the ministers however was not greed or incompetence or the choice of inappropriate investments but *suppressio veri*. Following a spate of rumours over the summer of 1912, the House of Commons in October was considering a motion to set up a Select Committee to investigate. Both Lloyd George and Isaacs intervened in the debate to deny categorically that they had ever had any interest, direct or indirect, in the English Marconi Company. What they said was formally correct but they signally omitted to inform the House of their American transactions. These came to light only in early 1913 when Isaacs and Samuel brought a successful libel action (in the English courts) against the Paris newspaper *Le Matin*. This new revelation created, to say the least, an unfavourable impression which considerably outweighed the effect of the success of the libel action. The Select Committee dragged on until the summer, when its Liberal majority eventually produced an exculpatory report which, aided by a generous and powerful speech from Asquith, was reluctantly accepted by the House, but only after a bitter debate and a division on straight party lines.

Churchill's role in the affair was at least threefold. First, he was the fifth minister against whom the finger of unsubstantiated rumour was turned. As a result he was summoned to appear before the Select Committee. Its members probably regretted this decision. Churchill vigorously denounced them:

am I to understand that every person, Minister or Member of Parliament, whose name is mentioned by current rumour and brought forward by a witness [the editor of the *Financial News*] who says he does not believe it, is to be summoned before you to give a categorical denial to charges which, as I have pointed out, have become grossly insulting by reason of the fact that the Minister in question, it is suggested, has concealed up to this moment what his position was? . . . I am grieved beyond words that a Committee of my fellow-members in the House of Commons should have thought it right to lend their sanction to the putting of such a question. Having said so much, I will proceed to answer your question. I have never at any time, in any circumstances, directly or indirectly, had any investments or any interests of any kind – however vaguely it may be described – in Marconi telegraphic shares, or any other shares of that description, in this or any other country in the inhabited globe.[2]

Churchill's second intervention in the affair was to bring off the inspired political coup of persuading F. E. Smith to appear for Samuel in the *Matin* libel action, which in turn led to the sardonic and silver-tongued Sir Edward Carson, the leader of Unionist intransigence in Ireland and himself a former Attorney-General, appearing for Isaacs. This not only took part of the politics out of a 'political' case (usually a wise thing to do before judges) but also half hobbled the Conservative exploitation of the issue. It ensured the House of Commons silence of two of the most effective Tory speakers and somewhat embarrassed their front-bench colleagues.

Third, and most importantly, Churchill exhibited both privately and publicly every manifestation of continued warm friendship for Lloyd George over this testing period. At the end of September 1912, just before the first difficult debate in the House of Commons, he appeared off Criccieth in *Enchantress* and took Lloyd George with his wife and daughter Megan for a west-coast cruise. In the following July, after the Select Committee report and the awkward debate in the House of Commons, he made a passionate speech in the Chancellor's defence (and incidentally that of the others implicated) at a dinner of the National Liberal Club:

But when we know on the evidence, on the mature conclusion even of their most bitter opponents, that no stain of any kind rests upon their integrity or upon their character, what kind of curs should we be if we allowed them to be trampled down by a campaign of calumny and slander unequalled in recent annals? And those who thought that this event and the cruel suffering it has entailed upon them would make any difference to their career of usefulness in public life and in the Liberal party, little knew the constant, discriminating and fearless loyalty of democracy to its leaders. They reckoned without the National Liberal Club; they reckoned without our noble chairman [the Marquess of Lincolnshire]; and they reckoned without the Prime Minister of this country. They reckoned without that broad yet searching justice which great peoples, and this people above all others, mete out to men who have served them well.[3]

After this general defence of his colleagues, which showed that Churchill knew how to play upon a National Liberal Club audience as did practically no one else until it came to the great oration in the same room of the Club, seven years later and after her father's victory in the Paisley bye-election, of his friend the more faithfully Liberal Violet Bonham Carter, he then turned specifically to the main object of his speech: 'the Chancellor of the Exchequer is more bitterly hated in certain powerful classes – certain great organized confederated group-ings of public opinion – he is more bitterly hated and more relentlessly pursued than even Mr Gladstone was in the great days of 1886.'

Churchill rounded the matter off with the most violent attack upon Lord Robert Cecil, the brother of his friend Hugh Cecil. Robert Cecil, later such a pillar of the League of Nations that he bequeathed his London house to the internationalist Labour MP Philip Noel-Baker, had apparently been going round saying that he had further substantial but unprovable evidence against Lloyd George which could not be put in the report but which he would impart privately to any MP who asked him. 'A more disgraceful statement never issued from the lips of a member of a Select Committee of the House of Commons,' Churchill thundered. 'And if anything could make it more odious and contempti-ble it is that it should be uttered by one who has been fraudulently posing as a fair-minded, impartial man, and lending a smooth pretence of gentlemanly culture to the dirty work he had set himself to do.'[4]

Lloyd George was very vulnerable at the time, but it was not Churchill's rhetoric which saved him. The crucial factor was the firm support of the Prime Minister. Asquith did not approve of the behaviour of the peccant ministers, although there is evidence that he became aware of the transactions in the American shares by the time of the October (1912) debate. It was 'lamentable' and 'so difficult to defend', he told the King;[5] and to Venetia Stanley he referred to 'certain follies wh. Rufus Isaacs and Ll. George have committed'.[6] He nonetheless did not regard it as a resigning matter. He was never very sympathetic towards money-making, although he liked a generous lifestyle and could not prevent his wife spending money they did not possess. His attitude was illustrated by his verbal precision during a wartime gathering of ministers when it was reported that a well-known trading firm had made a 'killing' on some commodity deal. 'Disgusting,' Asquith said, whereupon a more free-market colleague defended the deal, saying it was not disgraceful; it was how markets operated. 'I did not say "disgraceful",' was Asquith's concluding remark, 'I said disgusting.'[7] And so he found the Marconi activities. But he was never harsh towards the frailties of others, and no doubt he did not wish to weaken his government by losing a Chancellor of the exceptional flair of Lloyd George.

So he saved the man who, three and a half years later, was to bring his long premiership to an unwelcome end and to step into his shoes.* There is no doubt about the value of the protection which Asquith gave to Lloyd George. He did it with firmness and authority. But he did it without warmth. His tone was well caught by a post-Marconi remark recorded by Masterman, when both were sitting on the front bench listening to a Lloyd George intervention. 'I think the idol's wings are a bit chipped,' the Prime Minister said. 'A bit chipped,' he repeated with a characteristic shrug of the shoulders.[8]

Churchill, by contrast, performed his less crucial supporting act with warmth. It did not need the Celtic side of Lloyd George's kaleidoscopic nature to appreciate this, but it probably made him appreciate it the more, and for it to remain a crucial factor in their relationship both over the strains during the winter of 1913–14 when Churchill's estimates went above £50 million and during the days of late July and early August of the latter year when they began on differing sides as to whether Britain should enter the war.

Relevant to the effect of their relationship on Churchill getting his naval estimates through without resignation in early 1914 was an interesting exchange of Cabinet table notes (always a strong Churchill–Lloyd George habit) on 1 July of that year. Lloyd George wrote: 'Philip Snowden in his weekly letter today [presumably a published article] says that had there been any other Chancellor of the Exchequer your Naval Bill would have been cut by millions.' Churchill replied: 'There would also have been another First Lord of the Admiralty! And who can say – if such gaps were opened – that there would not have been another government, which does not necessarily mean lower estimates.'[9]

---

* It is a little reminiscent, although with many variations of character and circumstance, of Edward Heath's recollection of how he contemplated dropping Margaret Thatcher from his government when in 1971 she had a great bout of unpopularity as 'Mrs Thatcher, milk-snatcher'.

To be on friendly terms with the Chancellor (or, to put it in more brutal *Realpolitik* terms, to be a colleague whom the Chancellor does not wish to lose from the government) is a major asset for a heavy-spending minister. But more important still was Churchill's relationship with Asquith. Later events should not be allowed to obscure the fact that Asquith was a very powerful Prime Minister in 1914. He had been 'chief' for six years, had led the government through great storms to considerable achievements, and had repeatedly shown himself a resourceful arbiter of Cabinet disputes. This he mostly did not by petty manipulation but by the calm exercise of a natural authority. He was seen to have knowledge and judgement, insight and tolerance, never negligible qualities. This authority was as much recognized by his two subordinates who were to rise to a fame greater than his own, Lloyd George and Churchill, as by the other ministers. And insofar as there was a balance of power it had been temporarily tilted in Asquith's favour and away from Lloyd George by the Marconi affair. It is a mistake to think that when one person, years later, grows greater than the man to whom he was previously subordinate this must always have been apparent in their relationship.

During those pre-war ministerial years Churchill treated Asquith with spontaneous respect. There is only one seriously critical passage about him in all the vast outpouring of Churchillian notes, letters, memoranda and other writings. That related to alcohol, a subject on which Churchill both by inclination and by fear of throwing stones out of glasshouses was in general tolerant. While still Home Secretary he wrote to his wife on 22 April 1911:

> On Thursday night the P.M. was vy bad: & I squirmed with embarrass-ment. He could hardly speak: and many people noticed his condition. He continues most friendly & benevolent, & entrusts me with everything [in the House] after dinner. Up till that time he is at his best – but thereafter! It is an awful pity & only the persistent freemasonry of the House of Commons prevents a scandal. I like the old boy and admire both his intellect & his character. But what risks to run. . . . The next day he was serene efficient undisturbed.[10]

What was Asquith's attitude to Churchill? To what extent did he appreciate that he had on his hands a man with the potential to be the most massive political figure of the century? He thought such a flower-ing possible, but far from certain, perhaps not even likely, should probably be the answer. His real if partial admiration was tempered by amusement at Churchill's extravagances, and his appreciation, which was considerable, by bursts of exasperation. Despite these bursts and a persistent mild complaint that Churchill talked too much, certainly in Cabinet and often in social intercourse too, Asquith chose to spend more time in his company than in that of any other member of his government. Apart from three cruises in *Enchantress* (two in the Mediterranean and one in British waters) there were innumerable small dinner parties at 10 Downing Street or Admiralty House and frequent country Sundays. This, in spite or perhaps because of a twenty-year age gap, was far more than he saw of his old friends Haldane and Grey. Churchill's only rival as provider of and participant in *petit comité* entertainments for the Prime Minister was McKenna, and in McKenna's case, although Asquith put him number three in his order of Cabinet merit,* just above Churchill and Lloyd George, to which couple he gave a tied fourth place, it was his wife who was at least half the attraction. This did not apply in Churchill's case, for Clementine, as previously noted, although always a perfectly acceptable and coolly decorative companion, was never regarded as more than that in the Asquith pantheon. It was always her husband who was the centre of attraction, even when, as on 5 February 1914: 'I dined at the Churchills' last night. Winston slept placidly in his armchair while I played Bridge with Clemmie, Goonie [Lady Gwendeline Churchill] and the Lord Chief Justice [Rufus Isaacs, who had been promoted from Attorney-General, in spite of his peccadilloes].'[11]

Illustrative of Asquith's mild mockery of Churchill are the following comments:

> *May 1913* [during an *Enchantress* cruise in the Adriatic]. Winston is of course quite hopeless [at classical scholarship]: his most salient remark as

---

* This list, which he drew up as half as a joke for the amusement of Venetia Stanley, put Crewe at number one and Grey at number two. In the case of Crewe and McKenna at least it was a slightly depressing indication that causing no trouble to the Prime Minister is an easy route to Cabinet merit points.

This and many other Asquith comments come from his letters to Venetia Stanley (1887–1948), later Mrs Edwin Montague. She was the youngest daughter of Lord Sheffield, as Lord Stanley of Alderley at this stage chose to be known. Between 1912 and 1915 she attracted a flood of letters, at once romantic and gossipy, from the Prime Minister. Asquith rarely wrote less than twice and sometimes four times a day. The announcement of her engagement to Montagu on 12 May 1915 not only put an abrupt stop to this flood but also considerably upset the Prime Minister's judgement. Later in life Mrs Montague became a close but not so special a friend of Churchill, habitually giving a dinner party for his birthday.

we wandered through Diocletian's Palace at Spoleto was: 'I should like to bombard the swine.'

9 January 1914. He [Churchill] has been hunting the boar in Les Landes and has come back with his own tusks well whetted, and all his bristles in good order.

7 October 1914. His mouth waters at the sight and thought of K[itchener]'s new armies. 'Are those glittering commands to be entrusted to dug-out trash bred on the obsolete tactics of 25 years ago' – 'mediocrities, who have led a sheltered life mouldering in military routine' &c &c. For about ¼ of an hour he poured forth a ceaseless cataract of invective and appeal, and I much regretted that there was no shorthand writer within hearing – as some of his unpremeditated phrases were quite priceless. He was, however, quite three parts serious, and declared that a political career was nothing to him in comparison with military glory. . . . He is a wonderful creature, with a curious dash of schoolboy simplicity (quite unlike Edward Grey's) and what someone said of genius – 'a zigzag of lightning in the brain'.[12]

The last comment was of course on the borderline between Asquith being amused by Churchill and being deeply admiring of his idiosyncratic qualities. Another comment takes us further towards admiration. 'I can't help being fond of him,' the Prime Minister wrote on 27 October, still in that first autumn of the war, 'he is so resourceful and undismayed: two of the qualities I like best.'[13] To set against this, however, there was Churchill's unrelenting and self-centred loquaciousness. Thus on 8 December 1913: 'We had a Cabinet which lasted nearly 3 hours, 2¼ of which was occupied by Winston.' And on 1 August 1914, which was a very tense two-and-a-half-hour Saturday Cabinet with a batch of resignations looming as Britain edged towards war: 'It is no exaggeration to say that Winston occupied at least half the time.'[14] And as a more general comment on his conversational as opposed to his Cabinet habits: 'He never gets fairly alongside the person he is talking to because he is always much more interested in himself and his own preoccupations and his own topics. . . .'[15]

About Churchill's future Asquith was less than prescient. Yet in view of what happened to Churchill's career in the quarter-century from 1915 to 1940 Asquith's scepticism was nearly right, and would have been wholly so had the first German war not been followed by a second. The two most relevant passages in the Asquith letters are both from early 1915. 'It is not easy to see what W's career is going to be here,' he wrote on 9 February. 'He is to some extent blanketed by E. Grey and Ll George & has no personal following: he is always hankering after coalitions and odd regroupings, mainly designed (as one thinks) to bring in F. E. Smith & perhaps the Duke of Marlborough. I think his future one of the most puzzling enigmas in politics. . . .'[16] And again, on 25 March, when Asquith had been told that Churchill was intriguing to push Grey out of the Foreign Office and have Arthur Balfour brought in to replace him:

> He has him [Balfour] at the Admiralty night and day, and I am afraid tells him a lot of things which he ought to keep to himself, or at any rate to his colleagues. . . . It is a pity . . . that Winston hasn't a better sense of proportion and also a larger endowment of the instinct of loyalty. . . . I am really fond of him: but I regard his future with many misgivings. . . . He will never get to the top in English politics, with all his wonderful gifts; to speak with the tongues of men & angels, and to spend laborious days & nights in administration, is no good, if a man does not inspire trust.[17]

Despite these shafts of criticism, Churchill had a strong position with the Prime Minister up to and over the outbreak of war. Asquith had the sense and generosity to be proud of having both Lloyd George and Churchill in his government and was determined, subject to the preservation of his own proper authority, to lose neither of them. Even when the cards had been so thoroughly reshuffled that Churchill had first been profoundly disillusioned by Asquith in 1915–16, had then been a supplicator for office under Lloyd George, had become part of a government whose 'coupon' of endorsement (in the terminology of the time) had driven Asquith out of Parliament in 1918, and had effected a crab-like transition to the Conservative party which certainly did not command Asquith's support or admiration, the old Prime Minister was still subject to the dazzle of Churchill's company and conversation. 'The ennui of the long waits', he wrote after the wedding of Lady Elizabeth Bowes-Lyon and the Duke of York (the future King George VI) in 1923, 'were relieved for me by being next to Winston, who was in his best form and really amusing. Between two fugues (or whatever they are called) on the organ, he expounded to me his housing policy: "Build the house round the wife and mother: let her always have water on the boil: make her the central factor, the dominating condition of the situation", etc, etc – in his most rhetorical vein.'[18] And two years later, in 1925, Asquith again wrote benignly: 'At lunch we had amongst others,

Winston Churchill, who was in his best form: he is a Chimborazo or Everest among the sandhills of the Baldwin Cabinet.'[19]

In 1913–14 Churchill thus had the substantial advantages of an entente of affinity and to some extent of interest with Lloyd George and a secure store of affection, and half-respect, in the mind of Asquith. He needed them both, for he was far from popular with the tail of the Cabinet. His foremost enemy was Sir John Simon, a brilliant analytical lawyer whose sanctimonious appearance and manner constantly repelled friendship, and who had in October 1913 entered the Cabinet as Attorney-General. His junior position at the Cabinet table (it was indeed unusual for the Attorney to be there at all) did not prevent his offering Asquith advice about the dispensability of Churchill. 'The loss of W.C. though regrettable', he wrote in January 1914, 'is *not* by any means a splitting of party – indeed large Admiralty estimates may be capable of being carried *only* because W.C. has gone. The party would feel itself strengthened in its Radical element and among the Economists. . . .'[20]

Asquith was not inclined to take this complacent and narrow-sighted advice. Even though he had just promoted Simon, and was to do so again in May 1915, when he made him Home Secretary, he had his own by no means wholly favourable opinion of him. His private correspondence nicknames were 'the Impeccable' and 'Sir Sympne', neither of them obviously favourable. And 'the Impeccable' was made worse by the Prime Minister's liking for embroidering it with a little wordplay. 'The Impeccable, who . . . might almost be described as the Inevitable,'[21] he wrote after one or two doubtfully welcome social encounters. In the naval-estimates dispute his comment on Simon was that 'the Impeccable is the real & only Irreconcilable'.[22] There were however quite a few others who were prepared to climb on to Simon's high moral horse for at least a short journey. On 29 January 1914 he drafted an anti-naval-estimates letter to Asquith which he got co-signed by four other members of the Cabinet. A further two broadly agreed with the line, but did not want to be seen as too close to Simon.

The letter managed at once to undermine its own appeal for unity and to show a shrewd awareness of the way in which the wind was beginning to blow. It argued against not only the First Lord's figures but 'the plan now tentatively suggested by the Chancellor of the Exchequer for dealing with them'. This plan amounted to letting Churchill have most of what he wanted for 1914–15 in return for the promise and prospect of some reduction in subsequent years. This was the only basis on which the crisis could be resolved without resignations, for there can be no doubt that over his 1913–14 Christmas and New Year holiday in Italy and France Churchill had come fully to accept that he might well have to resign soon after his return. (Curiously enough, although resignations are much provoked by irritation at colleagues, it is easier to settle one's mind on intransigence when away, more or less alone, than when engaged in day-to-day arguments about a little more or a little less.) Churchill was determined to stick on his minimum central requirement of four new dreadnoughts to be laid down in 1914–15, and this is what the Lloyd George plan essentially enabled him to get. It was in many ways curiously similar to the famous 'compromise' of 1909, when the dispute between four or six led to the result of eight.

The promised economies of 1915–16 of course never took place, it being a different world by then. But there had in the meantime been a bewildering and not wholly creditable *chassé-croisé* by different members of the cast list. Only Asquith, consistently in favour of a strong navy, whether under McKenna or Churchill, but not thinking he could force it too roughly down the throats of his colleagues and followers, remained steady. He had a twenty-five-year commitment to Liberal Imperialism. Grey (with Haldane, who was on the same side) was his oldest friend in politics, Churchill was the young member of his Cabinet whose company he most enjoyed. He was not likely to go against all these affections.

A settlement was not achieved without a good deal of early-February brinkmanship and bad temper between Churchill and Lloyd George and even between Churchill and Asquith. It was Asquith who, building on the latent goodwill of Lloyd George, at this juncture saved Churchill. This was generously acknowledged by Churchill in *The World Crisis* where he wrote of the 'unwearying patience of the Prime Minister and ... his solid, silent support'.[23] The Prime Ministerial patience was fortified by an exceptional sense of when the opposing forces had exhausted themselves and would be willing to accept, with even an approach to goodwill, the settlement which Asquith had wanted from the beginning but against which some of them had been arguing so strenuously. This was achieved at the Cabinet of 11 February.

The only subject which, from the autumn of 1911 to August 1914, even started to compete with the navy for Churchill's attention was that of Irish Home Rule. It was the dominating domestic political issue of the period, at least from the time when the Home Rule Bill, freed from the certainty of futility but condemned to what proved to be the almost

equal frustration of a three-lap course by the Parliament Act, began
its first round of progress through the House of Commons with its
introduction on 11 April 1912. The Irish issue continued so strenuously
to dominate up to late July 1914 that ministers (and other politicians)
had great difficulty until a month after the Sarajevo assassination and
only a week or so before the plunge to Armageddon in turning their
attention from what Churchill described as 'the muddy by-ways of
Fermanagh and Tyrone' to the tyranny of mobilization schedules
encouraging first Austria against Serbia, then Russia against Austria,
then Germany against Russia, then France against Germany, and finally
Britain because of the invasion of Belgium and in fear of a German
crushing of France to move like zombies to the war which destroyed
Europe's world pre-eminence and killed sixty million of its citizens.

Churchill made three notable interventions in the Irish controversy.
The first was his visit to Belfast in February 1912. He had engaged
himself to speak in the Ulster Hall in that city, the citadel of Northern
Ireland Protestantism, and one which moreover had been the venue,
twenty-six years before, of his father's intransigent declaration of support for Ulster resistance. The original plan, to make matters worse,
was that Winston Churchill should there share the platform with John
Redmond, leader of the Irish Nationalist party (and also with Joseph
Devlin). As the object of his visit was to make the Home Rule Bill more
acceptable in the North, this did not seem sensible. Indeed the
impression is that Churchill had rashly entered into the commitment,
probably persuaded by the Chief Whip (the Master of Elibank had not
then departed for Bogotá), without giving much prior thought to the
consequences. His Cabinet colleague Augustine Birrell, who as Irish
Secretary was responsible for order in the whole of Ireland and had to
provide a vast security cover for the visit, was not consulted in advance
of the plans. Birrell wrote (on 28 January) a letter of fairly horrified
complaint of which the conciliatory crux was 'My own belief is that if
you hold a mid-day meeting in a tent, *no* blood will be shed. But the
moral is (for the Master's consumption): Leave Ireland alone in future.'[24]

By then the Ulster Unionist Council had met and had carried a
resolution noting 'with astonishment the deliberate challenge thrown
down by [the] intention to hold a Home Rule meeting in the centre of
the loyal city of Belfast', and expressing their 'resolve to take steps to
prevent its being held'.[25] This resolution it was assumed amounted to a
deliberate invitation to a major riot, and there were indeed menacing
police reports about 'great quantities of bolts and rivets having been

1. Lord and Lady Randolph Churchill in 1874, the year both of their marriage and of WSC's birth.

2. A very young cornet of hussars: 1895.

3. Blenheim Palace.

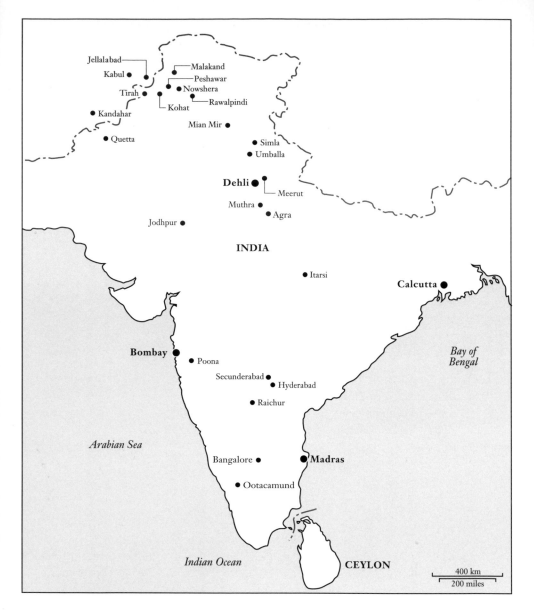

Jellalabad
Kabul ●
Malakand
Peshawar
Tirah
Nowshera
Kohat
Rawalpindi
● Kandahar
Mian Mir ●
● Quetta
● Simla
● Umballa
Dehli ●
Meerut
Muthra
● Agra
Jodhpur ●
INDIA
● Itarsi
Calcutta ●
Bay of Bengal
Bombay ●
● Poona
Secunderabad ●
● Hyderabad
● Raichur
Arabian Sea
Bangalore ●
●**Madras**
● Ootacamund
Indian Ocean
CEYLON
400 km
200 miles

4. Churchill's movements in India.

5. Unsuccessful candidate for Oldham, 1899.

6. A sulky prisoner of war in Pretoria.

7. The happy escaper arrives in Durban.

8. Churchill's escape route from
Pretoria, December 1899.

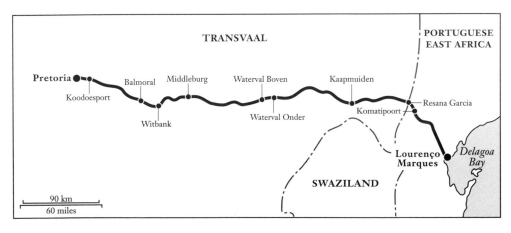

9. Future sovereign as boulevardier. King Edward VII two years before his accession.

10. With Consuelo, Duchess of Marlborough, at Blenheim (the only known mildly compromising photograph of WSC with a woman).

11. The budding Liberal statesman.

12. The Earl of Elgin who, as Colonial Secretary (1905–8), endeavoured to keep his under-secretary WSC under control.

13. Two earnest young men. WSC with his private secretary, Edward Marsh, in Malta, 1907.

14. Unsuccessful electioneering in Manchester at the 1908 bye-election.

15. Clementine Hozier at the time of her engagement to WSC in 1908.

16. Two Liberals in a hurry. Lloyd George and WSC, *circa* 1910.

17. Three Liberal ministers. Grey, WSC and Crewe leaving a Cabinet meeting in February 1910; they look very respectable revolutionaries.

18. WSC and his best man, Lord Hugh Cecil, arrive at St Margaret's, Westminster, for the wedding. Which looks more like the coachman?

19. WSC with the Kaiser at German army manoeuvres, 1909.

20. A day at the seaside. WSC and Clementine at Sandwich Bay on the eve of Armageddon, July 1914.

Above left and right: 21. WSC with two First Sea Lords: relaxed with 'Quite Concur' Prince Louis of Battenburg; chained together in tension with Lord Fisher.

22. On Horse Guards Parade with Arthur Balfour, 1915.

23. A December 1915 visit to the French army. WSC in his favourite and just acquired poilu's helmet with General Fayolle. Louis Spears third from the left.

Left: 24. WSC with his second-in-command, Sir Archibald Sinclair, on a visit to an Armentières photographer's studio, January 1916: the result achieving a texture worthy of Rodin's *Burghers of Calais.*

Above: 25. WSC unusually wearing his disliked Glengarry cap as a colonel commanding the 6th Battalion of the Royal Scots Greys.

26. Georges Clemenceau, *circa* 1917.

27. WSC with the Prince of Wales (later King Edward VIII), 1919. The beginning of a considerable but ultimately unrewarding friendship.

28. The cream of the coalition – all dressed up – to go where? *Left to right:* Worthington-Evans, WSC, Birkenhead, Lloyd George, Austen Chamberlain and Curzon. Churchill seems to have got for himself not merely more medals but a special Privy Counsellor's uniform, subtly different from the others.

29. The Cairo Conference, March 1921. Camel ride to the Sphinx. *Left to right:* Clementine, WSC, Gertrude Bell and Lawrence of Arabia.

30. Churchill's Middle Eastern 'durbar'. *Left to right:* Sir Herbert Samuel (High Commissioner in Palestine), WSC, Sir Perry Cox (High Commissioner in Mesopotamia) and General Aylmer Haldane.

31. Dundee, November 1922. A weak and emaciated Churchill
arrives only four days before the disastrous poll.

32. Narrow defeat in the Abbey division of Westminster, 20 March 1924.

33. A happy journey to Buckingham Palace for new seals of office, November 1924.

34. Parking his own car – almost for the last time – 1925.

35. Churchill, boar hunting at the Normandy house of the Duke of Westminster; pictured with Coco Chanel and his son, Randolph, 1927.

36. Bricklaying at Chartwell, 1928: WSC and his daughter Sarah.

37. Lunch party for Charlie Chaplin at Chartwell, September 1928. *Left to right:* Tom Mitford (the only brother of all those girls), Freddie Furneaux (later the 2nd Earl of Birkenhead), WSC, Clementine, Diana, Randolph and Chaplin.

38. Leaving 11 Downing Street to present his fifth budget, April 1929. Clementine is beside WSC, Randolph, Sarah and Robert Boothby are behind him.

39. Three Conservative ex-Chancellors after a Westminster Central Hall party meeting, October 1930: Austen Chamberlain, Robert Horne and WSC – formality, complacency and pugnacity.

40. WSC leaving hospital after his paratyphoid in September 1932, following his New York accident in December 1931.

41. WSC correcting proofs in his Chartwell study, February 1930.

42. The approach to war. WSC walking down Whitehall with his future Foreign Secretaries. *Right*, with Halifax, March 1938. *Above*, with Eden, August 1939.

abstracted from the [ship] yards'. This led to a very cold correspondence between Churchill and his second cousin the fifth Marquess of Londonderry, whose last appearance in the Churchill saga had been to try to hustle him out of the Carlton Club in 1904. The Belfast Unionist plan was however a little more subtle than a riot to destroy the meeting. The Ulster Hall had been booked by the local Liberals (of whom there were not very many) for 8 February. The Unionists retaliated by booking it for 7 February and planning a sit-in from which it would require great force to remove them over the next twenty-four hours.

Even Churchill came to recognize that a degree of tactical retreat was necessary. He had written on 13 January a long, careful letter to Redmond explaining that, while he would be happy to speak with him in an English city such as Manchester, he did not think it would be wise to do so together in Belfast. But ten days after that he was still telling Clementine that '*coûte que coûte* I shall begin punctually at 8 o'clock on the 8th of February to speak on Home Rule in Belfast'.[26] Two days later he started to move from that rigidity of time, and ended up, thanks to Birrell, at two o'clock on a Saturday afternoon in a vast marquee erected on the ground of the Celtic Football Club at the end of the Falls Road, in other words not in the city centre but deep in the working-class Catholic area. Fortunately it was a sodden Belfast afternoon, and the tent was not entirely waterproof. However an audience of 5,000, including the maybe slightly penitent Master of Elibank, Churchill's cousin Freddie Guest, who insisted on having a revolver in his pocket, and, somewhat surprisingly, Clementine Churchill, listened to him for over an hour.

The speech was not deliberately provocative, although it was highly courageous, by virtue both of being delivered at all and of taking head-on the comparison with his father's speech of 1886:

> It is in a different sense that I adopt and repeat Lord Randolph's words 'Ulster will fight and Ulster will be right'. Let Ulster fight for the dignity and honour of Ireland; let her fight for the reconciliation of races and for the forgiveness of ancient wrongs; let her fight for the unity and consolidation of the British empire; let her fight for the spreading of charity, tolerance and enlightenment among men. Then indeed Ulster will fight and Ulster will be right.[27]

This was a splendid attempt at squaring a circle and entirely to Churchill's credit. The question which remains is why Clementine was there. She had been having an early winter off, still semi-convalescing from the birth of Randolph, she was soon to have a miscarriage, and Churchill had been subject to a plea, at once passionate and rational, from 'the Master' that she should not go. 'It will be at once said by the enemy that we are all attempting to lessen *our* difficulties by her presence. Her great courage and *spirit* naturally impel her to accompany you – but I assure you it is a mistake.'[28] But she came, and a perfectly horrid time was had by all. They crossed from Stranraer by a night boat made hideous by suffragettes tramping round and round the boat and shouting 'votes for women' outside their cabin. They came into Belfast from Larne by train, with policemen every few yards along the track, and established themselves for four or five hours in the old Great Central Hotel. Fists were shaken as they passed through the lobby and a hostile crowd of 10,000 shouted in the street beneath their windows throughout the morning (the downpour had not then started). Their drive to the meeting was accompanied by even more venom until they crossed the religious divide and threats turned to friendly waves. Ulster has long been good at sectarianism, but it was curious although admirable that the son of Lord Randolph and the granddaughter of an East of Scotland Presbyterian countess should have got themselves so much on the 'wrong side of the tracks'. After the meeting they were smuggled by an unexpected route back to Larne, and so to the safety of Scotland. It could only have been that Clementine Churchill had insisted on coming, and that Winston Churchill had not wished to frustrate her. It would have been totally out of character for the intrepid hero of Swat, Omdurman and the South African armoured train to have brought her along as petticoat protection.

Perhaps unfortunately he did not proceed to London from Stranraer but turned north to Glasgow and there delivered a speech remarkably ill calculated to move the Germans towards the 'naval holiday' which he purported to be seeking. It was in a way quite a subtle but at the same time maddeningly bland argument which he there presented.

> The British Navy is to us a necessity and ... the German Navy is to them more in the nature of a luxury. Our naval power involves British existence. It is existence to us; it is expansion to them. We cannot menace the peace of a single continental hamlet, no matter how great and supreme our Navy may become. But, on the other hand, the whole fortunes of our race and Empire, the whole treasure accumulated during so many centuries of sacrifice and achievement, would perish and be swept utterly away if our naval supremacy were to be impaired. It is the British Navy which makes Great Britain a great power. But Germany was

a great power, respected and honoured all over the world, before she had a single ship. . . .[29]

The phrase *Luxus Flotte*, which may or may not have been an exact translation, was treated in Germany as a dismissive provocation, and Churchill himself when he got back to London detected a distinct chill among his Cabinet colleagues. His whole Celtic swing had been a hyper-typical Churchill enterprise: in Belfast a fearless radical provoking the Ulster Protestants, and in Glasgow a super-patriot provoking both the Germans and the pacific wing of the Liberal party; and it was also typical that the concentration of these two major and disparate speeches into thirty hours should have left little pause for intermediate reflection.

Churchill's second Irish intervention was in September 1913 when he was staying at Balmoral as minister in attendance and overlapped with Bonar Law, then in his second year as Conservative leader. (Monarchs in those days subjected themselves to more social intercourse with politicians.) In general Churchill, like Asquith, thought little of Law. A teetotaller whose favourite food was rice pudding was not likely to arouse his enthusiasm. On this visit, however, a combination of Highland air and royal hospitality led them to a constructive talk. Both, in their different styles, were more eager for an Irish accommodation than could have been easily guessed from their public pronouncements. Churchill reported to Asquith, and this led to three semi-secret meetings between the Prime Minister and Bonar Law. These meetings were devoted to exploring the possibility of some form of special treatment for Ulster, or at least for that part of the province that had a clear Protestant majority. This, Churchill claimed, had long been the solution he had advocated. In *The World Crisis*, for instance, he was to write: 'From the earliest discussions on the Home Rule bill in 1909 the Chancellor of the Exchequer and I had always advocated the exclusion of Ulster on a basis of county option or some similar process.'[30]

In a record which Austen Chamberlain made of a long Irish conversation when Churchill had taken him on a short *Enchantress* cruise in November 1913, the same point is made, with the additional information that in a Cabinet committee Loreburn, Lord Chancellor until 1912, had shot it down. The explanation does not entirely add up, for it is difficult to believe that Lloyd George and Churchill, two of the most powerful and certainly most eloquent members of the government, and dealing with an issue which was not the strict departmental business of any of them, would not have outgunned a dour Scottish lawyer who was more a relic of the Campbell-Bannerman leadership than a core member of the Asquith administration. What however is indisputable is that, by the autumn of 1913 at latest, Churchill in spite of his endemic tendency to revert to public truculence, was an active private seeker of an Ulster accommodation. Apart from his Bonar Law and Chamberlain talks he was, it need hardly be said, in close touch with F. E. Smith, who was in many respects his mirror image on the subject, acting as Carson's 'galloper' in Ulster but nonetheless fearful of the consequences if an accommodation was not reached.

In his third major Irish intervention Churchill reverted to public truculence. This was in March 1914. The Asquith–Bonar Law talks, like so many attempts to find Ulster solutions, had run into the sand, and attention switched to military matters. Were the Ulster Volunteers (a paramilitary anti-Home Rule Protestant organization) about to attempt some coup against the (official) arms depots in the province? And on 20 March there began the so-called mutiny at the Curragh (the main military depot of Ireland, close to Dublin), which was however much more an affair of bungling generals than of serious military insurrection against possible orders to enforce Home Rule on Ulster. Into this incendiary atmosphere Churchill threw the burning brand of his Bradford speech of 14 March. He had been engaged to speak there for some time, and it could not have been foreseen how apposite (or inappropriate) the timing was to be. He approached it with all the respect that he normally applied to a major oratorical occasion. There is an unforgettable description of his arriving at Bradford station late that afternoon, accompanied by two oxygen cylinders, as well as no doubt by a suitable retinue, the task of one member of which was to pump the oxygen into him before the meeting so as to secure an adequate level of exuberance.

In spite of this stimulus most of what he said was responsible. His central purpose was to warn those who might seek to challenge parliamentary decisions by force. If that was to be done, he concluded, 'let us go forward and put these grave matters to the proof'. Like many of the most famous phrases it contained a substantial element of imprecision. Who were 'we', to where were we to go forward, and how exactly were these matters, grave or otherwise, to be put to the proof? But it sounded suitably menacing on the side of constitutionalism, and was backed up by his ordering 'the forthcoming practice' of the 3rd Battle Squadron to take place off the Isle of Arran, in other words only an hour or so's sailing from the Northern Irish coast.

The speech and the naval deployment were regarded as highly

provocative by the Unionists. They formed the basis of a most virulent attack upon Churchill by Edward Carson in the House of Commons five days later, the prelude to Carson's finely timed and dramatic departure to catch the Belfast mail train, leaving deliberate doubt as to whether he had gone to proclaim an insurgent provisional government. (He had not, for Carson's command over gesture was, fortunately, always greater than his cold courage.) They added a few inches to the stalagmite of Conservative dislike and distrust of Churchill, which was already of a formidable length. Equally however the speech strongly reinforced his position with Liberal militants inside and outside the House of Commons. It showed that he was not just a minister of high naval estimates. The speech also did him good with the head of the government. It embedded itself in Asquith's memory sufficiently for him to include a long extract from it in his *Fifty Years of Parliament* (1926), admittedly a fairly scissors-and-paste compilation, 'as proof that the Twentieth Century can hold its own in an oratorical competition'.[31] The contrast between Churchill's search for compromise in private and his sabre-rattling in public was very characteristic of his style. He always believed in magnanimity from a position of strength.

The Irish problem ground on through a conference at Buckingham Palace on 21–24 July, which proved just as futile as the Asquith–Law conversations of eight months before. But the growing European crisis increasingly distracted attention from it, and finally overwhelmed it entirely. Amid the gathering storm, Churchill was a consistent force for intervention and ultimately for war. In successive – ever more tense – Cabinets, he resolutely supported Grey in arguing for intervention should the neutrality of Belgium be compromised and the security of France imperilled. On 28 July he ordered the Fleet to remain together at the end of the manoeuvres, and in the following days took a series of further on-the-edge-of-his-authority mobilization decisions. 'Winston very bellicose and demanding immediate mobilization', Asquith reported to Venetia Stanley after Cabinet on 1 August.[32]

Churchill also launched a sustained friendly bombardment of Lloyd George, to keep his erstwhile radical ally in government and prevent a serious Cabinet split. The anti-war resignations of Burns and Morley were of relatively minor importance. Lloyd George's departure, by contrast, would have been potentially catastrophic. 'Remember your part at Agadir. I implore you to come and bring your mighty aid to the discharge of our duty,' Churchill urged Lloyd George in a note across the Cabinet table on 1 August. He added a further argument –

'Afterwards by participating in the peace we can regulate the settlement and prevent a renewal of 1870 conditions'[33] – which was not to be one of his happier predictions. At Cabinet the following day there was another note from Churchill across the table: 'Together we can carry a wide social policy ... which you taught me. The naval war will be cheap: not more than 25 millions a year.'[34] These later predictions were no better than the first, but by now Lloyd George was moving behind Asquith and Grey towards a declaration of war should Germany invade Belgium.

Two days later German troops crossed the Belgian frontiers and set off a European conflagration without parallel in modern history. For Churchill there was no sense of foreboding, let alone gloom. Asquith wrote privately after the Cabinet meeting on 4 August which resolved to issue the midnight ultimatum to Berlin: 'Winston, who has got on all his war-paint, is longing for a sea fight in the early hours of tomorrow morning, resulting in the sinking of the Goeben.* The whole thing fills me with sadness.'[35] For Churchill it was a moment of exhilaration, the supreme contingency for which he had been consciously preparing himself since his teenage days as a subaltern and his subsequent involvement in war reporting from every colonial trouble spot he could get to. Yet even in his dreams he cannot have conceived of the role, good and bad, that two wars would play in the rest of his political life.

* A German battle cruiser which had been shelling French defences off the coast of Algeria.

PART THREE

THE NOONTIDE WAS BRONZE

1914–1918

13

A FLAILING FIRST LORD

IN THE FIRST DAYS of the war Churchill lived a super-charged life. Clementine remained in Norfolk in their rented house in Overstrand throughout August and into September as the birth of their third child, Sarah, approached. It was curious, in spite of her fragile pregnancies, that he did not persuade her to come back to London. She was on one of the most exposed bits of the east coast, and several of his pre-war Cabinet memoranda had been heavy with scenarios of German raids and even full-scale invasion.

However, she stayed at Overstrand, and he was therefore on his own in Admiralty House, working feverishly and sleeping little. When he was not at his desk he stalked about Whitehall and Horse Guards Parade totally engaged and with a mixture of scowls of destiny and beams of happiness on his face. He was the one minister who felt instinctively at home with war and with the politics of war. To the 'respectable Liberal politicians', as he was to describe them in *The World Crisis*, war, even if necessary, was a hideously unfamiliar landscape, and when Kitchener joined the Cabinet as Secretary for War on 6 August, occupying the seat between the Prime Minister and Churchill which had hitherto been John Morley's, he was obviously conversant with some types of war, but he was totally at sea with politics. Churchill therefore started from a position of unique strength. Even *The Times*, not normally his warmest press support, had written on the morning of 4 August that he was the one minister 'whose grasp of the situation and whose efforts to meet it have been above all praise'. He expressed his gratitude by having its editor Geoffrey Robinson (later to change his name to Dawson) to dinner at Admiralty House that evening, together with his own brother and mother, who, her marriage to Cornwallis-West having foundered the year before, had reverted to the designation of Lady Randolph Churchill. She was now sixty years old, and had become a rather minor figure in his life compared with her role as his central confidante around 1900. The choice of family company on this watershed evening pointed to a certain loneliness without Clementine and the addition of Robinson paid vivid testimony to the (short-term) national mood which Churchill was later to illustrate by quoting Dryden:

> Men met each other with erected look,
> The steps were higher that they took,
> Friends to congratulate their friends made haste,
> And long-inveterate foes saluted as they passed.[1]

All that Churchill needed for his position of strength and opportunity to consolidate itself was for the ships, many of which he had so expensively constructed, to secure the triumphs which were widely and confidently expected. This they mostly stubbornly failed to do. Fate, and maybe one or two other factors, ran against them. The first setback was in the Mediterranean, and came right at the beginning. The little humiliation was complete by 9–10 August. No British ships had been lost, but they and their senior officers had all been made to look like blundering players in a game of blind man's bluff by the new battle cruiser *Goeben*, with her escorting light cruiser consort *Breslau*, which were the only German warships in the Mediterranean. By 10 August, after a series of ineffective Royal Navy chases over much of that Sea, *Goeben* and *Breslau* were safely in Constantinople, which had been their destination throughout, although unsuspected by the British. There they were nominally sold to the Turks and made a more than nominal contribution to Turkish entry into the war on the German side on 1 November.

The whole chapter of events was an unfortunate beginning to the naval war. One admiral, Troubridge, was court-martialled, although acquitted. Another, Berkeley Milne, was placed on half-pay and remained on it for the rest of the war (Fisher thought, perhaps not very seriously, that he ought to have been shot). And Beatty, then Vice-Admiral commanding the Battle Cruiser Squadron of the Grand Fleet, well summed up the effect on naval morale when he wrote to his wife on 11 October: 'To think that it is to the Navy to provide the first and only instance of failure. God it makes me sick.'[2]

The clear impression left on a lay mind by the reading for the first time of the details of those unfortunate events is that the instructions from the Admiralty did nothing but harm. Had communications been ruptured the not very good Flag Officers on the spot could not have done worse and might have done better. Yet the responsibility for almost all the unfortunate messages lay directly with Churchill. And this was so not only in the formal sense that a departmental minister is nominally responsible for everything that happens within the department. It was true also in the much more specific sense that Churchill had deliberately created a highly centralized system for the exercise, jointly with the First Sea Lord, of personal operational authority. He described it with pride in *The World Crisis*: 'Robed in the august authority of centuries of naval tradition and armed with the fullest knowledge available, the Board of Admiralty wielded unchallenged power.' And within the Admiralty that 'unchallenged power' was exercised, not by the whole Board, but by a partnership of the civilian minister and the principal professional sailor, the First Lord and the First Sea Lord.

> I claimed and exercised an unlimited power of suggestion and initiative over the whole field, subject only to the approval and agreement of the First Sea Lord on all operative orders. . . . Within the limits of our agreed policy either he or I gave in writing* authority for telegrams and decisions which the Chief of the Staff might from hour to hour require. Moreover, it happened in a large number of cases that seeing what ought to be done and confident of the agreement of the First Sea Lord, I myself drafted the telegrams and decisions in accordance with our policy, and the Chief of the Staff took them personally to the First Sea Lord for his concurrence before despatch.[3]

This system, as Churchill himself points out, was in total contrast to that which prevailed in Germany. In Berlin the naval minister, despite the fact that he was Admiral von Tirpitz, the virtual creator of the Kaiser's navy, was confined to administrative matters and cut off from any operational control of the fleets. There may be room for doubt as to how far Prince Louis of Battenberg, steady if undynamic an admiral although he was, was able to provide a balanced partnership, particularly after xenophobia got at his throat. Not only was Churchill one of the most formidable personalities of the century but he was also argumentatively dexterous to an unusual degree. He had two barrels to his gun. He was famous and no doubt intimidated senior naval officers ('hypnotized' was the word employed by one), who were used to measuring

---

* One of the features of Churchill's administration, which persisted into and throughout the Second World War, was his devotion to written instructions. This made his pattern of administration tidier than it would otherwise have been. It was a surprising attitude for someone who liked talking so much. Fortunately he was as fluent and urgently energetic at dictation and with his own pen as he was in his conversation.

relative broadside capacity, with the amount of political firepower which he commanded. He also possessed an argumentative capacity, semi-polemical, which made him almost impossible to gainsay in any personal encounter. He must therefore be regarded as having been in full, almost unilateral control of the Admiralty during the first few months of the war.

Those months began badly. And, as is the way, the quiet triumph of ferrying unmolested the six divisions of the British regular army to France, which was complete by 19 August, attracted no comparable notice. This was a problem endemic in naval superiority. The 'inter-diction' role of the Royal Navy was not one to excite public plaudits. There was a basic contradiction between the sophisticated theory of seapower and the desire of the British press (and maybe public) to see victories won. The major purposes of naval superiority, which were to secure safe communication between England and the expeditionary force in Northern France, to render the German High Seas Fleet a verbal contradiction by bottling it up in its home ports, to deny western imports to Germany, and to maintain secure trade access from the outer world to Britain, were none of them headline-catching issues. They were crucial to the avoidance of defeat, but they did not produce setpiece victories. It was only in June 1916, when the German fleet came out to engage in the drawn Battle of Jutland, and in early 1917, when the U-boat threat nearly broke the North Atlantic link, that these major objectives were at serious risk. Churchill was instinctively nearer to the 'death and glory' boys of Fleet Street than to the most sophisti-cated naval strategists. Indeed there is a view that he always saw ships as cavalry squadrons whose role was to charge rather than to block.[4] Negative achievements therefore failed to satisfy and positive ones proved disappointingly elusive throughout the five months until the end of 1914.

On the morning of 22 September three elderly British armoured cruisers, known collectively as the 'Cressys', were sunk by submarine attacks off the Dutch coast within an hour or so. Almost 1,400 men were lost. The ships had been in a rash position and Admiralty instructions, conveyed in a telegram of 19 September were again to blame, although not on this occasion Churchill himself. He had not seen or approved the fatal telegram, although Battenberg had, and the dyarchy which Churchill had created for the Admiralty was therefore under test. The result was a double wound. Churchill got most of the public blame, at a time when his reputation was already on the decline.

And Battenberg suffered most of the private guilt, which together with the mounting attacks on his lack of 'Britishness' led to his resignation five weeks later. This coincided with the loss by mine or torpedo of the 1912 dreadnought *Audacious* off Lough Swilly on the coast of Northern Ireland and therefore deep in what should have been secure home waters. Half a week later Rear Admiral Cradock lost the Battle of Coronel, off the coast of Chile. He himself perished, as did 1,600 of his men and the cruisers *Monmouth* and *Good Hope*. This defeat was revenged in December by the Battle of the Falklands when Admiral Sturdee sank four German warships, including the armoured cruisers *Gneisenau* and *Scharnhorst*, with very light British casualties, but the five-week interval was uncomfortable waiting time.

On 3 November Yarmouth was lightly bombarded; and then on 16 December there was a more serious bombardment of Scarborough, Whitby and Hartlepool. The assault on Scarborough, that town of terraces and later of conferences, led to some casualties, a lot of rubble and Osbert Sitwell's temporarily famous book *Before the Bombardment*. Worse than the actual damage was the fear (misplaced as it turned out) that the bombardments were merely the preliminary to a more serious German onslaught on the coast of England, quite apart from the press and public affront at the impudence of the attacks against the shoreline of the greatest naval power in the world.

Altogether it was a disappointing autumn for the navy. Given its vast size – more than a thousand craft of one sort or another throughout the world – the losses were not serious and the setbacks were not defeat-threatening. But nor were they morale-enhancing for the 150,000 officers and men (in 1913; rising to 400,000 by 1918) who manned these thousand ships and their Admiralty headquarters. And none of them was as exposed to criticism as their civilian First Lord, who had a host of political enemies, and a number of naval ones too. It was not surprising that Churchill's beaming face and exhilarated step of early August did not entirely survive into the darkening days of mid-autumn. As he himself was subsequently to write, 'I do not remember any period when the weight of the War seemed to press more heavily on me than those months of October and November, 1914.'[5]

It should not be thought that this weight destroyed his courage and resilience. His Prime Minister's most notable tribute to him – 'he is so resourceful & undismayed: two of the qualities I like best' – was penned as late as 27 October. Nevertheless there was a general awareness that his star was not shining as brightly as it had been. After a Cabinet meeting of 4 November Asquith wrote to the King: 'The Cabinet are of opinion that this incident [the Coronel defeat], like the escape of the *Goeben*, the loss of the *Cressy* and her two sister-cruisers . . . is not creditable to the officers of the Navy.'[6] What however Churchill would probably have most minded was that at just about this time David Beatty, who in 1911–13 as his Naval Secretary had been an intimate part of his official family, was writing to his wife: 'If we only had a Kitchener at the Admiralty we could have done so much and the present state of chaos in naval affairs would never have existed. It is inconceivable the mistakes and blunders we have made and are making.'[7]

A curious feature of this first autumn of the war was that Churchill, who had been obsessed by the navy in peacetime and had become, in Lloyd George's already quoted words of complaint, 'a water creature, [forgetting] . . . that most of us live on land', allowed much of his attention to flicker back towards his early fascination with land campaigns. Not only did he assume an excessive responsibility for issuing detailed naval operational orders, but he believed that he could do it while reserving part of his attention for the clash of armies in France and Belgium and with even occasional yearning to be a general rather than First Lord of the Admiralty. 'No one department, hardly one war, was enough for him . . .' was a comment from his friend F. E. Smith.

This dichotomy most exhibited itself in Churchill's Antwerp adventure of 3–7 October. The French victory in the Battle of the Marne on 6–10 September had turned the German left flank and prevented Moltke's advance being a walkover as Rundstedt's was to be in 1940. There followed the so-called race to the sea, with digging in on both sides along a front which, in spite of tremendous efforts and appalling casualties, was not much to vary until 1918. What was crucial to British supply and communications generally was that when both sides got to the sea the essential ports should be left in Allied hands. The core needs were Boulogne, Calais and Dunkirk, although it would also have been desirable to keep the Germans out of Ostend and Antwerp. The last was hardly a Channel port, but it nonetheless had a special importance, because controlling the mouth of the Scheldt had been a cardinal objective of British policy for at least 200 years, and because the Belgian government had retreated there from Brussels. The fall of Antwerp would therefore mean the end of effective organized resistance on Belgian soil.

Churchill was already in the habit of paying frequent visits to Dunkirk, where he had established both a naval air squadron and several armoured car squadrons (under naval command), which he had grandly constituted by requisitioning all available Rolls-Royces. With some armour plating (of a sort familiar to British ambassadors in the late 1970s when terrorist attacks became a threat) and the provision of equipment for 'bridging small cuts in the road', Churchill saw them as early prototypes of the tank. On the night of 2 October Churchill was on one of his Dunkirk excursions when his special train was stopped and reversed in Kent. His own account[8] implies, a little implausibly in view of his commanding and indeed irascible temperament, that he was unaware of the reason until it arrived back at Victoria Station and he was summoned to a meeting in Kitchener's house in Carlton Gardens, at which Edward Grey, Battenberg and a senior Foreign Office official (Tyrrell) were also present. (Asquith was in Cardiff addressing a recruiting meeting; Prime Ministers, even ones as non-demagogic as Asquith, are always in danger of finding themselves deployed representationally rather than executively.) The Carlton Gardens conclave was prompted by the receipt of a telegram from the British minister to Belgium saying that 'the [Belgian] Superior Council of War in the presence of the King [Albert]' had decided to evacuate Antwerp on the next day and fall back on Ostend. Without reluctance Churchill accepted to go immediately to Antwerp to investigate the situation on the spot, and to try to rally the Belgian government. How little persuading he required can easily be imagined – by about 1.30 a.m. he was back at Victoria Station and in his waiting special train.

He may have been over-eager for this adventure, but there is no doubt that he went with the full blessing of the Secretary of State for War and, more reluctantly, of the Foreign Secretary. The Belgians were also promised substantial military reinforcements, although these included parts of the almost totally untrained Royal Naval Division, a private army of Churchill's. A battalion which went to Antwerp was commanded by his mother's ex-husband George Cornwallis-West, and contained the Prime Minister's second son, Arthur (or Oc), an exceptionally good soldier who rose to be a 'civilian' brigadier-general. Churchill took until 3.00 p.m. to arrive in one of his commandeered Rolls-Royces. But once in Antwerp he threw himself, with a mixture of galvanic energy, total indifference to his own safety and considerable concern for his own comfort, into organizing Belgium's resistance. He persuaded King Albert and his Prime Minister that they should try to hold out for ten days, a period which would be invaluable for the consolidation of the left of the British line between Lille and the sea.

In fact they managed to do so only for five, but these days Churchill considered to have been time well bought, for without them he believed that Dunkirk would have fallen. The counterbalancing risk was the loss of the bulk of the Belgian army, although at the end much of this was extricated and available to fight again further back. Some 2,500 British, including many of Churchill's untrained Naval Division, were either lost in battle, captured by the Germans or forced into internment in the Netherlands.

Churchill in retrospect became uncertain about the role which he himself had played. At the time he was swept along by the drama and the opportunity for conducting a little war of his own. His status was wholly ambiguous, well epitomized by the fact that he moved around Antwerp in a cloak and yachting cap, not only becoming a plenipotentiary for dealing with the Belgian King and the government but also assuming the temporary role of local commander-in-chief. He established his headquarters in the principal hotel, employed Admiral Oliver, the Chief of Naval Intelligence, as his private secretary, lay in bed in the mornings dictating telegrams for the Admiral to despatch in all directions, and spent the afternoons touring, often under heavy German shellfire, the defensive posts on the outskirts of the city, and the evenings and some part of the nights in conferences. It was a mini-dress rehearsal for the pattern of his life in 1940–1. And it also had some features of the comforts to which he was to cling, in Downing Street, at Chequers or at Ditchley, in those later dark days. 'Twenty minutes in a motor car', he was later to write of a return from a visit to the newly arrived Royal Marines in action around the village of Lierre, 'and we were back in the warmth and light of one of the best hotels in Europe, with its perfectly appointed tables and attentive servants all proceeding as usual.'[9] The picture of the indestructible quality of Flemish napery (with food to match) is a vivid and convincing one.

So much was Churchill enjoying himself that, after thirty-six hours, he telegraphed to Asquith suggesting that he be allowed to resign as First Lord and take over, with the necessary military rank, as authorized commander at Antwerp. Kitchener, who saw the telegram on its way through the War Office, annotated it to the effect that he was prepared in these circumstances to make Churchill a lieutenant-general. The civilian members of the Cabinet reacted less favourably. Asquith commented: 'W. is an ex-Lieutenant of Hussars, and would if his proposal had been accepted, have been in command of 2 distinguished Major Generals, not to mention Brigadiers, Colonels &c: while the Navy was only contributing its little brigades.... I regret to say', he reported, 'that it was received [in the Cabinet] by a Homeric laugh.'[10] But the 'regret' was not genuine, for Asquith at this stage certainly did not want to lose Churchill from the Admiralty or the Cabinet, and although he laughed at his impetuosity he also admired qualities which were so different from his own mature phlegmatism. General Rawlinson, a rapidly rising and highly professional soldier, was appointed in Churchill's stead, and after Rawlinson's arrival in Antwerp on 7 October Churchill wisely withdrew to London. This was as well, from a domestic in addition to a political point of view, for Clementine gave birth to Sarah on that day.

General political and press opinion was less generous to Churchill's adventure than was Asquith. His old (High Tory) outlet the *Morning Post* thought that he had rendered himself 'unfit for the office he now holds'. Beatty (despite this being the third hostile quotation from him, he was far from being obsessively anti-Churchill and in any event represented the sort of dashing just-below-the-top naval opinion which Churchill most wanted to keep on his side) held that 'the man must have been mad to have thought that he could relieve [Antwerp] ... by putting 8000 half-trained troops into it'.[11] Clementine Churchill, possibly slightly resentful that her husband did not get back from his excursion until after her baby had been born, thought he had temporarily lost his sense of proportion.[12] And Churchill himself subsequently penned a few strokes of mild self-reproof. In volume one of *The World Crisis* (1923) he wrote of the refusal of the Cabinet to let him accept the lieutenant-generalship: 'But other voices prevailed: and I certainly have no reason to regret that they did so.' And a little later in the text: 'No doubt had I been ten years older I should have hesitated long before accepting so unpromising a task [as the whole mission to Antwerp].'[13] A decade after that in *Thoughts and Adventures* (1932) in an essay entitled 'Second Chances' he singled out Antwerp as something which with hindsight he would have done differently, or not done at all.

That autumn was altogether a time of severe strain on Churchill's vast reserves of self-confidence. In late September he had gone to Liverpool and 'one unhappy phrase – true enough in thought – about "digging rats out of holes" ... had slipped from my tongue in a weary speech'.[14] The 'rats' were the Kaiser's capital ships and the 'holes' were their secure harbours near the mouths of the big rivers of north Germany. It created a reaction, particularly among service officers, very similar to that which followed Michael Portillo's Conservative party conference anti-European speech (as Defence Secretary) in 1995. In both cases the admirals and the captains felt that they were being made into tin cans on the tails of politicians' brash rhetoric. There does not now seem to be anything very surprising or objectionable about Churchill's words, except for a bit of routine bombast, which was apparently a considerable *sur place* success before an audience of 15,000. But why was he making a 'weary speech' in Liverpool or anywhere else at that time? The answer is almost certainly that he had too easily undertaken to do so a few weeks in advance without considering whether he would have anything useful to say, and found himself on the day thrashing around for resonant phrases. Such circumstances have been a frequent cause of trouble for many politicians less inherently rash than Churchill.

A month later Churchill had to face the need for a new First Sea Lord, who would be the fourth occupant of the post during his three years at the Admiralty. The press campaign of vilification of Battenberg, on the ground that he was of alien birth and maybe of German sympathies as well, was not endorsed by Churchill, but he offered little resistance to Battenberg's replacement. The same was true of Asquith. They both felt that Battenberg had become too easy-going to be the principal professional sailor in a desperate war. He had in particular become too pliant to Churchill's wishes to be a good vis-à-vis for such an assertive First Lord. He was to be seen sitting calmly in his office reading *The Times* for a large part of each morning, while Churchill poured out minutes and instructions. The eminent American naval historian A. J. Marder points out that in the first three months of the war there were remarkably few minutes or memoranda emanating from Battenberg. J. A. Sanders, Balfour's long-standing and powerful private secretary, claims that he was given the sobriquet of 'quite concur'. Fisher, writing to Jellicoe, commander of the Home Fleet, in that December, put it still more bluntly: 'Battenberg was a cipher and Winston's facile dupe!' Churchill's published reply to his letter of departure was in the best tradition of urbane acceptance of a welcome resignation. 'I must express publicly my deep indebtedness to you, and the pain I feel at the severance of our three years' official association. In all the circumstances you are right in your decision.'[15]

The truth was that Churchill needed an outstanding First Sea Lord after Antwerp and the loss of the three cruisers. Fisher fitted the bill. The prospect of bringing Fisher back also excited him. He thought that he would dilute the danger of Fisher's impetuosity if not of his age (seventy-three) by also bringing back as a special adviser Admiral Sir Arthur Wilson, the First Sea Lord of whom he had disposed in 1911. Wilson was seventy-two. Asquith did not resist this gerontophilia, but King George V did. The monarch's real reason was that he believed the navy did not trust Fisher. But he made the mistake of using a false argument with Churchill. The strain of the work, he argued, would kill a man of Fisher's age. 'I cannot think of a more glorious death for him' was Churchill's calm and conclusive rejoinder.

There was a good deal of scepticism in the higher ranks of the navy as to how long Churchill and Fisher would get on together. They were both stars of sufficient power that each needed a separate orbit. (The nearest they came to achieving this was that Churchill worked half the night and rose late, while Fisher went to bed at dinner time and was at his desk from the very early morning.) But up to Christmas nearly all was harmony and Churchill ended the year on a much higher note than he would have thought possible in October and November. 'Then suddenly all over the world the tension was relaxed,' as he wrote nine years later in *The World Crisis*. There followed an impressive catalogue of dangers that had been averted and of results that had been achieved. He continued:

> As December passed, a sense of indescribable relief stole over the Admiralty. . . . A feeling of profound thankfulness filled our hearts as this first Christmas of the war approached; and of absolute confidence in final victory. The mighty enemy, with all the advantages of preparation and design, had delivered his onslaught and had everywhere been brought to a standstill. It was our turn now. The initiative had passed to Britain – the Great Amphibian. . . . It was for us to say where we would strike and when.[16]

This meant that Churchill began 1915 in an over-confident and strategically restless mood.

14

LAST MONTHS AT THE ADMIRALTY

CHURCHILL'S STRATEGIC RESTLESSNESS found full expression in a post-Christmas letter to Asquith. Throughout his seven years as a Liberal Cabinet minister, whether in peace or war, Churchill rarely left his Prime Minister to face the New Year without a major missive of advice. For 1915 this was sent four days in advance, on 27 December 1914.

On this occasion Churchill was not unique in providing Asquith with such a budget of advice. On 28 December Colonel Maurice Hankey, the staff officer who created the Cabinet secretariat and presided over it for more than twenty years, composed a major memorandum. On the 31st Lloyd George, who was rarely a great man for paper, weighed in with a third *tour d'horizon*. It reads the best of them, and indeed so struck Asquith, who wrote that he had on New Year's day received 'two long mem^d – one from Winston, the other from Lloyd George (quite good, the latter)'[1] – but this may merely have expressed his surprise that the very oral Lloyd George should have been at least as good on paper as the habitually fluent-with-the-written-word Churchill. What was notable was that of these three strategic papers Churchill's was at that time the one least inclined to put its eggs in the basket of an Eastern strategy.

Churchill's premiss, which did not greatly differ from those of the other two, was that, for a variety of reasons, stasis had settled on all the main fronts. In France the opposing armies were dug in so completely that there were no flanks to turn, and the only prospect was for assaults as prodigal in casualties as they were likely to be exiguous in results. In the east the Russians were thrown back as soon as they came 'in contact with the German railway system' (a typically graphic Churchill touch), but when they withdrew into the vast recesses of their own country were as difficult to bring to decisive defeat as Napoleon had found them a century earlier. The British navy had established secure superiority, but was not likely to be given the chance to engage the German fleet. If a break-out from this impasse was to be achieved some bold new strategy had to be devised. 'Are there not other alternatives than sending our armies to chew barbed wire in Flanders?' No decisive result was likely to be achieved there, although, as he added in a slightly bitter throwaway, 'no doubt several hundred thousand men will be spent to satisfy the military mind on the point'.[2]

There were two possible routes out of the impasse, Churchill argued. The first was the bolder and the more hazardous: 'The invasion of Schleswig-Holstein from the seas would at once threaten the Kiel Canal and enable Denmark to join us. The accession of Denmark would throw open the Baltic. British naval command of the Baltic would enable the Russian armies to be landed within 90 miles of Berlin.'[3] One thing of which Churchill could never be accused was a failure to think big. However, big thoughts sometimes have to be concentrated on small initial objectives, and this became the seizure of the five-miles-by-two island of Borkum, just off the mouth of the Ems river, and only a few miles north of the Dutch frontier. Borkum was a favoured prize for both Arthur Balfour, who at this stage, much encouraged by Churchill, hovered over the Admiralty as a sort of shadow First Lord, and still more significantly for Fisher. It was also the favoured option put forward by Churchill in his New Year letter to Asquith.

The alternative was to force a passage through the Dardanelles and, either with or without an army occupation of the Gallipoli peninsula, to insert a fleet into the Sea of Marmora, which could then advance to the Golden Horn, intimidate Constantinople and induce the Turkish government to sue for peace, while at the same time bringing Greece, Bulgaria and Roumania into the war on the Allied side. This Aegean alternative was initially a bigger enterprise than the seizure of Borkum, although the ultimate hopes for the full Baltic strategy – with Russian troops, with or without snow on their boots, advancing across a short stretch of Pomeranian plain to seize the Imperial German capital – was a still more ambitious ultimate outcome. In both cases, however, there was much room for slips between cups and lips.

There was also an unfortunate ambiguity between the two directions. Churchill was responsible for having initially set Asquith's mind off across the North Sea. But Asquith, at least so far as he was willing to go along with Churchill's subsequent switch to the Dardanelles, was not the problem. Nor was Balfour. The problem was the still more formidable one of Fisher. The old First Sea Lord, rehabilitated by Churchill, fascinated by yet intensely jealous of him, was half persuaded to go along with an Aegean strategy yet was always harking back, whenever things went badly in the eastern Mediterranean, which they mostly did, to how much better it would have been to concentrate on defeating Germany across the North Sea. This stretch of cold grey water, in spite of his earlier Mediterranean exploits, had become the centre of Fisher's world after the early-twentieth-century creation of the German High Seas Fleet.

The real trouble between Fisher and Churchill, however (and it was very real trouble indeed, for it meant that the old Admiral ended his great service to the navy on a note of sour hysteria, and that the young statesman experienced the most crushing check of his long career), was not the difference between Borkum and the Dardanelles. It was much more that they were too strong meat for each other. They were like a husband and wife who could not live without each other but who could not live together either. In the spring of 1915, the latter aspect became more dominant. To vary the metaphor, it was a classic example of putting two scorpions together in a bottle, with the added complication that in the Fisher–Churchill case they not only had the capacity to inflict most venomous damage upon each other, but also had an intensity of emotional relationship, particularly on Fisher's side, which was more appropriate to a love affair than to a professional association at the head of the 'silent service' under the stress of a great war.

The lovers' tiff which Fisher had provoked in 1912 has already been cited. But that was when Fisher had no direct responsibilities, and was in any event as nothing compared with the emotional tensions which built up three years later. Sir Frederick Sturdee was a flag officer of whom Fisher thought little (which made him far from unique). A vice-admiral at the time, he had been lucky enough to be in command in the South Atlantic in November 1914 when a battle cruiser squadron (a formation which was very much Fisher's creation) had won the Battle of the Falklands. This did not prevent Fisher continuing to regard him as 'a pedantic ass'. What was of more relevance was the way Fisher wrote about him to Churchill on 25 April, only three weeks before the smash which brought them both down: 'Really yesterday had it not been for the Dardanelles forcing me to stick to you through thick and thin I would have gone out of the Admiralty yesterday never to return, and sent you a postcard to get Sturdee up *at once* in my place. You would *then* be quite happy!!!'[4] But at about the same time Fisher also wrote: 'I honestly believe that Winston loves me.'[5]

Even without the element of jealousy betrayed by this couple of sentences, the Churchill–Fisher partnership would have been doomed.

Fisher was an imperious commander. He had enjoyed remarkab. success in covering with charm an unusual mixture of eccentricity, insolence and solid administrative drive. As a young man he had made a considerable impact upon Gladstone and upon Garibaldi. He had been a favourite of both Queen Victoria and King Edward VII, an infrequent double, although he failed dismally with King George V. His success or failure with the royal wives matched that with their husbands. In spite of his fairly short stature (five feet seven inches) he was good at seizing Queen Alexandra round the waist and swirling her into one of his famous waltzes. With Queen Mary even he was too intimidated to try, or if he did, it did not work.

Broadly speaking his charm was even more successful with women than with men. This was not universal. Violet Asquith, in spite or perhaps because of her pre-breakfast dancing sessions off Malta in 1912, wrote in her diary for 1915, 'I consider that he has behaved in a lower – more cowardly and more unworthy way over this [resignation from the Admiralty] than any Englishman since the War [began].'[6] However, that was after he had greatly added to her beloved father's difficulties at a particularly testing time, and there were plenty of dancing partners and others to take a contrary view. In particular there were the Grand Duchess Olga, the Tsar's sister, who is recorded as having once said that she would walk to England (from where?) for another waltz with Fisher,[7] and above all Nina, Duchess of Hamilton, thirty-eight years his junior, who was the prop and pillow of his old age, on whom he subsided after the *dégringolade* of 1915, which resulted in his papers being deposited at Lennoxlove, the Hamiltons' romantically named house in East Lothian.

No doubt there was a touch of spoilt genius about him. He thought he was the greatest sailor since Nelson, but so did – and do – quite a lot of other people. He saw Kitchener exercising supreme power at the War Office. He thought, with justification, that he was at least as good an admiral as Kitchener was a general. His horizons were limitless. In a remarkably ill-judged letter to Asquith (on 19 May 1915), admittedly when he had gone into a deranged state, he set out megalomaniac terms for returning to the post he had deserted:

If the following conditions are agreed to, I can guarantee the successful termination of the war. . . .
    That Mr Winston Churchill is not in the Cabinet to be always circumventing me. . . .

That there shall be an entire new Board of Admiralty, as regards the Sea Lords and the Financial Secretary (who is utterly useless). *New measures* demand new men.

That I have complete professional charge of the war at sea, together with the absolute sole disposal of the Fleet and the appointment of all officers of all ranks whatsoever, and absolutely untrammelled sole command of all the sea forces whatsoever.

That the First Lord of the Admiralty should be absolutely restricted to policy and parliamentary procedure. . . .

That I should have the sole absolute authority for all new constructional and dockyard work of whatever sort whatsoever, and complete control of the Civil Establishments of the Navy.

These . . . conditions must be published verbatim so that the Fleet may know my position.[8]

Alongside this desire to rule absolutely there was the fact that when Fisher came back to office at the end of October 1914 he both owed his return to, and was confronted by, the most operationally interfering First Lord in the history of the Admiralty. During Fisher's previous periods of service in Whitehall, first as Second Naval Lord in 1902–3, and then in 1904–10 as First Sea Lord (Fisher himself was responsible for the replacement of 'Naval' by 'Sea'), he had served nominally under, but in fact with, or even over, four First Lords: Selborne, Cawdor, Tweedmouth and McKenna. None of this quartet had prepared him for dealing with Churchill, to whom he was indebted and by whom he was fascinated. It was the equivalent of taking a walk in a spring breeze along the seafront at Torquay as preparation for dealing with a hurricane in Havana.

Churchill had got into the habit when Prince Louis was First Sea Lord of himself drafting detailed instructions to fleet commanders and even individual ships. 'Quite concur' Battenberg provided the fiction that it was all being done jointly with the professional head of the service. But it was little more than a fiction. Battenberg could not resist Churchill in argument, and he was by no means alone among senior naval officers in this deficiency. Furthermore it became the habit, contrary to normal government practice, for the political minister himself to draft the minutes or instructions resulting from any meeting. Churchill's reversal of normal practice brings two adages to mind: that 'the devil is in the detail'; and that he who drafts the communiqué (or better still arrives with one already drafted) often controls the outcome of a conference. At the root of the matter was Churchill's phenomenal energy and fluency, and also by this stage his total immersion in and grasp of naval operational detail, if not always of high strategy. He worked long hours with great concentration. 'His power of work is absolutely amazing,' Fisher wrote to Jellicoe on 20 December.[9] Churchill did not, in the normal ministerial way, briefly sum up a discussion and ask for a draft to be prepared. He did the drafting himself, and often, choosing to believe that he had got agreement, sent it off before there could be any time for second thoughts.

These habits, combined with his habitual self-confidence, gave him a complete ascendancy over the Battenberg Admiralty. He must have felt some need for stronger tension on the rope, or he would not have brought in Fisher accompanied by 'old 'Ard 'Art' Wilson. It was always one of Churchill's strengths that, although he wanted to dominate those around him, he wanted to do it over first- and not second-rate people. But, although he no doubt felt he was inducting Fisher into an enthusiastic partnership, he did not propose to change his own habits. In particular, he persisted in believing that opposition verbally battered down was the same thing as a real meeting of minds. And he continued to do his own detailed drafting of operational instructions.

A good example of how far Churchill was prepared to go with his own pen, and to some considerable extent on his own responsibility, is the minute which he wrote on 14 May 1915, and which became very much the last straw on Fisher's camel's back:

> 1. The fifth 15-inch howitzer, with fifty rounds of ammunition, should go to the Dardanelles with the least possible delay, being sent by special train across France and re-embarked at Marseilles. Let me have a time table showing by what date it can arrive at the Dardanelles.
> The two 9.2 inch guns will go to the Dardanelles, either in the two monitors prepared for them or separately, for mounting on shore. This will be decided as soon as we hear from Vice-Admiral de Robeck.
> 2. The following nine heavy monitors should go in succession to the Dardanelles, as soon as they are ready:–
> *Admiral Faregut, General Grant, Stonewall Jackson, Robert E. Lee, Lord Clive, Prince Rupert, Sir John Moore, General Craufurd,* and *Marshal Ney*.'[10]

So it went on for another 300 or so words of assured but presumptuous detail.

What was Fisher's state of mind as these sad (both for him and for Churchill) early months of 1915 unfolded? Primarily he felt increasingly impotent. He was so used to blasting his way through any difficult defile. He was so used to charming King Edward VII, to getting his own way with four successive First Lords, two of one party, two of the other, to defeating his silver-spooned enemy Admiral Lord Charles Beresford, that he thought there was nothing he could not overcome. Like Churchill he had the confidence to welcome engagement with the most doughty champions. Churchill should have been by far the most exhilarating of the five First Lords whom he had subdued, the greatest of his conquests.

But Churchill was too much for him. This was partly because, at seventy-four, Fisher's powers were beginning to fade. He still got up at four in the morning and was at his desk in the Admiralty at an inordinately early hour. He closely oversaw the ordering of 600 new ships during his six months of Indian summer as First Sea Lord. He galvanized the Admiralty, and as Churchill said in their good pre-Christmas period together, 'made [it] quiver like one of his great ships at its highest speed'.[11] But his sustained application was not what it had been. He was once humiliated by Maurice Hankey, soon to be the first secretary of the Cabinet, coming into his room in the middle of one morning and finding him fast asleep.

Still more however was it that in Churchill he had at last more than met his match. 'He is always *convincing* me,' Fisher almost pathetically said.[12] It was as though one of the most powerful meteorites in the solar system had by singular chance met another head on. The result, not unnaturally, was mutual destruction. But before the crash took place the Fisher meteorite, if such suspended animation is possible, recognized that the Churchill one was still more powerful. And this produced anguish even more than apprehension. Fisher, who had himself crushed so much other opposition, could not stand up to Churchill in face-to-face argument. He therefore acquiesced when he did not agree. Cumulatively this left him unhappy and resentful. And there was the already noted emotional relationship. The result was a seething cauldron of Admiralty tensions. The surprising thing was, not that it blew up in mid-May 1915, but that it had not done so several months before.

From this over-heated cauldron, far more than from any temporary strategic differences between Borkum and the Dardanelles, or between a cautious policy of cutting losses and pressing on relentlessly to turn defeat into victory, there boiled up the upheaval of May 1915. If the protagonist and the antagonist had been men of the cool stamp of, say, Admiral Sir John Jellicoe and Arthur James Balfour there might well

have been hard-pounding argument, but the fissile material would h
lacked its ultimate destructive quality.

How much was Churchill to blame for the Dardanelles? Whether h
over-estimated the impact a decisive victory in the Near East woulc
have on the two main fronts is a question impossible to answer given
the actual outcome. The Dardanelles strategy was bold and imaginative, and its central premise, summed up in Churchill's famous phrase
of seeking an alternative to 'chew[ing] barbed wire in Flanders', was
undoubtedly legitimate – as half a million British graves in that flat and
sombre countryside bear eloquent testament.

The critical weakness was the failure to plan for an integrated naval
and military operation from the outset. Much of the blame for this lies
with Churchill. The planning in late December 1914 and early January
1915 assumed it would in fact be a joint operation. It was Churchill who
argued for a solely naval attack at the War Councils of 13 and 28
January, despite Fisher's obvious misgivings. Fisher had to be restrained
by Kitchener from walking out of a Defence Committee on 28 January,
and did so only to maintain 'an obstinate and ominous silence', as
Asquith noted afterwards.[13] Only in mid-February, six days before the
commencement of the naval bombardment, was a decision taken to send
troops. The detachment was too little and too late, and one of the First
World War's human catastrophes resulted.

Hankey, writing in his diary on 19 March, speculated that Churchill
planned a solely naval operation in order to recoup the prestige he had
lost at Antwerp.[14] Yet Churchill was First Lord of the Admiralty, not
Secretary of State for War, let alone Prime Minister. Kitchener and
Asquith ought to have had continual regard to the wider military
implications. Asquith in particular failed to elicit either Kitchener's full
commitment or the nature of Fisher's misgivings.

Churchill's later summing up was that the concept was overwhelmingly right, that it was only a singularly unfortunate accumulation of
narrowly missed chances which prevented it from working, but that it
was nonetheless a 'bridge too far' for him to attempt without supreme
power. Had he been Prime Minister, with the implication that he would
have run a very much more taut decision-making line of command
(as indeed he did a quarter-century later), he would have won a great
victory, substantially shortened the war and saved many hundreds of
thousands of lives. But it is difficult to find a serious military historian
who agrees.

He was not Prime Minister, however, but an exceptionally active though not always persuasive First Lord of the Admiralty, forced to operate through a War Council of at least ten, with a fairly sympathetic although naturally sceptical Prime Minister and a publicly heroic War Office vis-à-vis in the shape of Kitchener. Churchill's relations with Kitchener were mixed, and the bad elements in the mixture were often his own fault. In the run-up to Christmas 1914, one particularly pointless dispute was about the extent to which naval land forces serving in France (the Royal Naval Division and the armoured Rolls-Royce squadrons, which were in effect Churchill's freebooters) should be under Admiralty or War Office discipline. Another, more dangerous one, was about Churchill's semi-private correspondence with Sir John French, the Commander-in-Chief of the British Expeditionary Force, supplemented by his frequent visits to France, sometimes to his own private army at Dunkirk, but often rounded off by a night or so with French at his St Omer headquarters. French was constantly pressing Churchill to come over and have a thorough strategic talk. Kitchener was not unnaturally suspicious, particularly as he also had a vague idea of the correspondence. On one occasion, showing more sense of humour than that with which he is normally credited, Kitchener was recorded (19 December) in one of Asquith's letters to Venetia Stanley, as having 'for his own amusement, & the enlightenment of posterity . . . [drawn] up an imaginary account of how he secretly induced or bullied Jellicoe into taking 300 War Office steamers and stowing them away on the S.W. coast of Ireland'.[15] At about this time Churchill was positively vetoed from going to French's headquarters. 'These meetings', the Prime Minister wrote to Churchill, 'have in K's opinion already produced profound friction between French & himself, & between French's staff & his staff, which it is most desirable to avoid.'[16] In addition Churchill's naval flank became increasingly exposed to the broadsides of Fisher, who was always present at meetings of the War Council.

Churchill added to the exposure of his position with three specific faults, for which he paid heavily. First, he should never have brought Fisher back to the Admiralty in 1914 unless he intended to share power with him far more fully than he did. There was never a chance of the partnership working if he intended to continue on his Battenberg basis. Only a degree of infatuation, on his side this time, could have begun to make him think that it would.

Second, he ignored danger signals from Fisher. With a mixture of honesty and naivety they are nearly all recorded in Churchill's own *pièce justificative, The World Crisis.* In an early acknowledgement of the problem he wrote: 'It was not until the end of January [1915] . . . that Lord Fisher began to manifest an increasing dislike and opposition to the [Dardanelles] scheme.'[17] This however ignores the scene at the crucial War Council of 13 January when, after a passionate advocacy of the Dardanelles option by Churchill, Fisher suddenly rose and attempted to storm out of the room. He was prevented by Kitchener, who took him briefly for a muttered conversation at a window, which got him reluctantly back to the table. Then, after the ineffective naval attempt to force the straits into the Sea of Marmora on 18 March and the 'pressing-on' telegram which Churchill subsequently sent to Admiral de Robeck, the First Lord recorded: 'This telegram the First Sea Lord was induced, with some difficulty, to agree to.'[18]

In April the protests from Fisher became more vivid, partly because recorded in his own inimitable prose with its Queen Victoria-like emphases. On the 2nd of the month: *'We can't send another rope yarn even to de Robeck!* WE HAVE GONE TO THE VERY LIMIT! . . . *A failure or check in the Dardanelles would be nothing – a failure in the North Sea would be RUIN.'*[19] And on the 5 April he wrote to Churchill: 'You are just simply eaten up with the Dardanelles and can't think of anything else! Damn the Dardanelles! They'll be our grave!'[20]

Yet Churchill believed that an adequate counterpoise to these eruptions of discontent was that he had got Fisher in a very equivocal minute of 7 April to acknowledge, 'But, as you state, these high points of policy are to be decided by the Cabinet; and in this case the real advantages to be gained caused me eventually to consent to their view, subject to the strict limitation of the Naval Forces to be employed so that our position in the decisive theatre in the North Sea should not be jeopardized in any one arm.'[21] This Churchill used as a basis on which to state: 'The position of the First Sea Lord is thus very clearly defined. It is seen to be formally and deliberately identified with the enterprise.'[22]

Churchill ought also to have been worried by the fact that he turned Fisher – whose natural style over thirty and more years of increasingly senior command had been that of Evelyn Waugh's 'biff-'em' Brigadier Ritchie-Hook – into an extremely miserly admiral. He became almost the cautious Jellicoe's *alter ego*. The supreme object of naval policy, Fisher argued, should be to keep the odds so firmly in Britain's favour that if the German High Seas Fleet ever came out (which it did only once, and then it was a draw) it would be statistically incapable of victory. Even were Fisher the greatest servant (or ruler) of the navy since Nelson, this was not exactly Nelsonian. Fisher had not participated in a naval action since 1882, and perhaps Churchill was right to regard him as essentially a naval constructor.

The third of Churchill's mistakes in this period was to get himself into a position in which 'everyone was out of step except Winston'. All were on his side at some stage, but eventually everyone let him down. This is always a position in which some degree of self-doubt is called for. But self-doubt was never one of Churchill's attributes (thank God, one could perhaps say, looking forward to 1940). Yet it is remarkable, in his detailed retrospective justification of the whole Gallipoli enterprise, how much blame he attaches to others and how little to himself. This justification is set out in a series of chapters in the second volume of *The World Crisis*, published in 1923 and therefore written not under the immediate lash of frustration and dismay, but after the opportunity for nearly eight years of calm reflection. His governing thesis is that, had it not been for ill-luck, incompetence, bad nerve, a faulty appraisal of the strength of the enemy or some combination of these factors, the breakthrough by land or sea or both to the Sea of Marmora was very near to being achieved. This is itself highly debatable, but more doubtful still is his constant confidence, contrary to his general assumption that in war nearly everything is a matter of hazard, that had this breakthrough been achieved all the most beneficial consequences would have come with the certainty that night follows day. Constantinople would have been invested, the Turkish government would have sued for peace, Imperial Russia would have been sustained and, perhaps most problematical of all, the Balkan states of Serbia, Bulgaria, Roumania and Greece would have been melded into a pro-Allied harmony.

Among those to whom Churchill attaches varying degrees of blame, often accompanied by doubtfully assuaging statements about their political skill, their military authority, their courage in other circumstances and, in one case, their agreeable manners as a country gentleman, were the following, who had all to a greater or lesser extent let Churchill down. First there was Asquith, who although in general a supporter of Churchill's Eastern strategy had not pushed it through with nearly sufficient ruthlessness, being too concerned with the balance of political forces within first his Liberal and then his coalition Cabinet; he was also responsible for fatal lost weeks in May and early June because of the political upheaval involved in the formation of the new government. Then there was the Foreign Secretary Edward Grey, whose diplomacy failed to produce that happy band of Balkan brothers which Churchill persisted in believing possible. Next, on the borderline between a minister and a commander, there was Kitchener. Apart from his general fault of blowing hot and cold, he was specifically charged with having delayed the departure for the eastern Mediterranean of the 29th Division for a crucial three weeks, and for then having allowed it to be so haphazardly embarked that there could be no question of it assuming an order of battle for some time after arrival. Fisher, already dealt with, was also clearly a baleful influence, but so too was Jellicoe, the Commander-in-Chief of the Grand Fleet, whose nervousness made him a miser of ships; he was always pretending that his position vis-à-vis the Germans was weaker than it was, and thus resisting any detachment of ships for tasks more positive than lying in wait for the German High Seas Fleet.

On the (eastern Mediterranean) spot the first 'villain' was Vice-Admiral de Robeck. He was second-in-command to Admiral Carden of the considerable fleet, mainly British, but with some French reinforcement, which lay off the southern end of the Dardanelles. This contained a number of old battleships, which some (including Churchill) considered expendable, but also *Queen Elizabeth*, which with its 15-inch guns and oil-fuelled propulsion was the finest ship under the Admiralty, and maybe in the whole world. Carden, who was co-operating well with London plans, most unpropitiously fell ill two days before the 18 March attempt to force the passage of the straits by ships alone. De Robeck was appointed in his place, although Admiral Rosslyn Wemyss, who was also on the spot, was senior to him. This was very much Churchill's decision, and one which he came to regret. The 18 March action did not succeed, the seaborne fire failing to subdue the guns of the Turkish land forts. Two major ships, *Inflexible* and *Irrepressible*, were lost. De Robeck was not particularly blamed for this. Churchill's objection to him became increasingly based on the fact that, having been repulsed once, he was reluctant to try again. When de Robeck, in turn, was replaced on grounds of ill-health and by the previously passed over Wemyss in late November (1915), a more aggressive spirit was introduced. Wemyss was willing to have another go. But by then it was too late. As Churchill sadly put it: 'When the Admiralty was willing the Admiral was unwilling. Now the conditions were reversed.'[23] The Admiralty, by then under Balfour (who was thus embraced in the list of those who had disappointed Churchill), would not sanction a bold stroke. But it was Churchill who bore most responsibility for de Robeck having the power to spend eight crucial months sitting cautiously and comfortably off shore.

Of the army commanders Churchill was at least as critical. Ian Hamilton was his closest friend among generals, and he was delighted at his appointment. His enthusiasm did not extend either to Hamilton's principal subordinate Lieutenant-General Stopford (he of the gentlemanly manners), whose complacent indolence on the day after the Allied August landing at Suvla Bay on the Gallipoli peninsula Churchill regarded as almost criminal, or to Hamilton's October replacement, General Charles Monro. Of Monro, a hard-line Westerner, who believed the war could be won only by killing Germans in Flanders (even if as many or more Britons and Frenchmen were also killed), Churchill wrote with venom, 'He came, he saw, he capitulated,' and of Monro's sole visit to the invasion beaches, 'he familiarized himself in the space of six hours with the conditions prevailing in the 15-mile front of Anzac, Suvla and Helles, and spoke a few discouraging words to the principal officers at each point'.[24]

Even of Hamilton's command Churchill came to write coolly if not hostilely towards the end. It is a striking indication of how Gallipoli got Churchill out of sorts with himself that such a normally generous man should have written so sourly about nearly everyone involved, except for himself and a few junior and middle-ranking officers who performed individual feats of outstanding gallantry. Such almost universal complaint does not inspire confidence in his judgements on the issue.

During the early months of 1915 there was also mounting irritation with Churchill among his Cabinet colleagues, and most importantly on the part of the Prime Minister. Asquith's new exasperation with Churchill is most authentically expressed in his spate of letters of this period to Venetia Stanley. The dominant note is one of slightly weary tolerance, although this may have owed something to his knowledge that Churchill was fairly close to Venetia ('I did not know until your letter today that you liked Winston quite so much as all that,' he wrote on 4 February).[25] But it also stemmed from his own genuine (sometimes exasperated) affection. 'I am rather vexed with Winston'[26] (18 February) and 'Winston was rather trying today & I felt constrained to talk to him afterwards a little for his soul's good' (26 February)[27] are typical examples. There could however be some less benign comments, such as (also on 26 February, but in a different and prior letter) 'Winston was in some ways at his worst – having quite a presentable case. He was noisy, rhetorical, tactless and temperless – or full.'[28] Greater acerbity from 10 Downing Street is to be found in the diaries of Margot Asquith; on 29 January she reports herself as saying to Lloyd George (hardly in general a favourite of hers): 'Winston, like all really self-centred people, ends by boring people. He's as you say, such a child!'[29] For 19 February she recorded: 'Henry [her husband] said to me in the motor: Winston just now is absolutely maddening, how I wish Oc [Arthur Asquith] had not joined his beastly Naval Brigade! . . . He has just emerged from a fearful row with K[itchener] by the skin of his teeth and has now let himself into yet another. . . . Of course Winston is intolerable. It is all *vanity* – he is devoured by vanity.'[30]

Churchill in turn began to exhibit impatience at what he regarded as the Prime Minister's dilatoriness. To his credit he did so more in direct letters than in epistolatory complaint to others. Thus on 7 February:

> My dear Prime Minister,
>   More than three weeks ago you told me of the vital importance of Servia. Since then nothing has been done, & nothing of the slightest reality is being done. Time is passing. You may not yet feel the impact of the projectile. But it has already left the gun & is travelling along its road towards you. Three weeks hence you, Kitchener, Grey will all be facing a disastrous situation in the Balkans: & as at Antwerp it will be beyond your power to retrieve it.
>   Surely in your position you cannot be content to sit as a judge pronouncing on events after they have taken place.[31]

Before he sent this letter Churchill deleted the last sentence, but it was nonetheless a rough letter for a young minister to send to a Prime Minister who was twenty-two years his senior.

Churchill also got on to fairly tense terms with a number of other colleagues who were important to him. With his old ally and continuing tenant (in Eccleston Square) Edward Grey there was a considerable deterioration of relations during these months. On 20 February Grey pronounced himself 'aghast' at Churchill's proposal to appoint 'a Governor' of the Aegean island of Lemnos, which the Greeks were merely, and hesitantly, allowing the British navy to use as anchorage. On 4 March Grey and Churchill were again in dispute about possible naval violation of Chilean territorial waters, and on the 6th Churchill nearly made matters much worse by writing to Grey an intolerably patronizing and hectoring letter: 'I beseech you in this crisis [relations with Greece] not to make a mistake in falling below the head of events.

Half-hearted measures will ruin all – & a million will die through prolongation of the war. You must be bold and violent. . . .'[32] However this was another piece of his immortal (or at least intrepid) prose which he decided not to send; the draft survives only in his archives. Then in April he had a sharp row with Grey about the activities of a strangely named arms dealer, Captain de la Force, whom Churchill was using in an unsuccessful attempt to buy Brazilian rifles. Grey said these activities were upsetting Washington and endangering much larger arms supplies from the United States. All this must be seen against the background that in late March Edwin Montagu* told Asquith (and no doubt others too) that Churchill was intriguing to have Grey replaced by Balfour at the Foreign Office. Asquith was at first inclined to believe this, but was a little later impressed by the fervour of Churchill's denials and expressions of loyalty to him (Asquith) and respect for his full authority over Cabinet dispositions.

Churchill also had a series of rows with Kitchener, in February about the unwanted armoured-car squadrons and then a particularly bad one in mid-April about leaks of army strength, which provoked Kitchener to threaten resignation, although Lloyd George and indeed McKenna were probably more to blame. Asquith, as usual, was critical but half forgiving of Churchill: 'The people who ought to have known better showed themselves at their worst. Winston was pretty bad, but he is impulsive & borne along on the flood of his too copious tongue, and in the end was frankly regretful & made amends.'[33] In the meantime Churchill had had a bad-tempered but short row about Lloyd George's 'King's Pledge' scheme for the renunciation of alcohol for the duration of hostilities.† The row was not on the merits but was provoked by the

* Edwin Montagu (1879–1924), a rich Liberal, started his political career with four years as Asquith's parliamentary private secretary and ended it with five years as Lloyd George's Secretary of State for India. In the interval he married Venetia Stanley.
† The object was the somewhat fanciful one of setting an example to drunken munitions workers, whose excessive consumption was having a bad effect on production, particularly in areas of high ordnance-factory concentration, most notably around Carlisle. Lloyd George, who became temporarily obsessed with the issue, inveigled Haldane and Kitchener into taking the pledge. Haldane was thought by the Prime Minister to suffer a marked diminution of energy and spirit as a result. When he was excluded from the government six weeks later he regarded himself as discharged from his undertaking and received some consolation for the loss of the Woolsack. Kitchener rather gloomily stuck to his sacrifice until his death just over a year later. Asquith, like Churchill, took not the slightest notice of the gesture, and even Lloyd George, who admittedly was always a very light drinker, with skilful opportunism regarded himself as exempt from his own

explosive disdain with which Churchill treated what he called Lloyd George's 'wheeze'. He blustered that he did not see the point. The diaries of Frances Stevenson (then a very close aide to the Chancellor and much later to become the Countess Lloyd-George) recorded: '"You will see the point", [Lloyd George] rapped out, "when you begin to understand the conversation is not a monologue!" Churchill went very red. . . .'[34] This last was not a serious quarrel (they both wrote letters of apology to each other that same evening), but it was an indication that as things went worse in the Dardanelles and as Churchill approached his downfall at the Admiralty, so he let his tongue and his temper run away with him in dispute with all the Cabinet colleagues who were of most importance to him.

His position at the top of the Admiralty was also crumbling. Mount Fisher, from whom, as we have seen, dangerous rumblings and puffs of smoke had been emerging for several months, finally went into full eruption on Saturday, 15 May. Typically with Fisher it began very early in the morning. There had been a difficult meeting of the War Council on the previous day. Churchill described it as 'sulphurous' and most of the sulphur was directed against himself. 'Hamilton's army', he continued, 'had been definitely brought to a standstill on the Gallipoli Peninsula, was suspended there in circumstances of peril, was difficult to reinforce, and still more difficult to withdraw. The Fleet had relapsed into passivity.'[35] *Queen Elizabeth*, on Fisher's instructions, had been ordered home, which was such an obvious symbol of Dardanelles failure that de Robeck was instructed to pretend that she was merely going to Malta for a few days of maintenance.

In Flanders Sir John French had just lost 20,000 men in a predictably ineffective attack on entrenched German positions. During this battle French claimed to have come to the conclusion that the reason he could not attain his inherently unattainable objective was a shortage of shells, and felt himself justified by this alleged deficiency in mounting a press campaign against the government. His agent in stirring up the *Morning Post*, the *Observer* and above all *The Times* was his aide-de-camp, Captain Freddie Guest MP, who was also Churchill's cousin and a *bête noire* of Clementine's. Guest's efforts were sufficiently successful that, as an addition to the gaiety of that 14 May War Council, *The Times* had that morning been full of news of a great shells scandal. French and

---

scheme. The poor King was left almost alone to suffer without alcohol for three and a half years until the Armistice.

Northcliffe (the proprietor of *The Times*) thought it was that which brought down the last purely Liberal government (except for the non-political Kitchener) ever to rule in Britain. But a less partial view is that, while this was a contributory factor, it was the rupture in the Admiralty which was the more decisive cause. This had been injected into the War Council by Fisher suddenly announcing that he had been against the Dardanelles expedition from the beginning, and that Asquith and Kitchener (and presumably Churchill) knew this well. Again according to Churchill, 'This remarkable intervention was received in silence.'[36]

Later that day Churchill devoted himself to his usual occupation, in semi-accord with the First Sea Lord, of ordering fleet dispositions. There were to be reinforcements for the Dardanelles fleet, as in his already quoted minute, to compensate for the detachment, not only of *Queen Elizabeth*, but also of four light cruisers to join the Italian fleet at Taranto as part of a ploy (which proved successful on 23 May) to get Italy into the war on the Allied side. Churchill went to see Fisher in the early evening (in the Whitehall hierarchy it is always a conciliatory gesture for a superior to visit a nominal inferior, and one which sometimes, but not always, works), and thought he had got his broad agreement. Once again Churchill missed a warning sign. He complained that Fisher's intervention that morning had not been fair and then recorded: 'He [Fisher] looked at me in an odd way and said, "I think you are right – it isn't fair." '[37] Churchill's mistake was thinking that this was half an apology. In fact it was a declaration, perhaps sad, of incompatibility. It hardly needed the further exacerbation of Churchill working late that night and sending off detailed instructions, with the unfortunately worded codicil of 'First Sea Lord to see after action'.[38]

The next day at breakfast Churchill noticed that there was no normal early-morning round-up letter of the night's events from Fisher. He went to a meeting at the Foreign Office at nine and on walking back across Horse Guards Parade was intercepted by an agitated private secretary (Masterton-Smith) who told him that Fisher had resigned, and added, significantly, 'I think he means it this time.'[39] The comment was significant, as well as right, for it was Fisher's eighth resignation in six and a half months. The terms in which he did so, as the consequences were so great, are worth quoting:

> First Lord,
>   After further anxious reflection I have come to the regretted conclusion I am unable to remain any longer as your Colleague. It is undesirable in

the public interests to go into details – Jowett* said, 'never explain' – but I find it increasingly difficult to adjust myself to the increasingly daily requirements of the Dardanelles to meet yr views – As you truly said yesterday – I am in the position of continually veto-ing your proposals.

This is not fair to you besides being extremely distasteful to me.

I am off to Scotland at once so as to avoid all questionings.

Yrs truly,

Fisher[40]

Fisher, true to his ambivalence, did not in fact decamp to Scotland. He lurked in London, removing himself from his Queen Anne's Gate official residence to the Charing Cross Hotel (in which central but not very grand establishment, Jan Morris says, he almost certainly took a back room because of his well-known financial meanness).[41] However, a back room in that railway hotel suited him perfectly at the time. He was unobtrusively ensconced, but he was only 300 yards from the Admiralty and 800 yards from Downing Street. Even though this eighth resignation was much the most serious of the series, he expected summonses, and they of course were forthcoming.

Downing Street was more strenuous than the Admiralty in endeavouring to find him. This was partly because Churchill did not at first take Fisher's resignation more seriously than the previous seven, and, cocooned in his own enterprises, did not apprehend its political consequences. Asquith was more wary. He fully appreciated how precarious it might make the government, particularly in combination with the alleged shell shortage. Churchill did however walk across Horse Guards Parade for the third time that morning in order to give Asquith the news that Fisher had absconded. The Prime Minister immediately wrote by hand a note commanding Fisher, in the name of the King, to return to his duty, and instructed Maurice Bonham Carter, one of his private secretaries, to deliver it. This was easier said than done. It was a little reminiscent of the late 1940s dilettante Tory MP Michael Astor (third son of Waldorf and Nancy Astor), who sent a telegram (from the Ritz Hotel, Madrid) to his Chief Whip saying: 'You must take me as you find me; that is if you can find me.' Fisher's rather sad wife in his Norfolk manor house at Kilvertone was contacted, continental boat trains were checked, London was scoured. Within a couple of hours Fisher was tracked down (Downing Street has long been good at that),

* It is curious that Fisher, almost as formally uneducated as Churchill, should cite the old Master of Balliol, particularly as the usual attribution of the phrase is to Disraeli.

and agreed to present himself to the Prime Minister, although not to set foot within the Admiralty. Asquith in the meantime had rather characteristically been to a wedding, although to some extent a duty one, that of Geoffrey Howard MP, his former parliamentary private secretary, into whose firmly Liberal hands the formidable Rosalind Countess of Carlisle had diverted the great mansion of Castle Howard.

It was not until late afternoon that Fisher, in Violet Asquith's vivid if imaginative words, 'was caught – carried in in one of the retrievers' mouths & dropped bloodshot & panting at the door of the Cabinet room'.[42] Asquith found him 'mellow and friendly' but adamant that he could not work with Churchill. Churchill was nonetheless instructed to have a go at bringing him back and that evening produced a very good attempt at an emollient letter to Fisher, which was duly despatched. It did not work. Fisher wrote back the next day in terms which once again were friendly, but emotional or hysterical according to taste. Churchill had one more go the same (Sunday) morning, and received an even firmer reply ('Please don't wish to see me. I could say nothing as I am determined not to'),[43] which even Churchill accepted as definitive.

He set about preparing his new Board of Admiralty, persuading another septuagenarian (Sir Arthur Wilson) to take over as First Sea Lord and the junior ones to remain in place. Armed with this he set off at 5.30 p.m., doubtfully invited, but accompanied by Clementine, to be driven the fifty miles to the Wharf at Sutton Courtenay, to which Thames-side house Asquith had retreated the previous evening. Asquith's phlegm was remarkable. Fisher's flounce and the perceived threat to his government was allowed to do no more than postpone his weekend by a few hours. And on the Sunday morning he had motored over to Oxford to see his youngest son who was still at a preparatory school there. The late afternoon, however, tested even the Asquithian power of remaining calm at the centre of a vortex. And there were elements of French farce too. According to Violet Asquith's diary, the McKennas arrived for tea while 'Prince Paul of Servia was loose in the garden' and were only with difficulty 'tucked up in their motor and speeded off' before the Churchills arrived. When Violet came back from half an hour's boat trip she saw 'Winston ... standing at the bottom of the lawn on the river's brink looking like Napoleon at St Helena. ... He was very low. ... Poor Clemmie was certainly a good deal upset.'[44]

Churchill offered Asquith his resignation, and understood that it was refused, although what he reported Asquith as saying was that he 'did not wish it', but that the situation was sufficiently serious that the

Conservative leader would have to be consulted, which was rather different, and might have been interpreted as containing as much warning as reassurance. With his customary benignity towards the Churchills, 'Mr Asquith asked [us] to stay and dine, and we had a pleasant evening amid all our troubles.'[45] The Churchills drove back that night. Asquith came up only the following morning, to have a crucial but for him disagreeable meeting with Bonar Law before lunch.

It was crucial because in the interstices of all his engagements and journeys of the weekend, Asquith had come to the conclusion, typically in his pattern of rapid but reluctant decision-making, that a coalition government with the Conservatives was inevitable. And it was disagreeable both because Asquith never appreciated Law and because he approached the concept of coalition with distaste. Although he had always been a moderate in politics, he hated, in a way that would have been incomprehensible to Churchill or Lloyd George, the idea of bringing Tories into his Cabinet. It was not so much the policies as the political style and manners of the opposition which he disliked. It was his old Liberal mandarin spirit. 'To seem to welcome into the intimacy of the political household, strange, alien, hitherto hostile figures', he wrote, '[was] a most intolerable task.'[46] Probably there was much of the same feeling on the other side, and it was this approach of antipathy and reluctance which bedevilled from the start the nineteen months of the Asquith coalition government. A marriage should at least start with some degree of mutual enthusiasm, such as was certainly to be found in the Churchill coalition of twenty-five years later, and was to some extent present, at any rate in the small War Cabinet, in Lloyd George's 1916 government.

Asquith's decision caught Churchill in an appallingly exposed position. At least since 1910 he had been attracted by the idea of coalition ('hankering after coalitions and odd regroupings', in Asquith's words of a few months earlier), but now he was likely to be a victim of any such development. According to his own account in *The World Crisis* (which does not wholly make parliamentary sense) it was only on the Monday afternoon, and not at Sutton Courtenay on the Sunday, that he was fully alerted. He went to the House of Commons intending to see the Prime Minister and then announce the composition of his new Board of Admiralty in a ministerial statement. He looked in on Lloyd George on the way – rather a habit of his – and was told by the Chancellor (maybe self-exaggeratingly) that it was he who had put a pistol to Asquith's head on coalition. Churchill, in his own words as recollected much later, 'said that he [Lloyd George] knew I had always been in favour of such a Government and had pressed it at every possible opportunity, but that now it might be deferred until my Board was reconstructed and in the saddle at the Admiralty'. Lloyd George said delay was impossible. Then, when Churchill went along the short corridor and formally presented his Board to Asquith, he was told, 'No, this will not do. I have decided to form a national Government.' Asquith went on to ask Churchill if he would take office in the new government, or would he prefer a command in France? So, for the first time, Churchill realized that he was losing the Admiralty.[47]

To keep up the pace, all according to Churchill's account, Lloyd George then entered the room and suggested the Colonial Office for the displaced First Lord. Before that issue could even begin to be resolved there was a message that, for the most urgent operational reasons, Churchill was required back at the Admiralty. There was no doubt some fairly solid intelligence suggestion that the German High Seas Fleet might for the first time be coming out in full strength. Equally little doubt is there that Churchill seized on the news, at once portentous and exciting, with alacrity. It made him like a wounded man – he was himself to use the simile with a different gloss – who desperately wanted to have his mind diverted to a heightened aspect of the life he had previously lived. He had a spectacular afternoon and evening sending out signals of command without a First Sea Lord with whom he had even to pretend to clear them. From 3.55 p.m., when the signal 'Grand Fleet is to prepare for sea at once' went to Jellicoe, to 8.10 p.m. when the Commander-in-Chief was sent a personal message, 'It is not impossible that tomorrow may be The Day. All good fortune attend you,'[48] Churchill had a wonderful time. He even managed, without, as it were, feeling the pain, to write to the Prime Minister in the course of the same evening accepting his dismissal from the Admiralty, but saying that he would be glad to be offered any other position in the new government, provided it was in 'a military department'; otherwise he would prefer 'employment in the field'.[49]

He probably included the Colonial Office (and the India Office) within the range of 'military departments', but neither wish signified, for these were two of the semi-peripheral offices with which Asquith was unwisely determined to fob off the unesteemed Conservatives. Bonar Law, who ought for the balance of the government to have become Chancellor (particularly as Lloyd George was moving to create a new Ministry of Munitions), in fact became Colonial Secretary and

Austen Chamberlain Indian Secretary. Churchill's chances of the Colonies would probably in any event have been swept aside by these inter-party considerations, but even had these not applied they would not have been helped by a remarkably hard letter which Alfred Emmott (Churchill's fellow member for Oldham in the parliament of 1900 and much later a short-term member of the Liberal Cabinet) wrote to Asquith on the Thursday (20 May): 'I do implore you for the sake of the Dominions not to put Churchill [in the Colonial Office].... The effect on the Dominions would be lamentable and possibly disastrous. He has neither the temperament nor manners to fit him for the post.'[50] This was strongly supported by a letter from W. M. R. Pringle, a Scottish MP and a great supporter and favourite of Asquith's, who described Churchill's continuance in office as 'a public danger', adding that this was the view of a considerable number of Liberal MPs.[51] Such was the unpopularity which Churchill had accumulated in sections of the Liberal party as well as in almost the whole of the Conservative party except for F. E. Smith and, maybe, Arthur Balfour.

Churchill's numbed calm did not last long. The prospect of a great naval affray which might put party manoeuvres in their petty place was effectively over by the morning of Tuesday, 18 May. The German ships turned back to the east and Churchill could no longer call their immediate challenge in aid as a reason why he must remain in office. This did not mean that he kept quiet. Over the next four days, from Tuesday to Friday, 18 to 21 May, he wrote another five letters to Asquith, which pointed between them to violent alternations of mood. On the 18th he said that he would not refuse the Colonies, but pleaded to be allowed to stay 'to complete my work' at the Admiralty. On the 20th he produced what he obviously hoped was a new and decisive trump card: 'I have learned with great surprise that Sir Arthur Wilson yesterday informed the Naval Lords that while he was prepared to serve as First Sea Lord under me, he was not prepared to do so under anyone else. This is the greatest compliment I have ever been paid.'[52] On that same day Clementine Churchill added to the barrage with a letter to the Prime Minister of which the object was to seek a stay of execution but of which the form, so far from assuming a pleading note, was forthright almost to the point of insolence. It also contained the famous, because much quoted, sentence, 'Winston may in your eyes & in those with whom he has to work have faults but he has the supreme quality which I venture to say very few of your present or future Cabinet possess, the power, the imagination, the deadliness to fight Germany.'[53]

Asquith described this as 'the letter of a maniac',[54] which it was not. It was a heartfelt plea which hit at least one bull's-eye.

On 21 May Churchill himself sent a letter spread over six (small) sheets in which he tried to present himself as indispensable to the successful completion of the Dardanelles enterprise: 'It is no clinging to office or to this particular office or my own interest or advancement wh moves me. I am clinging to my *task* & to my *duty*. I am straining to make good the formidable undertaking in wh we are engaged; & wh I know – with Arthur Wilson – I can alone discharge.'[55] On that day he also wrote a still longer letter of justification and plea to Bonar Law.

Later that Friday there was probably a crossing of a deflated further letter from Churchill with a firm but considerate letter from Asquith. 'I have your letters,' the Prime Minister wrote. 'You must take it as settled that you are not to remain at the Admiralty. . . . I hope to retain your services as a member of the new Cabinet, being, as I am, sincerely grateful for the splendid work you have done both before and since the war.'[56] Churchill's punctured letter – the change of mood seems to have been spontaneous, for a subsequent letter strongly suggests that he had not then seen Asquith's definitive (so far as the Admiralty was concerned) missive – said, 'I am very sorry for yr troubles, and sorry to have been the cause of a situation wh has enabled others to bring them upon you – I will accept any office – the lowest if you like – that you care to offer me. . . .' Then, an hour or so later, when he had seen Asquith's letter, he wrote again, 'All right, I accept your decision. I shall not look back.'[57] Asquith immediately wrote yet again to express 'gratitude, but without surprise, [for] the spirit in which it is written'.[58] So this remarkable burst of correspondence came to an end.

The new government was not announced until 26 May, and the office which Churchill received was very near to being (within the Cabinet) 'the lowest', although it carried the consolation that he continued to be a member of the War Council, or Dardanelles Committee as it came to be called. He became Chancellor of the Duchy of Lancaster, the least regarded of the archaic sinecure offices, the two principal ones being the Lord Presidency of the Council and the Lord Privy Seal. Almost his only departmental duties were to appoint magistrates for the county of Lancashire. During the five months for which he held the office it gave him not a single occasion to make a speech in the House of Commons. But he had at least retained a position, although a peripheral and personally weakened one, from which he could go on arguing the case for the Dardanelles strategy.

15

FINISHED AT FORTY?

THE CHECK TO Churchill was severe, and in some ways, given his mercurial temperament, with strong depressive swings as well as magnificent and exuberant energy, the surprise is that he bounced back from it as well as he did. But the downswing should not be minimized. 'I am finished!' he told Lord Riddell, the proprietor of the *News of the World*, whom a surprising number of politicians chose as their confidant. 'Finished in respect of all I care for – the waging of war, the defeat of the Germans.'[1] And Clementine Churchill, reflecting much later (to Martin Gilbert) on the immediate aftermath of his downfall, said simply: 'I thought he would die of grief.'[2]

Whatever dark nights he went through on his own, his public demeanour was not that of a wounded animal wanting to crawl off and hide in the bushes. Rather was he keen to cling on to such public activities as were still at his disposal. Somewhat like his father, who after his 22 December 1886 resignation stayed in the Treasury Chambers writing letters over Christmas, so Churchill continued for five or six days after the announcement of the new government to direct his correspondence from the Admiralty. It was the not very glorious first of June 1915 before he began to write from what he regarded as the remote and unsatisfactory location of the Duchy of Lancaster Office on the northern approach to Waterloo Bridge. Typically, almost his first communication from there was a 4,000-word memorandum to his colleagues on the general strategic situation in both Western and Eastern theatres. And another of that day was to Jellicoe, who had written a gruff but proper letter of respect and restrained friendliness, not exactly regretting Churchill's departure, but saying how much he had done for the navy.

His great event of that week however was his Saturday visit to Dundee, where he delivered to a packed audience in the Caird Hall a short (half-hour) but powerful speech to his constituents. It was the first time that he had visited them since the beginning of the war, and it was to be a long time before they saw him again. But the speech was a great success, punctuated by frequent bursts of loud cheering, and appeared satisfactorily to seal up his constituency flank. It was half a justification of his naval policy, a quarter (surprisingly) a rejection of conscription for service in France (for less dangerous home duties, he implied, it might be acceptable), and a quarter a perorative demand for a government that would issue decisive calls to action and a people that would respond to these calls. There were foretastes of 1940. He concluded, not without grandiloquence but arousing no sense of bathos in the audience:

> Then turn again to your task. Look forward, do not look backward. Gather afresh in heart and spirit all the energies of your being, bend anew together for a supreme effort. The times are harsh, the need is dire, the agony of Europe is infinite, but the might of Britain hurled united into the conflict will be irresistible. We are the grand reserve of the Allied cause, and that grand reserve must now march forward as one man.[3]

One reason why the Churchills were slow to leave the Admiralty was that they had nowhere else to live in London. The Foreign Secretary was still their tenant in Eccleston Square and showed no eagerness to make it immediately available to them. Arthur Balfour, the new First Lord, showed no impatience to get his hands on Admiralty House – as a bachelor with his own house in Carlton Gardens it would have been grasping had he done so – and it was more Clementine's desire to escape from a background which had become odious which made their departure urgent. They accepted a few weeks of cousinly Arlington Street hospitality from Ivor Guest, who had just become Lord Wimborne. (In view of her well-known Guest antipathy, it must have been for Clementine a choice of evils.) Then at the end of June they decided to share the cavernous but commodious house at 41 Cromwell Road, opposite the Natural History Museum, where their sister-in-law Lady Gwendeline (or 'Goonie') Churchill had been installed with her two children by her husband Jack before his departure, as a staff officer, for the Dardanelles. The location, made hideous today by the traffic pounding down the main western exit from central London, was in marginally fashionable territory, but the house itself, while larger, had even less charm than Eccleston Square. Both families, who got on very well with each other – and continued to do so – were attracted by the economy of sharing. Churchill himself however does not appear to have been very keen on life in this conflated nursery. As he told his brother in a letter of 2 October, he spent most of his London nights in their mother's house at 72 Brook Street, Mayfair.

A mild addition to Winston Churchill's troubles was the reduction in his ministerial salary to £2,000 as a result of his transfer to the Duchy.* Money was a problem which he always believed in rising above, and the change did not prevent his taking a small country house that summer. This was Hoe Farm, near Godalming in Surrey, and had been rented before his débâcle. It was a Tudoresque minor manor house (recently 'Lutyenized'), rather than a farm, set in a secluded valley of that convoluted but already semi-suburbanized countryside. 'We live very simply [here],' he wrote to his brother on 19 June, 'but with all the essentials of life well understood & well provided for – hot baths, cold champagne, new peas, & old brandy.'[4]

Hoe Farm had a large garden which was the scene of one of the personal turning points of Churchill's life. One weekend in June, while he was still disorientated by his sudden loss of high executive office – 'like a sea-beast fished up from the depths, or a diver suddenly hoisted' was his own description[5] – he came upon the beautiful Goonie painting in watercolours. She persuaded him to take a brush and try for himself. He was captivated, although pictorial art had not previously played any part in his life.[†] The pale delicacies of watercolours were however not long for him. He was quickly on to the harder stuff of oils. Hazel Lavery, herself a painter and wife of the fashionable portraitist, came to visit and showed him both how to use turpentine and how to escape from inhibition into audacity by slapping on the paint in good bold colours. This greatly increased his enjoyment, and made painting an absorbing occupation until nearly the end of his remaining fifty years of life. He attained a considerable proficiency, and, as Violet Bonham Carter perceptively noticed over many years, it was the only occupation which he ever pursued in total silence. More immediately, this new

---

* Within a few months, however, a spirit of wartime fair shares seized the government, and all the Cabinet salaries were pooled, coming out at £4,057 for everyone (perhaps the equivalent of £150,000 today). After the war they reverted to the previous pattern, so that Stanley Baldwin, when he accepted the number-two position in the National government of 1931, although the leader of much the largest party, got only £2,000 as Lord President of the Council (as opposed to the £5,000 of most other ministers) at a time when his iron and steel wealth was seriously depleted.

† According to Clementine he had never up to that moment been in a picture gallery (Mary Soames, *Winston Churchill: His Life as a Painter*.)

pastime calmed his mind and helped him to come to some sort of terms with his reduced political prospects.

He was not contracting out from politics. On the contrary he was anxious to cling on to every bit of influence which he could exercise from his diminished little office, which in itself gave him practically nothing to do. It was redeemed only by his membership of the War Council, now renamed the Dardanelles Committee, with its numbers at first reduced to nine, although fairly quickly creeping up to thirteen or fourteen. There were still no Cabinet minutes, but Colonel Hankey was already meticulously keeping them for the subordinate body. These show that at the June meetings Churchill intervened only less frequently than Kitchener, significantly more so than Balfour (his Admiralty successor) and far more so than the Prime Minister or any of the other six members, among whom only Curzon, in the senior sinecure office of Lord Privy Seal, figures on the scoreboard.

In mid-June Churchill wrote to Edwin Montagu as Financial Secretary to the Treasury, asking for an advanced battle headquarters near Whitehall in which he could accommodate himself, a private secretary (he had retained Edward Marsh), a shorthand writer and a messenger, because 'the Duchy of Lancaster office is as you will know quite unsuitable' for his 'heavy' Cabinet and War Council work.[6] The 'heavy' may have been an exaggeration but the request was modest, and he got a small suite in 19 Abingdon Street, opposite the House of Lords. From a man who had so recently bestridden the Admiralty Board Room, the grand adjacent residence and the deck of *Enchantress*, it was a sad request.

In July he thought he was to go on a three-week mission to confer on the spot with General Hamilton and Admiral de Robeck, the local commanders in the Dardanelles theatre, and to report to the Cabinet. There might even be a possibility of extending the visit to comprise Bulgaria and Roumania, two countries which Churchill had long believed he had a special mission to bring into the war on the Allied side. It is not clear with whom the idea originated, probably with Churchill himself, but it was warmly supported, perhaps from a variety of motives, by Asquith, Balfour, Kitchener and Edward Grey. Churchill was excited at the prospect, although in a curiously apocalyptic way, given his normal indifference to personal danger. On 18 July he wrote to Asquith: 'I shall of course be careful to run no unnecessary risks; but it will not be possible for me to appreciate the position without landing on the Gallipoli peninsula and in consequence coming under fire. If any mischance shd occur I consider that my wife shd receive the pension prescribed for a general officer's widow; & I rely on you to see to this.'[7] The day before he had written a still more doom-laden letter to Clementine, to be delivered only after his death. The first two paragraphs were about money and consequently rather dull. The third paragraph was in a sense play-acting, certainly self-dramatization, but nonetheless providing a highly charged view as to how he saw himself and his marriage, all written in resounding prose:

> I am anxious that you shd get hold of all my papers, especially those wh refer to my Admiralty administration. I have appointed you my sole literary executor. . . . There is no hurry; but some day I shd like the truth to be known. Randolph will carry on the lamp. Do not grieve for me too much. I am a spirit confident of my rights. Death is only an incident, & not the most important wh happens to us in this state of being. On the whole, especially since I met you my darling one I have been happy, & you have taught me how noble a woman's heart can be. If there is anywhere else I shall be on the look out for you. Meanwhile look forward, feel free, rejoice in life, cherish the children, guard my memory. God bless you.
>   Good bye
>   W.[8]

Bathos followed, for he never went. On Monday, 19 July Churchill came to London from Hoe Farm, intending to leave for the eastern Mediterranean on the Tuesday. Hankey, by the desire of Kitchener, endorsed by Asquith, was to accompany him. This may not have been in accordance with Churchill's spontaneous wishes, for it was to some extent putting a guard dog on him, but it was a minor irritant which he was prepared to accept with a good grace. He was in Downing Street saying goodbye to Asquith, Kitchener and Grey when Curzon arrived and expressed surprise at the news of Churchill's mission, but added his good wishes. However, with the tendency to a forked tongue which marred Curzon's great gifts and greater ambitions, and which was certainly to be a factor in his not becoming Prime Minister in 1923, he then rushed to inform his Conservative Cabinet colleagues, which led to their imposing what was in effect a veto on Churchill going as a Cabinet emissary. As soon as he was appraised of this, Churchill withdrew. He would not go without a wholehearted Cabinet asking him to do so. His withdrawal was a relief for Asquith, who did not want a fight on the issue. It was a further humiliation for Churchill.

After this setback he was to remain in the government for another sixteen weeks. They were all in a sense part of a long downhill road to resignation, although it was one of varying gradients and of sufficient twists and turns for the destination to be frequently out of view. He was inclined to argue with himself as to whether he was justified in staying in London with a civilian lifestyle. Thus on 20 September he wrote to Colonel Jack Seely, the brave middle-aged boy scout who as Secretary of State for War had made such a mess of the Curragh 'mutiny' in the spring of 1914 but who was currently successfully commanding the Canadian Cavalry Brigade: 'It is odious to me to remain here watching sloth & folly with full knowledge & no occupation';[9] and in October to his brother: 'Here with full knowledge [a recurring phrase] & now lots of time on my hands it is damnable. But for the present this is my post.'[10]

He saw himself, naturally and reasonably in view of his initiating responsibility, as the Cabinet member for the Dardanelles strategy and for those from General Ian Hamilton downwards who engaged danger-ously in that ultimately futile enterprise, losing in some cases their reputations, and in too many others their lives. This gave him a purposeful role until well into August. On 25 April Hamilton had made his first Gallipoli landings with the 29th Division and the Australian and New Zealand army corps. They had suffered heavy casualties but had managed to maintain footholds until 6 August when the reinforcing landings of IX Corps took place at Suvla. Once again casualties were very heavy. Within four or five days it was obvious that, in Jack Churchill's on-the-spot words, 'the chance of a real coup has gone I am afraid'. Maybe through an almost criminal lack of initiative on the part of Hamilton's subordinate generals, the thrust became bogged down. All that had been secured was another precarious foothold. The supreme irony was that this great flanking strategy, which had adventurously dominated Churchill's cavalry-trained mind for the previous eight months, had resulted in a stalemate which, though minor, was as bloodstained as that on the Western Front, to which it was supposed to be the imaginative, fluid and light-casualty alternative.

Churchill's loyal reaction was to urge in the Dardanelles Committee the sending of further reinforcements to Hamilton. His interest in the Dardanelles had become so obsessive that he ignored the normally sound military precept of not reinforcing failure. Reading the minutes of those rambling and dismayed meetings of the Committee, however, it is difficult not to feel sympathy with the bleak and mordant comments of Bonar Law who had come to assume the role of chief sceptic. On 19

August he said that '[Sir Ian Hamilton] was always *nearly* winning.'[11] On the 27th August he asked if 'Hamilton was supposed to be acting on the defensive, or if he was going to continue his course of sacrificing men [casualties were already approximately 40,000] without a chance of success'.[12] Churchill must have realized this, yet was pinioned. He fell back on blaming the creakingly ineffective decision-taking capacity of the Dardanelles Committee, and still more so that of the Cabinet. Asquithian although I am, and sceptical of how much the direction of the war improved under Lloyd George, I am nonetheless shocked by reading the minutes of the Dardanelles Committee. This, more than its name implies, was the central strategic directing body of the time. There was certainly no other. Yet it was a forum for the undulating exchange of views rather than for taking any hard decisions. The undulations were good tempered when exceptionally there was favourable news, more often bad tempered when there was not.

The Committee did bring itself to recall Hamilton in mid-October. A considerable part in this was played by Keith Murdoch, then a young correspondent on the *Sydney Sun*, who himself became a major Australian newspaper proprietor and was the father of a more global press tycoon in the shape of his son Rupert, born in 1931, long after Keith Murdoch had returned from the hazards of the Dardanelles. Keith Murdoch's importance in the circumstances stemmed from the strong Australian presence (and casualties) in Gallipoli. Robert Donald, the editor of the (Liberal) *Daily Chronicle* wrote to Churchill about him in interesting but reserved terms:

> Mr Murdoch does not pretend to possess any military knowledge. When I questioned him on details of his report he gave me rather evasive replies. It is quite obvious that he has not seen the things which he described, nor has any personal knowledge of the men he has condemned. His information was largely second-hand. I do not say that much of it is not correct, or that some of his criticisms are not justified, but my personal feeling about him is that his statements must be accepted with caution.[13]

Tendentious or not, Murdoch's report, which he sent to Asquith, Lloyd George and the Prime Minister of Australia (Andrew Fisher), turned up the final heat on Ian Hamilton's goose. Churchill at the Dardanelles Committee of 14 October which took the decision to recall him (and Hamilton was never again given a general's command) was reduced to saying that his difficulties had been 'appalling' and that he trusted there would be no 'slur' associated with his recall.

It was almost as near the (temporary) end for Churchill as it was the (permanent) one for Hamilton. Churchill was still writing powerful Cabinet memoranda and/or letters to Asquith at the beginning of October. On the 4th he proposed that Kitchener, who had been a failure at the War Office, should replace Sir John French in command in France (where Churchill thought as little as possible should be attempted). French should command 'the British armies against the Turks'. Lloyd George should replace Kitchener at the War Office 'with the best & strongest general staff that can be formed. Sir Douglas Haig in spite of feeble powers of speech is incontestably the most highly educated and intellectually gifted soldier we possess.'[14]

The trouble was that, much though Churchill was coming to upbraid Asquith's lack of courage, he himself, lion though he normally was, suffered from something of the same disease. Perhaps there was some dreadful stultifying virus which hovered over Whitehall in the autumn of 1915. The last four paragraphs, and those the most effective, were cut out before the letter was sent. The same non-sending hesitation applied to his two resignation letters to Asquith, those of 22 and 29 October. The first was a simple threat to go if Kitchener was not removed from the War Office and replaced by 'a competent civilian Secretary of State for War responsible in a real sense to Parliament & sustained by the strongest general staff who can be formed'.[15] Kitchener was not deprived of the title of War Secretary, but he was shipped off on a month's visit to the Dardanelles and surrounding points, an arrangement which enabled Asquith to get his own hands on the War Office, as he had previously done between the Curragh trouble and the outbreak of war in 1914, and to give a remarkable late display of his deft administrative skill, which sits ill with the view that he had by this time become hopelessly lethargic and procrastinating. He lanced a number of boils which had long been festering under Kitchener, including the major one of recalling French from the Expeditionary Force in France and replacing him as Commander-in-Chief by Haig.

Before Kitchener left for the eastern Mediterranean Asquith also responded to a widespread Cabinet demand for a much smaller War Council. This intention the Prime Minister conveyed to his colleagues in a minute of 28 October, and it was this which provoked Churchill's second unsent letter of resignation. He was in a similar awkward position to that of the previous May. Then he had been in favour of a coalition in principle, but not if it involved his own exclusion, or at any rate semi-exclusion, from the seats of power. Now he was a great critic of the rambling indecisiveness of the inflated Dardanelles Committee, but realized that a small taut body would not include himself, and that he would be left in his sinecure with little other than his Lancashire magisterial appointments to occupy him. The letter he drafted showed some signs of bad temper:

> The views I have expressed on war policy are on record, and I have seen with deep regret the course which has been followed. Nor could I conscientiously accept responsibility without power. The long delays in coming to decisions have not been the only cause of our misfortunes. The faulty & lethargic execution and lack of scheme and combination over all military affairs, & of any effective concert with out Allies are evils wh will not be cured merely by the changes indicated in yr memorandum – good though these are in themselves. . . . There is one point however on which it would perhaps be well for us to have a talk. It is now necessary for the truth to be made public about the initiation of the Dardanelles expedition.[16]

It was as well that this letter, rather curiously drafted on Claridge's Hotel writing paper, was not sent, for he wrote a very much tauter (and definitive) one two weeks later. It avoided the note of peevish complaint which characterized the discarded draft, and it also put the vindication of his Admiralty policy in a more positive and self-confident way, thereby avoiding the slight hint of blackmail which there had been in the last sentence of the draft. In his semi-unemployed condition of the summer, Churchill had become obsessive about his wartime record as First Lord, and was constantly demanding that minutes, telegrams and other documents relating not only to shared responsibility (with Asquith, Kitchener and indeed the whole War Council) for the winter decision to go for the Dardanelles strategy, but also to the Antwerp affair, to the sinking of the three 'Cressys' and to Admiral Cradock's lost battle in the South Pacific, should be published.

There was no enthusiasm for this on the part of Asquith, Balfour (who had of course become departmentally responsible) or any other minister. They could hardly be expected, in the middle of a fairly desperate war, to give the same priority over security, morale and also, no doubt, an instinctive ministerial liking for secrecy to the vindication of Churchill's reputation that he himself did. As he could not secure a more general circulation he took to handing round, particularly to his new Conservative colleagues, who had of course not been privy to them at the time, copies of the relevant secret documents, rather as though they were especially salacious pieces of pornography, and awaiting with impatience their impressed reaction. It was not his finest hour.

However, in his real letter of resignation he cut himself free from this niggling self-justification and struck a more self-confident note. As a result this published statement was widely thought to have achieved a high tone and called forth letters of approval from, among many others, Violet Asquith (who even wrote him out a copy of Kipling's 'If', presumably less hackneyed then than it is today), Edward Grey and the colonel of the 4th Hussars. It makes a sufficiently important break in his life to be worth quoting in full.

Duchy of Lancaster Office
11 November 1915

My dear Asquith

When I left the Admiralty five months ago, I accepted an office with few duties in order at your request to take part in the work of the War Council, and to assist new Ministers with the knowledge of current operations which I then possessed in a special degree. The counsels which I have offered are upon record in the minutes of the Committee of Imperial Defence [a loose term for what was first the War Council and then the Dardanelles Committee], and in the Memoranda I have circulated to the Cabinet; and I draw your attention at the present time to these.

I am in cordial agreement with the decision to form a small War Council. I appreciated the intention you expressed to me six weeks ago to include me among its members. I foresaw then the personal difficulties which you would have to face in its composition, and I make no complaint at all that your scheme should be changed. But with the change my work in the Government comes naturally to a close.

Knowing what I do about the present situation, and the instrument of executive power [an obscure phrase], I could not accept a position of general responsibility for war policy without any effective share in its guidance & control. Even when decisions of principle are rightly taken, the speed and method of their execution are factors which determine the result. Nor do I feel able in times like these to remain in well-paid inactivity. I therefore ask you to submit my resignation to the King. I am an officer, and I place myself unreservedly at the disposal of the military authorities, observing that my regiment is in France.

I have a clear conscience which enables me to bear my responsibility for past events with composure.

Time will vindicate my administration of the Admiralty, and assign me my due share in the vast series of preparations and operations which have secured us the complete command of the seas.

With much respect, and unaltered personal friendship, I bid you good-bye.
Yours very sincerely,
Winston S. Churchill[17]

His resignation statement in the House of Commons on Monday, 15 November also went well, in great contrast with his next parliamentary intervention four months later. Once again Violet Asquith was to be free in her praise: 'I thought your speech *quite* flawless – I have seldom been more moved – It was a fine and generous speech – *How* thankful I am you said what you did about that wicked old lunatic.'[18] The 'wicked old lunatic' was, needless to say, Fisher and not her father, although Asquith soon became more the target of Churchill's criticism. From a different political angle Sunny Marlborough was almost equally enthusiastic, although taking a different view about the passage on the 'old lunatic'. 'It was an excellent exposition of your case and I rejoice,' the Duke wrote. 'I wish though that you had left out the part criticizing Fisher.'[19] It is not difficult to guess which of these two letters Churchill preferred, it being an almost absolute rule that when a letter of general praise contains a piece of criticism, it is the criticism and not the praise which remains in the mind of the recipient.

Churchill's speech, apart from his criticism of Fisher, which although severe was dignified ('I did not receive from the First Sea Lord either the clear guidance before the event or the firm support after which I was entitled to expect'), was unvindictive and resolute about the future. 'There is no reason to be discouraged about the progress of the War. We are passing through a bad time now, and it will probably be worse before it is better, but that it will be better, if we only endure and persevere, I have no doubt whatsoever.'[20] But it was in many ways the negative rather than the positive aspects of the speech which were most notable. It was Sherlock Holmes's dog that did not bark. He indulged in no vituperation against Asquith or any other of his late colleagues. As a result he went off, whatever bitterness there was in his heart and in that of Clementine, with superficial goodwill. He had not offended the Asquithians, nor indeed, recently, the Conservatives. Asquith himself, in the debate which followed the resignation statement, was urbanely friendly, and Bonar Law was rather more: 'I entered the Cabinet, to put it mildly, with no prejudice in favour of the right honourable gentleman ... but I say deliberately, in my judgement, in mental power and vital force he is one of the foremost men of our country. . . .'[21] And he wrote to Asquith suggesting that Churchill might be sent to East Africa, presumably as commander-in-chief, and therefore as a lieutenant-general.

The farewell luncheon at 41 Cromwell Road on the following day, while it had elements of a wake had even more those of a Churchill–Asquith *Fest*. Violet Asquith came, and so, more surprisingly, did Margot Asquith. Obviously Clementine did and there were also her sister Nellie Hozier, Goonie Churchill and Eddie Marsh. As Violet recorded, most had 'leaden hearts', but 'Winston alone was at his gayest and his best, and he and Margot held the table between them.'[22] It is difficult to think who, whatever the circumstances, could have competed with that duo.

On the morning of 18 November Churchill crossed the Channel to join his pre-1914 yeomanry regiment of the Oxfordshire Hussars. The speed with which he could arrange his embodiment and his transit was remarkable; it was his old Malakand Field Force or Omdurman touch. He went as a major. No one knew quite how far and how quickly he would rise once he arrived.

16

AN IMPROBABLE COLONEL AND A
MISJUDGED RE-ENTRY

CHURCHILL'S RECEPTION AT Boulogne was not exactly that of a run-of-the-mill major. He was met on the quayside by the driver of a motor car sent by the Commander-in-Chief to take him to General Headquarters at St Omer. With good sense he persuaded the chauffeur to divert via the headquarters of the Oxfordshire Hussars so that he at least made his number with the regiment whose insignia he was bearing, although in fact he never served with them.

That night he dined with Sir John French and slept 'in a fine chateau, with hot baths, beds, champagne & all the conveniences'. There were also almost excessive reminders that GHQ remained psychologically rather nearer to London politics than to the mud and squalor of the trenches. 'Redmond [pre-war and very moderate Irish Nationalist leader at Westminster] has been dining here. Very agreeable, & admits I am absolutely right to leave the Govt.'[1] The whole episode, balanced by several other quickly following and uncomfortable as well as moderately dangerous ones, is at once as vivid and as unreal as a scene in an opera or a medieval pageant. Of all periods of modern history I find the lives (and many deaths) of those in the British Expeditionary Force in France in 1914–18 the most difficult to comprehend. The assumptions of peacetime pre-1914 politics are easy to re-create. The physical circumstances of Gladstone's Midlothian campaign are not too difficult to understand. And even Wellington's one-day clash with Napoleon at Waterloo, now nearly 200 years ago, is not beyond the bounds of imagination. But those four years of suffering and slaughter, less than half as long ago, only forty or fifty miles from Dover, barely four or five hours' travel from Victoria or Charing Cross stations in the heart of London, are to me much more unreal. Even my four (admittedly fairly unhazardous) years in the Second World War army do not constitute much of a bridge to the much more unrelieved hardship and tragedy of the first war.

Equally unreal is this brief segment of Churchill's life. He was only in the army for five and a half months, just about as long as he endured the Duchy of Lancaster, and of this brief spell he was in England on either private or parliamentary leave for an aggregate of three weeks. It is a particularly well-documented few months, for there was no period of his life when his correspondence with his wife was more intensive, more affectionate, even passionate, or provided a more detailed picture of his circumstances and states of mind.* Nevertheless these months are to me a life in limbo, neither wholly in the world of squalor, sacrifice and of dogged acceptance of going on to the end, nor wholly in that of privilege, occasional semi-luxury and only conditional engagement. He was torn between three conflicting desires. The first was a determination to do his duty with his normal fearlessness. The second was a great ambition for military promotion. The higher up the hierarchy of army rank he could quickly get the more pleased he would be. Third, to some extent conflicting with both the other two, was a constant keeping of his eye on London politics. Even within a month of his arrival in France he was writing of his confidence that '[no] difficulty wd be placed in my way, if I required to return home for Parliamentary duties and the situation needed my presence'.[2]

On his second day in France he went to see Major-General (later Field Marshal) the Earl of Cavan, who was then commanding the Guards Division, and returned (from GHQ) the next day to lunch with him. Everything was done in a stately and hospitable order at these levels. Churchill was then told that he was to be attached, for familiarization with trench warfare, to the 2nd Battalion of the Grenadiers. This was a supernumerary attachment. He had no command duties. But it plunged him into rough and fairly dangerous conditions. Rats and waterlogged dug-outs entered his consciousness. He reacted to them reasonably well. It was sixteen years since he had experienced field soldiering in South Africa. But, as he wrote after a week in France: 'It is satisfactory to find that so many years of luxury have in no way impaired the tone of my system.'[3]

The welcome that he received from Cavan was not at first repeated at battalion level. The colonel was George Jeffreys, later to be a general, much later still to be Conservative MP for Petersfield for ten years and, in my overlapping House of Commons recollection of three years, to be

* Mary Soames's collection of their letters (*Speaking for Themselves*, 1998) provides a magnificent insight into this period above all others.

the nearest approach to a caricature of an *Oh! What a Lovely War* commander that I have ever seen. His greeting to Churchill when he arrived at the battalion was chilly. As Churchill (who subsequently made him a peer in 1952) remembered it, admittedly many years later in his 1932 *Thoughts and Adventures*, Colonel Jeffreys said: 'I think I ought to tell you that we were not at all consulted in the matter of your coming to join us.' And his adjutant encouragingly added: 'I am afraid we have had to cut your kit rather, Major. . . . We have found a servant for you, who is carrying a spare pair of socks and your shaving gear.'[4] I suspect an element of exaggeration here, for Churchill was writing to Clementine within twenty-four hours to demand:

(1) A warm brown leather waistcoat
(2) A pair of trench wading boots, brown leather bottoms, & waterproof canvas tops coming right up to the thigh
(3) A periscope (most important)
(4) A sheepskin sleeping bag. . . .
In addition please send me
(5) 2 pairs of khaki trousers (wh Morris [his valet] stupidly forgot to pack)
(6) 1 pair of my brown buttoned boots
(7) three small face towels[5]

A little later his requests became more concentrated on food and drink. These became more urgent and substantial the looser became his links with GHQ. On 23 November he merely ordered for 'once a week a *small* box of food to supplement the rations. Sardines, chocolate, potted meats, and other things which may strike your fancy. Begin as soon as possible. . . .' Two days later he wanted '2 bottles of my old brandy & a bottle of peach brandy. This consignment might be repeated at intervals of ten days.'[6] But by 27 January 1916: 'About food – the sort of things I want you to send me are these – large slabs of corned beef: stilton cheeses: cream: hams: sardines – dried fruits: you might almost try a big beef steak pie: but not tinned grouse or fancy tinned things.'[7]

More significantly however he quickly overcame the initial Grenadier hostility to his attachment. They were impressed by his seriousness of purpose, by his indifference to danger and by his ability to endure discomfort – although not in this case stemming from his indifference to it. And he in turn developed a high admiration for the senior regiment of Foot Guards. 'The discipline of this battalion is very strict,'

he wrote on 27 November, '. . . But the results are good. The spirit
is admirable. . . . A total indifference to death or casualties prevails.
What has to be done is done, & the losses accepted without fuss or
comment. . . .'[8]

He spent much of his time with the company commanded by Edward
Grigg (much later Lord Altrincham),* and acquired a quick familiarity
with trench life in the front line. Churchill's time with the Grenadiers
was effectively confined to the last ten days of November and forty-
eight or so hours in mid-December. On the 9th of that latter month
Jeffreys offered to make him his second-in-command, believing that he
might arrange a waiver of the rule that Grenadiers could be commanded
only by their own. Churchill was flattered, but he believed that he had
higher things firmly within his grasp. At times in the past – at Antwerp
or if he had gone to East Africa – even a lieutenant-general's rank had
floated before his eyes, but now his immediate ambitions were concentrated upon 'getting a brigade'. He believed that Asquith had promised
him this before he left London. And Field Marshal French certainly
intended that he should have it. By 10 December the proposal had
assumed precise form. On that day he wrote to Clementine: 'I am to
be given command of the 56th Brigade in the 19th Division. Bridges
will command the Division & the Bde I shall command comprises
4 Lancashire Battalions. . . . I hope to get Spiers as Brigade Major &
Archie [Sinclair] as Staff Captain. . . . Please order another khaki tunic
for me as a Brigadier General. Let the pockets be less baggy than the
other 2, & let the material be stouter.'[9]

It did not happen, and no doubt, given the detailed form of his
expectation and preparations, the result was a sense of dismay and even
humiliation. Yet his reaction to the disappointment was extreme and in
one direction unbalanced. There were clearly great turbulences in his
mind underneath a nominally calm surface at the time. At first in France
he was at pains to stress his sense and appearance of well-being. On 23
November, after his initial and very abrupt immersion in the trenches
(only five days out from London), he wrote: 'Amid these surroundings,

---

* There were a lot of peers and future peers about, apart from Grigg. Cavan and Jeffreys
have already been noted. The adjutant of the 2nd Grenadiers, who began by being at
least as unfriendly as Colonel Jeffreys, was to succeed as the third Lord Glanusk, and
French, Churchill's great initial friend at the head of the Expeditionary Force, became
Earl of Ypres. Soon, however, Churchill was to settle down in much more typical and
humble army circumstances, commanding middle-class officers and Ayrshire-coalfield
other ranks.

aided by wet & cold, & every minor discomfort, I have found happiness & content such as I have not known for many months.'[10] And on 4 December: 'They all say I look 5 years younger: & certainly I have never been in better health & spirits.'[11]

Furthermore there were several of those who had his best interests at heart who thought that immediate command of a brigade was rushing things and stultifying the good effect of his modestly working his passage in France. 'Do get a battalion *now* & a brigade later,' Clementine, so often wiser than her husband, wrote on 6 December, having two days earlier written: 'General Bridges [whom they both greatly respected] came to see me last night.... He said "I suppose Winston is going to get a brigade". I said I thought you would rather take a battalion first – His face lighted up & he said "I am *so* glad".'[12] And Churchill himself faithfully reported that when he had again lunched with Lord Cavan on 11 December: '[The General] strongly advised me to take a battalion before a Brigade: & this is what I think I shall do, if it is open to me.'[13]

French undoubtedly wanted his friend Churchill to have his brigade. But French was on the way out. Asquith had taken this decision before Kitchener came back from the eastern Mediterranean on 30 November; and French was aware of it. In mid-December the C-in-C was in London on a *nunc dimittis* mission. He told Asquith of his intention about Churchill's brigade, and the Prime Minister at first seemed pleased, but when a parliamentary storm threatened (had Churchill ever commanded even an infantry battalion; how many weeks had he been at the front?) he became cautious, wrote to French saying that it was probably unwise, and added 'Perhaps you might give him a Battalion.'[14]

French telephoned to Churchill at St Omer (where apart from his Guards interludes Churchill spent much of December waiting in 'days of absolute idleness' at GHQ) to tell him the bad news. It was for Churchill a terrible let-down (beyond having to cancel his brigadier's tunic), although it is difficult to see from outside and in retrospect what was the vast difference for an amateur soldier, who seven months before had commanded a whole service, between a battalion and a brigade, at least as a starting point. Yet Asquith's 'Perhaps you might give him a Battalion' rankled more than almost any phrase with which he had hitherto come into contact. His mind became obsessive about it. He regarded it as a gross betrayal. Previously he had been critical, perhaps with substantial justification, of Asquith's deft rather than dynamic conduct of the politics of the war. After it he became violent and unbalanced in his criticism. It sits ill with his own reiterated view that he was happy and calm in his new life in the field.

This led to a several-months-long running argument between him and Clementine about his future relations with Asquith. She wanted to keep lines of contact open, he wanted to descend into an offended bunker. She was a great deal more sensible than he was. In the first place his prior attitude was not such that Asquith, had he possessed full knowledge, could have been held to owe him much. Even before he had received the bad news, he had written to his wife: 'The hour of Asquith's punishment & K[itchener]'s exposure draws nearer. The wretched men have nearly wrecked our chances. It may fall to me to strike the blow. I shall do it without compunction.'[15] After this he wrote two letters which he asked her to destroy (as she did) because he was 'depressed & my thought not organized'. What they contained compared with what he wrote the next day, which he did not ask to be destroyed, is difficult to imagine. Then he wrote: 'Altogether I am inclined to think that his conduct reached the limit of meanness & ungenerousness. . . . Personally I feel that every link is severed: & while I do not wish to decide in a hurry – my feeling is that all relationship should cease.'[16]

As this husband-and-wife epistolary dispute wound on it became increasingly a matter of whether Asquith should be treated as a black-hearted betrayer or whether he should be regarded, maybe with a touch of critical cynicism, as the benign if sometimes complacent leader which he had been to both of them until seven months before. There was a sub-theme of Churchill being much attracted to Lloyd George (and hopeful that he might be the agent of his own return to office), whereas Clementine was firmly distrustful of him. This marital argument was conducted within a framework of great mutual friendliness and love, but it was nevertheless steadily there. On 10 January Churchill wrote to her with more analysis and less abuse of Asquith than was his habit of the time, but with a depressed finality: 'I cannot see any way in wh Asquith's interests can stand in need of me. However friendly his feelings his *interests* are best served by my effacement. If I were killed he wd be sorry: but it wd suit his political hand. Ll.G on the other hand wd not be sorry, but it wd not suit his political hand.'[17]

On 2 February, he was back to more obsessive complaint. 'My dislike of Asquith and all his works grows steadily.' But she wrote: 'Don't close your mind to the P.M. entirely. He is lazy but (or perhaps therefore) healthy & anyhow he is not a skunk tho' a wily old tortoise.' Of Lloyd

George at about the same time she wrote: 'I don't trust him one bit, fair of speech, shifty of eye, treacherous of heart. . . .'[18]

Clementine Churchill's relations with the Asquiths remained surprisingly close, particularly as, unlike her sister-in-law Goonie, she had never been a personal favourite. This reflected their continuing if sometimes exasperated friendship for her husband. On 30 November her four-and-a-half-year-old son Randolph had been a page at the wedding of Violet Asquith and Maurice Bonham Carter. She had gone to 10 Downing Street for the reception and gave quite a funny description to Churchill of the 'Block' (their mocking but not wholly unfriendly sobriquet for Asquith) coming across her and Haldane (a double embarrassment) together in the hall. '[He] muttered a few civil words & shuffled off sniffing nervously. . . .'[19] Margot Asquith plus her daughter Elizabeth (later Bibesco) came to tea at 41 Cromwell Road in the following week and Clementine and Goonie were bidden to luncheon at Downing Street on the Sunday after that. In the New Year she was again invited on 9 February and sat next to the Prime Minister. In mid-February she spent a weekend at Walmer Castle (which residence of the Lord Warden of the Cinque Ports the Asquiths had temporarily taken over because it was a good staging post for communication with the front), and played golf alone with the Prime Minister, just failing to beat him. At the end of the month both Asquiths came to dine in Cromwell Road, and on 6 March, during Churchill's first extended leave in England – he had had three days for Christmas – they again did so. It was not bad treatment from a Prime Minister for the wife of a semi-disgraced scapegoat, as Churchill regarded himself, left in London on her own.

Nor can it easily be sustained that Asquith, whatever may be thought of his deficiencies in pushing the Dardanelles campaign to determined victory (very difficult to do with Fisher against and Kitchener cautiously lukewarm), had personally treated Churchill badly. When Asquith was forced (largely because of Churchill's predictable inability to get on with the volcanic First Sea Lord whom Churchill had insisted on bringing back to the Admiralty) to form an unwelcome coalition with the Tories, he had at least provided him with a sinecure pulpit within the Cabinet, which was better than he did for Haldane, his oldest political friend. When in the autumn he was pressed (not least by Churchill) to form a war executive, in which there was no possible room for a Chancellor of the Duchy of Lancaster, he accepted Churchill's resignation, both publicly and privately, with regret and good grace.

The Prime Minister did not then in any way force Churchill to go out and find salvation in the field. But, when he did so, he was quite disposed to help him to a higher command of troops in action than any officer–politician, going out without any recent military experience, was to be given in either the First or the Second World Wars. Churchill got very near to achieving his desired brigade, but that was partly because of his over-close cultivation when a minister of the Commander-in-Chief (French) on whom the sun was setting, which had created a good deal of distrust between him and Kitchener, as well as with some other Cabinet colleagues. But when Churchill's too rapid promotion showed signs of becoming damagingly controversial, both for himself and for the government, Asquith did not wish to persist. It may not have been heroic but it was hardly heinous.

The Churchill–Clementine correspondence of these months was still more concerned with the general pattern of his short military life, its periods of hazards and of safety, its discomforts and occasional comforts, its adventures and its flatnesses, than with his grievance, obsessive although this was becoming. When his brigade evaporated he was left hanging around at GHQ, waiting for a battalion to command. St Omer had become a much less attractive place to him after he had seen off French on 19 December. This role he did literally and almost romantically perform. On the previous day they had driven out into the Flanders countryside together and picnicked in a small cottage. And on the very last day: '[French] saw a long succession of generals etc, & then opened his door & said "Winston, it is fitting that my last quarter of an hour here shd be spent with you". Then off he went with a guard of honour, saluting officers, cheering soldiers & townsfolk – stepping swiftly from the stage of history into the dull humdrum of ordinary life.'[20]

Haig was perfectly civil to Churchill, but not much more. As a result Churchill removed himself to stay with Max Aitken (soon to be Lord Beaverbrook), a member of Parliament who was temporarily in uniform and who had established what the guest described as 'a sort of Canadian War Office' in the town of St Omer, but not too near Haig's headquarters. This was the effective beginning of Churchill's close relations with Beaverbrook, which lasted until their respective deaths, within seven months of each other, and it began in a very typical way. Beaverbrook both cosseted and amused Churchill at a time when he had high need of these two assuagements. That continued to be Beaverbrook's habit, at least up to and over Churchill's severe 1953 stroke, when he was one of his first visitors. Beaverbrook's political influence was mostly bad (certainly in the view of Clementine Churchill) and he was by no means invariably on Churchill's side, but he knew how to massage Churchill and he appealed to his lifelong weakness for bounders.

Another new friend of these weeks was Edward (normally known as Louis) Spiers, who later changed his name to Spears, and whose forte from the time of Joffre to that of de Gaulle was to be a liaison officer with the French. He was completely bilingual, having been brought up in France, but he was much more than an interpreter. He was almost as good a talker as Churchill himself, although when at the age of thirty-one he first met the forty-one-year-old word master he was mostly willing to be a respectful listener. On 8 December (1915) Churchill wrote (somewhat self-regardingly but probably also accurately): 'I like him very much and he is entirely captivated.'[21] The captivation was both ways, for it led Churchill, when the brigade was beckoning, as we have seen, to want Spiers as brigade major, and, when he had to lower his sights, as second-in-command of his battalion. To both of these posts Spiers, a quintessential headquarters and liaison officer if ever there was one, would have been totally unsuited. But this did not prevent the force of Churchill's persuasion making him reluctantly available.

That December Spiers's more practical role was to take Churchill on two visits to the French armies, an experience curiously alien to most British officers, even those much senior to Churchill. The two sectors, due as much to the French taste for closed shutters as to British insularity, remained contiguous but almost hermetically sealed. The first visit, to General Fayolle and the Tenth Army in front of Arras on 5 December, was the more visually memorable. They gave him a bluish French steel helmet, the shape of which much suited his martial scowl. He hoped it would protect his 'valuable cranium'. He wore it, perhaps not closely in accord with regulations, whenever subsequently in the trenches (and quite often out of them). It became in a minor way almost as much his symbol as, a quarter of a century later, did Montgomery's beret.

He liked battening himself down (which the French helmet certainly did) and buttoning himself up. Both aspects are unforgettably illustrated by the picture of Churchill and Archibald Sinclair (the future Liberal leader), who unlike Spiers did actually become his second-in-command, that they had formally taken in a local photographic studio at Armentières on an afternoon in February 1916. It looks as though they were both carved in rain-sodden bronze, with all the sombre endurance of two of Rodin's Burghers of Calais. Churchill's trenchcoat, tightly strapped under his Sam Browne belt, gives a singular impression of force. The liking for being strapped up (without his trenchcoat) comes through even more clearly in a picture with Fayolle on the day he was given the helmet. It invokes a curious leap forward to the tight-buttoned black coats (always looking as though they were made for someone with a smaller waist) of his Second World War 'parliamentary' uniform.

The second visit to the French sector, again with Spiers, was to Vimy Ridge and the view down over the plain of Douai. Spiers recalled to Martin Gilbert many years later, after Churchill's death (before which his relations with him had considerably cooled), that the French commanders were polite to Churchill but, at that stage, did not take him seriously. When he expatiated on his ideas for developing the tank, one of them said: 'Wouldn't it be simpler to flood Artois and get your fleet here?'[22] Churchill took the military might and the capacity to absorb punishment of the French more seriously than they took him, and some of the faith which made him, as late as March 1933, cry out in the House of Commons, 'Thank God for the French army,' may have been implanted on these visits.

On New Year's Day 1916, Churchill learned that his battalion was to be the 6th Royal Scots Fusiliers. He arrived to take command on 5 January. The battalion was then in reserve at Meteren, near Bailleul, about five miles short of the Belgian frontier and ten miles back from the front line. Now it is even closer to another line along which Eurostars thunder from Lille (then in enemy occupation) to Calais. The battalion was distinguished only in the sense that in the previous September it had suffered appalling casualties in the Battle of Loos. It had lost half its other ranks and three-quarters of its officers. Since then it had had an uncomfortable time in the Ypres Salient. Not surprisingly, morale was fairly low. Churchill wrote about the battalion to Clementine in terms which sound fair but almost contradictory:

> This regiment is pathetic. The young officers are all small middle class Scotsmen – vy brave & willing & intelligent: but of course all quite new to soldiering. All the seniors & all the professionals have fallen. I have spent the morning watching each company in turn drill & handle their arms. They are vy good. The mess also is well managed – much better than with the Grenadiers. The regiment is full of life & strength, & I believe I shall be a help to them. Archie [his new second-in-command] is vy happy, & I hope he will be made a Major.[23]

How did the thoughts of the battalion about their new commanding officer develop? From junior commissioned level this is remarkably well documented. The officers may have been middle class and small – the latter a surprising point for Churchill to take, for his own height was hardly towering – but two of the handful on his headquarters staff were both interestingly successful in after-life and highly observant at the time. A. D. Gibb, the adjutant, was a Scottish lawyer, who after a mixture of academic jobs and practice at both the London and the Edinburgh bars became Regius Professor of Law in the University of Glasgow for twenty-four years from 1934. He was twice an unsuccessful Conservative candidate in the 1920s, but then became a Scottish Nationalist and, equally unsuccessfully, in the late 1930s contested the Scottish Universities three times as a parliamentary candidate in that interest. In 1924, he published (at first anonymously but later coming out of the closet) *With Winston Churchill at the Front*.

Gibb wrote this little book (it is barely 20,000 words long) in an agreeably mocking style. His two basic assumptions were that the army mostly operated on a series of 'cock-ups', and that, to some extent as a corollary of this, most orders given from a senior to a junior officer were more likely to be wrong than right. This applied particularly if the orders came from outside the battalion and there were staff officers involved. His cynicism was however good tempered, and he made life in and immediately behind the trenches sound more amusing than squalid. His irony embraced Colonel Churchill, although in this case it was accompanied by an amused admiration that a creature of such energy, confidence, fearlessness, self-indulgence and eccentricity could exist. And at the end he cast away his detachment and wrote:

I am fairly convinced that no more popular officer ever commanded troops. As a soldier he was hard-working, persevering and thorough. . . . He was out to work hard at tiresome but indispensable details and to make his unit efficient in the very highest possible degree. I say nothing of his tactical and strategic ability – these were not tested in our time, but I cannot conceive that exceptionally creative and fertile brain failing in any sphere of human activity to which it was applied. And moreover, he loved soldiering: it lay very near his heart and I think he could have been a very great soldier. How often have we heard him say by way of encouragement in difficult circumstances, 'War is a game to be played with a smiling face'. And never was precept more consistently practised than this. . . . He is a man who is apparently always to have enemies. He made none in his old regiment, but left behind him there men who will

always be his loyal partisans and admirers, and who are proud of having
served in the Great War under the leadership of one who is beyond
question a great man.[24]

And Gibb, from his whole tone, was a man whom it was difficult to
impress.

The other witness was Edward Hakewill Smith, then a chubby-faced
youth of nineteen but nonetheless the battalion's only regular officer,
who became a Second World War divisional general and ended as
Lieutenant-Governor of Windsor Castle. They both testify that the
battalion was not at all pleased to see Churchill. The general reaction
was: why couldn't he go elsewhere and leave their battle-ravaged
battalion in peace? The first day did not go tactfully or well. He and
Sinclair arrived, unconvincingly wearing the glengarries of the regiment
(to escape from them was no doubt part of his reason for his attachment
to his French helmet), on two black chargers, accompanied by two
grooms equally well mounted and a pile of luggage way above the
regulation weight including (a very typical Churchill touch) 'a long bath
and a boiler for heating the bath water'. He then summoned all the
officers (according to Hakewill Smith) to 'quite the most uncomfortable
lunch I have ever been at'. During the lunch Churchill glowered rather
than spoke. At the end he made a short speech: 'Gentlemen, I am now
your Commanding Officer. Those who support me I will look after.
Those who go against me I will break.' Then he attempted to drill a
parade of the whole battalion, but as he gave cavalry commands, and
fairly archaic ones at that, there was more farce than precision about the
result.[25]

The jarred note at the beginning was probably exaggerated by
Hakewill Smith, not out of malevolence, for he quickly became a great
Churchill fan, but in order to increase the Cinderella-like drama of the
transformation scene. And, as with Churchill's attachment to the Grenadiers, it did have something of a fairy-tale ending. Those who would
have jeered had they dared, quickly came to cheer. Churchill had two
weeks in which to prepare the battalion for its return to the trenches,
although to an easier and more static part of the line than they had
hitherto experienced. He undoubtedly did it with great vigour and
application to the details upon which he chose to concentrate.

He adopted a hearty approach. There were football matches and
sing-songs. Training was not made too obtrusive, although, Grenadier-
influenced, he was keen on smartening up their rather slovenly West of

Scotland drill. Where he was not Grenadier-influenced, however, was in his leniency of punishments by the sometimes frighteningly harsh standards of the First World War. It was his old Liberal Home Secretary's attitude coming out. He was indeed rebuked by his brigade commander (to whom perhaps he felt an instinctive antipathy because of his disappointment) for his softness in this respect. But Major-General Furse, commanding the 9th (Scottish) Division of which the 6th Royal Scots Fusiliers was part, whom he had not previously known, thought he had greatly smartened up and improved the morale of his battalion, and became in general a supporter, although once, in the spring, peremptorily summoning him back from parliamentary leave in London.

On 27 January Churchill led his battalion into the trenches, just across the Belgian frontier and in front of the village of Ploegsteert. From then until the beginning on 6 March of his seven-day leave in England (later extended to thirteen days at his request for parliamentary reasons) was the period of his real soldiering. During these five weeks there were alternating periods, at first forty-eight hours then six days in the front line, interspersed with short intervals in reserve, but there were no major offensives, by either the British or the Germans. As a result Churchill, fortunately for posterity, never participated in one of the terrible slaughters for a few yards of ground, of which he so deeply disapproved.

Within a quiet tactical situation, although with a fair amount of sporadic shelling, his inclination was always to risk himself beyond the call of duty in occasional rash and fearless expeditions into no-man's land. But how much real danger was he in? His letters to his wife, fascinating and informative though in this period they were, are unreliable on the subject for one identifiable reason. At first he was very concerned to reassure her and to discount the danger. Thus on 19 November, when he was about to go into the trenches with the Grenadiers for the first time, he wrote: 'But I do hope you will realize what a very harmless thing this is. To my surprise I learn they only have about 15 killed & wounded each day out of 8000 men exposed! It will make me vy sulky if I think you are allowing yourself to be made anxious by any risk like that.'[26] (The 8,000 referred to the Guards Division as a whole; and it may be thought that cumulatively the risk was far from negligible.)

Later however he became less disposed to shelter Clementine from the contemplation of danger. He was more inclined to describe disagreeable incidents, narrow escapes and future threats. On 16 February he wrote: 'I have now had 2 officers hit out of 5 in my H.Q. mess: & there is no doubt that we are rather a target.' And in the same letter, provoked into unusual frustration by news of a successful trial in England of the first caterpillar tank, very much his brainchild, he added in bitter complaint that he had not been given a directing job. 'And how powerless I am! Are they not fools not to use my mind – or knaves to wait for its destruction by some flying splinter? I do not fear death or wounds, & I like the daily life out here; but their impudence and complaisance makes me quite spiteful sometimes.'[27]

A possible reason for the change was that another division of opinion, beyond the issue of whether to place more trust in Asquith or Lloyd George, had opened up between the Churchills. Once he had got his battalion into better shape, had led it into the front and got it and himself settled down to trench life, and as too his hope of even an eventual brigade became remote, he was feeling unstretched and a little bored. The twitch upon the thread of London politics was drawing him back, not at all from fear but from a mixture of frustration and unrealistic ambition. 'The group I want to work with & form into an effective governing instrument', he wrote to Clementine in an undated February letter, 'is Ll.G:, F.E: [Smith], B.L: [Bonar Law], Carson & Curzon. Keep that steadily in mind. It is the alternative Government, when "wait & see" is over.'[28] He began intensely to look forward to his early March leave, even more for political than for recreational purposes. As has been seen he extended it by a week in order to stay on in the House of Commons, and after his return from it his mind was much more on politics in London than on soldiering in France. He was increasingly impatient to exercise his right to resign his commission and return full time to his parliamentary duties.

Clementine did not agree with him. Of course she was anxious for his return to safety, but she could also see how liable he was to rush his fences. Her dilemma was best expressed in a letter of 6 April, several weeks after he had gone back from his leave:

My Darling own Dear Winston I am so torn and lacerated over you. If I say 'stay where you are' a wicked bullet may find you which you would but for me escape. . . . If I were sure you would come through unscathed I would say: 'wait, wait, have patience, don't pluck the fruit before it is ripe – Everything will come to you if you don't snatch at it' – To be great one's actions must be able to be understood by simple people. Your motive for going to the Front was easy to understand – Your motive for coming back requires explanation.[29]

It was very robust advice, clearly given in his interests but against his increasingly urgent desires. As that spring went on he became convinced that his return would transform politics and open the way to his ministerial rehabilitation. Clementine's only hesitation about telling him that this was wrong lay in worry about his danger in France. Such was his inability to keep away from the falsely beckoning prospect that it pushed him, in contrast with November–December, towards a slight exaggeration of the risk. That was the tempting way to move Clementine's mind and to persuade her to give more palatable advice.

It is very difficult to see why Churchill's extended leave in early March should have moved his mind away from soldiering and towards a return to full-time London politics. Politically that leave was a near disaster. He saw plenty of people, but nobody, apart from his two editor friends, C. P. Scott of the *Manchester Guardian* and J. L. Garvin of the *Observer*, offered any sensible basis of support for an alliance to bring down the Asquith government or any realistic prospect of his return to office under it or any likely successor. And his own behaviour was to say the least erratic. He hunted with the hare as well as with the hounds. He allowed himself to be seduced into the most bizarre alliance. And towards the end of his eleven days away from his battalion, his fluctuating view about whether or not he wanted to return to it became a caricature of indecision.

The first contradiction was that on his first full evening in London, the Friday, he had got his mother to arrange a dinner party which was a nest of conspirators against the government. F. E. Smith (in spite of being Attorney-General) was the most prominent, but there were also Scott and Garvin. Carson would almost certainly have been procured had he not been ill. More surprising was the presence of Sir Francis Hopwood, Churchill's old reproving permanent secretary at the Colonial Office nine years before and a disloyal and intriguing civil lord at the Admiralty more recently. Roping him in pointed to a desperation for allies. Churchill had become aware as soon as he got back to London that on the following Tuesday and Wednesday there was to be a debate on the naval estimates which would provide him with a fine opportunity to attack the government through what he regarded as the quiescent policy of his successor, Arthur Balfour. He had indeed spent the first day of his leave in meticulous preparation (no sloth for him) of the main part of a speech for the occasion, which he proceeded that evening to rehearse to the assembled company.

On the Monday Clementine had arranged for the Asquiths to dine at 41 Cromwell Road. Not many battalion commanders had the Prime Minister and his wife to grace their first substantial leave, although it could equally be said that not many had been his Cabinet colleague for seven years. Churchill did not disguise the fact that he was going to speak and defend his own Admiralty record on the following day, but he almost certainly did not indicate how damaging he intended the speech to be, not only to Balfour, but to the government as a whole. Nor did he disclose the bizarre alliance which he had been engaged in reforging during the weekend.

This was with Fisher, the cause of his downfall eleven months previously. They each had an amazing and almost indestructible fascination for the other. The two editors, Scott and Garvin, had been promoting both Fisher and Churchill, and with a singular lack of judgement thought that they could usefully bring them back together. Both the ex-Admiralty chiefs were so thirsty for major re-employment that they could not resist the dangerously beckoning lights across the marsh. Fisher was invited to Saturday lunch at Cromwell Road, and Churchill saw him again on the Sunday evening. Clementine Churchill, as so often in this period, had much better sense. She was reported by both F. E. Smith (who was present at the luncheon) and Violet Bonham Carter (who was not) as in effect saying: 'Keep your hands off my husband. You have all but ruined him once. Leave him alone now.'[30] But Churchill and Fisher could never leave each other alone, and although Fisher wrote him a letter of manifest insanity at 4.00 a.m. on 6 March, Churchill amazingly became once again entwined within his embrace.

This destroyed the impact of Churchill's 7 March speech in the House of Commons. He spoke, using what were then regarded as his natural rights as a Privy Councillor, from the opposition despatch box and did so, unlike many serving officers in that war and even in the second war, in plain clothes, if a tail-coat can be so described. The earlier parts of his speech were impressive. He defended his own record well and fired some damaging but not obviously maliciously expressed shots against subsequent Admiralty policy. Then he launched into his final bewildering passage: 'I urge the First Lord of the Admiralty without delay to fortify himself, to vitalize and animate his Board of Admiralty by recalling Lord Fisher to his post as First Sea Lord.'[31]

This was comparable with the moment in July 1942 when Sir John Wardlaw-Milne, an unremembered figure except for his brief moment of fluffed glory, descended into farce when his much heralded motion of censure *against Churchill* collapsed into his suggestion that the Duke of Gloucester should be made Commander-in-Chief of the British forces. Churchill's concluding remarks in 1916 produced the same disastrous sense of bathos. The air suddenly seeped out of the balloon which he had been so strenuously blowing up for the previous forty minutes. He did not at first appreciate his failure. He left the chamber and the building almost immediately after he sat down. Balfour was not due to reply until the following day, and Churchill felt he had no spare time for listening to backbenchers. This was in itself an arrogant thing to do, and not one calculated to win friends. It also cut him off, for the moment, from appreciating how unfavourable to him was the future course of the debate. He missed in particular the excoriating reply of Admiral of the Fleet Sir Hedworth Meux. Meux, who as a son of an Earl of Durham had been born Lambton, had changed his name only in 1911 when he had bestowed upon him a vast brewing fortune by the Lady Meux who was the subject of one of Whistler's best portraits. This did not prevent his being an highly esteemed as well as very senior admiral. He was obviously also a man of quick debating skill. At the age of fifty-nine he had only just been elected to Parliament at a Portsmouth bye-election. He had not made his maiden speech and did not intend to do it on this occasion – until he heard Churchill.

Meux quickly seized on a point which Churchill seemed hardly to have considered: that if Fisher were to be made First Sea Lord the incumbent, Sir Henry Jackson, would have to be ignominiously disposed of. Meux used this as a vehicle for mounting a widely appreciated attack on what he regarded as the histrionic antics of both Churchill and Fisher:

> Let us put ourselves in the place of the Grand Fleet – Sir John Jellicoe, captains and officers – when they read this debate and see what the late First Lord has said. They will say, 'Here is a nice state of things. What has our present First Sea Lord of the Admiralty done? What is the matter with Sir Henry Jackson? What is his fault?' Shall I tell you what is his fault in the eyes of the people who want to turn him out? It is that he does not advertise. He does not have correspondents and newspaper people in his place all day. That is really the reason this agitation has been got up. It is because the present Board of Admiralty are doing their work to the satisfaction of the Navy and not boasting about it.

In the first few months of the War, whenever we had a success or whenever the enemy had a slight failure, the whole of the Navy were pained by the vulgar boasting that went on. . . . Anyone in the Navy knows what an unlucky thing it is to boast. When the present First Lord's speech is read we shall say 'Thank heaven, at last we have got a ruler who does not grate upon our nerves!' . . .

I am sorry the late First Lord is not in his place. . . . We all wish him a great deal of success in France, and we hope that he will stay there.[32]

By the next morning at least Churchill knew what a failure his speech had been. Not only did he have to read Meux and several other attacks, but he could also see that the London newspapers – and he always set a great deal of store by the press – were unanimously hostile. Only the then non-metropolitan *Manchester Guardian*, as well it might under Scott, found good words to say. Whether he was chagrined or defiant he could not slink away to lick his wounds. He had to go back to the House that afternoon and listen to Balfour's reply to him, and whatever his criticism of the former Tory leader's languid administration he was perfectly aware of Balfour's debating skills, based much more on the rapier than the bludgeon. Despite their early 1915 friendship (excessive in Asquith's view) Balfour had plenty of much earlier scores to settle with Churchill, and on this occasion he simply carved him up. He used Churchill's Fisher proposition to dismiss his seriousness to an extent which made it unnecessary for him to reply to Churchill's other criticisms.

My right hon. Friend [Colonel Churchill, as Hansard temporarily referred to him] has often astonished the House, but I do not think he ever astonished it so much as when he came down to explain that the remedy for all our ills, as far as the Navy is concerned, is to get rid of Sir Henry Jackson and to put in his place Lord Fisher. . . . What did he say when he made his farewell speech, when he exchanged a political for a military career? He told us that . . . Lord Fisher did not give him, when he was serving in the same Admiralty with him, either the clear guidance before the event or the firm support after it which he was entitled to expect.

I cannot follow the workings of the right hon. Gentleman's mind. He told us . . . that he told the Prime Minister when Prince Louis resigned . . . that the only man he could work with was Lord Fisher. He seems dogged by ill fortune. Is it not a most extraordinary and emphatic coincidence that the only man with whom my right hon. Friend could consent to work at the Admiralty was the most distinguished sailor who, after five months, refused to work with my right hon. Friend?[33]

This, presumably provoking a good deal of mocking laughter, reduced Churchill almost to pleading for mercy. He both thought it necessary to reply and was given the opportunity to do so. Balfour, he said, was 'a master of parliamentary sword-play and of every dialectical art'. This, together with his 'high position, his long standing in this House', enabled him to rebuke one 'so much younger than himself'.[34] On Fisher, Churchill defensively maintained his position, claiming that circumstances were different as the Dardanelles campaign was regrettably over, but he did so without impact.

The effect upon Churchill of this heavy setback was bewilderingly inconsequential. To retreat to France and to bury himself in the trenches and in the cosseting popularity which, according to Gibb and others, he had by this time achieved with his battalion might have seemed natural. Instead he did the reverse. He applied for an extension of his leave, cast his mind forward to the following Tuesday (14 March) when the army estimates were to be debated, and allowed himself to be at least half persuaded by his demented advisers (Fisher was the worst, but the two editors and two or three inconsiderable backbench MPs were not much better), who were telling him that another dose of the same disastrous medicine would bring the government crashing down and put him in a dominant position.

The two most extreme reactions were provided by Fisher on the one hand and Margot Asquith on the other: 'you have the Prime Ministership in your grasp', Fisher wrote on (of all days) that 8 March of the terrible press. Mrs Asquith wrote (on that same day and to Balfour): 'I hope and believe Winston will never be forgiven his yesterday's speeches. He is a hound of the lowest sense of political honour, a fool of the lowest judgement and contemptible.'[35] Her stepdaughter, by now Violet Bonham Carter, was more compassionate. She went to see Churchill (at his request) and recorded: 'He looked pale, defiant, on the defensive. I shall never forget the pain of the talk which followed. . . . What he had conceived as a great gesture of magnanimity – the forgiveness of the wrongs Fisher had done to him, for the sake of a greater aim, our naval supremacy . . . was regarded instead as a clumsy gambler's throw for his own ends. . . .'[36]

All on that same day Churchill himself wrote to Kitchener asking to 'be relieved of my command as soon as this can be done without disadvantage to the service', in the meantime requesting an extension of his leave, and suggesting that the letter be shown to the Prime Minister. On the following day he went to see Asquith in Downing Street for a substantial private talk – at whose initiative is not clear. For an account of what took place we are dependent upon Violet Bonham Carter, writing many years later, but giving a strong impression of verisimilitude. The Prime Minister was reproving but avuncular. He said he wanted to save Churchill from his father's fate of political suicide through impulsive action. He stressed his affection. He hinted at his desire to bring him back into the government if only animosities (mainly but not exclusively Tory) could be cooled. He advised him strongly to go back to France.[37] The next day Churchill wrote to say that he was accepting this advice, but asking in return for a written undertaking that he could permanently return to London whenever he thought that his 'sense of public duty' called him home. This he got, in Asquith's own hand, dated 11 March.[38]

So he recrossed the Channel on Monday, 13 March, eschewing the army debate on the following day. Clementine accompanied him to Dover. There is the strong impression that around this time she was tossed, torn and battered by his fluctuating mind, and perhaps even more by his obsession with his fortunes, political or military, and with the fact that these had dominated the leave more than any family relations. On 23 March she was to write: 'These grave public anxieties are very wearing. When next I see you I hope there will be a little time for us both alone. We are still young, but Time flies, stealing love away and leaving only friendship which is very peaceful but not very stimulating or warming.'[39]

That parting at Dover can hardly have reassured her. On the train he had changed his mind and written to Asquith asking immediately to be relieved of his command, as well as drafting a press statement explaining his new course, which his wife was to issue. From late morning to late afternoon he accomplished his journey from Dover to his battalion's forward position before Ploegsteert. It was a vivid illustration of how near and yet so far was the life of the trenches to and from that of English normality. When he got there he immediately began to change his mind – for about the fourth time – and telegraphed that night to Asquith withdrawing his letter. Asquith was wearily relieved, and with a shrewd wisdom sent a private secretary to Cromwell Road to gather in the press statement from Clementine and to make sure that it was not issued by mistake.

It is impossible to take any view other than that Churchill at this stage was completely disorientated and did not know from one twenty-four hours to another what he wanted to do. It is surprising that this equivocation did not communicate itself to his battalion and fatally mar the end of his command. But there is not the slightest indication from Gibb or any other sources that it did so. He maintained his authority and the loyalty of his subordinates. Yet there can be no doubt that the core of his ambition moved decisively and paradoxically after this brief and unsuccessful excursion back from the sandbags of the trenches to the despatch boxes of Westminster. He wrote almost frenziedly to a wide range of friends and acquaintances asking for advice as to what he should do. Most of them, including Sir George Ritchie, his constituency chairman in Dundee, thought he should stay where he was in France. But he had become too restless. Even a tentative Haig offer of a brigade towards the end of April, the goal which had so tantalized and infuriated him four months before, failed to tempt him.

Given his mood, he had a considerable final piece of luck. The depleted 6th and 7th battalions of the Scots Fusiliers were to be amalgamated. The colonel of the 7th was senior. Churchill was able to escape *en beauté*. On 6 May he gave his officers a well-remembered, and no doubt a well-lubricated, farewell luncheon in Armentières. On 7 May he recrossed the Channel and his short half-year of First World War military career were over.

17

LLOYD GEORGE'S AMBULANCE
WAGON ARRIVES A LITTLE LATE

EVEN GARVIN HAD counselled Churchill 'to spend a month after leaving the army before reappearing in the House'. Almost needless to say, he took no notice of this advice. He spoke within forty-eight hours of his arrival in London, and he spoke foolishly. The Conscription Bill, which had caused great upheaval within the Liberal elements in the coalition but of which Churchill (with Lloyd George) had been strongly in favour, was in the course of passage. Ireland, although strong on voluntary recruitment, was in a febrile state following the Dublin Easter Rebellion in April 1916. Asquith, who had himself accepted compulsion only with reluctance, decided illogically but wisely that Ireland should be excluded. Churchill, logically if an unrelenting Unionist view were accepted – but he had not been a Unionist in 1912–14 – joined with Carson in opposing this. It may have been logical but it was not wise. There was no way in which conscription in Ireland after Easter 1916, or maybe even before, could produce more men than trouble.

Throughout the remainder of May he went on speaking relentlessly. Any debate which had anything to do with the general conduct of the war called forth a Churchill oration – and they were none of them short. They contained very good passages, showing that he had in no way lost his capacity to shine an original light on to an argument and to express it with eloquence. Thus in the 17 May debate on the setting up of an Air Board under Curzon (Churchill wanted a fully fledged Air Ministry, preferably under himself), he routinely complained that air superiority had been lost but uniquely put its importance into an overall context:

At sea, the increased power of the defensive in mines and submarines has largely robbed the stronger Navy of its rights. On land, we are in the position of having lost our ground before the modern defensive was thoroughly understood, and having to win it back when the defensive has been elevated into a fine art. But the air is free and open. There are no entrenchments there. It is equal for the attack and for the defence. It is equal for all comers.[1]

He also spoke powerfully (23 May) about the terrible distinction between what he called the 'trench population' and the 'non-trench population' within the army. The former lived under constant danger and were often sent back to the same exposed positions after two and sometimes three wounds. The latter, by contrast, lived in almost complete safety and relative comfort, and got higher pay and more decorations. Here he was of course exploiting the age-old hostility of the front line for the staff (peculiarly acute in the static but murderous conditions of 1914–18), although he was also much concerned with the large numbers of more or less able-bodied British soldiers, both in England and in France, who were permanently employed on duties which could be equally well done by civilians, even female civilians. He accompanied this with an illusion that vast numbers of fighting troops could be obtained from Britain's dependent territories (31 May).

In general, his criticisms were searching and his remedies sensible during this re-entry stage, but their effect was vitiated by three factors. First, he spoke too often. There was an inevitableness about his determination to speak in every major debate (on 23 May for instance he was up immediately after the Prime Minister) which reduced his effect. Second, he was too concerned, feeling vulnerable, to defend every bit of his own record up to the previous May. Everything, in the Admiralty at any rate, had been right up till then. Everything had gone wrong subsequently. Third, he presented too easy a sitting target for those who wished to push him aside with dismissive *ad hominem* ripostes rather than to answer his arguments. The fashion set by Balfour in March was followed by Bonar Law in the Air Board debate and even by the War Office parliamentary secretary (H. J. Tennant) on 23 May. And his first 'civilian' intervention on 9 May, when he had been urging conscription for Ireland, had been torpedoed by a highly intelligent Nationalist MP employing the 'know nothing' technique and calling out 'What about the Dardanelles?' at what should have been Churchill's moment of maximum effect. He could have given a fine hour's answer, but could think of nothing effective to say within the compass of two sentences.

These experiences, together with two crucial war developments of early June led him into a substantial shift of tactics. The events were both at sea: the drawn Battle of Jutland on 1 June and the drowning of Kitchener on his way to Russia on 6 June. The first, apart from its more significant consequences, led to a curious involvement for Churchill. After a confused initial Admiralty statement on the battle had produced an adverse public reaction, Balfour asked him to come in and produce a more convincing second statement. This Churchill did with gusto, but also allowed it, accompanied as it was by an invitation from Curzon to attend the first meeting of his new Air Board, to rekindle in his mind hopes of an early return to office. These were fortified by Kitchener's death, which meant there would have to be a new Secretary of State for War. Churchill did not see himself as leaping direct into these shoes, but he rightly saw Lloyd George as the most likely candidate for the War Office and thought that he might follow him as Minister of Munitions.

This, perhaps together with a suspicion that he was straining the patience of the House, led to his going parliamentarily quiet during June. But he was still caught by a dilemma. He was desperately eager to get rid of the Dardanelles slur on his reputation, or at the very least to spread the guilt. He wanted to do this both in what he saw as the cause of justice and because he realized that, so long as he was regarded as the guilty man, there was a great obstacle to his getting back into the government. This obstacle he thought would be removed if the key documents relating to the Dardanelles could be published. Bonar Law, on behalf of the Prime Minister, had indicated in May that this might be done. But as June went on Asquith became increasingly reluctant to do so. In particular he could not agree to the publication of the minutes of meetings of the War Council, three of which, those of 13 and 28 January and 26 February 1915, Churchill regarded as crucial. This led to Churchill writing five substantial argumentative and complaining letters to Asquith in June and the first half of July. His ceasing to be a public nuisance in the House of Commons was replaced by his becoming a more direct private nuisance to the Prime Minister.

He did not get the Munitions post. When Lloyd George eventually became Secretary of State for War on 7 July, Munitions went to Edwin Montagu. Montagu's recent marriage to Venetia Stanley seemed less of a bar in Asquith's eyes than Churchill's fault of being temporarily unpopular with nearly all Tories and with a large part of the Liberal party too. This disappointment sent Churchill into a state of deep resentment and depression. A painting sojourn at Blenheim, accompanied by his wife and three children, failed for once to restore his

equanimity, and he even contemplated returning to France as a battalion
commander. What is a matter of written record is a letter of 15 July to
his brother Jack, to whom (although if anything with a slightly optimistic sheen) he often disclosed his frankest thoughts:

> Is it not damnable that I should be denied all real scope to serve this
> country in this tremendous hour? I cannot tell how things political will
> turn out: but great instability prevails and at any moment a situation
> favourable to me might come. Meanwhile Asquith reigns, supine, sodden
> and supreme. LG made a half-hearted fight [for me] about Munitions.
> He is very much alone and none too well qualified for the particular job
> he has claimed. . . .
>
> Tho' my life is full of comfort, pleasure and prosperity I writhe hourly
> not to be able to get my teeth effectively into the Boche. . . . Jack my dear
> I am learning to hate.[2]

The reason he felt so prosperous was that he had switched his attempt
to influence public opinion from making unpaid speeches in the House
of Commons to writing well-paid articles in the *Sunday Pictorial*. He did
four in July, for each of which he was paid £250, a formidable sum in
1916 money, the approximate equivalent of £7,000 today. This affluence
and the prospect of its continuance fed his natural generosity. Earlier in
the same letter he had told Jack Churchill: 'Money difficulties need not
weigh with you. I find myself able quite easily to earn ten or twelve
thousand pounds in the next six months. So that Cromwell [Road] and
all in it will be well supplied. Mind you let me know of anything that
wants paying.'[3] This journalism earned him some plaudits as well as
many pounds. Even so fastidious a mind (and unnatural reader of the
Sunday Pictorial) as Haldane wrote after the first two: 'These articles
contain far the most penetrating and accurate analysis of the situation
before the war that I have seen, & I agree with every word that you
have written in them.'[4]

This aspect of his life, although a substantial one, provided the only
shaft of light at the time. But it was at least accompanied by a stimulus.
The outcome of his long argument with Asquith about the publication
of Dardanelles papers was non-publication, accompanied by the sola-
tium of the setting up of a Commission of Enquiry. This was announced
on 18 July and was to be under the then ageing Earl of Cromer, the
Cairo proconsul with whom Churchill had enjoyed friendly intercourse
at the time of *The River War*. The remainder of the summer became for
Churchill a time of intensive preparation of his evidence. Thoughts of

returning to a battalion command in France, which had never been very serious, disappeared.

The Cromer Commission was neither a triumph nor a disaster for Churchill. On balance it somewhat improved his reputation and enabled him to escape from some of the guilt of the Dardanelles, but it did not do so in time for the most critical week in the politics of 1914–18, that at the beginning of December (1916), when Asquith fell and Lloyd George replaced him with a new shape of coalition. Despite his anger that Asquith would not publish the Dardanelles documents, Churchill began with high hopes of Cromer. There were only eight members, none of them obviously hostile to Churchill. 'It is a pretty good commission,' he wrote to his friend Colonel Seely on 13 August.[5] Churchill's relative enchantment with the Commission did not last long. Although he made one or two speeches to an inattentive and thin (for him) House of Commons which continued to sit during August, his main energies were directed to preparing his evidence for the Commission. Amazingly he spent a lot of time trying to co-ordinate his own with that of Fisher. With Kitchener in a hero's North Sea grave he was already inhibited in how much blame he could seek to attach to the vacillations of the former War Secretary – and was made more so on the advice of Sir Graham Greene, still permanent secretary of the Admiralty, to whom he submitted his draft. To try to keep in step with Fisher was to add a second encumbrance. At least equally serious, however, was the Commission's decision to take a different form from that which Churchill had confidently expected. He wrote to Cromer on 12 August saying: 'With regard to the procedure of the Commission, I presume that I shall be at liberty to be present during the course of the Enquiry. I have a number of witnesses to bring before the Commission. I propose to conduct the case, so far as I am concerned, myself, and not to ask leave to employ Counsel.'[6]

Cromer did not reply until 20 September,* and what he then said was deeply disappointing to Churchill. The Commission was to meet in secret and Churchill could not therefore be present for the examination of other witnesses, although a transcript of what they had said would, where relevant, be sent to him, and he could, if necessary, ask to be recalled. There was no question of his either employing counsel or representing himself. He could have no opportunity for cross-

* There is some indication that his grip was not nearly as firm as in his great Cairo days. He died on 27 January 1917 before the completion of even the interim report.

examination. Nonetheless he gave his evidence at an early stage, on 28 September. He concentrated on establishing what he called 'five distinct truths':

1) That there was full authority [in other words that he did not act unilaterally beyond his proper powers];
2) That there was a reasonable prospect of success;
3) That greater interests [that is the strength and safety of the Grand Fleet] were not compromised;
4) That all possible care and forethought were exercised in the preparation;
5) That vigour and determination were shown in the execution.[7]

He also submitted great quantities of supplementary written evidence (which he was disappointed that the Commission never published), and ensured that they saw several Admiralty witnesses whom he regarded as helpful, as well as himself making a number of reappearances. He thought he was making progress. He wrote to Spiers on 27 October: 'I am slowly triumphing in this Dardanelles Commission, and bit by bit am carrying the whole case. I am really hopeful that they will free me from the burden wh. cripples my action.'[8]

A good example of the 'crippling burden' which made him a political pariah was a *Daily Mail* article on 13 October. It was at a time when the vastly expensive Somme offensive, begun on 1 July and amounting in Churchill's mind to the supreme example of how the war should not be conducted, was grinding into manifest failure. Yet the gist of the *Daily Mail* article was that no politicians should be allowed to interfere with the relentless plans of Haig and the Chief of the Imperial General Staff, Robertson, and above all not 'a megalomaniac politician' who in the Dardanelles had 'risked the fate of our Army in France and sacrificed thousands of lives to no purpose'.

The *Daily Mail* was of course Northcliffe's popular journal, just as *The Times* was its upmarket companion. It was therefore ironical that almost Churchill's only press patron of the time should have been Northcliffe's younger brother, Harold Harmsworth, Lord Rothermere. The Harmsworths had a fraternity of money-making newspaper proprietorship, although not always an identity of view. It was Rothermere's *Sunday Pictorial* which gave Churchill his July affluence and, still more important, his sense that he could repeat the exercise as often as he wanted to. And it was Rothermere who, under his own name, wrote in the same *Sunday Pictorial*, on 12 November, almost the only puff, in the popular press at least, which Churchill received around this time. Moreover Rothermere commissioned in that summer of 1916 what, according to Jock Colville, Churchill's latter-day Eddie Marsh, became his favourite painting of himself and which adorned his London dining room until the end of his life. He gave William Orpen eleven sittings at what he subsequently described with only partial exaggeration as a very unhappy time of my life when I had nothing whatever to do'.[9]

In spite of the downturn of his political fortunes it was a fecund period for portraits of the politician who himself became probably the best and certainly the highest-valued landscape artist among politicians of the twentieth century. Lavery painted him in his famous *poilu*'s helmet during his time with the Royal Scots Fusiliers and Ernest Townsend, a little earlier, had done him in Privy Councillor's uniform for the National Liberal Club.* Of these three, Townsend was buoyant and verging on the glamorous, Lavery was martial and Orpen was sombre, and it is interesting, even surprising, that it should have been the sombre one which he most liked. This was particularly so in view of his intense dislike of Graham Sutherland's fine but undoubtedly sombre portrait with which Churchill was presented by the House of Commons nearly forty years later on his eightieth birthday. The difference was that Orpen made him look sombre because he was excluded from the power to which his energy entitled him, whereas Sutherland made him look sombre because the energy had flowed away.

The political crisis of December 1916 was a peculiarly esoteric one. It was so in the sense that the senior politicians and the press had it almost to themselves. This was not true of the other major upheavals of British politics in the last century and a little more. Eighteen-eighty-six turned on the failure of Gladstone to carry the first Home Rule Bill through the House of Commons. In 1922 the fall of the Lloyd George government was determined by a clear vote of the members of Parliament of the Conservative party, on which he overwhelmingly depended. In 1931 King George V played a surprisingly assertive and doubtfully

* This somewhat formal portrait has had a charged subsequent history. Churchill was to unveil it during his March 1916 leave. But he cancelled the occasion in favour of his frantic although unsuccessful politicizing. Perhaps because of that cavalier treatment, as well as of his drift towards Liberal unacceptability, the picture, which had remained visible but not formally unveiled until 1921, was then packed and stored. In 1941, as an ecumenical gesture (on both sides), it was not only resurrected but personally unveiled, twenty-five years late, by Churchill at the height of his prestige. Today it rivals Gladstone, Asquith and Lloyd George in its dominance of the Club's hall.

beneficial role in the formation of the National government. And in 1940 Churchill's own apotheosis was brought about by an open House of Commons vote. But in 1916 it all depended on the manoeuvrings of about fifteen front-rank politicians, somewhat excessively influenced by what they read from day to day in the principal but not necessarily very principled newspapers.

However the overture did take an open and parliamentary form. On 8 November, Edward Carson, a melodramatic but almost wholly destructive lawyer–politician, challenged the government in the division lobbies on the question of whether enemy property in Nigeria could be sold only to British buyers or to those of neutral citizenship as well. It was such a ludicrously peripheral issue that it could only have had symbolic interest and significance. But it was well aimed, for Bonar Law, a man with a great belief in party legitimacy, was both Colonial Secretary and Conservative leader, and only 73 out of 286 Conservative members voted with him. Sixty-five, aided by eleven disaffected Liberals, with Churchill prominently among them, voted against. The remainder did not vote.

This destabilized Bonar Law, and because of his position as the leader of the necessary coalition partner, even if not in Asquith's eyes a very esteemed one, the whole government. But it did not conduce to the alliance between Law and Lloyd George necessary to bring it down. Lloyd George on the evening of the vote was known to have been dining with Carson, the mover of the critical motion. But he did not bother to return to vote for the government, although his dining companion did so to vote against it. There then set in a period reminiscent of the atmosphere brilliantly created by the beginning of Verdi's *Ballo in Maschero*, where it is not clear who is on whose side but where each mistily circles the others with daggers in their hands.

According to Churchill's own appraisal, as expressed in volume two of *The World Crisis*, the two key figures were brought back into accord with each other 'through the offices of Sir Max Aitken'. Churchill had a great interest in this, for although his hopes of Bonar Law had considerably cooled since the time when he wrote to Clementine in February 1916 that the people with whom he wished to work were 'Ll.G:, F.E:, B.L:, Carson and Curzon', he nonetheless had strong faith that a Lloyd George premiership would bring his own return to high office.

From the point of his own general desires everything worked out admirably. By the evening of 5 December Asquith was out and Lloyd George poised to be in. It was an evening of excitement but also of bitter disappointment for Churchill. It began in the Turkish Baths of the Royal Automobile Club where he and F. E. Smith had jointly repaired, no doubt in the hope of counteracting some of their indulgences. It is a scene splendidly typical of the first third of the twentieth century. It is difficult to imagine Gladstone in a Turkish bath any more than Attlee, Home, Wilson or Major. But no doubt Smith and Churchill were perfectly at home in this essentially Edwardian ambience, sufficiently so at any rate for Smith to be able, seventy years before the 'mobile' age, to arrange a telephone call from there to Lloyd George to remind him that he was due to dine later that evening at Smith's house in Grosvenor Gardens. Max Aitken was also to be present. When Lloyd George heard that Churchill was with Smith he immediately suggested he should come along too. So, of course, Churchill did, and so would most politicians in the circumstances, although it is legitimate to wonder what his previous plans had been, whether another dinner party was disappointed or whether Clementine found herself condemned to an evening of unexpected loneliness.

The dinner must have been fairly brief, for Lloyd George departed early to meet Bonar Law, who had just come back from the King, at Carson's house in Eaton Place. And Aitken, who wanted to be treated as a major politician but who was mostly a voyeur of politics, went with him for the drive. During the brief dinner the conversation, in Aitken's so far wholly convincing words, 'turned entirely on the personnel of the new Ministry and all present . . . took part in the conversation on terms of equality'.[10] Churchill naturally assumed that he was to be included, more or less in the inner circle. This, ironically and equally naturally, was also Aitken's own assumption about himself. Indeed he was more specific about his hope than was Churchill: the Presidency of the Board of Trade was the post that he coveted. In fact his role was confined to preparing Churchill for the bad news:

> Thus I conveyed to him the hint Lloyd George had given me. I have a reason for saying that these are the exact words I used: 'The new Government will be very well disposed towards you. All your friends will be there. You will have a great field of common action with them.'
>
> Something in the very restraint of my language carried conviction to Churchill's mind. He suddenly felt he had been duped by his invitation to the dinner, and he blazed into righteous anger. I have never known him address his great friend Birkenhead in any other way except 'Fred' or 'F.E.'. On this occasion he said suddenly: 'Smith, this man knows that I am not to be included in the new Government.'

    With that Churchill walked out into the street carrying his coat and
hat on his arm. Birkenhead pursued him and endeavoured to persuade
him to return, but in vain.[11]

Lord Beaverbrook, as Aitken immediately became (his only compensation for not getting the Board of Trade and his only reward for acting
as a messenger of ill-tidings to Churchill was a peerage he did not want;
fortunately Lloyd George had the sense not to attempt the same ploy
with Churchill), published this account forty-four years after the events
described. How much he was drawing on written notes of the period
and how much on his always lively and sometimes imaginative memory
is not known. But there is no reason to doubt the general drift of the
account, and the precision of the detailed words give it (possibly falsely)
a gloss of verisimilitude.

    Lloyd George wanted Churchill in his government. Indeed in three
long pages of his *War Memoirs* he strongly implied that, not absolutely
for favourable reasons, he would have liked to have him in the small
War Cabinet (himself, Bonar Law, Curzon, Milner and Arthur Henderson as a representative of Labour) which he constituted. After a tribute
to 'his fertile mind, his undoubted courage, his untiring industry and his
thorough study of the art of war', he continued: 'Here [in the War
Cabinet] his more erratic impulses could have been kept under control
and his judgement supervised and checked, before plunging into
action.'[12] Whatever the reasons, membership of such a central directing
body would have given Churchill unalloyed joy. It would have blotted
out his sense of post-Dardanelles exclusion, it would have justified (not
least to Clementine) his anti-Asquith strictures, and it would have
endorsed the wisdom of his return from the front to seek greater service
at home. But it was not to be. Lloyd George wanted Churchill, but
he wanted much more to be Prime Minister and to form a viable
government.

    Churchill was simply unsaleable to most Conservatives who, with a
hostile Asquithian rump on his flank, it was essential that Lloyd George
should propitiate. Balfour and Carson would have accepted Churchill,
but no other leading Tory would, including, notably, the 'three Cs'
(Austen Chamberlain, Curzon and Robert Cecil) whose adhesion was
crucial to Lloyd George's ability to proceed. But the blocking Cerberus,
whom not even the desire of the great leader of the First World War and
the ambition of the even greater one of the Second World War could get
past, was Bonar Law. Lloyd George described in his *War Memoirs* how,

without overstating the case, he tried to persuade the Conservative leader with an analogy from his early legal life. He told how, in an important case, one of his most responsible duties as a solicitor was the choice of counsel. (In fact, as he can never have briefed outside the North Wales circuit, based on Chester, the choice can not have been very extensive.) There was the reliable man, who always did his steady best, and there was the brilliant man, who on his day was devastatingly effective, but who might also make some terrible gaffe. The danger was that if you played safe the brilliant man might be briefed by the other side. He went on: 'the question one always had to put to oneself was this: "Is he more dangerous when he is *for* you than when he is *against* you?"' It was not one of the most persuasive exercises of the Welsh wizard, that habitual master of persuasion. And it completely failed with the unimaginative but bluntly honest mind of Bonar Law. 'I would rather have him against us every time,' he said.[13] And that, for the time being, was that.

There then followed a period of Churchill's life which, objectively at least, was even flatter than those of which he had previously complained. Until December 1916, there was always the prospect that he might play a part – although he exaggerated how great a part – in bringing Asquith down and opening up a new political landscape for himself. Now the first objective had been achieved, but his outlook was even more enclosed. He did not wish to join a cave of the displaced Liberal ministers, with all of whom – Asquith, Grey, McKenna, Runciman – he was for a variety of reasons disenchanted. And, although he made a few mildly grumbling speeches and wrote for good money a few similar articles, he was inhibited from attacking the new government in a way that he had not been with the previous one.

Those early months of 1917 were also, Churchill's personal position apart, the nadir of the long agony of the First World War. In early January Roumania, which had entered the war on the Allied side in August, was effectively obliterated. Close to that date the Germans adopted a policy of unrestricted submarine warfare. Immediately it was devastatingly effective. British shipping losses were appalling, and there was a real threat of the severance of the North Atlantic link. In the medium term it lost the Germans the war, for it added the irresistible resources of the United States to the faltering Anglo-French effort. But this was not appreciated until President Woodrow Wilson secured the assent of Congress to a declaration of war on 6 April. This followed a frightening three weeks between the collapse of the Russian Empire on 16 March and the entry into the conflict of the United States.

In Britain, and still more in France, there was also the melancholy background of casualties affecting almost every family. The Churchills were relatively lucky. They did not suffer anything very close. But Asquith lost his eldest and almost too golden son Raymond on the Somme in September 1916, and to take two random other examples, Sir Frederick Cawley MP, a member of the Dardanelles Commission, had lost one son near Mons in the first month of the war, another a year later in Gallipoli, and was to lose a third in France in 1918; and Rothermere, who falsely sounds almost the epitome of those who from comfort urged sacrifice upon others, lost one son on the day after he had published his Churchill-friendly article in November 1916, and another in February 1918.

Churchill's fortunes began to turn in early May (1917). He had been advocating a secret session of the House of Commons for a few weeks, but nobody at first took much notice of him. However, as criticism of the government mounted, Churchill skilfully persuaded his versatile cousin Freddie Guest, who had moved from being French's aide-de-camp to being Lloyd George's joint Chief Whip, that a secret session would be the Prime Minister's best chance of re-establishing his parliamentary authority by explaining his problems and strategy more fully than he could in open sitting. Such a throw appealed to Lloyd George, and the occasion was set up for 10 May – several times an important date in Churchill's calendar, nine years after he had returned in victory after his first Dundee election, twenty-three years before he became Prime Minister.

No senior Asquithian showed an interest in exploiting the opportunity, and it therefore fell to Churchill to open the debate, paving the way for the Prime Minister who immediately followed him. In complete contrast with his experience fourteen months previously it appears to have been one of the most successful Commons speeches of the first half of his career, even though it lasted one and a quarter hours – no mere 'warm-up' job (but, the session being secret, it is not recorded in Hansard). In *The World Crisis*, however, Churchill reconstructed the core of this speech from his notes, which were always extensive. It emerges as a classic example of his ability to pick out the broad lines of a conjuncture, and to state them in terms which gripped his audience (a packed House) and made their minds receptive to the direction in which he wanted to lead them. Both because of the inherent interest of the speech and of its importance as one of the several turning points of his long political life, it is worth citing at length:

Since the beginning of the year two events have occurred, each of which has changed the whole situation and both of which must be taken into account in the policy of the Allies. The United States has entered and Russia has collapsed. On the one hand an ally Empire whose standing army comprised over seven million soldiers has been crushed by the German hammer. On the other, a nation comprising 120 million of the most active, educated and wealthy citizens, commanding instant and almost limitless resources of every kind, has engaged in our cause. But this nation is not ready. It has no large armies and no munitions. Its manhood is untrained to war. Its arsenals and factories, except in so far as they are engaged in producing munitions for the Allies, are unorganized. If time is given, nothing can stand against Great Britain and the United States together. . . . But a long time will be needed – a time measured not by months but by years – before this mighty force can be brought to bear.

There was another vital factor, he said: sea communications. 'When the Germans decided upon the unrestricted submarine campaign, they must also have known that they would bring the United States into the war against them. Must they not also have believed that by this same means they would prevent her effective intervention? We do not know, we do not wish to know how many ships are being sunk each week by submarines.' The proportion was serious, however, and was still increasing. That, Churchill asserted, was 'the first and decisive danger' which had to be mastered. 'Let the whole energies of Britain be directed upon this point. Let the Navy make of it its great victory in the war. Let every resource and invention be applied. Let the anti-submarine war claim priority and dominance over every form of British effort.' The British should make sure that the American armies were brought to Europe as to soon as they were fit to come.

Meanwhile what should be our policy on land? Is it not obvious from the primary factors which have been described, that we ought not to squander the remaining armies of France and Britain in precipitate offensives before the American power begins to be felt on the battlefields? We have not the numerical superiority necessary for such a successful offensive. We have no marked artillery preponderance over the enemy. We have not got the numbers of tanks which we need. We have not established superiority in the air. We have discovered neither the mechanical nor the tactical methods of piercing an indefinite succession of fortified lines defended by German troops. Shall we then in such circumstance cast away our remaining manpower in desperate efforts on the Western Front before large American forces are marshalled in France? Let the House implore the Prime Minister to use the authority which he wields, and all his personal weight, to prevent the French and British High Commands from dragging each other into fresh bloody and disastrous adventures. Master the U-boat attack. Bring over the American millions. And meanwhile maintain an active defensive on the Western Front, so as to economize French and British lives, and so as to train, increase and perfect our armies and our methods for a decisive effort in a later year.[14]

It was of course possible to dismiss Churchill's exciting generalizations as deceptively impressive, and this was precisely what was done by the shadowy but influential Lord Esher, a false friend if ever there was one, who left Sir Francis Hopwood looking ruggedly straightforward, when he wrote to General Haig later that month and immediately before a Churchill visit to GHQ at St Omer – his first for over a year. 'He handles great subjects in rhythmical language,' Esher wrote, 'and becomes quickly enslaved by his own phrases. He deceives himself into the belief that he takes broad views, when his mind is fixed upon one comparatively small aspect of the question.'[15] But this was not the view taken on 10 May by either that flickering entity, the general feeling of the House of Commons, or, perhaps more importantly, the Prime Minister, who also enjoyed a major parliamentary triumph that afternoon. 'Fortuitously', in Churchill's word, they met behind the Speaker's chair soon after their participation in a debate which had been highly satisfactory to both of them. Post-successful-oratorical *bonhomie* is a well-known experience of all politicians. They greeted each other with an enthusiasm reminiscent of Churchill's satirical description, written many years later and published in *Great Contemporaries* (1937), of Philip Snowden, his Labour predecessor and successor as Chancellor of the Exchequer: 'The Treasury mind and the Snowden mind embraced each other with the fervour of two long-separated kindred lizards, and the reign of joy began.'[16]

So indeed it did for Churchill, and from that day forward his relationship with Lloyd George almost reverted to that of the early days of the Asquith premiership, when they were the twin radical stars of the government. Its immediate manifestation was that Lloyd George facilitated a week's visit by Churchill to the French front, to Paris and to Haig at St Omer. It was the first time he had been in France for just over a year. Everywhere he went he was received at the highest level. He was emphatically back within the loop.

The spirit was made flesh when, on 18 July, ignoring substantial Conservative protests, Lloyd George made Churchill Minister of Munitions. Christopher Addison, much later to be one of Attlee's most dependable props in the Labour government of 1945, rather the equivalent of Crewe to Asquith, but at that time one of the most loyally Lloyd Georgeite of Liberals, conveniently moved to the hazardously vague job of Minister of Reconstruction to make room for Churchill. In itself Munitions was not a great post at that stage, even though Lloyd George himself had thought it worth while to leave the Treasury for it in May 1915. But it was indisputably linked to the war effort. It was somewhat the equivalent of Stafford Cripps in the autumn of 1942, after a heady but unsuccessful eight months during which, following his return from the ambassadorship to Moscow bearing, more accidentally than deservedly, clouds of temporary Soviet glory, he was effectively second man in the government and even a potential challenge to Churchill himself, then accepting an important but non-central role as Minister of Aircraft Production, and there performing a technically good job. In 1917 Churchill was of course delighted to be back in any role, provided it was not manifestly subordinate, and moved with enthusiasm into the Ministry's headquarters in the old Hotel Metropole at the Trafalgar Square end of Northumberland Avenue, premises which emphasized its extempore nature.

What were Lloyd George's motives for bringing him back in July 1917, having resiled from doing so seven months earlier? Partly it was that his own success in the Churchill-instigated secret session had made him more confident vis-à-vis his Conservative partners, who continued boringly to protest against Churchill's inclusion. Partly it was that Churchill's own performance in the secret session had impressed him with how formidable an opponent he could be, as well as bringing them together in a rekindling of their old friendship. But still more convincing than any of these reasons was the diary entry of 19 May of Frances Stevenson, as close to Lloyd George as anyone could be at the time: 'He says he wants someone who will cheer him up and help & encourage him, & who will not be continually coming to him with a long face and telling him that everything is going wrong. At present, he says, he has to carry the whole of his colleagues on his back.'[17] So, maybe, Captain Gibbs's attribution to Churchill of the precept and practice that 'war is a game to be played with a smiling face' served him well, even though he could often scowl too. In any event he was back, twenty-six months after he had been excluded from the Admiralty, twenty months after he had voluntarily excluded himself from a pointless Cabinet office, and with sixteen months of the war still to go, although most would have put it longer at the time.

18

MAKING THE MOST OF MUNITIONS

ALMOST THE FIRST THING Churchill had to do after his resurrection was to go to Dundee and fight a bye-election. The war did not set aside the old rule that those appointed to Cabinet rank (even if outside Lloyd George's small War Cabinet) had to resubmit themselves to their constituents. And Churchill, remembering his Manchester experience of 1908, cannot have been over-joyed at the prospect, particularly when it became clear that he was to be opposed. The indefatigable Edwin Scrymgeour was not going to let such an opportunity slip, and he duly came forward for the fourth of his anti-Churchill contests. On this occasion he called himself both 'Prohibitionist and Labour', although it was only the anti-war element of the Labour party and not the pro-war trades union leadership that he represented. 'My opponent proposes to seek peace with Germany in order to suppress the liquor traffic in Scotland'[1] was the best of Churchill's non-conciliatory remarks in a short but fairly rumbustious campaign. On a low poll, partly due to an electoral register which was three years out of date, he won by 7,302 to Scrymgeour's 2,036.

On 30 July 1917 Churchill was able to return to London with this hurdle behind him and to engage fully with his duties of 'a shopman at the orders of the War Cabinet', as he self-mockingly put it at the time. It had been his third bye-election, and there were to be two more, which gave him an unique campaigning record in the whole history of modern British electoral politics. This was a function both of his parliamentary longevity and also of the fact that changes of party and other hazards meant that, unlike some other 'long-termers', he did not always win, and had to fight again in the same parliament. He notched up twenty-one constituency contests.*

---

* His nearest rival in this respect was Gladstone, whose parliamentary span was within two years of Churchill's, who had a change of party in common and whose controversy-arousing capacity fully matched Churchill's. But Gladstone fought only sixteen contests, unless the two occasions when he was spontaneously elected for a second constituency

Dundee out of the way for the time being, Churchill settled into the physical framework within which he was to live for the remaining fifteen months of the war. In the spring of 1917 the Churchills had returned to live in Eccleston Square. Edward Grey, departing from the Foreign Office with the fall of Asquith, disenchanted by politics and with seriously failing eyesight (although he was to live another seventeen years, to be several times suggested as a possible Prime Minister of a centrist coalition, and to be elected unopposed as Chancellor of Oxford in 1929), had no further use for it. The Churchills did not however stay very long in Eccleston Square. At this stage in their lives at least they were congenitally restless in London. Furthermore they needed the rent from Eccleston Square. So they relet it after a year or so and adopted a regime of 'perching', in Asquith's old phrase, first at 16 Lower Berkeley Street (lent by the Horners of Mells), then at 3 Tenterden Street (lent by Churchill's aunt, Lady Wimborne, then at 1 Dean Trench Street (which they rented for a year in 1919), and finally in this phase at a Roehampton house called Templeton (lent by Lady Wimborne's son Freddie Guest). In the spring of 1920 the Churchills bought 2 Sussex Square, off the Bayswater Road, and had a London house of their own for the first time for two years.

Since the spring of 1917 they had possessed a country property just on the Kent side of the Sussex border near East Grinstead. Lullenden, as it was called, was bought for £6,000 and was a fairly modest fore-runner to Chartwell, a long, low, extended and improved farmhouse, but certainly not a 'cottage' as one of Churchill's biographers (William Manchester) almost obsessively refers to it. At first it was merely a weekend retreat, but as Zeppelin raids were mildly threatening Churchill encouraged Clementine and the three children (with a fourth, Marigold, born that November) to stay there more or less permanently. He took to sleeping frequently in his office – one advantage of its being the Hotel Metropole was that its bedroom facilities were presumably satisfactory – and from the summer of 1918 this became his established London habit. He was however much at Lullenden, partly because he

---

while campaigning in another (Greenwich as well as South-East Lancashire in 1868 and Leeds as well as Midlothian in 1880) are added. In the first case the 'back-up' constituency was necessary to him, for he was defeated in Lancashire. In the second case it was not, so he merely passed on Leeds to his already mentioned youngest son (Herbert), who kept it for thirty years, becoming both Liberal Chief Whip and Home Secretary on the inheritance. By Churchill's day such pluralism had ceased to be possible.

always liked, not exactly to have his weekends off, but to sustain the rhythm of his work by shifting its *mis-en-scène*, and partly because, as he took more and more to making his journeys to France, both to GHQ and to Paris, by air, so Lullenden became a convenient staging post.

This cross-Channel activity was a marked feature of his work at Munitions. As the head of that department, Lloyd George had been mobile, occasionally at the front but more frequently at Glasgow, Carlisle or Coventry. The same had been true of Montagu and Addison, although their movements attracted less attention than did those of either Lloyd George or Churchill. The latter did not neglect the home-front aspect of his ministerial responsibilities, and indeed conducted labour relations with some success, mostly based on the helpful approach of 'give 'em the money', accompanied by an instinctive distaste for profiteering employers. Nevertheless his built-in preference for the sound of gunfire over the rivet-hammering of those who were making the guns was indisputable. The reality was that, while he much preferred being a confined departmental minister to being no minister at all, and indeed evinced some continuing gratitude to Lloyd George for having braved Tory protests to give him this opportunity, he chafed at his 'shopman' status, shut out from the strategic discussions and decisions of the War Cabinet. He relieved his frustration by writing long letters to the Prime Minister, sometimes of complaint, sometimes giving his views on the broader questions of general strategy. A substantial proportion of these were drafts which he did not send. To the rest Lloyd George mostly did not reply, although this did not necessarily mean that he was not influenced by them.

Churchill was left with a lot of surplus energy. This, combined with several other factors, made him find excuses for crossing the Channel more often than did any other minister, British or French. The other factors were, first, an overwhelming desire to be where the action was; and second, his persistent francophilia. This was a never to be underestimated feature of Churchill's long life. Even though he began as a subaltern of empire, faced his greatest challenge (and also his greatest opportunity) as a result of the French collapse of 1940, and said semisatirically, later in the Second World War, that the heaviest cross he had to bear was that of Lorraine (that is, of General de Gaulle), France was always a magnet to him. From the days when he went to watch French army manoeuvres in 1907 to his very old age dozing away in either Beaverbrook's La Capponcina or La Pausa, the nearby villa of his cosseting American agent Emery Reves and his even more cosseting wife, he loved being in France. On 6 June 1918, when the Germans after their successful spring push were only forty-five miles away, he wrote to Clementine from the Paris Ritz: 'Next time I come here (if there is a "next time") you must really try to accompany me. You must prepare a good cause under the shelter of the Y.M.C.A. [with which she was much involved] . . . & spend a few jolly days in this menaced but always delightful city.'[2]

By March 1918, when he observed, and above all heard, the beginning of the last great German offensive, he was on his fifth visit to France of the previous six months, and several of them had lasted nearly two weeks. On this occasion he was very far forward for a minister, or indeed any civilian. Visiting the HQ of his old formation, the 9th Scottish Division, he spent a short night in quarters alongside the commanding general until at about 5.00 a.m. 'there rose in less than one minute the most tremendous cannonade I shall ever hear'.[3] He had reverted to his South African War habit of travelling with ducal escort, and Westminster was with him on this visit, as Marlborough (the old team) was to be a couple of months later. Westminster however performed a useful service. Churchill wanted to stay and see the battle. Westminster persuaded him they had better get out while they still could. The village of Nurlu, where they had been, was deep inside enemy territory within a few weeks.

Two days later Churchill was back in London with the great advantage of being thought to know more about the massive last German offensive of the war than anyone else. He got Lloyd George, accompanied by General Sir Henry Wilson, the newly appointed and somewhat serpentine Chief of the Imperial General Staff, and Sir Maurice Hankey, the increasingly well-established spider of the Whitehall web, to dine with him at Eccleston Square, on what Churchill described as never 'thro' the whole course of the war' exceeded as an 'anxious evening'.[4] It was the last occasion of glory (or glamour) for that house, which the Churchills abandoned very soon afterwards. Churchill was manifestly back, maybe temporarily, at the centre. A few days later, as the Allied armies reeled in retreat, he went again to France, this time at the specific request of the Prime Minister. At first Lloyd George wanted him to go direct to Marshal Foch, who was edging towards the position of Supreme Allied Commander. Henry Wilson managed to veto the Foch visit on grounds of military protocol. Generals must talk only to generals (officially at least) and Churchill's mission was therefore in a sense elevated to one of talking primarily to Clemenceau, the seventy-six-year-old 'tiger' who had at the end of 1917 emerged as the returning Prime Minister of France, an office which he had last occupied nine years before.

Being diverted to Paris (via Haig's new headquarters at Montreuil, St Omer having become over-exposed as a result of the German offensive) at least had the advantage of 'the luxuries of an almost empty Ritz'. It also led to Churchill's forming a good relationship with Clemenceau (probably the only man in the world at the time who could outbid Churchill both in martial spirit and in conversational fireworks), who took him on a remarkable fifteen-hour expedition. At eight o'clock on the morning of Saturday, 30 March Churchill was invited to present himself at Matignon, the office and residence of the French Prime Minister in the rue St Dominique. 'Five military motor cars all decorated with the small satin tricolours of the highest authority filled the courtyard,' Churchill subsequently wrote. He added that Clemenceau greeted him in fluent but slightly Gallic English in the following terms: 'I am delighted, my dear Mr Winston Churchill, that you have come. We shall show you everything. . . . We shall see Foch. We shall see Debeney [commanding the French First Army]. We shall see the Corps Commanders, and we will also go and see the illustrious Haig, and Rawlinson as well. Whatever is known you shall know.'[5]

They set off first for Beauvais where they were given a briefing at once dramatic and optimistic by Foch. He demonstrated the diminishing amount of ground which the Germans had gained on each successive day of the attack. As Churchill summed up the burden of his message:

> The hostile effort was exhausted. The mighty onset was coming to a standstill. The impulse which had sustained it was dying away. The worst was over. Such was the irresistible impression made upon every mind by his astonishing demonstration, during which every muscle and fibre of the General's being had seemed to vibrate with excitement and passion of a great actor on the stage.
>
> And then suddenly in a loud voice 'Stabilisation. Sure, certain, soon. And afterwards. Ah, afterwards. That is my affair.'
>
> He stopped. Everyone was silent.
>
> Then Clemenceau, advancing, 'Alors, Général, il faut que je vous embrasse.'[6]

The party then moved on to Drury, twelve miles south of Amiens, where they conferred and lunched with General Rawlinson, who was engaged in trying to rebuild and integrate the shattered Fifth Army, which had suffered appallingly in the German onslaught, into his own Fourth Army. Haig drove over from Montreuil to join them, and had an important conversation with Clemenceau at which it was agreed that the French response to the British appeal for help would be not the launch of a separate offensive further south but the pouring in of (relatively) fresh French troops to strengthen the British line where it was most under pressure. This seemed to satisfy both parties. Clemenceau then claimed his 'reward' from Rawlinson: this was to be allowed to go far forward into the battle zone. Churchill escorted him, which created a grave danger that they would try to outdo each other in acts of foolhardy courage. However, some sense of how important Clemenceau was to French fighting spirit restrained Churchill, and he led the party back with reasonable caution. They then went to see General Debeney beyond Amiens and then back to Beauvais, where they dined with Marshal Pétain in his 'sumptuous' train before regaining Paris at 1.00 a.m. Churchill wrote to Clementine on the following day:

> He [Clemenceau] is an extraordinary character. Every word he says – particularly general observations on life & morals – is worth listening to. His spirit & energy indomitable. 15 hours yesterday over rough roads at high speed in motor cars. I was tired out – & he is 76!
> He makes rather the same impression on me as Fisher: but much more efficient, & just as ready to turn round & bite! I shall be vy wary.[7]

Churchill's other achievement on that week-long visit to Paris with several excursions to the front (they were pretty close together at that time of retreat and crisis) was to persuade Clemenceau to join with Lloyd George in an appeal to President Wilson (rashly over the head of the American Commander-in-Chief General Pershing) to send a flood of American troops to Europe and to let their brigades be melded into French and British divisions, without waiting for Pershing's preference for the assembly of a great all-American *force de frappe*. Wilson accepted that 480,000 should cross the Atlantic over the next four months. So this visit of Churchill could be judged a great success. It may also – and in particular his day's tour with Clemenceau – have contributed to his sombre conviction, set down in a memorandum which he sent to Lloyd George on 18 April, that, in the Allies' still fairly desperate circumstances, if the British High Command had to make a Faustian choice between abandoning the Channel ports and being separated from the French formations in the south of Picardy, it would be less bad to stick to the union of the two armies, and let the ports go.

Churchill's other major war-probing views of the period were a mixture of hard and soft lines, with a strong streak of attractive unpredictability running through them. He was implacably opposed to any peace negotiations until the enemy had manifestly been defeated and German militarism, but not the German people, had been extirpated. But he was firmly against man-mangling offensives until the infusion of the Americans built up an irresistible superiority. He did not therefore expect victory until the summer of 1919. He could be brutally unsentimental on instruments of war, and was furious when the International Red Cross got the French to support them in an initiative to ban the use of poison gas. Its employment, he somewhat simplistically argued, was more favourable to the Allies because the prevailing wind was from the west. And he defeated the Red Cross proposal. On the other hand, at the end of the war and when he much needed his Prime Minister's support for satisfactory future ministerial employment, he did not hesitate to clash with him on the issue of hanging the German Kaiser. Lloyd George was in favour. Churchill, partly on general humanitarian grounds and partly maybe on grounds of the sanctity of rulers, was not.

All of these issues and all of these achievements with Clemenceau, with the possible exception of poison gas, were however well outside the departmental scope of a Minister of Munitions. He did not neglect his duties at the ministry. Indeed there was a widely held view that he regalvanized it (two years after Lloyd George had tried to do the same), and he greatly improved his relations with Haig by convincing him that he was the Father Christmas of abundant *matériel*. He also made two or three much publicized and photographed tours of weapons-production areas, most notably to Glasgow, Sheffield and Manchester in October 1918, when he still envisaged providing armaments for a 1919 campaign.

Yet the fact remains that, occupying a subordinate ministerial position, he tried to compensate for his exclusion from the highest seats of power at home by spending as much time as he could in France, where he was almost invariably the only minister on the spot, and which also had the advantage, a point by which he was always obsessed, of making him feel close to the centre of action. In May 1918 he conceived the idea that he ought to have a little headquarters of his own, close to but not on top of GHQ, and his relations with Haig, never as dangerously close as those with Sir John French, had improved sufficiently for the Commander-in-Chief to make available to him, from early August, the Château Verchocq, between St Omer and Montreuil and about twenty-five miles back from the British front, even when the Germans had surged through Bailleul and Armentières. It was, as he described it to Clementine, 'simple but clean ... the grounds contain[ing] avenues of the most beautiful trees'.[8] It was his base for twenty-six of the next forty days, with poor Eddie Marsh, the most civilian of private secretaries, whom he had peremptorily but irresistibly summoned back to the colours, being forced to fly hazardously to and fro over the Channel, to submit himself to shellfire during Churchill's frequent attempts to see as much of the battlefield as possible, and also having to act as major-domo of the house under a mostly good-humoured but exigent ministerial chief.

Churchill was a natural critic of the 'château-generalship' of the First World War (very different from that of the Second, when, apart from other styles having taken over, commanders were either retreating or advancing too fast to settle down in country-house comfort). Château Verchocq was his advanced headquarters (as thirty years later, when leader of the opposition, he came to describe the Savoy Hotel, two miles nearer to Westminster compared with his own house in Hyde Park Gate) through the last three approach-to-victory months of the war – even though, until well into the autumn, he cautiously refused to accept that German resistance was subsiding.

The question remains of what he was effectively doing at the Ministry of Munitions and of how the passing of half his time in France was compatible with the discharge of a major administrative but non-policy-making and non-strategic job in London. It was no doubt desirable that he should have a lively appreciation of the ordnance needs of the army, and should give the generals confidence that their problems in this respect were fully appreciated in London. But his dedication to semi-front-line life and to high Anglo-French relations went far beyond this.

Did this broader interest impair his efficiency as a departmental minister? The question is not subject to a simple answer. He inherited a cumbersome and non-traditional department, with a staff of 12,000 which expanded to 25,000 by the end of the war, mostly housed in commandeered hotels in Northumberland Avenue, off Trafalgar Square, with businessmen rather than civil servants in the key posts. There were fifty civilian divisions of the ministry, each operating semi-independently. Churchill quickly decided to reduce these to ten, with the surviving business chiefs contributing to a Munitions Council which was to meet daily (at least when he was in London) under his chairmanship. He brought in some key staff with whom he had been used to working, Sir Graham Greene and Masterton-Smith from his Admiralty days together with Marsh.

The writ of the Ministry of Munitions for the supply of material of war ran only for the army. Naval shipbuilding and naval guns remained strictly under the control of the Admiralty, as Churchill would have wished it to be had he still been First Lord. But he was always one for seeing issues through the departmental spectacles he was wearing at the time, and quickly got involved in a turf war with Sir Eric Geddes, one of Lloyd George's businessmen ministers, who was at the time presiding over the Admiralty with little naval knowledge. Churchill was brash – he was also soon engaged in rows with the Minister of Labour (G. O. Roberts) and with George Barnes, who had replaced Arthur Henderson as the representative of the trades union and Labour movement in the War Cabinet. Nor were his relations with Lord Derby, the Secretary of State of the department which he was engaged in supplying, altogether smooth. However, in the view both of Hankey, the secretary of the Cabinet, and still more importantly of Lloyd George, Churchill, particularly in his dispute with Geddes, had a lot of right on his side. And at least he satisfied Haig. The Commander-in-Chief's opinion of Churchill went steadily up during the latter's tenure of Munitions, as was indicated by his frequent welcome at GHQ and the 'gift' of a château. Churchill kept Haig well supplied with shells, bullets, guns and, increasingly, Churchill's own pet addition to the armoury of war, the tank, although he believed that Haig allowed this new weapon to be frittered away, rather than held back for a massive surprise attack, preferably in 1919. Churchill was always a 1919 man, to some extent foreshadowing his resistance to the opening of the Second Front in 1943, believing that the correct Western Front strategy was to remain on the defensive until the Americans had arrived in massive strength. This view was forestalled by the German offensive in the spring of 1918, which first removed the option of quiet defence and then, by its failure after initial success, led on to the unexpected German collapse of the autumn.

When he was not in France, the core of Churchill's work at Munitions was the handling of labour relations, for which many would have said that he was unsuited both by experience and by temperament. Nineteen-seventeen was the most discontented year of the war, with revolution in the streets of Petrograd and near mutiny in the French army being reflected, somewhat more mildly, in the arms factories of Clydeside and the Midlands. There was a wave of strikes that summer.

The definable cause, although there were also the less precise underlying ones of war-weariness and resentment at profiteering, was the erosion of the financial rewards of skilled workers organized in craft unions. They were mostly on 'time rates', with pay depending on the hours worked. But the new unskilled labour, whether male or female, which had increasingly been brought in, were on 'piece rates'. As extra output was strenuously sought, differentials were at best narrowed, and in some cases the take-home pay of the unskilled came to exceed that of the skilled. In addition skilled men were prevented, without obtaining a leaving certificate from the authorities, from leaving one munitions job to seek better pay in another.

Churchill's approach to these problems was a mixture of the sympathetic and the authoritarian. He took the risk of abolishing the disliked leaving certificate. Careless of inflationary implications he pushed through a 12.5 per cent increase in 'time rates' for skilled engineers, although this was not much more than a temporary relief for it quickly set a pattern for everyone else's wage claim. He also strongly advocated in Cabinet that the Excess Profits Tax should be put up from 80 to 100 per cent, but was defeated by Bonar Law. On the other hand he was impatient of workers striking in safety while soldiers were dying in France, and persuaded Lloyd George to threaten them with conscription, a threat which proved highly effective in the summer of 1918. His contribution was to draft a denunciatory warning against 'evil and subterranean influences', which he identified as 'Pacifism, Defeatism and Bolshevism'. Perhaps fortunately this statement was never issued.

Unlike the Prime Minister he was not a deft conciliator, but he nonetheless managed to find his way with a slapdash buoyancy through a fairly chaotic industrial scene. 'Here we have complete industrial disorder,' he encouragingly told a deputation of engineering employers in October 1918. When the war ended the general feeling was that he had been a more successful Minister of Munitions than either Edwin Montagu or Christopher Addison. The worst fears of the sixty Conservative MPs, who had met in horror when they heard of the prospect of his appointment, had not been realized. Their 1917 action, coupled with threats of individual resignation from Lord Derby, always an old walrus but usually a generous one, and Walter Long, the leading Tory country gentleman, made him realize for the first time, according to Hankey, just how unpopular he was.

So the end of 1918 was better for his stock than the middle of 1917. But he had not come near to regaining the position which he occupied towards the end of Asquith's peacetime ministry. He was then one of three or four best-known members of that memorable government, with a considerable age advantage over the others, combined with a wide experience of high office. He remained disliked and distrusted by the more partisan and unsophisticated members of the Conservative party which he had deserted – although not by Balfour, Curzon or F. E. Smith. But he compensated for this with the growing admiration, strong but not intimate, rather as sparrows and crows might regard an exotic bird which had flown in, of that great instrument of late-nineteenth- and early-twentieth-century government, the Liberal party. By 1918 that instrument was destroyed, with Churchill having played a minor role in its destruction. The amused but affectionate patronage of Asquith was no longer available, desired or of use to him. Even more than in the 1908–12 days when they were seen as the 'heavenly twins' of advanced radicalism, he had become a client of Lloyd George. An untrusted man himself, Churchill was dependent upon an undoubted star, but one for whom few, with Churchill not among them, would choose the word trustworthy as his most signal characteristic.

What would Lloyd George do with him in the new world after the German defeat? This became a preoccupation of Churchill's as the war moved towards its conclusion and peacetime politics became imminent. On 6 November Churchill and Montagu, as the two most senior Liberal ministers in the Coalition (which was in itself an indication of how much Lloyd George had allowed it to become Tory or allegedly non-party dominated), were summoned to luncheon at 10 Downing Street for a serious discussion about the political future. The first issue was an early general election, which Lloyd George wanted and with which desire Churchill was prepared go along. But Churchill was nonetheless in a cantankerous mood. Montagu expressed it pungently by recording that 'Winston began sulky, morose and unforthcoming.'[9]

Gradually the reason for Churchill's morosity came out. He much wanted to be in a peacetime coalition government but not without a full voice in the major policy decisions. In other words, the existing form of a small War Cabinet, with other ministers being only occasionally invited into it for isolated decisions relating to their own specific responsibilities, would not be acceptable to him in peacetime. Lloyd George apparently attempted to sweep this aside with a typical mixture of assuaging charm and semi-concession on the point of substance. The War Cabinet, he said, would be dissolved with the end of the war and he would revert to what he called 'a Gladstonian Cabinet' of about twelve members. What he in fact did for at least the next year or so while the Paris Peace Conference proceeded was not so much to broaden the Cabinet as effectively to abolish it. He left Bonar Law to look after politics at home while he paced the boards of European statesmanship, hardly ever attending either Cabinets or the House of Commons. He went a full year without attending Prime Minister's questions.

For the moment, Montagu thought, Churchill was fully appeased: 'The sullen look disappeared, smiles wreathed the hungry face, the fish was landed. . . .'[10] But, maybe in the dark recesses of the night, suspicion developed in Churchill's mind that he might once again be vetoed by Conservatives, on whom Lloyd George was obviously going to be heavily dependent, for inclusion even in such a wider body. On the following day he wrote to the Prime Minister a fairly rough letter, which Lloyd George chose to interpret even more roughly than its actual content justified. The key and hard half-sentence of Churchill's was 'I feel that I cannot choose my own course without knowing who your chief colleagues would be.'[11]

Lloyd George did not at all like Churchill's letter: 'Your letter came upon me as an unpleasant surprise. Frankly it perplexes me. It suggests that you contemplate the possibility of leaving the Government, and you give no reason for it beyond an apparent dissatisfaction with your own personal prospects.'[12] What was amazing about this correspondence was the length at which each wrote, for these letters were on the threshold of the Armistice, and those involved, certainly Lloyd George, should have been preoccupied by a multitude of other issues. Churchill began with a 600-word letter, Lloyd George replied with 1,200 words and Churchill came back with another 1,200. They are the more remarkable when the pressures of the time, particularly for the Prime Minister, are recalled, and there is no indication of any of the letters being drafted by private secretaries. They also point to an exceptionally close underlying relationship, whatever the day-to-day moods might be.

The essential umbilical cord, not necessarily producing amity or even mutual respect, was that, as already noted, they were the two Prime Ministers of near genius of the twentieth century. Although Churchill was in the context of history the superior of the two, it was in November 1918 of all months much more difficult for Lloyd George to appreciate Churchill's quality than vice versa, and it was much to Lloyd George's credit that, perhaps through a glass darkly, he at least half did. This is the only explanation of how little permanent, or indeed immediate, stain this tiresome correspondence left on their relationship. Churchill's letter of 7 November caused Lloyd George sharp but not dismissive irritation. Churchill was essentially trying to force his hand to a promise almost of a particular job in a peacetime government even before the war was formally over, well before the general election, and before Lloyd George could have been expected to have decided on the balance of his new government. And Lloyd George reacted very strongly: 'Surely this is an unprecedented demand! The choice of the Members of the Government must be left to the Prime Minister, and anyone who does not trust his leadership has but one course, and that is to seek leaders whom he can trust.' Then he legitimately twisted the knife in Churchill: 'I have fully recognized your capacity, and you know that at the cost of a great deal of temporary dissatisfaction amongst many of my supporters I placed you in the Ministry of Munitions. . . .'[13]

Three days later the war was over. Churchill described vividly in *The World Crisis* how he stood at his ministry window looking up Northumberland Avenue to Trafalgar Square as the chimes of Big Ben for the 11.00 a.m. cessation of hostilities rang out, and how his mind went back to similar chimes four years and fourteen weeks before. Then they were for eleven at night rather than in the morning, and had allowed him to signal hostilities to ships all over the world. 'I was conscious', he wrote of 1918, 'of reaction rather than elation.'[14] Then Clementine joined him, and they decided, or at least he did, to drive to 10 Downing Street and offer congratulations to Lloyd George. Most, after such a rough correspondence only half a week before, would have hesitated so to obtrude, uninvited, on to a Prime Minister at such a time. But Churchill's instinct was right. The upshot was that he was asked to return there for dinner that evening. The Prime Minister's only other guests were F. E. Smith and General Sir Henry Wilson, the Chief of the Imperial General Staff. To dine in such a select intimacy on that evening was obviously a mark of confidence, friendship and forgiveness for the letters. The only loser was Clementine, who was not asked to this all-male dinner and was left to 'celebrate' with her children but without her husband. There was something symbolic about this. In peace as in war the lure of high politics and the excitement of being at the centre of events were always to have priority.

The only thought which might have marred Churchill's pleasure at being in Downing Street on that watershed evening was the recollection of a similarly select dinner just under two years previously and almost on the eve of Lloyd George becoming Prime Minister, and his subsequent sense of let-down, almost of betrayal. That was not to be the case this time. On 29 December he was offered a choice between a return to the Admiralty and becoming Secretary of State for War, with ministerial responsibility for the air force thrown in. He could not begin to complain that he was not being treated up to the very top of his expectations. It made his requests for an advance guarantee look still more churlish, particularly as they were made from a very weak political base. He was lucky that Lloyd George did not make them the reason for a rift rather than merely for a long written rebuke.

Before Churchill could move back into full Cabinet rank, and with, for the first time in nearly four years, a proper established department behind him, the general election, the first since 1910, had to be fought and won. That did not present too much difficulty, either for Churchill at Dundee or for Lloyd George with the nation. In Dundee Churchill, running in alliance with a pro-war trades unionist, won by more than two to one, although, on a much higher poll than in the 1917 bye-election, the indefatigable Scrymgeour moved up to 10,000 votes. Nationally Lloyd George, with his 'coupon' of endorsement for those Conservatives and Liberals, plus a handful of Labour members, who were regarded as having been satisfactorily loyal to the government and the war effort, won on a landslide. But he did so at the price of destroying both the Liberal party, which between its formal inaugur-ation in Willis's Rooms in June 1859 and the end of 1916, had governed for thirty-two out of the fifty-seven years, and with it the balance of pre-1914 politics. The Liberal vote was down from 50 per cent in 1910 to 25 per cent, and it has since only once recovered above that figure, which was in alliance with the nascent Social Democratic party (with which it has since amalgamated) in 1983. And there has never since Asquith been any serious question of a purely Liberal government exercising power.

Lloyd George secured 478 seats, but no fewer than 335 of them were Conservatives, outnumbering the Coalition Liberals by two and a half to one. Perhaps even more indicative of how the old pattern had been shattered was the novel and fissiparous nature of the opposition. The largest group were seventy-three Sinn Feiners, who disdainfully stayed away from Westminster. Then came the Labour party, who with sixty-three seats constituted the official opposition, under a dour and little-remembered Scottish miner, William Adamson. All their known leaders, the pro-war Arthur Henderson and the anti-war Ramsay MacDonald and Philip Snowden, had lost their seats. Then came the shattered remnant of the old pre-war Liberal majority, equally bereft of their tallest poppies, most notably of Asquith, who after thirty-two years as MP for East Fife had there gone down to humiliating defeat. The others were twenty-five Irish Unionists (mainly from Ulster), twenty-three Conservatives who did not recognize Lloyd George's leadership and seven survivers from the old Redmondite Irish Nationalist party, an even more pathetic piece of flotsam than the 'wee free' Liberals.

Lloyd George had undoubtedly triumphed, but contained within his triumph was the replacement on the one hand of moderate Home Rulers by determined Republicans who had no desire to maintain any form of common polity for the British Isles, and on the other of the old Asquithians with whom Lloyd George had sat in Cabinet and reasonable amity for eleven years by, in Stanley Baldwin's immortal phrase, 'hard-faced men who looked as though they had done well out of the war', and who, within four years, were to bring Lloyd George's career to a crash so resounding that it proved irreversible in the remaining twenty-two years of his life.

Churchill's reaction to these developments had elements of Liberal nostalgia. He had no taste for a return to the political wilderness, and he knew that his only hope of avoiding it was to cling close to Lloyd George. Furthermore his 1915–16 experiences, as his letters only too vehemently expressed, had severed any links of loyalty to Asquith. Yet he felt a slightly patronizing sympathy for him in his vicissitudes. 'Asquith is having a very rough time in East Fife,' Churchill wrote to Clementine on 13 December, 'and is being subjected to abominable baiting by a gang of discharged soldiers. I do hope it will be all right for the poor old boy. I have been sorely tempted to take up the cudgels for him, but it would have caused many complications here and else-where. . . .'[15] It is difficult to imagine a more perfect expression of his retrospective generosity combined with a realistic appraisal of where his present and future interests lay.

Less sentimentally Churchill was anxious to make the Coalition manifesto as radical as possible, and certainly introduced such a note into his Dundee campaigning. He made a major issue of the nationali-zation of the railways, which aroused his full enthusiasm, even if it involved substantial government subsidy. 'It might even pay the State to run the railways at a loss,' he said, 'if by developing industries, creating new ones, reviving agriculture, and placing the trader in closer contact with his markets, they stimulated a great development at home.'[16] He was also a determined advocate of the creaming off of wartime profits:

'Why *should* anybody make a great fortune out of the war?' he wrote to Lloyd George in mid-November, and not demagogically, for the letter was not published. 'While everybody has been serving the Country, profiteers & contractors & shipping speculators have gained fortunes of a gigantic character. Why shd we be bound to bear the unpopularity of defending old Runciman's ill-gotten gains?* I would reclaim everything above say £10,000 (to let the small fry off) in reduction of the War Debt.' He also advanced a simple vision of all pulling together in a planned and to some extent state-directed economy to achieve the same efforts for the needs of peace as had been made for those of war. 'Why should peace have nothing but the squabbles and the selfishness and the pettiness of daily life? Why, if men and women, all classes, all parties, are able to work together for five years like a mighty machine to produce *destruction*, can they not work together for another five to produce *abundance*?'[17]

Where Churchill was moderate, perhaps too moderate for the wishes of many of his constituents, was in resisting demands for the dismemberment of Germany and in refusing to foster the illusion that the defeated nation could be made to pay for the total cost of the war: £2 billion of reparations for damage directly done was admissible but £40 billion for the total British cost of fighting the war was preposterous.

The campaign in Dundee was a rowdy one. 'The meeting last night', he wrote to his wife on 27 November, 'was the roughest I have ever seen in Dundee.' His detailed description suggests that his prominent supporters sometimes gave at least as good as they got:

We had a great struggle to get into the hall in a very hostile mob. I was afraid for a few moments that Sir George Ritchie [his Liberal chairman] would be knocked down. However with great agility he [Ritchie] seized his assailant by the throat and succeeded in forcing him under the wheels of a motor-car, whence he was rescued with some difficulty by Archie [Sinclair, who had loyally followed his former commanding officer to Dundee for the campaign].[18]

Churchill decided that he had done all that he could or need do by the middle of polling day and announced his intention of catching 'the 2.47 to Edinburgh, where I shall dine'[19] (presumably before taking

* It was not his Cabinet colleague of 1908–16 and former President of the Board of Trade but Walter Runciman's shipowing father to whom Churchill was referring, although he would no doubt not have minded had a few of his swipes at profits caught the son, never one of his favourites, as well as the father.

the sleeper south). Back in London, on the morning of 15 December he awaited the results with confidence (there was a Christmas gap of fourteen days between the polls and the counts, to allow the votes of soldiers overseas to come in), learned firmly of the satisfactory alternative posts that Lloyd George had in mind for him, and, with his own position secure, gave the Prime Minister the benefit of his advice on both the size and the individual composition of his Cabinet just as freely (and at just as great a length) as he had a few years before favoured Asquith with his views on similar subjects. He wrote six pages on 26 December. He thought the Cabinet should be not less than fourteen or fifteen, although the Lord Chancellor need not be included – he no doubt did not foresee that it would be his great friend F. E. Smith who was to be relegated. He suggested Isaacs (Reading) for Foreign Secretary, 'the Infant Samuel', echoing Asquith's satirical method of referring to him in his letters to Venetia Stanley, for Home Secretary – although, with Montagu (presumably) remaining at the India Office, he became worried that it might look bad if the Liberal side of the Cabinet were so predominantly Jewish. As a counterbalance he abandoned Samuel and wrote, 'For the Home Office I suggest Fisher.'[20] On reading this sentence my eyes, in the old cliché phrase, nearly popped out of my head. But it was not the old Admiral, trotted out once again for any available job, however inappropriate. It was H. A. L. Fisher, the historian and Warden of New College, Oxford, who had been President of the Board of Education since 1916 and was to remain so until 1922. As this example indicated, Churchill's advice was mostly not taken. But nor was it resented.

As for Churchill's own position, his mind moved increasingly towards the Admiralty, but that of the Prime Minister moved increasingly away from it and towards the War Office. With the power inherent in Lloyd George's office as well as his well-known capacity for cajolery, it hardly needed the bonus which he had up his sleeve of the Air Ministry as well as the War Office to make sure that Churchill not merely accepted, but did so with a good grace. Walter Long became a quiet First Lord of the Admiralty. These dispositions were obviously good sense. For Churchill to have gone back to the Admiralty would have been too much, to put it crudely, of a dog returning to its vomit, or to put it less crudely of an encouragement to him to go on fighting his old obsessive battles about the Dardanelles, Asquith and Kitchener. The War Office, his seventh office of state, and he was still only forty-four, gave him a much better chance of looking towards the future.

PART FOUR

HESITANT AFTERNOON

SUNSHINE

1919–1939

19

ANTI-BOLSHEVIK CRUSADER AND
IRISH PEACEMAKER

THE FORTY-SIX MONTHS of Lloyd George's peacetime Coalition were
one of the least creditable periods of Churchill's career. They were not
the most unhappy. He had office and power, by which he always set
high store. He found 1915–17, 1922–4 and the 'wilderness years' of the
1930s much more personally frustrating. Yet 1919–20 added the least to
his unparalleled collection of achievement and interest. He was not
alone in this period not being his finest hour. Although the Coalition
had some achievements, most notably perhaps the Irish Treaty of 1921,
there were few, and certainly not its Prime Minister, who came out
of that government with their reputation enhanced. There was something of a miasma about it, so that all who dwelt for long within the
atmosphere came out a little polluted.

Churchill was by no means the most mud-spattered of the somewhat
motley crew who clustered with varying and on the whole declining
allegiance around the Prime Minister. For the first two years Bonar
Law, the leader of three-quarters of the Coalition's majority, was the
key domestic anchor. While Lloyd George was absent for months at the
Paris Peace Congress leading to the Treaty of Versailles, it was Law
who filled in. He was Martha to Lloyd George's Mary. His background
was a mixture of Ulster Protestantism and Glasgow accountancy. He
was emphatically not louche, but nor was he either inspiring or inspiriting. His life, particularly after the early death of his wife in 1909, was
peculiarly joyless. Almost his only recreations were playing chess, eating
rice pudding and smoking cigars. He was a devastating debater 'on the
assumption' (in the words of Maynard Keynes) 'that the pieces visible
on the board constituted the whole premise of the argument'. His
somewhat lowering honesty was however tempered by an admiration
for success accompanied by an instinctive tendency to veer away when
it declined. This, aided by a fortuitous illness in the spring of 1921,
facilitated his retirement from the government. By the autumn of 1922

he had recovered sufficently to make a key contribution to delivering the *coup de grâce* to Lloyd George, and then to preside briefly over the first independent Conservative government for seventeen years. Churchill and Law had as little natural rapport with each other as did any two major political figures of the first half of this century.

In 1921 cautious, stiff, decent Austen Chamberlain took over as Conservative leader from Law. He quickly became more bedazzled by Lloyd George's wizardry than Law had been. But he was less successful at dealing either with Lloyd George himself or with the Conservative party on Lloyd George's behalf than his predecessor had been. With Law, Lloyd George's relationship, at least from 1916, had been not unlike that with his long-standing and long-suffering wife, Dame Margaret. Both of them enjoyed certain prerogatives because he was used to them and they were necessary supports, but these did not extend to an approach to equality or to a relationship infused by interest or excitement. With Austen Chamberlain, however, despite Chamberlain's unconditional loyalty, Lloyd George was both less at ease and less well protected. As a result October 1922 saw both of them crash, Lloyd George from a great height, and Chamberlain becoming the only Conservative leader, whose term both began and ended in the twentieth century, never to achieve 10 Downing Street. Once again, however, except for a certain tendency to like the company of those less respectable than himself (which he shared with Churchill), Chamberlain could hardly be described as louche.

From where, therefore, apart from the Prime Minister himself, half radical innovator and wartime leader of fortitude, but also half political manipulator of unexampled skill, did there stem the atmosphere of loucheness, or what would more recently be called sleaze? Hardly from Balfour, Foreign Secretary until October 1919, or from Curzon, his successor for the remaining three years of the government. Balfour could be coldly ruthless, and had an unrivalled capacity for stepping delicately away from any scene of squalor. But that did not make him remotely tawdry or corrupt. Nor was Curzon, even though he could sometimes be ridiculous and was on balance a less distinguished man than Balfour. He had a propensity for marrying rich American wives and using their fortunes to indulge his passion for acquiring and doing up more and more country houses. After the death of one wife this led to his quarrelling both with her American relations and with his own (and her) daughters. But if this was sleaze it had nothing to do with the public interest (except when it saved the houses) and was on such a grand scale as to be beyond the dreams of even the most grasping of modern political sinners. Lord Birkenhead, as F. E. Smith became on his 1919 appointment as Lord Chancellor, cannot be quite so easily acquitted – of loucheness at any rate. With all his great gifts of wit, and sometimes of wisdom, he always gave the impression of sailing close to several winds, and was eventually forced to leave office for the last time (in 1928) because of his total inability to live on his ministerial salary, and consequent attempts to earn money in ways thought inappropriate for a minister of the crown.

That left the other Chancellor (of the Exchequer), Sir Robert Horne, who came to the Treasury after Austen Chamberlain succeeded Law as Conservative anchor. Horne, like Bonar Law himself, was a son of the manse, but he rejected much more comprehensively than did the non-believing Law the values of Scots Presbyterianism. He was a nightclub-loving bachelor; in later life his only recorded address was 69 Arlington House, Piccadilly, a 1920s block of flats built on the site of the old Salisbury town house, where he was a fellow tenant of Beaverbrook. Baldwin memorably described him as 'that rare thing, a Scots cad'. This may have been based on mild commercial jealousy (it could hardly have been political jealousy on the part of the master of inter-war politics for a short-term Chancellor who never held office after the age of fifty-one) because Horne became chairman of the Great Western Railway, a post of high regional prestige which Baldwin's father had held, and which while appropriate for a Worcestershire ironmaster was less so for the MP for Glasgow, Hillhead. Horne was never seriously scandalous, but not could it be said that he had any spare store of respectability – as say with Edward Grey, Edward Halifax, Stafford Cripps or Peter Carrington – to throw over the government as a whole.

There was also the variegated collection of businessmen who passed through the Cabinet while leaving little more persistent trace on the face of politics than does an April snowfall. These businessmen were an odd addiction for Lloyd George, whose background was that of a pastoral radical. It is difficult now to see what was the special contribution of the Geddes brothers (Eric and Auckland) which entitled them to two places in the Cabinet of twenty-one – much bigger than Churchill had advocated – which in the course of 1919 took over from the small War Cabinet. An even more shadowy figure was Lord Inverforth, a Glasgow merchant and shipowner, who effectively disappeared from the scene after two years. The fourth member of this group was Hamar Greenwood, a Canadian who became Irish Chief Secretary in 1920.

Greenwood provided 'resolute government' for Ireland less elegantly than Balfour had done in 1887–92.

This was the government within which Churchill operated between the ages of forty-four and forty-eight. Although the clock ticked on for him, as for everybody else, he remained remarkably young for a minister of such long experience in senior office. It is difficult to say whether or not he found the ambience inspiriting. He began well because he quickly modified an unrealistic and potentially incendiary demobilization scheme. It had been worked out in 1917, under Lord Derby and without much political input and provided for the early release (almost exclusively) of those who were industrially the most necessary at home. As those in this category were often those who, for the same reason, had been the last to be called up, this provoked a great sense of unfairness, with among other manifestations of unrest a minor British mutiny at Calais and an ugly soldiers' demonstration in the heart of official London.

Churchill quickly saw the untenability of the scheme, and within ten days of taking office had produced an alternative founded on length of service, age and the number of times a man had been wounded. This resolved the issue more or less acceptably. Upon its basis he was within remarkably few months able to bring about a precipitate run-down of the army from over three million to one temporarily of 900,000 before going further down to a peacetime 370,000. Once the objective of saving money had been given the highest Cabinet priority, Churchill drove in this direction with enthusiasm, as throughout his career he did to nearly all departmental aims. He hit upon the happy solution of letting the majority of soldiers go while paying the retained core twice as much as they had received before.

Churchill had ministerial responsibility for the air force as well as the army. He had been enthusiastic about air power for nearly a decade, he believed strongly (in spite of his own dual role) that it should be developed as an independent service, and he got on well with General (soon to be Air Marshal) Hugh Trenchard, the effective professional creator of the RAF. Politicially his Air Ministry arrangements were less successful. He got General Seely MP to come in as parliamentary under-secretary, to answer for Air in the Commons and to be the only politician full-time in the Air Ministry. Seely was a close friend, as well as a gallant soldier. Some of Churchill's best letters during both his doldrums and his period as Minister of Munitions had been written to him in France. But Seely had also himself been a full Secretary of State (for War) five years before, until Asquith pushed him out for incompetence in handling the trouble at the Curragh.

Such previous elevation is never the best of preparation for a subordinate position, however great the degree of personal loyalty. Moreover though Seely was good both as a friend and as a soldier, he was not good as a minister. He quickly became unhappy and made somewhat contradictory complaints about Churchill: on the one hand that he tried to run the Air Ministry as a branch of the War Office, and on the other that he left Seely too much on his own, spending only an hour or so a week in the Secretary of State's room at the Air Ministry. In November 1919, Seely resigned, making a House of Commons statement along these lines, which caused Churchill some distress. He was replaced by the Marquess of Londonderry, a less attractive figure than Seely, even though he was, with Marlborough and Westminster, one of Churchill's high-titled cronies. For Londonderry it began a connection with the air force which continued until in the early 1930s he earned some derision (in left-wing circles at any rate) by claiming that he had only with difficulty prevented the outlawing of bombing aircraft at the Disarmament Conference (1931–3) because of the great need for them 'on the frontiers of empire'.

However few hours Churchill put in at the Air Ministry, he put in quite a number again trying to get his pilot's licence. This had been an ambition of his when he was First Lord of the Admiralty before the war, until after a number of hairy incidents he had been begged by Clementine to desist. No doubt the reliability of planes had somewhat improved in the meantime, but not to the extent of making them proof against Churchill. In June 1919 (when not at the controls) he experienced a crash landing at Buc airfield near Paris. Undeterred he went out to Croydon aerodrome from the War Office barely a month later for an hour's early-evening flying practice. It did not last that long. From a hesitant ninety feet some mechanical failure, maybe assisted by human error, put the plane precipitately back on the ground, with considerable damage to itself, heavy bruising and facial scratches for Churchill, and somewhat but not much worse injuries to his instructor. Churchill had thought that he was about to be killed, but he was able to pick himself up and go off to preside over a House of Commons dinner for General Pershing, the American commander in France.

Churchill may not have been one of nature's pilots, but he continued to be ludicrously fearless. Most would have been put off by his crash landing a month before. Few would have wanted to go on after this second narrow escape. It nonetheless required a lot of persuasion to make him abandon his quest for a licence, although he did ultimately and to widespread relief succumb to the pressure.

The dominant theme of Churchill's War Secretaryship was not however his deft if precipitate handling of demobilization, his fostering of the early RAF, or his personal adventures, but his dedicated attempt at strangling near to birth the Bolshevik regime in Russia. In this unsuccessful enterprise he showed no comprehension of the war-weariness of Britain. His pulsating energy made him rarely weary, and almost never of war. This separated him from the sentiment not only of the British people but also of the war-winning Prime Minister. Lloyd George knew that there was no heart for an anti-Bolshevik crusade. Nor was this surprising in the immediate aftermath of a war which had killed 750,000 British troops (and still more Russian, German and French ones) and which was being closely followed by a virulent influenza epidemic which was almost equally devastating. But such factors were irrelevant to Churchill. He regarded the Lenin regime as a disaster for Russia and a menace to the world. He used the most extravagant language about it. In *The Aftermath*, the last volume of *The World Crisis*, published after ten years of opportunity for calming down, he wrote of 'not a wounded Russia only, but a poisoned Russia, an infected Russia, a plague-bearing Russia; a Russia of armed hordes smiting not only with bayonet and with cannon, but accompanied and preceded by swarms of typhus-bearing vermin which slew the bodies of men, and political doctrines which destroyed the health and even the soul of nations'.[1]

He also vastly over-estimated the ease with which the West could overthrow the 'plague-bearing' regime. In the first chapter of *The Aftermath* he postulated an imaginary meeting (planned for some reason or other in the Isle of Wight or Jersey and taking place before the Paris peace negotiations) between Woodrow Wilson, Clemenceau and Lloyd George in which they made all the right decisions. Most of these decisions were very sensible and would have led to a much better post-1918 world. But when they came to Russia they decided to send for Marshal Foch and ask him how that country could be freed of the Bolsheviks and brought, not back but forward, to some form of constitutional democracy. Churchill had Foch reply:

> There is no great difficulty and there need be no serious fighting. A few hundred thousand American troops who are longing to play a part in events, together with volunteer units from the British ... and French

armies can easily with the modern railways obtain control of Moscow; and anyhow we hold already three parts of Russia. If you wish your authority to embrace the late Russian Empire ... you have only to give me the order. How easy this task will be to me and Haig and Pershing compared with restoring the battle of the 21st March [1918] or breaking the Hindenburg line![2]

It was horribly reminiscent of Churchill's Dardanelles illusions, the belief that will and optimism were more important than an adequacy of resources for the task envisaged. The idea that three-quarters of the enormous Russian territories were under effective Allied or counter-revolutionary control was a figment which Churchill's imagination made him put into the mouth of Foch. There were about 30,000 Allied troops, nearly half of them British, under General Ironside in the Arctic ports of Archangel and Murmansk. There were another 30,000 under the White Russian General Denikin in the south, and perhaps most formidably there were the troops of the Siberian Provisional Government, under the equally White Admiral Kolchak, with its headquarters at Omsk. They had a sort of control over the trans-Siberian railway, but the forces available to the Admiral were somewhat heterogeneous. There were some French, some Americans and some Japanese, as well as two British battalions, that had somehow or other got there from Hong Kong (still more bizarrely, one of them was under the command of Colonel John Ward, Labour MP for Stoke-on-Trent). Kolchak's main military resources, however, were 70,000 Czech troops who were vaguely on their way home to Prague from Vladivostok. It was not, in retrospect at any rate, a formidable array with which to overcome Leon Trotsky's revolutionary army, particularly as the latter was operating on interior lines of communication against a scattered opposition. But Churchill determined to put his faith and some considerable part of his reputation in backing these disparate elements. It did neither him nor them any good, and ended up in complete withdrawal and defeat. The result was a fairly quiet débâcle, from which he escaped without disaster, but with his reputation far from enhanced. For many it reinforced the Antwerp–Dardanelles view that he was a rash military adventurer. It also had some important consequences for his political orientation.

In the first place it soured his relations with Lloyd George. The Prime Minister had not the slightest intention of getting embroiled in a Russian civil war. But, perhaps because of his Peace Conference preoccupation, he played out too much rope to Churchill and to the others in his on the whole right-wing Cabinet who were inclined to support the Churchill line. This had several important consequences for the development of Churchill's political position and prospects. It reinforced Lloyd George's distrust of his judgement, which, battling with his admiration for Churchill's bold vigour and liking for his company, was always there. It made him anxious to transfer Churchill away from the War Office. He was moved to the Colonial Office in early 1921, replacing his old adversary Milner. This was no demotion, the two posts being of equal rank. But Lloyd George had no intention of promoting Churchill either, and when in March of that same year Bonar Law's retirement through ill-health led to Austen Chamberlain's promotion to the leadership of the Conservative party and vacating of the Treasury, Churchill did not get the Chancellorship. This was contrary to his hopes and expectations. His disappointment and resentment were exacerbated by Sir Robert Horne, who did get the job, being a far less experienced and prominent politician than himself – indeed he became one of the least-remembered Chancellors of the past century. There ensued a period when Churchill was at least as much off his Prime Minister as the Prime Minister was off him.

His Russian adventurism, however, even though it cost a lot of money by the budgetary standards of the day (£73 million was one estimate) and ended in the failure of the counter-revolution and withdrawal of British troops from its support, gave him for the first time for nearly twenty years something of a constituency on the right of the Conservative party. Just as the withdrawal after failure, although decided upon over Churchill's head and against his wishes, struck a dangerous echo of the Dardanelles, so his suddenly finding an issue which appealed to diehards foreshadowed his sustained early 1930s campaign against the hesitant moves of Baldwin, Samuel Hoare and Halifax (then called Irwin and the returning Viceroy) towards Indian self-government.

The Russian adventure also had the effect of digging a deeper ditch between him and Labour and trades union opinion than that which existed between them and many Conservatives, let alone other Liberal politicians of the day. It took a long time, for instance, for his relations with Ernest Bevin, the dominant trades union leader of the 1920s and 1930s and a crucial Second World War colleague of Churchill's, to recover from the *Jolly George* confrontation in May 1920. This curiously named ship was to convey arms from the East India Dock (in London) to Poland for use against the Red Army. Churchill, rather against the view of Lloyd George, was determined that the cargo should sail. Bevin was determined that it should not, and was prepared to use the industrial power of the newly amalgamated Transport and General Workers Union. Bevin won.

Even before this Churchill had been subject to heavy Labour criticism, and as was his habit responded in kind. 'Labour is quite unfitted for the responsibility of Government,' he said in January 1920,[3] a note he was frequently to repeat. It was very different from that which Baldwin was quite soon to be sounding. Furthermore, Churchill's confrontational policy, stemming out of his passion to crush the Bolsheviks, helped to undermine his support in the proletarian city of Dundee, where in 1918 he had won handsomely on a joint ticket with a trades unionist and where in 1922 he was to suffer a crushing defeat.

The exact Dundee effect is difficult to measure, but what is clear is that, during his twenty-five months at the War Office, Churchill crossed over the median line of politics. At the 1918 election he was still in spirit as well as in form part of the centre-left. By early 1921, although it was to be nearly another four years before he formally joined the Conservative party, he was on the rightward side of the line, where he was to remain (although always in his idiosyncratic way) some would say for his remaining four decades, although I would rather say until the late 1930s, when he began to transcend party politics.

His twenty months as Colonial Secretary were in some but by no means all ways a more felicitous period for him than his War Office years. They were dominated by two areas of the world which had been remote from the responsibilities of the Colonial Office during Churchill's two years there as under-secretary in 1905–8. The first was the Middle East, which had effectively passed from Turkish to British suzerainty, and the second was Ireland, which was moving from being an integral part of the United Kingdom to dominion status disguised as the Irish Free State, and hence, prior to the first appointment of a separate Dominions Secretary in 1930, a matter within his Colonial Office responsibility. As, towards the end of this period, the Coalition moved towards its downfall, Churchill's private expressions of view became increasingly detached about both its record and the Prime Minister's individual performance. But he nonetheless thought that his own record made the 1921–2 parliamentary session the most successful of his career.

Nineteen-twenty-one was also marked by the most searing succession of family deaths. On 15 April Bill Hozier, Clementine's thirty-three-year-old former naval officer brother committed suicide in a Paris hotel room. On 29 June Lady Randolph Churchill, a month after tripping downstairs in very high heels and after suffering a leg amputation in the meantime, succumbed, still after all her experiences aged only sixty-seven. In early August there came the death of Thomas Walden, who had begun his service with Lord Randolph and had been Churchill's 'man' since he went to South Africa with him in 1899. Then on 23 August there came by far the worst blow of the lot. This was the death from a diphtheria-like illness of the Churchills' youngest child, Marigold, aged just under four. She had become ill ten days before in seaside lodgings at Broadstairs, where all the children were under the care of a governess and nursemaids. Clementine was at Eaton Hall, the Cheshire mansion of the Duke of Westminster. She hastened to Kent, but her grief at the harrowing death was increased by remorse at not having been there in the early days of the illness.

Nor did the end of the year bring much of a pick-up. Churchill went to Cannes with Lloyd George (surprisingly in view of the froideur after Horne's appointment) on 26 December (with a compulsion familiar to some authors, Churchill made the Prime Minister read two manuscript chapters of *The World Crisis* in the train). The next day the whole household, left under Clementine's care in the new house in Sussex Square, began to be struck down by a second wave of influenza epidemic. First two maids and then Randolph and Diana were infected. On top of this a cousin of Clementine's who had arrived to help with the children fell ill with pneumonia. The whole house became a cottage hospital, fortunately with an adequate quota of temporarily hired nurses drafted in. So close to the 1919 killing influenza epidemic and so soon after the death of Marigold it is surprising that a greater panic than is evident in the correspondence to and from the South of France did not set in. However all recovered fairly quickly – although Clementine soon added to the invalid ranks by being ordered to her own bed with nervous exhaustion. She was at the beginning of her fifth and last pregnancy, perhaps an obvious replacement reaction, which resulted in the birth of Mary (later Lady Soames) in September 1922, the last, best balanced and longest-surviving of the Churchill children.

Churchill came back from the South of France on 7 January after twelve days and with 20,000 words of *The World Crisis* there written. A couple of weeks later Clementine, in urgent need of recuperation, both physical and psychological, replaced him in Cannes. She was accompanied by Venetia Montagu, Asquith's old penfriend, and stayed for four or five weeks. The Churchills, for a successfully married couple, spent a lot of time apart, although if anything less than the Gladstones, another outstanding example of a successful Prime Ministerial marriage, had done two-thirds of a century earlier. Perhaps a degree of separateness aids rather than contradicts the success. In any event, if both parties are fluent and literate, as with the Gladstones and the Churchills, periods of separation, and consequent correspondence, are a boon to the biographer.

The other thought aroused by this pattern of life is the extraordinary hold which the old French Riviera had upon the governing class of Britain during the 1920s, and to a somewhat lesser extent the 1930s too. Even naturally insular figures like Bonar Law were frequently there, while those who saw themselves as more cosmopolitan, Churchill, Lloyd George, F. E. Smith, Beaverbrook, crowded into the grand hotels of Monte Carlo, Nice and Cannes. And it was all done in the three winter months, during which, despite a great deal of contrary evidence, the British aficionados persisted in believing that the Côte d'Azur enjoyed a peculiarly benign climate. This was largely because sunnier and warmer winter resorts from North Africa to the West Indies were then difficult to get to. It was a few years before Scott Fitzgerald in *Tender is the Night* made Dick Diver act as a spearhead for the revolutionary view that the South of France might be better as a summer than a winter resort. This attachment to the Riviera was however very good for the Grands Express Européennes. It was the golden age of the Golden Arrow and a period of blue sky for the Train Bleu. And it did help to make the politicians of the 1920s a little less insular than Sir Edward Grey, who managed to be Foreign Secretary for nearly nine peacetime years without once crossing the Channel. Even so, when the British stepped sedately out of the *wagons-lits* at Cannes or Nice they proceeded to lead a very anglocentric life. The politicians, if they were grand enough, might see Clemenceau, Poincaré, Briand or Herriot on their way through Paris, but when they imbibed 'beakerfuls of the [fairly] warm south' they mostly did so in British enclaves. Clementine Churchill played very successfully in a lot of Riviera tennis tournaments, but her partners and vanquished victims were nearly all subjects of King George V rather than citizens of the Third French Republic.

How great a part did the forbidden fruit of the casinos (illegal in Britain for many decades to come, and even in France allowed at only a dozen or so resort towns) play in the attractions of the Riviera to the visitors? Even Clementine, particularly when Churchill was not there, indulged in an occasional mild flutter, while Venetia Montagu plunged somewhat more heavily. Churchill enjoyed serious gambling, although less so the losses in which it mostly resulted. And for this reason Clementine was more inclined to dip her toe into casinos in his absence. It was not that she was ashamed of her very modest indulgences but that she wished to give no encouragement to his tendency to more serious ones. One reason why she had strong reservations about F. E. Smith (although greatly liking his wife) was that his macho example encouraged Churchill to gamble heavily. It did not need the apparatus of croupiers and green-baize tables for this to happen: it had been a feature of life at the Oxfordshire Hussars' pre-1914 summer camps in Blenheim Park.*

She was more worried about the bad gambling influence of Smith than about his bad drinking influence. This was a wise judgement even though Birkenhead (as he had been since 1919) would in the last year or so of his life help to set her son Randolph (whose godfather he was) on an excessively alcoholic course. Winston Churchill, however, made alcohol much more his servant than Birkenhead (or Randolph) was able to do. In the first place, he did not drink as much as he was commonly thought to do, although this is not incompatible with his being a fairly heavy and consistent imbiber. But he was a sipper not a guzzler. Second, while not necessarily having a better head than Birkenhead, who could make remarkably lucid speeches while in a high state of intoxication, Churchill had a metabolism which enabled him to survive many years of an approach to the intake which finished off Birkenhead at the age of fifty-eight. Third, Churchill had no need of the occasional periods of abstinence with which Birkenhead tried to temper his excesses, and was somewhat dismissive of them. 'F.E. has gone absolute Pussyfoot for a year,' he wrote to Clementine on 9 February 1921. 'He drinks cider & ginger pop & looks ten years younger. Don't make a mock of this, as he is quite sensitive about it. He looks sad. Not for Pig.'[†4] And on 27 February he added: 'F.E. dined last night. Only cider! He is becoming vy fierce & calm – a formidable figure – rather morose – vy ambitious. Terrible results of intemperate self restraint.'[5]

---

* Margaret Smith (Lady Birkenhead) very late in her long life told Mary Soames that one reason why her husband had been bad for Churchill in this respect was that while he (Smith) could recoup his losses with a few days of highly paid court appearances, Churchill had no similar resources. If she was referring to the pre-1914 years, when Churchill was a young minister and not doing books or journalism, this was true. But by the 1920s Churchill had developed his literary gifts to be at least as remunerative as Smith's powers of advocacy had been.
† 'Cat' and 'Pig' were the Churchills' pet names for each other.

Good though he was at absorbing alcohol, Churchill led a surprisingly café-society, even rackety, life for a Secretary of State, particularly during the winters of 1921 and 1922 and the summer of the latter year when Clementine was a good deal away. Much of it centred around the future King Edward VIII or 'P. of W.' as Churchill mostly referred to him.* Thus on 9 February 1921: '[The Laverys] gave a vy amusing party on Tuesday to the P. of W. We danced in the studio & had an entertainment. Last night Philip [Sassoon] renewed the party – reinforced by Ll.G. Unhappily in dancing I trod with my heel upon the P. of W. toe & made him yelp. But he bore it vy well – & no malice. The little lady [Freda Dudley Ward] was vy much to the fore. I am booked almost every night for one of these tiny parties. . . .'[6] And again on 15 July 1922: 'I have had a vy tiring week with late sittings in the Commons, & last night a dance at Philip's [again Sassoon] at wh I stayed till 2. All my partners were there & I danced 8 times running. . . . My dinner to the Prince is expanding & will I think attain 16 or even 18. Don't be alarmed. I will organise it all with yr excellent staff.'[7]

These last years of the Coalition were also marked by two developments on the Churchill housing front, the first casting a long prior shadow on future events and the second leading much more quickly to a change in the family circumstances. On 6 February 1921 Churchill wrote from Chequers, the Chilterns country house which Lord Lee of Fareham had given 'as a place of recreation' for Prime Ministers and which had first been occupied by Lloyd George only a month beforehand. 'Here I am,' he wrote to Clementine. 'You would like to see this place – Perhaps you will some day! It is just the kind of house you admire – a panelled museum full of history, full of treasures – but insufficiently warmed – Anyhow a wonderful possession.'[8]

The second house, which first appeared on the horizon in the summer of 1922, was Chartwell, an unusually shaped and proportioned manor house which became the base of a large part of Churchill's life for his remaining four decades. It was only twenty-four miles from Westminster, just in Kent. Despite this semi-suburban location, it commanded a sequestered valley as well as one of the best distant views in the southeast of England. It was a Victorianized house of Elizabethan origin in a

---

* Thereby recalling the rather good joke of a 1920s don who issued invitations to the beau monde of Oxford for a luncheon party, saying that he had 'the P of W' coming, achieved an almost unanimous acceptance rate, and then explained that he had of course meant the Provost of Worcester (College).

somewhat dilapidated condition. Churchill had his eye on it from early
July 1922. Clementine had gone over to see it at the end of that month,
when she had been staying near by. Her first reaction had been
favourable: 'I can think of nothing but that heavenly tree-crowned Hill
– It is like a view from an aeroplane being up there – I do hope we shall
get it – If we do I feel that we shall live there a great deal & be very
very happy.'⁹ Later, however, she became reticent, even hostile, on
account of the cost of restoration, enlargement, and the general *train de
maison* which she (rightly) thought it likely to involve. Indeed she much
later told her daughter Mary, who entered the Churchill family at
almost exactly the same time as Chartwell Manor (September 1922) that
she thought, in relation to its purchase, it was the one occasion in fifty-
seven years of marriage when Churchill's candour with her had been
deficient.¹⁰

   He bought the house for £5,000 (say the equivalent of £120,000 in
today's money), less than he had paid for Lullenden, but with a vast
amount of work needing to be done. The fact that he could rationally
contemplate this (even allowing for his habitual view that income should
always be expanded to meet expenditure rather than that expenditure
should be tempered by the exigencies of income) was due to his having
recently inherited the Garron Towers estate in County Antrim. This
was contingently left to him by his grandmother, Frances Duchess of
Marlborough, a Londonderry daughter. For promise to become reality,
however, Lord Henry Vane-Tempest, only fifteen years Churchill's
senior, and an intervening beneficiary, had to die. This Lord Henry
conveniently did, aided by a railway accident in Wales, in January 1921.
The estate was thought to be worth the substantial sum in 1920s money
of £4,000 a year, although there was some subsequent doubt as to
whether the legacy wholly came up to expectations. The renovating of
Chartwell made heavy calls upon it.

   Churchill engaged Philip Tilden, a fashionable if slightly dilettante
young architect of the period, who had already refashioned Philip
Sassoon's Port Lympne and was soon to do Lloyd George's Bron-y-de
at Churt. Tilden's plans made Chartwell cost at least £20,000, a total
investment of nearly a modern half-million and took eighteen months
to implement, so that it was April 1924 before Churchill first spent a
night there.

   Tilden, as might have been expected from his work at Port Lympne,
still a millionaire's semi-modernistic showpiece worth visiting, gave the
reconstructed and enlarged Chartwell a sense of light and air contrasting

sharply with its Tudor beginnings. Indeed its dining room, jutting out over the valley (although this was a somewhat later addition) recalls the Verandah Grills on the old Cunard *Queens*. Tilden, plus his successor designer, plus decades of Churchill occupancy, plus waves of often personally executed dammings as well as bricklayings in the grounds, have had the cumulative effect of turning Chartwell into one of the two most evocative political shrines in the Western world. Its only rival is Hyde Park, the Hudson Valley family house of Franklin Roosevelt. In both of them it is easy to imagine, almost to feel, the physical presence of the authors of their fame. Clementine was however right in fearing that it was a bridge too far. Chartwell was a continuing strain on their resources and required two injections of friendly financial support, one in 1938–9 and one in 1946, for the Churchill occupation to continue.

The Middle Eastern aspects of Churchill's Colonial Secretaryship dominated its first few months just as, in a somewhat overlapping way, the Irish problem did the subsequent period. He was told by Lloyd George that he was to go to the Colonial Office on 1 January 1921, but it was another six weeks before he took over the seals of that office and surrendered those of the War Office, keeping however those of the Air Ministry for another two months until, in a somewhat incestuous way, they were passed to his ubiquitous cousin, Freddie Guest. During his already cited 9 February Chequers visit to Lloyd George they had jointly decided to summon the Cairo Conference of 12–22 March (1921). The conference was concerned not with Egypt, which remained a Foreign Office matter, but with the lands beyond the Suez Canal, between the Mediterranean and the Persian Gulf, and particularly with Iraq (then called Mesopotamia). *The Times* believed that the plan stemmed from Churchill's desire to hold a 'Durbar', and Curzon, who during his Indian Viceroyalty of twenty years before had himself been prince of such ostentatious pageants, expressed the same thought somewhat differently by suggesting that Churchill would 'be under an irresistible temptation to proclaim himself King in Babylon'.

That he did not do, but he nonetheless enjoyed himself enormously in an informal viceregal role. He picked up Clementine in the South of France, had a luxurious voyage with her from Marseille to Alexandria, was ineffectively stoned on arrival in Cairo by Egyptian nationalists, but presided satisfactorily over the conference in a closely guarded Hotel Semiramis, although escaping to visit (and be photographed) in a highly vulnerable group of English gentlemen (and a few ladies) uneasily seated on camels before the Sphinx and the pyramids. What he essentially secured was that the Emir Feisal should become a client king in Iraq, and that this historically famous area around and between the Tigris and Euphrates rivers should in reality be run by Britain on the cheap. The RAF was to provide the sole garrison. The army units there (which by an odd quirk were under the command of General Aylmer Haldane, Churchill's old companion in arms and in prison camp, but to whom at this stage he privately attributed 'slanderous malice') were to be withdrawn over the next year or so. Churchill was advised at the time and in this theatre by T. E. Lawrence, *alias* Aircraftman Shaw, for whom he had developed an admiration barely less than that which he had at times felt for Admiral Lord Fisher.

After Cairo Churchill went on to Jerusalem, where Herbert Samuel was already British High Commissioner charged with implementing the League of Nations mandate over Palestine which had been given to Britain under the Peace Treaties. Churchill there reaffirmed his moderate Zionism by committing the British government to some sort of Jewish national home in Palestine, which he symbolized by planting a tree on Mount Scopus, alongside the new Hebrew University. He also, then and subsequently, delivered himself of a number of well-phrased and semi-contradictory aphorisms. 'The British government is the greatest Moslem state in the world,' he said at the time, 'and it is well disposed to the Arabs and cherishes their friendship.'[11] Then, three months later, he told a Manchester cotton audience: 'In Africa, the population is docile and the country fruitful; in Mesopotamia and the Middle East the country is arid, and the population ferocious.' He did however succeed in establishing an Arab royal dynasty in Transjordan which has proved substantially longer lasting that that of Feisal in Baghdad. Sheik Abdullah, the father of King Hussein, under an agreement negotiated by Churchill set himself up in Amman with limited sovereignty vis-à-vis the British but without subordination to the High Commissioner in Jerusalem. Churchill and Clementine then made a holiday journey home, taking over two weeks to proceed via Alexandria, Sicily and Naples and reaching London only on 12 April, after six weeks of absence.

Churchill then shed his Air Ministry responsibilities, which he had incongruously carried to the Colonial Office with him. This did not mean that he had much time for the more traditional areas of Colonial Office concerns – Africa and the West Indies – because he almost immediately became deeply embroiled in the Irish question. The outer areas were mostly left to the permanent officials aided by the parliamentary under-secretary, then a thirty-nine-year old Yorkshire MP called Edward Wood. Wood later became Lord Irwin (when he went to India as Viceroy five years later) and then as Viscount Halifax was Chamberlain's Foreign Secretary and the man who might easily and disastrously have frustrated Churchill becoming Prime Minister in May 1940. Wood complained that he saw little of Churchill when he was his junior minister, although allowing that on the rare occasions when he did he was treated with courtesy. He was shipped off to do a detailed study of the problems of the West Indies between November 1921 and February 1922.

In May 1920 Churchill at the War Office had borne a heavy responsibility for the recruitment and deployment in Ireland of both the Black and Tans and their ex-officer supplement the Auxis. They were a sort of Freikorps of those for whom the war had not provided enough violence or the peace enough employment opportunity. They were given the task of trying to use force to suppress terrorism or, as became increasingly the case, meeting terror with terror. During 1920 the authority of British rule in Ireland disintegrated rapidly. The Chief Secretary, Hamar Greenwood, sang a song of persistent optimism. The defeat of the forces of disorder was just around the corner. His advice led Lloyd George at the Lord Mayor's banquet that November (1920) to make the singularly unfortunate boast that 'we have murder by the throat'. In fact the authority of Dublin Castle was becoming more and more limited to the old pale, the three or four counties around Dublin, and was far from secure even there. In October the lord mayor of Cork, not a Tammany-style alderman but a sensitive poet-intellectual, died in a London gaol after a seventy-four-day hunger strike. This led to a redoubling of violence, particularly in the south-west, with the proclamation of martial law in the counties of Tipperary, Cork, Kerry and Limerick as a counter-measure, one of the first fruits of which was the burning (by British forces) of a substantial part of the city of Cork on 11 December.

This and other incidents led to a very unfavourable international press for the British government, as well as to a great deal of criticism at home. Churchill, as might have been expected, was at first strongly in favour of establishing military superiority over Sinn Fein ('ourselves alone'), which had swept the old moderate Irish Nationalist party into oblivion at the 1918 election, and its military branch, the Irish Republican Army, before negotiating with them. 'In defeat (or against rebellion) defiance, in victory magnanimity' was one of his most strongly held lifelong maxims. And at the end of 1920 there was no British victory in sight, except in the perennially optimistic gaze of Greenwood. Churhill's instinctive aggressiveness against challenge was however undermined both by the inherent intractability of a deeply disaffected population, and by some trenchant criticism from very near to home (even if temporarily 600 miles away). On 18 February 1921 Clementine wrote from Beaulieu-sur-Mer one of her most forthright letters:

> Do my Darling use your influence *now* for some sort of moderation or at any rate justice in Ireland – Put yourself in the place of the Irish – if you were their leader, you would not be cowed by severity & certainly not by reprisals which fall like the rain from Heaven upon the Just & upon the Unjust. – You say (in a recent letter) that the confident assertions of Hamar [Greenwood] do not seem to be borne out by events. It makes me blush to think that men of the calibre of yourself & the P.M. should have listened to a man of the stamp of Hamar who is nothing but a blaspheming, hearty, vulgar, brave Knock-a-bout Colonial – I think he has done his executive part pluckily and efficiently (tho' considering he has had the whole resources of Scotland Yard for his protection I don't see why he should be much alarmed). . . . It always makes me unhappy & disappointed when I see you *inclined* to take for granted that the rough iron-fisted 'hunnish' way will prevail. . . .[12]

How much Churchill was influenced by this strong and persuasive letter is difficult to estimate. In Cabinet he continued as a supporter of a hard line until at least two, maybe three months after its receipt. But an increasing conflict began to arise in his mind. In *The Aftermath* he sets out the contrary emotions fighting within him. He had of course been a fairly determined Home Ruler before the war, although, perhaps partly on filial grounds, more sensitive to the problem of Ulster than were some of his colleagues. But the Ulster problem was now out of the way. Its own separate parliament (Stormont) had been set up under the Act of 1920. He was willing to concede to the Irish 'all that Gladstone had striven for', not apparently realizing that it was thirty years too late for a 'union of hearts' solution within an imperial polity. But any severance of Ireland's link with the Crown, which would raise the threat of a 'revolutionary Republic', was deeply repugnant to him. It was also his strong instinct that terrorism must be beaten before even its legitimate demands could be conceded. Yet such a victory was proving maddeningly elusive. This mood was retrospectively well represented in the prose of Churchill's relevant chapter in *The Aftermath*. The phrases were as richly redolent as ever, but they clanged atonally in different directions. He wrote like a vigorous but frustrated fly, banging itself first against one windowpane and then against another.

> It was clear by the early summer of 1921 that Britain was at the parting of the ways. It would have been quite easy [something of an overstatement] to quell the odious and shameful form of warfare by which we were assailed, and into which we were being increasingly drawn, by using the ruthlessness which the Russian communists adopted towards their fellow countrymen. The arrest of large numbers of persons believed by the police to be in sympathy with the rebels and the summary execution of four or five of these hostages (many of whom must certainly have been innocent) for any life taken of a Government servant, might have been a remedy at once sombre and efficacious. It was a course of which the British people in the hour of their deliverance [from the First World War] were utterly incapable. Public opinion recoiled with anger and irritation even from the partial measures into which our agents had been gradually drawn. The choice was by now clearly open: 'Crush them with iron and unstinted force, or try to give them what they want.' These were the only alternatives, and though each had ardent advocates, most people were unprepared for either.
>
> Here indeed was the Irish Spectre – horrid and inexorcizable.[13]

There then occurred what Churchill described as the most 'complete and sudden ... reversal of policy' in the modern history of British government. 'In May the whole power of the State and all the influence of the Coalition were used to "hunt down the murder gang": in June the goal was a lasting reconciliation with the Irish people.' Churchill did not play a major role in securing this historic shift in the opinion of the Cabinet. It was essentially Lloyd George who moved. Hitherto the Prime Minister had believed that he could depend absolutely on the Conservatives with whom he had stuffed his Cabinet to back a hard-line imperial-supremacy policy in Ireland. After all they were still called Unionists as frequently as they were called Conservatives. Then he suddenly discovered they were becoming lily-livered, or, put more attractively, had at least as sensitive a liberal conscience as himself. Churchill wrote a little cynically about this highly political shift on Lloyd George's part. He did not exactly assist it, but (contrary to his natural pugnacity) he did not resist it either, perhaps accepting it with some relief, which may well have owed something to the delayed-action effect of Clementine's February *démarche*.

Aided by a conciliatory speech, written by Edward Grigg for ministers, but pronounced by King George V at the inauguration of the

Northern Ireland Parliament on 22 June and undermined by discouraging reports from General Macready, who was finding the Irish command more intractable than his previous post as Commissioner of the (London) Metropolitan Police, the British government moved towards an Irish truce. It was a classic example of the fog of war beneficially conducing to peace. Neither side realized that the other was at least as exhausted as they were themselves. The truce took effect from 11 July 1921.

Eamon De Valera, the Sinn Fein leader, then aged thirty-eight, as tricky and in many ways deadening a man to deal with as ever entered the tangled web of Anglo-Irish negotiations, first visited Downing Street on 14 July. He blazed a path up that famous but in those days much less fortified street which has since been followed by seasoned terrorists nearly as well known as himself. That particular Lloyd George–De Valera meeting did not advance matters very far. Lloyd George indulged himself by showing that he had greater command over one branch of the Celtic tongue than had De Valera over its Hibernian cousin. However, an almost irreversible but also tortuous process of negotiation was set in train. It proceeded via such alarums and excursions as a special holiday Cabinet on 7 September in the Inverness town hall* (convenient for the Prime Minister and thought to be adequately so for others, such was then the early-autumn Highland propensity of British ministers) and the dismissal from Lloyd George's Gairloch retreat of two Irish envoys who had come with excessive republican demands from De Valera, to a serious and protracted conference of Irish and British delegations which assembled in London on 11 October. The delegation from Dublin was composed of Arthur Griffith, a European intellectual who was also a politician of integrity but of limited antennae; Michael Collins, the inspired clerk who by the age of thirty had become a sort of Bonaparte diminished only by the relative powerlessness of Ireland in relation to France, a revolutionary general who had in him an unusual talent for combining guerrilla war with an instinctive sense of when to fight and when to settle; and three others of much less importance, Barton, Duffy and Duggan. The great absentee was De Valera. With a fine feeling for politics if not for statesmanship he decided to stand

* Such Cabinet meetings away from London (where the Prime Minister's room in the House of Commons occasionally replaces Downing Street) are very rare. In 1966 I participated in one of these few, which took place in the Grand Hotel, Brighton. It was a peculiarly unsatisfactory meeting.

back, let his lieutenants take the strain and reserve the right to repudiate what they had done.

The British delegation was one member larger, although as the outcome was not going to be decided by a majority vote the purpose of this was not clear. It was composed of the Prime Minister, Austen Chamberlain as leader of the (hitherto) Unionists, Birkenhead as Lord Chancellor, Sir Laming Worthington-Evans, Churchill's successor as War Secretary, who is a one-man proof that length of name offers no guarantee of lasting fame, Hamar Greenwood as Chief Secretary for Ireland, and Churchill himself as Colonial Secretary. It was a very strong Cabinet committee, comprising, if cut another way, two of the strongest pre-1914 Unionist opponents of Home Rule (Chamberlain and Birkenhead) and three Coalition Liberals (Lloyd George, Churchill and Greenwood). This conference performed a stately minuet until early December, with the Irish delegates giving the curious impression that they were as cut off from Dublin as are Tamino and Papageno in the *Magic Flute* after their journey from Egypt to the court of the Queen of the Night – the last a role well suited to Lloyd George. This however had the result that in the long-drawn-out proceedings they began to form closer relationships with their English vis-à-vis than with the absent De Valera.

This was particularly true of Collins and Churchill. Churchill himself laid no claim to playing a great part in these negotiations – only 'of second rank', he uncharacteristically said of his own role, and gave the accolade to Birkenhead, Carson's galloper of 1912–14. Birkenhead was a great force for settlement in the negotiations, who in the subsequent debates delivered one of the most famous repudiations of old alliance of the first half of this century. In the House of Lords debate on 14 December (1921) he said: 'As for the speech of Lord Carson, as a constructive effort at statecraft it would have been immature on the lips of an hysterical schoolgirl.'[14] Churchill's closest friend, who in the days before his ennoblement as Birkenhead had been given the sobriquet 'Chuck it Smith', in the words of Chesterton's unforgettable ballad, could never be accused of pulling his punches. But the value of Churchill's own relationship with Collins, the centre of gravity of the Irish delegation, should not be under-estimated. He had him to Sussex Square. He showed him the 1899 Pretoria proclamation of a reward of £25 for his own head and flatteringly contrasted this with the £5,000 which Collins had become worth twenty years later. But it was not just a question of flattery. Churchill was always good at getting on with erstwhile adversaries. Botha and Smuts were the most obvious examples. Collins was rather in their category. Had he lived, Churchill might well have wanted to have him in the Other Club. And Collins might well have accepted membership and travelled to London, perhaps two or three times a year (the club met about eight times) to dine with a Churchillian (and until 1930 Birkenheadian) selection of British politicians, military commanders and other public servants.

Alas, however, Collins did not live. Nor for that matter did Griffith. When they eventually signed the Irish Treaty in December 1921 they were both aware that they might be signing their death warrants, which was true in the sense that, having got the Treaty through the Dáil (but against the bitter opposition of De Valera and only by sixty-four votes to fifty-seven) and set up a provisional government of the Irish Free State, they were both dead, Griffith aged fifty and Collins thirty-one, within nine months of the signature. Griffith died of a heart attack and Collins, who had survived so many dangers from the Black and Tans, in a murderous ambush mounted by his adversaries in the Irish civil war. Churchill, even if not crucial to the signature of the Treaty, had, as the Secretary of State in charge of relations with a new dominion, the major British responsibility for its implementation, and he maintained close relations with Collins. Undoubtedly a bond of respect and even friendship was established between them. Shortly before his death Collins sent an oral message via an intermediary: 'Tell Winston we could never have done anything without him.'[15] This pleased Churchill sufficiently for him to record it in *The Aftermath* and to supplement it with a realistic and unsentimental tribute to Collins: 'Successor to a sinister inheritance, reared among fierce conditions and moving through ferocious times, he supplied those qualities of action and personality without which the foundation of Irish nationhood would not have been re-established.'[16]

Churchill's 1922 actions in relation to Ireland were not always wise. When in April the rebels seized the symbolic majesty of the Four Courts in Dublin, thereby at once threatening the authority of the provisional government at its legal heart and involving the sacred memory of the occupation of the General Post Office during the Easter Rebellion only six years earlier, he wanted General Macready to shell them with British howitzers positioned in Phoenix Park. Macready was wiser. He said he did not have enough ammunition, and wisely left it to the Collins forces, to whom he lent the guns, later to blast them out.

In general however Churchill appreciated that there was no going back and did his best to make the settlement work. He was steady over the assassination by the IRA in June of Sir Henry Wilson, in field marshal's uniform and on the steps of his Eaton Square house. He was even-handed in dealing with incidents on the border with Ulster. And he conducted Irish business in the House of Commons with authority and aplomb. It was this essentially which led him to his self-congratulatory view of the 1921–2 session.

It was also the last session of the Coalition government and of the Lloyd George premiership. Churchill took the symptoms of disintegration with a degree of equanimity. Their Christmas journey to Cannes together had not restored his admiration for Lloyd George as the senior partner in a joint constructive partnership. 'The P.M. is singularly tame,' he wrote to Clementine from Cannes on 4 January (1922). 'I have never seen him quite like this. . . . He seems to me to have much less vitality then formerly.'[17] Then, three weeks later: 'I don't feel the slightest confidence in Ll.G.'s judgment or care for our rational naval position. Anything that serves the mood of the moment & the clatter of the ignorant & pliable newspapers is good enough for him.'[18] At the same time they lived remarkably closely, almost unhealthily, in each other's company. A week after that he was writing to Clementine, who in turn was in the South of France: 'I dined with Jack & Goonie [his brother and sister-in-law] the night before last, but usually (3 nights out of the last 4) the P.M., F.E. [Birkenhead], Max [Beaverbrook] & I dine together.'*[19]

Churchill did however fully retain his licence to offer the Prime Minister forthright and often wise advice. At one stage during the Irish negotiations Lloyd George, oppressed by both Tory opposition and Irish intrigue, was semi-tempted to throw his hand in and resign, no doubt partly actuated by the childish-tantrum reaction of 'they will be sorry when I am dead (or gone).' Churchill firmly told him: 'Most men sink into insignificance when they quit office. Very insignificant men acquire weight when they obtain it. . . . The delusion that an alternative government cannot be formed is perennial.'[20]

Then in April the Genoa Conference, designed to reach a settlement with Russia and to allow the economic rehabilitation of Germany, went

---

* *Per contra*, during the two and a half years when I was Harold Wilson's main adjutant (and possible replacement) in 1967–70, I never dined (or lunched) with him once, except at some large official banquet. Probably somewhere between the two would be the optimum.

so badly that the Germans and the Russians took a day excursion to Rapallo, twenty miles along the coast, and there concerted a separate trade agreement which greatly aroused Western fears. Churchill reminded Lloyd George of the advice he had given him two years earlier: 'Since the armistice my policy would have been "Peace with the German people, war on the Bolshevik tyranny!" Willingly or unavoidably you have followed something vy near the reverse.'[21]

In the next and last international contretemps of the Coalition government, however, Churchill was very much on Lloyd George's side, mainly because of his natural bellicosity in a crisis, although he did not prove a tactful auxiliary. This was the Chanak confrontation of September 1922. The Treaty of Sèvres with the Turks (one of the subsidiary treaties to Versailles) had given large parts of Asia Minor to the Greeks. Lloyd George was always excessively favourable to the Greeks, believing them to be an almost Celtic mountainous warrior race. Their warrior qualities, however, were not sufficient for this role and in the summer of 1922 Mustapha Kemal, the founder of modern Turkey, pushed most of the Greeks into the Aegean and threatened the small British garrison at Chanak on the Dardanelles, and with this went the implication that the Straits into the Sea of Marmora and then on to Constantinople and the Black Sea would be closed. There was no combination of land and water so vividly and traumatically imprinted upon Churchill's mind. The littorals were covered with the bones of those who had fallen in 1915, and also with the skeleton of his early and considerable reputation. But he was ready to support the Prime Minister, if necessary, in another conflict there. Once again, as in Russia, he greatly over-estimated the appetite of the British people, and even more that of the British Dominions, for another war (even if a little one) less than four years after the Armistice. Churchill's particular task was to rally Dominion support, and he did not handle it well. His only excuse was that the Prime Ministers, from Wellington to Ottawa, were rather slow with their deciphering machines. As a result a communiqué of commitment, issued by Lloyd George but drafted by Churchill, was published before they had taken in his telegrams. They were not pleased. Fortunately the Turks agreed to not to attack the British zone at Chanak without, in an old Churchillian phrase, 'these grave matters [being] put to the proof'.

It was the last spurt of Lloyd George adventurism. Five weeks later the Coalition was dead, killed by a Conservative 'peasants' revolt' against the Prime Minister pirouetting on the base of their majority. Churchill could play little part in this final drama. It was a matter for the Conservative party, and he was still at least nominally a Liberal. And he was further excluded by the fact that he had been stricken with an acutely inflamed appendix and that this organ was removed (no minor operation in those days) on the day before Lloyd George was deprived of the premiership. Lloyd George never held office again. Churchill's fate was much less absolute, but he never again did so as a Liberal.

20

A Politician without a
Party or a Seat

ON THE DAY OF Lloyd George's enforced resignation, Thursday, 19 October 1922, Churchill was in a small private hospital in Dorset Square, Marylebone, recovering from his appendicitis operation the previous evening. Not until 1 November, thirteen days after the operation, was he able to remove himself the short mile to his own house in Sussex Square. There, however, he remained heavily convalescent, unable to leave the house for another ten days.

Churchill's sudden illness not only took him from the scene of Lloyd George's demise. It also, and more damagingly for his political prospects, prevented him from campaigning in the general election which immediately followed. The election was called on 26 October. It was 11 November before Churchill was able to make a pale and emaciated appearance in Dundee, only four days before the poll. Clementine had gone earlier to hold the fort. Churchill, although physically weak, was not mentally inactive during his forced absence. From the West End of London, he bombarded Dundee with a rich stream of manifestos and political essays. One was a vast document of 2,000 words addressed to his new chairman, which *The Times* published in full on the following day. The other four, each of almost equal length, were entitled 'Winston S. Churchill: Notes for his Constituents', but they might more accurately have been called 'Our Present Discontents: Reflections from a London Sickbed'. They are still fascinating to read, but they were totally enmeshed in the assumptions of the inner circle of metropolitan politicians, and were far from being skilfully targeted upon Tayside. Dundee was for the most part a very poor city, and the Churchill forces in the campaign found themselves hard up against a sullen proletarianism. Churchill, while sensitive to the poverty ('If you saw the kind of lives the Dundee folk have to live, you would admit they have many excuses,' he wrote to H. A. L. Fisher after the result),[1] did not easily adjust himself to conciliating the deprived. Even his medical statement explaining his absence was hardly tactfully couched for those who were resentful of privilege: 'Mr Churchill's medical advisers, Lord Dawson, Sir Crisp English and Dr Hartigan, have consented to his fixing provisionally Saturday, November 11th, as the date when he can address a public meeting in Dundee. Whether in fact Mr Churchill will be able to fulfil this engagement must depend upon the progress made in the next four or five days, when a further consultation will be held.'[2]

Churchill, running in double harness with an elderly local employer who was the other National Liberal (that is, Lloyd Georgeite) candidate, had three candidates to the left of him, or perhaps four if the independent (Asquithian) Liberal is included. The real threat came from the combination of his faithful opponent Scrymgeour, still nominally an independent Prohibitionist but in fact increasingly allied with the sole Labour candidate, E. D. Morel, who as the founder of Union of Democratic Control, and also a notable anti-slavery campaigner in Africa, had been one of the more esteemed opponents of the war. Churchill made the mistake of thinking that Morel was in partnership not with Scrymgeour but with William Gallacher, who ran as a Communist and came bottom of the poll (when MP for East Fife from 1935 to 1950 he became the pet Communist of everybody, including Churchill, at least after the invasion of Russia in 1941). Churchill from his Dorset Square nursing home attacked them both in most extreme terms: 'A predatory and confiscatory programme fatal to the reviving prosperity of the country, inspired by class jealousy and the doctrines of envy, hatred and malice, is appropriately championed in Dundee by two candidates both of whom had to be shut up during the late war in order to prevent them further hampering the national defence.'[3]

Churchill at this stage, no doubt reacting to the frustrations of his sickbed, was pursuing a policy of attack *à tous azimuts* and not confining himself to the left. He proclaimed himself a true and old friend of Lloyd George, and when Reginald McKenna for the first time in several years put his head in criticism above the political parapet, Churchill rounded on him with a fine display of old animus:

> I was [Lloyd George's] friend before he was famous. I was with him when all were at his feet. And now today when men who fawned upon him, who praised even his errors, who climbed into place and Parliament upon his shoulders, have cast him aside, when Wee Free fanatics think the time has come to pay off old scores, when Mr McKenna, the political banker, emerges from his opulent seclusion to administer what he no doubt calculates is a finishing kick, I am still his friend and lieutenant.[4]

It was not only 'bolsheviks' and bankers who got the rough edge of his sickbed pen. Bonar Law, the new Prime Minister, got short shrift. But it was for Beaverbrook, Law's Sancho Panza and Churchill's old friend from St Omer to many intimate dinners with Lloyd George, that he reserved his greatest venom. He fired off a barrage (as a press statement) in this direction which, while somewhat indiscriminate in its field of fire, nonetheless managed to score several palpable hits:

> No credence should be attached to the tendentious misrepresentations of Lord Beaverbrook. His charges that public men who were recently his friends were anxious to bring about a war are false and wicked, and he knows better than anyone else how wicked and how false. The information on which these charges are based is in part the result of breaches of confidence distorted by malevolent invention. Mr Bonar Law will gain no advantage from support of this character. Lord Beaverbrook has for many months beslavered Lord Curzon with abuse in the column of his paper [the *Daily Express*] and his praise must be rated at the same value. In the last year he has boxed the entire political compass from extreme Tory to extreme Radical according to caprice, and an insatiable appetite for excitement and intrigue has carried him hither and thither. His trans-Atlantic methods have been equally harmful to British politics and to British journalism. It is high time that it became the subject of proper publicity.[5]

These metropolitan fireworks probably passed indifferently over the heads of most Dundonians. But the campaign was a fairly continuous nightmare for the Churchill forces. Clementine had got there on 5 November, and clearly had a perfectly horrid time both before and after Churchill arrived on the 11th. It was unfortunately appropriate that the supporters she at first stayed with lived in Dudhope Terrace. (After Churchill came she joined him in the Royal Hotel.) They had to rely excessively upon outside help, and their chosen imports did not seem well suited to Dundee. The star was intended to be the ex-Lord Chancellor, Birkenhead. About his performance Clementine was dismissive. 'He was no use at all,' she said. 'He was drunk.'[*6] Moreover his main platform piece was an attack on the French paternity of Morel who (with an English mother) had been born in Paris and christened

---

* A problem with Dundee in that transport era was that it was very difficult to arrive from the south for an evening meeting other than in the morning. Birkenhead had consequently fallen back on the hospitality of the Conservative Eastern Club to occupy most of his day.

Georges Edouard Pierre Achille Morel-de-Ville. Birkenhead apparently repeated this, in an exaggerated French accent, at least five times, imbuing it with as much moral reprobation as though he had been talking of Proust's Baron de Charlus' homosexual partner and draft-dodging violinist of the same Morel name rather than of a respectable Quaker pamphleteer and pacifist. The effect of this 'third-rate music-hall performance', as E. D. Morel quite reasonably called it, is well indicated by the newspaper reports of the response of Birkenhead's 3,000-strong audience in the Caird Hall. After his first repeat 'loud laughter' was recorded, after his second 'laughter', after his third 'diminished laughter', after his fourth 'some laughter, but many now joined in an embarrassed silence', and after his fifth nothing but silence.[8]

The other imports were General Spears, last encountered in France, and Lord Wodehouse, one of Churchill's secretaries and the son of the Earl of Kimberley. 'I knew nothing about politics,' Spears subsequently wrote. 'Jack Wodehouse knew nothing about politics. There we both were – rivals only in ignorance.'*[8] The only approach to an exception was John Pratt, MP for the Cathcart division of Glasgow and former under-secretary at the Scottish Office. He too had a rough time at a big meeting with Clementine on 6 November in the most working-class area of the city. But in general, no doubt benefiting from his Glasgow training, he was more streetwise with Scottish audiences than the Sassenach auxiliaries. Wodehouse retired hurt from the stricken field (although later returning to it), but Spears provided an admiring if not altogether optimistic escort for Clementine. 'Clemmie appeared with a string of pearls,' the General recorded on 7 November. 'The women spat on her.'

However he added, 'Clemmie's bearing was magnificent – like an aristocrat going to the guillotine in a tumbril.'[9] She had a series of rowdy and disagreeable meetings, hardly being able to make herself heard, and scoring remarkably few points for her gallantry in coming 500 miles with a barely two-month-old baby (Mary) to an unwelcoming northern strand to defend a sick husband. Unfortunately, and very out of character, Clementine allowed herself at a women's meeting on the afternoon of Wednesday the 8th to descend to the level of knocking anti-Morel propaganda which was too great a feature of the badly

* Spears, who had in 1919 changed the spelling of his name from Spiers, had, however, just been elected, unopposed, as MP for the Loughborough division of Leicestershire, and Wodehouse had been a Liberal MP for four years from 1906.

rattled Churchill campaign. 'Is it a fact that Mr Morel is not an Englishman but was born a Frenchman?' she asked. 'Is it true that he became an Englishman to avoid military service in the land of his birth? Did he, during the war, render any service to Britain?' It was an error which she quickly regretted even before Morel responded with considerable dignity:

> My father was a Frenchman, my mother an Englishwoman, and I was born in Paris. We do not select our parents or our place of birth. I am no more responsible for the fact that my father was French than Mr Churchill is responsible for the fact that his mother was an American. . . . My father died when I was an infant. My mother sent me to school in England when I was eight. . . . Very clever of me to come over here when I was eight in order to escape military service. . . .[10]

Churchill himself arrived wanly on the morning of 11 November, accompanied by a nurse and a detective. There was a good greeting party on the railway platform, but he was too weak to climb up the flight of stairs to the road level and had to be taken up in a goods lift. Later that morning he attended a civic Armistice Day ceremony, bedecked in his eleven campaign medals, which none of his rival candidates could begin to match, but which did not do him much good in the trough of poverty and disillusionment into which Dundee had descended. In the afternoon he had a 3,000-strong Caird Hall meeting. It was a largely monitored and ticketed audience, although this did not prevent a fair number of hecklers. But he was able to make a coherent speech, which, never one for moderation, he did for the Gladstonian length of one and a half hours. He delivered it sitting (except for the peroration) in a specially constructed elevated seat.

Two nights later, in the Drill Hall, bear-garden conditions revived. He had to abandon his speech with little more than a few paragraphs on the record. The meeting began at 8.00 and was over by 8.45. Then, on the Tuesday afternoon at a meeting of 300 ladies in the parish church hall of the genteel Dundee suburb of Broughty Ferry, within a half-mile of his target's residence, Churchill indulged in the doubtful tactic of launching a full-scale attack on D. C. Thomson, the local newspaper proprietor, whose base was in Dundee but whose tentacles spread wide over Scotland and indeed, with his mass-circulation *Sunday Post*, down into the north-east of England.* Thomson owned both the

---

* Thomson also created well-known 'comics', first *Rover* and then *Dandy* and *Beano*.

morning and Liberal *Dundee Advertiser* and the evening and Conservative *Dundee Courier*. This might have been held to point to a healthy even-handedness. They were, however, united on one thing and that was an animus against Churchill, for whom Thomson had come to feel a mixture of dislike and disapproval. Some countervailing feeling on Churchill's part was therefore wholly understandable, although whether he was wise to give public vent to it is another matter. Thomson he portrayed at Broughty Ferry as 'a narrow, bitter, unreasonable being eaten up with his own conceit, consumed with his own petty arrogance, and pursued from day to day and from year to year with an unrelenting bee in his bonnet'. The *Courier* responded by declaring, 'Whatever may be his chances at the poll today, there can be no doubt that Mr. Winston Churchill is in a vile temper.'[11]

The result was a crushing defeat for Churchill. He was out by a huge margin. Scrymgeour was top of the poll with over 32,000 votes, not a bad rate of progression from his 650 of the 1908 bye-election, his 2,000 of the 1917 one and his 10,000 of the 1918 general election. A Scottish joke of the period was that the electors of Dundee, well known to be heavy drinkers, came out of the pubs, staggered to the polls and voted for total prohibition. The reality was that Scrymgeour got the whole of the Labour vote, considerably swollen by anti-Churchill feeling, plus a couple of thousand of his own, probably made up of some ardent teetotallers but also of others who admired his perseverance. His victory was certainly a classic example of that quality. So far from supporting the theory that electoral losers rarely turn into winners, he had tried, tried, tried, tried, tried and tried again – and won. He remained a member for Dundee until 1931, when he went down to the National government landslide.

Morel was next with just over 30,000 votes and gained the second seat. Eight thousand behind was Churchill's little-known National Liberal running mate, who ought to have combined the disadvantages of being at once elderly and a tyro in politics. Yet Churchill was 1,800 votes behind him, nearly as big a gap as separated Scrymgeour and Morel. The Asquithian Liberal got 6,600 and then Gallacher, the Communist on whom Churchill had concentrated much of his early fire, 5,900.

Churchill had plunged, during less than four years of high office, from a better than two-to-one victory to a worse than three-to-two defeat. His 'life seat' of 1908 had crumbled in his hands. Perhaps fortunately it was not a swing-conscious age, with the outcome further

obscured by Dundee being a two-member seat, but it was surely one of
the heaviest swings in the country. Happily, Churchill kept his temper
in defeat. The count must have been an agony for him, both of physical
exhaustion and of mounting impatience with the slow advance to
humiliating defeat. It lasted over seven hours, with a slow recount taking
place not because he had any hope of winning but because a thousand
votes had been misplaced. The result was not delivered until just after
5.00 p.m. He sagged, and declined to speak at the declaration ceremony.
But he then went back to the Liberal Club and made a speech of
singular generosity. It was his last in Dundee. He told his supporters of
his heart being devoid 'of the slightest sense of regret, resentment or
bitterness'. He even had a good word to say for Scrymgeour who, he
thought, 'would have a useful part to play in representing Dundee,
where there was such fearful misery and distress and such awful contrast
between one class and another'.[12]

Within four hours he severed his connection with the city, and
departed for London by the 9.04 sleeping-car express. A large crowd of
noisy but friendly students (many apparently Irish) came to see him off
at the station, and he made his final crossing of the Tay Bridge
temporarily buoyed up by their cheers. But he was very down when he
got to London. He was still not at all well. He was left, as he was later
mordantly to write, 'without an office, without a seat, without a party,
and without an appendix'.[13] At a political dinner party given by Sir
Alfred Mond he was reported as being 'so down in the dumps that he
could scarcely speak the whole evening',[14] in his case an unusual
affliction.

He rallied, no doubt partly as a result of regaining physical strength.
The Churchills decided to go to the South of France for the winter.
Sussex Square was let and the Villa Rêve d'Or, near Cannes, was rented.
He turned as both a solace and a sustenance to his writing. The first
volume of *The World Crisis* was reasonably far advanced, but not
complete. However on 23 November he caused his agent, Curtis Brown,
to inform *The Times* that he should have enough material for serialization by the end of the year, and got urgently to work. On November
28th he had an audience of the King, both to take leave as Colonial
Secretary (which he had not been able to do in October) and to be
invested as a Companion of Honour, which recently established but
high order, to his considerable satisfaction, had been conferred upon
him in Lloyd George's resignation list. And on 30 November, his forty-
eighth birthday, he and Clementine left London for the Riviera. Seven

years after his journey to the front in 1915 it was just as symbolic a break with what had gone before, and his view of his immediate political prospects was equally gloomy.

The Churchills stayed in the South of France until mid-May (1923). Outwardly he was calm and even content. His assuagements were, first that he was steadily recovering his full health and vigour. Second he was painting well in the good Midi light which suited his love of strong colours. Third, volume one of *The World Crisis* (the title settled upon only with difficulty at the end of January, many less satisfactory choices having been played with; fortunately his London and New York publishers joined in vetoing *The Great Amphibian*) was well received, both when it was serialized in February and when it appeared as a book in April. Fourth, he was working hard at and making very good progress with the second volume, covering the year 1915. He could never contemplate a holiday without it being interspersed with a good deal of hard work and he travelled heavy in order to make this possible. Apart from his elaborate painting equipment, he had a lot of source material as well as a secretary and a research assistant with him at the Cannes villa.

No doubt these activities were intermingled with bursts of profound private gloom, but at least these did not make him unduly restless. He returned to England only three times (and briefly) during the five and a half months, and these were purposeful visits, triggered by taking his elder children to and from school, and occupied in settling book affairs and supervising the work on Chartwell, which was proceeding in a spacious and stately way. In London he stayed at the Ritz, no doubt subscribing to his mother's view that 'it was cheaper in the end'. He spent most of his first visit there in his room working furiously at his book. As he told Clementine (letter of 30 January 1923), 'I am so busy that I hardly ever leave the Ritz except for meals.'[15] For these, however, he was much in demand, and retained general high social and political prestige, in spite of his Dundee debâcle. On one day, for instance, he entertained J. L. Garvin, editor of the *Observer* as well as an enthusiastic reader of his proofs, and Edward Grey. On another he had the Prince of Wales to lunch at Buck's Club, together with Freddie Guest and the Dundee battle-scarred Lord Wodehouse, 'to talk polo and politics'. On an intermediate evening he dined with Haldane, the once and future (in the 1924 Labour government) Lord Chancellor.

It was noticeable that his political contacts still remained mildly left of centre. And he also recorded that Hilton Young (later the first Lord

Kennet), the new Chief Whip of the Lloyd George Liberals, wanted to call upon him about a new seat. Young however had hardly any at his disposal. The Lloyd George Liberals had won only fifty-seven (or according to another more optimistic estimate sixty-two), so their Chief Whip did not have much opportunity for easing out and easing in. But at least their Whip recognized that he had to court Churchill rather than vice versa. Clementine, however, who remained anchored on Cannes tennis tournaments during this half-year, wanted him, true to her steady orientation, to move back in an Asquithian direction. But the Asquithians had only sixty seats, or, according to the alternative classification, fifty-five. (The explanation of the discrepancies was that several Liberal MPs were uncertain which leader was more likely to lead them out of the wilderness.) Churchill himself was in a peculiarly unrooted mood. He still believed in Free Trade. He was still shocked by Dundee poverty and class alienation, but even more strongly was he coming to believe in the need to man the ramparts of the bourgeois state against the threat of Labour socialism, which he was only too inclined to equate with Leninist communism.

During the summer of 1923, however, after the return of the Churchills to England, these thoughts were not dominant. Churchill's mind was more concentrated on the second volume of *The World Crisis* than on where, and under whose banner, he would fight the next general election. The Conservative government had a secure parliamentary majority – its first for nearly twenty years. And Chartwell was a very absorbing, and expensive, pastime. He rented a nearby house called, improbably, Hosey Rigge, from where he could exercise close supervision. This, not surprisingly, resulted in his falling out with his architect, under whom costs mounted and progress was slow, although the ultimate result was satisfactory. But it was April 1924 before he was able to sleep his first night in Chartwell and date his first letter from there. It was to Clementine, who had gone to spend Easter with her mother in Dieppe. He was having some difficulty in convincing her that the amenities of Chartwell were worth the expense, and this letter, in conjunction with one seven months earlier, was very much directed to this end. On 2 September 1923 he had written from the Duke of Westminster's yacht in Bayonne harbour:

> My beloved – I do beg you not to worry about money, or to feel insecure.
> On the contrary the policy we are pursuing aims above all at *stability*. . . .
> Chartwell is to be our *home*. It will have cost us £20,000 and will be worth

at least £15,000 apart from a fancy price. [Not, it may be thought, a brilliant investment.] We must endeavour to live there for many years & hand it on to Randolph afterwards. We must make it in every way charming & as far as possible economically self-contained. It will be cheaper than London.

Eventually – though there is no hurry – we must sell Sussex [Square] and find a small flat for you and me. . . . Then with the motors we shall be well equipped for business or pleasure. If we go into office we will live in Downing Street!

The [Garron Towers] estate at this moment is at least as large as it was when I succeeded, but part is invested in Chartwell instead of in shares. You must think of it in this light. . . .[16]

Then on 17 April 1924 he was endeavouring to tackle the same problem from the other end:

We have had two glorious days. The children have worked like blacks; and Sergeant Thompson,* Aley [chauffeur], Waterhouse [semi-retired head gardener], one gardener & 6 men have formed a powerful labour corps. The weather has been delicious, & we are out all day toiling in dirty clothes & only bathing before dinner. I have just had my bath in your de luxe bathroom. I hope you have no amour propre about it! . . . I drink champagne at all meals & buckets of claret & soda in between, & the cuisine tho' simple is excellent. . . .

Your steps are nearly made in the centre of the bank. The front basement windows go on apace. . . . You will be pleased with the effect. It is majestic. . . . Everything is budding now that this gleam of deferred genial weather has come.

> Only one thing lack these banks of green –
> The Pussy Cat who is their Queen.[17]

This letter was perhaps more successful in painting a picture of the future amenities of Chartwell than of giving reassurance about the modesty and economy of the *train de maison* which it would involve.

By this time Churchill had (post-Dundee) already unsuccessfully fought one general election and one bye-election, as well as performing a considerable political zigzag. So it is necessary to turn from the private to the public scene, and also to revert to the summer of 1923 following his return from his half-year of voluntary exile. Baldwin was then in his first months as an unexpected Prime Minister. Churchill rightly

---

* No doubt because of his involvement with the Irish Treaty he kept a Scotland Yard detective during these two years out of office and Parliament.

preferred him to Bonar Law, on both objective and subjective grounds. The objective grounds were that Baldwin was a much more interesting and generous-minded politician than was Law. The subjective ground was that Baldwin had played no role comparable with Law's stubborn vetoing of Churchill from 1915 to 1917. Churchill in 1923 neither disliked nor respected Baldwin. He at first regarded him as a very jumped-up junior figure – despite the fact that he was seven years older than Churchill – to be Prime Minister. 'Bring out your Baldwins' was a disparaging cry (meaning your pawns) which he sometimes used when playing chess. However, as a fully paid-up member of the senior politicians' union, Churchill did respect Baldwin's office. It is not quite the same as in the United States where, the headship of state being combined with executive power, a certain sacerdotal quality is bestowed upon the presidency, sometimes against the personal record. Nevertheless I can think of no circumstances in which the grandest of senior politicians (let alone junior ones) would have refused, if summoned, to go and confer in 10 Downing Street with even the least regarded of Prime Ministers.

Such an encounter took place between Churchill and Baldwin on 14 August 1923. It is not clear on whose initiative, although it was probably on Churchill's because he had a semi-hidden agenda. He was incapable of making it more than half hidden, for whatever else were Churchill's faults he was a hopeless dissembler, his spontaneous exuberance always giving away his purpose. His half-hidden agenda, however, was to sound out Baldwin's attitude to a merger between Royal Dutch Shell, Burmah Oil and the majority-government-owned Anglo-Persian Oil Company, this public investment being largely due to Churchill's own 1913 initiative as First Lord of the Admiralty. Churchill had just been asked by the first two companies to represent them in their dealings with the government for a fee of £5,000. This was the equivalent of at least £125,000 in today's money, and, for someone trying to cope with the mounting bills for Chartwell and to still his wife's financial unease, was very tempting. Yet, private citizen though he was at the time, he was unhappy about its propriety. Masterton-Smith, who after being his private secretary at the Admiralty had become his permanent under-secretary of the Colonial Office and whom Churchill had consulted, had pronounced himself 'vy shy of it on large political grounds'.[18] So Churchill wanted to test Baldwin's reactions to the merits both of the issue itself and of his involvement in it.

The meeting went well. Baldwin could always switch on the beam of his fully engaged attention. 'My interview with the PM was most agreeable,' Churchill wrote to his wife the next day. 'He professed unbounded leisure & recd me with the utmost cordiality. We talked Ruhr, Oil, Admiralty & Air, Reparations, the American Debt & general politics. I found him thoroughly in favour of The Oil Settlement on the lines proposed. Indeed he might have been Waley Cohen [managing director of Shell] from the way he talked. I am sure it will come off. The only thing I am puzzled about is my own affair.'[19] Churchill also reported to Clementine that 'I entered Downing Street by the Treasury entrance [now the entrance to the Cabinet Office] to avoid comment.' 'This much amused Baldwin,' he added.[20]

This friendly meeting was of considerable importance, for Baldwin, while less dominant than either of the other two, was to occupy a position in relation to Churchill, superior and amicable in the second half of the 1920s, much less friendly in the 1930s, comparable only with that which first Asquith and then Lloyd George had done. The immediate practical outcome of this (or of a closely following contact) was that Churchill did accept his oil-company lobbying role, and with the Prime Minister's blessing went to see both the First Lord of the Admiralty (his old semi-enemy L. S. Amery) and the President of the Board of Trade (Lloyd-Graeme, who was soon to change his name to Cunliffe-Lister) about the matter. In mid-November, however, when a general election had been unexpectedly announced, he formally withdrew from any further work on the merger. Despite his perennial shortage of money it was almost the only foray into business which he made in the course of his long life. For the rest his money-making was confined to selling his enormous book and article output for the best prices he could get and speculating (not always wisely) on the stock exchange with part of the proceeds.

The general election of 1923 arose out of Baldwin's lurch to Protection (without which he said he could not fight unemployment) and his conviction that he could not introduce it without a new and specific electoral mandate. The general result was that he threw away a Tory majority of seventy-three seats (the first independent one since 1900) in a parliament which was only a year old. The result for Churchill was that it temporarily halted his progress across the political spectrum to the right. This had been gathering momentum for several years, and was no doubt reinforced by his Dundee punishment at the hands of the left. But he was still a Free Trader and the news that this citadel had again to be defended brought him back to the Liberal colours like an old soldier nostalgically inspired by looking at his campaign medals of the first years of the century. He issued a press statement in stirring terms: 'I have taken no part in opposing the Conservative Government, nor in disparaging the new Ministers. . . . But an aggressive attack has been levelled needlessly and wantonly at the foundations of the people's livelihood. A monstrous fallacy is erected against us. . . . Those who are opposed to this wild adventure and reckless experiment must stand together in real comradeship. . . .'[21]

For the first time since 1910 he was prepared to fight an election under Asquith's nominal leadership, although Lloyd George, who also rallied (perhaps without much conviction) to the old cause, was in reality co-leader. But where was Churchill to fight? Certainly not in Dundee, and he also firmly rejected an invitation from Glasgow Central. He had probably had enough of Scotland. Lancashire seemed the most obvious area, particularly if his mind was stirred by memories of the great days leading up to 1906. And his first speeches of the campaign were delivered in Manchester on 16 and 17 November, one in the Free Trade Hall and one in the city's Reform Club. Lancashire invitations were freely available. A perverse advantage of the Liberals having few seats was that there were plenty of constituencies, unencumbered by sitting members, on offer. Salford West and both the Rusholme and Mossley divisions of Manchester all made approaches to him. Then, almost incomprehensibly, he decided on 19 November to descend upon Leicester and to contest its West division. There is no evidence that he had ever before visited that historic but in its modern form somewhat anonymous East Midland city. Nor did it offer an enticing psephological prospect. Before 1918 Leicester as a whole had been a two-member constituency, like Dundee, but with an even stronger tradition of 'Lib–Labery'. In 1906 Henry Broadhurst, a trades unionist by origin but so absorbed into mainstream Liberalism that he had been a junior minister in Gladstone's third government, and Ramsay MacDonald were elected in double harness. In 1918 the city was split into three, and MacDonald had chosen the West division, presumably thinking it the best left-wing prospect of the three. He was in fact slaughtered there, but this was because of his wartime pacifism rather than on more general grounds of class politics, and Labour narrowly regained the seat in 1922.

Churchill's only real hope was if he did not have a Conservative opponent. But it is impossible to see why he should have thought this remotely likely. Baldwin was seeking a mandate for Protection. It would have made no sense for him to have allowed two Free Trade candidates to battle it out on their own in a semi-marginal constituency. Churchill's main opponent was not Captain Instone, the somewhat token Conservative candidate (although he got 7,700 votes, only 1,500 fewer than Churchill) but F. W. Pethick-Lawrence, one of the most quietly bizarre Labour figures of the first half of the twentieth century. His father is described in the *Dictionary of National Biography* as a 'carpenter', but he must have been a most successful follower of that occupation, because he made enough money not only to send his son to Eton, where he was captain of the Oppidans and won almost every possible prize, and to Trinity College, Cambridge, but also to leave him a substantial fortune. Pethick-Lawrence possessed an acute social conscience which first directed him towards ameliorative social work in the East End of London, rather as it was to do Clement Attlee, his junior by twelve years. But then after his 1901 marriage to Emmeline Pethick (a good suffragette Christian name) – which led to his making his surname double-barrelled, not as a mark of social climbing but as a gesture of sexual equality – he switched his attention to women's enfranchisement, for which cause he was once and she twice imprisoned. There is a distinct feeling that he was somewhat henpecked. He appeared to have had a contented if childless marriage for fifty-three years, but when Emmeline Pethick-Lawrence died he quickly (and at the age of eighty-six) married a friend of over forty years' standing.

Pethick-Lawrence's career was curiously if distantly intertwined with Churchill's. They were like two spacecraft tracking each other without communicating. Apart from the Leicester encounter, Lawrence moved into the Treasury when Churchill moved out in 1929 – but as Financial Secretary not as Chancellor. And during the Second World War coalition, as the senior Labour front-bencher not in the government, he acted as a formal leader of the opposition, with the function of maintaining the usages of Parliament rather than of making trouble for the government. And in 1945–7, sent up to the House of Lords, he was Secretary of State for India and did not earn Churchill's plaudits as he brought that (fairly) historic office to a close.

In Leicester Lawrence fought mainly on advocacy of a capital levy, and Churchill, having greatly changed his position over the five years since he had been talking about creaming off the 'ill-gotten gains' of 'old Runciman' (and others), devoted a good part of his local campaigning to refuting Lawrence's arguments on this. His country-wide speeches, however, following the success of his opening Manchester salvo in the Free Trade Hall, were directed to the traditional anti-

Protection case. The Leicester campaign, although somewhat rowdy but not in this respect rivalling the previous year in Dundee, seems to have been peculiarly without interest, and Churchill, during its two and a half weeks' duration, was in an uncommunicative mood. In contrast with his normal fluent and documented life he wrote practically no letters, which makes it difficult to unravel the mystery of why on earth he went to Leicester. There were no notable local figures who drew him there, no equivalent of Sir George Ritchie. The local press position was almost as unfavourable as in Dundee, with both the *Leicester Mercury* and the *Leicester Mail* against, although lacking the full animus of D. C. Thomson, so that he had to look to Nottingham, not the happiest position given the inevitable rivalry between the two cities, for any press support.

Furthermore he had had plenty of advice, from Clementine in particular, that he would have done much better to go to Manchester. She had been quite specific in her argument. In an undated letter from the summer of 1923 she had written: 'Instinctively, one of the reasons I wanted Rusholme was that if you were to lose a seat I felt it would be better for you to be beaten by a Tory (which would rouse Liberal sympathy) than by a Socialist.'[22] This was of course probing along an old fault line, she more resolutely Liberal, he beginning to feel increasing twitches upon the thread of his original and, as some thought, always underlying Toryism. Rusholme was won by the Liberals, and as Churchill moved towards a predictably routine defeat in Leicester he must have regretted, even though it might not have been in his long-term interests, that he had not taken his wife's advice. Pethick-Lawrence beat him by the solid figure of 13,624 to 9,236. He cannot even have got any real satisfaction out of the campaign. He was never within striking distance of winning, and he established no rapport with the constituency. In the latter respect, however, he was probably at least as good as Harold Nicolson, who emerged as its nervously remote National Labour member from 1935 to 1945.

Immediately after his Leicester defeat on 6 December Churchill was involved in a criminal libel case, in which, it being *criminal* libel, the Attorney-General (Sir Douglas Hogg) was the prosecutor, and Churchill, although the principal witness, was not financially at risk. It was perhaps as well that he had something to take his mind off the Leicester defeat for that carried with it the threat of something worse than Dundee. He was in danger of getting like his old Home Office under-secretary, Charles Masterman, who on being promoted to the

Cabinet in 1914 had lost three bye-elections running and scuppered his career, although Masterman had also, by a supreme irony, been adopted for Manchester, Rusholme when Churchill passed it up in 1923, and won it, although only to be defeated in 1924.

The criminal libel case was against Lord Alfred Douglas, Oscar Wilde's old 'Bosie', for having said that Churchill's reassuring statement about the Battle of Jutland in June 1916 had been corruptly done in order to manipulate the stock exchange in the interests of a Jewish syndicate, headed by Sir Ernest Cassel, who had given him a reward of £40,000. It was nonsense, Churchill was wholly vindicated, and when Lord Alfred was sentenced to six months' imprisonment there was a lot of surprise at the leniency of the punishment. More interesting were some of the messages of congratulations to Churchill. Sir Graham Greene, his former Admiralty permanent secretary, for instance, wrote, 'In all my life . . . I cannot recall the case of any public man who has suffered such abuse & misrepresentation.'[23]

Over Christmas and the New Year of 1923–4 Churchill proceeded to make a seismic political shift, although one which could have been seen coming. It was most accurately charted in correspondence with his old friend Violet Bonham Carter. The early-December general election had defeated Baldwin's attempt to get a majority for Protection. Pethick-Lawrence in his memoirs recorded that Churchill, with remarkable breadth of view in the circumstances, had greeted the Leicester, West result by saying to him, 'Well, anyhow it is a victory for Free Trade.'[24] It had destroyed the Conservative majority, but it had not provided a majority for anyone else. The Conservatives remained much the largest party with 258 seats, with Labour on 191 and the fragilely united Liberals on 157. In these circumstances it was the view of Asquith (in agreement for once with Lloyd George) and of a large majority of the Liberal MPs that they should join with Labour in defeating the Conservatives on the Address in reply to the King's Speech. The natural result of this, according to the rigidities of the British party system, would be a very weak minority Labour government. A more sensible and durable result would of course have been a Lib–Lab coalition. But this ran hard up against Labour tribalism, and the view that, while the party's leaders had no hope of, or perhaps desire for, the introduction of socialist policies, they must at least keep themselves from being defiled by overt collaboration with a bourgeois party.

Both Asquith and Baldwin were content to let in the socialists, as they were mostly then incongruously known, for MacDonald's vision of socialism was so misty as to be lost in a future of biological evolution, and that of Snowden, the prospective Chancellor of the Exchequer, was wholly subordinated to a Gladstonian view of budgetary probity. The view of the leaders of both the other parties was that the inevitable experiment of a Labour government could not be tried in safer circumstances.

Churchill's view was in sharp contradiction. As a follow-through from his anti-Bolshevik frenzy of 1919 and his understandable reaction to his disagreeable encounter with proletarian surliness in Dundee in 1922, he regarded a Labour government as a mixture between a sullying of the escutcheon of the British state and a letting in of the Trojan horse. On 28 December, in reply to a Boxing Day letter of Violet Bonham Carter, he wrote a letter sufficiently extreme that he decided not to send it. But on 8 January, realizing that Asquith was firmly set in the opposite direction to his desires, he wrote of 'the great misfortune of a Socialist Government being formed'. His recipe was that once the Liberals had defeated the Conservative government on Protection they should at the first opportunity vote against its Labour replacement on the ground that it would be 'composed exclusively of Ministers who are declared Socialists and whose policy of a Capital Levy has been decisively rejected by the majority of the electorate'. Its life could 'thus be terminated in a single day' with, he hoped, the outcome of an Asquith-led government with 'tacit support of the Conservative party'. The alternative, he believed, as opinion in the country hardened against 'the apparition of this Socialist monstrosity' would be a great accretion of strength to the Conservative party, with a distinct hint that he himself might be part of that accretion.[25]

A week later, and before Violet Bonham Carter had replied, Churchill incorporated a modified version of these ideas in a personal manifesto (nominally in the form of a letter to 'a correspondent') which *The Times* published in full. Asquith's daughter recognized this as a definite parting of the ways, and she replied sadly, and a little reproachfully, but above all loyally – although the loyalty was to her father rather than to the old friend for whom she had persistent affection: 'Father's speech on Thursday was masterly, as fine a thing as I have ever heard him do. Wise – generous – courageous – extremely dextrous & witty – the Labour men were genuinely & deeply moved. . . .' And she ended with a shrewder judgement of the future than Churchill had showed: 'I think the Labour Govt will suffer for the timidity & inefficiency of its members not for their violence.'[26]

Late on 21 January the watershed vote took place. Baldwin was defeated (in accordance with his expectations) by 328 to 256; 137 Liberals voted with the Labour party, ten with the Conservatives, and six abstained. The Churchill faction, if it was such, was small. The next day Ramsay MacDonald kissed hands as the first Labour Prime Minister, a remarkably short time after his party had emerged from being a small special-interest group under the wing of the Liberal party. It was an achievement on his part, a thrust to power (or at least office) beyond anything that could have been secured by any of his more stolid colleagues, and one which could not be entirely taken away by anything which happened from 1931 onwards. But Churchill, in spite of his somewhat hysterical reaction to the prospect of Labour in office, contrasting with the much greater calm of the Asquiths, father and daughter, and indeed of Baldwin, was nonetheless in a sense right. There was no threat to the social order, but nothing was politically quite the same again. It was the last chance for the Liberals of being a governing party. Thereafter, even in Labour's 1930s trough, if there was to be a realistic alternative to the Conservatives it was for the rest of the century, with the exception of a brief flicker in 1981–3, Labour rather than the Liberals who were to provide it. There was a new divide in politics and one which left Churchill firmly on the rightward side.

Before he could be very effective on either side, however, he had to get back in the House of Commons, and while he went about this with his habitual energy and panache, he also did it with a typical lack of restraint. 'Don't rush your fences' was the core advice which Clementine sent to him from the South of France, where she was on her habitual long February visit, just as she had done in 1916 when he was in Flanders and she was in England. That, however, was precisely what he proceeded to do, and under what she regarded as the most undesirable initial auspices.

J. S. Nicholson, gin distiller and brigadier-general, died on 21 February (1924), thereby precipitating a bye-election in the Abbey division of Westminster, the stretch of turf immediately in front of the political grandstand. Churchill wrote a wonderfully vivid, succinct and over-optimistic description of the area and of his prospects there to Clementine on 24 February:

It is an amazing constituency comprising – Eccleston Sq, Victoria Station, Smith Sq, Westminster Abbey, Whitehall, Pall Mall, Carlton House Terrace – part of Soho, the south side of Oxford Street, Drury Lane theatre & Covent Garden! It is of course one of the choicest preserves of the Tory Party. . . . There must be at least a hundred MP resident voters in the division, & I shall have no difficulty in securing a vy fine & representative platform. Grigg, L. Spears and other Liberal MPs will fight for me, and it is possible that E. Grey (a resident) will give me his support. McKenna too – I think. Then I hope to get a letter from AJB [Lord Balfour], also a resident – Altogether it is an exceedingly promising opportunity, & if it comes off I shd hold the seat for a long time. . . .

Less reassuring (to Clementine at any rate) were the opening sentences of this letter: 'This Westminster Abbey bye-election swooped down upon me like a thunderstorm. Rothermere and Max [Beaverbrook] offered the full support of their press, & it was necessary for me to let it be known straight away that my cap was in the ring.'[27]

Many prominent Conservatives, as Churchill hoped, were attracted by the glamorous colours of that cap and, at a time of great political uncertainty, by the reinforcement which it might bring. But there was also the deadweight orthodoxy of the local Tory machine. Whether they would have been prepared to have Churchill under a straight Conservative label is not clear. In any event he thought it was too early to be so uncompromising and would only stand under the title of 'Independent Anti-Socialist'. The Abbey Tories ought not to have been too worried about that, for the late Nicholson had run under the still more cumbersome title of 'Independent Conservative Anti-Waste' as recently as a 1921 bye-election. The Nicholsons had no long connection with the constituency, but the Conservative caucus nonetheless insisted on adopting a thirty-two-year old nephew of the former member rather than giving Churchill a clear run.

This created acute agitation in the highest Conservative circles. Baldwin drove fifty miles to have a Sunday-luncheon discussion about the matter with Austen Chamberlain, his predecessor in the leadership, with whom he was not on the easiest terms. Churchill never failed to infuse an issue with tension and excitement. Most of the top Conservatives, including Baldwin himself, probably wanted Churchill to be elected, but they did not want a row with the local Association. Austen Chamberlain summed up the mood well when he wrote to his wife: 'I shall vote quietly for Winston saying nothing about it, but it is amazing how unpopular he is. . . .'[28] Baldwin tried to hold a line that no member of the shadow Cabinet should support either of the right-wing candidates, but when L. S. Amery, so often the David with the catapult against Churchill's Goliath, broke ranks by coming out strongly for Nicholson, Baldwin agreed that a typically fine-shaded endorsement of Churchill from Balfour could be published.

Churchill's campaign had all the glamour that had been lacking in Leicester. He drove around the West End of London in a coach and four with a trumpeter on the box, a stunt organized by his new acolyte, Brendan Bracken, then aged twenty-three, who was to remain both close and faithful for the rest of his life. The chorus girls of Daly's Theatre were said to have sat up all night addressing envelopes for Churchill's election address, although a kernel of truth may here have become exaggerated into an often repeated myth. Was it all night and was it the whole chorus line? Better authenticated was his feat of getting a Conservative MP to preside over each of his nine ward committees. This was symptomatic of the upheaval which his campaign caused within the Tory party, both locally and nationally. The contest inevitably attracted tremendous attention, equally because of Churchill's fame and personality and because of its location. Bye-elections in unusual circumstances and with a contestant not in a run-of-the-mill party groove, as I discovered first in the industrial borough of Warrington and then in the West End of Glasgow in 1981–2, even far away from London, can attract persistent press interest, as well as unusually stimulating the candidate, who is operating on an uncharted sea without a reliable psephological compass. These factors must have been several times magnified in the Abbey division. It is not therefore surprising that, nearly ten years later, Churchill should have described it as 'incomparably the most exciting, stirring, sensational election I have ever fought'.[29]

He did not win, although on the morning of the count (20 March) London was swept by rumours that he had done so. On the first tally he was out by thirty-three. Then, when his agent had naturally but as it turned out mistakenly demanded a recount, he was out by forty-three. It was tantalizing but nonetheless a very good result for him. He had shown his vote-drawing power in a rich constituency, much better suited to him than Dundee or Leicester West, and he had done so without creating the mixture of bitterness and farce which would have arisen had he, under his chosen label of 'Independent and Anti-Socialist', let the socialist in. The Labour candidate was Fenner Brockway, later as a left-wing peer to address the House of Lords to the age of nearly a hundred, but who in this 1924 contest, despite his own considerable publicity-attracting powers, found it difficult to get much of a look-in. Brockway polled just over 6,000 votes against the figures in the 8,100s achieved by the two rivals. The seat was one of the few which was Conservative enough to allow such a joust without Labour coming through the middle.

Furthermore Churchill had performed the paradoxical feat of opposing an official Conservative (with many the most prominent Conservatives half wanting him to win) while moving himself in a more Conservative direction. In his eve-of-poll speech he had resiled from the idea of a Conservative–Liberal coalition to combat socialism, and moved a distinct stage further to advocating an united Conservative party 'with a Liberal wing'. For membership of that Liberal wing, within the Conservative party, he was obviously becoming an eager candidate.

He was well across the river, but he still had to negotiate some testing rapids close to the Conservative bank. For the last stage of the crossing he made a brilliant choice of boatman. Sir Archibald Salvidge was an unusual combination of a Tory city 'boss' (in Liverpool) and a man with real claims to statesmanship. He was an employee of a brewery who became its managing director. But his life's work had been the building up of the Liverpool Conservative Working Man's Association, founded on a mixture of Protestant Unionism and the beer trade, though with a considerable dash of civic pride thrown in. When Salvidge (born 1863) was a young man Lord Randolph Churchill, with his Tory Democracy, had been his natural hero. Despite this, Salvidge's early contacts with Winston Churchill did not go well, for when Churchill got him to attend a dinner of Unionist Free Traders in the House of Commons in 1903 Salvidge walked out saying that it was a conspiracy against Joseph Chamberlain, a leader who meant 'more to the masses of the Industrial Midlands and North than all of us put together'.[30] However in the years of the Lloyd George Coalition he and Churchill moved together. Salvidge supported both the fusion of the Conservative and Liberal elements in the government and the Irish Treaty of 1921, which was courageous for a Liverpool Unionist.

At the beginning of April (1924) Churchill asked Salvidge to dinner in London with a view to getting him to organize a joint Conservative–Liberal rally in Liverpool for an important Churchill speech. Salvidge said it would be better to have a straight Conservative occasion, which he guaranteed would be welcoming. On 11 April he duly provided a unanimous invitation from 'the Central Committee of the Liverpool

Conservative Working Man's Association, representing 23 branches in the 11 Parliamentary Divisions, and the Executive Committee of the Women's Unionist Federation',[31] which Churchill accepted for 7 May. He was asked to speak on 'Present Dangers of the Socialist Movement', and when the day came Churchill, it need hardly be said, provided a denunciatory oration. Salvidge well fulfilled his part of the bargain by providing an audience of 5,000.

Churchill handled the occasion easily, although he did not subsequently think it had been one of his best speeches. It was the first Conservative meeting he had addressed for over twenty years, although, as he pointed out, for nearly half that period he had been collaborating in Asquith's or Lloyd George's coalitions with the principal Conservatives. Clementine, who accompanied him, found the occasion more of a cultural shock, and it is unlikely that she sat up with him until two in the morning while he dazzled his hosts, over supper in the Adelphi Hotel, with a more extreme and indiscreet version of the speech he had just delivered. He was on the banks of the Mersey but a Rubicon had been recrossed.

He now had to get a Conservative seat which he could win at the next general election. It was uncertain how near this was. The Labour government, with Snowden's cautious yet skilful budget and MacDonald's high-style foreign policy performance, had started much better than even friendly Liberals, let alone Churchill himself, had expected. Nevertheless, few gave it a long run. Churchill turned down some immediate offers from Ashton-under-Lyme, Kettering and Royston. He was perhaps heeding some advice which Clementine had written to him three months before: 'Do not however let the Tories get you too cheap – They have treated you so badly in the past & they ought to be made to feel it.'[32] And he was still making difficulties about standing under a straight Conservative label. However, he knew that he had Sir Stanley Jackson, the chief Conservative agent, on his side.

During the summer Jackson told him that he had either Richmond-on-Thames or Epping in mind for him. Richmond evaporated, but Epping prospered. This was a mixture of fairly rich London outer suburbia and West Essex rural area. It was fundamentally safe Conservative territory, but the local officers had been made nervous by a strong Liberal challenge in 1923, which had reduced their majority to 1,600. This increased Churchill's attraction for them. Moreover they had an appropriately deferential attitude towards a statesman MP. When, in September, they wanted Churchill to meet the full Council of the

Conservative Association, the mountain came to Mahomet. The meeting was in the City of London not in what Curzon had called 'those benighted suburbs'. Their favourable decision was overwhelming, if not quite unanimous. The issue was complicated by the question of label. They did not want him to be an 'Independent'. It was agreed that he could be a 'Constitutionalist', whatever that meant. He did not for the moment join either the Conservative party or the Carlton Club.

In that same month of September 1924 an 'entry of the Queen of Sheba' occasion, with all trumpets blowing, was arranged for him in Edinburgh. He addressed Scottish Conservatives in the Usher Hall. Balfour introduced him. Edward Carson and Robert Horne were on the platform. The Labour government was defeated in the House of Commons on 8 October, and on the 30th, in the third general election within three years, Churchill was returned for Epping with 19,843 votes, against 10,080 for the Liberal and 3,768 for the Labour candidate. The menace of socialism was not very strong in Epping, which (later renamed Woodford) in contrast with Dundee did prove a seat for life, although there was to be in 1938–9 a little internal trouble from part of the Conservative Association. But this was a long way off in 1924.

21

GOLD AND STRIKES

AT THE BEGINNING of November 1924, Churchill's prospects looked much better than they had for the previous two years. He was safely back in the House of Commons and effectively part of a Conservative phalanx of 419 MPs, for the securing of which solid majority he was given minor credit. He undoubtedly hoped for substantial office. He was nonetheless bowled over by the offer which Baldwin made to him on 5 November. His comment that 'you have done more for me than Lloyd George ever did'[1] was exactly apposite. Lloyd George had disappointed him in 1921 by not offering him the Chancellorship of the Exchequer. Baldwin, in 1924, more than fulfilled his expectations by offering him this high post, often but not invariably the second position in a government.

There was an element of luck in the disposition. The Treasury had first been offered to Neville Chamberlain, who declined, preferring the workaday Ministry of Health with its then wider (housing, local government and the poor law, as well as 'health' itself) and reform–inviting responsibilities. Churchill was the next caller, and Baldwin splendidly illustrated his 'leap in the dark' propensity which Birkenhead had earlier attributed to him a few years earlier,* by offering the grand job to him. The story that, when Baldwin mentioned the Chancellorship, Churchill thought it was that of the Duchy of Lancaster, is false, but like much apocrypha not entirely without a tenuous connection with reality. Apart from anything else it would have been tactless of Baldwin to have offered Churchill a return to the position in which he had been singularly unhappy in 1915; and Baldwin was rarely lacking in personal sensitivity. What was the case was that when Churchill, his head unexpectedly up, left Baldwin, whom he had seen not in Downing Street but at Conservative Central Office, he passed through the room of his supporter, Sir Stanley Jackson who, when he heard the word Chancellor,

---

* 'He takes a leap in the dark, looks round and takes another,' was the then Lord Chancellor's by no means favourable appraisal of Baldwin.

assumed that it must be of the Duchy. He had not realized how high had flown the bird that he (at least as a Conservative) had helped to hatch.

It was therefore for Churchill a surprising, lucky and only marginally achieved appointment. All this might have been expected to have two consequences. One was a sense of gratitude towards Baldwin, and this, although at a gradually and inevitably declining level, was in fact lively for several years. The other – in most people – would have been a respect for the household gods of his new party and a caution in asserting himself in a new field of departmental authority of which he knew little.

A signal example of Churchill's impudent genius was that he showed no such respect or caution. He assumed the authority of the Treasury within the government as though he had the combined Exchequer experience of Gladstone, Disraeli, Lloyd George and Bonar Law, and he behaved towards his colleagues as though he had the most unassailable of Conservative credentials. Occasionally he overdid the self-confidence, as when, set to preside over a Cabinet committee during the General Strike, he began by assuring the two other principal members, the Home Secretary (Joynson-Hicks) and the Secretary for War (Worthington-Evans): 'I have done your job for eighteen months, Jix, and yours for two years, Worthy, so I had better unfold my plan.'[2] His general experience of government was rivalled in that administration only by Balfour, who did not join until April 1925 and who was in any event beginning to fail, and by Austen Chamberlain, who made himself remote as Foreign Secretary; but Churchill's experience had all been acquired within the bosom of the Conservative government's opponents.

This did not give him a moment's pause. The overwhelming impression which emerges from the records of his first few months at the Treasury is of the explosive release of a vast store of energy and the outpouring of a flood of memoranda and letters, which, whether internal to the department or directed to the Prime Minister or other colleagues, bore his unmistakable personal stamp. Most such communications within a government are written in a flat prose style which is sometimes called civil service-ese. This is somewhat unfair, for civil servants, asked to draft hurriedly, mostly have no knowledge of what style their ministers would adopt in the unlikely event that they attempted themselves to draft such documents. They therefore naturally cleave close to a safe coast without headlands or cliffs. Churchill, on the other hand, both did his own drafting and showed a remarkable capacity to dictate (for such had become his habit) resonant aphorisms which not even the most literary and self-confident civil servant would have dared to compose on his behalf.

Thus, when on 28 November 1924 he set out his views on direct taxation in a nine-page letter advocating remissions in the middle and at the lower end which he addressed to Sir Richard Hopkins, then chairman of the Board of Inland Revenue and later to be permanent secretary to the Treasury, he argued a little obscurely and certainly idiosyncratically:

> As the tide of taxation recedes it leaves the millionaires stranded on the peaks of taxation to which they have been carried by the flood. . . . Just as we have seen the millionaire left close to the high water mark and the ordinary Super Tax payer draw cheerfully away from him, so in their turn the whole class of Super Tax payer will be left behind on the beach as the great mass of the Income Tax payers subside into the refreshing waters of the sea. The harmonious and natural character of the process is graceful and pleasing in the last extreme.[3]

On 1 December he wrote to the Foreign Secretary saying that he proposed to demand payment of overdue French and Italian war debt obligations which 'will mean worry for you – sulky instead of smiling Ambassadors, etc'.[4] The next day he minuted the secretary of the Cabinet asking whether it was not provocative to increase the number of submarines based at Hong Kong from six to twenty-one. 'Suppose the Japanese owned the Isle of Man and started putting 21 submarines there.'[5] Two weeks later he wrote to Baldwin saying that to accept the construction demands currently being put forward by the Admiralty 'is to sterilize and paralyse the whole policy of the Government. There will be nothing for the taxpayer and nothing for social reform. We shall be a Naval Parliament busily preparing our Navy for some great imminent shock – Voilà tout!'[6] Then, on 22 February 1925, when he was vigorously contesting the determination of the official Treasury and the Bank of England to return to the Gold Standard at the pre-war parity, he wrote to Sir Otto Niemeyer (Treasury controller of finance): 'I would rather see Finance less proud and Industry more content.'[7]

This spate of highly personal outpouring and his general vibrating certainty struck people in differing ways. His wife's Christmas comment to Professor F. A. Lindemann (a moon who had come over Churchill's horizon at just about the same time as Brendan Bracken, the latter more in the nature of a comet; they were both to be very much part of his firmament for the next thirty-five years) was a good central judgement: 'Winston is immersed in thrilling new work with the Treasury officials whom he says are a wonderful lot of men.'[8] These Treasury officials and those of the Bank were stimulated by Churchill, although finding him less amenable and more time-consuming than his immediate predecessor Snowden had been. Among Churchill's senior colleagues Austen Chamberlain was determined to be friendly, and Birkenhead, as we have seen, had been for many years, despite their previous difference of party, his most compatible companion.

Earl Beatty (Admiral of the Fleet and current First Sea Lord) supplied, as the naval-estimates argument unfolded, a view of Churchill from a different angle. 'That extraordinary fellow Winston has gone mad,' he wrote to Lady Beatty on 26 January 1925. But ten days later he added: 'It takes a good deal out of me when dealing with a man of his calibre with a very quick brain. A false step, remark or even gesture is immediately fastened upon, so I have to keep my wits about me.'[9] However it was from Neville Chamberlain, whose self-abnegation had made Churchill Chancellor, that there came the most striking 'insider' portrait of Churchill's Cabinet performance in his early Conservative days. Chamberlain wrote to Baldwin at the end of August 1925:

> Looking back over our first session I think our Chancellor has done very well, all the better because he hasn't been what he was expected to be. He hasn't dominated the Cabinet, though undoubtedly he has influenced it. . . . He hasn't intrigued for the leadership, but he has been a tower of debating strength in the House of Commons. . . . What a brilliant creature he is! But there is somehow a great gulf between him and me which I don't think I shall ever cross. I like him. I like his humour and vitality. I like his courage. . . . But not for all the joys of Paradise would I be a member of his staff! Mercurial! A much abused word, but it is the literal description of his temperament.[10]

On Baldwin himself Churchill's influence was at that stage considerable. Churchill was linked to the Prime Minister by gratitude, and the Prime Minister, even though good at not being dazzled by Lloyd George, allowed himself to be temporarily dazzled by the man who was to be Britain's even greater war leader of the twentieth century. This came out in the tone of Baldwin's letters to Churchill. Their style was different from his usual ones. It was almost as though he was trying to rival his Chancellor's level of sophistication and verbal felicity. Thus, when Herbert Samuel had been summoned from the Tyrol to see the Prime Minister at Aix-les-Bains in the summer of 1925 in the hope that he would accept the chairmanship of the Royal Commission on the Coal Industry, Baldwin reported to Churchill at Chartwell:

> The infant Samuel duly arrived as the clock was striking six on Monday evening. Cool, competent, and precise as when he was first lent to this temporary world by an inscrutable providence, it was the work of a moment for him to grasp our problem in all its manifold implications. . . .
>
> Aix is very full: so are most of the people here [he amiably concluded his letter]. The hotel buses discharge 'em at the baths, and they look, many of them, as if you stuck a fork in them, a rich gravy would burst forth.[11]

In spite of this epistolary familiarity the social lives of Baldwin and Churchill did not much overlap. They nonetheless saw each other frequently, for Churchill developed the habit of walking from the Chancellor's traditional residence of 11 Downing Street through the two connecting doors of No. 10, on his morning progress to his room in the Treasury building, and mostly calling in for a few minutes' chat with the Prime Minister on the way. This greatly contributed to their never seriously quarrelling for the four and a half years of the government, although the peace did not long survive its defeat. The habit certainly helped to get Churchill through his first few months as a Conservative minister, when he was engaged in at least four major disputes within the government, as well as in the preparation of his first budget and in the conduct of delicate war-debt negotiations with the French.

The most dangerous of the disputes for Churchill was over the naval estimates. This was because here he not only performed an extraordinary volte face from his position twelve years before when he had almost broken the Asquith Cabinet with his demand for a *bigger* navy but also in his 1925 demand for a *smaller* navy took on Baldwin's closest friends within the government – Bridgeman, was First Lord of the Admiralty, and Davidson, its Financial and Parliamentary Secretary. A major Cabinet row rumbled on for nearly a year, with threats of resignation from these two ministers as well as from the admirals, but not from Churchill, which was perhaps part of his strength. Eventually Baldwin steered skilfully towards a solution which was somewhat more on the Admiralty's than on Churchill's side, but at least the Chancellor escaped without either humiliation or great ill-will.

The second dispute was with Steel-Maitland at the Ministry of Labour, and to a lesser extent with Neville Chamberlain at Health, about the provisions of the widows' and orphans' pension insurance scheme which Churchill was determined to introduce in his first budget. Steel-Maitland argued strongly that it was too generous and too early in the parliament, and on the latter point at least Chamberlain agreed. Churchill however got his way on both issues. The powers of a determined Chancellor on anything to do with his budget are great.

The third dispute was with the other Chamberlain (Austen), who was a much older friend of Churchill's than Neville, and who protested plaintively about lack of Churchill support at two unsatisfactory Cabinet meetings in early March 1925. Chamberlain was formulating his initiative for tying Britain, France, Germany, Italy and Belgium into a mutual security arrangement as part of what became the Locarno treaties, Baldwin was lying back, and the Chancellor, Chamberlain held, stirred up trouble rather than helping his colleague in the other senior department. Churchill at that stage was against any entangling commitment to France, who 'could stew in her own juice without its having any bad effect on anybody or anything. All we had to do was to go our own way and in a few years' time we should see France on her knees begging for our help.'[12] In Weimar Republic days there was a certain sense in this but it was certainly not an attitude calculated to make a Cabinet ally of Austen Chamberlain, who was however remarkably unresentful and gave Churchill a lot of budget support.

The fourth dispute was much the most interesting, even though it did not spill from the Treasury and the Bank into the Cabinet arena. Nearly all the *bien-pensant* sources of advice were unanimous that it was Britain's interest and duty to return to the Gold Standard (the British-led exchange rate system which had broken down under the strains of the First World War) and to do so at the pre-war parity. On this subject Churchill's minutes were masterpieces of pungent questioning whereas the replies took refuge in a misty higher wisdom. On 29 January 1925 Churchill wrote a minute and circulated it to Montagu Norman (Governor of the Bank of England from 1920 to 1944), Otto Niemeyer, R. G. Hawtrey (who in forty-one years in the Treasury made himself almost more of a legend even than Niemeyer as a pundit of international finance) and Lord Bradbury. Bradbury, retired and ennobled after being permanent secretary to the Treasury throughout the First World War, had recently become chairman of the joint Select Committee of both Houses of Parliament on Currency and Banking, which was specifically charged with pronouncing on the wisdom or otherwise of a return to Gold. The spirit in which this minute was received is well expressed by its becoming known in the Treasury as 'Mr Churchill's exercise', which combined a hint of admiration for its strenuousness with more than a hint of impatience at its naivety, and by Bradbury's comment: 'The writer ... appears to have his spiritual home in the Keynes–McKenna sanctuary [the Cambridge economist and the ex-Chancellor who had become Midland Bank chairman were the most prominent anti-Gold sceptics] but some of the trimmings of his mantle have been furnished by the *Daily Express* [that is, Beaverbrook].'[13]

The direct replies to the Churchill minute, as opposed to such oblique comments, were splendid examples of substituting superior wisdom for rational argument. Niemeyer said that to dodge the issue now would be to show that Britain had never really 'meant business' about the Gold Standard and that 'our nerve had failed when the stage was set'.[14] Norman, the great Governor, was even more sublimely bland. In the opinion 'of educated and reasonable men', he wrote, there was no alternative to a return to Gold. The Chancellor would no doubt be attacked whatever he did but: 'In the former case (Gold) he will be abused by the ignorant, the gamblers and the antiquated industrialists; in the latter case (not Gold) he will be abused by the instructed and by posterity.'[15]

Churchill's doubts took a lot of subduing. And his combination of energy and self-confidence made him a formidable fighter of a rearguard action. Niemeyer's reply to Churchill's first memorandum was written on a Saturday (21 February). Churchill in turn replied to this with the purest milk of expansionary doctrine:

> The Treasury has never, it seems to me, faced the profound significance of what Mr Keynes calls 'the paradox of unemployment amidst dearth'. The Governor shows himself perfectly happy in the spectacle of Britain possessing the finest credit in the world simultaneously with a million and a quarter unemployed. Obviously if these million and a quarter were usefully and economically employed, they would produce at least £100 a year a head, instead of costing up at least £50 a head in doles.

This reply he composed at length and with great speed. 'Forgive me adding to your labours', he concluded, 'by these Sunday morning reflexions.'[16] Whatever else Churchill was, he was not a lazy minister. Of the near-contemporary Chancellors, Snowden would have accepted the advice without argument; Baldwin might have mulled it over during a quiet Sunday morning walk with Dr Tom Jones, the gently influential deputy secretary of the Cabinet who became just as much his confidant as he had been that of Lloyd George; and Austen Chamberlain, tending his rock garden at the unfortunately named Twitt's Ghyll, might have complained in a letter to a sister that he was being pushed, but would never have provided a polemical riposte without an official draft.

Churchill encouraged the issue to take a face-to-face as well as a paper form. On 17 March he set up a dinner-table jousting ground. He always liked argument over the knives and forks. Despite his cavalry subaltern's background the traditional army convention of not talking shop in the mess was totally alien to him. He sought to combine his enthusiasms of the moment with his perennial indulgences. Champagne should be intermingled with controversy and brandy with a recipe for action, if it could be obtained. To this dinner he summoned Keynes and McKenna, the two sceptics on Gold, whose 'sanctuary' he was thought to inhabit, together with Bradbury and Niemeyer.

The sixth participant was P. J. Grigg, principal private secretary to five Chancellors before eventually becoming permanent under-secretary and then Secretary of State at the War Office. Grigg recorded that the encounter lasted until after midnight (mildly foreshadowing Churchill's later habits) and that at the end 'the ayes (that is the pro-Gold forces) had it'.[17] Keynes took a rather abstruse point about the discrepancy between American and British prices and also between American and British phases of economic development being too great for an open currency system. McKenna showed that *le trahison des clercs* could embrace not only clerks of banks but their chairmen as well. On the merits he supported Keynes but at the end he sold the pass by saying that as a matter of practical politics Churchill had no alternative but to go back to Gold. When the dinner broke up Churchill's last hope of resistance had crumbled.

It was the culmination of a two-month process. As the Gold battle unfolded there was a sense of even such a normally dominating minister as Churchill being swept downstream by the force of a compelling current, protesting but nonetheless essentially impotent. The Treasury was against him, the Bank was against him, the Select Committee presided over first by Austen Chamberlain and then by Bradbury was against him. Snowden, his Labour 'shadow', was against him. Baldwin, much respecting Montagu Norman, in fact played no part in the decision, but would have been very unhappy had Churchill decided against Gold. The two tufts of ground – Keynes and McKenna – on which Churchill attempted to stand proved, for varying reasons, unsatisfactory footholds. The momentum of conventional wisdom swept them away. After the 17 March dinner the decision was not so much formally taken as generally assumed within the inner circle, although not announced until the budget on 28 April.

The whole story was a remarkable example of a strong not a weak minister nonetheless reluctantly succumbing, grudgingly adjusting himself to the near unanimous, near irresistible flow of establishment opinion. Two further points are worth mention. The first was the secrecy with which the dispute was carried on. During two months of intensive argument, of minute and counter-minute, it hardly spread outside the Treasury, let alone outside the government. Such security is unimaginable today. The second was the ability of such a near unanimous concentration of advice to be wrong, or at least sufficiently myopic as to produce highly undesirable lateral consequences. This Churchill vaguely perceived: his corner-of-the-eye perspective was far superior to that of Norman or Niemeyer or Bradbury, Austen Chamberlain or Philip Snowden. But in dealing with economic affairs his confidence at that stage, perhaps always, while fully up to writing iconoclastic letters and minutes, did not extend to a persistent overruling of all the pundits.

As a result there was committed what is commonly regarded as the greatest mistake of that main Baldwin government, and the responsibility for it came firmly to rest upon Churchill. Keynes, for instance, wrote a pamphlet to which, playing on the resounding success of his 1919 *The Economic Consequences of the Peace*, he gave the title of *The Economic Consequences of Mr Churchill*. In a sense this allocation of blame was unfair, but only in a sense. Churchill was deliberately a very attention-attracting Chancellor. He wanted his first budget to make a great splash, which it did, and a considerable contribution to the spray was made by the announcement of the return to Gold. Reluctant convert although he had been, he therefore deserved the responsibility and, if it be so judged, a considerable part of the blame. An irony was that by upvaluing the pound Churchill threw a destructive spanner into the works of Baldwin's industrial policy, although had he not done so Baldwin would almost certainly have interfered for the only time in that government in financial policy and pushed him towards accepting Montagu Norman's advice.

The results of this advice however ran directly counter to the emollient policy towards the trades unions which the Prime Minister had proclaimed on 6 March (1925) – at the height of the internal

Treasury dispute – in one of his two outstandingly successful speeches in an oratorically quiet career.* This was his 'Give peace in our time, O Lord' speech, which led to the withdrawal of an anti-trades union Conservative private member's bill and sent his leadership to its apogee of repute. Churchill wrote of it to Clementine: 'I had no idea he could show such power.'[18] Yet almost the worst possible contribution to industrial 'peace in our time' was to make things more difficult for the already suffering traditional export trades, cotton, shipbuilding, steel and above all coal, which was precisely what was done by the return to Gold. Churchill's reluctant decision only a few weeks after the Baldwin speech which had so impressed him, and entirely in accord with Baldwin's own contradictory desires, meant that 'peace in our time' became the General Strike within fourteen months.

Under the Churchill regime budget days themselves were given even more of a sense of occasion than was habitual, with the surrounding ritual fully matched by the *élan* with which the budget speech itself was delivered. At these annual festivities he not merely did a routine display of the 'Gladstone box' (containing the budget secrets) at the door of 11 Downing Street, but then processed down Whitehall to the House of Commons, accompanied by his parliamentary private secretary, Robert Boothby (only for the 1926 budget onwards, for he was not appointed until the end of 1925, but thereafter as present and as top-hatted as Churchill himself), and by a rotating group of family members, a posse of policemen and a tail of respectful members of the public. On these occasions, despite all his budgets being well into April, Churchill displayed a fine variety of overcoats. His great astrakhan-collared one he appeared to put away after the equinox (although it reappeared surprisingly early in the autumn), but he had at least two others and rarely ventured out without one of them. He always believed in being well wrapped up, sometimes more so than anyone else in the picture, although in general matched by his fellow politicians of the 1920s and 1930s. President Kennedy-like lack of encumbrance, either around the body or on the head, was alien to Churchill and his contemporaries.

When the procession had safely arrived at the House, Churchill made a well-received entry into an expectant chamber, without the overcoat but with Boothby, the Gladstone box and the speech, and proceeded to deliver it for *circa* two hours. In form at least his budget speeches were

---

* The other was his abdication *pièce justificative*, gently devastating of the former King Edward VIII, which he delivered nearly twelve years later.

all successes. The oratorical style was lush and so characteristic that the words could hardly have come from any other lips, but was relieved by mordant pin-pricks, both of himself and of others.

He was determined to present the 1925 budget, despite its substantial remissions for high earners (and to a lesser extent for large owners) as a 'condition of the people' enterprise, well in the tradition of his pre-1914 partnership with Lloyd George. Indeed there was some inter-ministerial criticism of his poaching announcements which would have more appropriately come from the Minister of Health. Yet the terms in which he spoke, with genuine compassion, of the risks and sufferings of 'the little people' now strike a note of patrician condescension. The social assumptions of the 1920s were very different from those of the post-Second World War world. But even allowing for this, there were visible in the 1925 budget some of the archaisms which contributed to Churchill's electoral defeat in 1945.

> The average British workman in good health, full employment and standard wages does not regard himself and his family as an object of compassion. But when exceptional misfortune descends upon the cottage home with the slender margin upon which it is floated, or there is a year of misfortune, distress or unemployment, or above all the loss of the breadwinner, it leaves the once happy family in the grip of the greatest calamity. If I may change to a military metaphor, it is not the sturdy marching troops that need extra reward and indulgence; it is the stragglers, the exhausted, the weak, the wounded, the veterans, the widows and the orphans to whom the ambulances of state aid must be directed.[19]

The 'ambulances of state aid' amounted to the removal of an earnings restriction to the ten shillings a week old-age pensions available at sixty-five (as against the five shillings a week at seventy which Asquith had introduced in 1908); to a new ten shillings a week for widows for life; to five shillings a week for such a widow's eldest child and three shillings a week for her other children; and seven and sixpence a week for full orphans, all of these children's pensions to cease at the age of fourteen and a half. The long-term costs were complicated, and Churchill made them still more so by bringing in as an offset the future decline in war pensions, which he confidently announced (a supreme irony for the great warrior of the Second World War), should be down from the current £67 million to £32 million in 1945. For the moment however the costs were small, only about £5 million a year for the remainder of the parliament, and were handsomely covered by the surplus of £37 million, most of which had been bequeathed to him by Snowden's caution.

This surplus he needed for some fairly dramatic reductions in direct taxation. Super-tax (sometimes called surtax) he proposed to reduce by £10 million, which was substantial in relation to the total yield of the tax at £60 million. He balanced this rich-favouring concession by recouping an almost equivalent amount from an increase in death duties beginning with estates of £12,500 thousand (about £340,000 today) and falling with increasing severity up to estates of £1 million (£27 million plus today). He could therefore claim that he was transferring the rich man's burden from income to capital, from the living to the dead, and thus encouraging enterprise at the expense of the frozen hand of established property rights.

Such a balancing transaction eased the presentation of his major concession, which was a reduction of the standard rate of income tax from four shillings and sixpence to four shillings in the pound. This was of substantial benefit to the rich, not only as individual taxpayers but also in the capacity of many of them as shareholders, for income tax was then the principal form of company taxation. So far as an individual's tax was concerned Churchill juggled with allowances so as to give proportionately the biggest relief at around £500 a year, which was then a good lower-middle-class income, but the absolute relief, particularly when added to the super-tax change, was incomparably greater for the rich. Snowden denounced the effect in somewhat routine terms, but Arthur Ponsonby, the Labour son of Queen Victoria's long-term private secretary, was nearer the mark when he wrote that, while Churchill's 'sympathy for the poor was eloquent, his sympathy with the rich was practical'.[20]

Nevertheless the budget was on the whole well received and enhanced Churchill's prestige within the government. Even before it, Birkenhead, as Secretary of State for India, had written to Reading, the Viceroy, that 'Winston's position in the Government and Cabinet is very strong. He takes infinite trouble with the Prime Minister who likes him and for whom he feels a very sincere gratitude.'[21] This prestige made Churchill prominently concerned with the coal crisis, which in one form or another dominated the life of the government from the summer of 1925. He was, as we have seen, partly the cause of the trouble, for the return to Gold at the 1914 parity was devastating to the coal industry (because the higher pound further damaged its already declining exports), which then employed a million men. But he was also looked to as a provider of a possible solution. In July (1925) he was made chairman of a special Cabinet committee to consider the nationalization of mining royalties. But this was no solution to the immediate problem, which was that the employers – or the 'owners' as they were appropriately and collectively known, and who were, in Birkenhead's judgement of a year later, the most stupid body of men he had ever encountered* – reacted to the new sterling parity by announcing a national lock-out from 31 July unless the miners accepted a substantial reduction in wages.

The miners themselves, living largely in close-knit and isolated communities, were the most battle-scarred fighting troops of organized labour. They may not have been led with brilliant tactical skill, but they had their own solidarity and great emotional command over the Labour movement and were therefore dangerous adversaries. Baldwin, who had more foresight as well as greater social conscience than the coal-owners, did not want a conflict. Nor did Churchill. He proposed to Baldwin a Royal Commission on the future of the coal industry, which (under Herbert Samuel) deliberated for the next seven months, and he readily agreed that a subsidy, estimated at £10 million but which in fact turned out to be £19 million, should be paid to the industry over this period. By these means were both the miners' lock-out and the General Strike postponed from July 1925 to May 1926. 'We were not ready' (in 1925) Baldwin subsequently told G. M. Young, his chosen biographer.

When Churchill came to present his second budget on 26 April 1926, he was therefore suspended between the publication of the Coal Commission Report on 11 March and the outbreak of the General Strike on 4 May. The Report proposed the nationalization of mining royalties, amalgamations and more closures, government aid for research and marketing, considerable welfare provisions and a sharp rejection of the owners' typically Bourbon-like proposals for both longer hours and less pay. However, the Commission considered that, with the retention of the seven-hour day and with a falling price index, some reduction in wages was reasonable.

Churchill additionally had all the difficulties inherent in a second budget after a considerable triumph with the first. On top of that he himself was beginning to suffer from some of 'the economic consequences of Mr Churchill'. Before the revenue havoc of the General

---

* It should in fairness be said that until this encounter he reserved the honour for the leaders of the Miners' Federation.

Strike itself and the long six months of coal strike which persisted when
the central challenge had been called off, the budgetary position was
tight. The £19 million of coal subsidy turned a small surplus into an
awkward deficit. He had seen this tightness coming in his 1925 speech,
but the intervening year, the coal subsidy entirely apart, marked a
climacteric in thinking about public finance. Hitherto it was thought
that an £800 million budget was a post-war aberration, and that with a
determined Chancellor it could be got back, if not to the £197 million
of 1913–14, at least to somewhere approaching equidistance between
the two figures.

   This was always a pipe-dream. Apart from anything else the post-war
debt charges of over £300 million (compared with £24 million in
1913–14) rendered it totally impracticable. But impracticability does not
always dull aspiration. It was one of Churchill's perhaps inadvertent
services that he burst this illusion. After his great strivings at economy
the net effect, behind convoluted obfuscations and with the coal subsidy
excluded, was that actual expenditure had risen between 1924–5 and
1925–6 from £795 million to £805 million. This his predecessor Robert
Horne cruelly pointed out in the budget debate. Thereafter the £800
million was a fact of life – until it passed £2,000 million in the second
1939 budget and £100,000 million in 1981–2 and reached £375,000
million, even after several years of 'prudence', in the budget for 2000–1.

   Churchill's room for manoeuvre before this second budget was small.
He nonetheless prepared for it with great energy but no exclusive
concentration upon Treasury work. From November 1925 onwards he
was fighting a sustained even if not notably successful battle to get down
the departmental estimates of his colleagues. This did not preclude him
from advocating a sweeping measure of House of Lords reform (which
made short shrift of the rights of hereditary peers) to a November
Cabinet committee on the subject, with the resulting scheme to be
submitted to a referendum. He took a long Christmas holiday at
Chartwell, with several of his favourite people to stay, including Edward
Marsh, whose span of private-secretarial service with him now exceeded
twenty years, and Professor Lindemann, his new guru, and with his
recreational hours punctuated by a vigorous exchange of memoranda
with the Treasury. Then on 20 January 1926, having negotiated an
Italian war-debt settlement in the preceding week, he went to Leeds
and addressed the annual Chamber of Commerce dinner. For some
reason this Leeds banquet was a favourite occasion for Chancellors to
make their last major speech before the period of pre-budget purdah.

I used it in 1970 to dampen expectations following the turn-round of
the balance of payments and in the run-up to an election. Churchill
used it in 1926 for a more high-flown appraisal of the future:

> Prosperity, that errant daughter of our house who went astray in the
> Great War, is on our threshold. She has raised her hand to the knocker
> on the door. What shall we do? Shall we let her in, or shall we drive her
> away? Shall we welcome her once again to our own fireside settle, or
> banish her once more to roam about among the nations of the world?
> That is the choice that will be before the British people in these next few
> anxious months.[22]

These sentences sufficiently impressed the normally pedestrian and
often anti-Churchill mind of King George V that he sought Churchill's
permission to use them in a speech of his own.

On 31 January Clementine Churchill went to the South of France
for a long winter holiday (as was her habit at the time) but this had no
diminishing effect on the scale of her husband's political hospitality. For
the weekend of 6–7 February he had to stay two Cabinet colleagues
(the multi-syllabled Worthington-Evans and Cunliffe-Lister) and his
Financial Secretary at the Treasury (Ronald McNeill, a hard-line
Unionist who had thrown a book at him in the House of Commons at
the height of the Ulster tension in 1912). For the next weekend he
invited no fewer than six *prominenti*, including Sam Hoare, then Secretary of State for Air, who wrote a memorable account of his visit: 'I
had never seen Winston before in the role of landed proprietor. Most
of Sunday morning we inspected the property, and the engineering
works on which he is engaged. These engineering works consist of
making a series of ponds in a valley, and Winston appeared to be a good
deal more interested in them than in anything else in the world.'
Churchill was convinced, Hoare added, 'that he is to be the prophet to
lead us into the Promised Land in which there will be no income tax
and everyone will live happily ever afterwards. The trouble is that he
has got so many schemes tumbling over each other in his mind, that
I am beginning to wonder whether he will be able to pull any one of
them out of the heap.'[23]

The budget, ten weeks later, gave him very little opportunity for
pulling anything out of the heap. It was all juggling with small amounts
and adjustments to the sinking fund in order to preserve a reasonably
provident posture without going back on his major concessions of the
previous year. Nor were the opportunities for eloquence great, although

he did his best with poor material. No one except Churchill could have moved from reviewing both the performance of the exchange rate following the return to the Gold Standard and the working of the new silk duties by saying: 'Now, having lingered for a few moments in the regions of silk and gold, we proceed to the more severe stages of our journey.'[24]

The main severities were a betting tax of 5 per cent and a 'raid' upon the Road Fund, for which revenue had risen to the substantial sum of £21.5 million, and in relation to which the motoring lobby had succeeded in building up an assumption that, contrary to the doctrine against the hypothecation of revenue, it should all be reserved for roads. Churchill was rightly scornful of this. 'Such contentions', he had written in a Treasury memorandum, 'are absurd, and constitute at once an outrage upon the sovereignty of Parliament and upon commonsense.'[25] He brushed aside the special pleading of the Home Secretary (Joynson-Hicks) who was president of the Automobile Association, took £7 million that year, and arranged for what he regarded as a fair future allocation between the Exchequer and the Road Fund.

Most of this became of minor relevance only a week later when the General Strike began. Churchill, as we have seen, had been a moderate in the summer of 1925 when the question was that of curbing the intransigence of the coal-owners by the appointment of the Samuel Commission and the payment of a temporary subsidy. And he was to be a moderate again in the summer of 1926 when Baldwin, after a virtuoso performance during the eight days of the General Strike, fell into a state of exhausted lassitude and retired hurt to Aix-les-Bains. During this three-and-a-half-week sojourn he left Churchill, in no way exhausted, in charge of the negotiations to end the coal strike. This continued for six months after the end of the General Strike, of which it had been the cause. But during the General Strike itself Churchill's mood was of the utmost bellicosity and, some of his colleagues thought, utmost irresponsibility as well. 'He thinks he is Napoleon,'[26] Davidson wrote to Baldwin. It was perhaps more a throwback to his longing to be at the enemy which had made him at Antwerp in 1914 try to give up the Admiralty in order to take personal command of the Naval Division and the other troops there, a role for which he had no relevant training. However it was also a foretaste of the spirit which gave him his lion's roar of defiance in the terrible summer of 1940.

In 1926, against a less malevolent and menacing enemy, this spirit aroused more apprehension than admiration. When the first convoy brought food into central London from the docks Churchill wanted it to be escorted by tanks with machine guns strategically placed along the route. He wanted to commandeer the BBC and use it as a government propaganda agency. It was therefore a relief to his colleagues when his energies were corralled within his chosen task of running the *British Gazette*. This was an official publication produced from the offices and with the plant of the *Morning Post*, while it and the other newspapers were more or less on strike. By the last day he got the *Gazette*'s circulation up to 2,200,000, a formidable achievement.

He did this at the expense of tense relations with all the main newspaper proprietors (Burnham of the *Telegraph*, Astor of *The Times*, Berry of the *Sunday Times* and Cadbury of the *Daily News*), who did not like having their stocks of newsprint commandeered. H. A. Gwynne, the editor of the *Morning Post*, suffered more directly and accused Churchill of charging about the *Post* offices and upsetting both the editorial staff by 'changing commas and full stops' and the printing staff by pretending that he knew better than they how to work the machines. So far as the content was concerned he provoked even such an almost excessively moderate man as Walter (later Lord) Citrine, the general secretary of the Trades Union Council, who ten or twelve years later was happy to appear on anti-appeasement platforms with Churchill, to describe it as 'a poisonous attempt to bias the public mind'.[27]

Yet, when all these criticisms are made, there was probably no one else who could have mounted such a vigorous enterprise to fill a dangerous information gap. Two months later, in a retrospective House of Commons debate on the strike Churchill again performed as no one else could have done and delivered a wonderfully emollient piece of self-mockery. A Labour member had threatened a renewed trial of industrial strength against parliamentary legitimacy. In the closing minute or so of the debate Churchill began to reply to this in portentous terms: 'I have no wish to make threats which would disturb the House and cause bad blood. . . .' Everyone nonetheless waited for an horrendous announcement that the thunderbolts of Zeus were at the ready. 'But this I must say. Make your minds perfectly clear that if ever you let loose upon us again a General Strike, we will let loose upon you' – a pregnant pause – 'another *British Gazette*.'[28] It was a brilliant *coup de théâtre*. He sat down in a burst of laughter which was equally strong from both sides of the House, and the corner of what might have been a dangerously bitter recriminatory debate was at once confidently and self-deprecatingly turned.

There were three phases to the coal negotiations until, at last, both sides having resisted a settlement, the owners with consistent intransigence, the Miners' Federation more variably, the strike petered out, broadly on the owners' terms, on 20 November. During the first phase Baldwin was still in England and nominally in charge, although with his attitude best summed up by his mid-July remark, 'Leave it alone – we are all so tired,'[29] and with Churchill as usual, being more than willing to fill any adjacent vacuum. Then on 22 August Baldwin was medically ordered away in a state of nervous prostration and stayed at Aix for the next twenty-four days.

This was Churchill's great window of opportunity. He had two adjutants, Arthur Steel-Maitland, the not very effective Minister of Labour, and George Lane-Fox, a Yorkshire country gentleman who was much too close to the owners to be a good Secretary of Mines. Neither of them really agreed with Churchill's approach, which they thought was too interventionist for the government, too favourable to the miners, and too bullying towards the owners. But such was the force of his personality that he largely swept them along with him. Gusto took over.

The Harold Wilson 'beer and sandwiches in 10 Downing Street' approach to industrial disputes was foreshadowed forty years earlier by champagne and oysters at Chartwell and the Savoy Grill. A. J. Cook and Herbert Smith, the miners' leaders, were too dour to be so entertained, but everybody else, the reluctantly following ministerial colleagues, the leader of the opposition Ramsay MacDonald, coalowners from Lord Londonderry to D. R. Llewellyn, and relevant officials, above all the *éminence grise* and relentlessly diary-writing Tom Jones, were all swept into that regime of energetic optimism and indulgent hospitality. And the more champagne that he consumed with every party to the dispute except for the unclubbable union leaders, the more favourable Churchill became to the miners and the less well disposed to the owners.

There were tangled cross-currents. The owners believed in profits and Churchill believed in the authority of the state. When therefore Churchill wanted a tripartite conference with the government as the balancing force and the owners refused, he thought it was almost *lèse-majesté*. There was also a bitter dispute on the issue of a national as opposed to 'district' agreements. The terms have now faded, but they had great emotive impact at the time. The owners wanted to be free to pay lower wages in the less profitable districts with seams which were harder to work. The Miners' Federation were passionately attached to equality of treatment, both because they thought that natural justice demanded at least as great a reward for working a difficult seam as for working an easy one, and because they saw it as the key to their unity and strength.

Then there was a still more powerful undertow, which was based on the view (correct so far as it went) of the owners and of the majority of the government that the miners were on the brink of being starved into a crushing defeat. It was therefore better to wait a few months for this to happen than to seek a compromise solution. Churchill's contrary view was that the country was suffering debilitating economic bleeding and that it was the duty of government to staunch the flow at the earliest possible moment. It was during this phase that he was first recorded as having coined the aphorism 'defiance in defeat, magnanimity in victory'. And there was the final cross-current that several devoted Baldwinites (Davidson, who was with his hero in Aix, Hankey the secretary of the Cabinet, and even Tom Jones, who combined his love of Baldwin with a reluctant admiration of Churchill's brilliance and a somewhat sentimental commitment to the left and hence the cause of the miners) were worried that Churchill might achieve a too early settlement which would leave the Prime Minister upstaged by his too successful lieutenant. They were making plans to get Baldwin back to share in any glory which might be going. The same apprehension later informed a comment by Jones during a winding up by Churchill of a coal debate on 27 September, which Baldwin had opened rather pedestrianly: 'During [Churchill's] brilliant performance the PM's face was turned towards the official Gallery, and covered with one of his hands. He looked utterly wretched, much as Ramsay [MacDonald] does when L.G. is on his legs.'[30]

In fact the protective apprehension of the Baldwinites was misplaced. Early September offered Churchill's best hope of achieving a settlement, and by his late-September oration it was effectively extinct. When his hopes were high he had put heavy pressure on the coal-owners. At an afternoon and early-evening meeting on 6 September he had harangued and argued with them over fifty-six pages of official transcript. But he had failed to move them. And when several of Churchill's colleagues (including his friend Birkenhead) came back from holiday and read the transcript, they thought he had tried to exert illegitimate pressure and constituted a bloc against him on the Coal and other Cabinet committees. Churchill was able to keep some part of the reins in his hands for a little time after Baldwin's return of 15 September. But by the end of that month he was much less in the driving seat, except for his ability to make by far the best speeches in the House of Commons. And in the third phase, which extended throughout October and for most of November, he became a prisoner of the view of most of his colleagues (curiously only the shadowy figure of Sir Laming Worthington-Evans was consistently with him), who much preferred victory for the coal-owners to a negotiated settlement.

Nevertheless his sustained pacific effort stands in sharp contrast both to his bellicosity during the General Strike and to the reputation which had followed him in Labour and trades union circles since Tonypandy in 1911. His whole method of operation was such that, if a problem was set before him, he could not fail to try to solve it. He might do so wisely or unwisely. But to echo Baldwin's quietist July remark was simply outside his range of choice. At this stage in his life, and indeed in all others, except perhaps after 1951, he was irremediably proactive.

As soon as the miners' strike was over, he switched his attention away from government affairs and in a month and a half of strenuous writing finished the third volume of *The World Crisis*. The preface was dated 'Chartwell Manor, January 1st 1927'. (It was serialized in *The Times* in February and published as a book in March.) Then he went on a twenty-five-day restless and peripatetic January Mediterranean holiday. This included playing in Malta his last game of polo, witnessing a Vesuvius eruption from Naples, enjoying a quick winter view of the Parthenon in Athens, and having two encounters with Mussolini in Rome, after which he issued much too friendly statements. He got back to London only on 29 January and then applied himself vigorously to the preparation of his third budget.

This became a thing of shreds and patches presented with even more brio than its two predecessors. Baldwin showed both generosity and a perceptive edge of description when he wrote that evening to the King: 'The [crowded] scene was quite sufficient to show that Mr Churchill as a star turn has a power of attraction which nobody in the House of Commons can excel. . . . [The Chancellor] came into the House beam-ing with smiles, having apparently filled the rôle of Pied Piper of Hamelin from Downing Street. . . .'[31] Churchill's opening words had a pungent impact which at least postponed his crowded and distinguished audience from falling quickly to sleep: 'We meet this afternoon under the shadow of the disasters of last year. The Coal strike has cost the taxpayer £30 million. It is not the time to bewail the past. It is the time to pay the bill. It is not for me to apportion the blame. My task is to apportion the burden. I cannot present myself in the role of an impartial judge. I am only the public executioner.'[32]

As an executioner, however, he cut off very few heads, not at any rate those on necks famous or stiff enough to cause much commotion. Translucent pottery was to contribute £200,000, motor-car tyres £750,000, matches £700,000, wines (mainly by adjusting the borderline at which they came to count as fortified down from 27 to 25 degrees) £1.25 million, and tobacco £3.5 million. The Road Fund was again to be raided, but in a peculiarly complicated way, and various windfalls were to be procured by, in his own phrase of the previous year, 'a judicious shaking of the tree'. These, in the form of a speeding up of the dates of payment, yielded the surprisingly large sum of nearly £20 million. But they were unrepeatable, and thus a source of slightly bogus finance. By these and other ingenious twists he managed to turn a prospective deficit of £21.5 million into a prospective surplus of £16.5 million, nearly all of which he devoted to raising the sinking fund to the very high level of £65 million, while still leaving himself with the little scalp of a surplus of £1.5 million.

Baldwin summed it up as neatly as anyone could in that letter to the King by writing: 'His enemies will say that this year's budget is a mischievous piece of manipulation and juggling with the country's finance, but his friends will say that it is a masterpiece of ingenuity.'[33] For some of his colleagues, maybe smarting under his attempts at boisterous leadership during the strikes, there was too much tinsel. Lane-Fox in a letter to his Yorkshire neighbour Irwin, the Viceroy of India, called it 'a cheap jingle',[34] and L. S. Amery, true to his general attitude to Churchill, subsequently delivered a catalogue of complaint to Baldwin including a request for Churchill's removal from the Treasury.[35]

Churchill, well aware that this budget had little substance to it, already before the Finance Bill was law by the end of July had begun to cast his mind forward to the 1928 and indeed 1929 budgets, which it was assumed would fall within the parliament and within his Chancellorship, although they would obviously be the last two within the former and probably the latter as well. He was eager to make as big a splash as possible. In 1925 he had sought to mark a return to normality by a delayed removal of some of the burdens of direct taxation, the weight of which would never have been contemplated had not 1914 transformed the world of 1913. In 1926 and 1927 he had been heavily constrained by the threat or reality of industrial strife. Nineteen-twenty-eight was his first chance to make a cavalry advance across open country (he was always much given to thinking in such military metaphors), and he intended it to be a dashing and a massive one.

Following the return to Gold and in the aftermath of the strike the British economy was performing flaccidly. Churchill wanted to give some dramatic and wide-impacting stimulus to economic activity. The best route he could see was via a lightening of the burden of local rates – a tax upon real estate levied by the local authorities, town or county councils. This lightening was to be total in the case of agriculture, which was already 75 per cent favoured, and with a new relief of the same figure of 75 per cent for all industry, heavy or light, prosperous or failing, as well as for freight-carrying railways, canals, docks and harbours. This would require a *masse de manoeuvre* of approximately £30 million of central government money, a very big sum in relation to the budgetary aggregates of those days, and this he proposed to provide partly by enforcing economies upon the departments, particularly the Admiralty, and partly by a substantial new tax on petrol.

He saw this derating scheme as opening the way to a major reform of local government – certainly the most important since 1886, 'perhaps since 1834'. This was of course much more Neville Chamberlain's business than his own, but he was never a great respecter of departmental frontiers, and in any event hoped to make Chamberlain into an enthusiastic ally, which to some extent he did. The local government reorganization would gradually require finance beyond the £30 million, and it was therefore important to develop buoyant sources of revenue. Petrol taxation showed every sign of being this.

The scheme was obviously bold. It was also ingenious and to some substantial extent a product of his own fertile mind. The person with the best claim to be a co-parent was – surprisingly for the time – Harold Macmillan, who had made seminal suggestions along these lines to him about two years before. Churchill launched the internal consideration of his plans by firing off three major memoranda, one down, one up and one lateral. The downwards one went to A. W. Hurst, a then powerful Treasury official whose subsequent career did not match his promise. From him he demanded flesh for his bones. Two days later he addressed eleven pages to the Prime Minister. They were couched in terms of high political strategy. The government was becalmed, but with menace ahead. Only by seizing the initiative with his great scheme could the clouds be dispersed and the storms weathered: 'we have to

dominate events lest we be submerged by them'. The third memorandum, on the day after that, went to Neville Chamberlain, his most
important Cabinet ally and/or adversary. It was skilfully directed to the
strengthening of responsible and economical local government to which
the scheme could lead.

Having launched these three salvoes, Churchill then proceeded to
take a summer and autumn holiday the length of which exceeded even
one of Baldwin's Aix-les-Bains sojourns. He was effectively away from
the first week of August to the third week of October, mostly at
Chartwell. Both his pattern and purpose were the reverse of Baldwin's.
Baldwin went to Aix in order to cut himself off from his colleagues and
so far as he could shut political thoughts out of his mind. He made a
point of never reading a newspaper there. Churchill went to Chartwell
in order to lengthen the stride of his political work, but not greatly to
reduce its quantity, and, so far from shutting himself off, he persuaded
as many as possible of his colleagues and henchmen to visit him, to
receive his ever generous hospitality, to listen to his views and to watch
his manifold other activities, from painting to bricklaying.

He continued to push, with total determination, his derating scheme.
It was very much his own initiative. Treasury officials, apart from Hurst,
were to say the least cool. They would have preferred him to devote
any surplus which he could muster to debt reduction. He had some,
although not many, Cabinet allies and the general goodwill but not firm
commitment of the Prime Minister, who was still somewhat in thrall to
the force of Churchill's personality and also thought that the adventur-
ousness of the Chancellor's scheme might give a puff of revival to his
flagging government. But the exuberance of Churchill's undiscriminat-
ing attacks on the departmental estimates of his colleagues was not
calculated to make friends. 'No more airships, half the cavalry and only
one-third of the cruisers,' he wrote to his wife on 30 October (1927).
'Neville costing £2½ millions more and Lord 'Useless' Percy [Lord
Eustace Percy was President of the Board of Education] the same figure
and we are opening a heavy battery against them this week. It is really
intolerable the way these civil departments browse onwards like a horde
of injurious locusts. . . .'[36]

Much the most dangerous possible adversary was Neville Chamberlain, both because of his stubborn but impressive application to detail,
in direct contrast with the grand sweep of Churchill's style, and because
of his crucial departmental position. Chamberlain himself provided a
penetrating retrospective account of the struggle, as well as of his view

of Churchill, in a letter which he wrote to Irwin in India on 12 August 1928:

> When these proposals came to me I declared my approval of the principle that industry should be relieved of a part of its rates, but I strongly objected on Local Government grounds to any plan which completely severed all connection between industry and industrial interests and Local Government. It appeared to me to be most dangerous if a large part of the Community were given to understand that they were unaffected by any inefficiency, extravagance or corruption in Local Government. . . .
>
> Over this point we had numerous battles. I accused Winston of reckless advocacy of schemes the effects of which he himself did not understand. He accused me of pedantry and of personal jealousy of himself. At times feelings became rather acute. But I had one advantage over Winston of which he was painfully conscious. He could not do without me. Therefore in the end I was the sole judge of how far to go because whenever I put my foot down he was helpless. As a matter of fact I only put it down once and he gave way directly. But it was a very harassing time for me and to tell you the truth, Edward, Winston is a very interesting but d----d uncomfortable bed fellow. You never get a moment's rest and you never know at what point he'll break out. . . . In the consideration of affairs his decisions are never founded on exact knowledge, nor on careful prolonged considerations of the pros and cons. He seeks instinctively for the large and preferably the novel idea such as is capable of representation by the broadest brush. Whether the idea is practicable or impracticable, good or bad, provided he can see himself recommending it plausibly and success-fully to an enthusiastic audience, it commends itself to him.[37]

It was a perceptive description, even though obviously written with some bias, and it conveyed a good sense both of the strains of 1927–8 and of the reasons which in 1939 made Chamberlain so loath to take Churchill into his government until war had actually broken out. All winter long and into the early days of spring (1928) the noise of battle rolled, and the outcome was not wholly satisfactory to either side. Chamberlain got his way on preserving some financial link between industry and local government, and Churchill got his way, almost at the last moment, on extending derating to railways, to which Chamberlain and several others had been strongly opposed. The finally agreed scheme was sufficiently Churchill's own for him to be able to present it to Parliament with the flourish of a three-and-a-half-hour speech on 24 April. This fourth budget was again favourably received, although it and the preceding arguments had clearly drained the Chancellor's great but sometimes dramatically exhaustible reserves of energy to the limit, as was shown both by half an hour's suspension of the sitting (for the first time in a budget speech since Lloyd George's 1909 marathon), and by Churchill being struck down by a violent influenza four days later, which prevented his replying to the budget debate and which not only kept him in bed for more than a week but also required nearly a month of full convalescence. He was back however for the Finance Bill, which proved complicated to get through, and did not become law until 3 August.

There remained the 1929 budget. Churchill was unusual in getting through to a fifth budget. Only four previous Chancellors had attained such persistence. And he determined that, whatever the future held, he would make the most of the last scene of this act. He did not have much new to announce, not surprisingly after the major change of 1928. He abolished his own unsuccessful betting tax of 1926, he brought forward full agricultural derating by six months (in the hope no doubt of encouraging grateful farmers to rush to the polls), and to underpin his 'friend of the people' credentials he got rid of the tea duty, but only as it turned out for a couple of years.

This paucity of changes did not prevent him from delivering the most polemical of all his budget speeches. It lasted three hours, with no break. He filled out the time by a sweeping if tendentious survey of his whole record since 1924, accompanied by denunciations of both the Labour and the Liberal proposals for the next parliament. It was bricks without much straw. But it stimulated the normally flat and restrained chroniclers of British budgets (Mallet and George) to refer to its 'scintillating rhetoric' and the *Sunday Times* to call it 'the most brilliantly entertaining of modern Budget speeches'. So he concluded on a high note. But neither his new party's position with the electorate nor his own position within his party had much underlying security. As a result that fifth budget speech was his last government front-bench appearance in the House of Commons for nearly ten and a half years. It was a much longer wilderness period than that which either the Dardanelles or Dundee had inflicted upon him.

22

A RELENTLESS WRITER

WITH A MORE vigorous Prime Minister than Baldwin Churchill would probably have been reshuffled out of the Treasury before the 1929 election. The view of his old schoolfellow Amery that his replacement by Neville Chamberlain 'would be worth twenty or thirty seats at least'[1] may be discounted on the grounds of settled animus plus Amery's obsessive interest in getting a Baldwin manifesto commitment to general Protection, to which he saw Churchill as a major obstacle. But the view that it was time for a Treasury change was much more widespread than Amery, and embraced Chamberlain himself, Baldwin's close friends Davidson and Bridgeman, and to some extent even the Prime Minister.

Without a full acceptance of Amery's electoral arithmetic there was a feeling that, with the glamour of Churchill's coruscating phrases, both in memoranda and on his feet, beginning to wear off, he had been at the Treasury long enough, and that if he were allowed to stay he might be building up an unwelcome claim to be Baldwin's natural successor. Furthermore he had ruffled too many ministerial feathers by his aggressive Exchequer-centric assaults on everybody's estimates, civil and military. The previous July, for instance, he had played a major role, against the views of such a venerable figure as Arthur Balfour, in getting reaffirmed the 'ten-year rule', under which defence planning proceeded on the basis that no major war was threatened within ten years. Germany was of course still the Germany of the Weimar Republic and on a strict time chart ten years did not expire until July 1938, two months before Munich. It was nonetheless an ironical position for the alarm-bell of the 1930s to have taken up.

There was no serious suggestion that Churchill should be dropped from the government. He was too good a trumpet and too dangerous an adversary for that to be mooted. It was a shift to an equal or almost equal position which was under consideration. Probably the most canvassed idea was that he should become Secretary of State for India, but the Viceroy (and Irwin was always very influential with Baldwin) poured tepid water on this, which was probably as well in view of the deeply obscurantist position on India to which Churchill devoted most of the five years after the fall of that government. The Foreign Office was also a possibility. Clementine Churchill in a remarkable but undated letter of this period wrote to her husband of the need for a replacement for Austen Chamberlain, who was 'just an animated cardboard marionette' (a bit hard, although as some photographs show, it was not an ill-directed shaft). But, in what the future made a great irony, she continued, 'I am afraid your known hostility for America might stand in the way.'[2]

In the event Baldwin's indolence avoided all these awkward choices. He lacked the energy to do a major reshuffle before the 1929 election, and after it he lacked the power. On 30 May the Conservatives lost 150 seats and became for the first time a smaller parliamentary party than Labour. They had in fact polled 300,000 more votes, but the British electoral system was happy to override, one way or the other, such tiresome logicalities and produced a House of Commons of 289 Labour members, 260 Conservatives and 58 Liberals. The position was much clearer cut than after the 1923 election. Labour, although still without a majority, was clearly entitled to govern and Baldwin resigned immediately. Ramsey MacDonald became Prime Minister for the second time.

This result, in view of many of his previous private comments, cannot have been a shock to Churchill. Epping was adequately safe, although giving him a majority of only 4,000 over a Liberal. He spent the night of the poll declarations not there but in Downing Street, in a joint wake (as it turned out) with Baldwin. Tom Jones wrote a famous description of his typically pugnacious partisanship:

> At one desk sat Winston ... doing lists in red ink, sipping whisky and soda, getting redder and redder, rising and going out to glare at the [tape] machine himself, hunching his shoulders, bowing his head like a bull about to charge. As Labour gain after Labour gain was announced, Winston became more and more flushed with anger, left his seat and confronted the machine in the passage; with his shoulders hunched he glared at the figures, tore the sheets and behaved as though if any more Labour gains came along he would smash the whole apparatus. His ejaculations to the surrounding staff were quite unprintable.[3]

However truculent was Churchill's attitude to the unfortunate messenger in the shape of the teleprinter, he had less underlying reason to regret the loss of office than most of his colleagues. At the lower level this was because it removed from him the threat of a ministerial demotion. At the middle level it was because, still aged only fifty-four, and having at least survived four and a half years in the central department of government on top of his unique experience of six other departments, he could without undue bombast feel that as a hinge between the past and the future he was better placed than any other British politician. Furthermore, having safely passed his father's age and having got over his premonitions of early death, he could reasonably feel that he still had an expanding field of political activity ahead of him. (Leaving the Treasury in early middle age can be deceptive from this point of view.)

Above all, however, it was because he had so many more non-political resources and activities than almost any other major figure since Gladstone. It was amazing how much extracurricular work he had been able to get through even during his Chancellorship. When he took that office the first volume of *The World Crisis* dealing with 1911–14 had already been published, work was complete on volume two dealing with the year 1915, and was far advanced on volume three, dealing with 1916–18. This was divided into two short parts and came out in early 1927. The finishing touches and proof checking of this volume he had done in office, and against all the distractions of the Treasury and the Cabinet he had composed the 450 pages of the fifth separate book of *The World Crisis*, entitled *The Aftermath* which carried the story through from the Armistice to the Chanak incident with Turkey of September 1922. This was published in March 1929, just before his fifth budget.

As though this was not enough he had started, as soon as the first draft of *The Aftermath* was complete, on a much lighter, more ironic work of autobiography which became entitled *My Early Life*. Many consider this to be Churchill's best book, and some would put it as one of the outstanding works of the twentieth century. It covered, with a much greater economy of words than was his habit, his career from birth to his separation from the Conservative party in 1902–3. What most distinguished the book was that it was designed not to prove a point or to advance a theory but to entertain. In consequence there disappeared the somewhat portentous and tendentiously partial citation of documents, which, even though interspersed by pages of sparkling description and polemic, somewhat marred both *The World Crisis* and (twenty years later) *The Second World War*. They were replaced by a most agreeable mockery of himself and of others with whom he came into contact.

Just as finishing *The Aftermath* much occupied him during his eleven-week semi-holiday in the long recess of 1927, so did *My Early Life* in the late summer of 1928. On 2 September of that year he wrote to Baldwin: 'I have had a delightful month – building a cottage & dictating a book: 200 bricks & 2000 words per day.'[4] It was an output which should have satisfied anyone, particularly as these were not the limit of his 'leisure' activities. He was painting hard, and in the previous year, true to his recipe of always going to the top for advice, he had got Walter Sickert down to Chartwell to advise him upon his technique.

My Early Life was published in October 1930 by Thornton Butterworth, who were in that period Churchill's regular London publishers. They had done all the volumes of *The World Crisis* and they were to do three other books of his (although not the four volumes on his great ancestor the first Duke of Marlborough) up to 1938, when they unfortunately went into liquidation. There is no evidence that Churchill's terms, although stringently negotiated and favourable to the author, contributed significantly to this fate. His advances were moderate (£2,000 or £2,500 for each of the volumes of *The World Crisis* – the equivalent of £60,000 to £75,000 today) but his royalty rate was high, and his sales were solid rather than sensational. *My Early Life* eventually sold 11,200 of the first edition in England and 6,600 in America. And his books, even before his 1940s apotheosis, had good follow-through value. *My Early Life* was translated into thirteen languages, and eventually was also sold for a film script, although that was not until 1960.

In New York Charles Scribner's Sons supplemented Thornton Butterworth in London. True to a frequent American habit they changed the London titles. *My Early Life* became *A Roving Commission*, and a book of essays which Churchill published in 1932 was transformed from *Thoughts and Adventures* into *Amid These Storms* – it may be thought that neither title for his latter book was inspired. Scribner's did not at this stage do well out of Churchill. One volume of *The World Crisis*, for instance, sold only a thousand copies in America. But he had no difficulty in getting almost everything he wrote published in New York as well as in London, and eventually of course his American sales yielded vast royalties for himself and vast profits for his publishers – although they were not then Scribner's.

Once out of government in the first days of June (1929) Churchill applied his full energy first to making contractual arrangements for his next wave of writing (that is post *The Aftermath* and *My Early Life*), and then to getting it done. His central project was to be his life of Marlborough, which he began by envisaging as a one- or at most two-volume work of between 180,000 and 250,000 words. He acted as his own agent, for although the firm of A. P. Watt came into the picture at one stage he firmly dismissed them, saying that he had got a much better offer on his own than the £6,000 advance which they relayed from Hodder & Stoughton. This was a £10,000 advance for British and Commonwealth rights from Geo. Harrap & Sons. Thornton Butterworth were granted a month's stay of execution to see if they could match this, but they failed, and that firm and Churchill went into a period of temporary and reasonably amicable separation. He supplemented Harrap's £10,000 with £5,000 from Scribner's for the American rights and another £5,000 for the serial rights, negotiated direct with Lord Camrose, the proprietor of the *Daily Telegraph*, after *The Times*, which had paid this sum for *The World Crisis*, declined to repeat the offer.*

Churchill also took on, specifically for Marlborough, a young Oxford graduate named Maurice Ashley, who subsequently himself became a considerable seventeenth-century historian and biographer, including, curiously, publishing his own life of Marlborough in 1939. He worked half time for Churchill until 1933 at a salary of £300 a year. Churchill got him going during July, compiling with him a long list of books they would require and taking him to Blenheim for a night to familiarize him with the muniment room there. All this, and also a good deal of negotiation about several series of articles, kept Churchill busy for the short two months before the end of the parliamentary session of 1929.

His preoccupations were increased by Clementine having to undergo a nasty tonsils operation on 4 July and, once they had vacated 11 Downing Street, their having nowhere to live in London. They had Chartwell of course, and they occasionally perched at Philip Sassoon's house at 25 Park Lane. And for the slightly longer term they arranged to rent for November and December Venetia Montagu's house in Onslow Gardens, South Kensington. Churchill also managed to fit in a minimum of strictly political and parliamentary commitments, carrying on some perfectly friendly correspondence with Baldwin and even delivering one or two somewhat perfunctory Commons speeches. He

---

* It is, I think, appropriate to multiply all sums relating to the sale of books and articles in this period by a factor of thirty. Eventually all four volumes of Marlborough were serialized not in the *Daily Telegraph* but in the *Sunday Times*, then quite separate from *The Times*, and owned by Camrose; it did not pass to the proprietorship of Lord Kelmsley, Camrose's brother, until 1937.

was still a member of the 'shadow Cabinet', although that was a less formalized body than it has since become.

On 3 August he sailed from Southampton for a major three-month North America visit. His party consisted of his son Randolph, his brother Jack and Jack's son, known as Johnnie. Both Johnnie and Randolph were Oxford undergraduates. The firm intention was for Clementine to be of the party, but slow recovery from her operation made this impossible – as a result the long visit yielded a rich haul of marital correspondence.

Throughout they travelled *en prince*. On the *Empress of Australia*, which took them to Quebec City, Churchill had a grand cabin suite which encouraged him to write two major articles (one the portrait of John Morley which eventually found its way into *Great Contemporaries* (1937), a series of 4,000- or 5,000-word profiles). He also did a lot of preliminary reading for *Marlborough*. Altogether it was a calm and agreeable six-day voyage, although Churchill got very agitated about the news that Arthur Henderson, the new Foreign Secretary, was dismissing Lord Lloyd, the High Commissioner in Egypt, 'a prancing pro-consul' (to revive William Harcourt's good phrase of the early 1880s) if ever there was one. Randolph Churchill's diary entry for 7 August showed how at eighteen he had in him the makings of a great journalist, even if not of a great statesman: 'In the evening a concert. Bad. Papa had to preside. Made quite a speech. Met attractive Canadian girl. Hope tomorrow to see an iceberg. . . . PS. Papa called the company at dinner several times to bear record that soon there would be grave trouble in Egypt. He seemed very upset about this, but some 1865 brandy cheered him up.'[5]

Churchill was wrong on the personal Lloyd issue, for Lloyd had undoubtedly been behaving in a far more imperialist way than government policy justified, and Henderson had shown not a difference of desire from Austen Chamberlain, merely an ability to act more decisively than his predecessor. It marked the beginning of Churchill's swing to the far right on imperial policy, with much of his political energy in the next four years devoted to opposing the modest advance towards Indian self-government contained in what became the India Act of 1935.

He still remained true to his old Free Trade Liberal beliefs, which he was unwilling to modify in order to give preferential tariff treatment to the British Dominions. The tranquillity of the voyage was somewhat marred by the presence on board of that frequently turning-up 'bad penny' and old schoolfellow L. S. Amery, who was a passionate believer in Imperial Preference. There was a joint dinner and major argument on 4 August with Churchill, in Amery's very partial account, 'just repeat[ing] the old phrases of 1903'. This at least had the advantage of Amery confiding to his diary an interesting account of Churchill's current general state of mind:

> He was very friendly about it [the Free Trade–Protection argument], and only said that if I got my way he would retire from politics and devote himself to making money. He had been all that he wanted to be short of the highest post which he saw no prospect of, and anyhow politics were not what they had been. The level was lower; there no longer were great men like Gladstone or Salisbury or Morley or even Harcourt and Hicks Beach.[6]

After disembarking at Quebec, the Churchill party proceeded to a leisurely great-circle tour of Canada and the United States, and did it in very comfortable circumstances. The Canadian Pacific Railway took them in hand and provided a special saloon coach for the various stages of their journey across Canada. This aroused unusual enthusiasm in Churchill, who tended to assume luxury. 'The car is a wonderful habitation,' he wrote to Clementine on 12 August. 'Jack and I have large cabins with big double beds and private bath rooms. Randolph and Johnnie have something like an ordinary sleeping car compartment. There is a fine parlour with an observation room at the end and a large dining room which I use as the office and in which I am now dictating together with kitchen and quarters for the staff.'[7] (The staff included a shorthand-writing travelling secretary, with whom, showing high sensitivity to his needs and habits, the company had also provided him.) As the CPR were additionally to put him up in the green-roofed hotels which punctuated their line across the continent, he was able to write with satisfaction at Banff Springs, just into the Rockies from the eastern side, in a passage of general financial reassurance: 'Since we left Quebec till now (a fortnight) we have had no expense of any kind.' In return he had to make eleven speeches of varying degrees of weight and audience size.

This letter to Clementine (of 27 August) also expressed much enthusiasm for Canada and confirmed (and took a little further) Amery's diary impression of his very conditional attachment to politics:

> I have been wonderfully received in Canada. Never in my whole life have I been welcomed with so much genuine interest & admiration as throughout this vast country. . . .

Darling I am greatly attracted to this country. Immense developments are going forward. There are fortunes to be made in many directions. The tide is flowing strongly. I have made up my mind that if N.Ch. [Neville Chamberlain] is made leader of the C.P. [Conservative Party] or anyone else of that kind, I clear out of politics & see if I cannot make you & the kittens a little more comfortable before I die. Only one goal still attracts me, & if that were barred I shd quit the dreary field for pastures new. . . . However the time to take decision is not yet.[8]

Whether this threat of sloughing off British politics and seeking a new life and fortune in Canada was serious is doubtful. But it was something with which he played in a mixture of the gloomy prospect of 'N.Ch.' and the sparkling air in the neighbourhood of Lake Louise.

After twenty-six days on Canadian soil he turned south and crossed into the United States. Another twenty days were spent in California, then a state much more hidden to English eyes, except through the movies, than today, and with a population of barely four million. There he passed through San Francisco to perform what seemed the near miracle of speaking by telephone to Clementine at Chartwell, spent five days in Los Angeles with a lot of film-studio visiting and laying the foundations of an intermittent friendly acquaintance with Charlie Chaplin, before staying first with the newspaper magnate William Randolph Hearst in his hill-top extravaganza at San Simeon and then with William McAdoo, Woodrow Wilson's son-in-law and Secretary of the Treasury, at Santa Barbara.

From Santa Barbara he wrote to Clementine on 19 September a more detailed and, as it turned out, grossly over-optimistic but nonetheless from several points of view highly informative account of what he saw as their financial position and his work schedule. After asking her to engage extra servants for the house rented from Mrs Montagu, he continued:

Now my darling* I must tell you that vy gt & extraordinary good fortune has attended me lately in finances. Sir Harry McGowan [chairman of Imperial Chemical Industries and a very respectable businessman] asked me – rather earnestly – before I sailed whether he might if an opportunity came buy shares on my account without previous consultation. . . . he operated on about ten times my usual scale, & as I told you made a profit

---

* Although there is no reason to doubt that this affectionate expression was heartfelt and used in other contexts too, it is difficult not to be struck by the fact that it was peculiarly likely to occur as a preface to a passage designed to still her doubts about financial improvidence.

on our joint account of £2,000. . . . With my approval he reinvested this
. . . & sold at a further profit of £3,000. He thus has £5,000 in hand on
my account, & as he has profound sources of information about this vast
American market, something else may crop up. Since I left office the
following have come to hand as the profits of fortune & labour:-

Advance on £20,000 Marlborough	£6,000
Profits by American investment	
before sailing	£1,300
since sailing	£900
McGowan's profits	£5,000
Rise of Sherwoods from 17/6 to 22/6	£2,000
Article for *Answers*	£225
Article for Jewish Paper*	£300
3 articles on Rosebery, Morley & Trotsky for Nash[†]	£1,350
Butterworth advance payment on Royalties due Oct. 30[‡]	£1,700
Contract for articles on American tour (not yet done)[§]	£2,750
Proposed address to Economic Club of Worcester, Massachusetts	£300
	£21,825

. . . there is money enough to make us comfortable & well-mounted in
London this autumn. . . .[9]

So indeed there would have been had this highly tendentious schedule, a muddle between capital and income, a mixture of scoring for work
not yet done and assuming that a period of exceptional stock-markets
bubble was likely to continue indefinitely, been a stringently accurate
snapshot of what his annual income in opposition was likely to be.
As only three and a half months had passed since he had left office, it
suggested that a combination of his literary earnings and capital gains
was running at a rate of nearly £80,000 (£2.4 million using the factor of

* Written for the New York *Zionist Record* and republished in the London *Sunday
Times*.
† These were in the series already mentioned in connection with his shipboard writing
of the Morley one. They were for the *Pall Mall* magazine, owned by Nash. Rosebery
(done before the North American visit) was published in that October, Morley in
November, Trotsky (much less good) in December, and in early 1930 one on the Earl
of Ypres (formerly Field Marshal French) in January, and one on Joseph Chamberlain
in February. The last three were written after his return to England.
‡ On *The Aftermath*.
§ This related to an arrangement for twelve *Daily Telegraph* articles, which he also placed
in an American magazine, about the insights gained on his tour.

thirty) a year. Few accountants would have been willing to give this schedule a certificate of audit, and Churchill himself would certainly not have dared to look after the nation's finances with the same creative accounting that he applied to his own. There is however plenty of evidence that provident Chancellors from Pitt to Asquith, and there have been one or two subsequent examples as well, do not always apply the same care to their own finances.

Nemesis was close at hand. He spent a couple of early October weeks in Washington, partly to visit Civil War battlefields and partly to see President Hoover, the great apostle of the ever benevolent effects of free markets.* He returned to New York on 24 October, the day when Wall Street gave a fearsome preliminary shudder. Five days later the great crash began in earnest. Churchill claimed to have witnessed an early example of one of the fabled financial suicides, a body hurtling down past his window from a fifteenth floor. Such self-destructive pessimism (despite his 'black dog' periods of intermittent depression) was not in his nature, but he was nevertheless a severe casualty of the market collapse. His financial optimism was fatally punctured. He had speculated heavily and lost about half a million pounds at present-day prices. He was both impoverished and on the edge of not being able to meet his obligations. His writing for a time became more a treadmill of expiation than a joyful expansion of resources. He returned to London on 5 November, not in the glow of home-coming exhilaration to which he had been looking forward, but with his tail between his legs, and having to confess to Clementine at Waterloo Station that his financial optimism had been totally undermined.

However, once he had got the bad news off his chest, he reacted, true to his normal form, by indulging in a frenzy of profitable writing projects rather than by sinking into despondency. There were some economies. His daughter Mary wrote in one of the linking passages in her edited volume of her parents' correspondence: 'That winter of 1929 Chartwell was run down to a low ebb: the big house was dust-sheeted, only the study being left open so that Winston could work there. The charming small house, Wellstreet Cottage (which he had been building and which had been intended for a butler) now became our "slump" haven. . . . I remember it all being very cosy.'[10] On the other hand the

---

* He failed however to make what would have been a more useful contact with the Governor of New York State, Franklin D. Roosevelt, who could not be in New York City on Churchill's available dates.

Churchills continued to take quite grand houses in London on short
lets. For the first half of 1930 they rented Edward Grigg's house at
113 Eaton Square, although they also at this time sometimes confined
themselves to staying for a few nights in the discreet comfort of the
Goring Hotel, off Victoria Square. They did not acquire a London base
of their own until late 1932, and then it was only a relatively modest
duplex at the top of a block in the purlieus of Westminster Cathedral
(11 Morpeth Mansions).

Meanwhile his writing activities became so multifarious that there is
some problem in disentangling them from each other. Before he left
New York he had arranged to write six articles for *Colliers Weekly* and
another six for the *Saturday Evening Post*. These two magazines were
then very much the staple diet of suburban and rural America. Both of
these series were distinct from the twelve much shorter articles for the
Daily Telegraph, which had additionally been placed in the United States.
By early January 1930 he had written two of the *Colliers* articles about
what he rightly saw as the hidden topic (to English and American
readers) of the war of the Eastern Front in 1914–17. These inspired
him to think that the subject might make a sixth volume to the five of
The World Crisis already published. He wrote to Thornton Butterworth
on 12 January: 'While I have not made up my mind whether I can fit
this in with all my other work, I am at present quite favourably disposed
to the idea. . . . I might be able by considerable exertions to complete
this work in the summer and autumn of the present year in time for a
January [1931] publication. Naturally I come to you first.'[11] Butterworth
agreed, though he still had *My Early Life* to bring out and knew that
Churchill had gone elsewhere with the contract for *Marlborough*. *The
Eastern Front*, although a little late on Churchill's optimistic schedule,
was written with remarkable expedition. The advance was £2,500 and
the initial burst of sales (that is up to the end of the year) amounted to
4,768, which meant that Churchill would not quite have earned his
advance, but that the publisher would probably have made a modest
profit.

On 22 February he wrote to propose the same work to Charles
Scribner's in New York. Here he had to deal with a slightly different
problem, which was that Scribner's were not only contracted, like
Thornton Butterworth, to *My Early Life* but also, unlike Butterworths,
to *Marlborough*. This he endeavoured to deal with (and clearly did so
successfully, for Scribner's accepted *The Eastern Front*) by writing: 'The
preparation of this volume will not in any way conflict with or delay the

"Marlborough" book, on which work is steadily proceeding and which forms the staple of my reading.'[12] He had already told Scribner's that he had engaged 'a very able officer* at a salary of £500 to prepare the military part of the material' (for *The Eastern Front*) and that he was also getting a lot of assistance from General James Edmunds, the official war historian.

As, in addition to Maurice Ashley, who was proving a highly satisfactory research assistant on *Marlborough*, Churchill had taken on both Rear Admiral Kenneth Dewar (just retired from the navy) and a younger naval historian (Commander J. H. Owen) to provide material on the naval war under Queen Anne, the question arises whether he was not running more of a cottage literary industry (and quite a big cottage) rather than performing the lonely task of setting a pen to a bare sheet of paper which is normally the test of the writer of quality.

The charge in its most literal sense is irrefutable. From at least this stage onwards Churchill never wrote out a book *de novo*. He depended on having his factual material not merely checked after he had written it, but as carefully prepared for him in advance as was the laying out of the instruments for a famous surgeon. When he transformed the basic material, by adding insights, comparisons, metaphors and flights of oratorical fancy, he mostly did so by dictation, normally the enemy of succinctness, and not by pen. Sometimes, as with many articles and with *My Early Life*, he would dictate the whole draft out of his head, and then very carefully correct it.

He also acquired the odd habit of being unable to envisage the shape of a book without having it set up in printed proof at an early stage, and then hacking it about in a way that a modern publisher would regard as intolerably inflating his printing budget. Thus when, in February 1930, he was proposing to add about 40,000 new words to the 50,000 or more of *My Early Life* which he had already written (the number of literary balls he had in the air at that stage is staggering), he insisted that, at his own expense if necessary, the already written text must be set up in print – 'until I see the existing material in type I cannot make progress'.[13] Associated with this was his increasing desire to work standing up, for which purpose he acquired a sloping desk of appropriate height at the side of his Chartwell study. He needed the feel and look of printed proofs for his literary teeth, but he rarely worked at them seated at a writing table. It was nearly all done either upright or in bed.

---

* Lieutenant-Colonel (ret.) Charles Hordern, Royal Engineers.

Yet, in spite of his growing need for others to prepare the way for
him, it is impossible to regard his books (or most of his articles) as
factory products. They bear the indelible stamp of his idiosyncratic
style. Insofar as he was producing finishing touches rather than working
single-handedly at the raw material, the personal value added was
nonetheless immense and unmistakable. The disadvantage of this
method of work was that researchers naturally tend to provide exhaus-
tive material and that Churchill himself often added volume as well as
value. The result was that many of his books put one in mind of the
famous apology for excessive length: 'I am sorry this letter is so long;
I did not have time to make it shorter.' Thus the five volumes of *The
World Crisis* (without appendices or the semi-detached *Eastern Front*
sixth volume) amounted to 2,300 pages and little under a million words.
Marlborough, in its eventual four volumes, was almost exactly the same,
both in pages and words. So much for his original estimate of a work of
180,000 to 250,000 words. And then in the six volumes of *The Second
World War* the cup was even more abundantly to overflow. That ran to
3,600 pages and nearly 1.4 million words. No one could ever have
accused Churchill of giving short measure. The danger rather was that
he put in so much that, even if, particularly in the last case, his sales did
not suffer, he became more bought than read. That is one reason why
his more taut and personal works, most notably *My Early Life* but also
Great Contemporaries and *Painting as a Pastime* (1948) are like draughts
of clear spring water.

Nevertheless the energy and the power of literary organization with
which he marshalled the various building blocks that kept his manifold
writing enterprises moving along in a reasonably orderly way demand
the highest admiration. Occasionally some of his article projects foundered, partly because he had negotiated deals for subjects which were
too close together with different editors or proprietors who were
competitive with each other. Thus his arrangement with the *Saturday
Evening Post* did not survive when they discovered that he was hoping
to interleave his articles for them with contributions to *Colliers Weekly*.

His books however turned up in good order and with remarkable
punctuality. *My Early Life* appeared on 20 October (1930) and sold
around 10,000 copies by Christmas. It was received with considerable
contemporary acclaim as well as being the foundation of many subsequent editions and the gradual achievement of a reputation as a minor
classic. Churchill pursued his habit of a wide distribution to friends and
political colleagues. Some, as is often the way, took the easy precaution

of thanking him before they had read the book, but he nonetheless got letters of substance and enthusiasm from a fine spread which included Baldwin (who had read it in proof and was particularly warm), General Sir Binden Blood, G. M. Trevelyan, Austen Chamberlain, Robert Somervell (who first aroused his interest in English prose), Lady Lytton (his old rather slow-burning flame), Samuel Hoare (with whom he was soon to be locked in bitter dispute on the India Bill), Bishop Welldon (his old headmaster, who regretted that, as the book made only too clear, he had not been able to make him happier at Harrow), T. E. Lawrence, General Sir Ian Hamilton (who remained a friend, although they had neither of them done each other very well in the Dardanelles) and General Sir Reggie Barnes (with whom he had first been under fire in Cuba thirty-four years before).

The Eastern Front came out in November 1931, following an abridged edition of the first four volumes of *The World Crisis*, which had required a good deal of Churchill work, in February of that year. Then, just to fill in the time as it were, he put together a collection of reminiscent essays entitled *Thoughts and Adventures*, which came out in November 1932. This book immediately sold 7,000 copies, which was good for such a collection, as well as leading to several subsequent editions and to translations into eight languages. The first volume of *Marlborough* followed in the autumn of 1933, the second in 1934, the third in 1936 and the fourth in 1938.

Furthermore he continued to act as essentially his own literary agent. This was even though a lady called Miss Pearn came into the picture at the beginning of 1930. She was in charge of newspaper rights at Curtis Brown, and was later one of the founders of the (in its day) famous literary agency of Pearn, Pollinger and Higham. She, a little confusingly, did a lot of correspondence with Mrs Pearman, who, for a decade beginning in 1929, was Churchill's principal and dedicated dictating and literary secretary. But he did major negotiations, for books and serial rights, both in Britain and America, for himself. This involved the dictating of long, complicated, often argumentative and self-promoting letters. It also involved receiving 'kicks as well as ha'pence'. He was frequently turned down. The serial rights of *The Eastern Front*, for instance, were rejected by *The Times* on the ground that 'our readers . . . are responding less and less to War History',[14] and had to be touted around several other newspapers. But he also received a great number of 'ha'pence'. For the financial year 1930–1 he pushed his total income up to approximately £35,000, the equivalent of at least a full million pounds today. But it was a high-geared enterprise, every possible source exploited to an extent which was far from easily renewable, and also with a lot of expenses, mainly on salaries, so that if there was any faltering the net position could deteriorate heavily. However, by this immensely hard-working and risk-taking strategy he succeeded in retrieving his financial position from the near disaster of October 1929, to reopen Chartwell and fully to resume his extravagant lifestyle.

The miracle was that, amid this frenzy of authorship and journalism, he managed to find any time at all for parliamentary, let alone constituency, politics. The latter he took surprisingly diligently by the standards of the time, addressing no fewer than eight public meetings in different parts of the Epping constituency during a (1929) mid-autumn ten days. It might have been better, at any rate for his short- to medium-term future, had he been more detached from the parliamentary scene. By not being entirely so he managed, during this year of vast earnings, to ensure that his 1924–9 chunk of high office, which had so gratified him, was to be his last until the threshold of his sixty-fifth birthday.

23

CUCKOO OUT OF THE NEST

CONSERVATIVE MORALE WAS low for most of the two and a quarter years of the second MacDonald government. It was as bad as after the even heavier defeat of 1906, worse than after the equally massive one of 1945, but not quite as devastatingly so as after 1997 and 2001. In 1929–31, except for self-inflicted wounds, which in politics are both the most frequent and the most painful, there was in reality little reason for dismay. The defeat of 1929 had been narrow, the Labour government, as was clear within six months, had inherited a horrible world economic prospect, and there seemed little reason to doubt that if the Conservative party kept calm it could glide back into office under Baldwin within a few years.

Many Conservatives, however, did not want to glide back into office under Baldwin. His previous administration, in Robert Rhodes James's well-chosen phrase, had 'drifted placidly into retirement'.[1] They wanted more excitement, and they wanted more extreme policies than 'Honest Stan' Baldwin, who believed in consensus, was willing to provide. The malcontents were greatly stirred up and assisted by the two middle-market press lords, Rothermere with his *Daily Mail* and associated papers and Beaverbrook with his *Daily Express* and much smaller newspaper empire, although this was partly balanced by Beaverbrook's greater political knowledge and experience, if nearly equal lack of judgement. To match the two press lords there were two issues to be exploited. The first, on which Beaverbrook was much the stronger, was the desire to commit the Conservative party to full-scale Imperial Preference, with all-round import duties including taxes on food, although mitigated for the Dominions, and sweetened by the hope that they in turn would give preferential entry to United Kingdom manufactures. The second was opposition to the policy of a gradual advance towards self-rule for India, supported by Ramsay MacDonald and his Secretary of State for India, Wedgwood Benn, by Irwin, still the Viceroy, by Baldwin and by Samuel Hoare, his Indian spokesman, as well as by most moderate Conservative opinion from *The Times* to Lord

Derby. Rothermere on this aspect of the extremist agenda was stronger than Beaverbrook.

Churchill's position was not clear cut. He had inherited something of Lord Randolph's 'instinctive rowdyism', although avoiding his sulky immaturity. Over the previous five years he had come considerably to like Baldwin, perhaps more than to respect him, but his taste in political climate was the reverse of that of his nominal leader. Baldwin liked quiet and calm water. Churchill liked the clashing noise of great storms. But on the subjects on which Baldwin was under attack Churchill was extremely moderate on one (Imperial Preference versus Free Trade) and immoderately extreme on the other (India). He first threatened to resign from the Conservative Business Committee, as the shadow Cabinet was then called, in October 1930 against a policy of limited Protection with which Baldwin, beset from both sides, had endeavoured to placate his party. Following a rough meeting of the Committee he dictated one of his famous 'not sent' letters to Baldwin. In it he accepted – a big move on his part – 'a general tariff on foreign, imported, manufactured articles'. But he baulked at food: 'I refuse categorically to seek a mandate from the electorate to impose taxes upon the staple foods of this overcrowded island.'[2] He had said much the same things at the meeting of the Committee, so that Baldwin wrote him a letter referring to 'a real parting of the ways'. The rest of Baldwin's letter was however couched in such emollient terms of friendship that Churchill resiled from his threat of resignation, which was nonetheless remembered against him in later skirmishes by other members of the Committee such as Neville Chamberlain.[3]

It might have been better had Churchill gone on this issue, which, although it had become essentially nostalgic for him, would at least have kept intact his reputation as a liberal Conservative and a man of the centre. Instead he chose to relieve the political frustration which was clearly pumping round in his veins by resigning three months later on the more immediately explosive issue of India. He had been growling about this ever since he got back from America in November 1929, most notably through the columns of the *Daily Mail*, but he did not speak on it in the House of Commons until 26 January 1931, although he had detonated a preliminary bombardment at the Cannon Street Hotel on 11 December (1930). This speech, designed to rouse the City, was 'admirable' according to the sponsors but 'monstrous' according to the Viceroy. His not very distinguished Commons speech of six weeks later had three effects. First, it definitely separated him from Baldwin.

And it did so at a time when Baldwin, in one of the most courageous episodes of his life, was determinedly facing a lot of internal Conservative party criticism to support his friend the Viceroy in a cautious advance towards Indian self-government. Separation in such circumstances inevitably leaves heavy scars on an embattled leader. Baldwin's affectionate admiration for Churchill, which had built up from 1924 onwards and which culminated in the friendly envy of *My Early Life* which he had expressed in the previous autumn, perished over India in the late winter and early spring of 1931. Of course in the long run Churchill's view of Baldwin had more historical impact, but in the context of the government reconstructions of 1931 and 1935, when Churchill deeply felt his exclusion from office, Baldwin's view of Churchill was not without significance.

Second, it threw Churchill into several exposed debating positions. On this first 26 January occasion, he was carved up by Wedgwood Benn, in general a much less effective parliamentarian than his son Tony Benn was to become. The sad fact was that India, which Churchill chose to make the focus of his political activity between 1931 and the first months of 1935, was a subject about which he knew little. He had never been there since his essentially polo-playing visit at the end of his time as a subaltern of Hussars in 1899. Nor was his degree of briefed information about the India of thirty years later as good as that which he normally sought and achieved before one of his major campaigns, whether it was that of Free Trade in 1904, or relative naval strength in 1911–14, or rating reform in 1927–8. When he appeared before the joint Select Committee of both Houses in 1933 'his lack of detailed knowledge of the subject', according to Rhodes James, 'was most painfully exposed'.[4] He was forced to resort to repetitive rhetoric before an audience to which it was singularly ill suited.

Third, it threw him into the arms of the 'diehard' wing of the Conservative party, with which neither his past nor his future made a suitable embracing partner. Baldwin's old friend, J. C. C. Davidson, who had been Chairman of the Conservative party from 1927 to 1929, wrote a very good comment on this reversal of alliances to Lord Irwin in Delhi on 6 March (1931). This was after a Churchill-led deputation from the party's Indian Committee had been to see Baldwin.

> Winston's game, of course, has been obvious, as it always is. He is not the son of Randolph for nothing. . . . How Stanley [Baldwin] must have chuckled to think that when the door opened and the India Committee

came in. . . . There he saw the same faces that time and again during the last Parliament had come to beg him to get rid of Winston from the Government and who have recently been acclaiming him as the heaven born leader of the Party – on, of course, only one subject, namely India.[5]

Churchill, on the contrary, was exhilarated by his new friends, and by a sense of commitment to politics which he had not felt since, at the latest, his last budget in the spring of 1929. He was working in close temporary alliance with Rothermere, whose political judgement was even worse than that of Beaverbrook, without the latter's balloon-pricking wit. Rothermere wrote to Churchill on 31 January, appropriately from the Riviera Palace Hotel, Monte Carlo: 'You have really got your foot on the ladder that quite soon leads to the Premiership. If you go unswervingly forward, nothing can stand in your way. The country is sick to death of the duds that surround their dud Conservative leader.'[6]

Churchill, who with thirty years of political experience ought to have known better, was taken in by this grossly optimistic flattery. He set himself vigorously to promote and lead a national campaign. Already by early Feburary he had reported to Rothermere, who had removed to the Royal Hotel, San Remo, on 'crowded and most enthusiastic meetings' in the two 'finest halls in Lancashire',[7] the Free Trade Hall in Manchester and the Philharmonic Hall in Liverpool. He moved on, first to a full meeting of his constituency association (in London) on 23 February, of which he wrote (to Clementine), 'I met the constituency in full force. . . . It was loving, ardent and unanimous.'[8] On this last occasion Churchill indulged in some unfortunately memorable remarks about Gandhi, whom the Viceroy had let out of gaol and with whom Irwin was engaging in a series of talks with a view to getting him to call off his campaign of non-violent disobedience. 'It is alarming and nauseating to see Mr Gandhi, a seditious Middle Temple lawyer, now posing as a fakir of a type well known in the East, striding half-naked up the steps of the Vice-regal palace . . . to parley on equal terms with the representative of the King–Emperor.'[9]

Then Churchill moved to a successful mass rally in the Albert Hall in mid-March, and a few days after that was writing, 'the next point of attack would, I think, be Glasgow'.[10] He had a good if somewhat traditional instinct for how to mount a Gladstone-style national campaign, although he was also alive to the growing medium of wireless and had a running battle over several years with the chairman and director general of the BBC about their unwillingness, no doubt under pressure from both the government and the official opposition whips, to allow him to broadcast on India. It is easy to understand that the excitement of a new campaign, great press coverage, especially in Rothermere's *Daily Mail*, new allies and packed enthusiastic audiences had an inspiriting effect upon him. What is more difficult to comprehend is why, when he was leading himself up one of the most futile (and four-year-long) blind alleys of modern British politics, he persuaded himself, with all his experience, that he was riding a winning wave.

Of this he undoubtedly did persuade himself – for a short time at least. Clementine had gone to America on 8 February – her first journey across the Atlantic – where she spent nearly two months with Randolph, who was finding the prolongation of a lecture tour more enjoyable and less intellectually demanding than Oxford, although he did eventually go back to Christ Church. Churchill wrote to her, on 20 February and again six days later, in a mood of almost foolish euphoria. First: 'Politics develop in an increasingly favourable manner for me . . .';[11] and then: 'It is astonishing looking back over the last six weeks what a change has been brought in my position. Every speech that I have made, and step that I have taken has been well received beyond all expectation. The turning points were the first Indian speech and my separation from the Shadow Cabinet. Anything may happen now if opinion has time to develop.' He did, however, have the sensible caution to add, whether he meant it or not: 'If not I shall be quite happy.'[12]

What is truly surprising, in view of her general forthrightness with him and stability of liberal good sense, is that Clementine did not try to resist this lurch to the right. No doubt the Atlantic was a formidable barrier to her understanding exactly what was happening (even though British news then got much more coverage in the American press than is the case today), but she had been in England for the first two weeks after his shadow Cabinet resignation and over his two major Manchester and Liverpool meetings. Furthermore she was good at calming rebuke by letter, as there are many examples to show. But all that she wrote back after his 26 February letter was 'I was so glad to get your dear letter. . . . It sent a warm thrill through my heart – I'm bird happy here, but I wish I was at your side to enjoy with you enjoying watching your Barometer steadily rise – I watch it all from here, every shoot up, every flicker. . . .'[13]

Churchill's deep involvement in his India campaign coincided with the most over-charged period of his writing commitments. This was particularly true in relation to article series, although *The Eastern Front*, still far from complete, was due to be delivered at the end of August. A lot of the articles were pure pot-boiling. He published one on Moses, for which he had required a good deal of help from the not obviously relevant hand of Professor Lindemann, in a series for the *Sunday Chronicle* entitled 'Great Bible Stories Retold by the World's Best Writers'. He was playing, again with Lindemann's help, on another series called 'If They Had Lived Long Ago'. He proposed to see Henry Ford in Cromwellian days, Mussolini as a vis-à-vis to Henry VIII, and Ramsay MacDonald in the French Revolution. Fortunately this group never saw the light of day, but a profile of the just-deposed King Alfonso XIII of Spain, which he composed for the joint outlets of the *Strand Magazine* and *Colliers Weekly*, was completed by the summer of 1931. In February of that year, desperately seeking the assistance of his Irish cousin, Shane Leslie, he launched into another series which in the context of his Indian campaign was, with an irony which he did not seem to notice, entitled 'Great Fighters in Lost Causes'.

What was most striking, however, was not the bizarre nature of some of the commissions which Churchill accepted, but his ability, interspersed with demanding political schedules and mind-distracting political disputes, to switch his attention and concentrate on disparate tasks. 'Politics are becoming very exacting,' he wrote to one of his *Marlborough* literary advisers on 13 March (1931).[14] But he never allowed politics to make him miss his deadlines. He had very good nerve, under the fire of guns and of politics. He even added marginally to the burden by persuading Thornton Butterworth to bring out (on 27 May) an edited version of seven of his Indian speeches. 'They are very good speeches,' he assured his publisher, 'and there is no repetition in them.' Then he rather surprisingly added: 'Of course I have taken much more trouble with them than with any book I have ever written.'[15] The little volume sold about 4,000 copies, which was quite good for a collection of speeches, and earned Churchill £150 minus £76 for excessive proof corrections.

These speeches were all powerful polemics, depending too much on the backward-looking argument that progress towards self-government would be bad for British trade which needed India as a captive market. (That was one reason why he started his campaign with the City of London and the two great Lancashire metropolises.) But they lacked his normal sparkle and memorability of phrase. It was as though he had taken on something of the sullen portentousness of his new friends. We have seen that on 26 January he was worsted in the House of Commons by 'little Benn', as the Secretary of State for India was often called. An even smaller man than Wedgwood Benn, in the shape of 'this particular small insect',[16] as Churchill amiably referred to Leo Amery in a contemporary letter, rebuked him mightily after his Albert Hall speech for his lack of Conservative credentials. But above all it was Baldwin who outshone Churchill in the early stages of the Indian dispute. No phrase of Churchill's, the great phrase-maker, except for the unfortunate one of 'the half-naked fakir', echoes down the decades, whereas several of Baldwin's quiet, ruminative, rather tentative speeches do precisely that.

Churchill in the early and heady days of his Indian campaign had substantially contributed by early March to the near destruction of Baldwin's leadership. It was on a knife-edge. But such destruction would not have availed him much had he succeeded. He would not have had a chance of himself becoming leader. Apart from the old adage that he who wields the dagger never gets the crown, he had far too many enemies within the Conservative party, and far too rickety a basis of support with his new-found diehard alliance. He would almost certainly have deposed Baldwin merely to make Neville Chamberlain king, with Chamberlain, at least until 1939, a man less sympathetic to him, on grounds both of policy and of personality, than was Baldwin.

In any event, Baldwin did not fall. As *The Times* wrote on 13 March (1931): 'It is one of Mr Baldwin's most unfailing characteristics that he never rises to the heights of which he is capable till the causes for which he stands seem almost desperate. His spiritual home is always the last ditch.' However, even before he got to that fosse he fought, on India at least, with a courage which was almost disdainful. To an extent unprecedented since the great 1886 Home Rule split in the Liberal party, and never quite to be seen again, even in the Labour party's public exhibition of its internal quarrels between Aneurin Bevan and Hugh Gaitskell towards the end of Attlee's leadership, the Conservative party fought out its quarrels on the floor of the House of Commons. The government party watched fascinated but hardly involved. As early as November 1929, Baldwin had there pronounced: 'I will only add that if ever the time comes when the party which I lead ceases to attract to itself men of the calibre of Edward Wood [Irwin, later Halifax, the Viceroy], then I have finished with my party.'[17] In March 1931, when Baldwin had almost decided that all was up, he rallied strongly, announced that he was prepared to resign his safe Worcestershire constituency and fight a pending bye-election in the St George's division of Westminster,

nearly as exposed a jousting ground as Churchill had chosen in the
Abbey division seven years before, and brought forward a critical Indian
debate to 12 March. Then he was even more forthright than sixteen
months before:

> If there are those in our party who approach this subject in a niggling
> grudging spirit, who would have to have forced out of their reluctant
> hands one concession after another, if they be a majority, in God's name
> let them choose a man to lead them. If they are in a minority, then let
> them at least refrain from throwing difficulties in the way of those who
> have undertaken an almost superhuman task, on the successful fulfilment
> of which depends the well being, the prosperity and the duration of the
> whole British Empire.[18]

In the event he did not have to fight St George's. Duff Cooper came
forth as a young champion on his behalf. But Baldwin threw himself
whole-heartedly into the campaign. On 17 March in the Queen's Hall
he delivered his famous 'power without responsibility – the prerogative
of the harlot' attack on the press lords. Polling day, which yielded a
substantial Duff Cooper–Baldwin, anti-press-lords and anti-Churchill
victory, was on 19 March. This rendered Churchill's Albert Hall rally
on the same evening, for all its good attendance and his bombinating
oratory, an anti-climax. The late winter and spring of 1931, despite his
temporary exhilaration, was far from Churchill's finest hour. It margin-
alized him for the political upheaval in the late summer of that year.
And, worse still, unlike the Abdication crisis five and a half years later,
which also damaged his mid-life reputation, it did not quickly come and
quickly go. The Indian issue remained at the centre of Churchill's
politics, draining his energies, leading him further into a miasma of
impotent isolation, for at least another three years.

August 1931 saw the death throes of the second Labour government,
and the re-emergence of Ramsay MacDonald as Prime Minister of a
'National' government, which soon became a predominately Conservative one. Only a tiny handful of Labour MPs followed their leader.
Churchill was curiously detached, even as a spectator. After his Indian-
campaign distractions of the late winter he was urgently trying to keep
up with his writing commitments and made much progress, particularly
with *The Eastern Front*. Almost his only intruding political engagement
before the parliamentary holidays was on 21 July when he motored into
Surrey suburbia accompanied by Brendan Bracken for a strange gathering of political plotters. This was held in Archibald Sinclair's house at

Coombe, near Kingston-on-Thames. Lloyd George was there and so was Oswald Mosley, accompanied by Harold Nicolson. 'Tom' Mosley was not then a fascist. If he had been, he would hardly have been accompanied by Nicolson, or supported by such left-wing figures as John Strachey and Aneurin Bevan. He was still an impatient radical populist, an under-educated (in spite of Winchester), charismatic young man in a hurry, of whom there were several examples in the politics of the twentieth century, most of them ending in failure but in less disgrace than Mosley. The object of the meeting, convened by Sinclair at Lloyd George's behest, was to set up an effective national opposition (which in Lloyd George's optimistic view would not long remain in opposition) to the National government of MacDonald and Baldwin, which, with considerable prescience, they saw coming.

Churchill was reported (by Nicolson) as being 'very brilliant and amusing but not constructive'. Nicolson added: 'We all part on the assumption that although nothing has been said, the Great Coalition has been formed.'[19] But it was not. Lloyd George retired to hospital for a major operation before the end of that July, and remained effectively out of action for the whole of the 1931 reorientation. And Churchill left at about the same time for a full month's holiday in France. Exceptionally he was accompanied by Clementine and stayed mostly in hotels rather than as a welcome guest in the luxurious (and free) villas of his friends. However, he began at St Georges-Motel, near Dreux on the southern edge of Normandy. This, in spite of its name, was not an early motor lodge, but a rose-red sixteenth-century château occupied by Consuelo Vanderbilt, former Duchess of Marlborough, and her much more satisfactory second husband, Jacques Balsan. It was a frequent Churchill refuge during the 1930s, and was indeed the place where he spent his last painting holiday before, on 23 August 1939, Europe closed in and he returned to England for six years of toil and triumph.

In 1931 it was an exception to his hotel tour. From there he went to the faded Edwardian glory of Biarritz, where, true to the Pays Basque August weather pattern, he reported on the 7th of that month, 'Here we have had no sun for a whole week. . . . I am tired of painting low tone pictures.'[20] From Biarritz he went to Carcassonne and then to Avignon, from where he returned to London for an uncovenanted forty-eight hours, before going back for a final Juan-les-Pins fortnight of writing, painting and, no doubt, more sun than at Biarritz. His pattern during that August of financial crisis was similar to that of his far from similar erstwhile colleague Stanley Baldwin, who appeared in London from France on 12 August and then was back across the Channel for another ten days on the same evening. Baldwin's addiction to holidays had more political effect than did Churchill's. In any event Churchill only took 'half-holidays' – with a lot of hard work always thrown in. 'I never have holidays,' he had stiffly informed Rothermere, at the height of their alliance, when that press lord had been importunate enough to telegraph that Churchill should 'chuck holidays and live laborious days'.[21] Baldwin's desire to be gone again left Neville Chamberlain in charge and able to force through the formation of the National coalition, which was much against Baldwin's interests (he would otherwise have been quite quickly Prime Minister again) and more than arguably against those of the country too, for it upset the new political balance to the building of which Baldwin had devoted great 1920s effort. This gave Labour a constitutional role as a party of occasional and weak government.

Churchill had devoted no such effort to fostering the constitutionalism of the Labour party. But insofar as he applied himself to the politics of August 1931 he was of the Baldwin rather than the Chamberlain school of thought. As that shadowy but not uninfluential ex-Chancellor Robert Horne wrote to Chamberlain on 18 August: 'There is a very definite body of Conservative opinion which would prefer us to take no responsibility whatsoever for Government plans. Winston Churchill, who came back last night for forty-eight hours, is aggressively of that view. This perhaps you would expect and discount.'[22]

It was discountable on the ground that Churchill knew he had no chance of being part of any coalition government which might emerge. At first there was room only for Baldwin, because he had survived as leader, for Neville Chamberlain, because he had been the helmsman of the boat which had crossed the dark and dangerous waters of inter-party co-operation, and for Samuel Hoare and Cunliffe-Lister because they had been helpfully present in London at the crucial time. Even when a more normal and much more Conservative Cabinet was constructed two months later there was no question of Churchill being asked to join. Much more 'loyal' figures such as Austen Chamberlain and the 'insect' Amery were also left out.

Churchill's mid-August visit to London was primarily literary rather than political. Reverting from the Goring Hotel to the Ritz (probably because Clementine was not with him) he arranged a levée of researchers, publishers and secretaries there for the morning of 18 August. It was indicative of the shift of his interests. In spite of the false euphoria of the early spring, politics was not working for him. Literature, or at least money-making writing and lecturing, looked a better prospect. In October he fought Epping and won it with a much increased majority – but so did every Conservative candidate in that landslide election of 1931. However his interest was more on the publication that autumn of *The Eastern Front* and on the major American lecture tour which, postponed for a couple of months by that general election, was due to begin in early December.

Accompanied by Clementine and their daughter Sarah, Churchill reached New York on 11 December, prepared for a forty-lecture tour, which was to bring him in at least £10,000, and maybe more, according to attendances. On the next evening he went to Worcester and in that not very distinguished mid-Massachusetts town delivered his first talk, entitled 'Pathway of the English-Speaking People'. The evening after that he was back in New York at the Waldorf-Astoria Hotel on Park Avenue and, after a quiet dinner with Clementine, responded to an invitation from Bernard Baruch to go and meet a few friends at his Fifth Avenue apartment a mile or so further up-town. He set out by cab, without the exact address, but apparently thinking that the driver would know how to find it. On this basis he would have been lucky in New York to have got to the Plaza Hotel, let alone a private residence. The result was an hour's frustrating search. Eventually he thought he saw a familiar doorway, stopped the taxi on the Central Park side and endeavoured to cross Fifth Avenue on foot. On the way he was knocked down by a car travelling at rather more than thirty miles an hour.*

His injuries were highly disagreeable without being destructive of either life or limb. 'Temperature 100.6. Pulse normal. Head scalp wound severe. Two cracked ribs. Simple slight pleural irritation of right

---

* I find confusing the Martin Gilbert account of the accident, admirably precise although Gilbert nearly always is. Fifth Avenue, unlike today, was then two-way. As he stopped the taxi on the park side, the adjacent traffic would have been going down, and if he looked left, as Gilbert says he mistakenly did, that would have been in the correct direction for the first stage of the crossing. Maybe he ought to have embraced both ways, for it was at the second stage that he was caught by a car (not a taxi, as has been commonly written) coming up-town. His fault must therefore have been that he did not look both ways, and cannot be too easily attributed to the perverse habit of the Americans of driving on the right. In any event he was nastily hit and gallantly maintained to the quickly arriving 'cop' that it was entirely his own fault. As a result his Italo-American accidental assailant, a temporarily unemployed truck driver, not only visited Churchill in hospital, but also attended, somewhat beyond the call of guilt or duty, Churchill's first lecture of his resumed tour, in Brooklyn on 28 January.

side. Generally much bruised. Progress satisfactory,' Clementine cabled to Randolph thirty-six hours later.[23] After a painful period of lying, conscious, in the roadway, he had been taken to the Lennox Hill Hospital, where he remained for eight days. Then he was allowed back to the Waldorf-Astoria, and stayed there, semi-bed-bound, over Christmas and until New Year's Eve, when he and Clementine went by ship to Nassau in the West Indies, where they remained for another three weeks of convalescence.* There his spirits collapsed. They had been very good in New York: 'Prepared two articles . . . upon how it seems to be run over by a motor car. . . . Have complete recollection of whole event & can produce literary gem about 2,400 words,' he cabled within sixty hours of the accident to Esmond Harmsworth,[24] to whom his father, Rothermere, had delegated almost complete control of the *Daily Mail.* But the over-admired and enervating climate of the West Indies, compared with the stimulation of a New York Advent and Christmas, no doubt combined with other factors to take its toll. 'I have not felt like opening the paint box' (a bad sign), he wrote to Randolph on 20 January 1932.[25] And Clementine had written poignantly, also to Randolph, a few days before: 'Last night he was very sad and said that he had now in the last 2 years had 3 very heavy blows. First the loss of all that money in the crash, then the loss of his political position in the Conservative Party and now this terrible physical injury. He said he did not think he would ever recover completely from the three events.'[26]

The lecture agency managed to reschedule about half his engagements, which he fulfilled until 11 March. He moved intensively around the North-East and the Middle West, but he did not go beyond Chicago. Clementine thought that he was well enough by mid-February for her to go home on her own. Churchill got back on 18 March, after his second three and a half months' absence in little over two years. And he was even contemplating, in an early-February letter to Robert Boothby, a five-week return visit in the summer to observe both the Republican and the Democratic Conventions in Chicago. There was no doubt that he had been deeply but benignly bitten by an American bug. As his ship, the *Majestic*, approached European waters, he was welcomed

---

* Partly at an historic and elegant guest house, known after its proprietress as Polly Leath's and then, after the arrival of the new Governor, Sir Bede Clifford, whose greatest claim to fame was the beauty of his three daughters (but they were not then out of their perambulators) at Government House.

by a message from Clementine which gave a prospect of a much better arrival than in 1929, when he had to confess his Wall Street losses:

> Great excitement here at your return. Am longing to see you. New car and lorry for luggage will be at Paddington 7 ock tomorrow waiting for you to wake up. [He must have landed at Plymouth and come to London by overnight sleeper.] Hot bath and breakfast will be ready at Chartwell. Please telegraph if this is what you would like. Jack [Churchill] and Mr Bracken coming Chartwell week-end. Tender love.[27]

A 'lorry' at Paddington seemed rather excessive even for Churchill baggage, but the 'new car' was intended to be a warming 'welcome home' gift, although a somewhat curious one in view of his New York vicissitude. It might have been thought better to turn his mind away from automobiles. However it was a handsome gift, a Daimler, costing £2,000 (£60,000 today). The present had been organized by the active and dedicated Bracken, although the donors were requested to send their cheques to the eminently respectable and cross-party Sir Archibald Sinclair, then Secretary of State for Scotland in the government from which Churchill was firmly excluded. The subscribing friends were reported to number 140, which would have given an average subscription of only £14 per head, and to have included Beaverbrook, Camrose, Esmond Harmsworth, Edward Grey, Charlie Chaplin, Ian Hamilton, Samuel Hoare, Robert Horne, Maynard Keynes, Harold Macmillan, the Prince of Wales, Lord Moyne, Louis Spears, Duff Cooper, Lord Riddell and the Duke of Westminster.[28]

Churchill's health misfortunes were not over with his recovery from his Fifth Avenue contretemps. Until he got back to England in the spring of 1932 he had been almost totally distracted from *Marlborough*, which should have been his main literary task. Maurice Ashley and Churchill's various other military and naval advisers had been working away, but Harraps and Scribner's had not signed valuable contracts to secure the notes of research assistants. Churchill had needed to give much reassurance that the full beam of his attention was about to be directed on to this project. So, after Easter 1932, it was. He worked hard that summer, and in late August, accompanied by Lindemann and an appropriate military retinue, he set off for a tour of the battlefields of 'John Duke', as he had taken to referring to Marlborough, from Flanders to Bavaria. In south Germany, which should have been one of the healthier places in the world, he developed paratyphoid fever, and had to retreat across the Austrian border to a Salzburg sanatorium for two weeks. Just as he had assured the New York police that it was his fault and not that of the assaulting driver that he had been run down, so he generously said that it was an English bug which he had brought with him rather than a German bug which had infected him. He got back to Chartwell on 25 September, still rather weak.

It had not been a brilliant ten years for his health. His acute appendicitis in 1922, his severe influenza after his 1928 budget, his New York accident and his Bavarian infection amounted to quite a battering between his forty-eighth and fifty-eighth years. But the afflictions were too disparate to make a pattern. Like many who achieved great longevity he was not particularly robust over the middle stretches. But he was at least as healthy and a good deal less valetudinarian than was Gladstone, his main prior rival in the Prime Ministerial old-age stakes. He was not to have much further health trouble until deep into the Second World War.

24

UNWISDOM IN THE WILDERNESS

AFTER HIS RETURN from America Churchill was still physically battered. It was indeed a remarkable feat of endurance on his part to have gone through the bulk of his lectures; 'eight nights of tour in a train and twenty-five harangues in a month were a rough kind of convalescence', he very reasonably wrote. He was a little sorry for himself. 'You have no idea what I have been through,' he informed his publisher.[1]

Nor was he politically inspirited. It was depressingly clear that he had no chance of returning to office under the existing political circumstances. And, as one of these circumstances was the biggest government majority ever seen in the House of Commons, this effectively sealed off the whole length of the still only six-months-old parliament. He therefore switched off most aspects of politics. The Ottawa Imperial Preference conference of August–September 1932, for instance, and the subsequent resignations from the government of Philip Snowden, Herbert Samuel and Churchill's old and devoted friend Archibald Sinclair seem to have made no significant impact on his consciousness, certainly not on his correspondence. Admittedly all this coincided with his paratyphoid, with his weakened return from his Salzburg sanatorium, and with a relapse at the end of September leading to his removal from Chartwell to a London nursing home. None of this, however, prevented his engaging in a fresh burst of literary negotiation, organization and even writing. Nor, unfortunately, did it dilute his energy for the one political cause – the dead end of trying to preserve the Raj of 1896 – which temporarily engaged his attention, though for far too long, indeed for nearly another three years until the early summer of 1935.

Churchill's writing projects over the summer and autumn of 1932 assumed an even more bewildering extravagance than in 1929–30. *The Eastern Front* had been published on 2 November 1931, and Thornton Butterworth wrote as early as the 19th: 'I am sorry to say that [it] has not done as well as we expected.'[2] Churchill thought it had been upstaged by Lord Crewe's pedestrian life of his father-in-law, Rosebery. However it is a useful reminder that Churchill at this stage in his life was more a relentless than a successful writer. Sometimes his sales were small (as a curious method of argument for a better royalty he had written to Thornton Butterworth in February 1931 saying that 'Messrs Scribner have lost money on every book except the last two they have produced for me'),[3] but his output was so great that the cumulative earnings, for him even more than for his publishers, was substantial.

Post *The Eastern Front* he had *Marlborough* looming. A lot of work had been done by his assistants, but he had had very little opportunity to apply his own varnish. Yet in June 1932, when he had written no more than one chapter which 'will be better written later on in the work', he was urging Harraps both to have it set up in type and to contemplate publication, if not in the spring of 1933, certainly in the autumn of that year. With much help he got on with that first volume of *Marlborough* with remarkable expedition, and published on time. But his roving eye (in a literary not a sexual sense, for he was probably the least dangerously sexed major politician on either side of the Atlantic, let alone across the Channel, since the Younger Pitt) could not be content with only one book every eighteen months. In that summer of 1932 he was toying, both in New York and London, with three books which might be described as in the category of 'cashing in on past efforts'. The first, which actually appeared in 1932, was *Thoughts and Adventures* (*Amid These Storms* in America). The second was to be called *American Impressions*, which never reached print on either side of the Atlantic. The third was *Notable Contemporaries*, as it was provisionally entitled at that time. At first he wanted to publish it before *Thoughts and Adventures*. But then he changed his mind, and *Great Contemporaries*, as it was retitled, did not appear until 1937.

In December 1932, there also began the chequered story of Churchill's *History of the English-Speaking Peoples*. Cassells offered him an advance of £20,000 (at least £600,000 today) for a 400,000-word work to which they recognized that he could not be expected to apply himself until the second half of the 1930s. It was an offer he could not refuse, as Thornton Butterworth sadly accepted when Churchill informed him of it. The work was in fact written on time, that is by 1939, but was then put into cold storage, first by the war and then by the priority which Churchill wished to be given to the many volumes of *The Second World War*, and did not appear until 1957. It was not one of his best literary productions.

Above all, however, it was his magazine article series in this period which left the baroque behind and passed to the rococo. Beyond 'Great Bible Stories Retold', 'If They Had Lived Long Ago' and 'Great Fighters in Lost Causes', he moved on to a series entitled 'Great Stories of the World Retold', commissioned by Lord Riddell for the *News of the World*. They were to be of about 5,000 words each, and the price Churchill asked for and got was £2,000 for the series. This sounds quite modest, although it should be remembered that this was the equivalent of a modern £10,000 for each article. And, as he got the ever faithful and highly literate Edward Marsh to write most of them for an 'honorarium' of £25 (£750) an article, it was a very good deal for Churchill. The subjects suggested by Riddell were Dumas' *Count of Monte Cristo*, Wilkie Collins's *Moonstone*, Rider Haggard's *She*, Lew Wallace's *Ben Hur*, Anatole France's *Thaïs* and Harriet Beecher Stowe's *Uncle Tom's Cabin*. It was interesting that two French novels got into Riddell's original list, which would hardly be the case today. Only Proust would have a chance, and it would be difficult to imagine *A la recherche* being put into 5,000 words for *News of the World* readers. In fact however *Thaïs* failed to survive into the final list, where it was replaced by *A Tale of Two Cities*. In this form the series was also sold to the *Chicago Tribune* (for £1,800), and the *Sunday Graphic* in London also secured second publication rights. The series was a very considerable success, so much so that both the *News of the World* and the *Chicago Tribune* asked for a second half-dozen. These were based on George Eliot's *Adam Bede*, Scott's *Ivanhoe*, Charles Kingsley's *Westward Ho!*, Charlotte Brontë's *Jane Eyre*, F. Anstey's *Vice Versa* and Cervantes' *Don Quixote*. Edward Marsh, as previously, did most of the work. The series ended only on 26 March 1933, somewhat before which time Churchill himself had become heavily re-embroiled in his opposition to the government's Indian policy.

This was all when *Marlborough* ought to have been the solid core of his intellectual application. It was his first major work of biographical history since 1906. When accepting, with profit and pleasure, Lord Riddell's request for a second series of 'great tales' he wrote on 13 January 1933: 'I shall have to lay aside *Marlborough* in which I am breast-high.'[4] Despite these distractions *Marlborough* made remarkably good progress. In the second six months of 1932, even with his paratyphoid, he had produced another fifteen chapters. His literary energy and industry were astonishing. The full first volume of 557 pages was published on time in October 1933. Apart from his own energy he was relentless in mobilizing the services of others. In May (1933) he had sent to Marsh twenty-seven chapters for stylistic correction, accompanied by a perceptive list of criteria which he wanted applied:

> The points I want you particularly to mark are:-
> (1) Clumsy sentences where the meaning is obscure or the grammar is questionable.
> (2) Repetition of words. I have a good many favourites and they may crop up too often, e.g. vast, bleak, immense, formidable, etc.
> (3) Repetition of phrases, e.g. where we talk about Marlborough as a great man, wise, profound, imperturbable statesman etc. in several variances.
> (4) Repetitions of arguments.... My eye is blunted by much re-reading....
> (5) Dull boring stodgy passages. You are almost the first person who will have read this book straight off. You might ask yourself the question 'which ten thousand words would I cut?'
> (6) Cheap, vulgar, undignified references. I hope you will not find any. My mature view of style is that it should follow the thought and also that I belong to the modern age and write with their knowledge and modes.
> (7) Hyphens. I see Macaulay writes 'hotheaded' in one word. I am sure we ought not to have too many hyphens. . . .[5]

By the summer of 1933 he not merely produced 200,000 words of *Marlborough*, but had written 308 letters (mainly requests for information and seekings of opinion) about the book. How good was the work? To me, who had never read *Marlborough* until I came to construct this book, and who am also under-educated in late-Stuart history, it was a revelation. Apart from the first chapter, about John Churchill's antecedents, and in which he seemed primarily concerned to let Ashley establish the quality of his research rather than to grip attention, the central part is compulsive reading. One boring chapter on forebears, a notoriously soporific contribution to many biographies, is not excessive. But it was curious that Churchill, such an accomplished and indeed commercial writer, should have allowed this chapter to sit surlily at the entrance to his first major biography since his life of Lord Randolph Churchill.

From chapter two onwards, however, *Marlborough* soars into the air. Churchill's description of the England of the Restoration and even more of the Europe of Charles II are both exhilarating swoops. They have a strong personal imprint on every page. Rather like a passenger on an adventurous but newly established airline one looks out of the window, excited by the landscape but hoping without total assurance that the maintenance has been well done. Churchill, however, always had a good sense of the vulnerability of his assumption. He knew where the most dangerous spots were and moved in resources to protect them.

There were two aspects of his first-volume treatment which were of particular interest. First there was his violent partisanship. Almost his primary motivation, apart perhaps from the money, was to refute Thomas Babington Macaulay. That quintessential Whig historian, high exponent of the virtues of the Glorious Revolution of 1688, had been highly critical of the switch of sides from Charles II to William of Orange of John Churchill (as he still was at the time). Winston Churchill, 250 years later, was determined to blast Macaulay out of the water, which he did to some considerable effect. But he did it at the expense of being as partisan as Macaulay had been nearly a century before: 'But what a way to write history! ... Lord Macaulay stands convicted of deliberately falsifying facts and making the most revolting accusations upon evidence which he knew, and in other connections even admitted, was worthless, for the purpose of bringing more startling contrasts and colour into his imaginative picture and of making the crowds gape at it.'[6]

This was a well-directed blow. But in the same volume Churchill exposed himself to almost exactly the equivalent counter-criticism. Macaulay may have been prejudiced against the first Marlborough. But his prejudice did not excuse that of Churchill against Louis XIV. The Sun King no doubt had much to be said against him, but he hardly merited this passage of Churchillian invective:

> During the whole of his life Louis XIV was the curse and pest of Europe. No worse enemy of human freedom has ever appeared in the trappings of polite civilization. Insatiable appetite, cold, calculating ruthlessness, monumental conceit, presented themselves armed with fire and sword. The veneer of culture and good manners, of brilliant ceremonies and elaborate etiquette, only adds a heightening effect to the villainy of his life's story.[7]

The second aspect of interest was his treatment first of John Churchill's youthful, daring and profitable liaison with Barbara Villiers, Duchess of Cleveland, twelve years his senior, and then of his long-lasting and marriage-sanctified romance with Sarah Jennings, his wife and first chatelaine of Blenheim Palace. These two passages constituted

almost the only two attempts, in all the millions of words which he
wrote, of the certainly unprurient and maybe uninterested Churchill to
deal in print with the subject of sexual passion, which, with explicitness
varying according to the changing conventions of different ages, has
commanded so much of the literature of the world.

He is a little uneasy with Barbara Villiers, who was Charles II's
primary mistress at the time of the Restoration and came back from
Holland with him. Churchill describes her in 1666 at the age of twenty-
four: 'She was a woman of exceeding beauty and charm, vital and
passionate in an extraordinary degree. In the six years that had passed
she had borne the King several children. . . . [She] was the reigning
beauty of the palace. She held Charles in an intense fascination. Her
rages, her extravagances, her infidelities seemed only to bind him more
closely in her mysterious web.' Yet he gets very upset at the suggestion
that among 'her infidelities' was one with John Churchill, then a
seventeen- or eighteen-year-old and singularly good-looking page about
the palace. Winston Churchill describes this as 'a filthy tale'.[8]

John Churchill then went on vaguely active service in Spain and
Tangier for more than two years. But when he came back aged twenty
at the beginning of 1671 there is no dispute that he quickly acquired (or
reverted to) the position of one of the lovers of the then twenty-nine-
year-old Barbara Duchess of Cleveland, to which rank Lady Castle-
maine, as she was when John Churchill went to Spain, had in the
meantime been elevated. Winston Churchill does not dispute that his
illustrious ancestor was almost certainly the father of her last child,
another Barbara, or that in the course of the next few years his liaison,
daring in view of the King's persistent if by now mildly waning passion,
involved him in some Feydeau-farce-like situations, such as jumping out
of windows and hiding in cupboards. What is also not in dispute is that
he was the recipient of substantial cash gifts from the Duchess, who was
as generously profligate in money matters as in other ways. John
Churchill was far from profligate in his treatment of these gifts – acting
more like a middle-aged accountant than an insouciant young gallant.
One £5,000 he used to buy an annuity of £500 from the Marquess of
Halifax, who seemed to run an amateur assurance business around the
court. This proved a very good investment for John Churchill whose
life lasted much longer than the actuarial expectation for young soldiers
of the time. In these circumstances his biographer's elevation of the date
of commencement of the affair into a matter of principle seems to point

to an underlying censoriousness, or at least unease, about the whole matter.

John Churchill disengaged from the Duchess of Cleveland during 1675 when Sarah Jennings erupted on to the court scene and seized his imagination. As she was barely fifteen at the time it is not immediately obvious why Winston Churchill should have regarded this as a less heinous example of child snatching than the eight-years-earlier 'filthy tale' of Barbara Villiers's alleged behaviour with John Churchill. But the Sarah romance led on to life-long monogamy. 'It lasted for ever,' Winston Churchill wrote; 'neither of them thenceforward loved anyone else in their whole lives, though Sarah hated many.'⁹ That made Winston Churchill feel at home, and he was also impressed by the fact that, though at least as well born as John Churchill, she had no more money than he did. It took John Churchill three years to marry her, but both remained firm, he rejecting his father's suggestion of a wealthy but angular alternative (who nonetheless became a mistress of the Duke of York – James II) during an occasionally turbulent courtship. There was a fair amount of self-identification in Churchill's account of the relationship, which was not diminished by his admiration for the independence of character of Sarah, whom he described as a 'young lady [who] was eventually to play as large a part in English history as any woman not a sovereign'.

The rest of the first volume of *Marlborough* is a very considerable *tour de force*. There are occasional *longueurs* when Churchill feels that he has to buttress his grand and fascinating sweeps with displays of meticulous even if second-hand scholarship. There was also his persistent and too defensive desire to refute Macaulay at every possible point, but particularly about John Churchill's alleged treacherous (to William III) dealings with the exiled James II court in France. The residual feeling is that he wins the argument, but that, like the result for their clients of a bruising clash between two major legal eagles in a libel case, some dirt sticks to both sides.

The volume rather tails off in its last four (of thirty-two) chapters. Churchill's original intention had been to conclude it with the grand finale of the Battle of Blenheim (1704), which was a wise plan, for in such clashes he was at his best. And all this was to be encompassed within a volume of 150,000 words. However elephantiasis, aided by the work of too many research assistants, reaped its toll and a volume of 200,000 words ended more anti-climatically with the death of William

III in 1702, which while a climacteric for that sovereign provided a less dramatic intermediate curtain-fall in the story of Marlborough.

Marlborough (volume one) appeared at the beginning of October 1933, was quickly reprinted, re-emerged in a lightly revised edition fifteen months later, and was then again reissued in 1939, after the three subsequent volumes were complete and published. In its four printings volume one sold 17,000 copies, which was a solid but well short of sensational sale. The subsequent volumes sold on a gently declining slope, 15,000 of the second and 10,000 of each of the last two. The first volume, as was Churchill's habit, was given a wide distribution list for inscribed copies: eminent politicians, former private secretaries and other close and senior officials, as well as the many whose brains had been picked for the book. The politicians, notably Baldwin, Neville and Austen Chamberlain, treated him rather like Dr Johnson's comparison between dogs 'on their hinder legs' and women preaching; it was amazing that he did it at all and produced such an output. They also found expressions of gratitude and admiration a satisfactory way of pretending to keep personal relations while political differences deepened. Neville Chamberlain was typically the most explicit: 'I am very grateful. . . . that you have not yet cut me out of the list of your beneficiaries.'[10] And again, they nearly all took the precaution of writing letters of thanks before reading, although H. A. L. Fisher was here the exception and claimed to have read it twice within a week of publication.

The Indian issue, after a lay season occasioned partly by Churchill's health vicissitudes of the autumns of 1931 and 1932 and partly by a pause associated with the change of Viceroy from Irwin to Willingdon, re-erupted in the spring of 1933. For the next two years almost every step that Churchill took on the issue alienated support and weakened his position in the Conservative party, and indeed in the House of Commons as a whole. Superficially India sometimes looked a promising field for mischief because the gut reaction of many of those active in local Conservative Associations was in favour of the 'imperialist' line and therefore suspicious of the relative progressivism of Baldwin and Hoare, the latter having become Secretary of State for India. This resistance expressed itself in strong (although always minority) votes in various non-parliamentary gatherings of the party. Thus in February 1932 at a meeting of the National Union of Conservative Associations the 'rebels' got to 165 against 189, their high-water mark. In June, at the General Council (of the party) they were down to 316 against 838, and in October at the party conference it was 344 against 737.

The minority vote was always formidable but it did not gather momentum.

The Churchill position among the Conservative members of Parliament, despite the wave of surprised and inexperienced victors who had been swept in by the landslide of 1931, was never nearly as strong. The Conservative party of those days was basically a deferential party. The most that the constituency diehards were likely to do was to stage a few afternoon manifestations of discontent before going home to tea and leaving the leadership, so long as it was backed, as it was, by a strong majority of MPs, to get on with it. The most that Churchill and his allies were able to do in the period was to give a few loyalist MPs an uncomfortable time when their Associations carried resolutions against the government. But this was relatively light fire. No one came near to having an alternative candidate chosen in their place, and Churchill, experienced as a parliamentarian if not as a Conservative, and also a man very steady under light fire, ought fully to have appreciated this. What the light fire did, as is its way, was not to break the morale of its recipients but to make them more hostile to those, notably Churchill, who had organized it.

What, furthermore, ought to have given Churchill pause was the thought of with what an illiberal fringe his Indian policy was forcing him to operate. Lord Carson, Lord Lloyd, Colonel Gretton, Sir Henry Page Croft and Sir Alfred Knox are hardly names which shine forth from the 1930s history of the Conservative party.* Page Croft became a bad joke figure during Britain's finest hour, and Knox (member for Wycombe) wrote Churchill a letter which ought to have set every alarm bell ringing in the head of its recipient, seasoned warrior of the 1909–11 constitutional struggles that he was. 'I am more than ever determined to fight to the last ditch,' Knox wrote on 24 February (1933).[11] By contrast Churchill's India campaign seriously separated him from Anthony Eden, Harold Macmillan and Duff Cooper as well as a number of other lesser-known progressive Tory MPs who were potential allies of Churchill in his later fight against the appeasement of Hitler. Duff Cooper indeed wrote after twenty years of time for reflection, that he regarded Churchill's determination to block any move towards

* There were, however, one or two less consistently right-wing figures, most notably the Duchess of Atholl, who was MP for Kinross and West Perthshire from 1922 to 1938, and who latterly, because of her support for the Republican government in the Spanish civil war, became known as the 'red Duchess'.

dominion status for India as 'the most unfortunate event that occurred between the two wars'.[12]

Churchill's major alienating actions were mostly in relation to the Joint Select Committee of Lords and Commons which the government in early 1933 agreed should be set up. The government had just published a White Paper outlining what they thought had emerged from the second so-called Round Table conference, that of 1932. The Select Committee was to give detailed consideration to these proposals before they were embalmed in the bill which eventually became the Government of India Act of 1935. The setting up of the Committee was intended to be a conciliatory gesture, giving an opportunity for parliamentary input in accordance with the previously persistent demands of the Churchill faction, and so indeed it was widely interpreted to be. But not by Churchill. At first he was very concerned to get some substantial 'rebel' representation on the Select Committee, although accepting that 'the Government must have an effective majority'. Then, when this was conceded, including an offer of the chairmanship to the fourth Marquess of Salisbury, very much a Churchill ally on the issue, and an invitation to Churchill himself to be a member, he flounced. In spite of a very friendly letter from Hoare accompanying the official invitation he replied intransigently: 'I see no advantage in my joining your Committee merely to be voted down by an overwhelming majority of the eminent persons you have selected. . . . I will have neither part nor lot in the deed you seek to do.'[13] This non-cooperation, ironically worthy of Gandhi (Churchill's Indian *bête noire*) in one of his more difficult moods, was disapproved of by a considerable chunk of Churchill's not too numerous supporters.*

Shortly after Churchill's refusal of membership he was engaged in a substantial correspondence with the Marquess of Linlithgow. Linlithgow, who was to be Viceroy from 1936 to 1943, had just been appointed chairman (after Salisbury declined) of the Select Committee. He was thirteen years Churchill's junior and a firm opponent of his position on

---

* It is not easy to see that it was justified on the merits. On a distinguished committee of thirty-four, there were four members of the Labour opposition (tiny at that time) and eight members of the Churchill-inspired India Defence Committee, which left twenty-two broad but not wholly dependable supporters of the government line. Maybe generosity would have awarded the rebels a couple more members, but it is difficult to think of any government with a big majority, from Churchill's own to Blair's, which would have gone further than that.

India, although a friend and admirer on other matters, who wished to see him back in high office. He wrote with evident goodwill, engagingly signing himself 'Hopie', a diminutive of his young man's title of Lord Hopetoun. There was an exchange of five long letters in the first weeks of May (1932), the main interest of which was that it led to Churchill disclosing the underlying rationale for his India policy more completely than on any other occasion. Churchill wrote on 7 May:

I think we differ principally in this, that you assume that the future is a mere extension of the past whereas I find history full of unexpected turns and retrogressions. The mild and vague Liberalism of the early years of the twentieth century, the surge of fantastic hopes and illusions that followed the armistice of the Great War have already been superseded by a violent reaction against Parliamentary and electioneering procedure and by the establishment of dictatorships real or veiled in almost every country. Moreover the loss of our external connections, the shrinkage in foreign trade and shipping brings the surplus population of Britain within measurable distance of utter ruin. We are entering a period when the struggle for self-preservation is going to present itself with great intenseness to thickly populated industrial countries.

It is unsound reasoning therefore to suppose that England alone among the nations will be willing to part with her control over a great dependency like India. The Dutch will not do it; the French will not do it; the Italians will not do it. As for the Japanese, they are conquering a new empire. All the time you and your friends go on mouthing the bland platitudes of an easy safe triumphant age which has passed away, whereas the tide has turned and you will be engulfed by it.

In my view England is now beginning a new period of struggle and fighting for its life, and the crux of it will be not only the retention of India but a much stronger assertion of commercial rights. . . . Your schemes are twenty years behind the times.[14]

This memorable letter strikes several chords. It marks Churchill's total rejection of the optimism which was a feature of both Gladstonian and Asquithian Liberalism. Thomas Hobbes has replaced John Locke as the presiding philosopher. It also contains a firm hint as to why, around this time, Churchill was seen by some as wishing to be a British Mussolini. The harsh *Realpolitik*, the impatience with 'parliamentary and electioneering procedure' both point a little in this direction. So did his Oxford Romanes lecture (of 1931) with the corporatist undertones of its advocacy of a separate 'industrial parliament'. Even the famous scowl, so valuable when it was confronting Hitler, could be mobilized for a

Mussolini comparison when it was merely confronting Hoare and Baldwin.

Linlithgow, however, not normally thought of as a polemicist remotely in Churchill's class, came back very effectively. On 19 May he wrote:

> You envisage . . . an approaching period of red tooth and claw, a struggle for the means to live. I doubt it, Winston! I wonder whether you take sufficient cognizance of two basic changes of tendency. (a) Falling birth-rates, (b) enormously enhanced production, actual and potential, both of primary and manufactured products? I think it is difficult to overestimate the significance of (b). . . . Forgive me, then, if I say that it is not, it seems to me, so much I who am mouthing the bland platitudes of an age that has passed away, twenty years behind the times, but rather *you* who are hanging, hairy, from a branch, while you splutter the atavistic shibboleths of an age destined by some to retreat into the forgotten past. In conclusion, let me as one Tory to another, beseech you to see in time the errors of your mind, and to retract them, lest irretrievably you miss the bus.[15]

In the context, not merely of the twentieth century as whole but even of the remaining thirty-two years of Churchill's life, it is difficult to believe that Linlithgow did not show the greater wisdom in this revealing exchange.

The Joint Select Committee began work in that summer (of 1933), and everything to do with Churchill's relations with it was a misfortune. When he gave evidence in October he was blustering rather than persuasive. But this, as well as his refusal of membership, paled into insignificance compared with the débâcle of his attempt to frustrate its whole work by his ill-starred Committee of Privileges enterprise of the spring of 1934. It was at once spirited and disastrous, a real last-ditch effort, inspired by an underlying (and correct) feeling that his great campaign was slipping away, combined with, as can happen in such circumstances, an increasing self-righteousness. A crucial element in the evidence delivered to the Joint Select Committee was that of the Manchester Chamber of Commerce. Especially because of Churchill's somewhat ill-matched double-barrelled case, half a grand vision of the maintenance of a beneficent British Empire and half a view that India must be kept as a captive market for Lancashire textiles, it was vital that the Manchester Chamber should support the second barrel. Both in their written submissions, however, and in their appearance before the Committee on 3 November, the Manchester delegation had failed to come up to Churchill's mark. They had shown a regrettable tendency to accommodate themselves to the reality of an evolving world. Churchill attributed their supineness (as he saw it) to improper pressure exerted by Hoare through the agency of that great Lancashire political fixer Lord Derby. He held this to be a breach of parliamentary privilege and raised it with some portentousness on the floor of the House of Commons on 16 April 1934.

It was referred, as he wished, to the Committee of Privileges, which deliberated on the issue between 23 April and 6 June when its report was printed. The Committee of Privileges in those days was constituted at an almost unbelievably high level. The Prime Minister was chairman and the other nine members included one past and one future Prime Minister (Baldwin and Attlee), as well as the nearly Prime Minister Austen Chamberlain, and the Liberal leader Herbert Samuel. There were also Churchill's old friend Lord Hugh Cecil and the Attorney-General (Inskip, an ecclesiastical lawyer from Bristol, later as Lord Chancellor and Lord Chief Justice ennobled as Caldecote) who, although a little more rotund, performed the role of a notary in a Mozart opera. In particular, when Churchill appeared before the Committee on 23 April, Inskip despite his normal courteous if dispiriting demeanour was impelled to treat him like an unsatisfactory Law Courts witness and to urge him 'to try to answer my questions if you can without rhetoric'. Much worse, for Churchill's interests, was that Austen Chamberlain, old colleague, current ally on an early awareness of the dangers of Nazism and above all respectfully decent exponent of an old-world courtesy, should have thought it necessary, somewhat periphrastically but nonetheless with unmistakable disapproval, to rebuke Churchill for 'using his position, as a distinguished member of this House, to address a Committee of the House in a way that Committees are not accustomed to be addressed by those who are invited to give them the assistance of such evidence and information as they have'.[16]

After six weeks of frequent long sittings and wearisome labour, for Churchill inundated them with documents, the Committee, which included some of the busiest men in the kingdom, produced an unanimous report, utterly rejecting Churchill's case and saying that neither Hoare nor Derby had been guilty of any breach of privilege. At this stage, confronted with this united verdict, nearly everybody would have run for cover, kept their heads down and retired briefly from the political scene. Churchill, with a mixture of courage, self-righteousness and unwisdom, did exactly the reverse.

When the Report came before the House on 13 June he rose immediately after the Prime Minister had moved its acceptance and spoke for a little over an hour, intransigently contesting every finding of the Committee of Privileges. It was in a sense magnificent but it was not war conducted by means which the first Marlborough, who ought to have been near to the forefront of his mind at the time, would have recognized as skilful. So far from collecting allies he repelled them. Hoare, writing to the acting Viceroy in Delhi, got it about right: 'Winston made the worst of every world. The obvious course for him to have taken would have been to express his satisfaction that the enquiry had exonerated two of his old friends and colleagues but that in the public interest he had felt it his duty to raise the case. If he had done this he would have regained much of his lost position and would have had a very sympathetic House'.[17]

On the contrary Churchill continued to maintain his position as though the Privileges Committee had never deliberated. As a result he got an extremely unsympathetic House. At one point Sir Percy Harris, soon to become Liberal Chief Whip, interrupted to ask, 'Is that an attack on the Committee of Privileges?' 'No,' Churchill imperturbably answered, 'it is an attack on the Report.' Leo Amery, true to his habit of being on the scene at crucial moments in Churchill's life and being generally willing to put the boot in, spoke immediately after Churchill with great success. He accused Churchill of a reckless dislocation for months of the work of the Joint Select Committee, a desire to force Hoare's resignation and generally to cause all possible disruption in the Conservative party. He then moved to the culmination of this part of his argument: 'The right honourable gentleman wishes to be true to his chosen motto, *Fiat justitia ruat caelum.*' Churchill morosely called out, 'Translate.' Bad classicist though he was, it was a classic example of a misjudged interjection. Amery, who could hardly have done advance preparation for that particular interruption, immediately offered his own somewhat free version: 'If I can trip up Sam [Hoare], the Government's bust,'[18] and almost the whole House, in one of its collective fits, joined in a torrent of anti-Churchill laughter.

For Churchill the debate went from bad to worse. Attlee, as deputy leader of the opposition, and then Hugh Cecil rejected him. Even the faithful and beloved Archibald Sinclair welcomed the Report, and John Simon, Foreign Secretary at the time but with an Indian *locus* as the chairman of the Indian Statutory Commission of 1928–9, delivered a skilfully serpentine dissection of Churchill.* By this time it was clear that Churchill had no prospect of mustering even a rump group into the division lobby against the Report. He responded to this by deserting the stricken field before the end of the debate. It was a very bad House of Commons day for him.

Unfortunately he did not desist. His Indian campaign went on for another full year. This embraced his sixtieth birthday, which made it late to go on clinging to the wilderness. Over the summer and autumn of 1934 Churchill carried through a provincial Lancashire-centred campaign and had some sufficiently successful public meetings to keep his morale up. However he missed the Conservative party conference in October, preferring an eastern Mediterranean cruise on Walter Guinness's yacht, which was sensible from every point of view except that of a campaign *à outrance*. The conference was not however the crucial encounter with extra-parliamentary Conservatives, where Churchill's strength was thought to lie, for this was at a meeting of the National Union Council in the Queen's Hall (London) on 4 December. By then the eighteen-months-long labours of the Joint Select Committee had produced a report reasonably satisfactory to the government. All the big guns were deployed in the Queen's Hall. Baldwin, Austen Chamberlain and Amery spoke for the Report, Churchill and Salisbury against. The result was 1,102 votes in effect for Baldwin and 390 in effect for Churchill.

Just over a week later there was a replay in the House of Commons. On this occasion Churchill was widely judged to have achieved an oratorical triumph. He was at this stage remarkably *journalier* in his performances. He could move from success to abject failure with consummate ease. What was admirable was that the failures did not prevent his bouncing back with confidence. The votes however closely mirrored the National Union outcome. The government defeated an amendment hostile to the report of the Joint Select Committee by 410 votes to 127. But 53 of the 127 were Labour or Liberal members who wanted a more rapid handover of power. Churchill's diehards mustered only 74. In the Lords a similar amendment was defeated by 239 to 62,

* Simon's attitude had some significance for he, together with most of the other senior politicians who were thought to have close Indian experience – Birkenhead as Secretary of State in 1924–8, Reading as Viceroy 1921–6 and even Austen Chamberlain – inclined to Churchill's rather than to Baldwin's side at the beginning of the dispute. Birkenhead died in 1930, and by 1934 Churchill had alienated all the others.

a high vote for the quiescent and absentee House of Lords of the 1930s, but not for Churchill a favourable one.

Still Churchill did not accept it as the end of the road. He was determined to fight the huge Government of India Bill which Hoare brought forward as the staple and somewhat monotonous diet for 1935. He spoke so frequently in the spring that he was forced to abandon his habit of meticulous preparation. He wrote to Clementine (away on a much longer and more distant Guinness cruise than their joint one of the previous autumn) on 13 April: 'At sixty I am altering my method of speaking, largely under Randolph's tuition, and now talk to the House of Commons with garrulous unpremeditated flow. They seem delighted. But what a mystery the art of public speaking is! . . . There is apparently nothing in the literary effect I have sought for forty years!'[19]

Randolph Churchill, however, in spite of his success as an oratorical adviser, was not in good parental odour during this period. He was desperately trying to find for himself a political role as an auxiliary but not a subordinate of his father. In mid-January 1935 he announced, without consultation, that he proposed to contest a pending bye-election in the Wavertree division of Liverpool as an anti-India Bill independent Conservative. Churchill was not pleased (particularly at the lack of consultation), but decided that the only thing to do was to support. He addressed several Liverpool meetings, and rallied his friends to provide both money and endorsement. He was also impressed by Randolph's exuberant performance. However the campaign much exacerbated Churchill's relations with the Conservative party, especially as Randolph polled enough votes (10,000 against the official Conservative's 13,000) to let in the Labour candidate.

Hardly was this over than Randolph was off again, not himself standing, but promoting with all his vigour though without his father's involvement a surrogate candidate (Richard Findlay, who had to be incarcerated for his fascist views at the beginning of Churchill's premiership) in the Norwood (South London) bye-election which took place on 14 March. This time the rebel vote was only 2,700 and the seat was held for the Conservatives, which was as well, for the official candidate was Duncan Sandys, who not only became a staunch if dour Churchill supporter but also married Diana Churchill within the year. Apparently the couple caught first glimpses of each other from different sides of the campaign, but did not actually meet until a little later. Altogether it was rather a relief when Randolph was struck down in April by a mixture of jaundice and glandular fever.

That spring the committee stage of the India Bill ground its weary way through the House of Commons. It was probably Churchill's most diligent application to the minutiae of parliamentary business in the whole of his sixty-four-year span in Parliament. As he wrote to Clementine on 5 April: 'The only time I was away the Government got sixty clauses through in a twinkling'[20] – it was a massive bill of over 400 clauses. Eventually the committee stage was concluded on 15 May. Churchill had made sixty-eight speeches during these marathon proceedings. Sometimes flashes of his wit and oratory shone through, but he also came nearer in these weeks to being a parliamentary bore than at any other stage in his long years in that arena. Then there was the report stage and then there was the third reading at the beginning of June. Churchill went on to the end, but when he sat down at the conclusion of his last speech on the subject on 5 June, the 'insect' Leo Amery, who was always buzzing around Churchill's head, rose and said to a sympathetic House: 'Here endeth the last verse of the last chapter of the Book of Jeremiah.'[21] This dismissal was well received in most quarters – although it is a mistake to treat that floating kidney of 'the mood of the House' as a reliable guide to what is right and what is wrong. Churchill mustered a final vote of 122 against the bill, as against the 386 government votes. But because once again a third of his votes came from Labour members whose beliefs on the subject were the reverse of his own it was not an end result in which he could take much satisfaction. A more accurate count of his hard-core support was provided by the attendance list of a dinner which he gave at Claridge's Hotel on 31 May (1935). (He always liked 'war to the knife and fork'.) Fifty-one MPs and twelve peers attended. Any analysis of the names, however, provoked in an extreme form the thought of *Non tali auxilio nec defensoribus istis tempus eget* (Neither for such help nor for such allies does the hour call). Few of them were much use to Churchill in the greater battle which lay ahead.

25

An Early Alarm Clock

HISTORY BEST REMEMBERS Churchill in the 1930s – his wilderness years in the resonant title of a television series – as a relentless but unheeded critic of the pusillanimous behaviour of British government, successively presided over by MacDonald, Baldwin and Neville Chamberlain, in the face of the mounting aggression of fascist dictators. This is a broadly correct but over-simplified description of Churchill's beliefs and conduct between 1932 and 1939. His record of courage and foresight in standing up to threats to peace and democracy was more creditable than that of any other major British politician, with the exception of Austen Chamberlain. But that honourable old statesman, who always lacked Churchill's energy and self-confidence, died in March 1937 and was therefore lucky enough not to witness the appeasement policies of his half-brother.

Churchill's staunch record is however subject to two qualifications, neither of them by any means inexcusable. First, he always saw the threat to Britain's security as essentially a German threat. He was therefore equivocal on what he regarded as peripheral challenges to the world order, from the Japanese invasion of Manchuria in 1931 through Mussolini's Abyssinian adventure in 1935 to the civil war in Spain in 1936–9. This meant that he did not vote the straight collective-security League of Nations ticket, as did several of those with whom he had privately been closely connected: Archibald Sinclair, Robert Cecil, Violet Bonham Carter, Lord Lytton. But he had the merit over them, and indeed over the official Labour party even when the pacifist George Lansbury, leader from 1931 to 1935, had been replaced by 'Major Attlee, who had a fine war record' (in Churchill's words),[1] of having a much clearer appreciation that resistance to fascist force required weapons as well as words.

The second qualification was that the valour of Churchill's opposition to the government was sometimes moderated by his desire to regain high office within it. This, too, was more than comprehensible. He loved the exercise of power. It excited him as a young man when he became a

Cabinet minister at the age of thirty-three. It stimulated rather than oppressed him from 1940 to 1945 when, in his first quinquennial of pensionable age, he carried more awesome burdens than any other Prime Minister. And, even after he had become eighty, he found its appurtenances very difficult to renounce. He was deprived, partly but not entirely through his own intransigence, of the sustenance of power from the age of fifty-four to that of almost sixty-five. Furthermore he showed considerable signs of ageing in the second half of the 1930s, soon after his sixtieth birthday. Although he became one of only three British Prime Ministers to survive into his tenth decade, it would be a mistake to assume from this that he was always young for his years. Until the early 1930s he retained a middle-aged pugnacity and mobility. He could still have been a lieutenant-colonel striding round his battalion positions, as he had done fifteen years before. Some time around 1934–5, however, he had something approaching a *coup de vieux*. The pictures of him campaigning, whether with Randolph in Wavertree in February 1935, or in a notable speech at the City [of London] Carlton Club in September of that year or in his own constituency of Epping two months later, are those of an elderly man. The vitality of his conversation or of his extraordinary dictating output did not diminish, but that of his physical movement did.

There was a bizarre occasion in the House of Commons in May 1935 when Colonel Thomas Moore, a little jockey of a man who lingered on as member for Ayr until 1964, rose immediately after Churchill and attacked him 'for having permeated his entire speech with the atmosphere that Germany is arming for war'. Moore then attempted to modify this harshness by also saying, 'although one hates to criticize anyone in the evening of his days'.[2] Churchill was then exactly sixty years and five months, and had nearly nine years of premiership and thirty of life ahead of him (Moore, who was almost his equal in longevity if not in achievement or fame, had himself thirty-six to go). So Moore's statement on this occasion must count as one of the most premature and ludicrous valedictions in the columns of Hansard. Nevertheless what he said was symptomatic of how *passé* Churchill was coming to be regarded, at least by the less perceptive.

Churchill himself may have had a nasty suspicion that Moore was half right. Over ten years later he wrote an account, accurate in detail but maybe falsely elegiac in sum, of this stage of his life:

The years from 1931 to 1935, apart from my anxiety on public affairs, were personally very pleasant to me. I earned my livelihood by dictating articles which had a wide circulation not only in Great Britain and the United States but also, before Hitler's shadow fell upon them, in the most famous newspapers of sixteen European countries. I lived in fact from mouth to hand. I produced in succession the various volumes of the *Life of Marlborough*. I meditated constantly upon the European situation and the rearming of Germany. I lived mainly at Chartwell, where I had much to amuse me. I built with my own hands a large part of two cottages and extensive kitchen-garden walls, and made all kinds of rockeries and waterworks and a large swimming-pool which was filtered to limpidity and could be heated to supplement our fickle sunshine. Thus I never had a dull or idle moment from morning till midnight, and with my happy family around me dwelt at peace within my habitation.[3]

This is too contented a picture of his state of mind during many months of these and adjacent years. There was a sense of political impotence, of his talents wasted, of time passing him by, and of some periods of 'black dog', even though the incidence of these tends to be exaggerated. Maybe, even by the standards of his exceptional absorptive capacity, he was drinking too much. At the turn of the year 1935–6, he encountered Lord Rothermere (never a good influence in his life) first in Tangier (never a wholesome place) and then in Marrakech. Rothermere offered Churchill a bet of £2,000 (he had done a similar thing to Birkenhead before the collapse of that cancellarian liver) that he could not renounce alcohol for 1936. Churchill refused it ('life would not be worth living'), but he accepted one of £600 that he would 'not drink brandy or undiluted spirits' during the forthcoming year. Whether he won is obscure, but the fact that the issue arose points to a problem.

There is also to be set against his own roseate description of his Cincinattus-like life at Chartwell in the 1930s Robert Boothby's account, filtered through the vivid, maybe on this occasion over-dramatic, prose of Harold Nicolson of the weekend before the abdication of King Edward VIII at the end of 1936. 'I knew', Nicolson reports Boothby as saying, 'that Winston was going to do something dreadful. I had been staying the weekend with him. He was silent and restless and glancing into corners. Now when the dog does that, you know he is going to be sick on the carpet. It is the same with Winston. He managed to hold it for three days, and then comes up to the House and is sick right across the floor.'[4]

Boothby was always an uncertain ally of Churchill's or of anyone else, not cowardly but wild, and his testimony must therefore be treated with some reserve. But he was probably right in portraying Churchill as being at least as much in a mood of frustrated discontent as in one of calm complacency during those Chartwell years. In these circumstances it is neither surprising nor discreditable that when he thought there was a chance of major office, primarily from the summer of 1935 to the spring of 1936, he pulled his punches against the government. Nor was he just seeking place without power. Indeed one reason that he was kept out was the belief that, once in, he would dominate the government. 'He won't give others a chance of even talking,' Neville Chamberlain is reported (at a later stage) to have said to Hore-Belisha.[5] Asquith, had he not died twelve years before, would have at least half understood, even though he had been notably more tolerant than Chamberlain.

The beginning of the hideous descent to war, according to Churchill's retrospective late 1940s judgement, was in 1931–2. He could not put it much earlier because in the summer of 1928, as we have seen, he had taken the lead, against Arthur Balfour, in getting the Baldwin Cabinet to reaffirm the 'ten-year rule', which meant that defence planning should continue upon the basis that no major war was threatened within the period. Ironically it was the MacDonald Cabinet which in 1932–3 spontaneously receded from this planning rule, but as they at the same time accepted a memorandum from the Chancellor of the Exchequer (Neville Chamberlain) saying that 'financial and economic risks are by far the most serious and urgent that the country has to face', the formal change made little practical difference to defence expenditure.

In the spring of 1936, immediately after Hitler had marched German troops into the Rhineland, which the Versailles Treaty had made a demilitarized zone, Churchill specified the previous five years as the period of *descensus Averno*. He told the House of Commons on 26 March of that year:

> We cannot look back with much pleasure on our foreign policy in the last five years. They have been disastrous years.... We have seen the most depressing and alarming changes in the outlook of mankind which have ever taken place in so short a period. Five years ago all felt safe; five years ago all were looking forward to peace, to a period in which mankind would rejoice in the treasures which science can spread to all classes if conditions of peace and justice prevail. Five years ago to talk of war would have been regarded not only as a folly and a crime, but almost as a sign of lunacy....[6]

Some might have placed the retreat from the benign expectations of the 1920s a little earlier, with the economic downturn as a major factor.

But Churchill, temporarily shattered though his personal fortune had been by the end of that boom, was never strong on the lateral effects of economic or financial events. And by fixing on 1931 as the start of the slide he was at least near to the rise of Hitler, whom he rightly and from the beginning regarded as the central irreconcilable threat.

One of the several weaknesses of the Weimar constitution was that it provided for much too frequent elections. Those for the Reichstag took place every two years and were interspersed with both national plebiscites for the President of the Republic and provincial elections. At the 1928 Reichstag elections Hitler's National Socialists won only twelve seats in a chamber of approximately 480 members. In 1930, with the economic downturn already biting, they went to 107, and in July 1932, with German unemployment over four million, they surged to 230 seats with 37 per cent of the vote. In the presidential election a few months earlier, they had polled thirteen and a half million votes against Field Marshal Hindenburg's nineteen million. They had become a formidable force in the state, and Randolph Churchill, rampaging around Germany as a correspondent of the *Sunday Graphic*, managed to persuade himself both that Hitler's achievement of power on 30 January 1933 would ultimately mean war and that he deserved a message of congratulations for his remarkable success, and duly sent a telegram.

Randolph Churchill was also anxious that his father should meet Hitler, and the circumstances for such a rendezvous were dangerously propitious. For much of September 1932 Winston Churchill with an entourage was in south Germany. His primary purpose was to inspect the battlefield of Blenheim, but after that had been accomplished and before his attack of paratyphoid he spent nearly a week, for no very clear reason, in the Regina Hotel at Munich. There he was successfully cultivated by a man with the splendidly unreassuring name of 'Putzi' Hanfstaengl, a part-American Munich art publisher who was close to Hitler at the time, although he was wisely to spend the years from 1937 to 1945 in the United States. 'Putzi' got on very well with Churchill, who invited him to dine with his party. 'After dinner,' Churchill wrote,

> he went to the piano and played and sang many tunes and songs in such remarkable style that we all enjoyed ourselves immensely. He seemed to know all the English tunes that I liked. . . . He was a great entertainer, and at that time . . . a favourite of the Fuehrer. He said I ought to meet him, and that nothing would be easier to arrange. Herr Hitler came every day to the hotel about 5 o'clock, and would be very glad indeed to see me. I had no national prejudices against Hitler at this time. I knew little

of his doctrine or record and nothing of his character. I admire men who stand up for their country in defeat, even though I was on the other side. He had a perfect right to be a patriotic German if he chose.[7]

Then, according to Churchill, he told 'Putzi' that he could not understand the point of Hitler being so violent against the Jews: 'What is the sense of being against a man simply because of his birth?'[8] So Hitler did not come the next day or any subsequent day, and the meeting did not take place. Nor did any later Churchill–Hitler meeting ever occur. Churchill recorded that, much later and during Ribbentrop's 1936–8 embassy to London, that *Sekt* salesman-turned-diplomat twice suggested to him that he might go to Germany and be received by Hitler. 'I declined, or rather let lapse, both invitations,' he flatly commented. It is difficult to imagine that a meeting would have seriously inhibited the build-up of Churchill's hostility, even when allowance is made both for Churchill's own susceptibility to Mussolini in 1927 and for Hitler's ability to exercise a hoodwinking charm, as most strikingly and unfortunately on Lloyd George in 1936. Furthermore there were one or two indications at the time that Churchill, while apprehending the threat of German militarism, was also capable of romanticizing some aspects of the early Nazi impact on Germany. Most notable was an altogether unfortunate speech (in it he was much too friendly both to Mussolini and to the Japanese invaders of Manchuria) which he delivered to the twenty-fifth-anniversary meeting of the Anti-Socialist and Anti-Communist Union on 17 February 1933 (that is barely three weeks after Hitler had come to power). 'My mind turns across the narrow waters of the Channel and the North Sea,' he said, pointing a contrast with the recent and notorious Oxford Union 'King and Country' motion,* 'where great nations stand determined to defend their national glories or national existence with their lives. I think of Germany, with its splendid clear-eyed youth marching forward on the road of the Reich singing their ancient songs, demanding to be conscripted into an army; eagerly seeking the most terrible weapons of war; burning to suffer and die for their fatherland.'[9]

He was nevertheless quicker than almost anyone else in fastening on to the menace of Hitler, and he related it as much to the internal

---

* On 9 February the Oxford Union Society, an autonomous and historically famous debating club within the University, had carried by 275 votes to 153 a motion 'that this House declines to fight for King or Country'.

unacceptability of the Nazi regime as to its external challenge to British interests. Already by 13 April (1933) he was speaking in the House of Commons of the 'odious conditions' now ruling in Germany and of the threat of 'persecution and pogrom of Jews' being extended to areas (notably Poland) to which Nazi influence or conquest spread. He also began, a month before that, his long series of speeches attacking the inadequacy of Britain's defence provision, and particularly that for the air force, which he noted with dismay had been allowed to slip to be only the fifth strongest in the world. Churchill's speeches of warning along these lines met with greatly varying receptions in the House. Sometimes he got large audiences which listened sympathetically and almost spellbound, but sometimes too he rubbed heavily against the mood of the House and produced a jarring performance. And there could be this contrast of effect even when his speeches, alternating sharply between success and failure, were endeavouring to convey exactly the same central message. Like any orator he knew when he was speaking with and when against the grain, when he had failed and when he had succeeded. And, as with all speakers, he enjoyed success and disliked failure.

Yet one of his major virtues that he never allowed even dismal failure to drive him slinking into his bunker, cowed, with his tail between his legs, and unable to do anything except concentrate on his grievances and his battered ego for some time to come. His writing schedule was such that, as soon as he got home, whether to Chartwell or to Morpeth Mansions, even from one of his most abysmal parliamentary days, he had no option but to get down to dictating a passage of *Marlborough* or an urgently pressing article. Furthermore, his inbuilt self-confidence was such that he was back within a few weeks, or even a few days, addressing the House, often at length (he was occasionally up to the almost Gladstonian level of one and a half hours) without much alteration of message, but sometimes, such is the strange alchemy of these things, with a considerable *sur place* success, although not with much obvious effect upon government policy.

His two March (1933) speeches, the one on the air estimates on the 14th and the other on the proposals which MacDonald had tabled at the Geneva Disarmament Conference on the 23rd, were in the 'jarring' category. He might have been somewhat inhibited on air force matters, both because he had done little to foster the new arm, either as its Secretary of State in 1919–20 or as Chancellor in 1924–9, and because he was too closely linked with the two Air Ministry ministers. 'Charlie'

Londonderry, his quite close although not much admired friend and kinsman, was Secretary of State, and Philip Sassoon was the under-secretary and spokesman in the Commons. Sassoon was Churchill's frequent and generous host at Lympne Castle. It was indeed a compli-cation of Churchill's life in the 1930s that in a dominant, still largely upper-class Conservative party, and with the truncated Labour and Liberal parties hardly playing a central role in politics, a high proportion of those with whom he clashed were old friends if not cousinly connections. He endeavoured to rise above this by firmly taking the view that the discharge of public duty should neither be inhibited by nor impair private friendship. But there is some doubt about how much this was accepted by others, or indeed by himself when he was seriously pricked by some attack.

He did not include the Prime Minister of the National government, Ramsay MacDonald, within this circle of friendship. This was not on snobbish grounds. MacDonald was in looks, and maybe by blood, half a Scottish laird, and humble origins had never inhibited Churchill's relations with Lloyd George or subdued his admiration for that product of rustic cottage life. Furthermore Churchill ought to have had instinc-tive sympathy for MacDonald's floor-crossing. But he despised Mac-Donald as an india-rubber man and he disapproved of the sham of the National government, partly no doubt because he had not been invited to join it, but also more widely, and with some considerable justification, on grounds of the public interest.

One reason for the failure of Churchill's speech of 23 March was that his attack on MacDonald, whom he extravagantly accused of being personally responsible for the deterioration of the previous four years which 'had brought us nearer to war and . . . made us weaker, poorer and more defenceless', was so vicious as to help his victim rather than himself. It led several subsequent speakers to suspect that his motive stemmed from frustrated ambition. This note was struck from all sides of the House, by Geoffrey Mander, a respected Liberal MP of the period, by David Logan, an elderly and fuzzy Labour Liverpudlian, and most damningly by a very obscure government supporter who went for the jugular by describing Churchill's as a speech not 'of a statesman or a man who was willing to help his country but . . . of a man who had some personal vendetta against the Prime Minister and [was] . . . a disappointed office-seeker'. Even Stafford Cripps, who was himself something of an expert in mischief at the time, described the speech as 'thoroughly mischievous'. The final irony was that it was Anthony Eden, then under-secretary at the Foreign Office, who wound up for the government and rebuked Churchill for practising 'his quips and jests' in a serious debate and producing arguments of 'a fantastic absurdity'.[10]

Apart from a small coterie Churchill was very isolated, and the disapproval was increased by the fact that this speech came between several of his most intransigent India speeches. Contrary to his reputation for highly sporadic attendance in these years, he was speaking too frequently in the House. The trouble was that, having spoken, and he seemed to command more than a Privy Councillor's normal mild priority and was always allowed to be on his feet at the best time, he was very loath to stay and listen to anyone else. When George Lansbury, normally far from a favourite of the Conservative benches, directly attacked Churchill's parliamentary manners in July 1932, he was loudly cheered from both sides. Lansbury complained that Churchill's habit was 'to walk in, make his speech, walk out and leave the whole place as if God Almighty had spoken'.

The unfortunately received 23 March (1933) speech was the occasion when Churchill caused a frisson by saying, 'Thank God for the French army,' then by far the biggest in Europe west of the Soviet frontier. It was the bluntness rather than the substance of the statement which was jarring, but the substance was also out of tune with the spirit of the time, and indeed of the debate, which was about the British government's belated attempt to provide a formula for the Disarmament Conference that might reconcile the French desire for security with the German desire for equality. It had been a difficult enough quest from the beginning of the conference in February 1932, and probably became impossible when Hitler came to power a year later. But there was a strong attachment to the long-standing and eminently sensible post-1918 objective of multilateral arms limitation. This was felt not only on the moderate left, although accentuated by Arthur Henderson, ex-Foreign Secretary and one of the few successful senior ministers of the 1929–31 government, having been drafted by international acclaim as the President of the conference, but also by much liberal Conservative opinion.

Churchill did not understand this sentiment. In one sense he was harshly right. He was by no means a warmonger, but from his early days playing with soldiers in his father's house in Connaught Place, through his experiences as a subaltern of Hussars to his own brief experiences in the First World War trenches, and fortified by his work on the glories of the first Marlborough's battles, he was at home with military formations and did not fear the clash of arms. Once Britain had failed to lead the way to a settlement in the relatively easy days (for the world if not for Germany) of the Weimar Republic, the game was up. But deep-seated hopes needed some time to prepare themselves for death. And the climate of the time was profoundly anti-war and semi-pacifist. This sentiment had been aided a few years before by the publication of a cluster of high-quality works about the horrors of 1914–18. Robert Graves, Edmund Blunden, Siegfried Sassoon and R. C. Sherriff all contributed to this barrage.

It was quite different from the spate of Second World War memoirs which descended on the bookshops and on the serial columns of two or three Sunday newspapers *circa* 1960, with more or less the same gap from the ceasefire that the more literary and downbeat compositions of thirty years before had observed. The generals' memoirs of 1960 celebrated triumph and created a post-Suez atmosphere of regret for the greater Britain which had slipped away. The *circa* 1930 batch portrayed the squalor of the trenches and the pointlessness of the sacrifice. They were part of the same response which produced the emotional splurge of the Oxford Union motion, which Churchill took too seriously – many of those who voted not to fight 'for King and Country' gave their lives a decade later. Pacifism, or anti-war sentiment, also accounts for the famous or notorious East Fulham bye-election of October 1933, which so agitated Baldwin. A Conservative majority of 14,000 became a Labour one of 5,000 on 'no issue but the pacifist one', as Baldwin put it three years later.

It was a dramatic reversal, although not greater than some which have occurred in the 1980s and 1990s, but it is doubtful whether it represented any deep-seated pacifist feeling. The seat, half of the small south-west London borough of Fulham, was won back by the Conservatives in 1935 and the area stood up to severe wartime bombing as well as any other part of the metropolis. And the briefly victorious Labour candidate of 1933, John Wilmot, so far from being a 'total surrender' pacifist was in the war parliamentary private secretary to Hugh Dalton, the most sonorously militant of the Labour ministers in the Churchill government, and then, as Minister of Supply in 1947, Wilmot was one of a small ministerial committee of six which took the decision, without telling either the full Cabinet or Parliament, to manufacture Britain's independent atom bomb. And, to round off the catalogue of paradox, Fulham's MP for thirty years from 1945, the uncharismatic but dogged Labour Foreign Secretary Michael Stewart, was so dedicated to the

Western alliance that he gave firm support to the Americans throughout
the Vietnam War. Given what came to be known about Hitler, and
maybe what ought to have been assumed from the beginning, this
miasma of semi-pacifist wishful thinking clearly had to be dispersed, and
so it gradually was, but too slowly and never in close harmony with the
French.

Churchill at this stage was contemptuous of what he regarded as the
soggily utopian Geneva spirit. Maybe he was starkly right to shine a
beam of fierce scepticism into the 'mush, slush and gush' as he had not
very agreeably put it as early as May 1932. Later he came to see that he
could elide with that Geneva idealism to broaden his appeal. But in
1933 he was too abrasive to do that. Even without India he was less
effective in bringing the bulk of the Conservative party round to the
need for rearmament than was the softly nudging approach of flabby
old Baldwin, as he dismissively regarded him. Mainly because of India,
but also because of his clanging anti-utopianism, Churchill had got
himself into a box of isolation. He was an alarm clock, but he was a
rasping one, which made most listeners more anxious to turn it off than
to respond to its summons.

An example of a somewhat crude rushing of his fences was provided
by the Chartwell weekend for which he had the Austen Chamberlains
in late October 1933. Chamberlain provided two vignettes of the visit,
first in a letter to his sister Ida written when he was actually at Chartwell:
'I am spending the week-end with the W. Churchills. I discuss Marlborough as much & India as little as I can. Only the family here, with a
guest or at most two at meals – very pleasant but on the tiring side, for
both Winston & Randolph roar when excited in argument.'[11] The
second was six days later to his sister Hilda and, although less vivid in
its picture of Chartwell home life, was more revealing politically:

He [Churchill] anticipates that he and his India Die-Hards will continue
to hold about 1/3rd of the Party, that the India bill will be carried but
that the fight will leave such bitter memories that the Govt. will have to
be reconstructed. Only Ramsay, S.B., Sam Hoare, Irwin [about to become
Halifax] & perhaps the Lord Chancellor [Sankey] are so committed that
they would have to go. Simon could stay & it would still be a National
Government, but who is to lead it? Obviously, I am this man! And so he
led me up into a high place & showed me the kingdoms of the world. I
was not greatly tempted, I told him I saw the situation developing
differently. . . . We must fight out our Indian battle as friends and bury
the hatchet as soon as it was over. I did not see any reason for

resignations, I was not anxious, indeed was wholly averse to becoming P.M. at 70 or 71, & saw no reason why I should submit to such a burden. . . . Rather ticklish grounds! I don't want what he wants, but if I had replied bluntly I am too old & won't in any case look at it, I should have lost influence all along the line.[12]

This was a very typical Austen Chamberlain reaction: wishing never to leave the arena nor to deliver a killer blow within it, while forever urging decency and if possible reconciliation. Churchill, on the other hand, was always wishing to be at the opposing gladiators (even if they were nominally on his own side) and half deceiving himself that he had already slain them long before the conflict was resolved. Nevertheless there was something distinctly moving about the loose partnership between Chamberlain and Churchill which, in some form, lasted until the death of the old statesman, three and a half years later. They were closer together on the menace of Hitler (both were equivocal on Mussolini) and the urgent need for British rearmament than was either with any other leading Conservative.

They each wished to see the other brought in to a senior position in the government. In December 1935, after the Hoare–Laval plan for handing over much of Abyssinia to Italy forced the resignation of Hoare as Foreign Secretary, Churchill was unimpressed by the choice of Eden as his replacement. 'Eden's appointment does not inspire me with confidence,' he wrote to Clementine. 'I expect the greatness of his office will find him out. Austen wd have been far better; & I wonder why he was overlooked.'[13] And on 15 February, Chamberlain, always a wonderful correspondent to his spinster sisters, wrote to the elder of the two, when a new Defence appointment was thought pending: 'In my view there is only one man who by his studies & his special abilities and aptitudes is marked out for it, & that man is Winston Churchill! I don't suppose that SB will offer it to him, & I don't think that Neville would wish to have him back, but they are both wrong.'[14] Given their differences on India and on some other subjects, and given too that Churchill was not superficially Chamberlain's type of man, being too flamboyant and rumbustious for his somewhat prim taste and over-attachment to good form, Austen behaved with great generosity towards Churchill. And Churchill, although probably never wholly at ease in his company, treated Chamberlain with genuine respect and not merely as a useful ally, although that he also was.

Churchill's speeches of warning during the middle 1930s concentrated upon the threat of German air superiority. There was indeed some danger that, curiously in concert on the point with Baldwin (who was at pains to stress that 'the bomber will always get through'), he may have weakened British will to resist by exaggerating the vulnerability of London and other cities to devastation from the Luftwaffe. This reached its highest point in his House of Commons speeches in 1934. On 30 July he spoke of London being 'the greatest target in the world, a kind of tremendous, fat, valuable cow tied up to attract the beast of prey',[15] and on 28 November, the metaphor was less vivid but the prophecy of doom was still more apocalyptic:

> However calmly surveyed, the danger of an attack from the air must appear most formidable. . . . no one can doubt that a week or ten days' intensive bombing attack upon London would be a very serious matter indeed. One could hardly expect that less than 30,000 or 40,000 people would be killed or maimed. The most dangerous form of air attack is . . . by incendiary bombs. The incendiary thermite bomb . . . will . . . I am assured by persons who are acquainted with the science go through a series of floors in any building, igniting each one practically simultaneously. No less formidable than these material effects are the reaction which will be produced upon the mind of the civil population. We must expect that under the pressure of continuous air attack upon London at least 3,000,000 or 4,000,000 people would be driven out into the open country around the Metropolis.

Then he widened the scope of the possible terror:

> It ought not be supposed that the danger . . . would necessarily be confined to London. . . . Birmingham, Sheffield and the great manufacturing towns should all be made the object of special study. . . . The danger which might confront us would expose us not only to hideous suffering, but even to mortal peril, by which I mean peril of actual conquest and subjugation. . . . It is not much use planning to move our arsenals and factories over to the west side of the island. When one considers the enormous range of modern aeroplanes and the speeds at which they travel – 230 and 240 miles an hour – it is evident that every part of this small island is almost equally within range of attack. . . . The flying peril is not a peril from which one can flee. It is necessary to face it where we stand. We cannot possibly retreat. We cannot move London. We cannot move the vast population which is dependent on the estuary of the Thames. We cannot move the naval bases which are established along our southern coasts with the great hereditary naval populations living around them.

The scientific side of defence against air attack should not be neglected, but 'The fact remains that when all is said and done as regards defensive methods, pending some new discovery, the only direct measure of defence upon a great scale is *the certainty of being able to inflict simultaneously upon the enemy as great damage as he can inflict upon ourselves'* (my italics).[16] Hence the need for rapidly and greatly increased expenditure upon the air force.

This November 1934 speech, one of a series concentrated on the air challenge of Germany which Churchill delivered around this date, was perhaps the best received. Frances Stevenson, who was present in the Commons gallery, for Lloyd George also spoke in that debate, noted with surprise that he (Churchill) sat down to 'almost an ovation'. Her surprise was accentuated by the fact that she did not consider that the speech was up to his best form (and it does indeed contain a good deal of periphrases), but she thought it was perhaps a triumph of substance over form.[17] One result of the substance was that he obtained from Baldwin, who concluded the debate, an undertaking that the government would not allow the strength of the Royal Air Force to fall below that of the Luftwaffe. On this Churchill withdrew his critical amendment and voted in the Tory lobby against a Labour amendment opposed to any increase in the size of the RAF.

It was as well that this was for Churchill a successful occasion as opposed to one of those too frequent days when he left the House having aroused every hackle in sight. It was his last appearance before his sixtieth birthday, which fell two days later, and was celebrated by a small dance, with speeches and much champagne, organized by Randolph Churchill at the Ritz Hotel, as well as by the regular birthday dinner, which Venetia Montagu had given for many years, and which was attended, among others, by Violet Bonham Carter. His Liberal past was not entirely buried.

It could be held that the almost obsessive concentration on the air challenge in these speeches of Churchill's led to a certain distortion of the limited British rearmament effort. The army, in a very run-down state, was neglected, and even Churchill's old love, the navy, was left to languish. When he returned to the Admiralty as First Lord in September 1939, he re-encountered familiar shapes, for most of the ships in service had been laid down during his 1911–15 tenure. However, the Battle of Britain was crucial to the country's survival, and turned upon a narrow margin. The recurrent dispute in these mid-1930s debates about the relative sizes of the German and British air forces was consistently obfuscated by alternative systems of classification between front-line and reserve strengths, but looming through the fog is the general impression that Churchill's estimates were mostly but not invariably nearer the truth than the more complacent ones of the government, and that, in view of what happened in 1940, little harm was done if he occasionally exaggerated. In general, however, he was much against extravagant exaggeration, and when Rothermere talked wildly about Germany having 20,000 aircraft (when Churchill believed the figure to be between 1,000 and 1,500) he rebuked him with as much force as he dared deploy against someone who commanded some of his most lucrative journalistic outlets.

When Churchill, in his November 1934, speech, used the odd phrase of 'persons who are acquainted with the science' he was referring principally to F. A. Lindemann, who held the chair of Experimental Philosophy in the University of Oxford and was known in Churchill circles as 'the Prof'. He had been born in Baden-Baden (to his great regret, for he was violently anti-German) of a rich Alsatian father and an equally rich Anglo-American mother. He was a man of great lucidity of mind who up to the age of thirty-five or so had done scientific work of wide range and considerable originality, but who subsequently devoted his gifts more to expounding (or contradicting) the opinions of others, to the administrative task of building up Oxford's moribund Clarendon Laboratory to approach rivalry with the Cavendish at Cambridge, and to the cultivation of the grand social life which was his main form of self-indulgence. He dressed like a butler yet was a tremendous snob.

His acquaintanceship with Churchill began in 1921, with, satisfactorily for Lindemann, the Duke of Westminster as catalyst. Gradually throughout the 1920s and much more strongly in the early 1930s this acquaintanceship ripened into a total acolyteship on Lindemann's part and the enthusiastic acceptance of a useful satellite, who soon became almost indispensable, by Churchill. Lindemann was always available when needed for advice or support or company and by the mid-1930s was staying at Chartwell for ten or twelve weekends a year.

Lindemann's dietary habits were not such as naturally to commend him to Churchill. He lived mainly on the whites of eggs and drank no alcohol except for an occasional carefully measured glass of brandy. The unconditional nature of his loyalty and the usefulness of his scientific advice – delivered with brevity and mostly in full support of the desired line – more than made up for these eccentricities. The mordancy of his tongue was reserved for outside targets and never turned against the Churchill family, with all of whom he was a popular visitor, which was as well in view of the frequency of his visits. Clementine liked him much more than most of her husband's cronies and acolytes, because of both the quality of his social conversation and the excellence of his tennis.

The less amiable sides of Lindemann's character were shielded at Chartwell, but were often on full display in Oxford. His professorial fellowship was in Wadham, but he thought that Christ Church was more suitable to his status, and contrived to live there for nearly forty years. He was a notable but cantankerous member of the common room. When he stood as an independent Conservative candidate (his views on issues other than the menace of Nazism were well to the right of Churchill's) at a 1937 bye-election for one of the University seats he was heavily defeated. He was taken into Whitehall by Churchill in 1939, and was made a peer by him in 1941, assuming the grandly riparian name of Cherwell. This led to a mocking piece of Oxford satirical verse, *circa* 1945, which started: 'Long, long ago when first the war began, Lord Cherwell was just plain Professor Lindemann'.

Lindemann's own contribution to public scientific policy in the 1930s was severely limited by his intolerance. When Churchill in 1935 got him appointed to an official scientific committee to consider air defence, he quickly quarrelled with the chairman Sir Henry Tizard and the other members. Within a year the committee had to be wound up and reconstituted without Lindemann. As a direct adviser to Churchill, however, he was very effective. He had precision and few doubts. He was a crucial contributor to Churchill's pre-war defence speeches as well as a favoured 'familiar of the house' at Chartwell.

Lindemann's scientific advice was supplemented by two sources of official information: Desmond Morton, then the head of the Industrial Intelligence Centre, a somewhat misleadingly named agency set up by the Committee of Imperial Defence to keep an eye on German rearmament; and Ralph Wigram, a rising Foreign Office official who died young in 1937. Morton had attracted Churchill's attention when, as an aide-de-camp to Haig, he had looked after Churchill during one of the latter's many visits to the front as Minister for Munitions. Then, when Churchill was Secretary of State for War, he got Morton into military intelligence, where he remained in a position of high responsibility until 1940. Partly perhaps out of gratitude and partly out of his own view of the public duty, Morton in the 1930s leaked copiously to Churchill. He claimed that he had been given a special authority to do so by Ramsay MacDonald, renewed by Baldwin and then by Neville Chamberlain when they in turn became Prime Minister. This somewhat improbable claim is uncorroborated. The alternative view, that he just did it on his own responsibility because he approved of Churchill's line on British rearmament and the German menace much more than that of the government, was made plausible by his living barely a mile from Chartwell. He merely had to take an innocent walk across the fields in order to spill the beans.

Morton was Churchill's main source on what was happening inside Germany, and in particular on the rebuilding of the Luftwaffe. In 1940 he came into 10 Downing Street on Churchill's personal staff and for a time was the conduit to the Prime Minister of the Ultra decodes from Bletchley Park. Later in the war the Chiefs of Staff imposed a more structured arrangement and Morton, losing his position of special influence, drifted into disenchantment with Churchill.

Wigram also held firm views against appeasement, although that word did not achieve its special meaning until a couple of years later. He was married to the daughter of J. E. C. Bodley, historian of modern France, who as long ago as the 1880s had been private secretary to Sir Charles Dilke in the days of Dilke's rising political fortunes. The bird-like Ava Wigram lived on to surprise the political and official world by marrying the portentous Sir John Anderson in 1941, and later, elevated to be Ava Waverley, both as wife and then as widow, kept as close as she could to the social centre of politics during both the Churchill and the Macmillan eras. In the mid-1930s she encouraged her first husband, a potential diplomatic star in his own right, to keep Churchill well primed with Foreign Office information. Wigram, until the end of 1936, completed the trio of those who, legitimately or illegitimately but for patriotic motives, kept Churchill remarkably well informed for an MP who was not a minister.

26

ARMS AND THE COVENANT

NINETEEN-THIRTY-FIVE was a junction year for Churchill. He went out of it in a different direction from that in which he had been proceeding when he entered. He at last got rid of the incubus of India. On the other hand he came to realize that it was much more difficult, once that quarrel was over, to get back into office than he had blithely assumed. The replacement as Prime Minister of MacDonald by Baldwin at the mid-point of the year made him no more welcome in the government. However he retained some hopes until 13 March 1936 when Sir Thomas Inskip was made Minister for the Co-ordination of Defence. With that news Churchill's hope died. It was as though a signal had been run up announcing that any appointment, however inappropriate, was preferable to the leaders of the Conservative party than Churchill's inclusion in the government. Lindemann said it was the worst appointment since 'Caligula made his horse a Consul'.

Previous to that climacteric Churchill had undoubtedly pulled some punches against the government. In October he had gone to the Conservative party conference at Bournemouth with the object not of burying Baldwin but of praising him. He described him as 'a statesman who has gathered to himself a greater volume of confidence and goodwill than any public man I recollect in my long career'.[1] Baldwin, not unnaturally, expressed amazed pleasure, and Churchill replied to his note of thanks in a purring way. Then on the day after Christmas, he wrote from Morocco a note of almost desperate entreaty to the ever unreliable Randolph: 'It would in my belief be vy injurious to me at this juncture if you publish articles attacking the motives and character of Ministers, especially Baldwin and Eden. I hope therefore you will make sure this does not happen. If not, I shall not be able to feel confidence in yr loyalty & affection for me.'[2] This phase of hope and caution came to an end with Inskip's appointment, even though Churchill handled carefully his reaction to the news and left it to others to express outrage.

There was another and quite separate significant shift of emphasis in Churchill's attitude during 1935. Previously in his speeches of warning he had been concerned to prick the bloated bladder of soggy hopes, as he saw it, with the poniard of harsh reality. In the *contra mundum* mood which was a product of his India intransigence, he had been more eager to shock the House of Commons than to persuade it. He had trained his sullen guns with equal truculence on the massed ranks of the supporters of Ramsay MacDonald's National government, on the puny and extreme Labour opposition and on the Liberals, including even his close old friend Archibald Sinclair.

Gradually over the mid-decade year he became more concerned to broaden his appeal and, without abating his central message that Britain needed rearmament, to do so in a way that embraced those, many of them on the centre-left of politics, whose hopes were concentrated on the League of Nations and on collective security, the core doctrine of its Covenant. With the Disarmament Conference out of the way, Churchill began to see the League, not as a threat to the Royal Air Force and to the French army, but as a possible instrument for resistance to fascist aggression. He adopted a two-handed policy, which made it possible for a collection of his 1930s speeches, published in 1938, to be reasonably entitled *Arms and the Covenant*. Four years earlier he would neither have sought this title nor have been justified in using it.

For the evolution of Churchill's attitude the main events of 1935 were the Anglo-German Naval Treaty in June, which conceded to Hitler the right to build up to 35 per cent of British strength and offended the French; the replacement of MacDonald by Baldwin as Prime Minister and of Simon by Hoare as Foreign Secretary in the same month; the launch of the Italian attack on Abyssinia in the early autumn; and the general election in November, which resulted in the return of the National government by a reduced but still large majority. Then, in early March 1936, Hitler, setting the crown on his reintroduction of conscription and the drive to recreate a major German army, marched his troops into the demilitarized Rhineland zone.

Churchill opposed the Anglo-German Naval Treaty, despite his friend Wigram, 'off-message' for once, having strongly urged him to support it, and he did it in interesting terms: 'The League of Nations has been weakened by our action, the principle of collective security has been impaired. German treaty-breaking has been condoned and even extolled. The Stresa Front has been shaken, if not, indeed, dissolved.'[3] The Stresa Front, created at a conference in that Italian lakeside resort between Mussolini, Ramsay MacDonald and Pierre Laval in April 1935, has been cynically described by A. J. P. Taylor as a meeting between 'three renegade Socialists defending the results of "the war to end war and to make the world safe for democracy", two of whom [MacDonald and Laval] had opposed the war, while the third [Mussolini] had destroyed democracy in his own country'.[4] The position was made still more convoluted by it becoming clear within a few months of Stresa that the most immediate threat to the international rule of law, much greater though might be the medium-term menace of Nazi Germany, came from the host of the Stresa gathering. By the late summer there was no room for doubt that Mussolini was preparing an invasion of Abyssinia. That nominally Christian kingdom was full of paradoxes. It was the oldest-surviving monarchy in Africa and although its territory embraced many barbaric practices it was a member of the League of Nations and as such entitled to the full protection of collective security against attack. But its membership of the League had been achieved only in 1923 (after Mussolini had come to power) at the insistence of Italy and against the opposition of the British government, which did not consider that Abyssinia met the necessary tenets of civilized stability.

For Churchill the Abyssinian War created a dilemma. His excessive late-1920s respect for Mussolini he could easily have sloughed off. He subsequently dismissed Mussolini's African adventure as 'unsuited to the ethics of the twentieth century'. With his concentration on the German danger what worried him was that Italy, in contrast with the position in the First World War, would be forced on to the German side. This ran into sharp conflict with his new-found desire to strengthen the League, which may have been augmented by the 'Peace Ballot', arranged by the League of Nations Union (a private pro-League organization) during the early summer of 1935. The result, announced on 27 June, showed a remarkably high degree of participation. Over eleven million people responded to the postal ballot. On the key fifth question more than ten million voted in favour of economic sanctions against an aggressor, with only 600,000 against. On the second part of the question, as to whether military sanctions (that is war, or at least a naval blockade) should be applied, 6,750,000 voted 'yes' with 2,360,000 against.

The campaign to produce this massive private poll made little impact upon Churchill. There is no mention of it in his always voluminous correspondence. During its most active phase he was engaged with the final stages of his India Bill battle, and much involved with associates (as at his large 'celebration of defeat' dinner on 31 May) to whom the League of Nations Union and a peace campaign were distinctly alien.

Almost certainly he did not himself return a completed questionnaire, although it is, as always, difficult to prove a negative. But he was not displeased with the result. Many years later he wrote an undated and friendly fragment of recollection about the ballot, but this was very much from the perspective of hindsight. His more spontaneous reaction was better captured in the memoirs of Lord Cecil of Chelwood (ex-Lord Robert Cecil), the President of the League of Nations Union: 'I met Mr Churchill just after the Peace Ballot. He was very cordial about its success, and congratulated me very much upon it. But he asked for an assurance from me that I would support all necessary increase of armaments, an assurance which I gave him.'[5]

Churchill rightly saw that, while the Peace Ballot intimidated ministers approaching an early general election with the need to present such rearmament as they were undertaking in peace clothing, it also made it easier for the non-pacifist leaders of the Labour and Liberal parties to move to a more realistic view of collective security. 'Indeed,' he concluded his passage on the ballot in *The Gathering Storm*, 'within a year I was working with them in harmony upon the policy which I described as "Arms and the Covenant".'[6] At the same time, however, it increased Churchill's own difficulties about how far he was prepared to alienate Italy by resisting the Abyssinia adventure. Already by 11 July he had warned that Britain should not be ahead of the field on this issue and become 'a sort of bell-wether or fugleman to gather and lead opinion in Europe against Italy's Abyssinian designs. . . . We must do our duty, but we must do it only in conjunction with other nations. . . . We are not strong enough – I say it advisedly – to be the law-giver and the spokesman of the world.'[7]

Then, on 11 September, Samuel Hoare, the relatively new Foreign Secretary, went to Geneva and delivered to the General Assembly of the League the most resonant pro-collective-security speech made by any British minister during the 1930s. It followed the groundwork to build up a front of resistance to Italy which Anthony Eden as Minister of League of Nations Affairs had been doing there for the previous ten days. Hoare also struck a note which Baldwin regarded as necessary for a successful election campaign at home. 'In conformity with its precise and explicit obligations,' the key sentence ran, 'the League stands, and my country stands with it, for the collective maintenance of the Covenant in its entirety, and particularly for steady and collective resistance to all acts of unprovoked aggression.'[8] The next day it was announced that the battle cruisers *Hood* and *Renown*, accompanied by a supporting flotilla, had arrived at Gibraltar from home waters. It looked as though Britain meant business.

Churchill was at Maxine Elliott's Château de l'Horizon at Golfe Juan.* It was mainly a painting holiday, interspersed by occasional casino excursions. He subsequently wrote: 'In spite of my anxieties about Germany, and little as I liked the way our affairs were handled, I remember being stirred by [Hoare's] speech when I read it in Riviera sunshine. . . . It united all those forces in Britain which stood for a fearless combination of righteousness and strength. Here at least was a policy.'⁹ The stirring of his blood must also have been increased by the thought of the great grey shapes of the Royal Navy moving to what might be their battle stations. He was always in favour of resolute action, and here there seemed to be a chance of it. He could hardly contemplate being outflanked in firmness by Sam Hoare, the agent of scuttle, as he regarded it, in India. Furthermore he wished to close ranks with the Conservative leadership in the approach to the election, which he proposed to fight as a supporter of the government, with the lively hope of office within it as soon as the contest was over.

Yet his true feelings as the Italians approached the launch of their African attack on 4 October were perhaps better expressed in a letter which he wrote to Austen Chamberlain on the 1st of that month.

> . . . I am very unhappy. It would be a terrible deed to smash up Italy, and it will cost us dear. How strange it is that after all those years of begging France to make it up with Italy, we are now forcing her to choose between Italy and ourselves. I do not think we ought to have taken the lead in such a vehement way. If we had felt so strongly on the subject we should have warned Mussolini two months before.¹⁰

Thereafter the election came and went (on 14 November) reasonably smoothly, with satisfactory majorities for the government in the country and for Churchill in Epping. The government lost nearly a hundred seats as a natural recoil from the totally artificial shape of the 1931 House of Commons, but it still had a massive majority of 278 over Labour and nearly 250 over all other parties combined. Churchill in

---

* Maxine Elliott made her reputation and money as an American actress in the early years of the twentieth century. She was then a spirited *grande dame* of late-Edwardian and inter-war international society. Already by 1915 Louis Spears, who encountered her in Picardy where she was looking after Belgian refugees on a canal boat, described her as 'a nice clever woman, must have been very beautiful' (Egremont, *Under Two Flags*, p. 44).

Epping polled 34,849 votes against 14,430 for the Liberal and 9,758 for the Labour candidate. The aftermath was much less to his taste. He got a telegram of congratulation on his majority from Baldwin, but no offer of office. As he wrote with subsequent frankness: 'This was a very great and bitter disappointment to me.'[11]

After a week had gone by he decided that all was (at least temporarily) up, and that he had better go abroad to hide his chagrin and hope to recover his equanimity. He was reported (in Harold Nicolson's diary) to have got tickets for Bali, where Clementine, after her South-East Asian cruise of the previous winter, may well have wanted him to go. In fact he stuck to a more Mediterranean direction and left on 10 December for Majorca. He retained enough political interest to lunch on his way through Paris with Pierre-Etienne Flandin, then uneasily poised between the Prime Ministership, which he had just left, and the Foreign Ministry to which he was soon to be appointed. But Churchill's interest was not such as to cause his plans to be deflected by news of the Hoare–Laval peace (or sell-out) proposals on Abyssinia, which almost exactly coincided with the Churchills leaving London. They were then pursued by rain (although Clementine soon defected to a skiing holiday in Austria) from Majorca to Tamariu to Barcelona to Tangier, where Churchill spent Christmas. Only at the Mamounia Hotel in Marrakech, which he described on the first of his many visits there as being 'one of the best I have ever used', did Churchill find sunshine, wonderful colours for painting, enough recovery of spirits for a great deal of work on *Marlborough* and, as an added bonus, the presence not only of Lloyd George but also of the ever peripatetic Rothermere.

In the December Spanish rain Churchill had digested the political upheaval caused by the Hoare–Laval proposals. Brendan Bracken wrote to him on 11 December: 'We have had a political earthquake. . . . Baldwin, who was on a pinnacle three or four days ago, is now greatly discredited.'[12] This was certainly not unwelcome news to Churchill, any more than was the fact that in Baldwin's ignominious retreat from the Hoare-Laval pact Churchill's India Bill enemy Hoare had been forced into resignation after barely six months as Foreign Secretary. But it did not encourage him to go home. Nor was he advised to do so by his small coterie of friends and advisers. Randolph telegraphed to him at the Colon Hotel, Barcelona on Tuesday the 19th with the succinctness which was a happy product of that now defunct medium of communication:

Government standing firm on peace proposals, squared Austen, and bound obtain reasonable majority Thursday. Presume you do not wish support shameful surrender Mussolini, and any opposition bound to be misinterpreted. Even if you do not speak, you are bound vote for, against, or abstain. Nothing to be gained anyway. Though Government will get away with it, prestige fatally ruined in country. Heavy rearmaments inevitable, and this your best re-entry card. Earnestly beg you stay Barcelona. This course emphatically recommended by Brendan, Prof, Samurai, Major.* Even Bob [Boothby] leading revolt against Government, and longing your support, agrees.[13]

This was welcome advice, and when Churchill abandoned Barcelona on 20 December it was southwards and not northwards that he went. Even as January 1936 passed he was very reluctant to return to England. The news that Randolph had decided to contest the Ross and Cromarty bye-election against Malcolm MacDonald, who like his father had been defeated in November in their naturally Labour seats, and was the official government candidate, reinforced his desire to keep away. The news from the Highlands was not encouraging. Bracken telegraphed on 17 January even more succinctly than the irrepressible candidate had done himself a month before: 'Randolph's prospects very doubtful.[†] Socialist win probable. More stags than Tories in Cromarty.'[14] And Churchill, apart from his scepticism about Randolph's ability to turn stags into votes, had no desire at this stage to get embroiled in dispute with the government.

It required the death of King George V on 20 January to bring him back. And even this event inspired him more to write a 4,000-word survey of the reign for the *News of the World* than to make an excessively hurried return. This article was both highly paid and highly praised by the new chairman – Riddell having died at the end of 1934 – of that remarkable mass-circulation Sunday newspaper. Completed by Churchill before he left Marrakech, it was dutifully typed by the ever accompanying Mrs Pearman on the train to Tangier. It resurfaced in *Great Contemporaries*, and as an historical essay was worthy of its place in that book of quality. But today the article seems wholly unsuited to

---

* The urgency of Randolph's message seems to have caused him to invent supporters. 'Major' could have been Desmond Morton, but Samurai defies interpretation. Martin Gilbert omits these two mysterious names when citing the passage. Perhaps the Barcelona telegraph office managed to turn Sandys into Samurai.
† He came a bad third, Malcolm MacDonald winning comfortably with the Labour candidate, Hector McNeil, who achieved brief early-1950s fame, coming second.

the *News of the World*. It was impersonal about the King, with whom Churchill had not even enjoyed the up-and-down relations which he had had with Edward VII, and concerned itself, in grandiose language, with the sweep of historical events and foreign upheaval which had taken place during the reign of King George. The article praised him more by implication than in words of personal flattery for maintaining his throne intact while so many others had foundered. It would have been an austere obituary, although a fine pageant of history, for *The Times* or the *Morning Post*. The feat of dictating it at speed without any reference books was however considerable.

Churchill regained Chartwell only on 26 January, but in time, in his capacity as one of the most senior Privy Councillors, to convey to King Edward VIII on the following day the accession address of the House of Commons. Westminster politics in the early months of 1936 centred around settling into the new reign, speculating upon who, assuming the appointment was to be made, would be the new Minister of Defence, cogitating how Britain's commitment to the League and Abyssinia, which had started so gloriously in September and deflated so sadly in December, could with least damage be wound down, and wondering, not very urgently, what Hitler would do next. Churchill, while involved in all these activities, particularly the speculation about the new minister, was also absorbed in the detached occupation of getting on urgently with *Marlborough*, and on 6 February was able to report that, volume two having been published in the previous October, he had precisely 315½ pages of volume three set up in print.[15] In mid-March he was also to begin a new series of regular fortnightly articles for the *Evening Standard*.

In the first half of February he additionally engaged in another piece of extra-curricular activity from which he emerged as an arbiter of the London theatre scene. The chain of events was a powerful indication of the extent to which, although then out of government for nearly seven years, he retained with the general and non-political public exceptional force as a 'personality'. A play entitled *St Helena*, about Napoleon's final phase, was put on at the Old Vic. It was jointly written by R. C. Sherriff (the author of the anti-war *Journey's End*) and Jeanne de Casalis. On 5 February the production was unfavourably reviewed by Dudley Barker as 'inexpressibly tedious'. The next day Churchill wrote to Edward Marsh, for whom he had much literary and general cultural respect: 'There was a very depressing review on *St Helena* in the *Evening Standard*. I am glad to hear from you that you think I should be interested in it. I will see if I can have a night, but it would pain me to witness the death agony of a figure [Napoleon] about which I have thought so much.'¹⁶ On 13 February he found 'a night' and the next day he wrote to *The Times* to contradict the 'unappreciative descriptions' which he had read. 'In my humble judgement as a life-long but still voracious reader of Napoleonic literature, it is a work of a very high order. Moreover it is an entertainment which throughout rivets the attention of the audience.'

The impact was, in a minor way, sensational. In his 1968 memoirs Sherriff wrote:

> The takings on the night before this letter was published added up to £17–12–6d, which means about sixty people in a theatre that could seat a thousand. For the performance on the night following the letter more than five hundred people came, and on the next evening, the Saturday, the theatre was packed. Every seat sold, with people standing at the back of the pit and gallery. It must have been the most complete turnaround that had ever happened to a play before.¹⁷

It must also have been a unique example of a politician's recommendation overturning adverse notices with the theatre-going public. Even Gladstone, with his passion for the theatre because of his appreciation of the actor's art as being nearest to his own and with his later habit of overcoming his deafness by getting permission to sit in a hidden corner of the stage, could not have achieved such an effect.

On the issue of who was to be the new minister in charge of the rearmament effort, announced on a limited scale in a government White Paper of 3 March, Churchill speculated as hard and optimistically, if tentatively, as anyone. On that same day of 3 March he wrote to Clementine, who was having an extended skiing holiday at Zürs, in Austria, where she had gone before Christmas, in terms of almost pathetic hopefulness:

> Anyhow I seem to be still *en jeu*. . . . Betty Cranborne [later Lady Salisbury] . . . told me that Neville Ch said to her last week 'Of course if it is a question of military efficiency, Winston is no doubt the man.' Every other possible alternative is being considered & blown upon. Hoare because of his F.O. position & Hoare–Laval pact: Swinton and Hankey & Weir because Peers: Ramsay because all can see he is a walking ruin: Lord U. [Useless] Percy because of himself & his size: Neville because he sees the PM'ship not far off: K Wood because he hopes to be Ch of Exch then, & anyhow does not know a Lieutenant General from a Whitehead

torpedo: Horne because he will not give up his £25,000 a year director-
ships – etc. So at the end it may all come back to your poor [sketch of a
pig]. . . . I do not mean to break my heart whatever happens. Destiny
plays her part.

   If I get it, I will work faithfully before God & man for *Peace*, & not
allow pride or excitement to sway my spirit.

   If I am not wanted, we have many things to make us happy, my darling
beloved Clemmie.[18]

Ten days later that hope had evaporated. Churchill had to make do
with the 'many [other] things to make us happy'. The first half of March
was a bewilderingly animated period. On 7 March Hitler sent his troops
into the demilitarized Rhineland, thereby defying Locarno as well as
Versailles. Churchill's initial reaction was muted. He telegraphed to
Clementine that day, merely telling her that nothing was yet settled (by
which he meant his inclusion in the government), saying that he was
doubtful about speaking in the debate on the Defence White Paper on
the following Tuesday (10 March) and telling her that she must not
hurry home, but in any event should avoid travelling through Germany.
In fact he did speak on the Tuesday, but in a curiously tentative and
low-key way, never mentioning the Rhineland, half defending the White
Paper (against Labour criticism) and half regretting flaccidity in the
past.

   Three days later he knew that Inskip had been preferred over himself, but even then he reacted ambiguously. On the evening of his
disappointment he gave dinner in his Westminster flat to Flandin,
whom the French governmental merry-go-round had just made Foreign Minister and who was in London to rally support for doing
something, it was not clear what, to counter Germany's occupation of
the Rhineland, which many saw as its own 'back garden'. His other
guests were Austen Chamberlain, Robert Horne and (surprisingly)
Samuel Hoare.

   With hindsight Churchill attached crucial importance to Anglo-
French weakness at the time of Hitler's military occupation of the
Rhineland. In *The Gathering Storm* he propounded the view that, had
the French merely mobilized their hundred divisions and their reputedly
strong air force, Hitler would have been forced to withdraw, or, had he
not done so, would have been repudiated and probably deposed by the
German General Staff. Thereafter, to the massive disadvantage of the
Western democracies, the hereditary German generals came to believe
in the star of the upstart corporal and to accept that Hitler had a daring

43. *The Garden at Hoe Farm*, Winston Churchill, summer 1915. (One of the first pictures WSC painted; Lady Gwendeline Churchill in foreground.)

44. *Chartwell in Winter*, Winston Churchill, late 1930s.

45. *The Chateau at St. Georges-Motel*, Winston Churchill, mid to late 1930s.

47. *The Loup River, Provence*, Winston Churchill, 1936.

Left: 46. *Marrakech and the Atlas Mountains*, Winston Churchill, January 1943.
(The only picture WSC painted during the war.)

48. *A Church in the South of France*, Winston Churchill, mid 1930s.

Above: 49. Tea-time at Chartwell, August 1927. *Clockwise from the front:* WSC, Thérèse Sickert, Diana Mitford, Edward Marsh, Frederick Lindemann, Randolph Churchill, Diana Churchill, Clementine Churchill, Walter Richard Sickert. Painted up by WSC from a photograph by John Fergusson.

Right: 50. Mrs Winston Churchill at the Launch of HMS Indomitable, 1940 (painted up by WSC 1955).

51. *Winston Churchill,*
Sir John Lavery, 1916.

52. *Portrait of Winston
Churchill,* Sir John
Lavery, 1921.

53. *Sir Winston Churchill*,
W. R. Sickert, 1927.

54. *Winston Churchill*,
Ruskin Spear.

55. Sketch for a portrait of Sir Winston Churchill, Graham Sutherland.

and vision which transcended their rational military calculations. Churchill cited and blamed what Flandin was told by both Baldwin and Neville Chamberlain during that London visit as being responsible for quenching the somewhat flickering French will to resist. Flandin, no great man at the best of times although rather a Churchill favourite, decided that, if he could not get British support to control the Germans when they were still relatively weak, he had better try to make friends with them as they became strong. As a result he was placed on trial as a collaborationist after the war, and it required oral testimony from Randolph and written testimony from Churchill himself to get him acquitted.

Despite his hindsight, Churchill was far from being rampageously strong on the Rhineland issue at the time. On the Saturday (14 March), the day immediately after his final disappointment so far as early office was concerned, he went to Birmingham to address the annual Jewellers' Banquet, a very grand civic and national occasion through at least to the 1960s, and there delivered no message of doom but a considerable panegyric of Chancellor of the Exchequer Chamberlain (it was of course on Neville's home ground) in which he referred to him, in the Shakespearian phrase, as 'the pack-horse in our great affairs'.* He also said that Chamberlain would 'be for ever associated with the regeneration of our finances and our credit'.[19] On the Tuesday Churchill dined at the Belgian Embassy for the new Prime Minister (Van Zeeland) of that country and was reported by Harold Nicolson as being 'in superb form', in contrast with Anthony Eden, 'who looked haggard with exhaustion, his lovely eyes rimmed with red and puffy with sleeplessness'.[20]

On neither occasion was there an indication that Churchill thought irreversible disaster had struck either himself or the country. He did however think that Hitler getting away with his Rhineland venture left the French in urgent need of cosseting, and he deliberately set himself up as an audible 'friend of France' in Britain. On 17 April he wrote a vast letter to *The Times* rebutting (in courteous terms) his old friend Lord Hugh Cecil for an inadequate understanding of French fears of Germany and chided Cecil again in the same columns a month later. In the early autumn he took even more pains with Anglo-French relations. After two painting sojourns, one at the end of August at the château of

* This reference caused Chamberlain almost as much pleasure as his ability to write to Churchill and point out that the quotation was from *Richard III* and not, as Churchill falsely believed, from *Henry VI*.

Consuelo Balsan (née Vanderbilt, ex-Marlborough) near Dreux on the southern edge of Normandy and the other in early September a return to Maxine Elliott's Côte d'Azur villa, he made a complicated journey to spend twenty-four hours at Flandin's house in his constituency of the Yonne. He got out of his Train Bleu *wagon-lit* at Dijon at 7.30 on a Sunday morning and was driven sixty miles into the Burgundy country-side. That evening he reported to Clementine, who as so often was not with him, that he had 'exhausted the possibilities of conversation on politics, & [had] retired to bed'.[21]

He also fitted in a day at French army manoeuvres with General Gamelin, who was to be the first and fairly disastrous French Com-mander-in-Chief in 1939–40, as well as calling in Paris on Léon Blum, who had become Prime Minister of a Popular Front government in May. In contrast with his attitude to the not very dissimilar Popular Front in Spain, for which he showed little sympathy when it was confronted by General Franco's revolt in July, he treated Blum with high consideration, writing respectfully to him on several occasions. 'I hope you will allow me to offer my earnest congratulations upon all the great improvements that have taken place in French affairs since I first had the pleasure of meeting you at the Quay D'Orsai [*sic*],'[22] he wrote on 8 November (1936). Then, almost as soon as he got back to Chartwell after this three-week trip, Churchill turned round and went back to Paris to deliver (in English) a much publicized lecture at the Théâtre des Ambassadeurs on the need to defend parliamentary democ-racy and the liberal state. To judge from the letters of congratulation which he received from both sides of the Channel (not always of course a wholly objective guide) it appears to have been a major success. The very worldly and long-serving press attaché at the British Embassy (Sir Charles Mendl) wrote that 'there is no question that no foreigner has even given a Conference since I have been here that has been so enthusiastically received'.[23]

This spurt of francophilia fitted in with his central political activity of the year, which was an attempt to marry support for the League of Nations with a determined strengthening of Britain's defences. To do this required a considerable feat of political engineering, for barely a couple of years before those who had been most enthusiastic for the League saw one of its most important and hopeful manifestations as the *Disarmament* Conference, and those who were most vigorous propagan-dists for Britain's armed forces regarded the League as a namby-pamby organization for interfering in other countries' business. Most of

Churchill's India Bill allies were in this latter category, and when he sought to broaden his demand for arms with support for the League Covenant several of them wrote in bewildered protest. It was indeed an odd time for Churchill to move towards a new enthusiasm for the League because it had just, and with Churchill's feelings very ambiguous on the issue, sustained a major defeat by its failure to restrain Mussolini. Nor had the supine acceptance of Hitler's Rhineland coup, with its tearing up of both Versailles and Locarno, done much to strengthen the view that security could be found through the enforcement of treaties by an international rule of law. Furthermore Churchill's sensible desire to improve his relations with those in the centre and on the moderate left of British politics (which were to be crucial to him in 1940) was not helped by his attitude to the Spanish Civil War. While he did not wish to see Italian Fascism, and still less German Nazism, get a grip on the Iberian peninsula, there is no doubt that he was instinctively inclined to blame the Soviet Union (towards which on other grounds he was becoming more favourable) at least as much as the two fascist powers for fomenting the conflict. He somewhat more readily believed stories of Republican than of Nationalist atrocities.

One result of his modified sympathy for General Franco's revolt was that it caused a hiccup in his developing relations with Ivan Maisky, the half-Jewish and relatively pro-Western Soviet ambassador in London throughout the 1930s. The usually calm Maurice Hankey, secretary of the Cabinet, was undoubtedly exaggerating when, after a visit to Chartwell in April 1936, he described Churchill as a 'bosom friend of M. Maisky',[24] but there was a certain amount of *va-et-vient* between them, which did not however prevent Maisky from rebuking Churchill for marring an otherwise good November House of Commons speech by blaming Russia for the Spanish eruption.

Nonetheless Churchill's 1936 move towards the centre of British politics was a neat exercise, strategically wise and tactically well executed. It was achieved through a number of relatively minor organizations with confusing names which were made in sum into a considerable force mainly through the refulgence of Churchill's fame and personality. And it was this quality, combined with his oratory, which made him such a desirable catch for those by whom he had recently decided that he wanted to be caught.

Central to the enterprise was the so-called Focus Group. This began hesitantly as a luncheon club, meeting in the Hotel Victoria on the corner of Northumberland Avenue and only a few yards from the Hotel

Metropole, his office as Minister of Munitions twenty years earlier. There was some early doubt about who was to pay the bills for the repasts. This was quickly and satisfactorily resolved, mainly through the generosity of Eugen Spier, a rich German Jew, who was not exactly a refugee, for he had migrated to Britain as early as 1922. This length of residence did not prevent his being interned as an enemy alien in June 1940 and deported to Canada, which fate (of which no doubt a preoccupied Churchill was ignorant at the time) seems a poor reward for his anti-appeasement activities of the 1930s. Spier returned to Britain in 1945 and subsequently published some interesting insights into the Focus Group.

One of these insights was that Churchill at the luncheons always insisted on sitting next to Lady Violet Bonham Carter, who was a regular participant, and also on having his favourite port served. When asked if there was any connection between these two demands he replied that it was because both of them generated a special warmth.[25] This regaining of centre stage by Lady Violet was a good indication of a mild leftward movement on Churchill's part, although from this point of view there was one even more significant Focus participant, and that was Sir Walter Citrine, the general secretary of the Trades Union Congress.

Others closely associated with the group were: Wickham Steed, a former editor of *The Times*; Norman Angell, a leading 'peace' propagandist since he had published *The Great Illusion* in 1910, who had been briefly a Labour MP in 1929–31 and had won the Nobel Peace Prize in 1933; Philip Guedalla, a now under-estimated historian of insight, too fond of epigrams for his academic reputation, and who was to write a good short life of Churchill in 1941 before dying young in 1944; and Duncan Sandys, as a son-in-law adjutant to the central figure. Less core figures but occasionally participating were Archibald Sinclair, who had become leader of the Liberal party after the defeat of Herbert Samuel at the 1935 election, and two significant Labour MPs, Philip Noel-Baker and Hugh Dalton, both products of King's College, Cambridge but of contrasting personality, the first too idealistic, the second too harshly realistic, and sometimes clangingly so. However they were both fully alive to the Nazi danger and less bound by Labour tribalism than many of their party colleagues.

Towards the end of the year Attlee, the party leader who was always cautious in pre-war days of acting outside the confines set by his colleagues, was persuaded by Cecil of Chelwood to sign a League of

Nations Union manifesto of which Churchill was the principal author. Churchill indeed during this year of repositioning operated through a series of 'fronts' which in their cumulative effectiveness were reminiscent of the contemporary efforts of his sworn enemies – the British Communist party. Thus the Focus group evolved into the Anti-Nazi Council, with Citrine as President and Norman Angell, Sylvia Pankhurst (of suffragette fame), and Eleanor Rathbone, the much respected and left-leaning Independent MP for the Combined English Universities, as Vice-Presidents. But Churchill was very much the guiding spirit, as he was of the British Section of the New Commonwealth Society, of which Lord Davies a rich, public-spirited Welsh peer, persuaded him without undue difficulty to accept the presidency.

In June 1936 Davies wrote long and flattering but manifestly heartfelt letters to Churchill, urging him to use the New Commonwealth Society as a platform and to become himself the light of the world and to save Europe from disaster. Churchill responded with an enthusiasm which was only slightly wary. He was indeed very good in this phase at ecumenicism. He wrote to Cecil on 21 October, when yet another body called 'Freedom and Peace' was mooted, saying: 'There is no question of the eclipse of the New Commonwealth Society nor the League of Nations Union, but only for a fusion of practical working effort and for united advance.'[26] And when he had spoken at another somewhat expanded Focus Group occasion at the Savoy Hotel on 15 October, he had exhibited both a tact which was not normally thought to be the strongest weapon in his armoury and the *bonhomie* which is mostly in good supply when those who are not used to working together come into a spontaneous unity for a specific object. His handling of Citrine was brilliant: 'I see no reason why we should not now have our opening meeting at the Albert Hall or Queen's Hall and marshal the widest platform we can possibly get. . . . Of course Sir Walter Citrine must be in the chair. We cannot have the meeting until he can take the chair. I certainly would not speak under a lesser authority than Sir Walter in the chair.'[27]

Churchill on this occasion was also good at embracing the other participants and the doctrine which was of most appeal to his new allies: 'As to the question of policy, we have a most important statement issued by [Mr Wickham Steed], who has been working for the past three or four months upon it, and we have also a Draft Manifesto; and I have had a letter from Sir Norman Angell with whom I am in the most hearty accord. . . . Our policy is that we adhere to the

Covenant of the League of Nations; that is our rock. We do not in the slightest degree allow that to be departed from or whittled down in any respect.'[28]

This new orientation involved him in no weakening of his conviction that a more strongly armed Britain must be the cornerstone of any effective League policy. At the end of July he had organized a strong Conservative deputation which had waited upon the Prime Minister, accompanied by Halifax (as leader of the House of Lords) and Inskip (as Minister for the Co-ordination of Defence) and had engaged them for many hours on the deficiencies in Britain's defence effort. Churchill had got Austen Chamberlain and Lord Salisbury to act as front men for this deputation of eighteen, but this did not prevent his doing most of the talking himself. Indeed there had been a reference in the Cabinet minutes of a few weeks earlier to his threatening to make a speech lasting four hours, although this threat fortunately did not materialize. Not a great deal resulted from the two meetings, but they at least showed that the development of the softer half of his line involved no weakening of its harder aspect. He was showing a greater capacity to foster an opening to the left than for a long time past, perhaps indeed since his post-1911 fixation on the navy had overlaid his Board of Trade and Home Office liberalism. He had tried to make the July 1936 deputation an all-party one, but Attlee had stood back and Sinclair had followed suit.

Taken in the round Churchill's political position by November 1936 looked more favourably based than had seemed likely when his 1935 and early 1936 hopes for inclusion in the government had been three times disappointed. He made a fairly successful Commons foreign policy speech on 8 November, and another more memorable one on the 12th. This later speech was notable for a sustained piece of contrapuntal irony and also for the fact that it provoked Baldwin, in reply, to touch one of the several low points of his roller-coaster career with something very near to a damaging whine. Churchill's mocking passage was pegged upon the loose premiss of a remark of Duff Cooper, the First Lord of the Admiralty and soon to be one of Churchill's closer allies. Cooper had said, 'We are always reviewing the position.' Churchill pounced: 'Everything, [the First Lord] assured us, is entirely fluid. I am sure that is true. . . . The government cannot make up their mind, or they cannot get the Prime Minister to make up his mind. So they go on in strange paradox, decided only to be undecided, resolved to be irresolute, adamant for drift, solid for fluidity, all powerful to be impotent. So we go on preparing more months and years – precious, perhaps vital, to the greatness of Britain – for the locusts to eat.'[29] No one could pretend that Churchill's careful constructions were spontaneous, but at least they achieved a certain derisive grandeur, which was wholly lacking from Baldwin's notorious reply, in which he defended himself from the charge that Hitler had been allowed to get a two-year head start in rearmament.

> I put before the House my own views with an appalling frankness. You will remember at that time [1933–4] the Disarmament Conference was sitting in Geneva. You will remember that at that time there was probably a stronger pacifist feeling running through this country than at any time since the War. You will remember the election in Fulham . . . when a seat which the National government held was lost by about 7000 votes on no issue but the pacifist one. My position as leader of a great party was not altogether a comfortable one. I asked myself what chance was there – when the feeling which was given expression to in Fulham was common throughout the country – what chance there was of that feeling being so changed that the country would give a mandate for rearmament? Supposing I had gone to the country and said that Germany was rearming and that we must rearm, does anyone think that this pacific democracy would have rallied to that cry at that moment? I cannot think of anything that would have made the loss of the election from my point of view more certain.[30]

It was hardly an heroic Prime Ministerial lead, and it made Churchill's clarion call stand out in sharp contrast. Six days later 'Baffy' Dugdale, Arthur Balfour's favourite niece and chosen biographer, as well as being no political fool herself, wrote in her diary: 'I predict that Winston will take on LNU* and use it! Also that he will shortly form a Government, drawing the Right by his Armament programme, the Left by his support of the League.'[31]

On 25 November Churchill further fortified his position by a rousing speech to a New Commonwealth Society London hotel luncheon which attracted the splendid audience of 450. And everything seemed *en bonne voie* for an Albert Hall 'umbrella' rally bringing all the interlocking organizations together. This had been under consideration since the beginning of the Focus Group, but Churchill had been reluctant to hold it prematurely. Now, with confidence, it was to take place on Thursday,

---

* League of Nations Union with, 'take on' being presumably used in the sense of 'take over'.

3 December. Citrine was to take the chair and Churchill was to be the principal speaker. It was to symbolize the new unity of the anti-Nazi and pro-collective-security political centre.

Alas, by the time that the meeting took place, Churchill had got himself diverted down one of the most foolish and least rewarding branch lines of his life. At the end of November 'the King's matter', as Baldwin euphemistically referred to it, came out from the wraps which for months had protected it from the eyes of the British public. At least since the summer the infatuation of the new King with Wallis Simpson, a Baltimore lady of the same relatively mature years as himself who was moving towards the end of her second marriage, had been much commented on in the American and continental press, as well as gravely preoccupying the Prime Minister. The issue was not whether the King was transferring his interest and affections to a new lady. Even after the twenty-five puritanical years of King George V the memory of King Edward VII was sufficiently green for King Edward VIII not to be forbidden this degree of indiscretion. It was that his wilfulness and her ambition posed the threat of marriage with its queenly consequences. And behind this lay a growing doubt on the part of Baldwin and others as to whether the monarch's character and sense of public propriety made him in any event suitable for the demands of constitutional kingship.

All of this, despite the amazing (as it now appears) silence of the British press and the apparently naive ignorance even of some members of the Cabinet, was common gossip in Churchill's circle. He counted himself a friendly familiar of the King's. As already mentioned, he had in the early post-war years been a frequent guest at small supper and dancing parties assembled to amuse the then Prince of Wales. And in the summer that had just gone by the Churchills had been guests at an intriguing Blenheim weekend where the other visitors were the King, Mrs Simpson, still accompanied by her husband, the Duff Coopers, the newly succeeded Duke and Duchess of Buccleuch and Lady Cunard. Churchill, in spite of his own faithful monogamy, was rarely censorious of others whose habits were less concentrated. Furthermore he was responsive to the new King's boyish charm, which fitted in with his romantic view of monarchy, and found him much preferable to King George V, who was the only one of the five monarchs of his political career with whom he never really got on. Arising partly out of the Blenheim encounter, he drafted during that summer two commemorative speeches for the King, and received warm expressions of gratitude.

There was therefore a basis and history of friendship which made it not only plausible but natural that when, at the height of the crisis, the King sought and secured Baldwin's permission to consult with some independent political figure, it should have been to Churchill that he turned. What is less plausible – and not without importance in relation to Churchill's story rather than to that of the King – is Churchill's statement on the timing of his summons. It is indisputable that he dined with the King alone at Fort Belvedere (a house on the edge of Windsor Great Park which bore a curious resemblance to a cardboard toy castle) on the evening of Friday, 4 December. Churchill stated, in an account of the Abdication which he dictated on an unspecified date soon after the events, that, following no contact with the King throughout the autumn, he was only alerted to the possibility of this dinner by a telephone call from Walter Monckton* at 5.00 p.m. on the same day.[32]

There is no obvious motive for dissimulation in Churchill's account of the timing, but there is a double reason for suggesting that at least a warning summons might have been delivered on the previous day. First, it was a bold view that an English politician, even when summoned by a King, could be reliably found at 5.00 on a Friday afternoon for a crucial dinner that evening. Second, Churchill's demeanour on the previous evening (Thursday, 3 December) was highly suggestive of his having just received a summons for the following day which set his mind racing. It was the evening of the Albert Hall meeting, at which he was to be the star and towards which setpiece he had been resolutely yet cautiously working for several months past. Yet, according to the sober memoirs of Citrine, the chairman of the evening:

> All [the speakers] had assembled in a private room behind the platform except for Winston who was late. . . . I hate to keep an audience waiting and I am a firm believer in starting meetings at the advertised time. So I said to my colleagues, 'If Winston isn't here in three minutes we are going on the platform without him.' . . . I was relieved when a few moments later Churchill rushed up. 'I must speak to you,' he said rather excitedly calling me aside. 'What about?' I asked rather gruffly. 'About the King,' he replied. . . . 'What's that got to do with this meeting?' I demanded. 'People will expect a statement from me,' Churchill answered. 'I don't see that at all,' I said. 'We have come here

---

* Monckton, a highly successful advocate, was a very close adviser to the King at the time and, fifteen years later, was to become a conciliatory Minister of Labour in Churchill's last government.

to demonstrate our unity in standing up to the Nazis. We haven't come to talk about the King or anything else. If you make a statement others may want to do so. You will certainly be challenged, and if no one else does it I will.

So the long-awaited rally began with a coolness between Churchill and his carefully cultivated chairman, although Citrine also graciously recorded that 'the meeting passed off successfully without the least vestige of discord', and that 'Winston read his speech [confined to international affairs] . . . in the most masterly fashion.'[33]

At the Fort Belvedere dinner on the following evening Churchill was struck by the strain under which the King, who he claimed had two mental blackouts during the meal, was operating, and urged him to send for both those great and good doctors, Lords Dawson of Penn and Horder. Above all he urged the need for time, and advised both the King and Baldwin (in a subsequent letter) to proceed slowly. There can be little doubt, however, that in the course of an emotionally charged evening, Churchill did come very near to casting himself in the role of a potential leader of a 'King's party'.* This came out clearly in a most extraordinary letter which Churchill wrote to the King on the next (Saturday) evening. It was extraordinary both because of the rashness (and frequent inaccuracies) of the content and because of the jauntiness of tone, in sharp contrast with the note of measured respect in which, both before and subsequently, he normally addressed his sovereign. This jauntiness was indeed such as to cast doubt upon Churchill's even semi-sobriety when he wrote it, although this, partly because of regularity of intake, was not normally a problem with him. The letter is worth reproduction almost in full:

Sir,
News from all fronts! No pistol to be held at the King's head. No doubt that this request for time will be granted. Therefore no final decision or Bill till after Christmas – probably February or March.
2. *On no account must the King leave the country*. Windsor Castle is his battle station (poste de commandment). When so much is at stake, no

* This could have had devastating constitutional consequences. It would have left those who took the other view in an 'anti-King's party' position, and the subsequent battle between the two parties would have totally compromised the political neutrality of the Sovereign, which is essential to constitutional monarchy. The danger was averted, not because of Churchill's wisdom, but because he found no basis of support. Both Parliament and country were overwhelmingly on Baldwin's side on this issue.

minor inclinations can be indulged. It would be far better for Mrs Simpson to return to England for a day or two, than for the King to go abroad now. . . .

3. Lord Craigavon, Prime Minister of Northern Ireland, is deeply moved by loyalty to the King, and all for time. Could he not be invited to luncheon tomorrow? He has a constitutional right of access (I think) & anyhow there could be no objection. His visit should be made public. He shares my hopes such as they are of an ultimate happy ending. It's a long way to Tipperary.

4. Max [Beaverbrook]. The King brought him back across the world. He is a tiger to fight. I gave him the King's message & – please telephone or write – better telephone. I cannot see it would do harm to see him if it could be arranged. Important however to make contact with him. A *devoted* tiger! Very scarce breed.

5. For real wit Bernard Shaw's article in to-night's Evening Standard should be read. He is joyous.

Summary.

Good advance on all parts giving prospects of gaining good positions and assembling large force behind them.

Your Majesty's faithful devoted servant and subject,

WSC[34]

On the following day (Sunday, 6 December) Churchill issued a rather turgid press statement. Nominally it was just an appeal for 'time and patience'. But in the course of developing this case he edged towards a number of dangerous constitutional doctrines. No ministry, he said, had the right to advise the abdication of the sovereign. If ministers did not like the rejection of their advice 'they are of course free to resign', and it was quite improper of them to try to prevent in advance the formation of any alternative government. Furthermore the King could not possibly (because of the timetable of the Simpson divorce) perform the act of which ministers were so frightened – marrying Mrs Simpson – before the end of April at the earliest. Why not therefore let the discussion run in a leisurely way?

This last point brought him a particularly heavy rebuke from J. A. Spender, biographer of Campbell-Bannerman and of Asquith and a much respected Liberal editor: 'How can you suggest that the present state of things should be prolonged for five months – five months of raging & tearing controversy, quite possibly a King's party being formed against the Government, the Crown a centre of schism tearing Country and Commonwealth to pieces & all this at this moment in world affairs?' Nor was Spender the only one to write severely. Wickham

Steed warned on the same day that it may be necessary 'for those of us who have worked with you in the Freedom and Peace movement [an alternative name for the sponsors of the Albert Hall meeting] to dissociate ourselves publicly from your standpoint'. And Lord Salisbury, from a different angle wrote with quiet menace: 'I am watching your attitude now with great anxiety.'[35]

None of these letters, which he would have received on the Monday, had the effect of warning Churchill off. He went to the House of Commons on the Tuesday afternoon (8 December), having reputedly lunched well at an Anglo-French occasion, determined to dig in. Many members had returned from weekends in constituencies more provincial and remote than Epping (where Churchill had in any event not been) with their pro-Baldwin and anti-King sentiments strengthened by such local opinion as they had encountered. Baldwin merely made a conciliatory holding statement, promising more on the Thursday. This did not prevent Churchill from plunging in as though he had not heard what Baldwin said and had come with all his heavy guns primed. It was not so much what he said – indeed he was bludgeoned into silence before he could say very much – as that it was a classic example of running completely against the feeling of the House. This may not always be a bad thing to do, for the House of Commons can sometimes be at its worst when it is seized by a common gust of emotion. The cause of keeping King Edward VIII upon the throne does not however appear in retrospect (or much at the time) to be equivalent to the moral force which led Martin Luther to nail his notice to the church door at Wittenberg.

There can be little doubt about the scale of Churchill's débacle on that afternoon. Harold Nicolson, normally friendly, wrote: 'Winston collapsed utterly in the House yesterday. . . . He has undone in five minutes the patient reconstruction works of two years.'[36] Leo Amery, despite his frequent hostility, at that stage relatively friendly to Churchill, wrote that 'he [Churchill] was completely staggered by the unanimous hostility of the House, as well as by being called to order by Mr Speaker'.[37] 'Baffy' Dugdale, reversing her opinion of three weeks before and allowing Churchill only three instead of Nicolson's five minutes for the digging of his grave, wrote: 'Robert Bernays [a young liberal Tory MP, subsequently killed in the war] drove me home. He says Winston was absolutely howled down yesterday, and is in a very chastened mood today. . . . In three minutes his hopes of return to power and influence are shattered.'[38] And to round it off with an *et tu*,

Brute cut, Robert Boothby made sure that Churchill was immediately informed at a moment of maximum vulnerability that 'this afternoon you have delivered a blow to the King, both in the House in the country, far harder than Baldwin ever conceived of. You have reduced the number of potential supporters to the minimum possible – I should think now about seven in all.'[39] Boothby subsequently apologized for this letter and Churchill was habitually free of vindictiveness. Even so, when in 1940 Boothby was forced to resign from the (Churchill) government on account of a 'sleaze' allegation, and its chief was thought not to have striven officiously to save him, it is possible that the recollection of this crashingly insensitive letter might have floated into Churchill's recollection.

Humiliated on the floor, assailed in the smoking room by Boothby's poisoned missive and no doubt also by a general atmosphere of hostility, Churchill could not just slink away. He was engaged that evening, presumably about two hours after the horror in the chamber, to deliver a major speech on defence to the 1922 Committee of Conservative backbenchers. The whips' report to the Cabinet on the meeting said: 'There was a large attendance. . . . Little applause was forthcoming while Mr Churchill spoke. The general impression, however, was that it was a good speech and was well received.'[40] Its content required a whip's report of substance running to several thousand words. It was in the circumstances a feat of self-discipline to have delivered it at all. It showed that Churchill, as well as being an egotistical *prima donna*, was also a trouper. And he showed this again on the Thursday, the day of Baldwin's ruminative, gentle yet devastating account of his whole handling of 'the King's matter', explaining how the King had been brought himself to prefer the signing of a deed of abdication to any other practicable outcome.

This speech was Baldwin's last great triumph. Then Attlee, in support of Baldwin, delivered what was perhaps the first of his major exercises in clipped authority and well-judged wisdom. After Sinclair, thought a little long, Churchill tried to perform the difficult operation of a tactical withdrawal in most unfavourable circumstances. Even Amery thought that Churchill did it brilliantly 'in an admirably phrased little speech'.[41] What was done was done was his note. That and what had been left undone should be left to history. Now all those who believed in the monarchical principle 'must endeavour to fortify the throne and to give His Majesty's successor that strength which can only come from the love of a united nation and Empire'.[42]

How much damage did the Abdication do to Churchill's position and prospects? On 1 January 1937 he wrote to Bernard Baruch saying: 'I do not feel that my own political position is much affected by the line I took; but even if it were, I should not wish to have acted otherwise.'[43] To most people at the beginning of 1937 this would have been regarded as grossly complacent. But in view of what happened less than three and a half years later it is at least arguable that Churchill's medium-term perspective, and certainly his ability to sustain yet another dip of the big dipper, was steadier than the judgements of Nicolson, Amery, Bernays, Dugdale, Boothby *et al.*

The final irony, however, is that, had Churchill succeeded in keeping Edward VIII upon the throne, he might well have found it necessary in 1940–1 to depose and/or lock up his sovereign as the dangerously potential head of a Vichy-style state. Mrs Dugdale concluded her 8 December judgement by writing: 'But God is once more behind his servant Stanley Baldwin.' In the context of the next decade He might be regarded as being still more powerfully, if also more subtly, behind his servant Winston Churchill.

27

FROM THE ABDICATION TO MUNICH

NINETEEN-THIRTY-SEVEN was on the whole a quiet year. In the downward descent of the late 1930s it was one in which the angle of plunge was temporarily reduced. There was no new monstrosity on the part of Hitler or of Mussolini. They went on supporting General Franco's increasingly successful revolt, and indeed destroyed Guernica in July in an early rehearsal for the Luftwaffe's concentrated blitz on Coventry and other British cities three years later. But there was no clear crisis such as Abyssinia had provided in 1935, the Rhineland in 1936, and as first the Anschluss with Austria and then the relentless pressure upon Czechoslovakia were to do in 1938. Nineteen-thirty-seven was as a result in the short inter-war armistice the final year of superficial peace, defined in the sense that people of judgement and foresight could for the last time avoid acknowledging that war was inevitable. It was the equivalent of 1913 in the pre-1914 autumnal sunshine.

It was not a satisfactory year for Churchill. Viewed with hindsight there can be little doubt that he had already got himself into a position in which only war could bring him back to effective power. This did not mean that he wanted war. Although exhilarated by military problems, he was, as previously argued, never a warmonger. He disliked the loss of life in a way that Haig would have found soft-hearted, Stalin incomprehensible and even Roosevelt a little over-cautious, and in addition he did not clearly see war as the necessary resurrection of his political fortunes. He was constantly semi-optimistic that some new shake of the political dice would bring him back into senior office. He always protested his indifference to office, but with a caveat that, if he were given some real job, such as defence, he would have to accept. He even displayed a flicker of hope that the replacement of Baldwin by Neville Chamberlain in late May might open up a new prospect for him.

By 1937 Churchill was getting bored by his life of semi-retirement. Cincinattus was very attached to his farm, but not for too long. Charles de Gaulle found that eleven years at Colombey-les-deux-Eglises was more than enough. And Churchill by 1937 was beginning to approach both this limit and de Gaulle's sense, twenty years later, that he was sixty-seven and physically ageing. Churchill during 1937 was only sixty-two, but he too was coming to feel his age. There was also a sense that his almost frenzied commercial writing of the early and mid-1930s was beginning to exhaust both the author and his market. Did *Marlborough*, his central literary task of the period, move from being a labour of pietistic love to being an albatross? It is difficult to see why he had allowed it to expand so vastly, both over pages and over time. What had been conceived in the summer of 1929 as a one- or at most two-volume work of 180,000–250,000 words was, eight years later (and four years after the publication of the first volume), requiring a desperate concentration of effort to get it finally to bed in four volumes and just under a million words. Neither his London nor his New York publisher was particularly pleased with the expansion. To the former he had to write on 11 June apologizing that it could not be ready for the press by the end of August but only by December. And to Clementine he was writing in late July (she was on a cure in Austria) complaining that he was grossly overworked, with *Marlborough* constituting the bulk of the ten-ton weight which he felt was sitting on his head. Generally there was an impression that 'John Duke' had overstayed his welcome and that everyone would be glad to see the project finished.*

Furthermore *Marlborough* obtruded into the time when Churchill ought to have been working (for a different publisher) on his next major project of a *History of the English-Speaking Peoples*, and he had to write rather doubtfully reassuring letters to Cassells, from whom he had already received an advance, telling them how thoroughly the preparatory research work was being done. The outpouring of newspaper articles had to continue, for their remuneration was an essential part of the economy of the whole Churchill establishment, Chartwell and Morpeth Mansions, secretaries and research assistants. The press output for the year 1937, recorded by Martin Gilbert, with his usual precision, amounted to sixty-four articles, well over one a week. Thirty-three of them were done for Beaverbook's *Evening Standard*, which had become Churchill's main outlet. Of these the majority were straight political

---

* Nevertheless, when the fourth volume eventually came out on 2 September 1938, it was warmly received and eagerly read at least by the long list of friends to whom Churchill sent a copy.

pieces, published about once a fortnight throughout the year. But there was also, for the same newspaper, a more wide-ranging (and pot-boiling) series entitled 'The Great Reigns', which began with 'The Heroic Story of Alfred the Great' and ended with 'Victoria, Mother of Many Nations'.

The *News of the World* came second as an outlet with thirteen articles published during the year, although it was close run by the *Sunday Chronicle*, which took eleven. The *News of the World* articles were always received with great enthusiasm by its principal proprietor, Sir Emsley Carr. Indeed he wrote on 30 October (1937) a letter which was almost equally lyrical about Churchill's most recent article* and the standing and success of his newspaper:

> Hearty congratulations on this week's article. It is, I think, one of the most interesting so far as our general readers are concerned.
>
> Today our circulation exceeds four million net, and it requires no imagination on your part to realize what an enormous public – probably the largest in the world – you are addressing. Four readers to every paper issued – some say five – is the usual computation, and the power behind this number is what you will comprehend.
>
> I cannot say how delighted we are to have you as our chief contributor, and we are looking forward to your promise to dine with us one Saturday night and see our production in active operation.[1]

The *News of the World* was a great standby, particularly as it paid nearly £400 an article (£12,000 today) but the *Sunday Chronicle* was very good at taking the leftovers from Churchill's capacious kitchen. In February the *Chronicle* published 'Big Navy', in May 'A King's Command' and in June 'The Creed of the Devil' (equally hostile to communism and to fascism). Those working in the kitchen were remunerated, but not over-generously. A rather shadowy ghost called Adam Marshall Diston – he never seemed to appear at Chartwell – got £15 for doing most of the work on a successful *News of the World* article, and even the much esteemed and fastidious Eddie Marsh (who was retired from the civil service and knighted in 1937) after being set to summarize Tolstoy's *War and Peace* in a few thousand words – 'the most gruelling job I ever did'[2] – was lucky if he got 10 per cent of a Churchill fee. However they and the separate book researchers seemed content to work on the terms they were offered.

---

* Somewhat cumbersomely entitled 'Vision of the Future through the Eyes of Science'.

Where Churchill was weaker in 1937 than he had been earlier in the decade was in his writing for the lucrative American market. The *Saturday Evening Post* had disappeared from his list of outlets, as had the Hearst press; he wrote four articles for *Colliers* during the year, but they were not all published. However his frank but by no means wholly unfriendly profile of Neville Chamberlain, following Chamberlain's accession to the premiership, most certainly was, although only after the addition of a supplementary 400 or 500 words of 'description aloof personality and anecdotes of man' which a cable from his exigent editors asked him to supply.[3] At home the *Daily Mail* outlet (then, as now, a very well-paying newspaper) had dried up. Rothermere remained a reasonably amicable acquaintance but no longer a promoting ally.

At the end of 1936 Churchill had itemized, in a letter to his always worried bank manager, how his total income for the next year should be around £15,000,[4] which turned out with a few balancing pluses and minuses to be reasonably accurate and which in early twenty-first century prices was the equivalent of approximately £450,000, hardly a pittance, but nor, in relation to his lifestyle or to the resources of most of his friends, at all munificent. Today many City traders of thirty-five would expect more. And it raised serious doubt about whether Chartwell, important although it was to his life and pleasure, could be kept going. On 2 February (1937) he wrote to Clementine, who was on a long skiing holiday, in a letter full of financial worries and even of news of little economies:

> there is a lady nibbling around for a house like Chartwell. . . . Capon [an estate agent] said he would on no account mention any figure less than £30,000. If I could see £25,000 I should close with it. If we do not get a good price we can quite well carry on for a year or two more. But no good offer should be refused, having regard to the fact that our children are almost all flown, and my life is probably in its closing decade.[5]

Either the 'nibbling lady' evaporated or there was some uplift in the Churchill fortunes, for the thought of sale receded for a couple of years – his prediction was accurate in this respect – until crisis again loomed. A small 'white knight', who was to be very important in Churchill's later life, did appear on the scene at almost exactly the time of the sale-seeking letter to Clementine, but it is highly doubtful that he made enough immediate financial impact to solve the problem. The welcome horseman was Imre Revesz, a Hungarian settled in Paris from where he ran an agency called Co-operation, which specialized in the wide syndication throughout twenty-five countries of articles by leading political figures. He was recommended to Churchill, almost as a parting benefit, by Austen Chamberlain (who died five weeks later), which was surprising, for remunerative journalism was on the whole one of the games which that grand old gentleman–statesman 'played and [nearly] always lost'. At first Revesz was almost collecting pennies for Churchill. He got *Paris Soir* to pay £9 9s for Churchill's *Evening Standard* articles and the *Dagens Nyheter* in Stockholm no more than £4 4s, while a little Yiddish journal in Kaunas, Lithuania, got them for eight shillings, today worth about £12. Of these second rights payments Revesz took 40 per cent, which was high, but he worked hard for it, creating and maintaining a web of contacts, arranging for a multiplicity of translations, and trying to ensure simultaneous publication (to which local editors attached great importance) in a Europe without faxes or e-mails and with only rudimentary air services. In the single month of October 1937 he and Churchill exchanged nineteen letters. Nine of them were written by Churchill, who after initial caution had become very keen on the Revesz enterprise, which was achieving not only wide dissemination of his views, but also additional income of nearly £2,000 a year, without any additional writing.

Early in the war Revesz moved first to London,* where he was seriously wounded in an air raid, and then to New York, changing his name to Emery Reves and acquiring an appealing (to Churchill at any rate) Texan companion called Wendy, whom he later married. In the late 1940s he made Churchill and himself rich by negotiating the American royalties for *The Second World War* and buying all the foreign-language rights on his own account. Out of this enterprise he acquired La Pausa, Churchill's favourite South of France retreat from 1955 to 1960, when there was a severe social hiccup between them. Clementine Churchill did not like the Reveses, and this may have much to do with the end of his long visits.

The most spirit-lifting of Churchill's writing activities of 1937 was the assembling and publication of *Great Contemporaries* in the summer

---

* Personal intervention by Churchill was required first to get Revesz admitted to Britain in October 1939 and then to get him naturalized (remarkably quickly) in February, 1940. The French Deuxième Bureau reported that he was a 'very suspect pro-Nazi propagandist', apparently on the somewhat convoluted ground that he was living with the sister of the editor of the Communist newspaper *L'Humanité*. This caused an explosive letter from Churchill to Sir Vernon Kell, the head of MI5.

and early autumn. He began to focus sharply upon it in mid-July and there was a subsequent feeling of how strongly the light and pleasurable work of pulling it together and checking a few facts competed with the much heavier labour of digging *Marlborough* on to the light at the end of the long tunnel. *Great Contemporaries* came out at the beginning of September, and had an immediate and continuing moderate success. The first impression of 5,000 copies was quickly sold and was followed by five further impressions of 2,000 each, bringing the sales in the first wave to the highly respectable but far from sensational total of 15,000. Churchill was pleased with this result. 'You will be glad to hear that *Great Contemporaries* has gone like hot cakes,' he wrote to Marsh on 11 October.[6] As usual he presented many copies to old friends and political semi-enemies (Baldwin, Neville Chamberlain and John Simon in the latter category, for example) and got a crop of even warmer letters than such distribution normally evokes.

The reviews, many anonymous in those days, were also mostly good. Leonard Woolf – 'some of the essays are brilliant' – in the *New Statesman* was particularly apposite and favourable. The exception was J. C. Squire, powerfully influential at the time in the *Daily Telegraph*, which caused excessive dismay in Thornton Butterworth, the book's publisher. *Great Contemporaries* in its 1937 version consisted of twenty-two previously published but touched-up profiles, starting with Rose-bery and ending with the hurriedly Moroccan-written King George V. The eight on British politicians were much the best, but the other fourteen were all respectable portraits. The essays on Balfour, Asquith, Curzon and Birkenhead contain passages which remain engraved on the mind. Of Balfour Churchill wrote: 'He passed from one Cabinet to the other [from that of Asquith to that of Lloyd George], from the Prime Minister who was his champion to the Prime Minister who had been his most severe critic, like a powerful graceful cat walking delicately and unsoiled across a rather muddy street.' Of Asquith he said: 'He sat [in Cabinet] like the great judge he was, hearing with trained patience the case deployed on every side. . . . and when at the end he summed up it was very rarely that the silence he had observed till then did not fall on all. . . . With Asquith, either the Court was open or it was shut. If it was open, his whole attention was focussed on the case; and if it was shut there was no use knocking at the door.'

Of Curzon's career he wrote: 'The morning had been golden; the noontide was bronze; and the evening lead. But all were solid, each was polished till it shone after its fashion.' To Birkenhead (F. E. Smith), his great cross-party friend, he was unforgettably generous: 'In every affair, public or personal, if he was with you on the Monday, you would find him the same on the Wednesday, and on the Friday when things looked blue, he would still be marching forward with strong reinforcements.' There was throughout the whole collection a welcome feeling of freedom from the literary atelier, with the brushwork all being as truly *ipsissima* Churchill and free from *scuola di* as were his own paintings. *Great Contemporaries* remains a very bright star in the constellation of Churchill's literary work.

Apart from his vast literary and journalistic output (however much help he employed, the final imprimatur always had to be supplied by himself) Churchill also carried on a large correspondence in which he was rarely economical in the use of words. He bombarded ministers with letters and they were generally treated with the utmost consideration. This was partly because of the manners of the period, which were ministerially better than those of today, and partly because no one wanted unnecessarily to arouse Churchill's debating ire. After a November speech the *Daily Telegraph* commented: 'That Mr Churchill is still the best orator in the House he made plain. . . .' There was also a false *politesse* which, rather like the narrow vowels of those days, as striking in the broad-bottomed bucolic Baldwin as in the more primly buttoned-up and urban Neville Chamberlain, was preserved within the circle of senior Conservative politicians. Baldwin and Chamberlain, it seems more clear in retrospect than it did at the time, were resolved to keep Churchill out of their governments, at least in peacetime in Chamberlain's case. They gave, in private, various reasons for their resolution. Baldwin, for instance, observed to Dr Tom Jones, the epitome of a confidant, in May 1936:

> One of these days I'll make a few casual remarks about Winston. Not a speech – no oratory – just a few words in passing. I've got it all ready. I am going to say that when Winston was born lots of fairies swooped down on his cradle [with] gifts – imagination, eloquence, industry, ability, and then came a fairy who said 'No one person has a right to so many gifts', picked him up and gave him such a shake and twist that with all these gifts he was denied judgement and wisdom. And that is why while we delight to listen to him in this House we do not take his advice.[7]

A few months before Chamberlain succeeded Baldwin, a luncheon with the Prime Minister-to-be inspired 'Baffy' Dugdale to write: 'It seems clear that Winston will not be invited to join Chamberlain's

Cabinet. He [Chamberlain] quoted with approval a description of him made (I think) by Haldane when they were in Asquith's Cabinet: "It is like arguing with a Brass band."[8] Yet, in their differing styles, both Baldwin and Chamberlain responded with enthusiasm tinged with affection whenever the gifts of his successive books arrived. Admiring his literary output was an easy substitute for taking seriously his mostly uncomfortable views.

With lesser ministers within his field of interest his correspondence was as voluminous as it was self-confident. Sir Thomas Inskip's appointment as Minister for the Co-ordination of Defence in March 1936 was a bitter disappointment to Churchill. Inskip was a most unChurchillian figure, worthy, Evangelical, provincial, portentous. But within two months Churchill was writing him letters of criticism, detailed advice and vast length. And Inskip went on with unfailing plodding patience to compose at almost as great a length as Churchill did himself.

As a small and early reward for such diligence Inskip and his wife were invited to lunch at Chartwell on a weekday during the Whitsun recess (of 1936) and accepted with an excessive willingness to start early on the drive from London: 'We hope to reach you on Monday about 12 or perhaps a little earlier,' Inskip announced,[9] somewhat inconsiderately for Churchill's writing habits. His eagerness shone an interesting light, of which there are several other examples of the period, on Churchill's continuing social prestige in the Conservative party. He was widely distrusted politically and ministers complained to each other, and sometimes in the Cabinet minutes, that he was a tiresome and potentially dangerous nuisance, but they also enjoyed an opportunity to visit the fascinating ogre in his castle and to see where he produced the flesh-destroying speeches and articles. Maurice Hankey, the long-standing Cabinet secretary who was soon to be made a minister by Chamberlain, was another (and more frequent) visitor to Chartwell, who also came with a certain sense of daring and being very careful to make a full subsequent record for the Prime Minister.

Other ministers of the period who received substantial policy missives from Churchill included Neville Chamberlain, Swinton, Secretary of State for Air 1935–8, Hore-Belisha after he went to the War Office in 1937, even his old enemy of the India Bill, Samuel Hoare who rejoined the government as First Lord of the Admiralty in the summer of 1936, and Anthony Eden, Foreign Secretary since Hoare's resignation in December 1935. It is noticeable however that the correspondence with Eden was qualitatively different from and warmer than that with the other ministers. These letters were frequent but shorter, more informal, and on Eden's part more forthcoming and less defensive than was the habit of his colleagues. Whatever future tensions were in the pipeline they marked an important transition between Churchill's lack of enthusiasm for Eden's appointment at the end of 1935 to his dismay at his resignation in early 1938. This dismay was famously recorded in *The Gathering Storm*:

> Late in the night of February 20 a telephone message reached me as I sat in my old room at Chartwell . . . that Eden had resigned. . . . During all the war soon to come and in its darkest times I never had any trouble in sleeping. . . . I slept sound and awoke refreshed, and had no feelings except appetite to grapple with whatever the morning's boxes might bring. But now on this night of February 20, 1938, and on this occasion only, sleep deserted me. From midnight till dawn I lay in my bed consumed by emotions of sorrow and fear. There seemed one strong young figure standing up against long, dismal, drawling tides of drift and surrender, or wrong measurements and feeble impulses. My conduct of affairs would have been different from his in many ways; but he seemed to me at this moment to embody the life-hope of the British nation, the grand old British race that had done so much for men, and had yet some more to give. Now he was gone. I watched the daylight slowly creep in through the windows, and saw before me in mental gaze the vision of Death.[10]

This memorable if somewhat contrived piece of writing was probably penned during 1946 and obviously by Churchill himself. It no doubt owed something to the benefits of hindsight. By then Eden had been his sometimes creditably unsubservient Foreign Secretary for three and a half years, and Churchill was also currently dependent upon him to run the opposition during his own frequent absences from the House of Commons. But the passage was also clearly built upon a solid foundation of 1938 truth. Eden's resignation was publicly attributed to differences with Chamberlain over the latter's desire to propitiate Mussolini, a subject about which Churchill had long been equivocal on strategic grounds. But, as with most resignations, this issue did not stand alone. At least equally important was Chamberlain's unimaginative pouring of cold water upon a secret and tentative initiative from Roosevelt which might have opened the way to American involvement in Europe and against Hitler nearly four years before Pearl Harbor. Here Churchill was overwhelmingly on Eden's side. His instinctive sense of the movements of geo-politics far exceeded Chamberlain's clear but

narrow-sighted view of the chessboard (in the phrase brilliantly used by
Keynes about Bonar Law). And there was a third factor, which was a
mixture of sheer incompatibility of temperament and of Eden's prickly
defence of the prerogatives of the Foreign Office against Chamberlain's
depredation, with Sir Horace Wilson, nominally the industrial adviser
to the government, as the spearhead of his advance into diplomatic
territory. (There was to be more than an echo of this fifty years later
when Mrs Thatcher's reliance upon the anti-Treasury advice of Professor Alan Walters contributed substantially to the resignation from the
Chancellorship of Nigel Lawson.) On the question of Foreign Office
amour propre Churchill was more or less neutral. It was the one great
department of state over which he never presided, and during his two
governments he was far from following a Baldwinesque habit of foreign
policy quiescence. On the other hand Horace Wilson, both in style and
in policy, was as deeply antipathetic to him as at any rate some Foreign
Office officials – Wigram (dead at the beginning of 1937) and Vansittart
(shunted from permanent under-secretary to be chief diplomatic adviser
at the beginning of 1938) – were sympathetic.

On balance, however, and beyond the emotion of the moment, the
resignation of Eden (and his replacement by Halifax – another of his
old India Bill enemies) was a major breakpoint in Churchill's attitude
to the Chamberlain government. At first he had undoubtedly preferred
the new Prime Minister to Baldwin, against whom he had latterly
developed an almost obsessive animus. The memory of the great lift
which Baldwin had given him in 1924 had naturally faded. But they
had got on well together for the subsequent four and a half years when
they were Downing Street neighbours, and although Churchill had
resigned against him in 1930 they had preserved full civilities throughout the long Churchillian war of attrition over India. Baldwin had not
been prepared to put him in his government as soon as that war was
over, but nor was Chamberlain when it was two years past. Yet on 17
May (1937) Churchill wrote (to Sir Abe Bailey): 'I am very glad Baldwin is going. I think we shall come to some real and straightforward
politics now he is out of the way.'[11] On 31 May as the senior Privy
Councillor in the House of Commons he seconded the motion for
Chamberlain's election as leader of the Conservative party (Lord Derby
as his analogue in the Lords was the proposer). On 23 September
he wrote to Linlithgow, who had recently succeeded Willingdon as
Viceroy, 'Neville has begun very well and is certainly being given a
very fair chance by all parties.'[12] And on 7 October he went to the

Conservative conference at Scarborough and spoke in almost peniten-
tial terms: 'I used to come here year after year when we had some
differences between ourselves about rearmament and also about a place
called India. So I thought it would only be right that I should come
here when we are all agreed.'[13] The rest of his short speech was a
tribute to the government's foreign policy, which could largely be
regarded as that of Anthony Eden.

Eden's resignation in February 1938 was therefore understandably a
shock, particularly as it was followed by a year during which Nazi
expansionism became increasingly rampant and the policy of the Chamberlain government more firmly committed to pursuing peace by seeking accommodation with Hitler and Mussolini, a policy summed up by
the new label of 'appeasement'. Nonetheless Churchill was still inclined
to give Chamberlain some benefit of the doubt. In mid-March he caused
Harold Nicolson to record that 'never has any man inherited a more
ghastly situation than Neville Chamberlain and he [Churchill] places
the blame wholly on Mr Baldwin'.[14]

At about the same time a bizarre luncheon took place in 10 Downing
Street. Joachim von Ribbentrop, who had been German ambassador in
London since 1936, had been appointed Foreign Minister in place of
Neurath and was about to return to Berlin. On Friday, 11 March 1938
he and his wife were given a farewell luncheon by the Chamberlains.
This was rating him very high. Most departing ambassadors are lucky
to get a Foreign Secretary's luncheon party. Many of them, including
some of distinction, have today to be content with a farewell meal
presided over by a Foreign Office minister of state. Ribbentrop's unique
feat was that of first attracting a Prime Minister's farewell luncheon and
then, eight and a half years later, being hanged by order of a court
jointly set up by a government of the country to which he had been
accredited. To add to the bizarreness of the occasion the Churchills
were invited to be part of the fairly small luncheon party – about sixteen
– and accepted, although neither by virtue of any official position nor of
friendship or sympathy with the Ribbentrops were they natural guests.
And to round off the sense of macabre farce, the Foreign Office
permanent under-secretary Sir Alexander Cadogan, sitting next to Clementine Churchill, received in the course of the meal a message
indicating that German troops were beginning their movement into
Austria for the Anschluss, the incorporation of that small country into
the Greater German Reich. When Cadogan had quietly informed him,
even Chamberlain became politely keen for the Ribbentrops to be off.

However they blandly lingered for another half-hour, giving Frau von Ribbentrop the opportunity chidingly to suggest to Churchill that he should be careful not to spoil friendly Anglo-German relations.[15]

This was the last time that Churchill lunched (or dined) in 10 Downing Street until after the outbreak of war. Although he kept his small Focus Group going and, particularly after *Marlborough* was finally out of the way in March (for publication on 2 September), spoke often in the House of Commons during that last year of the deteriorating peace, he was still on the literary and journalistic treadmill of trying to keep his earnings within hailing distance of his outgoings. In late March (1938) he had to survive the considerable blow of the termination of his *Evening Standard* contract. This, it was made clear, was because his foreign policy views had come to diverge sharply from those of Lord Beaverbrook. Typically of newspaper proprietors, however, a man of business and not Beaverbrook himself, despite his quarter of a century of fluctuating friendship with Churchill, was made to deliver the ill-tidings. Within two weeks Churchill got Lord Camrose to step into the breach and to agree that henceforward his fortnightly political articles should be transferred, on similar terms, from the *Standard* to the *Daily Telegraph*.

Neither this nor a potentially highly profitable two-month American lecture tour, which he was negotiating for the autumn, was sufficient to offset a second series of devastating New York stock exchange losses which the recession of 1938 had just cost Churchill. Stocks which he had bought for over £18,000 had fallen to a value of barely £5,700, a loss in modern terms of about £375,000. In spite of what should have been expert advice from Bernard Baruch and others, Churchill was a singularly unfortunate Wall Street speculator.

These capital losses made him take the grave step of putting Chartwell definitively (as it appeared) on the market. Knight, Frank and Rutley were authorized to prepare a descriptive brochure, which, while not unnaturally enthusiastic about the property – 'Five reception rooms, nineteen bed and dressing rooms, eight bath rooms ... occupying a magnificent position in a valley on the southern slope of the Kentish hills'[16] – offered it for £20,000, well short of the £30,000 which another estate agent had suggested fifteen months before, or even of the £25,000 at which Churchill then said he would happily close. Yet the sale, even at one of these higher figures, would clearly have been a tremendous wrench, disorganizing not merely much of his pleasure but also his working regime, and coming too at a time when neither his own prospects nor those of his country and his continent gave much cause for optimism.

Happily he was once again spared the trauma. Another 'white knight', immediately more substantial but less long-lasting in Churchill's life than Imre Revesz, came over the horizon. He was Sir Henry Strakosch, like so many of both the good and bad figures of the first half of the twentieth century, an Anglo-South African financier. He was a near contemporary of Churchill's who had established himself many years before both as a banker and as a quiet public figure (member of a Royal Commission in the 1920s, adviser to several international conferences) and had been knighted as early as 1921, without any apparent intervention from Churchill. Later he was chairman of the *Economist*. In 1938, building upon an acquaintanceship with Churchill based mainly on supplying him by correspondence with detailed and authoritative facts about the effect of rearmament upon the German economy, and activated, it appears, by no motives beyond a firm anti-Nazism and personal admiration, he saved Chartwell for Churchill.

Strakosch did this indirectly and in a somewhat complicated way. He arranged through Brendan Bracken that he would take over all of Churchill's American stocks at the price Churchill had originally paid for them (which was nearly three times their current value) and hold them without risk to Churchill for at least three years, with the right to make switches and paying Churchill interest at the rate of about £800 a year. What happened at the end of the three years is not recorded. Strakosch had recouped some of the losses which he had voluntarily accepted. By the spring of 1941 not only was the main house at Chartwell closed, Churchill Prime Minister and Britain's position, before the entry into the war of either the Soviet Union or the United States, still semi-desperate, but British-owned American assets were (with compensation) requisitioned. In 1938, however, Strakosch's intervention was immensely beneficial to Churchill. Chartwell was again withdrawn from the market.

Under the harsh searchlight of modern parliamentary investigation the transaction would no doubt have appeared highly suspect. Strakosch would have been presented as a most sinister manipulative figure, bribing his way to great influence. In fact what was remarkable was that the benefit he had conferred seemed to make absolutely no difference to his relations with Churchill. He remained an arm's-length figure, never appearing at the house he had saved, occasionally writing respectfully and informatively about the European economic scene but without any change of tone from that which he had previously employed. His sole rewards appear to have been that, in the following year, he was made a member of the Other Club, and was occasionally invited to a meal in Downing Street or at Chequers during the early years of the Churchill government. When he died, in 1943, he left Churchill £20,000 in his will.

During the late spring and early summer of 1938 Churchill did some sustained anti-appeasement campaigning. As late as February he declined on grounds of his literary commitments an invitation from the New Commonwealth Society, to the presidency of which Lord Davies had without much difficulty enticed him, to address a late-winter rally in Birmingham. But by the end of March his attention switched from *Marlborough* to Manchester. He had a joint New Commonwealth and League of Nations Union meeting planned there for 9 May, and at first persuaded Lord Derby to take the chair at it. Derby subsequently ran out, saying that he was not really a supporter of the League of Nations and that in any event the prospect of the meeting was arousing controversy and even bitterness, with which as Lord Lieutenant of Lancashire he did not wish to be involved. Churchill accepted with surprising equanimity this striking further illustration of Derby's ability, so brilliantly described by Field Marshal Haig nearly two decades before, to be like a cushion and to bear the imprint of the last man who sat upon him. He wrote Derby an assuaging letter and fell back upon Alderman Toole, a temporary favourite of Churchill's who had been the local Labour lord mayor in the previous year. The success of the meeting, however, depended neither on Derby nor on Toole, but on Churchill himself, who made a considerable impact on Manchester as he did on Bristol a week later and on Sheffield and Birmingham about two weeks after that, having taken in a constituency speech at Chingford in the meantime. These meetings were like all successful political meetings, giving both the speaker and the audience a sense at the time of influencing events, perhaps depositing a residue of inspiration for future action upon a few of those present, but essentially leaving the currents of politics to go on much as before.

Churchill buttressed these orations with the publication in late June of a collection of his 1930s speeches (with one added from 1928) appropriately entitled, at least for those after 1935, *Arms and the Covenant*, although before that date there was much more of Arms than of the Covenant. They were compiled and introduced by Randolph

Churchill. This was a gracious paternal gesture on Churchill's part, for in February and into March he had had an appalling epistolatory row with his only son. It arose out of some allegedly offensive remark which Randolph had made to his father about Hore-Belisha. Both father and son possessed an infinite capacity for carrying on lengthy written exchanges, sometimes abusive, sometimes complaining, nearly always mutually uncomprehending, and which in this instance dragged on for nearly three weeks.

Randolph did the editing task competently, the speeches were prescient and mostly good, the title apposite and resonant in the context of the time. For a volume of speeches it sold not badly – about 4,000 – but below Churchill's hopes and expectations. Clementine wrote to him, loyally if Liberally, on 12 July from one of her many cures, this time in the Pyrenees: 'I'm sorry Darling you are disappointed at the sale of the Book. I'm sure it's the price – The sort of people who want to hear that the Government is all wrong are not the rich ones – The Tories don't want to be made to think!'[17] Nevertheless the book provided a filial reconciliation as well as a manifesto for his current campaign, and is of continuing interest.

Churchill was also paying a lot of attention to France in that year. He spent two nights in the Paris Embassy on his way south in early January. The ambassador, Sir Eric Phipps, had Blum to lunch on the first day and on the second Léger, Secretary-General of the Quai d'Orsay and in his spare time a poet who later won a Nobel prize for literature. Thereafter Churchill went for five weeks to two houses in the South of France, one belonging to Maxine Elliott, the other to Daisy Fellowes, daughter of the Duc Decazes and widow of Prince Jean de Broglie before she married the quietly gentlemanly Reggie Fellowes; she hovered over Churchill's life and generally over fashionable, slightly rakish Anglo-French society for fifty years. In these two refuges he worked hard – at *Marlborough* – although occasionally interrupting his literary regime to see the press of politicians who inhabited the Riviera in that epoch and at that time of the year. 'I do not get up till luncheon time,' he wrote to Clementine on 10 January, 'but work in bed and have a masseur. After lunch we play Mah Jong till 5 o'clock, when I again retire to rest and work.' Then, after describing a dinner *chez* Miss Elliott, to which the Duke and Duchess of Windsor and Lloyd George came, he continued: 'On Wednesday Anthony Eden and LG are coming to dine. To-morrow I am lunching with Rothermere and dining with

LG in the evening. I was going to lunch with Van[sittart], but his father died. . . . The dinner with Flandin was very depressing, the food lamentable . . . the account he gave of France was most pessimistic.'[18]

In late March Churchill was back again for another weekend at the Paris Embassy. On the face of it Phipps could hardly have been more accommodating. While accepting a short-notice postponement of a week he wrote to Churchill of the new visit: 'On Friday night I have Herriot* to dinner: on Saturday [Sir Charles] Mendl has Reynaud to lunch: on Saturday I have Blum and probably Paul-Boncour [current Foreign Minister] to dinner: on Sunday I have Daladier† to dinner. I will arrange meetings for you with Léger and Flandin besides.'[19] Phipps also wrote however and with some apprehension to his Secretary of State, Halifax, on the Monday after the weekend:

> Winston Churchill's stay here has continued in an increasingly kaleidoscopic manner. Almost every facet of French political life has been presented to him at and between meals. In addition to the interviews [with those already mentioned] . . . he has seen (mostly 'en tête à tête') Louis Marin, General Gamelin, Mandel, Chautemps, Chastenet of the *Temps*, Sauerwein of the *Paris-Soir* and others. He wanted to see a Communist but I strongly advised against this and he abstained. . . . it will be very useful for you and the Prime Minister to come over here and put things into somewhat better proportion than they have been left by Winston. His French is most strange and at times incomprehensible. . . . You will get a most eloquent first-hand account of this hectic and electric week-end from its brilliant animator. . . .[20]

Churchill's next visit to Paris was in the third week of July. This was occasioned by the state visit to France of King George VI and Queen Elizabeth, one of the great *Götterdämmerung* occasions of 1930s history. It was intended to symbolize the strength, unity and calm elegance of the two Western democracies in the face of the harsh challenge from across the Rhine. The spirit of Clemenceau and Lloyd George, Foch

---

* Edouard Herriot (1872–1957) was a leading Radical Socialist from his first premiership in 1924 until his death. Partly because he was out of office (although President of the National Assembly) during the lead-up to the débâcle, his reputation survived better than most of his fellow French politicians.

† Edouard Daladier (1884–1970), another Radical Socialist who had also been a minister as early as 1924, had the misfortune to be at the peak of his power at the worst possible time. He was Prime Minister from 1938 to 1940, had the sense to look miserable at Munich but was no more a good war leader than was Chamberlain. He was replaced by Reynaud three months before the fall of France.

and Haig was to be re-created. The new King, the Queen and the weather did their best, as did the more elderly and very Third Republican President Lebrun, forever in an evening tail-coat and white tie, morning and night, who was to be cast aside like an old glove within two years. The Churchills were not part of the royal suite but were invited to all the main events as the guests of the French government, an unusual French mark of esteem for an unofficial Briton. They were given high precedence at the Elysée banquet and Clementine sat next to Marshal Pétain, who was not to resume in the Second World War his hero status of the First. Churchill, by no means for the first time (that had been at least forty years before) but effectively for the last, combined the roles of honoured guest and newspaper correspondent. He wrote for the *Daily Telegraph* in elegiac terms:

> The entertainment offered to the British Sovereign had a charm and elegance, a quality of gentle peace and culture, of art and poetry, of music and dance, which only French genius can command. The scenes at Bagatelle, at the Opéra, in the chapel of Versailles, in the Bosquet d'Apollon, might well have been devised to show how much there is in human life above and beyond the blare of trumpets or the webs of diplomacy. . . . Poor indeed must be the heart which could not delight in this day-dream amid the mellow sunshine of Freedom and of France.[21]

Churchill was intending to make the visit, whatever it portended for the two countries, a few days of pleasure and festivity for himself. Clementine had written to him a week before, 'I hope you have got a lovely grey [morning] suit for Versailles etc,'[22] and he had organized an indulgent party for the visit. Yet what actually happened was a perfect vignette of how in these years he balanced on a narrow ridge between pleasure and duty, but how, if put to the test, duty won. His party for Paris comprised Venetia Montagu and Duff and Diana Cooper. They were due to leave London on Tuesday, 18 July by the newly inaugurated and currently fashionable Night Ferry, which brought blue *wagons-lits* into Victoria Station and deposited their passengers, maybe refreshed, in Paris at nine in the morning. Diana Cooper's diary recorded:

> We had a merry dinner with the Rothschildren [Victor, the newly succeeded third Lord Rothschild and his first wife Barbara, formerly Hutchinson later Ghika] and Winston and Venetia. Winston packed for the Ferry with bezique-cards in hand for plucking me. But a message came from the Chief Whip that trouble would be debated next day. Too disappointed to believe it, Winston tore round to the House, only to

meet us again at Victoria with the news endorsed. He'll start tomorrow
night instead.[23]

'Trouble' was the Sandys affair. In the summer of 1938 Duncan
Sandys, who had become a territorial army officer as well as an MP,
used secret information, which he had acquired in his military capacity,
to ask an embarrassing parliamentary question about the inadequacies
of London's anti-aircraft defences. When he was threatened with military discipline he raised the issue on the floor of the House as a breach
of parliamentary privilege. At first the complaint went well. Attlee,
Sinclair and Churchill all supported referral to the Committee of
Privileges, and this was carried without a division. Moreover the Committee found quickly that it was a breach of privilege for a military court
to interfere with an MP in the discharge of his parliamentary duties.
Within days, however, it emerged that the facts as laid before the
Committee were at least technically inaccurate. The issue then became
messy and dragged on without a clear result until the House went away
for the long recess. Not only did it disrupt the beginning of Churchill's
Paris trip, it became an unneeded exacerbating factor in his relations
with the government.

   The priority which he gave, not to parliamentary diligence in general
– for routine business he hardly attended the House – but to an issue in
which he felt on either personal or national grounds closely involved,
was illustrated on a bigger scale by his July decision to cancel his
scheduled America lecture tour for the autumn. By doing this before
August he incurred a contractual penalty of £400, as opposed to the
£600 he would have had to pay after that date. His reason for paying
this (in modern money) £12,000 of fine and for forgoing the substantial
profits to which he had been looking forward was that he judged the
European situation, and in particular the mounting German threat to
Czechoslovakia, to be such that he could no longer commit himself to
being away. The cancellation produced howls of agonized protest from
his New York lecture agent. Never before had such an important tour
been arranged. 'The prestige that will be destroyed can never be
remedied.' Did Churchill imagine that after such a let-down another
similar tour could ever be arranged? The £400 met the legal obligation
but: 'Your word, your assurance, Mr Churchill, [meant] more to me
than any legal agreement.'[24]

   Once Churchill had made the decision he was adamant against such
appeals. He wrote dismissively about the agent's agitation, 'Naturally he

is disappointed at losing the chance of making twenty-five thousand dollars out of my lecture tour,' but for the rest, 'I think it is all nonsense.'[25] It was a foretaste of the spirit which made him, within a few years, good at sacking generals when he believed it was in the public interest. This commitment somewhat ruthlessly cleared, he settled down at Chartwell for August and for his first real go at the *History of the English-Speaking Peoples*, which he was contracted to supply by the summer of 1939 for publication in 1940. Such was his fluency and application that in the next four or five weeks, despite the distraction of the developing Czech crisis, he had got 70,000 words, taking him from ancient Britons to the Norman Conquest, written and set up in print.

He had F. W. Deakin, later first head of the British military mission to Tito and then Warden of St Antony's College, Oxford, as his resident research assistant, but it is doubtful how much either of them knew about the early history to which they had to devote themselves that summer. Churchill called in aid the services of Mortimer Wheeler, already a well-known London University archaeologist. In July he wrote asking Wheeler to come to Chartwell for two weekends. 'Would you then be willing to give me three informal lectures or talks on (1) pre-Roman Britain, (2) Roman Britain and its downfall, and (3) the Saxon kingdoms to Alfred. Your audience would be attentive and select – Mr Deakin and me!'[26] Despite the political and psychological distractions of the last year of the peace, the *English-Speaking Peoples* was pushed on with at such speed – with the additional assistance for some phases of G. M. Young – that by 31 August 1939, a year later, a crucial terminal date as things turned out, the almost incredible, indeed somewhat excessive total of 530,000 words was written and set up in print. The work was not published until 1956–8. It was delayed first by the obstacle of the Second World War, and then by the author's determination (with the agreement of the publisher) to give priority to his six–volume account of those six years. But, by the day before Hitler invaded Poland, Churchill after barely thirteen months of effective work, had massively respected his contract with Cassells.

Churchill's intention had been to stay at Chartwell until 15 September (1938) and then to go once again, taking his work with him, to Maxine Elliott's Riviera villa. Already by early September, however, apprehension at the prospect of Nazi aggression and Anglo-French weakness leading to a Czech *dégringolade* destroyed the prospect of such a relaxed sojourn. He did go to France in mid-September, but only to Paris for twenty-four hours. Accompanied by Louis Spears he went by air to see the two most resolutely anti-Nazi figures in the current French government, Paul Reynaud and Georges Mandel. This visit was disapproved of both by Sir Eric Phipps in Paris and in London by Sir Maurice Hankey (just retired as Cabinet secretary), always snakily censorious of Churchill to others while almost cloyingly friendly in private. What, Hankey rhetorically asked of no one in particular, would we think if some French politicians came over and tried to stir up the 'anti-peace' members of the Cabinet?[27]

Throughout that September Churchill was highly agitated (as were many others), trying to exercise an influence on the government which he did not really possess, and as a result experiencing frequent moods of impotence and gloom. The miracle is that in these circumstances his Chartwell *villégiature*, interrupted by frequent excursions to London and with his composure always far from complete, yielded such rapid progress on *The English-Speaking Peoples*. On 19 September he wrote to Mortimer Wheeler: 'It has been a comfort to me in these anxious days to put a thousand years between my thoughts and the twentieth century.'[28] But this was more a throwaway remark than a real expression of detachment.

The timetable of the descent to Munich was that on 8 September Chamberlain came back from holiday and began an intensive period of Cabinet committee and full Cabinet discussions, the outcome of which was the first of his supplicatory missions to Hitler. He flew to Berchtesgaden on 15–16 September. On the 18th Daladier and Bonnet (French Prime Minister and Foreign Minister) came to London. On the 22nd Chamberlain went back to Germany. Hitler made the concession of coming to meet him at Godesberg in the Rhineland, but delivered a sharp metaphorical slap in the face when he got there, saying that the plans for the dismemberment of Czechoslovakia, which Chamberlain, following their Berchtesgaden understanding, had got the French and, very reluctantly, the Czechs to accept, were too dilatory and must be speeded up. Faced with this rubbing in of the humiliation, Chamberlain, when he got back to London on the 24th, prompted by Halifax in particular, showed some signs of stiffening. There were a few days when Cabinet and country prepared themselves for war.

On 28 September there followed the dramatic scene in the House of Commons when a sombre speech from the Prime Minister was interrupted by a note passed via Simon from the small gallery where officials sat, which enabled Chamberlain to announce that Hitler had agreed to a four-power conference (that is including France and Italy but not

Czechoslovakia) in Munich on the following day. The whole House, with the almost solitary exception of Harold Nicolson, rose to its feet in a gesture of ill-judged relief and sent Chamberlain off in a splurge of goodwill.

Did Churchill rise or not? Sir Martin Gilbert says that he, together with Eden and Amery, as well as Nicolson, did not.[29] Eden's non-participation is most implausible – he pulled many of his punches out of over-anxiety to show no pique towards Chamberlain; and Amery, although more naturally curmudgeonly, was so small that he might have been thought to be sitting down when he was in fact on his feet. What Churchill did was to rise (probably slowly) to walk across to Chamberlain, wish him God speed (possibly an ambiguous message) and tell him how lucky he had been, which, according to Nicolson, Chamberlain did not at all like. In Munich, over the next day and a half, Hitler got everything that he wanted, but Chamberlain flew back on 30 September to scenes of great enthusiasm which led him to make the disastrous mistake of proclaiming Munich as a triumph ('peace with honour') and not as a necessary playing for time, which would have been an arguable case.

Throughout these weeks Churchill enjoyed full access to the Foreign Secretary and the Prime Minister. He had substantial talks alone with Halifax at the end of August and on 11, 19 and 22 September. In addition he saw Chamberlain and Halifax together on 10 September and again on the 26th. There was no want of courtesy. The only trouble was that they took no notice of his advice, which was consistent throughout the month. He was not against giving a good deal of autonomy to the Sudetendeutsch as the Germans who inhabited a substantial fringe of Bohemia were known, and he was not particularly hostile to the Chamberlain-sponsored Runciman mission, which had gone to Czechoslovakia in late July to try to achieve such a settlement. What, however, he was adamant about was that it should be made clear to Hitler that Britain would if necessary fight for Czechoslovakia. This indeed was enshrined in the Cabinet minutes of the meeting on 12 September. 'The Secretary of State for Foreign Affairs reported that with the Prime Minister he had seen Mr Winston Churchill. . . . Mr Churchill's proposition was that we should tell Germany that if she set foot in Czechoslovakia we should at once be at war with her.'[30] Furthermore he was at pains to stress that to make strategic sense of such a threat required the closest possible collaboration with the Soviet Union. Harold Nicolson's diary for 26 September recorded: 'Winston says (and we all agree) that the fundamental mistake the P.M. has made is his refusal to take Russia into his confidence.'[31]

As his advice on these two central points went unheeded so Churchill moved into a mood which mingled contempt for the government with a slightly desperate defiance and pessimism. Three vignettes stand out. On 22 September Nicolson was summoned to a conclave of ten or so at Morpeth Mansions:

> While I wait for the lift to descend Winston appears from a taxi. We go up together. 'This', I say, 'is hell.' 'It is the end of the British Empire' [he replies].
> We gather in his drawing-room.... He [Churchill] stands there behind the fire-screen, waving a whisky-and-soda at us, rather blurry, rather bemused in a way, but dominant and in fact reasonable.[32]

Then Nicolson once more (but wholly endorsed by Violet Bonham Carter in a 1948 letter to Churchill) for 29 September, when Chamberlain was in Munich:

> At 7 p.m. we [the Focus Group] meet again in the Savoy Hotel. The idea had been to get Winston, Cecil [of Chelwood], Attlee, Eden, Archie Sinclair and [Lloyd] to join in a telegram to the P.M. begging him not to betray the Czechs. We had been busy at it all afternoon. But Anthony Eden refused to sign on the grounds that it would be interpreted as a vendetta against Chamberlain. Attlee refused to sign without the approval of his Party. There was thus no time. We sat there gloomily realizing that nothing could be done. Even Winston seemed to have lost his fighting spirit.[33]

Colin Coote, at that time on the staff of *The Times* but later for fourteen years editor of the *Daily Telegraph*, then took over the account of the evening, for the scene moved to a dinner of the Other Club, and neither Nicolson nor Violet Bonham Carter were for varying reasons members of that august body. Coote wrote:

> Churchill was in a towering rage and a deepening gloom.... he turned savagely upon the two ministers present, Duff Cooper and Walter Elliot. One could always tell when he was deeply moved, because a minor defect to his palate gave an echoing timbre to his voice. On this occasion it was not an echo, but a supersonic boom. How, he asked, could honourable men with wide experience and fine records in the Great War condone a policy so cowardly? It was sordid, squalid, sub-human and suicidal.[34]

Duff Cooper had to bear the lash of Churchill's tongue, the brunt of trying to defend the government from which he was to resign less than two days later. A hard core of members sat on until the first editions of the morning newspapers, which contained stop-press summaries of the Munich terms, were already on the streets and Coote went out to buy them in the Strand. (The Other Club of those days obviously had to accommodate itself to Churchillian hours as opposed to the 10.00 to 10.30 break-up of today.) When he returned they were all stunned by the completeness of the surrender to Hitler's demand. Duff Cooper slunk away. Churchill left even later, leaning, as it were, upon the arm of Richard Law, a son of his far from favourite former Prime Minister but a staunch anti-appeaser. On their way out of the hotel they passed a large private-party room full of gay (in the old sense) diners and dancers, Law later recalled. 'I was acutely conscious of the brooding figure beside me. As we turned away, he muttered "Those poor people! They little know what they will have to face."'[35]

The Munich debate was spread over four days of the following week. Churchill did not speak until the third day, Wednesday, 5 October. He was always good at the timing of his speeches so as to get a full House and major press attention. This restraint enabled him to achieve precisely that, without competition, as he would have had on the first two days from Duff Cooper's resignation speech, Chamberlain himself, Attlee and Lloyd George. He rose at 5.10 and spoke for forty-five minutes. It was a speech of power and intransigence. After a perfunctory disclaimer of personal animosity towards the Prime Minister, he moved into the substance of his message by stating that 'we have sustained a total and unmitigated defeat, and that France has suffered even more than we have'. All that the 'intense exertions of the Prime Minister' had been able to secure was that 'the German dictator, instead of snatching the victuals from the table, has been content to have them served to him course by course'.

This passage produced a rumble of dissent from the government benches behind him and even a recorded 'nonsense' from the irrepressible but generally wrong Lady Astor. He continued balloon-prickingly: 'The terms which the Prime Minister brought back with him could easily have been agreed, I believe, through the ordinary diplomatic channels at any time during the summer. . . . the Czechs, left to themselves and told they were going to get no help from the Western Powers, would have been able to make better terms than they have got after all this tremendous perturbation; they could hardly have been

worse. . . . All is over. Silent, mournful, abandoned, broken, Czechoslovakia recedes into the darkness. She has suffered in every respect from
her association with the Western democracies and with the League of
Nations, of which she has always been an obedient servant.'

He next moved on to a prophecy which proved only too quickly to
be vindicated: 'I venture to think that in future the Czechoslovak state
cannot be maintained as an independent entity. I think you will find
that in a period of time which may be measured by years, but which
may be measured only by months, Czechoslovakia will be engulfed in
the Nazi régime.' He proceeded to an indictment of the neglect or
squandering of British power in the previous five years: 'We have passed
an awful milestone in our history, when the whole equilibrium of
Europe has been deranged, and . . . the terrible words have for the time
being been pronounced against the Western democracies: "Thou art
weighed in the balance and found wanting." . . . I cannot believe that a
parallel exists in the whole course of history'; but he then could not
resist calling in aid his studies of the summer and introducing one in
the shape of Ethelred the Unready.

His next point was the more disputable one that France and Britain
could have much more successfully fought Germany in 1938, when its
army was 'not nearly so matured or perfected' as that of France, than at
any putative date in the future. Then he savaged the Prime Minister's
desire to have cordial relations with the German government. With the
German people, yes. 'But never will you have friendship with the present
German government. You must have diplomatic and correct relations,
but there can never be friendship between the British democracy and
the Nazi power, that power which spurns Christian ethics, which cheers
its onward course by a barbarous paganism, which vaunts the spirit of
aggression and conquest, which derives strength and perverted pleasure
from persecution, and uses, as we have seen, with pitiless brutality the
threat of murderous force. That power cannot ever be the trusted friend
of British democracy.'

He then denounced the idea of an early general election to cash in
on the nation's spurious sense of relief as a 'constitutional indecency'
before coming to his concluding warning: 'This is only the beginning
of the reckoning. This is only the first sip, the first foretaste of a bitter
cup which will be proffered to us year by year unless, by a supreme
recovery of moral health and martial vigour, we rise again and take our
stand for freedom as in the olden times.'[36]

It was a powerful, even a noble speech, and one which has withstood the passage of over sixty years. But it was not one which won many friends on the Conservative benches. They were more or less limited to the thirty who abstained when the division was called, of whom, according to Gilbert,[37] thirteen including Churchill but not Eden remained ostentatiously in their place as their more loyal or supine fellow members filed past. The other seventeen were more discreet about their defiance. To those unversed in the sophistries of parliamentary life, abstention, with or without flaunting, might in any event have seemed an anti-climax after the grand denunciations contained in the speeches of Churchill and of some others. But on this occasion it was all that was forthcoming, and even in Churchill's case it left him so exposed to constitutency and whips' disapproval that he was forced to row back a little if he was to maintain any base within the Conservative party. The fanfare of trumpets and clash of cymbals of Churchill's 5 October speech was followed not by a great advance but by a temporary sounding of the retreat and shortening of his exposed front. He had seen too much electoral vicissitude to contemplate with equanimity the losing of the Conservative nomination for Epping, which was the threat which, post the Munich debate, quickly arose.

28

THE LAST YEAR OF THE PEACE

IN RETROSPECT THE post-Munich trouble which Churchill had with his Conservative constituency association is almost incredible. Within a year he was to be back in office. Within eighteen months he was to be Prime Minister. Within two years he was to be elected, without opposition, leader of the Conservative party, and from this position he was to bestride British politics for a further fourteen and a half years. And then thirty years after the end of that period he was to be appropriated by Margaret Thatcher as the only authentic Tory among her batch of post-1945 predecessors.

Yet the hard fact is that for six weeks or so in the autumn of 1938, and then on a diminuendo basis for another four months, there was doubt if he would be able to continue to sit as a Conservative MP. There is no reason to think that the members of the Epping (or West Essex) Conservative Association were either peculiarly reactionary or tiresome. In 1924 they had taken in Churchill as a shipwrecked refugee. They had supported him as a rumbustious Chancellor of the Exchequer. They had sustained his resignation from the shadow Cabinet in 1930 and his long-drawn-out battle over the India Bill. They had not been heavily demanding of either his time or his money. They had been on the whole sympathetic to his mid-1930s campaign for rearmament. But when he assailed 'the prince of peace', as Chamberlain temporarily appeared to most local Conservatives, in the terms which Churchill had used in the Munich debate, unhappiness and some positive hostility set in.

Similar experiences beset the Duchess of Atholl in Kinross and West Perthshire, Robert Boothby in East Aberdeenshire, and Richard Law in Hull, which together with Epping formed a wide geographical spread. Some other anti-appeasers – Duncan Sandys in Streatham, Brendan Bracken in Paddington – seemed immune, but Duff Cooper was not without trouble in Westminster, St George's, nor were Cranborne in South Dorset and Wolmer in Aldershot. There is always a certain irrationality about where the lash of constituency disapproval falls.

Constituency militants are almost inevitably a force against sense and statesmanship. Politics, in any event a declining enthusiasm, could hardly function without militants. But the difficulty of sustaining enthusiasm without giving militants excessive power has been one of the perennial problems of democratic government. In 1909 Arthur Balfour delivered himself of the great *de haut en bas* aphorism: 'I have the greatest respect for the Conservative party conference, but I would no more consult it on a matter of high policy than I would my valet.' It was perhaps not an accident that within three years of this remark Balfour became one of the few Conservative leaders to be forced out of office.

While Churchill was never on record as being quite so provocative as Balfour he firmly believed that policy should be determined by leaders and not by local activists. In any event he regarded the points at issue between Chamberlain and himself as far transcending party loyalty. In spite or perhaps because of these views he took the Epping rumbles seriously but not weakly. His most explicit statement about them was contained in an 18 October (1938) reply to a spontaneous letter of support and appeal for resolute action from Ramsay Muir, a prolific historian and devoted Liberal party office-holder of roughly Churchill's own age who had sat briefly in the House of Commons in 1923–4. Churchill wrote: 'I am having trouble in my Constituency, and have let it be known that unless I am accorded a renewed expression of this confidence, I shall appeal to the electors. In that case a bye-election would occur which, from the character of the constituency, would greatly assist the developments you have in mind.' What the second, slightly ambiguous sentence meant was that, in such an event, Churchill would much welcome the support of the Liberals, who at the last election had provided his main even if not formidable challenge, in a contest against a pro-Chamberlain official Conservative. This was made more explicit by his concluding point. 'I am in close touch with Archie [Sinclair]. . . . I wonder if I could persuade you to come down and lunch with me [at Chartwell] one day next week.'[1] This letter shows both how seriously Churchill was taking the threat and that an element of return to his Liberal phase was part of his contingent strategy for combating it.

Another essential part of this strategy was to meet the 'loyalist' threat head-on. Indeed he had written a little impatiently to an agitated Boothby on 4 October: 'I do not think you will have any serious difficulty with your constituents if you let them know that whatever they say or do you will fight the seat.'[2] He had followed his 'head-on' precept by writing, very formally, to Hawkey, the chairman of the Epping Conservative Association, on 13 October:

My dear Sir James Hawkey,
I wish to consult the Association upon the grave events which have occurred. Upon India and National Defence we have always acted in common. War has only been averted by submission to wrong-doing. I am convinced that a supreme national effort must be made to place our country in a position of security.... Very great sacrifices and exertions will be required from all, if the name of England is not to fail.
Will you therefore kindly ask our friends to assemble, and take the necessary steps in accordance with the rules of the Association.
Yours very truly,
Winston S. Churchill[3]

Hawkey was a great support for Churchill, and a man whom he wisely treated with warm consideration. Hawkey was a locally educated and self-made master baker who held nearly every possible civic office in the constituency and who, perfectly respectably therefore, was knighted during Churchill's Chancellorship and advanced to a baronetcy at the end of his first premiership in 1945. He and Miss Hawkey, who was also locally active (Lady Hawkey seemed more retiring), were occasional overnight guests at Chartwell. Hawkey's only disadvantage from Churchill's point of view was that he could not abide the League of Nations. There are a few semi-jocular references to this in their correspondence, rather as though it were an aversion to bananas or strawberries. He was therefore much more in favour of the Arms than of the Covenant part of Churchill's policy: but above all he was devotedly but intelligently loyal to the great man whose local eyes and ears he had become.

On 4 November 1938 he duly brought together the Epping Conservatives at Winchester House in the City (where Churchill had first met them or their predecessors in 1924), having prepared the ground as carefully as he could beforehand. He and Churchill were right not to take anything for granted, because there was a lot of local muttering and worse. Several of the branches passed hostile resolutions, and the empoisoned atmosphere was well captured in a letter (of 20 October) which Sir Harry Goschen, an elderly City financier resident in a northern part of the constituency, wrote to Hawkey on 20 October:

> I cannot help thinking that it was rather a pity that he [Churchill] broke up the harmony of the House by the speech that he made. Of course he was not like a small ranting member, and his words were telegraphed all over the Continent and to America, and I think it would have been a great deal better if he had kept quiet and not made a speech at all. . . . a good many of the electors from some of the outlying divisions such as Harlow are up in arms about him. . . . A good many people have written to Douglas Pennant [Goschen's son-in-law] and others about him. There is to be a meeting against him in Epping I hear, and altogether it seems to be a jolly mess up.[4]

It was all a little vague, but the damaging intent was not in doubt. Lord Randolph Churchill had famously forgotten one Goschen, and although Sir Harry was not a direct descendent of George Joachim Goschen he was of the same ilk, and Winston Churchill was resolved to put the issue to the sword, either within the Epping Conservative party or, if that failed, in a joust before the whole local electorate. It did not fail, for at the 4 November meeting Churchill secured a vote of 100 to 44 in his favour, Goschen among others having swung to his side. The majority was clear, but the minority was nonetheless uncomfortably substantial, of a size likely to encourage its members to live to fight another day. Furthermore the resolution for which the 100 votes were cast was a masterpiece of propitiatory drafting:

> We express our gratitude to the Prime Minister [Chamberlain] for his continuous and courageous efforts in the cause of peace, but we regret that the warnings given during the last five years by the member for the Division, the Rt. Hon. Winston Churchill, endorsed as they have been by this association as well as by the National Union of Conservative Associations, about the proper and timely rearmament of our country, have not been hearkened to; because we feel that if their counsels had been heeded the Prime Minister would have found himself in a far better position to negotiate with the heads of the dictator States. We therefore urge Mr Churchill to continue his work for national unity and national defence, believing that this will be the surest foundation for that lasting peace which is our deepest desire.[5]

Who could have done the drafting? It is not Churchillian, either in style or in substance, for he would surely have avoided striking the even-handed note between Chamberlain and himself. Indeed, given this ambiguity in the resolution, it was probably as well that his real critics voted against – otherwise it could have been dismissed as meaningless. They were led by (later Colonel Sir) Colin Thornton-

Kemsley, then a thirty-five-year-old local Essex estate agent, who had married and double-barrelled into Scottish property and in 1939 became MP for Kincardine and West Aberdeenshire, for which east-coast Scottish constituency, allowing for a change of name and boundaries in 1950, he sat until 1964. I remember him as a small dark moustachioed Conservative backbencher trying without much success to make an impact upon the House of Commons. In 1938 however he had the effrontery and/or courage to attempt a direct repudiation of Churchill's whole appraisal of the diplomatic and military situation. It was not perhaps surprising that his parliamentary career did not greatly prosper during the Churchill leadership, and that even from Macmillan he only got a 'rations' knighthood after nineteen years of service.

What would have happened had thirty people (some of whom were no doubt among the mutterers) changed sides and the vote gone the other way? Churchill would clearly have forced a bye-election, but the timing would have been not in his hands but in those of his enemies among the Conservative whips, who could choose, within limits, when to move in the House of Commons the writs without such a contest could not start. Would he have won? Before Christmas, when relief that there was no war and Chamberlain's stock remained high, it might have been very doubtful. In early 1939, and particularly after Hitler made a mockery of Munich by swallowing the rump of Czechoslovakia, the prospect would have been brighter. The only anti-Munich rebel who did face a bye-election was the Duchess of Atholl, and she, in spite of a message of support from Churchill, was defeated on 21 December by an insignificant Chamberlainite and by a margin of 11,808 votes to 10,495. There were no Liberal or Labour candidates, which was very much the line-up which Churchill, had it come to a contest, would have liked to achieve in Epping. The Duchess was not of course Churchill, but her fate suggests that his enterprise would have been hazardous. Had he stood and been defeated, it would have been the most disastrously repercussive bye-election in history.

Did his constituency trouble induce any temporary caution in his public attitude? Not in the House of Commons, where for instance, on 17 November, he voted with the Labour party on a Liberal motion for the setting up of a Ministry of Supply. It was the first time since the India Bill that he had voted against the government as opposed to merely abstaining. He was joined in the opposition lobby only by

Harold Macmillan and Brendan Bracken. But outside the House he was far from fulfilling the somewhat maudlin threat which he had announced to Harold Nicolson at a moment of special exasperation with Chamberlain: 'At the next election I shall speak on every socialist platform in the country.'[6]

On the contrary he declined, unlike two of his successors as Conservative leader, Harold Macmillan and Edward Heath, to support A. D. Lindsay, the Master of Balliol, when he stood (unsuccessfully) as an Independent anti-Munich candidate in the famous Oxford bye-election of late October. Nor did he support Vernon Bartlett, the *News Chronicle* journalist, when he stood (successfully) on roughly the same ticket at Bridgwater in mid-December. Churchill worked out a sophisticated (some might say sophistical) theory which he expressed in a telegram of 26 October to Lord Cecil of Chelwood: 'As long as I accept the Conservative Whip it is not possible for me to take sides in a bye-election against them except where two Conservative candidates are standing.'[7]

He was mildly complaining against the caution of Anthony Eden at the time. 'I doubt if Mr Eden would come. He is very shy at present,'[8] he wrote to the Focus Group organizer on 12 November; but to some extent he emulated Eden. However no one who has ever been through the process of trying to remain within a party while disagreeing with its leadership on the central issue of the day should be inclined to criticize him for this. The minor votes against one's conviction, the attempts to set an artificial line and to confine rebellion to big issues, are all too familiar a feature of party politics, incomprehensible to those outside the game, but necessary, even to those who consider themselves brave, if they seek, however loosely, to operate within its frame.

Despite these displays of relative restraint on Churchill's part, relations between him and Chamberlain were worse during that post-Munich autumn than at any other time during the two decades over which, without much in the way of either intimacy or animosity, their political lives had impacted upon each other. Curiously it was a relatively minor issue immediately following the conclusion on 6 October of the Munich debate itself which appeared to cause the ill-feeling on both sides. The government wanted to send the House back into recess until 1 November. This was opposed by the Labour and Liberal parties and by Churchill, Macmillan and a few other Conservatives. In the course of this semi-procedural debate Churchill and Chamberlain got very bad-tempered with each other. The Prime Minister said that Churchill's arguments were 'unworthy' and then wrote him that same evening a distinctly peevish letter:

> I am sorry you think my remarks were offensive, but I must say that I think you are singularly sensitive for a man who so constantly attacks others.
>
> I consider your remarks highly offensive to me and to those with whom I have been working.
>
> I had not regarded these remarks, wounding as they were, as requiring a breach of personal relations, but you cannot expect me to allow you to do all the hitting and never hit back.[9]

Whether or not personal relations nominally held, Chamberlain made no attempt to restrain the attempts by his 'loyalist' enthusiasts in the Epping division to undermine Churchill's constituency position. And in the 17 November Ministry of Supply debate Chamberlain went out of his way, within a penumbra of flattery, to puncture Churchill's personal qualities rather than his arguments.

> I have the greatest admiration for my right honourable friend's many brilliant qualities. He shines in every direction. I remember once asking a Dominion statesman, who held high office for a great number of years, what in his opinion was the most valuable quality a statesman could possess. His answer was judgement. If I were asked whether judgement is the first of my right honourable friend's many admirable qualities I should have to ask the House of Commons not to press me too far.[10]

This rather arch smear no doubt produced a wave of mocking laughter from Chamberlain's still loyal cohorts. Nor was there any early sign of an improvement in relations over the winter, although, paradoxically, the froideur turned out to be the prelude, not to a continuing deterioration, but, once the war had broken out and Churchill had joined the government, to better relations than they had ever enjoyed before.

Churchill did not reply in the House of Commons to Chamberlain's attack. He was rarely good at quick improvisation on his feet – although his spontaneous conversation around the luncheon or dinner table was often both brilliant and memorable – but he did so most powerfully at a meeting in his constituency nearly a month later. To hold this meeting in Chingford on 9 December was a bold throw on Churchill's part, for it was a cross-party affair organized by the League of Nations Union, with a strong Liberal element on the platform. In the course of his speech Churchill demolished Chamberlain's attack on his lack of judgement.

> I would gladly submit my judgements about foreign affairs and national defence during the last five years to comparison with his own. In February he said that the tension in Europe had greatly relaxed; a few weeks later Nazi Germany seized Austria. I predicted that he would repeat this statement as soon as the shock of the rape of Austria passed away. He did so in the very same words at the end of July; by the middle of August Germany was mobilising for those bogus manoeuvres which after bringing us all to the verge of a world war, ended in the complete destruction and absorption of the republic of Czechoslovakia. At the Lord Mayor's Banquet in November at the Guildhall, he told us that Europe was settling down to a more peaceful state. The words were hardly out of his mouth before the Nazi atrocities upon the Jewish population [*Kristallnacht* took place on 9–10 November] resounded throughout the civilised world.[11]

The violence of the new wave of anti-Semitism which swept Germany, largely at the behest of its government, in late October and early November somewhat strengthened Churchill's position while weakening that of Chamberlain. On 28 October an edict for the expulsion of the 20,000 Polish Jews resident in Germany was issued. In response to this a junior German diplomat in Paris was assassinated by a Polish Jewish youth of seventeen. The terror of the early hours of 10 November was a contrived Nazi response. Jewish shops had their windows smashed and contents looted, synagogues were burnt and many Jews were violently assaulted. Then on 13 November the regime, so far from correcting this lawless vengeance, gave it the sanctity of law by promulgating a decree by which all Jews had to cease trading and other business activities by the end of the year.

Obviously this chain of events made it more difficult for Chamberlain to portray the Führer as a partner in peace. Hitler had obsessively devoted two successive speeches, one on 6 November and another two days later, to strong personal attacks on Churchill which prompted his main Nazi newspaper to accuse Churchill of being the instigator of the Paris murder. The German leader's hysteria and this ludicrous claim produced a natural British reaction in Churchill's favour. Even *The Times*, firmly entrenched in its appeasement groove, denounced the attacks as 'wholly intolerable' and as demanding 'official notice', whatever that meant.

That late autumn and Advent season was however by no means a time of steady upswing for Churchill. If Chamberlain was tetchy, so was he. After the Ministry of Supply debate he even managed to quarrel with Duff Cooper, notoriously short-tempered but also one of his few allies of the time and very much the innocent party. The award of a gold medal for *Marlborough* at the *Sunday Times* book fair on the same day somewhat cheered up Churchill, but then on 5 December, in the final act of the long-drawn-out Sandys saga, he experienced a medium-grade failure in the House of Commons. He was brought down, suprisingly, by Hore-Belisha. Nicolson's diary, with a striking final comment, recorded:

> Winston starts brilliantly and we are all expecting a great speech. He accuses Hore-Belisha of being too complacent. The latter gets up and says, 'When and where?' Winston replies, 'I have not come unprepared,' and begins to fumble among his notes, where there are some press cuttings. He takes time. He finds them. But they are not the best cuttings, and the ones he reads out excuse rather than implicate Hore-Belisha. Winston becomes confused. He tries to rally his speech, but the wind has gone out of his sails which flop wretchedly. 'He is becoming an old man' [my neighbour says]. He certainly is a tiger, who, if he misses his spring, is lost.[12]

Clementine was again away. She had left in late November for another long (but not from her point of view wholly successful) cruise on Lord Moyne's yacht, and did not return until February. Churchill was lonely – so was she, but that did not help much – and he and Mary (then aged sixteen) sent her a poignant joint telegram on 17 December: 'Do please send us messages. Distressed not hearing.'[13] On the 24th he wrote thanking a friend (Lord Craigavon) for a present: 'this time of trouble and misunderstanding in which I feel much alone, tho' constant . . .'.[14] That same afternoon he took Mary and Randolph for a three-day Christmas at Blenheim. Then at the end of the first week of January 1939 he set off for a Paris political weekend (meetings with Reynaud, Blum and former Foreign Minister Yvon Delbos) before settling down for another two-week hard-working (on the *English Speaking-Peoples*) sojourn at Maxine Elliott's Château de l'Horizon. He loved light and sun (although neither was in guaranteed supply on the Riviera in January) and was unappreciative of the deep snow with which Chartwell, Blenheim and much of England had been covered over that Christmas season. Also, although he had a strong apprehension that it was all being done for the last time, in that phase at any rate, he was determined, while he could, to keep up the routine of a pre-war English upper-class winter holiday: Blenheim, the Paris Ritz, the Train Bleu, a Golfe Juan villa, dinners with the Windsors, 'very long' but not 'foolish' gambling sessions at the Casino. The only things which broke the normal 'high life' pattern were his taste for Third Republican politicians and the hard work and relentless outpouring of written words which filled all the interstices between these various indulgences.

Nineteen-thirty-nine, after the clashes of 1938, was for Churchill a year of rowing back towards the shore of government, although he, with a degree of justification, regarded it as a period in which the shore of government moved more to meet him. The key event of the first quarter was Hitler's contemptuous absorption of the rump of Czechoslovakia on 15 March. That destroyed the idea of appeasement as a rationally arguable policy, although its spirit lingered for several months. This event considerably tilted the balance of influence towards Churchill and away from Chamberlain. But the new circumstances still left power firmly in the hands of the Prime Minister, who, however weak he might be vis-à-vis the dictators, was a lion of courage in resisting the encroachments of Attlee, Sinclair and, at that stage, Churchill.

The result was an oddly anomalous period, in which Churchill at least purported to believe that he had won, while Chamberlain accepted no such defeat. Thus, on 22 March, Churchill wrote to Margot Oxford (Asquith's irrepressible widow, but a lady of much less sound views than her stepdaughter Violet Bonham Carter): 'The Government have now adopted the foreign policy which I and most Liberals have long been pressing, and consequently I am in very good relations with them . . .'[15] This happy view from the great realist of the 1930s was based more on hope than on fact. It chimed ill with a letter of clanging intransigence which Chamberlain wrote to his sister Hilda three weeks later. It expresses how far he was from being able to lead a government of national unity. Referring to a debate on 13 April he wrote, 'Attlee behaved like the cowardly cur he is,' and continued, 'I had already given up Archie Sinclair & was not surprised by his speech which was a really lamentable exhibition on such an occasion, but I had hoped for a better speech from Winston . . . [who had] declared his intention of making a "not unhelpful" speech. But there was an acid undertone which brought many cheers from Labour benches & again I felt depressed when he sat down.'[16]

Churchill's belief that the government had come round to his policy led to a recrudescence of his ministerial correspondence. He wrote to the Prime Minister on 21 and 27 March and 9 April (1939) not having previously communicated with him since the tart exchange after the 17 November (1938) debate. The March–April letters were all directed to telling Chamberlain what he ought to do, but were amiably couched. Churchill also reverted to a bombardment of other ministers with advice – Kingsley Wood (Air) and Hore-Belisha (War) on semi-technical questions, and Halifax on broader policy issues. His energy and fluency were, as so often, formidable. All these ministers treated him with respectful courtesy. But they also showed signs of wishing he would calm down a little. This was particularly true of the Prime Minister, but also of Chatfield, Admiral of the Fleet, who had been appointed Inskip's successor as defence co-ordinator at the end of January. Chatfield, replying to Halifax, who had sent on to him a Churchill memorandum on naval deployment, almost perfectly captured the mixture of weariness, respect and complaint with which ministers greeted yet another missive from Churchill's flowing pen: 'Thank you for your letter from Winston. There is of course a good deal in all he says, though one wishes he would not be quite so restless, because it implies a want of confidence in the Admiralty and ignores certain important considerations altogether.'[17]

Easter day that year fell on 9 April. On Good Friday Churchill had Harold Macmillan to lunch at Chartwell, and Mussolini launched his invasion of Albania.* Macmillan later wrote a memorable portrait of Churchill's attempt to relieve his frustrations at not being a minister when yet another Axis attack was launched by trying to behave as though he was one:

It was a scene that gave me my first picture of Churchill at work. Maps were brought out; secretaries were marshalled; telephones began to ring. 'Where was the British fleet?' . . . That considerable staff which, even as a private individual, Churchill always maintained to support his tremendous outflow of literary and political effort was at once brought into play. . . . I shall always have a picture of that spring day and the sense of power and energy, the great flow of action, which came from Churchill, although he then held no public office. He alone seemed to be in command, when everyone else was dazed and hesitating.[18]

* Halifax, when given this news, was said to have underlined his position as a Christian gentleman by exclaiming, 'And on Good Friday too!'

Neville Chamberlain was less impressed by the additional disturbance of his Easter peace which resulted from Churchill's excitement. He wrote to a sister on the Sunday: 'It doesn't make things easier to be badgered for a meeting of pmt [parliament] by the two Oppositions & Winston who is the worst of the lot, telephoning almost every hour of the day. I suppose he has prepared a terrific oration which he wants to let off.'[19]

Churchill, who did not of course know of the tone about him in which Chamberlain carried on his ever diligent family correspondence, allowed his hopes for inclusion in the government to rise for the first time since early 1936. It had become inevitable, as was proved five months later, that his hope of office depended directly upon deteriorations in the prospects for both Britain and peace. On 13 April however, he thought it worth while to take David Margesson, Chamberlain's (and later his own) formidable Chief Whip, to dinner after a debate and to urge his own claims upon him. Margesson's report of this encounter was relayed by Chamberlain (again to a sister) on 15 April and, despite the double-hearsay nature of the evidence, rings on the whole true, although the interchange may have been given some anti-Churchill 'spin' in the transmission. Chamberlain wrote that at dinner Churchill:

> saying this was no time for mincing words informed him [David Margesson] bluntly of his strong desire to join the Govt. In reply to enquiries he assured David of his confidence that he could work amicably under the P.M. who had many admirable qualities some of which he did not possess himself. On the other hand he too had great qualities and could do much to help the P.M. to bear his intolerable burden, likely as it was to get worse as time went on. He would like the Admiralty but would be quite satisfied to succeed Runciman as Lord President. He thought Eden should be taken in too but observed that he could give much more help than Eden.[20]

Churchill's hopes were not fulfilled and he therefore returned to a mixture of the *English-Speaking Peoples*, journalism, the Focus Group and dealing with the tail-end of the Epping storm. In journalism he began a new and fairly short-lived love affair with the *Mirror* group. On 23 April the twenty-six-year-old Hugh Cudlipp devoted the first two pages of the *Daily Mirror*'s partner paper, the *Sunday Pictorial*, to an eulogy of Churchill and a demand for his inclusion in the Cabinet. Two days later Cudlipp wrote to inform Churchill that he had received 'an unqualified response' such as he had never previously known: 2,400 letters, of which only 73 were not favourable.[21] The goodwill thus engendered perhaps eased Churchill's passage to the *Daily Mirror* as his principal journalistic outlet when his *Daily Telegraph* contract came to an amicable end in May.

The *Daily Mirror* in those days did not carry the prestige, unprecedented until then and unmatched since for a tabloid, which it was to achieve under Cudlipp's editorship from 1959 to 1973. It did not match the *Telegraph* as a vehicle for conveying Churchill's views to the influential classes. But at least it meant that, as he bounced from the *Daily Mail* to the *Evening Standard* to the *Daily Telegraph* to the *Daily Mirror*, with the *News of the World* always hovering in reserve, he was not bereft. So far as secondary publication was concerned, however, Imre Revesz was finding it increasingly difficult to get Polish, Roumanian, Greek, even Swedish newspapers to take Churchill's articles. They were thought dangerous rather than dull. It was a vivid illustration of what Churchill described in his Munich-agreement speech as the new *sauve qui peut* attitude in Europe: 'It must now be accepted that all the countries of Central and Eastern Europe will make the best terms they can with the triumphant Nazi power.'[22] However, the resourceful Revesz balanced this by negotiating an American broadcasting contract for Churchill, by which he was to be paid £100 each for a series of ten-minute talks to the United States.

During 1939 the Focus Group activities seemed to move somewhat out of focus. Churchill, using the excuse of the pressure of the *English-Speaking Peoples* and a little disillusioned with the previous results (good meetings, but little influence on events), had given up provincial campaigning. There was a danger of the Focus meetings becoming not a spearhead of action but merely a luncheon discussion group, open to all opinions. On 9 February the group had entertained Lord Halifax. On 25 April there was a very well-attended occasion in honour of Joseph P. Kennedy, the defeatist American ambassador. Kennedy arrived accompanied by his second son, the future President of the United States. Harold Nicolson surprisingly recorded (as it was Joseph P. and not John F. who did it): 'Kennedy makes an excellent speech.'[23]

The Epping trouble continued through the spring. Right up to the time of his late-March Scottish bye-election the indefatigable Thornton-Kemsley pursued a vigorous campaign of recruiting new anti-Churchill members to the small outlying branches with the hope, those small branches being over-represented, of securing a majority at the annual general meeting of the Central (Epping) Association. Churchill wrote a furious letter to Sir Douglas Hacking, the party chairman, on 18 March, accusing Conservative Central Office of being party to these manoeuvres. Perhaps wisely, however, it joined the substantial file of his unsent correspondence. There were a few last gusts of the storm in late April when Sir James Hawkey, as chairman of the Association, became the exposed target, and Churchill had to defend him rather than vice versa.

A week after Churchill had joined the government on the outbreak of war, Thornton-Kemsley wrote a letter of apology: 'I want to say only this. You warned repeatedly about the German danger & you were right: a grasshopper under a fern is not proud now that he made the field ring with his importunate chink.'[24] It was an attempt at graciousness, but it was not appealing. Support when it is not needed is always easy to give. Churchill wrote back with surprising generosity: 'so far as I am concerned the past is dead'.[25]

Throughout the late spring and summer of 1939 Churchill was torn by conflicting desires and thoughts. First he believed that the government had at last accepted the policy which he had been urging for several years. Bracken, always his faithful mouthpiece, informed Bernard Baruch on 18 April: 'Winston has won his long fight. Our government are now adopting the policy that he advised three years ago';[26] and Churchill himself defined this policy (to Lord Lytton) as 'a Grand Alliance on the basis of the Covenant of the League'.[27] He could not oppose any British will to resist. Yet he believed that fighting for Poland (and maybe for Roumania), following Chamberlain's splurge of guarantees after Hitler's occupation of Prague, made much less strategic sense than fighting for Czechoslovakia would have done; 'the Prime Minister offered guarantees and contracted alliances in every direction still open, regardless of whether we could give any effective help to the countries concerned'. To the Polish guarantee was added a Greek and Roumanian guarantee, and to these an alliance with Turkey. Yet Churchill was convinced that none of these 'set[s] of assurances had any military value except within the framework of a general agreement with Russia'.[28]

The obstacle to such an agreement was not only the dilatoriness of Chamberlain and Halifax but also the unwillingness of the Poles and the Roumanians to contemplate any arrangement which involved Russian troops on their soil. They were very uncertain which they feared more, Hitler or Stalin. Churchill's differing desires would have been a difficult circle to square in any event, and it was further complicated by the fact that he was going through one of the phases when he wished to minimize his differences with the Conservative leadership. This was nothing to do with Epping. He had surmounted that trouble, and he had never weakened during the months when the threat was greatest. But his desire to be back in a senior office from where he could act and not merely pontificate was strong and far from ignoble.

There was yet a further complication. In retrospect at least, Churchill believed that the realistic prospect of a Soviet alliance of mutual interest disappeared that spring. In a debate of 19 May he, Lloyd George, Eden, Attlee and Sinclair all spoke firmly in favour of vigorously pursuing such an outcome. In terms which made his acceptance in June 1941 of the Soviet Union as an ally ('If Hitler invaded Hell, [I] would at least make a favourable reference to the Devil')[29] much less of a volte-face than is commonly assumed, he said, 'If you are ready to be an ally of Russia in time of war. . . .why should you shrink from being an ally now . . . ?'[30] But, again in retrospect, although maybe with a nasty suspicion at the time, he thought that Litvinov's replacement by Molotov as Soviet Foreign Minister on 3 May probably marked the moment when the Russian leadership lost hope of the West and began to move towards the Nazi–Soviet Pact of three and a half months later. Nevertheless, however dismally he viewed the strategic prospect, he thought the central objective was to get the British government to stand up and fight, even if it had stacked at least the immediate odds against itself.

Churchill had two assuagements that summer. On 27 June Thornton Butterworth published *Step by Step*, a collection of his *Evening Standard* and *Daily Telegraph* articles of the previous three years. It sold well, 7,500 in the first wave, with reprints of 1,500 and 1,800 in the following eight months, as well as a New York edition and six foreign-language translations. He distributed his usual raft of complimentary copies, but more to very old friends and possible new allies than to his previous list of Conservative recipients. Neither Chamberlain nor Baldwin, let alone Hoare or Simon, got one. But Attlee did, and wrote back a warm 'My dear Winston' letter. Churchill was also cultivating Sir Stafford Cripps, who had been expelled from the Labour party because of his relentless search for some new combination in politics. This was in contrast to his dismissive attitude towards Cripps just over two years previously, when Cripps vainly appealed for Churchill's help after the trustees of the Albert Hall had refused his application to hold a United Front (Labour, Communist and ILP) meeting there. Churchill saw Cripps for an hour on 22 June and there was subsequent correspondence in which Cripps urged Churchill to provide leadership of a progressive alliance.

At the beginning of July there was a remarkable wave of newspaper editorials, embracing such key Conservative journals as the *Daily Telegraph* and the *Daily Mail*, demanding Churchill's inclusion in the government. There was also an anonymous poster campaign, extending to 600 metropolitan sites. 'What Price Churchill?' was proclaimed by a dominating one in Piccadilly Circus. Chamberlain, although unenthusiastic, was beginning to recognize that such inclusion might become inevitable. Already in mid-April he had told his sisters when describing Churchill's head-on request to Margesson: 'I would let this suggestion simmer a bit. It caught me at a moment when I was certainly feeling the need of help, but I wanted to do nothing too quickly. The question is whether Winston, who would certainly help on the Treasury bench in the Commons, would help or hinder in Cabinet or in Council.'[31] On 3 July, immediately following the *Telegraph*'s most clamant demand for Churchill's inclusion, Chamberlain had seen Lord Camrose at length. While assuring the *Telegraph*'s proprietor that his relations with Churchill were much improved on those of the previous autumn, he still took a hesitant line. 'His [Chamberlain's] own responsibility at the present time was so onerous that he did not feel he would gain sufficiently from Winston's ideas and advice to counterbalance the irritation and disturbance which would inevitably be caused.'[32]

So matters drifted towards 4 August, when Parliament dispersed for its last recess of the short twenty-one-year peace. It was, by chance, the twenty-fifth anniversary of the beginning of the First World War. Churchill was at Chartwell, still struggling with the end of the *English-Speaking Peoples* until 14 August when he went to France for eight days. This was primarily a military visit, at the invitation of General Georges, a very senior figure in the French army. Indeed all Churchill's comments (to Clementine) on the trip combined notes of schoolboy excitement, over-optimism about the military strength of the French, and an elegiac sense of doing everything in great comfort, but for the last time in peace.

[Georges] met the aeroplane & drove me to the restaurant in the Bois where in divine sunshine we lunched; & talked 'shop' for a long time. . . . The General is coming here [the Ritz] in a few minutes to take me to the Gare de l'Est. We are to travel in a special Michelin train of extreme speed to Strasbourg, dining en route. We are to have 2 vy long days on the line. . . . We sleep tonight Strasbourg: tomorrow Colmar: & Wednesday Belfort.[33]

Then, after a very short holiday in Normandy:

> On my way through Paris I gave General Georges luncheon. He pro-
> duced all the figures of the French and the German Armies, and classified
> the divisions in quality. The result impressed me so much that for the
> first time I said: 'But you are the masters.' He replied 'The Germans have
> a very strong army, and we shall never be allowed to strike first. If they
> attack, both our countries will rally to their duty.'[34]

When Churchill invited General Ironside, about to be Chief of the
Imperial General Staff (CIGS), down to Chartwell for lunch in the
following week, Ironside recorded: 'Winston was full of Georges. . . .
I found that he had become very French in his outlook and had a
wonderful opinion of the whole thing he saw. . . . I told him that the
French had told him far more than they had told our General
Staff. . . .'[35]

His five-day Normandy holiday was at St Georges-Motel, the château
of Consuelo Balsan, ex-Duchess of Marlborough, which he always liked
visiting, although her views – pro-Munich, thankful for Chamberlain
and rather anti-Semitic[36] – were just as bad as had been those of her
former husband, Churchill's cousin Sunny Marlborough, of whom he
had also been fond. With people whom he had known a long time, who
were politically unimportant, whom he found socially agreeable and
who could entertain him in great comfort, he did not much care about
views. He was therefore content to spend what he was acutely aware
were his last days of French pleasure in 'the light of this lovely valley at
the confluence of the Eure and the Vesgre'. He wrote that he could
'feel the deep apprehension brooding over all' and 'found painting hard
work in the uncertainty'. He nonetheless impressed his companion
painter, the Anglo-French artist Paul Maze, with the intensity of his
concentration before he turned to Maze and said, 'This is the last
picture we shall paint in peace for a very long time.'[37]

He was at Chartwell for just over another week after his return from
France, partly working on the proofs of *The English-Speaking Peoples* (he
was writing detailed letters about them to Deakin and G. M. Young as
late as 29 and 31 August), but also deep in military politics. He went to
London for a special one-day sitting of Parliament on 25 August. By
then the Nazi–Soviet Pact had been announced, and the inevitability of
war became still greater. He had Kingsley Wood (separately) as well as
General Ironside down, and was even able to inform the latter at 10.00
on the morning of 1 September that the German invasion of Poland

had started at dawn before Ironside or anyone else at the War Office seemed to have heard. Later that day he moved from Chartwell to more advanced headquarters in Morpeth Mansions. This was the last, for six years, of his literary and peacetime life.

PART FIVE

THE SAVIOUR OF HIS
COUNTRY AND THE LIGHT
OF THE WORLD?

1939–1945

29

QUIET WAR WITH GERMANY AND
UNEASY PEACE WITH CHAMBERLAIN

ON THE AFTERNOON of Friday, 1 September 1939, a dozen hours after the launch of Hitler's invasion of Poland, Churchill was summoned to see Chamberlain and accepted the offer of a place in the War Cabinet. This offer was firm but not precise. Chamberlain at that stage was contemplating an entirely non-departmental War Cabinet and Churchill assumed that he was to be some sort of minister without portfolio. Nor was it clear when exactly he was to become a member of the government. Over that day and the next he was complaining that he had been left in limbo, not knowing whether he was already in office or not, but feeling inhibited from speaking either at the six o'clock session of the House (summoned back from recess) that Friday evening, or at the same time on the Saturday, when there was an eruption of revolt, led by Arthur Greenwood (acting leader of the Labour party in Attlee's absence through illness) and echoed by Leo Amery, at Chamberlain's apparent continuing equivocation.

However, following Britain's declaration of war against Germany at 11.00 on the Sunday morning, matters became clearer. First, when the House met at noon, Churchill threw off his inhibition and made his last-ever backbench speech. But it might have been better had he not done so. It lasted only six minutes, but it added nothing. Harold Nicolson wrote: 'Winston intervenes with a speech which misses fire since it is too like one of his articles.'[1] The pre-eminent characteristic of this brief speech was that it was a piece of over-prepared and otiose rhetoric, delivered because he thought he ought to speak rather than because he had something significant to say. Lloyd George, who followed, was in the same category. Nicolson indulgently added that, in any event the House was too preoccupied with the first (false) air-raid siren and the all-clear which sounded during the debate to take much notice of what anyone said.

Immediately after the brief exchange the House adjourned and

Churchill was again summoned to see Chamberlain. There is a conflict of evidence as to where this important meeting took place. The conflict is typical of the frailty of memory, without will to deceive, which renders unreliable so much personal reminiscence as opposed to hard, written records, particularly if made at the time or not long subsequently. Churchill himself in *The Gathering Storm* says that he went to 'his [Chamberlain's] room', which in the context would strongly imply the Prime Minister's room in the House of Commons. But Churchill's personal detective, Inspector W. H. Thompson, who had been called back into his service a few days before, provides a graphic description of how, immediately after the debate, Churchill came down to his car (a 'hearse-like Daimler') and said, '10, Downing Street, Thompson.' Then, when he emerged from seeing the Prime Minister, he climbed into the back beside Clementine, who had been waiting, and said, 'It's the Admiralty,' and added with a pleased chuckle, 'That's a lot better than I thought.'[2] Thompson, who subsequently wrote two books of memoirs about Churchill, had some motive for exaggerating his centrality to the action on this crucial day, but it is nonetheless difficult to believe that he made up the entire episode, particularly as he very well captured Churchill's mood.

It *was* the Admiralty, and the War Cabinet as well, for Chamberlain had changed his mind since the Friday and decided to include in the supreme body the ministerial heads of the service departments. The Admiralty both gave Churchill real executive power, which a brooding ministership without portfolio would not have done, and aroused in him tremendous, even dangerous, nostalgia for his role in the same office twenty-five years before in the late summer of 1914. In any event he was firmly appointed even though he did not receive the seals of office until two days later, attended his first (brief) War Cabinet meeting at 5.00 that afternoon and went immediately afterwards to take possession of his restored naval kingdom.

It was not an altogether easy return to office – after a gap of ten years. So much fuss had been made about whether he should or should not be readmitted that there was a danger of anti-climax. There was at once suspicion of him among most of his new ministerial colleagues and too much expectation of him among the press and public. How did he perform? Above all with enormous vigour, but also with some slapdashness. Internally in the Admiralty he started his habit, which he was to apply more widely after he became Prime Minister eight months later, of firing off departmental minutes, to the First Sea Lord, to the civilian

permanent secretary and to two or three other crucially placed or
specially favoured senior naval officers. These were brief, mostly courteous, occasionally witty, probing enquiries or comments. The picture
they give in *The Churchill War Papers*, as was to be the case in *The Second
World War*, is distorted by replies hardly every being allowed a place.
They had however both spontaneity and impact. He dictated them
without hesitation as soon as he read or physically observed something
which attracted his attention. There never has been a minister or a
writer more dependent upon the constant attendance of a stenographer.
He needed secretaries by day and far into the night, more even than
many great men need sycophants.

Internal Admiralty matters occupied only a portion of his time. He
was fecund in letters to his colleagues, particularly to Halifax as Foreign
Secretary and to the Prime Minister. To Neville Chamberlain he wrote
thirteen letters of substance in the first six weeks of the war. These do
not appear to have irritated, although not more than one of them was
directly answered, Chamberlain claiming that he saw the new First Lord
so frequently that there was no need to respond on paper. Churchill
also wrote a clutch of Cabinet papers, as well as figuring prominently in
the Cabinet minutes of the period.

Did he overplay his hand at the beginning of his return to government? Samuel Hoare expressed the early reaction of an old Chamberlain
Cabinet hand when he wrote to Beaverbrook on 1 October: 'Winston
has been much as you expected he would be, very rhetorical, emotional
and, most of all, very reminiscent. He strikes me as an old man who
easily gets tired. Certainly in the country he has a very big position. . . .
I should say that at the moment he is the one popular figure in the
Cabinet.'*[3]

The comment that Churchill was ageing (beyond the routine ticking
of the chronological clock) was frequent at the time, but there was
remarkably little support for it in the output of his working day, and
there is a strong suspicion more of wishful thinking than of hard
evidence.

Within the Admiralty most of his senior subordinates were amazed

---

* Hoare, who was at the time Lord Privy Seal and a member of the War Cabinet having
just ceased to be Home Secretary by changing places with Sir John Anderson, was paid
an annual subvention of £2,000 (about £55,000 at today's prices) by Beaverbrook, but
there is no reason to think that this payment, highly improper although it would now
be judged to be, influenced the appraisal which he delivered to his paymaster.

at his volume of work and at the long (if inconvenient) hours which he worked. Geoffrey Shakespeare – not an admiral but a junior Admiralty minister in that first year of the war, and one who had the comparative experience of having been a secretary to Lloyd George – wrote: 'Usually after dinner he held a Naval conference from 9 to 11 p.m. But after 11 p.m. he devoted himself to speech making. . . . He dictated directly and firmly to an expert typist who used a silent machine. One night he remarked: "Are you all ready? I'm feeling very fertile tonight."'[4] Churchill himself wrote on 24 September: 'During the last three weeks I have not had a minute to think of anything but my task. They are the longest three weeks I have ever lived.'[5] But as this was in a letter excusing himself from a request it should perhaps be taken with a pinch of salt. Clementine probably (as often) struck about the right note when she wrote, a few days earlier, 'Winston works night & day – He is well, Thank God & gets tired only if he does not get his 8 hours sleep – He does not need it at a stretch but if he does not get that amount in the 24 then he gets weary.'[6]

In fact, while he undoubtedly worked very hard for a minister of any age, he did manage to sustain a few links with his pre-war life. On Sundays 10 September and 8 October he was at Chartwell for short weekends, and he also managed to write a few letters to Deakin, Alan Bullock (another young Oxford research assistant) and G. M. Young about the polishing off of *The English-Speaking Peoples*. He also managed to keep up some vestiges of his pre-war London pattern. On 11 September he dined at the Other Club; on 16 October he lunched at the Savoy Grill with Stefan Lorant (then editor of the new and very successful *Picture Post*), with Samuel Hoare also present. Hoare, although an old half-enemy whom Churchill exiled to the Embassy in Madrid as soon as he formed his 1940 government, occasionally made similar surprising appearances in his semi-political semi-social life.

So his head was not totally buried, without any ability to come up for air, in Admiralty and other government business. But his official output was nonetheless formidable. On 16 October, for instance, the day of his Stefan Lorant luncheon, he dictated five separate minutes to admirals, as well as composing a major paper on Scandinavian strategy for the War Cabinet and another memorandum on aircraft manufacture (fairly wide of his departmental boundaries), and writing letters to President Roosevelt, General Georges and the French ambassador in London. The whole amounted to a total output of nearly 3,000 words, a good daily total for any full-time writer, although Churchill, in addition, kept an eye on all fleet dispositions as well as making a major contribution, which required many paragraphs of minutes, to an 11.30–1.00 meeting of the War Cabinet.

The correspondence with Roosevelt had been initiated by the President, who had written on 4 September, 'It is because you and I occupied similar positions in the World War that I want you to know how glad I am that you are back again at the Admiralty,' and suggesting that they should carry on a continuing correspondence through diplomatic pouches on naval and even wider matters. Churchill of course jumped at this invitation. But it required careful handling with Chamberlain. The Prime Minister might not unreasonably have thought that he was the correct vis-à-vis with F.D.R. However, the limitations of his judgement of individuals outweighed any tendency to jealousy. He never thought much of Roosevelt, regarding his restless urge for innovation as the sign of a rather flashy and unreliable fellow, a bit like his *bête noire* Lloyd George. If Churchill wanted to cultivate such a mountebank then Chamberlain, activated partly by sheer absence of imagination and partly by a gruff decency, was quite prepared to let him get on with it.

Nevertheless Churchill was wise enough to make sure that his Presidential correspondence was not done behind the Prime Minister's back. Indeed, throughout the whole of these early war months, he was at pains to treat Chamberlain with respect and circumspection, which is generally a wise tactic for ministers in relation to the head of the government, particularly when substantial sections of press and public are elevating the subordinate minister over his nominal chief. Thus describing an event on 13 October Churchill wrote:

> my relations with Mr Chamberlain had so far ripened that he and Mrs Chamberlain came to dine with us at Admiralty House, where we had a comfortable flat in the attics. We were a party of four. Although we had been colleagues under Mr Baldwin for five years, my wife and I had never met the Chamberlains in such circumstances before. By happy chance I turned the conversation on to his life in the Bahamas [in 1890–5], and I was delighted to find my guest expand in personal reminiscence to a degree I had not noticed before. He told us the whole story, on which I knew only the barest outline, of his six years' struggle to grow sisal on a barren West Indian islet near Nassau. . . . I was fascinated by the way Mr Chamberlain warmed as he talked, and by the tale itself, which was one of gallant endeavour. I thought to myself, 'What a pity Hitler did not know when he met this sober English politician with his umbrella at Berchtesgaden, Godesberg and Munich, that he was actually talking to a

hard-bitten pioneer from the outer marches of the British Empire!' This
was really the only intimate social conversation that I can remember with
Neville Chamberlain amid all the business we did together over nearly
twenty years.[7]

During the evening news was brought in, by instalments, of the
sinking of three U-boats. Mrs Chamberlain, not normally noted for
sagacity, enquired whether it had all been arranged on purpose. Alas, it
was a shrewd shaft, for as Churchill sadly subsequently noted, none of
these sinkings was borne out by subsequent records. What was true was
that the British battleship *Royal Oak* was sunk by torpedoes in Scapa
Flow soon after midnight. The Chamberlains' habits were not nearly
late enough for that to mar the proceedings, and there can be no doubt
that Churchill, curbing for once his own desire to dominate the
conversation, had handled brilliantly this rare social encounter. (There
is, however, just the faintest impression that he had been a little
artificially on his best behaviour.) The evening was, for differing reasons,
a success for both couples – although not an occasion to be frequently
repeated.

The respect and circumspection with which Churchill was determined to treat Chamberlain, and Chamberlain's generally friendly
response to this treatment, did not avoid some inevitable tensions. As
early as 12 September Churchill made strenuous efforts to get Brendan
Bracken appointed parliamentary secretary to the new Ministry of
Information, of which the unjournalistically minded Scottish law lord,
Macmillan, had been made chief. Chamberlain was unmoved and
appointed Edward Grigg. Then on the 26th Churchill made his first
substantial House of Commons speech since his return to the front
bench. He did so with the permission of the Prime Minister (it would
have been difficult for Chamberlain to have said 'no') and confined
himself to twenty minutes on the war at sea. Nevertheless the speech
was in unfortunately close juxtaposition to Chamberlain's opening of
the debate, and produced much drawing of comparisons in a way that
would have bruised Chamberlain. Nicolson wrote:

The effect of Winston's speech was infinitely greater than could be
derived from any reading of the text. His delivery was really amazing and
he sounded every note from deep preoccupation to flippancy, from
resolution to sheer boyishness. One could feel the spirits of the House
rising with every word. It was obvious afterwards that the Prime Minister's inadequacy and lack of inspiration had been demonstrated even to

his warmest supporters. In those twenty minutes Churchill brought himself nearer the post of Prime Minister than he has ever been before.[8]

Ronald Cartland, the soon-to-be-killed young Tory MP for the King's Norton division of Birmingham (his sister Barbara lived sixty years longer), wrote: 'Winston smashed and confounded the critics who had been whispering that the years had been taking their toll. He revealed to a delighted House all the weapons of leadership that his armoury contains.'[9] From the other side of the Conservative pre-war divide Henry 'Chips' Channon confirmed the cathartic nature of the two performances:

> The PM made his usual dignified statement: unfortunately he was fol-lowed by Winston, who executed a *tour-de-force*, a brilliant bit of acting and exposition, in describing in detail the work of the Admiralty. He amused and I fear impressed the House – he must have taken endless trouble with his speech, and it was a contrast, which was noticed, to the PM's colourless statement.
>
> I am sure Winston is angling for the Premiership, convinced of it: the moment is not yet ripe, but already today I noticed signs of the 'glamour boys' [a derisive Chamberlainite term for the young Tory MPs who were anti-appeasement] beginning to intrigue again. We must watch out.[10]

This was followed five days later by a Churchill broadcast on the general progress of the war at sea. It was the first of his wartime Sunday-evening wireless speeches, and the forerunner of what from eight months later became the most famous series of sound broadcast decla-mations (for they were that rather than 'talks') in the history of the medium. This 1 October broadcast was in its way as great a success as the House of Commons speech, and ranged rather more widely outside Admiralty business. J. R. (Jock) Colville wrote of 'Winston Churchill's inspiring speech on the wireless'.[11] This was noteworthy for, although Colville was later to be one of the best chroniclers of Churchill's premierships, he was then a Chamberlain private secretary and loyalist who in May 1940 was to be sceptical of the new man. But Chamberlain expressed himself as equally favourable, and was genuinely so, for the approval came not in a 'good relations' *billet doux* to his bounding colleague but at the beginning of one of his frank letters to a sister: 'I take the same view as Winston, to whose excellent broadcast we have just been listening.'[12]

Nevertheless there may have been some connection between Churchill's two successive triumphs and the Cabinet minute which the

Prime Minister sent round a few weeks later saying that he had asked the Lord Privy Seal (Sir Samuel Hoare) to exercise a general supervision over ministerial broadcasts and in effect instructing ministers to clear the matter with Hoare before accepting an invitation. Churchill was not submitting himself to any possible ukase from an old adversary whom he did not much respect. He was however good at stubbornness without rudeness and he wrote back to Chamberlain:

> Communications by Cabinet Ministers of their views on public events have always in my experience been left to their discretion and knowledge of Government policy. . . . I receive many letters and requests to broadcast, and from time to time – though certainly it is no pleasure – I feel I have something to say which might be useful. I am of course quite willing to be guided by your wishes in the matter: but I do not think I should like to address myself to the Lord Privy Seal on such a point. I shall therefore await your personal intervention before undertaking to broadcast; and should I feel it my duty to do so I will come and see you.[13]

Thus was Hoare firmly discarded from any possible supervisory role in relation to Churchill, and Chamberlain put on notice that if ever he sought to come between Churchill and his public he would have to face a potentially disagreeable interview. It was a good example of how strong ministers flex their muscles when they think the head of government is treating them too much as a subordinate rather than as a near-equal colleague. There is no suggestion that Churchill ever needed to have such a disagreeable interview with Chamberlain. This was despite the fact that only two weeks later he launched into another Sunday-evening broadcast which encroached far more on to general policy than had his 1 October one and was much less favourably received by official opinion than had been the earlier one. His central message amounted to a rather patronizing pinning of the colours of his Prime Minister to the mast:

> You know that I have not always agreed with Mr Chamberlain; though we have always been personal friends. But he is a man of very tough fibre, and I can tell you that he is going to fight as obstinately for victory as he did for peace. You may take it absolutely for certain that either all that Britain and France stand for in the modern world will go down, or that Hitler, the Nazi régime and the recurring German and Prussian menace to Europe will be broken and destroyed. That is the way the matter lies and everybody had better make up their minds to that solid, sombre fact.[14]

In that way he intended to block any possible veering towards a negotiated peace. Then he made some tendentious remarks about Italy and Japan being estranged from Germany by the Nazi–Soviet Pact, about American commitment to the Allied side, and about the threat of an early German attack upon Holland and Belgium, the whole carrying a flavour of braggadocio. Colville reacted and reported less favourably than following 1 October. 'We listened to Winston Churchill's wireless speech, very boastful, over-confident and indiscreet (especially about Italy and the U.S.A.), but certainly most amusing.' And then a day later: 'Winston's speech has made a very bad effect at No. 10 but the F.O. and the City take a favourable view. . . . The Italian and Dutch Representatives protested at the F.O. and Rab Butler tells me he thought it beyond words vulgar.'[15]

Despite these wider activities Churchill in the autumn months of 1939 was a dynamo at the Admiralty. On 14 September the previously quoted Channon wrote: 'I am told that Winston is already driving the Admiralty to distraction by his interference and energy.'[16] But on the next day, Kathleen Hill, Churchill's principal dictating secretary throughout the war, wrote: 'When Winston was at the Admiralty the place was buzzing with atmosphere, with electricity. When he was away on tour, it was dead, dead, dead.'[17] The truth was probably somewhere between these two conflictingly partial witnesses.

Churchill drew no distinction between his rights over administrative policy on the one hand and over operational matters on the other. In this context it is important that the Admiralty, by long tradition and unlike the War Office or the Air Ministry, was a control tower as well as an administrative bureaucracy. Operational instructions to remote fleets flashed out from the masts of the Admiralty in a way that their equivalents never were from the War Office or the Air Ministry. This degree of control from the centre was a standing temptation for Churchill. A revealing and relevant contrast emerged when he went on a four-day visit to France in early November. Although he also fitted in a visit to General Lord Gort's British Expeditionary Forces headquarters,* his primary purpose was to confer with the French on naval matters. As Churchill recalled well after the event:

---

* Two British divisions went to France in October and another two in November. Between the New Year and March another six followed, giving a total strength (including support troops) of nearly a quarter of a million men. Gort's headquarters in November were near Arras.

Before we went into the conference Admiral Darlan explained to me how Admiralty matters were managed in France. The Minister of Marine, M. Campinchi, was not allowed by him to be present when operational matters were under discussion. These fell into the purely professional sphere. I said that the First Sea Lord and I were one. Darlan said he recognised this, but in France it was different. 'However,' he said, 'Monsieur le Ministre will arrive for luncheon.'[18]

This stood in splendid juxtaposition to a minute Churchill had despatched five days earlier to the Chief and Deputy Chief of the Naval Staff:

We cannot allow ourselves to be driven out of the North Sea without failing in our prime duty of securing the Island against raid or invasion. No base on the West Coast can be accepted except for a brief and unexpected interval. *Nelson* and *Rodney*, 'The Captains of the Gate', must take their stations at Rosyth [on the Firth of Forth], and fight it out there when not at sea. *Warspite* and *Valiant* are available to replace casualties. There is no reason why they should not remain at Plymouth till they are needed.[19]

Churchill in Paris struck a counterblow for the rights of politicians against the pretensions of Admiral Darlan by inviting Campinchi to dinner that night in a private room at the Ritz. There he discerned the 'patriotism', 'ardour' and 'acute intelligence' of the minister, and preferred him to the Admiral 'who, jealous of his own position, was fighting on quite a different front from ours'.[20]

Churchill was not disdainful of professional naval opinion, although he was apt to pull rank in the shape of his senior 1914 experiences, when his 1939 advisers were junior officers or even midshipmen. Furthermore they were less formidable personalities than those he had dealt with in the age of the dreadnought, and he also had the advantage that, apart from the sinking of *Courageous* (torpedoed in the Bristol Channel on 17 September) and *Royal Oak* and a nasty spate of merchant ship losses when the Germans first developed magnetic mines, there were no naval vicissitudes in the autumn of 1939 comparable with those he had had to explain away in the analogous months of 1914.

Among his manifold activities in and around the Admiralty during the autumn were the following miscellany. He made two visits to Scapa Flow, the defences of which were causing him considerable concern. He observed the precipitate engagement and marriage within a week of Randolph to the nineteen-year-old Pamela Digby, who after an adventurous career became Mrs Averell Harriman and then in her Harriman widowhood American ambassador to Paris; it was a union which gave Churchill pleasure at the time. He fielded a tiresome letter from the Duke of Windsor[21] in which the former King tried to involve him in a dispute with his sovereign brother as well as with the high military authorities. In reply Churchill told him as circumspectly as he could that, having accepted the rank of major-general nominally to liaise with the French, he had better accept orders which came to him from higher up. This exchange probably marked the end both of Churchill's romantic attachment to the Duke, and of the Duke's belief that he could get Churchill to go on being as totally in his favour as he had been in December 1936.

Then there was the writing (with help) of a 10,000-word introduction to the *English-Speaking Peoples* and the delivery of what he thought was a completed proof of 500,000 words (a remarkable feat in the circumstances) to Cassells in mid-December. Throughout there were the demands of a regular and commanding presence at the very frequent meetings (twenty-four during November for instance) of the War Cabinet of nine members. From mid-November there were supplementary demands of the Military Co-ordination Committee, comprised of the service ministers with a few professional advisers, which also met frequently under Chatfield's chairmanship but Churchill's leadership, until form merged with reality and Churchill took over the chairmanship at the beginning of April 1940.

It was a formidable budget of activity for a man who had passed his sixty-fifth birthday and entered pensionable age at the end of November (1939), although less of course than six months later he was eagerly to undertake, and sustain for five years. That Advent season was made buoyant by the destruction of the *Graf Spee* pocket battleship off the coast of Uruguay on 17 December. It followed the first dramatic naval encounter of the war. Churchill allowed it to lead to no excessive Christmastide relaxation. He demanded from the navy no break or holiday period at Christmas or the New Year, and he set a good example from the top. He told the secretary to the Cabinet that he would be at the Admiralty 'all through Christmas or at the outside within an hour and a quarter [which presumably meant Chartwell], and that only for a few hours'.[22] But he did not go to Chartwell, at any rate not on Christmas Day, when according to his detective, 'he worked from early morning until dinner time'.[23] He produced over 4,000 words of dictation, ranging from a long letter to the Prime Minister and a pro-Zionist

Cabinet paper to a couple of jaunty one-line internal minutes ('How is *Rodney* getting on, and when can we expect her?' and 'Has the *Warspite* received its warm clothing yet? If not, on what date will it be provided?').[24]

On Boxing Day, again according to his detective, he 'unbended a little': 'He worked for fourteen hours and spent three hours in a local cinema.'[25] Inspector Thompson in his two volumes of reminiscence is good at capturing the heart of the matter but a little less reliable on exact dates, times and places than might have been hoped for from a meticulous detective, and there is room for doubt whether 'local' meant Westerham, a more natural meaning, rather than the West End of London. Nor does Thompson record the name of the film. But he provides another shot of detailed colour when on 30 December, after a day of naval inspections at Weymouth, Churchill went for a couple of nights with the Digbys, Randolph's new parents-in-law, at Cerne Abbas in Dorset. 'This', Thompson wrote, 'was the first day's relaxation that the First Lord had taken since the beginning of the war.'[26] It was probably made more relaxing by the absence of the happy couple. Then, on 4 January 1940, Churchill left for a four-and-a-half-day visit to France, where he again conferred with Darlan, inspected a new (to him) segment of the French line and a Royal Air Force unit before going to stay a night with Gort at the BEF headquarters. Churchill never allowed rigid inter-service divisions to stand in his way.

While in France a contretemps with his publisher reached near-crisis. Desmond Flower of Cassells was not nearly as satisfied with getting half a million words of *The English-Speaking Peoples* as either Churchill or an objective observer would have expected him to be. He had already written to complain that it ended most abruptly with the assassination of Abraham Lincoln, thereby leaving a large and important lacuna of over seventy years. Churchill, who was nearly always remarkably concili-atory in anything to do with his publishers or commissioning newspaper editors, reserving his acerbity for political colleagues, wrote back offer-ing to produce an epilogue of 10,000 words. Flower, who was to make immense profits out of Churchill's *The Second World War* (although he did not then know that), responded with a truculence as surprising as was Churchill's conciliation and said that it would not do:

> I am sorry, at a time like this, to have to put before you a more serious view for your consideration. We cannot feel that your MS, ending as it does with the close of the American Civil War, fulfils your contract with

us to write a History of the English Speaking peoples. . . . 10,000 words, of whatsoever nature they may be, cannot repair the omission of fifty years' vital history.[27]

Then Brendan Bracken, who appears to have intercepted this letter, gave a brilliant demonstration of his value as 'Mr Churchill's honorary man of business' (so he described it to Flower), as well as going on to illustrate why he remained, nearly until his death in 1958, so indispensable to Churchill. When Churchill got to the British Embassy in Paris he received via Miss Hill a message from Bracken saying:

> Cassell's sent you a long, rambling letter asking for supplements to your history. No indication was given of when the payment due under the contract [£7,500, nearly £200,000 at today's values] wd. be made.
> B[racken] had a very frank talk to Mr Desmond Flower. He told that publisher that you wd. round off the history. But no new material could be expected of you until June 30th, 1940. B. also required payment early tomorrow morning. The promise was given & B. expects a cheque by 11 a.m. Flower also agreed to give sympathetic consideration to B's proposal that Cassell's should reimburse you the amount [£1,100, or almost £30,000 today] spent on printing proofs.[28]

Bracken's performance had clearly been masterly. Fortunately it did not, as things turned out, involve Churchill spending most of the month of June 1940 writing about the Venezuelan border or the Canadian fisheries disputes between Britain and the United States.

Apart from the constant eye for detail (were there enough duffle coats for those on winter duty in destroyers; what was the position of the dependants of the gallant Captain Kennedy of the *Rawalpindi*; what facilities for 'rest and recreation' were there for ratings and indeed officers in Weymouth?), Churchill's main preoccupation over the turn-of-the-year season were two battles, in neither of which he was triumphant, one within the Admiralty and the other in the War Cabinet. The internal Admiralty one concerned where should be the base of the core of the Home Fleet. After the sinking at anchor on 14 October (1939) of *Royal Oak*, Scapa Flow, until substantially refortified, was judged unsafe. So was Rosyth, which was subject to a damaging air raid two days later. *Rodney* and *Nelson*, those 'Captains of the Gate' in Churchill's typically dramatic 29 October phrase, and their attendant protectors and supporters were moved to the Clyde.

It was a temporary move, but one which lasted until March 1940, and was cordially disliked by Churchill.* He thought the great ships ought to be facing the enemy at Rosyth on the Forth and not cowering in soft, protected western waters, long hours of steaming time from the North Sea. This led to many minutes of complaint from Churchill to Admiral Pound, the First Sea Lord. These were directed both to the slow pace of the refortification of Scapa Flow and to the disadvantages of the Clyde over the Forth. Apart from being on the wrong side of Britain it was difficult to enter and leave, it had feeble guns and harbour defences, and was even assailed on the ground of Glasgow's large Irish population, which provided an open channel for conveying intelligence about fleet movements and accidents to Germany via Dublin. The west coast did not even provide safety for the capital ships. *Nelson* was badly crippled by striking a mine at the mouth of Loch Ewe on 7 December. The whole long-drawn-out argument left two strong impressions. The first was that great battleships had already become like dinosaurs, formidable in shape but so vulnerable that the protection they required balanced any security that they could give. And the second was that even the most politically powerful and strategically uninhibited First Lord found it very difficult to push his admirals against the grain of their professional caution.

The War Cabinet battle was essentially over whether Britain should fight a war of initiative with all the risks inherently involved, or whether it was better to avoid provocation: both of neutrals and of Germany. This first manifested itself in relation to the Irish Treaty ports of Queenstown (later Cobh), Berehaven and Lough Swilly. Britain's rights over their naval use, retained in the Irish Treaty of 1921, in the negotiation of which Churchill had been actively concerned, were surrendered in the new settlement of 1938 under which the Irish Free State was rechristened Eire. This surrender was strongly but not very realistically opposed by Churchill. He raised little support on the issue and merely put strain on wider relations with his 'Arms and the Covenant' allies. By October 1939, under the pressure of U-boat activity in the western approaches, he reverted to the issue in the War Cabinet

* Stephen Roskill in his on the whole authoritative, although sometimes polemical *Churchill and the Admirals* (p. 118) says that Churchill was only persuaded of this view by a head-on argument with Admiral Forbes, the Commander-in-Chief of the Home Fleet in *Nelson* on 31 October. This is however wholly incompatible with his already cited 'Captains of the Gate' minute of two days before. Oral historical recollections are notoriously inaccurate, but even written records have a nasty habit of quite frequently contradicting each other.

on the 16th of the month: 'The First Lord emphasized the acute shortage of Destroyers. . . . the strain was very heavy. It would be a great help if we could obtain the use of Berehaven.'[29]

That view was no doubt of naval logistical validity but it did not convince the Cabinet that the Taoiseach (De Valera) could be cajoled by the Dominions Office or the Foreign Office into giving the ports back to Britain or that, if not, they should be reoccupied by force. Churchill was convinced that 'three-quarters of the people of southern Ireland are with us' and that it was only an 'implacable malignant minority' who intimidated De Valera. It is difficult not to feel that Anthony Eden (as Dominions Secretary) had more realism when he wrote to Halifax on 20 October: 'I fear that it has become every day clearer that it is scarcely possible for "Dev" to square neutrality with the grant of the facilities for which the Admiralty ask, and at least 80% of the Irish people favour neutrality.'[30] Churchill grudgingly accepted defeat.

During December and January however a bigger but not wholly dissimilar issue built up. It tried Churchill's patience even more. It also contained the seeds from which sprang the Norwegian campaign of April 1940, the least successful enterprise with which Churchill had been associated since the Dardanelles, but which, by a lucky paradox, so far from casting him once again into disregard, made him Prime Minister. This was the question of the interdiction of the supply to Germany of Scandinavian iron ore. It involved shipments from both the northern Norwegian port of Narvik and the Swedish port of Lulea on the Gulf of Bothnia. The latter, although well south of Narvik, was immune from gulf stream influences and was hard frozen and unusable for long winter months. Swedish ore therefore went in winter through Narvik.

Churchill persuaded himself and others, not without some rational foundation, that the blocking of these supplies could amount to a rapid crippling of the German war effort. At a Cabinet on 23 December he used a memorandum from Fritz Thyssen, who had recently turned against Hitler and fled temporarily to Switzerland and then to France, arguing that victory would accrue to the side which 'obtained mastery of the iron ores and magnetic iron in Northern Sweden'. It was a subject on which anyone bearing the name of Thyssen (and this one was head of the firm and family, although about to spend nearly five wartime years in concentration camps) was likely to be well informed. Churchill embellished the paper by saying that this interdiction would be 'worth all the rest of the blockade, and provides a great chance of shortening the war and possibly saving immeasurable bloodshed on the Western Front.'[31]

The War Cabinet 'wouldn't say yes but didn't say no'. It hovered for weeks between what was regarded as the narrower and the wider plans. The narrower one involved stopping traffic from Narvik down the west coast of Norway to Germany, which could be done by a combination of mine laying in Norwegian territorial waters and a continuous patrol of destroyers outside them. The wider one involved effective Allied possession of the Swedish ore fields, and would become urgent when Lulea ceased to be ice-bound by the end of April. Ideally this should be in response to overt German coercion of Sweden, but if this was not forthcoming (there seemed no particular reason why it should be), by an Allied military intervention, however shocking this might be to world neutral opinion from the United States to the Netherlands.

The central position of the Cabinet appeared to be that it willed the end without willing the means. The Prime Minister was recorded as saying on 22 December that: '[the decision] might be one of the turning points of the war. He was greatly impressed by the statements contained in Herr Thyssen's memorandum, and it certainly seemed as if there was a chance of dealing a mortal blow to Germany.'[32] As a result there evolved a nice theory that the narrower action alone should not be decided upon lest it pre-empt the wider course and that both options should be kept open. This stratagem, probably adopted as a means of restraining Churchill, had, as the weeks went by, the fairly predictable effect of infuriating him. Halifax was particularly good at deploying these delaying tactics, so much so that after a very negative meeting on 12 January (1940), he felt it necessary to write a conciliatory letter to Churchill. But the conciliation was all in the form and not in the substance. Churchill replied on 15 January:

> My disquiet at the decision taken was due mainly to the awful difficulties which our machinery of war-conduct presents to positive action. I see such immense walls of prevention, all built or building, that I wonder whether any plan will have a chance of climbing over them. . . . Pardon me, therefore, if I showed distress. One thing is absolutely certain, namely, that victory will never be found by taking the line of least resistance.[33]

His frustration also expressed itself in a minute to Admiral Pound on 16 January. It nominally related to the anti-aircraft defences of Scapa

Flow, but in fact fired off in a variety of directions, most of which had nothing to do with Pound:

> The squandering of our strength proceeds in every direction, everyone thinking he is serving the country by playing for safety locally. Our Army is puny as far as the fighting front is concerned; our Air Force is hopelessly inferior to the Germans; we are not allowed to do anything to stop them receiving their vital supplies of ore; we maintain an attitude of complete passivity dispersing our forces ever more widely. The Navy demands Scapa and Rosyth both to be kept at the highest point. Do you realize that perhaps we are heading for *defeat*?[34]

Churchill's main relief was the fourth of his Sunday evening broadcasts, which he delivered on 20 January. On naval matters in particular he struck a much more optimistic note ('It seems pretty certain tonight that half the U-boats with which Germany began the war have been sunk; the *Spee* still sticks up in the harbour of Montevideo as a grisly monument and measure of the fate in store for any Nazi warship which dabbles in piracy on the broad waters'; 'things are not going badly after all – indeed, they have never gone so well in any Naval war'), but what was even more striking was the breadth of the canvas he chose and the stridency of the colours with which he covered it. He was close to caricaturing his own style, metaphorically in painting and actually in oratory. He surveyed the neutral states:

> Look at the group of small but ancient and historic states which lie in the North. Or look again at that other group of anxious peoples in the Balkans or in the Danube Basin behind whom stands the resolute Turk. . . .The hardy Swiss arm and man their mountain passes. The Dutch, whose services to European freedom will be remembered long after the smear of Hitler has been wiped from the human path, stand along their dykes as they did against the tyrants of bygone days. Only Finland, superb, nay sublime, in the jaws of peril shows what free men can do.

Finland at the time was with some success resisting a Russian invasion, which had begun on 30 November, although its resistance was not to be sustained beyond March. This meant that Churchill spoke in more anti-Soviet Union terms than he had been doing for the two previous years or was to do again for several years after June 1941. 'They [the Finns] have exposed to all the world to see the military incapacity of the Red Army and of the Red Air Force.' Without Britain and France the smaller states of Europe would 'be divided between the opposite, though similar barbarisms of Nazidom and Bolshevism'. Then he moved into his 'all cymbals clashing' peroration:

> Very few wars have been won by mere numbers alone. Quality, will-power, geographical advantages, natural and financial resources, the command of the sea, and above all a cause which rouses the spontaneous surgings of the human spirit in millions of hearts – these have proved to be the decisive factors in the human story. If it was otherwise, how would the race of men have risen above the apes; how otherwise would they have conquered and extinguished the dragons and monsters of the prime; how would they have evolved the moral theme; how would they have marched forward across the centuries to broad conceptions of compassion, of freedom and of right? How would we have ever discerned those beacon lights which summon and guide us across the rough, dark waters, and presently across the flaming lines of battle towards the better days? The day will come when the joy-bells will ring again throughout Europe, and when victorious nations, masters not only of their foes, but of themselves, will plan and build in justice, in tradition and in freedom, a house of many mansions where there shall be room for all.[35]

Whatever the effect upon the enemy, the broadcast frightened the Foreign Office. Halifax waited five days and then sent under cover of a pained letter of rebuke a devastating collection of unfavourable press reactions from Norway, Holland, Switzerland, Denmark, Belgium and even Finland: 'It puts me in an impossible position if a member of the Gov. like yourself takes a line in public which differs from that taken by the PM or myself; and I think, as I have to be in daily touch with these tiresome neutrals, I ought to be able to predict how their minds will work.'[36] Churchill replied semi-contritely: 'This is undoubtedly a disagreeable bouquet. I certainly thought I was expressing your view and Neville's.'[37] But it did not prevent his making another spirited (and broadcast) speech in the Free Trade Hall at Manchester on the following Saturday.

In a flaccid period he had begun his 20 January broadcast with the brilliantly appropriate sentence of 'Everyone is wondering what is happening about the war.' He had without question made himself the orator of the government. The idea of Chamberlain or Halifax, whose views with somewhat tongue-in-cheek naivety he had claimed to be expressing, speaking in anything like the terms he employed was simply preposterous. He stirred hearts, but he also aroused animosities. He was far from always getting his way in the War Cabinet, or even from completely dominating the admirals, but his position was nonetheless unassailable. It was noticeable that Chamberlain stood back from any rebukes to his extravagances. And when the fifth meeting of the Supreme War Council (a somewhat grandiose title for a body so few of whose political heads were to survive the next few months) took place in Paris on 4–5 February, with a view to planning a more active phase of the war, Churchill was for the first time asked to participate.

30

THROUGH DISASTER IN THE FJORDS
TO TRIUMPH IN DOWNING STREET

<hr>

THERE WAS ANOTHER losing battle which Churchill fought in the early
spring of 1940. It was not with the enemy, which was hardly engaged
during this period, nor with the War Cabinet or the admirals, but with
the French. As early as mid-November 1939 he had become enthusiastic
about a project, which subsequently became known as Operation Royal
Marine, for suffusing the Rhine, the principal artery of west German
commerce, with a plague of floating mines. It was to be done between
Strasbourg and the River Lauter, just south of Karlsruhe, where the
left bank of the river was French territory. It was seen as a powerful
disruption of German internal communications which could be justified
as a legitimate and appropriate response to German attacks upon Allied
high-seas commerce. It would be primarily a British enterprise so far as
the supply and laying of the mines was concerned, but, in view of the
location, enthusiastic French co-operation was essential.

General Gamelin was in favour from an early stage, but French
politicians were more difficult to convince. The French government in
this phase were in favour of rash and distant operations but less keen on
anything which might stir up the Germans on the Western Front.
Before the Russo-Finnish armistice of 13 March they were disposed to
sending several Allied divisions to assist the Finns on their front with
the Russians. And as late as 26 March they were equally rashly in favour
of bombing the Russian oil installations at Baku. Nearer to metropolitan
France they were more cautious. However, at the Supreme War Council
in London on that same date agreement was reached on a two-handed
operation for early April. Operation Royal Marine was to begin on the
4th, and the exit from Narvik was to be mined on the 5th. Backsliding
soon set in. Daladier, who after he had been replaced as Prime Minister
by Paul Reynaud on 21 March became a surly but powerful Minister of
Defence, was the foot-dragger. He claimed that French aircraft factories
would be unacceptably exposed to German reprisals. (It is amazing in

retrospect, but so are a lot of other things from this perspective, that barely six weeks before the unleashing of the German *Blitzkrieg*, which cut through France like a dagger, the prospect of a few air raids should have aroused such transfixing terror.)

The timetable of both operations (which the British regarded as complementary) therefore began to slip. On 4 April Churchill went to Paris with the blessing of Chamberlain and the intention of bringing Daladier into line. He was accompanied by his old francophile and francophone friend General Spears, who recorded some fascinating vignettes, sour and sweet, of this visit, which well illustrated the mixture of occasional discomfort, even danger, and continuing indulgent luxury which was a characteristic of political life at the beginning of the war, and which, in Churchill's case, substantially continued throughout the next five years. Spears recorded that on the outward journey: 'We were shaken in our old de Havilland as if we were a salad in a colander manipulated by a particularly energetic cook.'¹ But he also recorded as the high spot of the visit a luncheon at Lapérouse, the Jacobean-fronted (in English architectural terms) restaurant on the Quai Grands-Augustins to which Proust's Swann was drawn because its name was the same as the street in which Odette de Crécy lived, and for which General Georges deserted his field GHQ in order to entertain Churchill (and Spears). 'That lunch *à trois*', Spears wrote, 'remains in my mind as one of the few pleasant occasions I experienced in the war. We were three friends enjoying each other's company and remarkable food and wine. Georges was tranquil, gay and confident.'²

The conviviality of the occasion, however, did not preclude some serious military conversation, in which Churchill stressed the dangers of delay, both in relation to Royal Marine and to a Scandinavian initiative. 'Nous allons perdre l'omnibus,' Spears recorded him as saying. This came a day after Chamberlain had made his disastrous statement to a Conservative National Union meeting that Hitler 'had missed the bus'. And on the very day of the Paris luncheon General Ironside, the CIGS, had also asserted at a press conference that Hitler had 'thank goodness' been late at the bus-stop. It was odd that these politicians and generals, none of whom had much recent experience of buses or bus-stops, should have become so obsessed with a particular piece of imagery.

The main purpose of Churchill's visit went less well. So far from persuading the French to remain faithful to the decisions of the London Supreme Council of the previous week, Churchill went native. On the first evening at the British Embassy he found Reynaud reluctantly loyal but wobbly. On the next morning he went to the rue St Dominique to persuade Daladier, and came out persuaded by him that it was more sensible to postpone the mine-laying operation to 1 July, by when the French would have removed their crucial aircraft factories to places of greater security. (In fact Royal Marine took place in early June, and, while temporarily disorganizing Rhine traffic, made only a small splash amid the catastrophe in France.) This volte-face enabled Chamberlain to make his only recorded witticism against Churchill. He said it reminded him of 'the story of the pious parrot which was bought to teach good language to the parrot which swore, but ended by itself learning to swear'.[3]

The other interesting residue of this Paris visit was that Spears recorded some general advice which he had received from Clementine Churchill about how to deal with her husband. 'Put what you have to say in writing,' Spears recorded her as advising. 'He often does not listen or does not hear if he is thinking of something else. But he will always consider a paper carefully and take in all its implications. He never forgets what he sees in writing.'[4] This was true; and it sharply, indeed surprisingly, in view of his lack of success in formal education, differentiated him from a wide range of non-intellectual politicians, whose formal education varied, but whose ears were more sensitive than their eyes.

Just before this Paris visit there had been an interesting illustration of the strength of Churchill's personality and of the varying impact which it produced, first upon a high American official and then upon a Foreign Office chain of command which embraced many names who were or became the stars of British diplomacy in the thirty years from 1940. Sumner Welles, a rich and sophisticated New Yorker and also a career diplomat of exceptional experience who was currently under-secretary (number two) at the State Department, where Roosevelt found him a useful counterbalance to the ornery but politically important Secretary of State (Cordell Hull), was sent to make an early-1940 tour of Europe as the President's special envoy. Welles went to Berlin and Rome as well as to London and Paris and other lesser capitals and was thought to have been a little too 'neutral'. His underlying purpose was to sound out whether there was a possibility of a tolerable negotiated peace.

On the afternoon of 12 March Welles had been received by Churchill, who had robustly told him, *inter alia*, that the war must be fought to a finish. Welles's account of the meeting came back to a

Foreign Office official (Berkeley Gage), who recorded in a departmental minute:

> Mr Welles was extremely impressed by Mr Winston Churchill. He was very tired when he saw Mr Churchill and expected to find difficulty in concentrating. The contrary turned out in fact to be the case. During an interview which lasted nearly three hours his interest in what Mr Churchill had to say became progressively keener and he left feeling mentally refreshed. Mr Welles expressed the opinion that Mr Churchill was one of the most fascinating personalities he had ever met.

As Gage's minute made its way up the hierarchy it attracted the following comments:

> Let us hope that Mr Churchill helped to efface the dangerously satisfactory impression previously made upon Mr Welles by Signor Mussolini. – F. Roberts*

> ? Inform Mr Churchill's Private Secretary – R. W. Makins†

> I think so. – W. Strang‡

> No, I don't think so. I couldn't authorize this without authority. I feel some delicacy about asking the S of S (or the PM) to authorize our telling Mr Churchill that he made a unique impression on Mr Welles. I take comfort from the fact that Mr C will already have that conviction, so nothing is lost. – AC§§

Thus did Cadogan belie his reputation for confining his waspish edge of comment to his posthumously published diaries.¶

Upon his return from France on 6 April Churchill was immediately plunged into the ill-fated (largely because ill-executed) Norwegian campaign. The mine-laying exercise at the mouth of Narvik harbour,

---

* (Sir) Frank Roberts (1907–97), sometimes known as 'the electric mouse,' was later ambassador to Moscow and Bonn.
† (Sir) Roger Makins (1904–96) was subsequently ambassador to Washington, permanent secretary of the Treasury and Lord Sherfield.
‡ (Sir) William (later Lord) Strang (1893–1978) became permanent under-secretary of the Foreign Office.
§ Sir Alexander Cadogan (1884–1968) was permanent under-secretary 1938–46, then ambassador to the United Nations and later chairman of the BBC.
¶ After all that Sumner Welles's report to Roosevelt was less favourable than is here implied. He said Churchill was 'unsteady, drinking too much'. (No doubt the three-hour conversation reqired a good deal of refreshment.) According to Professor Lukacs's *Five Days in London* (p. 72) this report was a factor in Roosevelt not placing full trust in Churchill's leadership during at least that crucial month of May.

which had been agonized over for at least four months, was subject to a final postponement from 5 to 8 April as a result of French resistance to the Rhine-mining operation. By then the Germans had moved against both Denmark and Norway, which rendered it largely irrelevant. Copenhagen had been seized by land forces without opposition. And every significant port in Norway from Oslo to Narvik had been smoothly occupied by the Germans, despite the much vaunted view of the British, and particularly of Churchill, that the Royal Navy had full command of the North Sea. The Germans made major strategic mis-judgements later in the war, but their tactical deployments of the spring of 1940, both in Scandinavia and in France, were carried out with a sureness of planning and of execution which made the Allies look bungling amateurs.

The minutes of the War Cabinet and of the Military Co-ordination Committee (over which Churchill presided) during the next few weeks of the Norwegian campaign convey a terrible impression of lack of advance planning, infirmity of purpose, ill-coordination between the services, and clutching now at one objective and then at another. The basic weakness in the Allied position was that the Germans commanded the Norwegian air and that, particularly as they had got their troops in first, this outweighed British command of the sea. In one sense this vindicated Churchill's croakings of the previous seven years. His expo-sures of British military weakness had been essentially directed to the air force against the Luftwaffe, and indeed he was sometimes criticized for having diverted limited resources away from the army and even the navy. He saw, and exaggerated, the air threat to cities more than to battlefields, whether naval or military. But this inferiority of British air power, limiting and even outweighing British naval supremacy, also made Churchill a less than triumphant First Lord of the Admiralty. If, a month or so later when Chamberlain fell, Churchill's claim to the succession had depended upon his conduct of the Norwegian campaign, his chances of success would hardly have been greater than those of, say, Sir Kingsley Wood. Fortunately his reputation was judged on a longer time-scale, as the prescient alarm clock of the 1930s, rather than as a civilian minister who, in an unsuccessful campaign, had made matters worse rather than better by constant operational arm-jogging of the professional commanders.

Even his gift for spirit-lifting oratory seemed to desert him during that dismal April. On the 11th, three days after the beginning of the Norwegian operations, he made an interim report to the House of

Commons. He began by saying that he had not had time to give to the speech 'that thorough and prolonged preparation which I have always endeavoured to give to any observations which I have had to offer to the House'. As a perverse result it was much longer – sixty-five minutes – than any previous speech which he had made in the House of Commons since his return to office, nearly three times as long for instance as his brilliantly successful report of the previous 26 September. Those who left written comments were struck by how tired Churchill looked and seemed. Harold Nicolson went further and wrote: 'he indulges in vague oratory coupled with tired gibes. I have seldom seen him to less advantage. . . . It is a feeble, tired speech and it leaves the House in a mood of grave anxiety.'[6] Others (General Spears and the Solicitor-General, Terence O'Connor) were more charitable and thought he had done well in difficult circumstances. Colville found him 'less polished than usual' but thought that he had 'made a good case for the navy's achievements during the last few days'.[7]

The German fleet did indeed suffer heavily in the Norwegian campaign, losing three cruisers and ten destroyers, while in addition two heavy cruisers and one of its two remaining pocket battleships were put temporarily out of action. It was left very weak over the summer of 1940, which contributed something to the relatively unmolested British escape from Dunkirk and to the calling off of the invasion (of Britain) plans three months later. British naval losses were also considerable (three cruisers, one sloop and seven destroyers sunk, plus three cruisers, two sloops and another seven destroyers damaged; in addition the aircraft carrier *Glorious* was sunk in Norwegian waters a month after Churchill had become Prime Minister). But the British melting was from a bigger iceberg.

It was the failure of combined navy–army operations to achieve any significant objectives which made the Norwegian campaign a medium-grade military catastrophe and a major political catalyst at home. Most of the War Cabinet believed that Trondheim, the old capital in central Norway, was a more important objective than Churchill's favourite of Narvik. For some time it was thought that Trondheim could and should be seized by direct assault. Then opinion swung round to the view that this was too hazardous and that it would be better to reinforce the small landings which had been successfully made in mid-April at Namsos to the north of Trondheim and Andalsnes to the south. This projected pincer movement failed completely. The British forces were withdrawn from these two fishing ports on 2 May, barely two weeks after they had been put ashore. Narvik was not captured until 28 May and then had to be evacuated on 8 June.

There was thus a dismal picture of failure and retreat which confronted the House of Commons and the nation in the first week of May. And overhanging the actual record of hesitations and withdrawals was the threat of a major German onslaught against the Low Countries and France. Churchill was prescient about this. His memoranda and statements to the War Cabinet contain many warnings that such an attack was probably imminent. He also had the advantage that his public reputation remained high. When the navy suffered sinkings and repulses the First Lord was not blamed by general opinion. He retained the image of a bulldog who would first bark and then put things right. He was, however, by no means the clear public choice for Prime Minister if and when Chamberlain went. In a public opinion poll published on 8 April (that is before the Norwegian setbacks) a question asking who, if Chamberlain 'retired', the public would like his successor to be, was answered in the following percentages: 28 for Eden, 25 for Churchill, 7 for Halifax, 6 for Attlee and 5 for Lloyd George.

Within the Whitehall machine Churchill's score would have been lower. On 16 April Sir Edward Bridges, the secretary of the Cabinet, recorded how crucial it was that the Prime Minister (Chamberlain) and not the First Lord of the Admiralty (Churchill) should preside over the next day's meeting of the Military Co-ordination Committee. This view had been strongly expressed to him by General Ismay, soon to be one of Churchill's most valued props and the hinge of his relations with the joint Chiefs of Staff. Ismay's view was that if Churchill presided (the projected attack on Trondheim was the subject) there was likely to be the most explosive and damaging row with resignations likely, either by the Chiefs of Staff or by other service ministers. This view was shared by Churchill's old Treasury private secretary, Sir James Grigg. Grigg had come back from India to be permanent secretary of the War Office. He was recorded by Colville as saying on 12 April, 'We must get the P.M. to take a hand in this before Winston and Tiny [Ironside, the Chief of the Imperial General Staff] go and bugger up the whole war.'[8] It is remarkable that, only a month before his fall and Churchill's rise, Chamberlain's 'grip' should have been yearned for by such a respectable clutch of high public servants, all of whom soon became Churchill devotees, although not entirely uncritical ones.

The 'inquest on Norway' House of Commons debate of Wednesday, 7 May and Thursday, 8 May 1940 was by a clear head both the most

dramatic and the most far-reaching in its consequences of any parliamentary debate of the twentieth century. It was also one in which nearly
every MP who occupied or sought first rank took part – almost the only
exception was Aneurin Bevan. Of its nineteenth-century rivals the
Don Pacifico debate of 8–11 July 1850, while comparable in the distinction of the speeches and the memorability of the speakers, falls on
the ground that nothing followed from it. The 1831 clash on the first
Reform Bill, with Lord John Russell's dramatic reading out of the list
of condemned boroughs and its culmination in a government majority
of one, is a stronger contender. So was the twelve-night second-reading
debate and subsequent rejection of Gladstone's first Home Rule Bill in
1886.

Even more flowed from the 1940 debate, which transformed the
history of the next five years. It was on an innocuous motion for the
adjournment of the House. The official Labour opposition were at first
doubtful about calling a vote, but were persuaded by the course of the
debate that this was the right thing to do. This decision was one of
the Labour party's two major contributions to securing a change of
Prime Minister. Neither, as will be seen, was in itself decisive to making
Churchill the inevitable successor, but in the absence of either of them
Chamberlain would have continued as Prime Minister, certainly beyond
10 May, and maybe until there was nothing for any successor to do
except sue for a peace as humiliating as that imposed upon France.

On the first day (Tuesday, 7 May) of the great debate Chamberlain
opened with a tired defensive speech which impressed nobody. Almost
his only hard point was an announcement that Churchill was to be
empowered 'on behalf of the Military Co-ordinating Committee to
give guidance and direction to the Chiefs of Staff Committee, who will
prepare plans to carry out the objectives which are given to them by
him'.[9] Even this significant devolution of power over the conduct of
the war was not well received. Attlee, who followed with a typical
sharp, deflating speech, did not like it. He thought it a lopsided
arrangement, unfair to Churchill, giving him half but not full power
while still requiring him to keep detailed control over one of the three
services. 'It is like having a man commanding an army in the field and
also commanding a division.' This comment expressed an attitude to
Churchill which emerged from several speeches during this debate.
The speakers did not feel that the conduct of the war had gone well
since he had been given more responsibility, but they preferred to
attribute such result to a misdirection of his talents rather than to any

personal weakness or incompetence. He was superficially as vulnerable as Chamberlain, but had the underlying strength of potential not fully used.

Attlee moved to a waspish conclusion. 'It is not Norway alone. Norway comes as the culmination of many other discontents. People are saying that those mainly responsible for the conduct of affairs [by which he meant Chamberlain, Simon and Hoare, but not Churchill] are men who have had an almost uninterrupted career of failure. Norway followed Czechoslovakia and Poland. Everywhere the story is "too late".' Then came Archibald Sinclair as Liberal leader, whose contribution was not notable as a speech but was firmly anti-Chamberlain. Next came a rodomontade from Admiral of the Fleet Sir Roger Keyes, who had been both a friend of Churchill's and a consistent advocate of the 'biff 'em' school of naval strategy since the Dardanelles. He was not in fact in a particularly pro-Churchill mood at the time, for he was bursting with frustration that naval forces, preferably under his own command, had not been allowed to attack and seize the principal Norwegian ports before the Germans could consolidate their hold on them. But he knew how to concentrate his guns, and it was on Chamberlain not on Churchill that he did so: 'I have great admiration and appreciation for my right honourable friend the First Lord of the Admiralty. I am longing to see proper use made of his great abilities.' To give more force to his bombardment Keyes was resplendent in the uniform of an Admiral of the Fleet, with a bullion store of gold braid upon his sleeves and six rows of medals upon his chest. This 'pulling of rank', so he said, was designed to symbolize the need 'to speak for some officers and men of the fighting, sea-going Navy who are very unhappy'. He ended by playing on the most obvious but nonetheless evocative chord in naval history: 'One hundred and forty years ago Nelson said, "I am of the opinion that the boldest measures are the safest", and that still holds good today.'[10]

Then came L. S. Amery, who although his speeches were mostly thought to be too long delivered the single most devastating missile of the two days. Eight months before, his pugnacity had led to his 'Speak for England, Arthur' call across the floor of the House to Greenwood on the day between Hitler's invasion of Poland and Britain's declaration of war, when Chamberlain seemed to be hesitating. The Prime Minister nonetheless thought of Amery as being bound to him by Birmingham constituency neighbourliness and even more by Amery as a young man having been one of the most dedicated supporters of Joseph Chamberlain's Imperial Preference campaign. Amery wrote a vivid diary description of his approach to the debate:

> I looked up my favourite old quotation of Cromwell's about his selection of Ironsides and then remembered his other quotation when he dismissed the Long Parliament. I doubted whether this was not too strong meat and only kept it by me in case the spirit should move me to use it as the climax to my speech, otherwise preparing a somewhat milder finish. . . . Down to the House . . . but it was not until after eight that I got up in a House of barely a dozen Members. However they steamed in pretty rapidly . . . and I found myself going on to an increasing crescendo of applause. . . . I cast prudence to the winds and ended full out with my Cromwellian injunction to the Government. . . . 'You have sat too long here for any good you have been doing. Depart, I say, and let us have done with you. In the name of God, go.'[11]

Lloyd George told Amery that it was the most dramatic climax of any speech he had ever heard. And Amery himself thought it helped push the Labour party to force a division at the end of the second day. The first day concluded with a robust Labour wind-up from Arthur Greenwood and an ineffective reply from the urbane but lightweight Secretary of State for War, Oliver Stanley.

Herbert Morrison opened for the opposition on the second day (Wednesday, 8 May). His speech reads diffusely, but it contained the hard kernel of news that the Labour party by its decision to divide was turning the routine adjournment motion into the equivalent of a vote of censure. This provoked the Prime Minister to rise and in a very few words to add more than a few inches to the depth of his own political grave: 'I do not seek to evade criticism, but I say this to my friends in the House – and I have friends in the House – I accept the challenge [what else could he have done, other than to resign immediately?]. I welcome it indeed. At least we shall see who is with us and who is against us, and I call upon my friends to support us in the lobby tonight.' The stress on 'friends' was thought to be narrowly partisan and deeply divisive at a time when the national mood was strong for unity and not for sectarianism.

Lloyd George, who rose immediately after Samuel Hoare as Secretary of State for Air had made a pedestrian reply to Morrison (his speech in any event would have been killed by the drama of the Prime Minister's one-minute intervention), seized on the appeal to friends to pay off more than twenty years of animosity to the man whom he had once described as reaching his ceiling by being lord mayor of Birmingham in a lean year. 'It is not a question of who are the Prime Minister's friends,' Lloyd George said.

> It is a far bigger issue. The Prime Minister must remember that he has met this formidable foe of ours in peace and in war. He has always been worsted. He is not in a position to appeal on the grounds of friendship. He has appealed for sacrifice. The nation is prepared for every sacrifice so long as it has leadership. . . . I say solemnly that the Prime Minister should give an example of sacrifice because there is nothing which can contribute more to victory in this war than that he should sacrifice the seals of office.[12]

These words were delivered as a scornful whiplash which recalled Lloyd George in his prime. It was the best speech he had delivered in the House of Commons for a long time, and although he remained a member for another five years it was also his last of any impact. It was also notable for a brilliant metaphor which he applied to Churchill. It may have been spontaneous, for it was in reply to a Churchill interjection. Lloyd George was trying to exonerate Churchill from blame for Norway. Churchill rose and said: 'I take complete responsibility for everything that has been done by the Admiralty, and I take my full share of the burden.' Lloyd George answered: 'The right honourable gentleman must not allow himself to be converted into an air-raid shelter to keep the splinters from hitting his colleagues.'[13]

A. V. Alexander wound up for the Labour party at about 9.30 p.m. Alexander was a product of the Co-operative Movement who sat in Parliament for a Sheffield constituency. Since 1929, when he became First Lord under MacDonald, Alexander had been almost entirely concentrated upon Admiralty matters. He was a bluff patriot of insular views who, although a Baptist lay preacher and teetotaller, tried to make himself a mini-Churchill. When he again became First Lord in the Churchill coalition government he liked appearing in the reefer jacket and dark yachting cap of an elder brother of Trinity House. However he was unlike Churchill in that he mostly did what the admirals told him, except when Churchill told him something different, and he then had an uncomfortable time.

Alexander had given Churchill very easy parliamentary passages in the previous eight months. To some extent his speech of 8 May was an exception. He asked with pith and directness some awkward questions. But he did so, as had others, within a framework of respect and regret that it was Churchill and not his more disliked colleagues who had to bear the brunt of speaking to such a crushingly bad brief:

> I say again publicly what I have said before, that I have very great respect for the ability, the determination and the fighting spirit of the First Lord of the Admiralty; but tonight he is to reply, at the end of two days' debate, as a member of the War Cabinet, which the Prime Minister indicated clearly to us yesterday had been at all times unanimous in its decisions about this campaign. Tonight, therefore, it is the War Cabinet, including the First Lord himself, which must make its reply to the criticisms which have been uttered in the House. If the First Lord will allow me to say so, the three colleagues of his [Chamberlain, Stanley and Hoare] who have addressed the House in the last two days have left him a pretty heavy job in the last lap.[14]

Churchill rose at 10.11 p.m. and spoke for forty-nine minutes. There was general agreement that his speech was a *tour de force*. Channon, from the pro-Chamberlain position, wrote: 'He [Churchill] made a slashing, vigorous speech, a magnificent piece of oratory.'[15] Nicolson, on the other side of the fence, recorded:

> [Winston] has an almost impossible task. On the one hand he has to defend the Services; on the other, he has to be loyal to the Prime Minister. One felt that it would be impossible for him to do this after the debate without losing some of his own prestige, but he manages with extraordinary force of personality to do both these things with absolute loyalty and apparent sincerity, while demonstrating by his brilliance that he really has nothing to do with this confused and timid gang.[16]

Churchill was heard with at least adequate attention for the first forty minutes. His speech, as read more than sixty years later, was more swashbuckling than scintillating. There were no great phrases and there was no sense of a relentless build-up of persuasive argument. He dealt skilfully with Chamberlain's unfortunate 'friends' intervention. 'He thought he had some friends, and I hope he has some friends. He certainly had a good many when things were going well.' Thus Churchill both contrasted his own position as a foul-weather friend with others running for cover, and delicately reminded his listeners that he had not been a Chamberlainite when the pre-war damage was done.

Towards the end, as the crucial division approached, there developed one of those scenes of faintly hysterical disorder with which the House of Commons has long been inclined to accompany its most serious decisions. It began with a few allegedly intoxicated Scottish Labour members, but was quickly reinforced by at least equally inebriated responses from the other side. Even Hugh Dalton, who echoed Lord Randolph Churchill's liking for rowdiness, was shocked and wrote that 'a good deal of riot, some of it rather stupid, developed towards the end of Winston's speech'.[17]

Following the great debate came the great division. Only 486 members out of a House of 615 voted. Deliberate abstentions on the Conservative side were thought to be sixty. In addition forty-one of those who were normally government supporters went into the Labour lobby. The result was that a nominal Conservative majority of 213 fell to 81. In most circumstances this was a perfectly sustainable position. Many governments have survived for years on less than a half of it. But in the circumstances of the time, with Britain on the road to losing the war, with the Prime Minister having been so assailed from all sides during the debate, and with a strong underlying desire for national unity and more inspiring leadership, it was devastating. Chamberlain left the House pale and grim. Between then and midnight he had Churchill to his room and told him that he did not think he could go on.

The forty-one who were shown by the division lists to have shifted their allegiance were not so much the traditional dissidents who had been used to working with Churchill or were part of Eden's troop of 'glamour boys'. (Brendan Bracken and Duncan Sandys, indeed, followed their master's example rather than his interest and voted with the government.) It was rather the unexpected rebels – Nancy Astor, the hostess of the pro-appeasement Cliveden set and Quintin Hogg, who eighteen months before had been the virulently pro-Munich victor of the Oxford bye-election, who made the impact. Dalton thought the 'no' or Labour division lobby was swirling with youngish Conservatives in service uniforms.*

* Among them, and (with Quintin Hogg) one of the only two of the forty-one to survive into the twenty-first century, was John Profumo who unexpectedly (almost to himself) voted with this crucial band. Then aged twenty-three, he had been elected without serious opposition as the pro-Chamberlain candidate at a Northamptonshire by-election as recently as April. He was currently serving in an army unit stationed in the far part of Essex. He had leave to come up to London for twenty-four hours and participate in the vote, although, as I once heard him recount in a riveting description of the occasion, most of his fellow officers thought that his main purpose was to go to a nightclub rather than to the House of Commons. In fact he did both, but the House of Commons came first. Suddenly at the end of the debate, when the division had been called, he thought it was his duty, in the interests of his country and his regiment, to vote against the government. It was a bold and even noble decision. The next morning,

Thirty hours after the vote Hitler launched his full offensive against the West, and terminated, insofar as Norway had not already done so, the so-called 'Phoney War'. The intervening day, that of Thursday, 9 May, was one of intensive political *va-et-vient*, although ministers did manage to fit in a distracted one-and-a-quarter-hour late-morning meeting of the War Cabinet. As is the way with animated days, recorded in the written memoirs or oral recollections of several participants, there are differences of nuance, although the broad sequence of events emerges fairly clearly. This is despite the fact that the main contributor to confusion was Churchill himself. Writing six years later for the first volume of his Second World War memoirs, he placed a most dramatic meeting between himself, Chamberlain and Halifax at 11.00 on the morning of Friday, 10 May, that is after the German offensive had been unleashed. He then described how Chamberlain, recognizing that he could not continue as Prime Minister, tried gently to slew the succession in favour of Halifax. Churchill memorably wrote: 'As I remained silent a very long pause ensued. It certainly seemed longer than the two minutes which one observes in the commemorations of Armistice Day. Then at length Halifax spoke.'[18] The Foreign Secretary in effect said that he was disqualified as a peer and threw the succession to Churchill.

This account is not without a certain central truth, but is wholly inaccurate as to times and participants. The crucial meeting took place not on the Friday morning but on the Thursday afternoon; Margesson was also present; and it required no determination not to break a long silence on Churchill's part to get Halifax to exclude himself. He had already done so at a 10.15 bilateral meeting with Chamberlain on the Thursday morning. There he stressed the great disadvantage he would suffer as a Prime Minister who was a peer, and for the first

---

somewhat bleary-eyed after the second of his night's activities, he was summoned to see Captain Margesson, the redoubtable Chief Whip. In an expletive-rich denunciation he was told that he had betrayed everything that he had been elected – or rather nominated – to support. But the aspect of the interview which remained most vividly in his mind when he recounted the tale over fifty years later was the long-term curse which Margesson had attempted to place upon him. 'And I can tell you this, you utterly contemptible little shit. On every morning that you wake up for the rest of your life you will be ashamed of what you did last night.' Rarely can a prophecy have been so quickly and completely confounded. To keep a sense of proportion about politics, however, it is necessary also to record Profumo's account of returning to his unit that afternoon. He was not sure whether he would be treated by his fellow officers as a hero or a villain. He had neither reception. The debate and vote had passed completely over their heads.

time used the phrase that the thought of being so 'left me with a bad stomach-ache'. This position he maintained at the 4.30 quadripartite meeting. As a Prime Minister in the Lords he would rapidly become a 'cipher' in the position to which Lloyd George had tried to relegate Asquith in 1916. 'I thought Winston was a better choice. Winston did not demur, was very kind and polite but showed that he thought this the right solution. Chief Whip and others think feeling in the House has been veering towards him.' This somewhat telegraphese account was recorded by the Foreign Office permanent under-secretary, Cadogan, who saw Halifax immediately on his return from 10 Downing Street. It gains conviction by the comment with which Cadogan's acerbic pen accompanied it. 'I said I personally welcomed this [decision], as it kept H. with us. (I think he is not the stuff of which a PM is made in such a crisis. We should lose a good S of S and get a doubtful PM. But I'm not at *all* sure of WSC.)'[19]

The next day, Rab Butler, who was Halifax's parliamentary under-secretary and very suspicious of Churchill, tried to get hold of his chief for a last-minute attempt to persuade him to change his mind. Butler was told that Halifax had gone to see his dentist, which suggested that his aches were not confined to his stomach, but also showed a high degree of disengagement. There is no doubt that Halifax was resolved not to become Prime Minister in the circumstances of 9–10 May 1940. Had he wished otherwise there is equally little doubt that he could have secured the appointment. He was the preferred establishment candidate. The position of the Labour party was equivocal. This was key, for it was Chamberlain's awareness that they would not serve under him which precipitated his decision to create a vacancy. Dalton was in favour of Halifax and, a little unreliably, reported Attlee as being so too. Morrison inclined that way. But, as Robert Blake has percipiently pointed out, they had 'not a choice but a veto'. The veto they would not have exercised against Halifax, but nor were they inclined to do so against Churchill.

What is more open to doubt is how self-abnegatory were Halifax's motives. He was not called the 'Holy Fox' for nothing. He believed he was wiser if not more energetic or militarily focused than Churchill. He believed he might exercise more control over this impetuous figure (to whom, together with some of his associates such as Beaverbrook and Bracken, he was known to refer as 'gangsters') from a strong Cabinet position and with the dignity of having declined the premiership than if he were jostling with him for control of what would have been nominally (but only nominally) a Halifax government. Furthermore the Churchill government might quickly fail. There were many who thought this at the beginning. In that event he (Halifax) could step in from a position of strength, unthreatened by a powerful rival, and pick up the pieces – although they would probably have been the fragments of an independent Britain as well as those of political power. Both these hypotheses were surmises, although there were a few hints in Halifax's private correspondence that they had some validity. And both proved false. Over the remainder of 1940, until he was sent as ambassador to Washington, Halifax's influence within the administration diminished rather than increased, and the Churchill government, so far from being 'nasty, brutish and short', survived for five years and became the most famous of the century, maybe indeed of the whole history of British Cabinets. For this we owe much to the fact that Halifax, who on 9 May could have become Prime Minister, wisely declined to do so.

The view that the Labour party made Churchill Prime Minister is therefore a myth. They were nevertheless a crucial piece on the chessboard. At 6.15 on the Thursday evening, after the crucial quadripartite meeting, Attlee and Greenwood came to see Chamberlain. In the meantime Halifax and Churchill had been despatched to the garden to have tea – never Churchill's favourite beverage at that or any other time of day. The *al fresco* ambience was typical of a paradoxical feature of that desperate late spring and summer for Britain. The more dreadful were the prospects the more splendid was the weather. There are frequent references from a multitude of sources to the poignant contrast between the beauty of the landscape and the awfulness of the threat.

While the garden tea was taking place Chamberlain saw Lord Camrose, the proprietor of the *Daily Telegraph*. Camrose's note of the meeting was precise, as was his habit:

> He [Chamberlain] had considered the question as to whom he should ask the King to send for, and had discussed the matter with Halifax and Winston. He was informed that feeling in the Labour Party had swung against Halifax; but, in any case, the latter had said he would prefer not to be sent for as he felt the position would be too difficult and troublesome for him. He (Neville) would therefore advise the King to send for Winston.[20]

Provided the Labour leaders behaved as they were expected to do the matter was therefore settled by the Thursday afternoon (9 May). Broadly they did so behave. Churchill described how Attlee and Greenwood sat on one side of the Cabinet table with Chamberlain, Halifax and himself on the other side. A note of Halifax's then takes up the story:

> The P.M. put the position to them [that is would they join a cross-party coalition of national unity] and they were a bit evasive, but eventually said that they did not think they could get their Party to agree to serve under the P.M. It was finally agreed that they should consult their Executive tomorrow on the two points; would the Labour Party join in principle (a) under Neville, (b) under someone else. They were to telephone tomorrow afternoon 'yes' or 'no' to both.[21]

The Labour party was about to hold its annual conference at Bournemouth. The full conference was not to meet until the Monday. But the National Executive Committee, in those days a very powerful body, assembled early for a series of intensive pre-conference meetings. The Labour party, an organization devoted to maintaining the rules of procedure, was not going to allow its habits to be upset by matters like defeat in Norway or the beginning of a *Blitzkrieg* a little more than a hundred miles away across the Channel. Attlee and his party took the 11.34 a.m. train from Waterloo Station to Bournemouth, duly assembled in a basement room of the Tollard Royal Hotel and, according to Dalton, although some members talked too much through over-excitement, an unanimous decision was reached with reasonable expedition. Attlee telephoned his bulletin to Downing Street at 5.00 p.m. Labour would serve in a coalition government, but not under Chamberlain. They would accept another Conservative Prime Minister, but they expressed no formal preference between Halifax and Churchill, the only effective possibilities. Upon receipt of the message Chamberlain went to Buckingham Palace, tendered his resignation and advised the King to send for Churchill, who was Prime Minister by six o'clock on the evening of Friday, 10 May. Attlee meanwhile was on his way back to London where he (and Greenwood) called on Churchill at the Admiralty later that night to discuss the shape of the new government.

Throughout those two days of crucial political adjustment there is no doubt that, unlike Halifax, Churchill very much wanted to be Prime Minister. On the Thursday morning immediately following the conclusion of the debate and his late-night interview with Chamberlain he had telephoned Eden and asked him to lunch with him that day. When Eden got there he was surprised to discover a third figure in the shape of Sir Kingsley Wood, then Lord Privy Seal and hitherto a firm

Chamberlain loyalist. But Wood had decided that, in Chamberlain's own interests as well as in those of the country, it was time for him to go, and he was firmly convinced, even before Halifax had contracted his 'stomach-ache', that Churchill was the essential successor. His views were not crucial on that Thursday, for Chamberlain and Halifax had already come to that conclusion without Wood's intervention. They may have been more so on the next day when, following the early-morning news of the German offensive in the West, Chamberlain was tempted to use this as an excuse for staying on 'until the French battle was finished'.[22] Wood's signal service then was to tell him, as a friend, that this was the reverse of sense. The unleashing of the onslaught made a change of leadership more and not less necessary.

On the Thursday morning Churchill had also seen Beaverbrook and Bracken, both of whom had strongly urged upon him the tactic of remaining silent whenever any question of a choice between him and Halifax arose. That evening Eden came back for dinner, and this time for a strict *tête-à-tête*. Clementine Churchill, as so often at vital times, although mostly for fairly good reasons, was away. The husband of her sister Nellie Romilly had died in Herefordshire and she had gone to be with her. Churchill, in her absence, was showing a good sense of priorities by not allowing any press of Admiralty responsibility to divert him from the vital political business of the moment.

The only hitch on the Labour party front occured when Churchill attempted to be too emollient towards Chamberlain. Attlee and Green-wood were more than satisfied with two non-portfolio posts in the War Cabinet of five, plus one service minister out of three (Alexander at the Admiralty), and senior posts outside the War Cabinet for Ernest Bevin, Morrison and Dalton. Simon and Hoare, the two 'ugly sisters', as they had come to seem to opposition parties as well as to some Conservatives, were satisfactorily disposed of. Simon, outside the War Cabinet, was made Lord Chancellor, where, Attlee said, 'he will be quite innocuous'. (Churchill, although allowing him to remain on the Woolsack, did not even put him in his normal-sized 'Caretaker' Cabinet of the summer of 1945.) Hoare was out of the government, although within the month he was sent as ambassador to Franco's Spanish government.

By contrast Churchill wished to show great consideration to Chamberlain. His original plan was to make him leader of the House of Commons and Chancellor of the Exchequer as well as retaining the leadership of the Conservative party, which last was not at Churchill's disposal. Churchill no doubt saw an analogy with Lloyd George's handling of Bonar Law, Chamberlain's predecessor but one as Tory leader, although there had then been the significant difference that Lloyd George was not a member of the majority party, whereas Churchill was.* These plans for Chamberlain were too much for the Labour party. Attlee made strong representations, although he accepted that the case for keeping Chamberlain 'somewhere in the government' was overwhelming. Kingsley Wood, the useful and cherubic messenger, became Chancellor of the Exchequer, and Churchill himself followed the Prime Ministerial habit and retained the nominal leadership of the House, with Attlee as the workaday deputy leader. Chamberlain became Lord President of the Council, a slightly senior sinecure office to that occupied by Attlee as Lord Privy Seal.

Apart from these dispositions, attempted and actual, Churchill showed early awareness of the possible weakness of his support within the Conservative party (as well perhaps as simple good manners) by immediately on his return from the Palace writing two substantial letters of appreciation and goodwill, one to Chamberlain and the other to Halifax.[†23] He was Prime Minister at last at the age of sixty-five, apart from his immediate predecessor the oldest person since Campbell-Bannerman to come to that office for the first time. It was also almost forty years after he had first been elected to Parliament. He took over in the most perilous circumstances in which any Prime Minister has ever come to office. And there were political as well as military perils. He was not the choice of the King. He was not the choice of the Whitehall establishment, which reacted with varying degrees of dismay to the prospect of his alleged wildness. And he was not the choice of the majority party in the House of Commons. In an inchoate way, however, he was, or quickly became, the accepted champion of the nation in the eyes of both public and press. And those who had initially been reluctant and suspicious, from Sovereign to permanent secretaries, fairly quickly came round to his indispensability.

---

* Lloyd George thought that Churchill in 1940 was afraid of Chamberlain (Lukacs, *Five Days in London*, p. 22), but, even if true, this was better than being afraid of Hitler, which Lloyd George himself had become; on 13 May he refused to join the new government, believing that Britain's prospects were hopeless.
† He also that same day of 10 May, with remarkable chivalry if an odd sense of priority, caused his private secretary to initiate an offer to the ex-Kaiser in Holland of asylum in Britain from the advancing Wehrmacht.

31

TWENTY-ONE DAYS IN MAY

THE LATE SPRING and early summer of 1940, not only in their effect upon the destiny of Britain but in the atmosphere through which lives were lived, was one of the most extraordinary, in some ways unreal, phases in the history of the nation. Maybe it was similar at the time of the Norman Conquest, or of the Armada, or of Napoleon's massed camps of invasion troops around Boulogne. But I doubt it. The means of communication were not good enough at any of these times for a sense of peril to become a nationwide emotion, and in the last case we are only too well informed, not least through Jane Austen's novels, about how calmly life went on in manor houses and nearby rectories.

In 1940 also a great deal of ordinary life ran along established channels. The nation was far from fully mobilized, which was part of the indictment against the previous government. There were still nearly a million unemployed, and the economy not yet stretched tight meant that for some much of the amenity of 1930s life continued. There was unimpeded travel by normally reliable train services, with the expresses bearing far more well-appointed restaurant cars than they do today. There was even a certain amount of petrol for private use. Food was still not tightly rationed and both town and country hotels and restaurants continued to serve as good meals (which was not saying a great deal) as they had done five years before, with wine and spirit supplies remaining adequate for some time to come. And all the superficialities of normality, as has been mentioned earlier, were experienced under one of the most persistent high-pressure weather systems ever to cover Britain. One beautiful summer's day succeeded another.

The national mood – insofar as it had cohesion, even at a time when it is thought to have been uniquely united – was not so much defiant as impregnable. The prospects were awful, but people pushed the consequences of defeat out of their collective mind. It was not a question of bravery. It was more that they chose to believe the worst would not happen. To what extent this was a product of the mesmerizing quality of Churchill's oratory is a difficult question to answer. His purpose and his method were to promote a mood of defiance. What he did, almost more in my recollection of my nineteen-year-old state of mind, was to produce a euphoria of irrational belief in ultimate victory. This at least stilled any paralysis of apprehension, and made it possible to pursue normal activity, some parts of which were more useful to the war effort than were others, and to live surprisingly happily on the edge of a precipice.

Churchill's accession to the premiership, even though long desired and eagerly seized by him, was at best the equivalent of an abrupt wartime marriage. He had a brief weekend of receiving enthusiastic letters from old friends (the ever faithful General Reggie Barnes – his companion in Cuba in 1896 – and Lady Violet Bonham Carter are good examples) and of government-making, the latter a naturally enjoyable pursuit for those who have for many years watched it being done worse than they would have accomplished it. This was his only brief honeymoon, and even for that he was criticized by the ever waspish and two-faced Hankey, who wrote to the dispossessed Samuel Hoare on Sunday, 12 May: 'I found complete chaos this morning. No one was gripping the war in its crisis. The Dictator, instead of dictating, was engaged in a sordid wrangle with the politicians of the left about secondary offices. N.C. [Chamberlain] was in a state of despair about it all.'[1] This short extract epitomized a whole raft of 1930s prejudices which confronted Churchill at the core of the old Whitehall establishment: Chamberlain was the man for orderly government; Churchill was a figure of bombast and political intrigue rather than of delivery, and a cross-party government was more a defiling of the nest than an achievement of national unity.

The next day Churchill encountered a less than enthusiastic reception from a House of Commons which had been summoned by individual telegram to meet at 2.30 on the afternoon of Whitsun bank holiday Monday. The diary of my father* described how, after an hour's formal appearance at the opening session of the Labour conference, Attlee and he were driven together to London. They were in Westminster by 1.30, in good time for the meeting of the House, for Attlee to symbolize the new political scene by taking his place on the government front bench,

---

* The author's father, Arthur Jenkins (1882–1946), was Labour MP for Pontypool in Monmouthshire from 1935 to his death and an unusually close parliamentary private secretary to Attlee from 1937 until early 1945, when he became a junior minister in the Churchill coalition government.

and for them both to observe the ensuing events. When Chamberlain came in he was given what Nicolson described as 'a terrific reception'[2] from the Conservative benches. Channon went further: 'MPs lost their heads; they shouted; they cheered; they waved their Order Papers, and his reception was a regular ovation.' Churchill by contrast, was 'not well received'.[3] His thin cheers came almost exclusively from the Labour and Liberal benches.

Churchill then made a very short statement, more a call to battle stations than a speech. It did however contain several phrases which have reverberated down the decades:

> I would say to the House, as I said to those who have joined this government, that I have nothing to offer but blood, toil, tears and sweat. We have before us an ordeal of the most grievous kind. . . . You ask, what is our policy? I will say: it is to wage war, by sea, land and air, with all our might and with all the strength that God can give us: to wage war against a monstrous tyranny, never surpassed in the dark, lamentable catalogue of human crime. That is our policy. You ask, what is our aim? I can answer in one word: It is victory, victory at all costs, victory in spite of all terror, victory, however long and hard the road may be; for without victory, there is no survival.[4]

Nicolson said it was 'to the point'.[5] Channon said, 'The new PM spoke well, even dramatically,'[6] and Colville, perhaps most significantly, for only sixty-eight hours before he had been drinking a champagne toast in company with Rab Butler, Alec Douglas-Home and Chips Channon 'to the king over the water' (that is to Chamberlain), wrote, 'He [Churchill] made a brilliant little speech.'[7] The forces of pro-Chamberlain, anti-Churchill conventional wisdom were beginning to melt, but in those early days there was a long way to go.

Churchill, who was the most clearly upper-class Prime Minister since the end of Balfour's premiership thirty-five years before, was also the one whose authority most stemmed from popular acclaim. On the day after his less than enthusiastic House of Commons reception (even though it granted without dissent a vote of confidence to his government), David Low, the outstanding left-of-centre political cartoonist of the 1930s and 1940s, published in the *Evening Standard* a memorable and opinion-forming drawing. Unusually, it was wholly without mockery. It showed Churchill, with his sleeves rolled up, marching resolutely forward and followed by Attlee, Bevin, Chamberlain, Greenwood, Halifax, Sinclair, Morrison, Eden, Amery, Duff Cooper, A. V. Alexander and a vast mass of anonymous supporters, all equally stripped for action. 'All behind you, Winston' was the caption. In a curious way it half caught and half formed the national mood, much more so than did the previous day's muted and backward-looking House of Commons.

That was the end of Churchill's brief and sombre honeymoon as Prime Minister. He had succeeded to the most appalling inheritance. He had never wavered in his desire for the job, although on the way back from his visit of appointment to the King he was recorded by his sometimes over-dramatizing detective as saying: 'I hope it is not too late. I am very much afraid it is.'[8] The next few weeks were a period of almost unmitigated disaster for France, for Britain – and for Churchill. The total self-confidence of the concluding passage of the first volume of his *The Second World War* is well known:

as I went to bed at about 3 a.m. [on the night he became Prime Minister], I was conscious of a profound sense of relief. At last I had the authority to give directions over the whole scene. I felt as if I were walking with destiny, and that all my past life had been but a preparation for this hour and for this trial.... I was sure I should not fail. Therefore, although impatient for the morning, I slept soundly and had no need for cheering dreams.[9]

In spite of this passage, which was written in the very different circumstances of six or seven years later, it is impossible to believe that Churchill did not in those next few weeks experience moments of almost crushing dismay, that there were not indeed mornings when he did not awake feeling that he must have been mistaken, nearly insane, to have sought such a burden of supreme responsibility at a time when everything seemed more likely than not to go down into the abyss. Colville recorded on 17 May that he went to meet the Prime Minister early at Hendon aerodrome on his return from a deeply discouraging visit to Paris: 'He looked quite cheerful, having slept and breakfasted well at the Embassy'; and a day later, 'Winston, who is full of fight and thrives on crisis and adversity'.[10] But on 21 May, 'I have not seen Winston so depressed....'[11] There were no doubt fluctuations of mood with occasional deep down-swings but there was little indication of the onset of any of his 'black dog' moods for which in any event there would have been little time. On one occasion he disappeared to Chartwell on his own for a day, where he did little more than sit feeding his black swans and his carp. This may have been an expression of gloom, but in general he possessed the great prophylactic against dejection of the vigour in all circumstances to dictate his innumerable short minutes, on big subjects and on small ones, and knowing that they would be obeyed. He loved the exercise of power.

On the other hand there are some strong but not surprising indications that his temper and even his courtesy suffered under the strain. Colville, after only a week working for Churchill,* recorded (but not as a complaint about his own treatment) that 'He is very inconsiderate with his staff.'[12] Of more substance, although from the following month (27 June), was a terrifying letter which Clementine wrote to him. Its impact may have been the greater because it is the only known letter which passed between them during the whole of 1940:

My Darling,
I hope you will forgive me if I tell you something that I feel you ought to know.
One of the men in your entourage (a devoted friend) has been to me & told me that there is danger of your being generally disliked by your colleagues & subordinates because of your rough sarcastic & overbearing manner – It seems your Private Secretaries have agreed to behave like schoolboys & 'take what's coming to them' & then escape out of your presence shrugging their shoulders – Higher up, if an idea is suggested (say at a conference) you are supposed to be so contemptuous that presently no ideas – good or bad – will be forthcoming. I was astonished & upset because in all these years I have been accustomed to all those who have worked with & under you, loving you – I said this & I was told 'No doubt it's the strain' –
My Darling Winston – I must confess I have noticed a deterioration in your manner; & you are not so kind as you used to be.
It is for you to give the Orders & if they are bungled – except for the King, the Archbishop of Canterbury & the Speaker you can sack anyone & everyone – Therefore with this terrific power you must combine urbanity, kindness and if possible Olympic calm. . . . I cannot bear that those who serve the Country & yourself should not love you as well as admire and respect you – Besides you won't get the best results by irascibility & rudeness. They will breed either dislike or a slave mentality – (Rebellion in War time being out of the question!)
Please forgive your loving devoted & watchful
Clemmie
I wrote this at Chequers last Sunday, tore it up, but here it is now.[13]

---

* Colville, seconded from his parent department of the Foreign Office, was inherited by Churchill from Chamberlain as a 10 Downing Street private secretary. Despite his early Chamberlain loyalty he soon became (and remained until 1955) Churchill's favourite private secretary, as well as the best diarist of official life in the later Churchill years.

The effect of this wise and courageous letter cannot be directly measured, but it is the case that most of those who worked closely with Churchill during the war did end up loving him, despite frequent bursts of exasperation.

Churchill's honeymoon as Prime Minister proved devastatingly short because early on the morning immediately after that happy Low cartoon, he was telephoned by Paul Reynaud, the head of the French government, and one of the French leaders whom Churchill most respected, regarding him as a vast improvement on his predecessor, Daladier. The note of the conversation reads: 'M. Reynaud was apparently in a very excited mood [a phrase which probably meant even more than it said]. He said that the counter-attack last night on the Germans who had broken through south of Sedan had failed and that the road to Paris was open and the battle was lost. He even talked about giving up the struggle.'[14]

This first serious warning for Churchill of the collapse of France was accompanied by a request for more British troops, which was not possible on any relevant time-scale, and for more fighter squadrons, which was possible, although only at the risk of reducing the number remaining at home below the minimum which Fighter Command considered essential for an effective defence of Britain. Behind the dilemma lay the crux question of the next five weeks. Should all resources be thrown into preventing a French collapse, or, as the signs of weak French will to resist became ever more pervading, was there not the still more transcendent purpose of preserving Britain's ability to fight on alone? Churchill had a greater emotional investment in the alliance with France and a greater initial faith in the French army than almost any British politician. On the other hand that faith began rapidly to diminish within days of his becoming Prime Minister. The possibility of a separate French peace lay uncomfortably at the back of his mind from that early-morning conversation with Reynaud. The note of this continued: 'He [Churchill] also said several times that, "*whatever the French did* [my italics], we would continue to fight to the last".'[15] The last point, as will soon be seen, was his dominating determination. This led to his thought, expressed through anodyne War Cabinet minutes, 'that we should hesitate before we denuded still further the heart of the Empire'.

This dilemma dominated all Churchill's dealings with the French for the next five weeks. The British, who had only ten divisions facing the enemy, were constantly urging the French generals to deploy their 103 divisions with more offensive spirit. The French, who instinctively resented this advice from David to Goliath, said a prior condition was that Britain should at least compensate for its pitiable land effort by throwing its available air resources into cover for the Allied armies in the decisive battle for France. This was not in itself an unreasonable proposition. It was supported by General Smuts, on whose strategic advice Churchill normally placed great reliance. Smuts signalled from South Africa in the first week of June that everything should be concentrated at the decisive point. This was good orthodox military doctrine. *Mutatis mutandis* it would certainly have been accepted by Lloyd George, supported by Churchill, in the later stages of the First World War. But then the will to resist of Clemenceau and Foch was not in doubt, nor broadly, in spite of the troubles of 1917, was the fighting spirit of the French army. The essential difference in 1940 was that this assumption was no longer accepted by Churchill, and with justification as things turned out. Nor is there any reason to think that greater profligacy with Britain's air resources would have produced a different outcome in France.

What it might have done was to produce a better atmosphere in the six visits which Churchill paid to France between his accession to the premiership and the French ceasefire (plus another two planned trips, one aborted because his colleagues dissuaded him and the other – on 16 June – because there was no French government which wanted to receive him) and one visit on 26 May of Reynaud to London. But a few weeks of French goodwill would hardly have been an adequate recompense for the narrow avoidance of defeat in the aerial Battle of Britain two and a half months later.

Three of Churchill's six French visits were in May. During the first on the 16th–17th he did in fact weaken to the extent of sending to France another ten fighter squadrons (to four of which the War Cabinet had already agreed, but were then pressurized into another six by compelling messages from Churchill in Paris). But that was the limit. The second visit on 22 May was the best of a bad bunch because the British took a favourable view of General Weygand who had replaced Gamelin, and who, in spite of being seventy-three, looked to Churchill 'like a man of fifty' and generally 'made a most favourable impression by his vigour and confidence'.[16] More specifically he had the 'Weygand Plan', by which the French First Army and the British Expeditionary Force near the Channel coast would strike south while a newly assembled French army group hastily put together from the Maginot Line,

North Africa and other miscellaneous sources would strike north from
the centre of the front with the hope of cutting off the German snout,
about fifty miles wide, somewhere around St Quentin, eighty miles to
the north-east of Paris on the main railway line to Brussels. It was not
very different from a previous Gamelin plan, except that Weygand for
the moment gave confidence that it might actually happen, which
Gamelin never did. It was an entirely false confidence. As little happened
under Weygand as under Gamelin. There was no French strike north
from the Somme. There was an ineffective British battle for Arras and
what Churchill subsequently regarded as a mistaken decision to evacuate
Boulogne by sea. On the evening of Saturday, 25 May, General Gort,
in command of the BEF, took the decision that the Weygand Plan was
dead and that his only option was to make for the sea and the remaining
ports of Calais and Dunkirk. Two days later the capitulation of the
Belgian King and army (although the ministers found their way through
France to England and became one of the Allied governments-in-exile)
hardly improved the prospect.

    The French, if only because of their great preponderance of numbers,
were at least as responsible as the British for the failure of the Weygand
Plan. Furthermore the French First Army was as cut off as were the
British between the German breakthrough and the sea. Everything
was dangerously in place for bitter recrimination between the two
floundering allies. Churchill was determined, compatibly with preserving Britain's ability to fight on alone, to do everything possible to avoid
this. His accession to supreme power over the British war machine, even
if hardly over events at this stage, noticeably improved his perspective.
He may, *pace* Clementine Churchill, have become more irascible to
subordinates, but he also became more willing to control his obsessions
and exasperations of the moment in pursuit of longer-term objectives.
This was notably so in his unsatisfactory exchanges with Roosevelt
during these weeks. It also applied in his attitude to the failing French.
He was desperately anxious to get as much as possible of the British
Expeditionary Force back to England. But he was also anxious not to
leave a bleeding scar on the French, who he still hoped might be
persuaded to fight, if not for and through Paris, at least behind it. It was
therefore urgent that he should get French endorsement of Gort's
decision. On 26 May the confidential annexe to the War Cabinet
minutes recorded the Prime Minister's view that 'it is important to
make sure that the French had no complaint against us on the score
that, by cutting our way to the coast, we were letting them down

militarily'.[17] And on the 31st when he flew to Paris for another meeting of the Supreme War Council, unusually taking Attlee, as well as Dill – the new CIGS – and Spears, with him, he was at pains to point out that the British would not embark first. We should go, he said, 'bras dessus, bras dessous' (arm in arm) and the British would provide the rearguard.

Nevertheless that was a chilling meeting. Pétain, recently appointed deputy Prime Minister, was present for the first time. Ismay* recorded that 'a dejected-looking old man in plain clothes shuffled towards me, stretched out his hand and said: "Pétain". It was hard to believe that this was the great Marshal of France whose name was associated with the epic of Verdun. . . . He now looked senile, uninspiring and defeatist.'[18] Reynaud still responded warmly to Churchill's 'magnificent peroration on the implacable will of the British people to fight on to the bitter end', in the words of the British ambassador, but who also thought that Reynaud's words 'came more from his head than his heart'.[19]

In the last days of May there were two great hazards which Churchill had to face, and which ran alongside each other at only a slight stagger. The evacuation from Dunkirk and adjacent beaches of more than 335,000 British and French troops took place between 27 May and 1 June with a little spillover until 4 June. The total far exceeded Churchill's expectations of a few days beforehand, when he thought the Allies would be lucky to get away with 50,000. Of the total, 224,000 were British and 111,000 Allied, mainly French but a few Poles and Belgians. It was a huge relief. The flower of the BEF was back behind the white cliffs of Dover, although without their equipment. Enough French troops had also been rescued to give a mild impression of continuing Allied solidarity. The return to the home shores by a quarter of a million of the still small British army was of hard practical importance. Without them, England would have been appallingly vulnerable to any German invasion force. But it had an even greater psychological significance. It amounted almost to a regathering of the family around the domestic hearth. It was Christmas come in early June. There was a seductive tendency to treat Dunkirk as a victory and not just as a deliverance. Churchill was good at not succumbing to that temptation. 'Wars are not won by evacuations,' he very properly told the House of Commons on 4 June.[20]

---

* General Sir Hastings ('Pug') Ismay had become, as he was to remain throughout the war, the essential and tactful link between Churchill as Minister of Defence and the Chiefs of Staff.

There remains a mystery as to whether, and if so why, Hitler failed to thwart the successful British evacuation by a final assault on the thinly held British positions. There might have been a symbolic reason. Even in his most enticingly pro-British moods and whatever role he was prepared to accord them in the wider world, he wanted the British, in the words of Gray's *Elegy*, to leave Europe 'to darkness and to me'. Few pageants could have better symbolized the German triumph in this respect, even if it was also reassuring for Britain, than the armada of little boats which contributed to bringing the BEF back to Kent through the calm seas of that late May and early June. But it was a little more complicated that that. Hitler undoubtedly held back the advance of German armour against the bridgehead.

He did this, after consultation with Rundstedt, the general commanding the forty-four divisions of Army Group A, at the end of the morning of 24 May. Rundstedt apparently agreed with the order. But German generals – and even field marshals – were very much disposed at that stage to agree with Hitler. Some nearer the spot were less pleased. General von Bock wrote reproachfully on 31 May: 'When we finally reach Dunkirk [the English] will be gone.' He was inclined to blame Rundstedt, who liked to spare his armour, rather than the Führer for the stand-off. There seems no reason to doubt that it was Hitler's order. Why? Partly, perhaps, because he believed that the British could be finished off by Göring's Luftwaffe. German aircraft did of course make life uncomfortable in Dunkirk harbour and on the beaches to the east of the town. But not much beyond that. Dunkirk provided an early example of how difficult it is to win campaigns from the air alone.

Was there more to it than that? Was there some inchoate thought in Hitler's mind that, if he wished to make an 'emperor of Europe and an emperor of the peripheral world' peace with Britain, too total a humiliation should not be inflicted and that Britain should be left with at any rate some troops with which to run the Empire? This is a question to which a definite answer will probably always prove elusive, although Ian Kershaw's *Hitler* discounts anything other than purely military considerations. But there is no doubt that hesitation on Hitler's part plus great good luck with the benign calmness of the weather contributed substantially to the success of the massive evacuation. It was the first, if negative, triumph of Churchill's premiership.

As a result Churchill's confidence was a good deal higher on 2 June, when the Dunkirk operation was effectively complete, than it had been a week before. 'The successful evacuation of the BEF has revolutionized the Home Defence position,'[21] he began a note to General Ismay on that morning. And the whole tone of that substantial and pungent minute was that of someone who had come out of a tunnel and was able to apply himself to the next phase – essentially a defence-of-Britain phase – of a journey across a new and more encouraging bit of countryside.

There was, however, another factor at work during those days which nearly but not quite coincided with the Dunkirk evacuation. On 26, 27 and 28 May nine tense meetings of the War Cabinet were held. This is an incidence of rare frequency. In January 1968 I participated in the key role of Chancellor of the Exchequer, for the issue was public expenditure, in eight meetings in eleven days. I doubt if there had been such intensity since 1940, and it was then (in 1968) regarded as an indication of the weakness of the Prime Minister's control over his Cabinet. Surprising though it may seem in retrospect, this may also have been true in May 1940. Churchill's resolution was not in doubt, but his political position was. The War Cabinet was then confined to five members, although it soon crept up to seven or eight. But at that stage there were only Churchill himself, Chamberlain, Halifax, Attlee and Greenwood. Halifax had a conversation which he regarded as important with Bastianini, the Italian ambassador, on the Saturday afternoon. Everyone at that stage wanted to direct full effort to keeping Italy out of the war. Britain – and France – had more than enough with which to cope without Italy tilting the European balance by coming in on the opposite side from that which it had supported in the First World War. But lurking behind Halifax's legitimate if optimistic desire to prevent Mussolini joining Hitler (which he did on 11 June) was a wish to use Italy as a mediating power to secure a peace which, while giving Hitler considerable gains, would nonetheless procure adequate autonomy for Britain and even its continuing imperial role. This would have been the equivalent of a second Munich twenty months after the first.

Such a prospect chimed with Halifax's Christian pessimism. He was not in the French sense a collaborationist. He would never have been a Laval. He thought himself a realist, which made him on India in the early 1930s much more liberal than was Churchill. But it also deprived him of Churchill's indomitable courage in the spring of 1940. Halifax had been half ashamed to be the apologist of appeasement. He never went as far in that direction as did Chamberlain, and he would not have made the terrible mistake of describing the Munich agreement as 'peace with honour'. He had a resigned desire to preserve as much as he could of the England that he knew and loved. There is a story, maybe only *ben trovato*, that he went to Garrowby, the lesser of his two Yorkshire houses, on one of the perfect spring weekends of the year. On the Saturday evening he sat on the terrace looking out over the smiling Vale of York and decided that his primary duty was to preserve as much of that as was humanly possible: the landscape, the ordered hierarchical society, the freedom from oppression or vulgar ostentation.

All these various factors attracted him to the possibility of a negotiated peace. It would mean Nazi dominance in Europe and acceptance by the British that their attempt to check Hitler by war had been a failure. But the Vale of York would be left alone. Britain might hope to be free from interference at least to the extent that was Franco's Spain. Halifax's views were not remotely those of Franco, but maybe the best that in 1940 Britain could hope for was to be left to live quietly beyond the Channel as Spain was behind the Pyrenees. Such a concept was utterly repugnant to Churchill. He was recorded at one of the early Cabinets of the series as saying that 'peace and security would not be achieved under a German domination of Europe. That we could never accept.'[22]

Europe was much more important to Churchill than it was to Halifax, or for that matter to Chamberlain. The latter two had in common a considerable insularity somewhat balanced by different experiences and concepts of empire. Churchill was much more Eurocentric. The writing of *Marlborough*, as well as his tastes and thought patterns, made continental Europe, and above all France, Britain's supplement as the centre of the world for him. While, as will be seen, there was considerable ambiguity about exactly the role that he envisaged for Britain in his post-war appeals for European unity, there is no doubt about the central importance which he attached to Europe uniting in the late 1940s and 1950s, and thus turning its back on the divided evils of the 1930s. Against this background of belief Churchill's order of priorities, even in the dreadful days before the relative success of Dunkirk, was clear and very different from Halifax's. His worst-case scenario was that it was better for Britain to go down fighting than to parley its way into another false and humiliating peace. His hope was that Britain could provide a bastion of resistance, even if not a springboard for victory, until 'in God's good time the new world with all its power and might, steps forth to the rescue and liberation of the old'.[23] Although the state of American public opinion at that stage was far from making it possible for Roosevelt to enter the war, Churchill, in his dealings both with the French and with Halifax, persisted in believing that it was something which would eventually happen.

Any apparent wavering on Churchill's part throughout the long series of nine meetings are to be explained not by there being little difference between the Churchill and the Halifax positions (as has unconvincingly been argued) but by the harsh reality that Churchill at the beginning of this three-day marathon, was by no means certain of an adequate majority within his own recently chosen War Cabinet. He could count upon the two Labour members to be unseduced by the prospect of dangerous negotiation. In argument, however, Attlee followed rather than led. He was laconically reliable. But it was that largely forgotten and, insofar as he is remembered, not much esteemed figure, Arthur Greenwood, who next to Churchill made most of the intransigent running.

Greenwood was then the sixty-year-old MP for Wakefield, who had been a lecturer in economics at Leeds University. A competent but not outstanding Minister of Health in the second MacDonald government, he had become deputy leader of the party under Attlee in 1935 and was a more outgoing personality and better speaker than his chief. He had done well during Attlee's long absence, following a serious operation, over the summer and early autumn of 1939. He had as great a propensity to alcohol as had Churchill himself, but he held it less well. He did not make an exhibition of himself, but alcohol did not energize him as it did Churchill. He was more a soak than a drunk. He also had a somewhat diffuse mind, which was accentuated by two Prime Ministers, first Churchill in 1940 and then Attlee in 1945, giving him posts of high prestige but little hard content. As a result of his not achieving much in these non-jobs they both, maybe unfairly, got rid of him after approximately two years. He did, however, have a couple of periods of glory, the one more public than the other. He led robustly from the opposition front bench in early September 1939. And he was Churchill's most articulate Cabinet ally at the end of May 1940.

The tightness of the issue was well illustrated by Churchill's ending the Sunday Cabinets by co-opting Archibald Sinclair for subsequent meetings. This was done on the ground that the issue was of sufficient importance that the Liberal party (even with only twenty-five seats) ought to be represented in the highest councils. The reality was that Churchill needed another reliable supporter, beyond Attlee and Greenwood, and that Sinclair, his second-in-command in France in 1916 and a consistent anti-appeasement voice, could be depended upon quietly to provide that.

The key figure, however, was Chamberlain. If he made common cause with Halifax the War Cabinet would be split along, for Churchill, a most uncomfortable fissure. And if both Halifax and Chamberlain were to resign on the issue his government would become untenable. (The big Conservative majority in the House of Commons, mostly still owing no loyalty to Churchill, could not simply be ignored.) Furthermore it is difficult to see what effective alternative administration could have emerged. Three weeks before, the Labour party had been willing to serve under Halifax. But Attlee and Greenwood, having witnessed at close hand the undermining of the Churchill position by Halifax arguments which they had firmly rejected, would hardly still have been content to serve under him. Nor would Sinclair. The outcome could hardly have been anything better than a narrowly and potentially defeatist government based on the less resistant sections of the Conservative party. Britain would have been very near to anticipating the French performance at Tours and Bordeaux a few weeks later, and with less excuse for there was not a single German soldier on British soil, and the disputing politicians were still in unchallenged possession of a calm capital city.

Although it would probably not have come exactly to this, for hypotheses are always highly hypothetical, the stakes for Churchill, and for Britain, were manifestly high. Had he from the beginning rejected with contumely all Halifax's arguments and propositions, his mind must have contemplated the unlocking of just such a series of events. Furthermore he had on his flank the weakness of the French government, staggering under the blows of Hitler and horrified at the prospect of the addition of a Mussolini attack on their south-eastern flank. The visit of Reynaud – the best of the actual and potential French ministers – on Sunday, 26 May, the first of the crucial three days of Cabinets, had made this clear. Churchill therefore had little option but to play for time – and for Chamberlain. As has been partly already recounted, he treated Chamberlain with great care from the moment that he succeeded him. On the occasion of his first visit to France Churchill asked him 'to mind the shop' and he generally at this stage looked to him more than to Attlee as his deputy. Chamberlain responded with loyalty and an approach to warmth. His deficiencies were a narrow-minded self-righteousness and an inability to respect the motives let alone to understand the arguments of his opponents. His virtues were also considerable. He was honourable and gruffly loyal. He clung to power while he could, but he then allowed remarkably little resentment at his supersession to show. He did not intrigue. And, most crucially, he eventually swung to Churchill's rather than to Halifax's side towards the end of these three days of marathon Cabinets.

Churchill had to achieve this without the assistance of the better news from Dunkirk. That came through only after he had successfully held the Cabinet position. At the third Cabinet of Sunday, 26 May, which took place from 5.00 p.m. to 6.30 – after Reynaud's departure – and which Halifax described as 'a very jumpy meeting',[24] Churchill brought the projected evacuation into the discussion, but essentially as a reason for not rushing fences: 'The Prime Minister thought that it was best to decide nothing until we saw how much of the Army we could re-embark from France. The operation might be a great failure. On the other hand our troops might well fight magnificently, and we might save a considerable portion of the Force.'[25] It was all very tentative at that stage. It was only on the following day (Monday, 27 May) that the first 7,000 got away. On the Tuesday it was 17,000 and then on the Wednesday, Thursday, Friday and Saturday (29 May to 1 June) came the great flood of over 50,000 a day. But all this was still in the future on the Sunday, which Chamberlain described in his diary as 'the blackest day of all'. As a minor addition to gloom it rained all day, for the first time in weeks. In the blackness the Cabinet minutes were not very illuminating. They 'lacked theme', to borrow a famous remark of Churchill's in a totally different context, and give the impression of five bewildered gentlemen firing off inconsequential remarks in a variety of haphazard directions. From these records it is not possible absolutely to confirm or deny Professor Lukacs's* two most important assertions from that evening's proceedings. The one was that 'Chamberlain now sat on the fence'; and the other was that 'Churchill, at least momentarily, thought that he had to make *some* kind of concession to Halifax'.[26] The balance of likelihood however seems on Lukacs's side on both statements.

There was no respite at the end of this dreadful day. That evening Churchill personally intervened to cause a 'fight to the death' instruction

---

* John Lukacs (b. 1924) went from Hungary to the United States as a young man and became a professor at Chestnut Hill College, Philadelphia. In 1990 he published *The Duel: Hitler v. Churchill* and in 1999 *Five Days in London, May 1940*.

to be sent to the brigadier commanding the small British force holding out in Calais. General Ismay who dined with Churchill that night wrote: 'The decision affected us all very deeply, especially perhaps Churchill. He was unusually silent during dinner that evening, and he ate and drank with evident distaste. As we rose from the table, he said, "I feel physically sick."'[27] His nausea may not have been caused only by the harsh order, for although hating mass slaughter he was never squeamish about sacrificing some lives in order to save more; and he regarded prolonging the Calais resistance for a couple of days as essential to improving the prospects of the Dunkirk evacuation. A day of three Cabinets in which he was far from being able to get his own way, plus several hours of trying to stiffen Reynaud, plus a specially organized morning's service of intercession in Westminster Abbey, at which Churchill was able to stay only for half the time, might on their own have been more than sufficient to produce a loss of appetite.

The next day, Monday, 27 May, provided little relief. There were Cabinets at 11.30 a.m., at 4.30 p.m. and at 10.00 p.m. Lest time should hang heavy on ministers' hands there was also a Defence Committee at 7.00 p.m. The morning meeting was long and large, for there were several additional ministers (beyond the usual five) present, as well as a number of officials. It was concerned with a range of naval and military affairs, such as the evacuation of Narvik, and not with the secret, central crunch issue. Equally the 10.00 p.m. meeting was almost exclusively concerned with the consequence of the Belgian surrender. It was in the one-and-a-half-hour meeting beginning at 4.30 that the previous day's issue was resumed by the five plus Sinclair. The tone is well captured by two contemporary comments. Halifax confided to his diary:

we had a long and rather confused discussion about, nominally, the approach to Italy, but also largely about general policy in the event of things going really badly in France. I thought Winston talked the most frightful rot, also Greenwood, and after bearing it for some time I said exactly what I thought of them, adding that if that really was their view, and if it came to the point, our ways must separate. Winston, surprised and mellowed, and when I repeated the same thing in the garden, was full of apologies and affection. But it does drive one to despair when he works himself up into a passion of emotion when he ought to make his brain think and reason.[28]

About the same session John Colville wrote: 'The Cabinet are feverishly considering our ability to carry on the war alone in such circumstances, and there are signs that Halifax is being defeatist. He says that our aim can no longer be to crush Germany but rather to preserve our own integrity and independence.'[29]

The 'walk in the garden' was Churchill's desperate but successful attempt, without conceding anything of substance, to move Halifax from his threatened separation of the ways. It was immediately after the meeting during which, according to the minutes, the differences between Prime Minister and Foreign Secretary, although still lightly cloaked in euphemism, came most starkly to the surface. The essence of the euphemism was that the Cabinet debate was conducted in terms of what the British government should say to Reynaud who certainly, with both his army and his government crumbling, would have clutched at Mussolini as an intermediary, rather than what his colleagues should say to Halifax, who, with less justification, was equally keen so to use the Italian dictator.

The salient points of the Cabinet minutes were as follows:

> The Prime Minister said the Foreign Secretary's note set out the kind of approach to Signor Mussolini which M. Reynaud wanted the French and British Governments to make. . . . It might be argued that an approach on the lines proposed by M. Reynaud was not unlike the approach which we had asked President Roosevelt to make to Signor Mussolini. There was, however, a good deal of difference between making the approach ourselves and allowing one to be made by President Roosevelt ostensibly on his own initiative.
>
> The Lord President [Chamberlain] . . . thought it would be unfortunate if [the French] were to add to this [their feeling that they had been let down by the BEF's march to the sea] that we had been unwilling even to allow them the chance of negotiations with Italy.
>
> The Prime Minister said that he was increasingly oppressed with the futility of the suggested approach to Signor Mussolini, which the latter would certainly regard with contempt. Such an approach would do M. Reynaud far less good than if he made a firm stand. . . .

This was when Halifax brought the difference between himself and Churchill most clearly to the surface:

> The Secretary of State for Foreign Affairs said that he saw no particular difficulty in taking the line suggested by the Lord President. Nevertheless he was conscious of certain profound differences of points of view which he would like to make clear. . . . In the discussion the previous day he had asked the Prime Minister whether, if he was satisfied that matters vital to the independence of this country were unaffected, he would be prepared

to discuss terms. The Prime Minister had said that he would be thankful to get out of our present difficulties on such terms, provided we retain the essentials and elements of our vital strength, even at the cost of some cession of territory. On the present occasion, however, the Prime Minister seemed to suggest that under no conditions would we contemplate any course except fighting to a finish. . . .

The Prime Minister said that he thought the issue which the War Cabinet was called upon to settle was difficult enough without getting involved in the discussion of an issue which was quite unreal and most unlikely to arise. If Herr Hitler was prepared to make peace on the terms of the restoration of German colonies and the overlordship of Central Europe, that was one thing. But it was quite unlikely that he would make any such offer.[30]

On such an indeterminate note that session concluded. The Cabinet minutes style was designed to cloak differences by avoiding sharp phrases, but it was nonetheless clear that they were there and unresolved. The minutes also gave the impression that ministers were potting different snooker balls in a series of fairly random directions rather than concentrating on a precise decision. But there was another day still to come. Tuesday, 28 May began to follow much the same pattern that Monday the 27th had done. There was a War Cabinet at 11.30 a.m., but mainly concerned with operational matters, and with outsiders beyond the five plus Sinclair present. Sir Roger Keyes was for instance present for an item concerned with the Belgian surrender. Then, immediately after lunch, Churchill made a short parliamentary statement, promising a fuller one in a week's time. 'Meanwhile the House should prepare itself for hard and heavy tidings.' No questions were raised and only two minuscule supportive comments were delivered.

At 4.00 p.m. the War Cabinet resumed the unresolved argument of the previous two days, meeting on this occasion not in Downing Street but in the Prime Minister's room in the House of Commons. Early on, Churchill was recorded as saying that 'the French were trying to get us on to the slippery slope. The position would be entirely different when Germany had made an unsuccessful attempt to invade this country.' Halifax replied 'that we must not ignore the fact that we might get better terms before France went out of the war and our aircraft factories were bombed, than we might get in three months' time'.

The Prime Minister then read out a draft which expressed his views. To him the essential point was that M. Reynaud [a.k.a. Lord Halifax] wanted to get us to the Conference-table with Herr Hitler. If we once got to the table, we should then find that the terms offered us touched our independence and integrity. When, at this point, we got up to leave the Conference-table, we should find that all the forces of resolution which were now at our disposal would have vanished.

That part of the meeting ended after about an hour and a half with a series of remarkably inconsequential remarks from different ministers. The snooker balls were still going off in different directions without much apparent hope of concentration:

The Foreign Secretary said that he still did not see what there was in the French suggestion of trying out the possibilities of mediation which the Prime Minister felt was so wrong.

The Lord President said that, on a dispassionate survey, it was right to remember that the alternative to fighting on [that is mediation] involved a considerable gamble.

The War Cabinet agreed that this was a true statement of the case.

The Prime Minister said that nations which went down fighting rose again, but those which surrendered tamely were finished.

The Foreign Secretary said that nothing in his suggestion could even remotely be described as ultimate capitulation.

The Prime Minister thought that the chance of decent terms being offered to us at the present time were a thousand to one against.[31]

Churchill then engaged in what could be regarded as either his most skilful ploy or his luckiest unplanned bonus of those peculiarly testing three days. He had summoned for six o'clock a meeting of the ministers of Cabinet rank who were not in the War Cabinet. If a planned ploy, it was a classic example of summoning the outer ring to redress the balance of the inner. In his war memoirs Churchill was to attach full importance to this gathering but was coolly uninformative about his motive for calling it: 'I had not seen many of my colleagues outside the War Cabinet, except individually, since the formation of the Government, and I thought it right to have a meeting. . . .' However he did not subsequently under-estimate the importance of the occasion. After he had said, ' "Of course whatever happens at Dunkirk, we shall fight on," there occurred a demonstration which, considering the character of the gathering – twenty-five experienced politicians and Parliament men, who represented all the different points of view, whether right or wrong, before the war – surprised me. Quite a number seemed to jump up from the table and come running to my chair, shouting and patting me on the back.'[32]

This mood was wholly confirmed by Hugh Dalton, whose diaries contain the fullest account of the meeting, and, less extensively but equally firmly, in the Leo Amery diaries. Dalton described Churchill as saying (in direct contradiction of the argument of the absent Halifax):

> It is idle to think that if we tried to make peace now we should get better terms from Germany than if we went on and fought it out. The Germans would demand our fleet – that would be called 'disarmament' – our naval bases and much else. We should become a slave state though a British Government which would be Hitler's puppet would be set up – 'under Mosley* or some such person'. And where should we be at the end of all that? On the other side, we had immense resources and advantages. Therefore, he said 'We shall go on and we shall fight it out, here or elsewhere, and if at the last the long story is to end, it were better it should end, not through surrender, but only when we are rolling senseless on the ground.'[33]

There was at the side a marginal note, added later by Dalton, that Churchill had also said: 'If this long island story of ours is to end at last, let it end only when each one of us lies choking in his own blood upon the ground.' It is impossible now to tell whether this last somewhat melodramatic phrase was Churchill's own or whether it was a Dalton pastiche of his style, which Dalton greatly admired and in which no phrase could be too 'over the top' for his taste. It was a pity that Churchill was never able to reciprocate the warm feelings of the able and courageous if sometimes clanging Dalton. Whatever the status of this phrase there seems no reason to doubt the accuracy of Dalton's description of the scene (in general confirmed by Churchill himself) or of his added detail that the three loudest cheerleaders were Amery (despite his old hostility), Lord Lloyd (one of Churchill's supporters in the India Bill dispute and in general a very right-wing Conservative) and Dalton himself (partisanly socialist, even if also robustly patriotic and anti-German).[34] It was a good spread and the whole encounter refreshed and inspirited Churchill.

At 7.00 p.m. he again met the inner group, who must by then have been formidably exhausted by each other's company and arguments. It was the ninth meeting of the three days and the fourth specifically devoted to the Halifax–Churchill encounters, which mostly took the

* Sir Oswald Mosley had turned his fairly respectable New party into the British Union of Fascists in 1932. He was placed under preventive detention first in Brixton Prison and then (joining his wife) in Holloway Prison from 1940 to 1943.

form of polite shadow boxing but, as the seriousness of the situation fully merited, with flashes of hard steel sometimes shining through. Churchill's mood was now that of *il faut en finir*. Whether it would have been so without the stimulus of the wider group is impossible to tell. At any rate he began by telling the War Cabinet bluntly of the quality of the nominally lesser ministers: they 'had expressed the greatest satisfaction when he had told them that there was no chance of our giving up the struggle. He did not remember having ever before heard a gathering of persons occupying high places in political life [perhaps they deserved higher ones, he may delicately have implied] express themselves so emphatically.'[35]

Halifax, who by now recognized that he was beaten, partly because Chamberlain had moved away from him and partly because he himself had been worn down by a mixture of Churchill's cajolery (in the garden) and determination (in the Cabinet room), resorted to a circumlocutionary retreat. Obviously Mussolini as mediator had become a fox that would not run. But there was still the hope of getting Roosevelt, a more respectable name, to try mediation: 'The Foreign Secretary again referred to the proposed appeal to the United States.' Churchill was justifiably brutal with this diplomatic minuet:

> The Prime Minister thought an appeal to the United States at the present time would be altogether premature. If we made a bold stand against Germany, that would command their admiration and respect; but a grovelling approach, if made now, would have the worst possible effect. He therefore did not favour making any approach on the subject at the present time.[36]

He then adjourned the meeting after barely twenty minutes. Back in Admiralty House (where he lived until 14 June, showing almost excessive consideration for Chamberlain, who even then only had to move from No. 10 to No. 11 Downing Street), his dinner appetite was better than two nights before. At 11.40 p.m. he sent Reynaud a message as firm as that which he had delivered to Halifax four hours earlier: 'In my view if we both stand out we may yet save ourselves from the fate of Denmark or Poland. Our success must depend first on our unity, then on our courage and endurance.'[37] The difference was that Churchill had been able, slowly, to rout Halifax, but that he was not able to rout the defeatism of the French government.

However he had won the first and one of the most important victories of his premiership, and it was immediately followed – not as a consequence, except in the semi-mystical sense that victories tend to gain elbow room whereas defeats tend to be crowded in upon with further failures – by the far better than expected news of the Dunkirk evacuation. Already by the routine Cabinet at 11.30 the next morning Churchill was able to report that 40,000 had been safely landed. In the next three days over another 200,000 got back, which transformed the home-defence prospects. This, together with his War Cabinet victory, much strengthened his self-confidence. On the morning after the conclusion of his Cabinet battle he caused the following minute to be sent to ministers and senior officials:

> In these dark days the Prime Minister would be grateful if all his colleagues in the Government, as well as high officials, would maintain a high morale in their circles; not minimizing the gravity of events, but showing confidence in our ability and inflexible resolve to continue the war till we have broken the will of the enemy to bring all Europe under his domination.'[38]

Churchill was in general good at not bearing grudges. But it is difficult to believe that the events of 26–28 May did not have much to do with his desire, when Lord Lothian died in Washington in the following December, to remove Halifax, with dignity, from the London scene. More senior ministers came to see Halifax off from King's Cross Station – for he went to Scapa Flow for a grand battleship crossing of the Atlantic – than can ever have been accorded, before or since, to a departing ambassador. After a hesitant start, he proved to be a dedicated and successful representative of Britain in a crucial post. But Churchill wanted Eden and not him as Foreign Secretary for the rest of the war. And Churchill, eight years later, wrote in his war memoirs, combining in almost equal parts charity (towards Halifax) and mendacity, the most breathtakingly bland piece of misinformation to appear in all those six volumes:

> Future generations may deem it noteworthy that the supreme question of whether we should fight on alone never found a place upon the War Cabinet agenda. It was taken for granted and as a matter of course by these men of all parties in the State, and we were much too busy to waste time upon such unreal, academic issues.[39]

32

THE TERRIBLE BEAUTY OF THE
SUMMER OF 1940

FOR THE BRITISH public the trauma of June 1940 was the collapse of France. For Churchill and those close to him it was more the fate of the several peripheral pieces of French power – the formidable French navy (fourth in the world) and the French Empire in North Africa – intertwined with the impact upon Anglo-American relations which were the crucial questions. Already by early June Churchill knew in his bones that metropolitan France was lost. He made strenuous efforts to keep it in the war, but there were about them elements of going through the motions and playing for these peripheral pieces.

On 4 June Churchill delivered one of his parliamentary setpieces of that summer. Unlike his holding statement of 26 May it was full-length (thirty-four minutes) and gave the impression of having been almost entirely composed by the Prime Minister himself.* How he found the time to produce these written reams almost challenges belief. His extraordinary dictating fluency was of course an asset, but even with it many hours of concentrated composition must have been involved. Yet it was time well spent, for that fateful summer, the climax of his whole

---

* This was most obviously although by no means exclusively true of the peroration, which, apart from anything else, must have been parodied at least a hundred times:

> Even though large tracts of Europe and many old and famous States have fallen or may fall into the grip of Gestapo and all the odious apparatus of Nazi rule, we shall not flag or fail. We shall go on to the end. We shall fight in France, we shall fight on the seas and oceans, we shall fight with growing confidence and growing strength in the air, we shall defend our island, whatever the cost may be. We shall fight on the beaches, we shall fight on the landing grounds, we shall fight in the fields and in the streets, we shall fight in the hills; we shall never surrender, and even if, which I do not for a moment believe, this island or a large part of it were subjugated and starving, then our Empire beyond the seas, armed and guarded by the British Fleet, would carry on the struggle, until, in God's good time, the new world, with all its power and might, steps forth to the liberation of the old. (Hansard, 5th series, vol. 361, cols 787–96)

long life, was measured out and given shape, like the intervention of choruses in a Greek play, by these Churchillian orations. With their high-flown eloquence, which in less dramatic times would have sounded overblown, they could be regarded as a form of self-indulgence. They not only matched the mood of the moment but have survived six decades etched in the memory of many who were young at the time and are old now. They were an inspiration for the nation, and a catharsis for Churchill himself. They raised his spirits and thus generated even more energy than was consumed in their composition. He was obviously and rightly pleased with his 4 June effort and its reception, although the Conservative benches were still cool. Channon, however, was moving perceptibly and wrote that 'he [Churchill] was eloquent and oratorical, and used magnificent English', adding, significantly, 'several Labour Members cried'.[1] Another Labour MP, the splendid but somewhat wild Colonel Josiah Wedgwood, wrote to Churchill, to whom he was an old cross-party ally and friendly acquaintance: 'That was worth 1,000 gns & [was] the speech of 1,000 years'.[2]

One effect on Churchill of this triumph (of words, not alas of arms, as he was well aware) was to make him benignly write by hand that evening one or two delayed letters of courtesy. He wrote to Baldwin, who had sent him warm wishes more than two weeks before. Churchill concluded: 'I do not feel the burden weigh too heavily, but I cannot say that I have enjoyed being Prime Minister vy much so far.'[3] And he wrote to the King thanking him for having agreed, again a week or so before, to the by some standards rather dubious list of Privy Councillors – Beaverbrook, Bracken etc. – which Churchill had put forward after forming his government. 'Better days will come – though not yet',[4] he concluded that letter.

The following two weeks until Churchill's next House of Commons oration on 18 June, after the French armistice, were dominated by relations with the French, and attempts, understandable but almost ludicrously optimistic, to persuade them that if they could hold on for only a few weeks longer America might voluntarily enter the war on the Allied side. There was never the slightest chance of this happening in the summer of 1940. Roosevelt had first to deal with his Democratic party convention in July and to get support for his unprecedented bid for a third term. Then, in November, he had actually to get re-elected. And in the course of that campaign he thought it necessary to declare in Boston on 30 October that 'your boys are not going to be sent into any foreign wars'. And, even after the 1940 campaign had been won, it required another thirteen months and the most direct form of attack, to get the United States into the war. In spite of a robust note struck by Roosevelt in a broadcast of 10 June when he said that 'we will extend to the opponents of force the material resources of this nation'.[5] Churchill was living in cloud-cuckoo land when he attempted to assure the French, politicians and generals alike, at a Supreme War Council near Briare on the 11th that 'in the British view the attack on the United Kingdom, when it came, would in all probability bring in the United States, who were already near the point of intervention'.[6] Equally the minutes record Churchill informing the British War Cabinet at a late-night meeting on 13 June:

> Since returning to the country [from his second French visit in two days] a ... remarkable message had been received [by Reynaud] from President Roosevelt.... This message, he said, came as near as possible to a declaration of war and was probably as much as the President could do without Congress. The President could hardly urge the French to continue the struggle, and to undergo further torture, if he did not intend to enter the war to support them. If the President was not disavowed by his country, then it was clear that he would bring them in on our side in the near future.[7]

To what extent was Churchill justified in attempting to deceive his allies and his colleagues with these fantasies, for such they were? The prior question is whether he first deceived himself, to which the answer probably is, up to a point. It was a time for clutching at straws. I can still pinpoint the telephone box in Oxford from which, three days earlier, after Roosevelt's broadcast, I had spoken to my father to ask for (and receive) his confirmation that this might herald exactly the development about which Churchill was wishfully thinking. Clutching at straws is only dangerous if, when they fail to offer support, the wishful-thinker abandons resistance and sinks with them. There was no danger of Churchill doing this. It may therefore be thought that if he wished to supply some false optimism both to French ministers (who particularly needed it) and to the British War Cabinet he was justified in so doing.

Nevertheless he must have been well aware in sober and downbeat moments just how much he was building on moonbeams. The harsh fact is that during that fateful month of June Roosevelt and America contributed practically nothing except for words – stirring and encouraging words, but nonetheless suggesting more than they delivered. More realistically Churchill had telegraphed to Mackenzie King, the Canadian Prime Minister, on 5 June:

> Although President is our best friend, no practical help has been forth-coming from the United States as yet. We have not expected them to send military aid, but they have not even sent any worthy contribution in destroyers or planes, or by a visit of a squadron of their Fleet to Southern Irish ports.* Any pressure you can supply in this direction would be invaluable.[8]

On 15 June (the day after the Germans had occupied Paris) and in sharp contrast with his optimistic appraisal of thirty-six hours before, Churchill was forced to inform the War Cabinet of a further and deflating message which he had received from Roosevelt: 'The President said that he hoped it was realized that the United States were doing all they could to furnish materials and supplies. His message of the 13th had in no sense been intended to commit the United States of America to military participation. This could only be done by Congress.'[9] And for good measure Roosevelt added that he was not willing to agree to the publication (on which both the French and the British were keen) of that message to Reynaud of the 13th.

There was no American naval visit to a Southern Irish port, and the semi-obsolete American destroyers which Churchill was so urgently requesting did not become available until late August,[†] and only in return for a toughly negotiated arrangement by which the Americans acquired rights over a series of bases in transatlantic British territories from the West Indies to Newfoundland. Churchill, however, had more than enough realism and sense of who was the *demandeur* to avoid any ill-calculated show of disappointment or impatience. Throughout the desperate weeks he maintained his urbanity in all his messages to Roosevelt. The most that he did was to point out to him how vulnerable the United States would be if Hitler acquired control, not merely of the

---

* This was a preoccupation of Churchill at the time. Having been forced to abandon his desire as First Lord of the Admiralty to seize the so-called Treaty Ports (see p. 564–5 above), partly because of the effect on American opinion, he thought the best substitute might be a US naval visit, which would help both to impress the Irish with the strength of support for the Allies and to warn the Germans off a possible invasion via Ireland. 'We are also worried about Ireland,' he telegraphed to Roosevelt on 11 June. 'An American squadron at Berehaven would do no end of good I am sure' (*Churchill War Papers*, II, p. 285).

† And were not of great use then. Only nine of them had been found serviceable by February 1941.

French navy but of the British navy as well. He looked into cataclysm more frankly, maybe even over-dramatically, in his correspondence with Roosevelt than anywhere else. He would never surrender, but, if he was defeated and a British collaborationist government came into existence, who could tell what pro-German subjugations they might make. 'If we go down,' he wrote on 15 June, 'you may have a United States of Europe under the Nazi command far more numerous, far stronger, far better armed than the New World'.[10] How much this prospect frightened Roosevelt is not clear, but gradually Churchill's mixture of friendly patience accompanied by occasional glimpses of contingent horror, produced the destroyers, a lot of arms, Lend–Lease in March 1941, and eventually, with help from the Japanese, full and decisive American commitment in December of that year.

Churchill's last two of his six 1940 early-summer visits to France were on 11–12 June and, separately, on 13 June. His last journey to Paris had been on 31 May. On 10 June he had wanted to go there again, but found that a French government preoccupied with packing up, burning archives and finding a destination for evacuation did not want to receive him. On 11 June, however, they gave him a rendezvous at Briare, near Orléans, seventy miles south of Paris, to where GQG (Grand Quartier Général) had moved. General Spears, accompanying together with Eden, Dill, Ismay and other more junior staff, gave a somewhat superior but nonetheless amusing account of their late-afternoon arrival at an airfield which seemed to be locked in a perpetual siesta:

> Three or four cars drove up at intervals, and the Prime Minister left in the first with a French Colonel, who, from his expression, might have been welcoming poor relations at a funeral reception. We drove a few kilometres to a hideous house [the Château du Muguet], the sort of building the *nouveau riche* French *bourgeoisie* delight in, a villa expanded by successful business in groceries or indifferent champagne into a large monstrosity of red lobster-coloured brick, and stone the hue of unripe Camembert. This was Weygand's abode, where the Prime Minister was to sleep.[11]

The Supreme War Council (a singularly inappropriate title in the circumstances of the Allies' total lack of supremacy) met at 7.00 p.m. For once the pen of Anthony Eden provided a vivid description: 'When the moment came for Mr. Churchill to tell the French that we would go on with the struggle, if necessary alone, I watched the expressions opposite. Reynaud was inscrutable and Weygand polite, concealing with difficulty his scepticism. Marshal Pétain was mockingly incredulous. Though he said nothing his attitude was obviously *C'est de la blague*.'[12] Weygand could not have been more blunt or more defeatist. 'I am helpless, I cannot intervene for I have no reserves, there are no reserves. *C'est la dislocation*,' he said (according to Spears's notes of the meeting).[13]

There was a further session over dinner that night and an extended breakfast one, beginning at 8.00 (a little early for Churchill to be fully dressed and ready for a multilateral discussion) the following day. By then Pétain had gone off in one direction and de Gaulle (a forty-nine-year-old brigadier-general just appointed under-secretary for war), who had made a favourable impression the previous evening, had, perhaps symbolically, gone off in another. The talks did not achieve much. There were two main points of disagreement. The French, as at previous meetings, wanted more air support from the British. The British, while giving a few assuagements like extra bomber sorties, were more determined than ever to hold back the bulk of their fighter squadrons for the next phase of the war, the assault on Britain. The British wanted the French to defend Paris to destruction. The Prime Minister asked: 'Will not the mass of Paris and its suburbs present an obstacle dividing and delaying the enemy as in 1914, or like Madrid [in the Spanish Civil War]?' Pétain's reply was deadening: 'To make Paris a city of ruins will not affect the issue.' Weygand added that 'he had already informed the Paris deputies that the city would be declared an open town and that no attempt at resistance would be made in it. It was full of defenceless people and he could not see it destroyed by German bombardment.'[14]

The Prime Minister and his party flew back to London for a War Cabinet at 5.00 p.m. Almost the only positive result of the visit was that Churchill believed he had got an assurance that Admiral Darlan would 'never surrender the French Navy to the enemy'. 'In the last resort,' Churchill reported, 'he would send it over to Canada. Nevertheless,' the Prime Minister cautiously added, 'there was, of course, the danger that he might be overruled by the politicians.'[15]

Despite the barren results of this Briare conference Churchill accepted a request from Reynaud (over a telephone line so bad it took Churchill some time to understand what he was saying) to fly over to France again on the following day, Thursday, 13 June, for an afternoon meeting in the Prefecture at Tours, the French government now moving ever westwards. He went with trepidation for he feared that this quick re-summons could only mean that the French wanted to be released from their obligation not to conclude a separate peace. The British party arrived over a bomb-pitted Tours airfield (from an attack of the night before), landed with difficulty in a thunderstorm, and found themselves without welcome or transport. With further difficulty they borrowed the aerodrome commander's Citroën and proceeded to the Prefecture, which seemed almost equally unprepared for their arrival. As Churchill later wrote: 'It being already nearly two o'clock, I insisted upon luncheon. . . .' Ismay, who together with Spears, was as habitually of the party (in addition Halifax and, somewhat incongruously, Beaverbrook were there on this occasion), filled in more accurate subsequent detail. A nearby restaurant was found which provided a private room and adequate but not sumptuous fare.*

Eventually Reynaud and co. turned up at the Prefecture and yet another session of the Supreme War Council began at 3.30. It was as Churchill feared. The French, with their army in disarray and with the will to fight having largely disappeared, wanted an armistice and wished to be free to seek it without incurring British obloquy. That Churchill was not, at this stage, willing to give. Instead he proposed a final appeal to Roosevelt, and got Reynaud, whose inclination was always that way although he was under terrible pressures from most of his generals and colleagues, to accept the marginal delay so involved. However a linguistic misunderstanding arose, and one which in the context of history became heavily ironic. Paul Baudouin, a somewhat serpentine French high official (but probably no more so than Hankey or Horace Wilson) was putting it about that Churchill, when asked in a private conversation with Reynaud what would be the British attitude to France's inability to continue the struggle, had said 'Je comprends.' But this, it was strenuously asserted on the British side, meant no more than that he had understood the dilemma which Reynaud was putting to him, maybe indeed no more that that he understood his French, and certainly not that he agreed to the abrogation of the solemn Anglo-French agreement against either ally making a separate peace.

When de Gaulle and a few others heard of this confusion they were

---

* It was not until the French government moved further on to Bordeaux that the famous but now extinct Chapon Fin restaurant became the stage for the last act of the tragedy of the Third Republic, with different political and military groups and the staff of various embassies occupying for a few days the same regular tables and going down to the catastrophe in gastronomic splendour.

horrified. If Churchill was agreeing so easily it undermined the position of those on the French side still advocating resistance. The episode was a classic example of the dangers of speaking at crucial moments a language of which the speaker is not in perfect command. The irony was that it was a foretaste of an ambiguity over the same French verb with which de Gaulle at the beginning of his return to eleven years of power was famously concerned. On 4 June 1958, he addressed in the main square of Algiers a vast crowd of French *colons* demonstrating in favour of *l'Algérie française*. 'Je vous ai compris,' he said with his deliberate pronunciation, like pebbles plopping into a clear stream. It was thought that he meant he was on their side. In fact he meant that he taken their measure, and proceeded to cut the albatross of Algeria from the neck of France. The difference was that de Gaulle, in his own language, used ambiguity to achieve his own ends whereas Churchill, eighteen years before, was in a minor way caught in a trap of only semi-familiarity with the words he was using.

When Churchill took off from the battered Tours airfield later that evening it was his last contact with French soil for four years less a day – until 12 June 1944 when, a week after D-day, he was allowed ashore in Normandy to visit (with Smuts and CIGS Alan Brooke) Montgomery in his Château de Creully headquarters. He did not envisage such a long separation at the time. Indeed for only three days later he planned a further meeting with Reynaud in a Brittany harbour. The Foreign Office was instructed to send a telegram to the British ambassador to France (then in Bordeaux) in which a sort of future present indicative tense was used with, as it turned out, singular inappropriateness: 'The P.M., accompanied by the Lord Privy Seal [Attlee], Secretary of State for Air [Sinclair], and their three Chiefs of Staff and certain others, arrives at Concarneau at twelve noon tomorrow, the 17th, in a cruiser for a meeting with M. Reynaud.'[16] Soon after this message was sent Churchill went to Waterloo Station to proceed by special train to Southampton for embarkation in the cruiser. A cryptic telegram came from Bordeaux: 'Meeting cancelled, message follows.' Churchill at first refused to accept the upset. He is reported as having petulantly sat for half an hour in his seat on the train, refusing to go back to Downing Street. Eventually, however, he had to recognize the defeat of his plan, and return.

The aborted Concarneau meeting was not just an attempt by Churchill to re-harangue Reynaud for the third or fourth time. The appeal for decisive intervention by Roosevelt had predictably failed. The last British throw to keep France in the war (or at least the French navy, French North Africa – and maybe a redoubt in Brittany) was one of the most extraordinary and, it might be said, benevolently half-baked plans ever to go through the British government decision-making machinery, which although often negative and unimaginative was mostly fine-combed and realistic. At a luncheon in the Carlton Club on 15 June the idea of amalgamating the British and French states in an indissoluble union had first effectively surfaced. Among those present were: Halifax, Corbin (French ambassador) and Sir Robert Vansittart. In the next twenty-four hours it gathered momentum out of desperation. The matter came before the War Cabinet at a 3.00 p.m. meeting on Sunday, 16 June. The day and timing of the meeting were themselves indicative of how critical the circumstances were seen to be. Churchill was surprised at the gust of wind which swept along such figures as Chamberlain and Attlee, who were both normally good at the pricking of hot-air balloons. The minutes recorded: 'The Prime Minister said that his first instinct had been against the idea, but in this grave crisis we must not let ourselves be accused of a lack of imagination. Some dramatic announcement was clearly necessary to keep the French going.'[17] So, with remarkably little detailed consideration, the offer was evolved: common citizenship, a single united War Cabinet, amalgamated armed forces, and maybe, although nothing was specifically said about this, a single polyglot parliament.

It was an amazing confection. In retrospect it is difficult to decide which was the more staggering: the presumption of the view that the disparate and complex mechanisms of the British and French states could be successfully put together by a document of barely 300 words; or the utterly heterogeneous nature of those who assisted at its hasty creation. Apart from Churchill himself, with his half reluctantly given but decisive final seal of approval, these were Halifax, Vansittart and on the French side Corbin, the very experienced ambassador, René Pleven, several times to be Prime Minister in the early 1950s, Jean Monnet, the founding father of the European Community, and Charles de Gaulle, who was subsequently, both in war and peace, to be the symbol and the sword of unnegotiable French sovereignty. De Gaulle indeed was responsible for telephoning the proposal through to Reynaud as soon as it had been agreed on the Sunday afternoon, and then for carrying the written document with him when he returned to Bordeaux that

evening.* Churchill's role at Concarneau was to have been that
of reinforcing it with his eloquence and argument, and the purpose of
taking with him Attlee and Sinclair was to underpin the seriousness
of the offer by showing that it came from all parties in Britain.

The motivation for this British action was half clear and half
muddled. No one in the War Cabinet wished, at a moment of high
crisis, to appear to be foot-dragging and below the level of events. They
seem, however, to have given singularly little hard-headed attention to
the effect which the scheme would have upon the growing majority in
French governing circles who desperately wanted an armistice and who
were becoming increasingly hostile to a Britain which gave them neither
the resources to withstand the Germans nor the freedom to seek a deal
with the conquerors. No doubt British ministers thought that de Gaulle,
Monnet, Pleven and Corbin could not all be wrong about their fellow
countrymen. But they were. The union scheme encouraged Reynaud
for an hour or so. It had the reverse effect upon most of those around
him. Some saw it as a plot to take over the French colonial Empire and
to turn France into the equivalent of a British dominion. Pétain said it
would be 'fusion with a corpse'. In the early evening (of 16 June)
Reynaud failed to carry acceptance of the union scheme through his
Cabinet. By 8.00 p.m. he had resigned, and Pétain proceeded to form a
government of surrender. That was the reason Churchill had been left
sulking in his train seat at Waterloo. There was no one left in office in
France who wanted to confer with him. The grand and rash scheme
appeared counter-productive. In reality it was just irrelevant. It was
swept quickly into the dustbin of history.

Apart from failing dismally to keep France in the war, the union ploy
had produced no results in relation to the future of the French navy. At
lunch time on 16 June (that is immediately before the War Cabinet
endorsed the union declaration) Churchill had sent Reynaud an insensitive and over-rigid message. After saying that a unilateral peace
involved 'the honour of France' it continued: 'Nevertheless, provided,
but only provided, that the French Fleet is sailed forthwith for British
harbours, pending negotiations, His Majesty's Government give their
full consent to enquiry by the French Government to ascertain the
terms of an armistice for France.'[18] Part of the object of the union

---

* He was to remain there for barely eighteen hours before making a last-minute decision
to board General Spears's plane and (metaphorically) to take the Cross of Lorraine to
London.

declaration was to preserve the substance while easing the harshness of this communication. However the French proceeded to the armistice while taking no notice of the condition. No French warship sailed for a British port, although it is equally true that neither then nor later was any such vessel allowed to be pressed into German service. But Churchill continued to blast away. Late at night on the following day (17 June) he telegraphed to Pétain and Weygand what Sir Alexander Cadogan, who tried to get him to tone it down, described as 'a scorching message'. He told them that any weakness vis-à-vis the Germans with the fleet would 'scarify their names for a thousand years of history'.[19] Such explosions, wise or not, were understandable in the circumstances and also illustrated Churchill's near obsession with the issue, which led to his most decisive action during the first weeks when Britain stood alone.

First he had to provide a trumpet voluntary for the new circumstances, and this he did brilliantly in the House of Commons on 18 June, the day after the final French collapse. There was a routine War Cabinet at 12.30, and Cadogan, with that faint air of disapproval which he always employed when dealing with the political activities of politicians, wrote: 'Winston not there – writing his speech.'[20] He might as well have complained that Lincoln did not apply himself to some minor piece of White House business on the morning of the Gettysburg Address. Churchill's 18 June forty-minute oration was however somewhat longer than Gettysburg but parts of it were almost as memorable:

> The battle of France is over. I expect that the battle of Britain is about to begin. Upon this battle depends the survival of Christian civilization. Upon it depends our own British life and the long continuity of our institutions and our Empire. The whole fury and might of the enemy must very soon be turned on us. Hitler knows that he will have to break us in this island or lose the war. If we can stand up to him all Europe may be free, and the life of the world will move forward into broad, sunlit uplands; but if we fail, then the whole world, including the United States, and all that we have known and cared for, will sink into the abyss of a new dark age made more sinister, and perhaps more prolonged, by the lights of a perverted science. Let us therefore brace ourselves to our duty and so bear ourselves that if the British Commonwealth and Empire lasts for a thousand years, men will still say, 'This was their finest hour.'[21]

Two days later there was a secret session of the House of Commons. Churchill's full notes survive, but no Hansard report exists. The notes (although he was always a very note-bound speaker) lack cohesion or vitality. They do not suggest that secret sessions, of which there were no fewer than another sixty-five, but with thirty-one of them concerned only with hours of sitting, during the remaining five years of the war, added much. Most MPs liked them because they contributed a sense of being privy to special knowledge. But Churchill wisely reserved his great efforts for the publicized occasions. Even in his most preoccupied periods he treated the House of Commons with high respect (much more than Lloyd George had done in the First World War), but he rightly wanted to deliver his most resonant words through Parliament and the BBC to the nation, and not merely to pander to the desire of MPs for special knowledge which they could with semi-discretion filter through to their constituency friends and neighbours.

Churchill saw the fate of the French fleet as the hinge of the world naval balance. Were it to fall into German or Italian hands the Mediterranean would become an Axis lake and the already doubtfully secure British command of the Atlantic would be undermined. The terms of the French armistice were in his view unsatisfactory from this standpoint. Article 8 provided that, except for some ships left for safeguarding French colonial interests, the bulk 'shall be collected in ports to be specified and there demobilized and disarmed under German or Italian control'. 'It was therefore clear', Churchill subsequently wrote, 'that the French war vessels would pass into that control while fully armed'. This article of the armistice also stated that the Germans would not use them for their own purposes. But how much reliance could be placed on Hitler's word? In any event there was an exception, in the German favour, of 'those units necessary for coast surveillance and mine-sweeping', which could be subject to very flexible interpretation. 'At all costs, at all risks, in one way or another',[22] Churchill determined, as many as possible of the French ships had either to be brought under British control or sunk. Although there had been occasional squawks from Halifax about the dangers of being too hostile to the new French government (he had, for instance, been against de Gaulle being allowed to broadcast to France from London on 18 June), Churchill had no real difficulty in carrying the support of the War Cabinet for this very hard line.

The dispersion of the French navy at the time of the armistice was surprisingly favourable to the British purpose. Two battleships, four light cruisers, eight destroyers, several submarines, including the large *Surcouf*, and no fewer than 200 minor craft were in British waters, mainly at Plymouth and Portsmouth. There was no real difficulty in assuming control of these. Only in the case of the *Surcouf* was there minor resistance, with one Briton and one Frenchman killed, and three other Britons wounded.

In Alexandria, at the eastern end of the Mediterranean, there was a French battleship, accompanied by four cruisers, three of them modern, and some small ships. They were adequately covered by a superior British force which lay outside. At Oran (or Mers el-Kebir, which was the alternative name for its adjacent military harbour) on the Mediterranean shores of Algeria, were two battleships, an aircraft carrier, three ordinary cruisers plus the battle cruisers *Dunkerque* and *Strasbourg* and sundry destroyers and submarines. The two battle cruisers, the pride of the French navy, were superior to the dreaded German raiders *Gneisenau* and *Scharnhorst*. Their only rival in French naval esteem were two new battleships, the *Jean Bart*, which lay at Casablanca and was still unarmed, and the *Richelieu* at Dakar, more armed but not wholly complete. There were also several cruisers at Algiers; and at Toulon – which was outside the scope of possible British action – there were four cruisers and a whole cluster of destroyers and submarines. The list shows that Churchill was not exaggerating when he talked about the pivotal capacity of the French navy.

It was judged that there were two key points for British action. Admiral Cunningham at Alexandria and Admiral Somerville, in command at Gibraltar – the base for action at Oran – were given orders which neither of them welcomed. They were to offer the French commanders four choices: (1) continue to fight against the enemy; (2) sail to a British port, where the ships would be interned although the crews repatriated to France; (3) sail to a French port in the West Indies where the ships could be demilitarized and perhaps entrusted to United States care; (4) scuttle the ships. If none of these choices was accepted the ships would be bombarded to destruction by the British. Cunningham, who was to be the key British admiral of the war, replacing Pound as First Sea Lord and Chief of the Naval Staff in 1943, managed to treat his orders with considerable flexibility and by so doing achieved an acceptable solution without firing on the French ships at Alexandria. Somerville was at least as unhappy with his task as was Cunningham. It was rendered even more poignant for him by his having been closely involved in the Dunkirk evacuation and taking particular pride in having successfully assisted the rescue of over 100,000 French soldiers. The signal which he received from London late at night on 2 July was therefore carefully drafted, maybe by Churchill himself. 'You are charged with one of the most disagreeable and difficult tasks that a British Admiral has ever been faced with, but we have complete confidence in you and rely on you to carry it out relentlessly.'[23]

On the following morning Somerville had his ships off Oran soon after 9.00. All day long he endeavoured unsuccessfully to negotiate an acceptable solution with the French admiral. Just before 6.30 p.m. he was sent a peremptory Admiralty signal telling him that he must settle the matter, if necessary by firing upon and sinking the French ships, before dark. The signal was otiose. He had already done so half an hour beforehand. The engagement lasted about ten minutes and was followed by heavy aerial attack from *Ark Royal* planes on the escaping *Strasbourg* and her two escorting destroyers. The result was moderate success. One French battleship was blown up and another beached. The *Dunkerque* ran aground, but the *Strasbourg* although damaged made Toulon. So did the three cruisers which had been at Algiers. (In a separate air action five days later the new *Richelieu* was severely damaged at Dakar.) At Oran 1,299 French sailors had been killed in the action, and another 350 wounded. This engagement had a rankling effect on Franco-British relations for many years.

It was brutal rather than glorious, and the French fleet had been crippled rather than definitively neutralized. There is also the feeling that, left more to his own judgement, Somerville might have achieved something closer to the bloodless victory of Cunningham at Alexandria. Nonetheless Churchill's ruthlessness had three points to be said in its favour, two of them more political than military. First, it showed immense cold courage to take such aggressive action against a former ally at a time when circumstances seemed so much against Britain. Nearly anyone else would have let sleeping ships lie, and hoped vaguely for the best. One cannot imagine a Halifax-led government giving the order for Oran.

Second, and somewhat surprisingly in view of their own caution at the time, the action produced a very good effect upon what Churchill described as 'high Government circles in the United States. . . . Henceforth there was no more talk about Britain giving in.'[24] Third, the news was received with equal enthusiasm in the House of Commons. On 4 July Churchill made a half-hour statement before the House went into secret session. His own later account ran:

The House was very silent during the recital, but at the end there occurred a scene unique in my own experience. Everybody seemed to stand up all around, cheering, for what seemed a long time. Up till this moment the Conservative Party had treated me with some reserve, and it was from the Labour benches that I received the warmest welcome when I entered the House or rose on serious occasions. But now all joined in solemn stentorian accord.[25]

This was wholly borne out by Harold Nicolson writing at the time: 'The House is at first saddened by this odious attack but is fortified by Winston's speech. The grand finale ends in an ovation, with Winston sitting there with the tears pouring down his cheeks.'[26] In its wider, if not perhaps wholly predictable, repercussions the Oran bombardment could therefore be held to be justifiable. For Churchill it marked a transition to a slightly more stable phase of the war. After the first days of July, in contrast with the previous two months, nothing got much worse for several weeks. The country was still living in imminent invasion danger, and Churchill wished to keep alive a sense of alert readiness. But, as there are many examples from his papers and recorded remarks to show, he did not really believe it – and he was right. He did not think the Germans, without naval supremacy, could invade until they had beaten the Royal Air Force. He knew that such an aerial battle was impending but he faced it with more confidence than the land battles in France. As a result he was able to lengthen his stride, and there are several indications of his morale substantially improving in the first half of July. Perhaps, recalling Clementine Churchill's letter of 26 June, his temper did too.

On 5 July Victor Cazalet MP, who walked every day with Halifax from the Dorchester Hotel to the Foreign Office, recorded that 'we are disturbed somewhat about Winston. He is getting very arrogant and hates criticism of any kind. H. says it's almost impossible to get 5 mins conversation with him.'[27] Maybe, in view of the May Cabinets there were reasons other than arrogance why he did not relish long conversations with Halifax. Moreover, Cazalet's view was semi-contradicted by several other reports. Colville wrote on 13 July, 'Winston showed greater animation and exuberance than I have seen before.... This week-end [he said] he felt more cheerful than at any time since he took office,'[28] and on the 18th Nicolson reported Brendan Bracken as saying that 'in the twenty years he has known Winston, he has never seen him as fit as he is today, and his responsibilities seem to have given him a new lease of life'.[29] This was partly because his 4 July parliamentary triumph led to a fresh confidence in his dealings with the House of

Commons. He answered a whole range of Prime Minister's questions on both Thursday 18 July and Tuesday the 23rd with zest and total command. Channon wrote of the latter occasion: 'Winston was in roaring spirits today, and gave slashing answers, which he had himself drafted, to foolish Questions, and generally convulsed the House. He is at the very top of his form now and the House is completely with him, as is the country. . . .'[30] In the course of the exchanges of 23 July he gave a very good example of how to withdraw with aplomb from a government proposal which had become embarrassing. It had been planned to set up 'silent columns' (known, more detrimentally, after the name of the Minister of Information, as 'Cooper's snoopers') with the duty of reporting on any examples of the spreading of alarm and despondency which they came across. When set down in black and white, Churchill said, 'it did not look by any means so attractive'. 'The movement to create a silent column has therefore passed into what is called in the United States innocuous desuetude.'[31] The House was pleased, Churchill was not discomfited.

Then, on 30 July, the House approached a secret-session debate on foreign affairs. A week earlier, Churchill said, this had appeared to be the strong desire of the House. Now, however, there was some wavering, partly under the influence of adverse newspaper comment about the secrecy, and many wanted an open debate. Accordingly, Churchill said, 'the Government are now in the embarrassing position of a servant receiving contradictory orders from those whom their only desire is to serve'. He would do whatever was wanted, but members really must make up their minds. He therefore proposed an immediate free vote, without whips and without ministers voting, on whether the debate should be closed or open. He concluded by announcing in that teasing manner which he often used, mostly in private, on this occasion in public, about Rab Butler, who as Foreign Office under-secretary was to open the debate: 'He has already, I believe, taken the precaution of preparing two speeches, both, I am sure, excellent, but one somewhat longer than the other.'[32] The session was secret, and the longer one was used.

At about 8.00 p.m. Churchill himself spoke. Dalton wrote: 'Winston in grand form both before and after. He now leads the whole House, unquestioned and ascendant.'[33] At 11.30 Churchill took a night train to the North-East to spend the next day inspecting troops and coastal defences. Before leaving he insisted to Halifax that an importunate message to Roosevelt should be despatched immediately. He had drafted a previous one on 5 July but had decided, perhaps under Foreign Office pressure, that the time was not opportune. The subject was always Britain's need for the semi-obsolete American destroyers. The core of the 30 July message was: 'I cannot understand why, with the position as it is, you do not send me at least 50 or 60 of your oldest destroyers. . . . Mr President, with great respect, I must tell you that in the long history of the world this is a thing to do now.'[34] There was a risk in deciding on such a peremptory tone, and the decision to take it, between the debate and the train, obviously added to the strains of the day, but it did no harm and maybe some good. The destroyer deal was announced on 3 September.

While Churchill was in the North-East, George Lambert, Liberal National MP and one of the very few whose parliamentary experience was longer than Churchill's (he had been first elected in 1891), wrote to him: 'As an old House of Commons man I am glad that you treat MPs as responsible individuals and not as irresponsible nobodies. Indeed, your leadership of the House is incomparably the most brilliant that I can remember, save perhaps that of Mr Gladstone. You have today the complete confidence of Parliament and the nation.'[35]

Had it, with July fading into August, been the end of a normal parliamentary session, with Churchill looking forward to long writing sojourns in the South of France, it would have been a good note on which to go away. It was hardly that, however. The next two months brought the greatest challenge. But at least Churchill's base was secure and his confidence was high.

Indeed during most of July itself Churchill had been able to apply himself to a number of matters, some of them hobby horses, which might not have qualified for attention in June. Prominent among them was the problem of the Duke of Windsor. With the collapse of France Churchill's former Prince Charming had got himself first to Madrid and then to Lisbon. He wanted to come back to England. Churchill was determined that he should not do so, and decided that the safest thing was to get him safely across the Atlantic as Governor of the Bahamas. But he was not willing to trust him in the United States at that stage, and had to issue some surprisingly detailed and strict instructions as to how the Duke should get to his domain via Bermuda and passages in two commercial ships. Then on 20 July he had to be even firmer on a different subject: 'I regret that there can be no question of releasing men from the Army to act as servants to your Royal Highness. Such a step would be viewed with general disapprobation in times like these. ...'[36] On the 27th Churchill wrote in an even more admonitory tone:

> Sir, may I venture upon a word of serious counsel. ... Many sharp and unfriendly ears will be pricked up to catch any suggestion that your Royal Highness takes a view about the war, or about the Germans, or about Hitlerism, which is different from that adopted by the British nation and Parliament. ... Even while you have been staying at Lisbon, conversations have been reported by telegraph through various channels which might have been used to your Royal Highness' disadvantage. ... I thought your Royal Highness would not mind these words of caution from your faithful and devoted servant. ...[37]

Nearer to home Churchill was giving trouble to Lord Woolton, the draper who had become the nation's grocer, over his sceptical attitude to food rationing. Tea rationing was the point immediately at issue, on which Churchill developed one of his 'cottage homes' positions. He had been told by Professor Lindemann that, together with bread, it was almost the only commodity of which the poorer classes consumed more than the richer, which indeed his own habits bore out. He therefore wanted tea to be in good supply. His more general and somewhat Falstaffian position was set out in a 14 July letter to Woolton at the Ministry of Food:

> I am glad you do not set too much store by the reports of the Scientific Committee. Almost all the food faddists I have ever known, nut-eaters and the like, have died young after a long period of senile decay. The British soldier is far more likely to be right than the scientists. All he cares about is beef. I do not understand why there should be these serious difficulties about food, considering the tonnages ... we are importing. The way to lose the war is to try to force the British public into a diet of milk, oatmeal, potatoes, etc, washed down on gala occasions with a little lime juice.[38]

Another issue on which he found time to expostulate was his hostility to the evacuation of (mostly well-connected) British children to the United States and Canada. He wrote to the Home Secretary (Sir John Anderson) on 18 July:

> I certainly do not propose to send a message by the senior child to Mr Mackenzie King, or by the junior child either. If I sent any message by anyone, it would be that I entirely deprecate any stampede from this country at the present time. I cannot conceive why Mr Shakespeare

[junior minister at the Dominions Office] should leave his duties in London to see off [from Liverpool] a hundred children.[39]

On the other hand when Tony Benn's younger brother (then aged eleven) wrote to *The Times* saying that he would 'rather be bombed to fragments than leave England', Churchill wrote to Labour MP Benn *père* saying 'A splendid letter from your boy.'[40]

Some other issues, more directly connected with the central direction of the war, to which Churchill applied himself during these months were, first, a directive that no decisions from him were valid unless they were given, or immediately confirmed, in writing; second, the replacement of Ironside (despite old friendship) by Alan Brooke as Commander-in-Chief of the Home Forces; and third, his instruction to Hugh Dalton, after confirming his authority as Minister of Economic Warfare to control the Special Operations Executive – an organization for sabotage in German-occupied territories – 'to go and set Europe ablaze'.[41]

Transcending all these, however, was his very bold July decision to reinforce the Middle East, including sending nearly half the available tanks on a slow and hazardous journey around the Cape of Good Hope. It was one of the few occasions throughout the war when he went against, as opposed to strenuously contending with but ultimately acquiescing in, the advice of the Chiefs of Staff. Without Churchill's nerve, Egypt might not have been held in 1941/early 1942, and the Western Desert could not have been the scene of Britain's first decisive land victory at the end of the latter year,

He also managed to get in a high state of excitement against what he considered to be unauthorized activity on the part of his old friend 'Hopey' Linlithgow as Viceroy and his still older half-friend (half-enemy) L. S. Amery towards offering India full self-government immediately after the war. Amery was subjected to a very heavy rebuke from the War Cabinet on 25 July – Linthithgow had the advantage of being 5,000 miles away. This at least was an illustration of Churchill's fine impartiality as head of the government. Amery had been a vociferous supporter of his at the crucial general meeting of ministers on 28 May. Eden and Sinclair, as Secretaries of the State for War and Air, were also frequent recipients of some of his most pained and therefore wounding letters. In the first month of his full authority as Prime Minister he exercised his power without fear or favour, with occasional irascibility and prejudice, but with these weaknesses nearly always redeemed by the wit, fluency and buoyancy of his flood of communications.

---— 33 ——---

THE BATTLE OF BRITAIN AND THE
BEGINNING OF THE BLITZ

THE BATTLE OF BRITAIN, although at least as decisive in its consequences as Blenheim or Waterloo, was a much less precise event. The
imprecision related to when it started and when it ended, as well as to
what actually happened. It was a very knightly contest in which few
more than a thousand young men on either side jousted with each other
at high altitude, high risk and for high stakes but without the squalor of
land battles, and also without a reliable scoreboard. Both sides grossly
exaggerated the other's losses and their own victories. The result was a
draw, but it was one of those draws which was much more valuable to
one side – the British – than to the Germans, who ought on the form
to have won overwhelmingly. A draw was all that Britain needed, in
combination with German naval weakness, to stave off invasion, for the
first time since 1066, across the narrow seas. It was therefore one of
the most decisive draws in history.

During July and into early August the Germans used their newly
acquired airfields in Normandy and Brittany to launch sporadic bombing
raids, without any clearly co-ordinated purpose, on the western parts of
England and South Wales. On 31 July, for instance, bombs are recorded
as having fallen on south-east Cornwall, Devon, Somerset, Gloucester-
shire, South Wales and Shropshire. It is difficult to see much pattern or
purpose to this, but it fits in with my own recollection that whenever I
stayed a few days at my family's house in Monmouthshire this involved
more time in our home-made but fairly comfortable air-raid shelter than
I was to spend in such circumstances in the whole of the rest of the war.
Relatively innocuous air-raid warnings were in operation for four or five
hours on most nights. There were sometimes bomb craters to inspect the
next day, but most of them were on mountainsides. A total of 258 civilians
were killed in those July raids, compared with 1,075 in August and over
6,500 in September, by which time the blitz on more easterly industrial
cities and on London had become much more concentrated.

Nevertheless it is difficult to count the beginning of the Battle of Britain as being in July or even in early August. When in March 1941 a thirty-two-page Air Ministry booklet was published, which sold a million copies and for the first time put the name Battle of Britain into general circulation (no one had quite seen it in that context when it was actually taking place), the starting date was put as 8 August and the finishing one as 31 October. These dates were arbitrarily chosen. One could say that 8 August was fairly near the mark, although some would put the great clash of 15 August as being the end of the overture and the true rising of the curtain. But 31 October is much more open to challenge. The essence of the Battle of Britain was that the Germans endeavoured to destroy the British fighter force either in the air or on the ground, and also to disrupt the output, mounting strongly during the summer months, of Hurricanes, Spitfires and bombers. It was a narrowly confined battle, partly because the main German fighter, the Messerschmitt 109, was brilliant at high altitudes (which did not avail them much if they could not get their adversaries to follow them into the high skies), but of severely limited range. The 109s could barely reach London from northern French bases, and certainly could not long sustain combat so far from these bases. The Battle of Britain could therefore be regarded as a somewhat grandiloquent name for a battle of Kent, Sussex and Surrey, almost a battle of the suburbs, although its repercussions of course extended far further.

Long before 31 October, however, the Germans had switched their objective, first to mass daylight bombing of London, which began on the afternoon of Saturday, 7 September, and to other cities, and then, when the losses from this became unacceptable, to night raids. These did not end on 31 October. November was a dreadful month for raids, both on London and on the provincial cities, with the most notorious of all such obliterations, at least until Dresden in 1944, shattering Coventry's monuments and shops but doing less damage to its aircraft factories, on 14 November.*

What was to become most striking about the Battle of Britain, however – apart from the gallantry with which on both sides it was fought – was not when it began and when it ended, but the ignorance on each side of what was happening on the other. The fog of battle was

---

* In fact, 1,353 were killed in Birmingham on the night of 19–20 November as opposed to the 554 who had been the fatal victims of the more notorious Coventry attack five days earlier.

truly pervasive. This was despite the fact that the Enigma decrypts of wireless traffic were already providing Churchill and the very restricted circle which was privy to this information with some insight into German dispositions. Almost the only piece of good news at the beginning of Churchill's premiership was that of an important crypto-graphic Enigma breakthrough at Bletchley on 11 May.

From an early stage of the war Bletchley Park's decrypts (codenamed Ultra) played a vital role. According to some commentators, they more or less won the war. Perhaps partly because I spent the last fifteen months before VE day endeavouring to break the daily traffic between Berlin and the principal commanders in the field, I put the results a little more cautiously. But they were certainly substantial. The naval Enigma, which linked U-boats with their home command, was perhaps the most crucial. The threat to the vital North Atlantic sealink went up or down according to how freely Bletchley was reading the U-boat instructions.

As an example of the fog of battle, the British constantly exaggerated both the preponderance of the German resources in planes and pilots, and, as a sort of unintentional offset, their own success, both absolutely and relatively, in destroying German raiders. The figures on aircraft availability are peculiarly difficult to disentangle,* both because of the complication between front-line and reserve strengths and because the Germans deployed a lot of bombers against first airfields and then London, whereas the British bomber force was engaged against more distant targets, and therefore not part of the Battle as such. What however does seem to have been the case is that in mid-August the British had 1,032 fighters available, whereas the Germans had margin-ally fewer at 1,011. Furthermore the number of available British pilots was 1,400, with several hundred fewer on the German side. This was in contrast with some British intelligence estimates which put the total number of pilots in Germany at 16,000, with at least 7,300 (including bomber pilots) deployed in Luftwaffe operational units.

---

* The relative strengths of German and British air power were even more perplexing to Churchill at the time than they have remained. Over Christmas and the New Year (1940–1), he borrowed a judge (Mr Justice Singleton) to try and weigh up the conflicting evidence. Singleton came to the surprisingly balanced conclusion that, overall, the German superiority was no more than four to three. The 'borrowing' of Singleton was almost the only occasion during the crux of the war when Churchill deigned to have any contact with Lord Chancellor Simon, thereby demonstrating how successfully he had made him 'innocuous' (in Attlee's word).

On Sunday, 15 September, which was the culmination of the daytime fighter battles, the British official claim, broadcast that night, was that 185 German aircraft had been destroyed, for a British loss of forty. In fact the German losses were sixty (thirty-four bombers and twenty-six fighters), with another twenty bombers seriously damaged, but able to get back to base. In general the 60/40 ratio, or even 50/50, for the attackers against the defenders was much nearer to the truth than the 4.5-to-1 claim seriously advanced, and believed by Churchill, or at least by his very sober-minded private secretary, John Martin. The motive was not deliberate deceit, although Churchill was very mocking of the Germans when they made exaggerated claims, but a certain understand-able tendency to wishful thinking, underpinned by many fighter pilots reporting the same victim as one of their near companions, with double- or treble-counting being a natural result.

Even more exaggerated was the German view of the damage they were inflicting upon Fighter Command and the general British strength. On 16 September, Göring announced that Fighter Command had been reduced to 177 aircraft. In fact it then had an operational strength of 656, with a strong flow of additional planes in reserve or in the pipeline. The battles of that summer never reduced the strength of Fighter Command or of the RAF generally. This was partly due to the success of Beaverbrook in his first months as Minister of Aircraft Production. He inherited a favourable upward swing, but his ruthless improvisa-tion considerably fortified this. The so-called Harrogate Programme of January 1940 provided for a year's output of 3,602 fighters (very precise). The total achieved was 4,283, which meant that nearly 352 fighters a month were forthcoming over the crucial summer and autumn months. The German output was barely a half of that.

This was a decisive factor and half justified Beaverbrook's promotion to the War Cabinet on 2 August, the first change in that body since the appointment of the five in early May. Churchill felt that he needed him, on both personal and political grounds. Chamberlain effectively ceased to function with his severe late-July stomach-cancer operation, although he remained nominally a member until 3 October, before his death on 9 November. Beaverbrook provided Churchill with another Conserva-tive to balance the two Labour members, but his character and style were so different from those of Chamberlain that his inclusion hardly amounted to a steadying of the ship. Those who had been most critical of the change of May 1940 felt that this was yet another example of the bounders taking over from the men of solid respectability. Only Halifax of the old guard remained. Two months later, when Chamberlain formally resigned, Halifax was offered Chamberlain's place as Lord President, with Eden moving to the Foreign Office, but wisely wished to retain the office which he knew.*

Kingsley Wood, as an ingenious but far from dominating Chancellor of the Exchequer, was brought in to balance the admission of Ernest Bevin, Minister of Labour, who had the reverse of Wood's qualities. Sir John Anderson, portentous but not at that stage politically partisan, also joined, in Chamberlain's old office of Lord President of the Council. To some extent this last appointment was a kicking upstairs, for as the London blitz became more severe Churchill decided that he needed a streetwise Londoner rather than Anderson as Home Secretary and Minister of Home Security. Herbert Morrison, who himself was to get into the War Cabinet in November 1942, was promoted from Minister of Supply to that post.

At different stages after October 1940, Anthony Eden, Stafford Cripps, Oliver Lyttelton and Lord Woolton also achieved membership of the inner group. Churchill's reward to Beaverbrook on 2 August therefore began a process which moved the War Cabinet well away from its original tight-knit group of non-departmental ministers (Halifax being the only exception to this) to a looser prefects' bench within the government. It might have been more sensible to give Beaverbrook the accolade of an earldom for his truly impressive departmental efforts, because he was never nearly enough of a team player to be either happy or useful in the War Cabinet. He was frequently wanting to resign, on grounds of either asthma or pique, and although he had several further notable escapades within the wartime government they were mostly directed to turf wars with colleagues (undermining Cripps in Moscow, quarrelling with Bevin about manpower allocation and with Sinclair about pilot training and trying to prise Coastal Command away from the Air Ministry) rather than to providing any steady contribution to the central direction of the war.

* Eden also was then offered the Lord Presidency of the Council, but showed a slight preference for remaining as Secretary of State for War, a preference which Churchill encouraged. Churchill then told him that the future was in any event with him (Eden). 'He reiterated that he was now an old man, that he would not make Lloyd George's mistake of carrying on after the war, that the succession must be mine' (Eden, *The Reckoning*, p. 145). In view of this it was not perhaps surprising that Eden grew impatient when, nearly a decade and a half later, the promised succession was still not made available to him.

Just as there is surprise, looking back, at the normality and amenity of life over the summer of 1940, so the rigours of existence in London (and a few other cities) as the nights drew in and the sirens wailed ever earlier are a sharp reminder that life when Britain stood alone was not just a matter of defiance and glory. At first the bombing onslaught was mainly on Docklands and the East End and the fight to keep up morale and maintain conditions of semi-civilized life had something of a soup-kitchen operation about it. Churchill was good at this, and after severe incidents made successful morale-boosting expeditions to parts of London in which he had hardly been since Sidney Street in 1910. He did not despise attention to presentation as opposed to substance and went accoutred in one of his 'funny' hats and never without a cigar. He was not given to waste quiet anonymity on the acrid air. But it worked, partly because he had the gift of communicable emotion. When his eyes filled with tears on 8 September at a scene of a dreadful carnage, a bomb-blasted local woman called out, 'Look, he really cares,' and the assembled crowd burst into spontaneous cheers.

Then the attacks spread much further west. The night of 15 October marked the most sustained attack on the governing centre of the capital. A bomb fell on the Treasury and killed three officials. The Downing Street cook and her assistant were saved only because Churchill had ordered them into the shelter a few minutes earlier. Pall Mall became a path of flames. The Carlton Club, then in that street and alongside the Reform, was effectively destroyed, although curiously without loss of life. The future Lord Chancellor Hailsham had carried his father, the former Lord Chancellor Hailsham, from the wreck upon his shoulders, like Aeneas bearing Pater Anchises from the ruins of Troy, as he typically but appropriately recorded. And Captain Margesson, the great whip, was even less effective in browbeating the bombers than he had been with John Profumo half a year earlier. He arrived rather forlorn and dirty to sleep the night at the Downing Street Annexe, but when the Prime Minister and his private secretary inspected the semi-wreckage of the Carlton Club on the next day they were much struck by the Margesson slippers being neatly set out at the door of his usual bedroom, like a dog's basket awaiting the return of its habitant.

At this stage London was more exposed than had been any undefeated seat of government in the civilized world. Moscow in 1812, Washington in 1814 and 1861, and Madrid as a Republican bastion in 1936–9 were the nearest rivals. But none of these was subject to the equivalent weight of shells or bombs. In these circumstances serious consideration had to be given to whether Britain, even in the absence of invasion, could continue to be governed from Whitehall and its purlieus. Even Chequers came to be regarded as unsafe on weekends of a high moon, when it was easier to locate from the air. As for 10 Downing Street, it was one of the most rickety large houses in London, built early in the eighteenth century, a well-known period for jerry-building. Churchill himself thought it unsafe, although his favourite occupation during air raids was to climb on to the nearest roof or turret and watch the action. He thought the fireworks should give off noise as well as light, and laid great store on keeping up anti-aircraft barrages, whether they hit anything or not; they were much better for civilian morale than an eerie silence while waiting for the next bomb explosion.

First the No. 10 dining room was moved into the former typing secretaries' room in the basement on the garden side. Three other premises were prepared for the Prime Minister, although two of them were little used. (This was apart from contingent and, with Churchill, highly unpopular plans for the removal of the whole seat of government to Worcestershire; he referred to this with repugnance as the 'Black Move'.) The serious and most used of the other premises was an above-ground corner of the old (but not very old – it had been solidly built in the first decade of the twentieth century) Board of Trade building facing St James's Park at Storey's Gate. It was above ground, indeed immediately on top of the new War Cabinet Rooms, and therefore had some light. It was reinforced with girders and steel shutters, but obviously did not provide full security, although a reasonable if fairly austere framework of amenity, within which quiet indulgence of food and drink could be sustained, and which from 21 October, when the move took place, was Churchill's main base for much of the war. It quickly became known as the No. 10 Annexe. It was also referred to as the 'Barn'. Nonetheless Churchill liked to go back and sleep in the real No.10 and also to hold Cabinet meetings in the traditional room whenever this was judged moderately safe.

In addition there was more secure accommodation provided by the London Passenger Transport Board beneath the disused Underground station at the corner of Down Street and Piccadilly (known in the government as the 'Burrow'). The station has never come back into tube use, but the twin semi-circular red arches, characteristic of early Underground architecture, can still be seen today. Surprisingly London Transport provided luxurious living for its occasional official visitors. Colville reported an unhappy visit there on 31 October: 'The P.M. felt ill, was sick, and went off to Down Street where he had no dinner.'[1] But on 19 November Colville reported more happily: 'I went with the P.M. to Down Street for the night and dined excellently, far beneath the level of the street. . . . The L.P.T.B. do themselves well: caviar (almost unobtainable in these days of restricted imports), Perrier Jouet 1928, 1865 brandy and excellent cigars.'[2]

A more suburban London retreat was also prepared at Dollis Hill, on the far edge of the borough of Willesden. It had good Prime Ministerial antecedents, for Gladstone had spent some substantial part of his last opposition years there, borrowing a villa of Lord Aberdeen's, in what is now called Gladstone Park. Churchill however had to embrace the prospect of a sojourn in less benign circumstances. On the morning of Sunday, 8 September (1940) he had gone to look at the Dollis Hill premises before paying his famous visit to the damage in the East End. As early as 3 October the War Cabinet held a 'rehearsal' meeting in the specially constructed 'citadel' (work began just after Munich) under-neath the Post Office Engineering Section, which had been built at Dollis Hill in 1933, 'and each Minister was requested to inspect and satisfy himself about his sleeping and working apartments'. They did not like what they saw. 'We celebrated this occasion', Churchill sub-sequently wrote, 'by a vivacious luncheon, and then returned to Whitehall.'[3] Churchill, whose war memoirs are not always factually accurate, wrote that they never went back to Dollis Hill. This was not true. Another War Cabinet meeting was held there on 10 March 1941, but under the chairmanship of Attlee not of Churchill, who was incapacitated by a heavy cold. His absence no doubt accounted for his lapse of memory.[4]

In early November it was also decided to move the House of Commons from Charles Barry's neo-gothic splendours, which particu-larly with its riverside location made it one of the most easily pinpointed buildings in London. The hours of sitting had already been changed from the habitual 2.45 until late at night to 11.00 a.m. until 5.00 p.m. From 7 November the locale was also changed to Church House, the headquarters of the Anglican Church, a Herbert Baker building com-pleted only a year before, adjacent to Westminster School and facing the Abbey. It was little more than a quarter of a mile from the Palace of Westminster and much less convenient in its facilities, but was also less conspicuous, and would, it was hoped, confuse the enemy. Most MPs would probably have preferred to stay where they were, and it was the government, very much prodded by Churchill himself, who were for movement. He did not want the risk of having two or three hundred simultaneous bye-elections.

The acoustics of the Church House hemicycle were bad, and it was thought that they substantially detracted from the immediate effect of the fine *éloge* of Neville Chamberlain which Churchill delivered there on 12 November. Its ten minutes of high-flown but warm and honest phrases (not disguising his earlier disagreements with Chamberlain) were certainly a remarkable production, every word evidently flowing from his own hand.* In spite of the limitations of Church House, Churchill used its subsidiary rooms for a few meetings of the War Cabinet. He became rather addicted to a policy of unpredicted movement in this phase, for which there was indeed something rationally to be said. But it meant that his private secretaries rarely knew in advance where he was going to settle for day or night work and had constantly to be prepared to scuttle with or after him, bearing as many relevant papers as they could hope hurriedly to gather.

The spirit of (fairly) affectionate exasperation which these habits provoked was brilliantly captured by a spoof minute which John Peck (the number-three private secretary) wrote on Thursday, 31 October:

Action This Day

Private Office
　　Pray let six new offices be fitted for my use, in Selfridge's, Lambeth Palace, Stanmore, Tooting Bec, the Palladium, and Mile End Road. I will inform you at 6 each evening at which office I shall dine, work and sleep. Accommodation will be required for Mrs Churchill, two shorthand writers, three secretaries and Nelson [the cat]. There should be shelter for all, and a place for me to watch air raids from the roof.
　　This should be completed by Monday. There is to be no hammering during office hours, that is between 7 a.m. and 3 a.m.
　　W.S.C.[5]

The circumstances of his London life being so restless it was not surprising that Churchill attached almost the solemnity of a religious observance to getting away for the weekend. But there was more to it

---

* Ronald Tree (via Harold Nicolson) recorded Churchill as saying 'that was not an insuperable task, since I admired many of Neville's great qualities. But I pray to God in his infinite mercy that I shall not have to deliver a similar oration on Baldwin. That indeed would be difficult to do' (Nicolson (ed.), *Harold Nicolson: Diaries and Letters, 1939–45*, p. 129). This was unfair to Baldwin. Chamberlain did more harm and was also a less attractive and narrower personality.

than a simple escape from the reinforced beams of the No. 10 Annexe. Probably because of his unrelenting habits of work, with dictation, whether of books in peacetime or of minutes in wartime enabling him to control the whole business of running a beleaguered country, he felt it the more necessary to vary the background against which he performed this heavy duty. It was a 1930s joke that Hitler and Mussolini always attacked at the weekend because, by so doing, they caught the English of the 'locust years' on the wrong foot. But Churchill was a far more inveterate weekender than Baldwin or Chamberlain or Halifax. Furthermore, he loved an audience at meals. He was not mostly good at bilateral conversation, but with a table he could often be brilliant. And his brilliance not only amused and inspired his guests (who were frequently generals, admirals and air marshals, as well as favourite ministers and officials, family and sometimes light social relief) but also provided an essential boost to his own zest and morale. Such audiences could hardly be assembled amid the constrictions and reinforcements of his London bunkers. There he had to make do with more limited audiences, such as was reported in Eden's diary note for 25 November: 'Dined with Winston. . . . We were alone. Champagne and oysters in his bedroom.'[6]

The Friday-afternoon (occasionally Saturday-morning) departure with entourage for Chequers came to assume the importance of an essential change of gear, or to continue the motoring metaphor, recharging of the batteries. It was therefore a grave matter when Chequers, in its Buckinghamshire hollow, was held to be unacceptably vulnerable at the time of the month 'when the moon was high'. Churchill reacted to this with a characteristic mixture of decision, buoyancy and self-centredness. On the afternoon of Tuesday, 5 November he sent for Ronald Tree, Conservative MP for Market Harborough, and informed him that, on the following Friday, he would like to arrive for the weekend at Ditchley, Tree's north Oxfordshire country house, with the full apparatus of Downing Street–Chequers secretarial and communications (but not domestic) staff, and possibly a few other guests as well, and to use it on this basis on future weekends of security need. He in fact did so on a total of fifteen weekends over the next year and a half, the last being in March 1942.

Tree was flattered and amenable. He was a forty-three-year-old Anglo-American of discriminating tastes, high good manners and large fortune, the last stemming from Marshall Field, the Chicago department store. He had been a strong Edenite in the last years of the peace, opposed to appeasement, but not close to Churchill. He was currently serving as parliamentary private secretary (the lowest form of semi-ministerial life) to Duff Cooper as Minister of Information, and was not one of nature's successful politicians. Ditchley is a fine mansion, rebuilt in the 1720s by a combination of Gibb and Kent for the second Earl of Lichfield, and acquired and delicately renovated by Tree in 1935. It is about seven miles north of Blenheim, Churchill's birthplace, and thirty-five miles or so further from London than Chequers.

The Trees, despite the abruptness of the notice, were on the whole pleased at the visitations. It strained their (considerable) resources but enhanced the interest of their lives. Mrs Tree, a Virginian who was a niece of Nancy Astor's, no sycophant, and a lady with a very sharp edge of comment, wrote to Churchill after the first weekend: 'I have always been one of your greatest if most humble admirers – and I meant to tell you how delighted and honoured we all were to have you come to Ditchley. If it is convenient for you at any time to use no matter how short the notice – it is at your disposal.'[7] Churchill appeared to like Ditchley. He extended the full moon over two of those initial mid-November weekends. The house was more elegant than Chequers (which was however nearer to the style of his own Chartwell), and the food was a good deal better. It was a pity that, at the end of the war, three years after the end of the (non-)paying-guest arrangement, when Tree lost his parliamentary seat, Churchill did not give more outward signs of gratitude.

The restless movements of workplaces not only made him a less predictable target but also raised his spirits. He liked arrivals and departures, and he also enjoyed taking a mischievous attitude towards the pompous and the pious. 'I should now like', he said to Colville as they approached Chequers on the evening of Friday, 1 November, 'to have dinner – at Monte Carlo – and then go and gamble!'[8] His morale was on the whole high, partly because of his natural buoyancy, particularly when provided with his vital mealtime stimulants of food, drink and an audience. Even in more sombre moments his strategic appraisals had become moderately favourable. He thought Britain's position was much better than four or five months previously. He believed the invasion threat had receded, but was loath to say so in public in case alertness diminished. Thanks again to Colville, from the next day of that same Chequers weekend, we know that 'He now thinks the invasion is off, but that can only be because of our constant vigilance.'[9]

He also believed that Britain had taken the strain of the German bombing onslaught, and that while it was a very disagreeable national wound it was not proving fatal, either in cracking the morale of the cities or in crippling the output of the aircraft and other munitions factories. Deaths from bombing settled down at somewhere between 3,000 and 5,000 a month, a sustainable haemorrhage. Nor did he think the destruction of property was such as to render impossible the continuation of structured urban life. 'It would take ten years at the present rate for half of the houses of London to be demolished,' he told the House of Commons on 8 October. 'After that, of course, progress would be much slower.'[10]

None of this meant that he saw clearly how Britain was going to win the war – without the intervention of the United States. The only central-front offensive action to which he could look was the bombing of German cities. It was curious, and ultimately damaging, particularly in view of Britain's own robust response to German attacks, that such a weight of optimism should have been placed upon this doubtful weapon. For an explanation it is probably unnecessary to go beyond the fact that there was nothing else. Such a concentration of hope was rendered the more bizarre by the failure of a Mannheim raid on 16–17 December (1940). At a War Cabinet on 12 December it had been decided, after some hesitation, that a concerted attempt should be made to break by aerial terror the morale of a single medium-sized German city. Mannheim was chosen. The result was disappointing. The *Stadtmitte* appears to have been missed. Only fourteen German males (plus eighteen women and two children) were killed, and seven out of 200 British bombers were lost. Few lessons were learned.

Beyond Churchill's wholly understandable failure in the autumn of 1940 to see the road to victory for a British Empire without allies, there was also one avenue to defeat which still haunted him – the deadly toll of shipping losses in the North Atlantic. That was a relatively hidden threat, which did not menace the public mind in a way that did the German Panzer divisions waiting to spring from northern France or the Luftwaffe bombers droning over the major cities. It was therefore imperative that Churchill saw it with such an X-ray penetration of clarity. He best expounded it in a (4,000-word) letter which he eventually sent to the most relevant destination of Roosevelt on 8 December. He had been working on the letter for several weeks and clearly regarded it as of crucial importance. The first mention of it was as early as 26 November.

When it came it was a powerful and sobering document. The North Atlantic sinking figures were ominous:

> Our shipping losses, the figures for which in recent months are appended, have been on a scale almost comparable with the worst year of the last war. . . . Our estimate of annual tonnage which ought to be imported in order to maintain our effort at full strength is 43 million tons; the tonnage entering in September was only at the rate of 37 million tons and in October at 38 million tons. Were this diminution to continue at this rate it would be fatal. The next six or seven months bring relative battleship strength in home waters to a smaller margin than is satisfactory. *Bismarck* and *Tirpitz* will certainly be in service by January.

The counteraction of these dangers depended upon a series of actions, just short of war, by the United States. 'If, as I believe, you are convinced, Mr President, that the defeat of the Nazi and Fascist tyranny is a matter of high consequence to the people of the United States and to the Western Hemisphere, you will regard this letter not as an appeal for aid, but as a statement of the minimum action necessary to achieve our common purpose.'[11]

Gradually over the next four months, with Lend–Lease and the enforcement by the American navy of freedom of commerce up to the 26th parallel of longitude, roughly two-thirds eastwards across the Atlantic, Churchill got most of his requests. The starkness with which he exposed his fear to Roosevelt worked. It was also an indication that his mind was far from easy on all fronts as 1940 drew towards its close. There was one November and one December boost to morale. The first was a successful Fleet Air Arm attack on a concentration of the Italian navy in Taranto harbour, and the second was the victory of General Wavell, the British Commander-in-Chief in the Middle East, over the Italians on the frontier of Egypt and Libya, with the freeing of Egypt from foreign troops and the capture of Sidi Barrani and 40,000 Italian prisoners-of-war. In fact this was merely the first stroke in the game of desert ping-pong which went on until El Alamein nearly two years later, but it was Britain's first land victory in fifteen months of war. It offset the fiasco of General de Gaulle's late-September failed attempt, with British assistance, to capture Dakar in French West Africa, and it was a vindication of Churchill's nerve, for the July 1940 decision to reinforce the Middle East while Britain remained under the heavy threat of invasion had been very much his own.

Churchill showed himself a little in occasional visits of inspection during that autumn, but it was nonetheless, with the exception of his Chequers and Ditchley weekends, his most static period of the entire war. There was no France as in the early summer and no America, no North Africa, no Russia as in the later years to draw him. He went to Dover and Ramsgate on 28 August and quite enjoyed himself by coinciding with an air raid on the latter. He was much struck by the effect of bomb blast on a small hotel-keeper's livelihood and in the train on the way back dictated a demand to the Chancellor of the Exchequer for a war-damage compensation scheme.

On the afternoon of Sunday, 8 September, the day after the first serious raid, Churchill made a famous and much photographed visit to the East End. On the 15th (another Sunday), the most intense day in the Battle of Britain, he drove over from Chequers to visit Air Vice-Marshal Park at his Uxbridge headquarters of Group Eleven of Fighter Command. The Group controlled the fighter squadrons covering the whole of Essex, Kent, Sussex and Hampshire. As they watched the lights on the key indicator boards it became apparent that there were no longer any reserve squadrons left on the board, and Churchill asked Park, 'What other reserves have we?' 'There are none,' Park answered.[12] Fortunately the German planes almost immediately began to go home.

Churchill was rightly obsessed by the need for reserves. When as early as 16 May he had asked General Gamelin, 'Où est votre masse de manoeuvre?' and had received the answer 'Aucune,' he had begun to have doubts both about Gamelin and about France. And in making dispositions for the defence of southern England against invasion in July and early August he had constantly been urging the generals not just to string out a thin line of troops along the beaches, but to make sure that they had mobile concentrations of the best units available inland and near by to strike at whatever point the Germans, if they had got ashore, were most vulnerable to counter-attack.

It is in one sense not surprising that Churchill, after the strain of observing the scoreboard of this classic air battle of 15 September (even if it gave a highly inaccurate result) when he got back to Chequers at 4.30 p.m. and in his own words 'tired by the drama of No. 11 Group'[13] went to sleep until eight o'clock. Yet in another sense it is remarkable that he could so compose himself on such a day. Then, on 7 October, Churchill went late at night with General Pile, in charge of Anti-Aircraft Command, to inspect guns in Richmond Park and afterwards searchlights near Biggin Hill. They lost the way between the two, and Churchill got his small, neat feet wet in the searchlight field, so that he arrived back in Downing Street (at 4.30 in the morning) in a doubtful temper. His next expedition was more to his taste, for it involved long-distance special train travel, which he always liked. From the early evening of 22 October to the morning of 24 October he was on a Scottish trip, looking at Rosyth dockyard and inspecting in Fifeshire the Polish troops who had somewhat circuitously arrived in Britain. On 1 November he inspected, in air commodore's uniform, which never suited him, a Hurricane squadron at Northolt.

That was it for the year, but probably quite enough. He was immensely busy. Most of his work was self-generated. It was not that he had to deal with a vast mass of paper which came up to him from subordinates. It was rather that he was constantly initiating, asking why programmes were not fulfilled, why there were so many on headquarter staffs, why so many more aircraft were manufactured than found their way into front-line service, why tank design kept on changing in a way that inhibited mass production, why the Admiralty could not appreciate that Britain needed good ships quickly rather than perfect ships which became available only when the war was over, and also taking up little examples of foolish bureaucracy which he gleaned from his voracious newspaper reading. It was no doubt very good for keeping ministers and departments on their toes, and it was noticeable, which was a good sign, that those ministers who were closest to him, notably Eden as Secretary of State for War and Sinclair as Secretary of State for Air, got the sharpest and most frequent rebukes. Eden received several letters beginning with phrases like 'I am unhappy with the way the War Office handled this French business' or 'This telegram shows the dead-alive way in which the Middle East campaign is being run.' Sinclair, who was a much longer-standing (even if cross-party) friend of Churchill's was than Eden, got a more teasing but also more devastating rebuke on 29 September:

> I am very glad to find that you are as usual completely satisfied. I merely referred the Foreign Office telegram to you in order to test once more that impenetrable armour of departmental confidence which you have donned since you ceased to lead an Opposition to the Government and became one of its pillars. Either you must have been very wrong in the old days, or we must all have improved enormously since the change.[14]

The Labour ministers he left almost entirely inviolate from this sort of treatment. A. V. Alexander, as First Lord of the Admiralty, got a little of it and often exasperated Churchill, but the personal edge was taken off by nearly all Prime Ministerial minutes to him being jointly addressed to Admiral Pound, the First Sea Lord. Bevin Churchill treated with a wary respect, as in a different way he did Attlee. Even Greenwood, who had become something of a fifth wheel on the War Cabinet coach, was spared any written lash. Morrison and Dalton, neither of whom unfortunately he could bring himself to like, were two useful and efficient ministers. Of Amery, in spite (jointly with Dalton) of his great support on 28 May, he was also instinctively impatient, at first hoping to demote him from the India Office to the Ministry of Health in the December reshuffle consequent upon Halifax going to Washington. Beaverbrook at this stage he also treated with a wariness equivalent to that which he gave Bevin, although (in Beaverbrook's case) additionally warmed by fluctuatingly close old acquaintanceship and a recurrent liking (almost an addiction and disapproved of by Clementine Churchill) for his company. Churchill thought Beaverbrook had performed prodigious feats in increasing the output of Hurricanes and Spitfires, and he was made unhappy by his frequent talk of resignation.

Churchill's busyness enabled him to avoid visitors he did not want. On 8 November he produced a fine letter of firm rejection in a cloak of respect to the exiled King Zog of Albania: 'Sir, I hope I shall not be thought discourteous if I say that in present circumstances the calls on my time are too pressing for me to have the honour of seeing Your Majesty. . . . Your Majesty's obedient servant, Winston S. Churchill'.[15] He also brushed off Sir Arthur Salter and even Admiral of the Fleet Sir Roger Keyes, who was always wanting to come to Chequers. By contrast he paid full attention to the House of Commons. Between 20 August and 19 December he spoke there on twelve separate occasions. These speeches varied a great deal both in length and in content. Two, after Taranto and Sidi Barrani, were just short statements of satisfaction, but most of the others were substantial and sober appraisals of the Battle of Britain, the blitz and other prospects. They did not attempt the high oratorical flights of the summer, although the 20 August one contained the famous: 'Never in the field of human conflict has so much been owed by so many to so few'; and concluded with the comparison between the advance of Anglo-American co-operation and the flow of a great river: 'I could not stop it if I wished; no one can stop it. Like the Mississippi it just keeps rolling along. Let it roll. Let it roll in full flood, inexorable, irresistible, benignant, to broader lands and better days.'[16] Even so, Colville wrote of that speech, 'It was less oratory than usual,'[17] and Nicolson added, 'He did not try to arouse enthusiasm but only to give guidance.'[18]

What was also noticeable was the extent to which he applied himself to some at least of the routine business of leadership of the House. He did not cocoon himself in the raiment of a remote war leader who could only make epic pronouncements. He took debates on the changed time of sittings and on the move to Church House. He made the normal Prime Ministerial speech in reply to the King's opening of the new session of Parliament on 21 November, and he took the adjournment for the Christmas recess of 19 December.

He spent his first Christmas at Chequers, and allowed himself more relaxation – little work after lunch on Christmas Day – than a year before. The prospects were undoubtedly better than they had been six months earlier but he had two major continuing half-hidden worries: the inexorable toll of shipping losses in the Western Approaches and rapidly dwindling financial resources with which to pay for essential *matériel* from America. On the latter subject he was locked in delicate exchanges with Roosevelt. And then, as if to make sure that the perils of the blitz were not forgotten, large parts of the City of London (Guildhall, eight Wren churches, St Paul's Cathedral just saved) were burned out in a massive incendiary raid on the night of 30 December. So ended Churchill's *annus mirabilis*.

34

NO LONGER ALONE

IN 1941 THE EUROPEAN WAR turned into a world war, and by so doing made it strongly likely that Britain, against the odds of June and July 1940, would be on the winning side, although not as splendidly the captain of victory as its period of solitary defiance might – in its own eyes at any rate – been held to deserve. Both Russia and America were pitchforked into war, Russia's involvement being more abrupt but paradoxically coming first, for America had been teetering on the semi-brink for nearly a year. Both developments raised Churchill's spirits, although they also both gradually made him a less pivotal world figure than he had been in the second half of 1940 and the first half of 1941. He nonetheless much welcomed both events, Japan's attack on America even more than Germany's attack on Russia, despite this adding Japan to the list of enemies, and leading, over the next two months, to the infliction of some of the most terrible imperial blows which Britain ever suffered and to the worst ebb-tide in the fortunes of the Churchill war government. Nevertheless his instinctive reaction to Pearl Harbor (7 December) – 'So we had won after all!'[1] – was correct.

It was an appropriate rounding off of the year 1941 which began with Churchill devoting overwhelming attention to the fostering of Anglo-American relations. This demonstrated his capacity to recognize and concentrate upon the essential, and showed itself in the pattern of his personal life, which although in many ways self-indulgent was also intertwined with and subordinate to his greater purposes.

The outstanding example of this was his treatment of Harry Hopkins, who paid a month's visit to Britain, beginning on Thursday, 9 January 1941. Hopkins was close to Roosevelt, and it might have been expected that Churchill would have extended to him the sort of courtesy – although it might be hoped with less equivocal results – that he had extended to Sumner Welles almost a year earlier. But the attention that he paid Hopkins was of a separate order, and the results were far from equivocal. Later in the war Churchill bestowed on Hopkins the two-thirds admiring, one-third satirical title of 'Lord Root-of-the-Matter'.

This was because of his ability, when Anglo-American conferences at the highest level had become bogged down in irrelevancies, to throw a glass of clear spring water (in Churchill's own phrase about Birkenhead) in everyone's face and say, The issue we have to decide is this. Churchill, however, in early 1941 had no experience of this quality. He nevertheless decided, going as much to the heart of the matter as Hopkins ever did, that Hopkins, in a no doubt Churchill-inspired phrase of Brendan Bracken's, 'was the most important American visitor to this country we had ever had'.[2]

Superficially Hopkins was not a natural Churchill crony. He was a poor boy from Sioux City, Iowa who had spent much of his life in welfare administration. His special relationship with Roosevelt extended back at least to F.D.R.'s election as Governor of New York State in 1928. He was a social-worker liberal who was also a very competent administrator. In Roosevelt's first two years as President he was credited with having disposed of $8.5 billion (a vast sum in 1930s money) without any major scandals. He had been elevated to be Secretary of Commerce in 1938 and was even thought to have post-Roosevelt Presidential ambitions (as did many), but when his never robust health took a sharp downward turn in early 1940 he settled for an *éminence grise* role. He was at Roosevelt's elbow in the third-term election of that year, and, his second wife having died in 1937, he became so much a 'familiar' that he moved into the White House, where he married his third wife in 1943. He never regained robust health and was to die in 1946, aged fifty-six. But he never until then relinquished an indomitable desire to promote the causes in which he believed, which in harmony with the President's, thereby contributing to his great influence, switched *circa* 1940 from the defeat of poverty to the defeat of Hitler. Beyond these credentials of influence, which might have given an entrée, Hopkins quickly acquired a personal position in the Churchill court. Essentially this stemmed from the fact that, like many of those whose company Churchill most enjoyed, he was a sophisticated outsider with a touch of loucheness. He had a mordant humour, he liked gambling and racetracks, and he was easily at home in any company where the tone was not too pious. He was ill dressed with a certain style.

Churchill sent Brendan Bracken to meet Hopkins at Poole Harbour, where he arrived by flying boat from Lisbon, and bring him to London. On the Friday Churchill gave him lunch alone in the Downing Street basement room and sat with him over port and brandy until four o'clock. On the day after that Hopkins was added to the Ditchley party (for it was a full-moon weekend) and stayed two nights there. On the Tuesday evening Churchill left by special train for the far north of Scotland, taking Hopkins, Clementine Churchill, his doctor and Lord and Lady Halifax with him. The nominal purpose of the journey was to see off Halifax on his way to Washington. He was certainly being given a 'first-class funeral' as Foreign Secretary. He was also met at sea by the 'all-highest' (F.D.R.) when he arrived on the other side.

The whole party crossed to Scapa Flow and spent the night in *King George V*, the new 'state of the art' battleship whose first assignment was to convey Halifax to Chesapeake Bay. There were however two subsidiary purposes to the tour. The first was to enable Churchill to pay his first visit for nearly a year to what in First World War terms (to which his mind only too easily reverted) was known as the Grand Fleet. The second was amiably to show off to Hopkins. From this point of view the trip was admirably organized. They skipped from ship to ship in a demonstration of the might of the Royal Navy, Clementine Churchill showing herself the most nimble and Hopkins, nearly falling into the sea, the least, but as he did not do so there was no bad effect on his morale. They then returned to the mainland and travelled overnight to the central belt of Scotland, where Churchill first inspected the Inverkeithing dockyard on the Forth, then picked up Tom Johnston, Labour MP for West Stirlingshire who was currently Regional Commissioner (for civil defence) but whom Churchill was about to appoint Secretary of State for Scotland, and travelled over a train luncheon to Glasgow. The commissariat was always well looked after on Churchill trips, and Glasgow was a key point of the expedition. Not only was it the centre of 'Red Clydeside', which had given Lloyd George a lot of trouble a quarter of a century before, it was also a vital shipbuilding and munitions area, and with its downriver neighbours one of the only three port complexes – the others being the Mersey and the Bristol Channel – which could be substantially used in the increasingly desperate Battle of the Atlantic, as Churchill was to christen it two months later.

Churchill alleged he was expecting only a quiet meeting with the Lord Provost and councillors, but instead found a large crowd and a platform set up in the City Chambers which faced George Square, one of the grandest civic sites of Britain with its statues of Queen Victoria and Prince Albert, Burns and Walter Scott, Peel and Gladstone, with other more local dignitaries. Churchill had no speech prepared but belied his reputation for being unable to speak impromptu by delivering a full-length and full-throated oration. He obviously played up the symbolism of Hopkins's presence as the representative of 'his famous chief', but perhaps the most impressive aspect of this speech was that, when he was seeking without preparation to stir his audience, he also had the skill and restraint to say nothing which might embarrass Hopkins – or Roosevelt. 'We do not require in 1941 large armies from overseas. What we do require are weapons, ships and aeroplanes.'[3]

Churchill got two rewards from this visit, one quick, the other more delayed. That evening Johnston gave the party dinner in the North British Hotel. Hopkins at the end of dinner, no doubt influenced by the emotion of the day and the quality of the hospitality, but nonetheless very committingly, quoted the Book of Ruth on the future of Anglo-American relations: 'Whither thou goest I will go; and where thou lodgest, I will lodge: thy people shall be my people and thy God my God.' 'Even to the end,'[4] Hopkins added. Churchill was in tears, never too difficult a result to achieve, but on this occasion more than justifiably so.

He had got Hopkins wholly on board, and he had done it by a mixture of daring embrace and calculated attention. Both his supreme self-confidence and his instinctive concentration on the nub of the matter were at work. At Ditchley he had exposed the New Deal welfare worker to his own distinctly non-austere life and his rakish social set. Colville wrote of that first evening: 'Dinner at Ditchley takes place in a magnificent setting. The dining-room is lit only by candles, in a large chandelier and on the walls. The table is not over-decorated, four gilt candle sticks with tall yellow tapers and a single gilt cup in the centre. The food is in keeping with the surroundings. . . .'[5] The company that evening included Venetia Montagu (Asquith's old epistolatory heart-throb) and the Marquesa de Casa Maury (as Mrs Dudley Ward, King Edward VIII's mistress until he mistakenly deserted her for Mrs Simpson, had implausibly become). On this and on eleven subsequent evenings, three weekends at Chequers, another visit to Ditchley, as well as a few evenings on the train or in Scotland, he was subjected to the full-blast late-night Churchillian treatment. At Ditchley there were films – *Brigham Young* on the Saturday and *Night Train to Munich* on the Sunday until two o'clock in the morning. At Chequers the cinema was not installed until later that winter, but Churchill's late-night dissertations, in which he ranged over subjects from the progress of the war, his non-hatred of the German people, his ideas for a post-war settlement both of states and of currencies, to the evil effects on British politics of Joseph Chamberlain and Stanley Baldwin (a curious and disparate couple), filled any gaps in the entertainment. Then, having without inhibition clutched Hopkins to his social and domestic bosom, he showed him both the strength of the fleet and the strength of his own ability to deal with the Glasgow Labour baillies. And Churchill's second reward for that Glasgow day came in the form of a defiant resistance to dreadful air raids on Clydeside in mid-March, killing over a thousand and seriously damaging several shipyards. One result was that a strike was called off.

When Hopkins eventually left for home on 10 February, having stayed over twice as long as had been his original intention, he had also been taken by Churchill to Dover to see the big cross-Channel gun and to peer across to enemy-held territory and on a post-raids visit to Portsmouth and Southampton, both of which had suffered heavy damage in the last week of January. But what was above all established was a relationship of close mutual trust, and indeed companionship, between him and Churchill. Hopkins's assessment of Churchill to Roosevelt, that he was 'the directing force behind the strategy and conduct of the war in all its essentials. He has an amazing hold on the British people of all classes and groups', was everything that Churchill could have desired.[6] This provided a vital link with the President, who at this stage Churchill had never effectively met. This relationship was still confined to the exchange of transatlantic messages and to a glancing London encounter in the days of the Lloyd George government. The paradox was that the link even more than the principal became the real friend. Hopkins and Churchill were more at ease in each other's company than Roosevelt and Churchill ever were. Just how good was the Hopkins–Churchill relationship is vividly illustrated by an incident six months later when, on a return visit to Britain, Hopkins was again at Chequers on a Sunday night. Churchill would not stop talking and allow the other guests, who included Attlee and Averell Harriman, two good yawners, to go to bed. It was Hopkins who dealt with the situation, mounting a great tease of Churchill and telling him that he 'went on so' that his staff were all leaving him, Colville into the RAF and Seal (the principal private secretary) on a posting to Washington, while 'you have to give that girl of yours [the redoubtable Mrs Kathleen Hill] a medal to have her stay'.[7]

The first (January) Hopkins's visit began two new patterns in Churchill's habits which became important features in his 1941 life. Hopkins was the first swallow of an American summer. Thereafter citizens of the great Republic were a fairly constant component of the Chequers and Ditchley guest lists. Wendell Wilkie, the Republican candidate at the 1940 election, but whose combination of a pro-British position and an ability to lose made him *persona grata* with Roosevelt, was at Chequers for the second half of one of Hopkins's visits there; Hopkins tactfully left on the Saturday of Wilkie's arrival and went to stay with Beaverbrook at Cherkley. Then, at the beginning of March, Gilbert Winant, ex-Republican Governor of New Hampshire, arrived in London as the new American ambassador. There had been an interval of nearly six months since the unlamented Joseph Kennedy had departed. The interests of the US government had been in the mean-time powerfully represented by Hershel Johnson, one of those career service 'number twos' who, at intervals over many decades, have held together American diplomacy in London when the system of awarding major embassies as rewards for past campaign contributions led either to a vacuum or to inadequate appointments.

Winant, however, was neither a vacuum nor a fat cat. His public presence was formidable, partly because he looked like Abraham Lincoln and partly because he said very little, and that very slowly, which meant that full weight was placed upon the few, mostly well-chosen words which he uttered. He was staunchly pro-British, a man of quiet, unpretentious but not unnoticeable charm and by any standards a vast improvement on his Kennedy predecessor. In spite of his taciturnity (a quality that put Churchill off General Wavell), he was quickly absorbed into the Prime Minister's inner circle. It was a great advantage to be an American during that period when things were still going only too wrong in the old world and almost all hope came from 'westward, look, the land is bright'.* Winant also had the advantage of looking in any photograph a perfect representation of the reserved, almost Puritan might of WASP America. Churchill first had him to dinner at Downing Street on 4 March and then for many subsequent country weekends.

Mrs Winant was an elegant, fey and shadowy presence on some of these occasions.† The Winants' marriage, which already seemed shaky

* The words concluded two whole stanzas of 'Say Not the Struggle Naught Availeth' by the Victorian poet Arthur Hugh Clough with which Churchill ended his broadcast of Sunday, 27 April (1941). After the broadcast he telephoned Violet Bonham Carter to tell her that she had first read the poem to him over thirty years before, and that it had remained at the back of his mind ever since.
† They both came, together with the Attlees, to stay with my parents for the weekend of 12–13 July 1941. I made a point of being present. Whether as a result of this or not Winant somewhat nepotically gave me a gentle research job in his staff for the last four months before, in February 1942, the army was ready to absorb me.

in 1941, foundered in 1944. Well before this, Winant had fallen rather ethereally in love with Sarah Churchill, then in her late twenties, which helped to attract him to the Churchill family, to the British cause in general and to Chequers in particular. He was a helpful ambassador, but his look of calm asceticism concealed inner seething. He committed suicide in 1947.

Hot upon Winant's heels Averell Harriman appeared on the London scene as a Lend–Lease expeditor. Harriman was two years younger than Winant and one year younger than Hopkins. He was one of that memorable generation of American proconsuls who served the 'imperial presidency' with authority and (mostly) wisdom. General George Marshall and Dean Acheson were perhaps the epitome of the genus, but those who were in London in 1941 did not do badly. Harriman became separated from Hopkins and Winant by his longevity (he lived to ninety-four as against fifty-six and fifty-eight), but this could hardly have been foreseen in 1941. Already, however, he was somewhat differentiated by his wealth. He was the son of the railroad magnate E. H. Harriman, and had in addition before 1939 achieved his own independent fortune as a founder of the New York banking firm of Brown Brothers, Harriman. To set against this was his extreme stinginess, in little things at any rate, so that one never felt in his presence the oppression of wealth, and also the pre-eminence which he accorded to public service over the values of Mammon.

In common with Winant, he succumbed to the erotic vapours which seem to have floated over Chequers when it was the command post of the free world. Maybe it was the pressure of great events which produced such romantic tension. Just as Winant fell dreamily in love with Sarah Churchill, so Harriman fell rather less dreamily in love with Pamela Digby, since October 1939 Mrs Randolph Churchill, who when Randolph went to Cairo in January 1941 was very much an *habituée de la maison* at Chequers. Already by 17 April, after one of the worst of the London air raids, they were encountered by Jock Colville together inspecting the damage, in circumstances which were not embarrassing but which nonetheless implied a quickly developed degree of close friendship.[8] Another forty years passed before Pamela Digby and Averell Harriman were married, and there were another fifteen years after that before his death left her to be a major player in late 1980s American Democratic politics and to end up with a successful if fatal ambassadorship to Paris, the only British-born individual, let alone woman, ever to be ambassador from the one great republic to the other.

The second new pattern in Churchill's 1941 life which followed (although not necessarily because of) the first Hopkins month was a much more vigorous pattern of provincial visiting. Towards the end of 1940 Churchill had not been exactly bunkered, but, with the small exceptions noted, he had travelled little about the country. Nineteen-forty-one was to be different. On 10–12 April he went to Swansea, Bristol and Plymouth, all of which had suffered horribly from bombing, but each of which he found worse than the previous city. At Bristol he performed an act of ceremonial defiance. He had been Chancellor of the University there since 1926, but his *deus ex machina* fully robed appearance in the Wills building on the hill up to Clifton to confer honorary degrees upon Winant, Menzies (Prime Minister of Australia) and President Conant of Harvard on the morning after a very rough night of attack on the old city centre, barely a mile away, was beyond the call of cancellarian duty. There was much (successful) gesture politics about it. Nor had he omitted first to visit some of the worst of the damage. Later that same month he spent twenty-four hours in Manchester and Liverpool, and on 1–2 May he was back in Plymouth, which in relation to its size was probably the most devastated of all the provincial cities. Typically of air raids, however, it was housing and the commercial centre which suffered worse, the dockyard areas escaping relatively lightly, as had the aircraft factories of Coventry five months earlier. Then there was a pause in this series of provincial bomb-damage visits until late September, when in a single combined expedition he visited Coventry, Birmingham and, again, Liverpool.

The pattern of air raids in 1941 was that for several early months London was left in relative peace. The House of Commons went back to its traditional home on 21 January, and 10 Downing Street itself became once more the main seat of Churchill's activities. Southern and south-western cities, Portsmouth, Cardiff and Swansea, continued to suffer somewhat, but it was not until the beginning of March that a systematic concentration began upon the ports: Manchester, Liverpool, Glasgow, Hull, Plymouth, Bristol and even Belfast were the main sufferers. Some of these onslaughts were kept up for six or seven successive nights. In Liverpool, in early May for example, 3,000 were killed and 76,000 rendered homeless over a week. London immunity also ceased. There were two very heavy raids on the capital on 16 and 17 April, and on 10 May, the anniversary of Churchill becoming Prime Minister, the worst of the lot. Among much other devastation the chamber of the House of Commons was destroyed.* Its sessions had gone back to Church House on 22 April, and as in any case the destruction was in the middle of the night there was no question of a heavy bye-election fall-out. But the chamber could not be used again until its rebuilding was completed in 1950. When 10 May proved to be the sting in the tail of the blitz and paved the way to nearly three years of London peace, the Commons moved into the chamber of the House of Lords, the peers modestly retreating to the dolls-house proportions of the semi-adjacent King's Robing Room.

It was a dreadful spring for Churchill and the British war prospect. The air raids, vicious though was the last lash of this phase, were containable. The nearest they came to securing an important military objective was probably the six successive nights of Liverpool bombardment in the first week of May when 69 out of 144 berths in the docks were put out of action and the tonnage landed at this vital west-coast port was cut for a time to a quarter. At sea, however, the losses were gently subsiding, thanks largely to the Americans effectively taking over responsibility for patrolling the westward half of the Atlantic Ocean, as far east as Iceland.

Almost everywhere else, however, things went wrong. On 6 April Hitler invaded Yugoslavia and Greece. By the 13th German troops were in Belgrade, the royal family had fled and Yugoslav resistance for the remaining four years of the war became a matter of increasingly powerful groups of guerrillas. They were wracked by bitter internal dissension until the Communist forces under Tito eventually came out on top. The Greeks took until 24 April to surrender. This surrender was much more traumatic for the British than the Yugoslav one. In early March a very difficult decision had been taken by the War Cabinet to strengthen the Greeks with 55,000 British troops, who had to come from Egypt where they could ill be spared. Wavell, the Middle East Commander-in-Chief, was at first distinctly hesitant but later fully accepted the London decision. However, when semi-disaster had occurred the view persisted in the Cairo military establishment that

* Churchill had last spoken there on 7 May, when he delivered a massive and pugnacious defence of the policy of the government at a time when nearly everything was going badly. He retained an unconditional admiration for the old chamber in which he had then performed for forty years. When questioned six weeks later about rebuilding he said: 'I cannot conceive that anyone would wish to make the slightest structural alterations in the House of Commons other than perhaps some improvement in ventilation . . .' (Hansard, 5th series, vol. 372, col. 814).

Wavell had been pushed into it by the politicians and by one in particular. Churchill insisted that he had not pressurized Wavell and he had himself undoubtedly been much agitated by the difficulty of the decision. Colville found his temper strained while it was in the balance, but much improved, together with his general morale, when it had been irrevocably taken.

The improvement in morale was not long maintained. Yet another evacuation had to take place in the last days of April. Of the 55,000 British troops in Greece, approximately 12,000 were lost. Worse was the feeling that the one military (and naval) act at which the British were superior to the Germans, mainly because they had more practice, was that of evacuation. And worse still was the subsequent experience in Crete, to which 26,000 of the escaping 43,000 were transferred. It was about a month before the next evacuation from there took place. As May turned into June about 16,000 got away to Alexandria. Starting with Norway, Crete was the most chaotic and the most humiliating of the four evacuations, just as Dunkirk was the least so. Both the features are unforgettably etched in the second volume (*Officers and Gentlemen*) of Evelyn Waugh's wartime trilogy. Not only can fiction frequently be more vivid than fact, but it can also sometimes capture as much of the truth.

Two weeks later British forces suffered a heavy reverse at the hands of Rommel in the North African desert war. Churchill wrote of this as being 'to me a most bitter blow'. That day he went to Chartwell – the main house 'all shut up' – which after a long interval he visited four times in that June and early July: 'I wandered about the valley disconsolately for some hours'.[9] It was one of his lowest points of the war. The only good news he had received for some time was that of the sinking of the *Bismarck* on 27 May. The downside was the loss (with more than 1,500 men) of the *Hood*, the largest and fastest British capital ship, and some damage to the *Prince of Wales*. Nonetheless *Bismarck*, the newest and more powerful battleship in the world (why was she so far in advance of the just completed *King George V* and *Prince of Wales*?), was regarded as a prize worth almost any price. In any event naval 'victories' seem almost always to involve nearly equal destruction on both sides.

The news of the sinking of the *Bismarck* provided a dramatic if temporary lightening of Churchill's mood. Cadogan wrote on 26 May of 'a very gloomy and unpleasant Cabinet',[10] a judgement entirely confirmed in Hugh Dalton's diaries. *Hood* had gone and *Bismarck* was still at large. Churchill in a *contra mundum* mood was insisting on extending conscription to Northern Ireland, which the Ulster Unionists wanted but which nearly everybody else in the Six Counties, London and Dublin thought would be disastrously divisive – far more trouble than it was worth. At the close of this dismal day Anthony Eden wrote Churchill a very good note:

> My dear Winston
>   This is a bad day; but tomorrow Baghdad will be entered, *Bismarck* sunk. On some day the war will be won, and you will have done more than any other man in history to win it.
>   No answer
>   Yours
>   Anthony[11]

By the 27th, when the *Bismarck* was gone, the mood had been transformed. Churchill quickly gave way on Ulster conscription and announced the decision to the House of Commons in emollient terms. And at a meeting of the Defence Committee late that evening his demeanour evoked a notable tribute from Alan Brooke, who was still C-in-C Home Forces and was not to become Chief of the Imperial General Staff for another six months. As Brooke was so often sharply critical of Churchill on later occasions, it is worth quoting his words of unmitigated praise on this occasion:

> PM in great form, and on the whole a very successful meeting. It is surprising how he maintains a light-hearted exterior in spite of the vast burden he is bearing. He is quite the most wonderful man I have ever met, and it is a source of never-ending interest studying him and getting to realize that occasionally such human beings make their appearance on this earth – human beings who stand out head and shoulders above all others.[12]

Churchill's temporary benignity was such that on 8 June he dictated from Ditchley a remarkable letter to his son Randolph, who was serving in Cairo. They are commonly thought to have got on badly, Randolph often an impossible son and Churchill a frequently irritated and resentful parent. But it is difficult to think of many fathers who, under the pressures and setbacks of that early summer, would have had the wit or the energy to produce a sparkling budget of 1,200 words adequately avoiding secrets but touching on nearly everything else of current interest. Of course his matchless dictating fluency helped but it was nonetheless a weighty bit of counter-evidence to the view that he was nearly as unsuccessful a father to Randolph as Lord Randolph had been to himself. And he followed it up, a month or so later, by acting on the suggestion, which came from Randolph, of appointing Oliver Lyttelton, until then President of the Board of Trade, as resident Minister of State in Cairo and a member of the War Cabinet.

During the first half of June, after his 'alone and palely loitering' afternoon in the valley at Chartwell, Churchill showed himself to be a great generalissimo by rallying from his mood of despair not himself to resign but to sack Wavell, in whose energy he had begun to express lack of confidence as early as 6 May. It was done decisively and with finesse on 21 June, and carried the agreement of the Chiefs of Staff, and to some extent of Wavell himself. He was made to change jobs with Auchinleck, the Commander-in-Chief in India, and the switch was presented on the ground not of Wavell's incompetence or lack of martial spirit but of his tiredness after an exacting period in a post with too many commitments and too few resources. The decision was accepted with grace by Wavell, but to many others just below him it appeared a poor reward for obeying over-demanding political orders.

The further trouble was that within a few weeks of General Auchinleck taking up his new command Churchill began to find him at least as stubbornly cautious as he had thought Wavell. Churchill's other late-June Middle East appointment was the Lyttelton one, already referred to. The confidence of *General* Auchinleck may or may not have been improved by the fact that, in a post-First World War archaism, Churchill referred in all communications about the appointment of the new local political supremo to *Captain* Oliver Lyttelton. Auchinleck, however, recovered some of his own and Churchill's confidence when he was summoned to London and Chequers at the end of July and made a good impression. The two years between the early desert victories against the Italians and Montgomery's victory at Alamein were not a happy time for the Cairo command.

All this was substantially overshadowed by Hitler's 22 June attack on Russia. Churchill believed from the early spring that this was impending. On 3 April he sent a personally drafted message for Cripps, as ambassador in Moscow, to deliver direct to Stalin. He believed that it should have great impact for it was the first communication that he had sent to Stalin for nine months. Most unusually for a Churchill communication, however, its words were strangely muddied. 'I have sure information from a trusted agent . . .', it began.[13]

Part of the explanation for this opaqueness was that the 'trusted agent' was no individual on the ground but Bletchley decrypts, about the existence of which Churchill was not willing to inform Stalin. Cripps, not unreasonably, thought that the opaque message was likely to be an anti-climax after his own clearer warnings about what was happening in the Balkans and was loath to deliver it with hurry or empressement. Churchill was irritably enquiring of Eden as late as 30 April when Cripps had performed his messenger-boy service. The answer was that he had done so on 19 April, but only through Vyshinsky, the deputy Soviet Foreign Minister. Churchill was reduced to writing slightly plaintively nine years later: 'I still regret that my instructions were not carried out effectively. If I had had any direct contact with Stalin I might perhaps have prevented him from having so much of his Air Force destroyed upon the ground.'[14]

It therefore followed that when Churchill was awakened on the morning of that midsummer Sunday with the news that a German onslaught on Russia had been launched in the early eastern dawn it was no surprise to him. His immediate response was that he would deliver a major wireless address. He had had such an initiative in mind at least since his drive down to Chequers on the Friday evening, but it was nonetheless a good early-morning response after a late night that, instead of bleating, as many might have done, 'What shall I say?', he at once fixed it for nine o'clock that Sunday evening. He had already told Colville on the Saturday evening what, even as an arch anti-Communist, his policy would be: 'If Hitler invaded Hell [I] would at least make a favourable reference to the Devil.'[15] Nor was he taking great risks by doing this, for his weekend guests included the Edens and the Winants. Winant assured him that assistance to Russia would command the support of the American government, and Eden, fortified by Beaverbrook, who came to lunch on the Sunday, gave him at least two supporters in a War Cabinet which was unlikely in any event to cause trouble.

Churchill rightly devoted to the broadcast all the working hours of the day – and some of the non-working ones too, for the Crippses, not altogether fortuitously home on leave, as well as Peter Fraser, the Prime Minister of New Zealand, also came to lunch, and stayed to dinner. The use of time was correct, for the reverberations of this and similar Churchill statements were immense. It was not that he spent the day laboriously producing successive drafts, but much more that he spent it taking soundings and, his policy making always being somewhat in thrall to his love of phrases, searching for those which would be appropriate, sustained by his confidence that he could always dictate out of his head a final version when the deadline was drawing near. On this occasion Churchill cut things fine and the text was not ready until twenty minutes before the appointed time. That narrowness of margin had the advantage that Eden, who was hovering with a desire to vet, could not get his phrase-destroying hands upon it.

Churchill's introduction was: 'No one has been a more consistent opponent of Communism for the past twenty-five years. I will unsay no word that I have spoken about it. But all this fades away before the spectacle that is now unfolding. The past, with its crimes, its follies, and its tragedies, flashes away.' And its main theme was: 'We have but one aim and one single irrevocable purpose. We are resolved to destroy Hitler and every vestige of the Nazi régime. From this nothing will turn us – nothing. . . . Any man or state who fights against Nazidom will have our aid. Any man or state who marches with Hitler is our foe. . . . It follows therefore that we shall give whatever help we can to Russia and the Russian people.'[16] Harold Nicolson wrote that the broadcast was a 'masterpiece', adding with a good touch of satirical insight into Churchill's style and quality that 'he does not conceal that Russia may be beaten quickly, but having indicated to us the approaching collapse of India and China, and, in fact, of Europe, Asia and Africa, he somehow leaves us with the impression that we are quite certain to win this war.'[17]

There is no doubt that almost all informed military opinion, whether in Britain or in America, expected the Red Army to be quickly smashed by the Wehrmacht. The main uncertainty was whether it would take one month or three. Nonetheless Churchill, by the grace of God an inveterate optimist, was very cheerful both at dinner and when he went to bed that night. Colville, who almost literally tucked him up, recorded that 'the P.M. kept on repeating how wonderful it was that Russia had come in against Germany when she might so easily have been with her'.[18] Eight years later, however, Churchill wrote: 'it is right to make it clear that for more than a year after Russia was involved in the war she presented herself to our minds as a burden and not as a help'.[19] Just when the British were becoming a little better equipped, large-scale diversions of weapons and scarce raw materials took the hazardous route to Murmansk or Archangel, with heavy losses both of *matériel* and of ships. Eventually, as Churchill freely admitted, the Russians took a toll of the hitherto invincible Wehrmacht, without which the British, even in co-operation with the full weight of a vast American army, would have found it almost impossible to break Hitler's intensely fortified West Wall.

As the summer went on, and still more as the autumn brought near the dead hand of the Russian winter – worse for the invaders than for the defenders – it became apparent that the Soviet armies were doing much better than had been expected. They had evacuated immense and valuable tracts of territory, although they had narrowly held both Moscow and Leningrad. But, just as their military performance and their value as military allies exceeded expectations, so political relations proved even more deadenly sullen. The aid diverted to Russia and the efforts made to get it there were greeted with more grumbling than gratitude, and with a total unwillingness to disclose information on strategy. From the beginning there were signs that the Kremlin was inclined to take the Americans, who were not in the war, more seriously than the British, who had been there from the beginning and alone for a year. Hopkins, who at the end of July made a dangerous trip to Moscow in a British-manned but American-built bomber, was treated by Stalin, with whom he had nearly six hours of talks, with far more consideration and frankness than Cripps ever received. It was the first indication, a sinister hint of the future for Churchill, of one landmass understanding another better than the Russians could comprehend a small island which thought its 1940 wound stripes entitled it to more continuing consideration than it received.

Very soon after Britain and Russia became co-belligerents, the question of a Second Front (in France) developed into a rock of Anglo-Russian discord. 'Second Front Now' quickly became as much of a slogan as a strategy, scrawled on walls, erected into a rallying cry for Communist-organized demonstrations, and attracting the support of such figures as Lord Beaverbrook and Michael Foot,* as well as, latterly, the United States Chiefs of Staff. The terrible casualties which the Russians inflicted (and suffered) made possible an ultimate and successful Second Front. In the meantime they could not understand why the British would not immediately throw their small army across the Channel and provide some relief. Curiously this was not far off Churchill's first reaction. He was quickly playing with the idea of 25,000-strong raids into northern France, and wrote a 23 June minute with the motto 'make hay while the sun shines'.[20] Something very

---

* The left-wing editor of the *Evening Standard* and, forty years later (1980–3), the leader of the Labour party.

similar to this happened fourteen months later with the August 1942 Dieppe raid, from which the casualties, mainly Canadian troops, were appalling. Long before that, however, Churchill had become convinced that a premature full-scale assault on the French coast would result not only in pointless slaughter, but in a hurling back into the sea, which would delay for several years the hope of Allied victory. He maintained this position for three years, playing out only small bits of rope at a time, for, had he at midsummer 1941 announced June 1944 as the first date by which an Anglo-American force could land in France, Russia's suspicious frostiness would have turned itself into a contemptuous ice age.

The highlight of August 1941 was the meeting between Roosevelt and Churchill in Placentia Bay, Newfoundland. Until after the event it was naturally shrouded in secrecy. Roosevelt went on a fishing trip up the coast of Maine, and then transferred to a US cruiser to get to the rendezvous. Churchill came from Scapa Flow in *Prince of Wales*, the second of the new British battleships. He was accompanied by two of the three Chiefs of Staff, by Sir Alexander Cadogan of the Foreign Office, by a large lesser retinue, and by Hopkins, who had just got back from Russia in time to scramble aboard. One of Hopkins's several engaging qualities was that, clutching his battered hat and a small suitcase mostly filled with pills and dirty laundry, he was always just managing to catch a ship or a plane or a train or to get out of hospital to give key advice at a crucial conference. Roosevelt was accompanied by General Marshall and Admirals King and Stark, as well as by Sumner Welles, and it may be that one of the most significant results of this maritime encounter was that it was the first time that the most senior American and British commanders had met each other. Beaverbrook joined the party halfway through, flying over from London.

Still more important was the impact which Roosevelt and Churchill made upon each other. Hopkins, acting as a duenna although he did not look at all like one, had been very anxious to bring them together. Quite how well the meeting went remains open to doubt. They were another couple of great stars (although Roosevelt was a much greater one than Fisher had been), and great stars always need their own orbits. They approached the encounter with curious imbalances. Churchill needed Roosevelt at this stage more than Roosevelt needed Churchill. But it was Roosevelt who, uncharacteristically, had a slight chip on his shoulder. They had met at a large banquet in Gray's Inn in 1918.

Churchill, already a famous minister, had not taken much notice of the young Navy Assistant Secretary and subsequently forgot the encounter. Roosevelt did not. To balance this there was the indisputable fact that in joint wartime photographs, from Placentia to Yalta, Roosevelt always looked Churchill's superior. He held his head higher, and his careless yet patrician civilian clothes suited him better than the fancy uniforms which Churchill was only too inclined to assume. At Placentia Bay it was as an Elder Brother of Trinity House (Frère Aîné de la Trinité as he on one occasion explained it to an amazed French statesman) and on subsequent occasions he appeared as an air commodore or a colonel of Hussars. None of those outfits suited him nearly as well as was Roosevelt by his loose-fitting dark suits, often enhanced by a long cigarette holder at a jaunty angle. In the nicotine stakes this was a more elegant symbol than Churchill's often spittle-sodden cigars.

On the other hand Churchill was a better if somewhat more portentous talker than Roosevelt. He liked rolling periods with an attentive audience. Roosevelt was more content with quiet reminiscence or with making plans for a retirement which he was never to attain, and needed no more than a single companion (preferably Hopkins) with whom so to muse, or even, like King George V, to stick stamps into his albums – although this pastime could be seen as no more eccentric than Churchill building his walls or feeding his black swans.

There was always the slight suspicion that Churchill talked – or rather orated – too much for Roosevelt's liking, and that Roosevelt was not reliably among his best listeners. On the other hand there was the striking and obviously personally composed compliment with which the President concluded a message of thanks to Churchill for sixtieth birthday congratulations on 30 January 1942, by which time he had had plenty of time to get to know Churchill: 'It is fun to be in the same decade with you.'[21] The only offsetting consideration here is that Roosevelt was singularly effective in the calculated use of well-chosen compliments. And at that shipboard conference of August 1941, Roosevelt of his own free initiative began by providing Churchill with an audience and inviting him to perform.

Churchill arrived in Newfoundland rested and relaxed. *Prince of Wales* had sailed from Scapa Flow on the evening of Monday, 4 August and arrived in Placentia Bay on the morning of Saturday the 9th. Churchill had been more idle on the voyage than on any day since he became Prime Minister. He read C. S. Forester's *Captain Hornblower RN*, he watched several films, including seeing *Lady Hamilton* (his favourite of all wartime films) for the fifth time and he lost £7 (£175 today) playing backgammon with Harry Hopkins.

On the first day at Placentia Bay Roosevelt was host at both luncheon and dinner in his cruiser to Churchill and the senior members of the British party. Between the two meals a preliminary session of the conference took place. After dinner, Roosevelt, primed by Hopkins, had asked Churchill if he would give one of his inimitable general appreciations of the war, not a lecture but a conversational setpiece to a somewhat wider audience of about twenty-five. Churchill of course agreed, but there remains a mystery as to whether the President and the senior American staff officers, who had never heard Churchill before, got full value. The unexciting dinner menu is recorded in full detail in Robert E. Sherwood's *White House Papers of Henry L. Hopkins*,* but on the subject of what they had to drink the account is silent. The US Navy is rigidly dry. Was the rigidity for once overridden by the Commander-in-Chief out of deference to the well-known habits of the distinguished visitor? And, if not, how much of the edge was taken off his late-night performance by the unaccustomed austerity?

The next morning the American party came across to the *Prince of Wales* where a 'church militant' service was held 'under the big guns'. Churchill said that he gave personal attention to the choice of hymns – 'For Those in Peril on the Sea', also known as 'Eternal Father Strong to Save', 'Onward Christian Soldiers' and 'O God, Our Help in Ages Past' – which were sung by the whole of the ship's company. The President's party then stayed to lunch, which, whatever the position the night before, would certainly not have been teetotal.

The conference culminated in a Roosevelt-given Tuesday lunch, attended, apart from the President himself, only by Churchill, Beaverbrook (who had arrived the previous day) and Hopkins. Hopkins thought this the most satisfactory session of the lot for fostering easy relations between the two principals. This apart, not much of substance came out of this naval meeting. The British had hoped that the communiqué would contain some strong American words of warning to the Japanese. It was not that the British wanted war with Japan, but more that they were convinced that only such a warning could prevent Japanese encroachments on British territories in the Far East which would lead inevitably to this end. Roosevelt, however, was very much in

* US title *Roosevelt and Hopkins*.

a 'two steps forward, one step back' mood. The rendezvous itself amounted to a full 'two steps' ration, and he was not going to make any further military commitments which might get him into trouble at home. Nor did anything hard come out of the staff talks, which had no well-prepared agenda, beyond the beginning of an important friendship between Generals Marshall and Dill. Dill was still CIGS, but four months later he was replaced by Alan Brooke and transferred to Washington, where his good relationship with Marshall was crucial.

The Placentia Bay communiqué was therefore dominated, in a way that had not previously been intended, on the British side at any rate, by what became known as the Atlantic Charter. This was a fairly imprecise eight-point statement of war aims, which was in itself an odd although not undesirable outcome, for Churchill instinctively thought that the aim of beating Hitler was enough, and Roosevelt could be accused of putting the cart before the horse by proclaiming the aims of a war which he was still reluctant to enter. Nor did the drafting prove smooth, even with the solvent that neither side wished to be too difficult with the other. The British would not have Point Four, which was about 'access on equal terms to the trade and raw materials of the world', without the insertion of what the Americans described as the niggling point of 'with due respect for their existing obligations'. This was intended to protect the Ottawa Imperial Preference Agreements, about which Churchill, as an old Free Trader, did not vastly care. But Beaverbrook certainly did, and was able to persuade the Prime Minister that he could not give this away without the approval of all the Dominion governments which was clearly impracticable in the time-scale. The Americans reluctantly gave in.

The British (this time with Churchill in the lead) were also unhappy about Point Three, which guaranteed 'the right of all peoples to choose the form of government under which they will live'. Churchill, as he subsequently told the House of Commons, thought of this as applying primarily to the 'nations of Europe now under the Nazi yoke' and only gradually realized that it might be regarded as pre-empting decisions about independence for India and the rest of the British Empire. Equally Roosevelt was unhappy about Point Eight relating to future world security, where the British draft referred to an 'effective international organization'. Remembering Woodrow Wilson, Roosevelt shied away from a commitment to a new League of Nations. On the other hand he was very happy with just about the only suggested amendment which came from London, where Attlee, taking very seriously his acting Prime

Ministerial function and receiving the draft Charter very late at night, had called a War Cabinet after midnight and replied to Churchill at 4.00 a.m. London time. This was to add a point related to social security, improved labour conditions and economic advancement. It was enthusiastically accepted by Roosevelt, who saw it was a useful filling-in of his Freedom from Want slogan, and became Point Five. It was also agreed that there should be a September joint Anglo-American mission to Moscow. Beaverbrook was to be the British member (which was the point of his presence), but it was only later, when it became obvious that Hopkins's health was not up to another immediate arduous flight via Archangel, that Harriman (who was also present at Placentia Bay) replaced him.

Prince of Wales, escorted by American destroyers, set off on the return eastward voyage on the Tuesday evening and was already some considerable part of the way to Iceland, where a stop was made, by the time that the communiqué, and indeed the existence of the conference, was announced to the world. The British party regained Scapa Flow on Monday (18 August), having been aboard for exactly two weeks. Churchill regarded it as time very well spent, and indeed, in spite of one or two disappointments, presented the outcome as a great achievement, hinting that there was more to it than met the eye. It was about this time that he began to use his at first ambiguous V-sign. Fame rapidly overtook ambiguity.

Between Churchill's return from the Atlantic meeting and the United States entry into the war there were 112 days. Despite the warmth and semi-commitment of Placentia Bay, it would be quite wrong to think of them as days of ineluctable steps in this direction. That was Churchill's hope and maybe belief, but it was not Roosevelt's settled desire. When Hopkins lunched with him in the Oval Office on Sunday, 7 December, and the first tentative news of the Japanese destruction of the American fleet at Pearl Harbor began to come in, he recorded Roosevelt's reaction as follows: 'The President discussed at some length his efforts to keep the country out of the war and *his earnest desire to complete his administration without war* [my italics], but that if this action of Japan's were true it would take the matter entirely out of his own hands, because the Japanese had made the decision for him'.[22]

Despite this persistent uncertainty about Churchill's great prize, with the uncertainty perhaps more than he himself realized, the intervening period had not gone badly for him. The Russians had held, the prospects of getting supplies to them, at first exclusively dependent upon the

Arctic convoys with their formidable losses, had been improved by a successful and almost bloodless British–Soviet takeover of Persia in late August. The shipping losses on the North Atlantic had declined enough for that battle to seem won. The cryptographers of Bletchley had played a sufficient part in this (by giving vital information about the location of U-boats) for Churchill to feel they deserved a personal visit of congratulation on 6 September. He also overruled some bureaucratic caution to ensure that they got everything they wanted in human and other resources. They were providing him not only with vital North Atlantic intelligence but with the certain knowledge that the invasion of Britain was off for the foreseeable future, as well as major pieces on German Eastern Front dispositions, of which he was pleased to inform Stalin, while endeavouring, probably unsuccessfully, to conceal the source. And Auchinleck in Egypt, tiresomely slow though Churchill thought he had been, had at last on 15 November launched his offensive, which, ten days later, achieved the substantial although limited success of raising the siege of Tobruk, a small Libyan port which Wavell had captured in January (1941) but which had been invested by the Italians (with a few Germans) since April.

Nevertheless Churchill saw no way of winning the war without full American participation. His 'give us the tools and we will finish the job' broadcast of 9 February 1941 was a piece of tactical phrasing and not of hard truth. The most that he really meant was 'give us the tools and we will hold on long enough for you to take your time about coming in'. It was therefore a moment of unalloyed joy when he heard the news of Pearl Harbor. He was at Chequers, dining with Winant and Harriman. This was typical of the priority which he was giving to Anglo-American relations and the timing was convenient as things turned out. Ironically they had to restrain him from immediately on hearing the first sound bulletin telephoning the Foreign Office and telling them to declare war on Japan. It was pointed out that he could hardly do this on the basis of an unconfirmed news item. It contrasted with Roosevelt's greater caution (although he did not have Churchill's unfettered executive powers in matters of peace or war) which meant that America was not at war with Germany – or Italy – until four days later, when it was Berlin and Rome – not Washington – which took the initiative to involve the United States in the European war.

Churchill's more mature reaction was expressed in the phrase of solid satisfaction with which this chapter began. After December 1941, whatever the vicissitudes, he did not doubt the ultimate outcome. Of

course he regretted the severe American naval losses. But they were as
nothing compared with the gain of having the full potential might of
the United States irreversibly committed to the cause for which he had
been fighting. His whole prospect appeared transformed as he immediately began preparing his second meeting with Roosevelt, to whom he
had already spoken on the telephone that Sunday evening. This time
however he would be meeting him not just as a greatly sought-after
friend whose commitment could vary but as an ally bound by hoops of
steel. Churchill, who had a young man's enthusiasm for journeys,
therefore set off on his 12 December expedition to Washington with
exceptional buoyancy. Ironically, however, the departure, so far from
marking a move into a more benign climate, began a period when
nearly everything went wrong. In the autumn of 1941 the war had been
getting along quite nicely. Over the turn of the year and in the winter
and spring of 1942 it went from one disaster to another.

THE ANGLO-AMERICAN
MARRIAGE CEREMONY

THE MISFORTUNES, great and small, had begun before Churchill and his large party left Chequers, by special train from Windsor to Gourock at the mouth of the Clyde, and continued during the slow journey to Washington. They crossed the Atlantic in the third new British battleship, *Duke of York*, embarkation in which was a vividly sad reminder that *Prince of Wales*, their carrier on the voyage to Newfoundland four months before, was already at the bottom of the sea, sunk by Japanese aircraft together with the *Repulse* off the coast of Malaya on 9 December 1941. This, on top of the American losses at Pearl Harbor, meant that command of every ocean except for the Atlantic had been lost to the Japanese.

This sombre reflection, combined with the weather, made the *Duke of York* transatlantic crossing far less pleasurable than the previous one had been. Rough weather persisted and they were heavily battened down for most of the voyage. 'We might as well be in a submarine,' Beaverbrook was reported as complaining. And they went slowly with a lot of anti-U-boat zigzagging, taking nine days to get to Hampton Roads, at the entrance to Chesapeake Bay. 'This voyage seems very long,' was Churchill's heartfelt conclusion of a message to Eden sent on the sixth day out.[1]

Again for security reasons the Prime Minister's party were allowed only limited wireless contact with the outside world, but such news as they received did little to lighten the atmosphere. Eden was in Russia and finding it very hard going. Stalin showed no gratitude for such supplies as the Russians were receiving and no appreciation of the difficulties of getting them there or of the difficulties of mounting an immediate Second Front in France. The Soviet Union's main political demand was that Britain and America should accept for a post-war settlement its June 1941 frontiers, which would mean recognizing their swallowing of the Baltic states, its share of the new partition of Poland

and its seizing of Bessarabia from Roumania. Eden's (and Churchill's) unwillingness to endorse this was slightly eased by his ability to point out that there was no chance of the United States accepting. At the time that was no doubt true, although in 1945–6 America was to accept, and to some extent aid, a division of Europe which left the Soviet Union with an even more hegemonic position in Eastern Europe than these demands would have involved.

The other main news which came through was of a heavily deteriorating situation in Malaya, and of Hong Kong approaching its last days of resistance (capitulation came on Christmas Day). There were also wider worries. America's entry into the war, vastly beneficial though were its long-term implications, initially meant a short-term concentration on the equipment of its own forces, with a consequent diminution of supplies across the Atlantic. Accompanied by the competing claim of Russia there was a threat of the flow to Britain being temporarily cut back. This proved a false fear, for the surge of American production following Pearl Harbor created the eighth wonder of the world, so that, from Californian shipyards to Detroit motor works – converted to less benign products than Fords and Buicks – provided enough for everybody.

The next fear was that the Americans would prove dedicated to the war against Japan and lukewarm about that against Germany. This might have been a natural reaction. It was the Japanese perpetration of 'the date which will live in infamy', in Roosevelt's personally inserted phrase in his message to Congress of 8 December, which had brought America into the war. Fortunately this fear also proved false. It was F.D.R.'s priority and also the great benefit which flowed from the staff talks following Placentia Bay. The American Chiefs (including even the far from Anglophile Admiral King) accepted a basic statement of position which had been drawn up by General Marshall and Admiral Stark: 'notwithstanding the entry of Japan into the war, our view remains that Germany is still the prime enemy and her defeat is the key to victory. Once Germany is defeated, the collapse of Italy and the defeat of Japan must follow.'[2]

The American acceptance of this comforting doctrine was not known on board the *Duke of York*. Churchill and the two British Chiefs of Staff (General Alan Brooke was at home settling in at the War Office) spent much of the slow and enclosed voyage exchanging memoranda as to how they could counter a contrary position. Churchill himself, almost as indefatigably dictating as ever – a naval shorthand writer, whom he kept with him for most of the rest of the war, had been specially provided – produced three major position papers. But he also spent most of the voyage in bed, although that did not preclude considerable output, as well as watching a film every night. His favourite of 'some very good ones' was *Blood and Sand*, a famously lush bull-fighting drama of the time, with Rita Hayworth and Clark Gable. He also read another C. S. Forester novel. But he felt incarcerated and cut off from general news. 'Being in a ship in such weather as this', he wrote to Clementine on the seventh day, 'is like being in a prison, with the extra chance of being drowned. . . . No one is allowed on deck, and we have two men with broken arms and legs.'[3]

The intention had been that *Duke of York* would sail up the Potomac and that Churchill would disembark only a short motor drive from the White House. But he had grown impatient during the long, slow westward progress and insisted on disembarking at Hampton Roads, and flying the 120 miles or so to Washington. When he arrived at the new National Airport Roosevelt was sitting in his car on the tarmac, waiting to greet him. It was not only a signal honour, which no visiting head of government would today get even from a non-crippled President. It was also a necessary boost to Churchill's morale after eight days of close confinement. 'I clasped his [Roosevelt's] strong hand with comfort and pleasure,' Churchill later wrote.[4] It was the sort of reassuring gesture at which F.D.R. was brilliantly good. With it he freed Churchill from the frustrations of the voyage and immediately made him feel that his journey had been worth while. While Roosevelt had at first been hesitant about such an early visit and grand strategy conference he quickly decided it was inevitable and decided to give it the warmest possible welcome. The formal invitation to stay in the White House came through Lord Halifax while Churchill was at sea. Churchill accepted on 18 December, saying that he wished only to be accompanied by a personal retinue of five: his principal private secretary (Martin), his naval aide, two detectives and his valet. The rest of the party could stay in the Mayflower Hotel.

This honour was again signal. The visitation, which with two intervals – two and a half days for Ottawa and a week in Florida – lasted three and a half weeks, was one of the most bizarre interludes in the history of relations between heads of state and government. It remains a standing contradiction of my view, expressed in the previous chapter, that great stars are only happy in their own unimpeded orbits. The White House, the Executive Mansion as it was more demurely known in the nineteenth century, is indeed a mansion, but to insert into it a second head of government with entourage was to make conditions almost hugger-mugger. At first Churchill had intended to stay only about a week, but as his visit lengthened he became near to a real-life version of *The Man Who Came to Dinner*.* There was no indication that his welcome wore thin.

On the other hand there were some signs, from Churchill's side at least, that he was almost artificially determined to be a good guest. Of his arrival he wrote: 'Here we were welcomed by Mrs. Roosevelt, who thought of everything that could make our stay agreeable'.[5] Eleanor Roosevelt had high qualities, and was the most independently considerable figure ever to be First Lady. But to elevate her into being a cosseting hostess was straining the truth. Indeed she imposed on the White House a regime of such austerity, of both food and drink, that there are several signs that the relatively abstemious F.D.R., let alone the indulgent Churchill, was more comfortable during her frequent absences and when his daughter-in-law Betsey, later Mrs John Hay Whitney, mostly presided over the domestic arrangements.

Churchill also recalled how before the thirteen dinners and almost as many luncheons which Roosevelt and Churchill had together, always accompanied by Hopkins and sometimes by a few others, 'the President punctiliously made the preliminary cocktails himself'.[6] Franklin Roosevelt was known to mix his dry martinis (his habitual cocktail) in proportions which sophisticated drinkers regarded as unfortunate. I once heard his third son, Franklin D. Roosevelt Junior, when Under-Secretary of Commerce in the Kennedy administration, describe his parents' style to the 1960s ruling family in terms which were at once modest and grand. 'My family were not at all international smart set,' he said. 'They were just Hudson Valley gentry. They thought the right proportions for a dry martini was one-third vermouth and only two-

---

* A late 1930s play under this name achieved great success in both New York and London. Written by George S. Kaufman and Moss Hart and acted in the title role by Monty Woolley, it portrays a great talker who arrives for a meal and maybe one night, has a fall which makes him take to a wheelchair and renders him unable to depart for several weeks. The difference was that in the play it is the host who has to push the guest everywhere, whereas in the White House over Christmas and the New Year of 1941–2 it was the guest who pushed the host. 'I wheeled him in his chair from the drawing room to the lift as a mark of respect, and thinking also of Sir Walter Raleigh spreading his cloak before Queen Elizabeth,' Churchill wrote (*Second World War*, III, p. 588).

thirds gin.' Perhaps fortunately Churchill did not normally drink gin, although it is possible that, such was his desire to be a good guest, he may have subordinated his tastes to participation in the cocktail ceremony over which Roosevelt enjoyed presiding and acting as bartender.

Roosevelt was in turn anxious to be a good host and to accommodate himself to at any rate some of Churchill's habits. Hopkins wrote that 'The food in the White House was always better when Churchill was there and, of course, the wine flowed more freely'.[7] President and Prime Minister also tried to adjust to the other's sleeping patterns. Roosevelt stayed up a little later than was his usual practice. Churchill pretended to go to bed earlier than he did, but then occupied himself with a mixture of sending messages to London via the indefatigable John Martin and talking to Hopkins, whose bedroom was across the corridor, and who was nearly as much of a night owl as was Churchill. Fortunately both Roosevelt and Churchill liked being late in the mornings, so there was no clash of habits there. Roosevelt, unlike Hopkins, also had the protection of being on a lower floor.

The extended visit passed off remarkably smoothly. Churchill's original intention was to go from Washington to Ottawa to address the Canadian Parliament and to go home direct from there at the New Year. The extension to 14 January 1942, which was when he finally left the White House, was occasioned mainly by the serious work being done in the well-structured and well-prepared sessions of the Arcadia conference, as it was known, and the sessions of which were attended typically by President and Prime Minister, Hopkins and Beaverbrook and ten or a dozen senior service officers. As the two high commands engaged with each other there was surprise on the American side at the constant air of bustle on the British side, with secretaries hurrying in and out bearing the heavy red despatch boxes with which British ministers, now to the mild bemusement of their European counterparts, try to impress the world with the urgency and importance of the business of the British Empire. The British, *per contra*, were struck by the atmosphere of relative calm which pervaded the White House and how Roosevelt operated in a much more isolated way than did Churchill, but sensibly attributed this, not to lethargy, but to the secure exercise of power. Churchill, who had always been an epicentre man – with a great urge to be where the action or the power or preferably both were – was perfectly content with his long White House sojourn over the turn of the year 1941–2. He already knew that it was the one place more crucial than 10 Downing Street as the command post of the free world.

After participating in the somewhat formalized White House festivities – the lighting of the Christmas tree in the garden accompanied by speeches from the balcony on Christmas Eve and going, accompanied by the President and a vast bevy of security guards to the Foundry Methodist Church on Christmas morning, where Churchill was much struck by the hymn 'O Little Town of Bethlehem', which he had never previously heard – he had a very serious speaking engagement on 26 December, when he addressed a joint session of both Houses of Congress. (The Americans have always believed in short holidays.) The speech was a considerable success, although Churchill noted with some concern that his anti-Japanese passages were received with more enthusiasm than his anti-German ones.

That night he suffered a mild heart attack. After struggling to open a window he had a dull pain over his heart which went down his left arm and he was very short of breath. For the first time the eminent physician, Sir Charles Wilson, soon to be Lord Moran, was part of Churchill's entourage. This had the advantage that Churchill was able to consult him the next morning but the disadvantage that Moran, as his 1966 book, *Winston Churchill: The Struggle for Survival*, showed, was so anxious to give himself a central role that he was not only an indiscreet but sometimes an unreliable witness of events. He also aroused in Churchill certain natural but contradictory emotions. First, he wanted to be assured that there was nothing much wrong with him. At the same time he was constantly requiring Moran to take his pulse and working himself up into a great state about the result. Moran's initial diagnosis was that Churchill was suffering from coronary deficiency, for which 'The textbook treatment . . . is at least six weeks in bed.'[8] This did not seem a feasible proposition, so he did not forbid Churchill's train trip to Ottawa a day and a half later, or his address to the Canadian Parliament on 30 December. That speech was notable for his 'some chicken, some neck' passage, delivered with brilliant timing after he had recalled the French generals' prediction that, within three weeks of deciding to fight on alone, Britain would have 'her neck wrung like a chicken'.

On the next day Churchill gave a Canadian press conference before returning to Washington by a train which started in 1941 and arrived in 1942. (He also found time to have the most famous of all his photographs – the bulldog with a scowl – taken by Karsh of Ottawa.)

The strain of the Ottawa press conference was not heavy. He had faced a more formidable Washington one on the day immediately after his arrival from Britain and had given a classic example of how to cloak evasion in buoyancy. Was Singapore the key to the whole situation from the Far East to Australia, he was asked? With nagging doubts about the security of Singapore he replied: 'The key to the whole situation is the resolute manner in which the British and American Democracies are going to throw themselves into the conflict.' Then he was asked how long it would take to achieve victory. 'If we manage it well, it will take only half as long as if we manage it badly.'[9] He was not easy to put on to the wrong foot.

Nevertheless the effort of his Canadian trip on top of his window-opening indisposition meant that he was thought to be looking tired by the President and others, and was persuaded to go to Florida for five days' rest, to an oceanside house lent by Edward Stettinius. There was also the thought by the Americans that they did not want him to go home before the Chiefs of Staff had completed their long series of twelve full meetings and there was a detailed joint policy for endorsement by him and the President. And on Churchill's part there was the view that to be a guest in the President's house for over three weeks, interrupted only by the three-day Canadian excursion, might be over-staying his welcome.

What was the substance of the Arcadia conference? First, on the political side, there was the setting up of the United Nations, not the organization for post-war security which was established at the San Francisco conference three and a half years later, but the framework of inter-Allied co-operation for waging the war. At first the flatter term of Associated Powers had been used. The change to United Nations came at a late stage as a result of a good personal 'wheeze' of Roosevelt's. There were more complications than that. Which countries should be included and in which order should they be listed? Originally the proposal was that it should begin with the United States (that was never in dispute) then have Britain and the four British Dominions, followed by the eight governments-in-exile, with China and the Soviet Union placed after those in exile. Then adjustments were made to bring Russia and China up to third and fourth place, with the Dominions being separated and merely placed in alphabetical order among the Belgians and the Greeks, together with eight Central American states which had loyally declared war on the axis powers.

The balancing adjustment, although not one which much aroused

Churchill's enthusiasm, was that India, on the strong advice of Halifax in Washington, Linlithgow, the current Viceroy, in Delhi, and
Eden, back in London from Moscow, would be included. The attempt
to include the Free French however foundered. Roosevelt was fairly
neutral, but Cordell Hull, the Secretary of State, was passionately
anti-de Gaulle, partly because of long-term prejudice and partly on the
immediate ground that he had just seized two minor fishing islands
off the coast of Newfoundland without American permission. The
State Department's admonitory statement referred to 'the so-called
Free French'. This led to Hull receiving a blast of American press
criticism, some of which referred to 'the so-called Secretary of State'.
This should have given Churchill full warning of how much trouble
de Gaulle was likely to have with America throughout the war,
primarily with the State Department, but with Roosevelt being loath,
except very infrequently, to override his senior Cabinet officer.
Finally, however, it was the rigidity of Litvinov, re-surfaced as Soviet
ambassador in Washington, which precluded the insertion of the
words 'and authorities' after 'governments', which would have let in
the Free French.

There was also mild trouble about a draft which committed the
Russians against the Japanese, with whom they were not at war.
The Russians were more concerned with this than with a clause, on
which the Americans were keen, about freedom of religion, particularly when Roosevelt argued that this embraced freedom to have no
religion. Eventually these and other difficulties were overcome and
the declaration was ready for a signing ceremony, mostly at ambassador level, in the White House on 1 January, immediately following
Churchill's return from Ottawa. What the ceremony and the declaration did, without formal proclamation, was to accept Washington's
position as the imperial capital of the Allied war effort, although with
Stalin maintaining a semi-independent position as the Emperor of
the East.

Even so, the Arcadia conference was for Churchill the one where he
was nearest to full equality with the Americans. At Placentia Bay he had
been too eager for United States entry into the war not to be almost
sycophantically attentive. As he was reported to have put it on the
voyage out to Washington: 'Previously we were trying to seduce them.
Now they are securely in the harem.' Or, as he more primly put the
same thought to King George VI at the first of their Tuesday luncheons
together after his return: 'Britain and America were now married after

many months of walking out.'*[10] Two days before he had told the War Cabinet: 'They [the Americans] were not above learning from us, provided that we did not set out to teach them.'[11]

On one point the Americans were inclined to give the British more than they wanted. Marshall converted Roosevelt to the view that it was essential to have a unified command for the whole vast south-west Pacific area and that the single commander-in-chief over all land, sea and air forces in the region should be General Wavell. They then proceeded, with considerable help from Beaverbrook and Hopkins, to bring an initially reluctant Churchill to this position. There was a faint suspicion that, concealed within the compliment, there was (to adapt a line from 'Politics and Poker', a song in a later American musical entitled *Fiorella*) a search for 'some qualified Britisher who's willing to lose'. In addition Churchill's confidence in Wavell's dynamism was far from total, and Wavell himself accepted the burden with more duty than enthusiasm, although discharging the thankless task with dogged skill. Balancing his supremacy (of command not of military power) in that theatre was the fact that his political authority was to stem from Washington, which meant the President, in frequent consultation with the British government, less frequent consultation with the Dutch and Australian governments and operating through the Joint (Anglo-American) Chiefs of Staff. Churchill recognized this when on 19 January he sent defence-of-Singapore suggestions to Wavell, adding 'I cannot of course [now] send you any instructions.'[12]

On the other hand, the British, together with this great prize of the spontaneous US acceptance of the 'Germany first' strategy, got their plans for an Anglo-American invasion of North Africa, codenamed first Gymnast, then Super-Gymnast, and finally Torch, given a fair wind. On this they had to overcome both some persistent suspicion of 'Dardanelles Churchill' as being an irremediable 'peripherist', and the instinctive American desire, which of course marched alongside constant pressure from Russia, to go for a central assault on Germany through France. Nevertheless the North African invasion, with 90,000 troops from America and another 90,000 from Britain, was optimistically

* As early as July 1940 this weekly luncheon *à deux* had been substituted for the traditional more formal early-evening audience, for which Churchill, during the desperate June days, several times turned up late and distracted. A luncheon engagement fitted more easily into his order of priorities, offering him the opportunity to talk freely and expansively. The new pattern contributed much to the steady build-up (after a shaky beginning) of confidence between Sovereign and Prime Minister.

planned for a date as early as the spring of 1942, and actually happened in November of that year.

There was also an arrangement by which American troops would move quickly into Northern Ireland, freeing the highly trained British troops there for deployment in more active theatres. The numbers at a late session of the conference had to be cut from 16,000 to 4,100 because of shipping constraints, but the primary objects were to make an early showing of US uniforms in the United Kingdom and to impress on the Southern Irish, to whom the United States was almost as much the fount of authority as it later became to the state of Israel, that they were not backing the right side. It was a delayed substitute for the US naval visit to Berehaven for which Churchill had unsuccessfully pressed hard in the spring and summer of 1940.

The Arcadia conference also encouraged Roosevelt, who was always a man for big and bold numbers, to set what seemed extravagantly high goals for American war production in his State of the Union speech to Congress on 6 January. Aircraft output was to be increased to 60,000 in 1942 and 125,000 in 1943. Tanks were to go up to 25,000 in 1942 and 75,000 in 1943. Anti-aircraft guns were to go to 20,000 and then to 35,000. And, perhaps most crucial of the lot, merchant shipping construction was to go from 6 million tons in 1942 (compared with 1.1 million in 1941) to 10 million tons in 1943. As these boasts not only became reality but were even surpassed they contained within them a large part of the secret of Allied victory, as well as easing on the way some part of the conflicting claims for equipment of Russia, Britain and the United States itself.

Churchill therefore, when he at last departed for home on 14 January, could feel considerable satisfaction. Although there had been items of bad news while he had been in America – further Japanese advances, particularly in Malaya, discouraging intelligence about Singapore defences and a check in the Western Desert, it was nonetheless one of his high points of the war. He departed in characteristic style. That evening he dined with Roosevelt and Hopkins alone. His scheduled time of departure was 8.45, but it was 9.45 before he rose from the table. Fortunately he had a special train waiting to take him to Norfolk, Virginia. The President drove with him to a private siding at 6th Street, and Hopkins put him into his sleeping car. Roosevelt returned to the White House, and Hopkins went to the Navy Hospital, where he collapsed with exhaustion.

The next day Churchill flew in an American flying boat to Bermuda, from where the party was intended to continue in *Duke of York*. On the three-hour flight Churchill took the controls for twenty minutes or so and made several (to him) exhilarating banking turns. What his passengers, including the Chief of Air Staff, thought is not recorded. He also persuaded the captain to fly him on to Plymouth – an eighteen-hour trip – during the next afternoon and night. *Duke of York* was left to bring the junior staff and heavy baggage.

Churchill was thoroughly aware that Britain would be dour after the excitement of early-wartime Washington. 'It was to no sunlit prospect that I must return.'[13] Everything was worse than he had expected. Events, from the Far East to Egypt to the English Channel, went almost uniformly badly. And the undercurrent of criticism of his government far exceeded anything that he had experienced in its previous twenty months. On the surface at least the prospect looked as discouraging as in June–July 1940, with the added difficulty that his words no longer sparked the electric currents which they had then done. Late January, February and March of 1942 were months of crisis of confidence both for the national coalition government and for Churchill personally.

36
THE HINGE YEAR

THE TROUBLES TO which Churchill got back after his prolonged North American visit were numerous rather than precise – and some of them were hidden to his critics, although not to himself. The December 1941 loss of the two great battleships and the almost unopposed advance of the Japanese through British territories in South-East Asia produced a sour parliamentary mood. For Churchill these were more than balanced by having the United States in the war. His geo-political sense, maybe aided by his Anglo-American provenance, made him see this as out-weighing any immediate setbacks. Others, with a less grand sweep, and maybe also a little jealous of his long absence in the luxuries of the New World, were more inclined to find that after twenty months of Churchill premiership there ought to be more positive results to show. Further-more, on the Western Desert battlefield in which, although distant, Churchill had invested much personal capital, disappointment was once again setting in. And there was a feeling, by no means discouraged by the friends, whether ideological or opportunistic, of the Soviet Union, that Britain (and America) were not doing much to assist Russia.

These were the overt troubles. There were another two which were more or less privy to Churchill and a small circle. First, the Bletchley decrypts of the U-boat cipher, which had played a major part in the North Atlantic 'victory' of the second half of 1941, suddenly dried up. The Germans added a new rotor in their naval Enigma coding machines and it was nearly a year before the vital signals were again readable by the cryptographers. This meant that the shipping losses on what Churchill regarded as Britain's most dangerous flank once again mounted to levels which, over any long period, would have been unsustainable.

The second issue was still more devastating in its implications. This was Churchill's mounting apprehension that British troops did not really have the stuff of battle in them, and that, man for man, they were not as good as the Germans. The seed of this thought had been sown in him as early as Norway in April 1940. During the campaign in France it had been obscured rather than confirmed or contradicted. If the British fought indifferently, the French fought worse. The Dunkirk evacuation was well conducted but it was an evacuation and not a victory, and the relative success owed a lot to Hitler holding back and to the generalship of Alan Brooke, rather than (Calais perhaps apart) to fighting quality. Greece and Crete had not done much to contradict this dismal judgement. Singapore, which surrendered on 15 February 1942, reinforced it. But already on 11 February he had left Violet Bonham Carter, to whom he always spoke with the frankness of very old friendship, with his fear 'that our soldiers are not as good fighters as their fathers were. In 1915 our men fought on even when they had only one shell left and were under a fierce barrage. Now they cannot resist dive-bombers. We have so many men in Singapore, so many men – they should have done better.'[1] Brooke, the relatively new CIGS, took the same view. 'If the Army cannot fight better than it is doing at present we shall deserve to lose our Empire!' he confided to his diary on 18 February.[2]

Almost coincidental with the fall of Singapore there came the escape from Brest on 12 February of the two battle cruisers *Gneisenau* and *Scharnhorst*, accompanied by the less powerful cruiser *Prinz Eugen*, and their insolently successful progress in daylight up the English Channel and through the Straits of Dover to their German home ports. This was a tremendous blow to British naval prestige. 'The country is more upset about the escape of the German battleships than over Singapore,' the perceptive bell-wether Chips Channon wrote in his diaries.[3] With this combination of events Churchill's morale sank to its lowest point of the whole war, and remained there for some time.

From a parliamentary point of view he was not in obvious danger. Soon after his return from America he had insisted on having a full, three-day vote of confidence debate. He opened with a speech of two hours and wound up with one of forty-two minutes, the length of his first intervention pointing to an unusual defensiveness. He somewhat trailed his coat: 'No one need be mealy-mouthed in debate, and no one should be chicken-hearted in voting.'[4] The tone of the debate was better than he had expected. He began, a little resentfully, mainly because there had been opposition to his request for the recording of his speech in order that it might be subsequently broadcast both at home and abroad. There had been some suggestion that in wireless addresses, following debates, he, the great broadcaster, had sounded tired and hesitant. He was therefore offended by a churlish response to his request, which, he subsequently wrote, 'would not have been denied in any other Parliament in the world'. However, he restrained his anger, and gradually as the long speech wore on he could feel his words carrying increasing weight: 'They took what they got without enthusiasm. But I had the impression that they were not unconvinced by the argument.'[5] Nicolson, so often a good judge of atmosphere even though himself an ineffective politician, confirmed this: 'by the time he finishes it is clear that there is really no opposition at all – only a certain uneasiness'.[6] And Churchill himself was surprised and relieved by the tone of the following debate, which 'was to me unexpectedly friendly'.[7] When he wound up he was anxious to see a division called, in order that the strength of his support should be arithmetically on record.

Fortunately, giving a superb example of why he was a much loved (in the House) toothless revolutionary, James Maxton, the leader of the Glasgow-based Independent Labour party, performed precisely this service. He went into the 'no' lobby alone, although his two party colleagues had to function as tellers (vote-counters) to enable him to do so. Churchill was then able to have recorded a positive vote of 466 (with tellers), which was very solid, if not brilliant, in a House of 640 – but many were necessarily away on various forms of war service. It was apropos of this debate and vote that he set down with interesting precision his attitude to intensive speech preparation: 'In spite of the shocks and stresses which each day brought, I did not grudge the twelve or fourteen hours of concentrated thought which ten thousand words of original composition on a vast, many-sided subject demanded. . . .'[8]

Yet this debate and vote did not wholly clear the air. The underlying parliamentary and press sourness persisted, which was a bad foundation for sustaining the setbacks of mid-February. For the first time the possibility began to enter Churchill's mind that he had run his course and might need to be replaced for the second half of the war. As early as 21 January Eden recorded that Churchill had said over a drink with himself, Beaverbrook and A. V. Alexander (a wide spread of witnesses) following a difficult Defence Committee that 'the bulk of the Tories hated him, that he had done all he could and would be happy to yield to another'.[9] There was probably an element of self-abnegatory rhetoric about this, aided by his having a heavy cold. Maybe there was also a touch of wishful thinking on Eden's part, although it was not until a decade later that his desire to succeed became urgent. Churchill's downbeat mood continued for a some time. On 10 February, before the 'mid-month disasters', Oliver Harvey, Eden's sober-minded private secretary, told his master that 'he must be prepared to take over'. Then, on the 15th, when Churchill had responded to the dreadful pieces of news with a Sunday-night broadcast Nicolson wrote that it 'was not liked. The country is too nervous and irritable to be fobbed off with fine phrases. Yet', he fairly added, 'what else could he have said?'[10]

Criticism of Churchill's rhetoric was nonetheless devastating, for it hit him at what should have been his strongest point. It was like saying that Mozart had lost the capacity to compose or Raphael the ability to draw. If he could not rally the nation with words he was not the man that he had been in 1940. Had he also lost the ability to govern? In the first week of March Cadogan recorded that Eden agreed that 'for the last fortnight there has been no central direction of the war. War Cabinet doesn't function – there hasn't been a meeting of Defence Committee. . . . There's no hand on the wheel.'[11] And in that same week even Mary Churchill noted in her diary that her father was 'saddened – appalled by events' and 'desperately taxed'.[12]

Apart from the defeats, Churchill was also exercised by the need to accommodate Sir Stafford Cripps. On 23 January Cripps had come back from a not very successful nineteen months as ambassador to Russia. His air of asceticism seemed to symbolize the valour and self-sacrifice of Soviet resistance, although asceticism was hardly Stalin's style. Cripps in any event had got on much less well with the Soviet leader than Beaverbrook or Harriman had done. Even so he was thought to have imbibed the secret of how to wage total war. He made a powerful and widely listened-to Sunday-evening broadcast on 8 February in which he said: 'There seems to be a lack of urgency in the atmosphere of the country. It is almost as if we were spectators rather than participants.' The criticism, although quietly delivered, was potentially very damaging. Cripps was coming nearer than anyone else to challenging Churchill as the voice of the nation.

Churchill, however, claimed with some justification always to like Cripps,[13] and had already at a Chequers luncheon on 25 January invited him to join the government – as Minister of Supply. Cripps at first seemed disposed to accept, but after four days of reflection wrote a letter of polite rejection on the terms offered. There is some evidence that he was influenced by a meeting with Ernest Bevin, hardly an old friend of his in the Labour party battles of the 1930s, but a minister for whose strength Cripps (like Churchill) had developed a great respect. If so, his refusal was tied up with a current home-front turf war which was raging at the time. Churchill had got back from America to find virulent relations between Bevin and Beaverbrook, two ministers whom he valued highly, although in differing ways. Brendan Bracken and Beaverbrook, his two most cherished companions among his ministers, both had a high capacity for treading on the toes of their colleagues; Bevin's row with Beaverbrook was about the latter's attempt, as Minister of Aircraft Production, to interfere with Bevin's heartland of labour allocation. And it was Churchill's intention to promote Beaverbrook, already a member of the War Cabinet of eighteen months' standing, to be Minister of Production, which would give him some 'overlord' powers (in the nomenclature of Churchill's 1951 government) over Cripps if he became Minister of Supply. Bevin was therefore pushing at a semi-open door when he advised Cripps to turn the job down.

There were then two developments, neither of which was clearly foreseen at the end of January. First Beaverbrook, having been Minister of Production for little more than a week, had what Churchill described as a 'nervous breakdown' and insisted on resigning all his offices. Second, largely as a result of his broadcast of 8 February and of the disasters of the following week, Cripps became stronger and the government weaker. Both he and Churchill danced a little minuet. Cripps at a meeting of his Bristol constituents on the day of his broadcast replied rather teasingly to a question about his joining the government by saying, 'You had better ask Mr Churchill.' Churchill wrote to him the following day half asking him to reconsider the Ministry of Supply. Oliver Lyttelton, brought back from Cairo, would become Minister of Production. Cripps was still not tempted, but both he and Churchill were in untenable positions. In time for an announcement on 19 February Churchill moved to making Cripps an offer which he could not refuse – the leadership of the House of Commons and membership of the War Cabinet, indeed number three in its hierarchy, after only himself and Attlee.

Was this accommodation of Cripps a major domestic political defeat for Churchill, coming on top of too many military setbacks? It was the first time that anyone had successfully bargained for a higher job in his government than Churchill instinctively wanted to give him. On the other hand it could be argued that he brilliantly corralled Cripps. At a time when, for those who were thinking about a possible successor Prime Minister, Cripps looked a more likely candidate than Eden, and incomparably more so than Attlee, Churchill gave him a job of very high prestige to which his talents were singularly ill suited. Like most successful King's Counsel Cripps was good at arguing a case but he had no feel for massaging the House of Commons, and he had no party phalanx behind him. He could never have played the House along, as Churchill in a good mood could and did, as in July 1940. He was too inclined to lecture. As leader of the Commons, he enjoyed a few weeks of honeymoon and then started to go rapidly downhill.

In relation to the central direction of the war as one of the supreme seven (Greenwood had been dropped from the government and Kingsley Wood from the War Cabinet but not from the Exchequer), Cripps gained a nominal position of strong influence. But, as he had no staff to help him to engage with military problems and as his ideas were in any event imprecise, his high position was more shell than kernel. The one specific job he was given to do, which chimed well with his inclinations, ended in failure although not in ignominy. For three weeks in March–April he took to India the first offer of ultimate independence. But this was so hedged around with reservations that, although Jawaharlal Nehru was tempted, Mahatma Gandhi was not and there set in a new period of intransigence from the Congress party, the main nationalist movement.

During the summer (of 1942) Cripps carried on a profound but surprisingly good-tempered battle with Churchill. Cripps wanted a small War Cabinet of four or five which would operate independently of the Chiefs of Staff and make strategic decisions. It was essentially a throwback to the Lloyd George organization of the last two years of the First World War. Churchill would preside over this body, but would give up his special role as Minister of Defence, by which the Chiefs of Staff advised him direct and he made the decisions, which were nominally endorsed by others – Attlee, Anderson, Eden, Bevin, Lyttelton – engrossed in strategically non-central departmental work. Such a solution as Cripps proposed was utterly unacceptable to Churchill. As he wrote in *The Second World War*, admittedly nearly eight years after these difficult issues had been transcended by triumph: 'I was entirely resolved to keep my full power of war-direction. . . . I should not . . . have remained Prime Minister for an hour if I had been deprived of the office of Minister of Defence.'[14]

By the early autumn their differences had become sufficiently serious that Cripps wanted to leave the War Cabinet – he was of course also influenced by his awareness as a sensitive man that he was not making a success of his leadership of the House – but not to go in dudgeon. Churchill persuaded him to stay until the impending battle (El Alamein) in the Western Desert was over. Once that was won, however, Cripps's position was fatally weakened. He eventually left the War Cabinet on 22 November with a good grace, freely accepting instead the important but peripheral office of Minister of Aircraft Production. This was very much the equivalent in rank and power of the Ministry of Supply he had refused in late January–early February of the same year, and he served with competence until the end of the war. In this phase his parabola through the sky had been a short one.

A week later, on Churchill's sixty-eighth birthday, one of the warmest of all the messages he received was from Cripps: 'However much we may differ in outlook on certain matters it has been a great joy to me to witness your tireless work for victory. . . . May God guard and guide you in the days to come.'[15] However unlike were their characters and habits there did appear to be an approach to a bond of mutual liking and respect. Even Churchill's best-known post-war joke about Cripps – 'There, but for the grace of God, goes God' – had an undertone of affectionate admiration about it.

Gradually, as the spring of 1942 wore on, Churchill's morale and spirits began to improve. There were no triumphs, but the defeats became further away and lost their full depressive impact. And Churchill's underlying settled belief was always that an alliance founded on Britain, the United States and Russia could not lose. His short-term doubts of February–March had only been about how long victory would take and whether he was the man to see it through.

On 8 April Harry Hopkins, accompanied on this occasion by General Marshall, arrived for his third substantial London visit. They were in England for ten days. Hopkins approached the visit with all the friendly enthusiasm of 1941. 'Will be seeing you soon, so please start the fire' (a reference to his bewildering the English by finding Chequers agonizingly cold), he cabled to Churchill. And Churchill was equally pleased to see him. 'Your visits always have a tonic effect,'[16] he told him. Once again five-star treatment was organized. There was an immediate Downing Street dinner and then a Chequers weekend. Furthermore these two staunch representatives of the American republic were even given the heady experience of a day when they lunched with the King and Queen at Buckingham Palace and then dined in Downing Street where the King was, unusually, a guest. The outcome of the mission was full nominal strategic agreement between the American and British governments, with which Roosevelt, when reported to, expressed strong satisfaction.

Yet the full warmth and spontaneous gaiety of January and July 1941 seemed to be missing. Perhaps, in the terms of Churchill's January (1942) remark to King George VI the transition from walking out to marriage was having a sobering effect. Perhaps it was the presence of Marshall. Although in the testimony of both Dean Acheson and Oliver Franks (the Oxford don who became a successful British ambassador to Washington from 1949 to 1953) the General had quiet charm, he was a less digestible social morsel than Hopkins; he would not have enjoyed the company of Venetia Montagu or the Marquesa de Casa Maury. And there was more to it than that. These April talks, while dealing with matters of the highest strategic importance, give more impression of shadow boxing in the dark than any other serious Anglo-American discussion in the whole war. Hopkins and Marshall had been sent by Roosevelt to convert Churchill to the idea that the next and early Allied engagement with Germany (for the Americans it would also be their first) should take place directly across the narrow seas, with a landing somewhere between the Pas-de-Calais and the mouth of the Seine.

Roosevelt's motive was primarily to provide a relief for the Russians, the collapse of whose front in the summer of 1942 was still regarded as only too likely, and secondly to show that the Americans were not just theoretically in the European war. It was never clear, however, what was the proposed date for this onslaught. Mostly it was discussed in terms of 1943, by which time the Americans could contribute thirty divisions as against the eighteen which were expected from the British. But it might be that German success in Russia would make a Second Front urgently necessary for September 1942. If so the American contribution would be limited to five divisions (or two and a half, which was all that Alan Brooke brutally estimated would actually be available).

Yet the British, either at Prime Minister or at Chiefs of Staff level, never clearly opposed the American proposals. Indeed they expressed enthusiastic general support, without ruling out the late 1942 possibility. Still less did they suggest that it might be June 1944 before anything serious would actually happen on the Channel front. This was wise, for any such suggestion would have been execrated by the Americans, to say nothing of the Russians. Nor did any sustained attention seem to be given to the fact that a direct assault on France in late 1942, or maybe even in the spring of 1943, would mean the abandonment of Torch, the North African landings, which had been agreed at the White House New Year conference. Torch was believed to command Roosevelt's strong personal support. Furthermore it ought on the original timetable to have been already taking place by the London April talks. But it seemed to have been temporarily forgotten, although Torch did take place only seven months later.

A further paradox was that the Americans showed almost total concentration on the war against Germany. The British, ironically, tried to remind them that there was also a war against Japan, that the loss of India could not be risked, any more than could that of Egypt. If both disasters occurred there would be a fearsome prospect of the two principal enemies joining up on a southern arc. The Americans did not take too seriously the threat to India, perhaps thinking that Churchill deliberately exaggerated it in order to frustrate the giving of immediate independence. On 12 April, as the Cripps mission moved towards failure, Roosevelt sent Churchill a very rough message and got back an equally unyielding reply. India was the one area, Hopkins noted, 'where the minds of Roosevelt and Churchill could never meet'.

The next major event in Churchill's calendar was Molotov's arrival in London on 20 May. He stayed until the 28th, when he departed for Washington. To appreciate the importance of this Western tour by the dour Soviet Foreign Minister who was in later Cold War days to become known as 'the abominable no-man', it should be remembered that at this stage neither Churchill nor Roosevelt had ever met Stalin. Beaverbrook and Eden, Hopkins and Harriman had been to Moscow and had seen Stalin (as well as Molotov), but that was the limit of high-level contact between Russia and its major allies. There was indeed some jockeying between Roosevelt and Churchill as to who should be the first to receive Molotov. Roosevelt thought it would be more natural if he went first to Washington, but Stalin had already proposed a London start and stuck to the plan. Churchill telegraphed a little smugly to Roosevelt: 'You will understand that I cannot now suggest to him a change in the order of his visits.'[17] This was an early hint that in the later stages of the war there would be some Anglo-American competition about relations with the Russians.

Molotov's instructions were to sign a treaty of friendship with Britain based on a recognition of Russia's pre-invasion frontiers (that is including the Baltic states and the part of Poland seized in 1939) and to get a promise of a 1942 Second Front in France. Given that he succeeded in neither objective, his visit went remarkably amicably. Churchill, feeling defensive on other issues, was willing to give way to the Russians on the frontiers issue, but received a firm negative from Roosevelt. Eden, whose earlier diplomatic skill and courage are in danger of being obscured by his Suez disaster, then conducted a brilliant negotiation as a result of which the Russians agreed to leave the question of frontiers in abeyance in return for a twenty-year treaty. It kept both the Russians and the Americans happy and was a 'great relief' to Churchill.

On the question of an early Second Front Churchill played Molotov along, as maybe he had done Roosevelt too. As an *aide-mémoire* given to Molotov on his second London visit, after his return from Washington, put it: 'We are making preparations for a landing on the Continent in August or September 1942.... Clearly however it would not further the Russian cause or that of the Allies as a whole if, for the sake of action at any price, we embarked on some operation which ended in disaster. ... *We can therefore give no promise in the matter.*'[18]

Still more interesting were the issues raised by Molotov, the ministerial representative of an unforthcoming regime, at a 22 May meeting. They were extraordinary questions for a secretive Foreign Minister of a secretive government to pose. He first asked for the views of Churchill on the prospects of Soviet success in the campaign of 1942. Churchill naturally gave a tentative answer. Then Molotov, probing even more awkward eventualities, asked what, if the Soviet army failed to hold, would be the position and attitude of the British government. Churchill's answer was masterly:

> Hitler would in all probability move as many troops and air forces as possible back to the West, with the object of invading Great Britain. ... Therefore our fortunes were bound up with the resistance of the Soviet Army. Nevertheless, if, contrary to expectation, they were defeated, and the worst came to the worst, we should fight on, and, with the help of the United States, hope to build up overwhelming air superiority, which in the course of the next eighteen months or two years would enable us to put down a devastating weight of air attack on the German cities and industries. We should moreover maintain the blockade and make landings on the Continent against an increasingly enfeebled opposition. Ultimately the power of Great Britain and the United States would prevail.[19]

Churchill in the course of these exchanges also made, gently, a powerful dialectical point against Molotov. The Soviet land-based attitude was that a cross-Channel landing should not be much more difficult than a river crossing. Churchill reminded him that in 1940–1 when Britain stood alone (a glancing anti-Russian point) and with much of its military equipment lost at Dunkirk, Hitler had been frightened to attempt an invasion in the opposite direction.

Molotov and his party, true to the Soviet dacha tradition, wished to stay out of London. Churchill, in mid-week, made Chequers available to them, and they also stayed over the weekend when he was himself present. Although they were not treated with marked inferiority to the Americans, they were prickly English country-house guests. They kept pistols under their pillows, brought their own bed-makers, the senior cousins of those formidable ladies who sat at the end of corridors in Moscow Cold War hotels, and were very reluctant to let any normal Chequers staff near the couches of repose of their masters. Nevertheless Churchill at this stage was over-impressed by Molotov. 'The treaty was signed yesterday afternoon, with great cordiality on both sides,' he reported to Roosevelt on 27 May. 'Molotov is a statesman, and has a freedom of action very different from what you and I saw with Litvinov.'[20]

On the night of 26–27 May Rommel launched his offensive (which Churchill thought Auchinleck ought to have anticipated) against the British forces in Libya. Although the first two weeks of a fluctuating (but mostly fluctuating the wrong way) battle went by no means well, Churchill did not feel that he ought to postpone or cancel his next visit to Roosevelt, for which he had arranged to leave on 17 June. This time he went direct by flying boat from Stranraer to Washington. It was comfortable and, by the standards of the time, quick (twenty-seven hours), but the risks of these wartime flights should not be minimized. Arthur Purvis, the very effective Anglo-Canadian head of the British purchasing mission in Washington, was killed on his way to the Placentia Bay conference in August 1941 (it was a toss-up whether he or Beaverbrook took the fatal plane), and Brigadier Stewart, War Office director of plans, who was with Churchill on the Washington flight, was killed seven months later on his way back from the Casablanca conference. There were elaborate precautions but no total security for VIPs on long-distance wartime flights.

Churchill, however, found his Hudson Valley experiences more frightening than the Atlantic hazards. After a night in the British Embassy, he proceeded to a small Dutchess County airfield in New York State, where Roosevelt, temporarily at his Hyde Park house, was waiting to meet him. The President, sitting in his car, watched imperturbably as the small incoming plane made what Churchill described as 'the roughest bump landing I have experienced'.[21] But this was no worse than the subsequent drive round the estate in Roosevelt's specially converted vehicle, with no foot controls, so that everything – steering, accelerator, brakes, gears – could be done with his arms, which did not prevent the President from manoeuvring the vehicle, sometimes backwards sometimes forward, very close to the great bluffs above the strong-flowing Hudson.

Churchill claimed that despite these distractions he and Roosevelt dealt with more serious business on the drive than they would have done in a comparable time and more formal circumstances. Certainly this was true of the thirty-hour Hyde Park visit as a whole, before the presidential train took them both back to Washington on the second night. After lunch on the second day they settled the broad lines of the arrangements for Tube Alloys, as the atomic bomb project was then codenamed in Britain. On the basis of pooling all information, working together on equal terms and sharing the results, it was decided that, for reasons of convenience and security, future developments (rechristened the Manhattan Project) should be in the United States, although up to that point at least as much progress had been made in Britain as in America. At the making of this momentous but sensible arrangement – there was, it should not be forgotten, the fear that the Germans might get there first – Churchill had no serious adviser with him, which showed great self-confidence. Even Roosevelt was almost alone, although the ubiquitous if benevolent Hopkins was present at the key moment.

Churchill also disclosed to Roosevelt his Second Front hand much more frankly than he had done to Marshall and Hopkins in London in April or in subsequent cabled exchanges. The key sentence in a paper which he had prepared for Roosevelt, and around which he no doubt talked most eloquently at Hyde Park, was as follows: 'No responsible British military authority has so far been able to make a plan for September 1942 which had any chance of success unless the Germans became utterly demoralised, of which there is no likelihood.' The paper added as an almost dismissive throwaway adjunct: 'Have the American Staffs a plan? At what points would they strike? What landing-craft and shipping are available? Who is the officer prepared to command such an enterprise?' But he continued: 'Can we afford to stand idle in the Atlantic theatre during the whole of 1942? . . . . It is in this setting and on this background that the French North-West Africa operation should be studied.'[22] He graciously threw in that he would be prepared to accept, in return for a concentration upon Algeria and Morocco, the sacrifice of 'Jupiter', a scheme for the invasion of northern Norway, which he, the incorrigible old peripherist, had been fostering during the

past ten weeks or so, but for which he had mustered little support.
Almost certainly this result, which is what actually happened, had been
Churchill's desired outcome since in April he had received the news of
Roosevelt's burst of enthusiasm for some early action in the West. But
he judged it wise to pour no early cold water in case this set the
President off on a course of Pacific priority, which was what much of
American public opinion would have preferred.

On these assumptions Churchill's tactics had been highly successful.
The low morale of the late winter and early spring had not diminished
his desire or ability up to this stage to get his own way in dealings with
the major allies. These developments also illustrated why he was so
determined not to surrender, as critics in both houses of Parliament
were urging, his powers as Minister of Defence and in effect as
generalissimo. Had he done so he would have greatly weakened his
position vis-à-vis Roosevelt and Stalin, both of whom exercised these
powers in states much larger than Britain in both population and land
area.

In the event the only assault on Fortress Europe which took place in
1942 was the Dieppe raid in mid-August, when 5,000 mainly Canadian
troops were briefly put ashore in that familiar cross-Channel terminal
and inflicted some damage on German lives and installations, but with
a devastating casualty rate. Nearly 1,000 were killed and another 2,000
were taken prisoner. The main result – maybe the main purpose – of
this action was to take the edge off the mounting obstreperousness
among idle Canadian troops in the South of England and to demonstrate how difficult was a landing on a fortified coast.

After his successful talks at Hyde Park, Churchill's luck did not hold.
On the morning of 21 June he got back to Washington following a slow
overnight journey (for some obscure reason Roosevelt would not allow
the Presidential train to travel at more than thirty-five miles an hour,
which was inconvenient for the railroad companies) and installed himself
in his familiar White House room. He then received what he subsequently described 'one of the heaviest blows I can recall during the war'.
This was the news that Tobruk with a garrison of 35,000 had surrendered to a lesser force of investing Germans. The humiliation was made
worse by his receiving the news from the hand of the President. They
were sitting in the Oval Office with Hopkins and Ismay when a message
was handed to Roosevelt. 'He passed it to me without a word,' Churchill
wrote with eloquent restraint. At first he could not believe it. He had

been assured by Auchinleck that enough forces and supplies had been put into Tobruk to sustain a long siege, as it had in the previous year.

When the news was confirmed it left Churchill temporarily disorientated. The worst aspect was that it confirmed his mounting suspicion that British troops, man for man or regiment for regiment, were not as good as the Germans. 'Defeat is one thing; disgrace is another.'[23] Roosevelt was very nice. 'What can we do to help?' was his immediate comment. There was at first a suggestion that an American division might be sent out to reinforce the British in the Western Desert. Churchill's gloomy reflection must have been that, however lacking in battle experience, the Americans could hardly fight worse, and might do better, than the British had done in Tobruk. In fact it was decided that extra weapons would be more useful. Three hundred Sherman tanks and a hundred howitzers were despatched in (relatively) fast convoys.

Full of practical sympathy though Roosevelt was, the receipt of the Tobruk news inevitably weakened Churchill's position in the White House. So far from being able to teach the Americans how to make war, he was left in desperate need of support in the theatre to which he had given a high priority and in which Britain's only land victories of thirty-two months of war had been secured. Moreover the American papers were full not merely of the news of the defeat but of suggestions that it called into question the survival of the Churchill government. This was an exaggeration, although on 25 June a motion of 'no confidence in the central direction of the war' was placed on the order paper of the House of Commons in the names of a cross-party spread of several by no means negligible MPs. It meant that when Hopkins saw Churchill into his flying boat at Baltimore that night, the latter's words of farewell were reported (by Ismay) as being 'Now for England, home, and a beautiful row.'[24]

His spirits were probably not as high as this jaunty valediction implied, for the parliamentary situation which he found was the nastiest of the entire war. There were other serious voting revolts – on the Beveridge Social Security Report in February 1943, when 119 voted against the government, on equal pay for women schoolteachers in March 1944, when at first a winning 120 did so, but then on a vote of confidence only 23 persisted, and on the alleged Yalta betrayal of the non-communist Poles in February 1945, when 23 of the Conservative right went into the lobby. But none of these so directly challenged Churchill as did the July (1942) censure debate. What was at issue was his competence to run the British war effort in his own way, and, although the voting outcome was broadly satisfactory, words were uttered about him in the course of the debate which were almost as wounding as those which had brought Chamberlain down in May 1940.

The debate was set down for 1 and 2 July. By the opening day Rommel had pressed forward to a point well inside the Egyptian frontier and only forty miles from Alexandria, and eighty from Cairo. As a reverse bonus the government had managed in the previous week to lose the Malden (Essex) bye-election. It was the first of a series of bye-elections in which substantial Conservative majorities were overturned in favour of almost anyone who presented himself as a vaguely radical anti-establishment independent candidate. This one began the long parliamentary career of Tom Driberg. Distinguished a gossip columnist though he was, and bizarre tribune of the Labour left that he subsequently became, this was hardly a recompense for the Libyan defeats.

Somewhat unctuously the putative mover of the motion of censure wrote to Churchill offering to postpone it until the crisis in the Western Desert had been resolved. Churchill wrote back pugnaciously:

> I brought your letter . . . before the War Cabinet this morning, and they desired me to inform you [Churchill was always very punctilious in getting constitutional cover for his bold and firmly unilateral decisions] that in view of the challenge to the competence and authority of the Government, which had now for some days been spread throughout the world, it is imperative that the matter should go forward to an immediate issue, and for this all arrangements have been made.[25]

Churchill's tactic for the debate was that of waiting until he saw the whites of the eyes of his opponents. There was only one government speech on the first day, even though the debate ran on until the House was 'counted out' (because there were fewer than a quorum of forty members present) at 2.40 a.m.* That one ministerial speech was from Oliver Lyttelton, and was not a success. It was interrupted twenty-nine times and Lyttelton was never quick on his feet in the House of Commons. This did not much matter for Churchill was determined to give the substantive answer himself and at a time when he could be guaranteed to have the last word. Nor did he make the mistake of thinking that effectiveness was to be achieved by a superfluity of words.

---

* The House of Commons, in the absence of air raids, even though the regular hours were still 11.00 a.m. to 5.00 p.m., when given an open end quickly reverted to nightclub timing.

In January, when his morale was becoming low, he had opened a debate with a speech of two hours. In April, when it was by no means wholly recovered, he addressed a secret session for 110 minutes. In July, at the end of a more potentially dangerous debate, he confined himself to forty-five minutes. It was a good sign.

Sir John Wardlaw-Milne, Conservative MP for Kidderminster since 1922, was one of those figures that 'struts and frets his hour upon the stage and then is heard no more'. He was a Scottish accountant, in spite of his Midlands constituency, who does not appear to have been proud of his early life, for he divulged neither his date of birth nor his education to reference books. Throughout the war he was however chairman both of the Conservative Foreign Affairs Committee and of a cross-party Select Committee on National Expenditure, which gave him backbench authority. He probably thought it ought to have been recognized by transferring him from the back benches to the government front bench. He was not a natural rebel, which made his choice and willingness to lead the attack the more menacing.

His speech, however, was a fiasco. He did not dodge the issue: 'The first vital mistake that we made in the war was to combine the offices of Prime Minister and Minister of Defence.' That went straight to the heart of Churchill's most cherished prerogative. He was listened to with attention. Harold Nicolson described him as 'an imposing man with a calm manner which gives the impression of solidity'. But Nicolson quickly added, 'He is in fact rather an ass.'[26] So Milne almost equally quickly proved himself to be. He sought to relegate the Prime Minister to an even less substantial role of authority than Lloyd George had wanted for Asquith in 1916. He demanded a dominating figure to run the war and also a generalissimo to command all the armed forces. It was not clear whether Milne wanted them to be the same person, or whether he wanted two rivals constantly to trip over each other's toes. However it did not greatly matter for he turned his whole argument into bathos by nominating the Duke of Gloucester, the third son of King George V, for either or both of these jobs. To quote Nicolson again: 'A wave of panic-embarrassment passes over the House.' Gloucester was an amiable figure of fun to those who knew him. Immediately after the war he was to find the responsibility of being Governor-General of Australia too demanding for his own or Australia's tastes. The idea that he could be turned into a dominating warrior prince scuppered both his own and Wardlaw-Milne's reputations.

Churchill was almost equally lucky that the seconder of the motion

was his old friend Admiral of the Fleet Sir Roger Keyes. In 1940 Keyes
had played a crucial part in putting Churchill in. Now in his semi-
dotage it appeared that he might be eager to complete the cycle by
playing an equally crucial part in putting him out. That was to under-
estimate his loyalty. Keyes's grievance was against the Chiefs of Staff,
who he thought (rightly) had removed him from the command of
Combined Operations in October 1941. The gravamen of his speech
was therefore that Churchill ought to interfere more with the Chiefs of
Staff. As Wardlaw-Milne's main point had been exactly the opposite, it
was obvious even to the collective mind of the House of Commons that
the rebels' case was not being built up with a relentless logic. Then, at
the end of his speech, when asked a specific question from the Labour
benches about Churchill's future, Keyes was unequivocal: 'It would be a
deplorable disaster if the Prime Minister had to go.'

Then came Lord Winterton, who had been Conservative MP for
Horsham since 1904 (as, like Palmerston, he held an Irish and not a
United Kingdom peerage he was eligible for the House of Commons)
and had over these long decades been associated with Churchill on
various issues, most notably the India Bill revolt in the early 1930s. This
did not prevent his launching the most direct assault. He had entered
into a loose political partnership with Emanuel Shinwell, the ex-
Clydeside revolutionary Labour MP who had refused office (admittedly
only a parliamentary secretaryship) at the beginning of Churchill's
government, and who felt that his self-denial gave him a special right to
be a bitter critic. The improbable pair had been given the sobriquet
of 'Arsenic and Old Lace', the title of a play currently running in the
West End, and Winterton showed that, although he was supposed to
perform the old-lace role, he could also contribute a touch of arsenic.
'If whenever we have disasters we get the same answer, that whatever
happens you must not blame the Prime Minister, we are getting very
close to the intellectual and moral position of the German people – The
Führer is always right. . . . During the thirty-seven years which I have
been in this House I have never seen such attempts to absolve a Prime
Minister from ministerial responsibility. . . . We never had anything in
the last war comparable with this series of disasters.'[27] Winterton's
solution was that Churchill should surrender the premiership to one of
his colleagues – there were several suitable ones – and by 'an act of self-
abnegation' take office under him, perhaps as Foreign Secretary.
Churchill did not stay to hear this hostile speech, although curiously he
reported it at length in his war memoirs. Nicolson recorded that 'the

P.M. strolls out deliberately with bowed shoulders'[28] as soon as Winterton began. No doubt he was in search of luncheon, as it was then well past one o'clock.

The next day opened with a *tour de force* from Aneurin Bevan, the South Wales Labour MP who was emerging as a major debater and political figure, although never commanding Churchill's admiration or liking. This was one of Bevan's most memorably destructive wartime speeches, including the damaging aphorism that 'the Prime Minister wins debate after debate and loses battle after battle'. Then, after a pause, and one can easily imagine the stoop, accusatory finger and slight stutter culminating in a rush of words with which he did it: 'The country is beginning to say that he fights debates like a war and the war like a debate.' He went on to accuse the army of being 'riddled with class prejudice'. Had Rommel, he said, 'been in the British Army he would still have been a sergeant'.[29] This precise claim – the specific always makes more debating impact than the general – no doubt rang like a pistol shot around the chamber, even though it ignored the fact that Imperial Army officer-cadet Rommel of 1910 had already passed through several commissioned ranks in the First World War, quite apart from subsequently. One of Bevan's solutions was not much more sensible than Wardlaw-Milne's chosen recipes. He thought there were brilliant Czech, Polish and French generals available. Let them be placed in command of British troops, and all would be well, or at least better.

Immediately before Churchill replied, Hore-Belisha wound up for the rebels with what should have been the authority of a former Secretary of State for War. Unfortunately (from his point of view), with the fatal instinct which leads many clever men to concentrate upon their weakest point, he made much of the inferiority of British military equipment, tanks and guns, most of which had been designed under his own War Office stewardship. Churchill missed some part of what he described as 'this powerful speech', for he was still putting last-minute touches to his own oration. He did not fail, however, to exploit the flank which Hore-Belisha had left exposed. To that extent he justified Bevan's claim that 'he fights debates like a war'. For the rest his speech was not one of his best. It was more effective than memorable. He made much of the somewhat tired point that every adverse vote would be welcomed by the enemies of Britain and every addition to the majority acclaimed by its friends. But it worked. The 25 adverse votes (27 with tellers) with 477 in favour was just about in accordance with the likely figure which he had mentioned to Roosevelt and Hopkins before leaving America. Walter Elliot won Churchill's considerable approval by pointing out in the debate that twenty-five was the maximum figure that, in 1799 and the darkest days of the Napoleonic War, the opposition had been able to mount against Pitt.

Churchill had firmly repulsed the strongest parliamentary challenge to his five years of wartime leadership. But it was not a triumph. His spirits were not noticeably high after the debate. He had to wait another four months before a real transformation occurred. Even had he wanted to, he was not able just to sit waiting. On 18 July a still more powerful American politico-military delegation than that of April descended upon London. Hopkins and Marshall were fortified by the addition of Admiral King, who was no anglophile. They were still pressing for some form of invasion of France in 1942 – Sledgehammer as against Torch in the code jargon of the time. Stalin of course was pressing even harder in the same direction. Churchill, however, aided by the Chiefs of Staff and the War Cabinet, held out. He had the advantage of military logic, which eventually the Americans accepted. Churchill had the secret weapon in this dispute that Roosevelt was half on his side. Roosevelt always liked Torch. Stalin did not and sent a fairly offensive telegram on 22 July.

Churchill's response was to decide to spend much of August on a journey of great courage to Egypt and Russia. It was courageous in two senses. First, it involved appreciable hazard and serious discomfort. The relatively luxurious flying boats of the North Atlantic could not operate either to Cairo or to Moscow. The austerities of long flights in large bombers had to be endured, which would have been agreeable for nobody and certainly not for an elderly gentleman of sybaritic habits. Even the cynical Cadogan (who went with Churchill) was full of admiration. Second, and more important, there was the inherent oppressiveness of the substance of Churchill's missions. In Cairo he had crucial and possibly damaging decisions of command to make. In Moscow he had to confront 'the ogre in his den' and to bring him a distinctly unwelcome message. It was a formidable undertaking.

Churchill arrived in Cairo on the morning of 4 August and on the night of 10 August he left for Teheran and Moscow. In his last days in Cairo he visited various army units (the front had stabilized around El Alamein) and tried to appraise the morale of troops and the vigour of generals. By the evening of 7 August he had decided that Ritchie, in command of the Eighth Army, should be replaced by Gott, and that

Auchinleck, although by no means disgraced in Churchill's view, should be replaced by Alexander, who had to be snatched away from Eisenhower's team for Torch. That same evening he was told that Gott had been killed by enemy action flying into Cairo for a quiet evening's rest on the same route which Churchill's plane had followed a day before. He then appointed Montgomery in Gott's place, a further decimating of the Eisenhower team, but one which, whether by luck or judgement, created, with Alexander, Britain's first winning combination of the war.

On the night of Monday, 10 August Churchill left Cairo in a Liberator bomber for Teheran, on the first leg of his journey to Moscow. He was accompanied, apart from his own large retinue, by Averell Harriman. He had hoped to get on to Moscow by the following evening after 'a bath at Teheran' (Churchill's most urgent request at any staging post), but there was an aeronautical hold-up, so that he spent the Tuesday lunching with the Shah and sitting in a 'delightful Persian garden'. He eventually reached Moscow at 5.00 on the Wednesday afternoon, after flights of six and a half hours to Teheran and ten and a half on. He was installed in State Villa No. 7, half an hour away from the Kremlin in pine woods. He was impressed with the totalitarian lavishness of his accommodation, and particularly pleased by the plumbing and the great tank of goldfish, which he assiduously fed during his three days there. In beautiful weather he also, and more surprisingly, enjoyed lying on the lawns or on the pine needles.

His first of four long meetings with Stalin was at seven that evening. For this he was accompanied only by Harriman, Sir Archibald Clark Kerr, who had replaced Cripps as British ambassador, and an interpreter. His accompanying generals and Cadogan had failed to arrive, having had to return to Teheran with engine trouble. This first, Wednesday-evening meeting lasted three hours and forty minutes. On the Thursday evening there was a second meeting beginning at 11.00 p.m., an unpropitious hour for nearly everyone except for Churchill and Stalin, and continuing for several hours, before concluding with Stalin inviting the whole British party to dinner on the Friday. This began at the semi-Western hour of 9.00 p.m. and turned out to be a caricature of a Soviet state banquet. There were about a hundred present, including most of the Russian generals who were not at the front. It was neither a restful nor an intimate occasion. From the moment of sitting down there was a constant succession of toasts, all proposed with little speeches. In addition Stalin spent much of his time walking round the table to clink glasses with various temporarily favoured subordinates. Churchill found it rather boring, as he was frequently left with Stalin's vacant place on one side of him and an interpreter on the other. At about 1.30 a.m. Stalin suggested a film, but Churchill declined, saying that he ought to get to bed. Stalin nevertheless paid him the signal honour of accompanying him through more long Kremlin corridors and down more staircases than he was remembered as doing with any previous visitor. The honours at that stage appeared to be about even.

The fourth and last meeting was on the Saturday (15 August) and was envisaged by Churchill as a round-up bilateral (with no one else present, except for interpreters) of an hour or so. He had indeed summoned General Anders, the Polish Commander, to dine with him at Villa No. 7, but at about 8.30 Stalin, after a not particularly amicable interchange, invited him to his private Kremlin apartment 'for some drinks'. The approach to intimacy was indicated by the presence there when they arrived of Stalin's daughter, who immediately set about laying the table. The only servant was an aged housekeeper, who however was the agent for producing the build-up to an elaborate meal, for which 'some drinks' had clearly been an euphemism. The prospect of an early night (Churchill was due to fly at 5.30 the next morning), or of Anders getting dinner, further receded when Stalin, as Churchill recorded it, said 'Why should we not have Molotov? . . . There is one thing about Molotov – he can drink'.[30]

This heralded a dinner-table session of nearly five hours. At first Stalin merely 'pecked and picked' at the food, until about 1.30, which Churchill thought was his normal dinner hour, when a sucking-pig was brought in which he attacked with solitary vigour. By this time Churchill had 'a splitting headache, which for me was very unusual',[31] but he managed to make a 2.30 getaway, debrief the ambassador and others, have a bath, get to the airport, remain upright to inspect a guard of honour, clamber into the plane and be off at 5.30 for the long day's flight to Teheran. There seems no doubt that Stalin managed to upstage him in the lateness of his hours, which must have given mild pleasure to Alan Brooke and others of the party who themselves suffered a good deal from Churchill's lesser ability to turn night into day.

Such was the framework of this formidable Moscow visit. The content was on the whole rough, although sometimes confusing, for Stalin's technique was to play the roles of both the hard cop and the friendly cop, and hope by these means to intimidate and bewilder, but at the same time to seduce his adversary, even if, to complete the paradox, the adversary was in fact a necessary ally. Churchill stood up to this bombardment with remarkable tenacity, patience and strength of personality. His most exasperated response to Stalin's taunts about the lack of fighting spirit of the Royal Navy, of British soldiers and indeed of Churchill himself was: 'I pardon that remark only on account of the bravery of the Russian troops.'[32] During the second meeting Harriman, whose *métier* at the time, like Beaverbrook, was to be pro-Russian, was shocked by the 'really insulting' nature of some of Stalin's comments. 'The violence of [his] attack was stunning to the British Prime Minister, who had come so far for this discussion, and who had done so much for the Allied cause for nearly three years.'[33]

Per contra, Harriman was enormously impressed by the force and sweep of Churchill's reply. He even rated it as the most brilliant of all Churchill's wartime utterances. Alas, he was the only non-Briton present on whom it was not wasted. The interpretation was appalling for such a high-level meeting. In the first place it was done the wrong way round. Putin, Stalin's Russian interpreter, rendered his remarks into an English which, in the view of Colonel Ian Jacob, Ismay's deputy and later director-general of the BBC, 'was crude in the extreme'. Churchill's English interpreter (Dunlop) was charged with translating his Prime Minister into Russian, and missed out many of his best points. He was replaced for the last meeting. But whatever Dunlop's personal deficiencies he and Putin were charged with inappropriate tasks. At the highest level interpreters should only be allowed to interpret *into* a maternal tongue. The position was made worse by Churchill's 'brilliant' response being so animated that he could not pause at appropriate interpretation intervals.*

Churchill, however, survived even this supremely frustrating experi-ence of his oratory being wasted on the Kremlin air and appears to have impressed Stalin by his 'spirit' and force of personality even if neither the impact of his phrases nor the logic of his arguments wholly got through. They both thought the meetings had been worth while and that they had even established a limited human rapport. It would have been a pity had they not done so, for the strain on Churchill, both the physical one of the air journeys and the emotional one of the tense encounters, must have been immense. He was back in Cairo on

* The art of *chuchotage*, by which the skilled interpreter whispers almost simultaneously into the ear of the other principal a translation of the speeches, did not then seem to have been developed.

17 August. There he observed with satisfaction, after several visits of inspection, that the Alexander–Montgomery combination was tautening the military spirit. He returned to England on 21 August, after a twenty-three-day absence. Second World War excursions were nearly all surprisingly long. Alan Brooke's mixture of affection for and exasperated criticism of Churchill was well encapsulated by his sigh of relief when he saw his plane climb away from Egypt soil. He did not doubt that Churchill had done well in Russia and had improved the command structure in Cairo, but he wanted him well out of the way before the beginning of Rommel's last desert attack, which started on 30 August.

Between Churchill's return from Cairo and the Sunday morning in mid-November, when (on his instructions) the church bells of Britain rang out for the first time for two and a half years,* there were eighty-three days. They were days of hope but also of great tension for him. They were in fact the turning point of the war. Until November 1942, after thirty-eight months of hostilities, either Britain and France, Britain alone or the 'United Nations' (to use that somewhat grandiose title) were always essentially on the defensive. After that November, for the remaining thirty months of the European war, it was the Germans who were in that position, although they maintained their resistance with a military tenacity which produced many setbacks for the Allies. Churchill, in spite of his enthusiasm for campanology, was cautious rather than boastful about the turn-round. At the traditional annual banquet of the Lord Mayor of London on 10 November, moved like the sittings of the House of Commons to daylight and luncheon rather than dinner, he was famously restrained: 'Now this is not the end. It is not even the beginning of the end. But it is, perhaps, the end of the beginning.' He also used the occasion to give a hostage to fortune and even to cock a mild snook at Roosevelt, which, in less favourable circumstances, he would not perhaps have dared to do: 'I have not become the King's First Minister in order to preside over the liquidation of the British Empire.'[34]

The run-up to Alamein was not a calm time for Churchill. He quickly discovered that the American Chiefs of Staff wanted both to put off (although only for a few weeks) and to reduce the scale and scope of

---

* Early in the Churchill government they had been silenced, except in the event of invasion when their peals would give a series of linked local warnings. Churchill typically missed these familiar sounds of an English Sunday, although there is no known instance of his responding to their summons when at Chartwell.

Torch. To this he was violently opposed. To postpone from 14 October was he thought a great mistake and the proposal to confine the landings to the Atlantic shore of North Africa and to abandon the softer, more crucial and Mediterranean targets of Algiers and Oran even worse. He would have regarded any scaling down as a betrayal of the importance he had given to the operation in his August talks with Stalin. Fortunately he had on his side the British Chiefs of Staff, the relevant American commanders, Eisenhower and Mark Clark, who were already in London, and maybe his own prestige with Roosevelt, who capitulated to the British point of view in early September.

Despite his victory with Roosevelt, Churchill's spirits were still not good in September or early October. On the favourable side was Montgomery's holding of the Rommel attack which petered out between 2 and 5 September, partly through lack of fuel, which Enigma decrypts had correctly predicted. (This was the battle before which Alan Brooke had been so relieved to see Churchill fly away on 21 August; by 8 September he was complaining about Churchill's harrying of Alexander and Montgomery and the Prime Minister's 'frightful impatience to get an attack launched' before it was ready.)[35] The German offensive against southern Russia continued to prosper at least until the last week of September. The difficulties of Arctic convoys for Anglo-American supplies, about which Stalin had been so dismissive, remained formidable. The September PQ 17, as the series was designated, required seventy-seven naval escort vessels, but nevertheless lost thirteen out of its forty supply-carrying merchant ships. This level of naval commitment could not be maintained if Torch was to be launched, and in October the alternative of sending off thirteen merchant ships independently was tried. Only five arrived. Early October was the nadir. 'If Torch fails,' Churchill was recorded by Oliver Harvey as telling Eden on 1 October, 'then I'm done for and must go and hand over to one of you.'[36] By this Churchill presumably meant one of his War Cabinet colleagues. And Harvey, although never good at capturing Churchill's phraseology, was an honest and highly intelligent observer who generally got the essence of the matter right.

Then everything began to change, and did so with all the suddenness but without the frivolity of a grand transformation scene in a pantomime. From the British point of view the Battle of El Alamein was crucial. In twelve hard-fought days starting on 23 October the Eighth Army secured a decisive victory over the opposing German and Italian forces. Rommel's front was broken – he was not on the battlefield at the time, but he returned and failed to restore the position. Over 20,000 prisoners and many tanks and guns were captured. The security of Alexandria and Cairo was never again threatened and the road westward along the Mediterranean shore was opened. Most important of all, Alamein broke the losing streak of British armies, about which Churchill had begun to become obsessive. This is what gave Montgomery, with all his boastfulness, angularities and self-righteous incompatibility with the Prime Minister's habits, a continuing place in Churchill's affections.

For the Americans the outstanding event was the successful, almost unopposed 8 November Torch landings, aided by their probably sensible but uninspiring willingness to use Vichy-tainted figures, from the lightly so General Giraud to the heavily so Admiral Darlan. For the Russians the Battle of Stalingrad took pre-eminence over everything and from a geo-political point of view was the most important. The mammoth slaughter of that battle, probably the worst in the history of warfare, made El Alamein look almost like a knightly joust. There were indeed only three German division deployed at Alamein, as opposed to *circa* 190 on the Russian front.

During October the apparently relentless German advance to the Caucasus and beyond was checked. In early November the bloody battle began hesitantly to flow in the Russians' favour. By the 23rd the German forces were encircled and by January 1943 were effectively destroyed. The Russians had far more to do with the turn-round than anyone else, but what was indisputable was that when 1942 ended, the Allies, still with a long way to go, were in an incomparably better position than could have been predicted even three months before. For Churchill these victories were a vindication of his defiance of 1940 and of his strategy of 1941–2, but also the beginning of his relative decline as Hitler's dominant opponent. He had provided the crucial centre for the formation of the Grand Alliance, but historic nodality was far from a guarantee of continuing dominance.

37

1943: FROM CASABLANCA
TO TEHERAN

DURING 1943 CHURCHILL's travelling became almost frenetic, and while his impact upon Roosevelt and Stalin, and upon major commanders, British and American, in the field remained high, his detailed application to British War Cabinet business declined sharply from what it had been in 1940–41. Illness, not surprisingly in view of the various strains to which he subjected his sixty-eight-year-old body, also began to take its toll.

The first conference of the year was at Casablanca in Morocco, soon to become better known as the name of a film, and lasted for the surprisingly long span of 15–24 January. It was famous for two things. First, it proclaimed the unwise doctrine of unconditional surrender of the enemy countries. This was essentially a doctrine against a separate peace or against a Halifax-style negotiated end to the war. But it would have been better expressed, and been more enticing to disaffected opinion in enemy countries, in terms of the extirpation of the enemy regimes without the implication that their polities were to be destroyed. Second, Casablanca procured the reluctant semi-reconciliation of two French generals. Giraud was able to ease the passage of the Allies into North Africa, but, apart from this, he suffered from ambiguities of record and flatness of personality which made it inevitable that he should be a bartered bride to de Gaulle, with his bold resistance record and strong if sometimes alienating charisma. The photograph of their formal nuptials, with Roosevelt and Churchill, like determined duennas, sitting on either side, is one of the classic images of the Second World War. Giraud, to whom Lloyd George's remark, 'he was brilliant – brilliant to the tops of his boots', would have been more appropriate than it was to the dour Douglas Haig at whom it was directed, was pushed by de Gaulle out of the unhappy nest within a year.

After the formal conference Roosevelt was taken to Marrakech by Churchill, whose mind went back to his successful peacetime visit of several years before, and who wished to show the President the view of the winter sun setting over the snow-topped Atlas mountains. Churchill, and maybe Roosevelt too, was in a mood of great benignity. If Lord Moran's testimony can be believed, he said to the President: 'It's the most lovely spot in the whole world.' And then when Roosevelt had temporarily disappeared: 'I love these Americans. They behave so generously.'[1] On the following afternoon he painted his only picture of the war years. And his benignity shone eastwards as well as westwards. Stalin had telegraphed requesting detailed information about the plans for the attack upon Italy which had been decided at Casablanca. This was asking for more than reciprocity, for Stalin was never willing to tell his Western allies of his own military intentions, but Churchill nevertheless argued to Roosevelt that the request should be granted, because 'no one can keep secrets better'.[2] It was also the period when Stalin gained a reputation with Churchill for always keeping his word. It was a somewhat delayed and not long-lasting honeymoon. Churchill–Stalin relations soon began to worsen. They had heavily deteriorated within six months, although they recovered again during and immediately after the November (1943) Teheran conference.

After Marrakech Churchill flew to Cairo for four days and then proceeded, at first by air, from there to south-eastern Turkey, where, in a railway siding near Adana, his special train 'docked' with that of President Inönü. Churchill always devoted great attention, both in his thoughts and in his travels, to trying to bring Turkey into the war on the Allied side. Perhaps this was a throwback to his First World War near obsession with trying to knock it out from the Central Powers' side. In neither case was much achieved, although Churchill claimed to have been rewarded by Inönü at their next meeting with a particularly warm embrace.

From Adana Churchill went to Cyprus, where he did not do much except inspect his old 4th Hussars, and then back to Cairo before a 2,000-mile North African littoral excursion to commanders and troops ending at Algiers. There he managed briefly to shore up the the marriage between de Gaulle and Giraud. Then he flew home in his Liberator bomber, which failed to start on the planned night, but which managed to get into the air, and indeed to Wiltshire, twenty-four hours later. When he reached London by train at Paddington Station there were thirteen ministers, headed by Attlee, Eden and Bevin, on the platform to greet his Sunday-afternoon return. He had been away for twenty-six days.

That evening he presided over a War Cabinet and a few days later addressed the House of Commons. The day after that (12 February) he became ill, took to his bed in the Downing Street Annexe, and was shortly afterwards diagnosed as having pneumonia. In the early days of sulphonamides, this was by no means a negligible illness for a man of his age, although he did a lot of work in the interstices of his fever, including dictating (when his temperature was still 102°) a very interesting seven-page appraisal of the war to King George VI on 22 February.[3] On 3 March Churchill was able to remove to Chequers, but it took another twelve days before he was back and fully active in London. Thirty-one days of illness and convalescence had been added to his twenty-six days of Mediterranean absence.

It was not long before he began to contemplate another Washington visit. On 28 March Montgomery's Eighth Army breached the Mareth Line in Tunisia, which marked the beginning of the end of the North Africa campaign. The question of what next therefore became urgent. Churchill strongly believed that the Allies should invade Sicily as a quick stepping-stone towards mainland Italy, rather than follow the enthusiasm of the American Chiefs of Staff for the dead-end of Sardinia. On 4 May he embarked in the *Queen Mary* at Greenock on the Clyde, and the ship, which carried 5,000 German prisoners-of-war plus the Prime Ministerial party, sailed for New York. Cunard, however, have always been good at segregation, so there was little problem of either group obtruding upon the other. Churchill was once more in the White House by the night of 11 May.

On this third Washington visit Churchill remained in the United States for fifteen days, during which time the conference codenamed Trident took place. It was conducted mainly at Chiefs of Staff level, although there were four plenary sessions at which both President and Prime Minister were present. In a message from the *Queen Mary* Churchill had demurred at again inflicting himself upon the White House, but Roosevelt brushed this aside, and insisted that he should at least begin there, although when Roosevelt was away from Washington Churchill moved to the British Embassy for some nights. The President continued to treat his guest with great punctiliousness. He was on the railroad platform to meet him when his train arrived from New York. He took him for the first weekend to Shangri-La, as what is today Camp David, the presidential 'simple life' retreat in the Maryland hills, was then called. He encouraged General Marshall to go back across the Atlantic in Churchill's flying boat, and he went down to the Potomac to see the party away. On this visit Churchill gave another full-scale address to Congress, seventeen months after his performance of Boxing Day 1941. This was again a success (as it should have been if the report of his accompanying typing secretary that he spent nine and a half hours dictating it to her is correct), and apparently commanded the approval of the President. Roosevelt may not however have been too pleased by subsequent Congressional comment that it was only by the British Prime Minister that they were told what was going on in the war.

There were no particularly sharp Anglo-American disagreements during Trident. The nearest approach to discord was caused first by the underlying American suspicion, particularly strong in Marshall's case, that while Churchill was always theoretically in favour of the direct assault on France his real hope, as defined by Hopkins's biographer, was 'that German power could be worn down by [peripheral] attrition to the point of collapse, whereupon the Anglo-American forces in the United Kingdom could perform a triumphal march from the Channel to Berlin with no more than a few snipers' bullets to annoy them';[4] second, by the tendency on most days of Roosevelt, primed by the State Department, to register a fresh anti-de Gaulle complaint, which would, however, have been more of an irritant had Churchill himself not been at that moment almost equally disenchanted by the aloof and lanky General; and, third, by a British suspicion that the Tube Alloys agreement of the previous June on atomic weapons research was coming apart. American officials took the view that it was a sound wartime principle that information should be furnished only to those who needed to know for the furtherance of the war effort. This ran directly counter to the agreement that the British, in return for sharing their own past research, should be equal beneficiaries of future advance.

None of these, except perhaps for the last, which was fairly quickly sorted out by Roosevelt taking a more generous view than his scientists, carried the seed of a rapidly germinating major quarrel. Nevertheless there is a strong impression that Trident was not the most joyous of Anglo-American occasions. The rapture of that first Christmas encounter, or the Hyde Park and Washington visit of June 1942, even of Casablanca, was beginning to wear off. The two principals, Roosevelt and Churchill, always fully preserved the convenances but it was noticeable that even such an agent of the partnership as Hopkins was more inclined to take seriously anti-British complaints than he had been earlier. And, within a few months of Trident, Winant was complaining from London that, over the spring and summer of 1943 not only had he been kept uninformed by the White House and State Department, but he had seen Churchill on only two occasions. It was very different from the wooing of 1941.

Probably the basic cause of the waning of romance was that Roosevelt was beginning to cast surreptitious glances over his shoulder in the direction of the third principal partner, 'Uncle Joe' or even 'UJ' as Churchill and Roosevelt frequently referred to him in their correspondence; the mutual use of mocking sobriquets for a third party is not however always proof against one of the partners being tempted in that direction. Relations between the Soviet Union and the Western powers were not going at all well in the summer of 1943. The sacrifices and successes of the Red Army had made Russia, no longer a half-drowned man crying out for help as in 1941 and even up to the autumn of 1942, but a massive presence in the world power balance. At the end of June Churchill told the British ambassador in Moscow that he believed he had come to the 'end of the Churchill–Stalin correspondence from which I fondly hoped some kind of personal contact might be created between our countries'.[5] And Hopkins's biographer refers to an atmosphere in July alarmingly reminiscent of that which had preceded the Molotov–Ribbentrop Pact of August 1939.[6] Roosevelt thought that he might do better with Stalin on his own, without the encumbrance of Churchill or the formality of a full tripartite meeting. A possible July Roosevelt–Stalin bilateral in Alaska was mooted, and Harriman was sent to London to try to take the edge off Churchill's hostility to such an arrangement. He reported back to Roosevelt with more blandness than frankness: 'There is no doubt in my mind as to his [Churchill's] sincere desire and determination to back you up in anything that you finally decide to do and, although I must emphasize his disappointment if he is not present, I am satisfied he would accept it in good part and that it would in the long run improve rather than adversely effect your relations with him.'[7] Martin Gilbert was far nearer the truth when he wrote that 'Churchill replied in anguish on the following morning.'[8]

Although Churchill could not in principle object to bilateral meetings – for he had had his own with Stalin in August 1942 and no fewer than five, plus a sixth planned, with Roosevelt – he nonetheless felt that his exclusion from a Roosevelt–Stalin meeting would be a major blow. Unlike the other two, he had become known as a 'have passport, will travel' man. His absence could only be due to the fact that he had not been invited, with the implication that the bigger boys were getting together over his head. They were both, in their different ways, doubtfully mobile. In Roosevelt's case there was his personal infirmity, as well as the tradition that American Presidents in office did not absent themselves from the great quadrilateral. The experience of the only two who had defied the convention was not encouraging. Woodrow Wilson's long absences at the Paris peace talks in 1919 coincided with a great loss of authority at home; and Warren Harding's expedition to Alaska in 1923 ended in his dying in the train on the way back. Furthermore there was some rational reinforcement for the convention, in that the President must within ten days sign or veto any bill sent up to him by Congress. On his way to the Teheran conference in November 1943, Roosevelt had to deal with twenty-nine bills in Cairo – twenty-seven signed and two vetoed, as well as another four during the conference itself. There were also the dangers of the journeys, even though the United States had already come the furthest towards achieving comfort and safety in the air. Nevertheless, when Roosevelt took off from Miami on the first stage of his flight to Casablanca it was the first time he had been exposed to the hazards of flying since taking office nearly ten years before. This did not cause him apprehension: Hopkins recorded that 'he acted like a sixteen-year-old'[9] and was determined to enjoy the trip.

Stalin's immobilism, by contrast, was said to be based on a physical fear of aeroplanes, buttressed by a sullen insularity, which made him at ease only against his own background with his own phalanx of security. Even when he ventured as far as Teheran he managed to get the conference held in the compound of the Soviet Embassy. The aviation experience of both these other two was very different from that of Churchill, who had been bouncing about in planes, large and small, over mountains and seas, in peacetime and in wartime, for the previous thirty years. This gave him the fantasy that he was going to entice Stalin to join himself and Roosevelt, who was little more enthusiastic, for a session of British hospitality at Scapa Flow, Edinburgh or London. At the end of June (1943), however, so far from the prospect of such benign hostmanship on his part, he had to come to terms with the possibility of his own temporary exclusion. He handled the threat with brilliant resource, sitting down late at night immediately after the disturbing visit from Harriman to prepare a counter-proposal and to send it off straightaway to Roosevelt. He suggested a preliminary conference of Foreign Ministers to pave the way for any meeting of principals. This, together with Stalin not jumping at Roosevelt's suggestion of an Alaskan weekend, turned a nasty corner. The big meeting, when it came, five months later at Teheran, was one of three not two, and Churchill by then had been able to have yet another bilateral summit with Roosevelt at Quebec in August, and also to get the President to preliminary talks in Cairo on the way to Teheran. None-theless several disturbing hints of American–Russian bilateralism did surface at Teheran.

In the meantime Churchill reverted to his relentless urge to move-ment. Accompanied by Marshall as well as his own entourage, he proceeded (by flying boat) from the Potomac to Newfoundland, from there to Gibraltar, and then after a night with the Governor, on to Algiers. They were flights of eight and a half, seventeen and three hours, a formidable budget by any standards, although no mishaps more serious than being struck by lightning in mid-Atlantic were suffered. The flying boat was very comfortable. Churchill slept for many hours in what he described as 'the large double bed in the bridal suite', and also devoted much attention to the timing of the meals (almost certainly better than anything available in the air today), which he ordered to be served at 'stomach-time', without regard to changing time zones. He arrived in good spirits. 'I have no more pleasant memories of the war than the eight days in Algiers and Tunis,' he subsequently wrote.[10] Others thought that he looked exhausted, but this did not prevent his mind darting off within three days to the possibility of going on to Moscow before returning to London. Fortunately a combination of Anthony Eden and Alan Brooke (two of those who had noticed his tiredness) was able to scotch the idea, partly because there would not have been much to discuss when he got there

His main aim in Algiers and Tunis was gently to get his way about Allied Mediterranean strategy after the invasion of Sicily. The assump-tion was that this invasion, due to take place in early July, would fairly quickly result in full conquest. 'Gently' is appropriate because Churchill fully realized that it was no good seeking merely to impose by the force of his personality a plan upon Eisenhower and Alexander which did not carry the approval of the American Chiefs of Staff or of Roosevelt. That was the reason that he had brought Marshall along with him. But he nonetheless had a very clear view as to what should be the next step. It should be the invasion of the Italian mainland on a scale sufficient to capture Rome and knock Italy out of the war. This he added with a touch of his persistent obsession, should bring Turkey in on the Allied side. This view was quite well received by the generals, although hedged around with several ifs, and Marshall remained uncommitted to anything which might weaken the concentration upon Overlord (the plan for the invasion of France).

There were three subsidiary purposes to this Churchill visit. There was a desire to celebrate with the troops, British and American, the great victory of clearing the enemy out of North Africa. The news of this achievement had reached him on 10 May as he approached the American shore. It was a fine contrast with receiving in the White House the news of the fall of Tobruk eleven months before. He ordered the church bells of England to be rung for the second time in six months. His own celebration a few weeks later took the form of an address to a mass gathering of troops in the amphitheatre at Carthage. The acoustics and the response appear to have been good. He thought the applause was as enthusiastic as would have been received by the victorious gladiators of 2,000 years before.

Then there was the business of putting some conjugality into the reluctant reconciliation which de Gaulle and Giraud had accepted at Casablanca. Progress was made at a meeting which culminated in a convivial luncheon on 4 June, even though de Gaulle was normally more than proof against such seductions. There was a feast of oratory. Churchill spoke in French ('an excellent speech', according to the critical pen of the nearly bilingual Alan Brooke), and was followed by Giraud, de Gaulle, Eden, whom Churchill had summoned from London to join the party, and General Georges, Churchill's friend of 1938–40, who had turned up in Algiers after some vicissitudes, and whose mind perhaps went back to his last 'immensely enjoyable' Paris luncheon with Churchill at Lapérousse in the spring of 1940. The setting up of the French Committee of National Liberation, on which de Gaulle had only two out of seven representatives, but with himself plus one proving more than a match for the other five, was a considerable achievement, although there was perhaps a note of warning in Churchill's comment to Roosevelt that this 'brings to an end my official connection with de Gaulle as leader of the Fighting French which was set out in the letters exchanged with him in 1940'.[11] And last, but not least, Churchill greatly enjoyed the sea-bathing on the Algerian shore. There was a certain porpoise-like quality about him, which meant that one of his keenest physical pleasures, second only to alcohol, was submerging himself in either hot bathwater or lukewarm seawater.

He wrote that he would have liked to stay another week, but he felt that he must reluctantly subject himself to London duty. He had been away for another full month. He flew back on the night of 4–5 June

(1943). The journey was without incident, except that the weather at Gibraltar was too bad for the intended transfer to the more comfortable flying boat, so that he had to continue by bomber. Later that same day however another Pan American flying boat did take off from Lisbon for Plymouth and was shot down with the deaths of a full load of passengers, including Leslie Howard of *Scarlet Pimpernel* fame. In the same month a Liberator bomber (a companion to Churchill's plane) flying from Gibraltar to England was also shot down, with the death of General Sikorski, the head of the Polish forces, and two accompanying British MPs. The cumulative risk to which Churchill's manifold journeys exposed him, even with the closest protection, can hardly, taking the war as a whole, have been less than 30 per cent.

Back in London he immediately presided over a Sunday-noon meeting of the War Cabinet and then made a Wednesday statement to the House of Commons. Both gatherings welcomed him, although there was becoming a touch of 'Prime Minister visits Britain' about his pattern. Nicolson, as usual a perceptive and friendly but not hagiographic parliamentary critic, thought his speech understated, but 'I think the House liked it better even than his most triumphant oratory. It was so eminently strong, powerful, sincere and confident.'[12]

That summer was marked by the launch of the last German offensive on the Eastern Front on 5 July and by the successful Anglo-American invasion of Sicily on the 9th. This was soon followed by King Victor Emmanuel's dismissal of Mussolini (25 July) and by his appointment of Marshal Badoglio in his place. Badoglio at once opened negotiations with the Allies, and these led to an armistice on 7 September and an immediate German offensive against Italy. In early July Churchill had got his way that it should be Sicily and not Sardinia which should be the object of the first engagement of American troops in Europe. Differences nonetheless persisted between London and Washington about where, after the conquest of Sicily (which was achieved by 17 August) the weight of Allied effort should be directed. Churchill wanted to drive straight up the Italian peninsula with the capture of Rome as an early and essential objective. Although he was always willing to spare a few divisions for eastern Mediterranean activity, whether in the Balkans or for the capture of the island of Rhodes, he remained unhappy about the planned withdrawal of seven divisions – four American and three British – from the force available for Italy in order to build up the strength available in England for a 1944 Overlord.

His reservations inevitably buttressed the suspicions of those, from

General Marshall to Marshal Stalin, who feared his heart was not in
Overlord. These suspicions would have been worse had they known
of his 19 July paper to the British Chiefs of Staff which advocated
that Jupiter, a plan for a landing in the north of Norway, should be
considered as a substitute for Overlord as the main non-Mediterranean
effort for the spring of 1944.

> I do not believe that 27 Anglo-American divisions are sufficient for
> 'Overlord' in view of the extraordinary fighting efficiency of the German
> Army, and the much larger forces they could so readily bring to bear
> against our troops even if the landings were successfully accomplished. It
> is right for many reasons to make every preparation with the utmost
> sincerity and vigour, but if later on it is realised by all concerned that the
> operation is beyond our strength in May and will have to be postponed
> till August 1944, then it is essential that we should have this other
> considerable operation up our sleeves.[13]

And in the same paper, as a piece of almost literal icing on the cake,
he advocated, for use in those northern waters, a device for transforming
icebergs, embellished with frozen wood pulp, into unsinkable air bases.

By this time he had secured a major political objective, which was
another bilateral meeting with Roosevelt, a very much happier prospect
than the Soviet–American bilateral which had been his fear three weeks
earlier. This became the first Quebec conference, codenamed Quadrant
(the second Quebec conference, codenamed Octagon, was in September
1944). Churchill left London for it on 4 August (exactly two months
after his return from North Africa and, although the conference itself
lasted only a week, interrupted by a Canadian country weekend, he was
away for nearly seven weeks. Once again *Queen Mary* was the chosen
means of transport, although he reverted to a battleship for the return.
He was accompanied by a total British contingent of over 200, including
(most unusually) Clementine Churchill and their daughter Mary. This
long visit had many social features, so that their presence was justified,
even if Churchill had not believed so firmly that the strains and
dedication of great leaders entitled them to high privilege.

From Halifax, Novia Scotia, where they landed, they went on a long
slow train journey to Quebec City, where they were installed in the
Citadel. Within twenty-four hours Churchill and Mary departed on
another long slow train journey to join the Roosevelts in the Hudson
Valley – Clementine was too exhausted after the previous travels to
come. They stayed two nights at Hyde Park. Quite a lot of useful

business was transacted and the party had picnic lunches each day at Eleanor Roosevelt's cottage in the woods. Churchill liked the rustic food and the open-air swimming pool, but found the weather stiflingly hot: '. . . I got up one night because I was unable to sleep and hardly to breathe, and went outside to sit on a bluff overlooking the Hudson River. Here I watched the dawn.'[14]

While it had been previously assumed, in London at any rate, that the Supreme Commander for Overlord would be British, Churchill fairly easily accepted Roosevelt's argument that the build-up of American forces would soon make the United States the predominant partner in France, and that this should be determining. Roosevelt at this stage wanted Marshall to have the job, although he later switched to Eisenhower, mainly on the tactfully expressed ground that he 'could not sleep at night with you [Marshall] out of the country'.[15] Churchill, who had promised the command to Alan Brooke just as much as Roosevelt had to Marshall, handled his CIGS's disappointment less tactfully when he got back to Quebec. 'He offered no sympathy, no regrets at having had to change his mind, and dealt with the matter as if it were one of minor importance!'[16] Brooke later wrote. At the same time it was freely agreed by the President that Mountbatten, then a somewhat junior admiral, who had succeeded Roger Keyes as Chief of Combined Operations, should be Supreme Commander in South-East Asia. The two commands were far from equal in importance.

At Hyde Park it was also decided to invite Stalin to an autumn tripartite meeting in Alaska. They got him for the autumn but not for Alaska. He suggested Archangel or Astrakhan. After several British rendezvous from Scapa Flow to Khartoum had been rejected almost as firmly by Roosevelt as by Stalin, the battle of the three As was eventually resolved in favour of Teheran. The Persian capital was at least four times as far for Roosevelt, who was the most infirm of the three, as it was for Stalin, and at least twice as far for Churchill, who was well the oldest.

Churchill having returned to Quebec, and Roosevelt and Hopkins having followed two days later, the conference proper started, although a lot of detailed work had been done between the Joint Chiefs of Staff during the Hyde Park interlude. There was not however much additional major outcome to Quadrant. Agreement on recognition of the French National Committee was secured, and Churchill, to Brooke's dismay, advocated the invasion of the northern tip of Sumatra (in the Dutch East Indies), amazingly hoping to strengthen his case by comparing it, 'in its promise of decisive consequences, with the Dardanelles operation of 1915'.[17] As Churchill failed to convince Roosevelt, Brooke was spared from having to put public spokes into his master's wheel.*

Of more practical interest was Churchill's continual rearguard action, under a cloak of general approval, against an unconditional commitment to Overlord. If, by the appointed day, there were more than twelve mobile German divisions in France, or the capacity to a build-up of more than another fifteen in the ensuing two months, he wanted a postponement. 'The old, old story of enormous casualties and the terrific strength of the German fortifications,'[18] Hopkins was recorded as saying. On this issue, unlike Sumatra, there was no division between Churchill and Brooke, which provided an additional argument for giving the Overlord command to Marshall, as was then the intention. Marshall's commitment to the invasion of France as the supreme Anglo-American objective for 1944 was greater than that of Churchill or any British general.

Although he had suffered no great setbacks Churchill was reported to be 'rather tired' (by himself) and 'peevish' (by Brooke) at the end of the conference and was glad to go on a five-day expedition to a fishing-lodge 4,000 feet up in the Laurentian mountains. He wrote of it, admittedly in a 'thank-you' letter, as being his 'first real holiday' since the war began. But such was his extraordinary metabolism that, three days after his arrival, he sat up talking (quite unnecessarily except for his reminiscent pleasure) until 3.45 a.m. with General Ismay and Leslie Rowan, one of his private secretaries. And at some of the (luxurious) log-cabin meals he made several of his entourage, including the fastidious Cadogan, take part in the collective singing of old music-hall songs.

In another leisurely train journey the core of the Churchill party then went to Washington, arriving on the evening of 1 September, and were once again installed in the White House. They stayed on North American soil for another eleven days before embarking at Halifax in the battleship *Renown* for the six-day return journey to the Clyde. Quite why this long extension was necessary is not clear. Churchill talked a lot

---

* This did not prevent Brooke from confiding to his diary one of his most acidulous comments about what he regarded as Churchill's obsession with this island. 'I had another row with him,' Brooke wrote in Quebec on 19 August. 'He refused to accept that any general plan [to defeat Japan] was necessary, recommended a purely opportunistic policy and behaved like a spoilt child that wants a toy in a shop irrespective of the fact that its parents [a rather grand view of the Chiefs of Staff vis-à-vis Churchill] tell it that it is no good' (*War Diaries, 1939–45: Field Marshal Lord Alanbrooke*, p. 444).

and on very good terms with Roosevelt. This was over the period of the Italian surrender, which took place after the Allied crossing of the Straits of Messina. An Allied landing at Salerno, thirty miles south of Naples, followed almost immediately. Churchill spent thirty-six hours on a round trip to Boston to get a Harvard honorary degree, which for some strange reason he decided to receive in Oxford DCL robes, borrowed with some difficulty from Princeton. In Harvard Yard he made a very successful speech, including a passage proposing in the post-war world the use 'of our common language even more widely throughout the globe'. This might not have pleased the French, but as a form of Anglo-Saxon imperialism it was much more realistic than endeavouring to cling on to the British Empire. And he spent the inside of another day at Hyde Park, with Clementine paying her first visit to the President's private domain. There the Churchills celebrated their thirty-fifth wedding anniversary with a Roosevelt dinner, before for the second night running they once again got into special sleeping compartments. Churchill liked both trains and being away from England.

Renown reached the Clyde on the morning of Sunday, 20 September and Churchill was in Downing Street by that evening. This time he had been away for forty-seven days. Not unnaturally therefore there was a press of domestic business awaiting him. On the Monday he addressed the House of Commons, starting at noon for an hour, and then after a luncheon break continuing for another one and a half hours. The tone of mild exasperation with which he began was well caught by the following simple anecdote. Perhaps he was learning homely imagery from Roosevelt. He tactically turned his complaint against the press, often a favourite target of Prime Ministers, rather than against his fellow MPs. He said that when he read the criticism in the Sunday papers at Greenock on the morning of his arrival (an interesting example of the priority he always gave to newspaper reading) he was reminded of the 'tale about the sailor who jumped into a dock, I think it was at Plymouth, to rescue a small boy from drowning. About a week later this sailor was accosted by a woman who asked, "Are you the man who picked my son out of the dock the other night?" The sailor replied modestly, "That is true ma'am." "Ah," said the woman, "you are the man I am looking for. Where is his cap?"'[19]

Nicolson thought Churchill began 'in a dull, stuffy manner' but loosened up, particularly after luncheon. He was impressed by the light and shade of the speech. 'It is the combination of great flights of oratory with sudden swoops into the intimate and conversational. Of all his

devices it is the one that never fails.'[20] On 21 September Kingsley
Wood, the only Chancellor of the Exchequer since the eighteenth
century to die in office, did so with total suddenness. Churchill
appointed John Anderson in his place and brought Attlee back from the
Dominions Office to be Lord President in Anderson's place; this did
not affect Attlee's position as Deputy Prime Minister, but it made him
more central to the network of Cabinet committees. In addition Beaverbrook rejoined the government as Lord Privy Seal, but not the War
Cabinet.

By the end of that month (September 1943), Churchill was reported
by his staff as being tired and bad-tempered. He blew up over an
ungracious message about Arctic convoys from Stalin. When the new
Soviet ambassador tried to deliver it he handed it back, unread, as *nul et
non avenu*. Cadogan, who had already read and informed Churchill of
the contents – otherwise it would have been difficult to see the basis on
which it was refused – was impressed by Churchill's knowledge of this
phrase from the handbooks of old-style diplomacy.

By 7 October, however, Churchill was prepared to fly to Tunis, if he
could persuade General Marshall to join him there. He wanted to
pursue his old loves of invading Rhodes and bringing Turkey into the
war, as well, maybe, as expressing some new doubts about Overlord.
But Marshall could not come. Then a strange anti-Overlord alliance
sprang up between Smuts and King George VI. Smuts lunched with the
King on 13 October, and they worked each other up into a considerable
state about the rashness of the operation. On the next day the King
wrote Churchill a letter of formidable length and some cogency expressing their fears, and concluding by asking if Churchill could dine with
him and Smuts that same evening. (Royal life was much more impro-
vised during the war than it was and is in peacetime.) Churchill went,
but not before he had sent the King a robust lesson in the facts of
life: 'There is no possibility of our going back on what is agreed. Both
the US Staff and Stalin would violently disagree with us.'[21] The fears
of both the King and Smuts were not due to cowardice. They were
attracted by other Mediterranean and Balkan objectives, but above all
they feared that the unbroken German fighting machine might hurl the
Allies back into the sea. Hitler would then, for the first time since 1942,
have a renewed chance of winning the war, or at least of greatly delaying
its end. This, in spite of his firmness before the dinner, was at least
half Churchill's view. He gently passed on these concerns to Roosevelt. 'Unless there is a German collapse,' he cabled on 17 October, 'the

campaign of 1944 will be by far the most dangerous we have undertaken, and personally I am more anxious about its success than I was about 1941, 1942 or 1943.'[22] Roosevelt, partly because of his own natural optimism and partly because of the firmness of his military advisers, remained undeflected.

Churchill next departed on his travels on 12 November. On the 11th he had not felt well enough to preside over a War Cabinet (mainly a heavy cold, a sore throat and the effects of cholera and typhoid inoculations), but he nonetheless set off at lunchtime the next day for Plymouth to embark in *Renown* for a voyage first to Algiers, then to Malta (where he disembarked for two days, spent mostly in bed), and then on to Alexandria (for Cairo) where he arrived on November 21st. His resolve to go was fortified by the news (via Roosevelt) before he left Downing Street that Stalin would come to Teheran for 27 November and that Roosevelt would arrive in Cairo on the 22nd. Throughout this journey Churchill was accompanied by his daughter Sarah (who had become Mrs Vic Oliver), which was a solace, for she was in many ways his favourite child, as well as by his son Randolph, who was liable to be less so. During the voyage out Captain Pim RNVR, his travelling map-room curator, helped to amuse him by calculating how much time he had spent both at sea and in the air, and what distance he had travelled, by ship or plane, since the beginning of the war. The answer was formidable: 110,000 miles and an aggregate of thirty-three days at sea and fourteen days and three hours in the air.

Although still not feeling well, Churchill was at Heliopolis airfield to meet Roosevelt on the morning after his own arrival, and attended him at both lunch and dinner that day. On the following morning (23 November) the first session of the Anglo-American Sextant conference took place, also at Roosevelt's villa, and was devoted to the war in the Far East. No hard decisions were taken, but no serious disagreements emerged. That afternoon Churchill and his daughter, having discovered that Roosevelt had never seen the Pyramids or the Sphinx and having made a personal dummy-run to ensure that the President could approach closely without getting out of his car, took him on a sight-seeing trip. 'I think he enjoyed himself – I think he appreciated the trouble that Papa took,' Sarah Churchill wrote to her mother.[23] It is tempting to think that Churchill was once again wooing Roosevelt as seductively as he had done before Pearl Harbor. But he always took great pleasure in showing what he regarded as his own domains to any new visitor, Blenheim to Clementine in 1908, his Chartwell building

and hydrological works to all who came in the 1930s, the Royal Navy
to Harry Hopkins in 1941. And he certainly regarded the sights of
wartime Cairo as within his domain. His own comment on the Sphinx
was that 'She told us nothing, and maintained her inscrutable smile,'[24]
which was curiously reminiscent of Gladstone's 1852 diary entry on
other ancient stoneworks at Stonehenge as 'telling much, telling too
that it conceals more'.[25]

The next morning's conference session covered familiar European
ground, Churchill not directly contesting Overlord but still putting the
weight of his emphasis on the Mediterranean. He expressed dismay at
the slow progress on the mainland of Italy (the Salerno landing was
bogged down) and at the German recapture of the island of Leros in
the Aegean. But this meant more not less Mediterranean effort. The
sequence he advocated was 'first Rome then Rhodes'. He also strongly
urged more Allied help for Tito's increasingly effective Yugoslav resistance. Churchill got some support from Eisenhower, still C-in-C Mediterranean and not yet designated Supreme Commander for Overlord,
and difficulties were circumnavigated by none of these desiderata being
rejected in advance of Teheran. Churchill cheerfully telegraphed to the
King: 'I am making good progress with the President and his high
officers, and I am pretty sure all will end up harmoniously.'[26] The
President equally cheerfully carved two vast Thanksgiving Day turkeys
for the top Anglo-American brass on 25 November.

At a more intimate British dinner on the following evening Churchill
was reported as having talked non-stop to the whole table for three
hours, and then for two more before going to bed, but being surprised
the next morning when, on departing for Teheran, he discovered he
had a bad sore throat. The five-and-a-half-hour flight did not do it
much good. Nor did the arrangements when they arrived. The British
stayed in their own Legation with its large compound. Adjacent to it
was the still bigger Soviet compound. The American Legation was
smaller and a mile away. The US stake in Iran, which since 1942 had
been under Soviet and British occupation, was less high. Churchill's
suggestion (to Stalin on 23 November) that Roosevelt should stay in the
British Legation – return hospitality for many nights in the White
House? – was ignored. After one inconvenient night installed in their
own Legation the Americans were persuaded to move to the Soviet
compound, which, the Russians said, was the only place where Roosevelt
could be safe from a possible assassination plot. The President acqui-

esced. 'The Soviets had once again got what they wanted,' General Ismay was bitterly to comment in his memoirs. 'I wonder if microphones had already been installed in anticipation.'[27]

Churchill had so completely lost his voice and was so generally exhausted that he was unable to join the tripartite dinner that first night in Teheran and had to have his in bed. The only consolation was that the engagement was therefore cancelled. The other two also dined separately. The next morning Churchill was much better, but his hopes of a private preliminary talk with Roosevelt were frustrated. And the President saw Stalin alone an hour before the formal opening of the conference at 4.30 p.m. That was superficially ungracious on Roosevelt's part in view of Churchill's disappointment of the night before. But it is possible to see his point. He had never met Stalin (Churchill of course had, in Moscow fifteen months before), and he had just spent three days with Churchill in Cairo. Furthermore the Russians skilfully nominated Roosevelt, who was the only head of state of the three, as the chairman of the conference. This, almost inevitably, encouraged him to equidistance in any dispute. Indeed in his preliminary meeting with Stalin he moved at least some way to this position, and somewhat away from Churchill's Cairo hopes, by indicating his sympathy for direct West Wall assault as opposed to a Mediterranean strategy.

Against this discouraging background Churchill performed with skill, although occasionally betraying signs of strain. In the Teheran conference there were three formal sessions, three dinners and two luncheons of the three principals. At the first session he felt himself somewhat isolated, mainly because Roosevelt conceded to Stalin that there should be no flexibility from the date of early May (1944) for the launch of Overlord. Churchill was sufficiently dimayed that he suggested a fairly early adjournment (to which Roosevelt readily agreed) and concluded on the warning note that 'while we are all great friends, it would be idle for us to delude ourselves that we see eye to eye on all matters. Time and patience are necessary.'[28]

The first dinner, given by Roosevelt, was somewhat subdued, for the President had taken over from Churchill as the sick man of Persia, and went to bed early. Churchill then led Stalin to two adjacent chairs and had some neither very productive nor, at this stage, disruptive conversation about the post-victory future of first Germany and then Poland. The next day Churchill again tried to get Roosevelt to lunch with him, and was once again politely repulsed. Harriman was sent to explain that the President did not want Stalin to feel that he and Churchill were ganging up against him. That afternoon Roosevelt again saw Stalin before the formal session.

In these circumstances the ceremony which immediately preceded that session must have seemed a somewhat anti-climactic presentation of an expensive bauble. The bejewelled Sword of Stalingrad had been specially made so that Churchill, on behalf of King George VI, could present it to Stalin 'in token of the homage of the British people . . . to the steel-hearted citizens of Stalingrad'. It had been on exhibition in Westminster Abbey for some weeks beforehand, where it had indeed attracted the homage of many filing-past members of the British public, as well as the bitter derision of Evelyn Waugh, whose hatred for the Soviet Union was at least as great as for Nazi Germany, and who later satirically adopted *Sword of Honour* as the overarching title for his wartime trilogy. Although Hopkins described the occasion as 'this impressive ceremony' it almost certainly meant more to the British than to the Russians.* King George VI must have been a shadowy figure to the defender of Stalingrad, and Stalin, although he made quite a gracious little speech before Marshal Voroshilov dropped the sword, was not disposed to regard a royal gift of a jewelled dagger as any substitute for an assault on the northern coast of France.

This was demonstrated by the rigour with which Stalin pursued this objective as soon as the formal conference was resumed. Churchill had to bear the brunt of it, although the first gun was turned on Roosevelt. 'Who will command Overlord' was the first demand, and when Roosevelt said it had not been decided, Stalin strongly implied that the operation could hardly be regarded as a serious intention until it was. (This Stalin threat may well have had a beneficial effect, for Roosevelt, who was not always the most resolute of decision-takers, made this momentous one six days later on Sunday, 5 December, and he made it in a bold or at least unorthodox direction, ignoring the strong advice of Hopkins and of War Secretary Stimson, as well as the known preferences of both Churchill and Stalin, in favour of Eisenhower over Marshall.)

Stalin then swung his guns in Churchill's direction, and after announcing that 'from the Russian point of view Turkey, Rhodes, Yugoslavia, and even the capture of Rome [all Churchill's pet objectives]

* The sword does however repose today in the museum at Stalingrad (renamed Volgograd).

were not important'[29] he asked him the direct and hostile question: did
he really believe in Overlord? Churchill's reply was not bad, but not
great either. It was a mixture of equivocation and rhetoric. Provided the
conditions* were met, he said, 'it will be our stern duty to hurl across
the Channel against the Germans every sinew of our strength'.[30]

It was not an easy day for Churchill. At the Russian-hosted dinner
that evening he got, untypically but in some ways to his credit, out
of the loop of the rather crude Stalin-led chaff about the post-war punishment of the Germans in which the Americans joined with ease.
As described by Churchill, writing nearly nine years later, it was an
unedifying scene, but there nonetheless remains a mystery as to why he,
the consummate circus master of witty, often deflating conversation, did
not handle it better. Stalin, maybe jocularly, said that the German
problem could be largely solved by rounding up and shooting the
50,000 foremost officers and technicians. (This could, by the standards
of some of his purges, be regarded as a relatively restrained affair.)
Churchill recorded: 'On this I thought it right to say, "The British
Parliament and public will never tolerate mass executions. . . . I would
rather . . . be taken out into the garden here and now and be shot myself
than sully my own and my country's honour by such infamy." '[31]

Then Roosevelt intervened and, presumably hoping to lighten the
atmosphere, said he wished to propose a compromise figure of 49,000.
Next Colonel Elliott Roosevelt, the President's second son who was
nepotically present, and who made Randolph Churchill, not there on
that occasion, seem almost like a scion of exquisite tact, rose and made
an uncalled-for (presumably somewhat inebriated) speech saying that he
strongly agreed with Stalin and so would the US Army. At that point
Churchill left the table to skulk in a dimly lit side room. 'I had not been
there a minute before hands were clapped upon my shoulders from
behind, and there was Stalin, with Molotov at his side, both grinning
broadly, and eagerly declaring that they were only playing, and that
nothing of a serious character had entered their heads. Stalin has a very
captivating manner when he chooses to use it, and I never saw him do
so to such an extent as at that moment. . . . I consented to return, and
the rest of the evening passed pleasantly.'[32]

---

* These were a 'satisfactory' prior reduction in the strength of German fighter forces,
not more than twelve mobile German divisions in France and the Low Countries; and
no possibility of the Germans transferring from other fronts more than another fifteen
divisions in the first sixty days.

Nevertheless Churchill, according to Moran, who is supported to some extent by Eden and Ambassador Clark Kerr, went to bed in a gloomy mood that night. There would probably be another war, in which mankind might well destroy itself. He would not be there. 'I want to sleep for billions of years.'[33] Sympathy is with Churchill on the events of the evening, but why did he handle them so unbuoyantly? Could it be that he had become so used to orchestrating all conversations that he found it difficult to handle one over which he did not wield the sole baton?

The next day went better. Churchill had an amicable but not particularly productive bilateral meeting with Stalin in the morning. They then both attended a Roosevelt luncheon. The third formal session that afternoon went reasonably well on the assumption that Overlord would take place at the appointed time and be preceded by a Russian offensive which would make it difficult if not impossible for the Germans to exceed the concentrations of force in the West laid down in Churchill's reiterated conditions. Communiqué drafting then began to occupy the principals, and at that Churchill's command of words made him the best. 'The note to be sounded', he said, 'was [that of] brevity, mystery, and a foretaste of impending doom for Germany.'[34] That night the dinner given by Churchill for his sixty-ninth birthday passed off smoothly, although it was not one of the most famous convivial occasions of the war. Churchill bestowed on his Russian table neighbour the accolade of 'Stalin the Great' and was happy to match the latter's semi-satirical toast to the Conservative party by saying, 'I drink to the proletarian masses.'[35]

There was a farewell luncheon on the following day, at which some issues were resolved. Part of the surrendered Italian navy was to be given to Russia. The Soviet Union was to be granted a 'warm-water' Baltic port. Königsberg, renamed Kaliningrad, was eventually decided upon. Poland's borders were to be shifted westwards, the Russians getting the territory up to the so-called Curzon line of 1919 and Poland receiving compensatory territory from German lands in Silesia and further north. This was amicably approved without the Poles being consulted. Roosevelt expatiated on his then favourite scheme for splitting Germany into five separate self-governing regions, with two more, called Kiel–Hamburg and Ruhr–Saar, placed under United Nations control. Churchill wisely confined himself to saying that the President had 'said a mouthful', which he thought a good American colloquialism, and indicating that he had some different ideas. There was general goodwill at the end, but Churchill's sunny message to Attlee was perhaps somewhat over the top: 'We have had a grand day here, and relations between Britain, United States and USSR have never been so cordial and intimate. All war plans are agreed and concerted.'[36]

On the following day (2 December) Churchill flew to Cairo, where he stayed in the villa of the Australian politician Richard Casey, who had replaced Oliver Lyttelton as British Minister Resident in the Middle East, until the 10th. Roosevelt was also in Cairo for three or four of these days. The interrupted (by Teheran) Anglo-American Sextant conference was resumed, and the decision was taken, most welcome to Churchill, that Buccaneer, an amphibious operation across the Bay of Bengal to seize the Andaman Islands, should be abandoned. This caused some gnashing of teeth among the American military and great bitterness in General 'Vinegar Joe' Stilwell, who made a speciality of that quality. This was accompanied by a general intimation to Mountbatten that he had to make do with what resources he had, for he was not for the foreseeable future going to get any more. For Churchill this meant that there was a good chance of preserving his Mediterranean strategy as well as assuaging the Americans and the Russians – and maybe winning the war – with Overlord.

While Roosevelt was still there Churchill also reverted to his old wooing of the Turks, whose leaders he had invited to Cairo for three days, but who proved as reluctant as previously to say either yes or no. He had to make do with Inönü kissing him goodbye at the airport. When Inönü (and Roosevelt) had gone he held a more heterogeneous series of meetings, with King Farouk of Egypt, with the exiled kings of Greece and of Yugoslavia, with the Regent of Iraq, with Harold Macmillan brought over from Algiers (where he was Minister Resident), and with Fitzroy Maclean and William Deakin, the latter his pre-war research assistant for *The English-Speaking Peoples* and now under Maclean his representative with Tito's partisans.

Churchill's morale and health made varying impressions. Macmillan thought on 8 December that he 'was in great form and holding forth to a circle of . . . young men',[37] who included George Jellicoe and Julian Amery – Churchill liked the sons more than he had or did the fathers. Alan Brooke also found him 'in tremendous form' on the previous night.[38] But he had been too unwell (with stomach ache) to attend the first dinner for the Turks. The ever present Smuts told Brooke that he was 'not at all happy about the condition of the PM'.[39] And Churchill himself noticed signs of his own exhaustion. He no longer had the energy to dry himself after his many baths, but lay on his bed until the air did it for him.

On the night of Friday, 10 December he made the eight-and-a-half-hour flight to Tunis, to stay a couple of days at Eisenhower's Carthage villa with the intention of going on to visit British troops in Italy. The arrival was a minor disaster. The plane went to the wrong airfield. Eisenhower was waiting with the welcoming cars forty miles away. Brooke, who had thought the Prime Minister already 'tired and flat' on the plane, left a haunting picture of his disconsolation after the false arrival. 'They took him out of the plane and he sat on his suitcase in a very cold morning wind, looking like nothing on earth. We were . . . there about an hour before we moved on and he was chilled by then.'[40] When eventually he was united with Eisenhower he said: 'I shall have to stay with you longer than I had planned. I am completely at the end of my tether.'[41]

He slept for most of the day of 11 December, although getting up for a dinner with Eisenhower, Tedder (the Supreme Allied Air Commander in the Mediterranean), Brooke and several members of his own entourage. During the night he became ill as opposed to merely exhausted. At four in the morning he blundered noisily into Brooke's room, thinking it was Moran's, and complaining that he had 'a terrible headache' – sinister shades of Roosevelt's affliction of sixteen months later. By the next morning this had subsided, but Churchill was left with a moderate fever. Moran then began a relentless but wise process of telegraphing for medical assistance from all directions. It made flesh of the joke of Colville being asked by a new junior private secretary what he should to if Churchill became ill while he was on solitary duty. Colville replied: 'You telephone Lord Moran and he will send for a real doctor.'[42] An X-ray machine was produced from Tunis, which showed a pneumonic patch on the lung. A pathologist (Colonel Pulvertaft) was summoned from Cairo, as a day or two later was a heart specialist (Brigadier Bedford) and a sulphonamide expert from Italy (Colonel Buttle). They were supplemented by Professor Scadding, the only one who did not seem to enjoy military rank, of the Brompton Hospital for Chest Diseases. In retrospect the profusion of red-tabs gives an impression of Mozartian physicians or notaries scurrying about the stage, but Moran was quite right to take matters seriously. Churchill was very ill for at least three days. Moran subsequently said that on the night of 14 December he had thought Churchill was going to die, and this was before the worst evening, which was that of the 15th, when his heart began to febrillate.

By the morning of the 16th he was better. On the afternoon of the following day Clementine Churchill arrived, accompanied by Jock Colville, who after two and a quarter years of salving his conscience as an RAF pilot, had made an immensely welcome return to Churchill's staff. He recorded that he found 'instead of a recumbent invalid a cheerful figure with a large cigar and a whisky and soda in his hand,'[43] though there is some contrary evidence that Churchill did not go back to cigars until later. There was a second but lesser attack of febrillation in the early morning of the 18th. After that Churchill slowly but steadily improved as Christmas approached. He managed an increasing budget of dictation and other work – he had never totally switched off for a full twenty-four hours – but he did not emerge from his bedroom until the late afternoon of Christmas Eve, when he presided, in his multi-coloured dressing-gown, over a meeting of generals and air-marshals concerned with the planned January landing at Anzio, just south of Rome. By Christmas Day however he was up for another conference and for a lunch at which no fewer than five major commanders were present, and which he did not allow to end until 4.00 p.m. He seemed to have become infected by Russian habits and spent much of the meal proposing a series of toasts.

On 27 December the whole Churchill party left by air for convalescence at Marrakech, his Shangri-La since 1936. It was a difficult flight for someone in Churchill's condition, over five hours in duration and involving mountains above 10,000 feet. On this visit he did not stay at his first favourite, the Mamounia Hotel, but at the Villa Taylor, a luxurious but ill-placed establishment belonging to an American lady, which had been placed at Roosevelt's disposal on the occasion of their post-Casablanca visit a year before. There he remained for eighteen days. For social purposes his chosen ministerial companion was Beaverbrook. The hold upon him of that mountebank (as Clementine Churchill saw him) was extraordinary, particularly as Beaverbrook was by no means a reliable supporter on issues.*

Churchill said that he did not feel strong enough to paint during these two and a half weeks, but he did see a number of visitors, of whom

---

* One advantage of Beaverbrook's presence was that it stimulated Churchill's reminiscent conversation. At dinner on 1 January 1944 it was reported by Colville that, when they had gone over almost the whole course of both the First and the Second World Wars, Churchill endearingly turned to his naval aide, Commander Thompson, and said: 'But, Tommy, you will bear witness that I do not repeat my stories so often as my dear friend, the President of the United States' (Colville, *The Fringes of Power*, p. 461).

at least two, President Beneš of Czechoslovakia, whom he saw for four
and a half hours and who was somewhat boring, and General de Gaulle,
whose attributes are too well known to need description, might have
been thought to require more strength than painting. The normal
routine for the Churchill party was to go out for luncheon picnics in
the foothills of the Atlas mountains. The convalescence was a success.
Churchill said that he would like to have stayed for another two weeks,
but he thought that he ought to be in London for the Anzio landing on
21 January. On the 14th he flew to Gibraltar and embarked in *King
George V* for the voyage back to Plymouth. He was in London on the
morning of the 18th, having been away for sixty-seven days. He had
been out of Britain for no fewer than 172 days, plus another thirty-one
days of pneumonic incapacitation in London and at Chequers, of the
year which had begun with his departure for the Casablanca conference
on 12 January, 1943.

Not surprisingly in the circumstances Churchill was met at Paddington by the entire Cabinet. More surprisingly he managed in his first
hours back to answer Prime Minister's questions in the House of
Commons, to preside over a War Cabinet and to lunch with the King
at Buckingham Palace. Nicolson's description of Churchill's Commons
performance on that day was one of his most memorable diary entries:

> We were dawdling through Questions . . . when I saw (*saw* is the word) a
> gasp of astonishment pass over the faces of the Labour Party opposite.
> Suddenly they jumped to their feet and started shouting, waving their
> papers in the air. We also jumped up and the whole House broke into
> cheer after cheer while Winston, very pink, rather shy, beaming with
> mischief, crept along the front bench and flung himself into his accus-
> tomed seat. . . .
>   A few minutes later he got up to answer questions. Most men would
> have been unable, on such an occasion, not to throw a flash of drama into
> their replies. But Winston answered them as if he were the youngest
> Under-Secretary, putting on his glasses, turning over his papers, respond-
> ing tactfully to supplementaries, and taking the whole thing as conscien-
> tiously as could be.[44]

Absence can indeed make the heart grow fonder, and with Churchill
it did not cause him to lose his House of Commons tricks, which he
had then been learning over forty-three years.

38

THE RETURN TO FRANCE

NINETEEN-FORTY-FOUR was a year of some weariness for Churchill, although no more than his illness and his age warranted. It was one of continuing close surface friendship with Roosevelt, although also one of more persistent Anglo-American difference of strategy than had previously been present. With Stalin it was one of curiously fluctuating relationship. The underlying trend was towards hostility, yet there was an upsurge of almost maudlin personal warmth when Churchill went to Moscow in October.

This was also however a much less restless year for Churchill than 1943 had been. Between his return from Marrakech and his departure for the Yalta conference on 29 January 1945 he was out of Britain for only sixty-three days. It was broadly a year of great triumph for the Allies, although with German resistance notably stiffening from September onwards. It was also one in which Churchill's problem was that he might become the half in an alliance of two and a half. This threat, which had just begun to surface in 1943, gained menacing strength. As a result the approach to Allied victory, which would have seemed such an incredible prize in 1940–1, and which he, above all, deserved to savour, became bittersweet. The great prospective triumph became tinged with melancholy and with apprehension about the post-war world.

The Anzio landing, forty miles south of Rome, took place three days after Churchill's return from Marrakech. It was a success to the limited extent that the bridgehead was secured and not dislodged. But as a means of unlocking the stalemate which had settled over the Italian front it was a disappointment. This became clear within a week or so and was memorably expressed by Churchill in a phrase which he repeated in several directions during February: 'I had hoped that we were hurling a wild cat on to the shore, but all we got was a stranded whale.'[1] Churchill was often in danger of being captured by his phrases. But this was a sufficiently true and vivid one that, having thought of it, he was fully justified in deploying it several times. The blame for immobilism fell mainly upon the American corps commander, General Lucas, but it may be that the difficulty of the terrain and the skill and tenacity of Kesselring's opposing generalship had at least as much to do with it. The Italian campaign was beginning to cost the attackers significantly greater resources than the defenders.

Meanwhile the central Allied thrust up the spine of southern Italy was unable to overcome the pivotal obstacle of Monte Cassino. Three unsuccessful offensives against that dominating monastery were launched between late January and mid-March. The casualties were considerable and the gains meagre. It was not until mid-May that the sanctuary of the Benedictine monks which inadvertently became one of the most formidable fortresses of the entire war was overcome and the road up the Liri valley to Rome was opened.

This Italian hold-up had a mixed impact upon Churchill's attitude to Overlord. It made him bemoan still more that Alexander's resources had been reduced by seven divisions (four American and three British) which returned to Britain in order to re-equip and be available for the cross-Channel assault. Even more did it make him resent the further weakening of the army in Italy necessarily involved in the American determination to pursue Anvil (the plan for an amphibious landing in the South of France), which was intended to coincide with Overlord, but which eventually took place two months after it. It may also, however, have made him realize that he should not put too many eggs in the Italian basket. Very soon after he got back to London he plunged into the detailed planning of Overlord. He set up and himself presided over a regular series of meetings of Chiefs of Staff and one or two ministers, at which either Eisenhower or his chief of staff General Bedell Smith was also present. The purpose of these meetings was to review progress on matters like the construction of the artificial Mulberry harbours and the best deployment of the now overwhelming Allied air power. He also instituted a regular weekly Downing Street luncheon between himself, Eisenhower and Bedell Smith.

Roosevelt might indeed have been tempted to think that there was a dangerous degree of asymmetry between the Prime Minister's on-the-spot interference and his own 3,000-mile detachment. But at least it could not be said that Churchill held himself aloof from the enterprise about which he had expressed so many doubts. When he sent a message to General Marshall on 20 February saying, about Overlord, 'I am hardening very much on the operation as the time approaches,'[2] and even more significantly adding that this was independent of whether or not the conditions he had laid down at Teheran were fully met, his words were compatible with his behaviour.

Nevertheless those late-winter and early-spring months of 1944 were not a good period for Churchill. His illness had aged and weakened him. On 2 February Marian Holmes, a devoted dictating secretary, wrote in her diary, 'Somehow today he looks 10 years older.'[3] This was echoed by Colville, who a fortnight later gave a picture of him 'sitting in a chair in his study at the [Downing Street] Annexe', where he 'looked old, tired and very depressed'.[4] This was immediately after the calamitous (for the government) West Derbyshire bye-election, where the Marquess of Hartington, the ill-fated heir to the dukedom of Devonshire, was defeated on a heavy swing by a local Labour worthy, standing as an independent, seven months before Hartington was killed in action in Belgium. This came only two weeks after an almost equally bad result in what should have been a safe Conservative seat in Brighton, and Churchill began to mutter (fortunately not more) that the appropriate response would be a general election.

Churchill had several other proximate things to depress him. One was the intransigence of the Russians towards any Poles who were not their helots. This was a dominating issue for Churchill throughout the year. He much liked getting on well with Stalin, as he thought he had done at Teheran, and was still more vehemently to accredit himself with doing when he went to Moscow in October (1944). But he could not forget that it was at least nominally to defend the Poles that Britain had entered the war in September 1939. He was willing to accede to Stalin's demand to move Poland westwards, like a mobile house, allowing the Russians to take over much of their eastward territory, including the city of Lvov, with recompense for the Poles from previously German lands. But he found the Russians' determination to have both this and a puppet Communist government in Warsaw hard to bear. (They had already set up one in Lublin, ninety miles south-east of the capital.) Furthermore his feelings were much exacerbated by the Russian treatment of two British sailors who, for what he regarded as no more than 'a drunken brawl' in Archangel, had been sentenced to long periods of imprisonment in Siberia. There was a striking contradiction, which preyed on Churchill's mind, between the Russians' desire for more British lives to be subjected to heavy risks in Arctic convoys and their unwillingness to exercise executive clemency in these two cases. The Soviet tradition was hardly that of the majesty of the law impartially taking its course.

Nor was Churchill vastly happier with the United States. Superficially their joint 'ship of state', in the words of the Longfellow poem which Roosevelt had sent Churchill in early 1941, sailed imperturbably along, but there was a lot of trouble ahead, some of which rose to the upper deck. When Churchill had a dinner of reconciliation with Alan Brooke on 25 February, after one of their roughest disagreements, he was reported, by Brooke, as having identified 'the President's unpleasant attitude lately'[5] as one of the hostile clouds on the horizon. One manifestation of this was that Roosevelt declined Churchill's invitation 'to spend Easter with me at Bermuda'. The President pleaded that he had 'flu. Churchill's medical reasons for not again crossing the Atlantic were stronger, but not strong enough to overcome his relentless appetite for summits and journeys.

He was in fact both physically and mentally jaded. When on 22 February he made his first major House of Commons speech since the previous September he told Colville that 'it was a great effort . . . to make these speeches now'.[6] Harold Nicolson, however, thought that 'He is looking well again, but he has a slight cough. He is not of course as vigorous or as pugnacious as in 1940. But he has no need to be. He is right to take the more sober tone of the elder statesman.'[7] There was also a nasty if sporadic recrudescence of London air raids, after a long quiet period, during that early spring. There were two in February, the first on the Sunday night of the 20th–21st, including a stick of bombs on Horse Guards Parade, which blew out the Downing Street windows. Churchill was at Chequers so was not exposed on this occasion, although he was in London for the subsequent February raids and for the four March attacks. According to his map-keeper, Captain Pim, he still greeted the raiders with high fighting spirits: 'The Prime Minister's only reaction was to have his coat and tin hat got ready so that as soon as the guns opened fire he might proceed to the roof of the building to get a better view.'[8] And in a 4 April letter to his son Randolph, who was then in Yugoslavia, plaguing the life out of the other members of the mission to Tito, he wrote: 'The bombing has been on a very modest scale. . . . Sometimes I go to Maria's battery [Mary Churchill, when she was not accompanying her father on major missions, was an anti-aircraft officer, then stationed in Hyde Park] and hear the child ordering the guns to fire.'[9]

Nevertheless this short burst of raids (in which 279 people were killed) was for Churchill an irritant superimposed upon a not very satisfactory general war situation. Colville, who well reflected Downing Street opinion, wrote early on that 'London seems disturbed by the raids and less ebullient than in 1940–41.'[10] And he also recorded Churchill, a week or so later, as indulging, late at night and in the great hall at Chequers in the, for him, extraordinary occupation of smoking Turkish cigarettes. It was the only time, for at least twenty-five years, when he was observed with such a modest source of nicotine in his hands. When asked why he was doing so he replied with a mixture of frivolity and depression that 'they were the only thing he got out of the Turks'.[11] A more comprehensive expression of strain and even gloom was contained in a telegram which he sent to Alexander, his favourite general at least so far as communality of outlook and therefore of frankness of phrase were concerned, saying: 'The war weighs very heavy on us all just now.'[12]

On 26 March Churchill delivered his first Sunday-evening broadcast for more than a year. It was not a great success. Colville referred to the Prime Minister broadcasting 'indifferently', and Nicolson wrote that many thought it that 'of a worn and petulant old man', although Nicolson himself was shocked by the ingratitude that a 'terribly war-weary' country was exhibiting towards the hero of 1940–1.[13] One reason why the broadcast did not go better was that Churchill devoted much of it to subjects in which he was not really interested – post-war reforms in housing, education and agriculture, and felt that he could not even mention the subjects which were on the top of his mind at the time. These were, first, the death on 23 March (in another air crash) of Orde Wingate, the unorthodox general whom he had swept off to Quebec with him in the previous August, and who he believed could bring a touch of genius to land-fighting in the war against Japan; and second his intense anger at the Russian treatment of the two Archangel sailors, combined with an intransigent and offensive message about the Polish dispute which he received from Stalin on the previous day.

He had two successful visits of troop inspection, one with Eisenhower of Americans in the south of England and the other of British units in Yorkshire. He slept, lunched and dined in his special train, which he always liked. But after a Chiefs of Staff meeting with him on 28 March Brooke wrote of the Prime Minister: 'I am afraid that he is losing ground rapidly. He seems quite incapable of concentrating for a few minutes on end, and keeps wandering dangerously. He kept yawning and saying he felt desperately tired.'[14]

Brooke's exasperation with Churchill, although combined with underlying respect, sometimes conjoined with his natural asperity to make his comments on the Prime Minister unduly harsh. Tiredness did not however make Churchill easily acquiescent. He nearly always accepted a clearly put Chiefs of Staff case, but this was more because he accepted the arguments than because he wearily subsided. Tiredness may have made him inconsequential, occasionally bad-tempered and quite frequently depressed, but it never sapped his pugnacious desire to engage with issues and to assert his power. There were three striking examples of this during the spring of 1944. On 21 March that epitome of official rectitude, Sir John Anderson, proposed to Churchill that the time had come to inform the War Cabinet about Tube Alloys (the atomic bomb project) and maybe, in very broad terms, the Russians too. To the first proposal Churchill responded, 'I do not agree. What can they do about it?'; and to the second, 'On no account.'[15]

A week later the government was defeated in the House of Commons for the first time since its formation nearly four years before. It was by the narrowest possible margin, on a very small vote (120 to 119) and on a subject of only peripheral concern to Churchill, that of whether or not equal pay for men and women teachers should be enshrined in the Education Bill, with which he had reluctantly allowed Rab Butler to proceed. He was immediately determined that the House should be forced to repudiate its impertinence. Two days later he got the previous vote erased by a majority of more than 400. Colville summed it up well: 'the P.M. was radiant. I thought it was cracking a nut with a sledge-hammer.'[16]

The third test of Churchill's resolution to command was the most difficult. In Greece, a resistance force second only to Tito's had been set up in the mountains, with EAM providing the political leadership and ELAS as its military arm. Their relationship was like that of Sinn Fein to the IRA. But unlike even the most extreme republicans of Ireland, they were both firmly under Communist control. In Churchill's own words they 'had formed a State within a State in the mountains of Central and Northern Greece'.[17] As the Soviet armies' advance to the borders of Roumania brought the prospect of a German retreat from the Balkans, the political ambitions of the Greek resistance quickened. On 26 March a Political Committee of National Liberation with pretensions to become a provisional government of Greece was proclaimed. This was a direct challenge to the Cairo government-in-exile under a little-remembered Greek politician named Tsouderos, which derived legitimacy from its allegiance to King George II of the Hellenes, and in consequence had the more tangible advantage of Churchill's support. Churchill's resolve was strengthened by Russian intransigence over Poland and the prospect of it being repeated in other eastern European lands in which he could bring little influence to bear. Greece at least should be within the sphere of British sea power, and one of Churchill's dominant purposes throughout the year 1944 became the prevention of its submission to a Communist takeover.

The Greek King was not an asset to this purpose. He was one of a gaggle of Mediterranean monarchs to whom Churchill felt a tentative commitment, but who were on the whole an embarrassment to him. King Peter of Yugoslavia was clearly within this category, and so to some extent, after the Italian surrender of September 1943, was King Victor Emmanuel III. And in Cairo itself, the subsidiary capital for governments-in-exile, King Farouk of Egypt was at least as much of a liability. The northern and London-based monarchs – King Haakon of Norway, Queen Wilhelmina of the Netherlands and the Grand Duchess of Luxembourg – were much less of a problem.

Churchill was an instinctive and somewhat romantic monarchist. He believed, for instance, that Germany would have been more able to resist the rise of Hitler had some Hohenzollern descendant, not tarnished with the Kaiser's personal aggressiveness, been head of state instead of the shadowy Social Democratic presidents of the early years of the Weimar Republic or even, nearer the edge of the cliff, Field Marshal von Hindenburg. Yet Churchill was essentially a Whig in his attitude to monarchs. He believed himself to be fully their social equal. In Britain itself, starting unpropitiously as a friend of King Edward VIII and as the supplanter of Chamberlain, who enjoyed much royal favour, he established an excellent relationship with King George VI. But although it was shrouded in Churchill's always employing the traditional formulae of a subject's respect, this partnership was in essence based on the King accepting a position as a royal adjunct to Churchill. He became a self-abnegatory but sometimes crucial and wise henchman to Churchill. He was an immensely dedicated sovereign, eager for duties, fearless of risks, and undemanding of his own leisure or prerogatives. It was symptomatic that when Churchill, having been often late for the traditional early-Tuesday-evening audiences, suggested a weekly luncheon instead the King responded with enthusiasm and then, later, accepted with alacrity the idea of coming in addition to Downing Street for a monthly dinner. Churchill was happy to talk with freedom to him about almost every aspect of the war, but not to allow him to make policy.

Churchill's other monarchs were less satisfactory and his loyalty to them much more conditional. If they assisted the prosecution of the war and the promotion in their countries of regimes helpful to Britain they should be supported, but if they got stubbornly in the way that support was withdrawn. King George of the Hellenes was in a marginal position. When the proclamation from the Greek mountains to the world of the Political Committee of National Liberation drastically destabilized the Cairo Greek government-in-exile, the King was in London. The Greek forces in Egypt began a revolt against this government – and the King. The British ambassador to the Cairo-based Greek government, a spirited but controversial Foreign Office figure (Rex Leeper), hoped the matter could be settled by the King keeping out of the way, preferably agreeing to a regency, and by a broadening of the government under a new Prime Minister, for which post Sophocles Venizelos (a good combination of names) was suggested.

In the absence of Eden on semi-sick leave, Churchill was temporarily in charge of the Foreign Office, and so had his hands even more directly on the levers of communication than was his habit. He used them to reject Leeper's advice and to send him an extraordinary series of teasing messages, which half pointed to Churchill having little confidence in him, although he paid him a notable tribute in a later volume of *The Second World War*. These messages also suggested that Churchill had been stimulated by his firm seizure of the controls into a temporary period of high spirits. On 7 April, the day that he received Leeper's advice, he had King George of the Hellenes to lunch in Downing Street and, totally contradicting the advice, told him that he was quite right to want to go back to Cairo and sustain his tottering government. He then cabled to Leeper telling him that the rebellion in the Greek forces must be put down with total determination. 'We are prepared to use the utmost force, but let us avoid slaughter if possible,' he told General Paget, the C-in-C Egypt,[18] and he concluded his message to Leeper, 'This is an occasion for you to show those qualities of imperturbability and command which are associated with the British Diplomatic Service.'[19] The next day he supplemented his instructions to Leeper with the following:

> For you yourself there is a great opportunity. You should stick to the line I have marked out and not be worried about the consequences. You speak of living on the lid of a volcano. Wherever else do you expect to live in times like these? Please however be careful to follow very exactly the instructions you are receiving from me, namely, first in priority, order and discipline to be maintained in the armed forces; secondly, the safety

of the King's person to be ensured; thirdly, every effort to be made to induce Tsouderos to hold office till the King returns and has had time to look around; fourthly, try to get Venizelos to remain with Tsouderos; fifthly, celebrate Easter Sunday in a manner pious and becoming.[20]

By the end of April Churchill's main objectives had been achieved, with no casualties on the Greek side and only one British officer lost. The King established himself for a time in Cairo and formed a new government under George Papandreou (father of the Prime Minister of the 1980s and 1990s), instead of Sophocles Venizelos, who on closer inspection was judged unsatisfactory. Greek politics were very hereditary. In these firm dealings Churchill received good distant support from Roosevelt. He was pleased by this, even though in one of his later instructions to Leeper he had written: 'On no account accept any assistance from American or Russian sources, otherwise than as specially enjoined by me.'[21] The Greek problem next erupted in December 1944, and very violently. Then it destroyed Churchill's last Chequers Christmas of his wartime premiership, and, ironically, forced him back to most of Leeper's recipes, as well as leaving him without any continuation of enthusiastic support from Roosevelt.

Meanwhile the date of the assault on Hitler's French fortress approached with, for Churchill, almost frightening speed. He may have 'hardened' but he remained apprehensive. In near defeat he had been the most splendidly and successfully defiant man in history, but in the approach to victory he remained notably more cautious than Roosevelt or General Marshall. This did not prevent his taking an active and encouraging role in the preparations. Ensconced in his special two-coach train, he was a frequent presence close to the embarkation points. Yet for that late spring of apprehensive waiting the strongest impression that comes through is that it was for Churchill a time of great fluctuation of mood, with bursts of energy and indeed brilliance of performance intervening in a general pattern of lassitude and gloom, stemming largely from an awareness that none of his interlocutors – Stalin, Roosevelt, de Gaulle – would do exactly what he wished, and a growing feeling of impotence to impose his will. He approached victory with much less buoyancy than he had confronted the menace of defeat four years before.

The essential reasons for his underground reservoir of gloom, which often but by no means always spurted to the surface, were threefold. First, he was becoming deeply worried about Soviet intentions and power in Europe after the war. There was always some ambiguity in his approach here. He greatly respected the fortitude of the Red Army, and largely as a result of this he was susceptible to Stalin's occasional charm and liked a personal partnership of titans with him. He half wanted to believe that Russia in its struggle for survival had been purged of its ideology and was becoming, if not a democracy, at least a respectable *état*. He told the House of Commons on 24 May that in Soviet Russia 'the Trotskyite form of Communism had been completely wiped out', without considering whether something worse might not have been erected in its place. But his attitude to the Soviet Union during that spring was one of increasing fear about its role in the post-war world. This did not prevent his sending to Stalin in the first days of the invasion accounts of what was happening in Normandy, which not only were upbeat, but divulged details he would have resisted disclosing to de Gaulle. When he drafted for Moscow telegrams of harsh complaint he nearly always addressed them to Molotov, whom he was nonetheless far from treating as either negligible or necessarily hostile. But when he was relaying Western hopes or actual successes he mostly did it to Stalin. Several of his bitter telegrams to Molotov were however consigned to the substantial volumes of Churchill's 'drafted but not sent' correspondence. This was sometimes on the advice of Eden and the Foreign Office and sometimes on that of the Chiefs of Staff.

Second among the factors fuelling Churchill's reservoir of gloom was that he could not turn from growing apprehension about the Russians to growing confidence that the United States would support him against them. On the contrary, Anglo-American strategic agreement, which had been almost miraculously well achieved between 1941 and mid-1943, came seriously apart at the end of that year and into 1944. It stemmed from an American feeling that Churchill never had his heart in Overlord and a corresponding British feeling that the Americans were equally deficient of commitment to the Italian campaign, and in particular that they did not share the British desire to push north-east as far as possible and pre-empt the arrival of the Russians in Vienna. On the ground, Anglo-American forces and commanders mostly continued to get on well together. But at the Chiefs of Staff level it was as though both sides had become dedicated to enterprises which the other did not like. The Americans were resolute for Anvil, the landing in the South of France, and would if necessary have been prepared to halt the advance in Italy, even before the capture of Rome, to make room for it. This was profoundly antipathetic to

Churchill, who increasingly thought that Anvil, even if it did not halt Alexander's advance in Italy, was misguided.

All of these military disputes more or less came out in the wash. Churchill had the assuagement that Alexander's offensive of mid-May was a success, although a hard-fought one, and resulted in the occupation of Rome. Anglo-American troops were outside the Palazzo Venezia, a symbolic point of occupation in view of Mussolini's orations from the central balcony there, by the evening of 4 June. This was a considerable boost to Churchill's morale in the immediate approach to D-day, but it did not obliterate the fact that, in the previous weeks of apprehensive waiting, so far from his quarrels with the Russians being balanced by perfect understanding across the Atlantic, the reverse had been the case.

Outweighing this, however, was Churchill's growing feeling that he was not the man he had been, certainly not physically and maybe not mentally either. On 7 May Brooke recorded a late-night conversation: 'He said that he could still always sleep well, eat well and especially drink well, but that he no longer jumped out of bed the way he used to, and felt as if he would be quite content to spend the whole day in bed.'[22] Allowance should be made for Brooke's savouring of downbeat remarks, but the point had been more graphically and objectively illustrated by the events of 26–29 April. Colville, although there were other confirming witnesses, set them out as follows:

Wednesday, April 26th. The P.M. made a fiasco of [parliamentary] Questions. He lost his place, answered the wrong question and forgot the name of the Maharajah of Kashmir [this last hardly the most heinous of crimes].

Friday, April 28th. The P.M. arrived [at Chequers] alone in his car, fast asleep with his black bandage over his eyes and remained asleep in the stationary car before the front door. There was then a dinner with Smuts, the statutory film following. Smuts went to bed, and the P.M. worked till 1.30, when the combined efforts of the Prof [Lindemann], Tommy [naval aide] and myself got him to bed too.

Saturday, April 29th. The P.M. did not wake till 11.35, which was strange.[23]

Yet this lassitude was interrupted by bursts of vitality. On 1 May, immediately following this weekend, there was, again in Colville's words, 'A mad rush to get to London by 12.00 noon in time for the opening of the meetings with the Dominion Prime Ministers at No. 10. The P.M. was late, of course, but the opening ceremony went off all right. . . .'[24] That afternoon he made what was variously described as a 'superb' and a 'brilliant' exposition to the assembled Prime Ministers of the whole war situation and prospects.

The Dominion Prince Ministers repaid him with an enthusiastic support which he had found recently lacking in the domestic press and Parliament. Smuts of South Africa had become almost excessively house-trained. He loved being at Churchill's side, whether in Cairo, London or Chequers. He gave wise advice, vitiated only by the fact that it was almost always exactly what Churchill wanted to hear. Mackenzie King of Canada was the head of government in the senior Dominion and because of its geographical position in relation to the United States was the only one which Churchill visited during the war. But King might have been put off by always being the *tertium quid* when Churchill was in North America, and the Canadians had also the tradition of leading the way to full Dominion independence. They were never in the sterling area and were the first to give up British titles. Nevertheless Mackenzie King was immensely supportive. 'It was perhaps the greatest of the many great things that Mr Churchill had done that he had withstood this [United States] pressure [for the Second Front] until the time was ripe,' he wrote.[25] Still more striking was the enthusiasm for Churchill of the two antipodeans. They were both Labour Prime Ministers. Fraser of New Zealand was in a semi-Smuts position. He had been much at Chequers. Curtin of Australia was more dour, and his country was nationally more suspicious of the Allied priority for the war against Germany over that against Japan, but he also showed an imaginative (given the geography) sympathy for Churchill's wariness about Soviet incursion into south-eastern Europe.

These expressions of admiring support were a great infusion for Churchill. Although the Dominion Prime Ministers remained for a full two weeks in England he was not impatient, and was happy to take them on various tours of troop inspection. His hold over them much sustained him. The Empire (or Commonwealth as it was becoming known, but it was never instinctively so thought of by Churchill) was fortified as an emotive force in his mind, creating in the late 1940s some conflict between his European federalism and his grand imperial view of Britain's position.

There were two other difficult issues for Churchill in the run-up to D-day. The first was bombing policy and the second was the handling of General de Gaulle in the new context of the Allied invasion of his country. They were not exactly inter-Allied disputes, for the issue of whether the great weight of bombs should be concentrated on French railway junctions was the brainchild of Solly Zuckerman (a young zoologist turned blast expert, whose versatile self-confidence was to play a major part in British defence policy for the next forty years) with Air Marshal Tedder, Eisenhower's deputy, as Zuckerman's convert and senior ranking advocate. Air Marshal Harris, head of Bomber Command, did not like it, for he could not take his eye off the obliteration of German cities. Nor, for different reasons, did Churchill. He thought that such a deployment would cause excessive French civilian casualties, and build up a strong anti-Allied resentment in France. He acknowledged that after D-day, 'when British and United States troops will probably be losing [men] at a much higher rate, a new proportion establishes itself',[26] but it was the intervening period which worried him. This was somewhat contrary to his general appraisal of the northern French battle, in which he rightly attached importance to the Germans not being able to reinforce quickly. The sundering of the French railway network was clearly a crucial contribution to this. On the other hand it fitted in with Churchill's dislike of slaughter and with his underlying francophilia. Roosevelt, however, felt no scruples and firmly took the view that whatever would assist the invasion should be done.

Even on casualties Churchill was full of ambiguity. He certainly did not wish to see another Somme, but he also believed that it was always the duty of troops to engage the enemy. He never liked quiet fronts or great quantities of staff officers ensconced in comfortable uselessness. Suddenly in early May he focused on those in Algiers, no longer a focal point of the war: 'The best thing would be to form a Sacred Legion of about 1,000 Staff officers and let them set an example to the troops in leading some particularly desperate attack.'[27] No such thing happened, of course, and nor in reality did he intend it to do. He was just blowing off against the excesses almost inevitably involved in any mass military organization.

The trouble in relation to de Gaulle was that neither the British nor the Americans were willing to give him much advance knowledge of where and when the landing was to take place. The Free French were regarded as congenitally insecure. Furthermore the Americans, even more than the British, who knew by this time the strength of de Gaulle's position with the resistance movements in France, were reluctant to accord to de Gaulle's Committee of National Liberation 'the title deeds of France'. De Gaulle was eventually invited over from Algiers to London and arrived in the early morning of Sunday, 4 June. He was greeted by a letter from Churchill asking him to join him for luncheon on his train in Hampshire. The train, lurking in sidings behind the south coast, had gone slightly to Churchill's head. It gave him a sense of advanced headquarters and almost of directing the invasion.

The previous evening he had come back from inspecting the embarkation of the Northumbrian Division at Southampton and of landing craft there and at Portsmouth, as well as paying a visit to Eisenhower's local headquarters. He had Smuts and Ernest Bevin with him on these visits (Bevin had been notably well received by the Tynesiders, which perhaps gave a thirteen-months early warning of the result of the 1945 general election) and Eden was waiting for him at the train. He then – Pierson Dixon, Eden's principal private secretary, is the witness – changed from his Trinity House navy serge into the lighter cavalry twill of a colonel of Hussars before presiding over 'a very convivial dinner' in the saloon. The food was 'admirable' and there was 1926 champagne and 'a grand old brandy out of balloon glasses'. The atmosphere was so relaxed, with Bevin and Eden expressing much mutual affection, that Churchill was tempted to say that 'he was ready to give up the leadership to either, or both of them, at any time'[28] – not perhaps the most precise of bequests.

The conviviality was by no means entirely repeated on the next day, even though Bevin, Eden and Smuts remained of the company and it was something that de Gaulle had agreed to come at all. De Gaulle's visit started fairly well. Churchill welcomed him with open arms on the railway track. But de Gaulle was not a man for easy intercourse, and on this occasion his reserve was easily comprehensible. He had been summoned first a thousand miles and then another eighty to an essentially theatrical setting. (Railway coaches in rural sidings had played a traumatic part, first one way in 1918 and then the other in 1940, in recent French history.)* There he was given thirty-six hours' notice of the invasion of his country. He was indeed lucky that it was thirty-six and not twelve for it was only the previous evening that weather forecasts had made Eisenhower order a postponement from 5 to 6 June. Churchill's other main message to him was that he ought to pay a Washington visit and try to improve his relations with Roosevelt over the crucial initial period of fighting in Normandy.

---

* The German surrender to Foch in November 1918 and the French surrender to Rundstedt in June 1940 had taken place in the same converted wagon-restaurant in the same siding in the forest of Compiègne.

Beyond this Churchill was recorded (by Eden) as having told de Gaulle that 'if after every effort had been exhausted the President [of the United States] was on one side and the French National Committee of Liberation on the other, he, Mr Churchill, would almost certainly side with the President, and that anyhow no quarrel would ever arise between Britain and the United States on account of France.'[29]

The record continued with de Gaulle saying that 'he quite understood that Britain would side with the United States'.[30] This was portrayed as being at least semi-conciliatory, although it was almost certainly said with more sarcasm than sympathy, and helped to form de Gaulle's view of nineteen years later when he vetoed Harold Macmillan's application to join the Common Market with the phrase that Britain belonged to 'le grand large' (the open sea) rather than in Europe. Churchill on 4 June was thought by his Cabinet colleagues present to have been too harsh to de Gaulle. Eden wrote in his 1965 volume of memoirs: 'I did not like this pronouncement, nor did Mr Bevin, who said so in a booming aside. The meeting was a failure.'[31] De Gaulle slowly took Churchill's advice to go to America, which he did from 6 to 11 July. He got on tolerably well with Roosevelt in Washington,* better paradoxically than he had with Churchill in Hampshire.

That evening Churchill went back to London, and stayed there over the next agonizingly tense few days. He had wanted to be much nearer to the scene of action, and in mid-May had bounced Admiral Ramsay into agreeing to a madcap plan. Ramsay, who as C-in-C Dover had been in charge of the Dunkirk evacuation, was in 1944, with a certain poetic justice, Allied naval commander (under Eisenhower) for the invasion. He reluctantly wrote to Churchill on 16 May.

> Briefly the plan is that you should embark in HMS Belfast ... in Weymouth Bay in the late afternoon of D minus 1, the ship being called

* This American visit of de Gaulle's was marked by one scene of almost total farce, in which de Gaulle conducted himself with a stiff propriety. Throughout the visit he stressed his military side, wore uniform the whole time, and, being also anxious not to be cosseted by Washington, expressed his determination to visit General Pershing, the American Commander in France of 1917–18. Pershing was eventually tracked down with difficulty to an old people's home in the Appalachians. When de Gaulle arrived Perhsing's semi-senile memory was stirred by his first sight of a French uniform and képi for many years. 'Tell me how is my old friend Marshal Pétain?' was therefore his first disconcerting remark to de Gaulle. 'La dernière fois que je l'ai vu, il se portait bien,' was de Gaulle's stiff but proper and formally accurate reply. That Pershing visit was not a success. (I am indebted for this recollection to Etienne Burin de Rozier, who accompanied de Gaulle to Washington and to Pershing.)

in on her passage from the Clyde for the purpose, and rejoining her squadron at full speed. I consider that nothing smaller than a cruiser is suitable for you during the night and the approach. . . . Next day it should be possible to transfer you to a destroyer which has completed her bombardment and which is due to return to England to re-ammunition. You could make a short tour of the beaches, with due regard to the unswept mine areas, before returning in her.[32]

Ramsay continued that he had respected Churchill's desire that the First Sea Lord should not be informed, but that he had thought it necessary to tell Eisenhower as Supreme Commander, 'and I must tell you that he is very averse to your going'.[33] Churchill's combination of courage and mischievousness pushed him towards irresponsibility at this supreme moment of the second half of the war. He told Colville on 25 April of his determination to be 'among the first on the bridgehead' and added, 'what fun it would be to get there before Monty'.[34] At least his Montgomery joke pointed to a considerable revival of spirits from the low points of the spring; and his determination appears to have been enough to sweep aside Eisenhower's opposition. Almost everyone was against Churchill's escapade. Certainly the Chiefs of Staff were when they heard. So was General Ismay, who made the rather clever point that the problem was not so much safety as being cut off from communications during a short period when crucial decisions might be necessary. Churchill boxed back, at least equally cleverly, by the whispered hint that if Ismay desisted, he would take him along.

It was however King George VI who eventually, and also with some subtlety, put a late block on the plan which was arousing such widespread consternation. At first the King treated it as a good idea and said that he would like to come too. Then, when he learned from his private secretary, Lascelles, of the strength of the opposition of the commanders, he withdrew from his own desire and devoted himself to trying to persuade Churchill also to do so. He was not prepared to issue a constitutional edict and formally to forbid the Prime Minister to go. But he used every other weapon in his armoury. It required two letters to undermine Churchill's resolve. In the second, sent as late as 4 June, the King wrote:

I want to make one more appeal to you not to go to sea on D Day. Please consider my own position. I am a younger man than you, I am a sailor, & as King I am the head of all three Services. There is nothing I would like to do better than to go to sea but I have agreed to stop at home; is it fair that you should then do exactly what I should have liked to do myself?[35]

   Churchill therefore had to spend the night of 5–6 June as 'a gentleman in England now abed'. Frustration combined with his persistent dislike of slaughter may have accounted for his alleged somewhat downbeat good-night comment to Clementine: 'Do you realize that by the time you wake up in the morning twenty thousand men may have been killed?'[36] This was not only macabre but pessimistic. In fact only about 3,000 Allied troops perished throughout the whole of D-day, and to the end of June the number killed did not exceed 8,000, of whom about two-thirds were American. At noon on D-day itself Churchill was able to give a tentatively favourable report to the House of Commons. He then lunched with the King and took him back to Allied Air Headquarters in St James's Square and the Eisenhower rear headquarters in Grosvenor Square. At 6.15 that evening, when he made a further and more confident statement to the House of Commons, he also paid a notable tribute to Eisenhower's 'courage'. This was evoked, although he did not say so, by the Supreme Commander's decision to go ahead with the invasion in spite of no more than doubtfully improving weather, after a postponement of only twenty-four hours. A further delay would have thrown the whole operation off balance, and in that bad summer, in sharp contrast with 1940, the year of defeat in France, a relentless search for a certain fair-weather period might have led to indefinite postponement.

39

THE BEGINNING OF THE END

CHURCHILL'S FIRST VISIT to the Normandy bridgehead was a day trip, accompanied by Smuts and Alan Brooke, to lunch at Montgomery's headquarters, then about five miles inland, on 12 June. Then there was a second and much longer one on 22–23 July, when he started with a visit to the Americans at Cherbourg and Utah Beach and then proceeded to the main British landing area at Arromanches, inspecting the Mulberry harbour and sleeping on the cruiser HMS *Enterprise*. On each of these July days he went to Montgomery's headquarters, and from there visited Caen and met the four British corps commanders as well as Omar Bradley, the principal American general under Eisenhower.

Churchill's return from each of these visits immediately preceded two separate but important events in the last summer of the war against Germany. On the evening of his return from the one-day visit the flying bombs or V1s first appeared over South-East England. Twenty-seven of these new and somewhat sinister weapons were launched that night, but only four reached the London area, and only one of them, landing at Bethnal Green, caused (two) fatal casualties. Thereafter there was a remarkably close one-to-one correlation between the number of these manless weapons – each about the size of a small fighter aircraft – launched and the fatalities they caused. On 6 July Churchill announced that in the first three weeks of the new assault 2,754 flying bombs had resulted in 2,752 deaths. By the end of August, when this particular threat died away, the number killed had risen to somewhat above 6,000. In addition nearly three-quarters of a million houses were damaged, but only 23,000 of them beyond repair.

These figures were well below those for the worst months of 1940–1, but they were sufficient to place a considerable strain on the worn nerves of a war-weary people. Many found the random threat, which could materialize at any hour of the day or night, in good or bad flying weather, more difficult to sustain than the more massive but more periodically predictable menace of the original blitz, three and a half years before. Churchill was not among those whose nerves frayed. He

56. Winston is back. Arriving at the Admiralty, 3 September 1939.

57. A War Cabinet for losing. *Left to right: seated*, Lord Halifax, Sir John Simon, Neville Chamberlain, Sir Samuel Hoare, Lord Chatfield; *back row*, Sir Kingsley Wood, WSC, Leslie Hore-Belisha, Lord Hankey.

58. A War Cabinet for winning. *Left to right: seated,* Sir John Anderson, WSC, Clement Attlee, Anthony Eden; *back row,* Arthur Greenwood, Ernest Bevin, Lord Beaverbrook, Sir Kingsley Wood.

59. A disparate trio. WSC leaving Neville Chamberlain's last Cabinet meeting on the morning of 10 May 1940, with his two best Cabinet allies on that day of decision, Kingsley Wood and Anthony Eden. (Churchill was Prime Minister by the evening.)

60. WSC and Clementine arriving at Westminster Abbey for a service of national prayer on 26 May 1940. It is his gas mask and not their lunch which Churchill is carrying. It is one of the rare photographs of him without a cigar.

61. WSC leaving 10 Downing Street on 20 August 1940 to deliver his 'never have so many owed so much to so few' speech to the House of Commons. Brendan Bracken is behind.

62. WSC and Clementine inspecting Thames-side bomb damage from the river, 25 September 1940. Not *pace* Ford Madox Ford's famous tondo of emigrants, 'the last of England', thanks largely to Churchill.

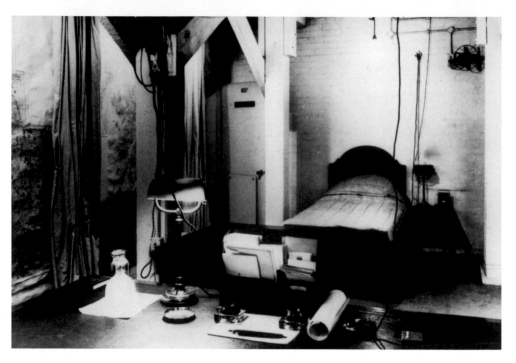

63. WSC's office/bedroom in the underground part of the Cabinet Annexe.

64. The dining room of the Annexe – at least an opportunity for conviviality was maintained, even under a lowering reinforced ceiling.

65. WSC as Chancellor of Bristol University conferring honorary degrees on Robert Menzies (Prime Minister of Australia) and Gilbert Winant (US Ambassador) on the day after that city's worst air raid, April 1941.

66. WSC working on his famous wartime train.

67. A rather stiff initial greeting on board USS *Augusta*, 9 August 1941. WSC hands over a letter from King George VI, who up to then knew Roosevelt much better than he did Churchill. FDR is supported by his son Elliott.

68. Sunday morning service under the guns of the *Prince of Wales*, on the following day.

69. WSC with Stalin (almost as friendly as with Consuelo Marlborough nearly four decades earlier) at a Kremlin banquet 16 August 1942.

70. 'The duennas arrange the match': the de Gaulle/Giraud reluctant handshake, Casablanca, 24 January 1943.

71. The big three at Teheran, November 1943.

72. Tunis, Christmas Day, 1943. WSC, perhaps aided by his multi-coloured
dressing gown, had recovered enough from his pneumonia to be able to lunch
with, among others, Generals Eisenhower and Alexander.

73. WSC with Montgomery on the Normandy beachhead, 12 June 1944.

74. WSC with Alexander in Italy, 26 August 1944.

75. WSC with Marshal Tito at Naples, 12 August 1944: the Communist Marshal is a little more formally dressed than the Conservative Prime Minister.

76. On the other hand, General de Gaulle rather upstages him on the Champs Elysées (Duff Cooper, Eden and Bidault behind), 11 November 1944.

77. WSC watching a battle in Italy, 26 August 1944 – the nearest (in the Second World War) to the front line he was ever allowed.

78. Archbishop
Damaskinos looks
down from a greater
height, Athens,
Christmas 1944.

79. WSC, a frail
Roosevelt and a
dour Stalin at Yalta,
February 1945.

80. A bleak picnic
beside the Rhine,
with Alanbrooke and
Montgomery, 26
March 1945.

81. WSC and Attlee leaving Westminster Abbey after Lloyd George's memorial service, 11 April 1945.

82. 8 May 1945: VE day in London.

Above: WSC ambushed by friendliness between Whitehall and the House of Commons.

Right: Sovereign and Prime Minister on the balcony of Buckingham Palace. After a hesitant start, five years of slow march to victory had made them unusually close.

Above: 83. WSC electioneering from the portico of the Red Lion Hotel, High Wycombe in June 1945. Many who came to listen and to applaud failed to vote for him. High Wycombe, typically, became a Labour seat.

Right: 84. WSC meeting President Truman for the first time. Potsdam, 15 July 1945.

Below: 85. On the reviewing stand for the Berlin victory parade, July 1945. *Left to right,* Montgomery, Lord Cherwell (over WSC's shoulder), WSC, General Ismay, Field Marshal Alexander, Anthony Eden.

86. Conservative front-benchers looking relaxed in the absence of their leader in the late 1940s. *Left to right*, Macmillan, Cranborne (later Salisbury), Crookshank, Woolton, Maxwell Fyfe, Eden, Butler.

87. WSC benignly contemplating his second term as Prime Minister. Woodford, 26 October 1951.

88. WSC dressed as for a polar expedition and taking leave of the Queen after staying at Balmoral, 30 September 1952. The children are now the Prince of Wales and the Princess Royal.

89. The tribulations of Anthony. WSC and Eden return from the United States, July 1954.

90. The last goodbye, (from office if not from the Queen), April 1955. Clementine and Prince Philip are in the doorway of 10 Downing Street.

91. Killing time in the South of France. WSC with his daughter Sarah and Emery Reves at La Pausa, February 1956.

92. WSC with Aristotle Onassis and others on board *Christina*.

was among the most war-weary, but he had unrelenting physical courage
and he took a perverse pleasure in big bangs. He imperturbably continued his dictation even when the V1s were close at hand. He assured
Stalin, perhaps with a touch of bravado, that the new weapon had 'no
appreciable effect upon the . . . life of London. . . . The streets and parks
remain full of people enjoying the sunshine when off work or duty.'[1]

The low one-per-bomb average casualty rate did not preclude a
number of nasty multiple incidents, for the average was lowered by
many of the V1s falling harmlessly in open country. On Sunday, 18
June sixty were killed in the Guards Chapel on Birdcage Walk when a
bomb fell on them during morning service; on 30 June what should
have been a harmless shortfall killed thirty-two at a children's home
within a mile of Chartwell; and in that same month a strike on the
eastern arm of Aldwych during the lunch hour of one of the few
beautiful days of that dismal summer produced a peculiarly vivid carnage
of office workers.

Churchill's Prime Ministerial reaction was not as indifferent as his
own stolidity or his message to Stalin implied. He was not tempted to
divert Allied strategy in France so as to get more quickly to the
launching sites, mostly in the Pas-de-Calais. But he played hard with
some wild schemes for inflicting retaliatory punishment on the Germans, who he thought had sacrificed all consideration by the manifestly
indiscriminate nature of the flying-bomb weapon against the civilian
population. Gas and even chemical warfare reprisals he caused to be
urgently studied, together with a scheme for the one-by-one obliteration
of a hundred medium-sized German towns. Eventually he was reluctantly persuaded by professional RAF advice that none of these would
work, and had to accept more passive endurance.

Underlying this reaction was a fear of the still greater menace of
Hitler's second secret weapon, the V2 rockets. The first of these was
launched on 8 September, just after the capture of the launching sites
brought release from the V1s. One fell in Chiswick and killed three.
The other was in Churchill's constituency, just north of Epping town
itself, and merely destroyed a few sheds. The government curiously
decided to try to envelop these attacks in a pall of secrecy – a gas main
was alleged to have exploded at Chiswick. Whether Churchill was a
party to (or even the instigator of) this dissimulation is not clear. He
was on his way to the second Quebec conference at the time. The *New
York Times* 'blew' the story on 12 September, but, as with the foreign
press on King Edward VIII and Mrs Simpson, this august organ did not

inform most people in Britain. The pretence of mystery was maintained for several weeks.

The V2 rockets carried a heavier high-explosive charge than the flying bombs and approached totally silently (unlike the V1s, which chugged noisily but safely overhead until their engines cut out). If you heard the explosion of a V2, someone else and not you were the victim. They were impossible to intercept and there was no defence other than the extirpation of the sites by bombing, which was very difficult, or by capture, which took until the last days of the war. The V2 ordeal thus lasted longer than did the V1s. During 177 days a total of 1,050 rockets fell on or around London. While the V2s also produced several mass carnages, the total fatalities were lower than with the flying bombs. But an average of seven unheralded rockets a day was an unwelcome accompaniment to the sixth, last and very cold winter of the war.

In France, in the summer of 1944, the result of the long-planned and long-argued-over invasion was first a secure bridgehead, which was a great relief. Next came a frustrating period of near stalemate that lasted for six weeks. Then, from 25 July there was a third phase of break-out and rapid advance, so that Paris was entered by Allied troops on 24 August and even Brussels was reached by 3 September. These successes were a vindication of the Roosevelt–Marshall determination on a full Second Front over the more hesitant Churchill–Brooke approach. The tilt in the Anglo-American balance which resulted from this was accentuated by the American troops under Omar Bradley getting most of the superficial glory from the advance. Montgomery's Twenty-First Army Group faced very hard if successful fighting around Caen and Falaise in order to provide a secure hub rotating on which Bradley's Twelfth Army was able to cover spectacular distances, sweeping down the Cotentin peninsula from Cherbourg and doing a right swing which took them within three weeks to Dreux, Chartres and Orléans.

Eisenhower, in the best sense of the word a political more than a fighting general, was brilliant at least until the autumn at preventing exacerbation between the two armies in the field. But at a still higher level the Anglo-American accord, which had held very strongly during the testing two and a half years of defeat followed by only peripheral attack, instead of being warmed by the sun of victory began badly to cool. The first issue, but it was only the first, was that of whether the Second Front should be supplemented by an Allied invasion of the South of France, first codenamed Anvil (as already discussed in the previous chapter), which the Americans claimed had been firmly agreed upon at Teheran. They were as dedicated to this as the British were opposed. The essential Churchill objection was that mounting this largely purposeless enterprise involved such a gross weakening of Alexander's forces in Italy as to inhibit his breaking through into the Po valley, destroying Kesselring's army and pressing on to reach Vienna, an objective on which for reasons of the Western Allies–Russian balance in central Europe, Churchill's heart was firmly set.

This dispute escalated between 21 June and 1 July from disagreements at Chiefs of Staff level to exchanges between Prime Minister and President which were far more acrimonious than anything which had previously passed between them. The Americans were absolutely unbudgeable on the issue and the British, rapidly becoming the junior military partners, ultimately had no option but to accept their decision. But not before (fortunately secretly) 'all [ten] day[s] long the noise of battle rolled'. The exceptional roughness of the exchanges can be gauged from Churchill's message to Roosevelt of 1 July. In reply to an unyielding response from the President to previous arguments he signalled: 'We are deeply grieved by your telegram ... [which], in my humble and respectful opinion, [insists on] the first major strategic and political error for which we two have to be responsible.'[2] In his final telegram of this series, sent the same day, Churchill wrote that he 'must enter a solemn protest' against a decision which left his hopes for the Italian campaign 'dashed to the ground'. 'It is with the greatest sorrow that I write to you in this sense,' he continued.[3]

Perhaps even more resented than the unshakeable American ukase were two of the arguments which were used from Washington in the course of the dispute. The British believed that a Bletchley decrypt of a 17 June instruction from Hitler provided their trump card in the argument for maintaining the Allied strength in Italy. The key sentence was: 'The Fuehrer has ordered the Apennine position as the final blocking line, since the enemy's entry into the Po plain would have incalculable military and political consequences.'[4] The British Chiefs of Staff took the view that this made it certain that the propping up of Kesselring's army against full-strength Alexander assaults would draw German divisions away from the Overlord front more effectively and more quickly than would an August-launched South of France landing. When they pressed the Americans on the point they (and Churchill) were deeply shocked when Marshall said that, while the Bletchley decrypts were of course very valuable, it must be remembered that, had absolute weight been given to them, it was doubtful whether Overlord would ever have been launched.[5]

The second 'insult' was what Churchill chose to interpret as a suggestion of Roosevelt's on 29 June that the British and the Americans should lay 'our respective cases before Stalin for arbitration'.[6] It is difficult to see that President's message bore this inference. What Roosevelt actually said was 'I am mindful of our agreement with Stalin as to an operation against the south of France and his frequently expressed views favouring such an operation and classifying all others in the Mediterranean of lesser importance . . .'; and 'In the event that you and I are unable to issue a direction to General [Sir Maitland] Wilson [the Allied C-in-C in the Mediterranean] by 1 July to launch Anvil at the earliest possible date, we must communicate with Stalin immediately.'[7] There may have been an element of implied threat here, but the specific proposal for arbitration was a figment of Churchill's imagination, which had become somewhat fevered on the issue. In one of his famous series of 'unsent' communications he drafted a message to Roosevelt on 30 June threatening to resign against Anvil.

This Anglo-American argument was traumatic enough in itself. Even after 1 July, when the British Chiefs of Staff, in Alan Brooke's words, succeeded in persuading Churchill that his only sensible attitude was 'All right, if you insist on being damned fools, sooner than falling out with you, which would be fatal, we shall be damned fools with you, and we shall see that we perform the role of damned fools damned well,'[8] Churchill insisted on returning to the issue in August and arguing, maybe sensibly but certainly ineffectively, that the landings should be on the west and not the south coast of France. Still more significant, however, was that, whether causally or coincidentally, the Anvil disagreement was the beginning of a new pattern. Before it the American and British Chiefs of Staff had rarely disagreed on a major issue. After it they were rarely on the same side of any issue, and the British side, because of the growing discrepancy of power, nearly always turned out to be the losing side.

Churchill's instinctive interim solution to any inter-Allied difficulty was to propose a summit meeting about it. At the height of his Anvil quarrel with Roosevelt he wrote almost plaintively: 'I am sure that if we could have met, as I so frequently proposed, we should have realized a happy agreement.'[9] He even had something of the same approach to Stalin, the bear in his den which he could hardly ever be persuaded to leave, but whom Churchill was always ready unilaterally to visit, and twice did so, as well as angling for invitations on several other occasions.

Why was Churchill so eager for these face-to-face encounters? It was not that he suffered from any inarticulateness on paper. On the contrary, there was his Whitehall rule, proclaimed at the beginning of his premiership, that all his instructions were to be written, and indeed there was a distinct impression that, both in his Anvil argument with Roosevelt and even more so in the spring of 1945 and the last weeks of Roosevelt's life, that his dictating fluency was leading him to smother the President in a flood of long messages. It was more to do with his almost obsessive love of travel, with his belief in the force of his own personality in a vis-à-vis situation, and with his desire, if there were more powerful men than himself in the world, of which he was becoming sombrely aware, to be frequently close to their powerhouses.

Normally these summit encounters went well. He established close and even warm relations with his interlocutors, not merely Roosevelt but also Stalin. He came away feeling that much had been achieved, that misunderstandings and even genuine differences had been straightened out, that his journey had been worth while. Yet the sad pattern was that, particularly in the second half of the war, the differences and difficulties quickly reasserted themselves and things went on much as before.

Churchill was almost always the visitor.* His efforts to get Roosevelt, still more Stalin, to London or Edinburgh or a shipboard conference in British waters always failed. And as the visitor he was to some extent always the *demandeur*. He had sought the encounter, and felt more than an equal share of the responsibility for making a success of it. The ambience of his own capital city always enhances the importance of the home head of state or government. With both Roosevelt and Stalin he was dealing with spiders at the centres of most formidable webs. Furthermore, if there were difficult crunches he did not have the cold immovability of a Stalin or a de Gaulle. He tended to break rather than to maintain silences. He could argue a case with resonance and even brilliance. But if he did not get his way he was not, at the highest level,

---

* The only two semi-neutral exceptions were when he and Roosevelt met at Casablanca and Cairo. At the two Quebec conferences Churchill came 'three thousand miles across the sea' whereas Roosevelt was within 400 miles of his family house at Hyde Park, where indeed he entertained Churchill in the surrounding days of both conferences.

very good at sulking ominously. As a result he tended to think that summits had achieved more than in fact they had.

The second half of 1944 provided plenty of opportunity for Churchill to assuage his travel lust, to experience the headiness and the disappointments of summits, and to suck the bittersweet fruit of realizing that, as Allied victory became nearer, Britain and he became less important among the Allies. In early August he failed to get Roosevelt, with or without Stalin, to come to Britain. 'I must deeply regret your inability to visit,' he cabled on 10 August, adding wistfully, 'The King seemed very disappointed when I told him.'[10] However he secured from the President the promise of a second bilateral Quebec conference (this one codenamed Octagon) and with this in his pocket he was able to enjoy an extended Italian visit which took him away from England from 10 to 29 August. It was a mixture of bathing holiday (with expeditions to the Capri Blue Grotto and to Ischia, and many immersions in various coves of the Bay of Naples), of serious conferences, and of movement up and down the peninsula, getting as near as possible to the firing lines. He even embarked on a destroyer and sailed for five hours to within a few miles of St Tropez in order to see as much as he could of the South of France landings which he had so bitterly opposed. It was a classic example of 'if you can't beat them, join them' and of his determination to get as near as he could to any scene of military action. It could have been regarded as an act of magnanimity, but he in no way abated his semi-private criticism of the reviled diversion.

On his way from London to Naples Churchill had stopped for a few hours in Algiers, where he asked de Gaulle to call upon him. The General refused. This produced great resentment: 'Naturally at times like this I do not let [it] influence my political judgment,' he a little implausibly wrote to Clementine Churchill, 'but I feel that de Gaullist France will be a France more hostile to England than any since Fashoda.'*[11] In Naples Tito was Churchill's first non-British visitor. He at least came, and there were two reasonably amicable meetings, although the Foreign Office official Pierson Dixon, who was then Eden's principal private secretary and who curiously accompanied Churchill throughout the long Italian visit, keeping a meticulous diary, wrote somewhat critically:

* The 1898 incident on the western borders of the Sudan, which produced great Franco-British bitterness.

Tito was cautious, nervous and sweating a good deal in his absurd Marshal's uniform of thick cloth and gold lace. . . . The P.M. pitched into Tito a good deal towards the end, and told him that we could not tolerate our war material being used against rival Yugoslavs. But Tito must have known that there was no real threat against him, since we have consistently done nothing but court him. . . .

We went straight from the conference into a lunch in Tito's honour, to which the Commander-in-Chief and Harold Macmillan came. The P.M., looking pasty and ill, lurched to his feet at the end and made a highly laudatory speech about Tito's exploits, welcoming him as an ally. This was a tactical mistake, which undid the good of the sermon at the conference.[12]

Churchill then moved into reminiscent mood, telling Tito how thirty-one years before he had visited the Dalmatian coast in the Admiralty yacht with Asquith and how politics had been mentioned only once 'during the forty days on tour'.[13] As the cruise lasted only nineteen days, and as Asquith's main complaint had been that Churchill never talked about anything but politics, this illustrated the frailty of reminiscent memory.

In the course of his Italian peregrinations (which were all in the form of several-day expeditions from his base in the Naples villa of General Wilson) Churchill looked down on Florence (still in German hands), stayed several nights at the newly reopened British Embassy in Rome and had an audience of Pope Pius XII. They agreed they were both against Communism. Churchill also put his toe into the muddy waters of post-Mussolini Roman politics. Almost at the end of his visit he got General Alexander to take him very near to the front line north of Ancona. 'This was the nearest I got to the enemy and the time I heard most bullets in the Second World War.'[14]

Churchill was back in England (where he arrived with a sudden temperature of 103° and a small patch on one lung) for only six days before departing in the *Queen Mary* for the Quebec conference. A mixture of the early antibiotic called M & B, anti-malaria tablets (which he had to take for four weeks after leaving Italy) and the ship ploughing for several days through the sticky heat of the Gulf Stream produced general testimony that Churchill was low during the voyage. He spent much of it in his cabin reading Trollope's *Phineas Finn* and *The Duke's Children*, although at dinner on the third night, according to Colville, he managed to work his way through 'oysters, consommé, turbot, roast turkey, ice with canteloupe melon, Stilton cheese and a great variety of fruit, petits fours etc, the whole washed down by champagne (Mumm 1929) and a very remarkable Liebfraumilch, followed by some 1870 brandy'.[15]

In spite of these diversions he remained either subdued or harshly critical throughout the voyage, which was normally one of his favourite ways of passing five days. He announced that, following an election, he 'would not regret the loss of any of his Labour colleagues except [Ernest] Bevin'.[16] But this may have been because he had just been having a sharp exchange with Attlee, who insisted on the War Cabinet reaching some decisions during Churchill's many and prolonged absences. The Prime Minister also succeeded in angering Alan Brooke at a staff conference on 9 September.

Once he had got to the relative freshness of Quebec City and the stimulus of a conference at the highest level, Churchill's spirits soared. 'The Conference has opened in a blaze of friendship,' he telegraphed to the War Cabinet on the evening of 13 September. 'The Staffs are in almost complete agreement already.'[17] In spite of this euphoria, Quebec II did not settle a great deal, and some of what was nominally settled was not sensible. This applied particularly to the Morgenthau Plan for turning post-war Germany into a primarily pastoral community. Henry Morgenthau Jr had been US Secretary to the Treasury since 1934 and, although a Jew, was a patrician landowning country neighbour of Roosevelt's in the Hudson Valley – an unusual combination at the time. He had also been a keen supporter of Roosevelt since his 1928 campaign for the governorship of New York State, and this again was unusual among F.D.R.'s neighbours. Morgenthau's influence was therefore considerable, and the President was temporarily attracted to his fairly crack-brained plan.

What was more surprising was that it temporarily captivated Churchill. Here Lord Cherwell was the foolish counsellor. Of the British who were present at the Quebec dinner when Morgenthau expounded his ideas only 'the Prof' was favourable. But Lindemann, who was always bitterly resentful that, largely by accident, he had been born in Germany, supported Morgenthau, and he, like his ally, carried great influence with his principal. In any event both Roosevelt and Churchill formally endorsed the Plan on 15 September. The Foreign Ministers of both countries were appalled. Eden told Churchill it would never get through the War Cabinet. Cordell Hull, exercising more strategic influence than usual, mobilized the full resources of the State

Department to kill the Plan. Just how unrealistic it was is well illustrated by the contrast between what actually happened in the 1950s and 1960s and one of the arguments put to Churchill by Cherwell: 'I explained to Winston that the plan would save Britain from bankruptcy by eliminating a dangerous competitor.'[18]

For the rest the strong impression emerges that the hard issues of strategic divergence were barely engaged with. The American Chiefs of Staffs, whose forces in Europe were rapidly becoming vastly superior in numbers to the British – by the end of the war they were approximately three million to one million – were naturally elevated by the success of Overlord, contrasting their consistent advocacy with the hesitations of the British. Dragoon (ex-Anvil), whatever the rights and wrongs of the strategic argument, had produced no setbacks and a rapid advance up the Rhône valley. Two days before the beginning of the Quebec conference there had been a meeting near Dijon of the Allied forces from Normandy with those from Provence. Even Churchill, in his opening statement at Quebec, felt constrained to say that the results of Dragoon had been 'most gratifying'.

Having got so much of what they wanted, the Americans were content to give general assurances that there would be no further weakening of Alexander's army in Italy until Kesselring's resistance had been overcome. But behind these courtesies there was a major underlying difference. The Americans were essentially interested in smashing the Wehrmacht on the central front and, provided this objective was achieved, did not much mind where they joined hands with the Soviet army. The British, on the other hand, were increasingly concerned about keeping Communism as far east as possible. They wanted to stop Tito seizing Trieste, to get to Vienna first, to encourage the Americans to do the same with Prague and above all to see either Montgomery or Bradley into the capital of the Third Reich before the Red Flag was hoisted there.

There was also some underlying difference about the approach to the war against Japan, which campaign was much discussed at Quebec. Churchill was determined to prevent the Americans thinking that the British were going quietly to contract out of this. Indeed he devoted much of the final press conference (joint with Roosevelt) to a semi-jocular rejection of the view that 'the British wish to shirk their obligations in the Japanese war. . . . And that [suggestion] astonished me very much, because, as a matter of fact, the conference has been marked by exactly the opposite tendency. If there was any point of difference which had to be adjusted, it was that we undoubtedly felt that the United States meant to keep too much of it to themselves. . . . You can't have all the good things to yourselves. You must share.'[19]

The British did not want their principal role to be that of fighting indefinitely in the appalling conditions of the jungles of Burma. They were eager that, once Germany had been defeated, their main fleet should be available for the central assault on Japan. But the Americans thought that Britain's essential interest was in the recovery of the imperial territories from which it had been so ignominiously ejected, and above all in a triumphant re-entry to Singapore. And the Americans, including the President, were far from enthusiastic about propping up the British Empire.

Such problems were not allowed to mar Churchill's favourite *bonne bouche* at the end of the Quebec conference, which was two days more or less alone with Roosevelt at Hyde Park. When asked by his egregious doctor on the way home whether he had found Quebec more or less tiring than the Cairo conference of the previous year, he was recorded as saying: 'What is this conference? Two talks with the Chiefs of Staff; the rest was waiting for the chance to put in a word with the President.'[20] However much he may have had to wait at Quebec his desires were abundantly met at Hyde Park. Except for his own entourage (never small, but disposable) and Harry Hopkins, whom he was delighted to see there, because he feared that Hopkins had fallen out of favour, there were no other guests. It was the last time that he ever had Roosevelt properly to himself. There was a brief encounter at Malta on the way to Yalta five months later, but at the Yalta conference itself Roosevelt, apart from his manifest exhaustion, was depressingly anxious to maintain equidistance between Stalin and Churchill.

This last Hyde Park visit, however, was sufficient to send Churchill back across the Atlantic in a much higher state of morale than that in which he had arrived. The testimony was unanimous, Colville, Moran, Cunningham and Marian Holmes, the dictating secretary. 'PM in excellent form', Admiral Cunningham, exhibiting a fine tolerance for reminiscence, noted, '& most interesting about his time at the Admiralty in the last war.'[21] The party got back to London on the morning of 26 September. That afternoon Churchill answered questions in the House of Commons and, although the main news on arrival was of the near annihilation of the 1st Airborne Division, which had attacked 'a bridge too far' by landing on the lower Rhine at Arnhem in Holland, he was reasonably upbeat both then and when he delivered a massive oration to the House two days later, an hour before lunch and another hour after it. Nicolson's verdict on this second occasion was: 'He is in fine form at the start, finding his words easily, thumping upon the box. But after three quarters of an hour his voice gets husky and his delivery hesitant.'[22]

Churchill's main next desire was to be off to Russia for another summit. His specific reason for going, as recorded by Colville, to whom he normally spoke frankly, was curious:

> The P.M.'s visit to Moscow, which is really very dangerous to his health, is, he assured me yesterday, entirely because he wants to discourage any idea that the U.K. and the U.S.A. are very close (as exemplified by the Quebec Conference) to the exclusion of Russia. His visit will make it quite clear that our counsels with Russia are close too, and that there is no tendency to leave her in the cold.[23]

The reason given was curious because it was exactly this attitude on Roosevelt's part which had affronted Churchill at the Teheran conference and was to do so again at Yalta. It was perhaps even more movement and summitry as such which attracted him, and also the hope that, face to face with Stalin, he could make progress on the future of Poland, Greece and other eastern European countries which the prospect of victory brought into sharp focus. He was off on the night of 7 October, in the relative luxury for the time of a York airliner, having prepared for his journey by taking Clementine, unusually, on two theatre expeditions, first to Shaw's *Arms and the Man* and then to Shakespeare's *Richard III*. After halts for refuelling, baths and brief conferences at Naples and Cairo, he arrived in Moscow on the morning of 9 October, unfortunately at the wrong airport (as at Tunis ten months before, but with less deleterious consequences) and had to make a corrective further flight of half an hour to encounter Vyshinsky and a welcoming guard of honour. Eden and Alan Brooke also came to Moscow but, at the urgent request of King George VI, in a separate plane.

Churchill began his *Second World War* account of this conference (codenamed Tolstoy) with a manifest inaccuracy: 'This time we were lodged in Moscow itself, with every care and comfort. I had one small, perfectly appointed house and Anthony [Eden] another near by.'[24] More detailed records, meticulously used by Martin Gilbert, make it clear however that he started at a dacha twenty-three miles and three-quarters of an hour's drive from the city, and there spent his first two nights in Russia, even travelling back between 2 and 3 a.m. on one of them. While this was typical of some of the minor errors of fact (together with occasional major ones) which marred the sometimes compelling narratives of Churchill's *pièce justificative*, there was happily a portion of the truth for everyone. The Russians lavishly provided both a country and a town house, and from the night of 11 October onwards, except for the 13th, he decided that he preferred urban convenience.

The lavishness of the Russian accommodation was paralled by Stalin's friendliness. And this in turn was more than equalled by Churchill's, as he set out to be pleasant and to establish a relationship with Stalin of two well-matched hard-boiled figures who having seen everything were up to anything, not even excluding a little ganging up against Roosevelt. Above all he wanted to put a seal of warmth on the talks. On 13 October he wrote to Clementine: 'The affairs go well.... I have had vy nice talks with the Old Bear. I like him the more I see him. *Now* they respect us here & I am sure they wish to work w. us.' Then in a semi-detached aside: 'I have to keep the President in constant touch & this is the delicate side.'[25]

Three days later he wrote in even more enthusiastic terms to King George VI (in the third person):

Here in Moscow the weather is brilliant but crisp, and the political atmosphere is extremely cordial.... The Prime Minister and Mr Eden in their various talks with Marshal Stalin and M. Molotov have been able to deal with the most delicate problems in a frank, outspoken manner without the slightest sign of giving offence. The Prime Minister attended a special performance of the ballet, which was very fine, and received a prolonged ovation from an enormous audience.... At or after the very lengthy feasts, and very numerous cordial toasts, it has been possible to touch on many grave matters in an easy fashion. The nights are very late, lasting till three or even four o'clock; but the Prime Minister also keeps late hours, and much work is done from about noon onwards....[26]

The first and most important meeting with Stalin was for about three hours at 10.00 on the evening of arrival, 9 October. Although it was perhaps the most indiscreet bilateral which Churchill ever held, he was not alone with his interlocutor. There were inevitably two interpreters present, and also Eden, Molotov and Clark Kerr, the British ambassador in Moscow. Nor could Churchill, even with his vast qualities of adrenaline-induced vitality, have been at his freshest. He had spent the previous two nights in an aeroplane, and was between his sixty-first and sixty-fourth hour without a proper night's rest. This may have accounted for some part of the indiscretion, although Churchill was almost as good at containing his tiredness as he was his alcohol, and even the combination of the two, which was no doubt present on this occasion.

The jauntiness was illustrated by some of his remarks about the Poles and the Italians and by one aside about Eden, which must have been intended as a joke in view of Eden's presence when it was made. One of the central purposes of the visit was to agree upon a Polish settlement, for which the key issues were the surrender of a lot of pre-war Polish territory to the Russians and a bringing together of the so-called Lublin Polish government, which was a Russian puppet, and the London Polish government, which the Russians no doubt thought, although with less justification, was a British puppet. To assist the process Churchill judged it wise to show the detachment of big boys dealing with small fry and hope that this would encourage Stalin to do the same. 'The difficulty about the Poles', he said, 'was that they had unwise political leaders. Where there were two Poles there was one quarrel.' Stalin capped this by saying, 'Where there was one Pole he would begin to quarrel with himself through sheer boredom.'[27]

Churchill's central indiscretion at this Kremlin meeting was his production of what he called the 'naughty document' which proposed *Realpolitik* spheres of influence in the Balkans. The record reported him as saying that 'the Americans would be shocked if they saw how crudely he had put it. Marshal Stalin was a realist. He himself was not sentimental while Mr Eden was a bad man [which presumably meant that he was liable to be unrealistically sentimental]. He [Churchill] had not consulted his Cabinet or Parliament.'[28] This led into the famous (or infamous) percentages deal with Stalin. As Churchill subsequently put it in the sixth volume of his war memoirs, published in 1954:

> The moment was apt for business, so I said, 'Let us settle about our affairs in the Balkans. Your armies are in Roumania and Bulgaria. We have interests, missions and agents there. Don't let us get at cross-purposes in small ways. So far as Britain and Russia are concerned, how would it do for you to have ninety per cent predominance in Roumania, for us to have ninety per cent of the say in Greece, and go fifty–fifty about Yugoslavia?' While this was being translated I wrote out on a half-sheet of paper:

Roumania
    Russia 90%
    The others 10%
Greece
    Great Britain (in accord with the U.S.A.) 90%
    Russia 10%
Yugoslavia 50–50%
Hungary 50–50%
Bulgaria
    Russia 75%
    The others 25%

I pushed this across to Stalin, who had by then heard the translation. There was a slight pause. Then he took his blue pencil and made a large tick upon it, and passed it back to us. It was all settled in no more time than it takes to set down.[29]

But how much was settled? The Polish issue, the most acute of the lot, was not included. The 50–50 arrangements for Yugoslavia and Hungary remained dead letters, and it would be very difficult to define to what the 10 per cent for the Western Allies in Roumania or the 25 per cent in Bulgaria amounted. What was of practical value to Britain was that, in return for the virtual Sovietization of the rest of the Balkans, Stalin rigidly refrained from using his vast trouble-making capacity in the Greek cauldron and left Churchill a free hand to deal with the Communist guerrillas there.

Churchill's account continued: 'After this [the tick] there was a long silence. The pencilled paper lay in the centre of the table. At length I said, "Might it not be thought rather cynical if it seemed we had disposed of these issues, so fateful to millions of people, in such an offhand manner? Let us burn the paper." "No, you keep it," said Stalin.'[30] Churchill at the time interpreted this as being a sign of friendliness and of willingness for him to have the evidence of commitment. As most things worked out, however, it could equally well have been interpreted as an indication of the small importance that Stalin attached to the exchange. Was Churchill proud of the deal that he thought he had done with Stalin? There are contradictory indications. First, he did not attempt concealment from his War Cabinet colleagues in London. He put them fairly fully in the picture in a telegram of 12 October, only hedging to the extent of saying that the percentages were intended to be no more 'than a guide'; and he received no remonstrance from them. In a prior telegram sent to Roosevelt on the 11th, however, while purporting to describe the previous evening's conversation, he did not make the picture at all clear. Furthermore he allowed heavy doctoring of the official secret Cabinet record of the Kremlin proceedings. The notes of the British interpreter (Birse), from which much of Churchill's 1954 account and effectively the whole of Martin Gilbert's 1986 one were taken, were heavily censored by Colonel Jacob, of Churchill's own staff, with the concurrence of Edward Bridges, the secretary of the Cabinet. 'I have sidelined certain passages,' Jacob wrote, 'which seem most inappropriate for a record of this importance. . . . [They might] give the impression to historians that these very important discussions were conducted in a most unfitting manner.'[31]

This Moscow visit was spread over ten days. Churchill did not leave until the afternoon of 19 October. He was unwell for nearly twenty-four hours from the morning of the 15th. It was becoming almost unknown for him to complete any major overseas expedition without some incapacity striking him. He took all these vicissitudes with remarkable equanimity, never appearing (except to his doctor) intimidated by soaring (clinical) temperatures in unpromising locations, and nearly always keeping up the paperwork through his fevers.

On the morning 15 October after his exhilarating Bolshoi visit he awoke with a severe stomach upset. Soviet doctors were called in and by noon he was able to get up and have a meeting with two of the recalcitrant London Poles. Whether or not as a result of their recalcitrance, he was worse again by the afternoon, with a temperature of 101°, and Moran decided to summon from Cairo three specialists, two of them the old Carthage team, and two nurses. By next morning, however, Churchill's temperature had declined to normal, the summonses were cancelled and he behaved with full vigour for the remaining three and a half days of the visit.

Although there was a good deal of discussion about purely military matters (which Churchill missed), about the speed with which the Russians would enter the war against Japan after the defeat of Germany (an early commitment which he wanted to bring back like a retrieved gamebird for Roosevelt), about post-war plans for Germany and about the French claim for a zone of occupation there, it was essentially the Polish issue which dominated the conference after the first 'naughty' session. One of Churchill's constant aims was a non-Communist Poland, and sensibly so, for when he failed to achieve this he had more trouble about it with the Conservative party in Britain than on any other issue. Furthermore he felt a moral commitment. He had enjoyed a good relationship with General Sikorski, the Polish C-in-C, until the latter was killed in a Gibraltar-to-London air crash in July 1943, and he had a great admiration for the bravery with which Polish exiled units had fought, first in the Battle of Britain and then in Italy. But by the second half of 1944 relations with Stalin and their victorious Russian armies had come to assume more importance in his eyes than those with any émigré groups.

He felt it his duty to do his best for the London Poles, but he judged that the most effective way to do this was to show understanding of Stalin's frontier demands and also to give the three London Poles who had come to Moscow at his request some hard lessons in *Realpolitik*. The latter he did with peculiar harshness at a British Embassy meeting on the morning of 14 October. According to the Polish record (not contradicted from the British side) he told them at one stage:

> You are no Government if you are incapable of taking any decisions. You are callous people who want to wreck Europe. I shall leave you to your own troubles. You have no sense of responsibility when you want to abandon your own people at home, to whose sufferings you are indifferent. You do not care about the future of Europe, you have only your own miserable interests in mind. I will have to call on the other Poles and this Lublin Government may function very well. It will be *the Government*. It is a criminal attempt to wreck, by your *Liberum Veto*, agreement between the Allies. It is cowardice on your part.

Then he dismissed an intervention from Mikolajczyk (the head of the London Polish government) with heavy irony: 'If you want to conquer Russia we shall leave you to do it. I feel as if I were in a lunatic asylum. I don't know whether the British Government will continue to recognize you.'[32]

The implausible sentiment was that 'this Lublin Government may function very well'. If Churchill was exasperated by the London Poles, he was contemptuous of the Lublin ones. He wrote to King George VI on 16 October: 'The day before yesterday was "all Poles day". Our lot from London are, as Your Majesty knows, a decent but feeble lot of fools but the delegation from Lublin seem to be the greatest villains imaginable.' It was however a sign of Churchill's semi-infatuation with Stalin that when, at a tripartite meeting these puppet Poles expressed their most craven sentiments, he looked across the table at Stalin and thought he caught a twinkle of cynical amusement 'in his expressive eyes'.[33]

Churchill's essential position was that he wanted the London Poles to accept the so-called Curzon Line of 1919 including the surrender of Lvov to the Russians, as Poland's eastern frontier, receiving territorial compensation in former German lands, and to co-operate in something like a fifty–fifty government with the Lublin Poles. In order to bring Stalin along he even went so far as to excuse Russian behaviour during the Warsaw uprising against the German occupation of the previous August, which had deeply affronted him at the time, saying that 'he accepted this view absolutely' (Stalin's claim that Soviet failure to assist the uprising, despite the proximity of Russian troops, had been 'due entirely to the enemy's strength and the difficulty of the terrain'). 'Serious persons in the United Kingdom had not credited the reports that failure had been deliberate. Criticism had only referred to the apparent unwillingness of the Soviet Government to send aircraft.'[34] He eventually thought he had got a settlement along roughly these lines. But it did not work, mainly because Stalin, as gradually became clear, had no intention of allowing political pluralism in Poland, and also because the Poles (except for the Soviet helots, whom the others hated even more) hated the Russians so much.

Churchill left Moscow on the morning of Thursday, 19 October and, after halts in the Crimea, Cairo and Naples, the first for a sumptuous Russian dinner and the other two for brief conferences, he was in London by the early evening of Sunday the 22nd. He had been a total of twenty-six hours in the air from Moscow.

No sooner was Moscow over than Churchill, after reporting to both the War Cabinet and the House of Commons* on his Russian activities, and unsuccessfully trying to get the London Poles to go back to Moscow and negotiate, was busy planning the next meeting of the Big Three, which was at first envisaged for December, with Jerusalem as Churchill's favoured location. He claimed that it had first-class hotels, government houses etc. and 'Stalin could come by special train'.[35] However there

---

* This was on 27 October, for which day that admirable diarist Alec Cadogan provides a fascinating glimpse of what were, by any normal standards, Churchill's bewildering habits. Cadogan was summoned to 'check some points' with the Prime Minister at 10.15 on the morning on which the speech was to be delivered at 11.00 and found him in bed (in Downing Street), from which 'he didn't upheave himself, . . . till 10.40' (Dilks (ed.), *Diaries of Sir Alexander Cadogan*, p. 675). What purpose of restful preparation, calm nerves for the occasion or unflustered arrival could have been served by this brinkmanship is impossible to imagine. But it was a good illustration of how difficult it is to judge Churchill by normal standards.

was no getting Stalin out of Russia, and by mid-November Roosevelt had decided he would prefer to delay the next summit until after his fourth inauguration on 20 January 1945. In the meantime Field Marshal Dill had died in Washington on 4 November, and Lord Moyne, who had replaced Casey as Minister of State in the Middle East, was assassinated by Jewish terrorists outside his house in Cairo – an event which would not have encouraged a Jerusalem or Egyptian venue even had Stalin been more graciously mobile. Churchill quickly replaced Dill with Maitland Wilson, the C-in-C in the Mediterranean, into whose shoes Alexander was promoted. Moyne was replaced by Sir Edward Grigg.

During those late October days Churchill also dealt, rather summarily, with the long-to-reverberate question of the return to Russia of Allied prisoners-of-war taken in Italy or on the Western Front who were presumed to be of Russian origin but who had been serving with the German armies. In Eden's absence in the Mediterranean he minuted to the Foreign Office: 'Are we not making unnecessary difficulties? It seems to me we work up fights about matters already conceded in principle. . . . I thought we had arranged to send all the Russians back to Russia.'[36]

On 10 November Churchill flew to Paris. It was a puny flight compared with his distant and hazardous journeys of the intervening years, but it was the first time that he had taken that previously familiar route since 31 May 1940. During the four and a half years since then his relations with de Gaulle had fluctuated violently, but mostly down rather than up. However de Gaulle had two, possibly three, substantial strengths which meant that no matter how much Churchill fulminated against him from the summer of 1941 to that of 1944, and indeed threatened completely to disown him, this never happened. First, on the personal and sentimental level, which always had a lot of force with Churchill, de Gaulle had a niche in the magical myth of the summer of 1940. And second, with every year which went by, de Gaulle's popularity in occupied France grew inexorably. In the second half of the war he could not have been jettisoned without the most appalling effect on the French internal resistance movement. And third, maybe, Churchill also apprehended that, for all his tiresome pirouetting on a slender power base, de Gaulle was genuinely a great man, perhaps the greatest statesman in Western Europe apart from himself.

Churchill was therefore disposed to remember his commitment to himself and to de Gaulle, given at one of the darkest times of the war, that 'one day we'll go down the Champs Elysées together'. On Armistice Day 1944 they did so. Whether the occasion was a total success is doubtful. Churchill was much acclaimed by the Parisians, he was ensconced in a grand apartment of the Quai d'Orsay with a bath (always an important piece of Churchill equipment) which was golden, and he made a thirty-six-hour trip in de Gaulle's special train to the French First Army front near Besançon. But at the parade itself he tried to look determinedly happy, while de Gaulle looked sour. This was a criticism of the General. He did not like sharing occasions, whereas Churchill was more generous. Moreover Churchill gave himself a handicap in the comparative appearance stakes by wearing his unbecoming air commodore's uniform with a heavy greatcoat, while de Gaulle strode along in his unencumbered and (still only) two-star general's tunic and képi. It was strange that Churchill did not realize how much more distinguished and authoritative he looked in civilian clothes, as in the photograph of him emerging five months later from Westminster Abbey after Lloyd George's memorial service.

The year by no means ended in a blaze of victorious glory. The Germans continued to resist with remarkable tenacity, both in Italy and on the threshold of their own country. And the strategic disputes within the Western Allies lost none of their edge. The British thought that the Americans were neglecting the northern axis of advance through the Netherlands and Montgomery became increasingly critical of Eisenhower. Churchill, while substantially endorsing Montgomery on the issue if not on the personal criticism, sent a half-plaintive message to Smuts on 1 December: 'You must remember . . . that our armies are only about one-half the size of the American and will soon be little more than one-third. . . . We musts now re-group and reinforce the armies for a spring offensive. . . . I am trying meanwhile to have Holland cleaned up behind us. But it is not so easy as it used to be for me to get things done.'[37] Five days later he complained to Roosevelt that, as the President would not agree to a pre-Christmas meeting, 'the time has come for me to place before you the serious and disappointing war situation which faces us at the close of the year'. Roosevelt responded calmly and a little chidingly: 'Perhaps I am not close enough to the picture to feel as disappointed about the war situation as you are, and perhaps also because six months ago I was not as optimistic as you were on the time element.'[38] All this was before the German Ardennes offensive, which became known in the West as the Battle of the Bulge. This was launched by Rundstedt on 16 December with a force of ten

Panzer and fourteen infantry divisions. It achieved remarkable success for just over a week. It nearly got to the Meuse at Dinant. In the Belgian village of Celles there is a commemorative swastikaed tank, the inscription on the stone base of which records that it was the most westerly point reached by the Rundstedt offensive, and that this occurred on the afternoon of Christmas Eve.

In the run-up to the last Christmas of the war, however, Churchill's preoccupation was not with the Ardennes but with Greece. As the Germans withdrew from Greece the ELAS guerillas made a determined attempt to take over the government of the country. One of Churchill's strongest resolves was that this should not be allowed to happen. A Communist Greece he thought would be a disaster for the Western Allies. As he pointed out in the 1954 volume of his war memoirs this had within a few years become firmly settled American policy. The United States commitment to sustain the democratic countries of Europe against Soviet expansionism could be dated almost precisely to the proclamation of the Truman Doctrine at the end of February 1947, when America took over British commitments for the defence of Greece and Turkey. In the next month Dean Acheson, a tough but liberal Secretary of State, baldly told a Congressional committee that 'a Communist-dominated Greece would be considered dangerous to United States security'.[39]

Two and a quarter years earlier, however, Churchill was remarkably isolated in his determination to hold Athens and as much of the hinterland as possible against Communist depredations. 'Having paid the price we have to Russia for freedom of action in Greece,' he told Eden at the beginning of November, 'we should not hesitate to use British troops.'[40] The price was indeed heavy – the sacrifice of almost every other country east of the German border, but Stalin remained faithful to the deal which he had made. The well-drilled Soviet press, unlike that of most of the rest of the world, never criticized Churchill for his resolute treatment of the Communist revolt in Greece at the end of 1944. Perhaps even more striking was the behaviour at the crucial time of the improbably named but apparently immaculately accoutred Colonel Popoff, the Soviet military attaché in Athens. He gave not the slightest encouragement to the insurgent Communist government.

Apart from Popoff on the spot and Stalin in the Kremlin, Churchill during December was uncomfortably bereft of support. On the credit side he held the War Cabinet, and Ernest Bevin in a *tour de force* carried the Labour party conference by the crushing vote of 2,488,000 to

137,000 (the Labour party liked to count its votes in big, mainly trades union, blocks.) Then Churchill faced the House of Commons on 8 December with a speech at once cogent and uncompromising, after which he got a nearly ten-to-one majority. The mostly left-wing rebels mustered a vote of thirty, which was relatively high. Moreover James Stuart, the Chief Whip, did not think that either the debate or the vote had cleared the air. Eleven days later he told Colville that it was the first time he had felt the House of Commons to be 'really irritated and impatient' with Churchill.[41]

Open opposition from Emanuel Shinwell, Aneurin Bevan *et al.* was by no means Churchill's most vulnerable flank. In England he faced sustained criticism from both *The Times* and the *Manchester Guardian*, but this was as nothing compared with the hostile excitement of the American press, which made the United States government a very quivering ally. In relation to the American press Churchill had bad luck. At the beginning of the period of crisis, when the Communist ministers had walked out of the ramshackle Greek government, when a general strike had been proclaimed, when ELAS had occupied half the police stations in Athens and civil war was about to start, he had in his own words taken 'a more direct control of the affair'. The immediate effect of this was that on the night of 4–5 December at one of his famous late sessions, noticing how tired Eden was, he sent him to bed at 2.00 a.m., saying 'Leave it to me.' He therefore drafted the crucial telegram of instruction to General Scobie, who was in command of 5,000 British troops in the Greek capital, telling him to open fire to contain the Communist guerrillas in Athens. It contained one harsh phrase of which the repercussions were heavy: 'Do not however hesitate to act as if you were in a conquered city where a local rebellion is in progress.'*[42]

This telegram went off to Scobie at 4.50 a.m., with a copy to General Wilson's headquarters in Italy. Telegrams sent there, unless governed by the key word 'Guard', which was a polite expression for 'don't show it to the Americans', were automatically repeated *inter alia* to the US ambassador in Rome. Perhaps because of the hour, 'Guard' was accidentally omitted from this message, of which the ambassador legitimately

---

* Churchill ought to have been thoroughly alert to the danger of clanging phrases in the Greek context for on the very day before his late-night or early-morning extravaganza Clementine had written him one of her famous warning letters. It was on a different but adjacent issue: 'Please do not, before ascertaining full facts, repeat to any one you meet today what you said to me this morning' (Mary Soames (ed.), *Speaking for Themselves*, p. 507).

informed the State Department. The State Department, perhaps less legitimately, leaked it to the famous columnist Drew Pearson, who published it, drawing particular attention to the offending sentence, in the *Washington Post* on 11 December.

This greatly exacerbated the bad Washington mood, and Stettinius, Cordell Hull's newly appointed replacement as Secretary of State, and even Harry Hopkins proved unsatisfactorily robust, while Admiral King, the US Chief of Naval Staff, tried to withdraw American landing craft which the British were using for transport to Greece. The President endeavoured to stand back from the wave of criticism, and sent Churchill one or two assuaging telegrams, but he did not disguise his uneasiness and produced a friendly but notably unheroic defence of his position to Churchill on 13 December: 'No one will understand better than yourself that I, both personally and as Head of State, am necessarily responsive to the state of public feeling. It is for these reasons that it has not been possible for this Government to take a stand along with you in the present course of events in Greece.'[43] The American attitude also somewhat disaffected Mackenzie King of Canada, normally a reliable supporter of Churchill's.

In addition to these transatlantic doubts Churchill also had some trouble with his own senior advisers on the spot. Harold Macmillan, Minister Resident in the Mediterranean, and Alexander, recently promoted both to field marshal and to Wilson's job as C-in-C for the whole area, arrived in Athens on 11 December. Rex Leeper, British ambassador to the Greek government, was already there, although he had spent most of his embassy time with the government-in-exile, either in Cairo or at Caserta in southern Italy. Leeper had long believed that the issue of the King (George II of the Hellenes, currently in London) was an obstacle to a solution, and that the best arrangement would be a regency under Archbishop Damaskinos, the Greek Orthodox Metropolitan. This quickly became the view of the others. Alexander in particular, to whom Churchill was always instinctively sympathetic, said that a political solution was essential because there was no force available to subdue the country outside Athens and Piraeus. This was more than enough to convert Eden and nearly every other member of the War Cabinet, but not Churchill. He had no regard for what little he knew of Damaskinos. He did not like the look (from a distance) of a political prelate with a black beard and a hat which elevated his already considerable height. He thought he would prove 'a dictator of the left'. But his distrust was more generalized and less rational than that. 'W[inston] has his knife into the Archbishop,' Eden wrote on 21 December, 'and is convinced that he is both a Quisling and a Communist. In fact, as Alec [Cadogan] puts it neatly, he had taken the place [in Churchill's gallery of demonology] of de Gaulle.'[44] The Greek King was also adamant against Damaskinos as regent, although he was prepared to try him as prime minister. But no one thought that would work.

There was in consequence a highly unsatisfactory Greek impasse (apart from worries about the German offensive in the Ardennes) as Christmas approached. Churchill had intended to go to Chequers on Friday evening, 22 December. But he stayed so late in the Downing Street Annexe that he decided that he had to sleep there and indeed stayed in bed there (working) until five o'clock in the afternoon of the following day. These changes of plan and (beyond his normal) idiosyncrasies of behaviour did not point to a very calm state of mind. By the time that he got to Chequers, however, he had firmly settled on one thing, which was that he would eat his Christmas luncheon not in the bosom of his family in the Buckinghamshire countryside but in a new and by the standards of those days comfortable C54 Skymaster aircraft on his approach to Athens from Naples.

His decision caused consternation in the Chequers household. A large, mainly family party had been bidden for what should have been the most relaxed (with victory around the corner) of the five wartime Christmases which the Churchills had spent there. The Prime Minister's arrival twenty-four hours late was enough of a disappointment. The news he brought with him, that he was to be off at the end of the next day (Christmas Eve) on a hazardous visit which would embrace the whole of the rest of the holiday period, was rough stuff. Clementine, who was usually good at taking in her stride both her own and her husband's absences, retired to her room in 'floods of tears'.[45]

Churchill was unbudgeable about his plans. Eden, although far from keen on having his own Christmas disrupted, offered to go in the Prime Minister's place. He was told that he could come too. The only person who made Churchill hesitate was Cranborne, Dominions Secretary and leader in the Lords, who came to lunch on the Sunday and argued cogently against the wisdom of the trip. But the hesitation was only momentary. The 'plans', which hardly existed in the morning, were relentlessly driven forward. As Colville's diary reported: 'A chaotic evening ensued, with the P.M. telling the King, Attlee, Bevin, Beaverbrook on one telephone and me warning the C.A.S. [Chief of Air Staff], Admiralty, Tommy [the Prime Minister's naval aide] on the other.'[46]

Eventually a small and (on Churchill's side) very personal entourage was airborne from Northolt just over an hour into the very early morning of Christmas Day. Churchill took his doctor, his favourite but not his senior private secretary, Colville, his naval aide, and 'the two best-looking' of the Downing Street dictating secretaries, Marian Holmes and Elizabeth Layton – the pulchritude point was noted by Colville rather than by Churchill himself. Eden had Pierson Dixon with him. Why was Churchill determined to make this visit which was disruptive of so many people's convenience? The obvious explanation is that it was the triumph of duty over pleasure, and that, in spite of his self-indulgent tastes, this was part of the pattern of his life. Whenever the two came into head-on conflict, if the issue was big enough, he always came down on the dutiful side. And this, like a lot of obvious explanations, contains a large part of the truth, although not all of it. Duty always had a most powerful ally in the shape of his desire to be at the centre of events, his preference for danger over boredom, for risk over inertia. Furthermore there was his faith, perhaps better placed in Athens than in Moscow, in his personal magnetism and in its ability to overcome problems which, from a distance, looked almost insuperable.

In Athens his personal intervention, because of its effect as much on himself as on objective circumstances, worked decisively. It changed his mind about Damaskinos. He first met him on the evening of Christmas Day. After arrival at the airport Churchill stayed on board the aircraft for a long conference with Alexander, Macmillan and Leeper. The cabin was cold and the wind was so strong that the aircraft bounced up and down on the tarmac. The party were then driven in armoured cars to Phaleron Bay, where they embarked on the cruiser *Ajax*, flagship of the Eastern Mediterranean Fleet, and five years earlier a hero vessel in the Battle of the River Plate. On board Churchill first saw Papand-reou, the *fainéant* Prime Minister, who he thought 'changes his mind about three times a day',[47] and who emerged from the Athens talks as very much the weak man of the past.

Then Churchill saw the emerging strong man of the future, the Archbishop. With one of his engaging lurches of opinion he suddenly found that all his prejudices against Damaskinos disappeared. 'Generally he impressed me with a good deal of confidence. He is a magnificent figure, and he immediately accepted the proposal of being chairman of the conference.'[48] Churchill thought that with his hat the Archbishop looked nearly seven feet tall and was even impressed that he had been a champion wrestler before entering the Church. He reserved his position only on the spirituality of his Beatitude, which he said he had not had time to test.

The conference over which Damaskinos so readily agreed to preside was intended to be one of all the Greek political leaders, including the leaders of ELAS, the desirability of which was decided upon at the gathering on board the Skymaster as soon as Churchill arrived. It was summoned for 6.00 p.m. on 26 December at the Greek Foreign Ministry – a fairly bleak building at the best of times. The bleakness was increased by the heating being almost non-existent, the lighting being by a few Hurricane lamps and the proceedings being enlivened, as was everything in Athens those days, by a background of sporadic gunfire and shell explosions which occasionally advanced to the foreground. At the appointed hour the old-guard Greek politicians were in their places but the ELAS representatives had not turned up. The meeting had to begin without them, and Churchill was halfway through his introductory speech when there was a mild commotion outside the room and, according to Colville, 'three shabby desperadoes' came in.[49] Churchill however described them as 'presentable figures in British battle dress', whom he thought looked 'a much better lot than the Lublin illegitimates'.[50] He was out to be pleasant, and was with difficulty (if doubtful wisdom) restrained from going forward to shake their hands. This, however, he was able to do on his way out after he had told them that he would be leaving Greeks to confer with Greeks under 'this most eminent and venerable citizen', the Archbishop.

It did not for the moment do much good. Some of the 'bourgeois' delegates tried to walk out rather than sit with the 'desperadoes', but their exit was barred by the British. Then ELAS, in the Archbishop's view, proved hopelessly intransigent, and in spite of their more prepossessing appearance, their delegates demanded as dominating a position in any coalition Greek government as did the Lublin Poles in any Warsaw one. The conference did not therefore achieve much in the way of a bridging result. Nor did much of substance occur in the remaining two days of Churchill's stay in Athens. He was there until the early afternoon of 28 December and then, after a night in Naples, was back in London on Friday the 29th, in time to give a report to an early-evening meeting of the War Cabinet and to spend half the night (with Eden) bludgeoning the stubborn Greek King into accepting a regency.

So ended Churchill's extraordinary Christmas adventure. He had not terminated the civil war. He had not secured an umbrella government of national unity. Yet, partly for intangible reasons, it was well worth while. It gave him the cover of action under which to move from an untenable position. It reunited his policy with that of Eden. It rallied the morale of the British forces, commanders and advisers on the spot. It left the Americans and others in no doubt about the importance that Churchill attached to the issue. It approached a breakthrough with the 'desperadoes', who were impressed with the attention that the great British warrior chief had bestowed upon them. Things were never quite as bad again. General Scobie held Athens and cleared most of Attica. The civil war subsided and Greece enjoyed nearly a quarter of a century of non-Communist and reasonably democratic government until the colonels took over in 1967.

Above all it was something which no one but Churchill could have done. It required his unique combination of world prestige and boy-scout enthusiasm. It is impossible to imagine Roosevelt or Stalin flying off on such a mission after midnight on Christmas Eve. It made a bizarre end to a year in which the destruction of Nazism became inevitable and imminent, yet curiously elusive of early achievement, and in which darkening world political clouds took much of the joy out of the approaching fulfilment of Churchill's wildest military hopes of four years before.

40

VICTORY IN EUROPE AND
DEFEAT IN BRITAIN

CHURCHILL GREETED sombrely the opening of 1945, the year of
victory. He wrote of 'this new, disgusting year'.[1] In a more considered
way he telegraphed to Roosevelt on 8 January of his fear that 'the end
of this war may prove to be more disappointing than was the last'.[2] It
was the European political scene which most worried him, but there
was not much short-term military comfort either. V2s continued to
harass London. American forces, with losses of 80,000, had blocked
the Ardennes offensive. But the crossing of the Rhine and the end of
effective German resistance in the West still seemed a long way off.
Alexander was bogged down in the flood plains of the Po. The weather
generally was appalling. When Churchill on 3 January went to visit
Eisenhower at his Versailles headquarters, and then on to see Montgomery at Ghent, a tedious night-train journey across the snow-bound
plains of northern France was involved. He had little good effect on
Montgomery, who three days later gave a bombastic press conference
which was immensely patronizing of the Americans who had just borne
the whole brunt of the last German offensive of the war. This caused so
much offence that Eisenhower doubted whether he could order any of
his generals to serve under Montgomery. The only front which was
going thoroughly well was the Eastern one. The Russians were sweeping
through southern Poland and on to the Oder. But that no longer caused
Churchill anything approaching unalloyed pleasure.

Churchill's gloom was not deadening. Gloom rarely was for him. On
1 January, when he believed that he had got Roosevelt for a preliminary
bilateral conference in Malta before they both proceeded to the Stalin-
imposed Crimean rendezvous of Yalta, he cabled a jingle to the President: 'No more let us falter! From Malta to Yalta! Let nobody alter.'
Even the Malta plan, however, turned largely to ashes. Churchill arrived
there with one of his too habitual temperatures and spent most of the
next two days in bed aboard the cruiser *Orion*. Roosevelt was only there

for the inside of a day, and although Churchill managed to drag himself to both lunch and dinner in the President's cruiser, Roosevelt was unwilling to apply himself to any serious pre-Yalta planning.

These vicissitudes and frustrations were not out of line with those which were only too regularly associated with summits in the second half of the war, apart, perhaps, from the President's new disinclination to apply himself to serious business. What should have been more disconcerting for Churchill were growing signs that he was losing control over his own government at home. This was not because of party politics, as with an election beginning to loom might have been feared. Nor was it on specific issues of policy. It essentially sprang from discontent with the way he had come to conduct the government. There had always been criticism about his long rather than decisive meetings, at which he rambled excessively around the wide horizon of his knowledge. Alan Brooke and Alexander Cadogan, both good diarists, specialized in complaining about these ramblings. But they, and others in the intimate circle, had always made it clear that their respect for Churchill as the indispensable leader far outweighed these faults, maddening in themselves though the faults could be.

Now Churchill was losing the support of his senior ministerial colleagues, not only because of his dilatoriness, but because he rarely read any papers other than his own before Cabinets, and because, on issues on which serious committee work had been done, he preferred the ill-informed prejudices of his cronies who commanded little wider confidence. Beaverbrook, Bracken and Lindemann were all in this category, and it was indeed his favourite physicist, become Lord Cherwell, who metaphorically produced the first nuclear explosion. The incident, together with some comment relevant to the broader problem, was made vivid in the Colville diary for 9 January:

After midnight, while Lord Beaverbrook and Brendan [Bracken] were closeted in the P.M.'s bedroom, having come no doubt on some nefarious intrigue (anti-Bevin, whom the P.M. cherishes above all Labour Ministers, I suspect), Anthony Eden rang up in a storm of rage. It was about a Minute from Lord Cherwell, forwarded by the P.M. to the F[oreign] O[ffice], in which Eden's assertions about the starvation confronting Europe were flatly denied. Eden told me he would resign if inexpert, academic opinions were sought on subjects to which he had given so much thought. I put him through to the P.M., to whom he ranted in a way that the P.M. nor I (who was listening in) had ever heard him before. The P.M. handled the storm in a very adept and paternal way. . . .[3]

Churchill may have been paternally adept, and Eden was well known to have an explosive temper, although practically never with Churchill. But it was nonetheless a serious matter for the Prime Minister to provoke such a reaction from his most important senior colleague, about whom indeed he was telling Harry Hopkins within two weeks that the pair of them 'were H.M.G., [and] that if for any reason we came into real conflict, the Government would break up'.[4]

Still more serious however was the Attlee *démarche* of 19 January. Attlee was never close to Churchill, who did not induct him into the Other Club, always a good test. But as leader of the Labour party and the deputy Prime Minister, who, as there were many to testify, performed miracles of chairmanship and administrative neatness when Churchill was (frequently) away, he was nodal to the functioning of the coalition government. Furthermore, if the future be allowed to cast its shadow, Attlee was to be judged one of the most successful of twentieth-century Prime Ministers, just as there were to be few competitors with Eden for the lowest position in this league.

Attlee's two most notable personal characteristics were first an economy in the use of words which made both his prose and his conversation verge on the jejune, and second a loyalty to institutions with which he worked so strong as sometimes to seem unimaginative. He certainly included the Churchill coalition among such institutions. It was therefore an amazing event when he sat down and wrote Churchill a letter of more than 2,000 words of remonstrance. A devoted but not accurate amateur typist, he hammered it all out on his private portable. Those who received letters from him in his later life can easily imagine the scattering of inadvertent asterisks and exclamation marks which enlivened the text. This should have given the missive more and not less force. It showed the trouble Attlee had taken to avoid even his personal staff knowing of the exasperation with which he had written. He wanted the message to hit its target but not be shouted from the housetops on its way.

By Attlee's standards the message was not particularly succinct, but that did not dilute its impact. The Prime Minister had set up a number of Cabinet committees (over several of which Attlee presided), carefully formed to represent a fair balance of political opinion. The committees worked hard, and generally managed to reach an agreement which 'subordinated party views to the general interest'. The conclusions were then submitted to the War Cabinet in reports which were kept as short as possible.

What happens then? Frequently a long delay before they can be considered. When they do come before the Cabinet it is very exceptional for
you to have read them. More and more often you have not read even the
note prepared for your guidance. Often half an hour or more is wasted in
explaining what could have been grasped by two or three minutes reading
of the document. Not infrequently a phrase catches your eye which gives
rise to a disquisition on an interesting point only slightly connected with
the subject matter. The result is long delays and unnecessarily long
Cabinets. . . .

I will give two recent instances: Instead of assuming that agreement
having been reached there is a prima facie case for the proposal, it is
assumed that it is due to the malevolent intrigues of socialist Ministers
who have beguiled their weak Conservative colleagues. This suggestion is
unjust and insulting to Ministers of both parties. . . .

Attlee's remonstrance then gained momentum:

But there is something worse than this. The conclusions agreed upon by
a Committee on which were sat five or six members of the Cabinet and
other experienced Ministers are then submitted with great deference to
the Lord Privy Seal [Beaverbrook] and the Minister of Information
[Bracken], two Ministers without Cabinet responsibility neither of whom
has given any serious attention to the subject. When they state their views
it is obvious they know nothing about it. Nevertheless an hour is
consumed in listening to their opinions. Time and again important
matters are delayed or passed in accordance with the decision of the Lord
Privy Seal. . . . There is a serious constitutional issue here. In the eyes of
the country and under our constitution the eight members of the War
Cabinet take responsibility for decisions. I have myself assured members
of both Parties who have been disturbed by the influence of the Lord
Privy Seal that this was so. But if the present practice continues I shall
not be able to do so in the future. It is quite wrong that there should be
a feeling amongst ministers and civil servants that it is more important to
have the support of the Lord Privy Seal and the Minister of Information
than of Cabinet Ministers, but I cannot doubt that that is a growing
impression.[5]

The letter arrived on Saturday, 20 January, when Attlee, who was no
doubt awaiting the reaction with some agitation, was attending my
wedding. In his typically laconic speech at the reception it is hardly
necessary to say that he made no reference to the delayed-action bomb
which he had despatched. Nor did he seem more tense than usual.
Churchill, because he had a bad cold, was exceptionally spending the
snow-bound weekend not at Chequers but in the bleak surroundings of

the Downing Street Annexe. Colville recorded that Churchill first reacted explosively: '[he] drafted and redrafted a sarcastic reply, said it was a socialist conspiracy, harped on nothing but the inadequate representation of the Tories in the Cabinet', and when he welcomed 'the typists, drivers, servants etc' to an after-dinner film show in an adjacent room he made the bad and surely mostly incomprehensible joke of inviting them not to 'bother about Attler or Hitlee'.[6] Worse still, in the view of Colville and of his senior John Martin, as devoted a pair of secretaries as are ever found even in the habitually loyal atmosphere of Whitehall private offices, was that he telephoned Beaverbrook and read the whole letter to him, thereby both confirming a part of Attlee's complaint and rendering otiose the care Attlee had taken with the secret typing.

Churchill's trouble was that nearly everyone close to him agreed with Attlee. Clementine did. Colville did, and recorded: 'Greatly as I love and admire the P.M. I am afraid there is much in what Attlee says, and I rather admire his courage in saying it. Many Conservatives,* and officials such as Cadogan and Bridges, feel the same.' Even Beaverbrook, apparently, thought it was 'a very good letter'.[7] Eventually, on the Monday, Churchill was reduced to sending Attlee a flat letter of acknowledgement:

My dear Lord President,
    I have to thank you for your Private and Personal letter of January 19.
You may be sure I shall always endeavour to profit by your counsels.
    Yours sincerely,
        W.S.C.[8]

If it be asked whether anything changed as a result of Attlee's boldness, and of the quiet support which it called forth, the answer is a little, but not much.

Amid this agitation about the conduct of government, Churchill's most controversial decision, taken in late January and founded on the belief that it would decisively shorten the war, was to intensify area bombing and to give Air Marshal Harris a largely free hand to unleash terror on Berlin and eastern German cities, leading to the obliteration of Dresden by some 1,200 British and US aircraft on 13/14 February. It would be wrong, however, to lay blame exclusively upon Harris. His

---

* These undoubtedly included the other Conservative or nominally 'independent' members of the War Cabinet, Eden, Anderson, Lyttelton and Woolton.

remit came from the top. But so too did the late-March decision to
restrict area bombing. 'Otherwise', Churchill minuted the Chiefs of
Staff on 28 March, 'we shall come into control of an utterly ruined
land. . . . The destruction of Dresden remains a serious query against
the conduct of Allied bombing.'[9]

Did Churchill regret the destruction, and was it a step too far? After
an evening of sombre reflection on 23 February, Colville recorded him
saying that, when Harris had finished his devastation of Germany,
'What will lie between the white snows of Russia and the white cliffs of
Dover?'[10] Foreboding was more pronounced than regret. But it is easy
to criticize with the hindsight of victory. The policy was no more
reprehensible than the use of the second atomic bomb by Truman six
months later.

The next major event was the Yalta conference, which took place
between 5 and 11 February, involving Churchill in another three-week
absence from England. It was the least successful of the wartime
summits for the essential reason that the only cement which held
together the Big Three, the need to defeat the massive German military
machine, was rapidly losing its adhesive power. Many previous features
were present, together with a few new ones, of which the most obvious
was the manifest decline in health and mental power of Roosevelt, and
it is unnecessary to go over the six days of argument and feasting with
the same detail which was applied to Teheran and to Churchill's various
westerly and easterly bi-laterals.

Two issues dominated Yalta. The first comprised the items which
remained in dispute from the preliminary Dumbarton Oaks (Washington) conference on the setting up of the United Nations Organization.
On this some considerable progress was made, although the central
issue, of whether the Security Council was to have effective power to
deal with a dispute in which one of its permanent members (the Big
Three plus China and possibly France) was involved, was dodged. For
the Assembly the Russians accepted that they should have only two or
three satraps from their subsidiary republics as opposed to the representation of the full sixteen which they had been demanding. This was seen
as a legitimate counter to the membership of the four British Dominions. The United States were left to make do with only one nominal
vote, but with what remained for a decade or so a fairly reliable batch
of client Latin American states. The arrangements, as was often the case
with summit agreements, came somewhat apart in a month or so and

produced a pre-San Francisco conference crisis. At the time, the issue eased rather than exacerbated the Yalta proceedings.

The second and more intractable one was the long-running and highly unsatisfactory saga of Poland. It was rightly regarded by Churchill – and to a lesser extent by Roosevelt – as a test case for the future of eastern Europe. From Teheran through Churchill's Moscow visit of October 1944 to Yalta, the issue sat oppressively at the centre of the stage. But with each conference the position of the West, and of the Poles, except for those who liked the puppet Lublin government, now transferred to Warsaw, became weaker. What had been haggled over in Moscow, a fifty–fifty 'Lublin–London government' for instance, would have been accepted with relief at Yalta. Churchill was throughout aware that, for whatever deal he succeeded in procuring from Stalin, he would be bitterly criticized. This he very quickly was in the House of Commons debate of 29 February to 1 March, at the end of which twenty-seven Tories voted against him, and many more were uneasy.

Nor was he merely criticized in the short term. John Charmley, for instance, in his hostile 'revisionist' biography published in 1993, argued strongly that Churchill's treatment of the Poles in 1944–5 was worse than Neville Chamberlain's treatment of the Czechs before and at the Munich settlement, which Churchill had so bitterly attacked at the time. Thus, Charmley argued, Churchill stands convicted not only of weakness but of hypocrisy. The argument ignores one salient fact. Churchill in 1938 was prepared to fight Germany over Czechoslovakia, and indeed propounded the view, with doubtful validity but full conviction, that it would have been a more favourable conjuncture at which to have gone to war than a year later. Declaring war on Russia, over Poland, in the spring of 1945, was simply not a feasible policy. It was advocated by no serious person in Britain, and was a course which would certainly have had to be followed without American support, and probably with American hostility at least as active as at the time of Suez eleven years later, and with still more devastating effect.

In these circumstances Churchill did as well as he could have done at Yalta. In the fourth plenary session, confronted by a Stalin still more determined in victory than he had been in near defeat, and aided only intermittently by a semi-comatose Roosevelt, Churchill delivered what Martin Gilbert describes with justification as 'one of the most difficult speeches, and advocacies, of his career'.[11] The issue of the frontiers, except for that of how far the Poles were to be allowed to penetrate into former German territory, had fallen away. What was now at issue was the meaning, in the words of the communiqué, of 'free and unfettered elections as soon as possible on the basis of universal suffrage and secret ballot'. No one wanted to be on record against these, but the lack of mutual comprehension about their meaning was vividly illustrated by a remark made by Stalin and an argument developed by Molotov and endorsed by his chief. At the third and least formal dinner Churchill was expatiating on the election he would soon have to face. 'You know we have two parties in England,' he said somewhat inconsequentially. 'One party is much better,' was Stalin's reply,[12] more amiable on the surface than in its implications. And when, in disputes about Western observers being allowed to supervise the 'free and unfettered elections' in Poland, Churchill argued that he would welcome reciprocal observers in Greece and northern Italy, Molotov produced (as he had done before) the splendidly breathtaking argument that such arrangements would be insulting to the sovereignty and dignity of the newly liberated peoples of Poland, and indeed of other relatively small countries.

There was one other remark made at Yalta which deserved equal resonance, and certainly achieved it in Churchill's mind. This was Roosevelt's almost casual statement at the first plenary session that the 'United States would take all reasonable steps to preserve peace, but not at the expense of keeping a large army indefinitely in Europe, 3,000 miles away from home. That was why the American occupation was limited to two years.'[13] Churchill's immediate reaction was to redouble his (successful) efforts to get France not only given an occupation zone in Germany but also made a full member of the Allied Control Commission to administer the defeated enemy country. His doubts about de Gaulle, who he was thankful was not at Yalta, were as nothing compared with his fear of an exhausted Britain being left, with the Americans gone home, as the only Western power trying to balance Russia across a devastated Germany. The French army again became necessary. The attempt either to live with or, preferably, to reverse that laconic statement of Roosevelt's on the afternoon of 5 February 1945 was a dominating factor in British foreign policy, whether under Churchill and Eden or Attlee and Bevin until the North Atlantic Treaty was signed fifty months later.

Churchill was on the whole on good form throughout the Yalta conference. His fever at Malta did not reassert itself, and his main trouble was with sore eyes. 'P.M. seems well,' the frequently downbeat Cadogan wrote in his diary for 9 February, 'though drinking buckets of

Caucasian champagne which would undermine the health of any ordinary man.'[14] Whether Churchill enjoyed being in the Crimea is doubtful. In advance he was disposed to agree with Harry Hopkins's view that 'we could not have found a worse place for a meeting if we had spent ten years looking for it'.[15] He hated the six-hour twisting and bumping drive from the airport; on one occasion he gazed out at the sea, sun and mountain view from his villa and said, 'the Riviera of Hades';[16] and when at the end he boarded a British liner in Sebastopol harbour he confounded the captain 'by wanting to get his clothes de-loused'.[17]

The Yalta accommodation was superficially luxurious: disused palaces, hurriedly filled with brittle furniture imported from Moscow. Yet the nightclub manager's hours suited Churchill well enough, much better than they did Roosevelt. The conference sessions habitually began between 4.00 and 5.00 p.m. They continued for four or even five hours, with a short break, during which Churchill was sustained with whisky and chicken soup. There was a *circa* 9.30 dinner, three of these being formal tripartite feasts given by each of the leaders in turn, which, with the usual pattern of extravagant toasts, lasted until well after midnight. In the course of the speeches some fairly embarrassing compliments were paid, not least by Churchill, because he was the most fluent. 'I walk through this world with greater courage and hope,' he said of Stalin at the Soviet dinner, 'when I find myself in a relation of friendship and intimacy with this great man, whose fame has gone out not only over all Russia, but the world.'[18] And at the final British dinner he paid tribute to Stalin's growing kindliness and added: 'We feel we have a friend whom we can trust.'[19] Allowance must obviously be made for the headiness of the circumstances, and it can also be pleaded in mitigation that Churchill was frank about his flattery (which was largely reciprocated), publishing the texts of the bouquets in his 1954 last volume of war memoirs.

On the four evenings when there was not an official dinner Churchill dined *en petit comité* in his own Vorontzov Villa, which meant with his daughter Sarah, who was a very successful companion at Yalta as she had been at Teheran (as well as providing a great source of 'pattern of life' detail in her letters to her mother), Anthony Eden and a varying supplement of generals, admirals and private secretaries. Such quiet occasions did not lead to early nights. The daily diplomatic pouch arrived by courier at about midnight and, after he had first rifled through that morning's London newspapers, Churchill then worked for several hours on its other contents. As a result he woke later than usual and there was a problem about fitting in his morning's work in bed, his substantial luncheon and his obligatory afternoon sleep before four o'clock. Sarah Oliver reported that it was solved by abandoning both breakfast and lunch, instituting a lavish bedroom brunch at 11.30, with Churchill staying in bed until the early afternoon. This regime seemed to suit him and he was reported as 'bearing up very well. . . . Physically . . . this conference does not seem as hard as the one last year.'[20]

Nevertheless, as soon as it was over, he was seized with an urgent desire to be off. It was like one of those scenes in an American musical when the hero (or heroine) says, 'Why don't we all go to New York?' Sarah described it brilliantly:

> Why do we stay here? Why don't we go tonight? . . . I leave in 50 minutes! . . . Naturally 50 minutes gave us time to change our minds six more times. We will spend the night here after all and leave tomorrow lunchtime. We will fly – We will leave tonight and go by sea – We will go to Athens – Alexandria – Cairo – Constantinople – We will not go to any of them – We will stay on board [the RMS *Franconia*, the liner which was waiting for them at Sebastopol] and read the newspapers. . . . Papa, genial and sprightly like a boy out of school, his homework done, walked from room to room saying 'Come on, come on'!
>   Believe it or not, 1 hour and 20 minutes later, about 5.30 p.m., saw a cavalcade of cars bulging with groaning suitcases winding its way to Sebastopol! And quick though we had been we were last. The President left an hour before us – but on an orderly plan laid days ago. Stalin, like some genie, just disappeared.[21]

In fact they spent the next two days resting in the *Franconia* and then flew to Athens to see how Archbishop Damaskinos was getting on. The answer was not at all badly, with the city considerably more settled than seven weeks before. Churchill was able to drive about the city, and be much acclaimed, in an open car as opposed to the armoured one of Christmas. Then he went to Alexandria, bidding goodbye to Roosevelt after a luncheon in the cruiser USS *Quincy* on 15 February. They never saw each other again.

After a few Cairo days of talks with an emperor, two kings and one president Churchill was back in England on 19 February, following a single flight of nearly fourteen hours. Air travel was assuming some of the convenience of the second half of the century. But this did not prevent his Skymaster being diverted by fog from Northolt, where the welcoming party, including Clementine Churchill, was waiting, to

Lyneham in Wiltshire. Eventually a surprising rendezvous was arranged in the hotel opposite the station in Reading. There he was sitting happily drinking whisky and soda when Clementine arrived. She thought he was looking 'marvellously well – much, much better than when he went off for this most trying and difficult of Conferences'.[22] They then went to dine with the King and Queen. Churchill found travel, almost independently of destination, and conferences at the highest level, almost independently of content or outcome, more restorative than exhausting.

Yalta was his last long-distance overseas excursion during the war. From 23 to 26 March he was with Montgomery for the final hazardous battle in the west, the crucial crossing of the Rhine, but that only involved being two hours' flight away from London. The puzzling question which inevitably arises is why, great traveller that he was, Churchill did not go to Roosevelt's funeral following the President's sudden but not unexpected death on 12 April. The obsequies took place partly in the White House on Saturday the 14th and partly at Hyde Park on Sunday the 15th, both of them for Churchill natural shrines to his relationship with Roosevelt. There was plenty of time for him to go to either or both, and their being on weekend days weakened the claim of competing business. His first instinct was to fly off on the Friday evening, and this remained an option right up to the planned 8.30 p.m. time of departure.

Why did he so uncharacteristically weaken? During the day he received a message from Halifax saying that both Harry Hopkins and Edward Stettinius (the fairly new Secretary of State) 'were much moved by my thought of possibly coming over, and both warmly agreed with my judgment of the immense effect for good that would be produced'; and later that Truman, the new President, had asked him to say 'how greatly he would personally value the opportunity of meeting me as early as possible. . . . Mr Truman's idea was that after the funeral I might have had two or three days' talk with him.'[23] This should surely have strengthened Churchill's desire. Yet he changed his mind, decided that Eden, who was on his way to the San Francisco conference, would do instead, and wrote one of his least convincing letters to the King explaining why he was not going:

> I was tempted during the day to go over for the funeral and begin relations with the new man. However so many of Your Majesty's Ministers are out of the country, and the Foreign Secretary had arranged to go

anyhow, and I felt the business next week in Parliament and also the ceremonies [essentially a St Paul's Cathedral service] connected with the death of Mr Roosevelt are so important that I should be failing in my duty if I left the House of Commons without my close personal attention. I had to consider the tribute which should be paid to the late President, which clearly it is my duty to deliver [this took place in the House of Commons on the afternoon of Tuesday, 17 April]. The press of work is also very heavy. Therefore I thought it better that I should remain here in charge at this juncture.[24]

Nothing hung together. In December 1941, at an incomparably more dangerous time in the war, Churchill had not hesitated to go to America when Eden was semi-incommunicado in Russia. But that was at a time when, as he later described it to Colville, 'No lover ever studied every whim of his mistress as I did those of President Roosevelt.' As far as other ministers being out of the country, Churchill hardly recognized the existence of most of them. As for the House of Commons tribute and even the St Paul's service, he could easily have been back for them, even if it meant cutting his talks with Truman a little short. And his Commons tribute, when it came, while thoroughly adequate, was not one of his most memorable *éloges*. Colville commented that it was in no way 'comparable to his epitaph on Neville Chamberlain in 1940'.[25]

So the mystery remains. Neither Churchill's own writing nor any contemporary source provides a clue to the real motive for his choice of the anti-climactic solution. None of the diaries which are often so full of insight into Churchill's moods and instinctive reactions are any help: not Cadogan, not Brooke, not Ismay, not Eden, not even Colville. All we know is that he hesitated all day on 13 April, but on the conflicting considerations which swayed his mind we can only surmise. Churchill's *ex post* judgement was that he wished he had come down the other way, but this he related entirely to his missing the opportunity to make early personal contact with Truman and not to his failure to be chief mourner at the obsequies of his great partner in the defence of the West.*

The question therefore arises as to whether Churchill had cooled on Roosevelt to an extent which had drained away the emotional impact of his death. Of course Roosevelt had not been much use to Churchill at Yalta. He had declined to have serious talks with him at Malta on the

---

* 'In the after-light I regret that I did not adopt the new President's suggestion. I had never met him, and I feel that there were many points on which personal talks would have been of the greatest value. . . .' (*The Second World War*, VI, p. 418).

way out, and he lay back during most of the conference sessions, partly because of his growing inertia and partly because of his desire to make a show of equidistance between the other two. There had also been a good deal of argumentative Churchill–Roosevelt correspondence during the eight weeks between their farewell off Alexandria and 12 April. The two main points at issue were first Churchill's belief that the American strategy in the last stages of the war against Germany gravely under-estimated the importance of the Western Allies getting to Berlin before or at least as soon as the Russians; and second how strong a Western reaction was called for by Soviet breaches of the Yalta undertakings on Poland. Hope of getting Western observers into Warsaw effectively perished with a message from Stalin on 7 April. Churchill urged a firm joint reaction on Roosevelt. Roosevelt however replied in a message transmitted on the day of his death, the penultimate of the more than 1,700 communications which passed between President and Prime Minister, in a distinctly deflating manner: 'I would minimize the general Soviet problem as much as possible, because these problems, in one form or another, seem to arise every day and most of them straighten out. . . .'[26]

This opened up a wide gulf of difference. But it is difficult to believe that Churchill, when confronted early the next morning with news of the sudden death which rocked the world, would have allowed it, even on top of the irritations of Yalta, to have blotted out nearly five years of the relationship by which he had set such store. It is more probable that the emotional link between Churchill and Roosevelt was never as close as was commonly thought. It was more a partnership of circum-stance and convenience than a friendship of individuals, each of whom, as was noted previously, was a star of a brightness which needed its own unimpeded orbit.

Churchill paid a certain price for his negative decision. It did not seriously damage his public repute, either in Britain or in America. But it did not enhance it either. There seemed something odd about his absence, and he certainly paid a price for not getting in on the ground floor in his relations with Truman. Truman was very much a tyro President and highly impressionable at that stage. Furthermore he had an instinctive hero worship of Churchill. When I went to see Truman (then just out of office) in Kansas City eight years later and hoped to get him to talk to me about Attlee, to whom some thought he was an American analogue, I could not get him to say anything of interest. All he wanted to do was to talk about Churchill, and in a laudatory way. So it is at least possible that, had they had 'two or three days' talk' together, some of Truman's early and to the British unhelpful decisions, most notably the abrupt termination of Lend–Lease, might have been avoided, and that Truman might have become the staunchest defender of Western security before 1947. Churchill also paid the penalty, if it is possible to pay an earthly one after death, that when his own funeral came, nearly twenty years later, President Johnson did not attend.

By the time of Roosevelt's death the war against Germany was nearly over. German resistance had not petered out after the Rhine was crossed by the Allies. Montgomery reported on 17 April that he had lost 5,180 men killed in the previous two months; and in Italy Alexander's army was still held outside Bologna. But from mid-April collapse gathered momentum and the end was clearly near. Triumph was on hand, but the dispositions of the Allied armies which were bringing it about were far from what Churchill would have wished. He set great political store by who got first to the capital cities. He had long wanted to drive through the Ljubljana Gap to Vienna, but when the Russians occupied the Austrian capital on 13 April the Anglo-American forces were still 500 miles away. Prague had come more recently into his sights, but his hopes for the Americans getting there first had disappeared by 24 April. Most important of all was Berlin. He hoped that at the least Allied troops could join hands with Russian across the rubble of Hitler's imperium. But he could not persuade the Americans of its symbolic and political significance. When Soviet troops reached the Berlin suburbs on 21 April Eisenhower seemed more concerned with Nuremberg and Leipzig. When the link-up of the Eastern and Western armies came on 25 April it was at the otherwise insignificant locality of Torgau, on the Elbe near Wittenberg. Only in the case of Copenhagen, on the occupation of which the Russians seemed to have their eye, did the Western Allies get there first, and that was by a fairly narrow margin.

As all of this showed, the pleasure for Churchill of victory, which five years before had been so much at the limit of his dreams yet at the centre of his determination, was heavily marred by his growing oppression with the thought of a Soviet-dominated Europe. As he telegraphed to Clementine, who was on a seven-week Red Cross tour of Russia:* 'Meanwhile I need scarcely tell you that beneath these triumphs lie

---

* For all her wifely wisdom and the persistent warm affection of their marriage, it was almost incredible how Clementine managed to be absent at nearly all the most important moments of Churchill's life.

poisonous politics and deadly international rivalries.'[27] Sometimes he thought he could get the new American President to see the threat and be prepared to join with him in putting up a strong front against it, but more often he thought not. He was unavailing in his attempts to get the Americans temporarily to hold what they had in Germany when this obtruded on parts of what had been agreed to be the Soviet zone of occupation. This embraced about 36,000 square miles of territory from Rostock to Leipzig. Churchill's idea was that the Americans should not fall back to the previously agreed line until satisfactory arrangements had been implemented for Austria (three Western zones plus quadri-partite control of Vienna) and for the four sectors of Berlin.

Truman was unpersuaded. He was told (rightly) that Roosevelt had agreed the zone boundaries with Churchill at Quebec and with Stalin at Yalta, and he thought the Americans should move smartly back to them. Churchill's attitude to Stalin remained ambiguous during this period. Essentially he thought the Russians were reneging on Yalta, particularly over Poland, and his deep anti-communism was sprouting up again, like spring bulbs coming through disappearing winter snow. He first used the phrase 'iron curtain' in a message to Truman on 12 May, and said that it was 'drawn down upon their [the Soviet] front'.

However he still half believed that he had a personal rapport with the Russian leader. His instinctive reaction to worsening relations within the Allies was to seek another early meeting of the Big Three. This was despite the post-Teheran and post-Yalta disappointments. The lure of summitry still took precedence over experience. He tried hard to persuade Truman to press for a meeting in late May or early June, which would hardly have been convenient for what became his British election timetable.

There was also an odd incident on 26 April described in the Colville diary:

> The P.M. returned from dining with Massigli, the French Ambassador, to find a nice telegram from Stalin, indeed the most friendly that U.J. has ever sent. This quite fascinated him (he was not altogether sober to begin with)* and I sat beside him in his room at the Annexe while he talked of nothing else, first of all to Brendan [Bracken] for one and a half hours and then to me for another one and a half. His vanity was astonishing

---

* This parenthesis was omitted from Colville's published version. Stalin's *bonhomie* was occasioned by Churchill assuring him that, despite feelers in this direction from various German sources, there was no question of the West agreeing to a separate peace.

and I am glad U.J. does not know what effect a few kind words, after so many harsh ones, might well have upon our policy toward Russia. . . . Further joy was caused by a generous message from de Gaulle. But no work was done and I felt both irritated and slightly disgusted by this exhibition of susceptibility to flattery. It was nearly 5.00 a.m. when I got to bed.[28]

The surprising harshness of the passage may be accounted for, not only by the time when Colville was allowed to go to bed, but also by Churchill in this phase sitting up gossiping later and later while getting through less and less of his paper work – at which he had previously been very good. Three days earlier Colville had written: 'The P.M's box is in a ghastly state. He does little work and talks far too long, as he did last December before his Greek adventures refreshed him.'[29] The reference to Churchill's Athens escapade having improved the diligence of his paperwork was an interesting insight into his metabolism. The reference to gossip with Bracken having consumed the first one and a half hours is symptomatic of the mild disapproval of the private secretaries as a whole, as well as of higher officials such as Bridges and Cadogan, of the excessive influence of Bracken (and of Beaverbrook) at the time.

Churchill's morale was not good in the hour of victory. Not only did he stay up further and further into the night, but he was also increasingly inclined to spend frequent days 'working in bed' until the early evening, with a solitary luncheon, for him a very bad sign. (And if he was not getting through his work, to what did 'working in bed' amount?) His physical condition was also notably poor for a man who, whatever vicissitudes of health and strain he had been through, was only just seventy. 'At this time,' by his own account, 'I was very tired and physically so feeble that I had to be carried upstairs in a chair by the Marines from the Cabinet meetings under the Annexe.'[30] This weakness contrasted with bursts of determined public duty, as on Victory in Europe Day itself when he lunched with the King, delivered his victory broadcast at 3.00, repeated the statement in the House of Commons at 3.30, led the members to St Margaret's for a service of thanksgiving, returned for a happy hour in the smoking room, then took the War Cabinet and the Chiefs of Staff to Buckingham Palace for royal congratulations, then spoke to a vast crowd from what was then the Ministry of Health balcony at the lower end of Whitehall, then dined with his daughters Sarah and Diana (plus the latter's husband, Duncan Sandys, and Lord Camrose), then made another speech to the Whitehall crowd, then went back to the Annexe to read the next morning's newspapers, of which, fortunately for Camrose who was still there, the *Daily Telegraph* pleased him, although the *Daily Mail* did not. His lassitude also contrasted with occasional nostalgic social relaxation. On 2 May he dined with Noël Coward and two long-standing women friends, Venetia Montagu and Juliet Duff, returning to the Downing Street Annexe only at 1.30 in the morning.

Domestically the dominant presence on the horizon was the break-up of the coalition government followed by an entrenched party conflict. The prospect of this produced further ambiguity of feeling in Churchill. On the whole he was proud of the coalition government of the past five years, his chieftainship of which was to make him in the context of history the greatest Prime Minister of the twentieth century. His impishness caused him to make occasional caustic remarks about it. On 24 September 1943, when the death of the Chancellor of the Exchequer, Kingsley Wood, necessitated a Cabinet reshuffle, he was reported in the acerbic diaries of Cadogan as having said to Anthony Eden: 'Except for you and me, this is the worst Government England ever had.'[31] At the other extreme he wrote in his 1954 volume of war memoirs, when he had fought three hard elections against the Labour party – and lost two of them: 'No Prime Minister could ever have wished for more loyal and steadfast colleagues then I had found in the Labour Party.'[32] Perhaps however his most authentic evaluation was given in a letter to Smuts on 3 December 1944. To Smuts, with whom he rarely dissimulated and with whom he was only six weeks later to describe his relationship as being that of 'two old love-birds moulting together on a perch but still able to peck',[33] he wrote: 'Meanwhile there approaches the shadow of the General Election, which before many months have passed will certainly break up the most capable Government England has had or is likely to have.'[34]

Partisanship began to gather momentum in the early spring. Churchill himself gave it a considerable kick-start by his speech to a Conservative party conference on 15 March. This speech foreshadowed several of the arguments equating the Labour programme with incipient totalitarianism, which were to disfigure his notorious 'Gestapo' election broadcast of 4 June. Less publicly he also provoked Ernest Bevin, his favourite Labour minister, by sending to the Trades Union Congress on 9 March an absolute refusal to amend the Trades Disputes Act of 1927. This Act, which was regarded even by moderate Labour opinion as a piece of vengeance for the General Strike of 1926, had become a

'King Charles's head'. It was more a matter of symbolism than of substance, but Churchill's total hostility to even a cosmetic amendment helped to provoke Bevin's Leeds speech of 7 April which Churchill described as 'very hostile' (to the Conservative party). So there accumulated signs of the approaching *déchirure*, which Churchill greeted with very mixed feelings. It was, and had always been, a complex part of his nature that, although he was mostly consensual, when he was partisan he was very very partisan.

Churchill was not enthusiastic about having the general election in the summer of 1945. He would have preferred the Labour ministers to have remained in the government until the war against Japan was won. They wanted to stay until October when there would be a fresh electoral register, but the Conservative ministers and the Central Office electoral strategists were against this. It was not so much that the Conservatives wanted a stale register, although the Labour vote being in general more transient there was some evidence that this favoured the Tories, but more that they wanted an early cashing in of the cheque of Churchill's victory popularity. He was therefore persuaded to offer the Labour ministers only the choices of staying until the end of the Japanese war or of the immediate break-up of the coalition.

This was a non-issue as it turned out. The desires of both sides could have been accommodated in an October election, with Japan two months out of the war, and Churchill, almost alone because of his full knowledge of nuclear progress, a knowledge which Attlee did not share, must have appreciated that this was at least a real possibility. But the non-issue led to some acrimony at the end of the political marriage. Attlee, at an 18 May encounter, immediately on his return from the San Francisco conference, asked Churchill to insert a sentence in his letter proposing continuance of the coalition until a Japanese surrender, promising that in the interim the united government would endeavour to implement social security and full-employment proposals. Churchill took this to mean that Attlee would then support the Labour party carrying on in government. But when two days later Attlee got to Blackpool, where the party conference was meeting, he discovered that the mood was strongly against. Morrison had always been against continuation, and Bevin and Dalton, who had previously been in favour, swung in that direction too. Attlee therefore turned down Churchill's proposition, and the Prime Minister felt that he had been cheated. It was essentially a difference in their concepts of leadership. Churchill believed a leader should be dominant. Attlee believed he should be representative.

The separation was by no means all acrimony. As is perhaps not unknown in more personal break-ups, there was an alternation between bickering over whose fault it was and an emotional recall of happier days. On 21 April, after the opening salvoes, Churchill, as Chancellor of the University there, had taken Ernest Bevin and A. V. Alexander to Bristol and conferred honorary degrees upon them. On 28 May, five days after he had resigned as coalition Premier and had received the King's commission to form a 'Caretaker' Conservative government, Churchill gave a farewell Downing Street party for the departing Labour ministers and under-secretaries. Hugh Dalton described how, 'with tears visibly running down his cheeks', Churchill addressed them. 'The light of history will shine on all your helmets,' he said.[35]

Yet exactly a week later Churchill delivered the most partisan and, in most people's view, the most ill-judged of all his famous wireless addresses. The 1945 election was very much a battle of the sound broadcasts. There was of course no television as a mass medium. But the possession of radio sets was almost universal, and in the war years people had got used to clustering around them for authoritative and trusted reports of what, good and bad, was happening. The BBC suspended all controversial programmes, such as the very popular *Brains Trust*, for the duration of the election, but night after night during June it presented a carefully balanced series of party political addresses. The Conservatives were allotted ten, as was the Labour party, the Liberals four, and two other groups, the Communists and the short-lived Commonwealth party, which had won a few bye-elections during the war, one each. Churchill himself decided to do four of the Conservative ten, including the first and the last. Six other ministers, including the nominally non-party Sir John Anderson and Lord Woolton, were given one shot each. Bracken but not Beaverbrook was included in the list. Labour spread its allocation more widely. Attlee did only one, but that perhaps his most effective performance to date. Morrison wound up for them.

During the weekend of 1–3 June at Chequers, Churchill prepared his first broadcast, which he delivered from there on the Monday. Neither Beaverbrook nor Bracken was present or had anything directly to do with the text. Nevertheless the cumulative effect of the many hours which he had recently spent in the company of one or both may have left its deposit on his electioneering stance. But the words were all his own. When the script was ready he showed it to Clementine, who, according to her daughter's biography, did not like it and 'begged [him] to delete the odious and invidious reference to the Gestapo. But he would not heed her.'[36]

The half-hour broadcast, which Churchill thought too short, contained several unobjectionable references to how much he regretted that the coalition had broken up, but 'the Socialists as a whole had been for some time eager to set out upon the political warpath, and when large numbers of people feel like that it is not good for their health to deny them the fight they want. We will therefore give it to them to the best of our ability.'

The trouble was that his idea of 'giving it to them' ran directly counter to his strenuously earned position as leader of the whole nation, which should have been his greatest electoral asset. The sound of the familiar voice, which had so often united and elevated the country, indulging in the exaggerated abuse of party politics made the shock the greater. The most complained-of passage – although there were several others which nearly matched it – went as follows:

> No Socialist government conducting the entire life and industry of the country could afford to allow free, sharp or violently worded expressions of public discontent. They would have to fall back on some sort of Gestapo, no doubt very humanely directed in the first instance. And this would nip opinion in the bud; it would stop criticism as it reared its head, and it would gather all the power to the supreme party leaders, rising like stately pinnacles above their vast bureaucracies of Civil Servants, no longer servants and no longer civil. . . .
>
> My friends, I must tell you that a Socialist policy is abhorrent to the British ideas of freedom. . . . A free Parliament – look at that – a Free Parliament is odious to the Socialist doctrinaire.[37]

The words, even if the ideas had not been so over the top, were infelicitous by Churchill's normal standards. Vita Sackville-West captured this well when she wrote to Harold Nicolson (her husband) much later in the campaign:

> You know I have an admiration for Winston amounting to idolatry, so I am dreadfully distressed by the badness of his broadcast Election speeches. What has gone wrong with him? They are confused, woolly, unconstructive and so wordy that it is impossible to pick out any concrete impression from them. If I were a wobbler, they would tip me over to

the other side. Archie Sinclair and Stafford Cripps were both infinitely better.[38]

By this time Churchill had come privately to agree with these strictures. 'He is very low, poor Darling,' Clementine wrote to her daughter Mary on 20 June. 'He thinks he has lost his "touch" & he grieves about it.'[39]

The immediate effect of his first broadcast was to lay himself open to a quietly devastating response from Attlee.

> When I listened to the Prime Minister's speech last night in which he gave such a travesty of the policy of the Labour party, I realized at once what was his object. He wanted the electors to understand how great was the difference between Winston Churchill, the great leader in war of a united nation, and Mr. Churchill, the party Leader of the Conservatives. He feared that those who had accepted his leadership in war might be tempted out of gratitude to follow him further. I thank him for having disillusioned them so thoroughly. The voice we heard last night was that of Mr. Churchill, but the mind was that of Lord Beaverbrook.[40]

This broadcast was the making of Attlee as a campaign leader. At the Blackpool conference, only two weeks before, he had been heavily eclipsed by the rhetoric of Morrison, Bevin and Dalton. He was never any good before a mass audience, and there were many in the Labour party who had their doubts about the quality of his leadership. On 5 June he had a still more mass audience – such was the concentrated authority of the BBC that between them 45 and 50 per cent of the adult population listened to these broadcasts – but the substitution of families in their own sitting rooms for the collective fervour of a large hall gave a great advantage to Attlee's 'tolerant schoolmaster' tone, in the phrase of the joint historians of the campaign.* Thereafter he handled the campaign with a new authority. Churchill had done the one thing which he should have been most anxious to avoid. He had built up instead of diminishing Attlee.

This also applied to Churchill's other campaign ploy, which was to indulge in a seemingly endless exchange of letters with Attlee on the

---

* R. B. McCallum, later Master of Pembroke College, Oxford, and Alison Redman, early psephologists, produced the first of the Nuffield College-sponsored histories of the post-war general elections. In a further passage they produced another campaign metaphor which, both because of the cricket allusion and because of the comparison, Attlee would have liked much more than would have Churchill: 'He [Attlee] had the air of a sound and steady batsman, keeping up his wicket with ease against a demon bowler who was losing both pace and length' (*The British General Election of 1945*, p. 175).

issue of whether a Labour Prime Minister would not be under the effective control of Professor Harold Laski and his allegedly 'polit-bureau'-style National Executive Committee. Laski was that year's chairman of the Labour party and was thought by the Tories to be a good bogeyman. He was a considerable irritant at this stage, trying to suggest that if Attlee accompanied Churchill to the July Potsdam three-power conference he could do so only as an 'observer', and generally endeavouring to undermine his leadership. Attlee dealt briskly with the pretentious professor. When he had received a 24 May letter from Laski urging him to resign the leadership, he wrote back: 'Thank you for your letter, contents of which have been noted.' And on another adjacent occasion he delivered to him the immortal rebuke, 'a period of silence from you would now be most welcome'.[41]

This aspect of Churchill's campaign was notably sterile. The vast majority of the public did not understand what he was on about, and he gave the impression of harping on about an unreal issue. Nevertheless there was some underlying constitutional validity to his point. The relationship of the Labour party machine to the party leadership was both confused and endowed with potential constitutional danger. It caused considerable difficulty both to Hugh Gaitskell when he was leader in opposition and to Harold Wilson when he was leader in government.

Despite the mistakes and failures of his campaign, Churchill was not seriously worried about its outcome. He could not easily believe that the country was about to entrust its destiny in what he saw as the immensely hazardous post-war world to Attlee rather than to himself. His party experts assured him that he would have a majority of at least sixty. He thought that if Roosevelt could win four elections, he could at least win one. And the evidence from his activities on the ground was superficially encouraging. He spent his nights, preceded by long hours of government work, in his special train, although leaving it for daily cavalcades in an open car followed by mass evening rallies. Crowds lined the roadsides to cheer him as he passed, and his arrival in town centres was a great local event. Attlee, by contrast, chugged around in a family saloon with his wife at the wheel from one moderate-sized meeting to another, with no spectators of his journeys.

Churchill fought aggressively on the ground as over the air. That was how he had been taught to electioneer as a young man, and he saw no reason to change his style. The Labour and Liberal parties did not oppose him in his own constituency (Epping had been split into two, and he chose the more residential and Conservative half, renamed Woodford), but this did not prevent him in his London open-air peregrinations from delivering fighting speeches in the constituencies of both Ernest Bevin and Herbert Morrison. In Attlee's Limehouse there were hardly enough inhabitants or intact buildings left to make it worth the trouble of a visit.

Throughout the campaign the press of official business weighed heavily on Churchill. Eden was ill (with a duodenal ulcer) and fulfilled only one election engagement – a notably moderate broadcast on 27 June. This meant that Churchill added the burdens of being temporarily in charge of the Foreign Office to those of the premiership and being party leader during an election. As he put it in his memoirs:

> The days were passed amid the clamour of multitudes, and when at night, tired out, I got back to my headquarters train, where a considerable staff and all the incoming telegrams awaited me, I had to toil for many hours. The incongruity of party excitement and clatter with the sombre background which filled my mind was in itself an affront to reality and proportion. I was glad indeed when polling day at last arrived. . . .[42]

The main government business was the preparation for the Big Three meeting at Potsdam, which was to start on 15 July, and Churchill's hope that he could there get Truman to join him in a stand which would halt the spread of the Communist tide across Europe. Polling day was 5 July, but, unprecedentedly since 1918, there was then an interval of three weeks before the votes were counted – so as to allow the service votes to come in. During this period the ballot boxes concealed their contents with a secrecy which would be the amazed envy of Whitehall today, and to some extent was so even in the much more disciplined climate of 1945. The interval enabled Churchill to take an eight-day painting and bathing holiday at Hendaye in the Pays Basque and just on the French side of the frontier with Spain.

He flew to Berlin for Potsdam on 15 July, and was joined there, not only by Eden but also by Attlee, who, in spite of his refutation of Laski was inevitably at this stage more of an 'observer' than a full participant. The Potsdam conference, appropriately from Churchill's point of view codenamed Terminal, was by far the longest of all the series of summits. Churchill, even before the break necessitated by his (and Attlee's) return to London for the election counts, was able to attend nine plenary sessions, spread over the same number of days; and when Attlee, accompanied this time by Ernest Bevin, the new Foreign

Secretary, returned to Potsdam on 28 July as head of the British delegation, there were another five days of conference.

Eden thought Churchill's opening performance was appalling:

> W. was very bad. He had read no brief & was confused & woolly & verbose. We had an anti-Chinese tirade from him. Americans not a little exasperated. . . . Alec [Cadogan] & I & Bob [Pierson Dixon] have never seen W. worse. . . . he is again under Stalin's spell. He kept repeating 'I like that man' & I am full of admiration of Stalin's handling of him.[43]

Whether it much mattered is open to doubt. By Potsdam there had set in a terrible sameness about the pattern of these summit meetings. It was like seeing the same not very good film several times round. Churchill would try to have a preliminary meeting to develop a common position with the Americans, and, whether it was Roosevelt or Truman, would be gently repulsed, on the grounds, as Truman more bluntly than Roosevelt put it, that he did not want to appear to be 'ganging up' against the Russians. Churchill would then arrive full of complaints against the Russians and mild discontent with the Americans. But his powerful and (in spite of his bad start at Potsdam) often sparkling performances in the conference chamber would quickly improve his morale. This would be further strengthened by a long tête-à-tête with Stalin – he had a five-hour dinner alone with him except for inter-preters at Potsdam – and he would believe a special rapport had been re-established. Then the old subjects, notably Poland, would be discussed and, with the assistance of the Americans who wanted a posi-tive outcome, a communiqué recording some slight progress would be agreed. This would come apart in the course of the next couple of months, which would dismay Churchill but also cause him to advocate a new summit. When this was arranged, sometimes quickly, sometimes more slowly, the procedure would begin again, often at almost exactly the same points. In reality, therefore summits were not the finest hours of Churchill, or of anybody else, and although he had many deprivations to face in that week, leaving Stalin and a summit for the last time should not have been one of them.

Churchill got back to London on the afternoon of Wednesday, 25 July, still uneasily hopeful that he had won the election. To say that he was calmly confident would not have been true. For that to be so he had made too many agitated requests, mainly to London by tele-phone, for reassurance while at Potsdam. Attlee, available on the spot but whom he did not consult, might have given him the most falsely steadying answer. The leader of the Labour party was much more certain that he had lost, although probably by a respectably small margin – perhaps forty or sixty seats – than was Churchill that he had won. The less perceptive members of Churchill's entourage were also of Attlee's view. Lord Moran was so certain of Churchill's and his return that he left all his luggage at Potsdam.

Churchill dined that evening, still in the constricted Downing Street Annexe, with only a family party of Clementine, Randolph, Mary and his brother Jack Churchill, although the inevitable Beaverbrook and Bracken, the two architects of his defeat as many thought, looked in, the one before and the other after dinner. He went to bed and to sleep at the early hour for him of 1.15. He subsequently wrote how 'just before dawn I woke suddenly with a sharp stab of almost physical pain. A hitherto subconscious conviction that we were beaten broke forth and dominated my mind.'[44] The dominance was not such however as to prevent his turning over and at once going to sleep again. He awoke only at nine, by which time the ballot boxes were beginning to yield their secrets, and he remained in his bed or his bath until after ten, when the first results were coming in. By 10.30 the outcome was clear to a psephologist with a slide-rule. One effect of the dominance of the broadcasts was that a remarkably similar pattern prevailed over the whole country. To know a few results was to know all, although this was not widely understood at the time.

Churchill got into his siren suit, lit a cigar and collapsed into his chair in his Map Room, where he remained as the dark picture became ever darker. It was quickly obvious to him that he had lost, but it took some time for the scale of the defeat to emerge. It was mammoth, one of the only three Conservative catastrophes of the twentieth century. The party was reduced to 210 seats, which was nonetheless better than its 156 seats of 1906 or its 165 of 1997. In all three cases its leftward challengers, the Liberals on the first occasion, the Labour party on the later two, won close to 400 seats. The reason that the Conservatives held around fifty more seats in the new House of Commons in 1945 than on the other two occasions was that there was no effective third-party pressure comparable with that of the nascent Labour party in 1906 or the Liberal Democrats in 1997.

It should also be recorded that, in spite of the many criticisms of Churchill's largely absentee and policy-indifferent leadership in opposition, the Conservative recovery from 1945 was more rapid, better tempered and more constructive in policy than the party performance after both the other two heavy defeats. In 1950, after four and a half years, most of the lost ground was won back, and twenty months later the Conservative party slithered back into government with a workable parliamentary majority, even if secured with fewer popular votes than the Labour party had polled. After 1906, by contrast, the Conservative party lost another two general elections, got rid of its leader and replaced him with a much less distinguished figure, participated in winning a third election but only under the coalition Prime Ministership of a man whom they had previously regarded as their bitterest political enemy, and took sixteen years to return to independent power.

On 26 July 1945 Churchill did not have these comforting thoughts to console him. Formally he behaved impeccably in defeat. Luncheon that day, mainly a family affair, was described by Mary Churchill as an occasion of Stygian gloom. When Clementine tried to tell him that the result might well be a blessing in disguise, he maintained his normal standards of mordant wit by replying that 'at the moment it's certainly very well disguised'.[45] The outside guests were Beaverbrook and Bracken, as well as, more surprisingly, the ennobled David Margesson, the ex-Chief Whip who had done so much to provide unshakeable parliamentary majorities for Baldwin and Neville Chamberlain.

After lunch, Lascelles, the King's private secretary, called to discuss the arrangements for the change of government. It was decided that Churchill would go to the Palace and resign at seven o'clock that evening. This involved a change of plan, for he had previously thought that, whatever the outcome, he would meet Parliament as Prime Minister. The decisiveness of the Labour majority made that inappropriate. He then wrote a courteous letter to Attlee informing him of the timetable. At the resignation audience the King, undoubtedly dismayed by the result,* offered Churchill the Order of the Garter, which he refused, suggesting that it should be offered to Anthony Eden instead.†

---

* But so he had been by the replacement of Chamberlain by Churchill, five years before.
† Eden also refused, although they both became 'Garters' in the early 1950s, no doubt thinking that the honour was more appropriate after the victory of 1951 than after the defeat of 1945. It was surprising that Churchill accepted even then, for it meant changing his style to the unPrime Ministerial Sir Winston Churchill, which was not in the tradition of Mr Pitt, Mr Gladstone, Mr Asquith or Mr Lloyd George. All previous Prime Ministers who had become KGs when in office had been peers, so that no change of style was involved. Churchill, however, accepted the Order of Merit in the New Year's Honours List for 1946, saying that this honour, coming direct from the Sovereign and not on ministerial advice, made it more attractive to him. But Attlee was just about

Churchill then issued a brief and dignified farewell statement, which was read on the nine o'clock news:

> The decision of the British people has been recorded in the votes counted today. . . . Immense responsibilities abroad and at home fall upon the new Government, and we must all hope that they will be successful in bearing them. It only remains for me to express to the British people, for whom I have acted in these perilous years, my profound gratitude for the unflinching, unswerving support which they have given me during my task, and for the many expressions of kindness which they have shown towards their servant.[46]

Dinner that evening (again in the unlovely Annexe) was a little less Stygian: still basically a family party plus the inevitable Bracken, but with the more emollient and responsible Eden substituted for Beaverbrook. Next day Churchill held a farewell Cabinet in the traditional room at noon. This must have been an occasion at once embarrassed and maudlin. On the way out Churchill told Eden that thirty years of his life had been passed in that room, and that he would never sit in it again. The heir apparent had the honesty not to express any desire that this view of the future should prove false, but assured Churchill that no return could add to the splendour of his place in history.

The afternoon was a succession of farewells. The most interesting was with the Chiefs of Staff. 'It was a very sad and very moving little meeting at which I found myself unable to say much for fear of breaking down,' Alanbrooke recorded.[47] Churchill's relationship with his generals – as with his ministers – had always been tense and often fraught. 'God knows where we would be without him, but God knows where we shall go with him!' had been Alanbrooke's diary reaction shortly after his appointment as CIGS in December 1941,[48] and that was the tone of his observations throughout the war. His final comment after Churchill's resignation was supremely ungrudging: 'I thank God that I was given an opportunity of working alongside of such a man, and of having my eyes opened to the fact that occasionally such supermen exist on this earth.'[49] Perhaps, however, the best epitome of the much discussed issue

---

to put the Garter into exactly the same royal category, and in any event it was the King and not the new Prime Minister who had offered it to Churchill in July. Membership of the Order of the Garter, which is limited to twenty-four, has since become almost routine for former Prime Ministers, but up to 1945 it had been more selectively bestowed. Of twentieth-century Prime Ministers only Salisbury, Balfour, Asquith and Baldwin had achieved it.

of Churchill–Alanbrooke relations was provided by their respective reactions to the Japanese attack on Pearl Harbor three and a half years before. Alanbrooke complained that it had undone forty-eight hours of staff work, while Churchill's response, as we have seen, was 'So we had won after all!'[50] That was the difference between a fine staff officer and a world statesman.

Churchill did not then slink away from officialdom to some private lair, partly perhaps because he had no nearly ready lair to which to go, but departed for a last weekend at Chequers, which Attlee had been glad to put at his disposal. There was some attempt at festivity, with a large enough party, to whom Winant, the American ambassador, was the most interesting addition, to produce fifteen round the table and a rehoboam of champagne for dinner on the Sunday evening. But the mood was perhaps more truly captured by Churchill appending his signature last to the visitors' book and writing 'Finis' underneath it.

PART SIX

WAS THE EVENING LEADEN?

1945–1965

41

'THE ENGLISH PATIENT'

ON MONDAY, 30 July 1945, Churchill and Clementine removed to a suite in Claridge's Hotel, and then after a week or so they perched in the Duncan Sandys' flat at Westminster Gardens in Marsham Street on the edge of Pimlico. On the first two weekends in August they went for 'camping out' weekends at Chartwell, but it took Clementine until the late autumn to get the main house there ready for reoccupation. The London house at 28 Hyde Park Gate, off Kensington Road, which they had bought a few months before, was ready in October. During most of Clementine's weeks of house preparation Churchill was away, first on Lake Como and then on the French Riviera. Before going he had been present at the opening of the new parliament and had made it clear to his colleagues that he intended, in opposition, to continue as leader of the Conservative party.

On 1 August, when the House of Commons assembled to elect a Speaker, Churchill was greeted with tumultuous enthusiasm by the embattled 200 Conservatives who sang For He's a Jolly Good Fellow. The Labour party responded by singing the Red Flag, which got the new parliament off to a divisive start. Competitive community singing was hardly good for inducting the 250 new Labour members into parliamentary proprieties. On 16 August, however, in the debate on the first King's speech of the new government a more healing note was struck. Churchill, speaking from the opposition front bench for the first time since his resignation from Baldwin's shadow Cabinet in 1930, delivered what his often critical wife described as 'a brilliant, moving, gallant speech'.[1] Attlee responded with a memorable tribute to Churchill's war leadership, which, among other more personal triumphs, had resulted in the end of the Japanese war on the previous day. The fact that it had required the dropping of two atom bombs, one on 6 August and one on the 9th, was not at that stage a matter of controversy, either between the Allies or between parties in Britain.

At this juncture Churchill's public face was more serene than his private one. On 26 August Clementine wrote to their daughter Mary a chilling description of home life in the still fairly chaotic Chartwell:

> I cannot explain how it is but in our misery we seem, instead of clinging to each other to be always having scenes. I'm sure it's all my fault, but I'm finding life more than I can bear. He is so unhappy & that makes him very difficult. He hates his food (hardly any meat). . . . I can't see any future. But Papa is going to Italy & then perhaps Nana [Clementine's cousin Maryott Whyte, who was always available both as companion and as factotum] can get this place straight. It looks impossible & one doesn't know where to start. . . .[2]

On 31 August Churchill managed to have a great row with his son Randolph (not the most difficult thing to achieve) at a Claridge's dinner with Brendan Bracken. It was time to be off, and on 2 September accompanied by his daughter Sarah, doctor, dictating secretary, detective and valet, he flew to Milan on his way to a villa on Lake Como, which Field Marshal Alexander had placed at his disposal. Alexander treated him with immense consideration throughout the visit. This was wholly deserved. The respect which any British general owed to his wartime chief and architect of victory was enhanced by the easy rapport and mutual sustenance which Churchill and Alexander had enjoyed throughout. But the treatment might nonetheless cause the raising of eyebrows if accepted for holiday purposes by any politician today. Alexander's personal Dakota was sent to London to bring out the Churchill party. The villa, although nominally a divisional headquarters, was put at the exclusive use of Churchill and his entourage during the seventeen-day stay. Two specially chosen aides-de-camp and a guard of twenty-four men from Churchill's own 4th Hussars regiment were seconded to him, and then Alexander himself came from Austria for a weekend visit and joined Churchill in painting sessions.

When Churchill moved on, first to a former Pirelli villa on the Riviera Levante and then into France, the ADCs accompanied him. One, who obviously had high travel-agent talents, went ahead to Monte Carlo and negotiated with a half-empty Hôtel de Paris a special full pension rate of four guineas (approximately £100 at present values) for his patron. Churchill, however, quickly moved again to an Antibes villa, to which General Eisenhower (*in absentia*) made him welcome. There is a story, recorded many years later by one of the ADCs, that Churchill, in Monte Carlo, after at first resisting the short walk across the square to the Casino, later succumbed and lost £7,000 (about £160,000 today), the cheque for which the manager did not cash but obligingly kept as a souvenir. It is however legitimate to suspect a strong element of retrospective *esprit de l'escalier* about this reminiscence. Churchill was not a gambler on that scale, least of all in his uncertain circumstances of 1945, before either the sale of his war memoirs was arranged or Lord Camrose rode over the horizon as the third and most permanently effective of the 'white knights' who came to the rescue of Chartwell.

Churchill returned to England in the first week of October, after a full five weeks of transalpine holiday. It had been good for him, both mentally and physically, although there was possibly an element of bravado about his early (5 September) claim to Clementine:

> It has done me no end of good to come out here and resume my painting. I am much better in myself, and am not worried about anything. We have had no newspapers since I left England, and I no longer feel any keen desire to turn their pages. This is the first time for very many years that I have been completely out of the world. The Japanese War being finished and complete peace and victory achieved, I feel a great sense of relief which grows steadily, others having to face the hideous problems of the aftermath. . . . It may all indeed be 'a blessing in disguise.'[3]

Physically he was not without his normal travelling ration of ailments, although on this visit they rarely interfered with Lord Moran's golf. A rupture, from which he had suffered as a child but which had been quiescent for sixty years, suddenly reasserted itself, and Moran had to perform his familiar wartime role of summoning an army consultant. Brigadier Harold Edwards, chief military surgeon in Italy, apparently came with great pleasure and fitted a truss, to which Churchill had to accommodate himself until he risked a hernia operation two years later. And at the end Churchill arrived back from Antibes with one of the heavy colds and sore throats which considerably agitated him. What was the clear gain of the long holiday was that, much more than at Hendaye in July, it had got him back into a settled and calming painting habit. He brought fifteen completed canvases back with him. The holiday regime also gave him plenty of time, if he so wished, to contemplate the reasons for his crushing electoral defeat. He need not have blamed himself unduly for his campaign, inept though much of this, particularly his crucial broadcasts, had been. For what it was worth the rudimentary psephological evidence indicated that the Conservatives had marginally improved their position during the month of electioneering. For several years previously the Gallup polls, published in the *News Chronicle*, had been indicating a steady Labour lead of approximately 10 per cent. The outcome gave them one of 8.5 per cent, enough under the trend-exaggerating British electoral system to produce the enormous Labour majority, but marginally down on the predictions – of which nobody had taken great notice.

Nor was there much indication that it was the service vote, brain-washed according to some Conservative apologists by the left-biased lectures of the Army Bureau of Current Affairs, which had done it. The percentage of the forces voting was low, helping to produce, together with a stale register and much wartime upheaval of residence, a weak overall participation of only 67 per cent. But a purely civilian vote, with those in the services excluded, would have produced just as clear a Labour majority. The fact was that there had been a settled view throughout most of the war and extending across a wide swathe of the British public, occupationally and geographically, that they did not wish to go back to the conditions of the 1930s, and they saw the Conservative party, with or without Churchill at its head, standing essentially for this. No doubt there were some who thought in a muddled way that they could both vote Labour and continue with Churchill as head of the government. Some of them may have cheered Churchill on his electoral peregrinations and then voted against him, but it is doubtful if they were many. And they were balanced by those whose animus against the Conservative party extended to Churchill himself, at any rate as a peacetime leader. This was illustrated by the Woodford result, when with the deliberate abstention of Labour or Liberal candidates a crazy independent, who advocated a one-day working week and got only 298 votes when he stood again in 1950, polled over 10,000 votes against Churchill.

In England that autumn he found nothing very soothing to balance these sombre reflections. He brooded over what he saw as the increasing menace of Soviet expansionism in Europe and the hesitant American resistance to it. He felt appallingly deprived by the absence of the traditional red boxes of British government, of the flow of secret information which they contained and of the services of a fleet of highly trained private secretaries. He needed three dictating or mail-opening secretaries of his own, and Clementine a fourth, and they acquired the adjacent house, 27 Hyde Park Gate, to house them. But that was different from the services, not merely of Colville, the favourite, but of Martin, Rowan, Peck and others who were in civil service rank Colville's senior. At the centre of his unease for the future, as opposed to his deprived nostalgia for the past, was his dilemma that he wanted neither to give up being leader of the opposition nor to perform on any regular basis the duties associated with that mostly unrewarding position. It is not clear whether at this stage his ambiguity was associated with a thought that it might lead him back to 10 Downing Street or whether, as he often implied but never acted upon, he was just looking for a favourable opportunity to hand over to Eden.

Even when he was in England his attendance in the House of Commons was fitful. Despite the priority he gave to writing his war memoirs, he mostly presided at the weekly meetings of the shadow Cabinet, which took place in the early evenings of Tuesdays, although as can easily be imagined he did so in a detached and rhetorical rather than a businesslike way. One of his idiosyncrasies was constantly to refer to David Maxwell Fyfe, later Home Secretary and, as Viscount Kilmuir, Lord Chancellor, whom he did not like, as 'Sir Donald', the insult being increased by the use of his knightly prefix, while more favoured members were addressed simply by their correct Christian names. Frequently, however, he was away for long periods, and Eden had to perform in his place. In early 1946, for example, Churchill was in America from early January to late March. He sometimes tried to compensate for this by switching the meetings from Westminster to luncheons at the Savoy Hotel, where the proceedings became more festive but also more meandering.

When Churchill was present in the chamber his interventions were frequent, and some of them, particularly the shorter and less prepared ones, were good-humoured and sparkling. His more portentous orations were treated with full respect by Attlee and Bevin at least, but were sometimes heard with impatience and even mockery by the brasher Labour MPs. Such speeches were better received by outside audiences, often outside not merely the House but the country. Then there was a sad occasion in December 1945, when he rashly tabled a motion of censure against the economic and social policy of the government, and found himself manifestly out-debated by a taut, deflating and witty reply from Attlee. This was a low moment of his life in opposition, and provoked many of his senior colleagues to think that the battered Conservative party would be better off without his unsteady leadership. That old walrus, the seventeenth Earl of Derby, who had been around in politics almost as long as Churchill himself, was always muttering for a change at the top, but there were other more serious figures who took the same view. Few, if any, were however prepared to tell Churchill so to his face.

A more regular parliamentary joust took place on Thursday afternoons between Churchill and Herbert Morrison, Lord President of the Council and leader of the House. This was when the parliamentary business for the following week was announced by the Lord President, and he and the leader of the opposition habitually engaged in short semi-spontaneous interventions over the sweep of government policy and intentions. Honours were frequently about even and tempers were sometimes but not invariably preserved. In general Churchill did not like Morrison, partly on account of his long-abandoned pacifism of the First World War, partly on account of his more contemporary party political skill. While recognizing his administrative competence as Home Secretary, he made more disparaging remarks about him than about any of his other Labour colleagues in the coalition. It was therefore surprising that, after Churchill's hernia operation in June 1947, Morrison not only called upon him at Hyde Park Gate but stayed for luncheon.* It was an interesting example of Churchill's fluctuations between sharpness of disapproval and generosity of forgiveness.

Churchill's best news at the end of 1945, before his early-January departure for his extended American visit, was his first knowledge of what he described as Lord Camrose's 'princely plan for making Chartwell a national possession'.+ This meant that for the third and last time that mixture of Churchill's haven and estate agents' tease was withdrawn from the market. It took Camrose another eight months to bring his plan to fruition, but by August 1946 he had raised enough money (£15,000 from himself and £5,000 from each of sixteen other donors) to buy the property from Churchill for £43,600 and to give it to the National Trust with an endowment of £35,000+ and the provision that Churchill should live in it for the remainder of his life at a rent of £350 a year plus rates and that after his death it should be a shrine to his memory. Churchill expressed enthusiasm for the project and promised to leave documents and mementoes to enhance the interest of the house.

---

* Attlee merely paid an afternoon call, after which he sent Churchill, in specific return for a similar present when he himself had been ill eight years before, a slim volume of his speeches which I had just edited. He wisely made it clear, however, that he did not expect Churchill to read them.

+ To obtain their modern requivalents all the figures should be multiplied by a factor of about twenty-three.

This undertaking he abundantly fulfilled. At that stage he also indicated that he would wish to be buried there, but he subsequently changed his mind, and his remains went to the Marlborough family church at Bladon, near Blenheim.

By the time the Chartwell transaction was complete Churchill had become much better off than when it was first mooted. Apart from the vast prospective profits from his war memoirs other sums had begun almost to pour in. Alexander Korda paid him £50,000 for the film rights of *The History of the English-Speaking Peoples*, a book which, although completed in a first draft just before the outbreak of war, was not published until 1956–8. Odhams Press paid him £25,000 for the residual value of all his pre-1940 book copyrights, and Henry Luce £12,000 for the American book rights to his wartime secret-sessions speeches in the House of Commons. A little ironically, therefore, he used the Camrose money not just to keep Chartwell but to buy several adjacent farms and to add considerably to the extent and agricultural content of the estate. As, following Mary Churchill's marriage to Christopher Soames in February 1947, the Soameses moved into the principal farm house and Christopher undertook the management of the estate, this came at a fortuitous time.

That winter of 1947 with all its privations of extreme cold (for England) and fuel shortages Churchill spent largely at Hyde Park Gate for which he had a special heating dispensation – Chartwell was mostly too cold. He devoted his main effort to the first volume, *The Gathering Storm*, of his war memoirs, but he was also able to spare some time for parliamentary politics. It was a contrast with the previous year when his long American sojourn, centred essentially on his 5 March carefully prepared speech at Fulton, Missouri, started with six weeks of sun-seeking and warm-water bathing, divided between Florida and Cuba. Clementine, who unusually was with him, found him difficult to get settled, either at writing or at painting. The few canvases he eventually produced did not suggest that the Caribbean suited his talents nearly as well as the Côte d'Azur or Marrakech. He also experienced one of the feverish bronchial infections which seemed an inevitable accompaniment to all his travels; Lord Moran had to be telephoned but not summoned.

The attraction of the invitation to deliver a major speech at the relatively unknown Westminster College in the small Mid-Western town of Fulton was that it came through President Truman. Fulton is in the middle of Missouri, the new President's home state, and he thought sufficiently highly of Westminster College to describe it as 'a wonderful school'. Moreover he offered to conduct Churchill to and from Fulton and to introduce him to the audience. That carried with it the enticement of two eighteen-hour train journeys in the company of Truman, whom Churchill had not seen since his own Potsdam presence was unexpectedly cut short and with whom he was eager to deepen his acquaintanceship. The journeys encompassed two sleeping-car nights in the Presidential train, but as, on the outward journey at least, the President and the former Prime Minister played poker until after 2.30 a.m., not much time was wasted on non-communal activities.

The original Fulton invitation envisaged three or four lectures, and Churchill was no doubt expected to indulge in some retrospective reminiscence. But that was not his way. There was no occasion in his whole life when he ever delivered a lecture series, as though it was a semi-academic exercise. He believed in single-shot salvoes and for Fulton he decided to put a great weight of explosive behind it. It became one of the most controversial, remembered and formative speeches of the post-war years. In the late 1940s only General Marshall's Harvard Commencement address in June 1947 and, maybe, Churchill's own Zurich speech in the autumn of 1946 could bear comparison with it.

The substance of Churchill's Fulton message, embellished with many typical rhetorical flourishes, was that an 'iron curtain' having descended across the continent of Europe 'from Stettin in the Baltic to Trieste in the Adriatic', peace and democracy in the post-war world could no longer be sustained by the three great powers of the wartime alliance performing as an equal trinity and offering the world a triangular leadership. He did not believe that the Russians wanted war, but he did think that their desire was for 'the fruits of war and the indefinite expansion of their power and doctrines'. This could be resisted without war only by America and Britain working ever more closely together.

> If the population of the English-speaking Commonwealth be added to that of the United States with all that such co-operation implies in the air, on the sea, all over the globe and in science and in industry, and in moral force, there will be no quivering, precarious balance of power to offer its temptation to ambition or adventure. On the contrary, there will be an overwhelming assurance of security.[5]

He was careful to say that it should all be done within the framework of strict adherence to the Charter of the United Nations, and that a Soviet Union which behaved in accordance with Western standards would always be welcome to enjoy the influence to which its wartime bravery and sacrifices entitled it. Nevertheless the core message was hard and clear. Whether or not it was given that name, a Western alliance was necessary, and there should no longer be any pretence that the leading members of the United Nations stood in an equally close relationship with each other. Within a very few years, of course, this became settled American and British policy, gratefully accepted by the non-Communist countries of Europe, not only by the core of France, Benelux and Italy but by others from Norway to Turkey and from Greece to Portugal. Truman and Marshall, Bevin and Acheson, achieved their greatest fame by being the architects of NATO, the alliance which, through forty years of cold war, achieved its central objective while never firing a shot.

In 1946, however, it was strong meat, not least for the American press. There is no reason to think that Churchill's words were other than well received by his Missouri audience. But that was far from the case with the next morning's newspapers. The *Wall Street Journal*, hardly a paper easily shocked by anti-Communist sentiment, stated bluntly that 'The United States wants no alliance, or anything that resembles an alliance, with any other nation.' The *New York Times* was highly critical. And the *Chicago Sun*, in general the liberal and internationalist answer to Colonel McCormick's *Chicago Tribune*, wrote so hostilely about what it described as the 'poisonous doctrines' of Fulton that Churchill withdrew from an arrangement, entered into only a week before, that the paper would serialize his *Secret Sessions Speeches*. Deep offence was necessary to make Churchill resile from a favourable publishing arrangement.

Outside America the London *Times* was predictably cool, and wrote about his 'perhaps less happy' passages. *Pravda* was obviously hostile, but it was Stalin who in a very rare 'interview' for that journal showed that he knew how to use the rapier as well as the bludgeon. He made two points, one a shrewd hit against Churchill's reiterated appeal for 'unity of the English-speaking peoples':

Now Mr Churchill is starting his process of unleashing war also [like Hitler] with a racial theory, declaring that only those people who speak English are full-blooded nations, whose vocation it is to control the fate of the whole world. . . . In point of fact Mr Churchill and his friends in England and in America are presenting those nations who do not speak English with a kind of ultimatum – recognize our supremacy over you, voluntarily, and all will be well – otherwise war is inevitable.

This cannot have been without some appeal to several countries, not least France.

Stalin's second point was a purely dialectical but spirited piece of *Alice Through the Looking Glass* audacity. It was built on Churchill's frequent complaints against the narrow political basis of governments in the Eastern bloc:

> In England today, the government of one party is ruling, the Labour Party, and the Opposition is deprived of the right to take part in the government. That is what Mr Churchill calls 'true democracy'. In Poland, Roumania, Yugoslavia, Bulgaria and Hungary, the government is made up of a bloc of several parties – from four to six parties – while the opposition, if it is more or less loyal, is assured of the right to take part in the government. That is what Mr Churchill calls 'totalitarianism, tyranny, police state'.[6]

At home, apart from *The Times*, the reaction to Fulton was mixed but not worrying. Attlee, urged from his back benches to dissociate himself and the government from Churchill's speech, declined to do so, although he did not endorse it either, saying that Churchill had spoken in an individual capacity on his own responsibility and that there was no obligation on the government to approve or disapprove. The Labour government were in fact well disposed towards Churchill's American visit. They, unlike many members of his own party, rather welcomed his long absence from the House of Commons; Bevin's foreign policy was moving very much in the direction of Fulton, even if a little more slowly; and Churchill, through his New York and Washington contacts, had been helpful in supporting the crucially necessary dollar loan to Britain following the termination of Lend–Lease which Keynes had negotiated in the previous autumn, and trying somewhat to soften its terms. Furthermore Churchill had been careful not to let the light of these activities hide under a bushel. British ministers had been kept very well informed about his conversations. Any such gratitude did not extend throughout the Labour MPs. Ninety-three of them, just under a quarter of the total, put down a motion of censure on Churchill. The list included some surprising names, notably James Callaghan and Woodrow Wyatt.

The key figure who, untypically, behaved more equivocally than Attlee or Bevin was Truman. A film of the Fulton occasion showed the President clapping vigorously during Churchill's most controversial passages, there was no hint of chill in his attitude to Churchill on the return journey, and he wrote a friendly letter as late as 12 March, when all the waves of the storm had broken, saying how much the people in Missouri had 'enjoyed what you had to say'.[7] But at a White House press conference on 8 March he had denied prior knowledge of Churchill's content (very doubtfully true) and had insisted that his presence implied no endorsement. And he even restrained Acheson, then Under-Secretary of State, from representing the US government at a New York reception for Churchill in the following week. However, this produced no impairment of relations. Churchill doubtless made full allowance for Truman being heir to the long Roosevelt tradition of advancing to great objectives by somewhat crab-like movements.

So far as the effect of Churchill's speech on the long-term direction of US policy was concerned, it had the luck to be fortified, although in private not in public, by the arrival in Washington at the end of February of George Kennan's famous 'long telegram' from Moscow. Kennan was essentially a moderate and not a sabre-rattler, but his analysis of the intentions of the Soviet Union and of the safest way for America to deal with them, bore a close but coincidental relationship to Churchill's prescripts. Kennan, currently chargé d'affaires in Moscow, was one of the most powerful influences on US foreign policy over a span of nearly fifty years, and his long telegram counts as a crucial state paper.

Churchill's second famous speech of 1946 was delivered to Zurich University on 19 September. It marked the opening of his campaign for a united Europe, which occupied much of his political time and interest from then until in the August of 1949 and 1950 he attended, with great *réclame*, the first two sessions, at Strasbourg, of the first and very rudimentary European institution. The Council of Europe was purely a sounding board, but it was nonetheless a symbolically powerful one, situated as it was at the junction of France and Germany in the city which had experienced four changes of suzerainty within a century. These changes had marked the victories and defeats over each other of the two greatest land powers in Europe, fluctuating in outcome but increasingly destructive not only of the two countries but of the world around them.

The great virtue of Churchill's Zurich speech was that it saw and faced head on the fact that an united Europe must be based on a Franco-German partnership: 'The first step in the re-creation of the European family must be a partnership between France and Germany. In this way only can France recover the moral leadership of Europe.

There can be no revival of Europe without a spiritually great France and a spiritually great Germany.' Once again, as at Fulton, he had proclaimed a doctrine which was at least premature to many people, but which was to become axiomatic within a few years. There were many in France in 1946 who could not contemplate the revival of an equal Germany. Churchill's son-in-law Duncan Sandys, who became the main organizer of the British European Movement, was sent to investigate de Gaulle's attitude, and reported back on 26 November:

[De Gaulle] said that the reference in Mr Churchill's Zurich speech to a Franco-German partnership had been badly received in France. Germany, as a state, no longer existed. All Frenchmen were violently opposed to recreating any kind of unified, centralized Reich, and were gravely suspicious of the policy of the American and British Governments. Unless steps were taken to prevent a resuscitation of German power, there was a danger that a United Europe would become nothing else than an enlarged Germany. He stressed that if French support was to be won for the idea of European union, France must come in as a founder partner with Britain. Moreover, the two countries must reach a precise understanding with one another upon the attitude to be adopted towards Germany before any approaches were made to the latter.[8]

Despite this discouraging early response (with de Gaulle, paradoxically in view of later events, wanting Britain in to help France deal with Germany), there can be no doubt that Churchill's vision gave a clearer direction. It led first to the somewhat misty old men's groping for friendship between Konrad Adenauer and de Gaulle himself, then to the clearer-cut mutual admiration society of Helmut Schmidt and Valéry Giscard d'Estaing, and finally the determination of Helmut Kohl and François Mitterrand to provide a joint motor for the European Community which gave to France (and to a lesser extent to Germany, the size of whose economy made it more effortlessly powerful) its greatest period of influence in post-war Europe.

Much of the early credit for this construction belongs to Churchill. Not only did he blaze the trail at Zurich but he followed it up with considerable organizational application. He was the initiator of The Hague conference of May 1948, which met with the specific objective of promoting a United Europe, and he used his full influence to ensure that statesmen of the quality of Blum, Monnet, Reynaud, Spaak and De Gasperi attended. He also tried hard to put together a strong all-party British delegation, but failed to move the Labour leadership beyond a reluctant tolerance of what they chose to regard as a rather frivolous event. Nonetheless, among the delegation of 140 which Churchill headed were twenty-two Labour MPs. The main thrust of the conference, which was graced with another powerful oration from Churchill, was to advance some form of European parliamentary coming together, and this, despite foot-dragging by the British government, was achieved by the setting up in Strasbourg of the Council of Europe Assembly by the summer of 1949. The first year it was without the Germans, but by the second year they too were present. 'They ought to have been here a year ago,' Churchill then told the Assembly.[9]

As has been already noted, Churchill played a full part in both these sessions. He endured the Strasbourgeois humidity for substantial sojourns in the two Augusts. He lived in a villa just outside the city and did a lot of multi-national entertaining there. He mingled freely and frequently in the corridors and delivered several speeches in the hemicycle. His most notable oratorical success was when, on 11 August 1949, he addressed an open-air crowd of 20,000 in the Place Kléber. Such spontaneous enthusiasm for the European cause had never been seen in Strasbourg before; nor has it been seen since.

In spite of all this there has long been doubt and argument about the extent to which Churchill was a committed British European. Did he intend Britain to be in or out? Was he merely telling others to unite, or was he willing to do so too? The evidence is generally held to be against a Churchill commitment to full British participation. I find it conflicting. There are passages in his carefully prepared speeches which are very difficult to reconcile with a role of merely cheering from the sidelines. In his speech at The Hague, for instance, he said, referring to the progress which had been made in the year and a half since his Zurich speech: 'Sixteen European states are now associated for economic purposes; five have entered into close economic and military relationship. We hope that this nucleus will in due course be joined by the people of Scandinavia, and of the Iberian peninsula, as well as by Italy....'[10] As he counted Britain not merely among the sixteen but among the five, he was obviously then regarding his country as not merely part of Europe but part of its core.

He went on to face the sovereignty issue directly. Mutual aid in the economic field and joint military defences, he said, must 'inevitably be accompanied step by step with a parallel policy of closer political unity'. 'It is said with truth', he continued, 'that this involves some sacrifice or merger of national sovereignty. But it is also possible and not less agreeable to regard it as the gradual assumption by all the nations concerned of that larger sovereignty which can also protect their diverse and distinctive customs and characteristics. . . .'[11] A little earlier (21 April) he had told an Albert Hall meeting of the Central Council of the Conservative party that 'there would be no hope for the world unless the peoples of Europe unite together to preserve their freedom, their culture, and their civilization founded upon Christian ethics'.[12] It would have been difficult in these circumstances to add, or even to harbour the thought, 'but of course I am only talking of others and not of Britain's unique position outside the culture and civilization of Christian ethics'.

Then, in 1950, when a practical issue of European integration arose with the launch of the Schuman Plan for a Coal and Steel Community, Churchill was strongly critical of the Labour party's insular line ('the Durham miners wouldn't like it', was a much mocked phrase of Herbert Morrison's) and was happy to lead the Conservative party into a pro-Schuman Plan debate and division. He did not absolutely commit himself to British participation but the whole thrust of his attitude was in that direction. Edward Heath was able to make an enthusiastically pro-European maiden speech in that debate without diverging from the official Conservative line. And the Treaty of Paris, which set up the Coal and Steel Community in 1952, was much more tightly supranational than the 1957 Treaty of Rome which created both the Economic Community and Euratom.

Balancing these pieces of detailed evidence, however, there is the undoubted fact that Churchill instinctively saw Britain's role in the post-war world as qualitatively different from that of Italy, Germany or even France. Still less did he see Europe or the world through a Benelux telescope. Perhaps he put the balance of his views most revealingly in a parliamentary speech on 26 June 1950. Britain's absence from the conference for the setting up of the Coal and Steel Community, he began, 'deranges the balance of Europe. . . . I am all for a reconciliation between France and Germany, and for receiving Germany back into the European family, but this implies, as I have always insisted, that Britain and France should in the main act together so as to be able to deal on equal terms with Germany which is so much stronger than France alone.' He then faced the question of 'whether I should have welcomed this event even if there had been no such thing as this Russian menace. . . . I should say, "Yes, certainly." The unity of France and Germany, whether direct or in a larger continental grouping, is a merciful and glorious forward step towards the revival of Europe and the peace of the world. The fact that there is a grave Soviet and Communist menace only adds to its value and urgency.' Next, however, came the beginning of the doctrine of three interlocking circles, Europe, the Commonwealth and a special relationship with the United States, and of Britain's role as belonging to all three:

> By our unique position in the world, Great Britain has an opportunity, if she is worthy of it, to play an important and possibly a decisive part in all the three larger groupings of the Western democracies. . . . The whole movement of the world is towards an interdependence of nations. We feel all around us the belief that it is our best hope. If independent, individual sovereignty is sacrosanct and inviolable, how is it that we are all wedded to a world organization?[13]

Churchill's Europeanism would not have made him contemplate sacrificing the closest possible link with the United States. But, as he himself pointed out, this was not at issue. It was a settled American policy – and remained so for many decades – to encourage the drive towards European unity, and Britain's reluctance to be part of it was an exacerbating rather than a helpful factor in London's relations with Washington. Nor did Churchill's ardent Atlanticism cut him off from most of the committed continental Europeans. Jean Monnet always set great store by good and close relations with America. Paul-Henri Spaak moved from being the first president of the Strasbourg Assembly and the driving force of the Treaty of Rome to becoming Secretary-General of NATO. Konrad Adenauer, 'little European' and Carolingian though he was, believing romantically that the finest date in history was the year 800 when Charlemagne was crowned Frankish Emperor at Aachen, nonetheless knew that the security behind which he was rebuilding West Germany was essentially provided by the Americans; he was accordingly very respectful in the 1950s to President Eisenhower and Secretary of State Dulles.

What did differentiate Churchill from these continental Europeans was the third of his circles, that of the British Commonwealth, which in those days essentially meant the white Commonwealth, although as early as 1949 he was beginning to move towards a sympathetic respect for Jawaharlal Nehru. His views on this were set out at a European Movement rally on 28 November 1949:

> Britain is an integral part of Europe, and we mean to play our part in the revival of her prosperity and greatness. But Britain cannot be thought of

as a single state in isolation. She is the founder and centre of a world-wide Empire and Commonwealth. We shall never do anything to weaken the ties of blood, of sentiment and tradition and common interest which unite us with the other members of the British family of nations.

But nobody is asking us to make such a desertion. For Britain to enter a European Union from which the Empire and Commonwealth would be excluded would not only be impossible but would, in the eyes of Europe, enormously reduce the value of our participation. The Strasbourg recommendations [that is of the first session of the Council of Europe Assembly] urged the creation of an economic system which will embrace not only the European States, but all those other States and territories elsewhere which are associated with them.[14]

This was undoubtedly a view which Churchill held as strongly at the time as he did the view that Britain's involvement in Europe would improve and not weaken its relations with America. The difference was that his view about America was reinforced with almost every future year which went by, whereas over this same period the economic cohesion of the Commonwealth was reduced and what remained became more difficult to meld with Europe. It may be that in the early 1950s Britain could have imported the Commonwealth, bag and baggage, and secured as favourable access for Australia or New Zealand products as France did for the exports of Senegal or the Ivory Coast. It fitted in with the view, widely based in England at any rate, that in the early post-war years Britain could have had the leadership of Europe on almost any terms which it chose. However neither the Attlee nor the second Churchill government, in which Eden was allowed to make most of the foreign policy running or – on Europe – limping, showed any desire to close on the offer, and by the time that first Macmillan and then Heath had to try to make up for lost time, harsher choices had to be faced.

It would be rash to guess what view Churchill would have taken had he still been responsible for policy decisions in the 1960s or 1970s. But what is certain is that his Europeanism of the late 1940s and very early 1950s was not superficial. It was one of his dominant political purposes of the time. Nor was it just a matter of cheering from the outside. He had a full sense of Britain's participatory European vocation. He combined this with a desire to preserve as much as possible of Britain's declining position in the triumvirate of world power. How could he not in view of the role that he had played from Dunkirk to Potsdam? The miracle is that his Europeanism was as deep-seated and far-sighted as it was.

During these years of opposition the tangled but remunerative story of the writing of *The Second World War* was as central to Churchill's life as was his politics. Nominally he took a little time to decide whether he was going to write these memoirs. But any hesitation was hardly serious. He had jocularly declared on several occasions during the war itself that, so far as the verdict of history was concerned, he was safe because he would write a large part of it himself. And his whole habit, from the days of the Malakand Field Force onwards, was a writing habit. It was his best protection against 'black dog'. The marshalling of proofs and of teams of researchers, advisers and ladies who took his dictation until far into the night was the best substitute for red boxes, the flow of telegrams in and out, and the constant availability of private secretaries supplemented by generals, admirals and air marshals. Furthermore he greatly needed the money. He ended the war with his finances as precarious as they had mostly been. His war memoirs made him securely rich and, because of the way in which he held taxation at bay and disposed of the money, made his descendants rich after him.

There were three key encounters on the road between Churchill's general predisposition to set down his own version of history and its evolution into a definite project with hard work in progress. The first was at the end of January 1946 when he invited Emery Reves (the Americanized version of the Imre Revesz who had been his European press agent at the end of the 1930s) to visit him in Miami. He still stuck a conditional note about whether he would write the memoirs, but together they roused each other's enthusiasm and he excited Reves by telling him that 'I shall want you to handle it.' Churchill then added the first knot to the tangled web of confusion by saying, according to Reves, that 'for private reasons and financial reasons he was going to carry out the transaction through Lord Camrose because he had to make a capital deal and contractually I [Reves] should have to deal with Lord Camrose'.[15]

Then Henry Luce, the owner of *Time-Life*, began nibbling hard at the prospect of serialization in *Life*, which was already investing heavily in Churchill by publishing both his *Secret Sessions Speeches* and a colour set of his paintings. Luce hoped that this would make him 'our author'. But although this became so in several exceptional ways (Luce even having the privilege of paying for his extended and luxurious writing sojourns abroad) in America Churchill also had contractual relations with Houghton Mifflin, the distinguished Boston publisher, and with the *New York Times*, which great journal accepted a surprisingly subordinate serialization role to *Life*. And in Britain he had contractual arrangements with the *Daily Telegraph* and with Cassells, to whose imprint, despite the roughness of his 1940 dealings with them over *The English-Speaking Peoples*, he seemed content to return.

So there were a lot of fingers in the pie, which however proved to contain plenty of gravy for everyone, including Emery Reves. Reves acquired for his own equity ownership the non-English-language rights in the memoirs and made a fortune out of them, as well as providing for Churchill handsome additions to his core receipts. Rich pickings although there were for others, Churchill was of course the central beneficiary. Exactly how much money the six volumes produced for the Chartwell Literary Trust is unfathomable. His pre-war writing transactions were complicated enough, but with determination it is possible to find a way through that marsh to a few flickering lights of certainty. These beacons disappear in the late 1940s. At the end of 1946 Camrose informed Churchill that *Life* would pay $1,150,000 for the first US serial rights and that Houghton Mifflin would provide an advance of $250,000 for American book rights. These were substantial sums, probably (in combination and going through both exchange rate and inflation adjustments) the equivalent of a modern £7 million. But it was not clear how many volumes of the projected work were to be covered by this. There were eventually six. This was an expansion from the original estimate of five. The first volumes became ready for serialization and book publication eighteen months after this offer, and it was seven and a half years before the last volume was complete. During these periods there were also occasional dollops of £35,000 (worth between £600,000 and £800,000 today) from Lord Camrose, presumably for *Daily Telegraph* serialization, although it may be that advances from Cassells were also involved in these payments.

What is certain is that the Chartwell Trust benefited to the extent of many millions of pounds. These sums escaped the full burden of direct taxation provided that the author lived for five years after the deed of settlement was drawn up, which hurdle was surmounted in the summer of 1951. His own spending needs, he told Camrose in 1946, amounted to not less than £12,000 a year. Given his lifestyle this was a surprisingly modest amount and must have been net of his heavy salaries bill for literary assistants of one sort or another. Everything else went to the

Trust, which sometimes indulged in peripheral activities such as buying a London house for Randolph Churchill, but which broadly accumulated for the future. Churchill's own needs crept up and in the summer of 1950 he told Walter Graebner of *Life*, 'I'm getting £35,000 out of Volume Five. That's plenty for me, but nothing of that will be left for the trust. Still the trust has had five whacks at the book already. Not so bad.'[16]

The book (nearly one and a half million words as it turned out) had to be composed as well as its financing arranged. From this point of view the third key meeting, comparable in its different way with Reves's visit to Florida and with the first serial discussions with Luce, was on 29 March 1946, when Captain William Deakin DSO, as he had become, came as a sole luncheon guest to Hyde Park Gate. Deakin, as a young history fellow of Wadham College, Oxford, had been with Churchill as a research assistant for three pre-war years, and had been largely responsible for the remarkable speed with which the first version of *The History of the English-Speaking Peoples* had been put together. Since then he had had an adventurous war including leading the first British military mission to Tito. In 1946 he returned to Wadham from the Croatian mountains. He had already proved himself the most effective of the Chartwell literary assistants, and when he agreed to come back into service for the war memoirs it increased Churchill's enthusiasm for the new project. But Deakin was to perform a much more demanding role in the late 1940s than ten years before. He assumed a general's rather than a captain's command, for Churchill took on many other high-ranking advisers whose work had to be co-ordinated if everything was not to run out of control. The core team was General Ismay, General Sir Henry Pownall, Commodore G. R. G. Allan RN, Air Chief Marshal Garrod, Denis Kelly, who became archivist of the Churchill papers in May 1947, Deakin and Churchill himself. And there was a wider circle of those who were consulted on specific issues and some of whom produced draft passages. These included Air Marshal Park (who had been in command at Uxbridge on the vital day of the Battle of Britain), Professor R. V. Jones, Duncan Sandys and Field Marshal Alexander.

There was never any shortage of material. Churchill obtained from a somewhat reluctant Cabinet Office (when it came up to the Cabinet itself Attlee was more helpful than Bevin) permission to use freely, except for those relating to the Ultra decrypts, his plethora of wartime official communications, Cabinet papers, telegrams, directives to

Chiefs of Staff etc. In addition Norman Brook, who had succeeded Bridges as secretary of the Cabinet, recommended that Churchill should also be allowed to cite some official documents written by others. If not, there would be 'some danger of creating the impression that no-one but he ever took an initiative'.[17] All this reproduction of official papers, together with long speech extracts, threatened to submerge the manuscript in a welter of quotations. This caused some considerable complaint from the serializers and book publishers, particularly in America, when they first saw what Churchill hoped was the finished version of volume one. Luce told him on 18 November 1947 that the abundance of quotation accompanied by too little 'analytical insight' marred 'the architectural sense'.[18] And Reves wrote even more chillingly a month later suggesting that volume one would have to be almost entirely rewritten. However Reves proved an easily soothed tiger, for only six weeks later, admittedly after some strenuous Christmas and New Year rearrangement by Deakin and Churchill himself, he telephoned to say that he now found the first volume, as revised, 'absolutely perfect'.[19]

It was not only Churchill's own documents which threatened a submerging tide. All the other authorities, whether half on the payroll or only voluntarily involved, thought they were performing their role generously if they provided long drafts which they hoped to see incorporated. The complications of the flood were increased by Churchill's liking for working on several volumes at once, for getting everything set up in type at the earliest possible moment, and for then making massive proof corrections. He began by starting the first and second volumes almost in double harness, and throughout the whole series queries and suggestions about one volume were coming in long after he had passed to the next, if not the one after that.

In these circumstances it required great organizational skill, mainly on Deakin's part, to prevent the whole enterprise dissolving into chaos, with narrative construction, fact-checking and proof-reading descending into one amorphous mass. It should not be thought that Churchill was merely a cipher in these processes. Denis Kelly gave a vivid and convincing picture of his editing skills. Seeing Churchill tightening and clarifying a paragraph, Kelly wrote, 'was like watching a skilful topiarist restoring a neglected and untidy garden figure to its true shape and proportions'.[20] There was also, throughout the six volumes, an adequate scattering of purple passages which could only have been written by Churchill himself. The rich rewards provided by Camrose and Luce, by

Cassells and Houghton Mifflin, supported a large-scale literary cottage industry, but they also called forth many *ipsissima verba* from the master himself.

More work on the memoirs was done at Chartwell than anywhere else, but Hyde Park Gate was a frequent hive of composing activity, and there were also the long nominally writing sojourns in sunnier climates, made possible in an era of tight British currency restrictions only by Henry Luce's sometimes reluctant generosity. Such expeditions became almost a dominant feature of these years in opposition. There were two six-week Christmas–New Year visits to Churchill's old haunt of the Mamounia Hotel in Marrakech, the first in 1946–7, the second in 1950–1.* There were a Swiss three weeks in August–September 1946 and a Provençal six weeks in the same months of 1948. Over the New Year of 1949 he was in the Hôtel de Paris at Monte Carlo for two and a half weeks. And in the following summer he went back to the Italian lakes and then, after a Strasbourg political interlude, to Beaverbrook's villa at Cap d'Ail. The following winter he went to Reid's Hotel in Madeira, but was brought back prematurely by news of the impending general election.

The sales of the war memoirs were more than sufficient to justify all the effort and expense put into them. Volume one came out in June 1948 in New York and four months later in London. By August Churchill was told that a 600,000 US sale was likely by Christmas, 350,000 of them accounted for by a Book of the Month Club purchase. There was nothing reprehensible there, particularly as that mammoth presence on the American publishing scene proceeded to take all five subsequent volumes. In England Cassells sold more than 200,000 first-edition copies, and when the second volume appeared in June 1949 they did a bigger first printing of 276,000.

The reviews of the first volume were sufficiently good to suggest that the previous fears of Luce, Reves and others about over-documentation were either misplaced or had been miraculously cured under the Marrakech winter sun. Gilbert firmly wrote that these reviews were a source of 'great personal satisfaction to Churchill in his capacity as an author'.[21] Furthermore, the reception of the subsequent volumes did not sag. Volume two, *Their Finest Hour*, dealt with the pinnacle of Churchill's

---

* On the first of them Deakin later recalled that Churchill 'didn't do very much work. He wanted company. He painted most of the time' (quoted in Gilbert, *Winston S. Churchill*, VIII, p. 383).

life. Volume three, *The Grand Alliance*, was the most profitable so far. Volume four, *The Hinge of Fate*, produced another spate of good reviews, including a very friendly first leader in *The Times*, so often cool about Churchill, but which on this occasion talked of the 'exhilaration many readers will find . . . as they turn the pages of this most graphic and revealing autobiography'.[22]

Nor were volumes five and six, *Closing the Ring* and *Triumph and Tragedy*, both of which came out while he was again in 10 Downing Street, anti-climaxes. The sales, in spite of the serious doubts from most of his sponsors about the need for a sixth volume, held up remarkably well. Partly, maybe, this was because of the desire of many purchasers to complete their set, the more so because it was a strength of the work that it penetrated into many houses of which books were not a prominent feature. This was equally true of Britain and America. Did the six volumes depend upon the great unread market? Up to a point this was no doubt so, although only to a point, for, especially if some of the larger quoted documents are skipped, the work has high readability. As Deakin recorded Churchill as saying on one occasion: 'This is not history, this is my case.'[23] It has suppressions and it has inaccuracies, it is less a work of literature than was *The World Crisis*, but it was the ultimate literary achievement of the outstanding author–politician of the twentieth century. It is an invaluable record, and it helped to give purpose to Churchill's life during what could have been for him a quinquennium with a crushing sense of being cast aside.

Politics, the war memoirs and his travels aside, Churchill's temper and morale fluctuated sharply during these years. He needed frequent doses of forthright advice from Clementine to prevent his committing a wide variety of acts which were a mixture of the unwise and the self-indulgent. She prevented him wearing his unbecoming air commodore's uniform for a Paris visit in May 1947: 'To me, air-force uniform except when worn by the Air Crews is rather bogus. . . . *I* am proud of my plain Civilian Pig.'[24] She made him attend Ambassador Winant's London memorial service in that November instead of just sending her in his stead. She prevented him going to stay with Beaverbrook in Jamaica in March 1949, at what she described as 'this moment of doubt and discouragement amongst your followers', a mood which she thought would be increased by a publicized sojourn with that deeply distrusted press lord.[25] But she failed, mainly because she was not present, to prevent Churchill from deeply offending his devoted daughter Sarah when in January 1949, having been divorced from Vic Oliver in early

1945, she brought her husband-to-be Anthony Beauchamp to stay in the Hôtel de Paris at Monte Carlo. Churchill, having instantly taken against him, treated him with considerable discourtesy.

He was also neurotically sensitive about books of reminiscence or revelation which he did not like. This applied to several early American books on the war, including one by H. C. Butcher, an Eisenhower military aide, and another by Elliott Roosevelt. They played a minor role in encouraging him to get on with his own version. He also took offence at a work on their joint Jerome forebears by his cousin Shane Leslie, and even managed to be very tetchy about some draft passages for the soon-to-be-famous *Eastern Approaches* sent to him by Fitzroy Maclean, a figure towards whom he would naturally be predisposed.

During these years when Churchill, while receiving almost every possible honour throughout the world, was half nursing his bruises and half looking forward with lively anticipation to defeating the Attlee government and returning to power, two highly self-revelatory reflections emerged from him. In both of them his father figured prominently. The first, when he had been persuaded to set it down in writing after telling it orally to two of his children, became known as 'The Dream'. 'One foggy afternoon in November 1947,' it began, 'I was painting in my studio at the cottage down the hill at Chartwell.' He had been sent a torn portrait of Lord Randolph, of which he was making a copy. 'I was just trying to give the twirl to his moustache when I suddenly felt an odd sensation. I turned round with my palette in my hand, and there, sitting in my red leather upright armchair, was my father. He looked just as I had seen him in his prime. . . .' There then followed 3,000 words of imaginary conversation between father and son, with the son trying to explain to an incredulous father the changes which had taken place in Britain and the world in the past half-century. Lord Randolph was at first inclined to assume that his son was either a retired soldier or a professional painter, and was consequently surprised by signs of relative affluence. At the end, when they had surveyed the first half of the twentieth century, he said:

> As I listened to you unfolding these fearful facts you seemed to know a great deal about them. I never expected that you would develop so far and so fully. Of course you are too old now to think about such things, but when I hear you talk I really wonder you didn't go into politics. You might have done a lot to help. You might even have made a name for yourself.[26]

Before there could be any question of Winston Churchill explaining his triumphs there was 'a tiny flash' and Lord Randolph vanished.

Barely two months later, at Marrakech, Churchill was asked which year of his life he would most like to relive, and replied, '1940 every time.' Then he added: 'I wish certain people could have been alive to see the events of the last years of the war; not many: my father and mother, and F. E. [Smith], and Arthur Balfour, and Sunny.'[27] The last named, the ninth Duke of Marlborough, may be thought to have added a touch of bathos to the list. But he and Churchill, first cousins, had undoubtedly been close, and his addition to the select group did not distract from Churchill's touching desire to let a few others – most of whom, certainly his father and Balfour, maybe his mother, had under-estimated his quality – see how spectacularly well he had done.

So the years of semi-rejection went by, interspersed with much activity, although with not quite the sustained personal concentration of the 1930s and early wartime years, some optimism, much gloom but that more about the world than about himself, some bad-temper and some engaging, rather petulant idiosyncrasy. On the night of 13 December 1946 when London was enveloped in one of the pea-soupers which embellished it from the days of Dickens to the mid-1950s, Churchill was endeavouring to make his way home from the Savoy Hotel, after a dinner of the Other Club. His car became fog-bound at Hyde Park Corner and after feeling his way on foot to Knightsbridge, about halfway to his house, he lost patience, went into the Hyde Park Hotel, took a room and having slept a satisfactory night remained in bed there for most of the next day, no doubt summoning secretaries, working papers, cigars, whisky and other necessary supplies.

42

TWO ELECTIONS AND A
RESURRECTION

THE GENERAL ELECTIONS of 1950 and 1951 were the two mass plebiscites of British electoral history. In the first, 83.9 per cent of those eligible voted, higher than at any other election since the arrival of universal suffrage. Twenty months later the turn-out declined only to 82.6 per cent, in sharp contrast with the 1910 experience, when two elections in one year resulted in 7 per cent of those who had voted in the first abstaining in the second. All of this pointed to Britain having a high degree of mid-twentieth-century satisfaction with its political system. The nation, as Churchill was perhaps too fond of alleging, may have been reduced to a sorry state of penury and weakness only five years after the great victory. But this was not reflected in constitutional discontent.

Moreover, in the second election 97 per cent of the 82.6 per cent voted either Labour or Conservative and they did so on an almost uniform pattern throughout Great Britain. The virtues or vices of individual candidates appeared to make little difference. Once a handful of constituency results was known it was possible to predict the overall outcome with a deadly accuracy. This pointed to a high degree of loyalty to the major parties, in contrast with the position in the 1980s and 1990s when they had difficulty in holding their combined share to 70 per cent of a much smaller participation. This loyalty had been almost equally present in 1950, the main difference being that the Liberals then polled 9 per cent instead of their 2.5 per cent of 1951. These facts had two consequences for party leaders. First, a peculiarly heavy responsibility lay upon their conduct of the campaign. If individual candidates could not pull in votes, the leaders had to do it for them. The sound broadcasts were not quite so dominating – or so numerous – as in 1945, but they were nonetheless important and so too, perhaps more so than in 1945, were the well-reported major campaign speeches of the leaders. These two elections were for Churchill more a matter of considered orations in big provincial halls than one of cavalcades through the cheering crowds of 1945.

Second, with a slight modification, it was still more the case than in 1882, when W. S. Gilbert wrote the libretto for *Iolanthe*, 'That every boy and gal, That's born into this world alive, Is either a little Labourite, Or else a little Conserva*tive*', and most strenuous efforts had to be made to shift a crucial but small segment of opinion. In the four and a half years of the parliament of 1945 the Conservatives, although often ahead in the opinion polls and doing well in local elections, had not reduced the bloated and vulnerable Labour parliamentary majority by a single bye-election victory.

The prospect which confronted Churchill at the beginning of 1950 was a far from easy one, and he was not nearly foolish enough to think otherwise. The Conservatives had an impressive team. Beneath the venerability of Churchill himself Eden was seen as experienced, moderate and vote-attracting. Butler and Macmillan in their different ways were major and persuasive figures. The two Olivers, Stanley and Lyttelton, the first quickly removed by death and the second less remembered than his ministerial service, particularly in war, deserves, had been front-rank parliamentary performers in opposition. And Lord Woolton, the draper from Liverpool who had nonetheless been Britain's grocer during the war, and was the twentieth century's answer to W. H. Smith (the nation's newsagent who rose to be First Lord of the Treasury under Salisbury), had brilliantly revitalized the moribund Conservative party organization. He had made it a veritable tribune of the middle classes who felt deprived of their 1930s status and comforts. The Young Conservatives became the most successful suburban tennis club and marriage bureau in history. The Housewives' League was a powerful but doubtfully disciplined auxiliary army.

All this however had to stand against a Labour party which had produced the most formidable ministerial team since the Asquith government in which Churchill had cut his teeth. For the 1950 election Bevin, Cripps, Morrison and Aneurin Bevan were all there. By 1951, Bevin was dead and Cripps had left the Treasury for a Swiss clinic, while Morrison had diminished himself by abandoning his role as a great marshal of parliamentary business in order, mistakenly, to succeed Bevin at the Foreign Office. But Gaitskell had emerged to the front rank, although only at the price of Bevan stalking out of the government. At both elections Attlee, the deftest cox in the history of parliamentary boat racing, presided over his more flamboyant supporters. Even more formidable than this team as an obstacle to Churchill's hopes was the solid Labour loyalty of the trades unions, of the great majority of the still numerous industrial working class (their wives a little less so), with the usual flavouring of socialist intellectuals, some with the highly administrative cast of mind of Gaitskell and Douglas Jay and some with the more maverick quality of Richard Crossman and Michael Foot.

Churchill returned from Madeira on 12 January 1950, with polling day already announced for 23 February, to a mixture of grindstone work and bad news. 'I have not thought of anything . . . since I returned except politics,' he wrote to Clementine on 19 January, 'particularly the Tory manifesto on which we have had prolonged discussions. One day we were nine hours in the dining room of No. 28 [Hyde Park Gate].' He also reported that the Gallup polls had 'taken a big dip' and that the Tories were now only three points ahead of Labour as against the nine points when he had gone away.[1] The net result of his efforts over the next five weeks was to see this already narrowed Conservative lead turn into a polling day Labour lead of 2.6 per cent. Fortunately, for him, the result in terms of seats was much narrower. This was because of the then strong pro-Tory bias in the British electoral system (since reversed), which meant that on a constituency victories-for-votes-basis Labour had a handicap against it of approximately fifty seats.

Some recovery on the part of the government would have been likely during the concentration of minds associated with an election, and there is no suggestion that Churchill fought a bad campaign. It was in many ways a better one than in 1945, more restrained, less energetic, no gaffes. But equally there were few memorable passages in his speeches. Perhaps the nearest that he came to them were in Edinburgh on 14 February and in the second of his only two broadcasts on the 17th. In the Scottish capital he said: 'It is my earnest hope that we may feel our way to some more exalted and august foundation for our safety than this grim and sombre balancing power of the bomb. We must not, however, cast away our only shield of safety unless we can find something surer and more likely to last.' And then, a moment or two later, he was back to one of his favourite themes of the last years of the war, as well as providing a glimpse of what was to be his dominant purpose in his last years of office a few years later: 'Still I cannot help coming back to the idea of another talk with Soviet Russia upon the highest level. The idea appeals to me of a supreme effort to bridge the gulf between the two worlds, so that each can live their life, if not in friendship, at least without the hazards of the cold war.'[2]

In his sound broadcast he was arguing the case for Britain 'with one heave of her shoulders' shaking herself free from what he saw as unnecessary constrictions imposed by the Labour government:

> I am reminded of the tale of the prisoner in the Spanish dungeon. For years he longed to escape from his bondage. He tried this, he tried that – all in vain. One day he pushed the door of his cell – it was open. It had always been open. He walked out free into the broad light of day. You can do that now on this very Thursday, and what a throng there will be to welcome us back in the forefront of the nations which now regard us with bewilderment and pity, but for whom only a few years ago we kept the flag of freedom flying amid all the winds that blew.[3]

The last sentence was well into the realm of hyperbole, and it could be thought that the 'Spanish dungeon' analogy was not the most appropriate one for Attlee's Britain, but it was election time, and at least it did not have the jarring quality of the 'Gestapo' speech of five years earlier.

One reason why Churchill's speeches in this campaign did not echo more resoundingly is that on the external front he basically agreed, although with a number of niggles, with the foreign policy of Ernest Bevin. And on the home front the battle was fought over a narrow and barren stretch of terrain. Churchill talked a lot about the evils of nationalization. But he had no intention of denationalizing the Bank of England (of which in its privatized form and under Montagu Norman he had had more than enough in 1925–9) or the railways (in the public ownership of which he had first believed nearly forty years before) or the coal mines (for the owners of which his sympathy had perished in the aftermath of the General Strike) or even British airways, gas and electricity, which did not arouse in him strong feelings one way or the other. In practical terms the issue was confined to the steel industry, an act for the nationalization of which was on the statute book but not fully operative, and road haulage, where the Conservatives did propose a reversal of what Labour had done. But the freedom of lorries, even if they were then less oppressively large than today, was not a natural subject for inspired oratory. And the Labour proposals for further public ownership – sugar refining, cement, meat wholesaling and industrial life assurance (the swine before the Pearl, as the programme was once satirically described)* was equally ill-tailored for stimulating great phrases. It was reminiscent of the passage in *Hamlet* when the Norwegian captain tells the Prince: 'We go to gain a little patch of ground that hath in it no profit but the name.'

Although he had, in addition to Edinburgh, major meetings in Leeds, Manchester, Cardiff and Plymouth (where his support failed to improve Randolph Churchill's unbroken record of never winning an election), he paid more attention to Woodford than in 1945. He delivered three full-scale speeches there, as well as spending polling day in the constituency. Then he returned to Hyde Park Gate to listen to the results, which at first were seriously misleading, at least to the psephologically uninitiated. It was the urban seats which counted more quickly, and overnight Labour seemed to be bounding ahead. But as the country results came in on the following morning the lead was heavily cut back. By lunch time it was clear that the massive Labour majority had been shattered, although Attlee was going to remain Prime Minister. The final tally gave him seventeen more seats than the Conservatives but an overall majority of only six.

The indications are that Churchill, although somewhat disappointed, was not remotely shattered, as he had been in 1945. Probably he had feared something worse, and consoled himself with the thought that, as he put it in a contemporary letter, 'another General Election in the next few months is inevitable'.[4] Time was of course running against him. He was seventy-five and three months, an age older than that at which no one other than Palmerston, Gladstone and Disraeli (only for his last two months) had been Prime Minister. But Churchill felt that he had brought the Conservative party far enough back for him to be entitled to give the final and early heave which he believed would dispose of the Labour government. There were many of his colleagues and followers who did not agree and thought the party could perform better under Eden. But there was little they could do about it once Churchill had made his intentions clear.

He indicated his resolve by private messages and by bouncing into the new Parliament full of partisan vigour. In a slightly perverse way he felt that the authority of the government had been more damaged by the election result than had his own. In the first day of debate there occurred a revealing little exchange between himself and the leader of the House. Hansard recorded it as follows:

* The Pearl was the name of Britain's second-largest industrial assurance company.

Mr Churchill. . . . I ask that an opportunity for a full debate [upon finance and economics] may be accorded to us in the next fortnight or so.

Mr Morrison indicated dissent.

Mr Churchill. It will take more than the oscillations of the Lord President's head in this Parliament necessarily to convince us that our desires must be put aside. . . .[5]

So began a parliament which, with only a few shafts of light, turned out to be both short and disagreeable. Churchill behaved very partisanly during these twenty months and extended scant respect to the tiring but not undistinguished ministers opposite to him. The efflux of time fed his impatience. He was giving a new reality to his father's most famous jibe that Gladstone was 'an old man in a hurry'. This may have encouraged him to pay a rare tribute to his hurrying predecessor in September 1950. 'What a light was the GOM,' he wrote in a letter. 'It encourages one to act with vigour in public.'[6] It was rare because he had never been much of a Gladstonian, even in his most strongly Liberal days. But if these considerations made him more pro-Gladstone they did not make him more pro-Attlee or Morrison or Bevin or even Cripps, with whom of the four, surprisingly, he had the most semi-intimate, semi-affectionate relations.

It may therefore be as well to start with the few shafts of cross-party light. October (1950) was a month of non-controversial parliamentary occasions. On the 1st Churchill celebrated the fiftieth anniversary of his election to Parliament, a rare but by no means unique event. On the 26th of the month the Commons returned from the red and the gold of the House of Lords to sit in their own more workaday chamber for the first time in nearly ten years. Churchill, who had been passionate in favour of retaining the shape and limited size of the old chamber, made a highly traditional parliamentary speech on the opening day. What was more personal to him was that the entrance from the members' lobby, reconstructed out of the stones of Charles Barry's original structure, was on the initiative of the government named the Churchill arch. 'Attlee has been very nice,' Churchill told Lord Camrose that evening.[7]

Then, when ill-health forced Bevin to leave the Foreign Office in March 1951, only a month before his death, Churchill imported an unusual cross-party note into a party political broadcast in order, 'as his war-time leader', to pay tribute. 'I feel bound to put on record', he said, 'that he takes his place among the great Foreign Secretaries of our country, and that, in his steadfast resistance to Communist aggression, in his strengthening of our ties with the United States and in his share of building up the Atlantic Pact, he has rendered services to Britain and to the cause of peace which will be long remembered.'[8]

There may have been a mild element of expiation about this tribute, for in the previous November a contretemps with Bevin had led Churchill to behave in a way both petty and pompous, two unusual peccadilloes for him. Bevin, who was neurotic about what he saw as the pro-federalist activities of the European Movement, had in the House of Commons accused the organization of 'semi-sabotage' of his negotiations, mostly with France. Churchill expostulated, 'You are the arch saboteur.' It was a minor parliamentary spat, of the sort that Churchill was in general prepared to take in his stride. But on the following evening he and Clementine were due to attend an official Bevin dinner for the departing and fairly distinguished American ambassador, Lew Douglas. Douglas was a right-wing Democrat, who had enjoyed a considerable social success in London, not least with Churchill, with whom, as leader of the opposition, he had in Bevin's also somewhat petty view become so close as to impair his effectiveness as an ambassador to the British government.

Nevertheless Bevin was giving a full-scale Foreign Office dinner for Douglas, which Churchill refused to attend. What he said to Bevin is not recorded, but to Douglas he wrote: 'After the incident in the House of Commons last night I do not feel it would be a good thing for us to dine with Mr and Mrs Bevin this evening, as it would be misunderstood abroad and also it would be embarrassing to meet him. This letter therefore is to bid you and your wife my affectionate Au revoir. . . .'[9]

Unfortunately relations between Churchill and his old wartime colleagues during this short parliament were more in accordance with this prickly letter than with his appreciation of Attlee's 'niceness' over the Churchill arch or with the generosity of his broadcast tribute to Bevin. This was perverse, for on the main event of the parliament, the June 1950 outbreak of the Korean War, following North Korea's invasion of the South, and Britain's decision to provide a fighting force auxiliary to the Americans, Churchill agreed with the Labour government. Even in that area, however, he was inclined to maximize rather than minimize peripheral differences. Before a July debate he made a major issue of the state of Britain's defences being so bad that he could deploy his full case only in a secret session. Second World War nostalgia no doubt played some part in his desire for such a reversion. When Attlee resisted on the ground that it would 'tend to cause the greatest amount of suspicion and uneasiness both at home and abroad', Churchill persisted and used the classic parliamentary formula for clearing the galleries by saying 'I spy strangers.' The Speaker then had to put the question which produced the slightly ludicrous result of 295 members voting for secrecy while 296 voted against.

Then, in a mid-September debate, again on defence, Churchill did some clever positioning by declaring: 'The Prime Minister has appealed to us for national unity on defence. That does not mean national unity on mismanagement of defence.' He went on to complain that the government had not put British troops into action alongside the Americans nearly soon enough, and received a tart answer. Churchill, Attlee said, 'has more experience in conducting military affairs than anyone in this House. He has been accustomed, no doubt, to receiving advice from those who are responsible for running a campaign. The campaign in Korea is being run by the Americans. We respond to their requests. If the request changes from what it was before it is not the fault of His Majesty's government. We have responded to the requests made to us.'[10]

Churchill also criticized the government for dilatoriness in the manufacture of British atomic weapons, although when he returned to office a year or so later he was surprised to discover how much had been done – including the decision in a very restricted group of ministers to make a British bomb – and was forced to admit that he had been wrong on this count. He was essentially uneasy because, although in favour of strenuous British rearmament and of equally strenuous support for the Americans in Korea, and if necessary elsewhere, above all in Germany, the more testing the times became, the more he disliked being excluded from the driving seat. The ministers, Attlee, Bevin, even the disliked Morrison, who had all served him well on the home front during the war, were now, he felt, elevated above their stations. The more perilous the world, the more frustrated he felt at not being in charge.

He was horrified at the military vacuum in western Europe, which meant that the Russians, if they so rashly chose, could send their tanks through to Paris and the Channel coast even more easily than Hitler had done in 1940. In these circumstances he believed that the American nuclear deterrent was the essential shield of the West. Yet he was as far as possible from being bomb-happy. Already he sensed to a greater extent than most political or military leaders that atomic weapons meant the destruction of civilization. And, while he had a total conviction that only the Americans could provide an adequate shield, he was far from having total faith in their ability to wield it with perfect discretion.

With these considerations no doubt in his mind, Churchill did not criticize what was certainly Attlee's most controversial intervention into Anglo-American relations in the whole course of his premiership. On 30 November 1950, President Truman appeared (falsely) at a press conference to be delegating to the local commander, General MacArthur, the decision whether to use atomic bombs against China in the Korean conflict. This set a lot of alarm bells ringing around the world. One of them rang in London at a particularly sensitive time. The House of Commons was holding a major foreign debate when news of the President's press conference came through in the late afternoon. The attendance in and around the chamber was augmented by the tense parliamentary situation of that short Parliament. The news from America, however, united rather than divided the House. Attlee was quickly confronted by a letter of dissociation with America signed by half his backbenchers. Churchill and Eden expressed slightly more measured dismay. Attlee calmed the House by proposing an immediate visit to Washington. This was a remarkable event, for he was no natural traveller. He mostly left such things to Bevin. But Bevin was too ill to go. Attlee flew to Washington on the evening of 3 December, and, despite the short notice and his being a doubtfully welcome visitor, had four full days of talks with the President, the Secretary of State (Acheson) and other relevant officials. This was a signal mark of the prestige which, despite frequent croakings from Churchill, Attlee's Britain still enjoyed. Even at ninety-six days' notice, let alone ninety-six hours', it was treatment which no allied head of government could now command in Washington.

There was no confrontation. The extreme British pro-Attlee version, which has almost become a myth, that Attlee gave Truman a great ticking-off, told him to dismiss thoughts of using the bomb from his mind, sack MacArthur and generally concentrate more on Europe than on Asia, is without foundation. But so is the extreme American view that Attlee came as a lugubrious and unwelcome guest at a time when the administration needed more encouragement than lectures, proceeded to whine a doctrine of total appeasement in the Far East, and was duly chastened by his more robust hosts until he departed, none too soon, with his tail between his legs. Acheson, although later speaking much more favourably of Attlee, inclined in his 1969 memoirs to the harsher second view.

The conjuncture might easily have tempted Churchill to make some disparaging comments about Attlee's 'panicky' visit. But he did not do so. When he next spoke in the House on 14 December he said: 'The Prime Minister's visit to Washington has done nothing but good.' And even when he added, 'The question we all have to consider this afternoon . . . is how much good,'[11] it was still a generous endorsement. Three days later he departed for nearly six weeks in Marrakech. In the previous summer he had had little holiday away from Chartwell. He had been pressing on hard to finish his fourth volume and to lay the foundations of the fifth and even the sixth of *The Second World War*, which he had become determined to impose upon his publishers. He also spent quite a chunk of the summer recess on politics: the second week of August at Strasbourg, a party political broadcast on 29 August, and an active participation in the two weeks of special parliamentary session in mid-September, speaking both on the defence programme and on steel nationalization. For the rest he stayed at Chartwell, concentrating on the memoirs and cancelling a planned painting holiday near Biarritz. But he fully made up for it, from both a holiday and a painting point of view, by his long Christmas–New Year sojourn in Morocco.

When he came back from there via Paris on 23 January 1951 he was more eager than ever to harry the government into an early election. They were tired and he intended to make them more so. And he had considerable success. By Easter Bevin was dead. Attlee had to spend a month in hospital with a duodenal ulcer, and three ministers were on the point of resigning. Partisan mischief-making became the keynote of the parliamentary tactics into which Churchill encouraged his followers. An example from mid-February remains fixed in my mind. On 14 and 15 February there was a major debate on the government's rearmament plans, including the recently announced decision to increase the £3,600 million programme to £4,700 million, both spread over three years.

The new figure was at or above the very limit to which it was possible to stretch British industrial capacity, as Churchill himself was to point out a year later when he had responsibility. This did not prevent his moving on the second day of the debate a motion of no confidence in the ability of the government with their record of 'vacillation and delay' to carry out an effective defence policy. His speech was long and quite powerful, marred however by an extended passage of arms with the Prime Minister about the latter's lack of success over five and a half years in making a British atomic bomb. Attlee, as Churchill would have been bound to admit a year later, behaved with great self-restraint, refusing on grounds of national security to disclose the details which would have torpedoed Churchill. Gaitskell, the new and young Chancellor of the Exchequer, who was passionately pro-NATO and rearmament (too much so for his own political good, many thought), rose in reply. Churchill, by a sustained piece of childish play-acting, completely wrecked the early part of Gaitskell's speech. He did it by the most simple tactic for destroying a speech, which is to create such a distraction that the speaker cannot concentrate and the audience cannot listen. Churchill began to turn and twist, looking on the ground and under his papers, searching his pockets and the crack between the seat and the back of the front bench to such an extent that Gaitskell was forced to pause and ask what was the trouble. Churchill slowly rose to his feet to answer. 'I was only looking for a jujube,'[12] he said, jujube being his somewhat archaic name for a throat pastille. Nearly the whole House dissolved in laughter.

It was not a wise or a gracious joke to play. It was one of Churchill's narrownesses that he was instinctively hostile to upper-middle-class intellectuals in the Labour party. The animus appeared to be increased by his belief that they had nearly all been at school at Winchester. At a time when, apart from Gaitskell himself, Cripps, Crossman, Douglas Jay and Kenneth Younger, not to mention D. N. Pritt from a very different wing of the party, were products of that academy, such a generalization was understandable. However Churchill gilded the lily by making constant not very funny anti-Wykehamical jokes in the House. 'I will translate for the benefit of any Wykehamists present' . . . 'I do not know whether French is taught at Winchester.'[13] Whether it was Harrovian jealousy or an affected anti-intellectualism was not clear.

What was clear was that from the spring of 1951 onwards few holds were barred for Churchill in his desire to get the government out. The opposition discovered that by a device of praying (a technical parliamentary term involving no devotional element) against almost every executive order they could keep the House of Commons sitting, night after night, far into the small hours of the morning and, not infrequently, through breakfast time and well into the next day. The advantage of this tactic was that it was far harder on the government MPs than on the opposition ones. For the opposition to win one of the dawn divisions was a bonus. For the government to lose one was, if not a disaster, at least a serious setback. Accordingly, with a majority of only six, Labour MPs, including ministers, had to be kept in constant attendance, and were never encouraged to speak, only to vote, for arguments merely delayed still further the hour of adjournment. The opposition could chose when to relax and when to mount a determined offensive. I remember 1951 as the most burdensome summer of all my thirty-four years in the House of Commons. The chamber was frequently a bear garden, and the lobbies, corridors and public rooms of the building were overcrowded with irritable and not notably sober MPs of both sides milling around like members of conscript armies who did their duty but had doubtful faith in their commanders.

Churchill was in a happier position. He could blow in when he liked and leave when he wanted to. Furthermore, he could speak whenever he wished, for the last obligation on him was to expedite government business. His object was to show vigour to his followers. On 7 June he dined at the Other Club and then went down to the House and for twenty-one hours actively led the opposition. Harold Macmillan left a good diary description of this night and of another a week later. Of the first he wrote: 'Churchill stuck it out, much to the delight of the party. . . .' For 14 June he recorded: 'he has used these days to give a demonstration of energy and vitality. He has voted in every division, made a series of brilliant little speeches, shown all his qualities of humour and sarcasm; and crowned all by a remarkable breakfast (at 7.30 a.m.) of eggs, bacon, sausages and coffee, followed by a large whisky and soda and a huge cigar. This latter feat commanded general admiration.'[14]

Whether this campaign of attrition, in which Churchill's participation was more symbolic than regular, was a major factor in forcing Attlee into an October election is open to argument. It certainly put a heavy strain upon a tired government, although the most obvious casualty was the elderly Speaker, who in his ninth year in the chair found intolerable the strain of presiding over a fractious House of Commons which rarely adjourned before the early hours of the morning, and temporarily retired hurt. Chuter Ede, the phlegmatic but uncharismatic Home Secretary, who had taken over from Morrison as leader of the House, battled on in a stubborn and grey-faced way, but those of more influence, or at any rate more ability to get their views recorded in diaries, were feeling by the early summer that an autumn election was inevitable. Attlee on 29 May told Dalton that it must in any event be before February (1952), when the King was due to go on an Australian tour.[15] It was a characteristically constitutional, almost military view from the Prime Minister. Gaitskell, the only front-rank figure still in the government who was not of pensionable age, lunched with the same source on 26 June, who recorded: 'We are both Octobrists. He says "everything is getting too difficult" to go on being handled in this Parliament, with the narrow majority and the Bevanites.'[16] As this indicated, the fissure in the Labour party ranks was as important as the Conservative attacks, but both were necessary to make it impossible for the parliament of 1950 to continue for anything like its full term.

In the summer recess of 1951 Churchill, who had been complaining about the rain at Chartwell, went to join his wife, who had come from one of her many convalescences, at Annecy, where he complained about it even more. As a result he moved to Venice, where he stayed at the Excelsior Hotel on the Lido for two weeks, then made a traditional return via Paris, with a couple of nights at the British Embassy. The only difference with the 1930s was that it was Jean Monnet who was the principal Frenchman summoned to dine with him, and that on the next day it was General Eisenhower, the NATO European Commander, rather than General Georges, the hope of the French army, who was his sole luncheon guest. He was back in London in good time to receive Attlee's letter of 20 September which gave him brief prior notice that he was about to announce an election for 25 October.

It was the last chance for Churchill if he was ever to get back to the stimulus of office. Yet there is no indication that this put him in a febrile mood during the campaign, which was his fourteenth general election and his seventeenth (three bye-elections) individual parliamentary contest. Maybe, much more than in 1950, he thought the walls of Troy were bound to fall. In fact the result was the closest thing imaginable. The merest flicker of public opinion could have sent it the other way. He showed some awareness of this by his great efforts in the preceding spring to form a Conservative–Liberal alliance. He rightly thought that there would be a lot of 1950 Liberal votes going begging in 1951, and that they might well determine the outcome. This sensible self-interest combined with an old man's nostalgia made him eager to hold out a hand of friendship to Violet Bonham Carter. He had written with satisfaction to his wife on 25 March: 'I have fixed it up all right for Violet in Colne Valley, but the voting of the Conservative Association (secret) was very close: 33 to 26.'[17]

The issue was whether the local Tories should withdraw their candidate and give Lady Violet a straight run against the sitting Labour member, Glenvil Hall, the chairman of the parliamentary Labour party, who had held the seat comfortably in 1950, but with slightly fewer votes than the combined Conservative and Liberal total. 'Once she gets down there and begins making her good speeches against the Socialists

I expect all will be well,'[18] Churchill added reassuringly. It was as well as could reasonably be expected, for her oratory plus his support (which included addressing a Huddersfield meeting with her at the peak of the campaign) succeeded in getting 95 per cent of the previous Conservative and Liberal votes into a single column. But it was not quite well enough. Hall survived with a majority of 2,189. However Churchill received an inspiriting letter of thanks a few days after his visit. 'The valley is still aglow with your presence,' Lady Violet wrote,[19] showing that her command of phrase was as good on paper as it was on the platform. And his ploy may have helped to swing to the Conservatives some more decisive ex-Liberal votes in other constituencies. A salient feature of the 1951 election compared with 1950 was that it saw a fall (partly because of fewer candidates) of 1.9 million in the Liberal vote, accompanied by an increase of 1.3 million for the Conservatives and of only 0.7 million for Labour. 'Disenfranchised' Liberals split, but not on an even basis, and therein lay much of the key to the outcome.

Churchill began his campaign in Liverpool on 2 October twenty-three days before the poll. As in Newcastle where he spoke in a boxing hall two weeks later and in Plymouth where he spoke on a football ground a week after that, Liverpool was not in a traditional hall but in the greyhound-racing stadium. This at least showed that the Conservatives were confident of attracting big audiences for their leader. He also spoke in the St Andrew's Hall in Glasgow, and on three occasions, necessarily in much smaller halls, in his own constituency. On the first of these Woodford occasions he dealt neatly with accusations that he was a warmonger. To some extent this was provoked by his advocating a response more robust than that of Morrison and Attlee to the decision of Dr Mossadeq, that tearful Iranian Prime Minister, to take over the Anglo-Persian refinery at Abadan and to force its employees out of the country within a week. Mossadeq's action was announced on 17 September, and the issue overhung the British election campaign without being central to it. But the attack on Churchill's alleged warmongering was on a wider front than the refinery in the Persian Gulf. 'The *Daily Mirror*', he said at Loughton in refutation,

> coined a phrase the other day, which is being used by the Socialist party, whom [it] supports. 'Whose finger', they asked, 'do you want on the trigger, Attlee's or Churchill's?' I am sure we do not want any finger on any trigger. Least of all do we want a fumbling finger.
>
> I do not believe that a Third World War is inevitable. I even think that the danger of it is less than it was before the immense rearmament

of the United States. But in any case I must now tell you that it will not be a British finger which will pull the trigger of a Third World War. It may be a Russian finger, or an American finger, or a United Nations Organization finger, but it cannot be a British finger. Although we should certainly be involved in a struggle between the Soviet Empire and the free world, the decision and the timing of that terrible event would not rest with us. Our influence in the world is not what it was in bygone days. I could wish indeed that it was greater. . . .[20]

This issue surfaced again on polling day when the *Mirror* covered its front page with a silhouette of Churchill, with a large cigar if any further identification were necessary, and the familiar legend of 'Whose finger on the trigger?' below it. Churchill sued and got a grovelling apology, but after the election of course.

More important than any of his platform speeches was Churchill's sound broadcast of 8 October. This was almost as moderate and vote-attracting as his 1945 one had been the reverse. David Butler, who in the following year published the first of his many authoritative surveys of post-war British general elections, wrote: 'In his moderation and vigour, in his clarity and technical adroitness in delivery, Mr Churchill gave the best Conservative broadcast of the election, perhaps the best broadcast for any party. It was thought by many to have been his finest personal effort since the war.'[21] He put his non-partisan appeal somewhat tendentiously, ignoring how exceptionally partisan the Conservative opposition had been during the preceding six months, but it was nonetheless skilfully done:

> We have lost a lot in the last two years by the party strife which belongs to electioneering times. We cannot go on like this with two party machines baying at each other in Parliament and grinding away all over the country. . . . We could not afford it for long even if the world were calm and quiet and if we were a self-supporting nation safer and more independent than we ever were before. . . . We shall endanger our very existence if we go on consuming our strength in bitter party or class conflicts. We need a period of several years of solid stable administration by a government not seeking to rub party dogma into everybody else.

He then turned to some of his Liberal social reforming imagery of forty years before and defined the essential difference between his and 'the Socialist outlook' as that 'between the ladder and the queue. We are for the ladder. Let us all do our best to climb. They are for the queue. Let each wait in his place until his turn comes.' His answer to the question of what happens if anyone slips off the ladder was: 'We shall have a good net and the finest social ambulance service in the world.'[22]

These were the keynotes, inevitably accompanied by a good number of jibes at socialist incompetence, which he continued to strike throughout the remainder of the campaign. In personal terms the results of the campaign were not particularly gratifying. Of his two special speaking excursions, we have seen the result in Colne Valley, and in the Devonport division of Plymouth Randolph Churchill went down by the usual small but decisive majority. Even in Woodford Churchill's majority went up by only 80 which meant that he had negligibly benefited from the national swing of 1.3 per cent. Perhaps the unwelcome news, which had reached him in Venice just before the beginning of the campaign, that a Gallup poll showed a distinct preference among Conservatives (and Liberals too) for Eden over him as leader, was showing itself well founded.

The overall outcome was however satisfactory, although by the narrowest possible margin, and was dependent on the quirkiness of the British electoral system. The Labour party polled 229,000 more votes than did the Conservatives. Indeed their total of 13,886,559 remained until 1997 the highest ever polled by any political party at any election. The limited but distinct pro-Conservative bias which then existed did the trick. It was the mirror image of the first 1974 election, when Edward Heath's party polled more votes but Harold Wilson became Prime Minister. The difference however was that Wilson had to form a minority government, whereas Churchill in 1951 had a small overall majority, which he handled with sufficient skill that it laid the foundation for thirteen years of Conservative power, under four different Prime Ministers, and reinforced by two subsequent general election victories.

In the new Parliament Churchill had 321 MPs against Attlee's 295. With the Liberals on only six, and others, including the Speaker, amounting to only three, it was sufficient. Attlee resigned on the Friday evening, Churchill kissed hands immediately afterwards, and began with gusto the task of reoccupying the seats of power and constructing a new administration. His last serious electoral throw – he was to be a quiet candidate at two more general elections, but this was the last which counted for him – had come off, if only just.

43

A CONSENSUAL GOVERNMENT

THE 1951 CHURCHILL government, in its early manifestations, was like the organization of a vast commemorative pageant for the great days of the war. There is a famous satirical passage in *Sybil* where Disraeli described how Pitt found the new peers to build up his majority in the House of Lords. 'He caught them in the alleys of Lombard Street and clutched them from the counting-houses of Cornhill,'[1] it ended. Those whom Churchill resummoned to the colours covered a wider spread, but 'clutch' was an appropriate word for the process. He would not take no for an answer, and when summoned they nearly all came.

Jock Colville was caught on Newmarket racecourse and told that he must come back as principal private secretary. As he had returned to his parent department for only two years (having been a private secretary to Princess Elizabeth from 1947 to 1949) after an effective absence of a decade, he was not keen to return to the night hours and weekend work of 10 Downing Street, thinking, rightly as it turned out, that it would be the effective end of his Foreign Office career. But his objections were overridden and he was very soon back in place, although Churchill was persuaded by civil service protocol that Colville should be joint principal secretary with David Pitblado of the Treasury, whom Attlee had recently appointed through regular channels. Colville's return not only provided Churchill with a further three and a half years of companionship (including endless games of bezique) but also ensured the 'Boswellization' of the second premiership, as of much of the first.

General Lord Ismay, who had recently been having a quietly impartial time, helping Churchill with his war memoirs and presiding over the Labour-nominated Council of the Festival of Britain, was awakened after midnight and summoned to Hyde Park Gate where he was pressed into being Secretary of State for Commonwealth Relations. He had no desire to be a minister and little feel for a fully political role. His hesitations were also swept aside, but at least he was able to escape within a year to be Secretary-General of NATO, a more congenial post for him.

Field Marshal Lord Alexander of Tunis was half luckier and half still more unlucky. He had the advantage of being 3,000 miles away on October 26–27. He had been Governor-General of Canada since 1946, and could not be precipitately withdrawn without considerable offence to the Canadians. Churchill was however determined that he should become Minister of Defence. His favourite wartime general must be the right man for that post. So he took that portfolio himself until Alexander reluctantly returned and accepted the office on 1 March 1952. In it he was resignedly miserable, for he had even fewer political gifts than Ismay, until October 1954 when he was delighted to be relieved by Harold Macmillan, his old collaborator in the Mediterranean, who certainly did not lack political or, for that matter, theatrical gifts.

Less interestingly there were the 'overlords'. Another of Churchill's throwbacks to the war was that he thought an intermediate level of these shadowy figures would help the co-ordination of departments. Lord Leathers was summoned to abandon innumerable boardrooms in order to supervise transport, fuel and power. Lord Woolton, who had remained much closer to the political scene, was to do the same thing for food, agriculture and the Conservative party machine. Leathers went in the autumn of 1953, but Woolton stayed on until the end, often critical of Churchill's longevity in office, but assuaged by rising effortlessly from baron to viscount and from viscount to earl. The third overlord was Lord Salisbury (the fifth Marquess, Cranborne when last encountered) on the external side, but exactly what he was supposed to supervise was less clear. It certainly did not include the Foreign Office, where Eden was, from the beginning and for too long in his own view, indisputably the second man in the government.

The most controversial overlord appointment was the one which did not take place. Churchill's idea was that the impressively portentous Sir John Anderson, still not a nominal Conservative but exuding experience and gravitas – 'Jehovah' as he had been known to his colleagues in his civil service days – should supervise the economic ministries. Rab Butler, even though he felt himself lucky to have become Chancellor at the age of forty-eight (Oliver Lyttelton was the rival and, many expected, the preferred candidate), thought this a very bad idea. Luckily for Butler, Anderson thought so too. He had restraint as well as portentousness, and preferred to remain chairman of both the Royal Opera House and the Port of London Authority, while becoming Viscount Waverley, which he would have done in any event. So was a great source of conflict at the centre of the government avoided.

The other principal appointments were: Harold Macmillan to the Ministry of Housing and Local Government, with a specific Tory manifesto commitment to produce 300,000 houses a year; the unesteemed (by Churchill) 'Sir Donald' Maxwell Fyfe to the Home Office; the rumbustious and more companionable even if parliamentarily maladroit Oliver Lyttelton to the Colonial Office; and Lord Simonds, a dry Wykehamist lawyer, as Lord Chancellor. Churchill had wanted to compensate for not getting Lady Violet Bonham Carter into the House of Commons by putting on the Woolsack her younger brother Cyril Asquith, already a Lord of Appeal in Ordinary, and thus getting the parliamentary adherence of at least one child of his old Liberal chief. But Asquith declined, mainly on grounds of health. Son-in-law Duncan Sandys, over the protests of Clementine, who thought it too nepotic an appointment, became Minister of Supply, specifically charged with steel denationalization.

The four days he spent putting together this personally stamped team were one of the happier times of Churchill's later life. There were present all the elements he had so greatly missed during his six and a half years in opposition: red boxes galore, bustling private secretaries to make telephone connections with the chosen ministers, messages of greeting to be exchanged with statesmen all over the world. He put on a great show. Indeed there was a feeling, throughout the second government, that he was asking all his principal interlocutors, his ageing crown prince Anthony Eden, first President Truman and then President Eisenhower, the members of the House of Commons, various insecure Prime Ministers of the Fourth French Republic, perhaps even the new Queen Elizabeth (when she succeeded her father in February 1952), much though she revered Churchill, to live up to a role which they thought a little over the top for the second half of the twentieth century.

It is impossible to re-read the details of Churchill's life as Prime Minister of this second government without feeling that he was gloriously unfit for office. The oxymoron is appropriate to the contradictions of his performance. The splendour of his personality, which infused everything he did with style and interest, is not in doubt. Yet many of the faults of his conduct of business, to which Attlee had so devastatingly drawn private attention in the last months of the war, were present in if anything exaggerated form. He became increasingly loath to read documents or to apply himself to any form of paperwork. He spent much of the time when he should have been doing so playing bezique, which became almost an obsession. Partly as a result Cabinets were rambling affairs, and Churchill was much inclined to treat them more as dinner-table audiences (it was now sixteen instead of the eight in wartime with which he was dealing) than as decision takers. Particularly in his last year he got into considerable trouble for doing things on his own without Cabinet approval.

With the exception of one issue which increasingly dominated his mind, the saving of the world from destruction in a reciprocal holocaust of H-bombs, his struggle to prolong his life in office became more important that any policy issue. The major milestones in his political year were occasions when he would endeavour to show the Cabinet or the Americans, the Conservative conference or the House of Commons, that he was fit to carry on. It was not so much what he said on these occasions, although he maintained his habit of meticulous preparation and sometimes produced speeches in which wit and vision were uniquely blended, as the fact that he was able to keep on his feet, and retain the resonance of his voice, long enough to say it at all.

This did not prevent his principal colleagues frequently wishing for his retirement. Fortunately for Churchill's tactics of delay they were not all impatient at the same time. Eden, the heir who had the strongest personal motive for impatience, was over a long middle stretch at least as physically incapacitated as Churchill. In the autumn of 1951 no one, probably including Churchill himself, contemplated his retaining the premiership for nearly three and a half years. A year, or at most two, was the assumption fostered. Then, throughout 1952 and 1953 and 1954, he conducted one of the most brilliant delaying actions in history. It was reminiscent of the way in which he had avoided unnecessary risk and Anglo-American carnage by postponing the Second Front until 1944. If he had announced this intention in the summer of 1941 he would have provoked louder explosions from Stalin than those which actually took place following each successive intimation that a further postponement was necessary. *Mutatis mutandis* Churchill pursued much the same tactics with Eden. To have announced in 1951 that he would still be Prime Minister in 1955 would have been intolerable, not only to the heir apparent, but to the majority of the Cabinet as well. Little by little it became acceptable, or at any rate unavoidable.

Compared with what might have been expected in 1951, his own condition made survival in office more difficult, but external circumstances made it easier. To balance Churchill's severe stroke of late June 1953, Eden's routine abdominal operation on 12 April of that same year was botched. A hazardous and corrective one on 29 April was followed by a period of incapacity before he left on 9 June for yet a third operation in Boston. American surgery did better than British had done, and gave him another twenty-four years of life, although he was never wholly well again, being subject to debilitating bile-induced fevers which marred his premiership. This apart, it took him until well into the autumn of 1953 to have even the temporary strength to be capable of succeeding Churchill.

Central features of Churchill's second premiership were his four official transatlantic visits. These were in January 1952, when he went primarily to see Truman, although he also addressed Congress for the third time (the first having been the day after Christmas 1941 and the second in May 1943), and fitted in a visit to Ottawa. The second was exactly a year later, when he had a long New York talk with the elected but uninstalled Eisenhower, as well as entertaining Truman to a 'rollicking' dinner at the British Embassy in Washington before going on a Jamaican holiday. The third was in December 1953 for the postponed tripartite Bermuda conference. This had been postponed because of Churchill's stroke in the previous summer, and it was tripartite because the French were included. The fourth and last visit (in office) was in late June–early July 1954 with a three-night stay in the White House and another detour to Ottawa.

Four of the crossings were made by air, and four by ship, three in the *Queen Mary* and one in the *Queen Elizabeth*. These were the last years of the full glory of the giant Cunarders – thereafter VIPs went by air – which were well matched with the last years of Churchill's power. The *Queen*s suited what might be called the 'Verandah Grill' side of his character.* The luxurious Cunard meals were almost as extensive as the seascape visible from the Grill's windows. He enjoyed them both to such an extent that his dining room at Chartwell bore more than a touch of 'Verandah' inspiration, with the Weald substituted for the ocean.

More seriously the importance of the four visits stemmed from his total conviction that peace and freedom could be preserved only on a

---

* The Verandah Grills were special restaurants in the *Queen*s, high up in the ships, with a fine view, charging a small supplement, and thought to be chicer than the general first-class restaurants.

foundation of unshakeable Anglo-American unity, ill matched, particularly after Eisenhower and Dulles took over from Truman and Acheson, with a gnawing lack of faith in the ability of the American administration to fulfil the awesome role which his romantic imagination had designed for it. Churchill's attempt to reconcile these two semi-irreconcilables was the key to most of his foreign policy attitudes and initiatives during his second premiership.

His cautiously hostile appraisal of Eisenhower was striking. They had got on thoroughly well together during the war, and Churchill had greatly welcomed Eisenhower's appointment as the NATO Supreme Commander in April 1951. But although he was an admirer of Eisenhower as a political general he was much more critical of him as a general in politics. Even in his pre-political days Eisenhower was always a little cold for Churchill's taste, with the famous smile barely skin-deep. And although Churchill could be ruthless he was never cold. He preferred Eisenhower with his much wider international experience to Taft as a 1952 Presidential candidate, but he was certainly not a Republican partisan. On the Sunday after the election he told Colville: 'For your private ear, I am greatly disturbed. I think that this makes war much more probable.'[2] And eight months later he put the same thought to the same source in more explicitly political terms. 'Very disappointed in Eisenhower whom he thinks both weak and stupid,' Colville recorded on 24 July (1953). 'Bitterly regrets that the Democrats were not returned at the last Presidential Election.'[3] Part, but by no means the whole, of the trouble was John Foster Dulles, the new Secretary of State. After a dinner with Eisenhower and Dulles at Bernard Baruch's New York apartment on 7 January (1953), the object of which was to promote warm and friendly relations with the incoming administration, Churchill on going to bed 'said some very harsh things about the Republican party in general and Dulles in particular, which Christopher [Soames] and I [Colville] thought both unjust and dangerous. He said he would have no more to do with Dulles whose "great slab of a face" he disliked and distrusted.'[4] How easily can benevolently planned dinner parties go wrong.

At this stage, even when he was getting on with him relatively well, there was an oddly competitive edge to Churchill's relations with Eisenhower. After a bilateral talk between the two leaders on this same New York visit, Colville noted, 'The P.M. told me . . . that he had felt on top of him this time: Ike had seemed to defer to his greater age and experience to a remarkable degree.'[5] This was an oddly unselfconfident remark. Churchill was at that stage, admittedly in a somewhat nostalgic sense, on top of the world.* He had been used to wooing Roosevelt but nonetheless had a guarded ease of relationship with him, while for Truman, although enjoying his tyro's reverence, Churchill probably had the most respect of the three Presidents.

The essence of the problem with Eisenhower, apart from his cold and even jejune personality, was that his imagination could not comprehend the horrors of the H-bomb in the way that Churchill did. This was most clearly expressed on 6 December 1953, towards the end of the Bermuda conference. Colville, having been sent to deliver to the President a letter from Churchill, recorded: 'He [Eisenhower] said several things that were noteworthy. The fact was that whereas Winston looked on the atomic weapon as something entirely new and terrible, he looked upon it as just the latest improvement in military weapons. He implied that there was in fact no distinction between conventional weapons and atomic weapons: all weapons in due course become conventional weapons.'[6]

This marked a big gulf. Churchill believed that an H-bomb exchange meant effectively the end of the human race. Eisenhower, with his much more limited imagination, thought that it would be the battle of the Rhine crossings writ larger. As Churchill also believed that there was no possibility of getting the Russians to talk sense about détente except on the basis of the strength of the American deterrent and a Washington willingness to negotiate seriously with them, it was a brave but delicate path which he tried to tread. Nor could he count upon Cabinet support. Eden, and several other members, most notably Salisbury, thought that he placed too much weight on the desire for summit talks, always a weakness of Churchill's, and too little on keeping close to the Americans. Yet the irony was that Churchill, despite irritations with Eisenhower, kept the Anglo-American relationship together, whereas Eden within eighteen months of becoming Prime Minister blew it wider apart than at any time since 1940, leaving Macmillan to try to put it together again.

On the home front the government's first year went reasonably well. As is the way with many incoming governments ministers exaggerated

---

* Nicholas Soames, the eldest child of the Soameses who was therefore brought up on the Chartwell estate, told me an engaging story. When he was about six (*circa* 1955) he broke through the valet-guard which normally defended Churchill's working room and said, 'Grandpapa, is it true that you are the greatest man in the world?' Churchill said: 'Yes, and now bugger off.'

the awfulness of the budgetary and foreign trade legacy they had been bequeathed. Churchill told the Lord Mayor's banquet two weeks after taking office that his inheritance was 'a tangled web of commitments and shortages, the like of which I have never seen before'.*7 The advantage of this approach was that it made room for manoeuvre for the government and for the Chancellor in particular. He wielded a bigger public expenditure threat over his spending colleagues, and he could try to put the blame for unpleasant interest rate and budgetary measures upon the preceding administration.

This Butler naturally did, first when he put up Bank Rate from 2 to 2.5 per cent in December and to 4 per cent in his March budget, the first moves since 1939. He also cut food subsidies by £160 million in that budget, thereby provoking Lord Woolton, who both disliked Butler and thought that he himself had a monopoly in anything to do with food, into a threat to resign because of a contrary pledge which he had given in his election broadcast. Churchill dismissed this idea with a wonderfully grand letter: 'Pray dismiss from your mind any idea of resigning from the Government because of mischievous debating points made by those who have brought the British community into deadly economic and financial peril.'8

The public temporarily took more notice of the 'debating points', and the Conservatives did disastrously in the local government elections that May. But politicians of any nerve are always good at sustaining casualties among their councillors, and the British economy was beginning to respond well to the relatively light surgery to which Butler subjected it, and the reputation of the surgeon rose correspondingly. In fact the early diagnosis was alarmist. There was Treasury talk of 'blood draining from the system and a collapse greater than had been foretold in 1931'.9 It was against this background that Churchill announced at the first Cabinet of the new government that ministers' salaries were for the period of rearmament to be reduced from £5,000 to £4,000 and that

* Much the same point was put more graphically by Harry Crookshank, whom Churchill had surprisingly made leader of the House of Commons as well as Minister of Health. When winding up the debate on the Address that November Crookshank said, 'We expected to find some skeletons in the cupboards, but they weren't even put in cupboards. They were hanging like candelabra from every ceiling in Whitehall' (Hansard, 5th Series, vol. 493, cols 936–44). It was a rare example of a highly partisan joke which convulsed the whole House. It was an even rarer example of quality from Crookshank. His main thanks for his over-promotion was to be always on the side of those who wanted to get rid of Churchill.

he himself would take a cut from £10,000 to £7,000. It was gesture politics, but as the ministers were mostly rich men they could take it with a stiff upper lip. Even closer to the bone but perhaps more relevantly, Churchill accepted Treasury proposals to reduce the overseas tourist allowance for British citizens first from £100 to £50 a year, and then, three months later, to £25. Henry Luce, if he rifled through old bills from the Mamounia in Marrakech or the Hôtel de Paris in Monte Carlo which he had settled for Churchill, could have permitted himself a smile that mixed sympathy and cynicism.

In fact the sickness of the British economy in the autumn of 1951 contained within itself the seeds of an almost automatic cure. The drive for massive American rearmament following the outbreak of the Korean War had produced a drastic inflation of world commodity prices, which turned the terms of trade sharply against Britain and produced what then seemed a massive external deficit – about £700 million a year. The budgetary and to some extent the inflationary consequences of this were exacerbated by Britain's own 1950–1 rearmament effort, which Churchill had strongly supported. Meanwhile the world commodity boom was beginning to correct itself. A major improvement in the terms of trade was a big economic bonus for the government.

As a result the haemorrhage of Britain's reserves, which was the main fear of the autumn, was reversed by the spring, and by the end of 1952 they were nearly 50 per cent above the worst Treasury predictions. This rendered somewhat irrelevant what was almost the last major dispute to be conducted within a British government in conditions of complete secrecy. Butler, taking too pessimistic a view of the outlook for sterling, bought a Bank of England scheme for floating the pound, blocking the accumulated sterling balances but making current sterling freely convertible and letting the exchange rate rather than the reserves take the strain. This plan was codenamed Robot. Butler wanted to announce it as the most dramatic feature of his early March budget. Curiously it was almost the exact mirror image of Churchill's experience with his first budget of 1925. Then the Bank of England, supported by official Treasury opinion, wanted to return the pound to the Gold Standard at a high fixed rate. Churchill at first resisted, then was overborne, and subsequently regarded it as the greatest mistake of his time as Chancellor. Now the Chancellor, backed by only half the Treasury and about the same proportion of the Cabinet, wanted to push ahead with a Bank scheme. All February long the noise of battle rolled. Churchill was at first favourable to Butler's idea. 'Setting the pound free' had an instinctive appeal to him. But he kept himself fairly detached. He was much preoccupied by the change of monarch on 6 February, and he did not delude himself that his four and a half years as Chancellor nearly three decades earlier gave him any special command over arcane currency issues. It was however Eden who, brought late into the picture, gave the *coup de grâce* to the scheme. The budget had to go forward without it. Whether or not Butler was lucky is difficult to say. Although a floating rate and fully convertible sterling are conventional wisdom today, they might have been a dangerously blinding light in the eyes of the long-restricted 'pit ponies' who ran the British economy in 1952.

What is indisputable is that the secrecy which covered such a sustained and intensively argued dispute was a tribute to the tribal loyalty of the Churchill government and of the Whitehall establishment.* At that time Hugh Gaitskell was shadow Chancellor and only six months out of the Treasury, and I was one of his two or three closest parliamentary collaborators. I knew nothing about the Robot dispute, and I believe Gaitskell knew very little either. Today such a dispute would reverberate from Downing Street out into Whitehall, along the Embankment to the 'counting houses' of Threadneedle Street, down to the newspaper offices of Wapping and back to Westminster within twenty-four hours.

As Butler's hand on the Treasury tiller (even if he was sometimes overridden) coincided with the restoration of stability in the British economy, so strengthened Churchill's hopes, which he expressed in his first House of Commons speech of the new parliament, of giving the country 'several years of quiet steady administration'. And, domestically, this was what his second administration essentially did. It relaxed the acerbities of Labour austerity under Sir Stafford Cripps without setting the clock back on most of the work of the Attlee government. How limited was the denationalization has already been seen. Equally unchallenged were the National Health Service and the main social security provisions. On constitutional change there was never any suggestion of reversing the provision of the second Parliament Act (of 1949), which halved the delaying powers of the House of Lords. And although Churchill had given a direct undertaking that he would restore the twelve university seats in the House of Commons, the last remaining

---

* This applied equally in the Attlee government. On 29 July 1949 the whole Cabinet considered and approved a devaluation which did not take place until 18 September, and did not leak in the meantime.

'fancy franchise', he decided that he would rather eat his own words, a form of diet which he had many years previously pronounced to be thoroughly wholesome, than get embroiled with a reversion so open to misrepresentation on simple democratic grounds.

Such cautious moves as were made towards a freer market and the liberalization from 'socialist' controls were skilfully done. The end of the remains of rationing proved to be little more than the dispersal of a thin layer of mist. Previously shortages had loomed up menacingly but a puff of wind produced sunshine and no sinister shapes. This approach was almost perfectly suited to the national mood of the early 1950s. There was no significant support for a counter-revolution and a return to the Britain of Neville Chamberlain. There was support for the knocking off of the rough edges and occasional spurts of class dogma of the previous administration, but for little more.

This was precisely what the Churchill government did. It showed a statesmanlike appreciation that, in circumstances where the country was divided almost exactly down the middle, the commander of the marginally and temporarily stronger side should not provoke too much conflict between the two main armies. In particular Churchill was determined not to get into head-on confrontation with the trades unions, then a massive force on the whole responsibly led. Churchill, it could be argued, long before Harold Wilson's 'beer and sandwiches' late-night negotiating sessions with leaders of the TUC, was too soft on union-backed wage claims. The appointment of the emollient Walter Monckton as Minister of Labour was a signal that all differences would be split, all disputes would be arbitrated and the seeds of the great inflation would be sown.

Whether or not any other Prime Minister of either party would have done better on this front may be doubtful. What is more certain is that the sin of omission of the second Churchill government was that it failed to impart any new dynamic into the post-war British economy. Throughout the 1950s Britain kept full employment, avoided (as did the whole developed world) any economic catastrophes, and drifted comfortably towards the reasonably distributed modest prosperity which enabled Harold Macmillan at the end of the decade to secure the unusual prize of a third election victory running for a single party, based it was thought upon the first introduction into many households of basic consumer goods – refrigerators, television sets, washing machines, vacuum cleaners and small cars. But it was a drift rather than a surge. Britain was still in the early 1950s the second-richest major country in

the world. All the other runners-up to the United States were peripheral: Sweden, Switzerland, Canada, Australia, New Zealand. France and
Germany were way behind, though they soon began to overtake, as did
Benelux and later northern Italy. About the mid-point in this second
Churchill premiership, Leicester was adjudged on some reputable scale
of measurement to have the highest average family income of any city
in Europe. (The then unusually high proportion of working women,
because of the demands of the hosiery trade, was the reason for its odd
pre-eminence over other British cities.) Twenty years later neither
Leicester nor any domestic rival would have been within the first
hundred. Whatever else it did, the mild freeing by the second Churchill
government of the Labour shackles around the British economy produced no bound forward in national output.

Once again, however, a comparative judgement may produce an
unenthusiastic acquittal, or at least a non-proven verdict. If there was
disappointment on this score after 1951, it was at least as great, and
more explicit, after 1964, after 1970 and for some time after 1979.
Where, and not entirely unconnected, there was more obvious room for
disappointment was in Churchill's resilement, once back in office, from
his European commitment in opposition. The Coal and Steel Community was going ahead without Britain, and the new government made
no attempt to reverse the 1950 decision of the Attlee government to
stay out, which Churchill and other leading Conservatives had harshly
criticized. By the autumn of 1951 the argument had shifted on to the
Pleven Plan for a European Defence Community. This was designed to
reconcile the pressing need of NATO for a German contribution with
French fears of the resurrection of the Wehrmacht, and to do so within
a framework which advanced the general cause of European unity. As
such it commanded strong American support. It involved the creation
of a multi-national European Army.

The Labour government had announced at the end of the summer
that the United Kingdom would become an associate but not a full
member of the Defence Community, the classic British position which,
mutatis mutandis, was to be repeated several times subsequently. So far
from reversing this, Churchill almost casually endorsed the mantra by
saying in a Commons defence debate on 6 December (1951): 'As far as
Britain is concerned, we do not propose to merge in the European
Army, but we are already joined to it.'[10] He was more explicit when
he told the Cabinet on 19 December following a visit with Eden to
Paris that 'the United Kingdom Government favoured the creation of a

European Defence Community, though they could not join it [but] were ready to associate themselves with it as closely as possible . . .'.[11] And then in a party political broadcast three evenings later he delivered himself of the wonderfully obfuscating statement: 'We shall work in true comradeship for and with United Europe.'[12] Thus, within two months of taking office, did the second Churchill government establish for itself the European role which was to be followed by every single British government, with the exception of that of Edward Heath, for the remainder of the twentieth century.

In fact Churchill did rather worse than this. Although he had moved, and carried, in the Strasbourg Assembly in August 1950 a resolution in favour of the principle of 'a unified European Army' he became obsessed with the weaknesses of the scheme which had emerged. 'A sludgy amalgam', he called it. These reservations dominated his conversation when he dined with Monnet and Reynaud at the Paris Embassy on his way back from Venice a few days before the beginning of the election campaign. Then, on 5 January 1952, on his first night in the United States as a restored Prime Minister, when being entertained on the Potomac in the Presidential yacht, he held forth to a distinguished company composed on the American side of Truman, Acheson, Harriman, Lovett and Snyder, in a sustained caricature of how a European army would or would not function. In Dean Acheson's subsequent account: 'He pictured a bewildered French drill sergeant sweating over a platoon made up of a few Greeks, Italians, Germans, Turks, and Dutchmen, all in utter confusion over the simplest orders. What he hoped to see were strong national armies marching to the defence of freedom singing their national anthems. No one could get up enthusiasm singing, "March NATO, march on!"'[13] Even such a very cool European as Eden was forced quickly to point out to the assembled company what a caricature that was. Integration was very unlikely to go much, if at all, below divisional level.

Churchill's performance on this issue that evening did not much impress the Americans. Maybe it was activated by a touch of guilt in view of the effort he had put into the European cause between 1946 and 1950. In the same way that the greatest nationalists are sometimes those who live nearest to the frontiers, so those who might have been expected to support a different position sustain the other with the most vehement arguments. Churchill's virtual acquiescence in the Attlee–Bevin position on Europe inevitably created a sense of let-down among those whom he had so vigorously summoned to the European colours

such a short time before. This extended to members of his government
and even of his family. In Cabinet Maxwell Fyfe and Harold Macmillan
were the two most committed Europeans. Outside it, but in the
government, were David Eccles and Duncan Sandys. Son-in-law Sandys had been specially charged with organizing the march of British
Europeans to the top of the hill. When the order came, in the strict
tradition of the 'grand old Duke of York', to march them down again,
he was naturally dismayed.

Macmillan was the key figure for pro-European resistance within the
Cabinet. Fyfe was nominally senior, but he had little influence with
Churchill and was a much less skilful political operator. Macmillan did
make something of a fight, but it was like one of the few spirited
actions of the French army in the débâcle of 1940 – gallant but without
hope of victory. He wrote a strong memorandum in February 1952.
He contemplated resignation in March, but only contemplated it. His
later *apologia* for the weakness of his stand had an engaging frankness
about it. He was a low-ranking member of the Cabinet with his future
reputation depending on whether he could fulfil the rash Conservative
party conference pledge to build 300,000 houses a year. Not unnaturally in the circumstances he succumbed to the well-known disease of
departmentalitis, very prevalent among ministers of that rank. 'My
immediate battle was with the Treasury,' he wrote in a 1969 volume
of memoirs. 'For this I needed an active alliance with No. 10 and at
least the benevolent neutrality of the Foreign Office.'[14] He was also
considerably reassured by the polite friendliness with which Eden
received his various papers and protests – while doing absolutely
nothing about them.

Furthermore, although Macmillan was in 1961 to promote Britain's
first application to join the European Community, he was only partially
a European. He possessed the vision to see the dangers of Britain being
excluded from a united Europe. But if Britain were outside, he did not
want Europe to achieve unity. He wanted the EDC to fail, and he
thought much the same about the early move towards the Economic
Community. Thus, as Foreign Secretary, he failed to see Britain
properly represented at the Messina conference of 1955, out of which
sprang the Economic Community or Common Market. In a sense his
position was the reverse of Churchill's. Churchill in government wanted
European unity to succeed with Britain benevolently on the outside.
Macmillan preferred it to fail unless Britain was satisfactorily even if
somewhat reluctantly on the inside.

Of greater interest, however, is what motivated Churchill to let the sand of his European commitment drain through his fingers during the early years of his second government. The conventional wisdom is that most of the blame rests with Anthony Eden. In order to maintain himself in office at such an advanced age, Churchill was forced to share his kingdom with his heir apparent, and Europe was judged to be within Eden's part of the divided realm. Eden, backed at this stage by the official Foreign Office, was undoubtedly cool on Europe. He had attended the Hague conference in 1948, but he had never joined the European Movement and he showed minimal interest in the Strasbourg proceedings. Then in December 1955 he welcomed an internal Foreign Office report which came to the conclusion that 'the United Kingdom cannot seriously contemplate joining in European integration'.[15] In January 1956 he added a touch of passion to this flat statement by telling a New York (Columbia University) audience that we know in our bones this was 'something which we cannot do'.[16]

Nevertheless a simple explanation of blaming Eden does not wholly convince. Anthony Montague Browne, who came to Churchill as a private secretary in October 1952 and devotedly stayed until his master's death more than twelve years later, subsequently recorded the Prime Minister as having told him 'that he had quite enough over which to fall out with Anthony Eden, without adding an issue which was not of urgent importance'.[17] But for several previous years Churchill had regarded Europe as an issue of high importance and had invested much political capital in the cause. And, particularly as he was aware of some if not majority ministerial support and was also aware that he was heavily disappointing several of those he cared about – Duncan Sandys and Violet Bonham Carter, to take two utterly contrasting personalities – Churchill would not normally have hesitated to make Eden at least argue the matter out in Cabinet. But he did not. The issue was not seriously debated that autumn. The view of Colville, who unlike Montagu Browne was there at the time, was that it just did not figure high enough in the Prime Minister's priorities. His primary purpose was to restore the 'special relationship' with America, which he believed, with doubtful accuracy, had languished under Attlee and Bevin. Later, as the government got into its stride, his priority became that of saving the world from the H-bomb through summitry. And here, once again, Washington was crucial, even though Churchill did not hesitate to try to impose his own wisdom over that of Eisenhower. The west Europeans, even the French at that stage, were not H-bomb players.

At the beginning of his second government Churchill was a month short of seventy-seven. Apart from the priceless asset of his indomitable will, he was not healthy. His only two British Prime Ministerial predecessors of that age, Palmerston and Gladstone, even without the benefits of twentieth-century medicine, had been more so at that stage in their lives. So were Adenauer, de Gaulle and Deng Xiaoping, to mention three who bore comparable responsibilities at comparable ages. Churchill was somewhat infirm of movement, deaf, and weakened by several minor but warning strokes. His capacities impressed different people in differing ways. This was partly because he had become very 'up and down', with his zest and tone sharply varying from day to day. But even more was there a division between those who had known him well at the zenith of his powers and those who came to him afresh in the evening light.

Clementine, who had known him longest, except perhaps for Violet Bonham Carter, firmly believed that he should not have been Prime Minister for a second time, but this was partly because she did not wish him to risk his unimprovable reputation, and partly because she felt a special responsibility for preserving his life. It was not the same as a straightforward judgement that, on national grounds, he was unfit for office. Colville thought that in some ways Churchill had improved: 'With the strain of war-time leadership relaxed, he was now less irascible and impatient than of old and readier to be convinced by argument, provided the right moment was chosen for the exercise. The charm and the lovable qualities were undiminished. . . .'[18] Six months into office, however, Colville wrote: 'Alone with the P.M. [at Chartwell] who is low. Of course the Government is in a trough, but his periods of lowness grow more frequent and his concentration less good. The bright and sparkling intervals still come, and they are still unequalled, but age is beginning to show.'[19] And another six months after that: 'He (W.) is getting tired and visibly ageing. He finds it hard work to compose a speech and ideas no longer flow.'[20]

Mountbatten and Leslie Rowan, the latter having been for four years one of Churchill's wartime private secretaries, provided roughly similar judgements from either end of the turn-of-the-year 1951–2 *Queen Mary* voyage. When a fouled anchor postponed the ship's departure, Mountbatten was summoned from his nearby house at Broadlands to dine aboard at Southampton. 'My impressions of this grand old man', he wrote, 'are that he is really past his prime. He was very deaf and kept having to have things repeated to him. He quoted poetry at great length.'*²¹ Rowan, meeting the party at New York, thought that Churchill had lost his tenacity – 'he no longer pushes a thing through. He has lost, too,' he added, 'his power of fitting in all the problems one to another.' And physically he had come to walk 'like an old man'.²² These Rowan judgements were filtered through the compelling but self-regarding pen of Dr Lord Moran. Moran always tended to exaggerate Churchill's infirmity in order to underline his own success in keeping him alive.

On the other hand David Hunt, a 1951–2 private secretary inherited from Attlee, who had not known Churchill during the war, was much impressed by his going down to the Cabinet room and working after dinner, as well as by the meticulousness of his speech preparation. 'One thing was certain,' he wrote: 'it was all his own work, which was not always the case with other Prime Ministers.'²³ Hunt also brought out an unusual attribute. Churchill, even at this late stage, was more than capable of original composition, but he liked doing it with an audience. He had no inhibition about searching for phrases while keeping waiting a succession of the Downing Street secretaries known as 'garden girls', relieved every quarter of an hour, so that Churchill might quickly see the typescript of his thoughts. A senior private secretary was also required to sit alongside both for company and to see that he did not stray too far away from the departmental brief – or indeed the facts.

Working after dinner was a mild throwback to his wartime habits, although hardly comparable with the small-hours conferences with the Chiefs of Staff, which often went on until 2.30 in the morning. In this second phase Churchill, although never early, was mostly safely in bed by 1.00 a.m., and the Chiefs of Staff, even before Field Marshal Alexander was interposed between him and them in the spring of 1952, became lay and remote figures. There were other changes of pattern. He mostly (but not invariably) preferred Chartwell to Chequers for weekends, and, although far from solitary, demanded less of a circus at either. Sometimes he would start at Chartwell on the Friday morning (or even the Thursday evening) and then transfer to Chequers in time for dinner on the Saturday, thereby satisfying his urge for movement, although also creating the maximum household inconvenience. And

---

* As this was an occasion where Mountbatten was regarded as having talked 'arrant political nonsense – he might have learned by heart a leader from the *New Statesman*', there may have been less than a meeting of minds between him and Churchill (Colville, *The Fringes of Power*, p. 637).

there was the growing grip of bezique. When Montague Browne
became a private secretary he was first instructed by Colville on what to
do if Churchill became ill and second on the rules of that arcane card
game.

Early in the second premiership came the death of King George VI.
Churchill's emotional nature was suffused with grief. After a brief sticky
start the wartime relations of Sovereign and Prime Minister had been
close and sustaining, combining to an exceptional degree mutual respect
and an easy equality of relationship. Churchill's tributes, both in a
broadcast and in the House of Commons, were among his finest *éloges*.
And the simple inscription of 'For Valour' (the words on the Victoria
Cross), which he wrote himself on the card with the government wreath,
were heartfelt. This did not prevent his getting strong satisfaction out
of being the first Prime Minister of the new Queen's reign. He was
imbued with romantic feelings both for the beginning of a new Elizabethan age and for the person of his new Sovereign. Perhaps because
Queen Elizabeth was a little older, already had a husband and because
he had more other things to do, it was less cloying than that of
Melbourne with the young Queen Victoria. And, of course, the change
of reign offered Churchill a wonderful excuse for pushing away any
thought of retirement until after the Coronation, arranged for sixteen
months later.

Altogether the second half of 1952 and the early months of 1953
were a period of calm and even sunlit weather for the second Churchill
premiership. His vigour and concentration were generally adjudged
better than a year previously. Stalin's death on 5 March (1953) not only
left him the sole survivor of the triumvirate of Allied wartime power but
opened his mind to the possibility of a new and more constructive
relationship with Soviet Russia. Nor did Eden's incapacity and effective
disappearance from the political scene at the beginning of April for his
three operations (two British and one American) lessen either
Churchill's sense of indispensability or his appetite for continuing
power. In February 1952 a conference of Lord Salisbury, Jock Colville
and the ubiquitous Moran had been planning to shunt Churchill to the
House of Lords, while graciously allowing him to remain Prime Minister. In April 1953, so far from easing his burdens, he enthusiastically
added to them by taking over the supervision of the Foreign Office.

Alas, nemesis was not far away. On 23 June there was a full-scale
Downing Street dinner for Alcide De Gasperi, the outstanding Prime
Minister of early republican Italy and one of the four or five major

architects of the European Community. After dinner Churchill, according to Colville, 'made a little speech in his best and most sparkling manner, mainly about the Roman Conquest of Britain'.[24] Shortly afterwards he had a severe stroke, much more serious than any of the previous eruptions. The Italians and others were quietly hustled away. The next day he managed a sadly drooping nominal chairmanship of a Cabinet. Then he departed for Chartwell, where he remained for a full month and was convalescent for much longer. Moran, always one for drama, thought he was going to die during the first weekend. But he did not. It was, however, the end of the first phase of his second premiership, and would have been its final end had not Eden been at least equally incapacitated and 3,000 miles away in Boston.

44

'AN AEROPLANE . . . WITH THE PETROL RUNNING OUT'

CHURCHILL'S RECOVERY FROM his 1953 stroke was slow but miraculously almost complete. The veil of secrecy about the nature and severity of his illness was another near miracle. Anyone without his will to live and to rule would never have wished to go on as Prime Minister. Without the conspiracy of silence, which was carefully contrived, he could not have continued, even with the bonus of Eden's absence. And there was another factor necessary to Churchill's political survival, which was a lack of deadliness in the ambition of Rab Butler, the Chancellor of the Exchequer and *tertium quid*, who exercised many Prime Ministerial functions over several months.

During this period of Churchill's recovery and slow convalescence there emerged to the surface, as though under an X-ray, a clear map of his personal relations, those whom he wanted to see and those whom he did not. He withdrew to Chartwell only at noon on Thursday, 25 June, thirty-eight hours after his attack. His deterioration was gradual. He had contemplated presiding over another Cabinet that morning and even answering House of Commons questions that afternoon, and his nadir was after he had got to Chartwell, over the Friday and the Saturday of 26 and 27 June. By the Sunday there was a glimmer of light through the clouds, and the very worst was over. On the Thursday on the drive to Chartwell he instructed Colville that the degree of his incapacity should be concealed, which pointed to a concern for maintaining the authority of the government, and maybe even his own, and not merely to apprehension about his illness. At his worst he remained coherent mentally, although his speech was slurred. The left side of his face sagged. He had difficulty in finding his mouth with his cigar, he stood only with the greatest effort, and he could walk only a few tottering steps.

Colville stayed at Chartwell for two weeks, and also on the spot and in more or less constant attendance were Clementine, Moran, Christopher and Mary Soames, two secretaries for typing and dictation (although for once there was not much of the latter) and soon a couple of nurses. There were also a few who were summoned, for reasons of state rather than of companionship, like prelates and counsellors called to the ante-rooms of a possibly dying king. Butler and Salisbury were pre-eminently in this category. They came on the Saturday, were party to a plan which Colville concocted with Lascelles, the Queen's principal secretary, by which if Churchill had to resign, which the Queen was advised was likely by Monday, a caretaker government should be formed, under the chairmanship rather than the Prime Ministership of Lord Salisbury, who would preside until Eden was well enough to take over. Against this arrangement of doubtful constitutional propriety and contrary to his interest, there is no evidence of a Butler protest. He modestly came down to Sevenoaks station by train in a clerkly fashion on the Saturday. He did not see Churchill. Nor did Salisbury, but together, as well as conferring on the constitutional arrangements, they toned down the medical bulletins which Moran and Sir Russell Brain, the neurological surgeon who had been called in, wanted to issue. A reference to 'a disturbance of the cerebral circulation' was cut out, and it was merely said that the Prime Minister needed a complete rest and had postponed his 9 July Bermuda rendezvous with Eisenhower. At a Monday (29 June) Cabinet meeting they jointly but elliptically reported on Churchill's condition.

Equally when three (or perhaps two and a half)* press lords came to Chartwell at Colville's urgent summons on 25 June, they too did not see Churchill but 'paced the lawn in urgent consultation' and hatched a benevolent conspiracy to gag the press. Camrose, Beaverbrook and Bracken managed to lead their fellow proprietors into constructing such a wall of silence that hardly a word of the true severity of Churchill's illness appeared in print until he himself casually mentioned the dread word 'stroke' in the House of Commons a year later. This was a business not a social visit, as in a sense was Bracken's first return on the Saturday morning (27 June) when he brought the most mobile and comfortable wheelchair that it was possible to procure in London. Bracken had the quality, useful but not wholly admired, which Evelyn Waugh ascribed in *Brideshead Revisited* to Rex Mottram (a character to some extent based on Bracken) of always instinctively knowing where best to procure any required device or service.

---

* Bracken was chairman but not owner of the *Financial Times*.

The chair was a great success, and enabled Churchill to begin moving about the house. As early as Sunday, 28 June, he used it to preside over a social dining-room luncheon with, almost inevitably, Beaverbrook as his first guest outside a circle of family and other attendants. Bracken came to dinner that same evening. On the Monday Sarah Churchill arrived from New York and Lord Camrose also came to luncheon. Moran reported that Camrose never seemed 'to have much to say' to Churchill, but that together they sat on the lawn for a long time.[1] On 30 June Lord Cherwell ('the Prof') was there for lunch and Norman Brook, the Cabinet secretary, for dinner. Of all the senior officials who had served Churchill, Brook was the one with whom he probably had the easiest relations. One subject on which he most wanted Brook's opinion was whether volume six of *The Second World War* was likely to offend the Americans. The terms in which he put it (again according to the not verbally reliable Moran) were of peculiar interest: 'If I am going to die, then I can say what I like ... but if I live and am still Prime Minister, then I must not say things which will anger Ike.'[2] And Churchill's action which most stuck in Brook's memory was his determination, in the drawing room after dinner, to stand upright without the support of the chair. By a tremendous effort, and with sweat pouring down his face, he achieved it.

On 2 July Harold Macmillan was bidden to dinner and found his host 'a sick but very gay man'.[3] On the 4th Churchill could walk a little unaided and Colville wrote that day to Clarissa Eden (she and the Foreign Secretary were still in America) with what was intended to be the reassuring message that thoughts of a caretaker government were disappearing. He did not add that it was a late rather than a premature retirement about which the Edens should now be more worried. On the 5th – the second Chartwell Sunday – Field Marshal Montgomery came to lunch, and stayed to dinner. The next day Sir William Strang, the permanent under-secretary of the Foreign Office, came to a business meeting. It is doubtful whether Strang got a meal, but had he stayed for the evening he might have heard Churchill display his distant memory by reciting almost faultlessly the first fifty lines of Longfellow's 'King Robert of Sicily', which he claimed he had last read 'about fifty years ago'.[4] With Eden away, Churchill was still nominally in supervisory control of the Foreign Office, although the ministerial work there was in practice divided between Salisbury and Selwyn Lloyd. On 7 July both Lord and Lady Salisbury came to dinner, she being the first spouse to penetrate to the convalescent home. 'Bobbity' Salisbury was not a special

friend. Churchill habitually referred to him as 'Old Sarum', and complained that, as a Cabinet colleague, he was either ill or awkward.

Butler, although he had paid the earlier working visit to Churchill,
had to wait until 19 July before he was invited to dinner. Meanwhile he
was quietly running the government. He presided over sixteen successive
meetings of the Cabinet between 29 June and mid-August, a high
frequency for a government which aspired to 'quiet steady administration'. During this period Butler made remarkably little attempt to
flex his political muscles. His one big Commons 'acting Prime Minister'
as opposed to Treasury speech, in a foreign affairs debate of 21 July,
was a very low-key affair. 'A dull speech yet more dully delivered' was
Colville's verdict.[5] It was a foretaste of how Butler threw away his
opportunity to rouse the Conservative conference at Blackpool ten years
later, at the time of his second contention for the leadership. In 1953 he
played his hand totally differently from the way Harold Macmillan
would have played it, and indeed did play it at a famous meeting of the
Conservative backbenchers (1922 Committee) in December 1956, when
Eden's leadership was obviously faltering. But Macmillan was not a
possible challenger in 1953. He was still in the lower half of the Cabinet
and in addition contributed to the general invalidism of the government
by spending much of July having a gall-bladder operation.

Yet, apart from the almost equally incapacitated Churchill and Eden,
Butler was the only possible Prime Minister in 1953. Cherwell, whose
political judgement was not his strongest suit but who had no possible
motive for wishing either to dispose of Churchill or to promote Butler,
thought that had the Chancellor of the Exchequer demanded title as
well as responsibility he could not have been resisted. Butler made no
such demand. Still barely fifty, he probably thought that time was on
his side, and that he had no need to hurry. Moreover he was one of
nature's intendants. Churchill, in a slightly teasing way, was quite fond
of him, despite his appeasement past. But he regarded him as of a
different species to himself, a servant rather than a ruler of the state,
almost an honorary Wykehamist, in spite of Butler coming from a
different academy.

By his lack of ruthless thrust at this zenith of his Treasury success
Butler set the pattern for his losing the premiership first to Macmillan
and then to Douglas-Home, in 1957 and 1963. How differently Lloyd
George, Harold Macmillan, and Mrs Thatcher, to take only a few
examples, would have behaved. Butler was the loser and Churchill (to
the substantial extent that longevity in office was his objective) was the

beneficiary, although such was his instinctive categorization of Butler that he did not recognize a debt. In early 1957 he repaid Butler ill by firmly, although maybe rightly, favouring Macmillan as Eden's successor.

On Friday, 24 July, four and a half weeks after his attack, Churchill removed from Chartwell to Chequers. According to Moran, semi-endorsed by Mary Soames, the Chartwell staff were on the verge of walking out unless there was a period of relief. He stayed at Chequers until 12 August, still more convalescent than governmental. He read more fiction than Cabinet papers, although his consumption of this showed considerable concentration and ability to absorb small print. For the first time he engaged with the Trollope political novels, and wisely thought *The Duke's Children* to be the best. He moved through Charlotte Brontë's *Jane Eyre* and Emily Brontë's *Wuthering Heights* to Disraeli's *Coningsby* and to an English translation of Voltaire's *Candide*. In September he had progressed to Balzac's *Père Goriot* in French, although by then he was deeply involved in the proofs of the sixth volume of his war memoirs, which as he grew stronger he found more absorbing and more satisfying to his sense of duty than even the most distinguished examples of other authors' fiction. So far as unavoidable business was concerned, the papers 'in the box' were dealt with by a fruitful combination of Jock Colville and Christopher Soames. The former had the authority of being a private secretary of long experience, the latter that of being a thirty-three-year-old backbench MP who had established a close relationship with his father-in-law. There is some ambiguity about whether they actually simulated the Prime Minister's initials, but it is not in dispute that they used their temporary power with restraint, endeavouring always to act as, with intimate knowledge, they thought Churchill in normal health would have done, rather than to impose their own views.

At Chequers the Edens, just back from New England surgery, came to lunch on Monday, 27 July. The Foreign Secretary was described by Colville as looking 'thin and frail ... but in good spirits'.[6] He earned good marks from Churchill by not raising the question of the succession. On the Wednesday Adlai Stevenson, who preserved his fame in defeat better than most unsuccessful American Presidential candidates, came to lunch, and the next day the Home Secretary and Lady Maxwell Fyfe. Churchill always had a soft spot for Stevenson, and regretted his defeat. The Fyfe visit indicated a reviving sense of duty on Churchill's part.

The following weekend there was a full-scale political and family gathering. The Edens, the Salisburys and the Soameses were there. Randolph and Sarah Churchill, as well as the Duff Coopers, came for the Bank Holiday Monday. On the Sunday Churchill was driven to Windsor for his first audience with the Queen since his illness. Given his respect for the institution of monarchy and near idolatry of the person of the just-crowned Queen, it was not possible for him to maintain with her the teasing silence about his intentions which he enjoyed doing with Eden. What he told the Queen was the truth, which was that he was uncertain whether he could go on until he saw if he could command the Conservative conference on 10 October, and then face Parliament.

A week or so later the Queen proffered an enticing but as it turned out controversial invitation for him and Clementine. She invited them to go with her to watch the St Leger at Doncaster on 12 September and then to go on by the royal train for a couple of nights at Balmoral. Churchill was determined to go, but Clementine was resolutely opposed on the ground that public exposure at the racecourse and the long train journeys would be too much for him. He went, and she dutifully accompanied him. He seems to have been right, for the expedition was such a success that, less than a week later, his doctors released him to go, without Clementine but accompanied by the Soameses, to stay in Beaverbrook's villa at Cap d'Ail.

Throughout August Churchill struggled hard to regain at least a loose grip on government business. On Saturday the 8th he took his first official meeting, at Chequers, where Butler, Salisbury and William Strang had been summoned to discuss a Soviet reply to a Western proposal for a four-power meeting of Foreign Ministers. Colville, who had taken the record, noted that 'The old man still gets his way.'[7] On the 18th of the month Churchill came up from Chartwell (to which base he had returned from Chequers on the 12th) to preside over an early-evening Cabinet, his first since 24 June. He had come to Downing Street in the morning and had Norman Brook to brief him while he lunched in bed. That Cabinet sounds a fairly desultory affair. It lasted an hour and forty minutes, and Churchill was reported as being unusually silent. Another Cabinet a week later produced a more animated performance from the Prime Minister.

Nonetheless, and despite the fact that he was far better than had seemed possible two months before, the early autumn was not a time of contentment for Churchill. Mary Soames described him between the two Cabinet meetings as 'dazed and grey'.[8] And Jane Portal, who had the unique distinction of being both Churchill's last favourite dictation secretary and Rab Butler's niece, wrote to her uncle from Cap d'Ail towards the end of September: 'The P.M. has been in the depths of depression. He broods continually whether to give up or not. . . . He is preparing a speech for the Margate [Conservative] conference but wonders how long he can be on his pins to deliver it. He has painted one picture in tempera from his bedroom window.'⁹

Why was he so anxious to use Margate to prove to himself and the world that he could go on? There was near unanimity of family, colleagues and medical advisers that he ought to do the reverse. He was nearly seventy-nine, his second premiership had almost doubled the span at which, in its beginning, he had strongly hinted. He was finding oppressive the burdens even of his very remote control. Without his unique *réclame* and the devoted covering-up service of his immediate staff, he could not possibly have sustained them. Furthermore he liked luxurious relaxation in the sun, interspersed with painting and putting books together, for which purposes he had accumulated an unique collection of welcoming houses.

There were several offsetting factors. The first and most obvious was his love not only of the appurtenances but of the reality of power. His sybaritic tastes only attained full satisfaction when they were superimposed on a period of high and testing achievement. He had not enjoyed his convalescence, and commented on it in an engaging way. 'I have not had much fun,' was his dismissal of July.¹⁰ He may have been a sybarite, but he was as far as it is possible to imagine from being a lotus-eater. He did not welcome old age, and he knew that the best way to stave off the effects was to postpone the time when power had gone for the last time. Thereafter it would be downhill all the way.

He also had genuine doubts about the succession. Eden was still several months short of being fit for immediate inheritance, and although, in the already cited letter to her uncle, Jane Portal reported to him that 'you are in high favour', Churchill did not instinctively believe that Butler was Prime Ministerial. He found it difficult to imagine a satisfactory younger successor. Such myopia has been by no means unique among the great statesmen. Outweighing all these other considerations, however, was his conviction that the world was in danger of nuclear destruction, and his mounting belief that his last service might be to save it from such a fate as could no one else.

Six weeks before his illness he had made a remarkable House of Commons speech. Throughout 1953 and 1954 his foreign affairs and defence speeches alternated, a little wildly, between those which infuriated the Labour opposition and those which dismayed a large part of the Cabinet and Conservative party. His 11 May speech, the thirteenth anniversary as it happened of his first full day as Prime Minister, was very much in the latter category. The key passage was:

> I must make it plain that, in spite of the uncertainties and confusion in which world affairs are plunged, I believe that a conference on the highest level should take place between the leading powers without any delay. This conference should not be overhung by a ponderous or rigid agenda, or led into mazes and jungles of technical details, zealously contested by hoards of experts and officials drawn up in vast, cumbrous array.[11]

The unfavourable impact may be measured by the comment which Anthony Eden wrote upon it eighteen months later, after plenty of time for mature consideration:

> It must be long in history since any one speech did so much damage to its own side. In Italy, as de Gasperi openly stated to Winston, & I believe elsewhere, it lost de Gasperi the election, i.e. his gamble for an increased majority. In Germany, Adenauer was exasperated. Worst of all it probably cost us EDC in France. At any rate, the whole summer was lost in wrangling. The speech was made without any consultation with the Cabinet. . . .[12]

In the six weeks between this speech and the beginning of his illness Churchill showed not the slightest sign of resiling under Foreign Office disapproval. The public reactions to the speech were strongly favourable, and in early June he got a reasonably fair wind from the Commonwealth Prime Ministers who were assembled in London for the Coronation. Then, in mid-August, just as Churchill was beginning hesitantly to recover strength, there came the news that Russia, only nine months behind the United States in this lap of the race, had graduated to thermo-nuclear status. H-bombs were about to replace A-bombs in the armouries of both the superpowers. The chances of a conflict destroying not merely a few cities but the whole of civilization were greatly increased. So were the horror and urgency of the problem in Churchill's mind. Put at its lowest it gave him a new excuse to try and stay on. Put at its highest it gave him his noblest sense of mission since 1940–1. But first he had to stand on his feet for fifty minutes at Margate on 10 October and then to take House of Commons questions on the 20th and to supplement this by making a full-length parliamentary speech in the 3 November debate on the Address.

All of these hurdles he surmounted satisfactorily, almost triumphantly. At the Conservative party conference his speech was inevitably
in many ways low-key. It opened on a very peripheral subject (British
Guiana). It contained no fewer than eleven separate tributes to government ministers, which, while fence-building and maybe well deserved,
were not the stuff of which high oratory is made. He struck a modest
note about the achievements of the government. 'Certainly we have
tried very hard to make our administration loyal, sober, flexible, and
thrifty, and to do our best to be worthy of the anxious responsibilities
confided to us.'[13] It was relatively unpartisan for a conference oration.
While he mentioned Attlee five times he did so with more respect than
venom, and his jokes about the 'Socialists' were good-humoured. He
stuck firmly to the line of his 11 May speech calling for a summit with
the Russians (his last previous speech – 'the first time in my political life
I have kept quiet for so long'), while not disguising that 'we have not
yet been able to persuade our trusted allies to accept it in the form I
suggested'. Even the peroration was quietly phrased: 'One word personally about myself. If I stay on for the time being bearing the burden at
my age it is not because of love for power or office. I have had an ample
share of both. If I stay it is because I have a feeling that I may through
things that have happened have an influence on what I care about above
all else, the building of a sure and lasting peace.'[14]

In spite of the phrases being somewhat flaccid by his own standards,
this speech fully achieved its purpose. It reasserted his command of his
party. At his first parliamentary question time two days later he had
some difficulty in hearing the supplementary questions, but otherwise
he was at ease in the House and verbally felicitous. When asked by
Moran afterwards whether jumping up and down for nearly a quarter of
an hour had tired him, he replied, somewhat inconsequentially: 'Oh no,
not at all; but it did make me rather short of breath.'[15] His greatest
triumph was his House of Commons speech of 3 November. It covered
the waterfront, as a Prime Minister's speech at the opening of a new
session must do, but its exceptional quality lay in the concluding
passages about the world prospect – and the bomb. His optimistic shaft
was that 'when the advance of destructive weapons enables everyone to
kill everybody else nobody will want to kill anyone at all. At any rate, it
seems pretty safe to say that a war which begins by both sides suffering
what they dread most – and that is undoubtedly the case at present – is
less likely to occur than one which dangles the lurid prizes of former
ages before ambitious eyes.'[16]

The speech went down well on all sides of the House, although the Labour diarists were unfortunately absent or silent for that day. 'Chips' Channon was ecstatic. He thought it immediately apparent that Churchill was making 'one of the speeches of his lifetime'. 'Brilliant,' he continued, 'full of cunning and charm, of wit and thrusts, he poured out his Macaulay-like phrases to a stilled and awed house. It was an Olympian spectacle. A supreme performance which we shall never see again from him or anyone else.'*[17] And Harold Macmillan, in a more measured way, confirmed Channon: '[Churchill's] performance on 3 November was really remarkable. . . . He was far more confident than at Margate. Indeed, he was complete master of himself and of the House. It seems incredible that this man was struck down by a second stroke at the end of June. I would not have believed it possible at any time in the summer or even in the early autumn.'[18]

After these efforts, whether at Margate or Westminster, Churchill was suffused with a mixture of exhaustion and euphoria. On the latter occasion he went happily to the smoking room for a session of refreshment and compliment. After that he was reported by Moran as saying: 'That's the last bloody hurdle. Now, Charles, we can think of Moscow.'†[19] Productive talks in Moscow, however, involved carrying Eisenhower with him, not literally in the aeroplane, but in the sense of securing at least the reluctant acquiescence of the President to a probing Churchill expedition. This meant the reinstatement of the Bermuda talks, which had been postponed from July. Churchill played with the idea of luring the President to an earlier meeting in the Azores, but there was no American enthusiasm for either the time or the place. Indeed there was some indication that Eisenhower, while solicitous for

---

* It is a great deprivation that for post-war Churchill speeches there were no Harold Nicolson comments to compare with Channon's. (Nicolson had lost his seat in 1945.) Nicolson and Churchill were more politically attuned than were Channon and Churchill, but Nicolson had a finer critical judgement than the sometimes cloying Channon.

† Moran was at this stage and for some time afterwards a rich mine of information about Churchill's attitudes and states of mind. The surrounding evidence suggests that, whatever may be thought of the medical ethics of his clinical revelations, he was mostly accurate in substance. But he rarely gets the rhythm of Churchill's words convincingly. It was partly that he was so anxious to stress the centrality of his own role that his christian name, 'Charles', had to be obsessively introduced into far too many sentences. Churchill rarely called those around him anything. Often he could not remember their names, and I much doubt if he treated his doctor differently in this respect from his ministers, private secretaries and stenographers.

Churchill's recovery, did not wish him to have too much energy for political initiatives. The arrival at the White House of a personal letter from Churchill, always very much his own composition (in contrast with the replies) and rather curiously beginning 'My dear Friend', was not in general warmly welcomed. Winthrop Aldrich, the current American ambassador in London, informed Harold Macmillan that 'Eisenhower was embarrassed by Churchill's attempt to revive, by personal correspondence, the old Churchill–Roosevelt relationship.' 'I said', Macmillan continued, 'that of course F.D.R., like Churchill, was an artist and a politician, and Eisenhower was neither. I agreed, however, that the informal correspondence between the Prime Minister and the President should be reserved for exceptional occasions. Like everything else, if it became common, it lost its value.'[20]

Nevertheless a four-day three-power Bermuda conference to start on 4 December was arranged without too much difficulty. The French were included on the initiative of the Americans, but with ready British acceptance. The British could do no other. If Churchill was so anxious to talk to the Russians he could hardly object to the presence of the transient Laniel (very briefly French Prime Minister) and the more permanent Bidault (for Foreign Ministers were invited too), into the cosy English-speaking gathering which he might have preferred. The journey to Bermuda (which still, with halts at Shannon and Gander, took seventeen hours of flying time) might have been regarded as the fourth hurdle which he had to surmount to remain Prime Minister, particularly as the purpose of his staying on was, west or east, to participate in summit meetings. Broadly, however, it had been accepted, with varying degrees of dismay from his family and colleagues, that he would continue until May 1954. The Queen's return then from a long tour of Australasia and the Pacific Commonwealth would form another of the 'stations of the cross' which he was so ingenious at discovering as props of postponement.

Churchill wisely spread his Bermuda absence over ten days rather than the four of the conference itself, and with this padding of leisure got through without too much difficulty. He approached the conference without the reverence of preparation, through either documents or discussion, which a decade earlier he would have devoted to such a gathering. Moran recorded how, at lunch on the plane between Gander and Bermuda, Churchill ignored his table companions (Eden, Cherwell and Moran himself) and voraciously read C. S. Forester's *Death to the French*, an unfortunate title if it was observed in his hand when he disembarked. His absorption in novel reading during these late 1953 months was on a scale which he had never previously experienced. After his July immersion in Trollope and the Brontës he became engrossed by Hardy's *The Dynasts* and Scott's *Quentin Durward*. He took a little time to get into *The Dynasts* but later told a mystified Lord Woolton that he had read it 'for hours on end'. By *Quentin Durward* he was so gripped that on 27 October he had to read another chapter rather than apply himself to a paper which was due for Cabinet discussion in half an hour. On 6 October he learned that he had been awarded the Nobel Prize for Literature, earned by his writing rather than his reading. He was later said to be disappointed that it was not the Peace Prize and, because he was in Washington at the time of the ceremony, got Clementine to go to Stockholm and receive it on his behalf. But at the time he sounded pleased enough: 'It is all settled about the Nobel Prize. £12,100 free of tax. Not so bad!'[21]

Bermuda was not an inspiring conference. Eisenhower was in his most unimaginative mood. He got Churchill's reluctant acceptance that, if the North Koreans and the Chinese went back on the truce lines which had been recently been agreed, the United States would feel free to use atomic weapons against them. Eden was horrified by this, and Churchill also became increasingly disturbed, although he at first thought of it as a sprat to catch the mackerel of American agreement to serious nuclear disarmament talks with the Russians. So far from the mackerel being landed, Eisenhower proclaimed his belief that atomic weapons were now coming to be thought of as a proper part of conventional armament, and also, in full plenary session, shocked the British delegation by his response to one of Churchill's grand *tours d'horizon*, full of a mixture of terror and hope, the predecessors of which had at least been listened to with respect by Roosevelt and Stalin. At Bermuda Colville, who had been used to these previous courtesies, wrote:

> Ike followed with a short, very violent statement, in the coarsest terms. He said that as regards the P.M.'s belief that there was a New Look in Soviet Policy, Russia was a woman of the streets and whether her dress was new, or just the old one patched, it was certainly the same whore underneath. America intended to drive her off her present 'beat' into the back streets. I doubt if such language has ever before been heard at an international conference. Pained looks all round. Of course, the French gave it all away to the press. Indeed some of their leaks were verbatim.
> To end on a note of dignity, when Eden asked when the next meeting

should be, the President replied, 'I don't know. Mine is with a whisky and soda' – and got up to leave the room.[22]

Churchill seemed curiously unfazed by this display of insensitivity verging on brutality. He was disposed to blame Dulles. Moran reported him as saying late on the last evening of the conference:

> It seems that everything is left to Dulles. It appears that the President is no more than a ventriloquist's doll. . . . This fellow [Dulles] preaches like a Methodist Minister, and his bloody text is always the same: That nothing but evil can come out of meeting with Malenkov [Stalin's successor]. . . . Dulles is a terrible handicap. . . . Ten years ago I could have dealt with him. Even as it is I have not been defeated by this bastard. I have been humiliated by my own decay.[23]

Moran's account makes the Prime Minister put too much blame upon Dulles, for whom Churchill had an almost chemical repugnance, rather than Eisenhower, who still possessed considerable wartime credit in his eyes. Furthermore he still believed, or at least hoped, that his own influence was such that all might come right in the end. 'Alle sal reg kom' is an Afrikaans phrase which he had picked up fifty-four years before and much liked quoting, mostly inaccurately it was said. And this, surprisingly, was at least half true. Churchill's next encounter with Eisenhower, in Washington in the summer of 1954, proved to be the most friendly in their relations since Eisenhower had progressed from General to President.

Most of Churchill's aspirations and energies between Bermuda and the Washington visit were devoted to seeking a summit with the Russians. The only rival for his attention was his eagerness to postpone the date of his retirement. Such solipsism he saw as fully justified because he alone possessed the philosopher's stone which might bring Eisenhower and Malenkov into some sort of limited harmony. In public he proclaimed the priority which he gave to the Anglo-American partnership, but in private and semi-private he was exasperated by the complacency of the United States towards the H-bomb and by its stubbornness in resisting summitry.

At the first Cabinets of the New Year of 1954 he was engaged in persuading his colleagues that trade with Russia in anything except manifest weapons of war should be fostered. The Americans wanted a much wider embargo, more or less on anything that might contribute to the manufacture of such weapons, which effectively covered everything that the Russians might wish to buy. He was also resistant to

France's appeals for British support in Indo-China, where its Asian empire was on its last legs, even though the final drama of the fall of Dien Bien Phu occurred only on 7 May. His guiding principle was that he did not wish to do anything which would increase the hostility of the Soviet leadership and make them less willing to talk.

His dedication was in no way diminished by the news on 1 March that the Americans had detonated a second H-bomb at Bikini Atoll. In the House of Commons he defended their right to do this, even welcoming the awesome power which it revealed, saying that American deterrent strength was the best safeguard for the peace of the world. But he was privately much less sanguine, referring to the H-bomb as 'the bloody invention'. Nevertheless he presided that summer over a meeting of the Defence Policy Committee of the Cabinet which took the decision, contrary to what he had told Eisenhower at Bermuda was his intention, to manufacture the British H-bomb.

There were several paradoxes about his attitude at this stage. He was pursuing a grand goal and his central purpose was, in British party political terms, essentially non-partisan. Yet he managed to embroil himself in a couple of petty but bitter parliamentary disputes with the Labour party. The first was over a new rifle, replacing the traditional .303 with which the British army had drilled and fought through two world wars. Was it to be a Belgian model, which the Americans (and Churchill) favoured and on which NATO might standardize, or a new British design? Although I recall vividly the rowdiness of the bad-tempered Commons debate on 1 February, during which Churchill was almost shouted down, the arguments on either side have long since dissolved into dust. But why on earth was any Prime Minister, let alone one aged seventy-nine, who was not only the most famous man in the world but was in pursuit of his last grail, participating at all in such a minor contretemps? What was the purpose of three War Office ministers if they could not handle such a matter?

Then on 5 April, having in the meantime made a thoroughly adequate foreign affairs speech on 25 February, he suffered a more serious parliamentary débâcle. The Labour party was complaining (ironically in view of Churchill's real beliefs and efforts) that he did not take a robust enough attitude to the Americans with their H-bomb-happy approach. Understandably irritated, Churchill told the Cabinet secretary (according to Moran) that he was going to 'put Attlee on his back'.[24] This he proposed to do by showing that the Labour government, by allowing the abrogation of the Quebec agreement (on the development of nuclear weapons) which Churchill had negotiated with Roosevelt in 1944, was responsible for the lack of British control over the use of the H-bomb, of which the opposition was now complaining.

Whatever the merits of the argument, the objective was misconceived. Even had he succeeded there was no profit at this stage for Churchill in putting Attlee 'on his back'. And the execution was dreadfully bungled. He simply lost the ear of the House. He was beset by Labour interruptions, with his own side sitting glum and unsupportive to his rear. 'Look at the faces behind you,' cruelly interrupted one MP. Meanwhile Churchill plodded woodenly on through his notes. It was the nightmare scene which all parliamentarians dread and which on a small scale nearly all of them have to endure once or twice in their careers. But in his case it was writ large, with a full House and the prospect of a devastating press the next morning. And then, to crown it all, that old but false friend Robert Boothby, perhaps still nursing the grievance of his dismissal in 1940, rose to his feet from the Tory bench below the gangway while Churchill was still speaking and sauntered down the floor and out of the chamber with insolent detachment. The Labour benches erupted in mockery. The Conservatives looked even glummer. The scene remains etched in my memory.

This was a terrible contrast with Churchill's commanding statesman's performance only five months before. Curiously he was not immediately cast down. 'It will be all right in the morning papers,' he consoled himself with misplaced complacency.[25] It was not. *The Times* said that his 'sense of occasion' had 'sadly deserted him'. It was his responsibility that the debate 'had degenerated into a sterile, angry and pitiful party wrangle'. The *Manchester Guardian*, in general at that stage more friendly to Churchill than *The Times*, said simply that 'he had blundered'.

To crown it all, Eden, winding up the debate at the end of the day, made an excellent speech, held the House, defended Churchill and underpinned his own claims to an early succession. It was ominously reminiscent of Churchill's winding up of the Norway debate fourteen years before, when he had defended Chamberlain so effectively that he succeeded him as Prime Minister within forty-eight hours. Whether Churchill ever fully appreciated the extent of his April 1954 debâcle is happily doubtful. 'Things didn't go as well as I expected,'[26] was his rather wistful understatement after he had read the following morning's press. But he was far from accepting, even if he was aware of, the lobby buzz that his performance rendered inevitable his early resignation.

Most of his Cabinet colleagues, while too used to him to believe in its inevitability, certainly wanted him to fix a firm, early date, and stick to it. The House of Commons misfortune had come close on the heels of frustrating Cabinets on 31 March. The Cabinet met twice during the day, mainly because of Churchill's feebleness of concentration on the points for decision. Eden was reported by his principal private secretary as saying: 'This simply cannot go on; he is gaga: he cannot finish his sentences.'*27

The *Daily Mirror*, almost the only mass-circulation newspaper not controlled by Churchill's 'friends', had added to the pressure by coming out on the next day with a front page skilfully headed 'Twilight of a Giant' and with a back page which found a sensitive flank by quoting a *New York Times* dismissal of Churchill as 'only a shadow of the great figure of 1940'. The *Times* further twisted the knife by contrasting him with Eden, who on a recent occasion had risen from beside Churchill 'precise, confident and clear'. The *Daily Mirror*, after its 1938–9 support, had ceased to be Churchill's friend. It had several times called for his resignation in the winter months of 1954. Churchill had not appeared to mind this much, showing more concern about a violent contemporary attack by Malcolm Muggeridge in *Punch*. This was accompanied by a cartoon depicting Churchill as a flaccid wreck of a man. '*Punch* goes everywhere,' Churchill had gloomily remarked, showing a surprising sensitivity to opinion in doctors' and dentists' waiting rooms.[28]

Churchill's own intentions were far from clear, perhaps not even to himself, during that spring. On 11 March he dined with Rab Butler and used the evocative words from which the title of this chapter is taken: 'I feel like an aeroplane at the end of its flight in the dusk, with the petrol running out, in search of a safe landing.' He added, according to Butler, that 'the only political interest he had left . . . was in high-level conversations with the Russians. He would be glad to retire to Hyde Park Gate and finish his *History of the English-Speaking Peoples*.'[29] On that same March day that he dined with Butler he talked alone with Eden and left him with the impression that he intended to go in May – 'or end of the summer at the latest'.[30] On 19 March he told Moran that he would resign at the end of June. Between those two March dates

* This private secretary, Evelyn Shuckburgh, was a compulsive and compelling diarist. But he was at this stage bitterly anti-Churchill, just as later at the time of Suez (but with more reason) he became bitterly anti-Eden. As with Moran, his words need to be treated with some caution. Colville's were more reliable than either.

Jock Colville found him on better form than he had been for years. Such surges in health and morale were dangerous to his resignation intentions, and if they were accompanied by a glint of summitry on the horizon the combination was nearly fatal. On 8 April he saw a new hope of talks with Malenkov. On the 22nd he perceived a chance of further talks with Eisenhower in late May and proposed himself to Washington for the 20th–24th. This did not work, but by early June he had got a firm invitation from Eisenhower for the second half of that month.

That was the end, for him, of any thought of resignation that summer. The Queen had been back from her Commonwealth tour since mid-May. Indeed Churchill had gone to meet her off the western point of the Isle of Wight and had sailed with her in the Royal Yacht round the south-eastern corner of England and up the Thames to the heart of the capital. Thirty-two years later it inspired her to a rare poetic reminiscence. 'One saw this dirty commercial river as one came up,' she recalled in a retrospective television programme, 'and he was describing it as the silver thread which runs through the history of Britain.'[31] But it did not inspire him to any thought that the silver thread should immediately extend to Anthony Eden as Prime Minister. Another 'station of the cross' had been passed, but Washington and what might follow provided him with grounds for a new extension of his duty.

He was indeed firm with one minister who suggested otherwise and sharp with another. Eden wrote on 7 June begging for a handover 'at least two weeks before the recess begins', which was normally in late July or early August.[32] Churchill replied on the 11th:

My dear Anthony,
    I am not able to commit myself to what you suggest in your letter. . . . I am increasingly impressed by the crisis and tension which is developing in world affairs and I should be failing in my duty if I cast away my trust at such a juncture or failed to use the influence which I possess in the causes we both have at heart. . . .[33]

That was as bland but clear a negative as it is easily possible to imagine. The only consolation was that Churchill hinted at the possibility (but no more) of an autumn handover before concluding: 'I am most anxious to give you the best opportunity to prepare for an election at the end of 1955 . . .' – a date which was nearly eighteen months away.[34] Harold Macmillan, who wrote on 18 June also urging a decision before the summer holidays, met equal determination but less blandness.

Churchill wrote (in his own hand as he had to Eden, and Eden to him) on 20 June:

> Dear Harold,
>   I received yr letter yesterday morning.
>   I do not think it ought to have been written except in yr own hand.
>   I was well aware of your views.
>   Yours sincerely,
>   Winston S. Churchill[35]

Had Macmillan's subsequent career not so strongly contradicted any such precept, his letter might have been regarded as a classic example of how not to get on in politics.

Before leaving for his last official visit to America, Churchill had two other preoccupations, neither of which figure large in the context of history. The first was the question of the salaries of members of Parliament. They were still paid only £1,000 a year, which even allowing for the 1950s value of money was a pittance, leaving those with no other income (many in the Labour party, a few in the Conservative party) in severely straitened circumstances. Having either to keep two houses or to stay in a hotel for much of the week, MPs were literally short of money for meals. A cross-party Select Committee of the House of Commons had unanimously recommended a substantial increase, a proposal which became the subject of violent political controversy. Conservative party activists hated the idea of paying MPs more. For a time it replaced hanging and flogging as the issue which most stirred local Conservatives, particularly the women's branches. It was therefore bold of Churchill to devote a large part of his last address to the Conservative Women's Conference in the Albert Hall on 27 May to this unpopular subject. It was however one which brought together his natural generosity, his sympathy for those worried about money, and his high constitutional respect for Parliament as an institution. 'I am sure it is a bad thing', he said, 'to have the tremendous affairs and responsibilities of the State discharged by men, a large number of whom are themselves seriously embarrassed.' The uphill nature of his task was underlined by the defensive way in which he presented his argument. 'I am not asking for your agreement,' he said. 'But I do ask for your patient consideration of the facts which I venture to give to you and the course which I have not hesitated to advise.'[36] He subsequently wrote to Clementine, who was on one of her cures, this time in Aix-les-Bains, saying that he had been 'received with the utmost goodwill and respect, though they did not like it'. He added, as a good indication of the atmosphere, that 'one poor lady (an M.P.'s wife) who pleaded the case for the increase was not only interrupted but *booed*, a procedure unusual at women's meetings'.[37]

The second issue, almost as trivial, but arousing less public hysteria, was that of his weight. There were several scales at Chartwell, one of which, in Clementine's bathroom and in which she had faith, showed him at fifteen stone (210 pounds) which was bad for his height of five feet seven inches. So he tried another, which showed fifteen and a half stone, even worse, and which machine he then claimed 'was a broken-down one'. Clementine had tried to put him on to a severe tomato regime. He wrote: 'I have no grievance against a tomato but I think one should eat other things as well.'[38] He tried other weighing machines until he found one which registered only fourteen and a half stone. Both the issue and the diet were then allowed to subside, and did not again seriously figure in his remaining decade of life.

On the night of 24 June Churchill, accompanied, *inter alia*, by Eden and Lord Cherwell, flew via Gander to Washington. Both the Americans and the British Cabinet had been loath to let him go without what they regarded as the restraining presence of Eden, although on nearly all current issues other than the central one of H-bomb talks with the Russians the Foreign Secretary was more critical of the Americans than was Churchill. The purpose of the visit was admirably summed up in Colville's diary:

> Primarily it was to convince the President that we must co-operate more fruitfully in the atomic and hydrogen sphere and that we, the Americans and British, must go and talk to the Russians in an effort to avert war, diminish the effect of Cold War and procure a ten years' period of 'easement' during which we can divert our riches and our scientific knowledge to ends more fruitful than the production of catastrophic weapons. Now, owing to Anglo-American disagreement over S.E. Asia, reflected very noticeably at the Geneva Conference [which had been meeting for several previous weeks under Eden's chairmanship in an attempt to deal with Indo-China], the meeting has become in the eyes of the world (and the Foreign Secretary) an occasion for clearing the air and re-creating good feeling. The main topics are to be: Indo-China, Germany if E.D.C. fails, Egypt and atoms.[39]

For Churchill the visit went well from the beginning. He was met at the airport by Vice-President Nixon and Secretary of State Dulles and swept off to the White House, where he was to stay for the first three nights. Eisenhower was determinedly out to be pleasant, perhaps regarding the weekend (for it was a Friday to Monday) as more in the nature of a respectful valediction than a basis of negotiation for the future. However, it was not all honours and no substance. At their first meeting, on the Friday morning, Eisenhower both flabbergasted and delighted Churchill by agreeing to talks with the Russians. He had expected to secure this (if at all) only after long hours and much eloquence. Nevertheless he regarded the issue as of such importance that he did not in the least mind having the wind taken out of his sails. He was reported (by Colville) that evening, after another successful session, mainly on Egypt, in the afternoon as being 'elated by success and in a state of excited good humour'.[40] And his euphoria persisted, in spite of some Dulles efforts to catch back on the President's broad approval for summitry. On the Sunday evening there was a 'very gay' White House dinner at which Eisenhower and Churchill both spoke warmly of the Germans, while Eisenhower, not necessarily endorsed by Churchill and contested by Eden, called the French by contrast 'a hopeless, helpless mass of protoplasm'.[41]

Roger Makins, the British ambassador, said that 'he never remembered a more riotous evening',[42] a comment which raises doubts about Makins's (not particularly) sheltered upbringing as well as arousing curiosity as to exactly what riotous activities took place in Eisenhower's staid and heavily furnished White House. Churchill, however, went to bed after the riot 'elated and cheerful' – 'buoyed up by the reception he has had here'.[43] He felt himself right back at the centre of world affairs, as much as he had been when he had paid his long visit to Roosevelt over the turn of the year 1941–2. Moreover he had got his 'green light' from Eisenhower, and however many 'yellows' subsequently flashed he was not going to be put off. He was hell-bent for Moscow – or at least for Berne, Stockholm or Vienna, which later became his proposed sites for a meeting with the Russians.

On the Tuesday afternoon (29 June) the Churchill party flew to Ottawa. There Churchill added a thirty-hour appendage to his American visit, as he had done on several previous occasions and as the admirably un-jealous Canadians seemed to like. He gave a small dinner for, among others, St Laurent, the French Canadian Prime Minister who had replaced Mackenzie King in 1945. The next morning Churchill attended a meeting of the Canadian Cabinet and addressed the Ottawa press corps. Colville wrote of the latter occasion: 'He did not do it as well as in Washington but it went down all right.'*⁴⁴ He then recorded a broadcast to the Canadian people before driving through cheering crowds in an open Cadillac to the Ottawa Country Club, where the Canadian government entertained him and his party to a dinner with speeches. From there he proceeded direct to the airport for New York, where 'a somewhat tired but very triumphant P.M.' boarded the *Queen Elizabeth* at 1.00 a.m.⁴⁵

The ship did not sail until noon, and that morning (1 July) Churchill held a shipboard levée at which various dignitaries from Baruch to Makins came to pay their respects. It was his last Atlantic liner voyage. He went to Washington again in 1959, doing the journey both ways by air, and in 1961, aboard Aristotle Onassis's yacht, he called in at New York. But this was the final time that he crossed the Atlantic by Cunarder or any other grand liner. Again according to Colville, it was about time. Colville thought that the food, even in the favoured Verandah Grill, was becoming depressingly Americanized, and that the general standard of service on the great ship was running down.⁴⁶

Nevertheless the voyage was a dramatic one, not from the elements, which were thoroughly well behaved, but because of the less disciplined conduct of the principal passengers. Eden had decided, against his desire and original intention, also to come back by ship in the hope of being able on the voyage to pin Churchill down to a definite date for retirement. (When Churchill heard of Eden's intention, he was tempted himself to switch to the air.) So there were two courts aboard, and the greater one more contented than the lesser with the way matters were evolving. Churchill, having cleared his Washington hurdle, was eager to get off a message to Moscow proposing his visit. He was unwilling to wait to consult his Cabinet, partly because he was impatient to get on with it, and partly because he had a nasty suspicion that they might make difficulties. Eden, deeply sceptical about the whole Moscow ploy, played the card of joint Cabinet responsibility, although delay was by no means wholly in his own interest. Unless Churchill had got his Russian initiative out of his system, there was little chance of his sticking

---

* At a Washington Press Club lunch, two days before, his answers to questions had met with such an enthusiastic reception as to fill him with a generalized beneficence which, when Colville came to collect his notes, caused Churchill warmly to shake his hand 'under the impression that [he] was a Senator or pressman endeavouring to congratulate him'. This at least was better than his confusion at Bermuda six months before, when he mistook the British diplomat (Sir) Frank Roberts, who combined high intellectual talent and certainty with an ability to irritate successive ministers, for one of John Foster Dulles's aides and proceeded to berate him for the errors of his supposed master.

to the 20 September handover to which Eden had got tentative agreement on the second day out from New York. However rational self-interest, sometimes to his credit, was not Eden's strongest suit. When Churchill's draft telegram was sent along the companionways for his approval he said firmly that the Cabinet ought first to be consulted. Churchill then offered a compromise. Butler would be telegraphed to seek Cabinet approval provided that Churchill could say that the telegram carried Eden's agreement in principle (which it certainly did not). Eden thought the message would be much better not sent, but weakly agreed. Then mild farce set in. Butler received the telegram in the country only on the Saturday afternoon and did not understand that he was to worry the whole Cabinet with it over a summer weekend. So he merely made one or two minor drafting amendments and despatched the summit proposal to Moscow. Churchill was content with this.

He and Eden however managed to keep the pot boiling by having what Colville described as 'a blood row' at dinner on the Sunday evening.[47] It was about a fairly peripheral matter and, Eden having slept it off until noon, they lunched together on the Monday in reasonable amity. Next day the *Queen Elizabeth* proceeded calmly from Cherbourg to Southampton, where she docked at 5.00 p.m. The calm did not long persist. There was a Cabinet on Wednesday, 7 July and also on each of the two following mornings, together with another four meetings before the 26th. Gradually over these meetings what had begun as a cave led by an affronted Salisbury supported by a yapping Crookshank broadened out into a majority including Eden, Macmillan and Butler. No member of the Cabinet gave Churchill unequivocal and articulate support.

Nor was Churchill assisted from overseas, looking either west or east. Eisenhower was obviously not pleased that Churchill had sent off his shipboard telegram to Molotov (reappointed Foreign Minister under Malenkov) without consulting him about the text. The terms in which he denied his displeasure could hardly have confirmed it more thoroughly, if politely: 'Of course I am not vexed. Personal trust based upon more than a dozen years of close association and valued friendship may occasionally permit room for amazement but never for suspicion.'[48] Then the Russians, having replied tentatively but encouragingly to Churchill's *Queen Elizabeth* communication, changed tack and fired a torpedo which was fatal to his summit plans. They chose 25 July to reply to a British note which had lain unanswered since 7 May, and did so in terms which would have made bilateral talks ridiculous. They demanded a thirty-two-power meeting to discuss the Soviet plan for European security – which would have involved NATO withdrawal from Germany.

When Churchill received this news, at Chequers on a Sunday afternoon, he first sought refuge in mordancy. 'Foreign Secretaries of the World unite; you have nothing to lose but your jobs.'[49] Dismay could not be far behind. When the Cabinet met on the Tuesday morning he had no alternative but to admit the defeat of his hopes. As his official biographer starkly put it: 'Churchill's last great foreign policy initiative was at an end.'[50]

He had paid a heavy price for no result. He had weakened the faith of the Eisenhower administration in his wisdom, and he had lost control of his own Cabinet. It was sadly reminiscent of Gladstone's final weeks as Prime Minister (aged eighty-four) when, with Irish Home Rule, the cause which had kept him in politics for the previous seven years, already dead, he found himself in a tiny Cabinet minority against increased naval expenditure. He regarded this as a major question – almost on a level with Churchill's brooding about the cataclysmic dangers of the H-bomb. 'If I stood alone in the world on this question, I could not be moved,' Gladstone said in 1894, 'so strongly am I convinced that this large increase to the Navy will lead to disaster in Europe. . . .'[51] And twenty years later who could say that he was clearly wrong?

The subsequent reactions of Gladstone and Churchill were, however, different. Gladstone retreated to Biarritz for a month. When he got back, after teasing his colleagues for nearly three weeks, he resigned for the last time and retreated to Hawarden for a final four years of life. Churchill retreated to Chartwell, also for a month, but there decided against his provisional September resignation and postponed it for a final half-year.

45

A Celebration and a Last Exit

CHURCHILL's *villégiature* at Chartwell in that August of 1954 was marked by dreadful weather – it rained almost every day – and by his growing determination to get out of his commitment to resign on 20 September. Clementine was in the South of France* for the first three weeks, but her absence was less exceptional than the rainfall, and Colville and the Soameses kept Churchill company for much of the time. He had several ministers down for luncheon or dinner and the night – Butler, Macmillan, Woolton and, a surprising addition to the circle, Osbert Peake, the Minister of Pensions and National Insurance, who at least enabled him to contribute a good satirical passage to one of his many long bulletins to Clementine, this one written in his own hand:

> Peake hates old people (as such) living too long and cast a critical eye on me. He told about his Father who was stone blind for 20 years and kept alive at gt expense by 3 nurses till he died *reluctantly* at 91; and of course the Death Duties were ever so much more than they wd have been if he had only been put out of the way earlier. I felt vy guilty. But in rejoinder I took him in to my study and showed him the 4 packets of proofs of the History of the E[nglish] S[peaking] Peoples wh bring 50,000 dollars a year into this island on my account alone. 'You don't keep me, I keep you.' He was rather taken aback. I think he will play a large part this coming year. . . . I think I may put him & his office in the Cabinet. . . .[1]

Some of the ministers more established than Peake thought that they were being picked off one by one to accept Churchill's continuance in office. He did not exactly get either Butler or Macmillan to endorse this but he did bring them to accept its inevitability without loud squawks of protest. The still more crucial figure, of course, was Eden. It was

---

* She was always reputed to dislike the Riviera, but she voluntarily went there several times on her own, thereby suggesting that it was more the friends with whom Churchill stayed and his propensity to casinos rather than hostility to the climate or landscape which mostly kept her from accompanying him.

always very difficult for him alone to fight an effective battle on his own behalf. His leverage depended upon the support of other senior members of the Cabinet. His 'hungry eyes', in Churchill's vivid and not very friendly phrase, grew 'ever more beseeching and more impatient'.[2] They irritated rather than propitiated the Prime Minister. During these last eight months of Churchill's premiership their relations came somewhat to resemble that of the two superpowers, each of whom had the ability to destroy the other, but only at the price of blowing up themselves – and the fortunes of the Conservative party – at the same time. Eden could not resign without throwing away the inheritance on which he had been counting for more than twelve years. On 27 August he nevertheless hinted weakly that he might do so, and on 2 October Macmillan did so on his behalf a little more strongly. Churchill, while not taking these particular hints very seriously, knew that he had to keep Eden's discontent within bounds. If Eden flounced, and he was rather a flouncing man, Churchill's final period of office would end in bitterness and ignominy. Furthermore the clashes of interest and policy between Prime Minister and Foreign Secretary were interleaved with tissue sheets of appreciation and respect built up over many years of working together – on the whole successfully. Also they both had good manners. As a result Churchill did not find it hard or too hypocritical to write Eden occasional warm notes of friendship, like the following on the eve of the Conservative party conference, at Blackpool that year:

> My dear Anthony,
>   I am so sorry for yr chill. . . . You are quite right to stay in bed and rest. We have a hard week before us. . . . I worry more than I used about speeches. If you and Clarissa are coming back by train *after* the Conference is over we cd dine together – a small party in my saloon and then an unhurried talk afterwards.
>   Everyone is singing yr praises – none more heartily than your sincere friend,
>   W[3]

When Colville wrote that in the last days of his premiership Churchill 'began to form a cold hatred of Eden',[4] he (so often right) was oversimplifying a more complex relationship. Undoubtedly Churchill had moments of high exasperation with Eden (and vice versa they were even higher), but that was by no means all there was to it. In mid-August he had taken immense trouble over a long letter to Eden explaining that he had 'no intention of abandoning my post at the present crisis in the world'. It went through six drafts, with both Butler and Macmillan being consulted. Almost the only new argument in it, however, was in the nature of things unlikely to be welcome to, or persuasive with, Eden. 'Fag-end Administrations have not usually been triumphant,' Churchill wrote. He recalled how he remembered Rosebery after Gladstone and Balfour after Salisbury. Neither had been saved by 'their ability, experience, and charm',[5] three words which, it might be thought, were well chosen in relation to Eden himself. The rule about 'tail-end Charlies' may be thought to have been subsequently reinforced by the experiences of Home after Macmillan, Callaghan after Wilson and Major after Mrs Thatcher, although with Eden after Churchill providing the most striking example of the lot.

Although this disaster was still in the future, Churchill's argument could be interpreted as referring not merely to the date of the handover but to its inherent undesirability. In general, however, he was at pains always to offer Eden shafts of hope, even if they were sometimes tactlessly phrased. At a *tête-à-tête* meeting on 27 August (1954) he was recorded by Eden as telling him that: 'It would be all mine before sixty.'[6] As Eden was not due to attain that milestone until June 1957, this was not the most encouraging of forecasts. On other occasions Churchill suggested that he might make way for Eden to fight a late-1955 election – or even that he might stay and fight it himself.

As the Conservative party conference passed (there were mixed views about the quality of Churchill's speech on this occasion, but none thought it a disaster) and a new session of Parliament began, there were several circles of view about the desirability of his retirement. At the epicentre, obviously, was Churchill himself. He was showing an increasing reluctance to concentrate on official papers or even on most of his speeches, to which he had previously devoted compulsive attention. And (writing a month or two later) Colville noted: 'During the winter months . . . I listened to many disquisitions of which the burden was: "I have lost interest; I am tired of it all".'[7] But for the greater part of the time Churchill much preferred being Prime Minister to the alternative, which was to accept that, save only for finishing off *A History of the English-Speaking Peoples*, his active life was effectively over. He also told Moran (16 December): 'I think I shall die quickly once I retire. There would be no purpose in living when there is nothing to do.'[8]

Then there was a second circle composed of Churchill's close family and of his almost equally close 'official family'. The former group on the whole wanted him to resign quickly. They wanted to preserve his life and reputation, and were fearful that continuance in office would endanger both. But this view was tempered by their intense desire to keep him as happy as possible. The 'official family' was equally indeterminate, although in a slightly different way. Once again it was best summed up by Colville. After describing several deteriorations in Churchill's performance, he wrote:

> And yet on some days the old gleam would be there, wit and good humour would bubble and sparkle, wisdom would roll out in telling sentences and still, occasionally, the sparkle of genius could be seen in a decision, a letter or a phrase. But was he the man to negotiate with the Russians and moderate the Americans? The Foreign Office thought not; the British public would, I am sure, have said yes. And I, who have been as intimate with him as anybody during these last years, simply do not know.[9]

The third circle was composed of his Cabinet colleagues. Their almost unanimous desire during this last seven or eight months was that Churchill should go as quickly as the handover could be arranged with proper respect for his dignity and proper appreciation for his past services. But few of them were prepared to beard him directly with their unwelcome views. They were also inhibited by fear that, if the operation were bungled, they would incur the wrath of the fourth and fifth circles, the fourth being the Conservative activists and the fifth the less committed public, who it was hoped would vote for the party at the general election which was beginning to loom.

The net result of these conflicting currents was that, in the absence of a firm will to resign on the part of Churchill himself, there was little more than making the best of it that anyone could do. Eden had to be satisfied with the Garter ribbon which the Queen conferred upon him that October. This acquiescence was reinforced by the imminent approach of Churchill's eightieth birthday on 30 November (1954). It was the first time for ninety years that a British Prime Minister had passed that climacteric in office. Gladstone was Prime Minister for the fourth time in his ninth decade but on his eightieth birthday he was in opposition; Palmerston in 1864 was Churchill's only predecessor who could have blown out eighty candles in Downing Street.

So the event was to say the least noteworthy, and nearly everyone joined in trying to make it memorable. On the whole they succeeded, although there were one or two jarring elements as well as the fact that Churchill himself, although he liked celebrations, was not entirely enthusiastic about becoming eighty. The first upset was that as he subsequently put it, 'I made a goose of myself at Woodford,'[10] an event (on 23 November) which was still repercussing a week later on the birthday itself. The constituency occasion should have been both gentle and innocuous. It was for the presentation of a portrait of Clementine. Churchill had no need to say more than a few gracious words, but he chose to make a foreign policy speech into which he inserted, by some quirk of false memory, a bombshell. In the context of defending his desire for summit talks with the Russians he suddenly said, referring back to 1945, 'I telegraphed to Lord Montgomery directing him to be careful in collecting the German arms, to stack them so that they could easily be issued again to the German soldiers whom we should have to work with if the Soviet advance continued.'[11]

There were several aspects to this statement which fully justified the question 'what on earth made him say it?' in a *Times* leader of the following morning. First, it was a singularly odd sentence for Churchill with his normal meticulous respect for English construction and words. Second, it made no sense in the context of a passage arguing for a rapprochement with Russia. Third, the despatch of any such telegram to Montgomery seems to have been a figment of his imagination. In 1954 he firmly believed not only that it had been sent in 1945 but that he had published it in volume six of *The Second World War*. This last belief was quickly dispelled. Searches of his own records and of those of Montgomery took longer but produced an equally negative result. Fourth, it provided ammunition for those who wished to portray him as an instinctive warmonger, imbued with an endemic hatred of the Soviet Union. *Pravda* took this line, which troubled Churchill more than criticism nearer home. He was still hankering for a last-minute reprieve for his summit hopes. The row rumbled on and cast a minor shadow over the birthday celebrations. On 26 November he paid his last degree-giving visit to Bristol as Chancellor of the University, and there referred to himself as 'supposed to be in a bit of a scrape', which made the enthusiasm of his welcome more gratifying.*[12] And on the day after his actual birthday he had to reply to a House of Commons attack on the Woodford speech from Emanuel Shinwell.

The second jarring note was the Graham Sutherland portrait, which was the main birthday gift from the House of Commons, and for which

* He was still wearing the robe which had been made for his father as Chancellor of the Exchequer in 1886, which must have been an economy for the University.

Churchill had begun sitting in August. Sutherland at first made a very favourable impression. 'Mr Graham Sutherland is a "Wow",'* Clementine wrote to Mary Soames on 1 September after the painter had been a guest at Chequers. 'He really is a most attractive man & one can hardly believe that the savage cruel designs which he exhibits come from his brush. Papa has given him 3 sittings & no one has seen the beginnings of the portrait except Papa & he is much struck by the power of his drawing.'[13] As the portrait advanced Sutherland became more secretive. Churchill was not allowed to observe its progress until he was shown the finished version two weeks before his birthday. Not only did he not like it. He hated it. 'I think it is malignant,' he told Moran.[14] His dislike, which passed the bounds of rationality, was based partly on the ground that it made him look old and spent, which it did, and partly that it showed his face as cruel and coarse, which it was not. At the presentation ceremony he contained his feelings and merely delivered himself of words which became famous for heavy ambiguity: 'The portrait is a remarkable example of modern art. It certainly combines force and candour.'[15] The picture quickly found its way to an attic until Clementine had it cut up and burned a year or so later. Sutherland was not again asked to Chequers – or Chartwell. A suggestion two months later that Churchill might pose for a portrait by Salvador Dali was quickly rejected.

The presentation ceremony was nevertheless splendid. Nearly all MPs, peers and other officers of state attended the Westminster Hall event. The other present from the Commons was a finely produced book beginning with a Bunyan quotation and containing the signatures of all the MPs who had subscribed to the unappreciated portrait. Only 26 of the 625 members declined to contribute. Attlee, who unusually was the only other living Prime Minister,[†] made an apt and generous speech. With the authority of an infantry captain on those dismal shores, he even praised Churchill's part in the Dardanelles campaign – 'the only imaginative strategic idea of the war'.[16] Relations with Attlee

* 'Wow' was a family word indicating great enthusiasm, I think originating with Sarah Churchill and much used by her. Churchill himself rarely if ever used it, but was certainly familiar with its meaning.
† This was largely due to the fact that he and Churchill had between them shared power for nearly fifteen years. It has been more usual for there to be a full hand of Prime Ministers surviving at any one time. Thirty years back from 1955, in 1925, for example, there were six alive. Thirty years forward in 1985, there was a total change in cast but another six were alive.

were very good during the last year of their two leaderships. The Attlees were invited to all major Downing Street events, both official and private, including not only the evening party for 200 close associates at the end of the November 1954 day of celebration, but also Clementine's seventieth birthday a few months later. In the interval Attlee caused Churchill perverse but understandable satisfaction by fainting 'in my arms' as he somewhat exaggeratedly put it,[17] at a Buckingham Palace dinner for Commonwealth Prime Ministers. Attlee was eight years younger than he was, and the fainting attack gave Churchill a sense of relative fitness, even if not of youth.

Between Churchill's birthday and Christmas there were seven Cabinet meetings, at only two of which Churchill presided, Eden being left to chair the other five. If Churchill was clinging to his responsibilities, he was taking them fairly lightly. On 23 December he went to Chequers. It was the tenth anniversary to the day of his late arrival for Christmas in 1944 and his immediate announcement that he proposed to leave on the next evening for Athens. In 1954 he took his family obligations more seriously. All nine grandchildren, among others, were at Chequers for that last Churchill Christmas in the house, and he stayed there until early January.

Some time early in the New Year of 1955, although with a few subsequent flickerings, Churchill moved towards a semi-settled acceptance of the imminence of resignation. On 22 December the day before he went to Chequers for Christmas, he had been confronted with a 'hanging jury' composed of seven of the most senior members of the Cabinet: Eden, Salisbury, Woolton, Butler, Crookshank, Macmillan and James Stuart (Secretary of State for Scotland and Churchill's wartime Chief Whip). Macmillan wrote of it as 'rather a painful occasion'.[18] The nominal purpose of the meeting was to discuss the date for the next election. But there was a prior question in which everyone was more interested. After a desultory beginning Churchill rounded on the assembled company (according to Eden), and said 'it was clear we wanted him out. Nobody contradicted him. . . . At the end W said menacingly that he would think over what his colleagues had said & let them know his decision. Whatever it was he hoped it would not affect their present relationship with him. Nobody quailed.'[19]

According to Moran Churchill had until then persisted in believing that Macmillan was his best ally. 'Captain of the Praetorian Guard', he once called him. After this meeting it was no longer possible for Churchill to take such a view. On 9 January, indeed, Macmillan took the trouble to invite Moran to lunch and to encourage him to say that Churchill was truly incapable of going on much longer. This defection may have had a powerful effect on Churchill during his Christmas-holiday broodings. By about the date of the Macmillan–Moran luncheon he seemed to have passed through a psychological divide and to have formed a serious, if not necessarily irrevocable, intention to go at the beginning of the Easter recess, which that year fell in early April. In the next week or so this became known in a tight circle, and, as is often the case with tight secrets, those in the know each told one or two, but not more, special confidants. Thus, on 17 January Bracken wrote to inform Beaverbrook. It was very similar to the way in which knowledge of Harold Wilson's 16 March 1976 resignation only marginally seeped out during the previous two or three months.

Twenty-one years earlier, in February 1955, Churchill was much occupied for the first two weeks with the entertainment and mind-moulding of the Commonwealth Prime Ministers. This was the conference in the interstices of which, showing that he could still give as much weight to the present and the future as to the past, he encouraged Jawaharlal Nehru to be 'The Light of Asia'.[20] On 8 February Malenkov was displaced as a result of a Moscow palace revolution and succeeded by a Bulganin–Krushchev dyarchy. Anything which suggested fluidity rekindled Churchill's appetite for summitry, and by the end of the month Butler reported to Macmillan that 'Winston is now trying to run out of his engagement to Anthony.'[21] He may have been so tempted, but in late February there were two developments which gave a better guarantee of his departure than any mere expressions of intent. First, he fixed for 4 April a grand farewell occasion when the Queen and Prince Philip would come to a Downing Street dinner. Second, he began to approach his 1 March speech in the debate introducing the annual Defence White Paper as though it might well be his last will and testament to the House of Commons, fifty-four years after he had first spoken there. So indeed it proved to be, for although he made two more speeches and answered some questions during his last month in office, they were not major orations. And he never spoke again during his nine years of post-Prime Ministerial membership of the House.

The attention he gave to this semi-swansong strongly implied that he realized how definitive it was likely to be. Jane Portal recorded that he spent a total of twenty hours preparing this speech and that 'He dictated it all himself,' a fact of which Miss Portal would have been the most reliable of all witnesses.[22] Did the speech merit the time and trouble? It announced the government's decision to manufacture a British H-bomb, but very much in a context of negotiation from strength. And, contradictory although this may seem to some, the emphasis was somewhat more on negotiation than on strength. In a real sense the British H-bomb, negligible in the East–West strategic balance, was seen as much a lever in dealing with the United States as a weapon against the Soviet Union. And this last Commons speech of Churchill's was notable for at least one unforgettable phrase which illuminated the dreadful prospect like a sheet of lightning on a desolate landscape: 'Which way shall we turn to save our lives and the future of the world? It does not matter so much to old people; they are going soon anyway; but I find it poignant to look at youth in all its activity and ardour . . . and wonder what would lie before them *if God wearied of mankind* [my italics]'. It was striking that a non-believer, at least in any conventional theological sense, should have thought of the most divinely apocalyptic phrase for depicting the terror. He ended after forty-five minutes on a more optimistic and almost too 'onward and upward' a note, although his last seven words were a good epitaph:

> The day may dawn when fair play, love for one's fellow men, respect for justice and freedom, will enable tormented generations to march forth serene and triumphant from the hideous epoch in which we have to dwell. Meanwhile, never flinch, never weary, never despair.[23]

He rarely if ever flinched, but during March he again twice flickered away from resignation on the appointed early-April day. On 11 March, almost as though to cause mischief, Eisenhower announced that he proposed to come to Paris on 8 May, the tenth anniversary of the end of the war with Germany, to endorse alternative arrangements for European defence which had been put together, largely by Eden, after the French rejection of the European Defence Community at the end of August 1954. The possible mischief lay in two sentences which were included in the telegram from Sir Roger Makins, outlining the President's plans. In Paris Eisenhower proposed 'solemnly [to] ratify the agreements in company with President Coty [of France], Adenauer and Sir Winston Churchill'. Moreover he might be prepared to 'lay plans for a meeting with the Soviets in a sustained effort to reduce tensions and the risk of war'.[24]

It was inevitable that these tempting prospects should unsettle Churchill's mind. If all his hopes were to be reopened by a meeting with Eisenhower in Paris on 8 May how could he be expected quietly to resign on 5 April? He began on the morning after he had read the Makins telegram by dictating an unfortunately phrased minute to Eden:

> Makins' tel[egram] is of prime importance. . . . This proposal of a meeting of Heads of Government which he [Eisenhower] would attend himself must be regarded as creating a new situation which will affect our personal plans and time-tables.
>
> It also complicates the question of a May Election to which I gather you are inclining. . . . [This] might be dangerous as it seems to suggest that the Party politics of a snap Election to take advantage of Socialist disunity would be allowed to weigh against a meeting of the Heads of Governments which would give a chance to the world of warding off its mortal peril. The British national reaction to that would not be favourable.[25]

Eden replied with deep affront: 'I was not aware that anything I had done in my public life would justify the suggestion that I was putting Party before country or self before either.'[26] He demanded an early Cabinet on the matter. This took place on the morning of Monday, 14 March, with a frigid atmosphere between Prime Minister and Foreign Secretary. On the substance Eden claimed to be as eager for four-power talks (including the Russians) as was Churchill, but on the handover timetable he was unyielding. When Churchill at one stage mentioned a possible further Eisenhower visit, this time to London in June, Eden coldly asked: 'Does that mean, Prime Minister, that the arrangements you have made with me are at an end?' And, with coldness turning into petulance, he added: 'I have been Foreign Minister for ten years. Am I not to be trusted?'[27] Churchill repulsed the attempt to raise the personal issue by saying that 'this was not a matter on which he required guidance or on which Cabinet discussion was usual'.[28]

Macmillan described the atmosphere in the Cabinet as 'queer'. Those ministers who knew about the promise for 5 April, he wrote, were 'very unhappy'. Those who did not were mystified.[29] That afternoon Churchill had to reply to a vote of censure in the House of Commons. It was not one of his most notable speeches, although, largely because of the rampaging Bevanite row within the Labour party, the government easily survived the attack. The Cabinet next met on Wednesday, 16 March. By that stage a further and clarifying telegram from Makins had arrived. Neither Eisenhower nor Dulles was seriously contemplating talks with the Russians. That let the air out of Churchill's balloon. Macmillan recorded that the Prime Minister 'made a gesture of disappointment' when he heard the news. However, Macmillan also recorded, it meant that 'The Cabinet crisis is over.'[30]

'From now till the "day",' Mary Soames wrote of her father three days later, 'it will be hard going. He minds *so* much. . . . It's the first death.'[31] The issue was complicated by the news of impending resignation beginning at about this stage to seep into the newspapers. What was remarkable was that the secret had until then held so well. Such publicity, however, did not prevent Churchill having one further lurch of indecision. On 27 March Bulganin had hinted that he favoured four-power talks. On the evening of the 28th, after entertaining Butler to a pre-budget dinner, Churchill told Colville that 'there was a crisis: two serious strikes (newspapers and docks); an important Budget; the date of the General Election to be decided; the Bulganin offer. He could not possibly go at such a moment just to satisfy Anthony's personal hunger for power. If necessary he would call a party meeting and let the party decide.'[32]

The consequences of this fresh hesitation were not made easier by the Churchills being engaged the next evening to attend a farewell dinner given in their honour by the Edens. Colville, admittedly only on his own testimony, gave Eden through Anthony Rumbold, his new private secretary, what proved to be a crucially good piece of advice: 'Amiability must the watchword: the Prime Minister thrived on opposition and show-downs, but amiability he could never resist.'[33] Before the dinner Churchill had been to see the Queen and had asked her if she had any objection to his postponing his resignation, to which question 'she had said no'.[34] She probably meant no more than that she did not regard her constitutional duty as extending to adjudicating between him and Eden, but he took it as an endorsement. However, Colville's advice triumphed. During the next day Churchill seems to have dismissed his last daydreams. He summoned Eden and Butler to see him at 6.30. Before they came he told Colville, 'I have been much altered and affected by Anthony's amiable manner.'[35] Then he gave them the definitive news that he would go on 5 April. After that, 'a sad old man', he asked Colville to dine with him. But Colville said that he had to go to the twenty-first birthday of a friend. In the circumstances, that seems one of his very few derelictions of duty during fifteen years of devoted if interrupted service.

There remained little except for the farewell ceremonies. The Churchills had already said goodbye to Chequers on the previous weekend. The final days they spent in Downing Street, Clementine preparing for the royal dinner party (of about fifty) on the Monday. It passed off very well and produced an appealing photograph of Churchill taking leave of the Queen on the doorstep of No. 10. Colville inserted a commentary which provided an antidote to a purely *Hello!* magazine or 'Jennifer's Diary' view of the event:

> the Duchess of Westminster put her foot through Clarissa [Eden's] train. . . . Randolph got drunk and insisted on pursuing Clarissa with a derogatory article about Anthony Eden he had written for *Punch*; Mrs Herbert Morrison [a second and rather Tory wife, not Peter Mandelson's grandmother] became much elated and could scarcely be made to leave the Queen's side. . . .[36]

More significant was Colville's description of Churchill's deflation after they had all gone: 'I went up with Winston to his bedroom. He sat on his bed, still wearing his Garter, Order of Merit and knee-breeches. For several minutes he did not speak and I, imagining that he was sadly contemplating that this was his last night at Downing Street, was silent. Then suddenly he stared at me and said with vehemence: "I don't believe Anthony can do it." '[37]

The next day Churchill held his last and rather formal Cabinet at noon, and went that afternoon, attired as he always was for such royal occasions in one of the last frock coats (as opposed to a cutaway) to be seen in London, to Buckingham Palace formally to resign. There was an extraordinary little charade about the offer of a dukedom. Earldoms had become 'routine' for Prime Ministers (if they wished to become peers) from the time of Lord John Russell a century before. The Queen rightly thought that Churchill rated something more. But she was probably not keen to create the first non-royal duke since Gladstone had elevated Westminster in 1874. Discreet enquiries were therefore made as to whether Churchill could be relied upon to refuse. Assured that he would, she made the offer. He duly refused, but only just. He was tempted, but restrained by his desire to stay in the Commons and perhaps even more by the thought of Randolph succeeding to the strawberry leaves of a ducal coronet, which Churchill politely disguised by pretending that it would interfere with Randolph's already hopeless political career. That corner turned, Churchill left Downing Street for the last time and on the afternoon of 6 April was driven to Chartwell, from where he quickly proceeded to a previously planned Sicilian holiday, accompanied only by Clementine, Cherwell and Colville. It was a small entourage by previous standards. The holiday was not a success, for it rained almost as much as it had done at Chartwell in the previous August. The party returned after two instead of three weeks.

Did Churchill's limpet-like attitude to the surrender of office harm his reputation or his future health and happiness? It would no doubt have been better had he retired in 1953. The first two years of his second government were a considerable success and played a constructive role in the acceptance by the Conservative half of Britain that in the post-war world the clock could not be put back to the 1930s. After that little was accomplished which, as summitry proved a wild-goose chase, could not have been done by others. But the fault in 1953 lay with Eden's illness and with Butler's lack of ruthless thrust. There was no one to push Churchill out. The effect on his reputation, whether domestic or international, was negligible. This was equally the case with his health, which would probably have been best preserved, so far as active life was concerned, by going on until, as Mary Soames put it in March 1955, 'he dropped in his tracks'.[38] The penalty he did perhaps pay for his adhesiveness was that, in retirement, he was less consulted by his one-time subordinate ministers and successors in the top office than he might have been had he gone more easily. That was a small price to set against his forty-seven-year span in Cabinet office and his one great and one better-than-average premiership.

— 46 —

THE SUN SINKS SLOW, HOW SLOWLY

OF THE EIGHTY-YEAR-OLD Prime Ministers, Palmerston was the luckiest. He died in office on 18 October 1865, two days short of his eighty-first birthday. Although not perfect, his health had been good for one of his age and period over the preceding summer, and in July he had won a general election. He liked climbing (until very recently vaulting) over railings, to demonstrate his continuing agility, and in the first week of October he had surmounted one at Brocket, his wife's Hertfordshire house. On the twelfth of the month, after a carriage drive, he was struck down by a fever, but during his four and a half days of illness rallied enough to enjoy a breakfast of mutton chops and port.

Gladstone, leaving office nearly four years older than Churchill and dying a year and a half younger than him, had a fairly miserable fifty months of retirement. He was half deaf and half blind. The deafness Churchill shared with him, but not the blindness. Churchill could and did read occasional books – mostly novels – until close to the end. In his final period Gladstone became as addicted to the South of France as Churchill had been throughout his life. Gladstone spent on aggregate nearly a year of his retirement in the Cannes villa of a rich acolyte. He was also taken on a cruise by a shipping magnate, although the host and the destinations – Hamburg, Kiel and Copenhagen – were less exotic than Churchill's excursions with Aristotle Onassis. For the last year of his life Gladstone was afflicted with terrible pain, from a cancer of the cheek. Churchill was spared any such agony. On the other hand Gladstone was sustained by a lively and literal religious faith, which except in the sense of a vague faith in a supreme being Churchill did not possess. Neither Gladstone's Apostolic certainties nor Churchill's mild Erastianism gave them much sense of purpose in life once temporal power had been sloughed off.

Churchill's ten-year retirement was long for one who had held power so late in life. It fell into three parts. There was the period up to and over the 1959 general election, which included his last publishing task, one or two notable speeches, and a semi-official American visit in which, as so often before, he was invited to stay at the White House. During those four and a half years his capacities, physical and mental, were not very different from what they had been during the post-1953-stroke phase of his premiership. Then there were the next two and a half years until in June 1962, at the age of eighty-seven, he fell in the Hôtel de Paris in Monte Carlo and broke his hip. He was flown home to the Middlesex Hospital and incarcerated there for three weeks. In the second phase he had devoted himself to getting what pleasure he could out of the fag end of his life, in which process cruises in Onassis's luxurious yacht had played a dominant role. After the summer of 1962 it was mainly a question of waiting, more or less patiently, for the end, which came after another two and a half years.

At the beginning of the first of these phases and following the unsuccessful Sicilian trip Churchill stayed in England mostly at Chartwell but sometimes in Hyde Park Gate, for the late spring and summer of 1955. The general election campaign filled most of May, but it did not fill Churchill's life. A little to his dismay he discovered that Eden, after so long a wait, wanted to establish his own unchallenged authority, and that he was not expected to play any central role. There was no suggestion of Churchill giving one of the Conservative broadcasts. He spoke only four times during the three weeks of the campaign. Two of these speeches were in his own constituency, a third in Bedford for Christopher Soames, and the fourth in West Walthamstow (outer London) where a former chairman of the Woodford Young Conservatives succeeded in overturning a narrow Labour majority and achieving one of the twenty-odd Conservative gains which underpinned Eden's position.

Churchill was mainly occupied with putting his *History of the English-Speaking Peoples* into final shape. It had been nominally completed, in spite of the complaints of Cassells about its abrupt end with the American Civil War, by the outbreak of war in 1939. But it had then been a hurried job and time had since moved on. He therefore supervised a very considerable recasting. Alan Hodge, the joint founding editor of *History Today*, was his chief agent for the task, although Denis Kelly, the shadowy figure who had first come to Chartwell to assemble documents for *The Second World War*, was also employed. Outside academics were flattered to be asked to help, and the rhythm of the enterprise was well captured by Hodge's wife when she reminisced that 'Immense drafts were turned in by J. H. Plumb and other historians and worked over by Churchill and Alan.'[1] Churchill did not have to work with anything like the intensity that he had applied to his pre-war bookwriting and journalism, or even to his late 1940s construction of his war memoirs. But the task provided him with some gentle intellectual exercise for the next two years, particularly in the South of France, by the end of which time the last of the four volumes was ready for the publishers.

By no stretch of the imagination was it the best of Churchill's books. But it sold well, and was highly profitable to both publisher and author. The British sales alone of the first volume were 130,000 on the first printing, with subsequent ones (of that edition) of another 90,000. This was entitled *The Birth of Britain* and took the story up to 1485. The subsequent three volumes – *The New World*, which covered two centuries of the Tudors and the Stuarts, *The Age of Revolution*, which took the story up to 1815, and *The Great Democracies*, which although he advanced from the original terminus of Abraham Lincoln, still did not go beyond 1900, for Churchill said he had no taste for writing about 'the woe and ruin of the terrible twentieth century'[2] – all started with a print-run of 150,000, but with fewer early reprints than in the case of volume one.

When the new 1955 Parliament met on 7 June Churchill advanced rather unsteadily to his new unofficial corner seat on the front bench below the gangway and got himself sworn in early. But although he occasionally voted he never spoke either in the four and a half years of that parliament or the five years of the next. Once, in July 1958, after the Iraq revolution and the murder of the King and Prime Minister, he prepared quite elaborate notes for a speech, but then decided that he had nothing to say which made it worth while to break his silence. He nonetheless delivered a number of successful outside addresses. In June of that first year out of office he spoke at the unveiling in the (London) Guildhall of a striking full-length statue of himself. It was by Oscar Nemon, a Jewish refugee from Yugoslavia who subsequently made something of a speciality of Churchill, producing several 'heads'.

In the month before Christmas 1955, Churchill made five speeches, two political ones in Woodford; one on his sixteenth consecutive visit to Harrow School Songs; and two in the City of London. Then in the following May he went to Aachen to receive the Charlemagne Prize and on that great European occasion made a far from platitudinous speech. He warned the West Germans that, if they too strenuously sought unification with Russian-occupied East Germany, it might be 'a unity of ashes and death'. This was not far off the private thoughts of Chancellor

Adenauer, who was much more interested in the integration of the Federal Republic into a Carolingian western Europe than in uniting with a Protestant and maybe socialist-voting East Germany. But it was nonetheless a hard doctrine to preach on a German ceremonial occasion.

These sporadic speeches combined with finishing off *The English-Speaking Peoples* left Churchill with plenty of time for boredom and even for loneliness. Although he had suffered yet another arterial spasm on 2 June, which made it temporarily difficult for him to hold his cigar – a serious deprivation – his health, despite his extra ten years, was on the whole better than Clementine's during that summer of 1955. 'Neuritis', as it was then called, was her great trouble, and on 4 August she flew to Switzerland, hoping that a special St Moritz cure would help her 'laborious effort to regain my health'.[3] This left Churchill semi-alone at Chartwell until he went to the South of France on 15 September. He had a lot of visitors, including such nostalgic ones as Pamela Lytton and Violet Bonham Carter, as well as a twenty-four-hour descent from the Edens (to whom he referred in a letter to Clementine as 'Anthony and Cleopatra'),[4] but he was also reduced to having seventeen dinners alone with the then thirty-two-year-old Anthony Montague Browne, which must have been a strain for both of them.

Montague Browne, who had been an assistant private secretary for Churchill's last two and a half years in Downing Street, had been re-seconded to him from the Foreign Service by decision of the new Foreign Secretary, Harold Macmillan, in mid-June (1955). It was thought that for a year or two, while Churchill still had a semi-diplomatic world role, Browne would help to steer him through such delicate waters. In fact he stayed for more than nine and a half years until Churchill's death, broadening his service from being a diplomatic counsellor to being the indispensable organizer of every aspect of Churchill's life. The arrangement ruined Browne's diplomatic career, but it greatly mitigated the trials of Churchill's last years. Montague Browne accompanied him almost everywhere, drafted his speeches and his letters, decided whom he wanted to see and whom he did not, as well as endeavouring to pick up any pieces of broken social china which Churchill left lying around. His salary was paid by Churchill and not by the Foreign Office, although he was kept on the Foreign Service list.

The most critical events which occurred during Churchill's first and most politically aware phase of retirement were the Anglo-French invasion of Suez at the beginning of November 1956 and the consequences which flowed from it. Churchill was in the South of France recovering from one of his small strokes until 28 October. Five days later, on request, he issued a statement of support for the action of the Eden government. He could hardly have done otherwise, for between 1951 and 1955 one of the most persistent issues of policy dispute between him and Eden had been his view that Eden was adopting too conciliatory an attitude to the Egyptian regimes of Neguib and Nassar. In his statement he had expressed his confidence that 'our American friends will come to realize that, not for the first time, we have acted independently for the common good'.[5]

He therefore neither had nor claimed to have any moral scruples about the Suez enterprise. He was however deeply shocked both by its being called off almost as soon as it had started and by the rupture with the Americans to which it led. For knowledge of his evolving attitude we are dependent upon subsequent conversations reported by Colville and Moran. The latter are subject to the reservations earlier expressed. On 29 November Colville asked Churchill whether, had he still been Prime Minister, he would have acted as Eden had done. His reply was: 'I would never have dared; and if I had dared, I would certainly never have dared stop.'[6] He added that in his view the operation was 'the most ill-conceived and ill-executed imaginable'.[7] Moran's testimony was that, on 26 November, Churchill expressed shock at Eden having retreated on health grounds for a West Indian rest, and said: 'I'd like to see Harold Macmillan Prime Minister.'[8] And then, on 6 December, he told Moran (as often from this source, the words but not the sentiment are unconvincing): 'Of course, one can't tell what one would have done, but one thing is certain, I wouldn't have done anything without consulting the Americans.'[9] When the sad adventure was over Churchill did everything he could, through letters to Eisenhower and on his visit to the White House two years later, to repair the damage to Anglo-American relations.

Churchill remained in England over the collapse of Eden's premiership in early January 1957. Montague Browne was worried that, as the succession hovered between Butler and Macmillan, Churchill was not being consulted. Other senior statesmen were known to have been called to Buckingham Palace to advise but not the most senior of all. Browne therefore telephoned Sir Michael Adeane, the Queen's principal secretary, who, superficially at least, had some of the qualities of an irascible major, and at first got a brush-off. Then Adeane offered to come to Chartwell and relay Churchill's views. No, Browne said, that would not do. Churchill must be *seen* to be consulted. Adeane gave way, and Churchill got out his top hat (which he found shabby) and his frock coat to proceed to a publicized audience. So the proprieties were observed, which was a tribute to Browne's persistence on behalf of his master, although not, it may be thought, a necessary prop to Churchill's prestige at that stage in his life.

Montague Browne's role was in general much more directed to saving Churchill from engagements than to forcing them upon him. The travelling-companion aspect of his duties became increasingly important, for Churchill's tastes, always inclined to a mixture of sun and luxury, turned more and more to the South of France and to Mediterranean – and occasionally Caribbean – cruises. Chartwell continued as his more frequent English base, although with Hyde Park Gate perhaps gaining over it as the years went by. At Chartwell, with his building and hydraulic works long since complete, with his last book finished and with his agricultural activities abandoned – the two outlying farms were sold in October 1957 – there was little left to do except gaze at the Weald of Kent. One of his last remaining English recreational interests was to see his racehorses run. They mostly lost, but not always. He came to prefer a seascape on which the sun at least sometimes shone, although he wrote many complaints about the uncertain Provençal winter weather. The Riviera life was based on two villas and, latterly, one hotel. The cruise life was based on one man and one quite small (less than 2,000 tons) but extravagently comfortable boat.

The first of the two villas was Beaverbrook's La Capponcina at Cap d'Ail. In 1939 Beaverbrook had bought this property, set on a rocky promontory about two miles west of Monte Carlo, from Captain Edward Molyneux, by which military designation that dress designer liked to be known. Beaverbrook had retrieved it more or less intact at the end of the war and was able to keep it lavishly functioning on his Canadian resources during the most stringent periods of British currency restrictions. Churchill had first visited La Capponcina in the summer of 1949, after a period of semi-estrangement from Beaverbrook. He might have been expected not to have the happiest memories of the place, for he had there experienced the first of his strokes, and been confined to the house for an extra week under the care of Lord Moran, who had been sent for and issued suitably misleading bulletins.

Despite this discouraging history, La Capponcina it was the scene of Churchill's first retirement visit to the South of France. He went there on 15 September (1955) and stayed – much longer than he had intended – until 15 November. He was accompanied at first by Clementine, who had come from Switzerland, and the Soameses, as well as by his regular small domestic entourage. Later not only his daughter Sarah, but Hodge and Kelly came out, and some fairly serious work on the *History* was done. Churchill was also still painting. Beaverbrook was not there, but he had left his excellent cook and other domestic staff. The Churchills went to La Capponcina for two other extended stays, including cele- brating their Golden Wedding anniversary there in September 1958. Churchill habitually stayed much longer than Clementine. Later, in the early 1960s, when he had removed his South of France base to the Hôtel de Paris at Monte Carlo, he took to visiting the garden of La Capponcina in the afternoons, doing some of his last paintings or just sitting in the sun.

Beaverbrook's villa, although rarely his presence, was therefore an important base for both the early and the late stages of Churchill's Riviera repose. But in the middle it was heavily superseded by another house, about ten miles away at Roquebrune, to the east of Monte Carlo. This villa was La Pausa, which had been built by Churchill's old friend Bendor, Duke of Westminster for Coco Chanel, and had been acquired only in 1954 by Emery Reves. Reves was back in France, from where he had syndicated Churchill's newspaper articles in the late 1930s, but as a very much richer man. His wealth had enabled him not only to buy La Pausa but to embellish it with paintings and furniture of the highest quality. As much of the wealth came from his highly profitable market- ing of Churchill's post-war writings there was a certain poetic justice in Churchill sharing the elegant luxury which it produced, and this between early 1956 and late 1959 he abundantly did.

On 26 Otober (1955) he wrote to Clementine from La Capponcina: 'I am bidden tomorrow to lunch with Reves and Madame R. at the St Pol Restaurant. . . . I will look at the Matisse Chapel after lunch.'[10] So the renewed acquaintance with the Reveses (Madame R was not Mrs Reves but Wendy Russell at that stage, although they were married less than a year later) began with a suitable mixture of gastron- omy and art. It ripened so rapidly that, when Churchill next went to the South of France on 11 January 1956, it was to La Pausa that he went. He stayed for a month and then returned for another eleven substantial visits during the next three and a half years, a total of fifty- four weeks.

He was made an immensely welcome guest, at least as much by Wendy as by Emery Reves. The central purpose of the Reveses' lives became the entertainment of Churchill. He was allowed to bring whoever he wanted with him – daughters, secretaries, valets, detectives, Lord Cherwell and even his publisher, Desmond Flower. And the Reveses would ask whom he wanted, and nobody he did not, to luncheons or dinners. Meal guests varying from the Windsors to Rab Butler and Paul Reynaud came over the years. But Churchill was mostly content with a quiet, almost domestic regime, broken by occasional excursions to grand restaurants or casinos. After his first three weeks at La Pausa he wrote about that pattern of life in almost infatuated terms:

> I spend the days mostly in bed, & get up for lunch and dinner. I am being taken through a course of Manet, Monet, Cézanne & Co by my hosts who are both versed in modern painting, and practise in the studio. . . . Also they have a wonderful form of gramophone wh. plays continuously Mozart and other composers of merit, and anything else you like on 10-fold discs. I am in fact having an artistic education with vy agreeable tutors.[11]

In the same letter he accepted with regret that Clementine, who had caught an infection in University College Hospital and been forced to remain there for three weeks, would not join him: 'I had hoped to persuade you to come out and convalesce out here & that you would meet Wendy who is a vy charming person. But I feel that with Sylvia [Henley] & the Ceylon sun your plan is a good one. . . .'*[12] Clementine was difficult to lure to La Pausa. There was an attempt to get her to come at the end of Churchill's second visit, when her ship, returning from Ceylon, docked at Marseille. But she thought the problems of packing tired clothes before disembarkation too great, and proceeded direct to England. She came only once to La Pausa, at the beginning of Churchill's third visit, in June 1956, and stayed no more than four days, leaving him (and Sarah) for another ten. Wendy's charm proved to be either too much or of the wrong sort for Clementine. She preserved the convenances and wrote several polite letters of regret and thanks 'for the affection and care you lavish upon Winston'.[13] But Lady Churchill's own affection for Mrs Reves was very limited, and while she probably did not have strong views one way or the other about Emery Reves, she did not wish to be a guest at La Pausa. By comparison, Beaverbrook's La Capponcina, particularly when he was not there, became an acceptable haven.

---

* Clementine went with her cousin Mrs Henley on a commercial cruise boat to Indian Ocean waters.

Out of Clementine's distaste, or maybe out of Churchill's own over-enthusiastic indulgence, there came the collapse of the idyll of La Pausa in 1959. In the meantime, however, there developed his cruising life, which was both a competitor to the attractions of La Pausa and a cause of the rupture with the Reveses. Furthermore, just as the pull of La Pausa developed out of an encounter during his 1955 La Capponcina visit, so the pull of Aristotle Onassis and of his yacht *Christina* began during Churchill's initial visit to La Pausa. Onassis's first appearance in the Churchill archive was on 17 January 1956 when Churchill wrote to Clementine: 'Randolph brought Onassis (the one with the big yacht) to dinner last night. He made a good impression upon me . . . & told us a bit about whales. He kissed my hand!'[14] Later on during that La Pausa visit Churchill and the Reveses dined on board *Christina*. Thereafter there was a fairly regular exchange of lunching or dining visits whenever Churchill was at Roquebrune, although it took another two and a half years before a full-scale cruise was arranged. In the meantime Churchill found Onassis entertaining – 'He was vy lively,' he wrote after one dinner[15] – and also very helpful. Churchill was nominally looking for a house of his own on the Riviera. How serious was this intention is open to question. In view of the eagerness of others to entertain him and of his liking for undemanding company it would seem to have made no sense. He was worried at first that he might be a burden at La Pausa, although his subsequent eleven visits suggest that his doubts on this score were quickly set at rest. But he went on vaguely looking for a year or so. Probably the nearest he came to an arrangement was for the Société de Bains de Mer of Monte Carlo to raze an old villa on a promontory above their Beach Hotel and to build a new one to Churchill's specifications, which they would rent to him for *circa* £1,500 a year. The controlling shareholder in the Société, which ran the Hôtel de Paris and the Casino as well as the Beach Hotel, was Aristotle Onassis. However, nothing came of the plan, and Churchill wisely settled down to be a perpetual guest.

The first *Christina* cruise, although it had been exhaustively discussed since the previous January, did not take place until September 1958. There was trouble about the guest list. Onassis had asked for guidance and was told that he should ask whoever he thought appropriate. Not realizing that this was the equivalent of Henry Ford telling his customers that they could have any model they liked provided it was black, Onassis asked the Duke and Duchess of Windsor and the Reveses. Churchill vetoed the Windsors. He had never recovered his opinion of that 'empty man' after 1940, and he also thought that their presence would involve a lot of 'jumping up and down'.[16] Clementine vetoed the Reveses. She would not come if they did. Churchill was determined that she should, so Montague Browne was set to deliver the ukase to Onassis. The Windsors appear to have taken it better than the Reveses. They got the story out of Onassis. It not unnaturally ignited a fire of resentment. But it was a slow burn. During 1959 Churchill paid another two visits to La Pausa. Then, having gone to stay at the Hôtel de Paris in January 1960, he again proposed himself to La Pausa for a September stay. This produced the most pained and painful refusal from Reves:

Your telegram suggesting to come to Pausaland [a poignant reminder of Churchill's affectionate name for the house when all was well] on the 6th September was a great surprise for us. Since last winter when you declined our repeated and even persistent invitation and went to the Hôtel de Paris we have been convinced that you had decided not to come back to us. We could understand that cruises had a greater attraction to you than our villa, but we could not interpret your decision to stay at a hotel rather than at Pausaland in any other way than that we had done something, or behaved in a manner which prevented you from returning to us. . . .

Our, perhaps foolish, dream was that during 1956, 1957 and 1958 . . . we had become friends. Both Wendy and I are devoted and dedicated to the idea of friendship which is for us the only real joy in life.

You cannot imagine how shocked we were when two years ago we suddenly remarked that all kinds of intrigue started destroying this friendship. . . . It is not possible for me to describe the humiliations and suffering we had to endure. . . . During the past two years Wendy has suffered deeply and dangerously from mental depressions. There is a certain way of disregarding other people's feelings which drives sensitive human beings to the borders of insanity. I am fully aware that all of this was not intended, and that you were a victim, perhaps even more than we were. . . . During my long life I developed the capacity to end a big cry with laughter and to-day I can only smile at the past two years. . . . But Wendy is not yet capable to master a deep emotional stress and her wounds are still open. She is a different woman, disillusioned and unbelieving. The doctors warned me most seriously to let her live a quiet life and to protect her from any possible emotional stress. . . . In October we are planning to go to New York. So this year, unfortunately, I cannot invite you. . . .[17]

This terrible letter, stemming from a supposed rejection of friendship built too high to last, hinted at things other than the Reveses' exclusion

from the cruise or Churchill preferring the Hôtel de Paris.* The
'intrigues' which had 'started destroying the friendship' probably related
to occasional complaints by Clementine that the Reveses were too fond
of attracting press publicity for themselves via Churchill and to Riviera
gossip, in which the Singer Sewing Machine heiress Mrs Reggie Fellowes played a prominent part, that Churchill had become besotted by
the over-cosseting charms of Wendy.

The letter might have been expected to have a devastating effect
upon Churchill, but, perhaps happily, he was past being devastated by
any emotional upset unless it involved a much longer-standing member
of his 'family' than Wendy or Emery Reves. After a gap of a month
Clementine wrote a cool but polite letter of acknowledgement and
regret to Emery Reves, asking them to lunch in Monte Carlo. Churchill
calmly took up his new quarters in a penthouse at the top of the Hôtel
de Paris. There was no complete rupture with the Reveses. Emery had
switched in his bitter missive to messages of esteem and of 'longing to
see you again'. Occasional meetings did take place, and Reves called
upon Churchill in London as late as June, 1964. But, so far from it ever
being 'glad confident morning' again, no more than the dank chill of a
late autumn twilight was achieved.

Reves was right in thinking that Churchill had come to prefer cruises.
To resurrect Lloyd George's words of nearly fifty years before, he had
again become a 'water creature'. In spite of its inauspicious beginning,
this first expedition with Onassis on board *Christina* was a great success
and was followed by no fewer than seven others between Churchill's
eighty-fourth and eighty-ninth years. The first started in Monte Carlo
and went via Majorca and Tangier and up the Guadalquivir river to
Seville, and then back to Gibraltar, from where the Churchills flew
home. The guests who had survived the purge were a curious collection:
Loel Guinness (an undistinguished Tory MP for Bath from 1931 to
1945, who had been a brave airman during the war) and his Mexican
third wife; Montague Browne and his wife; Tito Arias, the Panamanian
who was married to Margot Fonteyn and whom Onassis used as an
international lawyer; Theodore Garafilides, a Greek surgeon whose

---

* Reves himself (aged fifty-four) had suffered a severe heart attack at the end of August
1959, from which he took some months to recover. This may have influenced
Churchill's decision to go to the hotel rather than to La Pausa for his winter visit
(starting on 2 January 1960), although Clementine's intention to come with him was
probably a more potent factor.

medical skills were a less important qualification (even though the facilities of *Christina* included an operating theatre) than that his wife – also present – was Onassis's sister; and of course 'Ari' himself, as well as Tina Livanos (later becoming Churchill's kinswoman by marrying – for ten years – the eleventh Duke of Marlborough when he was Marquess of Blandford).

With this heterogeneous company the Churchills both seemed content. Clementine liked shipboard life and Churchill liked Onassis, who had an almost chemical knack of attracting his interest and indeed of interpreting his words to an assembled company. This Greek, born in Turkey, who had become an Argentinian citizen although living mostly in Monaco, seemed towards the end both to understand what Churchill was trying to say and to penetrate his deafness better than anyone else. There is a curious description of Onassis performing this role at a meeting of the Other Club in November 1962. Churchill had made him a member, despite some raising of eyebrows.* At his first meeting he sat between Churchill and Selwyn Lloyd, then a recently dismissed Chancellor of the Exchequer and ex-Foreign Secretary. 'The result was that, with this odd interpreter, Selwyn Lloyd had [with Churchill] quite a substantial talk about the Middle East.'[18]

On two of the seven further cruises the party crossed the Atlantic. The first of these (spring 1960) was purely Caribbean, but the second (spring 1961) proceeded up the east coast of the United States to anchor, during a great storm, in the Hudson River. On this latter occasion Adlai Stevenson (a persistent favourite), escorted by Marietta Tree, the second wife of Churchill's old Ditchley host, Ronald Tree, braved the elements to come aboard and dine. There was also a pressing invitation from the newly installed President Kennedy for Churchill to come to Washington and stay in the White House. Montague Browne refused this without consultation, believing that Churchill would be tempted but was no longer capable of acquitting himself as a rewarding guest in such circumstances. Four of the other five cruises were in central and eastern Mediterranean waters, embracing meals with Marshal Tito and with Konstantinos Karamanlis, the Prime Minister of Greece both before and after the Colonels.

The shipboard company, with a fairly constant Onassis family core, occasionally took in Lord and Lady Moran, the Colvilles, Diana Sandys,

---

* However, there was no real reason for complaint; he attended only twice and left the club well endowed with champagne.

Margot Fonteyn (a considerable success), Maria Callas (much less of a success), Lee Radziwill, who as Jacqueline Kennedy's sister provided the only window of the Churchill cruise years on to Onassis's future marriage and, on the last foray down the Dalmatian coast, Randolph Churchill, whose proximity to his father ended as usual in a colossal row.

The Onassis relationship, unlike the Reves one, did not end in tears. It just subsided, mainly because Churchill himself, after the June 1963 date of this final cruise, was in a state of quiet but not happy subsidence. During his 'Onassis period' Churchill had managed to fight, or more accurately to be a candidate, at the October 1959 election. He spoke only three times, twice in Woodford and once again in Walthamstow, somewhat inaudibly and with texts prepared by Montague Browne. Probably he ought not to have stood again. He had however survived a last Washington visit (both ways by air) in the spring of that year, when he had been Eisenhower's guest for three days. The Woodford Conservative Association were acquiescent rather than enthusiastic, the local electorate somewhat less so. At an election which increased the Conservative Commons majority from 54 to 100, Churchill's own majority fell by a thousand. It was natural that some of those who had not lived in their candidate's great past should be unenthusiastic about re-electing a member who never spoke in the House and could soon enter it only in a wheelchair.

More constructively, a week after the campaign he went to Cambridge to plant a commemorative tree and lay the foundation stone of the new Churchill College. Sir John Cockcroft, a nuclear physicist who combined in almost equal proportions academic repute and practical administrative experience (he had been director of the Atomic Energy Research Establishment at Harwell for twelve years), had just been appointed the first Master. The idea of Churchill College had arisen from discussions with Cherwell and Colville during the otherwise ill-fated holiday in Sicily immediately after Churchill's resignation. It was intended to provide a British answer to the Massachusetts Institute of Technology. Colville was very successful in raising the money (including £50,000 from the Transport and General Workers' Union). The college now stands as one of Cambridge's small cluster of post-war colleges. It has perhaps been more famous for sheltering the vast Churchill archive than for improving British technology.

A significant step in Churchill's slow decline was marked by a fall from his bed in late June 1962 which broke his thigh. This took place in his familiar penthouse in the Hôtel de Paris, and was highly disagreeable. He lay on the floor unable to move until he was found an hour later by one of the nurses who now accompanied him. Montague Browne reported that later that day Churchill insisted that he wanted to die in England.[19] An RAF Comet was sent to bring him back. From Northolt he was taken to the Middlesex Hospital, where he had to remain for many weeks.

It was a widely held view that he was never the same after this experience. But this was true of the many stages of decline through which he was alleged to have passed, beginning with his severe bronchial infection in Tunis over eighteen years before. This time, however, there was no subsequent upsurge. Churchill lived another two and a half years, but there was even more twilight in them than in the immediately previous period. He went back to Monte Carlo and the Hôtel de Paris once; he made his last Onassis cruise; he was created an honorary citizen of the United States (the first since Lafayette) but could not attend his installation; he was intermittently present in the House of Commons until the end of July 1964; he visited Chartwell for the last time in October of that year and did not again leave London; he quietly celebrated his ninetieth birthday on 30 November of that year; and he somnolently attended dinners of the Other Club until 10 December.

Christmas was as quiet as his birthday had been. On 12 January 1965 he suffered his last and most severe stroke. In the twelve days between then and his death there were many solicitous callers at Hyde Park Gate, ranging from Violet Bonham Carter, probably his oldest living friend and the relict of the Prime Minister under whom he had first sat in Cabinet, to Harold Wilson, who, newly in that office, was anxious to make his obeisance to his eminent predecessor. On the morning of Sunday, 24 January Churchill died. By a macabre coincidence it was the seventieth anniversary of the death of his father.

The funeral was six days later, the coffin having lain in state in Westminster Hall for the preceding three days. It was the first time since Gladstone in 1898 that any non-royal personage had been so treated. Gladstone's funeral had been the first great state burial since the Duke of Wellington's in 1852. Churchill's was the last in the British tradition of imperial ceremony. His funeral, like Wellington's but unlike Gladstone's, was in St Paul's Cathedral not Westminster Abbey. This offered more processional opportunities, enhanced by the coffin after the service being taken by boat along the Thames for transfer to Waterloo Station and transit by special train and special route for burial in Bladon churchyard on the edge of Blenheim Park.

Of more importance than a comparison of the different obsequies is a judgement between Gladstone, undoubtedly the greatest Prime Minister of the nineteenth century, and Churchill, undoubtedly the greatest of the twentieth century. When I started writing this book I thought that Gladstone was, by a narrow margin, the greater man, certainly the more remarkable specimen of humanity. In the course of writing it I have changed my mind. I now put Churchill, with all his idiosyncrasies, his indulgences, his occasional childishness, but also his genius, his tenacity and his persistent ability, right or wrong, successful or unsuccessful, to be larger than life, as the greatest human being ever to occupy 10 Downing Street.

References

CV refers to the series of *Companion Volumes* to the official biography, *Winston S. Churchill*, by Randolph Churchill and Martin Gilbert. From 1939, these volumes are rechristened *The Churchill War Papers* (referred to here as *War Papers*), of which three volumes, up to the end of 1941 only, have so far been published.

1. A DOUBTFUL PROVENANCE

1 David Cannadine, essay in Blake and Louis (eds), *Churchill*, p. 11
2 *CV*, I, pt 1, pp. 1–2
3 Winston S. Churchill, *Lord Randolph Churchill*, I, p. 44
4 *CV*, I, pt 1, p. 12
5 Winston S. Churchill, *My Early Life*, p. 19
6 *CV*, I, pt 1, pp. 78–160 *passim*
7 *Ibid.*, pp. 210–19 *passim*
8 *Ibid.*, p. 221
9 *Ibid.*, p. 207
10 *Ibid.*, p. 226
11 Information from Randolph Churchill via the late Lord Harris of Greenwich
12 Foster, *Lord Randolph Churchill*, p. 222
13 *Ibid.*, p. 130, quoting from a letter of Salisbury's to Lady John Manners
14 Queen Victoria's Journal, 25 July 1886, Royal Archives, Windsor
15 John Grigg, essay in Blake and Louis (eds), *Churchill*, pp. 97–8
16 Winston S. Churchill, *My Early Life*, pp. 30–1
17 *Ibid.*, p. 36
18 *Ibid.*, pp. 39–40
19 *Ibid.*, p. 76

2. Subaltern of Empire and Journalist of Opportunity

1 Winston S. Churchill, *My Early Life*, p. 118
2 *CV*, I, pt 2, p. 725
3 *Ibid.*, pp. 730 and 733
4 *Ibid.*, p. 726
5 *Ibid.*, p. 719
6 *Ibid.*, p. 734
7 *Ibid.*, p. 751
8 *Bath Daily Chronicle*, 27 July 1897
9 *CV*, I, pt 2, pp. 740–1
10 *Ibid.*, p. 743
11 *Ibid.*, pp. 751–2
12 Winston S. Churchill, *Thoughts and Adventures*, p. 32
13 *CV*, I, pt 1, p. 599
14 *Ibid.*, p. 597
15 Winston S. Churchill, *My Early Life*, p. 136
16 *Ibid.*, p. 137
17 *Ibid.*, pp. 137–8
18 *CV*, I, pt 2, p. 927
19 *Ibid.*, p. 930
20 Newman, *Idea of a University*, pp. 234–9
21 Winston S. Churchill, *Savrola*, p. 27
22 *Ibid.*, p. 28
23 *Ibid.*, p. 43
24 Balfour, *Foundations of Belief*, p. 19
25 Winston S. Churchill, *Savrola*, p. 47
26 *Ibid.*, p. 42
27 *CV*, I, pt 2, p. 971
28 *Ibid.*, p. 942
29 *Ibid.*, p. 870
30 *Ibid.*, p. 868
31 *Ibid.*, p. 906
32 *Ibid.*, p. 948
33 *Ibid.*, p. 952
34 *Ibid.*, p. 949
35 Winston S. Churchill, *My Early Life*, p. 182
36 *CV*, I, pt 2, p. 970
37 *Ibid.*, p. 979

38 Anglesey, *History of the British Cavalry*, III, p. 385
39 *CV*, I, pt 2, p. 979
40 Anglesey, *History of the British Cavalry*, III, p. 388
41 Winston S. Churchill, *My Early Life*, p. 211
42 *CV*, I, pt 2, p. 1015
43 *Ibid.*, p. 1012
44 *Ibid.*, p. 1003
45 *CV*, I, pt 2, p. 1017
46 *Ibid.*, p. 1019
47 *Ibid.*, p. 1017
48 *Ibid.*, pp. 1019–20
49 *Ibid.*, p. 1023

3. Oldham and South Africa

1 *CV*, I, pt 2, p. 1028
2 *Ibid.*, p. 1035
3 *Ibid.*, p. 1029
4 Winston S. Churchill, *My Early Life*, p. 237
5 *Ibid.*, p. 239
6 *Ibid.*, p. 240
7 *Ibid.*, pp. 240–1
8 *CV*, I, pt 2, p. 1052
9 Winston S. Churchill, *My Early Life*, pp. 257–8
10 *Ibid.*, p. 266
11 *CV*, I, pt 2, p. 1077
12 *Ibid.*, p. 1085
13 *Ibid.*, p. 1075
14 *Ibid.*, p. 1086
15 Winston S. Churchill, *My Early Life*, p. 319
16 *CV*, I, pt 2, p. 1091
17 *Ibid.*, p. 1090
18 *Ibid.*, pp. 1104, 1110 and 1115
19 *Ibid.*, pp. 1101–2
20 Sandys, *Churchill: Wanted Dead or Alive*, pp. 129–31
21 Winston S. Churchill, *My Early Life*, p. 319
22 *CV*, I, pt 2, p. 1147
23 *Ibid.*, p. 1143
24 *Ibid.*, p. 1164

4. Tory into Liberal

1 Winston S. Churchill, *My Early Life*, p. 373
2 *Letters of Theodore Roosevelt*, *passim*
3 Information from Professor Arthur M. Schlesinger Jr
4 *CV*, I, pt 2, p. 1224
5 *Ibid.*, p. 1225
6 *Ibid.*, p. 1228
7 *Ibid.*, p. 1225
8 Hansard, 4th Series, vol. 39, cols 407–15
9 Randolph S. Churchill, *Winston S. Churchill*, II, p. 15
10 Hansard, 4th Series, vol. 39, cols 1562–79
11 *CV*, II, pt 1, pp. 69–70
12 Winston S. Churchill, *My Early Life*, p. 383
13 Hansard, 5th Series, vol. 28, col. 1470
14 Winston S. Churchill, *My Early Life*, p. 385
15 Randolph S. Churchill, *Winston S. Churchill*, II, p. 51
16 *Ibid.*, p. 33
17 Winston S. Churchill, *Lord Randolph Churchill*, I, pp. 283–4
18 Randolph S. Churchill, *Winston S. Churchill*, II, p. 36
19 *Ibid.*, p. 31
20 *CV*, II, pt 1, p. 113
21 *Ibid.*, pp. 174–5
22 *Ibid.*, p. 184
23 *Ibid.*, pp. 242–4
24 Randolph S. Churchill, *Winston S. Churchill*, II, pp. 72–4
25 *Ibid.*, p. 75
26 *Ibid.*, p. 88
27 *Ibid.*, pp. 89–90
28 Hansard, 4th Series, vol. 132, cols 1028–9
29 *Ibid.*, vol. 133, cols 958–1001

5. Convert into Minister

1 *CV*, II, pt 1, pp. 164–5
2 *Ibid.*, p. 225
3 *Ibid.*, p. 371
4 Randolph S. Churchill, *Winston S. Churchill*, II, p. 161

5 Chilston MSS, Kent County Record Office, Maidstone
6 *CV*, II, pt 1, p. 341
7 *Ibid.*, p. 219
8 *Ibid.*, p. 311
9 *Ibid.*, pp. 392–3
10 *Ibid.*, p. 327
11 Hansard, 4th Series, vol. 92, cols 1577–9
12 Randolph S. Churchill, *Winston S. Churchill*, II, p. 99
13 Hansard, 4th Series, vol. 150, col. 119
14 *CV*, II, pt 1, pp. 399–400
15 Randolph S. Churchill, *Winston S. Churchill*, II, p. 100
16 *Ibid.*, pp. 101–3
17 *Ibid.*, p. 96
18 *CV*, II, pt 1, p. 441
19 Randolph S. Churchill, *Winston S. Churchill*, II, p. 133
20 *Ibid.*, p. 132
21 *Ibid.*, pp. 88–9
22 Winston S. Churchill, *Lord Randolph Churchill*, II, p. 56
23 Randolph S. Churchill, *Winston S. Churchill*, II, p. 111
24 *Ibid.*, p. 228
25 Chamberlain, *Politics from Inside*, p. 459
26 Randolph S. Churchill, *Winston S. Churchill*, II, p. 113
27 *Ibid.*, p. 122
28 *CV*, II, pt 1, p. 501
29 *Ibid.*, p. 417

6. An Upwardly Mobile Under-Secretary

1 Hansard, 4th Series, vol. 151, cols 554–71
2 *CV*, II, pt 1, p. 505
3 *Ibid.*
4 *Ibid.*, p. 500
5 *Ibid.*, p. 517
6 *Ibid.*, p. 605
7 Randolph S. Churchill, *Winston S. Churchill*, II, p. 207
8 Marsh, *A Number of People*, p. 152
9 Hansard, 4th Series, vol. 152, cols 487–99
10 Randolph S. Churchill, *Winston S. Churchill*, II, p. 184
11 *Ibid.*, p. 185

12 *Ibid.*, pp. 185–6
13 Hansard, 4th Series, vol. 162, cols 729–53
14 *CV*, II, pt 1, p. 571
15 *Ibid.*
16 *Ibid.*, p. 574
17 *CV*, II, pt 2, p. 755
18 Randolph S. Churchill, *Winston S. Churchill*, II, p. 243
19 *Ibid.*, p. 241

7. Two Hustings and an Altar

1 *CV*, II, pt 2, p. 782
2 Randolph S. Churchill, *Winston S. Churchill*, II, p. 253
3 *CV*, II, pt 2, p. 787
4 *Dundee Advertiser*, 5 May 1908
5 *Manchester Guardian*, 5 May 1908
6 Soames (ed.), *Speaking for Themselves*, p. 3
7 *Ibid.*
8 *Dictionary of National Biography*, *1912–21*, p. 382
9 Randolph S. Churchill, *Winston S. Churchill*, II, p. 210
10 Violet Bonham Carter, *Winston Churchill as I Knew Him*, p. 15
11 *Ibid.*, p. 18
12 *Ibid.*, pp. 217–18
13 Mark Bonham Carter and Mark Pottle (eds), *Lantern Slides: The Diaries and Letters of Violet Bonham Carter, 1904–14*, p. 162
14 *Ibid.*, pp. 162–3

8. The Sorcerer's Apprentice at the Board of Trade

1 Grigg, *Lloyd George*, II, p. 100
2 Wilson, *C-B: A Life of Sir Henry Campbell-Bannerman*, p. 463
3 Boothby, *Recollections of a Rebel*, p. 52
4 *CV*, II, pt 2, p. 755
5 *Ibid.*, p. 863
6 N. and J. MacKenzie (eds), *Diary of Beatrice Webb*, II, pp. 287–8
7 *Ibid.*, pp. 326–7
8 *Ibid.*, III, pp. 100–1
9 Soames (ed.), *Speaking for Themselves*, p. 21

10 Randolph S. Churchill, *Winston S. Churchill*, II p. 308
11 *Ibid.*, p. 305
12 *Ibid.*, pp. 295–316
13 *CV*, II, pt 2, p. 967
14 Randolph S. Churchill, *Winston S. Churchill*, II, p. 282
15 *CV*, II, pt 2, p. 814
16 *Ibid.*, p. 813
17 Randolph S. Churchill, *Winston S. Churchill*, II, p. 515
18 *CV*, II, pt 2, p. 943
19 Spender and Asquith, *Life of Lord Oxford and Asquith*, I, p. 254
20 *Ibid.*, p. 254
21 *CV*, II, pt 2, p. 889
22 *Ibid.*, pp. 898–900
23 Jenkins, *Asquith*, p. 199
24 *CV*, II, pt 2, p. 906
25 Grigg, *Lloyd George*, II, pp. 206–7
26 Cannadine (ed.), *Blood, Toil, Tears and Sweat: Winston Churchill's Famous Speeches*, p. 53
27 Hansard, 5th Series, vol. 4, cols 1190–3
28 *Ibid.*, vol. 13, cols 546–58
29 *Ibid.* (Lords), vol. 4, cols 1190–3
30 Scawen Blunt, *My Diaries*, p. 689

9. A Young Home Secretary

1 *CV*, II, pt 2, p. 914
2 *Ibid.*, pp. 968–71
3 Randolph S. Churchill, *Winston S. Churchill*, II, p. 363
4 *Ibid.*, p. 365
5 *Ibid.*, p. 437
6 *CV*, II, pt 2, p. 994
7 *Ibid.*, p. 1003
8 *Ibid.*, pp. 1036–7
9 Randolph S. Churchill, *Winston S. Churchill*, II, p. 434
10 *Ibid.*, pp. 434–6
11 *Ibid.*, p. 436
12 *Ibid.*, p. 437
13 *Ibid.*, p. 438
14 *Ibid.*, p. 439

15 *CV*, II, pt 2, p. 1032
16 Hansard, 5th Series, vol. 26, cols 493–510
17 *CV*, II, pt 2, p. 988
18 *Ibid.*, p. 973
19 *Ibid.*, p. 1141
20 Hansard, 5th Series, vol. 556, cols 1141–55
21 Randolph S. Churchill, *Winston S. Churchill*, II, p. 387
22 Hansard, 5th Series, vol. 522, cols 1853–6
23 Randolph S. Churchill, *Winston S. Churchill*, II, pp. 417–18
24 Winston S. Churchill, *Europe Unite: Speeches, 1947 and 1948*, p. 296
25 *CV*, II, pt 3, p. 1466
26 *Ibid.*, p. 1475
27 Randolph S. Churchill, *Winston S. Churchill*, II, p. 343
28 Jenkins, *Asquith*, p. 261
29 Randolph S. Churchill, *Winston S. Churchill*, II, p. 341

10. FROM PRISONS TO WARSHIPS

1 *CV*, II, pt 2, p. 1030
2 *Ibid.*, pp. 1031–3
3 Hansard, 5th Series, vol. 22, col. 55
4 *CV*, II, pt 2, p. 1172
5 *Ibid.*, p. 1168
6 *Ibid.*, p. 1172
7 *Ibid.*, pp. 1173–4
8 Jenkins, *Asquith*, p. 69
9 *CV*, II, pt 2, p. 1274
10 *Ibid.*
11 *Ibid.*, p. 1280
12 Hansard, 5th Series, vol. 29, cols 232–6
13 Winston S. Churchill, *World Crisis*, I, p. 31
14 Grigg, *Lloyd George*, II, p. 309
15 Soames (ed.), *Speaking for Themselves*, p. 23
16 Winston S. Churchill, *World Crisis*, I, p. 48
17 *Ibid.*, pp. 60–4
18 Haldane, *Autobiography*, p. 230

11. 'The Ruler of the King's Navee'

1 Soames (ed.), *Speaking for Themselves*, p. 48
2 Winston S. Churchill, *World Crisis*, I, p. 92
3 *Ibid.*, p. 70
4 Soames (ed.), *Speaking for Themselves*, p. 30
5 Grey of Falloden, *Twenty-Five Years*, I, p. 238
6 Margot Asquith, *My Autobiography*, II, p. 196
7 Winston S. Churchill, *World Crisis*, I, p. 62
8 *Ibid.*, p. 84
9 *Ibid.*, p. 85
10 *Ibid.*, p. 79
11 *Ibid.*, p. 78

12. Churchill in Asquithland

1 Riddell, *More Pages from my Diary, 1908–14*, p. 46
2 Randolph S. Churchill, *Winston S. Churchill*, II, p. 555
3 *The Times*, 2 July 1913
4 *Ibid.*
5 Nicolson, *King George V*, p. 210
6 M. and E. Brock (eds), *Asquith: Letters to Venetia Stanley*, p. 24
7 Jenkins, *Asquith*, p. 239
8 *Ibid.*, p. 253
9 *CV*, II, pt 3, p. 1873
10 Soames (ed.), *Speaking for Themselves*, p. 43
11 M. and E. Brock (eds), *Asquith: Letters to Venetia Stanley*, p. 45
12 *Ibid.*, *passim*
13 *Ibid.*, p. 287
14 *Ibid.*, p. 140
15 Jenkins, *Asquith*, p. 339
16 M. and E. Brock (eds), *Asquith: Letters to Venetia Stanley*, p. 423
17 *Ibid.*, p. 508
18 H. H. Asquith, *Letters to a Friend*, II, p. 53
19 *Ibid.*, p. 123
20 *CV*, II, pt 3, p. 1859
21 Jenkins, *Asquith*, p. 270
22 *Ibid.*, p. 43

23 Winston S. Churchill, *World Crisis*, I, pp. 142–3
24 *CV*, II, pt 3, p. 1389
25 *Belfast Telegraph*, 27 January 1913
26 Soames (ed.), *Speaking for Themselves*, p. 59
27 Rhodes James (ed.), *Complete Speeches of Winston Churchill*, III, p. 2233
28 *CV*, II, pt 3, p. 1390
29 Randolph S. Churchill, *Winston S. Churchill*, II, p. 563
30 Winston S. Churchill, *World Crisis*, I, p. 181
31 Oxford and Asquith, *Fifty Years of Parliament*, II, p. 148
32 M. and E. Brock (eds), *Asquith: Letters to Venetia Stanley*, p. 43
33 *CV*, II, pt 3, pp. 1996–7
34 *Ibid.*, p. 1997
35 M. and E. Brock (eds), *Asquith: Letters to Venetia Stanley*, pp. 150–1

13. A FLAILING FIRST LORD

1 *Threnodia Augustalis*, cited by Churchill in *World Crisis*, I, p. 221
2 See Richard Ollard's essay on Churchill and sea power in Blake and Louis (eds), *Churchill*
3 Winston S. Churchill, *World Crisis*, I, pp. 239–41
4 Marder, *From the Dreadnought to Scapa Flow*, II, p. 82
5 Winston S. Churchill, *World Crisis*, I, p. 397
6 *CV*, III, pt 1, p. 250
7 *Ibid.*, p. 206
8 Winston S. Churchill, *World Crisis*, I, p. 338
9 *Ibid.*, pp. 347–8
10 M. and E. Brock (eds), *Asquith: Letters to Venetia Stanley*, pp. 262–3
11 Gilbert, *Winston S. Churchill*, III, pp. 133–4
12 Soames, *Clementine Churchill*, pp. 113–14
13 Winston S. Churchill, *World Crisis*, I, p. 358
14 *CV*, III, pt 1, p. 320
15 Winston S. Churchill, *World Crisis*, I, p. 401
16 *Ibid.*, pp. 502–3

14. LAST MONTHS AT THE ADMIRALTY

1 M. and E. Brock (eds), *Asquith: Letters to Venetia Stanley*, p. 357
2 *CV*, III, pt 1, p. 344

3 *Ibid.*

4 *Ibid.*, p. 814

5 Morris, *Fisher's Face*, p. 214

6 Pottle (ed.), *Champion Redoubtable: The Diaries and Letters of Violet Bonham Carter, 1914–45*, p. 51

7 Morris, *Fisher's Face*, p. 58

8 *CV*, III, pt 2, pp. 906–7

9 *Ibid.*, pt 1, p. 319

10 *Ibid.*, pt 2, p. 885–6

11 Winston S. Churchill, *World Crisis*, I, p. 460

12 Morris, *Fisher's Face*, p. 211

13 M. and E. Brock (eds), *Asquith: Letters to Venetia Stanley*, p. 405

14 Hankey, *Supreme Command*, p. 293

15 M. and E. Brock (eds), *Asquith: Letters to Venetia Stanley*, p. 390

16 *CV*, III, pt 1, p. 313

17 Winston S. Churchill, *World Crisis*, II, p. 48

18 *Ibid.*, p. 235

19 *CV*, III, pt 1, p. 764

20 *Ibid.*, p. 770

21 Winston S. Churchill, *World Crisis*, II, p. 305

22 *Ibid.*

23 *Ibid.*, p. 505

24 *Ibid.*, p. 489

25 M. and E. Brock (eds), *Asquith: Letters to Venetia Stanley*, p. 415

26 *Ibid.*, p. 436

27 *Ibid.*, p. 450

28 *Ibid.,*. p. 449

29 Margot Asquith Papers

30 *CV*, III, pt 1, p. 504

31 *Ibid.*, p. 495

32 *Ibid.*, p. 645

33 M. and E. Brock (eds), *Asquith: Letters to Venetia Stanley*, p. 546

34 *CV*, III, pt 1, pp. 776–7

35 Winston S. Churchill, *World Crisis*, II, p. 350

36 *Ibid.*, p. 351

37 *Ibid.*, p. 357

38 *Ibid.*, p. 358

39 *Ibid.*, p. 559

40 *CV*, III, pt 2, p. 887

41 Morris, *Fisher's Face*, p. 216

42 Pottle (ed.), *Champion Redoubtable: The Diaries and Letters of Violet Bonham Carter, 1914–45*, p. 51

43 *CV*, III, pt 2 p. 893–4

44 Pottle (ed.), *Champion Redoubtable: The Diaries and Letters of Violet Bonham Carter, 1914–45*, p. 52

45 Winston S. Churchill, *World Crisis*, II, p. 364

46 Jenkins, *Asquith*, p. 360

47 Winston S. Churchill, *World Crisis*, II, p. 366

48 *CV*, III, pt 2, p. 901

49 *Ibid.*, p. 898

50 *Ibid.*, pt 2, p. 919

51 *Ibid.*

52 *Ibid.*, pp. 919–20

53 *Ibid.*, p. 921

54 *Ibid.*, p. 932

55 *Ibid.*, p. 925

56 *Ibid.*, p. 926

57 *Ibid.*, pp. 926 and 927

58 *Ibid.*, p. 927

15. Finished at Forty?

1 Gilbert, *Winston S. Churchill*, III, p. 457

2 *Ibid.*, p. 473

3 Rhodes James, (ed.), *Complete Speeches of Winston Churchill*, III, p. 2348

4 *CV*, III, pt 2, p. 1042

5 Winston S. Churchill, *Thoughts and Adventures*, p. 307

6 *CV*, III, pt 2, p. 1033

7 *Ibid.*, p. 1099

8 *Ibid.*, p. 1098

9 *Ibid.*, p. 1180

10 *Ibid.*, p. 1193

11 *Ibid.*, p. 1140

12 *Ibid.*, p. 1158

13 *Ibid.*, p. 1191

14 *Ibid.*, p. 1196

15 *Ibid.*, p. 1233

16 *Ibid.*, p. 1244

17 *Ibid.*, pp. 1249–50

18 *Ibid.*, p. 1272
19 *Ibid.*
20 Hansard, 5th Series, vol. 75, cols 1514–1515
21 *Ibid.*, col. 1570
22 Violet Bonham Carter, *Winston Churchill as I Knew Him*, pp. 429–30

16. An Improbable Colonel and a Misjudged Re-entry

 1 Soames (ed.), *Speaking for Themselves*, p. 113
 2 *Ibid.*, p. 137
 3 *Ibid.*, p. 118
 4 Winston S. Churchill, *Thoughts and Adventures*, p. 101
 5 Soames (ed.), *Speaking for Themselves*, p. 115
 6 *Ibid.*, pp. 117–19
 7 *Ibid.*, p. 164
 8 *Ibid.*, p. 120
 9 *Ibid.*, p. 130
10 *Ibid.*, p. 116
11 *Ibid.*, p. 127
12 *Ibid.*, p. 125
13 *Ibid.*, p. 124
14 Gilbert, *Winston S. Churchill*, III, p. 412
15 Soames (ed.), *Speaking for Themselves*, p. 133
16 *Ibid.*, p. 137
17 *Ibid.*, p. 150
18 *Ibid.*, p. 168
19 *Ibid.*, p. 125
20 *Ibid.*, p. 139
21 *Ibid.*, p. 129
22 Gilbert, *Winston S. Churchill*, III, p. 625
23 Soames (ed.), *Speaking for Themselves*, p. 148
24 Gibb, *With Winston Churchill at the Front.*
25 Gilbert, *Winston S. Churchill*, III, p. 632
26 Soames (ed.), *Speaking for Themselves*, p. 114
27 *Ibid.*, p. 178
28 *Ibid.*, p. 166
29 *Ibid.*, pp. 197–8
30 Violet Bonham Carter, *Winston Churchill as I Knew Him*, p. 449
31 Hansard, 7th Series, vol. 80, col. 1430

32 *Ibid.*, cols 1442–3
33 *Ibid.*, col. 1570–3
34 *Ibid.*, col. 1575
35 *CV*, III, pt 2, p. 1444
36 Violet Bonham Carter, *Winston Churchill as I Knew Him*, p. 452
37 *Ibid.*, pp. 454–5
38 *CV*, III, pt 2, p. 1450
39 Soames (ed.), *Speaking for Themselves*, p. 195

17. Lloyd George's Ambulance Wagon Arrives a Little Late

1 Hansard, 5th Series, vol. 82, col. 1589
2 *CV*, III, pt 2, pp. 1530–1
3 *Ibid.*, p. 1530
4 *Ibid.*, p. 1531
5 *Ibid.*, p. 1543
6 *Ibid.*, p. 1542
7 *Ibid.*, p. 1570
8 *Ibid.*, p. 1578
9 Gilbert, *Winston S. Churchill*, III, p. 793
10 Beaverbrook, *Politicians and the War*, p. 489
11 *Ibid.*, pp. 492–3
12 Lloyd George, *War Memoirs*, I, pp. 635–6
13 *Ibid.*, p. 636
14 Winston S. Churchill, *World Crisis*, III, pp. 253–4
15 *CV*, IV, pt 1, p. 64
16 Winston S. Churchill, *Great Contemporaries*, p. 293
17 Taylor (ed.), *Lloyd George: A Diary by Frances Stevenson*, p. 158

18. Making the Most of Munitions

1 Rhodes James (ed.), *Complete Speeches of Winston Churchill*, III, p. 2565
2 Soames (ed.), *Speaking for Themselves*, p. 207
3 Gilbert, *Winston S. Churchill*, IV, p. 79
4 Winston S. Churchill, *World Crisis*, III, pt 2, p. 423
5 Gilbert, *Winston S. Churchill*, IV, p. 92
6 *Ibid.*, pp. 93–4
7 Soames (ed.), *Speaking for Themselves*, p. 206

8 *Ibid.*, pp. 208–9
9 Gilbert, *Winston S. Churchill*, IV, p. 159
10 *Ibid.*, pp. 159–60
11 *CV*, IV, pt 1, p. 408
12 *Ibid.*, pp. 408–10
13 *Ibid.*, p. 410
14 Winston S. Churchill, *World Crisis*, III, pt 2, p. 541
15 *CV*, IV, pt 1, p. 437
16 Gilbert, *Winston S. Churchill*, IV, p. 173
17 *CV*, IV, pt 1, p. 429
18 *Ibid.*
19 *Ibid.*, p. 437
20 *Ibid.*, pp. 443–7

19. Anti-Bolshevik Crusader and Irish Peacemaker

1 Winston S. Churchill, *World Crisis*, V, p. 263
2 *Ibid.*, p. 24
3 Gilbert, *Winston S. Churchill*, IV, pp. 365–6
4 Soames (ed.), *Speaking for Themselves*, p. 227
5 *Ibid.*, pp. 234–5
6 *Ibid.*, p. 227
7 *Ibid.*, p. 256
8 *Ibid.*, p. 225
9 *Ibid.*, p. 239
10 Soames, *Clementine Churchill*, pp. 218–19
11 *CV*, IV, pt 2, p. 1420
12 Soames (ed.), *Speaking for Themselves*, p. 232
13 Winston S. Churchill, *World Crisis*, V, pp. 289–90
14 Hansard, 5th Series (Lords) vol. 48, col. 204
15 Winston S. Churchill, *World Crisis*, V, p. 348
16 *Ibid.*, p. 349
17 Soames (ed.), *Speaking for Themselves*, p. 246
18 *Ibid.*, pp. 247–8
19 *Ibid.*, p. 249
20 *CV*, IV, pt 3, pp. 1666–7
21 *Ibid.*, pt 2, p. 1053

20. A Politician without a Party or a Seat

1 *CV*, IV, pt 3, p. 2126
2 *Ibid.*, p. 2100n.
3 *Ibid.*, p. 2094
4 *Ibid.*, pp. 2095–6
5 *Ibid.*, pp. 2100
6 Gilbert, *Winston S. Churchill*, IV, p. 880
7 Patterson, *Churchill: A Seat for Life*, pp. 238–9
8 Gilbert, *Winston S. Churchill*, IV, p. 875
9 Egremont, *Under Two Flags: The Life of Sir Edward Spears*, p. 104
10 Patterson, *Churchill: A Seat for Life*, p. 235
11 Gilbert, *Winston S. Churchill*, IV, p. 886
12 *Ibid.*, p. 887
13 Winston S. Churchill, *Thoughts and Adventures*, p. 213
14 Gilbert, *Winston S. Churchill*, IV, p. 892
15 Soames (ed.), *Speaking for Themselves*, p. 268
16 *Ibid.*, p. 273
17 *Ibid.*, p. 281
18 *CV*, V, pt 1, p. 55
19 Soames (ed.), *Speaking for Themselves*, p. 271
20 *Ibid.*
21 Gilbert, *Winston S. Churchill*, V, pp.15–16
22 Soames (ed.), *Speaking for Themselves*, p. 269
23 *CV*, V, pt 1, p. 82
24 Pethick-Lawrence, *Fate Has Been Kind*, p. 129
25 *CV*, V, pt 1, pp. 92–4
26 *Ibid.*, pp. 97–8
27 Soames (ed.), *Speaking for Themselves*, p. 280
28 *CV*, V, pt 1, p. 120
29 Winston S. Churchill, *Thoughts and Adventures*, p. 213
30 Randolph S. Churchill, *Lord Derby*, p. 82
31 Salvidge, *Salvidge of Liverpool*
32 Soames (ed.), *Speaking for Themselves*, p. 278

21. GOLD AND STRIKES

1 Jones, *Whitehall Diary*, I, p. 303
2 Gilbert, *Winston S. Churchill*, V, p. 163
3 *CV*, V, pt 1, pp. 268–9
4 *Ibid.*, p. 280
5 *Ibid.*, p. 286
6 *Ibid.*, p. 304
7 *Ibid.*, p. 412
8 *Ibid.*, p. 316
9 *Ibid.*, p. 356
10 *Ibid.*, pp. 533–4
11 *Ibid.*, pp. 530–1
12 *Ibid.*, pp. 430–2 (not Churchill's own words but words attributed to him by the Foreign Office permanent under-secretary in a note prepared for Austen Chamberlain)
13 Gilbert, *Winston S. Churchill*, V, p. 94
14 *Ibid.*, p. 95
15 *Ibid.*
16 *CV*, V, pt 1, p. 411
17 *Ibid.*, pp. 437–8
18 Gilbert, *Winston S. Churchill*, V, p. 103
19 Hansard, 5th Series, vol. 183, col. 71
20 Gilbert, *Winston S. Churchill*, V, p. 118
21 *CV*, V, pt 1, p. 358
22 Rhodes James (ed.), *Complete Speeches of Winston Churchill*, IV, p. 3818
23 Gilbert, *Winston S. Churchill*, V, p. 145
24 Hansard, 5th Series, vol. 183, col. 69
25 Gilbert, *Winston S. Churchill*, V, p. 140
26 *CV*, V, pt 1, p. 708
27 Gilbert, *Winston S. Churchill*, V, p. 161
28 Hansard, 5th Series, vol. 197, col. 2218
29 Middlemas and Barnes, *Baldwin*, p. 432
30 Jones, *Whitehall Diary*, II, p. 88
31 *CV*, V, pt 1, pp. 984–5
32 Hansard, 5th Series, vol. 205, col. 59
33 *CV*, V, pt 1, p. 986
34 Gilbert, *Winston S. Churchill*, V, p. 236
35 Barnes and Nicholson (eds), *Leo Amery Diaries*, I, pp. 542–3

36 Soames (ed.), *Speaking for Themselves*, pp. 315–16
37 *CV*, V, pt 1, pp. 1328–9

22. A Relentless Writer

 1 *CV*, V, pt 1, p. 1469
 2 Soames (ed.), *Speaking for Themselves*, p. 332 (slighting reference to Austen Chamberlain omitted from this published version)
 3 Jones, *Whitehall Diaries*, II, p. 186
 4 *CV*, V, pt 1, p. 1333
 5 *Ibid.*, pt 2, p. 36
 6 Barnes and Nicholson (eds), *Leo Amery Diaries*, I, p. 49
 7 Soames (ed.), *Speaking for Themselves*, p. 337
 8 *Ibid.*, p. 341
 9 *Ibid.*, p. 345
10 *Ibid.*, p. 349
11 *CV*, V, pt 2, p. 133
12 *Ibid.*, p. 140
13 *Ibid.*, p. 141
14 *Ibid.*, p. 331

23. Cuckoo out of the Nest

 1 Rhodes James, *Churchill: A Study in Failure*, p. 181
 2 *CV*, V, pt 2, p. 192
 3 *Ibid.*, pp. 193–4
 4 Rhodes James, *Churchill: A Study in Failure*, p. 299
 5 *CV*, V, pt 2, p. 293
 6 *Ibid.*, p. 254
 7 *Ibid.*, p. 257
 8 *Ibid.*, p. 280
 9 *Ibid.*, p. 280n.
10 *Ibid.*, p. 307
11 *Ibid.*, p. 274
12 Soames (ed.), *Speaking for Themselves*, p. 354
13 *Ibid.*, p. 356
14 *CV*, V, pt 2, p. 302
15 *Ibid.*, p. 307

16 *Ibid.*, p. 308
17 Hansard, 5th Series, vol. 231, col. 1306
18 *Ibid.*, vol. 249, col. 1426
19 Nicolson (ed.), *Harold Nicolson: Diaries and Letters, 1930–39*, p. 82
20 *CV*, V, pt 2, p. 339
21 *Ibid.*, p. 265
22 *Ibid.*, p. 348
23 *Ibid.*, p. 382
24 *Ibid.*, p. 383
25 *Ibid.*, p. 396
26 *Ibid.*, p. 393
27 *Ibid.*, p. 407
28 *Ibid.*, p. 394n.

24. Unwisdom in the Wilderness

1 *CV*, V, pt 2, p. 412
2 *Ibid.*, p. 374
3 *Ibid.*, p. 276
4 *Ibid.*, p. 518
5 *Ibid.*, p. 601
6 Winston S. Churchill, *Marlborough*, I, p. 144
7 *Ibid.*, p. 258
8 *Ibid.*, p. 52
9 *Ibid.*, p. 117
10 *CV*, V, pt 2, p. 665
11 *Ibid.*, p. 532
12 Duff Cooper, *Old Men Forget*, p. 171
13 *CV*, V, pt 2, p. 566
14 *Ibid.*, pp. 595–6
15 *Ibid.*, pp. 602–3
16 Minutes of Evidence of the Committee on Privileges, June 1934
17 *CV*, V, pt 2, p. 809
18 Hansard, 5th Series, vol. 290, cols 1736–47
19 Soames (ed.), *Speaking for Themselves*, p. 399
20 *CV*, V, pt 2, p. 1129
21 Hansard, 5th Series, vol. 302, cols 1925–34

25. An Early Alarm Clock

1 Winston S. Churchill, *Second World War*, I, p. 157
2 Hansard, 5th Series, vol. 201, col. 666
3 Winston S. Churchill, *Second World War*, I, p. 62
4 Nicolson (ed.), *Harold Nicolson: Diaries and Letters, 1930–39*, p. 284
5 Pelling, *Winston Churchill*, p. 384
6 Hansard, 5th Series, vol. 310, col. 1526
7 Winston S. Churchill, *Second World War*, I, p. 65
8 *Ibid.*
9 Gilbert, *Winston S. Churchill*, V, p. 456
10 Hansard, 5th Series, vol. 287, cols 394–485
11 Self (ed.), *Austen Chamberlain Diary Letters*, p. 451
12 *Ibid.*
13 Soames (ed.), *Speaking for Themselves*, p. 402
14 Self (ed.), *Austen Chamberlain Diary Letters*, p. 499
15 Hansard, 5th Series, vol. 292, cols 2363–77
16 *Ibid.*, vol. 295, cols 857–72
17 Taylor (ed.), *Lloyd George: A Diary by Frances Stevenson*, p. 294

26. Arms and the Covenant

1 Gilbert, *Winston S. Churchill*, V, p. 675
2 *CV*, V, pt 2, p. 1364
3 Winston S. Churchill, *Arms and the Covenant*, p. 253
4 Taylor, *English History, 1914–1945*, p. 377
5 *CV*, V, pt 2, p. 1203
6 Winston S. Churchill, *Second World War*, I, p. 133
7 Winston S. Churchill, *Arms and the Covenant*, p. 251
8 *The Times*, 12 September 1935
9 Winston S. Churchill, *Second World War*, I, p. 135
10 *CV*, V, pt 2, p. 1279
11 *Ibid.*, p. 1324
12 *Ibid.*, pp. 1348–50
13 *Ibid.*, p. 1353
14 *Ibid.*, pt 3, p. 18
15 *Ibid.*, p. 37
16 *Ibid.*

17 Sherriff, *No Leading Lady*
18 Soames (ed.), *Speaking for Themselves*, p. 414
19 Rhodes James (ed.), *Complete Speeches of Winston Churchill*, VI, p. 5894
20 Nicolson (ed.), *Harold Nicolson: Diaries and Letters, 1930–39*, p. 252
21 Soames (ed.), *Speaking for Themselves*, p. 417
22 *CV*, V, pt 3, p. 392
23 *Ibid.*, p. 353
24 *Ibid.*, p. 108
25 *Ibid.*, pp. 387–8
26 *Ibid.*, p. 370
27 *Ibid.*, p. 363
28 *Ibid.*, p. 362
29 Hansard, 5th Series, vol. 317, cols 1098–1118
30 *Ibid.*, col. 1144
31 Rose (ed.), *Baffy: The Diaries of Blanche Dugdale*, 18 November 1936
32 *CV*, V, pt 3, p. 452
33 Citrine, *Men and Work*, pp. 356–7
34 *CV*, V, pt 3, pp. 455–6
35 *Ibid*, p. 457
36 Nicolson (ed.), *Harold Nicolson: Diaries and Letters, 1930–39*, p. 284
37 Barnes and Nicholson (eds), *Leo Amery Diaries*, II, p. 430
38 *CV*, V, pt 3, p. 465
39 *Ibid.*, pp. 466–72
40 *Ibid.*, pp. 480–1
41 Hansard, 5th Series, vol. 318, col. 2189–91
42 *CV*, V, pt 3, p. 521

27. From the Abdication to Munich

1 *CV*, V, pt 3, p. 822
2 *Ibid.*, p. 619
3 *Ibid.*, p. 709
4 *Ibid.*, p. 517
5 Soames (ed.), *Speaking for Themselves*, p. 426
6 *CV*, V, pt 3, p. 787
7 *Ibid.*, p. 166
8 Rose (ed.), *Baffy: The Diaries of Blanche Dugdale*, 27 February 1937
9 *CV*, V, pt 3, p. 188
10 Winston S. Churchill, *Second World War*, I, p. 201

11 *CV*, V, pt 3, p. 673
12 *Ibid.*, pp. 767–8
13 Rhodes James (ed.), *Complete Speeches of Winston Churchill*, VI, p. 5894
14 Nicolson (ed.), *Harold Nicolson: Diaries and Letters, 1930–39*, p. 332
15 Winston S. Churchill, *Second World War*, I, pp. 211–12
16 *CV*, V, pt 3, p. 973
17 Soames (ed.), *Speaking for Themselves*, p. 436
18 *Ibid.*, p. 433
19 *CV*, V, pt 3, pp. 951–2
20 *Ibid.*, pp. 963–4
21 *Daily Telegraph*, 26 July 1938
22 Soames (ed.), *Speaking for Themselves*, p. 436
23 *CV*, V, pt 3, p. 1104
24 *Ibid.*, pp. 1124–5
25 *Ibid.*, p. 1129
26 *Ibid.*, p. 1089
27 Gilbert, *Winston S. Churchill*, V, p. 978n.
28 *CV*, V, pt 3, p. 1166
29 Gilbert, *Winston S. Churchill*, V, pp. 986–7
30 *CV*, V, pt 3, p. 1156
31 Nicolson (ed.), *Harold Nicolson: Diaries and Letters, 1930–39*, p. 367
32 *Ibid.*, pp. 363–4
33 *Ibid.*, p. 372
34 Coote, *Editorial*, pp. 173–4
35 *CV*, V, pt 3, p. 1189n.
36 Hansard, 5th Series, vol. 339, cols 360–70
37 Gilbert, *Winston S. Churchill*, V, p. 1002

28. The Last Year of the Peace

1 *CV*, V, pt 3, pp. 1229–30
2 *Ibid.*, p. 1210
3 *Ibid.*, p. 1213
4 *Ibid.*, pp. 1232–3
5 Gilbert, *Winston S. Churchill*, V, p. 1015
6 Nicolson (ed.), *Harold Nicolson: Diaries and Letters, 1930–39*, p. 383
7 *CV*, V, pt 3, p. 1239
8 *Ibid.*, p. 1270
9 *Ibid.*, pp. 1204–5

10 Hansard, 5th Series, vol. 341, col. 1196
11 *CV*, V, pt 3, p. 1302
12 Nicolson (ed.), *Harold Nicolson: Diaries and Letters, 1930–39*, p. 382
13 *CV*, V, pt 3, p. 1316
14 *Ibid.*, p. 1325
15 *Ibid.*, p. 1402
16 *Ibid.*, p. 1455
17 *Ibid.*, p. 1464
18 Macmillan, *Winds of Change*, p. 592
19 *CV*, V, pt 3, p. 1439
20 *Ibid.*, p. 1461
21 *Ibid.*, p. 1475
22 Hansard, 5th Series, vol. 339, col. 361
23 Unpublished Harold Nicolson diary entry for 25 April 1939, Balliol College, Oxford
24 *CV*, V, pt 3, p. 1622
25 *Ibid.*, p. 1622
26 *Ibid.*, p. 1463
27 *Ibid.*, p. 1406
28 Hansard, 5th Series, vol. 347, cols 1840–9
29 Colville, *Fringes of Power*, p. 404
30 Hansard, 5th Series, vol. 347, cols 1840–9
31 *CV*, V, pt 3, p. 1456
32 *Ibid.*, p. 1545
33 Soames (ed.), *Speaking for Themselves*, p. 451
34 *CV*, V, pt 3, pp. 1592–3
35 *Ibid.*, p. 1597
36 *Ibid.*, pp. 1169 and 1232
37 *Ibid.*, p. 1591

29. Quiet War with Germany and Uneasy Peace with Chamberlain

1 Nicolson (ed.), *Harold Nicolson: Diary and Letters, 1930–39*, pp. 421–2
2 Thompson, *I Was Churchill's Shadow*, p. 20
3 *War Papers*, I, p. 187
4 *Ibid.*, p. 153
5 *Ibid.*, p. 146
6 *Ibid.*, p. 128

7 Winston S. Churchill, *Second World War*, I, pp. 388–9
8 Nicolson (ed.), *Harold Nicolson: Letters and Diaries, 1939–45*, p. 37
9 Cartland, *Ronald Cartland*, p. 232
10 *War Papers*, I, p. 160
11 Colville, *Fringes of Power*, p. 29
12 *War Papers*, I, p. 195
13 *Ibid.*, p. 304
14 *Ibid.*, p. 358
15 Colville, *Fringes of Power*, pp. 50–1
16 Rhodes James (ed.), *Chips*, p. 220
17 *War Papers*, I, p. 100
18 Winston S. Churchill, *Second World War*, I, p. 392
19 *War Papers*, I, p. 312
20 Winston S. Churchill, *Second World War*, I, p. 392
21 *War Papers*, I, pp. 369–70
22 *Ibid.*, p. 505
23 Thompson, *I Was Churchill's Shadow*, p. 25
24 *CV*, V, pt 3, p. 571
25 Thompson, *I Was Churchill's Shadow*, p. 25
26 *Ibid.*, pp. 26–7
27 *War Papers*, I, p. 611
28 *Ibid.*, pp. 611–12
29 *Ibid.*, p. 244
30 Gilbert, *Winston S. Churchill*, VI, pp. 67–8
31 *War Papers*, I, p. 553
32 *Ibid.*, p. 555
33 *Ibid.*, p. 642
34 *Ibid.*, p. 652
35 *Ibid.*, pp. 667–75
36 *Ibid.*, p. 689
37 *Ibid.*, p. 690

30. Through Disaster in the Fjords to Triumph in Downing Street

1 Spears, *Assignment to Catastrophe*, I, p. 97
2 *Ibid.*, p. 99
3 Colville, *Fringes of Power*, p. 95
4 Spears, *Assignment to Catastrophe*, I, p. 100

5 *War Papers*, I, pp. 922–3

6 Nicolson (ed.), *Harold Nicolson: Diaries and Letters, 1939–45*, p. 70

7 Colville, *Fringes of Power*, p. 101

8 *Ibid.*, p. 102

9 Hansard, 5th Series, vol. 360, cols 1073–86

10 *Ibid.*, cols 1094–1130

11 Barnes and Nicholson (eds), *Leo Amery Diaries*, I, p. 592

12 Hansard, 5th Series, vol. 360, cols 1250–83

13 *Ibid.*, col. 1283

14 *Ibid.*, cols 1320–9

15 Rhodes James (ed.), *Chips*, p. 246

16 Nicolson (ed.), *Harold Nicolson: Diaries and Letters, 1939–45*, p. 79

17 Pimlott (ed.), *Political Diary of Hugh Dalton, 1918–40, 1945–51*, p. 342

18 Winston S. Churchill, *Second World War*, I, pp. 523–4

19 Dilks (ed.), *Diaries of Sir Alexander Cadogan*, p. 280

20 *War Papers*, I, pp. 1260–1

21 *Ibid.*, pp. 1261–2

22 Templewood, *Nine Troubled Years*, p. 432

23 *War Papers*, I, pp. 1285–6

31. TWENTY-ONE DAYS IN MAY

1 *War Papers*, II, pp. 14–15

2 Nicolson (ed.), *Harold Nicolson: Diaries and Letters, 1939–45*, p. 85

3 Rhodes James (ed.), *Chips*, p. 252

4 *War Papers*, II, p. 22

5 Nicolson (ed.), *Harold Nicolson: Diaries and Letters, 1939–45*, p. 85

6 Rhodes James (ed.), *Chips*, p. 252

7 Colville, *Fringes of Power*, p. 129

8 Thompson, *Sixty Minutes with Winston Churchill*, p. 444

9 Winston S. Churchill, *Second World War*, I, pp. 526–7

10 Colville, *Fringes of Power*, p. 133–4

11 *Ibid.*, p. 138

12 *Ibid.*, p. 133

13 Soames (ed.), *Speaking for Themselves*, p. 454

14 *War Papers*, II, p. 35

15 *Ibid.*

16 *Ibid.*, pp. 110 and 116

17 *Ibid.*, pp. 156–7

18 Ismay, *Memoirs*, p. 133
19 *War Papers*, II, p. 220
20 Hansard, 5th Series, vol. 361, cols 787–96
21 *War Papers*, II, p. 226
22 *Ibid.*, p. 153
23 Hansard, 5th Series, vol. 361, col. 796
24 Lukacs, *Five Days in London*, pp. 117–18
25 *War Papers*, II, p. 158
26 Lukacs, *Five Days in London*, pp. 115–16
27 Ismay, *Memoirs*, p. 131
28 Birkenhead, *Halifax*, p. 458
29 Colville, *Fringes of Power*, pp. 140–1
30 *War Papers*, II, pp. 166–7
31 *Ibid.*, pp. 180–1
32 Winston S. Churchill, *Second World War*, II, pp. 87–8
33 Pimlott (ed.), *Second World War Diary of Hugh Dalton*, p. 28
34 *Ibid.*, p. 28 and n.
35 *War Papers*, II, p. 185
36 *Ibid.*
37 *Ibid.*, p. 187
38 *Ibid.*
39 Winston S. Churchill, *Second World War*, II, p. 157

32. THE TERRIBLE BEAUTY OF THE SUMMER OF 1940

1 Rhodes James (ed.), *Chips*, p. 256
2 *War Papers*, II, p. 248
3 *Ibid.*, pp. 248–9
4 *Ibid.*, p. 249
5 Sherwood (ed.), *The White House Papers of Harry L. Hopkins*, I, p. 145
6 *War Papers*, II, p. 294
7 *Ibid.*, p. 320
8 *Ibid.*, p. 255
9 *Ibid.*, p. 333
10 *Ibid.*, p. 338
11 Spears, *Assignment to Catastrophe*, II, pp. 137–8
12 Eden, *Reckoning*, p. 116
13 *War Papers*, II, p. 305
14 *Ibid.*, p. 305

15 Winston S. Churchill, *Second World War*, II, p. 158
16 *War Papers*, II, p. 349
17 *Ibid.*, p. 348
18 *Ibid.*, p. 346
19 *Ibid.*, p. 359
20 Dilks (ed.), *Diaries of Sir Alexander Cadogan*, 18 June 1940
21 Hansard, 5th Series, vol. 362, cols 51–61
22 Winston S. Churchill, *Second World War*, II, p. 205
23 *War Papers*, II, p. 458
24 Winston S. Churchill, *Second World War*, II, p. 212
25 *Ibid.*, p. 211
26 Nicolson (ed.), *Harold Nicolson: Diaries and Letters, 1939–45*, p. 100
27 *War Papers*, II, pp. 483–4
28 Colville, *Fringes of Power*, p. 193
29 Nicolson (ed.), *Harold Nicolson: Diaries and Letters, 1939–45*, p. 103
30 Rhodes James (ed.), *Chips*, p. 262
31 Hansard, 5th Series, vol. 363, cols 367–404
32 *Ibid.*, cols 1193–4
33 Pimlott (ed.), *Second World War Diary of Hugh Dalton*, p. 67
34 *War Papers*, II, p. 594
35 *Ibid.*, p. 595
36 *Ibid.*, p. 555
37 *Ibid.*, p. 579
38 *Ibid.*, p. 514
39 *Ibid.*
40 *Ibid.*, p. 493
41 Pimlott (ed.), *Second World War Diary of Hugh Dalton*, p. 67

33. THE BATTLE OF BRITAIN AND THE BEGINNING OF THE BLITZ

1 Colville, *Fringes of Power*, p. 280
2 *Ibid.*, p. 297
3 Winston S. Churchill, *Second World War*, II, pp. 324–5
4 Valentine, *Willesden at War*, passim
5 *War Papers*, II, p. 1017
6 Eden, *Reckoning*, p. 175
7 *War Papers*, II, pp. 1068–9
8 Colville, *Fringes of Power*, p. 283
9 *Ibid.*

10 Hansard, 5th Series, vol. 365, cols 766–78

11 *War Papers*, II, pp. 1189–97

12 *Ibid.*, p. 816

13 *Ibid.*

14 *Ibid.*, p. 883

15 *Ibid.*, pp. 1066–7

16 Hansard, 5th Series, vol. 364, cols 1159–71

17 Colville, *Fringes of Power*, p. 227

18 Nicolson (ed.), *Harold Nicolson: Diaries and Letters, 1939–45*, p. 109

34. No Longer Alone

1 Winston S. Churchill, *Second World War*, III, p. 539

2 Colville, *Fringes of Power*, p. 331

3 *War Papers*, III, p. 90

4 Moran, *Winston Churchill*, p. 6

5 Colville, *Fringes of Power*, p. 332

6 Sherwood (ed.), *White House Papers of Harry L. Hopkins*, I, p. 257

7 Colville, *Fringes of Power*, p. 417

8 *Ibid.*, p. 375

9 Winston S. Churchill, *Second World War*, III, pp. 307–8

10 Dilks (ed.), *Diaries of Sir Alexander Cadogan*, 26 May 1941

11 *War Papers*, III, p. 713

12 Danchev and Todman (eds), *War Diaries, 1939–45: Field Marshal Lord Alanbrooke*, pp. 160–1

13 *War Papers*, III, p. 447

14 Winston S. Churchill, *Second World War*, III, p. 323

15 Colville, *Fringes of Power*, p. 404

16 *War Papers*, III, pp. 835–8

17 Nicolson (ed.), *Harold Nicolson: Diaries and Letters, 1939–45*, p. 174

18 Colville, *Fringes of Power*, p. 406

19 Winston S. Churchill, *Second World War*, III, p. 352

20 *War Papers*, III, p. 841

21 Gilbert, *Winston S. Churchill*, VII, pp. 52–3

22 Sherwood (ed.), *White House Papers of Harry L. Hopkins*, I, p. 435

35. The Anglo-American Marriage Ceremony

1 *War Papers*, III, p. 1659
2 Sherwood (ed.), *White House Papers of Harry L. Hopkins*, I, p. 449
3 Soames (ed.), *Speaking for Themselves*, pp. 461 and 459
4 Winston S. Churchill, *Second World War*, III, p. 587
5 *Ibid.*
6 *Ibid.*, p. 588
7 Sherwood (ed.), *White House Papers of Harry L. Hopkins*, I, p. 446
8 Moran, *Winston Churchill*, pp. 16–17
9 Gilbert, *Winston S. Churchill*, VII, p. 25
10 Wheeler-Bennett, *King George VI*, p. 535
11 Gilbert, *Winston S. Churchill*, VII, p. 43
12 *Ibid.*, p. 47
13 Winston S. Churchill, *Second World War*, III, p. 625

36. The Hinge Year

1 Nicolson (ed.), *Harold Nicolson: Diaries and Letters, 1939–45*, p. 211
2 Danchev and Todman (eds), *War Diaries, 1939–45: Field Marshal Lord Alanbrooke*, p. 231
3 Rhodes James (ed.), *Chips*, p. 321
4 Hansard, 5th Series, vol. 377, cols 592–619 and 1006–17
5 Winston S. Churchill, *Second World War*, IV, pp. 57 and 61
6 Nicolson (ed.), *Harold Nicolson: Diaries and Letters, 1939–45*, p. 207
7 Winston S. Churchill, *Second World War*, IV, p. 62
8 *Ibid.*, p. 54
9 Eden, *Reckoning*, p. 319
10 Nicolson (ed.), *Harold Nicolson: Diaries and Letters, 1939–45*, p. 212
11 Dilks (ed.), *Diaries of Sir Alexander Cadogan*, p. 438
12 Gilbert, *Winston S. Churchill*, VII, p. 69
13 Winston S. Churchill, *Second World War*, IV, p. 56
14 *Ibid.*, p. 80
15 Gilbert, *Winston S. Churchill*, VII, p. 261
16 Sherwood (ed.), *White House Papers of Harry L. Hopkins*, II, p. 536
17 Winston S. Churchill, *Second World War*, IV, p. 296
18 *Ibid.*, p. 305
19 *Ibid.*, p. 299

20 *Ibid.*, p. 302
21 *Ibid.*, p. 338
22 Winston S. Churchill, *Second World War*, IV, pp. 342–3
23 *Ibid.*, pp. 343, 344
24 Ismay, *Memoirs*, p. 257
25 Winston S. Churchill, *Second World War*, IV, p. 353
26 Nicolson (ed.), *Harold Nicolson: Diaries and Letters, 1939–45*, p. 231
27 Hansard, 5th Series, vol. 381, cols 205–14
28 Nicolson (ed.), *Harold Nicolson: Diaries and Letters, 1939–45*, p. 231
29 Hansard, 5th Series, vol. 381, cols 552–8
30 Winston S. Churchill, *Second World War*, IV, p. 446
31 *Ibid.*, p. 449
32 Gilbert, *Winston S. Churchill*, VII, p. 187
33 *Ibid.*, p. 185
34 *Ibid.*, p. 254
35 Danchev and Todman (eds), *War Diaries, 1939–45: Field Marshal Lord Alanbrooke*, p. 319
36 Harvey (ed.), *War Diaries of Oliver Harvey*, 2 October 1942

37. 1943: FROM CASABLANCA TO TEHERAN

1 Moran, *Winston Churchill*, p. 82
2 Sherwood (ed.), *White House Papers of Harry L. Hopkins*, II, p. 762
3 Gilbert, *Winston S. Churchill*, VII, pp. 346–9
4 Sherwood (ed.), *White House Papers of Harry L. Hopkins*, II, p. 763
5 Gilbert, *Winston S. Churchill*, VII, p. 437
6 Sherwood (ed.), *White House Papers of Harry L. Hopkins*, II, p. 730
7 *Ibid.*, p. 734
8 Gilbert, *Winston S. Churchill*, VII, p. 436
9 Sherwood (ed.), *White House Papers of Harry L. Hopkins*, II, p. 668
10 Winston S. Churchill, *Second World War*, IV, p. 729
11 Kimball (ed.), *Churchill and Roosevelt: The Complete Correspondence*, II, p. 231
12 Nicolson (ed.), *Harold Nicolson: Diaries and Letters, 1939–45*, p. 299
13 Gilbert, *Winston S. Churchill*, VII, p. 445
14 Winston S. Churchill, *Second World War*, V, p. 73
15 Sherwood (ed.), *White House Papers of Harry L. Hopkins*, II, p. 793
16 Danchev and Todman (eds), *War Diaries, 1939–45: Field Marshal Lord Alanbrooke*, p. 442
17 Gilbert, *Winston S. Churchill*, VII, p. 478

18 *Ibid.*, p. 477

19 Hansard, 5th Series, vol. 392, cols 69–105

20 Nicolson (ed.), *Harold Nicolson: Diaries and Letters, 1939–45*, p. 320–1

21 Gilbert, *Winston S. Churchill*, VII, p. 531

22 Kimball (ed.), *Churchill and Roosevelt: The Complete Correspondence*, II, p. 541

23 Sarah Churchill, *Keep on Dancing*, p. 69

24 Winston S. Churchill, *Second World War*, V, p. 371

25 Foot and Matthew (eds), *Gladstone Diaries*, IV, p. 510

26 Gilbert, *Winston S. Churchill*, VII, p. 563

27 Ismay, *Memoirs*, p. 357

28 PRO: CAB 80/77, Record of 1st Plenary Meeting of the Teheran Conference

29 Gilbert, *Winston S. Churchill*, VII, p. 579

30 *Ibid.*

31 *Ibid.*, p. 580

32 Winston S. Churchill, *Second World War*, V, p. 330

33 Moran, *Winston Churchill*, pp. 136–41

34 Gilbert, *Winston S. Churchill*, VII, p. 585

35 *Ibid.*, p. 586

36 *Ibid.*, p. 593

37 Macmillan, *War Diaries*, p. 321

38 Danchev and Todman (eds), *War Diaries, 1939–45: Field Marshal Lord Alanbrooke*, p. 492

39 *Ibid.*, p. 493

40 *Ibid.*, p. 496

41 Gilbert, *Winston S. Churchill*, VII, p. 603

42 Montague Browne, *Long Sunset*, p. 142

43 Colville, *Fringes of Power*, p. 455

44 Nicolson, (ed.), *Harold Nicolson: Diaries and Letters, 1939–45*, pp. 344–5

38. THE RETURN TO FRANCE

1 Winston S. Churchill, *Second World War*, V, p. 432

2 Gilbert, *Winston S. Churchill*, VII, p. 706

3 *Ibid.*, p. 669

4 Colville, *Fringes of Power*, p. 474

5 Danchev and Todman (eds), *War Diaries, 1939–45: Field Marshal Lord Alanbrooke*, p. 525

6 Colville, *Fringes of Power*, p. 475

7 Nicolson (ed.), *Harold Nicolson: Diaries and Letters, 1939–45*, p. 352

8 Gilbert, *Winston S. Churchill*, VII, p. 697

9 *Ibid.*, p. 709–10

10 Colville, *Fringes of Power*, p. 475

11 *Ibid.*, p. 476

12 Gilbert, *Winston S. Churchill*, VII, p. 714

13 Nicolson (ed.), *Harold Nicolson: Diaries and Letters, 1939–45*, p. 356

14 Danchev and Todman (eds), *War Diaries, 1939–45: Field Marshal Lord Alanbrooke*, p. 535

15 Gilbert, *Winston S. Churchill*, VII, p. 715

16 Colville, *Fringes of Power*, p. 480

17 Winston S. Churchill, *Second World War*, V, p. 476

18 *Ibid.*, p. 485

19 *Ibid.*, p. 479

20 *Ibid.*, p. 480

21 *Ibid.*, p. 483

22 Danchev and Todman (eds), *War Diaries, 1939–45: Field Marshal Lord Alanbrooke*, p. 544

23 Colville, *Fringes of Power*, pp. 485–6

24 *Ibid.*, p. 487

25 Gilbert, *Winston S. Churchill*, VII, p. 765

26 Winston S. Churchill, *Second World War*, V, p. 467

27 Gilbert, *Winston S. Churchill*, VII, p. 759

28 Dixon, *Life of Sir Pierson Dixon*, pp. 89–90

29 Gilbert, *Winston S. Churchill*, VII, p. 789

30 *Ibid.*

31 Eden, *Reckoning*, p. 453

32 Gilbert, *Winston S. Churchill*, VII, p. 772

33 *Ibid.*, p. 773

34 Colville, *Fringes of Power*, p. 485

35 Bradford, *King George VI*, p. 359

36 Gilbert, *Winston S. Churchill*, VII, pp. 793–4

39. THE BEGINNING OF THE END

1 Gilbert, *Winston S. Churchill*, VII, p. 835

2 Kimball (ed.), *Churchill and Roosevelt: The Complete Correspondence*, III, pp. 227–9

3 *Ibid.*, p. 229

4 Gilbert, *Winston S. Churchill*, VII, p. 822

5 *Ibid.*, p. 825

6 Kimball (ed.), *Churchill and Roosevelt: The Complete Correspondence*, III, p. 229

7 *Ibid.*, p. 223

8 Danchev and Todman (eds), *War Diaries 1939–45: Field Marshal Lord Alanbrooke*, p. 565

9 Kimball (ed.), *Churchill and Roosevelt: The Complete Correspondence*, p. 229

10 *Ibid.*, p. 270

11 Soames (ed.), *Speaking for Themselves*, p. 501

12 Dixon, *Life of Sir Pierson Dixon*, pp. 99–100

13 *Ibid.*, p. 104

14 Winston S. Churchill, *Second World War*, VI, p. 107

15 Colville, *Fringes of Power*, p. 510

16 *Ibid.*, p. 509

17 Gilbert, *Winston S. Churchill*, VI, p. 961

18 Moran, *Winston Churchill*, p. 178

19 Gilbert, *Winston S. Churchill*, p. 967

20 Moran, *Winston Churchill*, pp. 177–8

21 Gilbert, *Winston S. Churchill*, VII, p. 971

22 Nicolson (ed.), *Harold Nicolson: Diaries and Letters, 1939–45*, p. 402

23 Colville's unpublished diary for 8 December 1944, Churchill College, Cambridge

24 Winston S. Churchill, *Second World War*, VI, p. 197

25 Soames (ed.), *Speaking for Themselves*, p. 506

26 Winston S. Churchill, *Second World War*, VI, p. 208

27 Gilbert, *Winston S. Churchill*, VII, p. 991

28 *Ibid.*, p. 992

29 Winston S. Churchill, *Second World War*, VI, p. 198

30 *Ibid.*

31 Gilbert, *Winston S. Churchill*, VII, p. 992n.

32 *Ibid.*, p. 1015

33 *Ibid.*, p. 1009

34 *Ibid.*, p. 1002

35 *Ibid.*, p. 1047

36 *Ibid.*, pp. 1041–2

37 *Ibid.*, pp. 1081–2

38 Kimball (ed.), *Churchill and Roosevelt: The Complete Correspondence*, III, pp. 434 and 448

39 Acheson, *Present at the Creation*, pp. 217–25

40 Gilbert, *Winston S. Churchill*, VII, p. 1055

41 Colville, *Fringes of Power*, p. 536
42 Winston S. Churchill, *Second World War*, VI, p. 252
43 *Ibid.*, p. 26
44 Eden, *Reckoning*, p. 499
45 Soames, *Clementine Churchill*, pp. 363–4
46 Colville, *Fringes of Power*, p. 538
47 Gilbert, *Winston S. Churchill*, VII, pp. 1132–3
48 Winston S. Churchill, *Second World War*, VI, p. 273
49 Colville, *Fringes of Power*, p. 541
50 Gilbert, *Winston S. Churchill*, VII, p. 1123

40. VICTORY IN EUROPE AND DEFEAT IN BRITAIN

1 Colville, *Fringes of Power*, p. 550
2 Kimball (ed.), *Churchill and Roosevelt: The Complete Correspondence*, III, p. 502
3 Colville, *Fringes of Power*, p. 550
4 Eden, *Reckoning*, p. 507
5 Published in full in Harris, *Attlee*, pp. 241–3
6 Colville, *Fringes of Power*, p. 554
7 *Ibid.*, pp. 554–5
8 Gilbert, *Winston S. Churchill*, VII, p. 1156
9 *Ibid.*, p. 1257
10 Colville, *Fringes of Power*, p. 563
11 Gilbert, *Winston S. Churchill*, VII, p. 1191
12 *Ibid.*, p. 1208
13 *Ibid.*, p. 1180
14 Dilks (ed.), *Diaries of Sir Alexander Cadogan*, p. 707
15 Sherwood (ed.), *White House Papers of Harry L. Hopkins*, II, p. 839
16 Sarah Churchill, letter to her mother, 7 February 1945
17 Gilbert, *Winston S. Churchill*, VII, p. 1215
18 Winston S. Churchill, *Second World War*, VI, p. 315
19 *Ibid.*, p. 343
20 Gilbert, *Winston S. Churchill*, VII, p. 1190
21 Sarah Churchill, *Keep on Dancing*, pp. 77–8
22 Soames, *Clementine Churchill*, p. 365
23 Winston S. Churchill, *Second World War*, VII, p. 418
24 Gilbert, *Winston S. Churchill*, VII, p. 1294
25 Colville, *Fringes of Power*, p. 589

26 Kimball (ed.), *Churchill and Roosevelt: The Complete Correspondence*, III, p. 630
27 Soames (ed.), *Speaking for Themselves*, p. 530
28 Colville, *Fringes of Power*, p. 593
29 *Ibid.*, pp. 591–2
30 Winston S. Churchill, *Second World War*, VI, pp. 512–13
31 Dilks (ed.), *Diaries of Sir Alexander Cadogan*, pp. 562–3
32 Winston S. Churchill, *Second World War*, VI, p. 508
33 Gilbert, *Winston S. Churchill*, VII, p. 1082
34 *Ibid.*, p. 1082
35 Pimlott (ed.), *Second World War Diary of Hugh Dalton*, p. 865
36 Soames, *Clementine Churchill*, p. 382
37 Cannadine (ed.), *Blood, Toil, Tears and Sweat: Winston Churchill's Famous Speeches*, pp. 270–7
38 Nicolson (ed.), *Harold Nicolson: Diaries and Letters, 1939–45*, p. 472
39 Soames, *Clementine Churchill*, p. 383
40 Jenkins (ed.), *Purpose and Policy: Selected Speeches of C. R. Attlee*, p. 3
41 Harris, *Attlee*, p. 252
42 Winston S. Churchill, *Second World War*, VI, p. 528
43 Rhodes James, *Anthony Eden*, p. 307
44 Winston S. Churchill, *Second World War*, VI, p. 583
45 Soames, *Clementine Churchill*, p. 386
46 Gilbert, *Winston S. Churchill*, VIII, p. 109
47 Danchev and Todman (eds), *War Diaries, 1939–45: Field Marshal Lord Alanbrooke*, p. 712
48 *Ibid.*, p. 207
49 *Ibid.*, p. 713
50 *Ibid.*, p. 209; Winston S. Churchill, *Second World War*, III, p. 539

41. 'THE ENGLISH PATIENT'

1 Soames, *Clementine Churchill*, p. 390
2 *Ibid.*, p. 391
3 Soames (ed.), *Speaking for Themselves*, p. 535
4 Gilbert, *Winston S. Churchill*, VIII, p. 176
5 Cannadine (ed.), *Blood, Toil, Tears and Sweat: Winston Churchill's Famous Speeches*, p. 308
6 Gilbert, *Winston S. Churchill*, VII, pp. 211–12
7 *Ibid.*, pp. 209–10

8 *Ibid.*, pp. 286–7
9 *Ibid.*, p. 542
10 Winston S. Churchill, *Europe Unite: Speeches 1947 and 1948*, pp. 310–11
11 *Ibid.*, p. 313
12 *Ibid.*, p. 294
13 Hansard, 5th Series, vol. 476, cols 2140–59
14 Winston S. Churchill, *In the Balance: Speeches, 1949 and 1950*, p. 152
15 Gilbert, *Winston S. Churchill*, VIII, p. 188
16 *Ibid.*, p. 534
17 *Ibid.*, p. 405
18 *Ibid.*, p. 357
19 *Ibid.*, p. 412
20 *Ibid.*, p. 344
21 *Ibid.*, p. 443
22 *The Times*, 3 August 1951
23 Gilbert, *Winston S. Churchill*, VIII, p. 315
24 *Ibid.*, pp. 328–9
25 Soames (ed.), *Speaking for Themselves*, p. 551
26 *Sunday Telegraph*, 30 January 1966
27 Moran, *Winston Churchill*, p. 324

42. Two Elections and a Resurrection

1 Soames (ed.), *Speaking for Themselves*, pp. 552–3
2 Winston S. Churchill, *In the Balance: Speeches, 1949 and 1950*, p. 206
3 *Ibid.*, p. 210
4 Gilbert, *Winston S. Churchill*, VIII, p. 512
5 Hansard, 5th Series, vol. 472, col. 890
6 Gilbert, *Winston S. Churchill*, VIII, p. 559
7 *Ibid.*, p. 564
8 Winston S. Churchill, *Stemming the Tide: Speeches, 1951 and 1952*, p. 29
9 Gilbert, *Winston S. Churchill*, VIII, p. 569
10 Hansard, 5th Series, vol. 478, cols 971–87
11 *Ibid.*, vol. 482, cols 1362–72
12 *Ibid.*, vol. 484, col. 642
13 *Ibid.*, cols 640–1
14 Macmillan, *Tides of Fortune*, p. 322
15 Pimlott (ed.), *Political Diary of Hugh Dalton, 1918–40, 1945–51*, p. 543
16 *Ibid.*, p. 547

17 Gilbert, *Winston S. Churchill*, VIII, p. 601
18 *Ibid.*
19 *Ibid.*, p. 647
20 Winston S. Churchill, *Stemming the Tide: Speeches, 1951 and 1952*, p. 130
21 D. E. Butler, *British General Election of 1951*, pp. 66–7
22 Winston S. Churchill, *Stemming the Tide: Speeches, 1951 and 1952*, p. 131

43. A CONSENSUAL GOVERNMENT

1 Disraeli, *Sybil, or The Two Nations*, p. 26
2 Colville, *Fringes of Power*, p. 654
3 *Ibid.*, p. 672
4 *Ibid.*, p. 662
5 *Ibid.*, p. 661
6 *Ibid.*, p. 685
7 Winston S. Churchill, *Stemming the Tide: Speeches, 1951 and 1952*, p. 189
8 Howard, *RAB: The Life of R. A. Butler*, p. 190
9 R. A. Butler, *Art of the Possible*, p. 157
10 Winston S. Churchill, *Stemming the Tide: Speeches, 1951 and 1952*, p. 199
11 Gilbert, *Winston S. Churchill*, VIII, p. 669
12 *Ibid.*, p. 670
13 Acheson, *Present at the Creation*, pp. 598–9
14 Macmillan, *Tides of Fortune*, p. 465
15 Dutton, *Anthony Eden*, p. 296
16 Rhodes James, *Anthony Eden*, p. 351
17 Montague Browne, *Long Sunset*, p. 138
18 Colville, *Fringes of Power*, p. 634
19 *Ibid.*, p. 647
20 *Ibid.*, p. 654
21 Ziegler, *Mountbatten*, pp. 502–3
22 Moran, *Winston Churchill*, p. 354
23 Hunt, *On the Spot: An Ambassador Remembers*, p. 63
24 Colville, *Fringes of Power*, p. 668

44. 'AN AEROPLANE . . . WITH THE PETROL RUNNING OUT'

1 Moran, *Winston Churchill*, p. 415
2 *Ibid.*, p. 417

3 Macmillan, *Tides of Fortune*, p. 517
4 Moran, *Winston Churchill*, pp. 425–6, 736
5 Colville, *Fringes of Power*, p. 671
6 *Ibid.*, p. 672
7 *Ibid.*, p. 674
8 Soames, *Clementine Churchill*, p. 436
9 R. A. Butler, *Art of the Possible*, p. 171
10 Moran, *Winston Churchill*, p. 441
11 Hansard, 5th Series, vol. 515, cols 883–98
12 Eden diary for 27 November 1954, quoted in Rhodes James, *Anthony Eden*, p. 365
13 Winston S. Churchill, *The Unwritten Alliance: Speeches, 1953 and 1954*, pp. 57–67
14 *Ibid.*, p. 67
15 Moran, *Winston Churchill*, p. 485
16 Hansard, 5th Series, vol. 515, cols 883–98
17 Rhodes James (ed.), *Chips*, p. 479
18 Macmillan, *Tides of Fortune*, pp. 526–7
19 Moran, *Winston Churchill*, p. 494
20 Macmillan, *Tides of Fortune*, p. 523
21 Soames (ed.), *Speaking for Themselves*, p. 575
22 Colville, *Fringes of Power*, p. 683
23 Moran, *Winston Churchill*, p. 508
24 *Ibid.*, p. 532
25 *Ibid.*, p. 536
26 *Ibid.*, p. 538
27 Shuckburgh, *Descent to Suez*, p. 157
28 Moran, *Winston Churchill*, p. 523
29 R. A. Butler, *Art of the Possible*, p. 173
30 Shuckburgh, *Descent to Suez*, p. 145
31 Gilbert, *Winston S. Churchill*, VII, p. 976
32 *Ibid.*, p. 989
33 *Ibid.*
34 *Ibid.*
35 *Ibid.*, p. 991
36 Winston S. Churchill, *The Unwritten Alliance: Speeches, 1953 and 1954*, p. 151
37 Soames (ed.), *Speaking for Themselves*, p. 580
38 *Ibid.*, p. 582
39 Colville, *Fringes of Power*, p. 691

40 *Ibid.*, p. 692
41 *Ibid.*, p. 693
42 *Ibid.*
43 *Ibid.*
44 *Ibid.*, p. 695
45 *Ibid.*, p. 696
46 *Ibid.*
47 *Ibid.*, p. 699
48 Gilbert, *Winston S. Churchill*, VIII, p. 1027
49 Colville, *Fringes of Power*, p. 702
50 Gilbert, *Winston S. Churchill*, VII, p. 1036
51 Jenkins, *Gladstone*, p. 610

45. A Celebration and a Last Exit

1 Soames (ed.), *Speaking for Themselves*, p. 596
2 Colville, *Fringes of Power*, p. 704
3 Gilbert, *Winston S. Churchill*, VIII, p. 1063
4 Colville, *Fringes of Power*, p. 706
5 Gilbert, *Winston S. Churchill*, VIII, pp. 1049–51
6 Rhodes James, *Anthony Eden*, pp. 385–6
7 Colville, *Fringes of Power*, p. 705
8 Moran, *Winston Churchill*, p. 623
9 Colville, *Fringes of Power*, p. 707
10 Moran, *Winston Churchill*, p. 617
11 Gilbert, *Winston S. Churchill*, VIII, p. 1070
12 *Ibid.*, p. 1071
13 Soames, *Clementine Churchill*, p. 445
14 Moran, *Winston Churchill*, p. 620
15 *Ibid.*, pp. 616–17
16 Gilbert, *Winston S. Churchill*, VIII, p. 1074
17 Moran, *Winston Churchill*, p. 630
18 Macmillan, *Tides of Fortune*, p. 550
19 Gilbert, *Winston S. Churchill*, VIII, p. 1086
20 *Ibid.*, p. 1094
21 *Ibid.*, p. 1097
22 *Ibid.*
23 Hansard, 5th Series, vol. 537, cols 1893–1905
24 Gilbert, *Winston S. Churchill*, VIII, p. 1103

25 *Ibid.*
26 *Ibid.*, p. 1104
27 *Ibid.*, p. 1107
28 *Ibid.*, pp. 1106–7
29 *Ibid.*, p. 1107
30 *Ibid.*, p. 1111
31 Soames, *Clementine Churchill*, p. 451
32 Colville, *Fringes of Power*, p. 707
33 *Ibid.*
34 Gilbert, *Winston S. Churchill*, VIII, p. 1115
35 Colville, *Fringes of Power*, p. 708
36 *Ibid.*
37 *Ibid.*
38 Moran, *Winston Churchill*, p. 640

46. The Sun Sinks Slow, How Slowly

1 Gilbert, *Winston S. Churchill*, VIII, p. 1148
2 Moran, *Winston Churchill*, p. 699
3 Soames (ed.), *Speaking for Themselves*, p. 593
4 *Ibid.*, p. 595
5 Gilbert, *Winston S. Churchill*, VIII, pp. 1220–1
6 Colville, *Fringes of Power*, p. 721
7 *Ibid.*
8 Moran, *Winston Churchill*, p. 709
9 *Ibid.*, p. 710
10 Soames (ed.), *Speaking for Themselves*, p. 598
11 *Ibid.*, p. 603
12 *Ibid.*
13 Gilbert, *Winston S. Churchill*, VIII, p. 1220, 1315
14 Soames (ed.), *Speaking for Themselves*, p. 601
15 Gilbert, *Winston S. Churchill*, VIII, p. 1279
16 Montague Brown, *Long Sunset*, p. 242
17 Gilbert (ed.), *Winston Churchill and Emery Reves: Correspondence, 1937–1964*, pp. 385–7
18 Coote, *Other Club*, p. 110
19 Gilbert, *Winston S. Churchill*, VIII, p. 1335

Select Bibliography

Books by Churchill

The Story of the Malakand Field Force (1898)
The River War, 2 vols (1899)
Savrola (1900)
Lord Randolph Churchill, 2 vols (1906)
The People's Rights (1909)
The World Crisis and the Aftermath, 5 vols (1923–31)
My Early Life (1930)
The Eastern Front (1931)
Thoughts and Adventures (1932)
Marlborough: His Life and Times, 4 vols (1933–8)
Great Contemporaries (1937)
Arms and the Covenant (1938)
Painting as a Pastime (1948)
The Second World War, 6 vols (1948–54)
A History of the English-Speaking Peoples, 4 vols (1956–8)

Books Directly About Churchill

Biographies

Randolph S. Churchill and Martin Gilbert: *Winston S. Churchill*, 2 vols by
    Churchill (1966–7), 6 vols by Gilbert (1971–88) [the official biography]
Geoffrey Best: *Churchill: A Study in Greatness* (2001)
Philip Guedalla: *Mr Churchill: A Portrait* (1941)
Martin Gilbert: *Churchill: A Life* (1991)
Henry Pelling: *Winston Churchill* (1974)

Collections of letters or speeches

The *Companion Volumes* to the official biography and their continuation as *The Churchill War Papers*,16 vols (1967–2000)

David Cannadine (ed.): *Blood, Toil, Tears and Sweat: Winston Churchill's Famous Speeches* (1989)

Winston S. Churchill: *Europe Unite: Speeches, 1947 and 1948*, ed. Randolph S. Churchill (1950)

Winston S. Churchill: *In the Balance: Speeches, 1949 and 1950*, ed. Randolph S. Churchill (1951)

Winston S. Churchill: *Stemming the Tide: Speeches, 1951 and 1952*, ed. Randolph S. Churchill (1953)

Winston S. Churchill: *The Unwritten Alliance: Speeches, 1953 and 1954*, ed. Randolph S. Churchill (1961)

Robert Rhodes James (ed.): *The Complete Speeches of Sir Winston Churchill, 1897–1963*, 10 vols (1974)

Martin Gilbert (ed.): *Winston Churchill and Emery Reves: Correspondence, 1937–1964* (1997)

Warren F. Kimball (ed.): *Churchill and Roosevelt: The Complete Correspondence*, 3 vols (1984)

Mary Soames (ed.): *Speaking for Themselves: The Personal Letters of Winston and Clementine Churchill* (1998)

Biographical essays or studies of Churchill from particular angles

Paul Addison: *Churchill on the Home Front, 1900–1955* (1993)

Robert Blake and William Roger Louis (eds): *Churchill* (1993)

Violet Bonham Carter: *Winston Churchill as I Knew Him* (1965)

A. D. Gibb: *With Winston Churchill at the Front* (1924)

John Keegan: *Churchill's Generals* (1991)

Anthony Montague Browne: *Long Sunset: Memoirs of Winston Churchill's Last Private Secretary* (1995)

Lord Moran: *Winston Churchill: The Struggle for Survival, 1940–1965* (1966)

R. A. C. Parker: *Churchill and Appeasement* (2000)

T. Patterson: *Churchill: A Seat for Life* (1930)

Robert Rhodes James: *Churchill: A Study in Failure, 1900–39* (1970)

Stephen Roskill: *Churchill and the Admirals* (1977)

Celia Sandys: *Churchill: Wanted Dead or Alive* (1999)

Mary Soames: *Winston Churchill: His Life as a Painter* (1990)

A. J. P. Taylor, Robert Rhodes James, J. H. Plumb, Basil Liddell Hart and Anthony Storr: *Churchill: Four Faces and the Man* (1969)

W. H. Thompson: *I Was Churchill's Shadow* (1951)
W. H. Thompson: *Sixty Minutes with Winston Churchill* (1953)

GENERAL

Dean Acheson: *Present at the Creation: My Years in the State Department* (1969)
John Barnes and David Nicholson (eds): *The Leo Amery Diaries*, 2 vols (1980–8)
Seventh Marquess of Anglesey: *A History of the British Cavalry, 1816–1919*, 8 vols (1973–97)
H. H. Asquith: *Letters to a Friend*, 2 vols (1934)
Margot Asquith: *Autobiography*, 2 vols (1920–2)
Arthur James Balfour: *The Foundations of Belief, Being Notes Introductory to the Study of Theology* (1895)
Lord Beaverbrook: *Politicians and the War, 1914–1916* (1959)
Second Earl of Birkenhead: *Halifax: The Life of Lord Halifax* (1965)
Mark Bonham Carter and Mark Pottle (eds): *Lantern Slides: The Diaries and Letters of Violet Bonham Carter, 1904–14* (1996)
Robert Boothby: *Recollections of a Rebel* (1978)
Sarah Bradford: *King George VI* (1989)
M. and E. Brock (eds): *H. H. Asquith: Letters to Venetia Stanley* (1982)
D. E. Butler: *The British General Election of 1951* (1952)
R. A. Butler: *The Art of the Possible* (1971)
Barbara Cartland: *Ronald Cartland* (1942)
Viscount Cecil of Chelwood: *A Great Experiment: Autobiography* (1941)
Sir Austen Chamberlain: *Politics from Inside: An Epistolary Chronicle, 1906–1914* (1936)
Randolph S. Churchill: *Lord Derby, 'King of Lancashire': The Official Life of Edward, Seventeenth Earl of Derby, 1865–1948* (1959)
Sarah Churchill: *Keep on Dancing* (1981)
Sarah Churchill: *A Thread in the Tapestry* (1967)
Walter Citrine: *Men and Work* (1964)
John Colville: *The Churchillians* (1981)
John Colville: *The Fringes of Power: Downing Street Diaries, 1939–1955* (1985)
Duff Cooper: *Old Men Forget* (1953)
Colin Coote: *Editorial: Memoirs* (1965)
Colin Coote: *The Other Club* (1971)
Alex Danchev and Daniel Todman (eds): *War Diaries, 1939–45: Field Marshal Lord Alanbrooke* (2001)
David Dilks (ed.): *The Diaries of Sir Alexander Cadogan, 1938–1945* (1971)

Benjamin Disraeli: *Sybil, or The Two Nations* (1845)

Piers Dixon: *Double Diploma: The Life of Sir Pierson Dixon, Don and Diplomat* (1968)

David Dutton: *Anthony Eden: A Life and Reputation* (1997)

Anthony Eden: *The Reckoning* (1965)

Max Egremont: *Under Two Flags: The Life of Major-General Sir Edward Spears* (1997)

M. R. D. Foot and H. C. G. Matthew (eds): *The Gladstone Diaries*, 14 vols (1968–94)

R. F. Foster: *Lord Randolph Churchill: A Political Life* (1981)

Viscount Grey of Falloden: *Twenty-Five Years*, 2 vols (1925)

John Grigg: *Lloyd George*, 3 vols (1973–85)

Viscount Haldane: *Autobiography* (1929)

Kenneth Harris: *Attlee* (1982)

Maurice Hankey: *Supreme Command, 1914–1918* (1961)

John Harvey (ed.): *The War Diaries of Oliver Harvey* (1978)

Anthony Howard: *RAB: The Life of R. A. Butler* (1987)

Sir David Hunt: *On the Spot: An Ambassador Remembers* (1975)

Lord Ismay: *The Memoirs of General the Lord Ismay* (1960)

Roy Jenkins: *Asquith* (1964)

Roy Jenkins: *Gladstone* (1995)

Roy Jenkins (ed.): *Purpose and Policy: Selected Speeches of C. R. Attlee* (1947)

Thomas Jones: *Whitehall Diary, 1916–1930*, ed. Keith Middlemas, 3 vols (1969–71)

Ian Kershaw: *Hitler*, 2 vols (1998–2000)

Letters of Theodore Roosevelt, 8 vols (1951–6)

David Lloyd George: *War Memoirs of David Lloyd George*, 2 vols (1938)

John Lukacs: *The Duel: Hitler v. Churchill, 10 May–31 July 1940* (1990)

John Lukacs: *Five Days in London, May 1940* (1999)

R. B. McCallum and Alison Redman: *The British General Election of 1945* (1947)

N. and J. MacKenzie (eds): *The Diary of Beatrice Webb*, 4 vols (1982–5)

Harold Macmillan: *Tides of Fortune, 1945–1955* (1969)

Harold Macmillan: *War Diaries: Politics and War in the Mediterranean, January 1943–May 1945* (1984)

Harold Macmillan: *Winds of Change, 1914–1939* (1966)

A. J. Marder: *From the Dreadnought to Scapa Flow: The Royal Navy in the Fisher Era, 1904–19*, 5 vols (1961–6)

Edward Marsh: *A Number of People* (1939)

Keith Middlemas and John Barnes: *Baldwin: A Biography* (1961)

Jan Morris: *Fisher's Face* (1995)

John Henry Newman: *The Idea of a University Defined and Illustrated* (1873)

Harold Nicolson: *King George V: His Life and Reign* (1952)

Nigel Nicolson (ed.): *Harold Nicolson: Diaries and Letters, 1930–39* (1966)

Nigel Nicolson (ed.): *Harold Nicolson: Diaries and Letters, 1939–45* (1967)

Earl of Oxford and Asquith: *Fifty Years of Parliament*, 2 vols (1926)

F. W. Pethick-Lawrence: *Fate Has Been Kind* (1943)

Ben Pimlott (ed.): *The Political Diary of Hugh Dalton, 1918–40, 1945–60* (1986)

Ben Pimlott (ed.): *The Second World War Diary of Hugh Dalton, 1940–45* (1987)

Mark Pottle (ed.): *Champion Redoubtable: The Diaries and Letters of Violet Bonham Carter, 1914–45* (1998)

Mark Pottle (ed.): *Daring to Hope: The Diaries and Letters of Violet Bonham Carter, 1946–69* (2000)

Robert Rhodes James: *Anthony Eden* (1986)

Robert Rhodes James (ed.): *'Chips': The Diaries of Sir Henry Channon* (1993)

Lord Riddell: *More Pages from my Diary, 1908–1914* (1934)

N. A. Rose (ed.): *Baffy: The Diaries of Blanche Dugdale, 1936–1947* (1973)

A. Salvidge: *Salvidge of Liverpool* (1934)

Wilfred Scawen Blunt: *My Diaries* (1965)

Robert Self (ed.): *The Austen Chamberlain Diary Letters* (1996)

R. C. Sherriff: *No Leading Lady* (1968)

Robert E. Sherwood (ed.): *The White House Papers of Harry L. Hopkins: An Intimate History*, 2 vols (1948–9)

Evelyn Shuckburgh: *Descent to Suez: Diaries, 1951–56* (1986)

Sikorski Historical Institute (ed.): *Documents on Polish–Soviet Relations, 1939–45*, 2 vols (1961)

Mary Soames: *Clementine Churchill* (1979)

E. L. Spears: *Assignment to Catastrophe*, 2 vols (1954)

J. A. Spender and Cyril Asquith: *Life of Herbert Henry Asquith, Lord Oxford & Asquith*, 2 vols (1932)

Graham Stewart: *Burying Caesar: Churchill, Chamberlain and the Battle for the Tory Party* (1999)

A. J. P. Taylor: *English History, 1914–1945* (1965)

A. J. P. Taylor (ed.): *Lloyd George: A Diary by Frances Stevenson* (1971)

Viscount Templewood (Samuel Hoare): *Nine Troubled Years* (1954)

Ronald Tree: *When the Moon was High* (1975)

K. J. Valentine: *Willesden at War* (1995)

J. W. Wheeler-Bennett: *King George VI: His Life and Reign* (1958)

John Wilson (second Lord Moran): *C-B: A Life of Sir Henry Campbell-Bannerman* (1973)

Philip Ziegler: *Mountbatten: The Official Biography* (1985)

Index

Index

Eden (*cont.*)
appointment as Prime Minister 586–7; WSC appoints wartime Foreign Secretary 610; accompanies WSC to Briare (France) 615; in War Cabinet 634, 685; WSC promises leadership succession to 634n, 682; dines with WSC 639; wartime relations with WSC 644; reports sinking of *Bismarck* to WSC 657; and Cripps in Moscow 659; and WSC's speech on Soviet entry into war 660; in Soviet Union 669–70; favours inclusion of India in United Nations 676; on WSC's perception of Tory hostility 682; on WSC's lack of direction (March 1942) 683; meets Stalin 688; and Suez crisis 688–9, 902; meets WSC on return from Casablanca 706; dissuades WSC from 1943 Moscow trip 711; in Algiers (1943) 712; at Teheran conference 724, 784; absence on sick leave (1944) 736; meets WSC with Bevin before D-day 742; and WSC's interview with de Gaulle before D-day 743; opposes Morgenthau plan 754, 861; visits Moscow (1944) 757–9; and WSC's policy on Greece 768–9, 772; accompanies WSC to Greece (1944) 770–1; Lindemann contradicts over potential European starvation 774; temper 775; post-war foreign policy 780; at Yalta conference 781; attends Roosevelt's funeral 783; illness during 1945 election campaign 795; attends Potsdam conference 796; declines then accepts Garter 798 & n; with WSC after 1945 election defeat 799; and WSC's leadership of Opposition 807; coolness on Europe 818; in 1950 election 828; as potential party leader 831; as Foreign Secretary in WSC's 1951 government 844–5; operation and ill-health (1953) 846–7, 862, 866, 897; succession delays and expectations 846, 863, 877–8, 882–3, 885–7, 891–2, 894; causes rift with USA 849; and 1952 economic crisis 852; on European army 855; attitude to united Europe 856–7; relations with Macmillan 856; nominated as WSC's successor 863; loses party leadership (1956) 865; visits WSC at Chequers 866–7; WSC's doubts on as leader 868, 896; criticizes WSC's Commons speech advocating summit 869; at Bermuda conference (1953) 871, 873–4; attends 1953 Bermuda conference 872–3; defends WSC in Commons (April 1954) 876; on WSC's increasing debility 877; accompanies WSC to Washington meeting (1954) 880, 882; returns from USA on *Queen Elizabeth* 882–3; and WSC's proposed visit to Moscow (1954) 883;

awarded Garter 888; chairs Cabinet meetings 891; European defence proposals 893; minute from WSC on proposed May 1955 election 894; WSC informs of resignation 895; premiership 899; premiership ends 902
Eden, Beatrice Helen (Anthony's first wife) 98
Eden, Clarissa (*later* Countess of Avon; Anthony's second wife) 864, 867, 886
Edmunds, General James 429
Education Bills: (1902) 21; (1907) 130, 147n; (1944) 734
Edward VII, King (*earlier* Prince of Wales): quarrel with Blandford 4, 7; congratulates WSC on *Malakand Field Force* 32; death and funeral 69, 172, 189; accession 71; relations with WSC 90–1, 106, 172, 488; criticizes WSC for speech against Milner 120; and WSC's visit to Kaiser 121–2; WSC offends 153, 162; and Lloyd George's Limehouse oration 163; parliamentary letters from WSC 172–3; behaviour 498
Edward VIII, King *see* Windsor, Edward, Duke of
Edwards, Alfred George, Bishop of St Asaph 140
Edwards, Brigadier Harold 805
Egypt: WSC visits 39, 44; in Second World War 629, 642, 694, 704; and Suez crisis (1956) 902
Eisenhower, General and President Dwight D.: commands in North Africa 699, 703; and British Mediterranean strategy 711, 721; as Supreme Commander for Overlord 715, 722, 730; in Tunis 726; WSC inspects US troops with 733; orders postponement of D-day 742, 745; opposes WSC's plan to witness D-day landings 744; WSC praises 745; diplomatic skills 748; Montgomery criticizes 765; WSC visits in Versailles 773; advance in Europe 786; makes Antibes villa available to WSC 804; Adenauer's respect for 817; WSC meets in Paris (1951) 839; and WSC's post-war premiership 845; presidency 847; WSC's criticisms of as politician 848–9; and nuclear weapons 849, 857, 873; at Bermuda conference (1953) 863, 871–4; in volume 6 of WSC's *Second World War* 864; WSC visits in Washington (1954) 874, 878, 881; agrees to talks with Russians 881, 883; announces visit to Paris (1955) 893–4; and Suez crisis 902
El Alamein, Battle of (October 1942) 685, 702–4
ELAS (Greek guerrilla force) 734, 766–7, 771
Elgin, Victor Alexander Bruce, 9th Earl of 26, 35, 104–6, 115–18, 122, 124

Index